D0643731

Principles of Economics 2e

SENIOR CONTRIBUTING AUTHORS

STEVEN A. GREENLAW, UNIVERSITY OF MARY WASHINGTON
DAVID SHAPIRO, PENNSYLVANIA STATE UNIVERSITY
TIMOTHY TAYLOR, MACALESTER COLLEGE

OpenStax
Rice University
6100 Main Street MS-375
Houston, Texas 77005

To learn more about OpenStax, visit https://openstax.org.
Individual print copies and bulk orders can be purchased through our website.

©**2018 Rice University.** Textbook content produced by OpenStax is licensed under a Creative Commons Attribution 4.0 International License (CC BY 4.0). Under this license, any user of this textbook or the textbook contents herein must provide proper attribution as follows:

- If you redistribute this textbook in a digital format (including but not limited to PDF and HTML), then you must retain on every page the following attribution:
  "Download for free at https://openstax.org/details/books/principles-economics-2e."
- If you redistribute this textbook in a print format, then you must include on every physical page the following attribution:
  "Download for free at https://openstax.org/details/books/principles-economics-2e."
- If you redistribute part of this textbook, then you must retain in every digital format page view (including but not limited to PDF and HTML) and on every physical printed page the following attribution:
  "Download for free at https://openstax.org/details/books/principles-economics-2e."
- If you use this textbook as a bibliographic reference, please include
  https://openstax.org/details/books/principles-economics-2e in your citation.

For questions regarding this licensing, please contact support@openstax.org.

Trademarks
The OpenStax name, OpenStax logo, OpenStax book covers, OpenStax CNX name, OpenStax CNX logo, OpenStax Tutor name, Openstax Tutor logo, Connexions name, Connexions logo, Rice University name, and Rice University logo are not subject to the license and may not be reproduced without the prior and express written consent of Rice University.

Portions of the Demand and Supply chapter were derived from "Why It Matters: Government in Action by Steve Greenlaw and Lumen Learning." Located at: https://courses.lumenlearning.com/waymakermacroxmasterfall2016/chapter/why-it-matters-government-action/. License: CC BY 4.0.

PRINT BOOK ISBN-10	1-947172-36-0
PRINT BOOK ISBN-13	978-1-947172-36-4
PDF VERSION ISBN-10	1-947172-37-9
PDF VERSION ISBN-13	978-1-947172-37-1
ENHANCED TEXTBOOK ISBN-10	1-947172-48-4
ENHANCED TEXTBOOK ISBN-13	978-1-947172-48-7
Revision Number	PE2-2017-002-(03/18)-LC
Original Publication Year	2017

Printed in Indiana, USA

OpenStax

OpenStax provides free, peer-reviewed, openly licensed textbooks for introductory college and Advanced Placement® courses and low-cost, personalized courseware that helps students learn. A nonprofit ed tech initiative based at Rice University, we're committed to helping students access the tools they need to complete their courses and meet their educational goals.

Rice University

OpenStax, OpenStax CNX, and OpenStax Tutor are initiatives of Rice University. As a leading research university with a distinctive commitment to undergraduate education, Rice University aspires to path-breaking research, unsurpassed teaching, and contributions to the betterment of our world. It seeks to fulfill this mission by cultivating a diverse community of learning and discovery that produces leaders across the spectrum of human endeavor.

Foundation Support

OpenStax is grateful for the tremendous support of our sponsors. Without their strong engagement, the goal of free access to high-quality textbooks would remain just a dream.

Laura and John Arnold Foundation (LJAF) actively seeks opportunities to invest in organizations and thought leaders that have a sincere interest in implementing fundamental changes that not only yield immediate gains, but also repair broken systems for future generations. LJAF currently focuses its strategic investments on education, criminal justice, research integrity, and public accountability.

The William and Flora Hewlett Foundation has been making grants since 1967 to help solve social and environmental problems at home and around the world. The Foundation concentrates its resources on activities in education, the environment, global development and population, performing arts, and philanthropy, and makes grants to support disadvantaged communities in the San Francisco Bay Area.

Calvin K. Kazanjian was the founder and president of Peter Paul (Almond Joy), Inc. He firmly believed that the more people understood about basic economics the happier and more prosperous they would be. Accordingly, he established the Calvin K. Kazanjian Economics Foundation Inc, in 1949 as a philanthropic, nonpolitical educational organization to support efforts that enhanced economic understanding.

Guided by the belief that every life has equal value, the Bill & Melinda Gates Foundation works to help all people lead healthy, productive lives. In developing countries, it focuses on improving people's health with vaccines and other life-saving tools and giving them the chance to lift themselves out of hunger and extreme poverty. In the United States, it seeks to significantly improve education so that all young people have the opportunity to reach their full potential. Based in Seattle, Washington, the foundation is led by CEO Jeff Raikes and Co-chair William H. Gates Sr., under the direction of Bill and Melinda Gates and Warren Buffett.

The Maxfield Foundation supports projects with potential for high impact in science, education, sustainability, and other areas of social importance.

Our mission at The Michelson 20MM Foundation is to grow access and success by eliminating unnecessary hurdles to affordability. We support the creation, sharing, and proliferation of more effective, more affordable educational content by leveraging disruptive technologies, open educational resources, and new models for collaboration between for-profit, nonprofit, and public entities.

The Bill and Stephanie Sick Fund supports innovative projects in the areas of Education, Art, Science and Engineering.

Table of Contents

PREFACE

Welcome to *Principles of Economics 2e* (2nd Edition), an OpenStax resource. This textbook was written to increase student access to high-quality learning materials, maintaining highest standards of academic rigor at little to no cost.

About OpenStax

OpenStax is a nonprofit based at Rice University, and it's our mission to improve student access to education. Our first openly licensed college textbook was published in 2012, and our library has since scaled to over 25 books for college and AP® courses used by hundreds of thousands of students. OpenStax Tutor, our low-cost personalized learning tool, is being used in college courses throughout the country. Through our partnerships with philanthropic foundations and our alliance with other educational resource organizations, OpenStax is breaking down the most common barriers to learning and empowering students and instructors to succeed.

About OpenStax resources

Customization

Principles of Economics 2e is licensed under a Creative Commons Attribution 4.0 International (CC BY) license, which means that you can distribute, remix, and build upon the content, as long as you provide attribution to OpenStax and its content contributors.

Because our books are openly licensed, you are free to use the entire book or pick and choose the sections that are most relevant to the needs of your course. Feel free to remix the content by assigning your students certain chapters and sections in your syllabus, in the order that you prefer. You can even provide a direct link in your syllabus to the sections in the web view of your book.

Instructors also have the option of creating a customized version of their OpenStax book. The custom version can be made available to students in low-cost print or digital form through their campus bookstore. Visit the Instructor Resources section of your book page on OpenStax.org for more information.

Errata

All OpenStax textbooks undergo a rigorous review process. However, like any professional-grade textbook, errors sometimes occur. Since our books are web based, we can make updates periodically when deemed pedagogically necessary. If you have a correction to suggest, submit it through the link on your book page on OpenStax.org. Subject matter experts review all errata suggestions. OpenStax is committed to remaining transparent about all updates, so you will also find a list of past errata changes on your book page on OpenStax.org.

Format

You can access this textbook for free in web view or PDF through OpenStax.org, and for a low cost in print.

About *Principles of Economics 2e*

Principles of Economics 2e (2nd edition) covers the scope and sequence of requirements for a two-semester introductory economics course. The authors take a balanced approach to micro-and macroeconomics, to both Keynesian and classical views, and to the theory and application of economics concepts. The text also includes many current examples, which are handled in a politically equitable way. The second edition has been thoroughly revised to increase clarity, update data and current event impacts, and incorporate the feedback from many reviewers and adopters.

Coverage and scope

To develop the first edition of *Principles of Economics*, we acquired the rights to Timothy Taylor's *Principles of Economics* and solicited ideas from economics instructors at all levels of higher education, from community colleges to PhD-granting universities. For the second edition, we received even more expansive and actionable feedback from hundreds of adopters who had used the book for several academic terms. These knowledgeable instructors informed the pedagogical courses, learning objective development and fulfillment, and the chapter arrangements. Faculty who taught from the material provided critical and detailed commentary.

The result is a book that covers the breadth of economics topics and also provides the necessary depth to ensure the course is manageable for instructors and students alike. We strove to balance theory and application, as well as the amount of calculation and mathematical examples.

The book is organized into eight main parts:

What is Economics? The first two chapters introduce students to the study of economics with a focus on making choices in a world of scarce resources.

Supply and Demand, Chapters 3 and 4, introduces and explains the first analytical model in economics: supply, demand, and equilibrium, before showing applications in the markets for labor and finance.

The Fundamentals of Microeconomic Theory, Chapters 5 through 10, begins the microeconomics portion of the text, presenting the theories of consumer behavior, production and costs, and the different models of market structure, including some simple game theory.

Microeconomic Policy Issues, Chapters 11 through 18, covers the range of topics in applied micro, framed around the concepts of public goods and positive and negative externalities. Students explore competition and antitrust policies, environmental problems, poverty, income inequality, and other labor market issues. The text also covers information, risk and financial markets, as well as public economy.

The Macroeconomic Perspective and Goals, Chapters 19 through 23, introduces a number of key concepts in macro: economic growth, unemployment and inflation, and international trade and capital flows.

A Framework for Macroeconomic Analysis, Chapters 24 through 26, introduces the principal analytic model in macro, namely the aggregate demand/aggregate supply model. The model is then applied to the Keynesian and Neoclassical perspectives. The expenditure-output model is fully explained in a stand-alone appendix.

Monetary and Fiscal Policy, Chapters 27 through 31, explains the role of money and the banking system, as well as monetary policy and financial regulation. Then the discussion switches to government deficits and fiscal policy.

International Economics, Chapters 32 through 34, the final part of the text, introduces the international dimensions of economics, including international trade and protectionism.

Alternate Sequencing

Principles of Economics 2e was conceived and written to fit a particular topical sequence, but it can be used flexibly to accommodate other course structures. One such potential structure, which will fit reasonably well with the textbook content, is provided below. Please consider, however, that the chapters were not written to be completely independent, and that the proposed alternate sequence should be carefully considered for student preparation and textual consistency.

Chapter 1 Welcome to Economics!
Chapter 2 Choice in a World of Scarcity
Chapter 3 Demand and Supply
Chapter 4 Labor and Financial Markets
Chapter 5 Elasticity
Chapter 6 Consumer Choices
Chapter 33 International Trade
Chapter 7 Cost and Industry Structure
Chapter 12 Environmental Protection and Negative Externalities
Chapter 13 Positive Externalities and Public Goods
Chapter 8 Perfect Competition
Chapter 9 Monopoly
Chapter 10 Monopolistic Competition and Oligopoly
Chapter 11 Monopoly and Antitrust Policy
Chapter 14 Poverty and Economic Inequality
Chapter 15 Issues in Labor Markets: Unions, Discrimination, Immigration
Chapter 16 Information, Risk, and Insurance
Chapter 17 Financial Markets
Chapter 18 Public Economy

This OpenStax book is available for free at http://cnx.org/content/col12122/1.4

Changes to the second edition

OpenStax only undertakes revisions when significant modifications to a text are necessary. In the case of *Principles of Economics 2e*, we received a wealth of constructive feedback. Many of the book's users felt that consequential movement in economic data, coupled with the impacts of national and global events, warranted a full revision. We also took advantage of the opportunity to improve the writing and sequencing of the text, as well as many of the calculation examples. The major changes are summarized below.

> Augmented explanations in chapters one through four provide a more comprehensive and informative foundation for the book.

> A clearer explanation, using a numerical example, has been given for finding the utility maximizing combination of goods and services a consumer should choose.

> The Theory of Production has been added to the chapter on costs & industry structure.

> A more complete treatment has been given to labor markets, including the theories of competitive and monopsonistic labor markets, and bilateral monopoly; and the labor markets chapter and the poverty and economic inequality chapter have been resequenced.

> Substantial revisions to the AD/AS model in chapters 24-26 present the core concepts of macroeconomics in a clearer, more dynamic manner.

> Case studies and examples have been revised and, in some cases, replaced to provide more relevant and useful information for students.

> Economic data, tables, and graphs, as well as discussion and analysis around that data, have been thoroughly updated.

Wherever possible, data from the Federal Reserve Economic Database (FRED) was included and referenced. In most of these uses, links to the direct source of the FRED data are provided, and students are encouraged to explore the information and the overall FRED resources more thoroughly.

Additional updates and revisions appear throughout the book. They reflect changes to economic realities and policies regarding international trade, taxation, insurance, and other topics. For issues that may change in the months or years following the textbook's publication, the authors often provided a more open-ended explanation, but we will update the text annually to address further changes.

The revision of *Principles of Economics 2e* was undertaken by Steven Greenlaw (University of Mary Washington) and David Shapiro (Pennsylvania State University), with significant input by lead reviewer Daniel MacDonald (California State University, San Bernardino).

Pedagogical foundation

Throughout the OpenStax version of *Principles of Economics 2e*, you will find new features that engage the students in economic inquiry by taking selected topics a step further. Our features include:

Bring It Home: This added feature is a brief case study, specific to each chapter, which connects the chapter's main topic to the real word. It is broken up into two parts: the first at the beginning of the chapter (in the intro module) and the second at chapter's end, when students have learned what's necessary to understand the case and "bring home" the chapter's core concepts.

Work It Out: This added feature asks students to work through a generally analytical or computational problem, and guides them step by step to find out how its solution is derived.

Clear It Up: This boxed feature, which includes pre-existing features from Taylor's text, addresses common student misconceptions about the content. Clear It Ups are usually deeper explanations of something in the main body of the text. Each CIU starts with a question. The rest of the feature explains the answer.

Link It Up: This added feature is a very brief introduction to a website that is pertinent to students' understanding and enjoyment of the topic at hand.

Questions for each level of learning

The OpenStax version of *Principles of Economics 2e* further expands on Taylor's original end of chapter materials by offering four types of end of module questions for students:

Self-Checks are analytical self-assessment questions that appear at the end of each module. They "click to reveal" an answer in the web view so students can check their understanding before moving on to the next module. Self-Check questions are not simple look-up questions. They push the student to think beyond what is said in the text. Self-Check questions are designed for formative (rather than summative) assessment. The questions and answers are explained so that students feel like they are being walked through the problem.

Review Questions have been retained from Taylor's version, and are simple recall questions from the chapter in open-response format (not multiple choice or true/false). The answers can be looked up in the text.

Critical Thinking Questions are new higher-level, conceptual questions that ask students to *demonstrate their understanding by applying* what they have learned in different contexts. They ask for outside-the-box thinking, for *reasoning* about the concepts. They push the student to places they wouldn't have thought of going themselves.

Problems are exercises that give students additional practice working with the analytic and computational concepts in the module.

Updated art

Principles of Economics 2e includes an updated art program to better inform today's student, providing the latest data on covered topics.

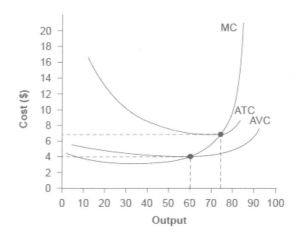

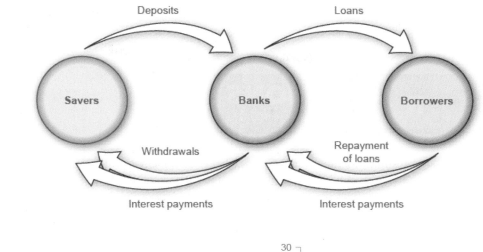

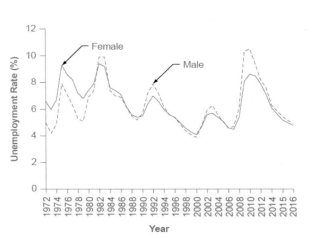

(a) Unemployment rates by gender

(b) Unemployment rates for women, by age

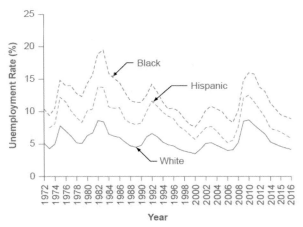

(c) Unemployment rates by race and ethnicity

Additional resources
Student and instructor resources

We've compiled additional resources for both students and instructors, including Getting Started Guides, an instructor solution manual, test bank, and PowerPoint slides. Instructor resources require a verified instructor account, which you can apply for when you log in or create your account on OpenStax.org. Take advantage of these resources to supplement your OpenStax book.

Community Hubs

OpenStax partners with the Institute for the Study of Knowledge Management in Education (ISKME) to offer Community Hubs on OER Commons – a platform for instructors to share community-created resources that support OpenStax books, free of charge. Through our Community Hubs, instructors can upload their own materials or download resources to use in their own courses, including additional ancillaries, teaching material, multimedia, and relevant course content. We encourage instructors to join the hubs for the subjects most relevant to your teaching and research as an opportunity both to enrich your courses and to engage with other faculty.

To reach the Community Hubs, visit www.oercommons.org/hubs/OpenStax.

Technology partners

As allies in making high-quality learning materials accessible, our technology partners offer optional low-cost tools that are integrated with OpenStax books. To access the technology options for your text, visit your book page on OpenStax.org.

About the authors
Senior contributing authors

Steven A. Greenlaw, University of Mary Washington

Steven Greenlaw has been teaching principles of economics for more than 30 years. In 1999, he received the Grellet C. Simpson Award for Excellence in Undergraduate Teaching at the University of Mary Washington. He is the author of *Doing Economics: A Guide to Doing and Understanding Economic Research*, as well as a variety of articles on economics pedagogy and instructional technology, published in the *Journal of Economic Education*, the *International Review of Economic Education*, and other outlets. He wrote the module on Quantitative Writing for *Starting Point: Teaching and Learning Economics*, the web portal on best practices in teaching economics. Steven Greenlaw lives in Alexandria, Virginia with his wife Kathy and their three children.

David Shapiro, Pennsylvania State University

David Shapiro is Professor Emeritus of Economics, Demography, and Women's, Gender, and Sexuality Studies at the Pennsylvania State University. He received a BA in economics and political science from the University of Michigan, and an MA as well as a PhD in economics from Princeton University. He began his academic career at Ohio State University in 1971, and moved to Penn State in 1980. His early research focused on women and youth in the United States labor market. Following a 1978-79 stint as a Fulbright professor at the University of Kinshasa in the Democratic Republic of the Congo, his research shifted focus to fertility in Kinshasa and more broadly, in sub-Saharan Africa. He has also received the top prize for teaching at both Ohio State and Penn State.

Timothy Taylor, Macalester College

Timothy Taylor has been writing and teaching about economics for 30 years, and is the Managing Editor of the *Journal of Economic Perspectives*, a post he's held since 1986. He has been a lecturer for The Teaching Company, the University of Minnesota, and the Hubert H. Humphrey Institute of Public Affairs, where students voted him Teacher of the Year in 1997. His writings include numerous pieces for journals such as the *Milken Institute Review* and *The Public Interest*, and he has been an editor on many projects, most notably for the Brookings Institution and the World Bank, where he was Chief Outside Editor for the *World Development Report 1999/2000, Entering the 21st Century: The Changing Development Landscape*. He also blogs four to five times per week at http://conversableeconomist.blogspot.com. Timothy Taylor lives near Minneapolis with his wife Kimberley and their three children.

Special thanks to Christian Potter from University of Mary Washington, who thoroughly researched and applied many of the data updates and provided the foundation for many new and revised illustrations.

Development editor

Thomas Sigel

Contributing authors

Eric Dodge, Hanover College
Cynthia Gamez, University of Texas at El Paso
Andres Jauregui, Columbus State University
Diane Keenan, Cerritos College
Dan MacDonald, California State University San Bernardino
Amyaz Moledina, The College of Wooster
Craig Richardson, Winston-Salem State University
David Shapiro, Pennsylvania State University
Ralph Sonenshine, American University

Reviewers

Bryan Aguiar, Northwest Arkansas Community College
Basil Al Hashimi, Mesa Community College
Emil Berendt, Mount St. Mary's University
Zena Buser, Adams State University
Douglas Campbell, The University of Memphis
Sanjukta Chaudhuri, University of Wisconsin - Eau Claire
Xueyu Cheng, Alabama State University
Robert Cunningham, Alma College
Rosa Lea Danielson, College of DuPage
Steven Deloach, Elon University
Michael Enz, Framingham State University
Debbie Evercloud, University of Colorado Denver
Reza Ghorashi, Richard Stockton College of New Jersey
Robert Gillette, University of Kentucky
Shaomin Huang, Lewis-Clark State College
George Jones, University of Wisconsin-Rock County
Charles Kroncke, College of Mount St. Joseph
Teresa Laughlin, Palomar Community College
Carlos Liard-Muriente, Central Connecticut State University
Heather Luea, Kansas State University
Steven Lugauer, University of Notre Dame
William Mosher, Nashua Community College
Michael Netta, Hudson County Community College
Nick Noble, Miami University
Joe Nowakowski, Muskingum University
Shawn Osell, University of Wisconsin-Superior
Mark Owens, Middle Tennessee State University
Sonia Pereira, Barnard College
Jennifer Platania, Elon University
Robert Rycroft, University of Mary Washington
Adrienne Sachse, Florida State College at Jacksonville
Hans Schumann, Texas A&M University
Gina Shamshak, Goucher College
Chris Warburton, John Jay College of Criminal Justice, CUNY
Mark Witte, Northwestern University

This OpenStax book is available for free at http://cnx.org/content/col12122/1.4

1 | Welcome to Economics!

Figure 1.1 Do You Use Facebook? Economics is greatly impacted by how well information travels through society. Today, social media giants Twitter, Facebook, and Instagram are major forces on the information super highway. (Credit: Johan Larsson/Flickr)

Bring it Home

Decisions ... Decisions in the Social Media Age

To post or not to post? Every day we are faced with a myriad of decisions, from what to have for breakfast, to which route to take to class, to the more complex—"Should I double major and add possibly another semester of study to my education?" Our response to these choices depends on the information we have available at any given moment. Economists call this "imperfect" because we rarely have all the data we need to make perfect decisions. Despite the lack of perfect information, we still make hundreds of decisions a day.

Now we have another avenue in which to gather information—social media. Outlets like Facebook and Twitter are altering the process by which we make choices, how we spend our time, which movies we see, which products we buy, and more. How many of you chose a university without checking out its Facebook page or Twitter stream first for information and feedback?

As you will see in this course, what happens in economics is affected by how well and how fast information disseminates through a society, such as how quickly information travels through Facebook. "Economists love nothing better than when deep and liquid markets operate under conditions of perfect information," says Jessica Irvine, National Economics Editor for News Corp Australia.

This leads us to the topic of this chapter, an introduction to the world of making decisions, processing information, and understanding behavior in markets —the world of economics. Each chapter in this book will start with a discussion about current (or sometimes past) events and revisit it at chapter's end—to "bring home" the concepts in play.

Introduction

In this chapter, you will learn about:

- What Is Economics, and Why Is It Important?
- Microeconomics and Macroeconomics
- How Economists Use Theories and Models to Understand Economic Issues
- How Economies Can Be Organized: An Overview of Economic Systems

What is economics and why should you spend your time learning it? After all, there are other disciplines you could be studying, and other ways you could be spending your time. As the Bring it Home feature just mentioned, making choices is at the heart of what economists study, and your decision to take this course is as much as economic decision as anything else.

Economics is probably not what you think. It is not primarily about money or finance. It is not primarily about business. It is not mathematics. What is it then? It is both a subject area and a way of viewing the world.

1.1 | What Is Economics, and Why Is It Important?

By the end of this section, you will be able to:
- Discuss the importance of studying economics
- Explain the relationship between production and division of labor
- Evaluate the significance of scarcity

Economics is the study of how humans make decisions in the face of scarcity. These can be individual decisions, family decisions, business decisions or societal decisions. If you look around carefully, you will see that scarcity is a fact of life. **Scarcity** means that human wants for goods, services and resources exceed what is available. Resources, such as labor, tools, land, and raw materials are necessary to produce the goods and services we want but they exist in limited supply. Of course, the ultimate scarce resource is time- everyone, rich or poor, has just 24 expendable hours in the day to earn income to acquire goods and services, for leisure time, or for sleep. At any point in time, there is only a finite amount of resources available.

Think about it this way: In 2015 the labor force in the United States contained over 158 million workers, according to the U.S. Bureau of Labor Statistics. The total land area was 3,794,101 square miles. While these are certainly large numbers, they are not infinite. Because these resources are limited, so are the numbers of goods and services we produce with them. Combine this with the fact that human wants seem to be virtually infinite, and you can see why scarcity is a problem.

Introduction to FRED

Data is very important in economics because it describes and measures the issues and problems that economics seek to understand. A variety of government agencies publish economic and social data. For this course, we will generally use data from the St. Louis Federal Reserve Bank's FRED database. FRED is very user friendly. It allows you to display data in tables or charges, and you can easily download it into spreadsheet form if you want to use the data for other purposes. The **FRED website (https://openstax.org/l/FRED/)** includes data on nearly 400,000 domestic and international variables over time, in the following broad categories:

- Money, Banking & Finance
- Population, Employment, & Labor Markets (including Income Distribution)

- National Accounts (Gross Domestic Product & its components), Flow of Funds, and International Accounts

- Production & Business Activity (including Business Cycles)

- Prices & Inflation (including the Consumer Price Index, the Producer Price Index, and the Employment Cost Index)

- International Data from other nations

- U.S. Regional Data

- Academic Data (including Penn World Tables & NBER Macrohistory database)

For more information about how to use FRED, see the variety of **videos (https://openstax.org/l/FRED_intro)** on YouTube starting with this introduction.

Figure 1.2 Scarcity of Resources Homeless people are a stark reminder that scarcity of resources is real. (Credit: "daveynin"/Flickr Creative Commons)

If you still do not believe that scarcity is a problem, consider the following: Does everyone require food to eat? Does everyone need a decent place to live? Does everyone have access to healthcare? In every country in the world, there are people who are hungry, homeless (for example, those who call park benches their beds, as **Figure 1.2** shows), and in need of healthcare, just to focus on a few critical goods and services. Why is this the case? It is because of scarcity. Let's delve into the concept of scarcity a little deeper, because it is crucial to understanding economics.

The Problem of Scarcity

Think about all the things you consume: food, shelter, clothing, transportation, healthcare, and entertainment. How do you acquire those items? You do not produce them yourself. You buy them. How do you afford the things you buy? You work for pay. If you do not, someone else does on your behalf. Yet most of us never have enough income to buy all the things we want. This is because of scarcity. So how do we solve it?

Link It Up ⚭⚭

Visit this website (http://openstax.org/l/drought) to read about how the United States is dealing with scarcity in resources.

Every society, at every level, must make choices about how to use its resources. Families must decide whether to spend their money on a new car or a fancy vacation. Towns must choose whether to put more of the budget into police and fire protection or into the school system. Nations must decide whether to devote more funds to national defense or to protecting the environment. In most cases, there just isn't enough money in the budget to do everything. How do we use our limited resources the best way possible, that is, to obtain the most goods and services we can? There are a couple of options. First, we could each produce everything we each consume. Alternatively, we could each produce some of what we want to consume, and "trade" for the rest of what we want. Let's explore these options. Why do we not each just produce all of the things we consume? Think back to pioneer days, when individuals knew how to do so much more than we do today, from building their homes, to growing their crops, to hunting for food, to repairing their equipment. Most of us do not know how to do all—or any—of those things, but it is not because we could not learn. Rather, we do not have to. The reason why is something called *the division and specialization of labor*, a production innovation first put forth by Adam Smith (**Figure 1.3**) in his book, *The Wealth of Nations*.

Figure 1.3 Adam Smith Adam Smith introduced the idea of dividing labor into discrete tasks. (Credit: Wikimedia Commons)

The Division of and Specialization of Labor

The formal study of economics began when Adam Smith (1723–1790) published his famous book *The Wealth of Nations* in 1776. Many authors had written on economics in the centuries before Smith, but he was the first to address the subject in a comprehensive way. In the first chapter, Smith introduces the concept of **division of labor**, which means that the way one produces a good or service is divided into a number of tasks that different workers perform, instead of all the tasks being done by the same person.

To illustrate division of labor, Smith counted how many tasks went into making a pin: drawing out a piece of wire, cutting it to the right length, straightening it, putting a head on one end and a point on the other, and packaging pins for sale, to name just a few. Smith counted 18 distinct tasks that different people performed—all for a pin, believe it or not!

Modern businesses divide tasks as well. Even a relatively simple business like a restaurant divides the task of serving meals into a range of jobs like top chef, sous chefs, less-skilled kitchen help, servers to wait on the tables, a greeter at the door, janitors to clean up, and a business manager to handle paychecks and bills—not to mention the economic

This OpenStax book is available for free at http://cnx.org/content/col12122/1.4

connections a restaurant has with suppliers of food, furniture, kitchen equipment, and the building where it is located. A complex business like a large manufacturing factory, such as the shoe factory (**Figure 1.4**), or a hospital can have hundreds of job classifications.

Figure 1.4 Division of Labor Workers on an assembly line are an example of the divisions of labor. (Credit: Nina Hale/Flickr Creative Commons)

Why the Division of Labor Increases Production

When we divide and subdivide the tasks involved with producing a good or service, workers and businesses can produce a greater quantity of output. In his observations of pin factories, Smith noticed that one worker alone might make 20 pins in a day, but that a small business of 10 workers (some of whom would need to complete two or three of the 18 tasks involved with pin-making), could make 48,000 pins in a day. How can a group of workers, each specializing in certain tasks, produce so much more than the same number of workers who try to produce the entire good or service by themselves? Smith offered three reasons.

First, **specialization** in a particular small job allows workers to focus on the parts of the production process where they have an advantage. (In later chapters, we will develop this idea by discussing comparative advantage.) People have different skills, talents, and interests, so they will be better at some jobs than at others. The particular advantages may be based on educational choices, which are in turn shaped by interests and talents. Only those with medical degrees qualify to become doctors, for instance. For some goods, geography affects specialization. For example, it is easier to be a wheat farmer in North Dakota than in Florida, but easier to run a tourist hotel in Florida than in North Dakota. If you live in or near a big city, it is easier to attract enough customers to operate a successful dry cleaning business or movie theater than if you live in a sparsely populated rural area. Whatever the reason, if people specialize in the production of what they do best, they will be more effective than if they produce a combination of things, some of which they are good at and some of which they are not.

Second, workers who specialize in certain tasks often learn to produce more quickly and with higher quality. This pattern holds true for many workers, including assembly line laborers who build cars, stylists who cut hair, and doctors who perform heart surgery. In fact, specialized workers often know their jobs well enough to suggest innovative ways to do their work faster and better.

A similar pattern often operates within businesses. In many cases, a business that focuses on one or a few products (sometimes called its "core competency") is more successful than firms that try to make a wide range of products.

Third, specialization allows businesses to take advantage of **economies of scale**, which means that for many goods, as the level of production increases, the average cost of producing each individual unit declines. For example, if a factory produces only 100 cars per year, each car will be quite expensive to make on average. However, if a factory produces 50,000 cars each year, then it can set up an assembly line with huge machines and workers performing specialized tasks, and the average cost of production per car will be lower. The ultimate result of workers who can focus on their preferences and talents, learn to do their specialized jobs better, and work in larger organizations is that society as a whole can produce and consume far more than if each person tried to produce all of his or her own goods and services. The division and specialization of labor has been a force against the problem of scarcity.

Trade and Markets

Specialization only makes sense, though, if workers can use the pay they receive for doing their jobs to purchase the other goods and services that they need. In short, specialization requires trade.

You do not have to know anything about electronics or sound systems to play music—you just buy an iPod or MP3 player, download the music, and listen. You do not have to know anything about artificial fibers or the construction of sewing machines if you need a jacket—you just buy the jacket and wear it. You do not need to know anything about internal combustion engines to operate a car—you just get in and drive. Instead of trying to acquire all the knowledge and skills involved in producing all of the goods and services that you wish to consume, the market allows you to learn a specialized set of skills and then use the pay you receive to buy the goods and services you need or want. This is how our modern society has evolved into a strong economy.

Why Study Economics?

Now that you have an overview on what economics studies, let's quickly discuss why you are right to study it. Economics is not primarily a collection of facts to memorize, although there are plenty of important concepts to learn. Instead, think of economics as a collection of questions to answer or puzzles to work. Most importantly, economics provides the tools to solve those puzzles. If the economics "bug" has not bitten you yet, there are other reasons why you should study economics.

- Virtually every major problem facing the world today, from global warming, to world poverty, to the conflicts in Syria, Afghanistan, and Somalia, has an economic dimension. If you are going to be part of solving those problems, you need to be able to understand them. Economics is crucial.

- It is hard to overstate the importance of economics to good citizenship. You need to be able to vote intelligently on budgets, regulations, and laws in general. When the U.S. government came close to a standstill at the end of 2012 due to the "fiscal cliff," what were the issues? Did you know?

- A basic understanding of economics makes you a well-rounded thinker. When you read articles about economic issues, you will understand and be able to evaluate the writer's argument. When you hear classmates, co-workers, or political candidates talking about economics, you will be able to distinguish between common sense and nonsense. You will find new ways of thinking about current events and about personal and business decisions, as well as current events and politics.

The study of economics does not dictate the answers, but it can illuminate the different choices.

1.2 | Microeconomics and Macroeconomics

By the end of this section, you will be able to:
- Describe microeconomics
- Describe macroeconomics
- Contrast monetary policy and fiscal policy

Economics is concerned with the well-being of *all* people, including those with jobs and those without jobs, as well as those with high incomes and those with low incomes. Economics acknowledges that production of useful goods and services can create problems of environmental pollution. It explores the question of how investing in education helps to develop workers' skills. It probes questions like how to tell when big businesses or big labor unions are operating in a way that benefits society as a whole and when they are operating in a way that benefits their owners or members at the expense of others. It looks at how government spending, taxes, and regulations affect decisions about production and consumption.

It should be clear by now that economics covers considerable ground. We can divide that ground into two parts: **Microeconomics** focuses on the actions of individual agents within the economy, like households, workers, and businesses. **Macroeconomics** looks at the economy as a whole. It focuses on broad issues such as growth of production, the number of unemployed people, the inflationary increase in prices, government deficits, and levels of exports and imports. Microeconomics and macroeconomics are not separate subjects, but rather complementary perspectives on the overall subject of the economy.

To understand why both microeconomic and macroeconomic perspectives are useful, consider the problem of studying a biological ecosystem like a lake. One person who sets out to study the lake might focus on specific topics: certain kinds of algae or plant life; the characteristics of particular fish or snails; or the trees surrounding the lake. Another person might take an overall view and instead consider the lake's ecosystem from top to bottom; what eats what, how the system stays in a rough balance, and what environmental stresses affect this balance. Both approaches are useful, and both examine the same lake, but the viewpoints are different. In a similar way, both microeconomics and macroeconomics study the same economy, but each has a different viewpoint.

Whether you are scrutinizing lakes or economics, the micro and the macro insights should blend with each other. In studying a lake, the micro insights about particular plants and animals help to understand the overall food chain, while the macro insights about the overall food chain help to explain the environment in which individual plants and animals live.

In economics, the micro decisions of individual businesses are influenced by whether the macroeconomy is healthy. For example, firms will be more likely to hire workers if the overall economy is growing. In turn, macroeconomy's performance ultimately depends on the microeconomic decisions that individual households and businesses make.

Microeconomics

What determines how households and individuals spend their budgets? What combination of goods and services will best fit their needs and wants, given the budget they have to spend? How do people decide whether to work, and if so, whether to work full time or part time? How do people decide how much to save for the future, or whether they should borrow to spend beyond their current means?

What determines the products, and how many of each, a firm will produce and sell? What determines the prices a firm will charge? What determines how a firm will produce its products? What determines how many workers it will hire? How will a firm finance its business? When will a firm decide to expand, downsize, or even close? In the microeconomics part of this book, we will learn about the theory of consumer behavior, the theory of the firm, how markets for labor and other resources work, and how markets sometimes fail to work properly.

Macroeconomics

What determines the level of economic activity in a society? In other words, what determines how many goods and services a nation actually produces? What determines how many jobs are available in an economy? What determines a nation's standard of living? What causes the economy to speed up or slow down? What causes firms to hire more workers or to lay them off? Finally, what causes the economy to grow over the long term?

We can determine an economy's macroeconomic health by examining a number of goals: growth in the standard of living, low unemployment, and low inflation, to name the most important. How can we use government macroeconomic policy to pursue these goals? A nation's central bank conducts **monetary policy**, which involves policies that affect bank lending, interest rates, and financial capital markets. For the United States, this is the Federal Reserve. A nation's legislative body determines **fiscal policy**, which involves government spending and taxes. For the United States, this is the Congress and the executive branch, which originates the federal budget. These are the government's main tools. Americans tend to expect that government can fix whatever economic problems we encounter, but to what extent is that expectation realistic? These are just some of the issues that we will explore in the macroeconomic chapters of this book.

1.3 | How Economists Use Theories and Models to Understand Economic Issues

By the end of this section, you will be able to:
- Interpret a circular flow diagram
- Explain the importance of economic theories and models
- Describe goods and services markets and labor markets

Figure 1.5 John Maynard Keynes One of the most influential economists in modern times was John Maynard Keynes. (Credit: Wikimedia Commons)

John Maynard Keynes (1883–1946), one of the greatest economists of the twentieth century, pointed out that economics is not just a subject area but also a way of thinking. Keynes (**Figure 1.5**) famously wrote in the introduction to a fellow economist's book: "[Economics] is a method rather than a doctrine, an apparatus of the mind, a technique of thinking, which helps its possessor to draw correct conclusions." In other words, economics teaches you how to think, not what to think.

Link It Up

Watch this video (http://openstax.org/l/Keynes) about John Maynard Keynes and his influence on economics.

Economists see the world through a different lens than anthropologists, biologists, classicists, or practitioners of any other discipline. They analyze issues and problems using economic theories that are based on particular assumptions about human behavior. These assumptions tend to be different than the assumptions an anthropologist or psychologist might use. A **theory** is a simplified representation of how two or more variables interact with each other. The purpose of a theory is to take a complex, real-world issue and simplify it down to its essentials. If done well, this enables the analyst to understand the issue and any problems around it. A good theory is simple enough to understand, while complex enough to capture the key features of the object or situation you are studying.

Sometimes economists use the term **model** instead of theory. Strictly speaking, a theory is a more abstract representation, while a model is a more applied or empirical representation. We use models to test theories, but for this course we will use the terms interchangeably.

For example, an architect who is planning a major office building will often build a physical model that sits on a tabletop to show how the entire city block will look after the new building is constructed. Companies often build models of their new products, which are more rough and unfinished than the final product, but can still demonstrate how the new product will work.

A good model to start with in economics is the **circular flow diagram** (**Figure 1.6**). It pictures the economy as consisting of two groups—households and firms—that interact in two markets: the **goods and services market** in which firms sell and households buy and the **labor market** in which households sell labor to business firms or other employees.

Figure 1.6 The Circular Flow Diagram The circular flow diagram shows how households and firms interact in the goods and services market, and in the labor market. The direction of the arrows shows that in the goods and services market, households receive goods and services and pay firms for them. In the labor market, households provide labor and receive payment from firms through wages, salaries, and benefits.

Firms produce and sell goods and services to households in the market for goods and services (or product market). Arrow "A" indicates this. Households pay for goods and services, which becomes the revenues to firms. Arrow "B" indicates this. Arrows A and B represent the two sides of the product market. Where do households obtain the income to buy goods and services? They provide the labor and other resources (e.g. land, capital, raw materials) firms need to produce goods and services in the market for inputs (or factors of production). Arrow "C" indicates this. In return, firms pay for the inputs (or resources) they use in the form of wages and other factor payments. Arrow "D" indicates this. Arrows "C" and "D" represent the two sides of the factor market.

Of course, in the real world, there are many different markets for goods and services and markets for many different types of labor. The circular flow diagram simplifies this to make the picture easier to grasp. In the diagram, firms produce goods and services, which they sell to households in return for revenues. The outer circle shows this, and represents the two sides of the product market (for example, the market for goods and services) in which households demand and firms supply. Households sell their labor as workers to firms in return for wages, salaries, and benefits. The inner circle shows this and represents the two sides of the labor market in which households supply and firms demand.

This version of the circular flow model is stripped down to the essentials, but it has enough features to explain how the product and labor markets work in the economy. We could easily add details to this basic model if we wanted to introduce more real-world elements, like financial markets, governments, and interactions with the rest of the globe (imports and exports).

Economists carry a set of theories in their heads like a carpenter carries around a toolkit. When they see an economic issue or problem, they go through the theories they know to see if they can find one that fits. Then they use the theory to derive insights about the issue or problem. Economists express theories as diagrams, graphs, or even as mathematical equations. (Do not worry. In this course, we will mostly use graphs.) Economists do not figure out the answer to the problem first and then draw the graph to illustrate. Rather, they use the graph of the theory to help them figure out the answer. Although at the introductory level, you can sometimes figure out the right answer without applying a model, if you keep studying economics, before too long you will run into issues and problems that you will need to graph to solve. We explain both micro and macroeconomics in terms of theories and models. The most well-known theories are probably those of supply and demand, but you will learn a number of others.

1.4 | How To Organize Economies: An Overview of Economic Systems

By the end of this section, you will be able to:
- Contrast traditional economies, command economies, and market economies
- Explain gross domestic product (GDP)
- Assess the importance and effects of globalization

Think about what a complex system a modern economy is. It includes all production of goods and services, all buying and selling, all employment. The economic life of every individual is interrelated, at least to a small extent, with the economic lives of thousands or even millions of other individuals. Who organizes and coordinates this system? Who insures that, for example, the number of televisions a society provides is the same as the amount it needs and wants? Who insures that the right number of employees work in the electronics industry? Who insures that televisions are produced in the best way possible? How does it all get done?

There are at least three ways that societies organize an economy. The first is the **traditional economy**, which is the oldest economic system and is used in parts of Asia, Africa, and South America. Traditional economies organize their economic affairs the way they have always done (i.e., tradition). Occupations stay in the family. Most families are farmers who grow the crops using traditional methods. What you produce is what you consume. Because tradition drives the way of life, there is little economic progress or development.

Figure 1.7 A Command Economy Ancient Egypt was an example of a command economy. (Credit: Jay Bergesen/ Flickr Creative Commons)

Command economies are very different. In a **command economy**, economic effort is devoted to goals passed down from a ruler or ruling class. Ancient Egypt was a good example: a large part of economic life was devoted to building pyramids, like those in **Figure 1.7**, for the pharaohs. Medieval manor life is another example: the lord provided the land for growing crops and protection in the event of war. In return, vassals provided labor and soldiers to do the lord's bidding. In the last century, communism emphasized command economies.

In a command economy, the government decides what goods and services will be produced and what prices it will charge for them. The government decides what methods of production to use and sets wages for workers. The government provides many necessities like healthcare and education for free. Currently, Cuba and North Korea have command economies.

This OpenStax book is available for free at http://cnx.org/content/col12122/1.4

Figure 1.8 A Market Economy Nothing says "market" more than The New York Stock Exchange. (Credit: Erik Drost/ Flickr Creative Commons)

Although command economies have a very centralized structure for economic decisions, market economies have a very decentralized structure. A **market** is an institution that brings together buyers and sellers of goods or services, who may be either individuals or businesses. The New York Stock Exchange (**Figure 1.8**) is a prime example of a market which brings buyers and sellers together. In a **market economy**, decision-making is decentralized. Market economies are based on **private enterprise**: the private individuals or groups of private individuals own and operate the means of production (resources and businesses). Businesses supply goods and services based on demand. (In a command economy, by contrast, the government owns resources and businesses.) Supply of goods and services depends on what the demands. A person's income is based on his or her ability to convert resources (especially labor) into something that society values. The more society values the person's output, the higher the income (think Lady Gaga or LeBron James). In this scenario, market forces, not governments, determine economic decisions.

Most economies in the real world are mixed. They combine elements of command and market (and even traditional) systems. The U.S. economy is positioned toward the market-oriented end of the spectrum. Many countries in Europe and Latin America, while primarily market-oriented, have a greater degree of government involvement in economic decisions than the U.S. economy. China and Russia, while over the past several decades have moved more in the direction of having a market-oriented system, remain closer to the command economy end of the spectrum. The Heritage Foundation provides information about how free and thus market-oriented different countries' are, as the following Clear It Up feature discusses. For a similar ranking, but one that defines freedom more broadly, see the Cato Foundation's Human Freedom **Index (https://openstax.org/l/cato)** .

What countries are considered economically free?

Who is in control of economic decisions? Are people free to do what they want and to work where they want? Are businesses free to produce when they want and what they choose, and to hire and fire as they wish? Are banks free to choose who will receive loans, or does the government control these kinds of choices? Each year, researchers at the Heritage Foundation and the *Wall Street Journal* look at 50 different categories of economic freedom for countries around the world. They give each nation a score based on the extent of economic freedom in each category.

The 2016 Heritage Foundation's Index of Economic Freedom report ranked 178 countries around the world: Table 1.1 lists some examples of the most free and the least free countries. Several additional countries were not ranked because of extreme instability that made judgments about economic freedom impossible. These countries include Afghanistan, Iraq, Libya, Syria Somalia, and Yemen.

The assigned rankings are inevitably based on estimates, yet even these rough measures can be useful for discerning trends. In 2015, 101 of the 178 included countries shifted toward greater economic freedom, although 77 of the countries shifted toward less economic freedom. In recent decades, the overall trend has been a *higher level of economic freedom around the world*.

Most Economic Freedom	Least Economic Freedom
1. Hong Kong	167. Timor-Leste
2. Singapore	168. Democratic Republic of Congo
3. New Zealand	169. Argentina
4. Switzerland	170. Equatorial Guinea
5. Australia	171. Iran
6. Canada	172. Republic of Congo
7. Chile	173. Eritrea
8. Ireland	174. Turkmenistan
9. Estonia	175. Zimbabwe
10. United Kingdom	176. Venezuela
11. United States	177. Cuba
12. Denmark	178. North Korea

Table 1.1 Economic Freedoms, 2016   (Source: The Heritage Foundation, 2016 Index of Economic Freedom, Country Rankings, http://www.heritage.org/index/ranking)

Regulations: The Rules of the Game

Markets and government regulations are always entangled. There is no such thing as an absolutely free market. Regulations always define the "rules of the game" in the economy. Economies that are primarily market-oriented have fewer regulations—ideally just enough to maintain an even playing field for participants. At a minimum, these laws govern matters like safeguarding private property against theft, protecting people from violence, enforcing legal contracts, preventing fraud, and collecting taxes. Conversely, even the most command-oriented economies operate using markets. How else would buying and selling occur? The government heavily regulates decisions of what to produce and prices to charge. Heavily regulated economies often have **underground economies** (or black markets), which are markets where the buyers and sellers make transactions without the government's approval.

The question of how to organize economic institutions is typically not a black-or-white choice between all market or all government, but instead involves a balancing act over the appropriate combination of market freedom and government rules.

This OpenStax book is available for free at http://cnx.org/content/col12122/1.4

Figure 1.9 Globalization Cargo ships are one mode of transportation for shipping goods in the global economy. (Credit: Raul Valdez/Flickr Creative Commons)

The Rise of Globalization

Recent decades have seen a trend toward **globalization**, which is the expanding cultural, political, and economic connections between people around the world. One measure of this is the increased buying and selling of goods, services, and assets across national borders—in other words, international trade and financial capital flows.

Globalization has occurred for a number of reasons. Improvements in shipping, as illustrated by the container ship in **Figure 1.9**, and air cargo have driven down transportation costs. Innovations in computing and telecommunications have made it easier and cheaper to manage long-distance economic connections of production and sales. Many valuable products and services in the modern economy can take the form of information—for example: computer software; financial advice; travel planning; music, books and movies; and blueprints for designing a building. These products and many others can be transported over telephones and computer networks at ever-lower costs. Finally, international agreements and treaties between countries have encouraged greater trade.

Table 1.2 presents one measure of globalization. It shows the percentage of domestic economic production that was exported for a selection of countries from 2010 to 2015, according to an entity known as The World Bank. **Exports** are the goods and services that one produces domestically and sells abroad. **Imports** are the goods and services that one produces abroad and then sells domestically. **Gross domestic product (GDP)** measures the size of total production in an economy. Thus, the ratio of exports divided by GDP measures what share of a country's total economic production is sold in other countries.

Country	2010	2011	2012	2013	2014	2015
Higher Income Countries						
United States	12.4	13.6	13.6	13.5	13.5	12.6
Belgium	76.2	81.4	82.2	82.8	84.0	84.4
Canada	29.1	30.7	30.0	30.1	31.7	31.5
France	26.0	27.8	28.1	28.3	29.0	30.0
Middle Income Countries						
Brazil	10.9	11.9	12.6	12.6	11.2	13.0
Mexico	29.9	31.2	32.6	31.7	32.3	35.3
South Korea	49.4	55.7	56.3	53.9	50.3	45.9

Table 1.2 The Extent of Globalization (exports/GDP)   (Source: http://databank.worldbank.org/data/)

Country	2010	2011	2012	2013	2014	2015
Lower Income Countries						
Chad	36.8	38.9	36.9	32.2	34.2	29.8
China	29.4	28.5	27.3	26.4	23.9	22.4
India	22.0	23.9	24.0	24.8	22.9	-
Nigeria	25.3	31.3	31.4	18.0	18.4	-

Table 1.2 The Extent of Globalization (exports/GDP)   (Source: http://databank.worldbank.org/data/)

In recent decades, the export/GDP ratio has generally risen, both worldwide and for the U.S. economy. Interestingly, the share of U.S. exports in proportion to the U.S. economy is well below the global average, in part because large economies like the United States can contain more of the division of labor inside their national borders. However, smaller economies like Belgium, Korea, and Canada need to trade across their borders with other countries to take full advantage of division of labor, specialization, and economies of scale. In this sense, the enormous U.S. economy is less affected by globalization than most other countries.

Table 1.2 indicates that many medium and low income countries around the world, like Mexico and China, have also experienced a surge of globalization in recent decades. If an astronaut in orbit could put on special glasses that make all economic transactions visible as brightly colored lines and look down at Earth, the astronaut would see the planet covered with connections.

Despite the rise in globalization over the last few decades, in recent years we've seen significant pushback against globalization from people across the world concerned about loss of jobs, loss of political sovereignty, and increased economic inequality. Prominent examples of this pushback include the 2016 vote in Great Britain to exit the European Union (i.e. Brexit), and the election of Donald J. Trump for President of the United States.

Hopefully, you now have an idea about economics. Before you move to any other chapter of study, be sure to read the very important appendix to this chapter called **The Use of Mathematics in Principles of Economics**. It is essential that you learn more about how to read and use models in economics.

Bring it Home

Decisions ... Decisions in the Social Media Age

The world we live in today provides nearly instant access to a wealth of information. Consider that as recently as the late 1970s, the *Farmer's Almanac*, along with the Weather Bureau of the U.S. Department of Agriculture, were the primary sources American farmers used to determine when to plant and harvest their crops. Today, farmers are more likely to access, online, weather forecasts from the National Oceanic and Atmospheric Administration or watch the Weather Channel. After all, knowing the upcoming forecast could drive when to harvest crops. Consequently, knowing the upcoming weather could change the amount of crop harvested.

Some relatively new information forums, such as Facebook, are rapidly changing how information is distributed; hence, influencing decision making. In 2014, the Pew Research Center reported that 71% of online adults use Facebook. This social media forum posts topics ranging from the National Basketball Association, to celebrity singers and performers, to farmers.

Information helps us make decisions as simple as what to wear today to how many reporters the media should send to cover a crash. Each of these decisions is an economic decision. After all, resources are scarce. If the media send ten reporters to cover an accident, they are not available to cover other stories or complete other tasks. Information provides the necessary knowledge to make the best possible decisions on how to utilize scarce resources. Welcome to the world of economics!

KEY TERMS

circular flow diagram a diagram that views the economy as consisting of households and firms interacting in a goods and services market and a labor market

command economy an economy where economic decisions are passed down from government authority and where the government owns the resources

division of labor the way in which different workers divide required tasks to produce a good or service

economics the study of how humans make choices under conditions of scarcity

economies of scale when the average cost of producing each individual unit declines as total output increases

exports products (goods and services) made domestically and sold abroad

fiscal policy economic policies that involve government spending and taxes

globalization the trend in which buying and selling in markets have increasingly crossed national borders

goods and services market a market in which firms are sellers of what they produce and households are buyers

gross domestic product (GDP) measure of the size of total production in an economy

imports products (goods and services) made abroad and then sold domestically

labor market the market in which households sell their labor as workers to business firms or other employers

macroeconomics the branch of economics that focuses on broad issues such as growth, unemployment, inflation, and trade balance

market interaction between potential buyers and sellers; a combination of demand and supply

market economy an economy where economic decisions are decentralized, private individuals own resources, and businesses supply goods and services based on demand

microeconomics the branch of economics that focuses on actions of particular agents within the economy, like households, workers, and business firms

model see theory

monetary policy policy that involves altering the level of interest rates, the availability of credit in the economy, and the extent of borrowing

private enterprise system where private individuals or groups of private individuals own and operate the means of production (resources and businesses)

scarcity when human wants for goods and services exceed the available supply

specialization when workers or firms focus on particular tasks for which they are well-suited within the overall production process

theory a representation of an object or situation that is simplified while including enough of the key features to help us understand the object or situation

traditional economy typically an agricultural economy where things are done the same as they have always been done

underground economy a market where the buyers and sellers make transactions in violation of one or more government regulations

KEY CONCEPTS AND SUMMARY

1.1 What Is Economics, and Why Is It Important?

Economics seeks to solve the problem of scarcity, which is when human wants for goods and services exceed the available supply. A modern economy displays a division of labor, in which people earn income by specializing in what they produce and then use that income to purchase the products they need or want. The division of labor allows individuals and firms to specialize and to produce more for several reasons: a) It allows the agents to focus on areas of advantage due to natural factors and skill levels; b) It encourages the agents to learn and invent; c) It allows agents to take advantage of economies of scale. Division and specialization of labor only work when individuals can purchase what they do not produce in markets. Learning about economics helps you understand the major problems facing the world today, prepares you to be a good citizen, and helps you become a well-rounded thinker.

1.2 Microeconomics and Macroeconomics

Microeconomics and macroeconomics are two different perspectives on the economy. The microeconomic perspective focuses on parts of the economy: individuals, firms, and industries. The macroeconomic perspective looks at the economy as a whole, focusing on goals like growth in the standard of living, unemployment, and inflation. Macroeconomics has two types of policies for pursuing these goals: monetary policy and fiscal policy.

1.3 How Economists Use Theories and Models to Understand Economic Issues

Economists analyze problems differently than do other disciplinary experts. The main tools economists use are economic theories or models. A theory is not an illustration of the answer to a problem. Rather, a theory is a tool for determining the answer.

1.4 How To Organize Economies: An Overview of Economic Systems

We can organize societies as traditional, command, or market-oriented economies. Most societies are a mix. The last few decades have seen globalization evolve as a result of growth in commercial and financial networks that cross national borders, making businesses and workers from different economies increasingly interdependent.

SELF-CHECK QUESTIONS

1. What is scarcity? Can you think of two causes of scarcity?

2. Residents of the town of Smithfield like to consume hams, but each ham requires 10 people to produce it and takes a month. If the town has a total of 100 people, what is the maximum amount of ham the residents can consume in a month?

3. A consultant works for $200 per hour. She likes to eat vegetables, but is not very good at growing them. Why does it make more economic sense for her to spend her time at the consulting job and shop for her vegetables?

4. A computer systems engineer could paint his house, but it makes more sense for him to hire a painter to do it. Explain why.

5. What would be another example of a "system" in the real world that could serve as a metaphor for micro and macroeconomics?

6. Suppose we extend the circular flow model to add imports and exports. Copy the circular flow diagram onto a sheet of paper and then add a foreign country as a third agent. Draw a rough sketch of the flows of imports, exports, and the payments for each on your diagram.

7. What is an example of a problem in the world today, not mentioned in the chapter, that has an economic dimension?

This OpenStax book is available for free at http://cnx.org/content/col12122/1.4

8. The chapter defines *private enterprise* as a characteristic of market-oriented economies. What would *public enterprise* be? *Hint*: It is a characteristic of command economies.

9. Why might Belgium, France, Italy, and Sweden have a higher export to GDP ratio than the United States?

REVIEW QUESTIONS

10. Give the three reasons that explain why the division of labor increases an economy's level of production.

11. What are three reasons to study economics?

12. What is the difference between microeconomics and macroeconomics?

13. What are examples of individual economic agents?

14. What are the three main goals of macroeconomics?

15. How did John Maynard Keynes define economics?

16. Are households primarily buyers or sellers in the goods and services market? In the labor market?

17. Are firms primarily buyers or sellers in the goods and services market? In the labor market?

18. What are the three ways that societies can organize themselves economically?

19. What is globalization? How do you think it might have affected the economy over the past decade?

CRITICAL THINKING QUESTIONS

20. Suppose you have a team of two workers: one is a baker and one is a chef. Explain why the kitchen can produce more meals in a given period of time if each worker specializes in what they do best than if each worker tries to do everything from appetizer to dessert.

21. Why would division of labor without trade not work?

22. Can you think of any examples of *free* goods, that is, goods or services that are not scarce?

23. A balanced federal budget and a balance of trade are secondary goals of macroeconomics, while growth in the standard of living (for example) is a primary goal. Why do you think that is so?

24. Macroeconomics is an aggregate of what happens at the microeconomic level. Would it be possible for what happens at the macro level to differ from how economic agents would react to some stimulus at the micro level? *Hint:* Think about the behavior of crowds.

25. Why is it unfair or meaningless to criticize a theory as "unrealistic?"

26. Suppose, as an economist, you are asked to analyze an issue unlike anything you have ever done before. Also, suppose you do not have a specific model for analyzing that issue. What should you do? *Hint:* What would a carpenter do in a similar situation?

27. Why do you think that most modern countries' economies are a mix of command and market types?

28. Can you think of ways that globalization has helped you economically? Can you think of ways that it has not?

This OpenStax book is available for free at http://cnx.org/content/col12122/1.4

2 | Choice in a World of Scarcity

Figure 2.1 Choices and Tradeoffs In general, the higher the degree, the higher the salary, so why aren't more people pursuing higher degrees? The short answer: choices and tradeoffs. (Credit: modification of work by "Jim, the Photographer"/Flickr Creative Commons)

Bring it Home

Choices ... To What Degree?

In 2015, the median income for workers who hold master's degrees varies from males to females. The average of the two is $2,951 weekly. Multiply this average by 52 weeks, and you get an average salary of $153,452. Compare that to the median weekly earnings for a full-time worker over 25 with no higher than a bachelor's degree: $1,224 weekly and $63,648 a year. What about those with no higher than a high school diploma in 2015? They earn just $664 weekly and $34,528 over 12 months. In other words, says the Bureau of Labor Statistics (BLS), earning a bachelor's degree boosted salaries 54% over what you would have earned if you had stopped your education after high school. A master's degree yields a salary almost double that of a high school diploma.

Given these statistics, we might expect many people to choose to go to college and at least earn a bachelor's degree. Assuming that people want to improve their material well-being, it seems like they would make those choices that provide them with the greatest opportunity to consume goods and services. As it turns out, the analysis is not nearly as simple as this. In fact, in 2014, the BLS reported that while almost 88% of the population in the United States had a high school diploma, only 33.6% of 25–65 year olds had bachelor's degrees, and only 7.4% of 25–65 year olds in 2014 had earned a master's.

This brings us to the subject of this chapter: why people make the choices they make and how economists explain those choices.

Introduction to Choice in a World of Scarcity

In this chapter, you will learn about:

- How Individuals Make Choices Based on Their Budget Constraint

- The Production Possibilities Frontier and Social Choices

- Confronting Objections to the Economic Approach

You will learn quickly when you examine the relationship between economics and scarcity that choices involve tradeoffs. Every choice has a cost.

In 1968, the Rolling Stones recorded "You Can't Always Get What You Want." Economists chuckled, because they had been singing a similar tune for decades. English economist Lionel Robbins (1898–1984), in his *Essay on the Nature and Significance of Economic Science* in 1932, described not always getting what you want in this way:

> The time at our disposal is limited. There are only twenty-four hours in the day. We have to choose between the different uses to which they may be put. ... Everywhere we turn, if we choose one thing we must relinquish others which, in different circumstances, we would wish not to have relinquished. Scarcity of means to satisfy given ends is an almost ubiquitous condition of human nature.

Because people live in a world of scarcity, they cannot have all the time, money, possessions, and experiences they wish. Neither can society.

This chapter will continue our discussion of scarcity and the economic way of thinking by first introducing three critical concepts: opportunity cost, marginal decision making, and diminishing returns. Later, it will consider whether the economic way of thinking accurately describes either how we *make* choices and how we *should* make them.

2.1 | How Individuals Make Choices Based on Their Budget Constraint

By the end of this section, you will be able to:
- Calculate and graph budget constraints
- Explain opportunity sets and opportunity costs
- Evaluate the law of diminishing marginal utility
- Explain how marginal analysis and utility influence choices

Consider the typical consumer's budget problem. Consumers have a limited amount of income to spend on the things they need and want. Suppose Alphonso has $10 in spending money each week that he can allocate between bus tickets for getting to work and the burgers that he eats for lunch. Burgers cost $2 each, and bus tickets are 50 cents each. We can see Alphonso's budget problem in **Figure 2.2**.

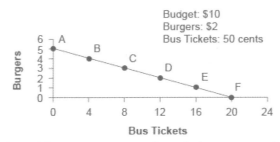

Figure 2.2 The Budget Constraint: Alphonso's Consumption Choice Opportunity Frontier Each point on the budget constraint represents a combination of burgers and bus tickets whose total cost adds up to Alphonso's budget of $10. The relative price of burgers and bus tickets determines the slope of the budget constraint. All along the budget set, giving up one burger means gaining four bus tickets.

The vertical axis in the figure shows burger purchases and the horizontal axis shows bus ticket purchases. If Alphonso spends all his money on burgers, he can afford five per week. ($10 per week/$2 per burger = 5 burgers per week.) However, if he does this, he will not be able to afford any bus tickets. Point A in the figure shows the choice (zero bus tickets and five burgers). Alternatively, if Alphonso spends all his money on bus tickets, he can afford 20 per week. ($10 per week/$0.50 per bus ticket = 20 bus tickets per week.) Then, however, he will not be able to afford any burgers. Point F shows this alternative choice (20 bus tickets and zero burgers).

If we connect all the points between A and F, we get Alphonso's **budget constraint**. This indicates all the combination of burgers and bus tickets Alphonso can afford, given the price of the two goods and his budget amount.

If Alphonso is like most people, he will choose some combination that includes both bus tickets and burgers. That is, he will choose some combination on the budget constraint that is between points A and F. Every point on (or inside) the constraint shows a combination of burgers and bus tickets that Alphonso can afford. Any point outside the constraint is not affordable, because it would cost more money than Alphonso has in his budget.

The budget constraint clearly shows the tradeoff Alphonso faces in choosing between burgers and bus tickets. Suppose he is currently at point D, where he can afford 12 bus tickets and two burgers. What would it cost Alphonso for one more burger? It would be natural to answer $2, but that's not the way economists think. Instead they ask, how many bus tickets would Alphonso have to give up to get one more burger, while staying within his budget? Since bus tickets cost 50 cents, Alphonso would have to give up four to afford one more burger. That is the true cost to Alphonso.

The Concept of Opportunity Cost

Economists use the term **opportunity cost** to indicate what one must give up to obtain what he or she desires. The idea behind opportunity cost is that the cost of one item is the lost opportunity to do or consume something else. In short, opportunity cost is the value of the next best alternative. For Alphonso, the opportunity cost of a burger is the four bus tickets he would have to give up. He would decide whether or not to choose the burger depending on whether the value of the burger exceeds the value of the forgone alternative—in this case, bus tickets. Since people must choose, they inevitably face tradeoffs in which they have to give up things they desire to obtain other things they desire more.

Link It Up

View this website (http://openstaxcollege.org/l/linestanding) for an example of opportunity cost—paying someone else to wait in line for you.

A fundamental principle of economics is that every choice has an opportunity cost. If you sleep through your economics class, the opportunity cost is the learning you miss from not attending class. If you spend your income on video games, you cannot spend it on movies. If you choose to marry one person, you give up the opportunity to marry anyone else. In short, opportunity cost is all around us and part of human existence.

The following Work It Out feature shows a step-by-step analysis of a budget constraint calculation. Read through it to understand another important concept—slope—that we further explain in the appendix **The Use of Mathematics in Principles of Economics**.

Work It Out ─O─O─O

Understanding Budget Constraints

Budget constraints are easy to understand if you apply a little math. The appendix **The Use of Mathematics in Principles of Economics** explains all the math you are likely to need in this book. Therefore, if math is not your strength, you might want to take a look at the appendix.

Step 1: The equation for any budget constraint is:

$$\text{Budget} = P_1 \times Q_1 + P_2 \times Q_2$$

where P and Q are the price and quantity of items purchased (which we assume here to be two items) and Budget is the amount of income one has to spend.

Step 2. Apply the budget constraint equation to the scenario. In Alphonso's case, this works out to be:

$$
\begin{aligned}
\text{Budget} &= P_1 \times Q_1 + P_2 \times Q_2 \\
\$10 \text{ budget} &= \$2 \text{ per burger} \times \text{quantity of burgers} + \$0.50 \text{ per bus ticket} \times \text{quantity of bus tickets} \\
\$10 &= \$2 \times Q_{\text{burgers}} + \$0.50 \times Q_{\text{bus tickets}}
\end{aligned}
$$

Step 3. Using a little algebra, we can turn this into the familiar equation of a line:

$$y = b + mx$$

For Alphonso, this is:

$$\$10 = \$2 \times Q_{\text{burgers}} + \$0.50 \times Q_{\text{bus tickets}}$$

Step 4. Simplify the equation. Begin by multiplying both sides of the equation by 2:

$$
\begin{aligned}
2 \times 10 &= 2 \times 2 \times Q_{\text{burgers}} + 2 \times 0.5 \times Q_{\text{bus tickets}} \\
20 &= 4 \times Q_{\text{burgers}} + 1 \times Q_{\text{bus tickets}}
\end{aligned}
$$

Step 5. Subtract one bus ticket from both sides:

$$20 - Q_{\text{bus tickets}} = 4 \times Q_{\text{burgers}}$$

Divide each side by 4 to yield the answer:

$$5 - 0.25 \times Q_{\text{bus tickets}} = Q_{\text{burgers}}$$
$$\text{or}$$
$$Q_{\text{burgers}} = 5 - 0.25 \times Q_{\text{bus tickets}}$$

Step 6. Notice that this equation fits the budget constraint in **Figure 2.2**. The vertical intercept is 5 and the slope is –0.25, just as the equation says. If you plug 20 bus tickets into the equation, you get 0 burgers. If you plug other numbers of bus tickets into the equation, you get the results (see **Table 2.1**), which are the points on Alphonso's budget constraint.

Point	Quantity of Burgers (at $2)	Quantity of Bus Tickets (at 50 cents)
A	5	0
B	4	4
C	3	8
D	2	12

Table 2.1

Point	Quantity of Burgers (at $2)	Quantity of Bus Tickets (at 50 cents)
E	1	16
F	0	20

Table 2.1

Step 7. Notice that the slope of a budget constraint always shows the opportunity cost of the good which is on the horizontal axis. For Alphonso, the slope is −0.25, indicating that for every bus ticket he buys, he must give up 1/4 burger. To phrase it differently, for every four tickets he buys, Alphonso must give up 1 burger.

There are two important observations here. First, the algebraic sign of the slope is negative, which means that the only way to get more of one good is to give up some of the other. Second, we define the slope as the price of bus tickets (whatever is on the horizontal axis in the graph) divided by the price of burgers (whatever is on the vertical axis), in this case $0.50/$2 = 0.25. If you want to determine the opportunity cost quickly, just divide the two prices.

Identifying Opportunity Cost

In many cases, it is reasonable to refer to the opportunity cost as the price. If your cousin buys a new bicycle for $300, then $300 measures the amount of "other consumption" that he has forsaken. For practical purposes, there may be no special need to identify the specific alternative product or products that he could have bought with that $300, but sometimes the price as measured in dollars may not accurately capture the true opportunity cost. This problem can loom especially large when costs of time are involved.

For example, consider a boss who decides that all employees will attend a two-day retreat to "build team spirit." The out-of-pocket monetary cost of the event may involve hiring an outside consulting firm to run the retreat, as well as room and board for all participants. However, an opportunity cost exists as well: during the two days of the retreat, none of the employees are doing any other work.

Attending college is another case where the opportunity cost exceeds the monetary cost. The out-of-pocket costs of attending college include tuition, books, room and board, and other expenses. However, in addition, during the hours that you are attending class and studying, it is impossible to work at a paying job. Thus, college imposes both an out-of-pocket cost and an opportunity cost of lost earnings.

Clear It Up

What is the opportunity cost associated with increased airport security measures?

After the terrorist plane hijackings on September 11, 2001, many steps were proposed to improve air travel safety. For example, the federal government could provide armed "sky marshals" who would travel inconspicuously with the rest of the passengers. The cost of having a sky marshal on every flight would be roughly $3 billion per year. Retrofitting all U.S. planes with reinforced cockpit doors to make it harder for terrorists to take over the plane would have a price tag of $450 million. Buying more sophisticated security equipment for airports, like three-dimensional baggage scanners and cameras linked to face recognition software, could cost another $2 billion.

However, the single biggest cost of greater airline security does not involve spending money. It is the opportunity cost of additional waiting time at the airport. According to the United States Department of Transportation (DOT), there were 895.5 million systemwide (domestic and international) scheduled service passengers in 2015. Since the 9/11 hijackings, security screening has become more intensive, and consequently, the procedure takes longer than in the past. Say that, on average, each air passenger spends an extra 30 minutes in the airport per trip. Economists commonly place a value on time to convert an opportunity cost in time into a monetary figure. Because many air travelers are relatively high-paid business people, conservative estimates set the average price of time for air travelers at $20 per hour. By these back-of-the-envelope calculations, the opportunity cost of delays in airports could be as much as 800 million × 0.5 hours × $20/hour, or $8 billion per year. Clearly, the opportunity costs of waiting time can be just as important as costs that involve direct spending.

In some cases, realizing the opportunity cost can alter behavior. Imagine, for example, that you spend $8 on lunch every day at work. You may know perfectly well that bringing a lunch from home would cost only $3 a day, so the opportunity cost of buying lunch at the restaurant is $5 each day (that is, the $8 buying lunch costs minus the $3 your lunch from home would cost). Five dollars each day does not seem to be that much. However, if you project what that adds up to in a year—250 days a year × $5 per day equals $1,250, the cost, perhaps, of a decent vacation. If you describe the opportunity cost as "a nice vacation" instead of "$5 a day," you might make different choices.

Marginal Decision-Making and Diminishing Marginal Utility

The budget constraint framework helps to emphasize that most choices in the real world are not about getting all of one thing or all of another; that is, they are not about choosing either the point at one end of the budget constraint or else the point all the way at the other end. Instead, most choices involve **marginal analysis**, which means examining the benefits and costs of choosing a little more or a little less of a good. People naturally compare costs and benefits, but often we look at total costs and total benefits, when the optimal choice necessitates comparing how costs and benefits change from one option to another. You might think of marginal analysis as "change analysis." Marginal analysis is used throughout economics.

We now turn to the notion of **utility**. People desire goods and services for the satisfaction or utility those goods and services provide. Utility, as we will see in the chapter on **Consumer Choices**, is subjective but that does not make it less real. Economists typically assume that the more of some good one consumes (for example, slices of pizza), the more utility one obtains. At the same time, the utility a person receives from consuming the first unit of a good is typically more than the utility received from consuming the fifth or the tenth unit of that same good. When Alphonso chooses between burgers and bus tickets, for example, the first few bus rides that he chooses might provide him with a great deal of utility—perhaps they help him get to a job interview or a doctor's appointment. However, later bus rides might provide much less utility—they may only serve to kill time on a rainy day. Similarly, the first burger that Alphonso chooses to buy may be on a day when he missed breakfast and is ravenously hungry. However, if Alphonso has a burger every single day, the last few burgers may taste pretty boring. The general pattern that consumption of the first few units of any good tends to bring a higher level of utility to a person than consumption of later units is a common pattern. Economists refer to this pattern as the **law of diminishing marginal utility**, which means that as a person receives more of a good, the additional (or marginal) utility from each additional unit of the good declines. In other words, the first slice of pizza brings more satisfaction than the sixth.

The law of diminishing marginal utility explains why people and societies rarely make all-or-nothing choices. You would not say, "My favorite food is ice cream, so I will eat nothing but ice cream from now on." Instead, even if you get a very high level of utility from your favorite food, if you ate it exclusively, the additional or marginal utility from those last few servings would not be very high. Similarly, most workers do not say: "I enjoy leisure, so I'll never work." Instead, workers recognize that even though some leisure is very nice, a combination of all leisure and no income is not so attractive. The budget constraint framework suggests that when people make choices in a world of scarcity, they will use marginal analysis and think about whether they would prefer a little more or a little less.

A rational consumer would only purchase additional units of some product as long as the marginal utility exceeds the opportunity cost. Suppose Alphonso moves down his budget constraint from Point A to Point B to Point C and further. As he consumes more bus tickets, the marginal utility of bus tickets will diminish, while the opportunity cost, that is, the marginal utility of foregone burgers, will increase. Eventually, the opportunity cost will exceed the marginal utility of an additional bus ticket. If Alphonso is rational, he won't purchase more bus tickets once the marginal utility just equals the opportunity cost. While we can't (yet) say exactly how many bus tickets Alphonso will buy, that number is unlikely to be the most he can afford, 20.

Sunk Costs

In the budget constraint framework, all decisions involve what will happen next: that is, what quantities of goods will you consume, how many hours will you work, or how much will you save. These decisions do not look back to past choices. Thus, the budget constraint framework assumes that **sunk costs**, which are costs that were incurred in the past and cannot be recovered, should not affect the current decision.

Consider the case of Selena, who pays $8 to see a movie, but after watching the film for 30 minutes, she knows that it is truly terrible. Should she stay and watch the rest of the movie because she paid for the ticket, or should she leave? The money she spent is a sunk cost, and unless the theater manager is sympathetic, Selena will not get a refund. However, staying in the movie still means paying an opportunity cost in time. Her choice is whether to spend the next 90 minutes suffering through a cinematic disaster or to do something—anything—else. The lesson of sunk costs is to forget about the money and time that is irretrievably gone and instead to focus on the marginal costs and benefits of current and future options.

For people and firms alike, dealing with sunk costs can be frustrating. It often means admitting an earlier error in judgment. Many firms, for example, find it hard to give up on a new product that is doing poorly because they spent so much money in creating and launching the product. However, the lesson of sunk costs is to ignore them and make decisions based on what will happen in the future.

From a Model with Two Goods to One of Many Goods

The budget constraint diagram containing just two goods, like most models used in this book, is not realistic. After all, in a modern economy people choose from thousands of goods. However, thinking about a model with many goods is a straightforward extension of what we discussed here. Instead of drawing just one budget constraint, showing the tradeoff between two goods, you can draw multiple budget constraints, showing the possible tradeoffs between many different pairs of goods. In more advanced classes in economics, you would use mathematical equations that include many possible goods and services that can be purchased, together with their quantities and prices, and show how the total spending on all goods and services is limited to the overall budget available. The graph with two goods that we presented here clearly illustrates that every choice has an opportunity cost, which is the point that does carry over to the real world.

2.2 | The Production Possibilities Frontier and Social Choices

By the end of this section, you will be able to:
- Interpret production possibilities frontier graphs
- Contrast a budget constraint and a production possibilities frontier
- Explain the relationship between a production possibilities frontier and the law of diminishing returns
- Contrast productive efficiency and allocative efficiency
- Define comparative advantage

Just as individuals cannot have everything they want and must instead make choices, society as a whole cannot have everything it might want, either. This section of the chapter will explain the constraints society faces, using a model called the **production possibilities frontier (PPF)**. There are more similarities than differences between individual choice and social choice. As you read this section, focus on the similarities.

Because society has limited resources (e.g., labor, land, capital, raw materials) at any point in time, there is a limit to the quantities of goods and services it can produce. Suppose a society desires two products, healthcare and education. The production possibilities frontier in **Figure 2.3** illustrates this situation.

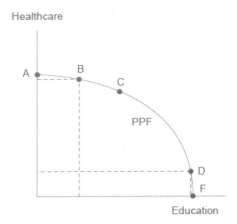

Figure 2.3 A Healthcare vs. Education Production Possibilities Frontier   This production possibilities frontier shows a tradeoff between devoting social resources to healthcare and devoting them to education. At A all resources go to healthcare and at B, most go to healthcare. At D most resources go to education, and at F, all go to education.

Figure 2.3 shows healthcare on the vertical axis and education on the horizontal axis. If the society were to allocate all of its resources to healthcare, it could produce at point A. However, it would not have any resources to produce education. If it were to allocate all of its resources to education, it could produce at point F. Alternatively, the society could choose to produce any combination of healthcare and education on the production possibilities frontier. In effect, the production possibilities frontier plays the same role for society as the budget constraint plays for Alphonso. Society can choose any combination of the two goods on or inside the PPF. However, it does not have enough resources to produce outside the PPF.

Most importantly, the production possibilities frontier clearly shows the tradeoff between healthcare and education. Suppose society has chosen to operate at point B, and it is considering producing more education. Because the PPF is downward sloping from left to right, the only way society can obtain more education is by giving up some healthcare. That is the tradeoff society faces. Suppose it considers moving from point B to point C. What would the opportunity cost be for the additional education? The opportunity cost would be the healthcare society has to forgo. Just as with Alphonso's budget constraint, the **slope** of the production possibilities frontier shows the opportunity cost. By now you might be saying, "Hey, this PPF is sounding like the budget constraint." If so, read the following Clear It Up feature.

What's the difference between a budget constraint and a PPF?

There are two major differences between a budget constraint and a production possibilities frontier. The first is the fact that the budget constraint is a straight line. This is because its slope is given by the relative prices of the two goods, which from the point of view of an individual consumer, are fixed, so the slope doesn't change. In contrast, the PPF has a curved shape because of the law of the diminishing returns. Thus, the slope is different at various points on the PPF. The second major difference is the absence of specific numbers on the axes of the PPF. There are no specific numbers because we do not know the exact amount of resources this imaginary economy has, nor do we know how many resources it takes to produce healthcare and how many resources it takes to produce education. If this were a real world example, that data would be available.

Whether or not we have specific numbers, conceptually we can measure the opportunity cost of additional education as society moves from point B to point C on the PPF. We measure the additional education by the horizontal distance between B and C. The foregone healthcare is given by the vertical distance between B and C. The slope of the PPF between B and C is (approximately) the vertical distance (the "rise") over the horizontal distance (the "run"). This is the opportunity cost of the additional education.

The Shape of the PPF and the Law of Diminishing Returns

The budget constraints that we presented earlier in this chapter, showing individual choices about what quantities of goods to consume, were all straight lines. The reason for these straight lines was that the relative prices of the two goods in the **consumption budget constraint** determined the slope of the budget constraint. However, we drew the production possibilities frontier for healthcare and education as a curved line. Why does the PPF have a different shape?

To understand why the PPF is curved, start by considering point A at the top left-hand side of the PPF. At point A, all available resources are devoted to healthcare and none are left for education. This situation would be extreme and even ridiculous. For example, children are seeing a doctor every day, whether they are sick or not, but not attending school. People are having cosmetic surgery on every part of their bodies, but no high school or college education exists. Now imagine that some of these resources are diverted from healthcare to education, so that the economy is at point B instead of point A. Diverting some resources away from A to B causes relatively little reduction in health because the last few marginal dollars going into healthcare services are not producing much additional gain in health. However, putting those marginal dollars into education, which is completely without resources at point A, can produce relatively large gains. For this reason, the shape of the PPF from A to B is relatively flat, representing a relatively small drop-off in health and a relatively large gain in education.

Now consider the other end, at the lower right, of the production possibilities frontier. Imagine that society starts at choice D, which is devoting nearly all resources to education and very few to healthcare, and moves to point F, which is devoting *all* spending to education and none to healthcare. For the sake of concreteness, you can imagine that in the movement from D to F, the last few doctors must become high school science teachers, the last few nurses must become school librarians rather than dispensers of vaccinations, and the last few emergency rooms are turned into kindergartens. The gains to education from adding these last few resources to education are very small. However, the opportunity cost lost to health will be fairly large, and thus the slope of the PPF between D and F is steep, showing a large drop in health for only a small gain in education.

The lesson is not that society is likely to make an extreme choice like devoting no resources to education at point A or no resources to health at point F. Instead, the lesson is that the gains from committing additional marginal resources to education depend on how much is already being spent. If on the one hand, very few resources are currently committed to education, then an increase in resources used can bring relatively large gains. On the other hand, if a large number of resources are already committed to education, then committing additional resources will bring relatively smaller gains.

This pattern is common enough that economists have given it a name: the **law of diminishing returns**, which holds that as additional increments of resources are added to a certain purpose, the marginal benefit from those additional increments will decline. (The law of diminishing marginal utility that we introduced in the last section is a more specific case of the law of diminishing returns.) When government spends a certain amount more on reducing crime, for example, the original gains in reducing crime could be relatively large. However, additional increases typically cause relatively smaller reductions in crime, and paying for enough police and security to reduce crime to nothing at all would be tremendously expensive.

The curvature of the production possibilities frontier shows that as we add more resources to education, moving from left to right along the horizontal axis, the original gains are fairly large, but gradually diminish. Thus, the slope of the PPF is relatively flat. By contrast, as we add more resources to healthcare, moving from bottom to top on the vertical axis, the original gains are fairly large, but again gradually diminish. Thus, the slope of the PPF is relatively steep. In this way, the law of diminishing returns produces the outward-bending shape of the production possibilities frontier.

Productive Efficiency and Allocative Efficiency

The study of economics does not presume to tell a society what choice it should make along its production possibilities frontier. In a market-oriented economy with a democratic government, the choice will involve a mixture of decisions by individuals, firms, and government. However, economics can point out that some choices are unambiguously better than others. This observation is based on the concept of efficiency. In everyday usage, efficiency refers to lack of waste. An inefficient machine operates at high cost, while an efficient machine operates at lower cost, because it is not wasting energy or materials. An inefficient organization operates with long delays and high costs, while an efficient organization meets schedules, is focused, and performs within budget.

The production possibilities frontier can illustrate two kinds of efficiency: productive efficiency and allocative efficiency. **Figure 2.4** illustrates these ideas using a production possibilities frontier between healthcare and education.

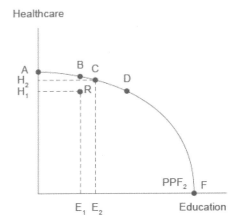

Figure 2.4 Productive and Allocative Efficiency   Productive efficiency means it is impossible to produce more of one good without decreasing the quantity that is produced of another good. Thus, all choices along a given PPF like B, C, and D display productive efficiency, but R does not. Allocative efficiency means that the particular mix of goods being produced—that is, the specific choice along the production possibilities frontier—represents the allocation that society most desires.

Productive efficiency means that, given the available inputs and technology, it is impossible to produce more of one good without decreasing the quantity that is produced of another good. All choices on the PPF in **Figure 2.4**, including A, B, C, D, and F, display productive efficiency. As a firm moves from any one of these choices to any other, either healthcare increases and education decreases or vice versa. However, any choice inside the production possibilities frontier is productively inefficient and wasteful because it is possible to produce more of one good, the other good, or some combination of both goods.

For example, point R is productively inefficient because it is possible at choice C to have more of both goods: education on the horizontal axis is higher at point C than point R (E_2 is greater than E_1), and healthcare on the vertical axis is also higher at point C than point R (H_2 is great than H_1).

We can show the particular mix of goods and services produced—that is, the specific combination of selected healthcare and education along the production possibilities frontier—as a ray (line) from the origin to a specific point on the PPF. Output mixes that had more healthcare (and less education) would have a steeper ray, while those with more education (and less healthcare) would have a flatter ray.

Allocative efficiency means that the particular combination of goods and services on the production possibility curve that a society produces represents the combination that society most desires. How to determine what a society desires can be a controversial question, and is usually a discussion in political science, sociology, and philosophy classes as well as in economics. At its most basic, allocative efficiency means producers supply the quantity of each product that consumers demand. Only one of the productively efficient choices will be the allocatively efficient choice for society as a whole.

Why Society Must Choose

In **Welcome to Economics!** we learned that every society faces the problem of scarcity, where limited resources conflict with unlimited needs and wants. The production possibilities curve illustrates the choices involved in this dilemma.

Every economy faces two situations in which it may be able to expand consumption of all goods. In the first case, a society may discover that it has been using its resources inefficiently, in which case by improving efficiency and producing on the production possibilities frontier, it can have more of all goods (or at least more of some and less of none). In the second case, as resources grow over a period of years (e.g., more labor and more capital), the economy grows. As it does, the production possibilities frontier for a society will tend to shift outward and society will be able to afford more of all goods.

This OpenStax book is available for free at http://cnx.org/content/col12122/1.4

However, improvements in productive efficiency take time to discover and implement, and economic growth happens only gradually. Thus, a society must choose between tradeoffs in the present. For government, this process often involves trying to identify where additional spending could do the most good and where reductions in spending would do the least harm. At the individual and firm level, the market economy coordinates a process in which firms seek to produce goods and services in the quantity, quality, and price that people want. However, for both the government and the market economy in the short term, increases in production of one good typically mean offsetting decreases somewhere else in the economy.

The PPF and Comparative Advantage

While every society must choose how much of each good or service it should produce, it does not need to produce every single good it consumes. Often how much of a good a country decides to produce depends on how expensive it is to produce it versus buying it from a different country. As we saw earlier, the curvature of a country's PPF gives us information about the tradeoff between devoting resources to producing one good versus another. In particular, its slope gives the opportunity cost of producing one more unit of the good in the x-axis in terms of the other good (in the y-axis). Countries tend to have different opportunity costs of producing a specific good, either because of different climates, geography, technology, or skills.

Suppose two countries, the US and Brazil, need to decide how much they will produce of two crops: sugar cane and wheat. Due to its climatic conditions, Brazil can produce quite a bit of sugar cane per acre but not much wheat. Conversely, the U.S. can produce large amounts of wheat per acre, but not much sugar cane. Clearly, Brazil has a lower opportunity cost of producing sugar cane (in terms of wheat) than the U.S. The reverse is also true: the U.S. has a lower opportunity cost of producing wheat than Brazil. We illustrate this by the PPFs of the two countries in Figure 2.5.

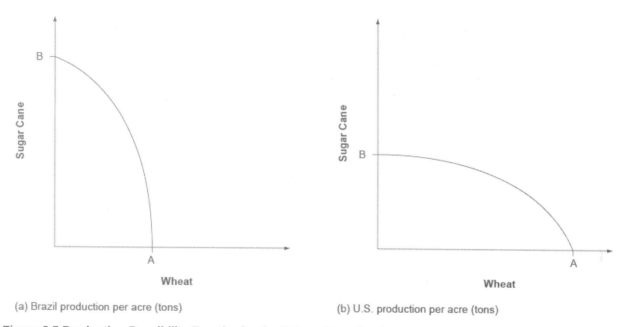

(a) Brazil production per acre (tons)   (b) U.S. production per acre (tons)

Figure 2.5 Production Possibility Frontier for the U.S. and Brazil   The U.S. PPF is flatter than the Brazil PPF implying that the opportunity cost of wheat in terms of sugar cane is lower in the U.S. than in Brazil. Conversely, the opportunity cost of sugar cane is lower in Brazil. The U.S. has comparative advantage in wheat and Brazil has comparative advantage in sugar cane.

When a country can produce a good at a lower opportunity cost than another country, we say that this country has a **comparative advantage** in that good. Comparative advantage is not the same as absolute advantage, which is when a country can produce more of a good. Comparative advantage is not the same as absolute advantage, which is when a country can produce more of a good. In our example, Brazil has an absolute advantage in sugar cane and the U.S. has an absolute advantage in wheat. One can easily see this with a simple observation of the extreme production points in the PPFs of the two countries. If Brazil devoted all of its resources to producing wheat, it would be producing at point A. If however it had devoted all of its resources to producing sugar cane instead, it would be producing a much larger amount than the U.S., at point B.

The slope of the PPF gives the opportunity cost of producing an additional unit of wheat. While the slope is not constant throughout the PPFs, it is quite apparent that the PPF in Brazil is much steeper than in the U.S., and therefore the opportunity cost of wheat generally higher in Brazil. In the chapter on **International Trade** you will learn that countries' differences in comparative advantage determine which goods they will choose to produce and trade. When countries engage in trade, they specialize in the production of the goods in which they have comparative advantage, and trade part of that production for goods in which they do not have comparative advantage. With trade, manufacturers produce goods where the opportunity cost is lowest, so total production increases, benefiting both trading parties.

2.3 | Confronting Objections to the Economic Approach

By the end of this section, you will be able to:
- Analyze arguments against economic approaches to decision-making
- Interpret a tradeoff diagram
- Contrast normative statements and positive statements

It is one thing to understand the economic approach to decision-making and another thing to feel comfortable applying it. The sources of discomfort typically fall into two categories: that people do not act in the way that fits the economic way of thinking, and that even if people did act that way, they should try not to. Let's consider these arguments in turn.

First Objection: People, Firms, and Society Do Not Act Like This

The economic approach to decision-making seems to require more information than most individuals possess and more careful decision-making than most individuals actually display. After all, do you or any of your friends draw a budget constraint and mutter to yourself about maximizing utility before you head to the shopping mall? Do members of the U.S. Congress contemplate production possibilities frontiers before they vote on the annual budget? The messy ways in which people and societies operate somehow doesn't look much like neat budget constraints or smoothly curving production possibilities frontiers.

However, the economics approach can be a useful way to analyze and understand the tradeoffs of economic decisions. To appreciate this point, imagine for a moment that you are playing basketball, dribbling to the right, and throwing a bounce-pass to the left to a teammate who is running toward the basket. A physicist or engineer could work out the correct speed and trajectory for the pass, given the different movements involved and the weight and bounciness of the ball. However, when you are playing basketball, you do not perform any of these calculations. You just pass the ball, and if you are a good player, you will do so with high accuracy.

Someone might argue: "The scientist's formula of the bounce-pass requires a far greater knowledge of physics and far more specific information about speeds of movement and weights than the basketball player actually has, so it must be an unrealistic description of how basketball passes actually occur." This reaction would be wrongheaded. The fact that a good player can throw the ball accurately because of practice and skill, without making a physics calculation, does not mean that the physics calculation is wrong.

Similarly, from an economic point of view, someone who shops for groceries every week has a great deal of practice with how to purchase the combination of goods that will provide that person with utility, even if the shopper does not phrase decisions in terms of a budget constraint. Government institutions may work imperfectly and slowly, but in general, a democratic form of government feels pressure from voters and social institutions to make the choices that are most widely preferred by people in that society. Thus, when thinking about the economic actions of groups of people, firms, and society, it is reasonable, as a first approximation, to analyze them with the tools of economic analysis. For more on this, read about behavioral economics in the chapter on **Consumer Choices**.

Second Objection: People, Firms, and Society Should Not Act This Way

The economics approach portrays people as self-interested. For some critics of this approach, even if self-interest is an accurate description of how people behave, these behaviors are not moral. Instead, the critics argue that people should be taught to care more deeply about others. Economists offer several answers to these concerns.

This OpenStax book is available for free at http://cnx.org/content/col12122/1.4

First, economics is not a form of moral instruction. Rather, it seeks to describe economic behavior as it actually exists. Philosophers draw a distinction between **positive statements**, which describe the world as it is, and **normative statements**, which describe how the world should be. Positive statements are factual. They may be true or false, but we can test them, at least in principle. Normative statements are subjective questions of opinion. We cannot test them since we cannot prove opinions to be true or false. They just are opinions based on one's values. For example, an economist could analyze a proposed subway system in a certain city. If the expected benefits exceed the costs, he concludes that the project is worthy—an example of positive analysis. Another economist argues for extended unemployment compensation during the Great Depression because a rich country like the United States should take care of its less fortunate citizens—an example of normative analysis.

Even if the line between positive and normative statements is not always crystal clear, economic analysis does try to remain rooted in the study of the actual people who inhabit the actual economy. Fortunately however, the assumption that individuals are purely self-interested is a simplification about human nature. In fact, we need to look no further than to Adam Smith, the very father of modern economics to find evidence of this. The opening sentence of his book, *The Theory of Moral Sentiments*, puts it very clearly: "How selfish soever man may be supposed, there are evidently some principles in his nature, which interest him in the fortune of others, and render their happiness necessary to him, though he derives nothing from it except the pleasure of seeing it." Clearly, individuals are both self-interested and altruistic.

Second, we can label self-interested behavior and profit-seeking with other names, such as personal choice and freedom. The ability to make personal choices about buying, working, and saving is an important personal freedom. Some people may choose high-pressure, high-paying jobs so that they can earn and spend considerable amounts of money on themselves. Others may allocate large portions of their earnings to charity or spend it on their friends and family. Others may devote themselves to a career that can require much time, energy, and expertise but does not offer high financial rewards, like being an elementary school teacher or a social worker. Still others may choose a job that does consume much of their time or provide a high level of income, but still leaves time for family, friends, and contemplation. Some people may prefer to work for a large company; others might want to start their own business. People's freedom to make their own economic choices has a moral value worth respecting.

Is a diagram by any other name the same?

When you study economics, you may feel buried under an avalanche of diagrams. Your goal should be to recognize the common underlying logic and pattern of the diagrams, not to memorize each one.

This chapter uses only one basic diagram, although we present it with different sets of labels. The consumption budget constraint and the production possibilities frontier for society, as a whole, are the same basic diagram. **Figure 2.6** shows an individual budget constraint and a production possibilities frontier for two goods, Good 1 and Good 2. The tradeoff diagram always illustrates three basic themes: scarcity, tradeoffs, and economic efficiency.

The first theme is scarcity. It is not feasible to have unlimited amounts of both goods. Even if the budget constraint or a PPF shifts, scarcity remains—just at a different level. The second theme is tradeoffs. As depicted in the budget constraint or the production possibilities frontier, it is necessary to forgo some of one good to gain more of the other good. The details of this tradeoff vary. In a budget constraint we determine, the tradeoff is determined by the relative prices of the goods: that is, the relative price of two goods in the consumption choice budget constraint. These tradeoffs appear as a straight line. However, a curved line represents the tradeoffs in many production possibilities frontiers because the law of diminishing returns holds that as we add resources to an area, the marginal gains tend to diminish. Regardless of the specific shape, tradeoffs remain.

The third theme is economic efficiency, or getting the most benefit from scarce resources. All choices on the production possibilities frontier show productive efficiency because in such cases, there is no way to increase the quantity of one good without decreasing the quantity of the other. Similarly, when an individual makes a choice along a budget constraint, there is no way to increase the quantity of one good without decreasing the quantity of the other. The choice on a production possibilities set that is socially preferred, or the choice on an individual's budget constraint that is personally preferred, will display allocative efficiency.

The basic budget constraint/production possibilities frontier diagram will recur throughout this book. Some examples include using these tradeoff diagrams to analyze trade, environmental protection and economic output, equality of incomes and economic output, and the macroeconomic tradeoff between consumption and investment. Do not allow the different labels to confuse you. The budget constraint/production possibilities frontier diagram is always just a tool for thinking carefully about scarcity, tradeoffs, and efficiency in a particular situation.

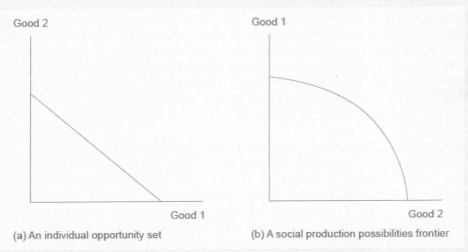

Figure 2.6 The Tradeoff Diagram   Both the individual opportunity set (or budget constraint) and the social production possibilities frontier show the constraints under which individual consumers and society as a whole operate. Both diagrams show the tradeoff in choosing more of one good at the cost of less of the other.

Third, self-interested behavior can lead to positive social results. For example, when people work hard to make a living, they create economic output. Consumers who are looking for the best deals will encourage businesses to offer goods and services that meet their needs. Adam Smith, writing in *The Wealth of Nations*, named this property the **invisible hand**. In describing how consumers and producers interact in a market economy, Smith wrote:

> Every individual…generally, indeed, neither intends to promote the public interest, nor knows how much he is promoting it. By preferring the support of domestic to that of foreign industry, he intends only his own security; and by directing that industry in such a manner as its produce may be of the greatest value, he intends only his own gain. And he is in this, as in many other cases, led by an invisible hand to promote an end which was no part of his intention…By pursuing his own interest he frequently promotes that of the society more effectually than when he really intends to promote it.

The metaphor of the invisible hand suggests the remarkable possibility that broader social good can emerge from selfish individual actions.

Fourth, even people who focus on their own self-interest in the economic part of their life often set aside their own narrow self-interest in other parts of life. For example, you might focus on your own self-interest when asking your employer for a raise or negotiating to buy a car. Then you might turn around and focus on other people when you volunteer to read stories at the local library, help a friend move to a new apartment, or donate money to a charity. Self-interest is a reasonable starting point for analyzing many economic decisions, without needing to imply that people never do anything that is not in their own immediate self-interest.

This OpenStax book is available for free at http://cnx.org/content/col12122/1.4

Bring it Home

Choices ... To What Degree?

What have we learned? We know that scarcity impacts all the choices we make. An economist might argue that people do not obtain a bachelor's or master's degree because they do not have the resources to make those choices or because their incomes are too low and/or the price of these degrees is too high. A bachelor's or a master's degree may not be available in their opportunity set.

The price of these degrees may be too high not only because the actual price, college tuition (and perhaps room and board), is too high. An economist might also say that for many people, the full opportunity cost of a bachelor's or a master's degree is too high. For these people, they are unwilling or unable to make the tradeoff of forfeiting years of working, and earning an income to earn a degree.

Finally, the statistics we introduced at the start of the chapter reveal information about intertemporal choices. An economist might say that people choose not to obtain a college degree because they may have to borrow money to attend college, and the interest they have to pay on that loan in the future will affect their decisions today. Also, it could be that some people have a preference for current consumption over future consumption, so they choose to work now at a lower salary and consume now, rather than postponing that consumption until after they graduate college.

KEY TERMS

allocative efficiency when the mix of goods produced represents the mix that society most desires

budget constraint all possible consumption combinations of goods that someone can afford, given the prices of goods, when all income is spent; the boundary of the opportunity set

comparative advantage when a country can produce a good at a lower cost in terms of other goods; or, when a country has a lower opportunity cost of production

invisible hand Adam Smith's concept that individuals' self-interested behavior can lead to positive social outcomes

law of diminishing marginal utility as we consume more of a good or service, the utility we get from additional units of the good or service tends to become smaller than what we received from earlier units

law of diminishing returns as we add additional increments of resources to producing a good or service, the marginal benefit from those additional increments will decline

marginal analysis examination of decisions on the margin, meaning a little more or a little less from the status quo

normative statement statement which describes how the world should be

opportunity cost measures cost by what we give up/forfeit in exchange; opportunity cost measures the value of the forgone alternative

opportunity set all possible combinations of consumption that someone can afford given the prices of goods and the individual's income

positive statement statement which describes the world as it is

production possibilities frontier (PPF) a diagram that shows the productively efficient combinations of two products that an economy can produce given the resources it has available.

productive efficiency when it is impossible to produce more of one good (or service) without decreasing the quantity produced of another good (or service)

sunk costs costs that we make in the past that we cannot recover

utility satisfaction, usefulness, or value one obtains from consuming goods and services

KEY CONCEPTS AND SUMMARY

2.1 How Individuals Make Choices Based on Their Budget Constraint

Economists see the real world as one of scarcity: that is, a world in which people's desires exceed what is possible. As a result, economic behavior involves tradeoffs in which individuals, firms, and society must forgo something that they desire to obtain things that they desire more. Individuals face the tradeoff of what quantities of goods and services to consume. The budget constraint, which is the frontier of the opportunity set, illustrates the range of available choices. The relative price of the choices determines the slope of the budget constraint. Choices beyond the budget constraint are not affordable.

Opportunity cost measures cost by what we forgo in exchange. Sometimes we can measure opportunity cost in money, but it is often useful to consider time as well, or to measure it in terms of the actual resources that we must forfeit.

Most economic decisions and tradeoffs are not all-or-nothing. Instead, they involve marginal analysis, which means they are about decisions on the margin, involving a little more or a little less. The law of diminishing marginal utility points out that as a person receives more of something—whether it is a specific good or another resource—the

This OpenStax book is available for free at http://cnx.org/content/col12122/1.4

additional marginal gains tend to become smaller. Because sunk costs occurred in the past and cannot be recovered, they should be disregarded in making current decisions.

2.2 The Production Possibilities Frontier and Social Choices

A production possibilities frontier defines the set of choices society faces for the combinations of goods and services it can produce given the resources available. The shape of the PPF is typically curved outward, rather than straight. Choices outside the PPF are unattainable and choices inside the PPF are wasteful. Over time, a growing economy will tend to shift the PPF outwards.

The law of diminishing returns holds that as increments of additional resources are devoted to producing something, the marginal increase in output will become increasingly smaller. All choices along a production possibilities frontier display productive efficiency; that is, it is impossible to use society's resources to produce more of one good without decreasing production of the other good. The specific choice along a production possibilities frontier that reflects the mix of goods society prefers is the choice with allocative efficiency. The curvature of the PPF is likely to differ by country, which results in different countries having comparative advantage in different goods. Total production can increase if countries specialize in the goods in which they have comparative advantage and trade some of their production for the remaining goods.

2.3 Confronting Objections to the Economic Approach

The economic way of thinking provides a useful approach to understanding human behavior. Economists make the careful distinction between positive statements, which describe the world as it is, and normative statements, which describe how the world should be. Even when economics analyzes the gains and losses from various events or policies, and thus draws normative conclusions about how the world should be, the analysis of economics is rooted in a positive analysis of how people, firms, and governments actually behave, not how they should behave.

SELF-CHECK QUESTIONS

1. Suppose Alphonso's town raised the price of bus tickets to $1 per trip (while the price of burgers stayed at $2 and his budget remained $10 per week.) Draw Alphonso's new budget constraint. What happens to the opportunity cost of bus tickets?

2. Return to the example in **Figure 2.4**. Suppose there is an improvement in medical technology that enables more healthcare with the same amount of resources. How would this affect the production possibilities curve and, in particular, how would it affect the opportunity cost of education?

3. Could a nation be producing in a way that is allocatively efficient, but productively inefficient?

4. What are the similarities between a consumer's budget constraint and society's production possibilities frontier, not just graphically but analytically?

5. Individuals may not act in the rational, calculating way described by the economic model of decision making, measuring utility and costs at the margin, but can you make a case that they behave approximately that way?

6. Would an op-ed piece in a newspaper urging the adoption of a particular economic policy be a positive or normative statement?

7. Would a research study on the effects of soft drink consumption on children's cognitive development be a positive or normative statement?

REVIEW QUESTIONS

8. Explain why scarcity leads to tradeoffs.

9. Explain why individuals make choices that are directly on the budget constraint, rather than inside the budget constraint or outside it.

10. What is comparative advantage?

11. What does a production possibilities frontier illustrate?

12. Why is a production possibilities frontier typically drawn as a curve, rather than a straight line?

13. Explain why societies cannot make a choice above their production possibilities frontier and should not make a choice below it.

14. What are diminishing marginal returns?

15. What is productive efficiency? Allocative efficiency?

16. What is the difference between a positive and a normative statement?

17. Is the economic model of decision-making intended as a literal description of how individuals, firms, and the governments actually make decisions?

18. What are four responses to the claim that people should not behave in the way described in this chapter?

CRITICAL THINKING QUESTIONS

19. Suppose Alphonso's town raises the price of bus tickets from $0.50 to $1 and the price of burgers rises from $2 to $4. Why is the opportunity cost of bus tickets unchanged? Suppose Alphonso's weekly spending money increases from $10 to $20. How is his budget constraint affected from all three changes? Explain.

20. During the Second World War, Germany's factories were decimated. It also suffered many human casualties, both soldiers and civilians. How did the war affect Germany's production possibilities curve?

21. It is clear that productive inefficiency is a waste since resources are used in a way that produces less goods and services than a nation is capable of. Why is allocative inefficiency also wasteful?

22. What assumptions about the economy must be true for the invisible hand to work? To what extent are those assumptions valid in the real world?

23. Do economists have any particular expertise at making normative arguments? In other words, they have expertise at making positive statements (i.e., what *will* happen) about some economic policy, for example, but do they have special expertise to judge whether or not the policy *should* be undertaken?

PROBLEMS

Use this information to answer the following 4 questions: Marie has a weekly budget of $24, which she likes to spend on magazines and pies.

24. If the price of a magazine is $4 each, what is the maximum number of magazines she could buy in a week?

25. If the price of a pie is $12, what is the maximum number of pies she could buy in a week?

26. Draw Marie's budget constraint with pies on the horizontal axis and magazines on the vertical axis. What is the slope of the budget constraint?

27. What is Marie's opportunity cost of purchasing a pie?

This OpenStax book is available for free at http://cnx.org/content/col12122/1.4

3 | Demand and Supply

Figure 3.1 Farmer's Market Organic vegetables and fruits that are grown and sold within a specific geographical region should, in theory, cost less than conventional produce because the transportation costs are less. That is not, however, usually the case. (Credit: Modification of work by Natalie Maynor/Flickr Creative Commons)

Bring it Home

Why Can We Not Get Enough of Organic?

Organic food is increasingly popular, not just in the United States, but worldwide. At one time, consumers had to go to specialty stores or farmers' markets to find organic produce. Now it is available in most grocery stores. In short, organic is part of the mainstream.

Ever wonder why organic food costs more than conventional food? Why, say, does an organic Fuji apple cost $1.99 a pound, while its conventional counterpart costs $1.49 a pound? The same price relationship is true for just about every organic product on the market. If many organic foods are locally grown, would they not take less time to get to market and therefore be cheaper? What are the forces that keep those prices from coming down? Turns out those forces have quite a bit to do with this chapter's topic: demand and supply.

Introduction to Demand and Supply

In this chapter, you will learn about:

- Demand, Supply, and Equilibrium in Markets for Goods and Services

- Shifts in Demand and Supply for Goods and Services

- Changes in Equilibrium Price and Quantity: The Four-Step Process

- Price Ceilings and Price Floors

An auction bidder pays thousands of dollars for a dress Whitney Houston wore. A collector spends a small fortune for a few drawings by John Lennon. People usually react to purchases like these in two ways: their jaw drops because they think these are high prices to pay for such goods or they think these are rare, desirable items and the amount paid seems right.

Link It Up

Visit this website (http://openstaxcollege.org/l/celebauction) to read a list of bizarre items that have been purchased for their ties to celebrities. These examples represent an interesting facet of demand and supply.

When economists talk about prices, they are less interested in making judgments than in gaining a practical understanding of what determines prices and why prices change. Consider a price most of us contend with weekly: that of a gallon of gas. Why was the average price of gasoline in the United States $3.71 per gallon in June 2014? Why did the price for gasoline fall sharply to $1.96 per gallon by January 2016? To explain these price movements, economists focus on the determinants of what gasoline buyers are willing to pay and what gasoline sellers are willing to accept.

As it turns out, the price of gasoline in June of any given year is nearly always higher than the price in January of that same year. Over recent decades, gasoline prices in midsummer have averaged about 10 cents per gallon more than their midwinter low. The likely reason is that people drive more in the summer, and are also willing to pay more for gas, but that does not explain how steeply gas prices fell. Other factors were at work during those 18 months, such as increases in supply and decreases in the demand for crude oil.

This chapter introduces the economic model of demand and supply—one of the most powerful models in all of economics. The discussion here begins by examining how demand and supply determine the price and the quantity sold in markets for goods and services, and how changes in demand and supply lead to changes in prices and quantities.

3.1 | Demand, Supply, and Equilibrium in Markets for Goods and Services

By the end of this section, you will be able to:
- Explain demand, quantity demanded, and the law of demand
- Identify a demand curve and a supply curve
- Explain supply, quantity supplied, and the law of supply
- Explain equilibrium, equilibrium price, and equilibrium quantity

First let's first focus on what economists mean by demand, what they mean by supply, and then how demand and supply interact in a market.

Demand for Goods and Services

Economists use the term **demand** to refer to the amount of some good or service consumers are willing and able to purchase at each price. Demand is fundamentally based on needs and wants—if you have no need or want for something, you won't buy it. While a consumer may be able to differentiate between a need and a want, but from an economist's perspective they are the same thing. Demand is also based on ability to pay. If you cannot pay for it, you have no effective demand. By this definition, a homeless person probably has no effective demand for shelter.

What a buyer pays for a unit of the specific good or service is called **price**. The total number of units that consumers would purchase at that price is called the **quantity demanded**. A rise in price of a good or service almost always decreases the quantity demanded of that good or service. Conversely, a fall in price will increase the quantity demanded. When the price of a gallon of gasoline increases, for example, people look for ways to reduce their consumption by combining several errands, commuting by carpool or mass transit, or taking weekend or vacation trips closer to home. Economists call this inverse relationship between price and quantity demanded the **law of demand**. The law of demand assumes that all other variables that affect demand (which we explain in the next module) are held constant.

We can show an example from the market for gasoline in a table or a graph. Economist call a table that shows the quantity demanded at each price, such as **Table 3.1**, a **demand schedule**. In this case we measure price in dollars per gallon of gasoline. We measure the quantity demanded in millions of gallons over some time period (for example, per day or per year) and over some geographic area (like a state or a country). A **demand curve** shows the relationship between price and quantity demanded on a graph like **Figure 3.2**, with quantity on the horizontal axis and the price per gallon on the vertical axis. (Note that this is an exception to the normal rule in mathematics that the independent variable (x) goes on the horizontal axis and the dependent variable (y) goes on the vertical. Economics is not math.)

Table 3.1 shows the demand schedule and the graph in **Figure 3.2** shows the demand curve. These are two ways to describe the same relationship between price and quantity demanded.

Price (per gallon)	Quantity Demanded (millions of gallons)
$1.00	800
$1.20	700
$1.40	600
$1.60	550
$1.80	500
$2.00	460
$2.20	420

Table 3.1 Price and Quantity Demanded of Gasoline

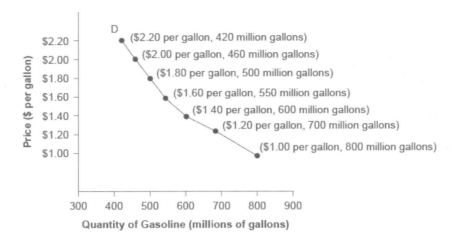

Figure 3.2 A Demand Curve for Gasoline The demand schedule shows that as price rises, quantity demanded decreases, and vice versa. We graph these points, and the line connecting them is the demand curve (D). The downward slope of the demand curve again illustrates the law of demand—the inverse relationship between prices and quantity demanded.

Demand curves will appear somewhat different for each product. They may appear relatively steep or flat, or they may be straight or curved. Nearly all demand curves share the fundamental similarity that they slope down from left to right. Demand curves embody the law of demand: As the price increases, the quantity demanded decreases, and conversely, as the price decreases, the quantity demanded increases.

Confused about these different types of demand? Read the next Clear It Up feature.

Is demand the same as quantity demanded?

In economic terminology, demand is not the same as quantity demanded. When economists talk about demand, they mean the relationship between a range of prices and the quantities demanded at those prices, as illustrated by a demand curve or a demand schedule. When economists talk about quantity demanded, they mean only a certain point on the demand curve, or one quantity on the demand schedule. In short, demand refers to the curve and quantity demanded refers to the (specific) point on the curve.

Supply of Goods and Services

When economists talk about **supply**, they mean the amount of some good or service a producer is willing to supply at each price. Price is what the producer receives for selling one unit of a good or service. A rise in price almost always leads to an increase in the **quantity supplied** of that good or service, while a fall in price will decrease the quantity supplied. When the price of gasoline rises, for example, it encourages profit-seeking firms to take several actions: expand exploration for oil reserves; drill for more oil; invest in more pipelines and oil tankers to bring the oil to plants for refining into gasoline; build new oil refineries; purchase additional pipelines and trucks to ship the gasoline to gas stations; and open more gas stations or keep existing gas stations open longer hours. Economists call this positive relationship between price and quantity supplied—that a higher price leads to a higher quantity supplied and a lower price leads to a lower quantity supplied—the **law of supply**. The law of supply assumes that all other variables that affect supply (to be explained in the next module) are held constant.

Still unsure about the different types of supply? See the following Clear It Up feature.

This OpenStax book is available for free at http://cnx.org/content/col12122/1.4

Clear It Up

Is supply the same as quantity supplied?

In economic terminology, supply is not the same as quantity supplied. When economists refer to supply, they mean the relationship between a range of prices and the quantities supplied at those prices, a relationship that we can illustrate with a supply curve or a supply schedule. When economists refer to quantity supplied, they mean only a certain point on the supply curve, or one quantity on the supply schedule. In short, supply refers to the curve and quantity supplied refers to the (specific) point on the curve.

Figure 3.3 illustrates the law of supply, again using the market for gasoline as an example. Like demand, we can illustrate supply using a table or a graph. A **supply schedule** is a table, like **Table 3.2**, that shows the quantity supplied at a range of different prices. Again, we measure price in dollars per gallon of gasoline and we measure quantity supplied in millions of gallons. A **supply curve** is a graphic illustration of the relationship between price, shown on the vertical axis, and quantity, shown on the horizontal axis. The supply schedule and the supply curve are just two different ways of showing the same information. Notice that the horizontal and vertical axes on the graph for the supply curve are the same as for the demand curve.

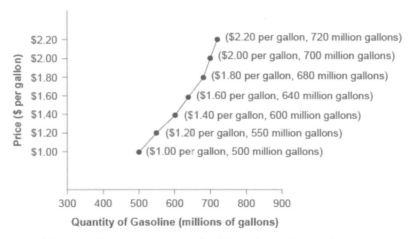

Figure 3.3 A Supply Curve for Gasoline The supply schedule is the table that shows quantity supplied of gasoline at each price. As price rises, quantity supplied also increases, and vice versa. The supply curve (S) is created by graphing the points from the supply schedule and then connecting them. The upward slope of the supply curve illustrates the law of supply—that a higher price leads to a higher quantity supplied, and vice versa.

Price (per gallon)	Quantity Supplied (millions of gallons)
$1.00	500
$1.20	550
$1.40	600
$1.60	640
$1.80	680
$2.00	700

Table 3.2 Price and Supply of Gasoline

Price (per gallon)	Quantity Supplied (millions of gallons)
$2.20	720

Table 3.2 Price and Supply of Gasoline

The shape of supply curves will vary somewhat according to the product: steeper, flatter, straighter, or curved. Nearly all supply curves, however, share a basic similarity: they slope up from left to right and illustrate the law of supply: as the price rises, say, from $1.00 per gallon to $2.20 per gallon, the quantity supplied increases from 500 gallons to 720 gallons. Conversely, as the price falls, the quantity supplied decreases.

Equilibrium—Where Demand and Supply Intersect

Because the graphs for demand and supply curves both have price on the vertical axis and quantity on the horizontal axis, the demand curve and supply curve for a particular good or service can appear on the same graph. Together, demand and supply determine the price and the quantity that will be bought and sold in a market.

Figure 3.4 illustrates the interaction of demand and supply in the market for gasoline. The demand curve (D) is identical to **Figure 3.2**. The supply curve (S) is identical to **Figure 3.3**. **Table 3.3** contains the same information in tabular form.

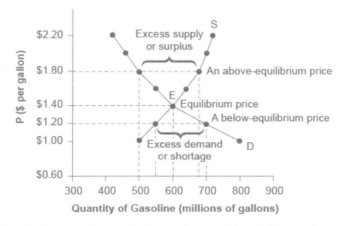

Figure 3.4 Demand and Supply for Gasoline   The demand curve (D) and the supply curve (S) intersect at the equilibrium point E, with a price of $1.40 and a quantity of 600. The equilibrium is the only price where quantity demanded is equal to quantity supplied. At a price above equilibrium like $1.80, quantity supplied exceeds the quantity demanded, so there is excess supply. At a price below equilibrium such as $1.20, quantity demanded exceeds quantity supplied, so there is excess demand.

Price (per gallon)	Quantity demanded (millions of gallons)	Quantity supplied (millions of gallons)
$1.00	800	500
$1.20	700	550
$1.40	**600**	**600**
$1.60	550	640
$1.80	500	680

Table 3.3 Price, Quantity Demanded, and Quantity Supplied

Price (per gallon)	Quantity demanded (millions of gallons)	Quantity supplied (millions of gallons)
$2.00	460	700
$2.20	420	720

Table 3.3 Price, Quantity Demanded, and Quantity Supplied

Remember this: When two lines on a diagram cross, this intersection usually means something. The point where the supply curve (S) and the demand curve (D) cross, designated by point E in **Figure 3.4**, is called the **equilibrium**. The **equilibrium price** is the only price where the plans of consumers and the plans of producers agree—that is, where the amount of the product consumers want to buy (quantity demanded) is equal to the amount producers want to sell (quantity supplied). Economists call this common quantity the **equilibrium quantity**. At any other price, the quantity demanded does not equal the quantity supplied, so the market is not in equilibrium at that price.

In **Figure 3.4**, the equilibrium price is $1.40 per gallon of gasoline and the equilibrium quantity is 600 million gallons. If you had only the demand and supply schedules, and not the graph, you could find the equilibrium by looking for the price level on the tables where the quantity demanded and the quantity supplied are equal.

The word "equilibrium" means "balance." If a market is at its equilibrium price and quantity, then it has no reason to move away from that point. However, if a market is not at equilibrium, then economic pressures arise to move the market toward the equilibrium price and the equilibrium quantity.

Imagine, for example, that the price of a gallon of gasoline was above the equilibrium price—that is, instead of $1.40 per gallon, the price is $1.80 per gallon. The dashed horizontal line at the price of $1.80 in **Figure 3.4** illustrates this above equilibrium price. At this higher price, the quantity demanded drops from 600 to 500. This decline in quantity reflects how consumers react to the higher price by finding ways to use less gasoline.

Moreover, at this higher price of $1.80, the quantity of gasoline supplied rises from the 600 to 680, as the higher price makes it more profitable for gasoline producers to expand their output. Now, consider how quantity demanded and quantity supplied are related at this above-equilibrium price. Quantity demanded has fallen to 500 gallons, while quantity supplied has risen to 680 gallons. In fact, at any above-equilibrium price, the quantity supplied exceeds the quantity demanded. We call this an **excess supply** or a **surplus**.

With a surplus, gasoline accumulates at gas stations, in tanker trucks, in pipelines, and at oil refineries. This accumulation puts pressure on gasoline sellers. If a surplus remains unsold, those firms involved in making and selling gasoline are not receiving enough cash to pay their workers and to cover their expenses. In this situation, some producers and sellers will want to cut prices, because it is better to sell at a lower price than not to sell at all. Once some sellers start cutting prices, others will follow to avoid losing sales. These price reductions in turn will stimulate a higher quantity demanded. Therefore, if the price is above the equilibrium level, incentives built into the structure of demand and supply will create pressures for the price to fall toward the equilibrium.

Now suppose that the price is below its equilibrium level at $1.20 per gallon, as the dashed horizontal line at this price in **Figure 3.4** shows. At this lower price, the quantity demanded increases from 600 to 700 as drivers take longer trips, spend more minutes warming up the car in the driveway in wintertime, stop sharing rides to work, and buy larger cars that get fewer miles to the gallon. However, the below-equilibrium price reduces gasoline producers' incentives to produce and sell gasoline, and the quantity supplied falls from 600 to 550.

When the price is below equilibrium, there is **excess demand**, or a **shortage**—that is, at the given price the quantity demanded, which has been stimulated by the lower price, now exceeds the quantity supplied, which had been depressed by the lower price. In this situation, eager gasoline buyers mob the gas stations, only to find many stations running short of fuel. Oil companies and gas stations recognize that they have an opportunity to make higher profits by selling what gasoline they have at a higher price. As a result, the price rises toward the equilibrium level. Read **Demand, Supply, and Efficiency** for more discussion on the importance of the demand and supply model.

3.2 | Shifts in Demand and Supply for Goods and

Services

By the end of this section, you will be able to:
- Identify factors that affect demand
- Graph demand curves and demand shifts
- Identify factors that affect supply
- Graph supply curves and supply shifts

The previous module explored how price affects the quantity demanded and the quantity supplied. The result was the demand curve and the supply curve. Price, however, is not the only factor that influences demand, nor is it the only thing that influences supply. For example, how is demand for vegetarian food affected if, say, health concerns cause more consumers to avoid eating meat? How is the supply of diamonds affected if diamond producers discover several new diamond mines? What are the major factors, in addition to the price, that influence demand or supply?

Visit this website (http://openstaxcollege.org/l/toothfish) to read a brief note on how marketing strategies can influence supply and demand of products.

What Factors Affect Demand?

We defined demand as the amount of some product a consumer is willing and able to purchase at each price. That suggests at least two factors in addition to price that affect demand. Willingness to purchase suggests a desire, based on what economists call tastes and preferences. If you neither need nor want something, you will not buy it. Ability to purchase suggests that income is important. Professors are usually able to afford better housing and transportation than students, because they have more income. Prices of related goods can affect demand also. If you need a new car, the price of a Honda may affect your demand for a Ford. Finally, the size or composition of the population can affect demand. The more children a family has, the greater their demand for clothing. The more driving-age children a family has, the greater their demand for car insurance, and the less for diapers and baby formula.

These factors matter for both individual and market demand as a whole. Exactly how do these various factors affect demand, and how do we show the effects graphically? To answer those questions, we need the *ceteris paribus* assumption.

The *Ceteris Paribus* Assumption

A demand curve or a supply curve is a relationship between two, and only two, variables: quantity on the horizontal axis and price on the vertical axis. The assumption behind a demand curve or a supply curve is that no relevant economic factors, other than the product's price, are changing. Economists call this assumption **ceteris paribus**, a Latin phrase meaning "other things being equal." Any given demand or supply curve is based on the *ceteris paribus* assumption that all else is held equal. A demand curve or a supply curve is a relationship between two, and only two, variables when all other variables are kept constant. If all else is not held equal, then the laws of supply and demand will not necessarily hold, as the following Clear It Up feature shows.

When does *ceteris paribus* apply?

We typically apply *ceteris paribus* when we observe how changes in price affect demand or supply, but we can apply *ceteris paribus* more generally. In the real world, demand and supply depend on more factors than just price. For example, a consumer's demand depends on income and a producer's supply depends on the cost of producing the product. How can we analyze the effect on demand or supply if multiple factors are changing at the same time—say price rises and income falls? The answer is that we examine the changes one at a time, assuming the other factors are held constant.

For example, we can say that an increase in the price reduces the amount consumers will buy (assuming income, and anything else that affects demand, is unchanged). Additionally, a decrease in income reduces the amount consumers can afford to buy (assuming price, and anything else that affects demand, is unchanged). This is what the *ceteris paribus* assumption really means. In this particular case, after we analyze each factor separately, we can combine the results. The amount consumers buy falls for two reasons: first because of the higher price and second because of the lower income.

How Does Income Affect Demand?

Let's use income as an example of how factors other than price affect demand. **Figure 3.5** shows the initial demand for automobiles as D_0. At point Q, for example, if the price is $20,000 per car, the quantity of cars demanded is 18 million. D_0 also shows how the quantity of cars demanded would change as a result of a higher or lower price. For example, if the price of a car rose to $22,000, the quantity demanded would decrease to 17 million, at point R.

The original demand curve D_0, like every demand curve, is based on the *ceteris paribus* assumption that no other economically relevant factors change. Now imagine that the economy expands in a way that raises the incomes of many people, making cars more affordable. How will this affect demand? How can we show this graphically?

Return to **Figure 3.5**. The price of cars is still $20,000, but with higher incomes, the quantity demanded has now increased to 20 million cars, shown at point S. As a result of the higher income levels, the demand curve shifts to the right to the new demand curve D_1, indicating an increase in demand. **Table 3.4** shows clearly that this increased demand would occur at every price, not just the original one.

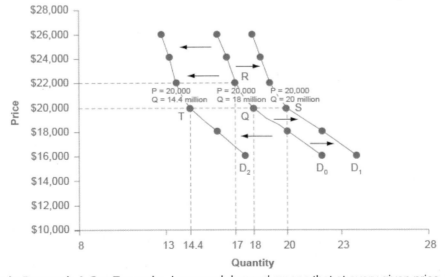

Figure 3.5 Shifts in Demand: A Car Example   Increased demand means that at every given price, the quantity demanded is higher, so that the demand curve shifts to the right from D_0 to D_1. Decreased demand means that at every given price, the quantity demanded is lower, so that the demand curve shifts to the left from D_0 to D_2.

Price	Decrease to D_2	Original Quantity Demanded D_0	Increase to D_1
$16,000	17.6 million	22.0 million	24.0 million
$18,000	16.0 million	20.0 million	22.0 million
$20,000	14.4 million	18.0 million	20.0 million
$22,000	13.6 million	17.0 million	19.0 million
$24,000	13.2 million	16.5 million	18.5 million
$26,000	12.8 million	16.0 million	18.0 million

Table 3.4 Price and Demand Shifts: A Car Example

Now, imagine that the economy slows down so that many people lose their jobs or work fewer hours, reducing their incomes. In this case, the decrease in income would lead to a lower quantity of cars demanded at every given price, and the original demand curve D_0 would shift left to D_2. The shift from D_0 to D_2 represents such a decrease in demand: At any given price level, the quantity demanded is now lower. In this example, a price of $20,000 means 18 million cars sold along the original demand curve, but only 14.4 million sold after demand fell.

When a demand curve shifts, it does not mean that the quantity demanded by every individual buyer changes by the same amount. In this example, not everyone would have higher or lower income and not everyone would buy or not buy an additional car. Instead, a shift in a demand curve captures a pattern for the market as a whole.

In the previous section, we argued that higher income causes greater demand at every price. This is true for most goods and services. For some—luxury cars, vacations in Europe, and fine jewelry—the effect of a rise in income can be especially pronounced. A product whose demand rises when income rises, and vice versa, is called a **normal good**. A few exceptions to this pattern do exist. As incomes rise, many people will buy fewer generic brand groceries and more name brand groceries. They are less likely to buy used cars and more likely to buy new cars. They will be less likely to rent an apartment and more likely to own a home. A product whose demand falls when income rises, and vice versa, is called an **inferior good**. In other words, when income increases, the demand curve shifts to the left.

Other Factors That Shift Demand Curves

Income is not the only factor that causes a shift in demand. Other factors that change demand include tastes and preferences, the composition or size of the population, the prices of related goods, and even expectations. A change in any one of the underlying factors that determine what quantity people are willing to buy at a given price will cause a shift in demand. Graphically, the new demand curve lies either to the right (an increase) or to the left (a decrease) of the original demand curve. Let's look at these factors.

Changing Tastes or Preferences

From 1980 to 2014, the per-person consumption of chicken by Americans rose from 48 pounds per year to 85 pounds per year, and consumption of beef fell from 77 pounds per year to 54 pounds per year, according to the U.S. Department of Agriculture (USDA). Changes like these are largely due to movements in taste, which change the quantity of a good demanded at every price: that is, they shift the demand curve for that good, rightward for chicken and leftward for beef.

Changes in the Composition of the Population

The proportion of elderly citizens in the United States population is rising. It rose from 9.8% in 1970 to 12.6% in 2000, and will be a projected (by the U.S. Census Bureau) 20% of the population by 2030. A society with relatively more children, like the United States in the 1960s, will have greater demand for goods and services like tricycles and day care facilities. A society with relatively more elderly persons, as the United States is projected to have by 2030, has a higher demand for nursing homes and hearing aids. Similarly, changes in the size of the population can affect the demand for housing and many other goods. Each of these changes in demand will be shown as a shift in the demand curve.

Changes in the prices of related goods such as substitutes or complements also can affect the demand for a product. A

This OpenStax book is available for free at http://cnx.org/content/col12122/1.4

substitute is a good or service that we can use in place of another good or service. As electronic books, like this one, become more available, you would expect to see a decrease in demand for traditional printed books. A lower price for a substitute decreases demand for the other product. For example, in recent years as the price of tablet computers has fallen, the quantity demanded has increased (because of the law of demand). Since people are purchasing tablets, there has been a decrease in demand for laptops, which we can show graphically as a leftward shift in the demand curve for laptops. A higher price for a substitute good has the reverse effect.

Other goods are **complements** for each other, meaning we often use the goods together, because consumption of one good tends to enhance consumption of the other. Examples include breakfast cereal and milk; notebooks and pens or pencils, golf balls and golf clubs; gasoline and sport utility vehicles; and the five-way combination of bacon, lettuce, tomato, mayonnaise, and bread. If the price of golf clubs rises, since the quantity demanded of golf clubs falls (because of the law of demand), demand for a complement good like golf balls decreases, too. Similarly, a higher price for skis would shift the demand curve for a complement good like ski resort trips to the left, while a lower price for a complement has the reverse effect.

Changes in Expectations about Future Prices or Other Factors that Affect Demand

While it is clear that the price of a good affects the quantity demanded, it is also true that expectations about the future price (or expectations about tastes and preferences, income, and so on) can affect demand. For example, if people hear that a hurricane is coming, they may rush to the store to buy flashlight batteries and bottled water. If people learn that the price of a good like coffee is likely to rise in the future, they may head for the store to stock up on coffee now. We show these changes in demand as shifts in the curve. Therefore, a **shift in demand** happens when a change in some economic factor (other than price) causes a different quantity to be demanded at every price. The following Work It Out feature shows how this happens.

Work It Out ⊙—⊙—⊙

Shift in Demand

A shift in demand means that at any price (and at every price), the quantity demanded will be different than it was before. Following is an example of a shift in demand due to an income increase.

Step 1. Draw the graph of a demand curve for a normal good like pizza. Pick a price (like P_0). Identify the corresponding Q_0. See an example in **Figure 3.6**.

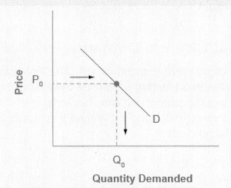

Figure 3.6 Demand Curve   We can use the demand curve to identify how much consumers would buy at any given price.

Step 2. Suppose income increases. As a result of the change, are consumers going to buy more or less pizza? The answer is more. Draw a dotted horizontal line from the chosen price, through the original quantity demanded, to the new point with the new Q_1. Draw a dotted vertical line down to the horizontal axis and label the new Q_1. **Figure 3.7** provides an example.

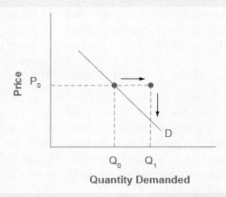

Figure 3.7 Demand Curve with Income Increase   With an increase in income, consumers will purchase larger quantities, pushing demand to the right.

Step 3. Now, shift the curve through the new point. You will see that an increase in income causes an upward (or rightward) shift in the demand curve, so that at any price the quantities demanded will be higher, as **Figure 3.8** illustrates.

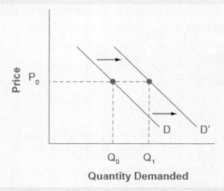

Figure 3.8 Demand Curve Shifted Right   With an increase in income, consumers will purchase larger quantities, pushing demand to the right, and causing the demand curve to shift right.

Summing Up Factors That Change Demand

Figure 3.9 summarizes six factors that can shift demand curves. The direction of the arrows indicates whether the demand curve shifts represent an increase in demand or a decrease in demand. Notice that a change in the price of the good or service itself is not listed among the factors that can shift a demand curve. A change in the price of a good or service causes a movement along a specific demand curve, and it typically leads to some change in the quantity demanded, but it does not shift the demand curve.

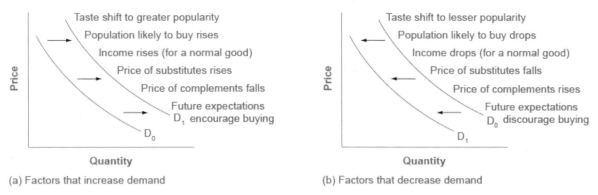

Figure 3.9 Factors That Shift Demand Curves (a) A list of factors that can cause an increase in demand from D_0 to D_1. (b) The same factors, if their direction is reversed, can cause a decrease in demand from D_0 to D_1.

When a demand curve shifts, it will then intersect with a given supply curve at a different equilibrium price and quantity. We are, however, getting ahead of our story. Before discussing how changes in demand can affect equilibrium price and quantity, we first need to discuss shifts in supply curves.

How Production Costs Affect Supply

A supply curve shows how quantity supplied will change as the price rises and falls, assuming *ceteris paribus* so that no other economically relevant factors are changing. If other factors relevant to supply do change, then the entire supply curve will shift. Just as we described a shift in demand as a change in the quantity demanded at every price, a **shift in supply** means a change in the quantity supplied at every price.

In thinking about the factors that affect supply, remember what motivates firms: profits, which are the difference between revenues and costs. A firm produces goods and services using combinations of labor, materials, and machinery, or what we call **inputs** or **factors of production**. If a firm faces lower costs of production, while the prices for the good or service the firm produces remain unchanged, a firm's profits go up. When a firm's profits increase, it is more motivated to produce output, since the more it produces the more profit it will earn. When costs of production fall, a firm will tend to supply a larger quantity at any given price for its output. We can show this by the supply curve shifting to the right.

Take, for example, a messenger company that delivers packages around a city. The company may find that buying gasoline is one of its main costs. If the price of gasoline falls, then the company will find it can deliver messages more cheaply than before. Since lower costs correspond to higher profits, the messenger company may now supply more of its services at any given price. For example, given the lower gasoline prices, the company can now serve a greater area, and increase its supply.

Conversely, if a firm faces higher costs of production, then it will earn lower profits at any given selling price for its products. As a result, a higher cost of production typically causes a firm to supply a smaller quantity at any given price. In this case, the supply curve shifts to the left.

Consider the supply for cars, shown by curve S_0 in **Figure 3.10**. Point J indicates that if the price is $20,000, the quantity supplied will be 18 million cars. If the price rises to $22,000 per car, *ceteris paribus*, the quantity supplied will rise to 20 million cars, as point K on the S_0 curve shows. We can show the same information in table form, as in **Table 3.5**.

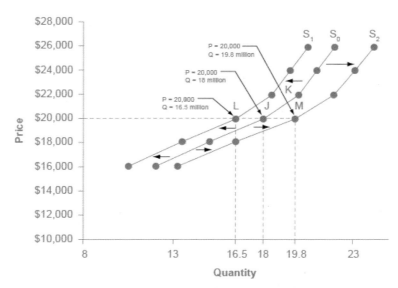

Figure 3.10 Shifts in Supply: A Car Example Decreased supply means that at every given price, the quantity supplied is lower, so that the supply curve shifts to the left, from S_0 to S_1. Increased supply means that at every given price, the quantity supplied is higher, so that the supply curve shifts to the right, from S_0 to S_2.

Price	Decrease to S_1	Original Quantity Supplied S_0	Increase to S_2
$16,000	10.5 million	12.0 million	13.2 million
$18,000	13.5 million	15.0 million	16.5 million
$20,000	16.5 million	18.0 million	19.8 million
$22,000	18.5 million	20.0 million	22.0 million
$24,000	19.5 million	21.0 million	23.1 million
$26,000	20.5 million	22.0 million	24.2 million

Table 3.5 Price and Shifts in Supply: A Car Example

Now, imagine that the price of steel, an important ingredient in manufacturing cars, rises, so that producing a car has become more expensive. At any given price for selling cars, car manufacturers will react by supplying a lower quantity. We can show this graphically as a leftward shift of supply, from S_0 to S_1, which indicates that at any given price, the quantity supplied decreases. In this example, at a price of $20,000, the quantity supplied decreases from 18 million on the original supply curve (S_0) to 16.5 million on the supply curve S_1, which is labeled as point L.

Conversely, if the price of steel decreases, producing a car becomes less expensive. At any given price for selling cars, car manufacturers can now expect to earn higher profits, so they will supply a higher quantity. The shift of supply to the right, from S_0 to S_2, means that at all prices, the quantity supplied has increased. In this example, at a price of $20,000, the quantity supplied increases from 18 million on the original supply curve (S_0) to 19.8 million on the supply curve S_2, which is labeled M.

Other Factors That Affect Supply

In the example above, we saw that changes in the prices of inputs in the production process will affect the cost of production and thus the supply. Several other things affect the cost of production, too, such as changes in weather or other natural conditions, new technologies for production, and some government policies.

Changes in weather and climate will affect the cost of production for many agricultural products. For example, in

This OpenStax book is available for free at http://cnx.org/content/col12122/1.4

2014 the Manchurian Plain in Northeastern China, which produces most of the country's wheat, corn, and soybeans, experienced its most severe drought in 50 years. A drought decreases the supply of agricultural products, which means that at any given price, a lower quantity will be supplied. Conversely, especially good weather would shift the supply curve to the right.

When a firm discovers a new technology that allows the firm to produce at a lower cost, the supply curve will shift to the right, as well. For instance, in the 1960s a major scientific effort nicknamed the Green Revolution focused on breeding improved seeds for basic crops like wheat and rice. By the early 1990s, more than two-thirds of the wheat and rice in low-income countries around the world used these Green Revolution seeds—and the harvest was twice as high per acre. A technological improvement that reduces costs of production will shift supply to the right, so that a greater quantity will be produced at any given price.

Government policies can affect the cost of production and the supply curve through taxes, regulations, and subsidies. For example, the U.S. government imposes a tax on alcoholic beverages that collects about $8 billion per year from producers. Businesses treat taxes as costs. Higher costs decrease supply for the reasons we discussed above. Other examples of policy that can affect cost are the wide array of government regulations that require firms to spend money to provide a cleaner environment or a safer workplace. Complying with regulations increases costs.

A government subsidy, on the other hand, is the opposite of a tax. A subsidy occurs when the government pays a firm directly or reduces the firm's taxes if the firm carries out certain actions. From the firm's perspective, taxes or regulations are an additional cost of production that shifts supply to the left, leading the firm to produce a lower quantity at every given price. Government subsidies reduce the cost of production and increase supply at every given price, shifting supply to the right. The following Work It Out feature shows how this shift happens.

Work It Out ○—○—○

Shift in Supply

We know that a supply curve shows the minimum price a firm will accept to produce a given quantity of output. What happens to the supply curve when the cost of production goes up? Following is an example of a shift in supply due to a production cost increase.

Step 1. Draw a graph of a supply curve for pizza. Pick a quantity (like Q_0). If you draw a vertical line up from Q_0 to the supply curve, you will see the price the firm chooses. **Figure 3.11** provides an example.

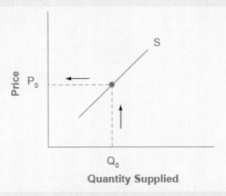

Figure 3.11 Supply Curve   You can use a supply curve to show the minimum price a firm will accept to produce a given quantity of output.

Step 2. Why did the firm choose that price and not some other? One way to think about this is that the price is composed of two parts. The first part is the cost of producing pizzas at the margin; in this case, the cost of producing the pizza, including cost of ingredients (e.g., dough, sauce, cheese, and pepperoni), the cost of the pizza oven, the shop rent, and the workers' wages. The second part is the firm's desired profit, which is determined, among other factors, by the profit margins in that particular business. If you add these two parts together, you get the price the firm wishes to charge. The quantity Q0 and associated price P0 give you one point on the firm's supply curve, as **Figure 3.12** illustrates.

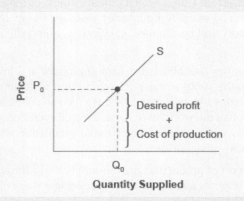

Figure 3.12 Setting Prices   The cost of production and the desired profit equal the price a firm will set for a product.

Step 3. Now, suppose that the cost of production increases. Perhaps cheese has become more expensive by $0.75 per pizza. If that is true, the firm will want to raise its price by the amount of the increase in cost ($0.75). Draw this point on the supply curve directly above the initial point on the curve, but $0.75 higher, as **Figure 3.13** shows.

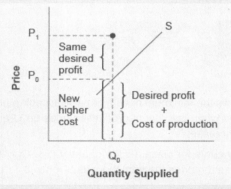

Figure 3.13 Increasing Costs Leads to Increasing Price   Because the cost of production and the desired profit equal the price a firm will set for a product, if the cost of production increases, the price for the product will also need to increase.

Step 4. Shift the supply curve through this point. You will see that an increase in cost causes an upward (or a leftward) shift of the supply curve so that at any price, the quantities supplied will be smaller, as **Figure 3.14** illustrates.

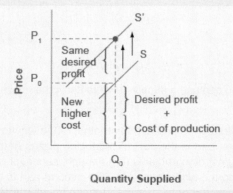

Figure 3.14 Supply Curve Shifts   When the cost of production increases, the supply curve shifts upwardly to a new price level.

This OpenStax book is available for free at http://cnx.org/content/col12122/1.4

Summing Up Factors That Change Supply

Changes in the cost of inputs, natural disasters, new technologies, and the impact of government decisions all affect the cost of production. In turn, these factors affect how much firms are willing to supply at any given price.

Figure 3.15 summarizes factors that change the supply of goods and services. Notice that a change in the price of the product itself is not among the factors that shift the supply curve. Although a change in price of a good or service typically causes a change in quantity supplied or a movement along the supply curve for that specific good or service, it does not cause the supply curve itself to shift.

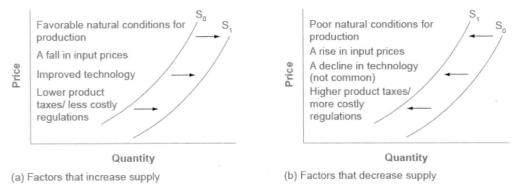

(a) Factors that increase supply   (b) Factors that decrease supply

Figure 3.15 Factors That Shift Supply Curves   (a) A list of factors that can cause an increase in supply from S_0 to S_1. (b) The same factors, if their direction is reversed, can cause a decrease in supply from S_0 to S_1.

Because demand and supply curves appear on a two-dimensional diagram with only price and quantity on the axes, an unwary visitor to the land of economics might be fooled into believing that economics is about only four topics: demand, supply, price, and quantity. However, demand and supply are really "umbrella" concepts: demand covers all the factors that affect demand, and supply covers all the factors that affect supply. We include factors other than price that affect demand and supply are included by using shifts in the demand or the supply curve. In this way, the two-dimensional demand and supply model becomes a powerful tool for analyzing a wide range of economic circumstances.

3.3 | Changes in Equilibrium Price and Quantity: The Four-Step Process

By the end of this section, you will be able to:
- Identify equilibrium price and quantity through the four-step process
- Graph equilibrium price and quantity
- Contrast shifts of demand or supply and movements along a demand or supply curve
- Graph demand and supply curves, including equilibrium price and quantity, based on real-world examples

Let's begin this discussion with a single economic event. It might be an event that affects demand, like a change in income, population, tastes, prices of substitutes or complements, or expectations about future prices. It might be an event that affects supply, like a change in natural conditions, input prices, or technology, or government policies that affect production. How does this economic event affect equilibrium price and quantity? We will analyze this question using a four-step process.

Step 1. Draw a demand and supply model before the economic change took place. To establish the model requires four standard pieces of information: The law of demand, which tells us the slope of the demand curve; the law of supply, which gives us the slope of the supply curve; the shift variables for demand; and the shift variables for supply. From this model, find the initial equilibrium values for price and quantity.

Step 2. Decide whether the economic change you are analyzing affects demand or supply. In other words, does the event refer to something in the list of demand factors or supply factors?

Step 3. Decide whether the effect on demand or supply causes the curve to shift to the right or to the left, and sketch the new demand or supply curve on the diagram. In other words, does the event increase or decrease the amount consumers want to buy or producers want to sell?

Step 4. Identify the new equilibrium and then compare the original equilibrium price and quantity to the new equilibrium price and quantity.

Let's consider one example that involves a shift in supply and one that involves a shift in demand. Then we will consider an example where both supply and demand shift.

Good Weather for Salmon Fishing

Supposed that during the summer of 2015, weather conditions were excellent for commercial salmon fishing off the California coast. Heavy rains meant higher than normal levels of water in the rivers, which helps the salmon to breed. Slightly cooler ocean temperatures stimulated the growth of plankton, the microscopic organisms at the bottom of the ocean food chain, providing everything in the ocean with a hearty food supply. The ocean stayed calm during fishing season, so commercial fishing operations did not lose many days to bad weather. How did these climate conditions affect the quantity and price of salmon? **Figure 3.16** illustrates the four-step approach, which we explain below, to work through this problem. **Table 3.6** also provides the information to work the problem.

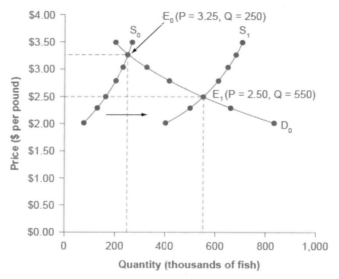

Figure 3.16 Good Weather for Salmon Fishing: The Four-Step Process   Unusually good weather leads to changes in the price and quantity of salmon.

Price per Pound	Quantity Supplied in 2014	Quantity Supplied in 2015	Quantity Demanded
$2.00	80	400	840
$2.25	120	480	680
$2.50	160	550	550
$2.75	200	600	450
$3.00	230	640	350
$3.25	250	670	250

Table 3.6 Salmon Fishing

This OpenStax book is available for free at http://cnx.org/content/col12122/1.4

Price per Pound	Quantity Supplied in 2014	Quantity Supplied in 2015	Quantity Demanded
$3.50	270	700	200

Table 3.6 Salmon Fishing

Step 1. Draw a demand and supply model to illustrate the market for salmon in the year before the good weather conditions began. The demand curve D_0 and the supply curve S_0 show that the original equilibrium price is $3.25 per pound and the original equilibrium quantity is 250,000 fish. (This price per pound is what commercial buyers pay at the fishing docks. What consumers pay at the grocery is higher.)

Step 2. Did the economic event affect supply or demand? Good weather is an example of a natural condition that affects supply.

Step 3. Was the effect on supply an increase or a decrease? Good weather is a change in natural conditions that increases the quantity supplied at any given price. The supply curve shifts to the right, moving from the original supply curve S_0 to the new supply curve S_1, which **Figure 3.16** and **Table 3.6** show.

Step 4. Compare the new equilibrium price and quantity to the original equilibrium. At the new equilibrium E_1, the equilibrium price falls from $3.25 to $2.50, but the equilibrium quantity increases from 250,000 to 550,000 salmon. Notice that the equilibrium quantity demanded increased, even though the demand curve did not move.

In short, good weather conditions increased supply of the California commercial salmon. The result was a higher equilibrium quantity of salmon bought and sold in the market at a lower price.

Newspapers and the Internet

According to the Pew Research Center for People and the Press, increasingly more people, especially younger people, are obtaining their news from online and digital sources. The majority of U.S. adults now own smartphones or tablets, and most of those Americans say they use them in part to access the news. From 2004 to 2012, the share of Americans who reported obtaining their news from digital sources increased from 24% to 39%. How has this affected consumption of print news media, and radio and television news? **Figure 3.17** and the text below illustrates using the four-step analysis to answer this question.

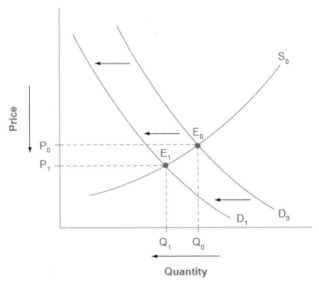

Figure 3.17 The Print News Market: A Four-Step Analysis   A change in tastes from print news sources to digital sources results in a leftward shift in demand for the former. The result is a decrease in both equilibrium price and quantity.

Step 1. Develop a demand and supply model to think about what the market looked like before the event. The demand curve D_0 and the supply curve S_0 show the original relationships. In this case, we perform the analysis without specific numbers on the price and quantity axis.

Step 2. Did the described change affect supply or demand? A change in tastes, from traditional news sources (print, radio, and television) to digital sources, caused a change in demand for the former.

Step 3. Was the effect on demand positive or negative? A shift to digital news sources will tend to mean a lower quantity demanded of traditional news sources at every given price, causing the demand curve for print and other traditional news sources to shift to the left, from D_0 to D_1.

Step 4. Compare the new equilibrium price and quantity to the original equilibrium price. The new equilibrium (E_1) occurs at a lower quantity and a lower price than the original equilibrium (E_0).

The decline in print news reading predates 2004. Print newspaper circulation peaked in 1973 and has declined since then due to competition from television and radio news. In 1991, 55% of Americans indicated they received their news from print sources, while only 29% did so in 2012. Radio news has followed a similar path in recent decades, with the share of Americans obtaining their news from radio declining from 54% in 1991 to 33% in 2012. Television news has held its own over the last 15 years, with a market share staying in the mid to upper fifties. What does this suggest for the future, given that two-thirds of Americans under 30 years old say they do not obtain their news from television at all?

The Interconnections and Speed of Adjustment in Real Markets

In the real world, many factors that affect demand and supply can change all at once. For example, the demand for cars might increase because of rising incomes and population, and it might decrease because of rising gasoline prices (a complementary good). Likewise, the supply of cars might increase because of innovative new technologies that reduce the cost of car production, and it might decrease as a result of new government regulations requiring the installation of costly pollution-control technology.

Moreover, rising incomes and population or changes in gasoline prices will affect many markets, not just cars. How can an economist sort out all these interconnected events? The answer lies in the *ceteris paribus* assumption. Look at how each economic event affects each market, one event at a time, holding all else constant. Then combine the analyses to see the net effect.

A Combined Example

The U.S. Postal Service is facing difficult challenges. Compensation for postal workers tends to increase most years due to cost-of-living increases. At the same time, increasingly more people are using email, text, and other digital message forms such as Facebook and Twitter to communicate with friends and others. What does this suggest about the continued viability of the Postal Service? **Figure 3.18** and the text below illustrate this using the four-step analysis to answer this question.

This OpenStax book is available for free at http://cnx.org/content/col12122/1.4

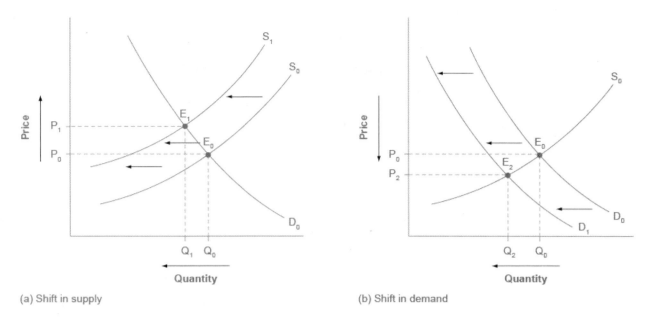

(a) Shift in supply   (b) Shift in demand

Figure 3.18 Higher Compensation for Postal Workers: A Four-Step Analysis (a) Higher labor compensation causes a leftward shift in the supply curve, a decrease in the equilibrium quantity, and an increase in the equilibrium price. (b) A change in tastes away from Postal Services causes a leftward shift in the demand curve, a decrease in the equilibrium quantity, and a decrease in the equilibrium price.

Since this problem involves two disturbances, we need two four-step analyses, the first to analyze the effects of higher compensation for postal workers, the second to analyze the effects of many people switching from "snail mail" to email and other digital messages.

Figure 3.18 (a) shows the shift in supply discussed in the following steps.

Step 1. Draw a demand and supply model to illustrate what the market for the U.S. Postal Service looked like before this scenario starts. The demand curve D_0 and the supply curve S_0 show the original relationships.

Step 2. Did the described change affect supply or demand? Labor compensation is a cost of production. A change in production costs caused a change in supply for the Postal Service.

Step 3. Was the effect on supply positive or negative? Higher labor compensation leads to a lower quantity supplied of postal services at every given price, causing the supply curve for postal services to shift to the left, from S_0 to S_1.

Step 4. Compare the new equilibrium price and quantity to the original equilibrium price. The new equilibrium (E_1) occurs at a lower quantity and a higher price than the original equilibrium (E_0).

Figure 3.18 (b) shows the shift in demand in the following steps.

Step 1. Draw a demand and supply model to illustrate what the market for U.S. Postal Services looked like before this scenario starts. The demand curve D_0 and the supply curve S_0 show the original relationships. Note that this diagram is independent from the diagram in panel (a).

Step 2. Did the change described affect supply or demand? A change in tastes away from snail mail toward digital messages will cause a change in demand for the Postal Service.

Step 3. Was the effect on demand positive or negative? A change in tastes away from snailmail toward digital messages causes lower quantity demanded of postal services at every given price, causing the demand curve for postal services to shift to the left, from D_0 to D_1.

Step 4. Compare the new equilibrium price and quantity to the original equilibrium price. The new equilibrium (E_2) occurs at a lower quantity and a lower price than the original equilibrium (E_0).

The final step in a scenario where both supply and demand shift is to combine the two individual analyses to determine what happens to the equilibrium quantity and price. Graphically, we superimpose the previous two diagrams one on top of the other, as in **Figure 3.19**.

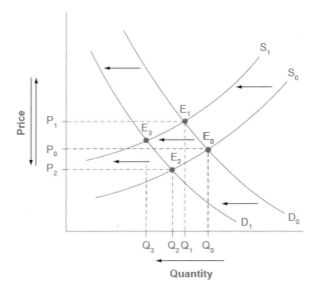

Figure 3.19 Combined Effect of Decreased Demand and Decreased Supply   Supply and demand shifts cause changes in equilibrium price and quantity.

Following are the results:

Effect on Quantity: The effect of higher labor compensation on Postal Services because it raises the cost of production is to decrease the equilibrium quantity. The effect of a change in tastes away from snail mail is to decrease the equilibrium quantity. Since both shifts are to the left, the overall impact is a decrease in the equilibrium quantity of Postal Services (Q_3). This is easy to see graphically, since Q_3 is to the left of Q_0.

Effect on Price: The overall effect on price is more complicated. The effect of higher labor compensation on Postal Services, because it raises the cost of production, is to increase the equilibrium price. The effect of a change in tastes away from snail mail is to decrease the equilibrium price. Since the two effects are in opposite directions, unless we know the magnitudes of the two effects, the overall effect is unclear. This is not unusual. When both curves shift, typically we can determine the overall effect on price or on quantity, but not on both. In this case, we determined the overall effect on the equilibrium quantity, but not on the equilibrium price. In other cases, it might be the opposite.

The next Clear It Up feature focuses on the difference between shifts of supply or demand and movements along a curve.

What is the difference between shifts of demand or supply versus movements along a demand or supply curve?

One common mistake in applying the demand and supply framework is to confuse the shift of a demand or a supply curve with movement along a demand or supply curve. As an example, consider a problem that asks whether a drought will increase or decrease the equilibrium quantity and equilibrium price of wheat. Lee, a student in an introductory economics class, might reason:

"Well, it is clear that a drought reduces supply, so I will shift back the supply curve, as in the shift from the original supply curve S_0 to S_1 on the diagram (Shift 1). The equilibrium moves from E_0 to E_1, the equilibrium quantity is lower and the equilibrium price is higher. Then, a higher price makes farmers more likely to supply the good, so the supply curve shifts right, as shows the shift from S_1 to S_2, shows on the diagram (Shift 2), so that the equilibrium now moves from E_1 to E_2. The higher price, however, also reduces demand and so causes demand to shift back, like the shift from the original demand curve, D_0 to D_1 on the diagram (labeled

This OpenStax book is available for free at http://cnx.org/content/col12122/1.4

Shift 3), and the equilibrium moves from E_2 to E_3."

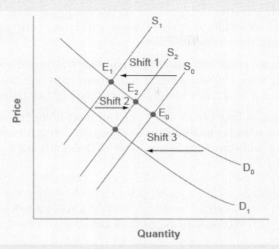

Figure 3.20 Shifts of Demand or Supply versus Movements along a Demand or Supply Curve A shift in one curve never causes a shift in the other curve. Rather, a shift in one curve causes a movement along the second curve.

At about this point, Lee suspects that this answer is headed down the wrong path. Think about what might be wrong with Lee's logic, and then read the answer that follows.

Answer: Lee's first step is correct: that is, a drought shifts back the supply curve of wheat and leads to a prediction of a lower equilibrium quantity and a higher equilibrium price. This corresponds to a movement along the original demand curve (D_0), from E_0 to E_1. The rest of Lee's argument is wrong, because it mixes up shifts in supply with quantity supplied, and shifts in demand with quantity demanded. A higher or lower price never shifts the supply curve, as suggested by the shift in supply from S_1 to S_2. Instead, a price change leads to a movement along a given supply curve. Similarly, a higher or lower price never shifts a demand curve, as suggested in the shift from D_0 to D_1. Instead, a price change leads to a movement along a given demand curve. Remember, a change in the price of a good never causes the demand or supply curve for that good to shift.

Think carefully about the timeline of events: What happens first, what happens next? What is cause, what is effect? If you keep the order right, you are more likely to get the analysis correct.

In the four-step analysis of how economic events affect equilibrium price and quantity, the movement from the old to the new equilibrium seems immediate. As a practical matter, however, prices and quantities often do not zoom straight to equilibrium. More realistically, when an economic event causes demand or supply to shift, prices and quantities set off in the general direction of equilibrium. Even as they are moving toward one new equilibrium, a subsequent change in demand or supply often pushes prices toward another equilibrium.

3.4 | Price Ceilings and Price Floors

By the end of this section, you will be able to:
- Explain price controls, price ceilings, and price floors
- Analyze demand and supply as a social adjustment mechanism

To this point in the chapter, we have been assuming that markets are free, that is, they operate with no government intervention. In this section, we will explore the outcomes, both anticipated and otherwise, when government does intervene in a market either to prevent the price of some good or service from rising "too high" or to prevent the price of some good or service from falling "too low".

Economists believe there are a small number of fundamental principles that explain how economic agents respond in different situations. Two of these principles, which we have already introduced, are the laws of demand and supply.

Governments can pass laws affecting market outcomes, but no law can negate these economic principles. Rather, the principles will become apparent in sometimes unexpected ways, which may undermine the intent of the government policy. This is one of the major conclusions of this section.

Controversy sometimes surrounds the prices and quantities established by demand and supply, especially for products that are considered necessities. In some cases, discontent over prices turns into public pressure on politicians, who may then pass legislation to prevent a certain price from climbing "too high" or falling "too low."

The demand and supply model shows how people and firms will react to the incentives that these laws provide to control prices, in ways that will often lead to undesirable consequences. Alternative policy tools can often achieve the desired goals of price control laws, while avoiding at least some of their costs and tradeoffs.

Price Ceilings

Laws that government enact to regulate prices are called **price controls**. Price controls come in two flavors. A **price ceiling** keeps a price from rising above a certain level (the "ceiling"), while a **price floor** keeps a price from falling below a given level (the "floor"). This section uses the demand and supply framework to analyze price ceilings. The next section discusses price floors.

A price ceiling is a legal maximum price that one pays for some good or service. A government imposes price ceilings in order to keep the price of some necessary good or service affordable. For example, in 2005 during Hurricane Katrina, the price of bottled water increased above $5 per gallon. As a result, many people called for price controls on bottled water to prevent the price from rising so high. In this particular case, the government did not impose a price ceiling, but there are other examples of where price ceilings did occur.

In many markets for goods and services, demanders outnumber suppliers. Consumers, who are also potential voters, sometimes unite behind a political proposal to hold down a certain price. In some cities, such as Albany, renters have pressed political leaders to pass rent control laws, a price ceiling that usually works by stating that landlords can raise rents by only a certain maximum percentage each year. Some of the best examples of rent control occur in urban areas such as New York, Washington D.C., or San Francisco.

Rent control becomes a politically hot topic when rents begin to rise rapidly. Everyone needs an affordable place to live. Perhaps a change in tastes makes a certain suburb or town a more popular place to live. Perhaps locally-based businesses expand, bringing higher incomes and more people into the area. Such changes can cause a change in the demand for rental housing, as **Figure 3.21** illustrates. The original equilibrium (E_0) lies at the intersection of supply curve S_0 and demand curve D_0, corresponding to an equilibrium price of $500 and an equilibrium quantity of 15,000 units of rental housing. The effect of greater income or a change in tastes is to shift the demand curve for rental housing to the right, as the data in **Table 3.7** shows and the shift from D_0 to D_1 on the graph. In this market, at the new equilibrium E_1, the price of a rental unit would rise to $600 and the equilibrium quantity would increase to 17,000 units.

This OpenStax book is available for free at http://cnx.org/content/col12122/1.4

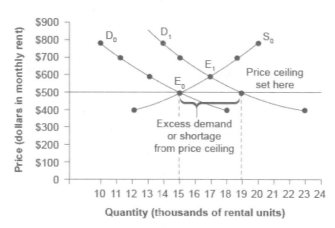

Figure 3.21 A Price Ceiling Example—Rent Control The original intersection of demand and supply occurs at E_0. If demand shifts from D_0 to D_1, the new equilibrium would be at E_1—unless a price ceiling prevents the price from rising. If the price is not permitted to rise, the quantity supplied remains at 15,000. However, after the change in demand, the quantity demanded rises to 19,000, resulting in a shortage.

Price	Original Quantity Supplied	Original Quantity Demanded	New Quantity Demanded
$400	12,000	18,000	23,000
$500	15,000	15,000	19,000
$600	17,000	13,000	17,000
$700	19,000	11,000	15,000
$800	20,000	10,000	14,000

Table 3.7 Rent Control

Suppose that a city government passes a rent control law to keep the price at the original equilibrium of $500 for a typical apartment. In **Figure 3.21**, the horizontal line at the price of $500 shows the legally fixed maximum price set by the rent control law. However, the underlying forces that shifted the demand curve to the right are still there. At that price ($500), the quantity supplied remains at the same 15,000 rental units, but the quantity demanded is 19,000 rental units. In other words, the quantity demanded exceeds the quantity supplied, so there is a shortage of rental housing. One of the ironies of price ceilings is that while the price ceiling was intended to help renters, there are actually fewer apartments rented out under the price ceiling (15,000 rental units) than would be the case at the market rent of $600 (17,000 rental units).

Price ceilings do not simply benefit renters at the expense of landlords. Rather, some renters (or potential renters) lose their housing as landlords convert apartments to co-ops and condos. Even when the housing remains in the rental market, landlords tend to spend less on maintenance and on essentials like heating, cooling, hot water, and lighting. The first rule of economics is you do not get something for nothing—everything has an opportunity cost. Thus, if renters obtain "cheaper" housing than the market requires, they tend to also end up with lower quality housing.

Price ceilings are enacted in an attempt to keep prices low for those who need the product. However, when the market price is not allowed to rise to the equilibrium level, quantity demanded exceeds quantity supplied, and thus a shortage occurs. Those who manage to purchase the product at the lower price given by the price ceiling will benefit, but sellers of the product will suffer, along with those who are not able to purchase the product at all. Quality is also likely to deteriorate.

Price Floors

A price floor is the lowest price that one can legally pay for some good or service. Perhaps the best-known example of a price floor is the minimum wage, which is based on the view that someone working full time should be able to afford a basic standard of living. The federal minimum wage in 2016 was $7.25 per hour, although some states and localities have a higher minimum wage. The federal minimum wage yields an annual income for a single person of $15,080, which is slightly higher than the Federal poverty line of $11,880. As the cost of living rises over time, the Congress periodically raises the federal minimum wage.

Price floors are sometimes called "price supports," because they support a price by preventing it from falling below a certain level. Around the world, many countries have passed laws to create agricultural price supports. Farm prices and thus farm incomes fluctuate, sometimes widely. Even if, on average, farm incomes are adequate, some years they can be quite low. The purpose of price supports is to prevent these swings.

The most common way price supports work is that the government enters the market and buys up the product, adding to demand to keep prices higher than they otherwise would be. According to the Common Agricultural Policy reform passed in 2013, the European Union (EU) will spend about 60 billion euros per year, or 67 billion dollars per year (with the November 2016 exchange rate), or roughly 38% of the EU budget, on price supports for Europe's farmers from 2014 to 2020.

Figure 3.22 illustrates the effects of a government program that assures a price above the equilibrium by focusing on the market for wheat in Europe. In the absence of government intervention, the price would adjust so that the quantity supplied would equal the quantity demanded at the equilibrium point E_0, with price P_0 and quantity Q_0. However, policies to keep prices high for farmers keeps the price above what would have been the market equilibrium level—the price Pf shown by the dashed horizontal line in the diagram. The result is a quantity supplied in excess of the quantity demanded (Qd). When quantity supplied exceeds quantity demanded, a surplus exists.

Economists estimate that the high-income areas of the world, including the United States, Europe, and Japan, spend roughly $1 billion per day in supporting their farmers. If the government is willing to purchase the excess supply (or to provide payments for others to purchase it), then farmers will benefit from the price floor, but taxpayers and consumers of food will pay the costs. Agricultural economists and policy makers have offered numerous proposals for reducing farm subsidies. In many countries, however, political support for subsidies for farmers remains strong. This is either because the population views this as supporting the traditional rural way of life or because of industry's lobbying power of the agro-business.

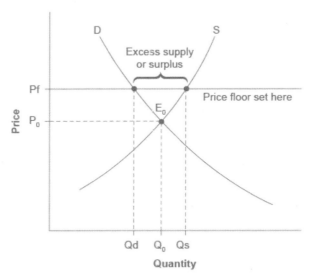

Figure 3.22 European Wheat Prices: A Price Floor Example   The intersection of demand (D) and supply (S) would be at the equilibrium point E_0. However, a price floor set at Pf holds the price above E_0 and prevents it from falling. The result of the price floor is that the quantity supplied Qs exceeds the quantity demanded Qd. There is excess supply, also called a surplus.

This OpenStax book is available for free at http://cnx.org/content/col12122/1.4

3.5 | Demand, Supply, and Efficiency

By the end of this section, you will be able to:

- Contrast consumer surplus, producer surplus, and social surplus
- Explain why price floors and price ceilings can be inefficient
- Analyze demand and supply as a social adjustment mechanism

The familiar demand and supply diagram holds within it the concept of economic efficiency. One typical way that economists define efficiency is when it is impossible to improve the situation of one party without imposing a cost on another. Conversely, if a situation is inefficient, it becomes possible to benefit at least one party without imposing costs on others.

Efficiency in the demand and supply model has the same basic meaning: The economy is getting as much benefit as possible from its scarce resources and all the possible gains from trade have been achieved. In other words, the optimal amount of each good and service is produced and consumed.

Consumer Surplus, Producer Surplus, Social Surplus

Consider a market for tablet computers, as **Figure 3.23** shows. The equilibrium price is $80 and the equilibrium quantity is 28 million. To see the benefits to consumers, look at the segment of the demand curve above the equilibrium point and to the left. This portion of the demand curve shows that at least some demanders would have been willing to pay more than $80 for a tablet.

For example, point J shows that if the price were $90, 20 million tablets would be sold. Those consumers who would have been willing to pay $90 for a tablet based on the utility they expect to receive from it, but who were able to pay the equilibrium price of $80, clearly received a benefit beyond what they had to pay. Remember, the demand curve traces consumers' willingness to pay for different quantities. The amount that individuals would have been willing to pay, minus the amount that they actually paid, is called **consumer surplus**. Consumer surplus is the area labeled F—that is, the area above the market price and below the demand curve.

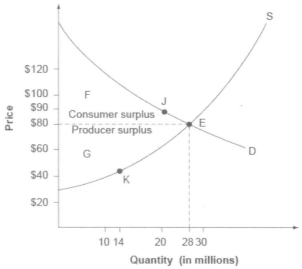

Figure 3.23 Consumer and Producer Surplus The somewhat triangular area labeled by F shows the area of consumer surplus, which shows that the equilibrium price in the market was less than what many of the consumers were willing to pay. Point J on the demand curve shows that, even at the price of $90, consumers would have been willing to purchase a quantity of 20 million. The somewhat triangular area labeled by G shows the area of producer surplus, which shows that the equilibrium price received in the market was more than what many of the producers were willing to accept for their products. For example, point K on the supply curve shows that at a price of $45, firms would have been willing to supply a quantity of 14 million.

The supply curve shows the quantity that firms are willing to supply at each price. For example, point K in **Figure**

3.23 illustrates that, at $45, firms would still have been willing to supply a quantity of 14 million. Those producers who would have been willing to supply the tablets at $45, but who were instead able to charge the equilibrium price of $80, clearly received an extra benefit beyond what they required to supply the product. The amount that a seller is paid for a good minus the seller's actual cost is called **producer surplus**. In Figure 3.23, producer surplus is the area labeled G—that is, the area between the market price and the segment of the supply curve below the equilibrium.

The sum of consumer surplus and producer surplus is **social surplus**, also referred to as **economic surplus** or **total surplus**. In Figure 3.23 we show social surplus as the area F + G. Social surplus is larger at equilibrium quantity and price than it would be at any other quantity. This demonstrates the economic efficiency of the market equilibrium. In addition, at the efficient level of output, it is impossible to produce greater consumer surplus without reducing producer surplus, and it is impossible to produce greater producer surplus without reducing consumer surplus.

Inefficiency of Price Floors and Price Ceilings

The imposition of a price floor or a price ceiling will prevent a market from adjusting to its equilibrium price and quantity, and thus will create an inefficient outcome. However, there is an additional twist here. Along with creating inefficiency, price floors and ceilings will also transfer some consumer surplus to producers, or some producer surplus to consumers.

Imagine that several firms develop a promising but expensive new drug for treating back pain. If this therapy is left to the market, the equilibrium price will be $600 per month and 20,000 people will use the drug, as shown in Figure 3.24 (a). The original level of consumer surplus is T + U and producer surplus is V + W + X. However, the government decides to impose a price ceiling of $400 to make the drug more affordable. At this price ceiling, firms in the market now produce only 15,000.

As a result, two changes occur. First, an inefficient outcome occurs and the total surplus of society is reduced. The loss in social surplus that occurs when the economy produces at an inefficient quantity is called **deadweight loss**. In a very real sense, it is like money thrown away that benefits no one. In Figure 3.24 (a), the deadweight loss is the area U + W. When deadweight loss exists, it is possible for both consumer and producer surplus to be higher, in this case because the price control is blocking some suppliers and demanders from transactions they would both be willing to make.

A second change from the price ceiling is that some of the producer surplus is transferred to consumers. After the price ceiling is imposed, the new consumer surplus is T + V, while the new producer surplus is X. In other words, the price ceiling transfers the area of surplus (V) from producers to consumers. Note that the gain to consumers is less than the loss to producers, which is just another way of seeing the deadweight loss.

This OpenStax book is available for free at http://cnx.org/content/col12122/1.4

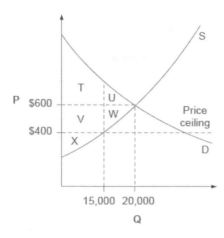 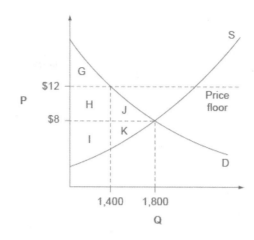

(a) Reduced social surplus from a price ceiling   (b) Reduced social surplus from a price floor

Figure 3.24 Efficiency and Price Floors and Ceilings (a) The original equilibrium price is $600 with a quantity of 20,000. Consumer surplus is T + U, and producer surplus is V + W + X. A price ceiling is imposed at $400, so firms in the market now produce only a quantity of 15,000. As a result, the new consumer surplus is T + V, while the new producer surplus is X. (b) The original equilibrium is $8 at a quantity of 1,800. Consumer surplus is G + H + J, and producer surplus is I + K. A price floor is imposed at $12, which means that quantity demanded falls to 1,400. As a result, the new consumer surplus is G, and the new producer surplus is H + I.

Figure 3.24 (b) shows a price floor example using a string of struggling movie theaters, all in the same city. The current equilibrium is $8 per movie ticket, with 1,800 people attending movies. The original consumer surplus is G + H + J, and producer surplus is I + K. The city government is worried that movie theaters will go out of business, reducing the entertainment options available to citizens, so it decides to impose a price floor of $12 per ticket. As a result, the quantity demanded of movie tickets falls to 1,400. The new consumer surplus is G, and the new producer surplus is H + I. In effect, the price floor causes the area H to be transferred from consumer to producer surplus, but also causes a deadweight loss of J + K.

This analysis shows that a price ceiling, like a law establishing rent controls, will transfer some producer surplus to consumers—which helps to explain why consumers often favor them. Conversely, a price floor like a guarantee that farmers will receive a certain price for their crops will transfer some consumer surplus to producers, which explains why producers often favor them. However, both price floors and price ceilings block some transactions that buyers and sellers would have been willing to make, and creates deadweight loss. Removing such barriers, so that prices and quantities can adjust to their equilibrium level, will increase the economy's social surplus.

Demand and Supply as a Social Adjustment Mechanism

The demand and supply model emphasizes that prices are not set only by demand or only by supply, but by the interaction between the two. In 1890, the famous economist Alfred Marshall wrote that asking whether supply or demand determined a price was like arguing "whether it is the upper or the under blade of a pair of scissors that cuts a piece of paper." The answer is that both blades of the demand and supply scissors are always involved.

The adjustments of equilibrium price and quantity in a market-oriented economy often occur without much government direction or oversight. If the coffee crop in Brazil suffers a terrible frost, then the supply curve of coffee shifts to the left and the price of coffee rises. Some people—call them the coffee addicts—continue to drink coffee and pay the higher price. Others switch to tea or soft drinks. No government commission is needed to figure out how to adjust coffee prices, which companies will be allowed to process the remaining supply, which supermarkets in which cities will get how much coffee to sell, or which consumers will ultimately be allowed to drink the brew. Such adjustments in response to price changes happen all the time in a market economy, often so smoothly and rapidly that we barely notice them.

Think for a moment of all the seasonal foods that are available and inexpensive at certain times of the year, like fresh corn in midsummer, but more expensive at other times of the year. People alter their diets and restaurants alter their menus in response to these fluctuations in prices without fuss or fanfare. For both the U.S. economy and the world economy as a whole, markets—that is, demand and supply—are the primary social mechanism for answering the basic questions about what is produced, how it is produced, and for whom it is produced.

Bring it Home

Why Can We Not Get Enough of Organic?

Organic food is grown without synthetic pesticides, chemical fertilizers or genetically modified seeds. In recent decades, the demand for organic products has increased dramatically. The Organic Trade Association reported sales increased from $1 billion in 1990 to $35.1 billion in 2013, more than 90% of which were sales of food products.

Why, then, are organic foods more expensive than their conventional counterparts? The answer is a clear application of the theories of supply and demand. As people have learned more about the harmful effects of chemical fertilizers, growth hormones, pesticides and the like from large-scale factory farming, our tastes and preferences for safer, organic foods have increased. This change in tastes has been reinforced by increases in income, which allow people to purchase pricier products, and has made organic foods more mainstream. This has led to an increased demand for organic foods. Graphically, the demand curve has shifted right, and we have moved up the supply curve as producers have responded to the higher prices by supplying a greater quantity.

In addition to the movement along the supply curve, we have also had an increase in the number of farmers converting to organic farming over time. This is represented by a shift to the right of the supply curve. Since both demand and supply have shifted to the right, the resulting equilibrium quantity of organic foods is definitely higher, but the price will only fall when the increase in supply is larger than the increase in demand. We may need more time before we see lower prices in organic foods. Since the production costs of these foods may remain higher than conventional farming, because organic fertilizers and pest management techniques are more expensive, they may never fully catch up with the lower prices of non-organic foods.

As a final, specific example: The Environmental Working Group's "Dirty Dozen" list of fruits and vegetables, which test high for pesticide residue even after washing, was released in April 2013. The inclusion of strawberries on the list has led to an increase in demand for organic strawberries, resulting in both a higher equilibrium price and quantity of sales.

KEY TERMS

ceteris paribus other things being equal

complements goods that are often used together so that consumption of one good tends to enhance consumption of the other

consumer surplus the extra benefit consumers receive from buying a good or service, measured by what the individuals would have been willing to pay minus the amount that they actually paid

deadweight loss the loss in social surplus that occurs when a market produces an inefficient quantity

demand the relationship between price and the quantity demanded of a certain good or service

demand curve a graphic representation of the relationship between price and quantity demanded of a certain good or service, with quantity on the horizontal axis and the price on the vertical axis

demand schedule a table that shows a range of prices for a certain good or service and the quantity demanded at each price

economic surplus see social surplus

equilibrium the situation where quantity demanded is equal to the quantity supplied; the combination of price and quantity where there is no economic pressure from surpluses or shortages that would cause price or quantity to change

equilibrium price the price where quantity demanded is equal to quantity supplied

equilibrium quantity the quantity at which quantity demanded and quantity supplied are equal for a certain price level

excess demand at the existing price, the quantity demanded exceeds the quantity supplied; also called a shortage

excess supply at the existing price, quantity supplied exceeds the quantity demanded; also called a surplus

factors of production the resources such as labor, materials, and machinery that are used to produce goods and services; also called inputs

inferior good a good in which the quantity demanded falls as income rises, and in which quantity demanded rises and income falls

inputs the resources such as labor, materials, and machinery that are used to produce goods and services; also called factors of production

law of demand the common relationship that a higher price leads to a lower quantity demanded of a certain good or service and a lower price leads to a higher quantity demanded, while all other variables are held constant

law of supply the common relationship that a higher price leads to a greater quantity supplied and a lower price leads to a lower quantity supplied, while all other variables are held constant

normal good a good in which the quantity demanded rises as income rises, and in which quantity demanded falls as income falls

price what a buyer pays for a unit of the specific good or service

price ceiling a legal maximum price

price control government laws to regulate prices instead of letting market forces determine prices

price floor a legal minimum price

producer surplus the extra benefit producers receive from selling a good or service, measured by the price the producer actually received minus the price the producer would have been willing to accept

quantity demanded the total number of units of a good or service consumers are willing to purchase at a given price

quantity supplied the total number of units of a good or service producers are willing to sell at a given price

shift in demand when a change in some economic factor (other than price) causes a different quantity to be demanded at every price

shift in supply when a change in some economic factor (other than price) causes a different quantity to be supplied at every price

shortage at the existing price, the quantity demanded exceeds the quantity supplied; also called excess demand

social surplus the sum of consumer surplus and producer surplus

substitute a good that can replace another to some extent, so that greater consumption of one good can mean less of the other

supply the relationship between price and the quantity supplied of a certain good or service

supply curve a line that shows the relationship between price and quantity supplied on a graph, with quantity supplied on the horizontal axis and price on the vertical axis

supply schedule a table that shows a range of prices for a good or service and the quantity supplied at each price

surplus at the existing price, quantity supplied exceeds the quantity demanded; also called excess supply

total surplus see social surplus

KEY CONCEPTS AND SUMMARY

3.1 Demand, Supply, and Equilibrium in Markets for Goods and Services

A demand schedule is a table that shows the quantity demanded at different prices in the market. A demand curve shows the relationship between quantity demanded and price in a given market on a graph. The law of demand states that a higher price typically leads to a lower quantity demanded.

A supply schedule is a table that shows the quantity supplied at different prices in the market. A supply curve shows the relationship between quantity supplied and price on a graph. The law of supply says that a higher price typically leads to a higher quantity supplied.

The equilibrium price and equilibrium quantity occur where the supply and demand curves cross. The equilibrium occurs where the quantity demanded is equal to the quantity supplied. If the price is below the equilibrium level, then the quantity demanded will exceed the quantity supplied. Excess demand or a shortage will exist. If the price is above the equilibrium level, then the quantity supplied will exceed the quantity demanded. Excess supply or a surplus will exist. In either case, economic pressures will push the price toward the equilibrium level.

3.2 Shifts in Demand and Supply for Goods and Services

Economists often use the *ceteris paribus* or "other things being equal" assumption: while examining the economic impact of one event, all other factors remain unchanged for analysis purposes. Factors that can shift the demand curve for goods and services, causing a different quantity to be demanded at any given price, include changes in tastes, population, income, prices of substitute or complement goods, and expectations about future conditions and prices. Factors that can shift the supply curve for goods and services, causing a different quantity to be supplied at any given price, include input prices, natural conditions, changes in technology, and government taxes, regulations, or subsidies.

3.3 Changes in Equilibrium Price and Quantity: The Four-Step Process

When using the supply and demand framework to think about how an event will affect the equilibrium price and quantity, proceed through four steps: (1) sketch a supply and demand diagram to think about what the market looked like before the event; (2) decide whether the event will affect supply or demand; (3) decide whether the effect on supply or demand is negative or positive, and draw the appropriate shifted supply or demand curve; (4) compare the new equilibrium price and quantity to the original ones.

3.4 Price Ceilings and Price Floors

Price ceilings prevent a price from rising above a certain level. When a price ceiling is set below the equilibrium price, quantity demanded will exceed quantity supplied, and excess demand or shortages will result. Price floors prevent a price from falling below a certain level. When a price floor is set above the equilibrium price, quantity supplied will exceed quantity demanded, and excess supply or surpluses will result. Price floors and price ceilings often lead to unintended consequences.

3.5 Demand, Supply, and Efficiency

Consumer surplus is the gap between the price that consumers are willing to pay, based on their preferences, and the market equilibrium price. Producer surplus is the gap between the price for which producers are willing to sell a product, based on their costs, and the market equilibrium price. Social surplus is the sum of consumer surplus and producer surplus. Total surplus is larger at the equilibrium quantity and price than it will be at any other quantity and price. Deadweight loss is loss in total surplus that occurs when the economy produces at an inefficient quantity.

SELF-CHECK QUESTIONS

1. Review **Figure 3.4**. Suppose the price of gasoline is $1.60 per gallon. Is the quantity demanded higher or lower than at the equilibrium price of $1.40 per gallon? What about the quantity supplied? Is there a shortage or a surplus in the market? If so, how much?

2. Why do economists use the *ceteris paribus* assumption?

3. In an analysis of the market for paint, an economist discovers the facts listed below. State whether each of these changes will affect supply or demand, and in what direction.
   a. There have recently been some important cost-saving inventions in the technology for making paint.
   b. Paint is lasting longer, so that property owners need not repaint as often.
   c. Because of severe hailstorms, many people need to repaint now.
   d. The hailstorms damaged several factories that make paint, forcing them to close down for several months.

4. Many changes are affecting the market for oil. Predict how each of the following events will affect the equilibrium price and quantity in the market for oil. In each case, state how the event will affect the supply and demand diagram. Create a sketch of the diagram if necessary.
   a. Cars are becoming more fuel efficient, and therefore get more miles to the gallon.
   b. The winter is exceptionally cold.
   c. A major discovery of new oil is made off the coast of Norway.
   d. The economies of some major oil-using nations, like Japan, slow down.
   e. A war in the Middle East disrupts oil-pumping schedules.
   f. Landlords install additional insulation in buildings.
   g. The price of solar energy falls dramatically.
   h. Chemical companies invent a new, popular kind of plastic made from oil.

5. Let's think about the market for air travel. From August 2014 to January 2015, the price of jet fuel increased roughly 47%. Using the four-step analysis, how do you think this fuel price increase affected the equilibrium price and quantity of air travel?

6. A tariff is a tax on imported goods. Suppose the U.S. government cuts the tariff on imported flat screen televisions. Using the four-step analysis, how do you think the tariff reduction will affect the equilibrium price and quantity of flat screen TVs?

7. What is the effect of a price ceiling on the quantity demanded of the product? What is the effect of a price ceiling on the quantity supplied? Why exactly does a price ceiling cause a shortage?

8. Does a price ceiling change the equilibrium price?

9. What would be the impact of imposing a price floor below the equilibrium price?

10. Does a price ceiling increase or decrease the number of transactions in a market? Why? What about a price floor?

11. If a price floor benefits producers, why does a price floor reduce social surplus?

REVIEW QUESTIONS

12. What determines the level of prices in a market?

13. What does a downward-sloping demand curve mean about how buyers in a market will react to a higher price?

14. Will demand curves have the same exact shape in all markets? If not, how will they differ?

15. Will supply curves have the same shape in all markets? If not, how will they differ?

16. What is the relationship between quantity demanded and quantity supplied at equilibrium? What is the relationship when there is a shortage? What is the relationship when there is a surplus?

17. How can you locate the equilibrium point on a demand and supply graph?

18. If the price is above the equilibrium level, would you predict a surplus or a shortage? If the price is below the equilibrium level, would you predict a surplus or a shortage? Why?

19. When the price is above the equilibrium, explain how market forces move the market price to equilibrium. Do the same when the price is below the equilibrium.

20. What is the difference between the demand and the quantity demanded of a product, say milk? Explain in words and show the difference on a graph with a demand curve for milk.

21. What is the difference between the supply and the quantity supplied of a product, say milk? Explain in words and show the difference on a graph with the supply curve for milk.

22. When analyzing a market, how do economists deal with the problem that many factors that affect the market are changing at the same time?

23. Name some factors that can cause a shift in the demand curve in markets for goods and services.

24. Name some factors that can cause a shift in the supply curve in markets for goods and services.

25. How does one analyze a market where both demand and supply shift?

26. What causes a movement along the demand curve? What causes a movement along the supply curve?

27. Does a price ceiling attempt to make a price higher or lower?

28. How does a price ceiling set below the equilibrium level affect quantity demanded and quantity supplied?

29. Does a price floor attempt to make a price higher or lower?

30. How does a price floor set above the equilibrium level affect quantity demanded and quantity supplied?

31. What is consumer surplus? How is it illustrated on a demand and supply diagram?

32. What is producer surplus? How is it illustrated on a demand and supply diagram?

33. What is total surplus? How is it illustrated on a demand and supply diagram?

34. What is the relationship between total surplus and economic efficiency?

35. What is deadweight loss?

CRITICAL THINKING QUESTIONS

36. Review Figure 3.4. Suppose the government decided that, since gasoline is a necessity, its price should be legally capped at $1.30 per gallon. What do you anticipate would be the outcome in the gasoline market?

37. Explain why the following statement is false: "In the goods market, no buyer would be willing to pay more than the equilibrium price."

38. Explain why the following statement is false: "In the goods market, no seller would be willing to sell for less than the equilibrium price."

39. Consider the demand for hamburgers. If the price of a substitute good (for example, hot dogs) increases and the price of a complement good (for example, hamburger buns) increases, can you tell for sure what will happen to the demand for hamburgers? Why or why not? Illustrate your answer with a graph.

40. How do you suppose the demographics of an aging population of "Baby Boomers" in the United States will affect the demand for milk? Justify your answer.

41. We know that a change in the price of a product causes a movement along the demand curve. Suppose consumers believe that prices will be rising in the future. How will that affect demand for the product in the present? Can you show this graphically?

42. Suppose there is a soda tax to curb obesity. What should a reduction in the soda tax do to the supply of sodas and to the equilibrium price and quantity? Can you show this graphically? *Hint:* Assume that the soda tax is collected from the sellers.

43. Use the four-step process to analyze the impact of the advent of the iPod (or other portable digital music players) on the equilibrium price and quantity of the Sony Walkman (or other portable audio cassette players).

44. Use the four-step process to analyze the impact of a reduction in tariffs on imports of iPods on the equilibrium price and quantity of Sony Walkman-type products.

45. Suppose both of these events took place at the same time. Combine your analyses of the impacts of the iPod and the tariff reduction to determine the likely impact on the equilibrium price and quantity of Sony Walkman-type products. Show your answer graphically.

46. Most government policy decisions have winners and losers. What are the effects of raising the minimum wage? It is more complex than simply producers lose and workers gain. Who are the winners and who are the losers, and what exactly do they win and lose? To what extent does the policy change achieve its goals?

47. Agricultural price supports result in governments holding large inventories of agricultural products. Why do you think the government cannot simply give the products away to poor people?

48. Can you propose a policy that would induce the market to supply more rental housing units?

49. What term would an economist use to describe what happens when a shopper gets a "good deal" on a product?

50. Explain why voluntary transactions improve social welfare.

51. Why would a free market never operate at a quantity greater than the equilibrium quantity? *Hint:* What would be required for a transaction to occur at that quantity?

PROBLEMS

52. Review Figure 3.4 again. Suppose the price of gasoline is $1.00. Will the quantity demanded be lower or higher than at the equilibrium price of $1.40 per gallon? Will the quantity supplied be lower or higher? Is there a shortage or a surplus in the market? If so, of how much?

53. **Table 3.8** shows information on the demand and supply for bicycles, where the quantities of bicycles are measured in thousands.

Price	Qd	Qs
$120	50	36
$150	40	40
$180	32	48
$210	28	56
$240	24	70

Table 3.8

a. What is the quantity demanded and the quantity supplied at a price of $210?
b. At what price is the quantity supplied equal to 48,000?
c. Graph the demand and supply curve for bicycles. How can you determine the equilibrium price and quantity from the graph? How can you determine the equilibrium price and quantity from the table? What are the equilibrium price and equilibrium quantity?
d. If the price was $120, what would the quantities demanded and supplied be? Would a shortage or surplus exist? If so, how large would the shortage or surplus be?

54. The computer market in recent years has seen many more computers sell at much lower prices. What shift in demand or supply is most likely to explain this outcome? Sketch a demand and supply diagram and explain your reasoning for each.
a. A rise in demand
b. A fall in demand
c. A rise in supply
d. A fall in supply

55. **Table 3.9** illustrates the market's demand and supply for cheddar cheese. Graph the data and find the equilibrium. Next, create a table showing the change in quantity demanded or quantity supplied, and a graph of the new equilibrium, in each of the following situations:

a. The price of milk, a key input for cheese production, rises, so that the supply decreases by 80 pounds at every price.
b. A new study says that eating cheese is good for your health, so that demand increases by 20% at every price.

Price per Pound	Qd	Qs
$3.00	750	540
$3.20	700	600
$3.40	**650**	**650**
$3.60	620	700
$3.80	600	720
$4.00	590	730

Table 3.9

56. Table 3.10 shows the supply and demand for movie tickets in a city. Graph demand and supply and identify the equilibrium. Then calculate in a table and graph the effect of the following two changes.

    a. Three new nightclubs open. They offer decent bands and have no cover charge, but make their money by selling food and drink. As a result, demand for movie tickets falls by six units at every price.

    b. The city eliminates a tax that it placed on all local entertainment businesses. The result is that the quantity supplied of movies at any given price increases by 10%.

Price per Pound	Qd	Qs
$5.00	26	16
$6.00	24	18
$7.00	22	20
$8.00	21	21
$9.00	20	22

Table 3.10

57. A low-income country decides to set a price ceiling on bread so it can make sure that bread is affordable to the poor. Table 3.11 provides the conditions of demand and supply. What are the equilibrium price and equilibrium quantity before the price ceiling? What will the excess demand or the shortage (that is, quantity demanded minus quantity supplied) be if the price ceiling is set at $2.40? At $2.00? At $3.60?

Price	Qd	Qs
$1.60	9,000	5,000
$2.00	8,500	5,500
$2.40	8,000	6,400
$2.80	**7,500**	**7,500**
$3.20	7,000	9,000
$3.60	6,500	11,000
$4.00	6,000	15,000

Table 3.11

This OpenStax book is available for free at http://cnx.org/content/col12122/1.4

4 | Labor and Financial Markets

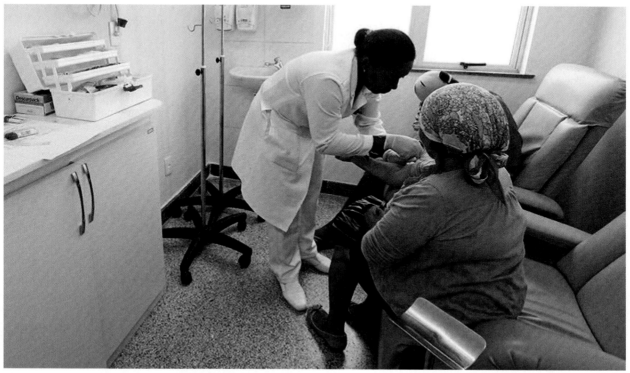

Figure 4.1 People often think of demand and supply in relation to goods, but labor markets, such as the nursing profession, can also apply to this analysis. (Credit: modification of work by "Fotos GOVBA"/Flickr Creative Commons)

Bring it Home

Baby Boomers Come of Age

The Census Bureau reports that as of 2013, 20% of the U.S. population was over 60 years old, which means that almost 63 million people are reaching an age when they will need increased medical care.

The baby boomer population, the group born between 1946 and 1964, is comprised of approximately 74 million people who have just reached retirement age. As this population grows older, they will be faced with common healthcare issues such as heart conditions, arthritis, and Alzheimer's that may require hospitalization, long-term, or at-home nursing care. Aging baby boomers and advances in life-saving and life-extending technologies will increase the demand for healthcare and nursing. Additionally, the Affordable Care Act, which expands access to healthcare for millions of Americans, has further increase the demand, although with the election of Donald J. Trump, this increase may not be sustained.

According to the Bureau of Labor Statistics, registered nursing jobs are expected to increase by 16% between 2014 and 2024. The median annual wage of $67,490 (in 2015) is also expected to increase. The BLS forecasts that 439,000 new nurses will be in demand by 2022.

These data tell us, as economists, that the market for healthcare professionals, and nurses in particular, will face several challenges. Our study of supply and demand will help us to analyze what might happen in the labor market for nursing and other healthcare professionals, as we will discuss in the second half of this case at the end of the chapter.

Introduction to Labor and Financial Markets

In this chapter, you will learn about:

- Demand and Supply at Work in Labor Markets

- Demand and Supply in Financial Markets

- The Market System as an Efficient Mechanism for Information

The theories of supply and demand do not apply just to markets for goods. They apply to any market, even markets for things we may not think of as goods and services like labor and financial services. Labor markets are markets for employees or jobs. Financial services markets are markets for saving or borrowing.

When we think about demand and supply curves in goods and services markets, it is easy to picture the demanders and suppliers: businesses produce the products and households buy them. Who are the demanders and suppliers in labor and financial service markets? In labor markets job seekers (individuals) are the suppliers of labor, while firms and other employers who hire labor are the demanders for labor. In financial markets, any individual or firm who saves contributes to the supply of money, and any who borrows (person, firm, or government) contributes to the demand for money.

As a college student, you most likely participate in both labor and financial markets. Employment is a fact of life for most college students: According to the National Center for Educational Statistics, in 2013 40% of full-time college students and 76% of part-time college students were employed. Most college students are also heavily involved in financial markets, primarily as borrowers. Among full-time students, about half take out a loan to help finance their education each year, and those loans average about $6,000 per year. Many students also borrow for other expenses, like purchasing a car. As this chapter will illustrate, we can analyze labor markets and financial markets with the same tools we use to analyze demand and supply in the goods markets.

4.1 | Demand and Supply at Work in Labor Markets

By the end of this section, you will be able to:
- Predict shifts in the demand and supply curves of the labor market
- Explain the impact of new technology on the demand and supply curves of the labor market
- Explain price floors in the labor market such as minimum wage or a living wage

Markets for labor have demand and supply curves, just like markets for goods. The law of demand applies in labor markets this way: A higher **salary** or **wage**—that is, a higher price in the labor market—leads to a decrease in the quantity of labor demanded by employers, while a lower salary or wage leads to an increase in the quantity of labor demanded. The law of supply functions in labor markets, too: A higher price for labor leads to a higher quantity of labor supplied; a lower price leads to a lower quantity supplied.

Equilibrium in the Labor Market

In 2015, about 35,000 registered nurses worked in the Minneapolis-St. Paul-Bloomington, Minnesota-Wisconsin metropolitan area, according to the BLS. They worked for a variety of employers: hospitals, doctors' offices, schools, health clinics, and nursing homes. **Figure 4.2** illustrates how demand and supply determine equilibrium in this labor market. The demand and supply schedules in **Table 4.1** list the quantity supplied and quantity demanded of nurses at different salaries.

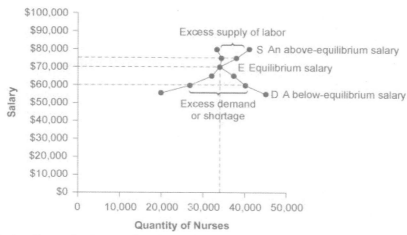

Figure 4.2 Labor Market Example: Demand and Supply for Nurses in Minneapolis-St. Paul-Bloomington The demand curve (D) of those employers who want to hire nurses intersects with the supply curve (S) of those who are qualified and willing to work as nurses at the equilibrium point (E). The equilibrium salary is $70,000 and the equilibrium quantity is 34,000 nurses. At an above-equilibrium salary of $75,000, quantity supplied increases to 38,000, but the quantity of nurses demanded at the higher pay declines to 33,000. At this above-equilibrium salary, an excess supply or surplus of nurses would exist. At a below-equilibrium salary of $60,000, quantity supplied declines to 27,000, while the quantity demanded at the lower wage increases to 40,000 nurses. At this below-equilibrium salary, excess demand or a shortage exists.

Annual Salary	Quantity Demanded	Quantity Supplied
$55,000	45,000	20,000
$60,000	40,000	27,000
$65,000	37,000	31,000
$70,000	34,000	34,000
$75,000	33,000	38,000
$80,000	32,000	41,000

Table 4.1 Demand and Supply of Nurses in Minneapolis-St. Paul-Bloomington

The horizontal axis shows the quantity of nurses hired. In this example we measure labor by number of workers, but another common way to measure the quantity of labor is by the number of hours worked. The vertical axis shows the price for nurses' labor—that is, how much they are paid. In the real world, this "price" would be total labor compensation: salary plus benefits. It is not obvious, but benefits are a significant part (as high as 30 percent) of labor compensation. In this example we measure the price of labor by salary on an annual basis, although in other cases we could measure the price of labor by monthly or weekly pay, or even the wage paid per hour. As the salary for nurses rises, the quantity demanded will fall. Some hospitals and nursing homes may reduce the number of nurses they hire, or they may lay off some of their existing nurses, rather than pay them higher salaries. Employers who face higher nurses' salaries may also try to replace some nursing functions by investing in physical equipment, like computer monitoring and diagnostic systems to monitor patients, or by using lower-paid health care aides to reduce the number of nurses they need.

As the salary for nurses rises, the quantity supplied will rise. If nurses' salaries in Minneapolis-St. Paul-Bloomington are higher than in other cities, more nurses will move to Minneapolis-St. Paul-Bloomington to find jobs, more people will be willing to train as nurses, and those currently trained as nurses will be more likely to pursue nursing as a full-time job. In other words, there will be more nurses looking for jobs in the area.

At **equilibrium**, the quantity supplied and the quantity demanded are equal. Thus, every employer who wants to hire a nurse at this equilibrium wage can find a willing worker, and every nurse who wants to work at this equilibrium salary can find a job. In **Figure 4.2**, the supply curve (S) and demand curve (D) intersect at the equilibrium point (E). The equilibrium quantity of nurses in the Minneapolis-St. Paul-Bloomington area is 34,000, and the equilibrium salary is $70,000 per year. This example simplifies the nursing market by focusing on the "average" nurse. In reality, of course, the market for nurses actually comprises many smaller markets, like markets for nurses with varying degrees of experience and credentials. Many markets contain closely related products that differ in quality. For instance, even a simple product like gasoline comes in regular, premium, and super-premium, each with a different price. Even in such cases, discussing the average price of gasoline, like the average salary for nurses, can still be useful because it reflects what is happening in most of the submarkets.

When the price of labor is not at the equilibrium, economic incentives tend to move salaries toward the equilibrium. For example, if salaries for nurses in Minneapolis-St. Paul-Bloomington were above the equilibrium at $75,000 per year, then 38,000 people want to work as nurses, but employers want to hire only 33,000 nurses. At that above-equilibrium salary, excess supply or a surplus results. In a situation of excess supply in the **labor market**, with many applicants for every job opening, employers will have an incentive to offer lower wages than they otherwise would have. Nurses' salary will move down toward equilibrium.

In contrast, if the salary is below the equilibrium at, say, $60,000 per year, then a situation of excess demand or a shortage arises. In this case, employers encouraged by the relatively lower wage want to hire 40,000 nurses, but only 27,000 individuals want to work as nurses at that salary in Minneapolis-St. Paul-Bloomington. In response to the shortage, some employers will offer higher pay to attract the nurses. Other employers will have to match the higher pay to keep their own employees. The higher salaries will encourage more nurses to train or work in Minneapolis-St. Paul-Bloomington. Again, price and quantity in the labor market will move toward equilibrium.

Shifts in Labor Demand

The demand curve for labor shows the quantity of labor employers wish to hire at any given salary or wage rate, under the *ceteris paribus* assumption. A change in the wage or salary will result in a change in the quantity demanded of labor. If the wage rate increases, employers will want to hire fewer employees. The quantity of labor demanded will decrease, and there will be a movement upward along the demand curve. If the wages and salaries decrease, employers are more likely to hire a greater number of workers. The quantity of labor demanded will increase, resulting in a downward movement along the demand curve.

Shifts in the demand curve for labor occur for many reasons. One key reason is that the demand for labor is based on the demand for the good or service that is produced. For example, the more new automobiles consumers demand, the greater the number of workers automakers will need to hire. Therefore the demand for labor is called a "derived demand." Here are some examples of derived demand for labor:

- The demand for chefs is dependent on the demand for restaurant meals.

- The demand for pharmacists is dependent on the demand for prescription drugs.

- The demand for attorneys is dependent on the demand for legal services.

As the demand for the goods and services increases, the demand for labor will increase, or shift to the right, to meet employers' production requirements. As the demand for the goods and services decreases, the demand for labor will decrease, or shift to the left. **Table 4.2** shows that in addition to the derived demand for labor, demand can also increase or decrease (shift) in response to several factors.

Factors	Results
Demand for Output	When the demand for the good produced (output) increases, both the output price and profitability increase. As a result, producers demand more labor to ramp up production.

Table 4.2 Factors That Can Shift Demand

This OpenStax book is available for free at http://cnx.org/content/col12122/1.4

Factors	Results
Education and Training	A well-trained and educated workforce causes an increase in the demand for that labor by employers. Increased levels of productivity within the workforce will cause the demand for labor to shift to the right. If the workforce is not well-trained or educated, employers will not hire from within that labor pool, since they will need to spend a significant amount of time and money training that workforce. Demand for such will shift to the left.
Technology	Technology changes can act as either substitutes for or complements to labor. When technology acts as a substitute, it replaces the need for the number of workers an employer needs to hire. For example, word processing decreased the number of typists needed in the workplace. This shifted the demand curve for typists left. An increase in the availability of certain technologies may increase the demand for labor. Technology that acts as a complement to labor will increase the demand for certain types of labor, resulting in a rightward shift of the demand curve. For example, the increased use of word processing and other software has increased the demand for information technology professionals who can resolve software and hardware issues related to a firm's network. More and better technology will increase demand for skilled workers who know how to use technology to enhance workplace productivity. Those workers who do not adapt to changes in technology will experience a decrease in demand.
Number of Companies	An increase in the number of companies producing a given product will increase the demand for labor resulting in a shift to the right. A decrease in the number of companies producing a given product will decrease the demand for labor resulting in a shift to the left.
Government Regulations	Complying with government regulations can increase or decrease the demand for labor at any given wage. In the healthcare industry, government rules may require that nurses be hired to carry out certain medical procedures. This will increase the demand for nurses. Less-trained healthcare workers would be prohibited from carrying out these procedures, and the demand for these workers will shift to the left.
Price and Availability of Other Inputs	Labor is not the only input into the production process. For example, a salesperson at a call center needs a telephone and a computer terminal to enter data and record sales. If prices of other inputs fall, production will become more profitable and suppliers will demand more labor to increase production. This will cause a rightward shift in the demand curve for labor. The opposite is also true. Higher prices for other inputs lower demand for labor.

Table 4.2 Factors That Can Shift Demand

Link It Up ⊂∞⊃

Click here (http://openstaxcollege.org/l/Futurework) to read more about "Trends and Challenges for Work in the 21st Century."

Shifts in Labor Supply

The supply of labor is upward-sloping and adheres to the law of supply: The higher the price, the greater the quantity supplied and the lower the price, the less quantity supplied. The supply curve models the tradeoff between supplying labor into the market or using time in leisure activities at every given price level. The higher the wage, the more labor is willing to work and forego leisure activities. **Table 4.3** lists some of the factors that will cause the supply to increase or decrease.

Factors	Results
Number of Workers	An increased number of workers will cause the supply curve to shift to the right. An increased number of workers can be due to several factors, such as immigration, increasing population, an aging population, and changing demographics. Policies that encourage immigration will increase the supply of labor, and vice versa. Population grows when birth rates exceed death rates. This eventually increases supply of labor when the former reach working age. An aging and therefore retiring population will decrease the supply of labor. Another example of changing demographics is more women working outside of the home, which increases the supply of labor.
Required Education	The more required education, the lower the supply. There is a lower supply of PhD mathematicians than of high school mathematics teachers; there is a lower supply of cardiologists than of primary care physicians; and there is a lower supply of physicians than of nurses.
Government Policies	Government policies can also affect the supply of labor for jobs. Alternatively, the government may support rules that set high qualifications for certain jobs: academic training, certificates or licenses, or experience. When these qualifications are made tougher, the number of qualified workers will decrease at any given wage. On the other hand, the government may also subsidize training or even reduce the required level of qualifications. For example, government might offer subsidies for nursing schools or nursing students. Such provisions would shift the supply curve of nurses to the right. In addition, government policies that change the relative desirability of working versus not working also affect the labor supply. These include unemployment benefits, maternity leave, child care benefits, and welfare policy. For example, child care benefits may increase the labor supply of working mothers. Long term unemployment benefits may discourage job searching for unemployed workers. All these policies must therefore be carefully designed to minimize any negative labor supply effects.

Table 4.3 Factors that Can Shift Supply

A change in salary will lead to a movement along labor demand or labor supply curves, but it will not shift those curves. However, other events like those we have outlined here will cause either the demand or the supply of labor to shift, and thus will move the labor market to a new equilibrium salary and quantity.

Technology and Wage Inequality: The Four-Step Process

Economic events can change the equilibrium salary (or wage) and quantity of labor. Consider how the wave of new information technologies, like computer and telecommunications networks, has affected low-skill and high-skill workers in the U.S. economy. From the perspective of employers who demand labor, these new technologies are often a substitute for low-skill laborers like file clerks who used to keep file cabinets full of paper records of transactions. However, the same new technologies are a complement to high-skill workers like managers, who benefit from the technological advances by having the ability to monitor more information, communicate more easily, and juggle a wider array of responsibilities. How will the new technologies affect the wages of high-skill and low-skill workers? For this question, the four-step process of analyzing how shifts in supply or demand affect a market (introduced in **Demand and Supply**) works in this way:

Step 1. What did the markets for low-skill labor and high-skill labor look like before the arrival of the new technologies? In **Figure 4.3** (a) and **Figure 4.3** (b), S_0 is the original supply curve for labor and D_0 is the original demand curve for labor in each market. In each graph, the original point of equilibrium, E_0, occurs at the price W_0 and the quantity Q_0.

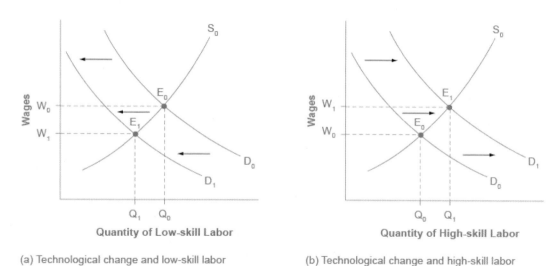

(a) Technological change and low-skill labor

(b) Technological change and high-skill labor

Figure 4.3 Technology and Wages: Applying Demand and Supply (a) The demand for low-skill labor shifts to the left when technology can do the job previously done by these workers. (b) New technologies can also increase the demand for high-skill labor in fields such as information technology and network administration.

Step 2. Does the new technology affect the supply of labor from households or the demand for labor from firms? The technology change described here affects demand for labor by firms that hire workers.

Step 3. Will the new technology increase or decrease demand? Based on the description earlier, as the substitute for low-skill labor becomes available, demand for low-skill labor will shift to the left, from D_0 to D_1. As the technology complement for high-skill labor becomes cheaper, demand for high-skill labor will shift to the right, from D_0 to D_1.

Step 4. The new equilibrium for low-skill labor, shown as point E_1 with price W_1 and quantity Q_1, has a lower wage and quantity hired than the original equilibrium, E_0. The new equilibrium for high-skill labor, shown as point E_1 with price W_1 and quantity Q_1, has a higher wage and quantity hired than the original equilibrium (E_0).

Thus, the demand and supply model predicts that the new computer and communications technologies will raise the pay of high-skill workers but reduce the pay of low-skill workers. From the 1970s to the mid-2000s, the wage gap widened between high-skill and low-skill labor. According to the National Center for Education Statistics, in 1980, for example, a college graduate earned about 30% more than a high school graduate with comparable job experience, but by 2014, a college graduate earned about 66% more than an otherwise comparable high school graduate. Many economists believe that the trend toward greater wage inequality across the U.S. economy is due to improvements in technology.

Link It Up

Visit this website (http://openstaxcollege.org/l/oldtechjobs) to read about ten tech skills that have lost relevance in today's workforce.

Price Floors in the Labor Market: Living Wages and Minimum Wages

In contrast to goods and services markets, price ceilings are rare in labor markets, because rules that prevent people from earning income are not politically popular. There is one exception: boards of trustees or stockholders, as an example, propose limits on the high incomes of top business executives.

The labor market, however, presents some prominent examples of price floors, which are an attempt to increase the wages of low-paid workers. The U.S. government sets a **minimum wage**, a price floor that makes it illegal for an employer to pay employees less than a certain hourly rate. In mid-2009, the U.S. minimum wage was raised to $7.25 per hour. Local political movements in a number of U.S. cities have pushed for a higher minimum wage, which they call a **living wage**. Promoters of living wage laws maintain that the minimum wage is too low to ensure a reasonable standard of living. They base this conclusion on the calculation that, if you work 40 hours a week at a minimum wage of $7.25 per hour for 50 weeks a year, your annual income is $14,500, which is less than the official U.S. government definition of what it means for a family to be in poverty. (A family with two adults earning minimum wage and two young children will find it more cost efficient for one parent to provide childcare while the other works for income. Thus the family income would be $14,500, which is significantly lower than the federal poverty line for a family of four, which was $24,250 in 2015.)

Supporters of the living wage argue that full-time workers should be assured a high enough wage so that they can afford the essentials of life: food, clothing, shelter, and healthcare. Since Baltimore passed the first living wage law in 1994, several dozen cities enacted similar laws in the late 1990s and the 2000s. The living wage ordinances do not apply to all employers, but they have specified that all employees of the city or employees of firms that the city hires be paid at least a certain wage that is usually a few dollars per hour above the U.S. minimum wage.

Figure 4.4 illustrates the situation of a city considering a living wage law. For simplicity, we assume that there is no federal minimum wage. The wage appears on the vertical axis, because the wage is the price in the labor market. Before the passage of the living wage law, the equilibrium wage is $10 per hour and the city hires 1,200 workers at this wage. However, a group of concerned citizens persuades the city council to enact a living wage law requiring employers to pay no less than $12 per hour. In response to the higher wage, 1,600 workers look for jobs with the city. At this higher wage, the city, as an employer, is willing to hire only 700 workers. At the price floor, the quantity supplied exceeds the quantity demanded, and a surplus of labor exists in this market. For workers who continue to have a job at a higher salary, life has improved. For those who were willing to work at the old wage rate but lost their jobs with the wage increase, life has not improved. **Table 4.4** shows the differences in supply and demand at different wages.

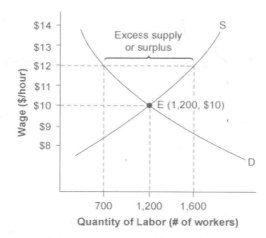

Figure 4.4 A Living Wage: Example of a Price Floor The original equilibrium in this labor market is a wage of $10/hour and a quantity of 1,200 workers, shown at point E. Imposing a wage floor at $12/hour leads to an excess supply of labor. At that wage, the quantity of labor supplied is 1,600 and the quantity of labor demanded is only 700.

Wage	Quantity Labor Demanded	Quantity Labor Supplied
$8/hr	1,900	500
$9/hr	1,500	900
$10/hr	1,200	1,200
$11/hr	900	1,400
$12/hr	700	1,600
$13/hr	500	1,800
$14/hr	400	1,900

Table 4.4 Living Wage: Example of a Price Floor

The Minimum Wage as an Example of a Price Floor

The U.S. minimum wage is a price floor that is set either very close to the equilibrium wage or even slightly below it. About 1% of American workers are actually paid the minimum wage. In other words, the vast majority of the U.S. labor force has its wages determined in the labor market, not as a result of the government price floor. However, for workers with low skills and little experience, like those without a high school diploma or teenagers, the minimum wage is quite important. In many cities, the federal minimum wage is apparently below the market price for unskilled labor, because employers offer more than the minimum wage to checkout clerks and other low-skill workers without any government prodding.

Economists have attempted to estimate how much the minimum wage reduces the quantity demanded of low-skill labor. A typical result of such studies is that a 10% increase in the minimum wage would decrease the hiring of unskilled workers by 1 to 2%, which seems a relatively small reduction. In fact, some studies have even found no effect of a higher minimum wage on employment at certain times and places—although these studies are controversial.

Let's suppose that the minimum wage lies just slightly *below* the equilibrium wage level. Wages could fluctuate according to market forces above this price floor, but they would not be allowed to move beneath the floor. In this situation, the price floor minimum wage is *nonbinding* —that is, the price floor is not determining the market outcome. Even if the minimum wage moves just a little higher, it will still have no effect on the quantity of employment in the economy, as long as it remains below the equilibrium wage. Even if the government increases minimum wage by enough so that it rises slightly above the equilibrium wage and becomes binding, there will be only a small excess supply gap between the quantity demanded and quantity supplied.

These insights help to explain why U.S. minimum wage laws have historically had only a small impact on employment. Since the minimum wage has typically been set close to the equilibrium wage for low-skill labor and sometimes even below it, it has not had a large effect in creating an excess supply of labor. However, if the minimum wage increased dramatically—say, if it doubled to match the living wages that some U.S. cities have considered—then its impact on reducing the quantity demanded of employment would be far greater. As of 2017, many U.S. states are set to increase their minimum wage to $15 per hour. We will see what happens. The following Clear It Up feature describes in greater detail some of the arguments for and against changes to minimum wage.

What's the harm in raising the minimum wage?

Because of the law of demand, a higher required wage will reduce the amount of low-skill employment either in terms of employees or in terms of work hours. Although there is controversy over the numbers, let's say for the sake of the argument that a 10% rise in the minimum wage will reduce the employment of low-skill workers by 2%. Does this outcome mean that raising the minimum wage by 10% is bad public policy? Not necessarily.

If 98% of those receiving the minimum wage have a pay increase of 10%, but 2% of those receiving the minimum wage lose their jobs, are the gains for society as a whole greater than the losses? The answer is not clear, because job losses, even for a small group, may cause more pain than modest income gains for others. For one thing, we need to consider which minimum wage workers are losing their jobs. If the 2% of minimum wage workers who lose their jobs are struggling to support families, that is one thing. If those who lose their job are high school students picking up spending money over summer vacation, that is something else.

Another complexity is that many minimum wage workers do not work full-time for an entire year. Imagine a minimum wage worker who holds different part-time jobs for a few months at a time, with bouts of unemployment in between. The worker in this situation receives the 10% raise in the minimum wage when working, but also ends up working 2% fewer hours during the year because the higher minimum wage reduces how much employers want people to work. Overall, this worker's income would rise because the 10% pay raise would more than offset the 2% fewer hours worked.

Of course, these arguments do not prove that raising the minimum wage is necessarily a good idea either. There may well be other, better public policy options for helping low-wage workers. (The Poverty and Economic Inequality chapter discusses some possibilities.) The lesson from this maze of minimum wage arguments is that complex social problems rarely have simple answers. Even those who agree on how a proposed economic policy affects quantity demanded and quantity supplied may still disagree on whether the policy is a good idea.

4.2 | Demand and Supply in Financial Markets

By the end of this section, you will be able to:
- Identify the demanders and suppliers in a financial market
- Explain how interest rates can affect supply and demand
- Analyze the economic effects of U.S. debt in terms of domestic financial markets
- Explain the role of price ceilings and usury laws in the U.S.

United States' households, institutions, and domestic businesses saved almost $1.3 trillion in 2015. Where did that savings go and how was it used? Some of the savings ended up in banks, which in turn loaned the money to individuals or businesses that wanted to borrow money. Some was invested in private companies or loaned to government agencies that wanted to borrow money to raise funds for purposes like building roads or mass transit. Some firms reinvested their savings in their own businesses.

In this section, we will determine how the demand and supply model links those who wish to supply **financial capital** (i.e., savings) with those who demand financial capital (i.e., borrowing). Those who save money (or make financial investments, which is the same thing), whether individuals or businesses, are on the supply side of the financial market. Those who borrow money are on the demand side of the financial market. For a more detailed treatment of the different kinds of financial investments like bank accounts, stocks and bonds, see the **Financial Markets** chapter.

Who Demands and Who Supplies in Financial Markets?

In any market, the price is what suppliers receive and what demanders pay. In financial markets, those who supply financial capital through saving expect to receive a rate of return, while those who demand financial capital by receiving funds expect to pay a rate of return. This rate of return can come in a variety of forms, depending on the type of investment.

The simplest example of a rate of return is the **interest rate**. For example, when you supply money into a savings account at a bank, you receive interest on your deposit. The interest the bank pays you as a percent of your deposits is the interest rate. Similarly, if you demand a loan to buy a car or a computer, you will need to pay interest on the money you borrow.

Let's consider the market for borrowing money with credit cards. In 2015, almost 200 million Americans were cardholders. Credit cards allow you to borrow money from the card's issuer, and pay back the borrowed amount plus interest, although most allow you a period of time in which you can repay the loan without paying interest. A typical credit card interest rate ranges from 12% to 18% per year. In May 2016, Americans had about $943 billion outstanding in credit card debts. About half of U.S. families with credit cards report that they almost always pay the full balance on time, but one-quarter of U.S. families with credit cards say that they "hardly ever" pay off the card in full. In fact, in 2014, 56% of consumers carried an unpaid balance in the last 12 months. Let's say that, on average, the annual interest rate for credit card borrowing is 15% per year. Thus, Americans pay tens of billions of dollars every year in interest on their credit cards—plus basic fees for the credit card or fees for late payments.

Figure 4.5 illustrates demand and supply in the financial market for credit cards. The horizontal axis of the financial market shows the quantity of money loaned or borrowed in this market. The vertical or price axis shows the rate of return, which in the case of credit card borrowing we can measure with an interest rate. **Table 4.5** shows the quantity of financial capital that consumers demand at various interest rates and the quantity that credit card firms (often banks) are willing to supply.

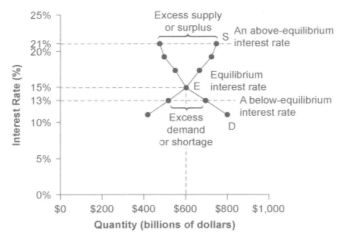

Figure 4.5 Demand and Supply for Borrowing Money with Credit Cards In this market for credit card borrowing, the demand curve (D) for borrowing financial capital intersects the supply curve (S) for lending financial capital at equilibrium E. At the equilibrium, the interest rate (the "price" in this market) is 15% and the quantity of financial capital loaned and borrowed is $600 billion. The equilibrium price is where the quantity demanded and the quantity supplied are equal. At an above-equilibrium interest rate like 21%, the quantity of financial capital supplied would increase to $750 billion, but the quantity demanded would decrease to $480 billion. At a below-equilibrium interest rate like 13%, the quantity of financial capital demanded would increase to $700 billion, but the quantity of financial capital supplied would decrease to $510 billion.

Interest Rate (%)	Quantity of Financial Capital Demanded (Borrowing) ($ billions)	Quantity of Financial Capital Supplied (Lending) ($ billions)
11	$800	$420
13	$700	$510
15	$600	$600
17	$550	$660
19	$500	$720
21	$480	$750

Table 4.5 Demand and Supply for Borrowing Money with Credit Cards

The laws of demand and supply continue to apply in the financial markets. According to the **law of demand**, a higher rate of return (that is, a higher price) will decrease the quantity demanded. As the interest rate rises, consumers will reduce the quantity that they borrow. According to the law of supply, a higher price increases the quantity supplied. Consequently, as the interest rate paid on credit card borrowing rises, more firms will be eager to issue credit cards and to encourage customers to use them. Conversely, if the interest rate on credit cards falls, the quantity of financial capital supplied in the credit card market will decrease and the quantity demanded will fall.

Equilibrium in Financial Markets

In the financial market for credit cards in **Figure 4.5**, the supply curve (S) and the demand curve (D) cross at the equilibrium point (E). The equilibrium occurs at an interest rate of 15%, where the quantity of funds demanded and the quantity supplied are equal at an equilibrium quantity of $600 billion.

If the interest rate (remember, this measures the "price" in the financial market) is above the equilibrium level, then an excess supply, or a surplus, of financial capital will arise in this market. For example, at an interest rate of 21%, the quantity of funds supplied increases to $750 billion, while the quantity demanded decreases to $480 billion. At this

This OpenStax book is available for free at http://cnx.org/content/col12122/1.4

above-equilibrium interest rate, firms are eager to supply loans to credit card borrowers, but relatively few people or businesses wish to borrow. As a result, some credit card firms will lower the interest rates (or other fees) they charge to attract more business. This strategy will push the interest rate down toward the equilibrium level.

If the interest rate is below the equilibrium, then excess demand or a shortage of funds occurs in this market. At an interest rate of 13%, the quantity of funds credit card borrowers demand increases to $700 billion, but the quantity credit card firms are willing to supply is only $510 billion. In this situation, credit card firms will perceive that they are overloaded with eager borrowers and conclude that they have an opportunity to raise interest rates or fees. The interest rate will face economic pressures to creep up toward the equilibrium level.

The FRED database publishes some two dozen measures of interest rates, including interest rates on credit cards, automobile loans, personal loans, mortgage loans, and more. You can find these at the FRED website (https://openstax.org/l/FRED_stlouis) .

Shifts in Demand and Supply in Financial Markets

Those who supply financial capital face two broad decisions: how much to save, and how to divide up their savings among different forms of financial investments. We will discuss each of these in turn.

Participants in financial markets must decide when they prefer to consume goods: now or in the future. Economists call this **intertemporal decision making** because it involves decisions across time. Unlike a decision about what to buy from the grocery store, people make investment or savings decisions across a period of time, sometimes a long period.

Most workers save for retirement because their income in the present is greater than their needs, while the opposite will be true once they retire. Thus, they save today and supply financial markets. If their income increases, they save more. If their perceived situation in the future changes, they change the amount of their saving. For example, there is some evidence that Social Security, the program that workers pay into in order to qualify for government checks after retirement, has tended to reduce the quantity of financial capital that workers save. If this is true, Social Security has shifted the supply of financial capital at any interest rate to the left.

By contrast, many college students need money today when their income is low (or nonexistent) to pay their college expenses. As a result, they borrow today and demand from financial markets. Once they graduate and become employed, they will pay back the loans. Individuals borrow money to purchase homes or cars. A business seeks financial investment so that it has the funds to build a factory or invest in a research and development project that will not pay off for five years, ten years, or even more. Thus, when consumers and businesses have greater confidence that they will be able to repay in the future, the quantity demanded of financial capital at any given interest rate will shift to the right.

For example, in the technology boom of the late 1990s, many businesses became extremely confident that investments in new technology would have a high rate of return, and their demand for financial capital shifted to the right. Conversely, during the 2008 and 2009 Great Recession, their demand for financial capital at any given interest rate shifted to the left.

To this point, we have been looking at saving in total. Now let us consider what affects saving in different types of financial investments. In deciding between different forms of financial investments, suppliers of financial capital will have to consider the rates of return and the risks involved. Rate of return is a positive attribute of investments, but risk is a negative. If Investment A becomes more risky, or the return diminishes, then savers will shift their funds to Investment B—and the supply curve of financial capital for Investment A will shift back to the left while the supply curve of capital for Investment B shifts to the right.

The United States as a Global Borrower

In the global economy, trillions of dollars of financial investment cross national borders every year. In the early 2000s, financial investors from foreign countries were investing several hundred billion dollars per year more in the U.S. economy than U.S. financial investors were investing abroad. The following Work It Out deals with one of the macroeconomic concerns for the U.S. economy in recent years.

Work It Out ⊷⊶⊶

The Effect of Growing U.S. Debt

Imagine that foreign investors viewed the U.S. economy as a less desirable place to put their money because of fears about the growth of the U.S. public debt. Using the four-step process for analyzing how changes in supply and demand affect equilibrium outcomes, how would increased U.S. public debt affect the equilibrium price and quantity for capital in U.S. financial markets?

Step 1. Draw a diagram showing demand and supply for financial capital that represents the original scenario in which foreign investors are pouring money into the U.S. economy. Figure 4.6 shows a demand curve, D, and a supply curve, S, where the supply of capital includes the funds arriving from foreign investors. The original equilibrium E_0 occurs at interest rate R_0 and quantity of financial investment Q_0.

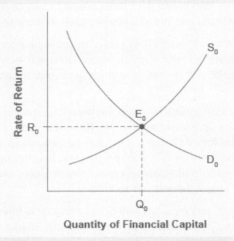

Figure 4.6 The United States as a Global Borrower Before U.S. Debt Uncertainty The graph shows the demand for financial capital from and supply of financial capital into the U.S. financial markets by the foreign sector before the increase in uncertainty regarding U.S. public debt. The original equilibrium (E_0) occurs at an equilibrium rate of return (R_0) and the equilibrium quantity is at Q_0.

Step 2. Will the diminished confidence in the U.S. economy as a place to invest affect demand or supply of financial capital? Yes, it will affect supply. Many foreign investors look to the U.S. financial markets to store their money in safe financial vehicles with low risk and stable returns. Diminished confidence means U.S. financial assets will be seen as more risky.

Step 3. Will supply increase or decrease? When the enthusiasm of foreign investors' for investing their money in the U.S. economy diminishes, the supply of financial capital shifts to the left. Figure 4.7 shows the supply curve shift from S_0 to S_1.

This OpenStax book is available for free at http://cnx.org/content/col12122/1.4

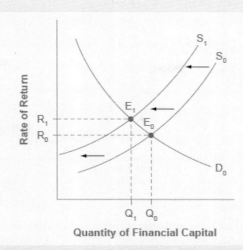

Figure 4.7 The United States as a Global Borrower Before and After U.S. Debt Uncertainty The graph shows the demand for financial capital and supply of financial capital into the U.S. financial markets by the foreign sector before and after the increase in uncertainty regarding U.S. public debt. The original equilibrium (E_0) occurs at an equilibrium rate of return (R_0) and the equilibrium quantity is at Q_0.

Step 4. Thus, foreign investors' diminished enthusiasm leads to a new equilibrium, E_1, which occurs at the higher interest rate, R_1, and the lower quantity of financial investment, Q_1. In short, U.S. borrowers will have to pay more interest on their borrowing.

The economy has experienced an enormous inflow of foreign capital. According to the U.S. Bureau of Economic Analysis, by the third quarter of 2015, U.S. investors had accumulated $23.3 trillion of foreign assets, but foreign investors owned a total of $30.6 trillion of U.S. assets. If foreign investors were to pull their money out of the U.S. economy and invest elsewhere in the world, the result could be a significantly lower quantity of financial investment in the United States, available only at a higher interest rate. This reduced inflow of foreign financial investment could impose hardship on U.S. consumers and firms interested in borrowing.

In a modern, developed economy, financial capital often moves invisibly through electronic transfers between one bank account and another. Yet we can analyze these flows of funds with the same tools of demand and supply as markets for goods or labor.

Price Ceilings in Financial Markets: Usury Laws

As we noted earlier, about 200 million Americans own credit cards, and their interest payments and fees total tens of billions of dollars each year. It is little wonder that political pressures sometimes arise for setting limits on the interest rates or fees that credit card companies charge. The firms that issue credit cards, including banks, oil companies, phone companies, and retail stores, respond that the higher interest rates are necessary to cover the losses created by those who borrow on their credit cards and who do not repay on time or at all. These companies also point out that cardholders can avoid paying interest if they pay their bills on time.

Consider the credit card market as **Figure 4.8** illustrators. In this financial market, the vertical axis shows the interest rate (which is the price in the financial market). Demanders in the credit card market are households and businesses. Suppliers are the companies that issue credit cards. This figure does not use specific numbers, which would be hypothetical in any case, but instead focuses on the underlying economic relationships. Imagine a law imposes a price ceiling that holds the interest rate charged on credit cards at the rate Rc, which lies below the interest rate R_0 that would otherwise have prevailed in the market. The horizontal dashed line at interest rate R_c in **Figure 4.8** shows the price ceiling. The demand and supply model predicts that at the lower price ceiling interest rate, the quantity demanded of credit card debt will increase from its original level of Q_0 to Qd; however, the quantity supplied of credit card debt will decrease from the original Q_0 to Qs. At the price ceiling (Rc), quantity demanded will exceed quantity supplied. Consequently, a number of people who want to have credit cards and are willing to pay the prevailing interest rate will find that companies are unwilling to issue cards to them. The result will be a credit shortage.

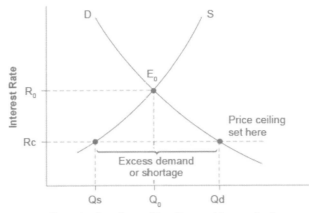

Figure 4.8 Credit Card Interest Rates: Another Price Ceiling Example   The original intersection of demand D and supply S occurs at equilibrium E_0. However, a price ceiling is set at the interest rate Rc, below the equilibrium interest rate R_0, and so the interest rate cannot adjust upward to the equilibrium. At the price ceiling, the quantity demanded, Qd, exceeds the quantity supplied, Qs. There is excess demand, also called a shortage.

Many states do have **usury laws**, which impose an upper limit on the interest rate that lenders can charge. However, in many cases these upper limits are well above the market interest rate. For example, if the interest rate is not allowed to rise above 30% per year, it can still fluctuate below that level according to market forces. A price ceiling that is set at a relatively high level is nonbinding, and it will have no practical effect unless the equilibrium price soars high enough to exceed the price ceiling.

4.3 | The Market System as an Efficient Mechanism for Information

By the end of this section, you will be able to:
- Apply demand and supply models to analyze prices and quantities
- Explain the effects of price controls on the equilibrium of prices and quantities

Prices exist in markets for goods and services, for labor, and for financial capital. In all of these markets, prices serve as a remarkable social mechanism for collecting, combining, and transmitting information that is relevant to the market—namely, the relationship between demand and supply—and then serving as messengers to convey that information to buyers and sellers. In a market-oriented economy, no government agency or guiding intelligence oversees the set of responses and interconnections that result from a change in price. Instead, each consumer reacts according to that person's preferences and budget set, and each profit-seeking producer reacts to the impact on its expected profits. The following Clear It Up feature examines the **demand and supply models**.

Why are demand and supply curves important?

The demand and supply model is the second fundamental diagram for this course. (The opportunity set model that we introduced in the Choice in a World of Scarcity chapter was the first.) Just as it would be foolish to try to learn the arithmetic of long division by memorizing every possible combination of numbers that can be divided by each other, it would be foolish to try to memorize every specific example of demand and supply in this chapter, this textbook, or this course. Demand and supply is not primarily a list of examples. It is a model to analyze prices and quantities. Even though demand and supply diagrams have many labels, they are fundamentally the same in their logic. Your goal should be to understand the underlying model so you can use it to analyze *any* market.

Figure 4.9 displays a generic demand and supply curve. The horizontal axis shows the different measures of quantity: a quantity of a good or service, or a quantity of labor for a given job, or a quantity of financial capital. The vertical axis shows a measure of price: the price of a good or service, the wage in the labor market, or the rate of return (like the interest rate) in the financial market.

The demand and supply model can explain the existing levels of prices, wages, and rates of return. To carry out such an analysis, think about the quantity that will be demanded at each price and the quantity that will be supplied at each price—that is, think about the shape of the demand and supply curves—and how these forces will combine to produce equilibrium.

We can also use demand and supply to explain how economic events will cause changes in prices, wages, and rates of return. There are only four possibilities: the change in any single event may cause the demand curve to shift right or to shift left, or it may cause the supply curve to shift right or to shift left. The key to analyzing the effect of an economic event on equilibrium prices and quantities is to determine which of these four possibilities occurred. The way to do this correctly is to think back to the list of factors that shift the demand and supply curves. Note that if more than one variable is changing at the same time, the overall impact will depend on the degree of the shifts. When there are multiple variables, economists isolate each change and analyze it independently.

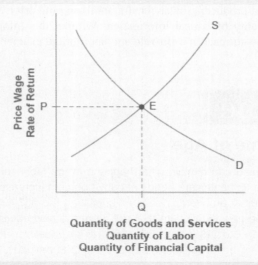

Figure 4.9 Demand and Supply Curves   The figure displays a generic demand and supply curve. The horizontal axis shows the different measures of quantity: a quantity of a good or service, a quantity of labor for a given job, or a quantity of financial capital. The vertical axis shows a measure of price: the price of a good or service, the wage in the labor market, or the rate of return (like the interest rate) in the financial market. We can use the demand and supply curves explain how economic events will cause changes in prices, wages, and rates of return.

An increase in the price of some product signals consumers that there is a shortage; therefore, they may want to economize on buying this product. For example, if you are thinking about taking a plane trip to Hawaii, but the ticket turns out to be expensive during the week you intend to go, you might consider other weeks when the ticket might be cheaper. The price could be high because you were planning to travel during a holiday when demand for traveling is high. Maybe the cost of an input like jet fuel increased or the airline has raised the price temporarily to see how many people are willing to pay it. Perhaps all of these factors are present at the same time. You do not need to analyze the market and break down the price change into its underlying factors. You just have to look at the ticket price and decide whether and when to fly.

In the same way, price changes provide useful information to producers. Imagine the situation of a farmer who grows oats and learns that the price of oats has risen. The higher price could be due to an increase in demand caused by a new scientific study proclaiming that eating oats is especially healthful. Perhaps the price of a substitute grain, like corn, has risen, and people have responded by buying more oats. The oat farmer does not need to know the details. The farmer only needs to know that the price of oats has risen and that it will be profitable to expand production as a result.

The actions of individual consumers and producers as they react to prices overlap and interlock in markets for goods, labor, and financial capital. A change in any single market is transmitted through these multiple interconnections to other markets. The vision of the role of flexible prices helping markets to reach equilibrium and linking different markets together helps to explain why price controls can be so counterproductive. Price controls are government laws that serve to regulate prices rather than allow the various markets to determine prices. There is an old proverb: "Don't kill the messenger." In ancient times, messengers carried information between distant cities and kingdoms. When they brought bad news, there was an emotional impulse to kill the messenger. However, killing the messenger did not kill the bad news. Moreover, killing the messenger had an undesirable side effect: Other messengers would refuse to bring news to that city or kingdom, depriving its citizens of vital information.

Those who seek price controls are trying to kill the messenger—or at least to stifle an unwelcome message that prices are bringing about the equilibrium level of price and quantity. However, price controls do nothing to affect the underlying forces of demand and supply, and this can have serious repercussions. During China's "Great Leap Forward" in the late 1950s, the government kept food prices artificially low, with the result that 30 to 40 million people died of starvation because the low prices depressed farm production. This was communist party leader Mao Zedong's social and economic campaign to rapidly transform the country from an agrarian economy to a socialist society through rapid industrialization and collectivization. Changes in demand and supply will continue to reveal themselves through consumers' and producers' behavior. Immobilizing the price messenger through price controls will deprive everyone in the economy of critical information. Without this information, it becomes difficult for everyone—buyers and sellers alike—to react in a flexible and appropriate manner as changes occur throughout the economy.

Bring it Home

Baby Boomers Come of Age

The theory of supply and demand can explain what happens in the labor markets and suggests that the demand for nurses will increase as healthcare needs of baby boomers increase, as Figure 4.10 shows. The impact of that increase will result in an average salary higher than the $67,490 earned in 2015 referenced in the first part of this case. The new equilibrium (E_1) will be at the new equilibrium price (Pe_1). Equilibrium quantity will also increase from Qe_0 to Qe_1.

This OpenStax book is available for free at http://cnx.org/content/col12122/1.4

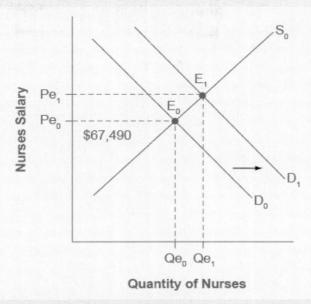

Figure 4.10 Impact of Increasing Demand for Nurses 2014-2024 In 2014, the median salary for nurses was $67,490. As demand for services increases, the demand curve shifts to the right (from D_0 to D_1) and the equilibrium quantity of nurses increases from Qe_0 to Qe_1. The equilibrium salary increases from Pe_0 to Pe_1.

Suppose that as the demand for nurses increases, the supply shrinks due to an increasing number of nurses entering retirement and increases in the tuition of nursing degrees. The leftward shift of the supply curve in **Figure 4.11** captures the impact of a decreasing supply of nurses. The shifts in the two curves result in higher salaries for nurses, but the overall impact in the quantity of nurses is uncertain, as it depends on the relative shifts of supply and demand.

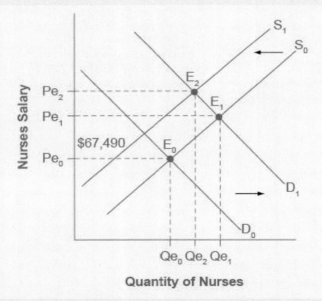

Figure 4.11 Impact of Decreasing Supply of Nurses between 2014 and 2024 The increase in demand for nurses shown in Figure 4.10 leads to both higher prices and higher quantities demanded. As nurses retire from the work force, the supply of nurses decreases, causing a leftward shift in the supply curve and higher salaries for nurses at Pe_2. The net effect on the equilibrium quantity of nurses is uncertain, which in this representation is less than Qe_1, but more than the initial Qe_0.

While we do not know if the number of nurses will increase or decrease relative to their initial employment, we know they will have higher salaries.

This OpenStax book is available for free at http://cnx.org/content/col12122/1.4

KEY TERMS

interest rate the "price" of borrowing in the financial market; a rate of return on an investment

minimum wage a price floor that makes it illegal for an employer to pay employees less than a certain hourly rate

usury laws laws that impose an upper limit on the interest rate that lenders can charge

KEY CONCEPTS AND SUMMARY

4.1 Demand and Supply at Work in Labor Markets

In the labor market, households are on the supply side of the market and firms are on the demand side. In the market for financial capital, households and firms can be on either side of the market: they are suppliers of financial capital when they save or make financial investments, and demanders of financial capital when they borrow or receive financial investments.

In the demand and supply analysis of labor markets, we can measure the price by the annual salary or hourly wage received. We can measure the quantity of labor various ways, like number of workers or the number of hours worked.

Factors that can shift the demand curve for labor include: a change in the quantity demanded of the product that the labor produces; a change in the production process that uses more or less labor; and a change in government policy that affects the quantity of labor that firms wish to hire at a given wage. Demand can also increase or decrease (shift) in response to: workers' level of education and training, technology, the number of companies, and availability and price of other inputs.

The main factors that can shift the supply curve for labor are: how desirable a job appears to workers relative to the alternatives, government policy that either restricts or encourages the quantity of workers trained for the job, the number of workers in the economy, and required education.

4.2 Demand and Supply in Financial Markets

In the demand and supply analysis of financial markets, the "price" is the rate of return or the interest rate received. We measure the quantity by the money that flows from those who supply financial capital to those who demand it.

Two factors can shift the supply of financial capital to a certain investment: if people want to alter their existing levels of consumption, and if the riskiness or return on one investment changes relative to other investments. Factors that can shift demand for capital include business confidence and consumer confidence in the future—since financial investments received in the present are typically repaid in the future.

4.3 The Market System as an Efficient Mechanism for Information

The market price system provides a highly efficient mechanism for disseminating information about relative scarcities of goods, services, labor, and financial capital. Market participants do not need to know why prices have changed, only that the changes require them to revisit previous decisions they made about supply and demand. Price controls hide information about the true scarcity of products and thereby cause misallocation of resources.

SELF-CHECK QUESTIONS

1. In the labor market, what causes a movement along the demand curve? What causes a shift in the demand curve?

2. In the labor market, what causes a movement along the supply curve? What causes a shift in the supply curve?

3. Why is a living wage considered a price floor? Does imposing a living wage have the same outcome as a minimum wage?

4. In the financial market, what causes a movement along the demand curve? What causes a shift in the demand curve?

5. In the financial market, what causes a movement along the supply curve? What causes a shift in the supply curve?

6. If a usury law limits interest rates to no more than 35%, what would the likely impact be on the amount of loans made and interest rates paid?

7. Which of the following changes in the financial market will lead to a decline in interest rates:
a. a rise in demand
b. a fall in demand
c. a rise in supply
d. a fall in supply

8. Which of the following changes in the financial market will lead to an increase in the quantity of loans made and received:
a. a rise in demand
b. a fall in demand
c. a rise in supply
d. a fall in supply

9. Identify the most accurate statement. A price floor will have the largest effect if it is set:
a. substantially above the equilibrium price
b. slightly above the equilibrium price
c. slightly below the equilibrium price
d. substantially below the equilibrium price

Sketch all four of these possibilities on a demand and supply diagram to illustrate your answer.

10. A price ceiling will have the largest effect:
a. substantially below the equilibrium price
b. slightly below the equilibrium price
c. substantially above the equilibrium price
d. slightly above the equilibrium price

Sketch all four of these possibilities on a demand and supply diagram to illustrate your answer.

11. Select the correct answer. A price floor will usually shift:
a. demand
b. supply
c. both
d. neither

Illustrate your answer with a diagram.

12. Select the correct answer. A price ceiling will usually shift:
a. demand
b. supply
c. both
d. neither

REVIEW QUESTIONS

13. What is the "price" commonly called in the labor market?

14. Are households demanders or suppliers in the goods market? Are firms demanders or suppliers in the goods market? What about the labor market and the financial market?

15. Name some factors that can cause a shift in the demand curve in labor markets.

16. Name some factors that can cause a shift in the supply curve in labor markets.

17. How do economists define equilibrium in financial markets?

This OpenStax book is available for free at http://cnx.org/content/col12122/1.4

18. What would be a sign of a shortage in financial markets?

19. Would usury laws help or hinder resolution of a shortage in financial markets?

20. Whether the product market or the labor market, what happens to the equilibrium price and quantity for each of the four possibilities: increase in demand, decrease in demand, increase in supply, and decrease in supply.

CRITICAL THINKING QUESTIONS

21. Other than the demand for labor, what would be another example of a "derived demand?"

22. Suppose that a 5% increase in the minimum wage causes a 5% reduction in employment. How would this affect employers and how would it affect workers? In your opinion, would this be a good policy?

23. Under what circumstances would a minimum wage be a nonbinding price floor? Under what circumstances would a living wage be a binding price floor?

24. Suppose the U.S. economy began to grow more rapidly than other countries in the world. What would be the likely impact on U.S. financial markets as part of the global economy?

25. If the government imposed a federal interest rate ceiling of 20% on all loans, who would gain and who would lose?

26. Why are the factors that shift the demand for a product different from the factors that shift the demand for labor? Why are the factors that shift the supply of a product different from those that shift the supply of labor?

27. During a discussion several years ago on building a pipeline to Alaska to carry natural gas, the U.S. Senate passed a bill stipulating that there should be a guaranteed minimum price for the natural gas that would flow through the pipeline. The thinking behind the bill was that if private firms had a guaranteed price for their natural gas, they would be more willing to drill for gas and to pay to build the pipeline.
   a. Using the demand and supply framework, predict the effects of this price floor on the price, quantity demanded, and quantity supplied.
   b. With the enactment of this price floor for natural gas, what are some of the likely unintended consequences in the market?
   c. Suggest some policies other than the price floor that the government can pursue if it wishes to encourage drilling for natural gas and for a new pipeline in Alaska.

PROBLEMS

28. Identify each of the following as involving either demand or supply. Draw a circular flow diagram and label the flows A through F. (Some choices can be on both sides of the goods market.)
   a. Households in the labor market
   b. Firms in the goods market
   c. Firms in the financial market
   d. Households in the goods market
   e. Firms in the labor market
   f. Households in the financial market

29. Predict how each of the following events will raise or lower the equilibrium wage and quantity of oil workers in Texas. In each case, sketch a demand and supply diagram to illustrate your answer.
   a. The price of oil rises.
   b. New oil-drilling equipment is invented that is cheap and requires few workers to run.
   c. Several major companies that do not drill oil open factories in Texas, offering many well-paid jobs outside the oil industry.
   d. Government imposes costly new regulations to make oil-drilling a safer job.

30. Predict how each of the following economic changes will affect the equilibrium price and quantity in the financial market for home loans. Sketch a demand and supply diagram to support your answers.

    a. The number of people at the most common ages for home-buying increases.

    b. People gain confidence that the economy is growing and that their jobs are secure.

    c. Banks that have made home loans find that a larger number of people than they expected are not repaying those loans.

    d. Because of a threat of a war, people become uncertain about their economic future.

    e. The overall level of saving in the economy diminishes.

    f. The federal government changes its bank regulations in a way that makes it cheaper and easier for banks to make home loans.

31. Table 4.6 shows the amount of savings and borrowing in a market for loans to purchase homes, measured in millions of dollars, at various interest rates. What is the equilibrium interest rate and quantity in the capital financial market? How can you tell? Now, imagine that because of a shift in the perceptions of foreign investors, the supply curve shifts so that there will be $10 million less supplied at every interest rate. Calculate the new equilibrium interest rate and quantity, and explain why the direction of the interest rate shift makes intuitive sense.

32. Imagine that to preserve the traditional way of life in small fishing villages, a government decides to impose a price floor that will guarantee all fishermen a certain price for their catch.

    a. Using the demand and supply framework, predict the effects on the price, quantity demanded, and quantity supplied.

    b. With the enactment of this price floor for fish, what are some of the likely unintended consequences in the market?

    c. Suggest some policies other than the price floor to make it possible for small fishing villages to continue.

33. What happens to the price and the quantity bought and sold in the cocoa market if countries producing cocoa experience a drought and a new study is released demonstrating the health benefits of cocoa? Illustrate your answer with a demand and supply graph.

Interest Rate	Qs	Qd
5%	130	170
6%	135	150
7%	140	140
8%	145	135
9%	150	125
10%	155	110

Table 4.6

5 | Elasticity

Figure 5.1 Netflix On-Demand Media   Netflix, Inc. is an American provider of on-demand Internet streaming media to many countries around the world, including the United States, and of flat rate DVD-by-mail in the United States. (Credit: modification of work by Traci Lawson/Flickr Creative Commons)

Bring it Home

That Will Be How Much?

Imagine going to your favorite coffee shop and having the waiter inform you the pricing has changed. Instead of $3 for a cup of coffee, you will now be charged $2 for coffee, $1 for creamer, and $1 for your choice of sweetener. If you pay your usual $3 for a cup of coffee, you must choose between creamer and sweetener. If you want both, you now face an extra charge of $1. Sound absurd? Well, that is similar to the situation Netflix customers found themselves in—they faced a 60% price hike to retain the same service in 2011.

In early 2011, Netflix consumers paid about $10 a month for a package consisting of streaming video and DVD rentals. In July 2011, the company announced a packaging change. Customers wishing to retain both streaming video and DVD rental would be charged $15.98 per month, a price increase of about 60%. In 2014, Netflix also raised its streaming video subscription price from $7.99 to $8.99 per month for new U.S. customers. The company also changed its policy of 4K streaming content from $9.00 to $12.00 per month that year.

How would customers of the 18-year-old firm react? Would they abandon Netflix? Would the ease of access to other venues make a difference in how consumers responded to the Netflix price change? We will explore the answers to those questions in this chapter, which focuses on the change in quantity with respect to a change in price, a concept economists call elasticity.

Introduction to Elasticity

In this chapter, you will learn about:

- Price Elasticity of Demand and Price Elasticity of Supply

- Polar Cases of Elasticity and Constant Elasticity

- Elasticity and Pricing

- Elasticity in Areas Other Than Price

Anyone who has studied economics knows the law of demand: a higher price will lead to a lower quantity demanded. What you may not know is how much lower the quantity demanded will be. Similarly, the law of supply states that a higher price will lead to a higher quantity supplied. The question is: How much higher? This chapter will explain how to answer these questions and why they are critically important in the real world.

To find answers to these questions, we need to understand the concept of elasticity. **Elasticity** is an economics concept that measures responsiveness of one variable to changes in another variable. Suppose you drop two items from a second-floor balcony. The first item is a tennis ball. The second item is a brick. Which will bounce higher? Obviously, the tennis ball. We would say that the tennis ball has greater elasticity.

Consider an economic example. Cigarette taxes are an example of a "sin tax," a tax on something that is bad for you, like alcohol. Governments tax cigarettes at the state and national levels. State taxes range from a low of 17 cents per pack in Missouri to $4.35 per pack in New York. The average state cigarette tax is $1.69 per pack. The 2014 federal tax rate on cigarettes was $1.01 per pack, but in 2015 the Obama Administration proposed raising the federal tax nearly a dollar to $1.95 per pack. The key question is: How much would cigarette purchases decline?

Taxes on cigarettes serve two purposes: to raise tax revenue for government and to discourage cigarette consumption. However, if a higher cigarette tax discourages consumption considerably, meaning a greatly reduced quantity of cigarette sales, then the cigarette tax on each pack will not raise much revenue for the government. Alternatively, a higher cigarette tax that does not discourage consumption by much will actually raise more tax revenue for the government. Thus, when a government agency tries to calculate the effects of altering its cigarette tax, it must analyze how much the tax affects the quantity of cigarettes consumed. This issue reaches beyond governments and taxes. Every firm faces a similar issue. When a firm considers raising the sales price, it must consider how much a price increase will reduce the quantity demanded of what it sells. Conversely, when a firm puts its products on sale, it must expect (or hope) that the lower price will lead to a significantly higher quantity demanded.

5.1 | Price Elasticity of Demand and Price Elasticity of Supply

By the end of this section, you will be able to:
- Calculate the price elasticity of demand
- Calculate the price elasticity of supply

Both the demand and supply curve show the relationship between price and the number of units demanded or supplied. **Price elasticity** is the ratio between the percentage change in the quantity demanded (Qd) or supplied (Qs) and the corresponding percent change in price. The **price elasticity of demand** is the percentage change in the quantity *demanded* of a good or service divided by the percentage change in the price. The **price elasticity of supply** is the percentage change in quantity *supplied* divided by the percentage change in price.

This OpenStax book is available for free at http://cnx.org/content/col12122/1.4

We can usefully divide elasticities into three broad categories: elastic, inelastic, and unitary. An **elastic demand** or **elastic supply** is one in which the elasticity is greater than one, indicating a high responsiveness to changes in price. Elasticities that are less than one indicate low responsiveness to price changes and correspond to **inelastic demand** or **inelastic supply**. **Unitary elasticities** indicate proportional responsiveness of either demand or supply, as Table 5.1 summarizes.

If . . .	Then . . .	And It Is Called . . .
% change in quantity > % change in price	$\frac{\% \text{ change in quantity}}{\% \text{ change in price}} > 1$	Elastic
% change in quantity = % change in price	$\frac{\% \text{ change in quantity}}{\% \text{ change in price}} = 1$	Unitary
% change in quantity < % change in price	$\frac{\% \text{ change in quantity}}{\% \text{ change in price}} < 1$	Inelastic

Table 5.1 Elastic, Inelastic, and Unitary: Three Cases of Elasticity

Link It Up

Before we delve into the details of elasticity, enjoy this article (http://openstaxcollege.org/l/Super_Bowl) on elasticity and ticket prices at the Super Bowl.

To calculate elasticity along a demand or supply curve economists use the average percent change in both quantity and price. This is called the Midpoint Method for Elasticity, and is represented in the following equations:

$$\% \text{ change in quantity} = \frac{Q_2 - Q_1}{(Q_2 + Q_1)/2} \times 100$$

$$\% \text{ change in price} = \frac{P_2 - P_1}{(P_2 + P_1)/2} \times 100$$

The advantage of the Midpoint Method is that one obtains the same elasticity between two price points whether there is a price increase or decrease. This is because the formula uses the same base (average quantity and average price) for both cases.

Calculating Price Elasticity of Demand

Let's calculate the elasticity between points A and B and between points G and H as Figure 5.2 shows.

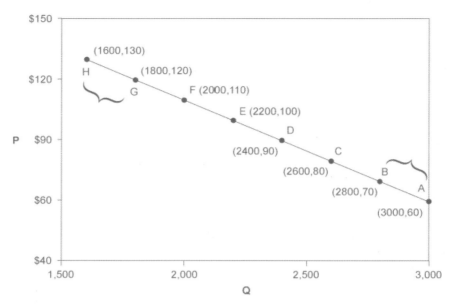

Figure 5.2 Calculating the Price Elasticity of Demand We calculate the price elasticity of demand as the percentage change in quantity divided by the percentage change in price.

First, apply the formula to calculate the elasticity as price decreases from $70 at point B to $60 at point A:

$$\% \text{ change in quantity} = \frac{3{,}000 - 2{,}800}{(3{,}000 + 2{,}800)/2} \times 100$$

$$= \frac{200}{2{,}900} \times 100$$

$$= 6.9$$

$$\% \text{ change in price} = \frac{60 - 70}{(60 + 70)/2} \times 100$$

$$= \frac{-10}{65} \times 100$$

$$= -15.4$$

$$\text{Price Elasticity of Demand} = \frac{6.9\%}{-15.4\%}$$

$$= 0.45$$

Therefore, the elasticity of demand between these two points is $\frac{6.9\%}{-15.4\%}$ which is 0.45, an amount smaller than one,

showing that the demand is inelastic in this interval. Price elasticities of demand are *always* negative since price and quantity demanded always move in opposite directions (on the demand curve). By convention, we always talk about elasticities as positive numbers. Mathematically, we take the absolute value of the result. We will ignore this detail from now on, while remembering to interpret elasticities as positive numbers.

This means that, along the demand curve between point B and A, if the price changes by 1%, the quantity demanded will change by 0.45%. A change in the price will result in a smaller percentage change in the quantity demanded. For example, a 10% *increase* in the price will result in only a 4.5% *decrease* in quantity demanded. A 10% *decrease* in the price will result in only a 4.5% *increase* in the quantity demanded. Price elasticities of demand are negative numbers indicating that the demand curve is downward sloping, but we read them as absolute values. The following Work It Out feature will walk you through calculating the price elasticity of demand.

This OpenStax book is available for free at http://cnx.org/content/col12122/1.4

Work It Out ⊢O─O─O

Finding the Price Elasticity of Demand

Calculate the price elasticity of demand using the data in **Figure 5.2** for an increase in price from G to H. Has the elasticity increased or decreased?

Step 1. We know that:

$$\text{Price Elasticity of Demand} = \frac{\% \text{ change in quantity}}{\% \text{ change in price}}$$

Step 2. From the Midpoint Formula we know that:

$$\% \text{ change in quantity} = \frac{Q_2 - Q_1}{(Q_2 + Q_1)/2} \times 100$$

$$\% \text{ change in price} = \frac{P_2 - P_1}{(P_2 + P_1)/2} \times 100$$

Step 3. So we can use the values provided in the figure in each equation:

$$\% \text{ change in quantity} = \frac{1,600 - 1,800}{(1,600 + 1,800)/2} \times 100$$

$$= \frac{-200}{1,700} \times 100$$

$$= -11.76$$

$$\% \text{ change in price} = \frac{130 - 120}{(130 + 120)/2} \times 100$$

$$= \frac{10}{125} \times 100$$

$$= 8.0$$

Step 4. Then, we can use those values to determine the price elasticity of demand:

$$\text{Price Elasticity of Demand} = \frac{\% \text{ change in quantity}}{\% \text{ change in price}}$$

$$= \frac{-11.76}{8}$$

$$= 1.47$$

Therefore, the elasticity of demand from G to is H 1.47. The magnitude of the elasticity has increased (in absolute value) as we moved up along the demand curve from points A to B. Recall that the elasticity between these two points was 0.45. Demand was inelastic between points A and B and elastic between points G and H. This shows us that price elasticity of demand changes at different points along a straight-line demand curve.

Calculating the Price Elasticity of Supply

Assume that an apartment rents for $650 per month and at that price the landlord rents 10,000 units are rented as **Figure 5.3** shows. When the price increases to $700 per month, the landlord supplies 13,000 units into the market. By what percentage does apartment supply increase? What is the price sensitivity?

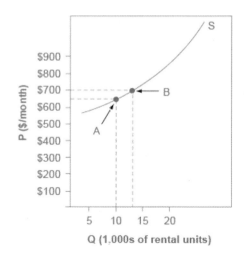

Figure 5.3 Price Elasticity of Supply We calculate the price elasticity of supply as the percentage change in quantity divided by the percentage change in price.

Using the Midpoint Method,

$$
\text{\% change in quantity} = \frac{13,000 - 10,000}{(13,000 + 10,000)/2} \times 100
$$

$$
= \frac{3,000}{11,500} \times 100
$$

$$
= 26.1
$$

$$
\text{\% change in price} = \frac{\$700 - \$650}{(\$700 + \$650)/2} \times 100
$$

$$
= \frac{50}{675} \times 100
$$

$$
= 7.4
$$

$$
\text{Price Elasticity of Supply} = \frac{26.1\%}{7.4\%}
$$

$$
= 3.53
$$

Again, as with the elasticity of demand, the elasticity of supply is not followed by any units. Elasticity is a ratio of one percentage change to another percentage change—nothing more—and we read it as an absolute value. In this case, a 1% rise in price causes an increase in quantity supplied of 3.5%. The greater than one elasticity of supply means that the percentage change in quantity supplied will be greater than a one percent price change. If you're starting to wonder if the concept of slope fits into this calculation, read the following Clear It Up box.

Is the elasticity the slope?

It is a common mistake to confuse the slope of either the supply or demand curve with its elasticity. The slope is the rate of change in units along the curve, or the rise/run (change in y over the change in x). For example, in **Figure 5.2**, at each point shown on the demand curve, price drops by $10 and the number of units demanded increases by 200 compared to the point to its left. The slope is –10/200 along the entire demand curve and does not change. The price elasticity, however, changes along the curve. Elasticity between points A and B was 0.45 and increased to 1.47 between points G and H. Elasticity is the *percentage* change, which is a different calculation from the slope and has a different meaning.

When we are at the upper end of a demand curve, where price is high and the quantity demanded is low, a small change in the quantity demanded, even in, say, one unit, is pretty big in percentage terms. A change in price of, say, a dollar, is going to be much less important in percentage terms than it would have been at the bottom of the demand curve. Likewise, at the bottom of the demand curve, that one unit change when the quantity demanded is high will be small as a percentage.

Thus, at one end of the demand curve, where we have a large percentage change in quantity demanded over a small percentage change in price, the elasticity value would be high, or demand would be relatively elastic. Even with the same change in the price and the same change in the quantity demanded, at the other end of the demand curve the quantity is much higher, and the price is much lower, so the percentage change in quantity demanded is smaller and the percentage change in price is much higher. That means at the bottom of the curve we'd have a small numerator over a large denominator, so the elasticity measure would be much lower, or inelastic.

As we move along the demand curve, the values for quantity and price go up or down, depending on which way we are moving, so the percentages for, say, a $1 difference in price or a one unit difference in quantity, will change as well, which means the ratios of those percentages and hence the elasticity will change.

5.2 | Polar Cases of Elasticity and Constant Elasticity

By the end of this section, you will be able to:
- Differentiate between infinite and zero elasticity
- Analyze graphs in order to classify elasticity as constant unitary, infinite, or zero

There are two extreme cases of elasticity: when elasticity equals zero and when it is infinite. A third case is that of constant unitary elasticity. We will describe each case. **Infinite elasticity** or **perfect elasticity** refers to the extreme case where either the quantity demanded (Qd) or supplied (Qs) changes by an infinite amount in response to any change in price at all. In both cases, the supply and the demand curve are horizontal as **Figure 5.4** shows. While perfectly elastic supply curves are for the most part unrealistic, goods with readily available inputs and whose production can easily expand will feature highly elastic supply curves. Examples include pizza, bread, books, and pencils. Similarly, perfectly elastic demand is an extreme example. However, luxury goods, items that take a large share of individuals' income, and goods with many substitutes are likely to have highly elastic demand curves. Examples of such goods are Caribbean cruises and sports vehicles.

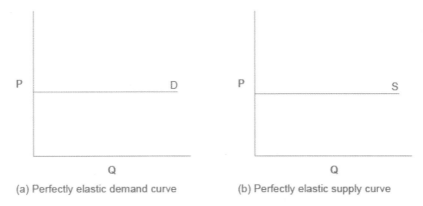

(a) Perfectly elastic demand curve   (b) Perfectly elastic supply curve

Figure 5.4 Infinite Elasticity The horizontal lines show that an infinite quantity will be demanded or supplied at a specific price. This illustrates the cases of a perfectly (or infinitely) elastic demand curve and supply curve. The quantity supplied or demanded is extremely responsive to price changes, moving from zero for prices close to P to infinite when prices reach P.

Zero elasticity or **perfect inelasticity**, as **Figure 5.5** depicts, refers to the extreme case in which a percentage change in price, no matter how large, results in zero change in quantity. While a perfectly inelastic supply is an extreme example, goods with limited supply of inputs are likely to feature highly inelastic supply curves. Examples include diamond rings or housing in prime locations such as apartments facing Central Park in New York City. Similarly, while perfectly inelastic demand is an extreme case, necessities with no close substitutes are likely to have highly inelastic demand curves. This is the case of life-saving drugs and gasoline.

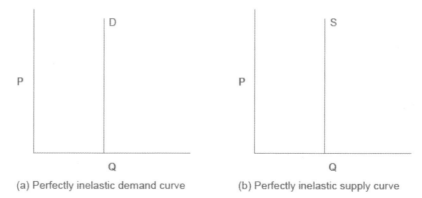

(a) Perfectly inelastic demand curve   (b) Perfectly inelastic supply curve

Figure 5.5 Zero Elasticity The vertical supply curve and vertical demand curve show that there will be zero percentage change in quantity (a) demanded or (b) supplied, regardless of the price.

Constant unitary elasticity, in either a supply or demand curve, occurs when a price change of one percent results in a quantity change of one percent. **Figure 5.6** shows a demand curve with constant unit elasticity. Constant unitary elasticity, in either a supply or demand curve, occurs when a price change of one percent results in a quantity change of one percent. Figure 5.6 shows a demand curve with constant unit elasticity. Using the midpoint method, you can calculate that between points A and B on the demand curve, the price changes by 28.6% and quantity demanded also changes by 28.6%. Hence, the elasticity equals 1. Between points B and C, price again changes by 28.6% as does quantity, while between points C and D the corresponding percentage changes are 22.2% for both price and quantity. In each case, then, the percentage change in price equals the percentage change in quantity, and consequently elasticity equals 1. Notice that in absolute value, the declines in price, as you step down the demand curve, are not identical. Instead, the price falls by $2.00 from A to B, by a smaller amount of $1.50 from B to C, and by a still smaller amount of $0.90 from C to D. As a result, a demand curve with constant unitary elasticity moves from a steeper slope on the left and a flatter slope on the right—and a curved shape overall. Notice that in absolute value, the declines in price, as you step down the demand curve, are not identical. Instead, the price falls by $23 from A to B, by a smaller amount of $1.50 from B to C, and by a still smaller amount of $.90 from C to D. As a result, a demand curve with constant unitary elasticity has a steeper slope on the left and a flatter slope on the right—and a curved shape overall.

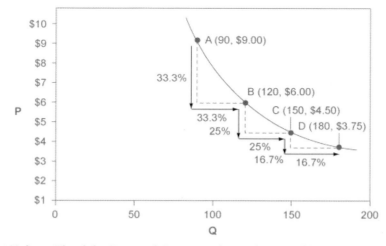

Figure 5.6 A Constant Unitary Elasticity Demand Curve A demand curve with constant unitary elasticity will be a curved line. Notice how price and quantity demanded change by an identical percentage amount between each pair of points on the demand curve.

Unlike the demand curve with unitary elasticity, the supply curve with unitary elasticity is represented by a straight line, and that line goes through the origin. In each pair of points on the supply curve there is an equal difference in quantity of 30. However, in percentage value, using the midpoint method, the steps are decreasing as one moves from left to right, from 28.6% to 22.2% to 18.2%, because the quantity points in each percentage calculation are getting increasingly larger, which expands the denominator in the elasticity calculation of the percentage change in quantity.

Consider the price changes moving up the supply curve in **Figure 5.7**. From points D to E to F and to G on the supply curve, each step of $1.50 is the same in absolute value. However, if we measure the price changes in percentage change terms, using the midpoint method, they are also decreasing, from 28.6% to 22.2% to 18.2%, because the original price points in each percentage calculation are getting increasingly larger in value, increasing the denominator in the calculation of the percentage change in price. Along the constant unitary elasticity supply curve, the percentage quantity increases on the horizontal axis exactly match the percentage price increases on the vertical axis—so this supply curve has a constant unitary elasticity at all points.

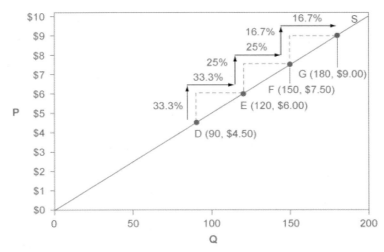

Figure 5.7 A Constant Unitary Elasticity Supply Curve   A constant unitary elasticity supply curve is a straight line reaching up from the origin. Between each pair of points, the percentage increase in quantity supplied is the same as the percentage increase in price.

5.3 | Elasticity and Pricing

By the end of this section, you will be able to:
- Analyze how price elasticities impact revenue
- Evaluate how elasticity can cause shifts in demand and supply
- Predict how the long-run and short-run impacts of elasticity affect equilibrium
- Explain how the elasticity of demand and supply determine the incidence of a tax on buyers and sellers

Studying elasticities is useful for a number of reasons, pricing being most important. Let's explore how elasticity relates to revenue and pricing, both in the long and short run. First, let's look at the elasticities of some common goods and services.

Table 5.2 shows a selection of demand elasticities for different goods and services drawn from a variety of different studies by economists, listed in order of increasing elasticity.

Goods and Services	Elasticity of Price
Housing	0.12
Transatlantic air travel (economy class)	0.12
Rail transit (rush hour)	0.15
Electricity	0.20
Taxi cabs	0.22
Gasoline	0.35
Transatlantic air travel (first class)	0.40
Wine	0.55
Beef	0.59
Transatlantic air travel (business class)	0.62
Kitchen and household appliances	0.63
Cable TV (basic rural)	0.69
Chicken	0.64
Soft drinks	0.70
Beer	0.80
New vehicle	0.87
Rail transit (off-peak)	1.00
Computer	1.44
Cable TV (basic urban)	1.51
Cable TV (premium)	1.77
Restaurant meals	2.27

Table 5.2 Some Selected Elasticities of Demand

Note that demand for necessities such as housing and electricity is inelastic, while items that are not necessities such as restaurant meals are more price-sensitive. If the price of a restaurant meal increases by 10%, the quantity demanded will decrease by 22.7%. A 10% increase in the price of housing will cause only a slight decrease of 1.2% in the quantity of housing demanded.

Read this article (http://openstaxcollege.org/l/Movietickets) for an example of price elasticity that may have affected you.

This OpenStax book is available for free at http://cnx.org/content/col12122/1.4

Does Raising Price Bring in More Revenue?

Imagine that a band on tour is playing in an indoor arena with 15,000 seats. To keep this example simple, assume that the band keeps all the money from ticket sales. Assume further that the band pays the costs for its appearance, but that these costs, like travel, and setting up the stage, are the same regardless of how many people are in the audience. Finally, assume that all the tickets have the same price. (The same insights apply if ticket prices are more expensive for some seats than for others, but the calculations become more complicated.) The band knows that it faces a downward-sloping demand curve; that is, if the band raises the ticket price and, it will sell fewer seats. How should the band set the ticket price to generate the most total revenue, which in this example, because costs are fixed, will also mean the highest profits for the band? Should the band sell more tickets at a lower price or fewer tickets at a higher price?

The key concept in thinking about collecting the most revenue is the price elasticity of demand. Total revenue is price times the quantity of tickets sold. Imagine that the band starts off thinking about a certain price, which will result in the sale of a certain quantity of tickets. The three possibilities are in **Table 5.3**. If demand is elastic at that price level, then the band should cut the price, because the percentage drop in price will result in an even larger percentage increase in the quantity sold—thus raising total revenue. However, if demand is inelastic at that original quantity level, then the band should raise the ticket price, because a certain percentage increase in price will result in a smaller percentage decrease in the quantity sold—and total revenue will rise. If demand has a unitary elasticity at that quantity, then an equal percentage change in quantity will offset a moderate percentage change in the price—so the band will earn the same revenue whether it (moderately) increases or decreases the ticket price.

If Demand Is . . .	Then . . .	Therefore . . .
Elastic	% change in Qd > % change in P	A given % rise in P will be more than offset by a larger % fall in Q so that total revenue (P × Q) falls.
Unitary	% change in Qd = % change in P	A given % rise in P will be exactly offset by an equal % fall in Q so that total revenue (P × Q) is unchanged.
Inelastic	% change in Qd < % change in P	A given % rise in P will cause a smaller % fall in Q so that total revenue (P × Q) rises.

Table 5.3 Will the Band Earn More Revenue by Changing Ticket Prices?

What if the band keeps cutting price, because demand is elastic, until it reaches a level where it sells all 15,000 seats in the available arena? If demand remains elastic at that quantity, the band might try to move to a bigger arena, so that it could slash ticket prices further and see a larger percentage increase in the quantity of tickets sold. However, if the 15,000-seat arena is all that is available or if a larger arena would add substantially to costs, then this option may not work.

Conversely, a few bands are so famous, or have such fanatical followings, that demand for tickets may be inelastic right up to the point where the arena is full. These bands can, if they wish, keep raising the ticket price. Ironically, some of the most popular bands could make more revenue by setting prices so high that the arena is not full—but those who buy the tickets would have to pay very high prices. However, bands sometimes choose to sell tickets for less than the absolute maximum they might be able to charge, often in the hope that fans will feel happier and spend more on recordings, T-shirts, and other paraphernalia.

Can Businesses Pass Costs on to Consumers?

Most businesses face a day-to-day struggle to figure out ways to produce at a lower cost, as one pathway to their goal of earning higher profits. However, in some cases, the price of a key input over which the firm has no control may rise. For example, many chemical companies use petroleum as a key input, but they have no control over the world market price for crude oil. Coffee shops use coffee as a key input, but they have no control over the world market price of coffee. If the cost of a key input rises, can the firm pass those higher costs along to consumers in the form of higher prices? Conversely, if new and less expensive ways of producing are invented, can the firm keep the benefits in the form of higher profits, or will the market pressure them to pass the gains along to consumers in the form of lower prices? The price elasticity of demand plays a key role in answering these questions.

Imagine that as a consumer of legal pharmaceutical products, you read a newspaper story that a technological breakthrough in the production of aspirin has occurred, so that every aspirin factory can now produce aspirin more cheaply. What does this discovery mean to you? **Figure 5.8** illustrates two possibilities. In **Figure 5.8** (a), the demand curve is highly inelastic. In this case, a technological breakthrough that shifts supply to the right, from S_0 to S_1, so that the equilibrium shifts from E_0 to E_1, creates a substantially lower price for the product with relatively little impact on the quantity sold. In **Figure 5.8** (b), the demand curve is highly elastic. In this case, the technological breakthrough leads to a much greater quantity sold in the market at very close to the original price. Consumers benefit more, in general, when the demand curve is more inelastic because the shift in the supply results in a much lower price for consumers.

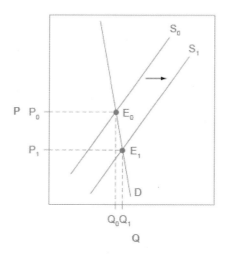
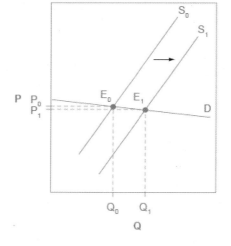

(a) Cost-saving with inelastic demand   (b) Cost-saving with elastic demand

Figure 5.8 Passing along Cost Savings to Consumers   Cost-saving gains cause supply to shift out to the right from S_0 to S_1; that is, at any given price, firms will be willing to supply a greater quantity. If demand is inelastic, as in (a), the result of this cost-saving technological improvement will be substantially lower prices. If demand is elastic, as in (b), the result will be only slightly lower prices. Consumers benefit in either case, from a greater quantity at a lower price, but the benefit is greater when demand is inelastic, as in (a).

Aspirin producers may find themselves in a nasty bind here. The situation in **Figure 5.8**, with extremely inelastic demand, means that a new invention may cause the price to drop dramatically while quantity changes little. As a result, the new production technology can lead to a drop in the revenue that firms earn from aspirin sales. However, if strong competition exists between aspirin producer, each producer may have little choice but to search for and implement any breakthrough that allows it to reduce production costs. After all, if one firm decides not to implement such a cost-saving technology, other firms that do can drive them out of business.

Since demand for food is generally inelastic, farmers may often face the situation in **Figure 5.8** (a). That is, a surge in

This OpenStax book is available for free at http://cnx.org/content/col12122/1.4

production leads to a severe drop in price that can actually decrease the total revenue that farmers receive. Conversely, poor weather or other conditions that cause a terrible year for farm production can sharply raise prices so that the total revenue that the farmer receives increases. The Clear It Up box discusses how these issues relate to coffee.

How do coffee prices fluctuate?

Coffee is an international crop. The top five coffee-exporting nations are Brazil, Vietnam, Colombia, Indonesia, and Ethiopia. In these nations and others, 20 million families depend on selling coffee beans as their main source of income. These families are exposed to enormous risk, because the world price of coffee bounces up and down. For example, in 1993, the world price of coffee was about 50 cents per pound. In 1995 it was four times as high, at $2 per pound. By 1997 it had fallen by half to $1.00 per pound. In 1998 it leaped back up to $2 per pound. By 2001 it had fallen back to 46 cents a pound. By early 2011 it rose to about $2.31 per pound. By the end of 2012, the price had fallen back to about $1.31 per pound.

The reason for these price fluctuations lies in a combination of inelastic demand and shifts in supply. The elasticity of coffee demand is only about 0.3; that is, a 10% rise in the price of coffee leads to a decline of about 3% in the quantity of coffee consumed. When a major frost hit the Brazilian coffee crop in 1994, coffee supply shifted to the left with an inelastic demand curve, leading to much higher prices. Conversely, when Vietnam entered the world coffee market as a major producer in the late 1990s, the supply curve shifted out to the right. With a highly inelastic demand curve, coffee prices fell dramatically. **Figure 5.8** (a) illustrates this situation.

Elasticity also reveals whether firms can pass higher costs that they incur on to consumers. Addictive substances, for which demand is inelastic, are products for which producers can pass higher costs on to consumers. For example, the demand for cigarettes is relatively inelastic among regular smokers who are somewhat addicted. Economic research suggests that increasing cigarette prices by 10% leads to about a 3% reduction in the quantity of cigarettes that adults smoke, so the elasticity of demand for cigarettes is 0.3. If society increases taxes on companies that produce cigarettes, the result will be, as in **Figure 5.9** (a), that the supply curve shifts from S_0 to S_1. However, as the equilibrium moves from E_0 to E_1, governments mainly pass along these taxes to consumers in the form of higher prices. These higher taxes on cigarettes will raise tax revenue for the government, but they will not much affect the quantity of smoking.

If the goal is to reduce the quantity of cigarettes demanded, we must achieve it by shifting this inelastic demand back to the left, perhaps with public programs to discourage cigarette use or to help people to quit. For example, anti-smoking advertising campaigns have shown some ability to reduce smoking. However, if cigarette demand were more elastic, as in **Figure 5.9** (b), then an increase in taxes that shifts supply from S_0 to S_1 and equilibrium from E_0 to E_1 would reduce the quantity of cigarettes smoked substantially. Youth smoking seems to be more elastic than adult smoking—that is, the quantity of youth smoking will fall by a greater percentage than the quantity of adult smoking in response to a given percentage increase in price.

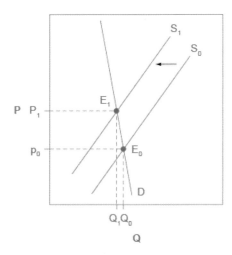

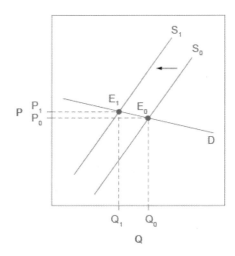

(a) Higher costs with inelastic demand   (b) Higher costs with elastic demand

Figure 5.9 Passing along Higher Costs to Consumers Higher costs, like a higher tax on cigarette companies for the example we gave in the text, lead supply to shift to the left. This shift is identical in (a) and (b). However, in (a), where demand is inelastic, companies largely can pass the cost increase along to consumers in the form of higher prices, without much of a decline in equilibrium quantity. In (b), demand is elastic, so the shift in supply results primarily in a lower equilibrium quantity. Consumers suffer in either case, but in (a), they suffer from paying a higher price for the same quantity, while in (b), they suffer from buying a lower quantity (and presumably needing to shift their consumption elsewhere).

Elasticity and Tax Incidence

The example of cigarette taxes demonstrated that because demand is inelastic, taxes are not effective at reducing the equilibrium quantity of smoking, and they mainly pass along to consumers in the form of higher prices. The analysis, or manner, of how a tax burden is divided between consumers and producers is called **tax incidence**. Typically, the tax incidence, or burden, falls both on the consumers and producers of the taxed good. However, if one wants to predict which group will bear most of the burden, all one needs to do is examine the elasticity of demand and supply. In the tobacco example, the tax burden falls on the most inelastic side of the market.

If demand is more inelastic than supply, consumers bear most of the tax burden, and if supply is more inelastic than demand, sellers bear most of the tax burden.

The intuition for this is simple. When the demand is inelastic, consumers are not very responsive to price changes, and the quantity demanded reduces only modestly when the tax is introduced. In the case of smoking, the demand is inelastic because consumers are addicted to the product. The government can then pass the tax burden along to consumers in the form of higher prices, without much of a decline in the equilibrium quantity.

Similarly, when a government introduces a tax in a market with an inelastic supply, such as, for example, beachfront hotels, and sellers have no alternative than to accept lower prices for their business, taxes do not greatly affect the equilibrium quantity. The tax burden now passes on to the sellers. If the supply was elastic and sellers had the possibility of reorganizing their businesses to avoid supplying the taxed good, the tax burden on the sellers would be much smaller. The tax would result in a much lower quantity sold instead of lower prices received. **Figure 5.10** illustrates this relationship between the tax incidence and elasticity of demand and supply.

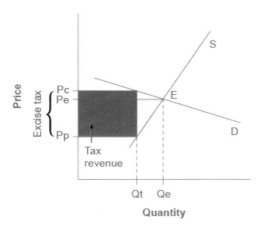
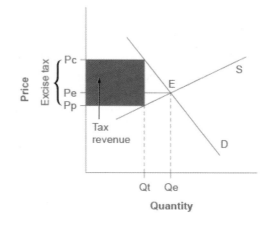

(a) Elastic demand and inelastic supply   (b) Elastic supply and inelastic demand

Figure 5.10 Elasticity and Tax Incidence An excise tax introduces a wedge between the price paid by consumers (Pc) and the price received by producers (Pp). The vertical distance between Pc and Pp is the amount of the tax per unit. Pe is the equilibrium price prior to introduction of the tax. (a) When the demand is more elastic than supply, the tax incidence on consumers Pc – Pe is lower than the tax incidence on producers Pe – Pp. (b) When the supply is more elastic than demand, the tax incidence on consumers Pc – Pe is larger than the tax incidence on producers Pe – Pp. The more elastic the demand and supply curves, the lower the tax revenue.

In **Figure 5.10** (a), the supply is inelastic and the demand is elastic, such as in the example of beachfront hotels. While consumers may have other vacation choices, sellers can't easily move their businesses. By introducing a tax, the government essentially creates a wedge between the price paid by consumers Pc and the price received by producers Pp. In other words, of the total price paid by consumers, part is retained by the sellers and part is paid to the government in the form of a tax. The distance between Pc and Pp is the tax rate. The new market price is Pc, but sellers receive only Pp per unit sold, as they pay Pc-Pp to the government. Since we can view a tax as raising the costs of production, this could also be represented by a leftward shift of the supply curve, where the new supply curve would intercept the demand at the new quantity Qt. For simplicity, **Figure 5.10** omits the shift in the supply curve.

The tax revenue is given by the shaded area, which we obtain by multiplying the tax per unit by the total quantity sold Qt. The tax incidence on the consumers is given by the difference between the price paid Pc and the initial equilibrium price Pe. The tax incidence on the sellers is given by the difference between the initial equilibrium price Pe and the price they receive after the tax is introduced Pp. In **Figure 5.10** (a), the tax burden falls disproportionately on the sellers, and a larger proportion of the tax revenue (the shaded area) is due to the resulting lower price received by the sellers than by the resulting higher prices paid by the buyers. **Figure 5.10** (b) describes the example of the tobacco excise tax where the supply is more elastic than demand. The tax incidence now falls disproportionately on consumers, as shown by the large difference between the price they pay, Pc, and the initial equilibrium price, Pe. Sellers receive a lower price than before the tax, but this difference is much smaller than the change in consumers' price. From this analysis one can also predict whether a tax is likely to create a large revenue or not. The more elastic the demand curve, the more likely that consumers will reduce quantity instead of paying higher prices. The more elastic the supply curve, the more likely that sellers will reduce the quantity sold, instead of taking lower prices. In a market where both the demand and supply are very elastic, the imposition of an excise tax generates low revenue.

Some believe that excise taxes hurt mainly the specific industries they target. For example, the medical device excise tax, in effect since 2013, has been controversial for it can delay industry profitability and therefore hamper start-ups and medical innovation. However, whether the tax burden falls mostly on the medical device industry or on the patients depends simply on the elasticity of demand and supply.

Long-Run vs. Short-Run Impact

Elasticities are often lower in the short run than in the long run. On the demand side of the market, it can sometimes be difficult to change Qd in the short run, but easier in the long run. Consumption of energy is a clear example. In the short run, it is not easy for a person to make substantial changes in energy consumption. Maybe you can carpool to work sometimes or adjust your home thermostat by a few degrees if the cost of energy rises, but that is about all.

However, in the long run you can purchase a car that gets more miles to the gallon, choose a job that is closer to where you live, buy more energy-efficient home appliances, or install more insulation in your home. As a result, the elasticity of demand for energy is somewhat inelastic in the short run, but much more elastic in the long run.

Figure 5.11 is an example, based roughly on historical experience, for the responsiveness of Qd to price changes. In 1973, the price of crude oil was $12 per barrel and total consumption in the U.S. economy was 17 million barrels per day. That year, the nations who were members of the Organization of Petroleum Exporting Countries (OPEC) cut off oil exports to the United States for six months because the Arab members of OPEC disagreed with the U.S. support for Israel. OPEC did not bring exports back to their earlier levels until 1975—a policy that we can interpret as a shift of the supply curve to the left in the U.S. petroleum market. **Figure 5.11** (a) and **Figure 5.11** (b) show the same original equilibrium point and the same identical shift of a supply curve to the left from S_0 to S_1.

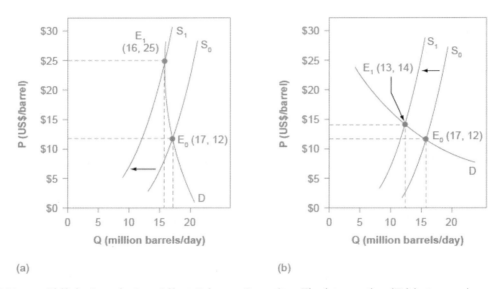

(a)   (b)

Figure 5.11 How a Shift in Supply Can Affect Price or Quantity The intersection (E_0) between demand curve D and supply curve S_0 is the same in both (a) and (b). The shift of supply to the left from S_0 to S_1 is identical in both (a) and (b). The new equilibrium (E_1) has a higher price and a lower quantity than the original equilibrium (E_0) in both (a) and (b). However, the shape of the demand curve D is different in (a) and (b), being more elastic in (b) than in (a). As a result, the shift in supply can result either in a new equilibrium with a much higher price and an only slightly smaller quantity, as in (a), with more inelastic demand, or in a new equilibrium with only a small increase in price and a relatively larger reduction in quantity, as in (b), with more elastic demand.

Figure 5.11 (a) shows inelastic demand for oil in the short run similar to that which existed for the United States in 1973. In **Figure 5.11** (a), the new equilibrium (E_1) occurs at a price of $25 per barrel, roughly double the price before the OPEC shock, and an equilibrium quantity of 16 million barrels per day. **Figure 5.11** (b) shows what the outcome would have been if the U.S. demand for oil had been more elastic, a result more likely over the long term. This alternative equilibrium (E_1) would have resulted in a smaller price increase to $14 per barrel and larger reduction in equilibrium quantity to 13 million barrels per day. In 1983, for example, U.S. petroleum consumption was 15.3 million barrels a day, which was lower than in 1973 or 1975. U.S. petroleum consumption was down even though the U.S. economy was about one-fourth larger in 1983 than it had been in 1973. The primary reason for the lower quantity was that higher energy prices spurred conservation efforts, and after a decade of home insulation, more fuel-efficient cars, more efficient appliances and machinery, and other fuel-conserving choices, the demand curve for energy had become more elastic.

On the supply side of markets, producers of goods and services typically find it easier to expand production in the long term of several years rather than in the short run of a few months. After all, in the short run it can be costly or difficult to build a new factory, hire many new workers, or open new stores. However, over a few years, all of these are possible.

In most markets for goods and services, prices bounce up and down more than quantities in the short run, but quantities often move more than prices in the long run. The underlying reason for this pattern is that supply and demand are often inelastic in the short run, so that shifts in either demand or supply can cause a relatively greater change in prices. However, since supply and demand are more elastic in the long run, the long-run movements in prices are more muted, while quantity adjusts more easily in the long run.

5.4 | Elasticity in Areas Other Than Price

By the end of this section, you will be able to:
- Calculate the income elasticity of demand and the cross-price elasticity of demand
- Calculate the elasticity in labor and financial capital markets through an understanding of the elasticity of labor supply and the elasticity of savings
- Apply concepts of price elasticity to real-world situations

The basic idea of elasticity—how a percentage change in one variable causes a percentage change in another variable—does not just apply to the responsiveness quantity supplied and quantity demanded to changes in the price of a product. Recall that quantity demanded (Qd) depends on income, tastes and preferences, the prices of related goods, and so on, as well as price. Similarly, quantity supplied (Qs) depends on factors such as the cost of production, as well as price. We can measure elasticity for any determinant of quantity supplied and quantity demanded, not just the price.

Income Elasticity of Demand

The income elasticity of demand is the percentage change in quantity demanded divided by the percentage change in income.

$$\text{Income elasticity of demand } = \frac{\%\text{ change in quantity demanded}}{\%\text{ change in income}}$$

For most products, most of the time, the income elasticity of demand is positive: that is, a rise in income will cause an increase in the quantity demanded. This pattern is common enough that we refer to these goods as normal goods. However, for a few goods, an increase in income means that one might purchase less of the good. For example, those with a higher income might buy fewer hamburgers, because they are buying more steak instead, or those with a higher income might buy less cheap wine and more imported beer. When the income elasticity of demand is negative, we call the good an inferior good.

We introduced the concepts of normal and inferior goods in **Demand and Supply**. A higher level of income causes a demand curve to shift to the right for a normal good, which means that the income elasticity of demand is positive. How far the demand shifts depends on the income elasticity of demand. A higher income elasticity means a larger shift. However, for an inferior good, that is, when the income elasticity of demand is negative, a higher level of income would cause the demand curve for that good to shift to the left. Again, how much it shifts depends on how large the (negative) income elasticity is.

Cross-Price Elasticity of Demand

A change in the price of one good can shift the quantity demanded for another good. If the two goods are complements, like bread and peanut butter, then a drop in the price of one good will lead to an increase in the quantity demanded of the other good. However, if the two goods are substitutes, like plane tickets and train tickets, then a drop in the price of one good will cause people to substitute toward that good, and to reduce consumption of the other good. Cheaper plane tickets lead to fewer train tickets, and vice versa.

The **cross-price elasticity of demand** puts some meat on the bones of these ideas. The term "cross-price" refers to the idea that the price of one good is affecting the quantity demanded of a different good. Specifically, the cross-price elasticity of demand is the percentage change in the quantity of good A that is demanded as a result of a percentage change in the price of good B.

$$\text{Cross-price elasticity of demand } = \frac{\%\text{ change in Qd of good A}}{\%\text{ change in price of good B}}$$

Substitute goods have positive cross-price elasticities of demand: if good A is a substitute for good B, like coffee and tea, then a higher price for B will mean a greater quantity consumed of A. Complement goods have negative cross-price elasticities: if good A is a complement for good B, like coffee and sugar, then a higher price for B will mean a lower quantity consumed of A.

Elasticity in Labor and Financial Capital Markets

The concept of elasticity applies to any market, not just markets for goods and services. In the labor market, for example, the **wage elasticity of labor supply**—that is, the percentage change in hours worked divided by the percentage change in wages—will reflect the shape of the labor supply curve. Specifically:

$$\text{Elasticity of labor supply} \ = \ \frac{\text{\% change in quantity of labor supplied}}{\text{\% change in wage}}$$

The wage elasticity of labor supply for teenage workers is generally fairly elastic: that is, a certain percentage change in wages will lead to a larger percentage change in the quantity of hours worked. Conversely, the wage elasticity of labor supply for adult workers in their thirties and forties is fairly inelastic. When wages move up or down by a certain percentage amount, the quantity of hours that adults in their prime earning years are willing to supply changes but by a lesser percentage amount.

In markets for financial capital, the **elasticity of savings**—that is, the percentage change in the quantity of savings divided by the percentage change in interest rates—will describe the shape of the supply curve for financial capital. That is:

$$\text{Elasticity of savings} \ = \ \frac{\text{\% change in quantity of financial savings}}{\text{\% change in interest rate}}$$

Sometimes laws are proposed that seek to increase the quantity of savings by offering tax breaks so that the return on savings is higher. Such a policy will have a comparatively large impact on increasing the quantity saved if the supply curve for financial capital is elastic, because then a given percentage increase in the return to savings will cause a higher percentage increase in the quantity of savings. However, if the supply curve for financial capital is highly inelastic, then a percentage increase in the return to savings will cause only a small increase in the quantity of savings. The evidence on the supply curve of financial capital is controversial but, at least in the short run, the elasticity of savings with respect to the interest rate appears fairly inelastic.

Expanding the Concept of Elasticity

The elasticity concept does not even need to relate to a typical supply or demand curve at all. For example, imagine that you are studying whether the Internal Revenue Service should spend more money on auditing tax returns. We can frame the question in terms of the elasticity of tax collections with respect to spending on tax enforcement; that is, what is the percentage change in tax collections derived from a given percentage change in spending on tax enforcement?

With all of the elasticity concepts that we have just described, some of which are in Table 5.4, the possibility of confusion arises. When you hear the phrases "elasticity of demand" or "elasticity of supply," they refer to the elasticity with respect to price. Sometimes, either to be extremely clear or because economists are discussing a wide variety of elasticities, we will call the elasticity of demand or the demand elasticity the price elasticity of demand or the "elasticity of demand with respect to price." Similarly, economists sometimes use the term elasticity of supply or the supply elasticity, to avoid any possibility of confusion, the price elasticity of supply or "the elasticity of supply with respect to price." However, in whatever context, the idea of elasticity always refers to percentage change in one variable, almost always a price or money variable, and how it causes a percentage change in another variable, typically a quantity variable of some kind.

$$\text{Income elasticity of demand} \ = \ \frac{\text{\% change in Qd}}{\text{\% change in income}}$$

$$\text{Cross-price elasticity of demand} \ = \ \frac{\text{\% change in Qd of good A}}{\text{\% change in price of good B}}$$

Table 5.4 Formulas for Calculating Elasticity

Wage elasticity of labor supply $=$	$\dfrac{\%\text{ change in quantity of labor supplied}}{\%\text{ change in wage}}$
Wage elasticity of labor demand $=$	$\dfrac{\%\text{ change in quantity of labor demanded}}{\%\text{ change in wage}}$
Interest rate elasticity of savings $=$	$\dfrac{\%\text{ change in quantity of savings}}{\%\text{ change in interest rate}}$
Interest rate elasticity of borrowing $=$	$\dfrac{\%\text{ change in quantity of borrowing}}{\%\text{ change in interest rate}}$

Table 5.4 Formulas for Calculating Elasticity

Bring it Home

That Will Be How Much?

How did the 60% price increase in 2011 end up for Netflix? It has been a very bumpy ride.

Before the price increase, there were about 24.6 million U.S. subscribers. After the price increase, 810,000 infuriated U.S. consumers canceled their Netflix subscriptions, dropping the total number of subscribers to 23.79 million. Fast forward to June 2013, when there were 36 million streaming Netflix subscribers in the United States. This was an increase of 11.4 million subscribers since the price increase—an average per quarter growth of about 1.6 million. This growth is less than the 2 million per quarter increases Netflix experienced in the fourth quarter of 2010 and the first quarter of 2011.

During the first year after the price increase, the firm's stock price (a measure of future expectations for the firm) fell from about $33.60 per share per share to just under $7.80. By the end of 2016, however, the stock price was at $123 per share. Today, Netflix has more than 86 million subscribers million subscribers in fifty countries.

What happened? Obviously, Netflix company officials understood the law of demand. Company officials reported, when announcing the price increase, this could result in the loss of about 600,000 existing subscribers. Using the elasticity of demand formula, it is easy to see company officials expected an inelastic response:

$$= \frac{-600,000/[(24\text{ million} + 24.6\text{ million})/2]}{\$6/[(\$10 + \$16)/2]}$$

$$= \frac{-600,000/24.3\text{ million}}{\$6/\$13}$$

$$= \frac{-0.025}{0.46}$$

$$= -0.05$$

In addition, Netflix officials had anticipated the price increase would have little impact on attracting new customers. Netflix anticipated adding up to 1.29 million new subscribers in the third quarter of 2011. It is true this was slower growth than the firm had experienced—about 2 million per quarter.

Why was the estimate of customers leaving so far off? In the more than two decades since Netflix had been founded, there was an increase in the number of close, but not perfect, substitutes. Consumers now had choices ranging from Vudu, Amazon Prime, Hulu, and Redbox, to retail stores. Jaime Weinman reported in *Maclean's* that Redbox kiosks are "a five-minute drive for less from 68 percent of Americans, and it seems that many people still find a five-minute drive more convenient than loading up a movie online." It seems that in 2012, many consumers still preferred a physical DVD disk over streaming video.

What missteps did the Netflix management make? In addition to misjudging the elasticity of demand, by failing to account for close substitutes, it seems they may have also misjudged customers' preferences and tastes. Yet, as the population increases, the preference for streaming video may overtake physical DVD disks. Netflix, the source of numerous late night talk show laughs and jabs in 2011, may yet have the last laugh.

KEY TERMS

constant unitary elasticity when a given percent price change in price leads to an equal percentage change in quantity demanded or supplied

cross-price elasticity of demand the percentage change in the quantity of good A that is demanded as a result of a percentage change in good B

elastic demand when the elasticity of demand is greater than one, indicating a high responsiveness of quantity demanded or supplied to changes in price

elastic supply when the elasticity of either supply is greater than one, indicating a high responsiveness of quantity demanded or supplied to changes in price

elasticity an economics concept that measures responsiveness of one variable to changes in another variable

elasticity of savings the percentage change in the quantity of savings divided by the percentage change in interest rates

inelastic demand when the elasticity of demand is less than one, indicating that a 1 percent increase in price paid by the consumer leads to less than a 1 percent change in purchases (and vice versa); this indicates a low responsiveness by consumers to price changes

inelastic supply when the elasticity of supply is less than one, indicating that a 1 percent increase in price paid to the firm will result in a less than 1 percent increase in production by the firm; this indicates a low responsiveness of the firm to price increases (and vice versa if prices drop)

infinite elasticity the extremely elastic situation of demand or supply where quantity changes by an infinite amount in response to any change in price; horizontal in appearance

perfect elasticity see infinite elasticity

perfect inelasticity see zero elasticity

price elasticity the relationship between the percent change in price resulting in a corresponding percentage change in the quantity demanded or supplied

price elasticity of demand percentage change in the quantity *demanded* of a good or service divided the percentage change in price

price elasticity of supply percentage change in the quantity *supplied* divided by the percentage change in price

tax incidence manner in which the tax burden is divided between buyers and sellers

unitary elasticity when the calculated elasticity is equal to one indicating that a change in the price of the good or service results in a proportional change in the quantity demanded or supplied

wage elasticity of labor supply the percentage change in hours worked divided by the percentage change in wages

zero inelasticity the highly inelastic case of demand or supply in which a percentage change in price, no matter how large, results in zero change in the quantity; vertical in appearance

KEY CONCEPTS AND SUMMARY

5.1 Price Elasticity of Demand and Price Elasticity of Supply

Price elasticity measures the responsiveness of the quantity demanded or supplied of a good to a change in its price. We compute it as the percentage change in quantity demanded (or supplied) divided by the percentage change in price. We can describe elasticity as elastic (or very responsive), unit elastic, or inelastic (not very responsive). Elastic demand or supply curves indicate that quantity demanded or supplied respond to price changes in a greater than proportional manner. An inelastic demand or supply curve is one where a given percentage change in price will cause a smaller percentage change in quantity demanded or supplied. A unitary elasticity means that a given percentage change in price leads to an equal percentage change in quantity demanded or supplied.

5.2 Polar Cases of Elasticity and Constant Elasticity

Infinite or perfect elasticity refers to the extreme case where either the quantity demanded or supplied changes by an infinite amount in response to any change in price at all. Zero elasticity refers to the extreme case in which a percentage change in price, no matter how large, results in zero change in quantity. Constant unitary elasticity in either a supply or demand curve refers to a situation where a price change of one percent results in a quantity change of one percent.

5.3 Elasticity and Pricing

In the market for goods and services, quantity supplied and quantity demanded are often relatively slow to react to changes in price in the short run, but react more substantially in the long run. As a result, demand and supply often (but not always) tend to be relatively inelastic in the short run and relatively elastic in the long run. A tax incidence depends on the relative price elasticity of supply and demand. When supply is more elastic than demand, buyers bear most of the tax burden, and when demand is more elastic than supply, producers bear most of the cost of the tax. Tax revenue is larger the more inelastic the demand and supply are.

5.4 Elasticity in Areas Other Than Price

Elasticity is a general term, that reflects responsiveness. It refers to the change of one variable divided by the percentage change of a related variable that we can apply to many economic connections. For instance, the income elasticity of demand is the percentage change in quantity demanded divided by the percentage change in income. The cross-price elasticity of demand is the percentage change in the quantity demanded of a good divided by the percentage change in the price of another good. Elasticity applies in labor markets and financial capital markets just as it does in markets for goods and services. The wage elasticity of labor supply is the percentage change in the quantity of hours supplied divided by the percentage change in the wage. The elasticity of savings with respect to interest rates is the percentage change in the quantity of savings divided by the percentage change in interest rates.

SELF-CHECK QUESTIONS

1. From the data in **Table 5.5** about demand for smart phones, calculate the price elasticity of demand from: point B to point C, point D to point E, and point G to point H. Classify the elasticity at each point as elastic, inelastic, or unit elastic.

Points	P	Q
A	60	3,000
B	70	2,800
C	80	2,600
D	90	2,400
E	100	2,200
F	110	2,000
G	120	1,800
H	130	1,600

Table 5.5

2. From the data in **Table 5.6** about supply of alarm clocks, calculate the price elasticity of supply from: point J to point K, point L to point M, and point N to point P. Classify the elasticity at each point as elastic, inelastic, or unit elastic.

Point	Price	Quantity Supplied
J	$8	50
K	$9	70
L	$10	80
M	$11	88
N	$12	95
P	$13	100

Table 5.6

3. Why is the demand curve with constant unitary elasticity concave?

4. Why is the supply curve with constant unitary elasticity a straight line?

5. The federal government decides to require that automobile manufacturers install new anti-pollution equipment that costs $2,000 per car. Under what conditions can carmakers pass almost all of this cost along to car buyers? Under what conditions can carmakers pass very little of this cost along to car buyers?

6. Suppose you are in charge of sales at a pharmaceutical company, and your firm has a new drug that causes bald men to grow hair. Assume that the company wants to earn as much revenue as possible from this drug. If the elasticity of demand for your company's product at the current price is 1.4, would you advise the company to raise the price, lower the price, or to keep the price the same? What if the elasticity were 0.6? What if it were 1? Explain your answer.

7. What would the gasoline price elasticity of supply mean to UPS or FedEx?

8. The average annual income rises from $25,000 to $38,000, and the quantity of bread consumed in a year by the average person falls from 30 loaves to 22 loaves. What is the income elasticity of bread consumption? Is bread a normal or an inferior good?

9. Suppose the cross-price elasticity of apples with respect to the price of oranges is 0.4, and the price of oranges falls by 3%. What will happen to the demand for apples?

REVIEW QUESTIONS

10. What is the formula for calculating elasticity?

11. What is the price elasticity of demand? Can you explain it in your own words?

12. What is the price elasticity of supply? Can you explain it in your own words?

13. Describe the general appearance of a demand or a supply curve with zero elasticity.

14. Describe the general appearance of a demand or a supply curve with infinite elasticity.

15. If demand is elastic, will shifts in supply have a larger effect on equilibrium quantity or on price?

16. If demand is inelastic, will shifts in supply have a larger effect on equilibrium price or on quantity?

17. If supply is elastic, will shifts in demand have a larger effect on equilibrium quantity or on price?

18. If supply is inelastic, will shifts in demand have a larger effect on equilibrium price or on quantity?

19. Would you usually expect elasticity of demand or supply to be higher in the short run or in the long run? Why?

20. Under which circumstances does the tax burden fall entirely on consumers?

21. What is the formula for the income elasticity of demand?

22. What is the formula for the cross-price elasticity of demand?

23. What is the formula for the wage elasticity of labor supply?

24. What is the formula for elasticity of savings with respect to interest rates?

CRITICAL THINKING QUESTIONS

25. Transatlantic air travel in business class has an estimated elasticity of demand of 0.62, while transatlantic air travel in economy class has an estimated price elasticity of 0.12. Why do you think this is the case?

26. What is the relationship between price elasticity and position on the demand curve? For example, as you move up the demand curve to higher prices and lower quantities, what happens to the measured elasticity? How would you explain that?

27. Can you think of an industry (or product) with near infinite elasticity of supply in the short term? That is, what is an industry that could increase Qs almost without limit in response to an increase in the price?

28. Would you expect supply to play a more significant role in determining the price of a basic necessity like food or a luxury like perfume? Explain. *Hint*: Think about how the price elasticity of demand will differ between necessities and luxuries.

This OpenStax book is available for free at http://cnx.org/content/col12122/1.4

29. A city has built a bridge over a river and it decides to charge a toll to everyone who crosses. For one year, the city charges a variety of different tolls and records information on how many drivers cross the bridge. The city thus gathers information about elasticity of demand. If the city wishes to raise as much revenue as possible from the tolls, where will the city decide to charge a toll: in the inelastic portion of the demand curve, the elastic portion of the demand curve, or the unit elastic portion? Explain.

30. In a market where the supply curve is perfectly inelastic, how does an excise tax affect the price paid by consumers and the quantity bought and sold?

31. Economists define normal goods as having a positive income elasticity. We can divide normal goods into two types: Those whose income elasticity is less than one and those whose income elasticity is greater than one. Think about products that would fall into each category. Can you come up with a name for each category?

32. Suppose you could buy shoes one at a time, rather than in pairs. What do you predict the cross-price elasticity for left shoes and right shoes would be?

PROBLEMS

33. The equation for a demand curve is P = 48 – 3Q. What is the elasticity in moving from a quantity of 5 to a quantity of 6?

34. The equation for a demand curve is P = 2/Q. What is the elasticity of demand as price falls from 5 to 4? What is the elasticity of demand as the price falls from 9 to 8? Would you expect these answers to be the same?

35. The equation for a supply curve is 4P = Q. What is the elasticity of supply as price rises from 3 to 4? What is the elasticity of supply as the price rises from 7 to 8? Would you expect these answers to be the same?

36. The equation for a supply curve is P = 3Q – 8. What is the elasticity in moving from a price of 4 to a price of 7?

37. The supply of paintings by Leonardo Da Vinci, who painted the *Mona Lisa* and *The Last Supper* and died in 1519, is highly inelastic. Sketch a supply and demand diagram, paying attention to the appropriate elasticities, to illustrate that demand for these paintings will determine the price.

38. Say that a certain stadium for professional football has 70,000 seats. What is the shape of the supply curve for tickets to football games at that stadium? Explain.

39. When someone's kidneys fail, the person needs to have medical treatment with a dialysis machine (unless or until they receive a kidney transplant) or they will die. Sketch a supply and demand diagram, paying attention to the appropriate elasticities, to illustrate that the supply of such dialysis machines will primarily determine the price.

40. Assume that the supply of low-skilled workers is fairly elastic, but the employers' demand for such workers is fairly inelastic. If the policy goal is to expand employment for low-skilled workers, is it better to focus on policy tools to shift the supply of unskilled labor or on tools to shift the demand for unskilled labor? What if the policy goal is to raise wages for this group? Explain your answers with supply and demand diagrams.

This OpenStax book is available for free at http://cnx.org/content/col12122/1.4

6 | Consumer Choices

Figure 6.1 Investment Choices We generally view higher education as a good investment, if one can afford it, regardless of the state of the economy. (Credit: modification of work by Jason Bache/Flickr Creative Commons)

Bring it Home

"Eeny, Meeny, Miney, Moe"—Making Choices

The 2008–2009 Great Recession touched families around the globe. In too many countries, workers found themselves out of a job. In developed countries, unemployment compensation provided a safety net, but families still saw a marked decrease in disposable income and had to make tough spending decisions. Of course, non-essential, discretionary spending was the first to go.

Even so, there was one particular category that saw a universal increase in spending world-wide during that time—an 18% uptick in the United States, specifically. You might guess that consumers began eating more meals at home, increasing grocery store spending; however, the Bureau of Labor Statistics' Consumer Expenditure Survey, which tracks U.S. food spending over time, showed "real total food spending by U.S. households declined five percent between 2006 and 2009." So, it was not groceries. What product would people around the world demand more of during tough economic times, and more importantly, why? (Find out at chapter's end.)

That question leads us to this chapter's topic—analyzing how consumers make choices. For most consumers, using "eeny, meeny, miney, moe" is not how they make decisions. Their decision-making processes have been educated far beyond a children's rhyme.

Introduction to Consumer Choices

In this chapter, you will learn about:

- Consumption Choices

- How Changes in Income and Prices Affect Consumption Choices

- How Consumer Choices Might Not Always be Rational

Microeconomics seeks to understand the behavior of individual economic agents such as individuals and businesses. Economists believe that we can analyze individuals' decisions, such as what goods and services to buy, as choices we make within certain budget constraints. Generally, consumers are trying to get the most for their limited budget. In economic terms they are trying to maximize total utility, or satisfaction, given their budget constraint.

Everyone has their own personal tastes and preferences. The French say: *Chacun à son goût*, or "Each to his own taste." An old Latin saying states, *De gustibus non est disputandum* or "There's no disputing about taste." If people base their decisions on their own tastes and personal preferences, however, then how can economists hope to analyze the choices consumers make?

An economic explanation for why people make different choices begins with accepting the proverbial wisdom that tastes are a matter of personal preference. However, economists also believe that the choices people make are influenced by their incomes, by the prices of goods and services they consume, and by factors like where they live. This chapter introduces the economic theory of how consumers make choices about what goods and services to buy with their limited income.

The analysis in this chapter will build on the budget constraint that we introduced in the **Choice in a World of Scarcity** chapter. This chapter will also illustrate how economic theory provides a tool to systematically look at the full range of possible consumption choices to predict how consumption responds to changes in prices or incomes. After reading this chapter, consult the appendix **Indifference Curves** to learn more about representing utility and choice through indifference curves.

6.1 | Consumption Choices

By the end of this section, you will be able to:
- Calculate total utility
- Propose decisions that maximize utility
- Explain marginal utility and the significance of diminishing marginal utility

Information on the consumption choices of Americans is available from the Consumer Expenditure Survey carried out by the U.S. Bureau of Labor Statistics. **Table 6.1** shows spending patterns for the average U.S. household. The first row shows income and, after taxes and personal savings are subtracted, it shows that, in 2015, the average U.S. household spent $48,109 on consumption. The table then breaks down consumption into various categories. The average U.S. household spent roughly one-third of its consumption on shelter and other housing expenses, another one-third on food and vehicle expenses, and the rest on a variety of items, as shown. These patterns will vary for specific households by differing levels of family income, by geography, and by preferences.

Average Household Income before Taxes	$62,481
Average Annual Expenditures	**$48.109**
Food at home	$3,264
Food away from home	$2,505
Housing	$16,557
Apparel and services	$1,700

Table 6.1 U.S. Consumption Choices in 2015   (Source: http://www.bls.gov/cex/csxann13.pdf)

Transportation	$7,677
Healthcare	$3,157
Entertainment	$2,504
Education	$1,074
Personal insurance and pensions	$5,357
All else: alcohol, tobacco, reading, personal care, cash contributions, miscellaneous	$3,356

Table 6.1 U.S. Consumption Choices in 2015   (Source: http://www.bls.gov/cex/csxann13.pdf)

Total Utility and Diminishing Marginal Utility

To understand how a household will make its choices, economists look at what consumers can afford, as shown in a **budget constraint (or budget line)**, and the **total utility** or satisfaction derived from those choices. In a budget constraint line, the quantity of one good is on the horizontal axis and the quantity of the other good on the vertical axis. The budget constraint line shows the various combinations of two goods that are affordable given consumer income. Consider José's situation, shown in **Figure 6.2**. José likes to collect T-shirts and watch movies.

In **Figure 6.2** we show the quantity of T-shirts on the horizontal axis while we show the quantity of movies on the vertical axis. If José had unlimited income or goods were free, then he could consume without limit. However, José, like all of us, faces a budget constraint. José has a total of $56 to spend. The price of T-shirts is $14 and the price of movies is $7. Notice that the vertical intercept of the budget constraint line is at eight movies and zero T-shirts ($56/$7=8). The horizontal intercept of the budget constraint is four, where José spends of all of his money on T-shirts and no movies ($56/14=4). The slope of the budget constraint line is rise/run or –8/4=–2. The specific choices along the budget constraint line show the combinations of affordable T-shirts and movies.

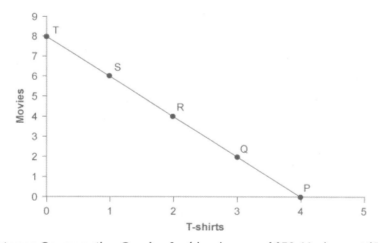

Figure 6.2 A Choice between Consumption Goods   José has income of $56. Movies cost $7 and T-shirts cost $14. The points on the budget constraint line show the combinations of affordable movies and T-shirts.

José wishes to choose the combination that will provide him with the greatest utility, which is the term economists use to describe a person's level of satisfaction or happiness with his or her choices.

Let's begin with an assumption, which we will discuss in more detail later, that José can measure his own utility with something called *utils*. (It is important to note that you cannot make comparisons between the utils of individuals. If one person gets 20 utils from a cup of coffee and another gets 10 utils, this does not mean than the first person gets more enjoyment from the coffee than the other or that they enjoy the coffee twice as much. The reason why is that utils are subjective to an individual. The way one person measures utils is not the same as the way someone else does.) **Table 6.2** shows how José's utility is connected with his T-shirt or movie consumption. The first column of the table shows the quantity of T-shirts consumed. The second column shows the total utility, or total amount of satisfaction, that José receives from consuming that number of T-shirts. The most common pattern of total utility, in this example, is that consuming additional goods leads to greater total utility, but at a decreasing rate. The third column shows **marginal utility**, which is the additional utility provided by one additional unit of consumption. This equation for marginal utility is:

$$\text{MU} = \frac{\text{change in total utility}}{\text{change in quantity}}$$

Notice that marginal utility diminishes as additional units are consumed, which means that each subsequent unit of a good consumed provides less *additional* utility. For example, the first T-shirt José picks is his favorite and it gives him an addition of 22 utils. The fourth T-shirt is just something to wear when all his other clothes are in the wash and yields only 18 additional utils. This is an example of the law of **diminishing marginal utility**, which holds that the additional utility decreases with each unit added. Diminishing marginal utility is another example of the more general law of diminishing returns we learned earlier in the chapter on **Choice in a World of Scarcity**.

The rest of **Table 6.2** shows the quantity of movies that José attends, and his total and marginal utility from seeing each movie. Total utility follows the expected pattern: it increases as the number of movies that José watches rises. Marginal utility also follows the expected pattern: each additional movie brings a smaller gain in utility than the previous one. The first movie José attends is the one he wanted to see the most, and thus provides him with the highest level of utility or satisfaction. The fifth movie he attends is just to kill time. Notice that total utility is also the sum of the marginal utilities. Read the next Work It Out feature for instructions on how to calculate total utility.

T-Shirts (Quantity)	Total Utility	Marginal Utility	Movies (Quantity)	Total Utility	Marginal Utility
1	22	22	1	16	16
2	43	21	2	31	15
3	63	20	3	45	14
4	81	18	4	58	13
5	97	16	5	70	12
6	111	14	6	81	11
7	123	12	7	91	10
8	133	10	8	100	9

Table 6.2 Total and Marginal Utility

Table 6.3 looks at each point on the budget constraint in **Figure 6.2**, and adds up José's total utility for five possible combinations of T-shirts and movies.

Point	T-Shirts	Movies	Total Utility
P	4	0	81 + 0 = 81
Q	3	2	63 + 31 = 94
R	2	4	43 + 58 = 101
S	1	6	22 + 81 = 103

Table 6.3 Finding the Choice with the Highest Utility

This OpenStax book is available for free at http://cnx.org/content/col12122/1.4

Point	T-Shirts	Movies	Total Utility
T	0	8	0 + 100 = 100

Table 6.3 Finding the Choice with the Highest Utility

Work It Out ─○─○─○

Calculating Total Utility

Let's look at how José makes his decision in more detail.

Step 1. Observe that, at point Q (for example), José consumes three T-shirts and two movies.

Step 2. Look at **Table 6.2**. You can see from the fourth row/second column that three T-shirts are worth 63 utils. Similarly, the second row/fifth column shows that two movies are worth 31 utils.

Step 3. From this information, you can calculate that point Q has a total utility of 94 (63 + 31).

Step 4. You can repeat the same calculations for each point on **Table 6.3**, in which the total utility numbers are shown in the last column.

For José, the highest total utility for all possible combinations of goods occurs at point S, with a total utility of 103 from consuming one T-shirt and six movies.

Choosing with Marginal Utility

Most people approach their utility-maximizing combination of choices in a step-by-step way. This approach is based on looking at the tradeoffs, measured in terms of marginal utility, of consuming less of one good and more of another.

For example, say that José starts off thinking about spending all his money on T-shirts and choosing point P, which corresponds to four T-shirts and no movies, as **Figure 6.2** illustrates. José chooses this starting point randomly as he has to start somewhere. Then he considers giving up the last T-shirt, the one that provides him the least marginal utility, and using the money he saves to buy two movies instead. **Table 6.4** tracks the step-by-step series of decisions José needs to make (*Key*: T-shirts are $14, movies are $7, and income is $56). The following Work It Out feature explains how marginal utility can effect decision making.

Try	Which Has	Total Utility	Marginal Gain and Loss of Utility, Compared with Previous Choice	Conclusion
Choice 1: P	4 T-shirts and 0 movies	81 from 4 T-shirts + 0 from 0 movies = 81	–	–
Choice 2: Q	3 T-shirts and 2 movies	63 from 3 T-shirts + 31 from 0 movies = 94	Loss of 18 from 1 less T-shirt, but gain of 31 from 2 more movies, for a net utility gain of 13	Q is preferred over P

Table 6.4 A Step-by-Step Approach to Maximizing Utility

Try	Which Has	Total Utility	Marginal Gain and Loss of Utility, Compared with Previous Choice	Conclusion
Choice 3: R	2 T-shirts and 4 movies	43 from 2 T-shirts + 58 from 4 movies = 101	Loss of 20 from 1 less T-shirt, but gain of 27 from two more movies for a net utility gain of 7	R is preferred over Q
Choice 4: S	1 T-shirt and 6 movies	22 from 1 T-shirt + 81 from 6 movies = 103	Loss of 21 from 1 less T-shirt, but gain of 23 from two more movies, for a net utility gain of 2	S is preferred over R
Choice 5: T	0 T-shirts and 8 movies	0 from 0 T-shirts + 100 from 8 movies = 100	Loss of 22 from 1 less T-shirt, but gain of 19 from two more movies, for a net utility loss of 3	S is preferred over T

Table 6.4 A Step-by-Step Approach to Maximizing Utility

Work It Out

Decision Making by Comparing Marginal Utility

José could use the following thought process (if he thought in utils) to make his decision regarding how many T-shirts and movies to purchase:

Step 1. From Table 6.2, José can see that the marginal utility of the fourth T-shirt is 18. If José gives up the fourth T-shirt, then he loses 18 utils.

Step 2. Giving up the fourth T-shirt, however, frees up $14 (the price of a T-shirt), allowing José to buy the first two movies (at $7 each).

Step 3. José knows that the marginal utility of the first movie is 16 and the marginal utility of the second movie is 15. Thus, if José moves from point P to point Q, he gives up 18 utils (from the T-shirt), but gains 31 utils (from the movies).

Step 4. Gaining 31 utils and losing 18 utils is a net gain of 13. This is just another way of saying that the total utility at Q (94 according to the last column in Table 6.3) is 13 more than the total utility at P (81).

Step 5. Thus, for José, it makes sense to give up the fourth T-shirt in order to buy two movies.

José clearly prefers point Q to point P. Now repeat this step-by-step process of decision making with marginal utilities. José thinks about giving up the third T-shirt and surrendering a marginal utility of 20, in exchange for purchasing two more movies that promise a combined marginal utility of 27. José prefers point R to point Q. What if José thinks about going beyond R to point S? Giving up the second T-shirt means a marginal utility loss of 21, and the marginal utility gain from the fifth and sixth movies would combine to make a marginal utility gain of 23, so José prefers point S to R.

However, if José seeks to go beyond point S to point T, he finds that the loss of marginal utility from giving up the first T-shirt is 22, while the marginal utility gain from the last two movies is only a total of 19. If José were to choose point T, his utility would fall to 100. Through these stages of thinking about marginal tradeoffs, José again concludes that S, with one T-shirt and six movies, is the choice that will provide him with the highest level of total utility. This step-by-step approach will reach the same conclusion regardless of José's starting point.

We can develop a more systematic way of using this approach by focusing on satisfaction per dollar. If an item costing $5 yields 10 utils, then it's worth 2 utils per dollar spent. **Marginal utility per dollar** is the amount of additional utility José receives divided by the product's price. **Table 6.5** shows the marginal utility per dollar for José's T shirts and movies.

$$\text{marginal utility per dollar} = \frac{\text{marginal utility}}{\text{price}}$$

If José wants to maximize the utility he gets from his limited budget, he will always purchase the item with the greatest marginal utility per dollar of expenditure (assuming he can afford it with his remaining budget). José starts with no purchases. If he purchases a T-shirt, the marginal utility per dollar spent will be 1.6. If he purchases a movie, the marginal utility per dollar spent will be 2.3. Therefore, José's first purchase will be the movie. Why? Because it gives him the highest marginal utility per dollar and is affordable. Next, José will purchase another movie. Why? Because the marginal utility of the next movie (2.14) is greater than the marginal utility of the next T-shirt (1.6). Note that when José has no T- shirts, the next one is the first one. José will continue to purchase the next good with the highest marginal utility per dollar until he exhausts his budget. He will continue purchasing movies because they give him a greater "bang for the buck" until the sixth movie which gives the same marginal utility per dollar as the first T-shirt purchase. José has just enough budget to purchase both. So in total, José will purchase six movies and one T-shirt.

Quantity of T-Shirts	Total Utility	Marginal Utility	Marginal Utility per Dollar	Quantity of Movies	Total Utility	Marginal Utility	Marginal Utility per Dollar
1	**22**	**22**	**22/\$14=1.6**	1	16	16	16/\$7=2.3
2	43	21	21/\$14=1.5	2	31	15	15/\$7=2.14
3	63	20	20/\$14=1.4	3	45	14	14/\$7=2
4	81	18	18/\$14=1.3	4	58	13	13/\$7=1.9
5	97	16	16/\$14=1.1	5	70	12	12/\$7=1.7
6	111	14	14/\$14=1	**6**	**81**	**11**	**11/\$7=1.6**
7	123	12	12/\$14=1.2	7	91	10	10/\$7=1.4

Table 6.5 Marginal Utility per Dollar

A Rule for Maximizing Utility

This process of decision making suggests a rule to follow when maximizing utility. Since the price of T-shirts is twice as high as the price of movies, to maximize utility the last T-shirt that José chose needs to provide exactly twice the marginal utility (MU) of the last movie. If the last T-shirt provides less than twice the marginal utility of the last movie, then the T-shirt is providing less "bang for the buck" (i.e., marginal utility per dollar spent) than José would receive from spending the same money on movies. If this is so, José should trade the T-shirt for more movies to increase his total utility.

If the last T-shirt provides more than twice the marginal utility of the last movie, then the T-shirt is providing more "bang for the buck" or marginal utility per dollar, than if the money were spent on movies. As a result, José should buy more T-shirts. Notice that at José's optimal choice of point S, the marginal utility from the first T-shirt, of 22 is exactly twice the marginal utility of the sixth movie, which is 11. At this choice, the marginal utility per dollar is the same for both goods. This is a tell-tale signal that José has found the point with highest total utility.

We can write this argument as a general rule: If you always choose the item with the greatest marginal utility per dollar spent, when your budget is exhausted, the utility maximizing choice should occur where the marginal utility per dollar spent is the same for both goods.

$$\frac{MU_1}{P_1} = \frac{MU_2}{P_2}$$

A sensible economizer will pay twice as much for something only if, in the marginal comparison, the item confers twice as much utility. Notice that the formula for the table above is:

$$\frac{22}{\$14} = \frac{11}{\$7}$$

$$1.6 = 1.6$$

The following Work It Out feature provides step by step guidance for this concept of utility-maximizing choices.

Work It Out ─○─○─○

Maximizing Utility

The general rule, $\frac{MU_1}{P_1} = \frac{MU_2}{P_2}$, means that the last dollar spent on each good provides exactly the same marginal utility. This is the case at point S. So:

Step 1. If we traded a dollar more of movies for a dollar more of T-shirts, the marginal utility gained from T-shirts would exactly offset the marginal utility lost from fewer movies. In other words, the net gain would be zero.

Step 2. Products, however, usually cost more than a dollar, so we cannot trade a dollar's worth of movies. The best we can do is trade two movies for another T-shirt, since in this example T-shirts cost twice what a movie does.

Step 3. If we trade two movies for one T-shirt, we would end up at point R (two T-shirts and four movies).

Step 4. Choice 4 in Table 6.4 shows that if we move to point R, we would gain 21 utils from one more T-shirt, but lose 23 utils from two fewer movies, so we would end up with less total utility at point R.

In short, the general rule shows us the utility-maximizing choice, which is called the **consumer equilibrium**.

There is another equivalent way to think about this. We can also express the general rule as *the ratio of the prices of the two goods should be equal to the ratio of the marginal utilities.* When we divide the price of good 1 by the price of good 2, at the utility-maximizing point this will equal the marginal utility of good 1 divided by the marginal utility of good 2.

$$\frac{P_1}{P_2} = \frac{MU_1}{MU_2}$$

Along the budget constraint, the total price of the two goods remains the same, so the ratio of the prices does not change. However, the marginal utility of the two goods changes with the quantities consumed. At the optimal choice of one T-shirt and six movies, point S, the ratio of marginal utility to price for T-shirts (22:14) matches the ratio of marginal utility to price for movies (of 11:7).

Measuring Utility with Numbers

This discussion of utility began with an assumption that it is possible to place numerical values on utility, an assumption that may seem questionable. You can buy a thermometer for measuring temperature at the hardware store, but what store sells an "utilimometer" for measuring utility? While measuring utility with numbers is a convenient assumption to clarify the explanation, the key assumption is not that an outside party can measure utility but only that individuals can decide which of two alternatives they prefer.

To understand this point, think back to the step-by-step process of finding the choice with highest total utility by comparing the marginal utility you gain and lose from different choices along the budget constraint. As José compares each choice along his budget constraint to the previous choice, what matters is not the specific numbers that he places on his utility—or whether he uses any numbers at all—but only that he personally can identify which choices he prefers.

In this way, the step-by-step process of choosing the highest level of utility resembles rather closely how many people make consumption decisions. We think about what will make us the happiest. We think about what things cost. We think about buying a little more of one item and giving up a little of something else. We choose what provides us with the greatest level of satisfaction. The vocabulary of comparing the points along a budget constraint and total and marginal utility is just a set of tools for discussing this everyday process in a clear and specific manner. It is welcome news that specific utility numbers are not central to the argument, since a good utilimometer is hard to find. Do not worry—while we cannot measure utils, by the end of the next module, we will have transformed our analysis into something we can measure—demand.

6.2 | How Changes in Income and Prices Affect Consumption Choices

By the end of this section, you will be able to:
- Explain how income, prices, and preferences affect consumer choices
- Contrast the substitution effect and the income effect
- Utilize concepts of demand to analyze consumer choices
- Apply utility-maximizing choices to governments and businesses

Just as we can use utility and marginal utility to discuss making consumer choices along a budget constraint, we can also use these ideas to think about how consumer choices change when the budget constraint shifts in response to changes in income or price. Because we can use the budget constraint framework to analyze how quantities demanded change because of price movements, the budget constraint model can illustrate the underlying logic behind demand curves.

How Changes in Income Affect Consumer Choices

Let's begin with a concrete example illustrating how changes in income level affect consumer choices. **Figure 6.3** shows a budget constraint that represents Kimberly's choice between concert tickets at $50 each and getting away overnight to a bed-and-breakfast for $200 per night. Kimberly has $1,000 per year to spend between these two choices. After thinking about her total utility and marginal utility and applying the decision rule that the ratio of the marginal utilities to the prices should be equal between the two products, Kimberly chooses point M, with eight concerts and three overnight getaways as her utility-maximizing choice.

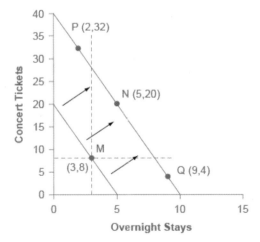

Figure 6.3 How a Change in Income Affects Consumption Choices   The utility-maximizing choice on the original budget constraint is M. The dashed horizontal and vertical lines extending through point M allow you to see at a glance whether the quantity consumed of goods on the new budget constraint is higher or lower than on the original budget constraint. On the new budget constraint, Kimberly will make a choice like N if both goods are normal goods. If overnight stays is an inferior good, Kimberly will make a choice like P. If concert tickets are an inferior good, Kimberly will make a choice like Q.

Now, assume that the income Kimberly has to spend on these two items rises to $2,000 per year, causing her budget constraint to shift out to the right. How does this rise in income alter her utility-maximizing choice? Kimberly will again consider the utility and marginal utility that she receives from concert tickets and overnight getaways and seek her utility-maximizing choice on the new budget line, but how will her new choice relate to her original choice?

We can replace the possible choices along the new budget constraint into three groups, which the dashed horizontal and vertical lines that pass through the original choice M in the figure divide. All choices on the upper left of the new budget constraint that are to the left of the vertical dashed line, like choice P with two overnight stays and 32 concert tickets, involve less of the good on the horizontal axis but much more of the good on the vertical axis. All choices to the right of the vertical dashed line and above the horizontal dashed line—like choice N with five overnight getaways and 20 concert tickets—have more consumption of both goods. Finally, all choices that are to the right of the vertical dashed line but below the horizontal dashed line, like choice Q with four concerts and nine overnight getaways, involve less of the good on the vertical axis but much more of the good on the horizontal axis.

All of these choices are theoretically possible, depending on Kimberly's personal preferences as expressed through the total and marginal utility she would receive from consuming these two goods. When income rises, the most common reaction is to purchase more of both goods, like choice N, which is to the upper right relative to Kimberly's original choice M, although exactly how much more of each good will vary according to personal taste. Conversely, when income falls, the most typical reaction is to purchase less of both goods. As we defined in the chapter on **Demand and Supply** and again in the chapter on **Elasticity**, we call goods and services normal goods when a rise in income leads to a rise in the quantity consumed of that good and a fall in income leads to a fall in quantity consumed.

However, depending on Kimberly's preferences, a rise in income could cause consumption of one good to increase while consumption of the other good declines. A choice like P means that a rise in income caused her quantity consumed of overnight stays to decline, while a choice like Q would mean that a rise in income caused her quantity of concerts to decline. Goods where demand declines as income rises (or conversely, where the demand rises as income falls) are called "inferior goods." An inferior good occurs when people trim back on a good as income rises, because they can now afford the more expensive choices that they prefer. For example, a higher-income household might eat fewer hamburgers or be less likely to buy a used car, and instead eat more steak and buy a new car.

How Price Changes Affect Consumer Choices

For analyzing the possible effect of a change in price on consumption, let's again use a concrete example. **Figure 6.4** represents Sergei's consumer choice, who chooses between purchasing baseball bats and cameras. A price increase for baseball bats would have no effect on the ability to purchase cameras, but it would reduce the number of bats Sergei could afford to buy. Thus a price increase for baseball bats, the good on the horizontal axis, causes the budget constraint to rotate inward, as if on a hinge, from the vertical axis. As in the previous section, the point labeled M represents the originally preferred point on the original budget constraint, which Sergei has chosen after contemplating his total utility and marginal utility and the tradeoffs involved along the budget constraint. In this example, the units along the horizontal and vertical axes are not numbered, so the discussion must focus on whether Sergei will consume more or less of certain goods, not on numerical amounts.

This OpenStax book is available for free at http://cnx.org/content/col12122/1.4

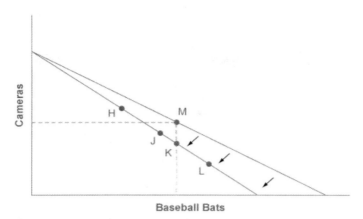

Figure 6.4 How a Change in Price Affects Consumption Choices The original utility-maximizing choice is M. When the price rises, the budget constraint rotates clockwise. The dashed lines make it possible to see at a glance whether the new consumption choice involves less of both goods, or less of one good and more of the other. The new possible choices would be fewer baseball bats and more cameras, like point H, or less of both goods, as at point J. Choice K would mean that the higher price of bats led to exactly the same quantity of bat consumption, but fewer cameras. Theoretically possible, but unlikely in the real world, we rule out choices like L because they would mean that a higher price for baseball bats means a greater consumption of baseball bats.

After the price increase, Sergei will make a choice along the new budget constraint. Again, we can divide his choices into three segments by the dashed vertical and horizontal lines. In the upper left portion of the new budget constraint, at a choice like H, Sergei consumes more cameras and fewer bats. In the central portion of the new budget constraint, at a choice like J, he consumes less of both goods. At the right-hand end, at a choice like L, he consumes more bats but fewer cameras.

The typical response to higher prices is that a person chooses to consume less of the product with the higher price. This occurs for two reasons, and both effects can occur simultaneously. The **substitution effect** occurs when a price changes and consumers have an incentive to consume less of the good with a relatively higher price and more of the good with a relatively lower price. The **income effect** is that a higher price means, in effect, the buying power of income has been reduced (even though actual income has not changed), which leads to buying less of the good (when the good is normal). In this example, the higher price for baseball bats would cause Sergei to buy fewer bats for both reasons. Exactly how much will a higher price for bats cause Sergei's bat consumption to fall? **Figure 6.4** suggests a range of possibilities. Sergei might react to a higher price for baseball bats by purchasing the same quantity of bats, but cutting his camera consumption. This choice is the point K on the new budget constraint, straight below the original choice M. Alternatively, Sergei might react by dramatically reducing his bat purchases and instead buy more cameras.

The key is that it would be imprudent to assume that a change in baseball bats will only or primarily affect the good's price whose price is changed, while the quantity consumed of other goods remains the same. Since Sergei purchases all his products out of the same budget, a change in the price of one good can also have a range of effects, either positive or negative, on the quantity consumed of other goods.

In short, a higher price typically causes reduced consumption of the good in question, but it can affect the consumption of other goods as well.

Link It Up ⛓️

Read this article (http://openstaxcollege.org/l/vending) about the potential of variable prices in vending machines.

The Foundations of Demand Curves

Changes in the price of a good lead the budget constraint to rotate. A rotation in the budget constraint means that when individuals are seeking their highest utility, the quantity that is demanded of that good will change. In this way, the logical foundations of demand curves—which show a connection between prices and quantity demanded—are based on the underlying idea of individuals seeking utility. **Figure 6.5** (a) shows a budget constraint with a choice between housing and "everything else." (Putting "everything else" on the vertical axis can be a useful approach in some cases, especially when the focus of the analysis is on one particular good.) We label the preferred choice on the original budget constraint that provides the highest possible utility M_0. The other three budget constraints represent successively higher prices for housing of P_1, P_2, and P_3. As the budget constraint rotates in, and in, and in again, we label the utility-maximizing choices M_1, M_2, and M_3, and the quantity demanded of housing falls from Q_0 to Q_1 to Q_2 to Q_3.

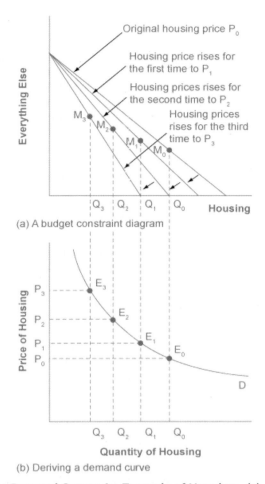

(a) A budget constraint diagram

(b) Deriving a demand curve

Figure 6.5 The Foundations of a Demand Curve: An Example of Housing   (a) As the price increases from P_0 to P_1 to P_2 to P_3, the budget constraint on the upper part of the diagram rotates clockwise. The utility-maximizing choice changes from M_0 to M_1 to M_2 to M_3. As a result, the quantity demanded of housing shifts from Q_0 to Q_1 to Q_2 to Q_3, *ceteris paribus*. (b) The demand curve graphs each combination of the price of housing and the quantity of housing demanded, *ceteris paribus*. The quantities of housing are the same at the points on both (a) and (b). Thus, the original price of housing (P_0) and the original quantity of housing (Q_0) appear on the demand curve as point E_0. The higher price of housing (P_1) and the corresponding lower quantity demanded of housing (Q_1) appear on the demand curve as point E_1.

Thus, as the price of housing rises, the budget constraint rotates clockwise and the quantity consumed of housing falls, *ceteris paribus* (meaning, with all other things being the same). We graph this relationship—the price of housing rising from P_0 to P_1 to P_2 to P_3, while the quantity of housing demanded falls from Q_0 to Q_1 to Q_2 to Q_3—on the demand curve in **Figure 6.5** (b). The vertical dashed lines stretching between the top and bottom of **Figure 6.5** show that the quantity of housing demanded at each point is the same in both (a) and (b). We ultimately determine the shape of a demand curve by the underlying choices about maximizing utility subject to a budget constraint. While economists may not be able to measure "utils," they can certainly measure price and quantity demanded.

Applications in Government and Business

The budget constraint framework for making utility-maximizing choices offers a reminder that people can react to a change in price or income in a range of different ways. For example, in the winter months of 2005, costs for heating homes increased significantly in many parts of the country as prices for natural gas and electricity soared, due in large part to the disruption caused by Hurricanes Katrina and Rita. Some people reacted by reducing the quantity demanded of energy; for example, by turning down the thermostats in their homes by a few degrees and wearing a heavier sweater inside. Even so, many home heating bills rose, so people adjusted their consumption in other ways, too. As you learned in the chapter on **Elasticity**, the short run demand for home heating is generally inelastic. Each household cut back on what it valued least on the margin. For some it might have been some dinners out, or a vacation, or postponing buying a new refrigerator or a new car. Sharply higher energy prices can have effects beyond the energy market, leading to a widespread reduction in purchasing throughout the rest of the economy.

A similar issue arises when the government imposes taxes on certain products, such as on gasoline, cigarettes, and alcohol. Say that a tax on alcohol leads to a higher price at the liquor store. The higher price of alcohol causes the budget constraint to pivot left, and alcoholic beverage consumption is likely to decrease. However, people may also react to the higher price of alcoholic beverages by cutting back on other purchases. For example, they might cut back on snacks at restaurants like chicken wings and nachos. It would be unwise to assume that the liquor industry is the only one affected by the tax on alcoholic beverages. Read the next Clear It Up to learn about how who controls the household income influences buying decisions.

The Unifying Power of the Utility-Maximizing Budget Set Framework

An interaction between prices, budget constraints, and personal preferences determine household choices. The flexible and powerful terminology of utility-maximizing gives economists a vocabulary for bringing these elements together.

Not even economists believe that people walk around mumbling about their marginal utilities before they walk into a shopping mall, accept a job, or make a deposit in a savings account. However, economists do believe that individuals seek their own satisfaction or utility and that people often decide to try a little less of one thing and a little more of another. If we accept these assumptions, then the idea of utility-maximizing households facing budget constraints becomes highly plausible.

Does who controls household income make a difference?

In the mid-1970s, the United Kingdom made an interesting policy change in its "child allowance" policy. This program provides a fixed amount of money per child to every family, regardless of family income. Traditionally, the child allowance had been distributed to families by withholding less in taxes from the paycheck of the family wage earner—typically the father in this time period. The new policy instead provided the child allowance as a cash payment to the mother. As a result of this change, households have the same level of income and face the same prices in the market, but the money is more likely to be in the mother's purse than in the father's wallet.

Should this change in policy alter household consumption patterns? Basic models of consumption decisions, of the sort that we examined in this chapter, assume that it does not matter whether the mother or the father receives the money, because both parents seek to maximize the family's utility as a whole. In effect, this model assumes that everyone in the family has the same preferences.

In reality, the share of that the father or mother controls does affect what the household consumes. When the mother controls a larger share of family income a number of studies, in the United Kingdom and in a wide variety of other countries, have found that the family tends to spend more on restaurant meals, child care, and women's clothing, and less on alcohol and tobacco. As the mother controls a larger share of household resources, children's health improves, too. These findings suggest that when providing assistance to poor families, in high-income countries and low-income countries alike, the monetary amount of assistance is not all that matters: it also matters which family member actually receives the money.

The budget constraint framework serves as a constant reminder to think about the full range of effects that can arise from changes in income or price, not just effects on the one product that might seem most immediately affected.

This OpenStax book is available for free at http://cnx.org/content/col12122/1.4

6.3 | Behavioral Economics: An Alternative Framework for Consumer Choice

By the end of this section, you will be able to:
- Evaluate the reasons for making intertemporal choices
- Interpret an intertemporal budget constraint
- Analyze why people in America tend to save such a small percentage of their income

As we know, people sometimes make decisions that seem "irrational" and not in their own best interest. People's decisions can seem inconsistent from one day to the next and they even deliberately ignore ways to save money or time. The traditional economic models assume rationality, which means that people take all available information and make consistent and informed decisions that are in their best interest. (In fact, economics professors often delight in pointing out so-called "irrational behavior" each semester to their new students, and present economics as a way to become more rational.)

However, a new group of economists, known as behavioral economists, argue that the traditional method omits something important: people's state of mind. For example, one can think differently about money if one is feeling revenge, optimism, or loss. These are not necessarily irrational states of mind, but part of a range of emotions that can affect anyone on a given day. In addition, actions under these conditions are predictable, if one better understands the underlying environment. **Behavioral economics** seeks to enrich our understanding of decision-making by integrating the insights of psychology into economics. It does this by investigating how given dollar amounts can mean different things to individuals depending on the situation. This can lead to decisions that appear outwardly inconsistent, or irrational, to the outside observer.

The way the mind works, according to this view, may seem inconsistent to traditional economists but is actually far more complex than an unemotional cost-benefit adding machine. For example, a traditional economist would say that if you lost a $10 bill today, and also received an extra $10 in your paycheck, you should feel perfectly neutral. After all, –$10 + $10 = $0. You are the same financially as you were before. However, behavioral economists have conducted research that shows many people will feel some negative emotion, such as anger or frustration, after those two things happen. We tend to focus more on the loss than the gain. We call this loss aversion, where a $1 loss pains us 2.25 times more than a $1 gain helps us, according to the economists Daniel Kahneman and Amos Tversky in a famous 1979 article in the journal *Econometrica*. This insight has implications for investing, as people tend to "overplay" the stock market by reacting more to losses than to gains. This behavior looks irrational to traditional economists, but is consistent once we understand better how the mind works, these economists argue.

Traditional economists also assume human beings have complete self control, but, for instance, people will buy cigarettes by the pack instead of the carton even though the carton saves them money, to keep usage down. They purchase locks for their refrigerators and overpay on taxes to force themselves to save. In other words, we protect ourselves from our worst temptations but pay a price to do so. One way behavioral economists are responding to this is by establishing ways for people to keep themselves free of these temptations. This includes what we call "nudges" toward more rational behavior rather than mandatory regulations from government. For example, up to 20 percent of new employees do not enroll in retirement savings plans immediately, because of procrastination or feeling overwhelmed by the different choices. Some companies are now moving to a new system, where employees are automatically enrolled unless they "opt out." Almost no-one opts out in this program and employees begin saving at the early years, which are most critical for retirement.

Another area that seems illogical is the idea of mental accounting, or putting dollars in different mental categories where they take different values. Economists typically consider dollars to be **fungible**, or having equal value to the individual, regardless of the situation.

You might, for instance, think of the $25 you found in the street differently from the $25 you earned from three hours working in a fast food restaurant. You might treat the street money as "mad money" with little rational regard to getting the best value. This is in one sense strange, since it is still equivalent to three hours of hard work in the restaurant. Yet the "easy come-easy go" mentality replaces the rational economizer because of the situation, or context, in which you attained the money.

In another example of mental accounting that seems inconsistent to a traditional economist, a person could carry a credit card debt of $1,000 that has a 15% yearly interest cost, and simultaneously have a $2,000 savings account that pays only 2% per year. That means she pays $150 a year to the credit card company, while collecting only $40 annually in bank interest, so she loses $130 a year. That doesn't seem wise.

The "rational" decision would be to pay off the debt, since a $1,000 savings account with $0 in debt is the equivalent net worth, and she would now net $20 per year. Curiously, it is not uncommon for people to ignore this advice, since they will treat a loss to their savings account as higher than the benefit of paying off their credit card. They do not treat the dollars as fungible so it looks irrational to traditional economists.

Which view is right, the behavioral economists' or the traditional view? Both have their advantages, but behavioral economists have at least identified trying to describe and explain behavior that economists have historically dismissed as irrational. If most of us are engaged in some "irrational behavior," perhaps there are deeper underlying reasons for this behavior in the first place.

Bring it Home

"Eeny, Meeny, Miney, Moe"—Making Choices

In what category did consumers worldwide increase their spending during the Great Recession? Higher education. According to the United Nations Educational, Scientific, and Cultural Organization (UNESCO), enrollment in colleges and universities rose one-third in China and almost two-thirds in Saudi Arabia, nearly doubled in Pakistan, tripled in Uganda, and surged by three million—18 percent—in the United States. Why were consumers willing to spend on education during lean times? Both individuals and countries view higher education as the way to prosperity. Many feel that increased earnings are a significant benefit of attending college.

U.S. Bureau of Labor Statistics data from May 2012 supports this view, as **Figure 6.6** shows. They show a positive correlation between earnings and education. The data also indicate that unemployment rates fall with higher levels of education and training.

Why spend the money to go to college during recession? Because if you are unemployed (or underemployed, working fewer hours than you would like), the opportunity cost of your time is low. If you're unemployed, you don't have to give up work hours and income by going to college.

This OpenStax book is available for free at http://cnx.org/content/col12122/1.4

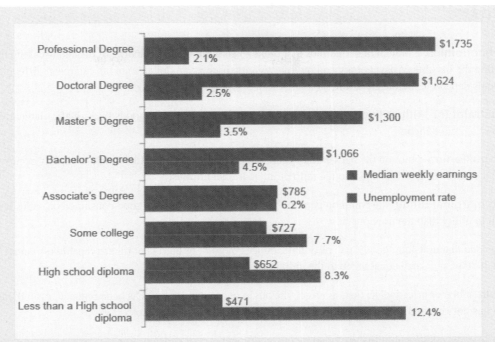

Figure 6.6 The Impact of Education on Earnings and Unemployment Rates, 2012 Those with the highest degrees in 2012 had substantially lower unemployment rates; whereas, those with the least formal education suffered from the highest unemployment rates. The national median average weekly income was $815, and the nation unemployment average in 2012 was 6.8%. (Source: U.S. Bureau of Labor Statistics, May 22, 2013)

KEY TERMS

behavioral economics a branch of economics that seeks to enrich the understanding of decision-making by integrating the insights of psychology and by investigating how given dollar amounts can mean different things to individuals depending on the situation

budget constraint (or budget line) shows the possible combinations of two goods that are affordable given a consumer's limited income

consumer equilibrium point on the budget line where the consumer gets the most satisfaction; this occurs when the ratio of the prices of goods is equal to the ratio of the marginal utilities.

diminishing marginal utility the common pattern that each marginal unit of a good consumed provides less of an addition to utility than the previous unit

fungible the idea that units of a good, such as dollars, ounces of gold, or barrels of oil are capable of mutual substitution with each other and carry equal value to the individual

income effect a higher price means that, in effect, the buying power of income has been reduced, even though actual income has not changed; always happens simultaneously with a substitution effect

marginal utility the additional utility provided by one additional unit of consumption

marginal utility per dollar the additional satisfaction gained from purchasing a good given the price of the product; MU/Price

substitution effect when a price changes, consumers have an incentive to consume less of the good with a relatively higher price and more of the good with a relatively lower price; always happens simultaneously with an income effect

total utility satisfaction derived from consumer choices

KEY CONCEPTS AND SUMMARY

6.1 Consumption Choices

Economic analysis of household behavior is based on the assumption that people seek the highest level of utility or satisfaction. Individuals are the only judge of their own utility. In general, greater consumption of a good brings higher total utility. However, the additional utility people receive from each unit of greater consumption tends to decline in a pattern of diminishing marginal utility.

We can find the utility-maximizing choice on a consumption budget constraint in several ways. You can add up total utility of each choice on the budget line and choose the highest total. You can select a starting point at random and compare the marginal utility gains and losses of moving to neighboring points—and thus eventually seek out the preferred choice. Alternatively, you can compare the ratio of the marginal utility to price of good 1 with the marginal utility to price of good 2 and apply the rule that at the optimal choice, the two ratios should be equal:

$$\frac{MU_1}{P_1} = \frac{MU_2}{P_2}$$

6.2 How Changes in Income and Prices Affect Consumption Choices

The budget constraint framework suggest that when income or price changes, a range of responses are possible. When income rises, households will demand a higher quantity of normal goods, but a lower quantity of inferior goods. When the price of a good rises, households will typically demand less of that good—but whether they will demand a much lower quantity or only a slightly lower quantity will depend on personal preferences. Also, a higher price for one good can lead to more or less demand of the other good.

This OpenStax book is available for free at http://cnx.org/content/col12122/1.4

6.3 Behavioral Economics: An Alternative Framework for Consumer Choice

People regularly make decisions that seem less than rational, decisions that contradict traditional consumer theory. This is because traditional theory ignores people's state of mind or feelings, which can influence behavior. For example, people tend to value a dollar lost more than a dollar gained, even though the amounts are the same. Similarly, many people over withhold on their taxes, essentially giving the government a free loan until they file their tax returns, so that they are more likely to get money back than have to pay money on their taxes.

SELF-CHECK QUESTIONS

1. Jeremy is deeply in love with Jasmine. Jasmine lives where cell phone coverage is poor, so he can either call her on the land-line phone for five cents per minute or he can drive to see her, at a round-trip cost of $2 in gasoline money. He has a total of $10 per week to spend on staying in touch. To make his preferred choice, Jeremy uses a handy utilimometer that measures his total utility from personal visits and from phone minutes. Using the values in Table 6.6, figure out the points on Jeremy's consumption choice budget constraint (it may be helpful to do a sketch) and identify his utility-maximizing point.

Round Trips	Total Utility	Phone Minutes	Total Utility
0	0	0	0
1	80	20	200
2	150	40	380
3	210	60	540
4	260	80	680
5	300	100	800
6	330	120	900
7	200	140	980
8	180	160	1040
9	160	180	1080
10	140	200	1100

Table 6.6

2. Take Jeremy's total utility information in Exercise 6.1, and use the marginal utility approach to confirm the choice of phone minutes and round trips that maximize Jeremy's utility.

3. Explain all the reasons why a decrease in a product's price would lead to an increase in purchases.

4. As a college student you work at a part-time job, but your parents also send you a monthly "allowance." Suppose one month your parents forgot to send the check. Show graphically how your budget constraint is affected. Assuming you only buy normal goods, what would happen to your purchases of goods?

REVIEW QUESTIONS

5. Who determines how much utility an individual will receive from consuming a good?

6. Would you expect total utility to rise or fall with additional consumption of a good? Why?

7. Would you expect marginal utility to rise or fall with additional consumption of a good? Why?

8. Is it possible for total utility to increase while marginal utility diminishes? Explain.

9. If people do not have a complete mental picture of total utility for every level of consumption, how can they find their utility-maximizing consumption choice?

10. What is the rule relating the ratio of marginal utility to prices of two goods at the optimal choice? Explain why, if this rule does not hold, the choice cannot be utility-maximizing.

11. As a general rule, is it safe to assume that a change in the price of a good will always have its most significant impact on the quantity demanded of that good, rather than on the quantity demanded of other goods? Explain.

12. Why does a change in income cause a parallel shift in the budget constraint?

CRITICAL THINKING QUESTIONS

13. Think back to a purchase that you made recently. How would you describe your thinking before you made that purchase?

14. The rules of politics are not always the same as the rules of economics. In discussions of setting budgets for government agencies, there is a strategy called "closing the Washington Monument." When an agency faces the unwelcome prospect of a budget cut, it may decide to close a high-visibility attraction enjoyed by many people (like the Washington Monument). Explain in terms of diminishing marginal utility why the Washington Monument strategy is so misleading. *Hint*: If you are really trying to make the best of a budget cut, should you cut the items in your budget with the highest marginal utility or the lowest marginal utility? Does the Washington Monument strategy cut the items with the highest marginal utility or the lowest marginal utility?

15. Income effects depend on the income elasticity of demand for each good that you buy. If one of the goods you buy has a negative income elasticity, that is, it is an inferior good, what must be true of the income elasticity of the other good you buy?

PROBLEMS

16. Praxilla, who lived in ancient Greece, derives utility from reading poems and from eating cucumbers. Praxilla gets 30 units of marginal utility from her first poem, 27 units of marginal utility from her second poem, 24 units of marginal utility from her third poem, and so on, with marginal utility declining by three units for each additional poem. Praxilla gets six units of marginal utility for each of her first three cucumbers consumed, five units of marginal utility for each of her next three cucumbers consumed, four units of marginal utility for each of the following three cucumbers consumed, and so on, with marginal utility declining by one for every three cucumbers consumed. A poem costs three bronze coins but a cucumber costs only one bronze coin. Praxilla has 18 bronze coins. Sketch Praxilla's budget set between poems and cucumbers, placing poems on the vertical axis and cucumbers on the horizontal axis. Start off with the choice of zero poems and 18 cucumbers, and calculate the changes in marginal utility of moving along the budget line to the next choice of one poem and 15 cucumbers. Using this step-by-step process based on marginal utility, create a table and identify Praxilla's utility-maximizing choice. Compare the marginal utility of the two goods and the relative prices at the optimal choice to see if the expected relationship holds. *Hint*: Label the table columns: 1) Choice, 2) Marginal Gain from More Poems, 3) Marginal Loss from Fewer Cucumbers, 4) Overall Gain or Loss, 5) Is the previous choice optimal? Label the table rows: 1) 0 Poems and 18 Cucumbers, 2) 1 Poem and 15 Cucumbers, 3) 2 Poems and 12 Cucumbers, 4) 3 Poems and 9 Cucumbers, 5) 4 Poems and 6 Cucumbers, 6) 5 Poems and 3 Cucumbers, 7) 6 Poems and 0 Cucumbers.

17. If a 10% decrease in the price of one product that you buy causes an 8% increase in quantity demanded of that product, will another 10% decrease in the price cause another 8% increase (no more and no less) in quantity demanded?

This OpenStax book is available for free at http://cnx.org/content/col12122/1.4

7 | Production, Costs, and Industry Structure

Figure 7.1 Amazon is an American international electronic commerce company that sells books, among many other things, shipping them directly to the consumer. Until recently there were no brick and mortar Amazon stores. (Credit: modification of work by William Christiansen/Flickr Creative Commons)

Bring it Home

Amazon

In less than two decades, Amazon.com has transformed the way consumers sell, buy, and even read. Prior to Amazon, independent bookstores with limited inventories in small retail locations primarily sold books. There were exceptions, of course. Borders and Barnes & Noble offered larger stores in urban areas. In the last decade, however, independent bookstores have mostly disappeared, Borders has gone out of business, and Barnes & Noble is struggling. Online delivery and purchase of books has overtaken the more traditional business models. How has Amazon changed the book selling industry? How has it managed to crush its competition?

A major reason for the giant retailer's success is its production model and cost structure, which has enabled Amazon to undercut the competitors' prices even when factoring in the cost of shipping. Read on to see how firms great (like Amazon) and small (like your corner deli) determine what to sell, at what output, and price.

Introduction to Production, Costs, and Industry Structure

In this chapter, you will learn about:

- Explicit and Implicit Costs, and Accounting and Economic Profit

- Production in the Short Run

- Costs in the Short Run

- Production in the Long Run

- Costs in the Long Run

This chapter is the first of four chapters that explores the *theory of the firm*. This theory explains how firms behave. What does that mean? Let's define what we mean by the firm. A **firm** (or producer or business) combines inputs of labor, capital, land, and raw or finished component materials to produce outputs. If the firm is successful, the outputs are more valuable than the inputs. This activity of **production** goes beyond manufacturing (i.e., making things). It includes any process or service that creates value, including transportation, distribution, wholesale and retail sales.

Production involves a number of important decisions that define a firm's behavior. These decisions include, but are not limited to:

- What product or products should the firm produce?

- How should the firm produce the products (i.e., what production process should the firm use)?

- How much output should the firm produce?

- What price should the firm charge for its products?

- How much labor should the firm employ?

The answers to these questions depend on the production and cost conditions facing each firm. That is the subject of this chapter. The answers also depend on the market structure for the product(s) in question. Market structure is a multidimensional concept that involves how competitive the industry is. We define it by questions such as these:

- How much market power does each firm in the industry possess?

- How similar is each firm's product to the products of other firms in the industry?

- How difficult is it for new firms to enter the industry?

- Do firms compete on the basis of price, advertising, or other product differences?

Figure 7.2 illustrates the range of different market structures, which we will explore in **Perfect Competition**, **Monopoly**, and **Monopolistic Competition and Oligopoly**.

Figure 7.2 The Spectrum of Competition   Firms face different competitive situations. At one extreme—perfect competition—many firms are all trying to sell identical products. At the other extreme—monopoly—only one firm is selling the product, and this firm faces no competition. Monopolistic competition and oligopoly fall between the extremes of perfect competition and monopoly. Monopolistic competition is a situation with many firms selling similar, but not identical products. Oligopoly is a situation with few firms that sell identical or similar products.

Let's examine how firms determine their costs and desired profit levels. Then we will discuss the origins of cost, both in the short and long run. Private enterprise, which can be private individual or group business ownership, characterizes the U.S. economy. In the U.S. system, we have the option to organize private businesses as sole proprietorships (one owner), partners (more than one owner), and corporations (legal entitles separate from the owners.

When people think of businesses, often corporate giants like Wal-Mart, Microsoft, or General Motors come to mind. However, firms come in all sizes, as **Table 7.1** shows. The vast majority of American firms have fewer than 20 employees. As of 2010, the U.S. Census Bureau counted 5.7 million firms with employees in the U.S. economy.

This OpenStax book is available for free at http://cnx.org/content/col12122/1.4

Slightly less than half of all the workers in private firms are at the 17,000 large firms, meaning they employ more than 500 workers. Another 35% of workers in the U.S. economy are at firms with fewer than 100 workers. These small-scale businesses include everything from dentists and lawyers to businesses that mow lawns or clean houses. Table 7.1 does not include a separate category for the millions of small "non-employer" businesses where a single owner or a few partners are not officially paid wages or a salary, but simply receive whatever they can earn.

Number of Employees	Firms (% of total firms)	Number of Paid Employees (% of total employment)
Total	5,734,538	112.0 million
0–9	4,543,315 (79.2%)	12.3 million (11.0%)
10–19	617,089 (10.8%)	8.3 million (7.4%)
20–99	475,125 (8.3%)	18.6 million (16.6%)
100–499	81,773 (1.4%)	15.9 million (14.2%)
500 or more	17,236 (0.30%)	50.9 million (49.8%)

Table 7.1 Range in Size of U.S. Firms   (Source: U.S. Census, 2010 www.census.gov)

7.1 | Explicit and Implicit Costs, and Accounting and Economic Profit

By the end of this section, you will be able to:
- Explain the difference between explicit costs and implicit costs
- Understand the relationship between cost and revenue

Each business, regardless of size or complexity, tries to earn a profit:

$$\text{Profit} = \text{Total Revenue} - \text{Total Cost}$$

Total **revenue** is the income the firm generates from selling its products. We calculate it by multiplying the price of the product times the quantity of output sold:

$$\text{Total Revenue} = \text{Price} \times \text{Quantity}$$

We will see in the following chapters that revenue is a function of the demand for the firm's products.

Total cost is what the firm pays for producing and selling its products. Recall that production involves the firm converting inputs to outputs. Each of those inputs has a cost to the firm. The sum of all those costs is total cost. We will learn in this chapter that short run costs are different from long run costs.

We can distinguish between two types of cost: explicit and implicit. **Explicit costs** are out-of-pocket costs, that is, actual payments. Wages that a firm pays its employees or rent that a firm pays for its office are explicit costs. **Implicit costs** are more subtle, but just as important. They represent the opportunity cost of using resources that the firm already owns. Often for small businesses, they are resources that the owners contribute. For example, working in the business while not earning a formal salary, or using the ground floor of a home as a retail store are both implicit costs. Implicit costs also include the depreciation of goods, materials, and equipment that are necessary for a company to operate. (See the Work It Out feature for an extended example.)

These two definitions of cost are important for distinguishing between two conceptions of profit, accounting profit, and economic profit. **Accounting profit** is a cash concept. It means total revenue minus explicit costs—the difference between dollars brought in and dollars paid out. **Economic profit** is total revenue minus total cost, including both explicit and implicit costs. The difference is important because even though a business pays income taxes based on its accounting profit, whether or not it is economically successful depends on its economic profit.

Work It Out ─○─○─○

Calculating Implicit Costs

Consider the following example. Fred currently works for a corporate law firm. He is considering opening his own legal practice, where he expects to earn $200,000 per year once he establishes himself. To run his own firm, he would need an office and a law clerk. He has found the perfect office, which rents for $50,000 per year. He could hire a law clerk for $35,000 per year. If these figures are accurate, would Fred's legal practice be profitable?

Step 1. First you have to calculate the costs. You can take what you know about explicit costs and total them:

Office rental :	$50,000
Law clerk's salary :	+$35,000
Total explicit costs :	$85,000

Step 2. Subtracting the explicit costs from the revenue gives you the accounting profit.

Revenues :	$200,000
Explicit costs :	−$85,000
Accounting profit :	$115,000

However, these calculations consider only the explicit costs. To open his own practice, Fred would have to quit his current job, where he is earning an annual salary of $125,000. This would be an implicit cost of opening his own firm.

Step 3. You need to subtract both the explicit and implicit costs to determine the true economic profit:

$$\text{Economic profit} = \text{total revenues} - \text{explicit costs} - \text{implicit costs}$$
$$= \$200,000 - \$85,000 - \$125,000$$
$$= -\$10,000 \text{ per year}$$

Fred would be losing $10,000 per year. That does not mean he would not want to open his own business, but it does mean he would be earning $10,000 less than if he worked for the corporate firm.

Implicit costs can include other things as well. Maybe Fred values his leisure time, and starting his own firm would require him to put in more hours than at the corporate firm. In this case, the lost leisure would also be an implicit cost that would subtract from economic profits.

Now that we have an idea about the different types of costs, let's look at cost structures. A firm's cost structure in the long run may be different from that in the short run. We turn to that distinction in the next few sections.

7.2 | Production in the Short Run

By the end of this section, you will be able to:
- Understand the concept of a production function
- Differentiate between the different types of inputs or factors in a production function
- Differentiate between fixed and variable inputs
- Differentiate between production in the short run and in the long run
- Differentiate between total and marginal product
- Understand the concept of diminishing marginal productivity

In this chapter, we want to explore the relationship between the quantity of output a firm produces, and the cost of producing that output. We mentioned that the cost of the product depends on how many inputs are required to produce the product and what those inputs cost. We can answer the former question by looking at the firm's production function.

Figure 7.3 The production process for pizza includes inputs such as ingredients, the efforts of the pizza maker, and tools and materials for cooking and serving. (Credit: Haldean Brown/Flickr Creative Commons)

Production is the process (or processes) a firm uses to transform inputs (e.g. labor, capital, raw materials) into outputs, i.e. the goods or services the firm wishes to sell. Consider pizza making. The pizzaiolo (pizza maker) takes flour, water, and yeast to make dough. Similarly, the pizzaiolo may take tomatoes, spices, and water to make pizza sauce. The cook rolls out the dough, brushes on the pizza sauce, and adds cheese and other toppings. The pizzaiolo uses a peel—the shovel-like wooden tool-- to put the pizza into the oven to cook. Once baked, the pizza goes into a box (if it's for takeout) and the customer pays for the good. What are the inputs (or factors of production) in the production process for this pizza?

Economists divide factors of production into several categories:

- **Natural Resources (Land and Raw Materials)** - The ingredients for the pizza are raw materials. These include the flour, yeast, and water for the dough, the tomatoes, herbs, and water for the sauce, the cheese, and the toppings. If the pizza place uses a wood-burning oven, we would include the wood as a raw material. If the establishment heats the oven with natural gas, we would count this as a raw material. Don't forget electricity for lights. If, instead of pizza, we were looking at an agricultural product, like wheat, we would include the land the farmer used for crops here.

- **Labor** – When we talk about production, labor means human effort, both physical and mental. The pizzaiolo was the primary example of labor here. He or she needs to be strong enough to roll out the dough and to insert and retrieve the pizza from the oven, but he or she also needs to know **how** to make the pizza, how long it cooks in the oven and a myriad of other aspects of pizza-making. The business may also have one or more people to work the counter, take orders, and receive payment.

- **Capital** – When economists uses the term capital, they do not mean financial capital (money); rather, they mean physical capital, the machines, equipment, and buildings that one uses to produce the product. In the case of pizza, the capital includes the peel, the oven, the building, and any other necessary equipment (for example, tables and chairs).

- **Technology** – Technology refers to the process or processes for producing the product. How does the pizzaiolo combine ingredients to make pizza? How hot should the oven be? How long should the pizza cook? What is the best oven to use? Gas or wood burning? Should the restaurant make its own dough, sauce, cheese, toppings, or should it buy them?

- **Entrepreneurship** – Production involves many decisions and much knowledge, even for something as simple as pizza. Who makes those decisions? Ultimately, it is the entrepreneur, the person who creates the business, whose idea it is to combine the inputs to produce the outputs.

The cost of producing pizza (or any output) depends on the amount of labor capital, raw materials, and other inputs required and the price of each input to the entrepreneur. Let's explore these ideas in more detail.

We can summarize the ideas so far in terms of a **production function**, a mathematical expression or equation that explains the engineering relationship between inputs and outputs:

$$Q = f[NR, L, K, t, E]$$

The production function gives the answer to the question, how much output can the firm produce given different amounts of inputs? Production functions are specific to the product. Different products have different production functions. The amount of labor a farmer uses to produce a bushel of wheat is likely different than that required to produce an automobile. Firms in the same industry may have somewhat different production functions, since each firm may produce a little differently. One pizza restaurant may make its own dough and sauce, while another may buy those pre-made. A sit-down pizza restaurant probably uses more labor (to handle table service) than a purely take-out restaurant.

We can describe inputs as either **fixed** or **variable**.

Fixed inputs are those that can't easily be increased or decreased in a short period of time. In the pizza example, the building is a fixed input. Once the entrepreneur signs the lease, he or she is stuck in the building until the lease expires. Fixed inputs define the firm's maximum output capacity. This is analogous to the potential real GDP shown by society's production possibilities curve, i.e. the maximum quantities of outputs a society can produce at a given time with its available resources.

Variable inputs are those that can easily be increased or decreased in a short period of time. The pizzaiolo can order more ingredients with a phone call, so ingredients would be variable inputs. The owner could hire a new person to work the counter pretty quickly as well.

Economists often use a short-hand form for the production function:

$$Q = f[L, K],$$

where L represents all the variable inputs, and K represents all the fixed inputs.

Economists differentiate between short and long run production.

The **short run** is the period of time during which at least some factors of production are fixed. During the period of the pizza restaurant lease, the pizza restaurant is operating in the short run, because it is limited to using the current building—the owner can't choose a larger or smaller building.

The **long run** is the period of time during which all factors are variable. Once the lease expires for the pizza restaurant, the shop owner can move to a larger or smaller place.

Let's explore production in the short run using a specific example: tree cutting (for lumber) with a two-person crosscut saw.

This OpenStax book is available for free at http://cnx.org/content/col12122/1.4

Figure 7.4 Production in the short run may be explored through the example of lumberjacks using a two-person saw. (Credit: Wknight94/Wikimedia Commons)

Since by definition capital is fixed in the short run, our production function becomes

$$Q = f[L, \bar{K}] \text{ or } Q = f[L]$$

This equation simply indicates that since capital is fixed, the amount of output (e.g. trees cut down per day) depends only on the amount of labor employed (e.g. number of lumberjacks working). We can express this production function numerically as **Table 7.2** below shows.

# Lumberjacks	1	2	3	4	5
# Trees (TP)	4	10	12	13	13
MP	4	6	2	1	0

Table 7.2 Short Run Production Function for Trees

Note that we have introduced some new language. We also call Output (Q) Total Product (TP), which means the amount of output produced with a given amount of labor and a fixed amount of capital. In this example, one lumberjack using a two-person saw can cut down four trees in an hour. Two lumberjacks using a two-person saw can cut down ten trees in an hour.

We should also introduce a critical concept: **marginal product**. Marginal product is the additional output of one more worker. Mathematically, Marginal Product is the change in total product divided by the change in labor: $MP = \Delta TP / \Delta L$. In the table above, since 0 workers produce 0 trees, the marginal product of the first worker is four trees per day, but the marginal product of the second worker is six trees per day. Why might that be the case? It's because of the nature of the capital the workers are using. A two-person saw works much better with two persons than with one. Suppose we add a third lumberjack to the story. What will that person's marginal product be? What will that person contribute to the team? Perhaps he or she can oil the saw's teeth to keep it sawing smoothly or he or she could bring water to the two people sawing. What you see in the table is a critically important conclusion about production in the short run: It may be that as we add workers, the marginal product increases at first, but sooner or later additional workers will have decreasing marginal product. In fact, there may eventually be no effect or a negative effect on output. This is called the **Law of Diminishing Marginal Product** and it's a characteristic of production in the short run. Diminishing marginal productivity is very similar to the concept of diminishing marginal utility that we learned about in the chapter on consumer choice. Both concepts are examples of the more general concept of diminishing marginal returns. Why does diminishing marginal productivity occur? It's because of fixed capital. We will see this more clearly when we discuss production in the long run.

We can show these concepts graphically as **Figure 7.5** and **Figure 7.6** illustrate. **Figure 7.5** graphically shows the data from **Table 7.2**. **Figure 7.6** shows the more general cases of total product and marginal product curves.

This OpenStax book is available for free at http://cnx.org/content/col12122/1.4

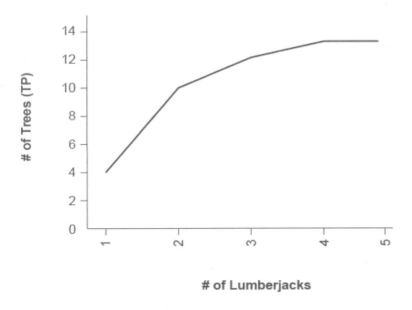

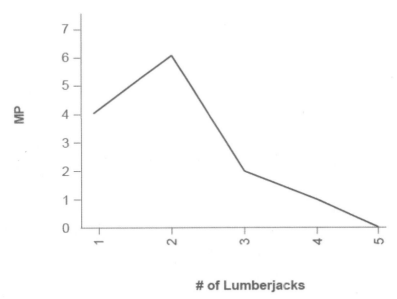

Figure 7.5

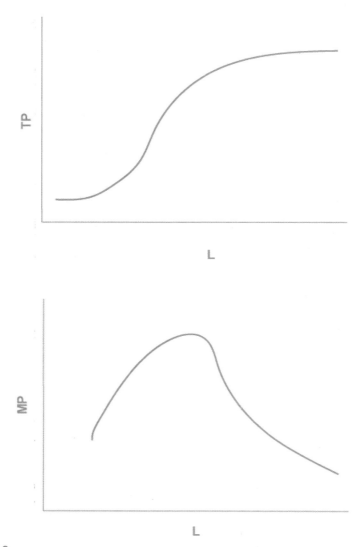

Figure 7.6

7.3 | Costs in the Short Run

By the end of this section, you will be able to:
- Understand the relationship between production and costs
- Understand that every factor of production has a corresponding factor price
- Analyze short-run costs in terms of total cost, fixed cost, variable cost, marginal cost, and average cost
- Calculate average profit
- Evaluate patterns of costs to determine potential profit

We've explained that a firm's total costs depend on the quantities of inputs the firm uses to produce its output and the cost of those inputs to the firm. The firm's production function tells us how much output the firm will produce with given amounts of inputs. However, if we think about that backwards, it tells us how many inputs the firm needs to produce a given quantity of output, which is the first thing we need to determine total cost. Let's move to the second

This OpenStax book is available for free at http://cnx.org/content/col12122/1.4

factor we need to determine.

For every factor of production (or input), there is an associated factor payment. **Factor payments** are what the firm pays for the use of the factors of production. From the firm's perspective, factor payments are costs. From the owner of each factor's perspective, factor payments are income. Factor payments include:

- **Raw materials prices** for raw materials

- **Rent** for land or buildings

- **Wages and salaries** for labor

- **Interest and dividends** for the use of financial capital (loans and equity investments)

- **Profit** for entrepreneurship. Profit is the residual, what's left over from revenues after the firm pays all the other costs. While it may seem odd to treat profit as a "cost", it is what entrepreneurs earn for taking the risk of starting a business. You can see this correspondence between factors of production and factor payments in the inside loop of the circular flow diagram in **Figure 1.6**.

We now have all the information necessary to determine a firm's costs.

A cost function is a mathematical expression or equation that shows the cost of producing different levels of output.

Q	1	2	3	4
Cost	$32.50	$44	$52	$90

Table 7.3 Cost Function for Producing Widgets

What we observe is that the cost increases as the firm produces higher quantities of output. This is pretty intuitive, since producing more output requires greater quantities of inputs, which cost more dollars to acquire.

What is the origin of these cost figures? They come from the production function and the factor payments. The discussion of costs in the short run above, **Costs in the Short Run**, was based on the following production function, which is similar to **Table 7.3** except for "widgets" instead of trees.

Workers (L)	1	2	3	3.25	4.4	5.2	6	7	8	9
Widgets (Q)	0.2	0.4	0.8	1	2	3	3.5	3.8	3.95	4

Table 7.4

We can use the information from the production function to determine production costs. What we need to know is how many workers are required to produce any quantity of output. If we flip the order of the rows, we "invert" the production function so it shows $L = f(Q)$.

Widgets (Q)	0.2	0.4	0.8	1	2	3	3.5	3.8	3.95	4
Workers (L)	1	2	3	3.25	4.4	5.2	6	7	8	9

Table 7.5

Now focus on the whole number quantities of output. We'll eliminate the fractions from the table:

Widgets (Q)				1	2	3				4

Table 7.6

Workers (L)				3.25	4.4	5.2				9

Table 7.6

Suppose widget workers receive $10 per hour. Multiplying the Workers row by $10 (and eliminating the blanks) gives us the cost of producing different levels of output.

Widgets (Q)	1.00	2.00	3.00	4.00
Workers (L)	3.25	4.4	5.2	9
× Wage Rate per hour	$10	$10	$10	$10
= Cost	$32.50	$44.00	$52.00	$90.00

Table 7.7

This is same cost function with which we began! (shown in Table 7.3)

Now that we have the basic idea of the cost origins and how they are related to production, let's drill down into the details.

Average and Marginal Costs

The cost of producing a firm's output depends on how much labor and physical capital the firm uses. A list of the costs involved in producing cars will look very different from the costs involved in producing computer software or haircuts or fast-food meals.

We can measure costs in a variety of ways. Each way provides its own insight into costs. Sometimes firms need to look at their cost per unit of output, not just their total cost. There are two ways to measure per unit costs. The most intuitive way is average cost. Average cost is the cost on average of producing a given quantity. We define **average cost** as total cost divided by the quantity of output produced. $AC = TC / Q$ If producing two widgets costs a total of $44, the average cost per widget is $\$44 / 2 = \$22$ per widget. The other way of measuring cost per unit is marginal cost. If average cost is the cost of the average unit of output produced, marginal cost is the cost of each individual unit produced. More formally, marginal cost is the cost of producing one more unit of output. Mathematically, **marginal cost** is the change in total cost divided by the change in output: $MC = \Delta TC / \Delta Q$. If the cost of the first widget is $32.50 and the cost of two widgets is $44, the marginal cost of the second widget is $\$44 - \$32.50 = \$11.50$. We can see the Widget Cost table redrawn below with average and marginal cost added.

Q	1	2	3	4
Total Cost	$32.50	$44.00	$52.00	$90.00
Average Cost	$32.50	$22.00	$17.33	$22.50
Marginal Cost	$32.50	$11.50	$8.00	$38.00

Table 7.8 Extended Cost Function for Producing Widgets

Note that the marginal cost of the first unit of output is always the same as total cost.

Fixed and Variable Costs

We can decompose costs into fixed and variable costs. Fixed costs are the costs of the fixed inputs (e.g. capital). Because fixed inputs do not change in the short run, fixed costs are expenditures that do not change regardless of the level of production. Whether you produce a great deal or a little, the fixed costs are the same. One example is the rent on a factory or a retail space. Once you sign the lease, the rent is the same regardless of how much you produce, at least until the lease expires. Fixed costs can take many other forms: for example, the cost of machinery or equipment to produce the product, research and development costs to develop new products, even an expense like advertising to popularize a brand name. The amount of fixed costs varies according to the specific line of business: for instance, manufacturing computer chips requires an expensive factory, but a local moving and hauling business can get by with almost no fixed costs at all if it rents trucks by the day when needed.

Variable costs are the costs of the variable inputs (e.g. labor). The only way to increase or decrease output is by increasing or decreasing the variable inputs. Therefore, variable costs increase or decrease with output. We treat labor as a variable cost, since producing a greater quantity of a good or service typically requires more workers or more work hours. Variable costs would also include raw materials.

Total costs are the sum of fixed plus variable costs. Let's look at another example. Consider the barber shop called "The Clip Joint" in **Figure 7.7**. The data for output and costs are in **Table 7.9**. The fixed costs of operating the barber shop, including the space and equipment, are $160 per day. The variable costs are the costs of hiring barbers, which in our example is $80 per barber each day. The first two columns of the table show the quantity of haircuts the barbershop can produce as it hires additional barbers. The third column shows the fixed costs, which do not change regardless of the level of production. The fourth column shows the variable costs at each level of output. We calculate these by taking the amount of labor hired and multiplying by the wage. For example, two barbers cost: $2 \times \$80 = \$160$. Adding together the fixed costs in the third column and the variable costs in the fourth column produces the total costs in the fifth column. For example, with two barbers the total cost is: $160 + $160 = $320.

Labor	Quantity	Fixed Cost	Variable Cost	Total Cost
1	16	$160	$80	$240
2	40	$160	$160	$320
3	60	$160	$240	$400
4	72	$160	$320	$480
5	80	$160	$400	$560
6	84	$160	$480	$640
7	82	$160	$560	$720

Table 7.9 Output and Total Costs

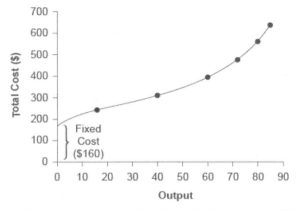

Figure 7.7 How Output Affects Total Costs   At zero production, the fixed costs of $160 are still present. As production increases, variable costs are added to fixed costs, and the total cost is the sum of the two.

At zero production, the fixed costs of $160 are still present. As production increases, we add variable costs to fixed costs, and the total cost is the sum of the two. **Figure 7.7** graphically shows the relationship between the quantity of output produced and the cost of producing that output. We always show the fixed costs as the vertical intercept of the total cost curve; that is, they are the costs incurred when output is zero so there are no variable costs.

You can see from the graph that once production starts, total costs and variable costs rise. While variable costs may initially increase at a decreasing rate, at some point they begin increasing at an increasing rate. This is caused by diminishing marginal productivity which we discussed earlier in the **Production in the Short Run** section of this chapter, which is easiest to see with an example. As the number of barbers increases from zero to one in the table, output increases from 0 to 16 for a marginal gain (or marginal product) of 16. As the number rises from one to two barbers, output increases from 16 to 40, a marginal gain of 24. From that point on, though, the marginal product diminishes as we add each additional barber. For example, as the number of barbers rises from two to three, the marginal product is only 20; and as the number rises from three to four, the marginal product is only 12.

To understand the reason behind this pattern, consider that a one-man barber shop is a very busy operation. The single barber needs to do everything: say hello to people entering, answer the phone, cut hair, sweep, and run the cash register. A second barber reduces the level of disruption from jumping back and forth between these tasks, and allows a greater division of labor and specialization. The result can be increasing marginal productivity. However, as the shop adds other barbers, the advantage of each additional barber is less, since the specialization of labor can only go so far. The addition of a sixth or seventh or eighth barber just to greet people at the door will have less impact than the second one did. This is the pattern of diminishing marginal productivity. As a result, the total costs of production will begin to rise more rapidly as output increases. At some point, you may even see negative returns as the additional barbers begin bumping elbows and getting in each other's way. In this case, the addition of still more barbers would actually cause output to decrease, as the last row of **Table 7.9** shows.

This pattern of diminishing marginal productivity is common in production. As another example, consider the problem of irrigating a crop on a farmer's field. The plot of land is the fixed factor of production, while the water that the farmer can add to the land is the key variable cost. As the farmer adds water to the land, output increases. However, adding increasingly more water brings smaller increases in output, until at some point the water floods the field and actually reduces output. Diminishing marginal productivity occurs because, with fixed inputs (land in this example), each additional unit of input (e.g. water) contributes less to overall production.

Average Total Cost, Average Variable Cost, Marginal Cost

The breakdown of total costs into fixed and variable costs can provide a basis for other insights as well. The first five columns of **Table 7.10** duplicate the previous table, but the last three columns show average total costs, average variable costs, and marginal costs. These new measures analyze costs on a per-unit (rather than a total) basis and are reflected in the curves in **Figure 7.8**.

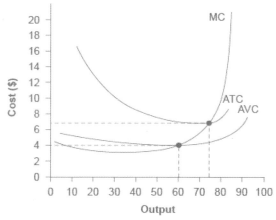

Figure 7.8 Cost Curves at the Clip Joint We can also present the information on total costs, fixed cost, and variable cost on a per-unit basis. We calculate average total cost (ATC) by dividing total cost by the total quantity produced. The average total cost curve is typically U-shaped. We calculate average variable cost (AVC) by dividing variable cost by the quantity produced. The average variable cost curve lies below the average total cost curve and is also typically U-shaped. We calculate marginal cost (MC) by taking the change in total cost between two levels of output and dividing by the change in output. The marginal cost curve is upward-sloping.

This OpenStax book is available for free at http://cnx.org/content/col12122/1.4

Labor	Quantity	Fixed Cost	Variable Cost	Total Cost	Marginal Cost	Average Total Cost	Average Variable Cost
1	16	$160	$80	$240	$15.00	$15.00	$5.00
2	40	$160	$160	$320	$3.33	$8.00	$4.00
3	60	$160	$240	$400	$4.00	$6.67	$4.00
4	72	$160	$320	$480	$6.67	$6.67	$4.44
5	80	$160	$400	$560	$10.00	$7.00	$5.00
6	84	$160	$480	$640	$20.00	$7.62	$5.71

Table 7.10 Different Types of Costs

Average total cost (sometimes referred to simply as average cost) is total cost divided by the quantity of output. Since the total cost of producing 40 haircuts is $320, the average total cost for producing each of 40 haircuts is $320/40, or $8 per haircut. Average cost curves are typically U-shaped, as **Figure 7.8** shows. Average total cost starts off relatively high, because at low levels of output total costs are dominated by the fixed cost. Mathematically, the denominator is so small that average total cost is large. Average total cost then declines, as the fixed costs are spread over an increasing quantity of output. In the average cost calculation, the rise in the numerator of total costs is relatively small compared to the rise in the denominator of quantity produced. However, as output expands still further, the average cost begins to rise. At the right side of the average cost curve, total costs begin rising more rapidly as diminishing returns come into effect.

We obtain **average variable cost** when we divide variable cost by quantity of output. For example, the variable cost of producing 80 haircuts is $400, so the average variable cost is $400/80, or $5 per haircut. Note that at any level of output, the average variable cost curve will always lie below the curve for average total cost, as **Figure 7.8** shows. The reason is that average total cost includes average variable cost and average fixed cost. Thus, for Q = 80 haircuts, the average total cost is $8 per haircut, while the average variable cost is $5 per haircut. However, as output grows, fixed costs become relatively less important (since they do not rise with output), so average variable cost sneaks closer to average cost.

Average total and variable costs measure the average costs of producing some quantity of output. Marginal cost is somewhat different. **Marginal cost** is the additional cost of producing one more unit of output. It is not the cost per unit of *all* units produced, but only the next one (or next few). We calculate marginal cost by taking the change in total cost and dividing it by the change in quantity. For example, as quantity produced increases from 40 to 60 haircuts, total costs rise by 400 − 320, or 80. Thus, the marginal cost for each of those marginal 20 units will be 80/20, or $4 per haircut. The marginal cost curve is generally upward-sloping, because diminishing marginal returns implies that additional units are more costly to produce. We can see small range of increasing marginal returns in the figure as a dip in the marginal cost curve before it starts rising. There is a point at which marginal and average costs meet, as the following Clear it Up feature discusses.

Where do marginal and average costs meet?

The marginal cost line intersects the average cost line exactly at the bottom of the average cost curve—which occurs at a quantity of 72 and cost of $6.60 in Figure 7.8. The reason why the intersection occurs at this point is built into the economic meaning of marginal and average costs. If the marginal cost of production is below the average cost for producing previous units, as it is for the points to the left of where MC crosses ATC, then producing one more additional unit will reduce average costs overall—and the ATC curve will be downward-sloping in this zone. Conversely, if the marginal cost of production for producing an additional unit is above the average cost for producing the earlier units, as it is for points to the right of where MC crosses ATC, then producing a marginal unit will increase average costs overall—and the ATC curve must be upward-sloping in this zone. The point of transition, between where MC is pulling ATC down and where it is pulling it up, must occur at the minimum point of the ATC curve.

This idea of the marginal cost "pulling down" the average cost or "pulling up" the average cost may sound abstract, but think about it in terms of your own grades. If the score on the most recent quiz you take is lower than your average score on previous quizzes, then the marginal quiz pulls down your average. If your score on the most recent quiz is higher than the average on previous quizzes, the marginal quiz pulls up your average. In this same way, low marginal costs of production first pull down average costs and then higher marginal costs pull them up.

The numerical calculations behind average cost, average variable cost, and marginal cost will change from firm to firm. However, the general patterns of these curves, and the relationships and economic intuition behind them, will not change.

Lessons from Alternative Measures of Costs

Breaking down total costs into fixed cost, marginal cost, average total cost, and average variable cost is useful because each statistic offers its own insights for the firm.

Whatever the firm's quantity of production, total revenue must exceed total costs if it is to earn a profit. As explored in the chapter **Choice in a World of Scarcity**, fixed costs are often sunk costs that a firm cannot recoup. In thinking about what to do next, typically you should ignore sunk costs, since you have already spent this money and cannot make any changes. However, you can change variable costs, so they convey information about the firm's ability to cut costs in the present and the extent to which costs will increase if production rises.

Why are total cost and average cost not on the same graph?

Total cost, fixed cost, and variable cost each reflect different aspects of the cost of production over the entire quantity of output produced. We measure these costs in dollars. In contrast, marginal cost, average cost, and average variable cost are costs per unit. In the previous example, we measured them as dollars per haircut. Thus, it would not make sense to put all of these numbers on the same graph, since we measure them in different units ($ versus $ per unit of output).

It would be as if the vertical axis measured two different things. In addition, as a practical matter, if they were on the same graph, the lines for marginal cost, average cost, and average variable cost would appear almost flat against the horizontal axis, compared to the values for total cost, fixed cost, and variable cost. Using the figures from the previous example, the total cost of producing 40 haircuts is $320. However, the average cost is $320/40, or $8. If you graphed both total and average cost on the same axes, the average cost would hardly show.

Average cost tells a firm whether it can earn profits given the current price in the market. If we divide profit by the quantity of output produced we get **average profit**, also known as the firm's *profit margin*. Expanding the equation for profit gives:

$$\text{average profit} = \frac{\text{profit}}{\text{quantity produced}}$$
$$= \frac{\text{total revenue} - \text{total cost}}{\text{quantity produced}}$$
$$= \frac{\text{total revenue}}{\text{quantity produced}} - \frac{\text{total cost}}{\text{quantity produced}}$$
$$= \text{average revenue} - \text{average cost}$$

However, note that:

$$\text{average revenue} = \frac{\text{price} \times \text{quantity produced}}{\text{quantity produced}}$$

$$= \text{price}$$

Thus:

$$\text{average profit} = \text{price} - \text{average cost}$$

This is the firm's **profit margin**. This definition implies that if the market price is above average cost, average profit, and thus total profit, will be positive. If price is below average cost, then profits will be negative.

We can compare this marginal cost of producing an additional unit with the marginal revenue gained by selling that additional unit to reveal whether the additional unit is adding to total profit—or not. Thus, marginal cost helps producers understand how increasing or decreasing production affects profits.

A Variety of Cost Patterns

The pattern of costs varies among industries and even among firms in the same industry. Some businesses have high fixed costs, but low marginal costs. Consider, for example, an internet company that provides medical advice to customers. Consumers might pay such a company directly, or perhaps hospitals or healthcare practices might subscribe on behalf of their patients. Setting up the website, collecting the information, writing the content, and buying or leasing the computer space to handle the web traffic are all fixed costs that the company must undertake before the site can work. However, when the website is up and running, it can provide a high quantity of service with relatively low variable costs, like the cost of monitoring the system and updating the information. In this case, the total cost curve might start at a high level, because of the high fixed costs, but then might appear close to flat, up to a large quantity of output, reflecting the low variable costs of operation. If the website is popular, however, a large rise in the number of visitors will overwhelm the website, and increasing output further could require a purchase of additional computer space.

For other firms, fixed costs may be relatively low. For example, consider firms that rake leaves in the fall or shovel snow off sidewalks and driveways in the winter. For fixed costs, such firms may need little more than a car to transport workers to homes of customers and some rakes and shovels. Still other firms may find that diminishing marginal returns set in quite sharply. If a manufacturing plant tried to run 24 hours a day, seven days a week, little time remains for routine equipment maintenance, and marginal costs can increase dramatically as the firm struggles to repair and replace overworked equipment.

Every firm can gain insight into its task of earning profits by dividing its total costs into fixed and variable costs, and then using these calculations as a basis for average total cost, average variable cost, and marginal cost. However, making a final decision about the profit-maximizing quantity to produce and the price to charge will require combining these perspectives on cost with an analysis of sales and revenue, which in turn requires looking at the market structure in which the firm finds itself. Before we turn to the analysis of market structure in other chapters, we will analyze the firm's cost structure from a long-run perspective.

7.4 | Production in the Long Run

By the end of this section, you will be able to:

- Understand how long run production differs from short run production.

In the long run, all factors (including capital) are variable, so our production function is $Q = f[L, K]$.

Consider a secretarial firm that does typing for hire using typists for labor and personal computers for capital. To start, the firm has just enough business for one typist and one PC to keep busy for a day. Say that's five documents. Now suppose the firm receives a rush order from a good customer for 10 documents tomorrow. Ideally, the firm would like to use two typists and two PCs to produce twice their normal output of five documents. However, in the short turn, the firm has fixed capital, i.e. only one PC. The table below shows the situation:

# Typists (L)	1	2	3	4	5	6	
Letters/hr (TP)	5	7	8	8	8	8	For K = 1PC
MP	5	2	1	0	0	0	

Table 7.11 Short Run Production Function for Typing

In the short run, the only variable factor is labor so the only way the firm can produce more output is by hiring additional workers. What could the second worker do? What can they contribute to the firm? Perhaps they can answer the phone, which is a major impediment to completing the typing assignment. What about a third worker? Perhaps he or she could bring coffee to the first two workers. You can see both total product and marginal product for the firm above. Now here's something to think about: At what point (e.g. after how many workers) does diminishing marginal productivity kick in, and more importantly, why?

In this example, marginal productivity starts to decline after the second worker. This is because capital is fixed. The production process for typing works best with one worker and one PC. If you add more than one typist, you get seriously diminishing marginal productivity.

Consider the long run. Suppose the firm's demand increases to 15 documents per day. What might the firm do to operate more efficiently? If demand has tripled, the firm could acquire two more PCs, which would give us a new short run production function as Table 7.4 below shows.

# Typists (L)	1	2	3	4	5	5	
Letters/hr (TP)	5	6	8	8	8	8	For K = 1PC
MP	5	2	1	0	0	0	
Letters/hr (TP)	5	10	15	17	18	18	For K = 3PC
MP	5	5	5	2	1	0	

Table 7.12 Long Run Production Function for Typing

With more capital, the firm can hire three workers before diminishing productivity comes into effect. More generally, because all factors are variable, the long run production function shows the most efficient way of producing any level of output.

7.5 | Costs in the Long Run

By the end of this section, you will be able to:
- Calculate long run total cost
- Identify economies of scale, diseconomies of scale, and constant returns to scale
- Interpret graphs of long-run average cost curves and short-run average cost curves
- Analyze cost and production in the long run and short run

The long run is the period of time when all costs are variable. The long run depends on the specifics of the firm in question—it is not a precise period of time. If you have a one-year lease on your factory, then the long run is any period longer than a year, since after a year you are no longer bound by the lease. No costs are fixed in the long run. A firm can build new factories and purchase new machinery, or it can close existing facilities. In planning for the long run, the firm will compare alternative **production technologies** (or processes).

This OpenStax book is available for free at http://cnx.org/content/col12122/1.4

In this context, technology refers to all alternative methods of combining inputs to produce outputs. It does not refer to a specific new invention like the tablet computer. The firm will search for the production technology that allows it to produce the desired level of output at the lowest cost. After all, lower costs lead to higher profits—at least if total revenues remain unchanged. Moreover, each firm must fear that if it does not seek out the lowest-cost methods of production, then it may lose sales to competitor firms that find a way to produce and sell for less.

Choice of Production Technology

A firm can perform many tasks with a range of combinations of labor and physical capital. For example, a firm can have human beings answering phones and taking messages, or it can invest in an automated voicemail system. A firm can hire file clerks and secretaries to manage a system of paper folders and file cabinets, or it can invest in a computerized recordkeeping system that will require fewer employees. A firm can hire workers to push supplies around a factory on rolling carts, it can invest in motorized vehicles, or it can invest in robots that carry materials without a driver. Firms often face a choice between buying a many small machines, which need a worker to run each one, or buying one larger and more expensive machine, which requires only one or two workers to operate it. In short, physical capital and labor can often substitute for each other.

Consider the example of local governments hiring a private firm to clean up public parks. Three different combinations of labor and physical capital for cleaning up a single average-sized park appear in **Table 7.13**. The first production technology is heavy on workers and light on machines, while the next two technologies substitute machines for workers. Since all three of these production methods produce the same thing—one cleaned-up park—a profit-seeking firm will choose the production technology that is least expensive, given the prices of labor and machines.

Production technology 1	10 workers	2 machines
Production technology 2	7 workers	4 machines
Production technology 3	3 workers	7 machines

Table 7.13 Three Ways to Clean a Park

Production technology 1 uses the most labor and least machinery, while production technology 3 uses the least labor and the most machinery. **Table 7.14** outlines three examples of how the total cost will change with each production technology as the cost of labor changes. As the cost of labor rises from example A to B to C, the firm will choose to substitute away from labor and use more machinery.

Example A: Workers cost $40, machines cost $80

	Labor Cost	Machine Cost	Total Cost
Cost of technology 1	10 × $40 = $400	2 × $80 = $160	$560
Cost of technology 2	7 × $40 = $280	4 × $80 = $320	$600
Cost of technology 3	3 × $40 = $120	7 × $80 = $560	$680

Example B: Workers cost $55, machines cost $80

	Labor Cost	Machine Cost	Total Cost
Cost of technology 1	10 × $55 = $550	2 × $80 = $160	$710
Cost of technology 2	7 × $55 = $385	4 × $80 = $320	$705
Cost of technology 3	3 × $55 = $165	7 × $80 = $560	$725

Table 7.14 Total Cost with Rising Labor Costs

Example C: Workers cost $90, machines cost $80

	Labor Cost	Machine Cost	Total Cost
Cost of technology 1	10 × $90 = $900	2 × $80 = $160	$1,060
Cost of technology 2	7 × $90 = $630	4 × $80 = $320	$950
Cost of technology 3	3 × $90 = $270	7 × $80 = $560	$830

Table 7.14 Total Cost with Rising Labor Costs

Example A shows the firm's cost calculation when wages are $40 and machines costs are $80. In this case, technology 1 is the low-cost production technology. In example B, wages rise to $55, while the cost of machines does not change, in which case technology 2 is the low-cost production technology. If wages keep rising up to $90, while the cost of machines remains unchanged, then technology 3 clearly becomes the low-cost form of production, as example C shows.

This example shows that as an input becomes more expensive (in this case, the labor input), firms will attempt to conserve on using that input and will instead shift to other inputs that are relatively less expensive. This pattern helps to explain why the demand curve for labor (or any input) slopes down; that is, as labor becomes relatively more expensive, profit-seeking firms will seek to substitute the use of other inputs. When a multinational employer like Coca-Cola or McDonald's sets up a bottling plant or a restaurant in a high-wage economy like the United States, Canada, Japan, or Western Europe, it is likely to use production technologies that conserve on the number of workers and focuses more on machines. However, that same employer is likely to use production technologies with more workers and less machinery when producing in a lower-wage country like Mexico, China, or South Africa.

Economies of Scale

Once a firm has determined the least costly production technology, it can consider the optimal scale of production, or quantity of output to produce. Many industries experience economies of scale. Economies of scale refers to the situation where, as the quantity of output goes up, the cost per unit goes down. This is the idea behind "warehouse stores" like Costco or Walmart. In everyday language: a larger factory can produce at a lower average cost than a smaller factory.

Figure 7.9 illustrates the idea of economies of scale, showing the average cost of producing an alarm clock falling as the quantity of output rises. For a small-sized factory like S, with an output level of 1,000, the average cost of production is $12 per alarm clock. For a medium-sized factory like M, with an output level of 2,000, the average cost of production falls to $8 per alarm clock. For a large factory like L, with an output of 5,000, the average cost of production declines still further to $4 per alarm clock.

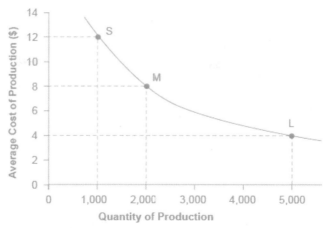

Figure 7.9 Economies of Scale A small factory like S produces 1,000 alarm clocks at an average cost of $12 per clock. A medium factory like M produces 2,000 alarm clocks at a cost of $8 per clock. A large factory like L produces 5,000 alarm clocks at a cost of $4 per clock. Economies of scale exist when the larger scale of production leads to lower average costs.

The average cost curve in Figure 7.9 may appear similar to the average cost curves we presented earlier in this chapter, although it is downward-sloping rather than U-shaped. However, there is one major difference. The economies of scale curve is a long-run average cost curve, because it allows all factors of production to change. The short-run average cost curves we presented earlier in this chapter assumed the existence of fixed costs, and only variable costs were allowed to change.

One prominent example of economies of scale occurs in the chemical industry. Chemical plants have many pipes. The cost of the materials for producing a pipe is related to the circumference of the pipe and its length. However, the cross-section area of the pipe determines the volume of chemicals that can flow through it. The calculations in Table 7.15 show that a pipe which uses twice as much material to make (as shown by the circumference) can actually carry four times the volume of chemicals because the pipe's cross-section area rises by a factor of four (as the Area column below shows).

	Circumference ($2\pi r$)	Area (πr^2)
4-inch pipe	12.5 inches	12.5 square inches
8-inch pipe	25.1 inches	50.2 square inches
16-inch pipe	50.2 inches	201.1 square inches

Table 7.15 Comparing Pipes: Economies of Scale in the Chemical Industry

A doubling of the cost of producing the pipe allows the chemical firm to process four times as much material. This pattern is a major reason for economies of scale in chemical production, which uses a large quantity of pipes. Of course, economies of scale in a chemical plant are more complex than this simple calculation suggests. However, the chemical engineers who design these plants have long used what they call the "six-tenths rule," a rule of thumb which holds that increasing the quantity produced in a chemical plant by a certain percentage will increase total cost by only six-tenths as much.

Shapes of Long-Run Average Cost Curves

While in the short run firms are limited to operating on a single average cost curve (corresponding to the level of fixed costs they have chosen), in the long run when all costs are variable, they can choose to operate on any average cost curve. Thus, the **long-run average cost (LRAC) curve** is actually based on a group of **short-run average cost (SRAC) curves**, each of which represents one specific level of fixed costs. More precisely, the long-run average cost curve will be the least expensive average cost curve for any level of output. Figure 7.10 shows how we build the long-run average cost curve from a group of short-run average cost curves. Five short-run-average cost curves appear on the diagram. Each SRAC curve represents a different level of fixed costs. For example, you can imagine $SRAC_1$ as a small factory, $SRAC_2$ as a medium factory, $SRAC_3$ as a large factory, and $SRAC_4$ and $SRAC_5$ as very large and ultra-large. Although this diagram shows only five SRAC curves, presumably there are an infinite number of other SRAC curves between the ones that we show. Think of this family of short-run average cost curves as representing different choices for a firm that is planning its level of investment in fixed cost physical capital—knowing that different choices about capital investment in the present will cause it to end up with different short-run average cost curves in the future.

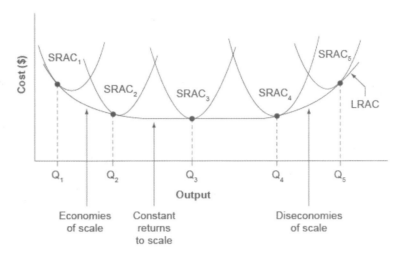

Figure 7.10 From Short-Run Average Cost Curves to Long-Run Average Cost Curves   The five different short-run average cost (SRAC) curves each represents a different level of fixed costs, from the low level of fixed costs at $SRAC_1$ to the high level of fixed costs at $SRAC_5$. Other SRAC curves, not in the diagram, lie between the ones that are here. The long-run average cost (LRAC) curve shows the lowest cost for producing each quantity of output when fixed costs can vary, and so it is formed by the bottom edge of the family of SRAC curves. If a firm wished to produce quantity Q_3, it would choose the fixed costs associated with $SRAC_3$.

The long-run average cost curve shows the cost of producing each quantity in the long run, when the firm can choose its level of fixed costs and thus choose which short-run average costs it desires. If the firm plans to produce in the long run at an output of Q_3, it should make the set of investments that will lead it to locate on $SRAC_3$, which allows producing q_3 at the lowest cost. A firm that intends to produce Q_3 would be foolish to choose the level of fixed costs at $SRAC_2$ or $SRAC_4$. At $SRAC_2$ the level of fixed costs is too low for producing Q_3 at lowest possible cost, and producing q_3 would require adding a very high level of variable costs and make the average cost very high. At $SRAC_4$, the level of fixed costs is too high for producing q_3 at lowest possible cost, and again average costs would be very high as a result.

The shape of the long-run cost curve, in **Figure 7.10**, is fairly common for many industries. The left-hand portion of the long-run average cost curve, where it is downward- sloping from output levels Q_1 to Q_2 to Q_3, illustrates the case of economies of scale. In this portion of the long-run average cost curve, larger scale leads to lower average costs. We illustrated this pattern earlier in **Figure 7.9**.

In the middle portion of the long-run average cost curve, the flat portion of the curve around Q_3, economies of scale have been exhausted. In this situation, allowing all inputs to expand does not much change the average cost of production. We call this **constant returns to scale**. In this LRAC curve range, the average cost of production does not change much as scale rises or falls. The following Clear It Up feature explains where diminishing marginal returns fit into this analysis.

This OpenStax book is available for free at http://cnx.org/content/col12122/1.4

How do economies of scale compare to diminishing marginal returns?

The concept of economies of scale, where average costs decline as production expands, might seem to conflict with the idea of diminishing marginal returns, where marginal costs rise as production expands. However, diminishing marginal returns refers only to the short-run average cost curve, where one variable input (like labor) is increasing, but other inputs (like capital) are fixed. Economies of scale refers to the long-run average cost curve where all inputs are allowed to increase together. Thus, it is quite possible and common to have an industry that has both diminishing marginal returns when only one input is allowed to change, and at the same time has economies of scale when all inputs change together to produce a larger-scale operation.

Finally, the right-hand portion of the long-run average cost curve, running from output level Q_4 to Q_5, shows a situation where, as the level of output and the scale rises, average costs rise as well. We call this situation **diseconomies of scale**. A firm or a factory can grow so large that it becomes very difficult to manage, resulting in unnecessarily high costs as many layers of management try to communicate with workers and with each other, and as failures to communicate lead to disruptions in the flow of work and materials. Not many overly large factories exist in the real world, because with their very high production costs, they are unable to compete for long against plants with lower average costs of production. However, in some planned economies, like the economy of the old Soviet Union, plants that were so large as to be grossly inefficient were able to continue operating for a long time because government economic planners protected them from competition and ensured that they would not make losses.

Diseconomies of scale can also be present across an entire firm, not just a large factory. The leviathan effect can hit firms that become too large to run efficiently, across the entirety of the enterprise. Firms that shrink their operations are often responding to finding itself in the diseconomies region, thus moving back to a lower average cost at a lower output level.

Link It Up

Visit this website (http://openstaxcollege.org/l/Toobig) to read an article about the complexity of the belief that banks can be "too-big-to-fail."

The Size and Number of Firms in an Industry

The shape of the long-run average cost curve has implications for how many firms will compete in an industry, and whether the firms in an industry have many different sizes, or tend to be the same size. For example, say that the appliance industry sells one million dishwashers every year at a price of $500 each and the long-run average cost curve for dishwashers is in **Figure 7.11** (a). In **Figure 7.11** (a), the lowest point of the LRAC curve occurs at a quantity of 10,000 produced. Thus, the market for dishwashers will consist of 100 different manufacturing plants of this same size. If some firms built a plant that produced 5,000 dishwashers per year or 25,000 dishwashers per year, the average costs of production at such plants would be well above $500, and the firms would not be able to compete.

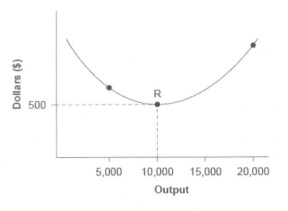
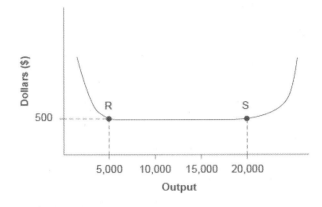

(a) LRAC curve with a clear minimum point   (b) A flat-bottomed LRAC curve

Figure 7.11 The LRAC Curve and the Size and Number of Firms (a) Low-cost firms will produce at output level R. When the LRAC curve has a clear minimum point, then any firm producing a different quantity will have higher costs. In this case, a firm producing at a quantity of 10,000 will produce at a lower average cost than a firm producing, say, 5,000 or 20,000 units. (b) Low-cost firms will produce between output levels R and S. When the LRAC curve has a flat bottom, then firms producing at any quantity along this flat bottom can compete. In this case, any firm producing a quantity between 5,000 and 20,000 can compete effectively, although firms producing less than 5,000 or more than 20,000 would face higher average costs and be unable to compete.

Clear It Up $

How can we view cities as examples of economies of scale?

Why are people and economic activity concentrated in cities, rather than distributed evenly across a country? The fundamental reason must be related to the idea of economies of scale—that grouping economic activity is more productive in many cases than spreading it out. For example, cities provide a large group of nearby customers, so that businesses can produce at an efficient economy of scale. They also provide a large group of workers and suppliers, so that business can hire easily and purchase whatever specialized inputs they need. Many of the attractions of cities, like sports stadiums and museums, can operate only if they can draw on a large nearby population base. Cities are big enough to offer a wide variety of products, which is what appeals to many shoppers.

These factors are not exactly economies of scale in the narrow sense of the production function of a single firm, but they are related to growth in the overall size of population and market in an area. Cities are sometimes called "agglomeration economies."

These agglomeration factors help to explain why every economy, as it develops, has an increasing proportion of its population living in urban areas. In the United States, about 80% of the population now lives in metropolitan areas (which include the suburbs around cities), compared to just 40% in 1900. However, in poorer nations of the world, including much of Africa, the proportion of the population in urban areas is only about 30%. One of the great challenges for these countries as their economies grow will be to manage the growth of the great cities that will arise.

If cities offer economic advantages that are a form of economies of scale, then why don't all or most people live in one giant city? At some point, agglomeration economies must turn into diseconomies. For example, traffic congestion may reach a point where the gains from being geographically nearby are counterbalanced by how long it takes to travel. High densities of people, cars, and factories can mean more garbage and air and water pollution. Facilities like parks or museums may become overcrowded. There may be economies of scale for negative activities like crime, because high densities of people and businesses, combined with the greater impersonality of cities, make it easier for illegal activities as well as legal ones. The future of cities, both in the United States and in other countries around the world, will be determined by their ability to benefit from the economies of agglomeration and to minimize or counterbalance the corresponding diseconomies.

We illustrate a more common case in **Figure 7.11** (b), where the LRAC curve has a flat-bottomed area of constant returns to scale. In this situation, any firm with a level of output between 5,000 and 20,000 will be able to produce at about the same level of average cost. Given that the market will demand one million dishwashers per year at a price of $500, this market might have as many as 200 producers (that is, one million dishwashers divided by firms making 5,000 each) or as few as 50 producers (one million dishwashers divided by firms making 20,000 each). The producers in this market will range in size from firms that make 5,000 units to firms that make 20,000 units. However, firms that produce below 5,000 units or more than 20,000 will be unable to compete, because their average costs will be too high. Thus, if we see an industry where almost all plants are the same size, it is likely that the long-run average cost curve has a unique bottom point as in **Figure 7.11** (a). However, if the long-run average cost curve has a wide flat bottom like **Figure 7.11** (b), then firms of a variety of different sizes will be able to compete with each other.

We can interpret the flat section of the long-run average cost curve in **Figure 7.11** (b) in two different ways. One interpretation is that a single manufacturing plant producing a quantity of 5,000 has the same average costs as a single manufacturing plant with four times as much capacity that produces a quantity of 20,000. The other interpretation is that one firm owns a single manufacturing plant that produces a quantity of 5,000, while another firm owns four separate manufacturing plants, which each produce a quantity of 5,000. This second explanation, based on the insight that a single firm may own a number of different manufacturing plants, is especially useful in explaining why the long-run average cost curve often has a large flat segment—and thus why a seemingly smaller firm may be able to compete quite well with a larger firm. At some point, however, the task of coordinating and managing many different plants raises the cost of production sharply, and the long-run average cost curve slopes up as a result.

In the examples to this point, the quantity demanded in the market is quite large (one million) compared with the quantity produced at the bottom of the long-run average cost curve (5,000, 10,000 or 20,000). In such a situation, the market is set for competition between many firms. However, what if the bottom of the long-run average cost curve is at a quantity of 10,000 and the total market demand at that price is only slightly higher than that quantity—or even somewhat lower?

Return to **Figure 7.11** (a), where the bottom of the long-run average cost curve is at 10,000, but now imagine that the total quantity of dishwashers demanded in the market at that price of $500 is only 30,000. In this situation, the total number of firms in the market would be three. We call a handful of firms in a market an "oligopoly," and the chapter on **Monopolistic Competition and Oligopoly** will discuss the range of competitive strategies that can occur when oligopolies compete.

Alternatively, consider a situation, again in the setting of **Figure 7.11** (a), where the bottom of the long-run average cost curve is 10,000, but total demand for the product is only 5,000. (For simplicity, imagine that this demand is highly inelastic, so that it does not vary according to price.) In this situation, the market may well end up with a single firm—a monopoly—producing all 5,000 units. If any firm tried to challenge this monopoly while producing a quantity lower than 5,000 units, the prospective competitor firm would have a higher average cost, and so it would not be able to compete in the longer term without losing money. The chapter on **Monopoly** discusses the situation of a monopoly firm.

Thus, the shape of the long-run average cost curve reveals whether competitors in the market will be different sizes. If the LRAC curve has a single point at the bottom, then the firms in the market will be about the same size, but if the LRAC curve has a flat-bottomed segment of constant returns to scale, then firms in the market may be a variety of different sizes.

The relationship between the quantity at the minimum of the long-run average cost curve and the quantity demanded in the market at that price will predict how much competition is likely to exist in the market. If the quantity demanded in the market far exceeds the quantity at the minimum of the LRAC, then many firms will compete. If the quantity demanded in the market is only slightly higher than the quantity at the minimum of the LRAC, a few firms will compete. If the quantity demanded in the market is less than the quantity at the minimum of the LRAC, a single-producer monopoly is a likely outcome.

Shifting Patterns of Long-Run Average Cost

New developments in production technology can shift the long-run average cost curve in ways that can alter the size distribution of firms in an industry.

For much of the twentieth century, the most common change had been to see alterations in technology, like the assembly line or the large department store, where large-scale producers seemed to gain an advantage over smaller ones. In the long-run average cost curve, the downward-sloping economies of scale portion of the curve stretched over a larger quantity of output.

However, new production technologies do not inevitably lead to a greater average size for firms. For example, in recent years some new technologies for generating electricity on a smaller scale have appeared. The traditional coal-burning electricity plants needed to produce 300 to 600 megawatts of power to exploit economies of scale fully. However, high-efficiency turbines to produce electricity from burning natural gas can produce electricity at a competitive price while producing a smaller quantity of 100 megawatts or less. These new technologies create the possibility for smaller companies or plants to generate electricity as efficiently as large ones. Another example of a technology-driven shift to smaller plants may be taking place in the tire industry. A traditional mid-size tire plant produces about six million tires per year. However, in 2000, the Italian company Pirelli introduced a new tire factory that uses many robots. The Pirelli tire plant produced only about one million tires per year, but did so at a lower average cost than a traditional mid-sized tire plant.

Controversy has simmered in recent years over whether the new information and communications technologies will lead to a larger or smaller size for firms. On one side, the new technology may make it easier for small firms to reach out beyond their local geographic area and find customers across a state, or the nation, or even across international boundaries. This factor might seem to predict a future with a larger number of small competitors. On the other side, perhaps the new information and communications technology will create "winner-take-all" markets where one large company will tend to command a large share of total sales, as Microsoft has done producing of software for personal computers or Amazon has done in online bookselling. Moreover, improved information and communication technologies might make it easier to manage many different plants and operations across the country or around the world, and thus encourage larger firms. This ongoing battle between the forces of smallness and largeness will be of great interest to economists, businesspeople, and policymakers.

Bring it Home

Amazon

Traditionally, bookstores have operated in retail locations with inventories held either on the shelves or in the back of the store. These retail locations were very pricey in terms of rent. Until recently, Amazon had no retail locations. It only sold online and delivered by mail. Amazon now has retail stores in California, Oregon and Washington State and retail stores are coming to Illinois, Massachusetts, New Jersey, and New York. Amazon offers almost any book in print, convenient purchasing, and prompt delivery by mail. Amazon holds its inventories in huge warehouses in low-rent locations around the world. The warehouses are highly computerized using robots and relatively low-skilled workers, making for low average costs per sale. Amazon demonstrates the significant advantages economies of scale can offer to a firm that exploits those economies.

This OpenStax book is available for free at http://cnx.org/content/col12122/1.4

KEY TERMS

accounting profit total revenues minus explicit costs, including depreciation

average profit profit divided by the quantity of output produced; also known as profit margin

average total cost total cost divided by the quantity of output

average variable cost variable cost divided by the quantity of output

constant returns to scale expanding all inputs proportionately does not change the average cost of production

diminishing marginal productivity general rule that as a firm employs more labor, eventually the amount of additional output produced declines

diseconomies of scale the long-run average cost of producing output increases as total output increases

economic profit total revenues minus total costs (explicit plus implicit costs)

economies of scale the long-run average cost of producing output decreases as total output increases

economies of scale the long-run average cost of producing output decreases as total output increases

explicit costs out-of-pocket costs for a firm, for example, payments for wages and salaries, rent, or materials

factors of production (or inputs) resources that firms use to produce their products, for example, labor and capital

firm an organization that combines inputs of labor, capital, land, and raw or finished component materials to produce outputs.

fixed cost cost of the fixed inputs; expenditure that a firm must make before production starts and that does not change regardless of the production level

fixed inputs factors of production that can't be easily increased or decreased in a short period of time

implicit costs opportunity cost of resources already owned by the firm and used in business, for example, expanding a factory onto land already owned

long run period of time during which all of a firm's inputs are variable

long-run average cost (LRAC) curve shows the lowest possible average cost of production, allowing all the inputs to production to vary so that the firm is choosing its production technology

marginal cost the additional cost of producing one more unit; mathematically, $MC = \Delta TC / \Delta L$

marginal product change in a firm's output when it employees more labor; mathematically, $MP = \Delta TP / \Delta L$

private enterprise the ownership of businesses by private individuals

production the process of combining inputs to produce outputs, ideally of a value greater than the value of the inputs

production function mathematical equation that tells how much output a firm can produce with given amounts of the inputs

production technologies alternative methods of combining inputs to produce output

revenue income from selling a firm's product; defined as price times quantity sold

short run period of time during which at least one or more of the firm's inputs is fixed

short-run average cost (SRAC) curve the average total cost curve in the short term; shows the total of the average
fixed costs and the average variable costs

total cost the sum of fixed and variable costs of production

total product synonym for a firm's output

variable cost cost of production that increases with the quantity produced; the cost of the variable inputs

variable inputs factors of production that a firm can easily increase or decrease in a short period of time

KEY CONCEPTS AND SUMMARY

7.1 Explicit and Implicit Costs, and Accounting and Economic Profit
Privately owned firms are motivated to earn profits. Profit is the difference between revenues and costs. While
accounting profit considers only explicit costs, economic profit considers both explicit and implicit costs.

7.2 Production in the Short Run
Production is the process a firm uses to transform inputs (e.g. labor, capital, raw materials, etc.) into outputs. It
is not possible to vary fixed inputs (e.g. capital) in a short period of time. Thus, in the short run the only way to
change output is to change the variable inputs (e.g. labor). Marginal product is the additional output a firm obtains
by employing more labor in production. At some point, employing additional labor leads to diminishing marginal
productivity, meaning the additional output obtained is less than for the previous increment to labor. Mathematically,
marginal product is the slope of the total product curve.

7.3 Costs in the Short Run
For every input (e.g. labor), there is an associated factor payment (e.g. wages and salaries). The cost of production for
a given quantity of output is the sum of the amount of each input required to produce that quantity of output times the
associated factor payment.

In a short-run perspective, we can divide a firm's total costs into fixed costs, which a firm must incur before producing
any output, and variable costs, which the firm incurs in the act of producing. Fixed costs are sunk costs; that is,
because they are in the past and the firm cannot alter them, they should play no role in economic decisions about
future production or pricing. Variable costs typically show diminishing marginal returns, so that the marginal cost of
producing higher levels of output rises.

We calculate marginal cost by taking the change in total cost (or the change in variable cost, which will be the same
thing) and dividing it by the change in output, for each possible change in output. Marginal costs are typically rising.
A firm can compare marginal cost to the additional revenue it gains from selling another unit to find out whether its
marginal unit is adding to profit.

We calculate average total cost by taking total cost and dividing by total output at each different level of output.
Average costs are typically U-shaped on a graph. If a firm's average cost of production is lower than the market price,
a firm will be earning profits.

We calculate average variable cost by taking variable cost and dividing by the total output at each level of output.
Average variable costs are typically U-shaped. If a firm's average variable cost of production is lower than the market
price, then the firm would be earning profits if fixed costs are left out of the picture.

7.4 Production in the Long Run
In the long run, all inputs are variable. Since diminishing marginal productivity is caused by fixed capital, there are
no diminishing returns in the long run. Firms can choose the optimal capital stock to produce their desired level of
output.

This OpenStax book is available for free at http://cnx.org/content/col12122/1.4

7.5 Costs in the Long Run

A production technology refers to a specific combination of labor, physical capital, and technology that makes up a particular method of production.

In the long run, firms can choose their production technology, and so all costs become variable costs. In making this choice, firms will try to substitute relatively inexpensive inputs for relatively expensive inputs where possible, so as to produce at the lowest possible long-run average cost.

Economies of scale refers to a situation where as the level of output increases, the average cost decreases. Constant returns to scale refers to a situation where average cost does not change as output increases. Diseconomies of scale refers to a situation where as output increases, average costs also increase.

The long-run average cost curve shows the lowest possible average cost of production, allowing all the inputs to production to vary so that the firm is choosing its production technology. A downward-sloping LRAC shows economies of scale; a flat LRAC shows constant returns to scale; an upward-sloping LRAC shows diseconomies of scale. If the long-run average cost curve has only one quantity produced that results in the lowest possible average cost, then all of the firms competing in an industry should be the same size. However, if the LRAC has a flat segment at the bottom, so that a firm can produce a range of different quantities at the lowest average cost, the firms competing in the industry will display a range of sizes. The market demand in conjunction with the long-run average cost curve determines how many firms will exist in a given industry.

If the quantity demanded in the market of a certain product is much greater than the quantity found at the bottom of the long-run average cost curve, where the cost of production is lowest, the market will have many firms competing. If the quantity demanded in the market is less than the quantity at the bottom of the LRAC, there will likely be only one firm.

SELF-CHECK QUESTIONS

1. A firm had sales revenue of $1 million last year. It spent $600,000 on labor, $150,000 on capital and $200,000 on materials. What was the firm's accounting profit?

2. Continuing from Exercise 7.1, the firm's factory sits on land owned by the firm that it could rent for $30,000 per year. What was the firm's economic profit last year?

3. The WipeOut Ski Company manufactures skis for beginners. Fixed costs are $30. Fill in Table 7.16 for total cost, average variable cost, average total cost, and marginal cost.

Quantity	Variable Cost	Fixed Cost	Total Cost	Average Variable Cost	Average Total Cost	Marginal Cost
0	0	$30				
1	$10	$30				
2	$25	$30				
3	$45	$30				
4	$70	$30				
5	$100	$30				
6	$135	$30				

Table 7.16

4. Based on your answers to the WipeOut Ski Company in **Exercise 7.3**, now imagine a situation where the firm produces a quantity of 5 units that it sells for a price of $25 each.

    a. What will be the company's profits or losses?

    b. How can you tell at a glance whether the company is making or losing money at this price by looking at average cost?

    c. At the given quantity and price, is the marginal unit produced adding to profits?

5. If two painters can paint 200 square feet of wall in an hour, and three painters can paint 275 square feet, what is the marginal product of the third painter?

6. Return to the problem explained in **Table 7.13** and **Table 7.14**. If the cost of labor remains at $40, but the cost of a machine decreases to $50, what would be the total cost of each method of production? Which method should the firm use, and why?

7. Suppose the cost of machines increases to $55, while the cost of labor stays at $40. How would that affect the total cost of the three methods? Which method should the firm choose now?

8. Automobile manufacturing is an industry subject to significant economies of scale. Suppose there are four domestic auto manufacturers, but the demand for domestic autos is no more than 2.5 times the quantity produced at the bottom of the long-run average cost curve. What do you expect will happen to the domestic auto industry in the long run?

REVIEW QUESTIONS

9. What are explicit and implicit costs?

10. Would you consider an interest payment on a loan to a firm an explicit or implicit cost?

11. What is the difference between accounting and economic profit?

12. What is a production function?

13. What is the difference between a fixed input and a variable input?

14. How do we calculate marginal product?

15. What shapes would you generally expect a total product curve and a marginal product curve to have?

16. What are the factor payments for land, labor, and capital?

17. What is the difference between fixed costs and variable costs?

18. How do we calculate each of the following: marginal cost, average total cost, and average variable cost?

19. What shapes would you generally expect each of the following cost curves to have: fixed costs, variable costs, marginal costs, average total costs, and average variable costs?

20. Are there fixed costs in the long-run? Explain briefly.

21. Are fixed costs also sunk costs? Explain.

22. What are diminishing marginal returns as they relate to costs?

23. Which costs are measured on per-unit basis: fixed costs, average cost, average variable cost, variable costs, and marginal cost?

24. What is a production technology?

25. In choosing a production technology, how will firms react if one input becomes relatively more expensive?

26. What is a long-run average cost curve?

27. What is the difference between economies of scale, constant returns to scale, and diseconomies of scale?

28. What shape of a long-run average cost curve illustrates economies of scale, constant returns to scale, and diseconomies of scale?

29. Why will firms in most markets be located at or close to the bottom of the long-run average cost curve?

CRITICAL THINKING QUESTIONS

30. Small "Mom and Pop firms," like inner city grocery stores, sometimes exist even though they do not earn economic profits. How can you explain this?

31. A common name for fixed cost is "overhead." If you divide fixed cost by the quantity of output produced, you get average fixed cost. Supposed fixed cost is $1,000. What does the average fixed cost curve look like? Use your response to explain what "spreading the overhead" means.

32. How does fixed cost affect marginal cost? Why is this relationship important?

33. Average cost curves (except for average fixed cost) tend to be U-shaped, decreasing and then increasing. Marginal cost curves have the same shape, though this may be harder to see since most of the marginal cost curve is increasing. Why do you think that average and marginal cost curves have the same general shape?

34. What is the relationship between marginal product and marginal cost? (Hint: Look at the curves.) Why do you suppose that is? Is this relationship the same in the long run as in the short run?

35. It is clear that businesses operate in the short run, but do they ever operate in the long run? Discuss.

36. Return to **Table 7.2**. In the top half of the table, at what point does diminishing marginal productivity kick in? What about in the bottom half of the table? How do you explain this?

37. How would an improvement in technology, like the high-efficiency gas turbines or Pirelli tire plant, affect the long-run average cost curve of a firm? Can you draw the old curve and the new one on the same axes? How might such an improvement affect other firms in the industry?

38. Do you think that the taxicab industry in large cities would be subject to significant economies of scale? Why or why not?

PROBLEMS

39. A firm is considering an investment that will earn a 6% rate of return. If it were to borrow the money, it would have to pay 8% interest on the loan, but it currently has the cash, so it will not need to borrow. Should the firm make the investment? Show your work.

40. Return to **Figure 7.7**. What is the marginal gain in output from increasing the number of barbers from 4 to 5 and from 5 to 6? Does it continue the pattern of diminishing marginal returns?

41. Compute the average total cost, average variable cost, and marginal cost of producing 60 and 72 haircuts. Draw the graph of the three curves between 60 and 72 haircuts.

42. A small company that shovels sidewalks and driveways has 100 homes signed up for its services this winter. It can use various combinations of capital and labor: intensive labor with hand shovels, less labor with snow blowers, and still less labor with a pickup truck that has a snowplow on front. To summarize, the method choices are:

Method 1: 50 units of labor, 10 units of capital

Method 2: 20 units of labor, 40 units of capital

Method 3: 10 units of labor, 70 units of capital

If hiring labor for the winter costs $100/unit and a unit of capital costs $400, what is the best production method? What method should the company use if the cost of labor rises to $200/unit?

This OpenStax book is available for free at http://cnx.org/content/col12122/1.4

8 | Perfect Competition

Figure 8.1 Depending upon the competition and prices offered, a wheat farmer may choose to grow a different crop. (Credit: modification of work by Daniel X. O'Neil/Flickr Creative Commons)

Bring it Home

A Dime a Dozen

When you were younger did you babysit, deliver papers, or mow the lawn for money? If so, you faced stiff competition from many other competitors who offered identical services. There was nothing to stop others from also offering their services.

All of you charged the "going rate." If you tried to charge more, your customers would simply buy from someone else. These conditions are very similar to the conditions agricultural growers face.

Growing a crop may be more difficult to start than a babysitting or lawn mowing service, but growers face the same fierce competition. In the grand scale of world agriculture, farmers face competition from thousands of others because they sell an identical product. After all, winter wheat is winter wheat, but if they find it hard to make money with that crop, it is relatively easy for farmers to leave the marketplace for another crop. In this case, they do not sell the family farm, they switch crops.

Take the case of the upper Midwest region of the United States—for many generations the area was called "King Wheat." According to the United States Department of Agriculture National Agricultural Statistics Service, statistics by state, in 1997, 11.6 million acres of wheat and 780,000 acres of corn were planted in North Dakota. In the intervening 20 or so years has the mix of crops changed? Since it is relatively easy to switch crops, did farmers change what they planted in response to changes in relative crop prices? We will find out at chapter's end.

In the meantime, let's consider the topic of this chapter—the perfectly competitive market. This is a market in which entry and exit are relatively easy and competitors are "a dime a dozen."

Introduction to Perfect Competition

In this chapter, you will learn about:

- Perfect Competition and Why It Matters
- How Perfectly Competitive Firms Make Output Decisions
- Entry and Exit Decisions in the Long Run
- Efficiency in Perfectly Competitive Markets

Most businesses face two realities: no one is required to buy their products, and even customers who might want those products may buy from other businesses instead. Firms that operate in perfectly competitive markets face this reality. In this chapter, you will learn how such firms make decisions about how much to produce, how much profit they make, whether to stay in business or not, and many others. Industries differ from one another in terms of how many sellers there are in a specific market, how easy or difficult it is for a new firm to enter, and the type of products that they sell. Economists refer to this as an industry's **market structure**. In this chapter, we focus on perfect competition. However, in other chapters we will examine other industry types: **Monopoly** and **Monopolistic Competition and Oligopoly**.

8.1 | Perfect Competition and Why It Matters

By the end of this section, you will be able to:
- Explain the characteristics of a perfectly competitive market
- Discuss how perfectly competitive firms react in the short run and in the long run

Firms are in **perfect competition** when the following conditions occur: (1) many firms produce identical products; (2) many buyers are available to buy the product, and many sellers are available to sell the product; (3) sellers and buyers have all relevant information to make rational decisions about the product that they are buying and selling; and (4) firms can enter and leave the market without any restrictions—in other words, there is free entry and exit into and out of the market.

A perfectly competitive firm is known as a **price taker**, because the pressure of competing firms forces it to accept the prevailing equilibrium price in the market. If a firm in a perfectly competitive market raises the price of its product by so much as a penny, it will lose all of its sales to competitors. When a wheat grower, as we discussed in the Bring It Home feature, wants to know the going price of wheat, he or she has to check on the computer or listen to the radio. Supply and demand in the entire market solely determine the market price, not the individual farmer. A perfectly competitive firm must be a very small player in the overall market, so that it can increase or decrease output without noticeably affecting the overall quantity supplied and price in the market.

A perfectly competitive market is a hypothetical extreme; however, producers in a number of industries do face many competitor firms selling highly similar goods, in which case they must often act as price takers. Economists often use agricultural markets as an example. The same crops that different farmers grow are largely interchangeable. According to the United States Department of Agriculture monthly reports, in 2015, U.S. corn farmers received an average price of $6.00 per bushel. A corn farmer who attempted to sell at $7.00 per bushel, would not have found any buyers. A perfectly competitive firm will not sell below the equilibrium price either. Why should they when they can sell all they want at the higher price? Other examples of agricultural markets that operate in close to perfectly competitive markets are small roadside produce markets and small organic farmers.

This OpenStax book is available for free at http://cnx.org/content/col12122/1.4

Link It Up @&

Visit this website (http://openstaxcollege.org/l/commodities) that reveals the current value of various commodities.

This chapter examines how profit-seeking firms decide how much to produce in perfectly competitive markets. Such firms will analyze their costs as we discussed in the chapter on **Production, Costs and Industry Structure**. In the short run, the perfectly competitive firm will seek the quantity of output where profits are highest or, if profits are not possible, where losses are lowest.

In the long run, positive economic profits will attract competition as other firms enter the market. Economic losses will cause firms to exit the market. Ultimately, perfectly competitive markets will attain long-run *equilibrium* when no new firms want to enter the market and existing firms do not want to leave the market, as economic profits have been driven down to zero.

8.2 | How Perfectly Competitive Firms Make Output Decisions

By the end of this section, you will be able to:
- Calculate profits by comparing total revenue and total cost
- Identify profits and losses with the average cost curve
- Explain the shutdown point
- Determine the price at which a firm should continue producing in the short run

A perfectly competitive firm has only one major decision to make—namely, what quantity to produce. To understand this, consider a different way of writing out the basic definition of profit:

$$\text{Profit} = \text{Total revenue} - \text{Total cost}$$
$$= (\text{Price})(\text{Quantity produced}) - (\text{Average cost})(\text{Quantity produced})$$

Since a perfectly competitive firm must accept the price for its output as determined by the product's market demand and supply, it cannot choose the price it charges. This is already determined in the profit equation, and so the perfectly competitive firm can sell any number of units at exactly the same price. It implies that the firm faces a perfectly elastic demand curve for its product: buyers are willing to buy any number of units of output from the firm at the market price. When the perfectly competitive firm chooses what quantity to produce, then this quantity—along with the prices prevailing in the market for output and inputs—will determine the firm's total revenue, total costs, and ultimately, level of profits.

Determining the Highest Profit by Comparing Total Revenue and Total Cost

A perfectly competitive firm can sell as large a quantity as it wishes, as long as it accepts the prevailing market price. The formula above shows that total revenue depends on the quantity sold and the price charged. If the firm sells a higher quantity of output, then total revenue will increase. If the market price of the product increases, then total revenue also increases whatever the quantity of output sold. As an example of how a perfectly competitive firm decides what quantity to produce, consider the case of a small farmer who produces raspberries and sells them frozen for $4 per pack. Sales of one pack of raspberries will bring in $4, two packs will be $8, three packs will be $12, and so on. If, for example, the price of frozen raspberries doubles to $8 per pack, then sales of one pack of raspberries will be $8, two packs will be $16, three packs will be $24, and so on.

Table 8.1 graphically shows total revenue and total costs for the raspberry farm, also appear in **Figure 8.2**. The horizontal axis shows the quantity of frozen raspberries produced in packs. The vertical axis shows both total revenue and total costs, measured in dollars. The total cost curve intersects with the vertical axis at a value that shows the level of fixed costs, and then slopes upward. All these cost curves follow the same characteristics as the curves that we covered in the **Production, Costs and Industry Structure** chapter.

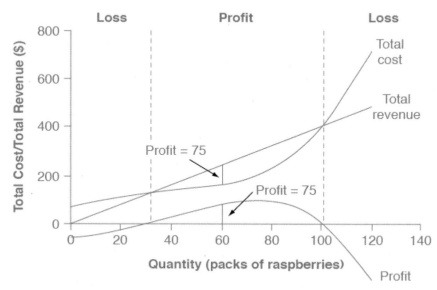

Figure 8.2 Total Cost and Total Revenue at the Raspberry Farm Total revenue for a perfectly competitive firm is a straight line sloping up. The slope is equal to the price of the good. Total cost also slopes up, but with some curvature. At higher levels of output, total cost begins to slope upward more steeply because of diminishing marginal returns. The maximum profit will occur at the quantity where the difference between total revenue and total cost is largest.

Quantity (Q)	Total Cost (TC)	Total Revenue (TR)	Profit
0	$62	$0	−$62
10	$90	$40	−$50
20	$110	$80	−$30
30	$126	$120	−$6
40	$138	$160	$22
50	$150	$200	$50
60	$165	$240	$75
70	$190	$280	$90
80	$230	$320	$90
90	$296	$360	$64

Table 8.1 Total Cost and Total Revenue at the Raspberry Farm

This OpenStax book is available for free at http://cnx.org/content/col12122/1.4

Quantity (Q)	Total Cost (TC)	Total Revenue (TR)	Profit
100	$400	$400	$0
110	$550	$440	$–110
120	$715	$480	$–235

Table 8.1 Total Cost and Total Revenue at the Raspberry Farm

Based on its total revenue and total cost curves, a perfectly competitive firm like the raspberry farm can calculate the quantity of output that will provide the highest level of profit. At any given quantity, total revenue minus total cost will equal profit. One way to determine the most profitable quantity to produce is to see at what quantity total revenue exceeds total cost by the largest amount. **Figure 8.2** shows total revenue, total cost and profit using the data from **Table 8.1**. The vertical gap between total revenue and total cost is profit, for example, at Q = 60, TR = 240 and TC = 165. The difference is 75, which is the height of the profit curve at that output level. The firm doesn't make a profit at every level of output. In this example, total costs will exceed total revenues at output levels from 0 to approximately 30, and so over this range of output, the firm will be making losses. At output levels from 40 to 100, total revenues exceed total costs, so the firm is earning profits. However, at any output greater than 100, total costs again exceed total revenues and the firm is making increasing losses. Total profits appear in the final column of **Table 8.1**. Maximum profit occurs at an output between 70 and 80, when profit equals $90.

A higher price would mean that total revenue would be higher for every quantity sold. A lower price would mean that total revenue would be lower for every quantity sold. What happens if the price drops low enough so that the total revenue line is completely below the total cost curve; that is, at every level of output, total costs are higher than total revenues? In this instance, the best the firm can do is to suffer losses. However, a profit-maximizing firm will prefer the quantity of output where total revenues come closest to total costs and thus where the losses are smallest.

(Later we will see that sometimes it will make sense for the firm to close, rather than stay in operation producing output.)

Comparing Marginal Revenue and Marginal Costs

The approach that we described in the previous section, using total revenue and total cost, is not the only approach to determining the profit maximizing level of output. In this section, we provide an alternative approach which uses marginal revenue and marginal cost.

Firms often do not have the necessary data they need to draw a complete total cost curve for all levels of production. They cannot be sure of what total costs would look like if they, say, doubled production or cut production in half, because they have not tried it. Instead, firms experiment. They produce a slightly greater or lower quantity and observe how it affects profits. In economic terms, this practical approach to maximizing profits means examining how changes in production affect marginal revenue and marginal cost.

Figure 8.3 presents the marginal revenue and marginal cost curves based on the total revenue and total cost in **Table 8.1**. The **marginal revenue** curve shows the additional revenue gained from selling one more unit. As mentioned before, a firm in perfect competition faces a perfectly elastic demand curve for its product—that is, the firm's demand curve is a horizontal line drawn at the market price level. This also means that the firm's marginal revenue curve is the same as the firm's demand curve: Every time a consumer demands one more unit, the firm sells one more unit and revenue increases by exactly the same amount equal to the market price. In this example, every time the firm sells a pack of frozen raspberries, the firm's revenue increases by $4. **Table 8.2** shows an example of this. This condition only holds for price taking firms in perfect competition where:

$$\text{marginal revenue} = \text{price}$$

The formula for marginal revenue is:

$$\text{marginal revenue} = \frac{\text{change in total revenue}}{\text{change in quantity}}$$

Price	Quantity	Total Revenue	Marginal Revenue
$4	1	$4	-
$4	2	$8	$4
$4	3	$12	$4
$4	4	$16	$4

Table 8.2

Notice that marginal revenue does not change as the firm produces more output. That is because under perfect competition, the price is determined through the interaction of supply and demand in the market and does not change as the farmer produces more (keeping in mind that, due to the relative small size of each firm, increasing their supply has no impact on the total market supply where price is determined).

Since a perfectly competitive firm is a price taker, it can sell whatever quantity it wishes at the market-determined price. We calculate marginal cost, the cost per additional unit sold, by dividing the change in total cost by the change in quantity. The formula for marginal cost is:

$$\text{marginal cost} = \frac{\text{change in total cost}}{\text{change in quantity}}$$

Ordinarily, marginal cost changes as the firm produces a greater quantity.

In the raspberry farm example, in **Figure 8.3**, **Figure 8.4** and **Table 8.3**, marginal cost at first declines as production increases from 10 to 20 to 30 to 40 packs of raspberries—which represents the area of increasing marginal returns that is not uncommon at low levels of production. At some point, though, marginal costs start to increase, displaying the typical pattern of diminishing marginal returns. If the firm is producing at a quantity where MR > MC, like 40 or 50 packs of raspberries, then it can increase profit by increasing output because the marginal revenue is exceeding the marginal cost. If the firm is producing at a quantity where MC > MR, like 90 or 100 packs, then it can increase profit by reducing output because the reductions in marginal cost will exceed the reductions in marginal revenue. The firm's profit-maximizing choice of output will occur where MR = MC (or at a choice close to that point).

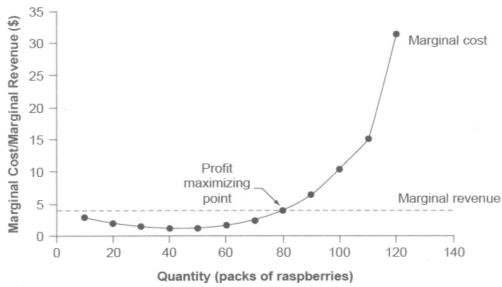

Figure 8.3 Marginal Revenues and Marginal Costs at the Raspberry Farm: Individual Farmer For a perfectly competitive firm, the marginal revenue (MR) curve is a horizontal line because it is equal to the price of the good, which is determined by the market, as **Figure 8.4** illustrates. The marginal cost (MC) curve is sometimes initially downward-sloping, if there is a region of increasing marginal returns at low levels of output, but is eventually upward-sloping at higher levels of output as diminishing marginal returns kick in.

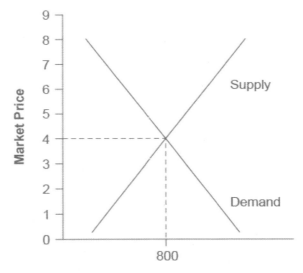

Market Quantity (packs of raspberries)

Figure 8.4 Marginal Revenues and Marginal Costs at the Raspberry Farm: Raspberry Market The equilibrium price of raspberries is determined through the interaction of market supply and market demand at $4.00.

Quantity	Total Cost	Marginal Cost	Total Revenue	Marginal Revenue	Profit
0	$62	-	$0	$4	-$62
10	$90	$2.80	$40	$4	-$50
20	$110	$2.00	$80	$4	-$30

Table 8.3 Marginal Revenues and Marginal Costs at the Raspberry Farm

Quantity	Total Cost	Marginal Cost	Total Revenue	Marginal Revenue	Profit
30	$126	$1.60	$120	$4	-$6
40	$138	$1.20	$160	$4	$22
50	$150	$1.20	$200	$4	$50
60	$165	$1.50	$240	$4	$75
70	$190	$2.50	$280	$4	$90
80	$230	$4.00	$320	$4	$90
90	$296	$6.60	$360	$4	$64
100	$400	$10.40	$400	$4	$0
110	$550	$15.00	$440	$4	-$110
120	$715	$16.50	$480	$4	-$235

Table 8.3 Marginal Revenues and Marginal Costs at the Raspberry Farm

In this example, the marginal revenue and marginal cost curves cross at a price of $4 and a quantity of 80 produced. If the farmer started out producing at a level of 60, and then experimented with increasing production to 70, marginal revenues from the increase in production would exceed marginal costs—and so profits would rise. The farmer has an incentive to keep producing. At a level of output of 80, marginal cost and marginal revenue are equal so profit doesn't change. If the farmer then experimented further with increasing production from 80 to 90, he would find that marginal costs from the increase in production are greater than marginal revenues, and so profits would decline.

The profit-maximizing choice for a perfectly competitive firm will occur at the level of output where marginal revenue is equal to marginal cost—that is, where MR = MC. This occurs at Q = 80 in the figure.

Work It Out

Does Profit Maximization Occur at a Range of Output or a Specific Level of Output?

Table 8.1 shows that maximum profit occurs at any output level between 70 and 80 units of output. But MR = MC occurs only at 80 units of output. How can do we explain this slight discrepancy? As long as MR > MC. a profit-seeking firm should keep expanding production. Expanding production into the zone where MR < MC reduces economic profits. It's true that profit is the same at Q = 70 and Q = 80, but it's only when the firm goes beyond that that see that profits fall. Thus, MR = MC is the signal to stop expanding, so that is the level of output they should target.

Because the marginal revenue received by a perfectly competitive firm is equal to the price P, we can also write the profit-maximizing rule for a perfectly competitive firm as a recommendation to produce at the quantity of output where P = MC.

Profits and Losses with the Average Cost Curve

Does maximizing profit (producing where MR = MC) imply an actual economic profit? The answer depends on the relationship between price and average total cost, which is the average profit or **profit margin**. If the market price is higher than the firm's average cost of production for that quantity produced, then the profit margin is positive and the firm will earn profits. Conversely, if the market price is lower than the average cost of production, the profit margin is negative and the firm will suffer losses. You might think that, in this situation, the firm may want to shut

This OpenStax book is available for free at http://cnx.org/content/col12122/1.4

down immediately. Remember, however, that the firm has already paid for fixed costs, such as equipment, so it may continue to produce for a while and incur a loss. **Table 8.3** continues the raspberry farm example. **Figure 8.5** illustrates the three possible scenarios: (a) where price intersects marginal cost at a level above the average cost curve, (b) where price intersects marginal cost at a level equal to the average cost curve, and (c) where price intersects marginal cost at a level below the average cost curve.

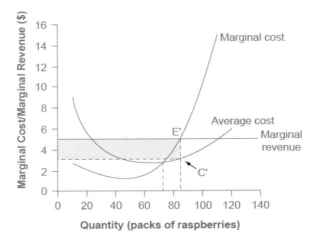

(a) Price is above average cost

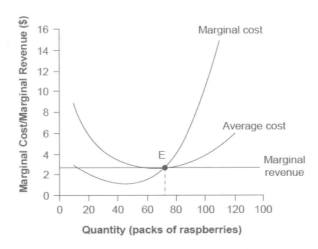

(b) Price equals cost

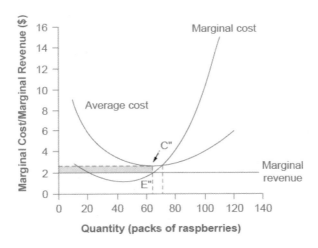

(c) Price is below average cost

Figure 8.5 Price and Average Cost at the Raspberry Farm In (a), price intersects marginal cost above the average cost curve. Since price is greater than average cost, the firm is making a profit. In (b), price intersects marginal cost at the minimum point of the average cost curve. Since price is equal to average cost, the firm is breaking even. In (c), price intersects marginal cost below the average cost curve. Since price is less than average cost, the firm is making a loss.

First consider a situation where the price is equal to $5 for a pack of frozen raspberries. The rule for a profit-maximizing perfectly competitive firm is to produce the level of output where Price= MR = MC, so the raspberry farmer will produce a quantity of approximately 85, which is labeled as E' in **Figure 8.5** (a). Remember that the area of a rectangle is equal to its base multiplied by its height. The farm's total revenue at this price will be shown by the rectangle from the origin over to a quantity of 85 packs (the base) up to point E' (the height), over to the price of $5, and back to the origin. The average cost of producing 80 packs is shown by point C or about $3.50. Total costs will be the quantity of 85 times the average cost of $3.50, which is shown by the area of the rectangle from the origin to a quantity of 90, up to point C, over to the vertical axis and down to the origin. The difference between total revenues and total costs is profits. Thus, profits will be the blue shaded rectangle on top.

We calculate this as:

$$\begin{aligned} \text{profit} &= \text{total revenue} - \text{total cost} \\ &= (85)(\$5.00) - (85)(\$3.50) \\ &= \$170 \end{aligned}$$

Or, we can calculate it as:

$$\begin{aligned} \text{profit} &= (\text{price} - \text{average cost}) \times \text{quantity} \\ &= (\$5.00 - \$3.50) \times 85 \\ &= \$170 \end{aligned}$$

Now consider **Figure 8.5** (b), where the price has fallen to $2.75 for a pack of frozen raspberries. Again, the perfectly competitive firm will choose the level of output where Price = MR = MC, but in this case, the quantity produced will be 75. At this price and output level, where the marginal cost curve is crossing the average cost curve, the price the firm receives is exactly equal to its average cost of production. We call this the **break even point**.

The farm's total revenue at this price will be shown by the large shaded rectangle from the origin over to a quantity of 75 packs (the base) up to point E (the height), over to the price of $2.75, and back to the origin. The height of the average cost curve at Q = 75, i.e. point E, shows the average cost of producing this quantity. Total costs will be the quantity of 75 times the average cost of $2.75, which is shown by the area of the rectangle from the origin to a quantity of 75, up to point E, over to the vertical axis and down to the origin. It should be clear that the rectangles for total revenue and total cost are the same. Thus, the firm is making zero profit. The calculations are as follows:

$$\begin{aligned} \text{profit} &= \text{total revenue} - \text{total cost} \\ &= (75)(\$2.75) - (75)(\$2.75) \\ &= \$0 \end{aligned}$$

Or, we can calculate it as:

$$\begin{aligned} \text{profit} &= (\text{price} - \text{average cost}) \times \text{quantity} \\ &= (\$2.75 - \$2.75) \times 75 \\ &= \$0 \end{aligned}$$

In **Figure 8.5** (c), the market price has fallen still further to $2.00 for a pack of frozen raspberries. At this price, marginal revenue intersects marginal cost at a quantity of 65. The farm's total revenue at this price will be shown by the large shaded rectangle from the origin over to a quantity of 65 packs (the base) up to point E" (the height), over to the price of $2, and back to the origin. The average cost of producing 65 packs is shown by Point C" or shows the average cost of producing 50 packs is about $2.73. Total costs will be the quantity of 65 times the average cost of $2.73, which the area of the rectangle from the origin to a quantity of 50, up to point C", over to the vertical axis and down to the origin shows. It should be clear from examining the two rectangles that total revenue is less than total cost. Thus, the firm is losing money and the loss (or negative profit) will be the rose-shaded rectangle.

The calculations are:

$$\begin{aligned} \text{profit} &= (\text{total revenue} - \text{total cost}) \\ &= (65)(\$2.00) - (65)(\$2.73) \\ &= -\$47.45 \end{aligned}$$

Or:

$$\begin{aligned} \text{profit} &= (\text{price} - \text{average cost}) \times \text{quantity} \\ &= (\$2.00 - \$2.73) \times 65 \\ &= -\$47.45 \end{aligned}$$

If the market price that perfectly competitive firm receives leads it to produce at a quantity where the price is greater than average cost, the firm will earn profits. If the price the firm receives causes it to produce at a quantity where price equals average cost, which occurs at the minimum point of the AC curve, then the firm earns zero profits. Finally, if the price the firm receives leads it to produce at a quantity where the price is less than average cost, the firm will earn losses. **Table 8.4** summarizes this.

This OpenStax book is available for free at http://cnx.org/content/col12122/1.4

If...	Then...
Price > ATC	Firm earns an economic profit
Price = ATC	Firm earns zero economic profit
Price < ATC	Firm earns a loss

Table 8.4

Clear It Up

Which intersection should a firm choose?

At a price of $2, MR intersects MC at two points: Q = 20 and Q = 65. It never makes sense for a firm to choose a level of output on the downward sloping part of the MC curve, because the profit is lower (the loss is bigger). Thus, the correct choice of output is Q = 65.

The Shutdown Point

The possibility that a firm may earn losses raises a question: Why can the firm not avoid losses by shutting down and not producing at all? The answer is that shutting down can reduce variable costs to zero, but in the short run, the firm has already paid for fixed costs. As a result, if the firm produces a quantity of zero, it would still make losses because it would still need to pay for its fixed costs. Therefore when a firm is experiencing losses, it must face a question: should it continue producing or should it shut down?

As an example, consider the situation of the Yoga Center, which has signed a contract to rent space that costs $10,000 per month. If the firm decides to operate, its marginal costs for hiring yoga teachers is $15,000 for the month. If the firm shuts down, it must still pay the rent, but it would not need to hire labor. Table 8.5 shows three possible scenarios. In the first scenario, the Yoga Center does not have any clients, and therefore does not make any revenues, in which case it faces losses of $10,000 equal to the fixed costs. In the second scenario, the Yoga Center has clients that earn the center revenues of $10,000 for the month, but ultimately experiences losses of $15,000 due to having to hire yoga instructors to cover the classes. In the third scenario, the Yoga Center earns revenues of $20,000 for the month, but experiences losses of $5,000.

In all three cases, the Yoga Center loses money. In all three cases, when the rental contract expires in the long run, assuming revenues do not improve, the firm should exit this business. In the short run, though, the decision varies depending on the level of losses and whether the firm can cover its variable costs. In scenario 1, the center does not have any revenues, so hiring yoga teachers would increase variable costs and losses, so it should shut down and only incur its fixed costs. In scenario 2, the center's losses are greater because it does not make enough revenue to offset the increased variable costs, so it should shut down immediately and only incur its fixed costs. If price is below the minimum average variable cost, the firm must shut down. In contrast, in scenario 3 the revenue that the center can earn is high enough that the losses diminish when it remains open, so the center should remain open in the short run.

Scenario 1

If the center shuts down now, revenues are zero but it will not incur any variable costs and would only need to pay fixed costs of $10,000.

Table 8.5 Should the Yoga Center Shut Down Now or Later?

$$\text{profit} = \text{total revenue} - (\text{fixed costs} + \text{variable cost})$$
$$= 0 - \$10,000$$
$$= -\$10,000$$

Scenario 2

The center earns revenues of $10,000, and variable costs are $15,000. The center should shut down now.

$$\text{profit} = \text{total revenue} \ - \ (\text{fixed costs} + \text{variable cost})$$
$$= \$10,000 \ - \ (\$10,000 + \$15,000)$$
$$= -\$15,000$$

Scenario 3

The center earns revenues of $20,000, and variable costs are $15,000. The center should continue in business.

$$\text{profit} = \text{total revenue} \ - \ (\text{fixed costs} + \text{variable cost})$$
$$= \$20,000 \ - \ (\$10,000 + \$15,000)$$
$$= -\$5,000$$

Table 8.5 Should the Yoga Center Shut Down Now or Later?

Figure 8.6 illustrates the lesson that remaining open requires the price to exceed the firm's average variable cost. When the firm is operating below the break-even point, where price equals average cost, it is operating at a loss so it faces two options: continue to produce and lose money or shutdown. Which option is preferable? The one that loses the least money is the best choice.

At a price of $2.00 per pack, as Figure 8.6 (a) illustrates, if the farm stays in operation it will produce at a level of 65 packs of raspberries, and it will make losses of $47.45 (as explained earlier). The alternative would be to shutdown and lose all the fixed costs of $62.00. Since losing $47.45 is preferable to losing $62.00, the profit maximizing (or in this case the loss minimizing) choice is to stay in operation. The key reason is because price is above average variable cost. This means that at the current price the farm can pay all its variable costs, and have some revenue left over to pay some of the fixed costs. So the loss represents the part of the fixed costs the farm can't pay, which is less than the entire fixed costs. However, if the price declined to $1.50 per pack, as **Figure 8.6** shows (b), and if the firm applied its rule of producing where P = MR = MC, it would produce a quantity of 60. This price is below average variable cost for this level of output. If the farmer cannot pay workers (the variable costs), then it has to shut down. At this price and output, total revenues would be $90 (quantity of 60 times price of $1.50) and total cost would be $165, for overall losses of $75. If the farm shuts down, it must pay only its fixed costs of $62, so shutting down is preferable to selling at a price of $1.50 per pack.

This OpenStax book is available for free at http://cnx.org/content/col12122/1.4

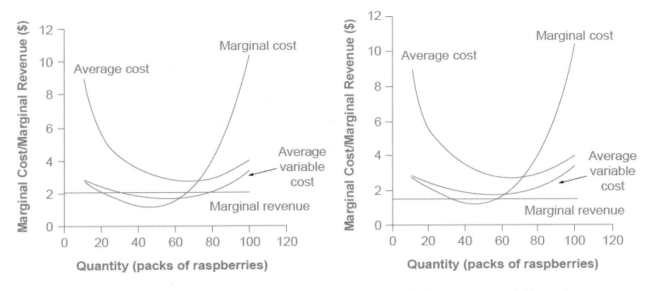

(a) Price is above average variable cost

(b) Price is below average variable cost

Figure 8.6 The Shutdown Point for the Raspberry Farm In (a), the farm produces at a level of 65. It is making losses of $47.50, but price is above average variable cost, so it continues to operate. In (b), total revenues are $90 and total cost is $165, for overall losses of $75. If the farm shuts down, it must pay only its fixed costs of $62. Shutting down is preferable to selling at a price of $1.50 per pack.

Looking at **Table 8.6**, if the price falls below about $1.65, the minimum average variable cost, the firm must shut down.

Quantity Q	Average Variable Cost AVC	Average Cost AC	Marginal Cost MC
0	-	-	-
10	$2.80	$9.00	$2.80
20	$2.40	$5.50	$2.00
30	$2.13	$4.20	$1.60
40	$1.90	$3.45	$1.20
50	$1.76	$3.00	$1.20
60	$1.72	$2.75	$1.50
70	$1.83	$2.71	$2.50
80	$2.10	$2.88	$4.00
90	$2.60	$3.29	$6.60
100	$3.38	$4.00	$10.40
110	$4.44	$5.00	$15.00
120	$5.44	$5.96	$31.50

Table 8.6 Cost of Production for the Raspberry Farm

The intersection of the average variable cost curve and the marginal cost curve, which shows the price below which the firm would lack enough revenue to cover its variable costs, is called the **shutdown point**. If the perfectly competitive firm faces a market price above the shutdown point, then the firm is at least covering its average variable costs. At a price above the shutdown point, the firm is also making enough revenue to cover at least a portion of fixed costs, so it should limp ahead even if it is making losses in the short run, since at least those losses will be smaller than if the firm shuts down immediately and incurs a loss equal to total fixed costs. However, if the firm is receiving a price below the price at the shutdown point, then the firm is not even covering its variable costs. In this case, staying open is making the firm's losses larger, and it should shut down immediately. To summarize, if:

- price < minimum average variable cost, then firm shuts down

- price > minimum average variable cost, then firm stays in business

Short-Run Outcomes for Perfectly Competitive Firms

The average cost and average variable cost curves divide the marginal cost curve into three segments, as **Figure 8.7** shows. At the market price, which the perfectly competitive firm accepts as given, the profit-maximizing firm chooses the output level where price or marginal revenue, which are the same thing for a perfectly competitive firm, is equal to marginal cost: P = MR = MC.

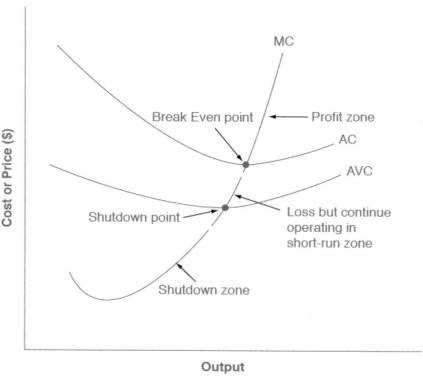

Figure 8.7 Profit, Loss, Shutdown We can divide marginal cost curve into three zones, based on where it is crossed by the average cost and average variable cost curves. We call the point where MC crosses AC the break even point. If the firm is operating where the market price is at a level higher than the break even point, then price will be greater than average cost and the firm is earning profits. If the price is exactly at the break even point, then the firm is making zero profits. If price falls in the zone between the shutdown point and the break even point, then the firm is making losses but will continue to operate in the short run, since it is covering its variable costs, and more if price is above the shutdown-point price. However, if price falls below the price at the shutdown point, then the firm will shut down immediately, since it is not even covering its variable costs.

First consider the upper zone, where prices are above the level where marginal cost (MC) crosses average cost (AC) at the zero profit point. At any price above that level, the firm will earn profits in the short run. If the price falls exactly on the break even point where the MC and AC curves cross, then the firm earns zero profits. If a price falls into the zone between the break even point, where MC crosses AC, and the shutdown point, where MC crosses AVC, the firm will be making losses in the short run—but since the firm is more than covering its variable costs, the losses

This OpenStax book is available for free at http://cnx.org/content/col12122/1.4

are smaller than if the firm shut down immediately. Finally, consider a price at or below the shutdown point where MC crosses AVC. At any price like this one, the firm will shut down immediately, because it cannot even cover its variable costs.

Marginal Cost and the Firm's Supply Curve

For a perfectly competitive firm, the marginal cost curve is identical to the firm's supply curve starting from the minimum point on the average variable cost curve. To understand why this perhaps surprising insight holds true, first think about what the supply curve means. A firm checks the market price and then looks at its supply curve to decide what quantity to produce. Now, think about what it means to say that a firm will maximize its profits by producing at the quantity where $P = MC$. This rule means that the firm checks the market price, and then looks at its marginal cost to determine the quantity to produce—and makes sure that the price is greater than the minimum average variable cost. In other words, the marginal cost curve above the minimum point on the average variable cost curve becomes the firm's supply curve.

Link It Up

Watch this video (http://openstaxcollege.org/l/foodprice) that addresses how drought in the United States can impact food prices across the world. (Note that the story on the drought is the second one in the news report. You need to let the video play through the first story in order to watch the story on the drought.)

As we discussed in the chapter on **Demand and Supply**, many of the reasons that supply curves shift relate to underlying changes in costs. For example, a lower price of key inputs or new technologies that reduce production costs cause supply to shift to the right. In contrast, bad weather or added government regulations can add to costs of certain goods in a way that causes supply to shift to the left. We can also interpret these shifts in the firm's supply curve as shifts of the marginal cost curve. A shift in costs of production that increases marginal costs at all levels of output—and shifts MC upward and to the left—will cause a perfectly competitive firm to produce less at any given market price. Conversely, a shift in costs of production that decreases marginal costs at all levels of output will shift MC downward and to the right and as a result, a competitive firm will choose to expand its level of output at any given price. The following Work It Out feature will walk you through an example.

Work It Out

At What Price Should the Firm Continue Producing in the Short Run?

To determine the short-run economic condition of a firm in perfect competition, follow the steps outlined below. Use the data in **Table 8.7**.

Q	P	TFC	TVC	TC	AVC	ATC	MC	TR	Profits
0	$28	$20	$0	-	-	-	-	-	-
1	$28	$20	$20	-	-	-	-	-	-
2	$28	$20	$25	-	-	-	-	-	-
3	$28	$20	$35	-	-	-	-	-	-
4	$28	$20	$52	-	-	-	-	-	-
5	$28	$20	$80	-	-	-	-	-	-

Table 8.7

Step 1. Determine the cost structure for the firm. For a given total fixed costs and variable costs, calculate total cost, average variable cost, average total cost, and marginal cost. Follow the formulas given in the **Production, Costs, and Industry Structure** chapter. These calculations are in **Table 8.8**.

Q	P	TFC	TVC	TC (TFC+TVC)	AVC (TVC/Q)	ATC (TC/Q)	MC $(TC_2-TC_1)/(Q_2-Q_1)$
0	$28	$20	$0	$20+$0=$20	-	-	-
1	$28	$20	$20	$20+$20=$40	$20/1=$20.00	$40/1=$40.00	($40−$20)/(1−0)= $20
2	$28	$20	$25	$20+$25=$45	$25/2=$12.50	$45/2=$22.50	($45−$40)/(2−1)= $5
3	$28	$20	$35	$20+$35=$55	$35/3=$11.67	$55/3=$18.33	($55−$45)/(3−2)= $10
4	$28	$20	$52	$20+$52=$72	$52/4=$13.00	$72/4=$18.00	($72−$55)/(4−3)= $17
5	$28	$20	$80	$20+$80=$100	$80/5=$16.00	$100/5=$20.00	($100−$72)/(5−4)= $28

Table 8.8

Step 2. Determine the market price that the firm receives for its product. Since the firm in perfect competition is a price taker, the market price is constant With the given price, calculate total revenue as equal to price multiplied by quantity for all output levels produced. In this example, the given price is $28. You can see that in the second column of **Table 8.9**.

Quantity	Price	Total Revenue (P × Q)
0	$28	$28×0=$0

Table 8.9

This OpenStax book is available for free at http://cnx.org/content/col12122/1.4

Quantity	Price	Total Revenue (P × Q)
1	$28	$28×1=$28
2	$28	S28×2=$56
3	$28	$28×3=$84
4	$28	$28×4=$112
5	$28	$28×5=$140

Table 8.9

Step 3. Calculate profits as total cost subtracted from total revenue, as **Table 8.10** shows.

Quantity	Total Revenue	Total Cost	Profits (TR−TC)
0	$0	$20	$0−$20=−$20
1	$28	$40	$28−$40=−$12
2	$56	$45	$56−$45=$11
3	$84	$55	$84−$55=$29
4	$112	$72	$112−$72=$40
5	$140	$100	$140−$100=$40

Table 8.10

Step 4. To find the profit-maximizing output level, look at the Marginal Cost column (at every output level produced), as **Table 8.11** shows, and determine where it is equal to the market price. The output level where price equals the marginal cost is the output level that maximizes profits.

Q	P	TFC	TVC	TC	AVC	ATC	MC	TR	Profits
0	$28	$20	$0	$20	-	-	-	$0	−$20
1	$28	$20	$20	$40	$20.00	$40.00	$20	$28	−$12
2	$28	$20	$25	$45	$12.50	$22.50	$5	$56	$11
3	$28	$20	$35	$55	$11.67	$18.33	$10	$84	$29
4	$28	$20	$52	$72	$13.00	$18.00	$17	$112	$40
5	**$28**	$20	$80	$100	$16.40	$20.40	**$28**	$140	**$40**

Table 8.11

Step 5. Once you have determined the profit-maximizing output level (in this case, output quantity 5), you can look at the amount of profits made (in this case, $40).

Step 6. If the firm is making economic losses, the firm needs to determine whether it produces the output level where price equals marginal revenue and equals marginal cost or it shuts down and only incurs its fixed costs.

Step 7. For the output level where marginal revenue is equal to marginal cost, check if the market price is greater than the average variable cost of producing that output level.

- If P > AVC but P < ATC, then the firm continues to produce in the short-run, making economic losses.
- If P < AVC, then the firm stops producing and only incurs its fixed costs.

In this example, the price of $28 is greater than the AVC ($16.40) of producing 5 units of output, so the firm continues producing.

8.3 | Entry and Exit Decisions in the Long Run

By the end of this section, you will be able to:
- Explain how entry and exit lead to zero profits in the long run
- Discuss the long-run adjustment process

It is impossible to precisely define the line between the short run and the long run with a stopwatch, or even with a calendar. It varies according to the specific business. Therefore, the distinction between the short run and the long run is more technical: in the short run, firms cannot change the usage of fixed inputs, while in the long run, the firm can adjust all factors of production.

In a competitive market, profits are a red cape that incites businesses to charge. If a business is making a profit in the short run, it has an incentive to expand existing factories or to build new ones. New firms may start production, as well. When new firms enter the industry in response to increased industry profits it is called **entry**.

Losses are the black thundercloud that causes businesses to flee. If a business is making losses in the short run, it will either keep limping along or just shut down, depending on whether its revenues are covering its variable costs. But in the long run, firms that are facing losses will cease production altogether. The long-run process of reducing production in response to a sustained pattern of losses is called **exit**. The following Clear It Up feature discusses where some of these losses might come from, and the reasons why some firms go out of business.

Why do firms cease to exist?

Can we say anything about what causes a firm to exit an industry? Profits are the measurement that determines whether a business stays operating or not. Individuals start businesses with the purpose of making profits. They invest their money, time, effort, and many other resources to produce and sell something that they hope will give them something in return. Unfortunately, not all businesses are successful, and many new startups soon realize that their "business venture" must eventually end.

In the model of perfectly competitive firms, those that consistently cannot make money will "exit," which is a nice, bloodless word for a more painful process. When a business fails, after all, workers lose their jobs, investors lose their money, and owners and managers can lose their dreams. Many businesses fail. The U.S. Small Business Administration indicates that in 2011, 534,907 new firms "entered," and 575,691 firms failed.

Sometimes a business fails because of poor management or workers who are not very productive, or because of tough domestic or foreign competition. Businesses also fail from a variety of causes. For example, conditions of demand and supply in the market may shift in an unexpected way, so that the prices that a business charges for outputs fall or the prices for inputs rise. With millions of businesses in the U.S. economy, even a small fraction of them failing will affect many people—and business failures can be very hard on the workers and managers directly involved. However, from the standpoint of the overall economic system, business exits are sometimes a necessary evil if a market-oriented system is going to offer a flexible mechanism for satisfying customers, keeping costs low, and inventing new products.

This OpenStax book is available for free at http://cnx.org/content/col12122/1.4

How Entry and Exit Lead to Zero Profits in the Long Run

No perfectly competitive firm acting alone can affect the market price. However, the combination of many firms entering or exiting the market will affect overall supply in the market. In turn, a shift in supply for the market as a whole will affect the market price. Entry and exit to and from the market are the driving forces behind a process that, in the long run, pushes the price down to minimum average total costs so that all firms are earning a zero profit.

To understand how short-run profits for a perfectly competitive firm will evaporate in the long run, imagine the following situation. The market is in **long-run equilibrium**, where all firms earn zero economic profits producing the output level where P = MR = MC and P = AC. No firm has the incentive to enter or leave the market. Let's say that the product's demand increases, and with that, the market price goes up. The existing firms in the industry are now facing a higher price than before, so they will increase production to the new output level where P = MR = MC.

This will temporarily make the market price rise above the minimum point on the average cost curve, and therefore, the existing firms in the market will now be earning economic profits. However, these economic profits attract other firms to enter the market. Entry of many new firms causes the market supply curve to shift to the right. As the supply curve shifts to the right, the market price starts decreasing, and with that, economic profits fall for new and existing firms. As long as there are still profits in the market, entry will continue to shift supply to the right. This will stop whenever the market price is driven down to the zero-profit level, where no firm is earning economic profits.

Short-run losses will fade away by reversing this process. Say that the market is in long-run equilibrium. This time, instead, demand decreases, and with that, the market price starts falling. The existing firms in the industry are now facing a lower price than before, and as it will be below the average cost curve, they will now be making economic losses. Some firms will continue producing where the new P = MR = MC, as long as they are able to cover their average variable costs. Some firms will have to shut down immediately as they will not be able to cover their average variable costs, and will then only incur their fixed costs, minimizing their losses. Exit of many firms causes the market supply curve to shift to the left. As the supply curve shifts to the left, the market price starts rising, and economic losses start to be lower. This process ends whenever the market price rises to the zero-profit level, where the existing firms are no longer losing money and are at zero profits again. Thus, while a perfectly competitive firm can earn profits in the short run, in the long run the process of entry will push down prices until they reach the zero-profit level. Conversely, while a perfectly competitive firm may earn losses in the short run, firms will not continually lose money. In the long run, firms making losses are able to escape from their fixed costs, and their exit from the market will push the price back up to the zero-profit level. In the long run, this process of entry and exit will drive the price in perfectly competitive markets to the zero-profit point at the bottom of the AC curve, where marginal cost crosses average cost.

The Long-Run Adjustment and Industry Types

Whenever there are expansions in an industry, costs of production for the existing and new firms could either stay the same, increase, or even decrease. Therefore, we can categorize an industry as being (1) a constant cost industry (as demand increases, the cost of production for firms stays the same), (2) an increasing cost industry (as demand increases, the cost of production for firms increases), or (3) a decreasing cost industry (as demand increases the costs of production for the firms decreases).

For a constant cost industry, whenever there is an increase in market demand and price, then the supply curve shifts to the right with new firms' entry and stops at the point where the new long-run equilibrium intersects at the same market price as before. This is the case of constant returns to scale, which we discussed earlier in the chapter on Production, Costs, and Industry Structure. However, why will costs remain the same? In this type of industry, the supply curve is very elastic. Firms can easily supply any quantity that consumers demand. In addition, there is a perfectly elastic supply of inputs—firms can easily increase their demand for employees, for example, with no increase to wages. Tying in to our Bring it Home discussion, an increased demand for ethanol in recent years has caused the demand for corn to increase. Consequently, many farmers switched from growing wheat to growing corn. Agricultural markets are generally good examples of constant cost industries.

For an increasing cost industry, as the market expands, the old and new firms experience increases in their costs of production, which makes the new zero-profit level intersect at a higher price than before. Here companies may have to deal with limited inputs, such as skilled labor. As the demand for these workers rise, wages rise and this increases the cost of production for all firms. The industry supply curve in this type of industry is more inelastic.

For a decreasing cost industry, as the market expands, the old and new firms experience lower costs of production, which makes the new zero-profit level intersect at a lower price than before. In this case, the industry and all the firms in it are experiencing falling average total costs. This can be due to an improvement in technology in the entire industry or an increase in the education of employees. High tech industries may be a good example of a decreasing cost market.

Figure 8.8 (a) presents the case of an adjustment process in a constant cost industry. Whenever there are output expansions in this type of industry, the long-run outcome implies more output produced at exactly the same original price. Note that supply was able to increase to meet the increased demand. When we join the before and after long-run equilibriums, the resulting line is the long run supply (LRS) curve in perfectly competitive markets. In this case, it is a flat curve. **Figure 8.8** (b) and **Figure 8.8** (c) present the cases for an increasing cost and decreasing cost industry, respectively. For an increasing cost industry, the LRS is upward sloping, while for a decreasing cost industry, the LRS is downward sloping.

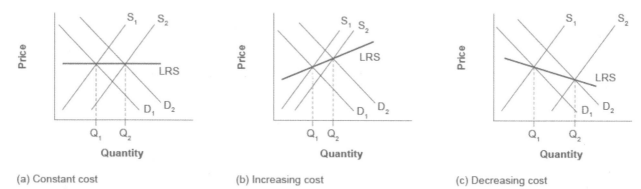

(a) Constant cost   (b) Increasing cost   (c) Decreasing cost

Figure 8.8 Adjustment Process in a Constant-Cost Industry In (a), demand increased and supply met it. Notice that the supply increase is equal to the demand increase. The result is that the equilibrium price stays the same as quantity sold increases. In (b), notice that sellers were not able to increase supply as much as demand. Some inputs were scarce, or wages were rising. The equilibrium price rises. In (c), sellers easily increased supply in response to the demand increase. Here, new technology or economies of scale caused the large increase in supply, resulting in declining equilibrium price.

8.4 | Efficiency in Perfectly Competitive Markets

By the end of this section, you will be able to:
- Apply concepts of productive efficiency and allocative efficiency to perfectly competitive markets
- Compare the model of perfect competition to real-world markets

When profit-maximizing firms in perfectly competitive markets combine with utility-maximizing consumers, something remarkable happens: the resulting quantities of outputs of goods and services demonstrate both productive and allocative efficiency (terms that we first introduced in (**Choice in a World of Scarcity**) .

Productive efficiency means producing without waste, so that the choice is on the production possibility frontier. In the long run in a perfectly competitive market, because of the process of entry and exit, the price in the market is equal to the minimum of the long-run average cost curve. In other words, firms produce and sell goods at the lowest possible average cost.

Allocative efficiency means that among the points on the production possibility frontier, the chosen point is socially preferred—at least in a particular and specific sense. In a perfectly competitive market, price will be equal to the marginal cost of production. Think about the price that one pays for a good as a measure of the social benefit one receives for that good; after all, willingness to pay conveys what the good is worth to a buyer. Then think about the marginal cost of producing the good as representing not just the cost for the firm, but more broadly as the social cost of producing that good. When perfectly competitive firms follow the rule that profits are maximized by producing at the quantity where price is equal to marginal cost, they are thus ensuring that the social benefits they receive from producing a good are in line with the social costs of production.

To explore what economists mean by allocative efficiency, it is useful to walk through an example. Begin by assuming

This OpenStax book is available for free at http://cnx.org/content/col12122/1.4

that the market for wholesale flowers is perfectly competitive, and so P = MC. Now, consider what it would mean if firms in that market produced a lesser quantity of flowers. At a lesser quantity, marginal costs will not yet have increased as much, so that price will exceed marginal cost; that is, P > MC. In that situation, the benefit to society as a whole of producing additional goods, as measured by the willingness of consumers to pay for marginal units of a good, would be higher than the cost of the inputs of labor and physical capital needed to produce the marginal good. In other words, the gains to society as a whole from producing additional marginal units will be greater than the costs.

Conversely, consider what it would mean if, compared to the level of output at the allocatively efficient choice when P = MC, firms produced a greater quantity of flowers. At a greater quantity, marginal costs of production will have increased so that P < MC. In that case, the marginal costs of producing additional flowers is greater than the benefit to society as measured by what people are willing to pay. For society as a whole, since the costs are outstripping the benefits, it will make sense to produce a lower quantity of such goods.

When perfectly competitive firms maximize their profits by producing the quantity where P = MC, they also assure that the benefits to consumers of what they are buying, as measured by the price they are willing to pay, is equal to the costs to society of producing the marginal units, as measured by the marginal costs the firm must pay—and thus that allocative efficiency holds.

We should view the statements that a perfectly competitive market in the long run will feature both productive and allocative efficiency with a degree of skepticism about its truth. Remember, economists are using the concept of "efficiency" in a particular and specific sense, not as a synonym for "desirable in every way." For one thing, consumers' ability to pay reflects the income distribution in a particular society. Thus, a homeless person may have no ability to pay for housing because he or she has insufficient income.

Perfect competition, in the long run, is a hypothetical benchmark. For market structures such as monopoly, monopolistic competition, and oligopoly, which are more frequently observed in the real world than perfect competition, firms will not always produce at the minimum of average cost, nor will they always set price equal to marginal cost. Thus, these other competitive situations will not produce productive and allocative efficiency.

Moreover, real-world markets include many issues that are assumed away in the model of perfect competition, including pollution, inventions of new technology, poverty which may make some people unable to pay for basic necessities of life, government programs like national defense or education, discrimination in labor markets, and buyers and sellers who must deal with imperfect and unclear information. We explore these issues in other chapters. However, the theoretical efficiency of perfect competition does provide a useful benchmark for comparing the issues that arise from these real-world problems.

Bring it Home

A Dime a Dozen

A quick glance at Table 8.12 reveals the dramatic increase in North Dakota corn production—more than double. Taking into consideration that corn typically yields two to three times as many bushels per acre as wheat, it is obvious there has been a significant increase in bushels of corn. Why the increase in corn acreage? Converging prices.

Year	Corn (millions of acres)	Wheat (millions of acres)
2014	91.6	56.82

Table 8.12 (Source: USDA National Agricultural Statistics Service)

Historically, wheat prices have been higher than corn prices, offsetting wheat's lower yield per acre. However, in recent years wheat and corn prices have been converging. In April 2013, *Agweek* reported the gap was just 71 cents per bushel. As the difference in price narrowed, switching to the production of higher yield per acre of corn simply made good business sense. Erik Younggren, president of the National Association of Wheat Growers said in the *Agweek* article, "I don't think we're going to see mile after mile of waving amber fields [of wheat] anymore." (Until wheat prices rise, we will probably be seeing field after field of tasseled corn.)

This OpenStax book is available for free at http://cnx.org/content/col12122/1.4

KEY TERMS

break even point level of output where the marginal cost curve intersects the average cost curve at the minimum point of AC; if the price is at this point, the firm is earning zero economic profits

entry the long-run process of firms entering an industry in response to industry profits

exit the long-run process of firms reducing production and shutting down in response to industry losses

long-run equilibrium where all firms earn zero economic profits producing the output level where P = MR = MC and P = AC

marginal revenue the additional revenue gained from selling one more unit

market structure the conditions in an industry, such as number of sellers, how easy or difficult it is for a new firm to enter, and the type of products that are sold

perfect competition each firm faces many competitors that sell identical products

price taker a firm in a perfectly competitive market that must take the prevailing market price as given

shutdown point level of output where the marginal cost curve intersects the average variable cost curve at the minimum point of AVC; if the price is below this point, the firm should shut down immediately

KEY CONCEPTS AND SUMMARY

8.1 Perfect Competition and Why It Matters

A perfectly competitive firm is a price taker, which means that it must accept the equilibrium price at which it sells goods. If a perfectly competitive firm attempts to charge even a tiny amount more than the market price, it will be unable to make any sales. In a perfectly competitive market there are thousands of sellers, easy entry, and identical products. A short-run production period is when firms are producing with some fixed inputs. Long-run equilibrium in a perfectly competitive industry occurs after all firms have entered and exited the industry and seller profits are driven to zero.

Perfect competition means that there are many sellers, there is easy entry and exiting of firms, products are identical from one seller to another, and sellers are price takers.

8.2 How Perfectly Competitive Firms Make Output Decisions

As a perfectly competitive firm produces a greater quantity of output, its total revenue steadily increases at a constant rate determined by the given market price. Profits will be highest (or losses will be smallest) at the quantity of output where total revenues exceed total costs by the greatest amount (or where total revenues fall short of total costs by the smallest amount). Alternatively, profits will be highest where marginal revenue, which is price for a perfectly competitive firm, is equal to marginal cost. If the market price faced by a perfectly competitive firm is above average cost at the profit-maximizing quantity of output, then the firm is making profits. If the market price is below average cost at the profit-maximizing quantity of output, then the firm is making losses.

If the market price is equal to average cost at the profit-maximizing level of output, then the firm is making zero profits. We call the point where the marginal cost curve crosses the average cost curve, at the minimum of the average cost curve, the "zero profit point." If the market price that a perfectly competitive firm faces is below average variable cost at the profit-maximizing quantity of output, then the firm should shut down operations immediately. If the market price that a perfectly competitive firm faces is above average variable cost, but below average cost, then the firm should continue producing in the short run, but exit in the long run. We call the point where the marginal cost curve crosses the average variable cost curve the shutdown point.

8.3 Entry and Exit Decisions in the Long Run

In the long run, firms will respond to profits through a process of entry, where existing firms expand output and new firms enter the market. Conversely, firms will react to losses in the long run through a process of exit, in which existing firms cease production altogether. Through the process of entry in response to profits and exit in response to losses, the price level in a perfectly competitive market will move toward the zero-profit point, where the marginal cost curve crosses the AC curve at the minimum of the average cost curve.

The long-run supply curve shows the long-run output supplied by firms in three different types of industries: constant cost, increasing cost, and decreasing cost.

8.4 Efficiency in Perfectly Competitive Markets

Long-run equilibrium in perfectly competitive markets meets two important conditions: allocative efficiency and productive efficiency. These two conditions have important implications. First, resources are allocated to their best alternative use. Second, they provide the maximum satisfaction attainable by society.

SELF-CHECK QUESTIONS

1. Firms in a perfectly competitive market are said to be "price takers"—that is, once the market determines an equilibrium price for the product, firms must accept this price. If you sell a product in a perfectly competitive market, but you are not happy with its price, would you raise the price, even by a cent?

2. Would independent trucking fit the characteristics of a perfectly competitive industry?

3. Look at **Table 8.13**. What would happen to the firm's profits if the market price increases to $6 per pack of raspberries?

Quantity	Total Cost	Fixed Cost	Variable Cost	Total Revenue	Profit
0	$62	$62	-	$0	−$62
10	$90	$62	$28	$60	−$30
20	$110	$62	$48	$120	$10
30	$126	$62	$64	$180	$54
40	$144	$62	$82	$240	$96
50	$166	$62	$104	$300	$134
60	$192	$62	$130	$360	$168
70	$224	$62	$162	$420	$196
80	$264	$62	$202	$480	$216
90	$324	$62	$262	$540	$216
100	$404	$62	$342	$600	$196

Table 8.13

This OpenStax book is available for free at http://cnx.org/content/col12122/1.4

4. Suppose that the market price increases to $6, as **Table 8.14** shows. What would happen to the profit-maximizing output level?

Quantity	Total Cost	Fixed Cost	Variable Cost	Marginal Cost	Total Revenue	Marginal Revenue
0	$62	$62	-	-	$0	-
10	$90	$62	$28	$2.80	$60	$6.00
20	$110	$62	$48	$2.00	$120	$6.00
30	$126	$62	$64	$1.60	$180	$6.00
40	$144	$62	$82	$1.80	$240	$6.00
50	$166	$62	$104	$2.20	$300	$6.00
60	$192	$62	$130	$2.60	$360	$6.00
70	$224	$62	$162	$3.20	$420	$6.00
80	$264	$62	$202	$4.00	$480	$6.00
90	$324	$62	$262	**$6.00**	$540	**$6.00**
100	$404	$62	$342	$8.00	$600	$6.00

Table 8.14

5. Explain in words why a profit-maximizing firm will not choose to produce at a quantity where marginal cost exceeds marginal revenue.

6. A firm's marginal cost curve above the average variable cost curve is equal to the firm's individual supply curve. This means that every time a firm receives a price from the market it will be willing to supply the amount of output where the price equals marginal cost. What happens to the firm's individual supply curve if marginal costs increase?

7. If new technology in a perfectly competitive market brings about a substantial reduction in costs of production, how will this affect the market?

8. A market in perfect competition is in long-run equilibrium. What happens to the market if labor unions are able to increase wages for workers?

9. Productive efficiency and allocative efficiency are two concepts achieved in the long run in a perfectly competitive market. These are the two reasons why we call them "perfect." How would you use these two concepts to analyze other market structures and label them "imperfect?"

10. Explain how the profit-maximizing rule of setting P = MC leads a perfectly competitive market to be allocatively efficient.

REVIEW QUESTIONS

11. A single firm in a perfectly competitive market is relatively small compared to the rest of the market. What does this mean? How "small" is "small"?

12. What are the four basic assumptions of perfect competition? Explain in words what they imply for a perfectly competitive firm.

13. What is a "price taker" firm?

14. How does a perfectly competitive firm decide what price to charge?

15. What prevents a perfectly competitive firm from seeking higher profits by increasing the price that it charges?

16. How does a perfectly competitive firm calculate total revenue?

17. Briefly explain the reason for the shape of a marginal revenue curve for a perfectly competitive firm.

18. What two rules does a perfectly competitive firm apply to determine its profit-maximizing quantity of output?

19. How does the average cost curve help to show whether a firm is making profits or losses?

20. What two lines on a cost curve diagram intersect at the zero-profit point?

21. Should a firm shut down immediately if it is making losses?

22. How does the average variable cost curve help a firm know whether it should shut down immediately?

23. What two lines on a cost curve diagram intersect at the shutdown point?

24. Why does entry occur?

25. Why does exit occur?

26. Do entry and exit occur in the short run, the long run, both, or neither?

27. What price will a perfectly competitive firm end up charging in the long run? Why?

28. Will a perfectly competitive market display productive efficiency? Why or why not?

29. Will a perfectly competitive market display allocative efficiency? Why or why not?

CRITICAL THINKING QUESTIONS

30. Finding a life partner is a complicated process that may take many years. It is hard to think of this process as being part of a very complex market, with a demand and a supply for partners. Think about how this market works and some of its characteristics, such as search costs. Would you consider it a perfectly competitive market?

31. Can you name five examples of perfectly competitive markets? Why or why not?

32. Your company operates in a perfectly competitive market. You have been told that advertising can help you increase your sales in the short run. Would you create an aggressive advertising campaign for your product?

33. Since a perfectly competitive firm can sell as much as it wishes at the market price, why can the firm not simply increase its profits by selling an extremely high quantity?

34. Many firms in the United States file for bankruptcy every year, yet they still continue operating. Why would they do this instead of completely shutting down?

35. Why will profits for firms in a perfectly competitive industry tend to vanish in the long run?

36. Why will losses for firms in a perfectly competitive industry tend to vanish in the long run?

37. Assuming that the market for cigarettes is in perfect competition, what does allocative and productive efficiency imply in this case? What does it not imply?

38. In the argument for why perfect competition is allocatively efficient, the price that people are willing to pay represents the gains to society and the marginal cost to the firm represents the costs to society. Can you think of some social costs or issues that are not included in the marginal cost to the firm? Or some social gains that are not included in what people pay for a good?

PROBLEMS

39. The AAA Aquarium Co. sells aquariums for $20 each. Fixed costs of production are $20. The total variable costs are $20 for one aquarium, $25 for two units, $35 for the three units, $50 for four units, and $80 for five units. In the form of a table, calculate total revenue, marginal revenue, total cost, and marginal cost for each output level (one to five units). What is the profit-maximizing quantity of output? On one diagram, sketch the total revenue and total cost curves. On another diagram, sketch the marginal revenue and marginal cost curves.

40. Perfectly competitive firm Doggies Paradise Inc. sells winter coats for dogs. Dog coats sell for $72 each. The fixed costs of production are $100. The total variable costs are $64 for one unit, $84 for two units, $114 for three units, $184 for four units, and $270 for five units. In the form of a table, calculate total revenue, marginal revenue, total cost and marginal cost for each output level (one to five units). On one diagram, sketch the total revenue and total cost curves. On another diagram, sketch the marginal revenue and marginal cost curves. What is the profit maximizing quantity?

41. A computer company produces affordable, easy-to-use home computer systems and has fixed costs of $250. The marginal cost of producing computers is $700 for the first computer, $250 for the second, $300 for the third, $350 for the fourth, $400 for the fifth, $450 for the sixth, and $500 for the seventh.

a. Create a table that shows the company's output, total cost, marginal cost, average cost, variable cost, and average variable cost.

b. At what price is the zero-profit point? At what price is the shutdown point?

c. If the company sells the computers for $500, is it making a profit or a loss? How big is the profit or loss? Sketch a graph with AC, MC, and AVC curves to illustrate your answer and show the profit or loss.

d. If the firm sells the computers for $300, is it making a profit or a loss? How big is the profit or loss? Sketch a graph with AC, MC, and AVC curves to illustrate your answer and show the profit or loss.

This OpenStax book is available for free at http://cnx.org/content/col12122/1.4

9 | Monopoly

Figure 9.1 Political Power from a Cotton Monopoly In the mid-nineteenth century, the United States, specifically the Southern states, had a near monopoly in the cotton that they supplied to Great Britain. These states attempted to leverage this economic power into political power—trying to sway Great Britain to formally recognize the Confederate States of America. (Credit: modification of work by "ashleylovespizza"/Flickr Creative Commons)

Bring it Home

The Rest is History

Many of the opening case studies have focused on current events. This one steps into the past to observe how monopoly, or near monopolies, have helped shape history. In spring 1773, the East India Company, a firm that, in its time, was designated "too big to fail," was experiencing financial difficulties. To help shore up the failing firm, the British Parliament authorized the Tea Act. The act continued the tax on teas and made the East India Company the sole legal supplier of tea to the American colonies. By November, the citizens of Boston had had enough. They refused to permit the unloading of tea, citing their main complaint: "No taxation without representation." Several newspapers, including *The Massachusetts Gazette*, warned arriving tea-bearing ships, "We are prepared, and shall not fail to pay them an unwelcome visit by The Mohawks."

Step forward in time to 1860—the eve of the American Civil War—to another near monopoly supplier of historical significance: the U.S. cotton industry. At that time, the Southern states provided the majority of the cotton Britain imported. The South, wanting to secede from the Union, hoped to leverage Britain's high dependency on its cotton into formal diplomatic recognition of the Confederate States of America.

This leads us to this chapter's topic: a firm that controls all (or nearly all) of the supply of a good or service—a monopoly. How do monopoly firms behave in the marketplace? Do they have "power?" Does this power potentially have unintended consequences? We'll return to this case at the end of the chapter to see how the tea and cotton monopolies influenced U.S. history.

Introduction to a Monopoly

In this chapter, you will learn about:

- How Monopolies form: Barriers to Entry

- How a Profit-Maximizing Monopoly Chooses Output and Price

Many believe that top executives at firms are the strongest supporters of market competition, but this belief is far from the truth. Think about it this way: If you very much wanted to win an Olympic gold medal, would you rather be far better than everyone else, or locked in competition with many athletes just as good as you? Similarly, if you would like to attain a very high level of profits, would you rather manage a business with little or no competition, or struggle against many tough competitors who are trying to sell to your customers? By now, you might have read the chapter on **Perfect Competition**. In this chapter, we explore the opposite extreme: monopoly.

If perfect competition is a market where firms have no market power and they simply respond to the market price, monopoly is a market with no competition at all, and firms have a great deal of market power. In the case of **monopoly**, one firm produces all of the output in a market. Since a monopoly faces no significant competition, it can charge any price it wishes, subject to the demand curve. While a monopoly, by definition, refers to a single firm, in practice people often use the term to describe a market in which one firm merely has a very high market share. This tends to be the definition that the U.S. Department of Justice uses.

Even though there are very few true monopolies in existence, we do deal with some of those few every day, often without realizing it: The U.S. Postal Service, your electric, and garbage collection companies are a few examples. Some new drugs are produced by only one pharmaceutical firm—and no close substitutes for that drug may exist.

From the mid-1990s until 2004, the U.S. Department of Justice prosecuted the Microsoft Corporation for including Internet Explorer as the default web browser with its operating system. The Justice Department's argument was that, since Microsoft possessed an extremely high market share in the industry for operating systems, the inclusion of a free web browser constituted unfair competition to other browsers, such as Netscape Navigator. Since nearly everyone was using Windows, including Internet Explorer eliminated the incentive for consumers to explore other browsers and made it impossible for competitors to gain a foothold in the market. In 2013, the Windows system ran on more than 90% of the most commonly sold personal computers. In 2015, a U.S. federal court tossed out antitrust charges that Google had an agreement with mobile device makers to set Google as the default search engine.

This chapter begins by describing how monopolies are protected from competition, including laws that prohibit competition, technological advantages, and certain configurations of demand and supply. It then discusses how a monopoly will choose its profit-maximizing quantity to produce and what price to charge. While a monopoly must be concerned about whether consumers will purchase its products or spend their money on something altogether different, the monopolist need not worry about the actions of other competing firms producing its products. As a result, a monopoly is not a price taker like a perfectly competitive firm, but instead exercises some power to choose its market price.

9.1 | How Monopolies Form: Barriers to Entry

By the end of this section, you will be able to:
- Distinguish between a natural monopoly and a legal monopoly.
- Explain how economies of scale and the control of natural resources led to the necessary formation of legal monopolies
- Analyze the importance of trademarks and patents in promoting innovation
- Identify examples of predatory pricing

Because of the lack of competition, monopolies tend to earn significant economic profits. These profits should attract vigorous competition as we described in **Perfect Competition**, and yet, because of one particular characteristic of monopoly, they do not. **Barriers to entry** are the legal, technological, or market forces that discourage or prevent potential competitors from entering a market. Barriers to entry can range from the simple and easily surmountable, such as the cost of renting retail space, to the extremely restrictive. For example, there are a finite number of radio frequencies available for broadcasting. Once an entrepreneur or firm has purchased the rights to all of them, no new competitors can enter the market.

In some cases, barriers to entry may lead to monopoly. In other cases, they may limit competition to a few firms. Barriers may block entry even if the firm or firms currently in the market are earning profits. Thus, in markets with significant barriers to entry, it is *not* necessarily true that abnormally high profits will attract new firms, and that this entry of new firms will eventually cause the price to decline so that surviving firms earn only a normal level of profit in the long run.

There are two types of monopoly, based on the types of barriers to entry they exploit. One is **natural monopoly**, where the barriers to entry are something other than legal prohibition. The other is **legal monopoly**, where laws prohibit (or severely limit) competition.

Natural Monopoly

Economies of scale can combine with the size of the market to limit competition. (We introduced this theme in **Production, Cost and Industry Structure**). **Figure 9.2** presents a long-run average cost curve for the airplane manufacturing industry. It shows economies of scale up to an output of 8,000 planes per year and a price of P_0, then constant returns to scale from 8,000 to 20,000 planes per year, and diseconomies of scale at a quantity of production greater than 20,000 planes per year.

Now consider the market demand curve in the diagram, which intersects the long-run average cost (LRAC) curve at an output level of 5,000 planes per year and at a price P_1, which is higher than P_0. In this situation, the market has room for only one producer. If a second firm attempts to enter the market at a smaller size, say by producing a quantity of 4,000 planes, then its average costs will be higher than those of the existing firm, and it will be unable to compete. If the second firm attempts to enter the market at a larger size, like 8,000 planes per year, then it could produce at a lower average cost—but it could not sell all 8,000 planes that it produced because of insufficient demand in the market.

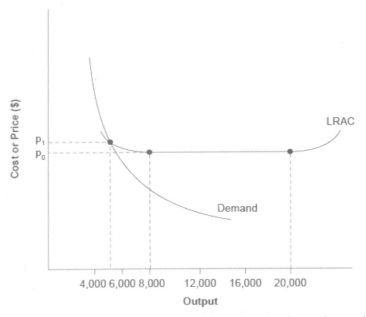

Figure 9.2 Economies of Scale and Natural Monopoly In this market, the demand curve intersects the long-run average cost (LRAC) curve at its downward-sloping part. A natural monopoly occurs when the quantity demanded is less than the minimum quantity it takes to be at the bottom of the long-run average cost curve.

Economists call this situation, when economies of scale are large relative to the quantity demanded in the market, a natural monopoly. Natural monopolies often arise in industries where the marginal cost of adding an additional customer is very low, once the fixed costs of the overall system are in place. This results in situations where there are substantial economies of scale. For example, once a water company lays the main water pipes through a neighborhood, the marginal cost of providing water service to another home is fairly low. Once the electric company installs lines in a new subdivision, the marginal cost of providing additional electrical service to one more home is minimal. It would be costly and duplicative for a second water company to enter the market and invest in a whole second set of main water pipes, or for a second electricity company to enter the market and invest in a whole new set of electrical wires. These industries offer an example where, because of economies of scale, one producer can serve the entire market more efficiently than a number of smaller producers that would need to make duplicate physical capital investments.

A natural monopoly can also arise in smaller local markets for products that are difficult to transport. For example, cement production exhibits economies of scale, and the quantity of cement demanded in a local area may not be much larger than what a single plant can produce. Moreover, the costs of transporting cement over land are high, and so a cement plant in an area without access to water transportation may be a natural monopoly.

Control of a Physical Resource

Another type of natural monopoly occurs when a company has control of a scarce physical resource. In the U.S. economy, one historical example of this pattern occurred when ALCOA—the Aluminum Company of America—controlled most of the supply of bauxite, a key mineral used in making aluminum. Back in the 1930s, when ALCOA controlled most of the bauxite, other firms were simply unable to produce enough aluminum to compete.

As another example, the majority of global diamond production is controlled by DeBeers, a multi-national company that has mining and production operations in South Africa, Botswana, Namibia, and Canada. It also has exploration activities on four continents, while directing a worldwide distribution network of rough cut diamonds. Although in recent years they have experienced growing competition, their impact on the rough diamond market is still considerable.

Legal Monopoly

For some products, the government erects barriers to entry by prohibiting or limiting competition. Under U.S. law, no organization but the U.S. Postal Service is legally allowed to deliver first-class mail. Many states or cities have laws or regulations that allow households a choice of only one electric company, one water company, and one company to pick up the garbage. Most legal monopolies are utilities—products necessary for everyday life—that are socially beneficial. As a consequence, the government allows producers to become regulated monopolies, to insure that customers have access to an appropriate amount of these products or services. Additionally, legal monopolies are often subject to economies of scale, so it makes sense to allow only one provider.

Promoting Innovation

Innovation takes time and resources to achieve. Suppose a company invests in research and development and finds the cure for the common cold. In this world of near ubiquitous information, other companies could take the formula, produce the drug, and because they did not incur the costs of research and development (R&D), undercut the price of the company that discovered the drug. Given this possibility, many firms would choose not to invest in research and development, and as a result, the world would have less innovation. To prevent this from happening, the Constitution of the United States specifies in Article I, Section 8: "The Congress shall have Power . . . to Promote the Progress of Science and Useful Arts, by securing for limited Times to Authors and Inventors the Exclusive Right to their Writings and Discoveries." Congress used this power to create the U.S. Patent and Trademark Office, as well as the U.S. Copyright Office. A **patent** gives the inventor the exclusive legal right to make, use, or sell the invention for a limited time. In the United States, exclusive patent rights last for 20 years. The idea is to provide limited monopoly power so that innovative firms can recoup their investment in R&D, but then to allow other firms to produce the product more cheaply once the patent expires.

A **trademark** is an identifying symbol or name for a particular good, like Chiquita bananas, Chevrolet cars, or the Nike "swoosh" that appears on shoes and athletic gear. Roughly 1.9 million trademarks are registered with the U.S. government. A firm can renew a trademark repeatedly, as long as it remains in active use.

A **copyright**, according to the U.S. Copyright Office, "is a form of protection provided by the laws of the United States for 'original works of authorship' including literary, dramatic, musical, architectural, cartographic, choreographic, pantomimic, pictorial, graphic, sculptural, and audiovisual creations." No one can reproduce, display, or perform a copyrighted work without the author's permission. Copyright protection ordinarily lasts for the life of the author plus 70 years.

Roughly speaking, patent law covers inventions and copyright protects books, songs, and art. However, in certain

This OpenStax book is available for free at http://cnx.org/content/col12122/1.4

areas, like the invention of new software, it has been unclear whether patent or copyright protection should apply. There is also a body of law known as **trade secrets**. Even if a company does not have a patent on an invention, competing firms are not allowed to steal their secrets. One famous trade secret is the formula for Coca-Cola, which is not protected under copyright or patent law, but is simply kept secret by the company.

Taken together, we call this combination of patents, trademarks, copyrights, and trade secret law **intellectual property**, because it implies ownership over an idea, concept, or image, not a physical piece of property like a house or a car. Countries around the world have enacted laws to protect intellectual property, although the time periods and exact provisions of such laws vary across countries. There are ongoing negotiations, both through the World Intellectual Property Organization (WIPO) and through international treaties, to bring greater harmony to the intellectual property laws of different countries to determine the extent to which those in other countries will respect patents and copyrights of those in other countries.

Government limitations on competition used to be more common in the United States. For most of the twentieth century, only one phone company—AT&T—was legally allowed to provide local and long distance service. From the 1930s to the 1970s, one set of federal regulations limited which destinations airlines could choose to fly to and what fares they could charge. Another set of regulations limited the interest rates that banks could pay to depositors; yet another specified how much trucking firms could charge customers.

What products we consider utilities depends, in part, on the available technology. Fifty years ago, telephone companies provided local and long distance service over wires. It did not make much sense to have many companies building multiple wiring systems across towns and the entire country. AT&T lost its monopoly on long distance service when the technology for providing phone service changed from wires to microwave and satellite transmission, so that multiple firms could use the same transmission mechanism. The same thing happened to local service, especially in recent years, with the growth in cellular phone systems.

The combination of improvements in production technologies and a general sense that the markets could provide services adequately led to a wave of **deregulation**, starting in the late 1970s and continuing into the 1990s. This wave eliminated or reduced government restrictions on the firms that could enter, the prices that they could charge, and the quantities that many industries could produce, including telecommunications, airlines, trucking, banking, and electricity.

Around the world, from Europe to Latin America to Africa and Asia, many governments continue to control and limit competition in what those governments perceive to be key industries, including airlines, banks, steel companies, oil companies, and telephone companies.

Link It Up

Vist this website (http://openstaxcollege.org/l/patents) for examples of some pretty bizarre patents.

Intimidating Potential Competition

Businesses have developed a number of schemes for creating barriers to entry by deterring potential competitors from entering the market. One method is known as **predatory pricing**, in which a firm uses the threat of sharp price cuts to discourage competition. Predatory pricing is a violation of U.S. antitrust law, but it is difficult to prove.

Consider a large airline that provides most of the flights between two particular cities. A new, small start-up airline decides to offer service between these two cities. The large airline immediately slashes prices on this route to the bone, so that the new entrant cannot make any money. After the new entrant has gone out of business, the incumbent firm can raise prices again.

After the company repeats this pattern once or twice, potential new entrants may decide that it is not wise to try to compete. Small airlines often accuse larger airlines of predatory pricing: in the early 2000s, for example, ValuJet accused Delta of predatory pricing, Frontier accused United, and Reno Air accused Northwest. In 2015, the Justice Department ruled against American Express and Mastercard for imposing restrictions on retailers that encouraged customers to use lower swipe fees on credit transactions.

In some cases, large advertising budgets can also act as a way of discouraging the competition. If the only way to launch a successful new national cola drink is to spend more than the promotional budgets of Coca-Cola and Pepsi Cola, not too many companies will try. A firmly established brand name can be difficult to dislodge.

Summing Up Barriers to Entry

Table 9.1 lists the barriers to entry that we have discussed. This list is not exhaustive, since firms have proved to be highly creative in inventing business practices that discourage competition. When barriers to entry exist, perfect competition is no longer a reasonable description of how an industry works. When barriers to entry are high enough, monopoly can result.

Barrier to Entry	Government Role?	Example
Natural monopoly	Government often responds with regulation (or ownership)	Water and electric companies
Control of a physical resource	No	DeBeers for diamonds
Legal monopoly	Yes	Post office, past regulation of airlines and trucking
Patent, trademark, and copyright	Yes, through protection of intellectual property	New drugs or software
Intimidating potential competitors	Somewhat	Predatory pricing; well-known brand names

Table 9.1 Barriers to Entry

9.2 | How a Profit-Maximizing Monopoly Chooses Output and Price

By the end of this section, you will be able to:
- Explain the perceived demand curve for a perfect competitor and a monopoly
- Analyze a demand curve for a monopoly and determine the output that maximizes profit and revenue
- Calculate marginal revenue and marginal cost
- Explain allocative efficiency as it pertains to the efficiency of a monopoly

Consider a monopoly firm, comfortably surrounded by barriers to entry so that it need not fear competition from other producers. How will this monopoly choose its profit-maximizing quantity of output, and what price will it charge? Profits for the monopolist, like any firm, will be equal to total revenues minus total costs. We can analyze the pattern of costs for the monopoly within the same framework as the costs of a perfectly competitive firm—that is, by using total cost, fixed cost, variable cost, marginal cost, average cost, and average variable cost. However, because a monopoly faces no competition, its situation and its decision process will differ from that of a perfectly competitive firm. (The Clear It Up feature discusses how hard it is sometimes to define "market" in a monopoly situation.)

Demand Curves Perceived by a Perfectly Competitive Firm and by a Monopoly

A perfectly competitive firm acts as a price taker, so we calculate total revenue taking the given market price and multiplying it by the quantity of output that the firm chooses. The demand curve *as it is perceived by a perfectly competitive firm* appears in **Figure 9.3** (a). The flat perceived demand curve means that, from the viewpoint of the perfectly competitive firm, it could sell either a relatively low quantity like Ql or a relatively high quantity like Qh at the market price P.

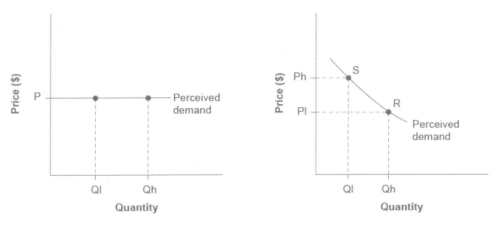

(a) Perceived demand for a perfect competitor   (b) Perceived demand for a monopolist

Figure 9.3 The Perceived Demand Curve for a Perfect Competitor and a Monopolist (a) A perfectly competitive firm perceives the demand curve that it faces to be flat. The flat shape means that the firm can sell either a low quantity (Ql) or a high quantity (Qh) at exactly the same price (P). (b) A monopolist perceives the demand curve that it faces to be the same as the market demand curve, which for most goods is downward-sloping. Thus, if the monopolist chooses a high level of output (Qh), it can charge only a relatively low price (Pl). Conversely, if the monopolist chooses a low level of output (Ql), it can then charge a higher price (Ph). The challenge for the monopolist is to choose the combination of price and quantity that maximizes profits.

What defines the market?

A monopoly is a firm that sells all or nearly all of the goods and services in a given market. However, what defines the "market"?

In a famous 1947 case, the federal government accused the DuPont company of having a monopoly in the cellophane market, pointing out that DuPont produced 75% of the cellophane in the United States. DuPont countered that even though it had a 75% market share in cellophane, it had less than a 20% share of the "flexible packaging materials," which includes all other moisture-proof papers, films, and foils. In 1956, after years of legal appeals, the U.S. Supreme Court held that the broader market definition was more appropriate, and it dismissed the case against DuPont.

Questions over how to define the market continue today. True, Microsoft in the 1990s had a dominant share of the software for computer operating systems, but in the total market for all computer software and services, including everything from games to scientific programs, the Microsoft share was only about 14% in 2014. The Greyhound bus company may have a near-monopoly on the market for intercity bus transportation, but it is only a small share of the market for intercity transportation if that market includes private cars, airplanes, and railroad service. DeBeers has a monopoly in diamonds, but it is a much smaller share of the total market for precious gemstones and an even smaller share of the total market for jewelry. A small town in the country may have only one gas station: is this gas station a "monopoly," or does it compete with gas stations that might be five, 10, or 50 miles away?

In general, if a firm produces a product without close substitutes, then we can consider the firm a monopoly producer in a single market. However, if buyers have a range of similar—even if not identical—options available from other firms, then the firm is not a monopoly. Still, arguments over whether substitutes are close or not close can be controversial.

While a monopolist can charge *any* price for its product, nonetheless the demand for the firm's product constrains the price. No monopolist, even one that is thoroughly protected by high barriers to entry, can require consumers to purchase its product. Because the monopolist is the only firm in the market, its demand curve is the same as the market demand curve, which is, unlike that for a perfectly competitive firm, downward-sloping.

Figure 9.3 illustrates this situation. The monopolist can either choose a point like R with a low price (Pl) and high quantity (Qh), or a point like S with a high price (Ph) and a low quantity (Ql), or some intermediate point. Setting the price too high will result in a low quantity sold, and will not bring in much revenue. Conversely, setting the price too low may result in a high quantity sold, but because of the low price, it will not bring in much revenue either. The challenge for the monopolist is to strike a profit-maximizing balance between the price it charges and the quantity that it sells. However, why isn't the perfectly competitive firm's demand curve also the market demand curve? See the following Clear It Up feature for the answer to this question.

What is the difference between perceived demand and market demand?

The demand curve as perceived by a perfectly competitive firm is not the overall market demand curve for that product. However, the firm's demand curve as perceived by a monopoly is the same as the market demand curve. The reason for the difference is that each perfectly competitive firm perceives the demand for its products in a market that includes many other firms. In effect, the demand curve perceived by a perfectly competitive firm is a tiny slice of the entire market demand curve. In contrast, a monopoly perceives demand for its product in a market where the monopoly is the only producer.

Total Cost and Total Revenue for a Monopolist

We can illustrate profits for a monopolist with a graph of total revenues and total costs, with the example of the hypothetical HealthPill firm in **Figure 9.4**. The total cost curve has its typical shape that we learned about in **Production, Costs and Industry Structure**, and that we used in **Perfect Competition**; that is, total costs rise and the curve grows steeper as output increases, as the final column of **Table 9.2** shows.

This OpenStax book is available for free at http://cnx.org/content/col12122/1.4

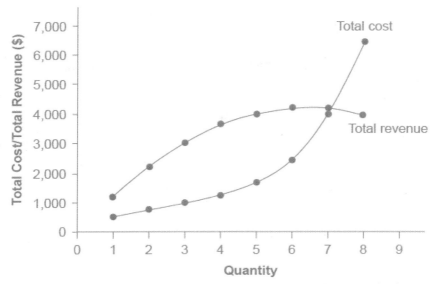

Figure 9.4 Total Revenue and Total Cost for the HealthPill Monopoly Total revenue for the monopoly firm called HealthPill first rises, then falls. Low levels of output bring in relatively little total revenue, because the quantity is low. High levels of output bring in relatively less revenue, because the high quantity pushes down the market price. The total cost curve is upward-sloping. Profits will be highest at the quantity of output where total revenue is most above total cost. The profit-maximizing level of output is not the same as the revenue-maximizing level of output, which should make sense, because profits take costs into account and revenues do not.

Quantity Q	Price P	Total Revenue TR	Total Cost TC
1	1,200	1,200	500
2	1,100	2,200	750
3	1,000	3,000	1,000
4	900	3,600	1,250
5	800	4,000	1,650
6	700	4,200	2,500
7	600	4,200	4,000
8	500	4,000	6,400

Table 9.2 Total Costs and Total Revenues of HealthPill

Total revenue, though, is different. Since a monopolist faces a downward sloping demand curve, the only way it can sell more output is by reducing its price. Selling more output raises revenue, but lowering price reduces it. Thus, the shape of total revenue isn't clear. Let's explore this using the data in **Table 9.2**, which shows quantities along the demand curve and the price at each quantity demanded, and then calculates total revenue by multiplying price times quantity at each level of output. (In this example, we give the output as 1, 2, 3, 4, and so on, for the sake of simplicity. If you prefer a dash of greater realism, you can imagine that the pharmaceutical company measures the pharmaceutical company measures these output levels and the corresponding prices per 1,000 or 10,000 pills.) As the figure illustrates, total revenue for a monopolist has the shape of a hill, first rising, next flattening out, and then falling. In this example, total revenue is highest at a quantity of 6 or 7.

However, the monopolist is not seeking to maximize revenue, but instead to earn the highest possible profit. In the

HealthPill example in **Figure 9.4**, the highest profit will occur at the quantity where total revenue is the farthest above total cost. This looks to be somewhere in the middle of the graph, but where exactly? It is easier to see the profit maximizing level of output by using the marginal approach, to which we turn next.

Marginal Revenue and Marginal Cost for a Monopolist

In the real world, a monopolist often does not have enough information to analyze its entire total revenues or total costs curves. After all, the firm does not know exactly what would happen if it were to alter production dramatically. However, a monopolist often has fairly reliable information about how changing output by small or moderate amounts will affect its marginal revenues and marginal costs, because it has had experience with such changes over time and because modest changes are easier to extrapolate from current experience. A monopolist can use information on marginal revenue and marginal cost to seek out the profit-maximizing combination of quantity and price.

Table 9.3 expands **Table 9.2** using the figures on total costs and total revenues from the HealthPill example to calculate marginal revenue and marginal cost. This monopoly faces typical upward-sloping marginal cost and downward sloping marginal revenue curves, as **Figure 9.5** shows.

Notice that marginal revenue is zero at a quantity of 7, and turns negative at quantities higher than 7. It may seem counterintuitive that marginal revenue could ever be zero or negative: after all, doesn't an increase in quantity sold not always mean more revenue? For a perfect competitor, each additional unit sold brought a positive marginal revenue, because marginal revenue was equal to the given market price. However, a monopolist can sell a larger quantity and see a decline in total revenue. When a monopolist increases sales by one unit, it gains some marginal revenue from selling that extra unit, but also loses some marginal revenue because it must now sell every other unit at a lower price. As the quantity sold becomes higher, at some point the drop in price is proportionally more than the increase in greater quantity of sales, causing a situation where more sales bring in less revenue. In other words, marginal revenue is negative.

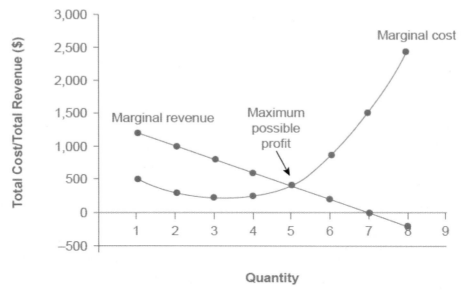

Figure 9.5 Marginal Revenue and Marginal Cost for the HealthPill Monopoly For a monopoly like HealthPill, marginal revenue decreases as it sells additional units of output. The marginal cost curve is upward-sloping. The profit-maximizing choice for the monopoly will be to produce at the quantity where marginal revenue is equal to marginal cost: that is, MR = MC. If the monopoly produces a lower quantity, then MR > MC at those levels of output, and the firm can make higher profits by expanding output. If the firm produces at a greater quantity, then MC > MR, and the firm can make higher profits by reducing its quantity of output.

This OpenStax book is available for free at http://cnx.org/content/col12122/1.4

Quantity Q	Total Revenue TR	Marginal Revenue MR	Total Cost TC	Marginal Cost MC
1	1,200	1,200	500	500
2	2,200	1,000	775	275
3	3,000	800	1,000	225
4	3,600	600	1,250	250
5	4,000	400	1,650	400
6	4,200	200	2,500	850
7	4,200	0	4,000	1,500
8	4,000	−200	6,400	2,400

Table 9.3 Costs and Revenues of HealthPill

A monopolist can determine its profit-maximizing price and quantity by analyzing the marginal revenue and marginal costs of producing an extra unit. If the marginal revenue exceeds the marginal cost, then the firm should produce the extra unit.

For example, at an output of 4 in **Figure 9.5**, marginal revenue is 600 and marginal cost is 250, so producing this unit will clearly add to overall profits. At an output of 5, marginal revenue is 400 and marginal cost is 400, so producing this unit still means overall profits are unchanged. However, expanding output from 5 to 6 would involve a marginal revenue of 200 and a marginal cost of 850, so that sixth unit would actually reduce profits. Thus, the monopoly can tell from the marginal revenue and marginal cost that of the choices in the table, the profit-maximizing level of output is 5.

The monopoly could seek out the profit-maximizing level of output by increasing quantity by a small amount, calculating marginal revenue and marginal cost, and then either increasing output as long as marginal revenue exceeds marginal cost or reducing output if marginal cost exceeds marginal revenue. This process works without any need to calculate total revenue and total cost. Thus, a profit-maximizing monopoly should follow the rule of producing up to the quantity where marginal revenue is equal to marginal cost—that is, MR = MC. This quantity is easy to identify graphically, where MR and MC intersect.

Work It Out ─O─O─O

Maximizing Profits

If you find it counterintuitive that producing where marginal revenue equals marginal cost will maximize profits, working through the numbers will help.

Step 1. Remember, we define marginal cost as the change in total cost from producing a small amount of additional output.

$$MC = \frac{\text{change in total cost}}{\text{change in quantity produced}}$$

Step 2. Note that in **Table 9.3**, as output increases from 1 to 2 units, total cost increases from $1500 to $1800. As a result, the marginal cost of the second unit will be:

$$MC = \frac{\$775 - \$500}{1}$$
$$= \$275$$

Step 3. Remember that, similarly, marginal revenue is the change in total revenue from selling a small amount of additional output.

$$MR = \frac{\text{change in total revenue}}{\text{change in quantity sold}}$$

Step 4. Note that in Table 9.3, as output increases from 1 to 2 units, total revenue increases from $1200 to $2200. As a result, the marginal revenue of the second unit will be:

$$MR = \frac{\$2200 - \$1200}{1}$$
$$= \$1000$$

Quantity Q	Marginal Revenue MR	Marginal Cost MC	Marginal Profit MP	Total Profit P
1	1,200	500	700	700
2	1,000	275	725	1,425
3	800	225	575	2,000
4	600	250	350	2,350
5	400	400	0	2,350
6	200	850	−650	1,700
7	0	1,500	−1,500	200
8	−200	2,400	−2,600	−2,400

Table 9.4 Marginal Revenue, Marginal Cost, Marginal and Total Profit

Table 9.4 repeats the marginal cost and marginal revenue data from Table 9.3, and adds two more columns: **Marginal profit** is the profitability of each additional unit sold. We define it as marginal revenue minus marginal cost. Finally, total profit is the sum of marginal profits. As long as marginal profit is positive, producing more output will increase total profits. When marginal profit turns negative, producing more output will decrease total profits. Total profit is maximized where marginal revenue equals marginal cost. In this example, maximum profit occurs at 5 units of output.

A perfectly competitive firm will also find its profit-maximizing level of output where MR = MC. The key difference with a perfectly competitive firm is that in the case of perfect competition, marginal revenue is equal to price (MR = P), while for a monopolist, marginal revenue is not equal to the price, because changes in quantity of output affect the price.

Illustrating Monopoly Profits

It is straightforward to calculate profits of given numbers for total revenue and total cost. However, the size of monopoly profits can also be illustrated graphically with Figure 9.6, which takes the marginal cost and marginal revenue curves from the previous exhibit and adds an average cost curve and the monopolist's perceived demand curve. Table 9.5 shows the data for these curves.

Quantity Q	Demand P	Marginal Revenue MR	Marginal Cost MC	Average Cost AC
1	1,200	1,200	500	500
2	1,100	1,000	275	388
3	1,000	800	225	333
4	900	600	250	313
5	800	400	400	330
6	700	200	850	417
7	600	0	1,500	571
8	500	−200	2,400	800

Table 9.5

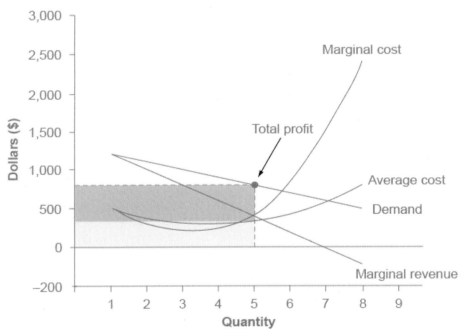

Figure 9.6 Illustrating Profits at the HealthPill Monopoly This figure begins with the same marginal revenue and marginal cost curves from the HealthPill monopoly from **Figure 9.5**. It then adds an average cost curve and the demand curve that the monopolist faces. The HealthPill firm first chooses the quantity where MR = MC. In this example, the quantity is 5. The monopolist then decides what price to charge by looking at the demand curve it faces. The large box, with quantity on the horizontal axis and demand (which shows the price) on the vertical axis, shows total revenue for the firm. The lighter-shaded box, which is quantity on the horizontal axis and average cost of production on the vertical axis shows the firm's total costs. The large total revenue box minus the smaller total cost box leaves the darkly shaded box that shows total profits. Since the price charged is above average cost, the firm is earning positive profits.

Figure 9.7 illustrates the three-step process where a monopolist: selects the profit-maximizing quantity to produce; decides what price to charge; determines total revenue, total cost, and profit.

Step 1: The Monopolist Determines Its Profit-Maximizing Level of Output

The firm can use the points on the demand curve D to calculate total revenue, and then, based on total revenue, calculate its marginal revenue curve. The profit-maximizing quantity will occur where MR = MC—or at the last possible point before marginal costs start exceeding marginal revenue. On **Figure 9.6**, MR = MC occurs at an output of 5.

Step 2: The Monopolist Decides What Price to Charge

The monopolist will charge what the market is willing to pay. A dotted line drawn straight up from the profit-maximizing quantity to the demand curve shows the profit-maximizing price which, in **Figure 9.6**, is $800. This price is above the average cost curve, which shows that the firm is earning profits.

Step 3: Calculate Total Revenue, Total Cost, and Profit

Total revenue is the overall shaded box, where the width of the box is the quantity sold and the height is the price. In **Figure 9.6**, this is 5 x $800 = $4000. In **Figure 9.6**, the bottom part of the shaded box, which is shaded more lightly, shows total costs; that is, quantity on the horizontal axis multiplied by average cost on the vertical axis or 5 x $330 = $1650. The larger box of total revenues minus the smaller box of total costs will equal profits, which the darkly shaded box shows. Using the numbers gives $4000 - $1650 = $2350. In a perfectly competitive market, the forces of entry would erode this profit in the long run. However, a monopolist is protected by barriers to entry. In fact, one obvious sign of a possible monopoly is when a firm earns profits year after year, while doing more or less the same thing, without ever seeing increased competition eroding those profits.

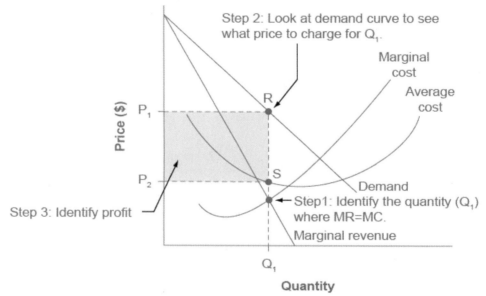

Figure 9.7 How a Profit-Maximizing Monopoly Decides Price In Step 1, the monopoly chooses the profit-maximizing level of output Q_1, by choosing the quantity where MR = MC. In Step 2, the monopoly decides how much to charge for output level Q_1 by drawing a line straight up from Q_1 to point R on its perceived demand curve. Thus, the monopoly will charge a price (P_1). In Step 3, the monopoly identifies its profit. Total revenue will be Q_1 multiplied by P_1. Total cost will be Q_1 multiplied by the average cost of producing Q_1, which point S shows on the average cost curve to be P_2. Profits will be the total revenue rectangle minus the total cost rectangle, which the shaded zone in the figure shows.

Why is a monopolist's marginal revenue always less than the price?

The marginal revenue curve for a monopolist always lies beneath the market demand curve. To understand why, think about increasing the quantity along the demand curve by one unit, so that you take one step down the demand curve to a slightly higher quantity but a slightly lower price. A demand curve is not sequential: It is not that first we sell Q_1 at a higher price, and then we sell Q_2 at a lower price. Rather, a demand curve is conditional: If we charge the higher price, we would sell Q_1. If, instead, we charge a lower price (on all the units that we sell), we would sell Q_2.

When we think about increasing the quantity sold by one unit, marginal revenue is affected in two ways. First, we sell one additional unit at the new market price. Second, all the previous units, which we sold at the higher price, now sell for less. Because of the lower price on all units sold, the marginal revenue of selling a unit is less than the price of that unit—and the marginal revenue curve is below the demand curve. *Tip*: For a straight-line demand curve, MR and demand have the same vertical intercept. As output increases, marginal revenue decreases twice as fast as demand, so that the horizontal intercept of MR is halfway to the horizontal intercept of demand. You can see this in the Figure 9.8.

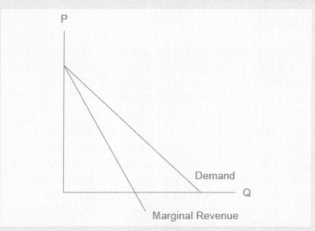

Figure 9.8 The Monopolist's Marginal Revenue Curve versus Demand Curve Because the market demand curve is conditional, the marginal revenue curve for a monopolist lies beneath the demand curve.

The Inefficiency of Monopoly

Most people criticize monopolies because they charge too high a price, but what economists object to is that monopolies do not supply enough output to be allocatively efficient. To understand why a monopoly is inefficient, it is useful to compare it with the benchmark model of perfect competition.

Allocative efficiency is an economic concept regarding efficiency at the social or societal level. It refers to producing the optimal quantity of some output, the quantity where the marginal benefit to society of one more unit just equals the marginal cost. The rule of profit maximization in a world of perfect competition was for each firm to produce the quantity of output where P = MC, where the price (P) is a measure of how much buyers value the good and the marginal cost (MC) is a measure of what marginal units cost society to produce. Following this rule assures allocative efficiency. If P > MC, then the marginal benefit to society (as measured by P) is greater than the marginal cost to society of producing additional units, and a greater quantity should be produced. However, in the case of monopoly, price is always greater than marginal cost at the profit-maximizing level of output, as you can see by looking back at Figure 9.6. Thus, consumers will suffer from a monopoly because it will sell a lower quantity in the market, at a higher price, than would have been the case in a perfectly competitive market.

The problem of inefficiency for monopolies often runs even deeper than these issues, and also involves incentives for efficiency over longer periods of time. There are counterbalancing incentives here. On one side, firms may strive for new inventions and new intellectual property because they want to become monopolies and earn high profits—at least for a few years until the competition catches up. In this way, monopolies may come to exist because of competitive pressures on firms. However, once a barrier to entry is in place, a monopoly that does not need to fear competition can just produce the same old products in the same old way—while still ringing up a healthy rate of profit. John Hicks, who won the Nobel Prize for economics in 1972, wrote in 1935: "The best of all monopoly profits is a quiet life." He did not mean the comment in a complimentary way. He meant that monopolies may bank their profits and slack off on trying to please their customers.

When AT&T provided all of the local and long-distance phone service in the United States, along with manufacturing most of the phone equipment, the payment plans and types of phones did not change much. The old joke was that you could have any color phone you wanted, as long as it was black. However, in 1982, government litigation split up AT&T into a number of local phone companies, a long-distance phone company, and a phone equipment manufacturer. An explosion of innovation followed. Services like call waiting, caller ID, three-way calling, voice mail through the phone company, mobile phones, and wireless connections to the internet all became available. Companies offered a wide range of payment plans, as well. It was no longer true that all phones were black. Instead, phones came in a wide variety of shapes and colors. The end of the telephone monopoly brought lower prices, a greater quantity of services, and also a wave of innovation aimed at attracting and pleasing customers.

Bring it Home

The Rest is History

In the opening case, we presented the East India Company and the Confederate States as a monopoly or near monopoly provider of a good. Nearly every American schoolchild knows the result of the "unwelcome visit" the "Mohawks" bestowed upon Boston Harbor's tea-bearing ships—the Boston Tea Party. Regarding the cotton industry, we also know Great Britain remained neutral during the Civil War, taking neither side during the conflict.

Did the monopoly nature of these business have unintended and historical consequences? Might the American Revolution have been deterred, if the East India Company had sailed the tea-bearing ships back to England? Might the southern states have made different decisions had they not been so confident "King Cotton" would force diplomatic recognition of the Confederate States of America? Of course, it is not possible to definitively answer these questions. We cannot roll back the clock and try a different scenario. We can, however, consider the monopoly nature of these businesses and the roles they played and hypothesize about what might have occurred under different circumstances.

Perhaps if there had been legal free tea trade, the colonists would have seen things differently. There was smuggled Dutch tea in the colonial market. If the colonists had been able to freely purchase Dutch tea, they would have paid lower prices and avoided the tax.

What about the cotton monopoly? With one in five jobs in Great Britain depending on Southern cotton and the Confederate States as nearly the sole provider of that cotton, why did Great Britain remain neutral during the Civil War? At the beginning of the war, Britain simply drew down massive stores of cotton. These stockpiles lasted until near the end of 1862. Why did Britain not recognize the Confederacy at that point? Two reasons: The Emancipation Proclamation and new sources of cotton. Having outlawed slavery throughout the United Kingdom in 1833, it was politically impossible for Great Britain, empty cotton warehouses or not, to recognize, diplomatically, the Confederate States. In addition, during the two years it took to draw down the stockpiles, Britain expanded cotton imports from India, Egypt, and Brazil.

Monopoly sellers often see no threats to their superior marketplace position. In these examples did the power of the monopoly blind the decision makers to other possibilities? Perhaps. As a result of their actions, this is how history unfolded.

This OpenStax book is available for free at http://cnx.org/content/col12122/1.4

KEY TERMS

allocative efficiency producing the optimal quantity of some output; the quantity where the marginal benefit to society of one more unit just equals the marginal cost

barriers to entry the legal, technological, or market forces that may discourage or prevent potential competitors from entering a market

copyright a form of legal protection to prevent copying, for commercial purposes, original works of authorship, including books and music

deregulation removing government controls over setting prices and quantities in certain industries

intellectual property the body of law including patents, trademarks, copyrights, and trade secret law that protect the right of inventors to produce and sell their inventions

legal monopoly legal prohibitions against competition, such as regulated monopolies and intellectual property protection

marginal profit profit of one more unit of output, computed as marginal revenue minus marginal cost

monopoly a situation in which one firm produces all of the output in a market

natural monopoly economic conditions in the industry, for example, economies of scale or control of a critical resource, that limit effective competition

patent a government rule that gives the inventor the exclusive legal right to make, use, or sell the invention for a limited time

predatory pricing when an existing firm uses sharp but temporary price cuts to discourage new competition

trade secrets methods of production kept secret by the producing firm

trademark an identifying symbol or name for a particular good and can only be used by the firm that registered that trademark

KEY CONCEPTS AND SUMMARY

9.1 How Monopolies Form: Barriers to Entry

Barriers to entry prevent or discourage competitors from entering the market. These barriers include: economies of scale that lead to natural monopoly; control of a physical resource; legal restrictions on competition; patent, trademark and copyright protection; and practices to intimidate the competition like predatory pricing. Intellectual property refers to legally guaranteed ownership of an idea, rather than a physical item. The laws that protect intellectual property include patents, copyrights, trademarks, and trade secrets. A natural monopoly arises when economies of scale persist over a large enough range of output that if one firm supplies the entire market, no other firm can enter without facing a cost disadvantage.

9.2 How a Profit-Maximizing Monopoly Chooses Output and Price

A monopolist is not a price taker, because when it decides what quantity to produce, it also determines the market price. For a monopolist, total revenue is relatively low at low quantities of output, because it is not selling much. Total revenue is also relatively low at very high quantities of output, because a very high quantity will sell only at a low price. Thus, total revenue for a monopolist will start low, rise, and then decline. The marginal revenue for a monopolist from selling additional units will decline. Each additional unit a monopolist sells will push down the overall market price, and as it sells more units, this lower price applies to increasingly more units.

The monopolist will select the profit-maximizing level of output where MR = MC, and then charge the price for that quantity of output as determined by the market demand curve. If that price is above average cost, the monopolist earns positive profits.

Monopolists are not productively efficient, because they do not produce at the minimum of the average cost curve. Monopolists are not allocatively efficient, because they do not produce at the quantity where P = MC. As a result, monopolists produce less, at a higher average cost, and charge a higher price than would a combination of firms in a perfectly competitive industry. Monopolists also may lack incentives for innovation, because they need not fear entry.

SELF-CHECK QUESTIONS

1. Classify the following as a government-enforced barrier to entry, a barrier to entry that is not government-enforced, or a situation that does not involve a barrier to entry.
   a. A patented invention
   b. A popular but easily copied restaurant recipe
   c. An industry where economies of scale are very small compared to the size of demand in the market
   d. A well-established reputation for slashing prices in response to new entry
   e. A well-respected brand name that has been carefully built up over many years

2. Classify the following as a government-enforced barrier to entry, a barrier to entry that is not government-enforced, or a situation that does not involve a barrier to entry.
   a. A city passes a law on how many licenses it will issue for taxicabs
   b. A city passes a law that all taxicab drivers must pass a driving safety test and have insurance
   c. A well-known trademark
   d. Owning a spring that offers very pure water
   e. An industry where economies of scale are very large compared to the size of demand in the market

3. Suppose the local electrical utility, a legal monopoly based on economies of scale, was split into four firms of equal size, with the idea that eliminating the monopoly would promote competitive pricing of electricity. What do you anticipate would happen to prices?

4. If Congress reduced the period of patent protection from 20 years to 10 years, what would likely happen to the amount of private research and development?

5. Suppose demand for a monopoly's product falls so that its profit-maximizing price is below average variable cost. How much output should the firm supply? *Hint*: Draw the graph.

6. Imagine a monopolist could charge a different price to every customer based on how much he or she were willing to pay. How would this affect monopoly profits?

REVIEW QUESTIONS

7. How is monopoly different from perfect competition?

8. What is a barrier to entry? Give some examples.

9. What is a natural monopoly?

10. What is a legal monopoly?

11. What is predatory pricing?

12. How is intellectual property different from other property?

13. What legal mechanisms protect intellectual property?

14. In what sense is a natural monopoly "natural"?

15. How is the demand curve perceived by a perfectly competitive firm different from the demand curve perceived by a monopolist?

16. How does the demand curve perceived by a monopolist compare with the market demand curve?

17. Is a monopolist a price taker? Explain briefly.

This OpenStax book is available for free at http://cnx.org/content/col12122/1.4

18. What is the usual shape of a total revenue curve for a monopolist? Why?

19. What is the usual shape of a marginal revenue curve for a monopolist? Why?

20. How can a monopolist identify the profit-maximizing level of output if it knows its total revenue and total cost curves?

21. How can a monopolist identify the profit-maximizing level of output if it knows its marginal revenue and marginal costs?

22. When a monopolist identifies its profit-maximizing quantity of output, how does it decide what price to charge?

23. Is a monopolist allocatively efficient? Why or why not?

24. How does the quantity produced and price charged by a monopolist compare to that of a perfectly competitive firm?

CRITICAL THINKING QUESTIONS

25. ALCOA does not have the monopoly power it once had. How do you suppose their barriers to entry were weakened?

26. Why are generic pharmaceuticals significantly cheaper than name brand ones?

27. For many years, the Justice Department has tried to break up large firms like IBM, Microsoft, and most recently Google, on the grounds that their large market share made them essentially monopolies. In a global market, where U.S. firms compete with firms from other countries, would this policy make the same sense as it might in a purely domestic context?

28. Intellectual property laws are intended to promote innovation, but some economists, such as Milton Friedman, have argued that such laws are not desirable. In the United States, there is no intellectual property protection for food recipes or for fashion designs. Considering the state of these two industries, and bearing in mind the discussion of the inefficiency of monopolies, can you think of any reasons why intellectual property laws might hinder innovation in some cases?

29. Imagine that you are managing a small firm and thinking about entering the market of a monopolist. The monopolist is currently charging a high price, and you have calculated that you can make a nice profit charging 10% less than the monopolist. Before you go ahead and challenge the monopolist, what possibility should you consider for how the monopolist might react?

30. If a monopoly firm is earning profits, how much would you expect these profits to be diminished by entry in the long run?

PROBLEMS

31. Return to **Figure 9.2**. Suppose P_0 is $10 and P_1 is $11. Suppose a new firm with the same LRAC curve as the incumbent tries to break into the market by selling 4,000 units of output. Estimate from the graph what the new firm's average cost of producing output would be. If the incumbent continues to produce 6,000 units, how much output would the two firms supply to the market? Estimate what would happen to the market price as a result of the supply of both the incumbent firm and the new entrant. Approximately how much profit would each firm earn?

32. Draw the demand curve, marginal revenue, and marginal cost curves from **Figure 9.6**, and identify the quantity of output the monopoly wishes to supply and the price it will charge. Suppose demand for the monopoly's product increases dramatically. Draw the new demand curve. What happens to the marginal revenue as a result of the increase in demand? What happens to the marginal cost curve? Identify the new profit-maximizing quantity and price. Does the answer make sense to you?

33. Draw a monopolist's demand curve, marginal revenue, and marginal cost curves. Identify the monopolist's profit-maximizing output level. Now, think about a slightly higher level of output (say $Q_0 + 1$). According to the graph, is there any consumer willing to pay more than the marginal cost of that new level of output? If so, what does this mean?

This OpenStax book is available for free at http://cnx.org/content/col12122/1.4

10 | Monopolistic Competition and Oligopoly

Figure 10.1 Competing Brands? The laundry detergent market is one that is characterized neither as perfect competition nor monopoly. (Credit: modification of work by Pixel Drip/Flickr Creative Commons)

Bring it Home

The Temptation to Defy the Law

Laundry detergent and bags of ice—products of industries that seem pretty mundane, maybe even boring. Hardly! Both have been the center of clandestine meetings and secret deals worthy of a spy novel. In France, between 1997 and 2004, the top four laundry detergent producers (Proctor & Gamble, Henkel, Unilever, and Colgate-Palmolive) controlled about 90 percent of the French soap market. Officials from the soap firms were meeting secretly, in out-of-the-way, small cafés around Paris. Their goals: Stamp out competition and set prices.

Around the same time, the top five Midwest ice makers (Home City Ice, Lang Ice, Tinley Ice, Sisler's Dairy, and Products of Ohio) had similar goals in mind when they secretly agreed to divide up the bagged ice market.

If both groups could meet their goals, it would enable each to act as though they were a single firm—in essence, a monopoly—and enjoy monopoly-size profits. The problem? In many parts of the world, including the European Union and the United States, it is illegal for firms to divide markets and set prices collaboratively.

These two cases provide examples of markets that are characterized neither as perfect competition nor monopoly. Instead, these firms are competing in market structures that lie between the extremes of monopoly and perfect competition. How do they behave? Why do they exist? We will revisit this case later, to find out what happened.

Introduction to Monopolistic Competition and Oligopoly

In this chapter, you will learn about:

- Monopolistic Competition
- Oligopoly

Perfect competition and monopoly are at opposite ends of the competition spectrum. A perfectly competitive market has many firms selling identical products, who all act as price takers in the face of the competition. If you recall, price takers are firms that have no market power. They simply have to take the market price as given.

Monopoly arises when a single firm sells a product for which there are no close substitutes. We consider Microsoft, for instance, as a monopoly because it dominates the operating systems market.

What about the vast majority of real world firms and organizations that fall between these extremes, firms that we could describe as **imperfectly competitive**? What determines their behavior? They have more influence over the price they charge than perfectly competitive firms, but not as much as a monopoly. What will they do?

One type of imperfectly competitive market is **monopolistic competition**. Monopolistically competitive markets feature a large number of competing firms, but the products that they sell are not identical. Consider, as an example, the Mall of America in Minnesota, the largest shopping mall in the United States. In 2010, the Mall of America had 24 stores that sold women's "ready-to-wear" clothing (like Ann Taylor and Urban Outfitters), another 50 stores that sold clothing for both men and women (like Banana Republic, J. Crew, and Nordstrom's), plus 14 more stores that sold women's specialty clothing (like Motherhood Maternity and Victoria's Secret). Most of the markets that consumers encounter at the retail level are monopolistically competitive.

The other type of imperfectly competitive market is **oligopoly**. Oligopolistic markets are those which a small number of firms dominate. Commercial aircraft provides a good example: Boeing and Airbus each produce slightly less than 50% of the large commercial aircraft in the world. Another example is the U.S. soft drink industry, which Coca-Cola and Pepsi dominate. We characterize oligopolies by high barriers to entry with firms choosing output, pricing, and other decisions strategically based on the decisions of the other firms in the market. In this chapter, we first explore how monopolistically competitive firms will choose their profit-maximizing level of output. We will then discuss oligopolistic firms, which face two conflicting temptations: to collaborate as if they were a single monopoly, or to individually compete to gain profits by expanding output levels and cutting prices. Oligopolistic markets and firms can also take on elements of monopoly and of perfect competition.

10.1 | Monopolistic Competition

By the end of this section, you will be able to:
- Explain the significance of differentiated products
- Describe how a monopolistic competitor chooses price and quantity
- Discuss entry, exit, and efficiency as they pertain to monopolistic competition
- Analyze how advertising can impact monopolistic competition

Monopolistic competition involves many firms competing against each other, but selling products that are distinctive in some way. Examples include stores that sell different styles of clothing; restaurants or grocery stores that sell a variety of food; and even products like golf balls or beer that may be at least somewhat similar but differ in public perception because of advertising and brand names. There are over 600,000 restaurants in the United States. When products are distinctive, each firm has a mini-monopoly on its particular style or flavor or brand name. However, firms producing such products must also compete with other styles and flavors and brand names. The term "monopolistic competition" captures this mixture of mini-monopoly and tough competition, and the following Clear It Up feature

This OpenStax book is available for free at http://cnx.org/content/col12122/1.4

introduces its derivation.

Clear It Up

Who invented the theory of imperfect competition?

Two economists independently but simultaneously developed the theory of imperfect competition in 1933. The first was Edward Chamberlin of Harvard University who published *The Economics of Monopolistic Competition*. The second was Joan Robinson of Cambridge University who published *The Economics of Imperfect Competition*. Robinson subsequently became interested in macroeconomics and she became a prominent Keynesian, and later a post-Keynesian economist. (See the Welcome to Economics! and The Keynesian Perspective chapters for more on Keynes.)

Differentiated Products

A firm can try to make its products different from those of its competitors in several ways: physical aspects of the product, location from which it sells the product, intangible aspects of the product, and perceptions of the product. We call products that are distinctive in one of these ways **differentiated products**.

Physical aspects of a product include all the phrases you hear in advertisements: unbreakable bottle, nonstick surface, freezer-to-microwave, non-shrink, extra spicy, newly redesigned for your comfort. A firm's location can also create a difference between producers. For example, a gas station located at a heavily traveled intersection can probably sell more gas, because more cars drive by that corner. A supplier to an automobile manufacturer may find that it is an advantage to locate close to the car factory.

Intangible aspects can differentiate a product, too. Some intangible aspects may be promises like a guarantee of satisfaction or money back, a reputation for high quality, services like free delivery, or offering a loan to purchase the product. Finally, product differentiation may occur in the minds of buyers. For example, many people could not tell the difference in taste between common varieties of ketchup or mayonnaise if they were blindfolded but, because of past habits and advertising, they have strong preferences for certain brands. Advertising can play a role in shaping these intangible preferences.

The concept of differentiated products is closely related to the degree of variety that is available. If everyone in the economy wore only blue jeans, ate only white bread, and drank only tap water, then the markets for clothing, food, and drink would be much closer to perfectly competitive. The variety of styles, flavors, locations, and characteristics creates product differentiation and monopolistic competition.

Perceived Demand for a Monopolistic Competitor

A monopolistically competitive firm perceives a demand for its goods that is an intermediate case between monopoly and competition. Figure 10.2 offers a reminder that the demand curve that a perfectly competitive firm faces is perfectly elastic or flat, because the perfectly competitive firm can sell any quantity it wishes at the prevailing market price. In contrast, the demand curve, as faced by a monopolist, is the market demand curve, since a monopolist is the only firm in the market, and hence is downward sloping.

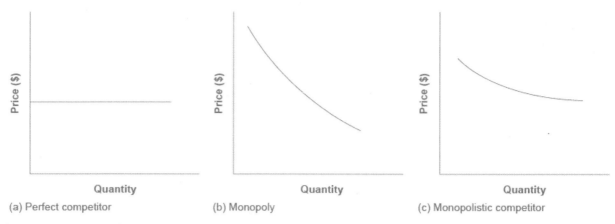

(a) Perfect competitor   (b) Monopoly   (c) Monopolistic competitor

Figure 10.2 Perceived Demand for Firms in Different Competitive Settings   The demand curve that a perfectly competitive firm faces is perfectly elastic, meaning it can sell all the output it wishes at the prevailing market price. The demand curve that a monopoly faces is the market demand. It can sell more output only by decreasing the price it charges. The demand curve that a monopolistically competitive firm faces falls in between.

The demand curve as a monopolistic competitor faces is not flat, but rather downward-sloping, which means that the monopolistic competitor can raise its price without losing all of its customers or lower the price and gain more customers. Since there are substitutes, the demand curve facing a monopolistically competitive firm is more elastic than that of a monopoly where there are no close substitutes. If a monopolist raises its price, some consumers will choose not to purchase its product—but they will then need to buy a completely different product. However, when a monopolistic competitor raises its price, some consumers will choose not to purchase the product at all, but others will choose to buy a similar product from another firm. If a monopolistic competitor raises its price, it will not lose as many customers as would a perfectly competitive firm, but it will lose more customers than would a monopoly that raised its prices.

At a glance, the demand curves that a monopoly and a monopolistic competitor face look similar—that is, they both slope down. However, the underlying economic meaning of these perceived demand curves is different, because a monopolist faces the market demand curve and a monopolistic competitor does not. Rather, a monopolistically competitive firm's demand curve is but one of many firms that make up the "before" market demand curve. Are you following? If so, how would you categorize the market for golf balls? Take a swing, then see the following Clear It Up feature.

Are golf balls really differentiated products?

Monopolistic competition refers to an industry that has more than a few firms, each offering a product which, from the consumer's perspective, is different from its competitors. The U.S. Golf Association runs a laboratory that tests 20,000 golf balls a year. There are strict rules for what makes a golf ball legal. A ball's weight cannot exceed 1.620 ounces and its diameter cannot be less than 1.680 inches (which is a weight of 45.93 grams and a diameter of 42.67 millimeters, in case you were wondering). The Association also tests the balls by hitting them at different speeds. For example, the distance test involves having a mechanical golfer hit the ball with a titanium driver and a swing speed of 120 miles per hour. As the testing center explains: "The USGA system then uses an array of sensors that accurately measure the flight of a golf ball during a short, indoor trajectory from a ball launcher. From this flight data, a computer calculates the lift and drag forces that are generated by the speed, spin, and dimple pattern of the ball. ... The distance limit is 317 yards."

Over 1800 golf balls made by more than 100 companies meet the USGA standards. The balls do differ in various ways, such as the pattern of dimples on the ball, the types of plastic on the cover and in the cores, and other factors. Since all balls need to conform to the USGA tests, they are much more alike than different.

This OpenStax book is available for free at http://cnx.org/content/col12122/1.4

In other words, golf ball manufacturers are monopolistically competitive.

However, retail sales of golf balls are about $500 million per year, which means that many large companies have a powerful incentive to persuade players that golf balls are highly differentiated and that it makes a huge difference which one you choose. Sure, Tiger Woods can tell the difference. For the average amateur golfer who plays a few times a summer—and who loses many golf balls to the woods and lake and needs to buy new ones—most golf balls are pretty much indistinguishable.

How a Monopolistic Competitor Chooses Price and Quantity

The monopolistically competitive firm decides on its profit-maximizing quantity and price in much the same way as a monopolist. A monopolistic competitor, like a monopolist, faces a downward-sloping demand curve, and so it will choose some combination of price and quantity along its perceived demand curve.

As an example of a profit-maximizing monopolistic competitor, consider the Authentic Chinese Pizza store, which serves pizza with cheese, sweet and sour sauce, and your choice of vegetables and meats. Although Authentic Chinese Pizza must compete against other pizza businesses and restaurants, it has a differentiated product. The firm's perceived demand curve is downward sloping, as **Figure 10.3** shows and the first two columns of **Table 10.1**.

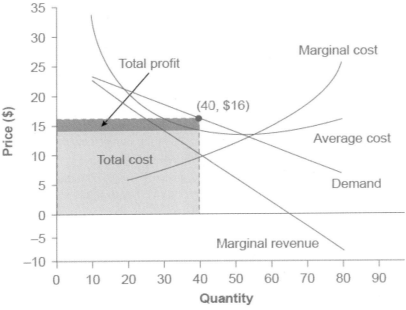

Figure 10.3 How a Monopolistic Competitor Chooses its Profit Maximizing Output and Price   To maximize profits, the Authentic Chinese Pizza shop would choose a quantity where marginal revenue equals marginal cost, or Q where MR = MC. Here it would choose a quantity of 40 and a price of $16.

Quantity	Price	Total Revenue	Marginal Revenue	Total Cost	Marginal Cost	Average Cost
10	$23	$230	$23	$340	$34	$34
20	$20	$400	$17	$400	$6	$20
30	$18	$540	$14	$480	$8	$16
40	$16	$640	$10	$580	$10	$14.50

Table 10.1 Revenue and Cost Schedule

Quantity	Price	Total Revenue	Marginal Revenue	Total Cost	Marginal Cost	Average Cost
50	$14	$700	$6	$700	$12	$14
60	$12	$720	$2	$840	$14	$14
70	$10	$700	–$2	$1,020	$18	$14.57
80	$8	$640	–$6	$1,280	$26	$16

Table 10.1 Revenue and Cost Schedule

We can multiply the combinations of price and quantity at each point on the demand curve to calculate the total revenue that the firm would receive, which is in the third column of **Table 10.1**. We calculate marginal revenue, in the fourth column, as the change in total revenue divided by the change in quantity. The final columns of **Table 10.1** show total cost, marginal cost, and average cost. As always, we calculate marginal cost by dividing the change in total cost by the change in quantity, while we calculate average cost by dividing total cost by quantity. The following Work It Out feature shows how these firms calculate how much of their products to supply at what price.

Work It Out

How a Monopolistic Competitor Determines How Much to Produce and at What Price

The process by which a monopolistic competitor chooses its profit-maximizing quantity and price resembles closely how a monopoly makes these decisions process. First, the firm selects the profit-maximizing quantity to produce. Then the firm decides what price to charge for that quantity.

Step 1. The monopolistic competitor determines its profit-maximizing level of output. In this case, the Authentic Chinese Pizza company will determine the profit-maximizing quantity to produce by considering its marginal revenues and marginal costs. Two scenarios are possible:

- If the firm is producing at a quantity of output where marginal revenue exceeds marginal cost, then the firm should keep expanding production, because each marginal unit is adding to profit by bringing in more revenue than its cost. In this way, the firm will produce up to the quantity where MR = MC.

- If the firm is producing at a quantity where marginal costs exceed marginal revenue, then each marginal unit is costing more than the revenue it brings in, and the firm will increase its profits by reducing the quantity of output until MR = MC.

In this example, MR and MC intersect at a quantity of 40, which is the profit-maximizing level of output for the firm.

Step 2. The monopolistic competitor decides what price to charge. When the firm has determined its profit-maximizing quantity of output, it can then look to its perceived demand curve to find out what it can charge for that quantity of output. On the graph, we show this process as a vertical line reaching up through the profit-maximizing quantity until it hits the firm's perceived demand curve. For Authentic Chinese Pizza, it should charge a price of $16 per pizza for a quantity of 40.

Once the firm has chosen price and quantity, it's in a position to calculate total revenue, total cost, and profit. At a quantity of 40, the price of $16 lies above the average cost curve, so the firm is making economic profits. From **Table 10.1** we can see that, at an output of 40, the firm's total revenue is $640 and its total cost is $580, so profits are $60. In **Figure 10.3**, the firm's total revenues are the rectangle with the quantity of 40 on the horizontal axis and the price of $16 on the vertical axis. The firm's total costs are the light shaded rectangle with the same quantity of 40 on the horizontal axis but the average cost of $14.50 on the vertical axis. Profits are total revenues minus total costs, which is the shaded area above the average cost curve.

This OpenStax book is available for free at http://cnx.org/content/col12122/1.4

Although the process by which a monopolistic competitor makes decisions about quantity and price is similar to the way in which a monopolist makes such decisions, two differences are worth remembering. First, although both a monopolist and a monopolistic competitor face downward-sloping demand curves, the monopolist's perceived demand curve is the market demand curve, while the perceived demand curve for a monopolistic competitor is based on the extent of its product differentiation and how many competitors it faces. Second, a monopolist is surrounded by barriers to entry and need not fear entry, but a monopolistic competitor who earns profits must expect the entry of firms with similar, but differentiated, products.

Monopolistic Competitors and Entry

If one monopolistic competitor earns positive economic profits, other firms will be tempted to enter the market. A gas station with a great location must worry that other gas stations might open across the street or down the road—and perhaps the new gas stations will sell coffee or have a carwash or some other attraction to lure customers. A successful restaurant with a unique barbecue sauce must be concerned that other restaurants will try to copy the sauce or offer their own unique recipes. A laundry detergent with a great reputation for quality must take note that other competitors may seek to build their own reputations.

The entry of other firms into the same general market (like gas, restaurants, or detergent) shifts the demand curve that a monopolistically competitive firm faces. As more firms enter the market, the quantity demanded at a given price for any particular firm will decline, and the firm's perceived demand curve will shift to the left. As a firm's perceived demand curve shifts to the left, its marginal revenue curve will shift to the left, too. The shift in marginal revenue will change the profit-maximizing quantity that the firm chooses to produce, since marginal revenue will then equal marginal cost at a lower quantity.

Figure 10.4 (a) shows a situation in which a monopolistic competitor was earning a profit with its original perceived demand curve (D_0). The intersection of the marginal revenue curve (MR_0) and marginal cost curve (MC) occurs at point S, corresponding to quantity Q_0, which is associated on the demand curve at point T with price P_0. The combination of price P_0 and quantity Q_0 lies above the average cost curve, which shows that the firm is earning positive economic profits.

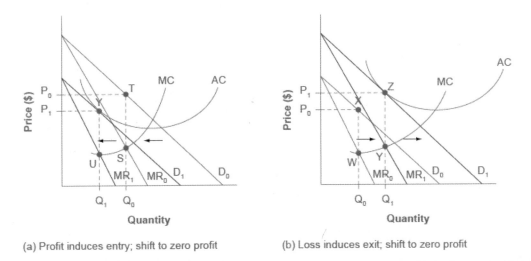

(a) Profit induces entry; shift to zero profit

(b) Loss induces exit; shift to zero profit

Figure 10.4 Monopolistic Competition, Entry, and Exit (a) At P_0 and Q_0, the monopolistically competitive firm in this figure is making a positive economic profit. This is clear because if you follow the dotted line above Q_0, you can see that price is above average cost. Positive economic profits attract competing firms to the industry, driving the original firm's demand down to D_1. At the new equilibrium quantity (P_1, Q_1), the original firm is earning zero economic profits, and entry into the industry ceases. In (b) the opposite occurs. At P_0 and Q_0, the firm is losing money. If you follow the dotted line above Q_0, you can see that average cost is above price. Losses induce firms to leave the industry. When they do, demand for the original firm rises to D_1, where once again the firm is earning zero economic profit.

Unlike a monopoly, with its high barriers to entry, a monopolistically competitive firm with positive economic profits will attract competition. When another competitor enters the market, the original firm's perceived demand curve shifts to the left, from D_0 to D_1, and the associated marginal revenue curve shifts from MR_0 to MR_1. The new profit-maximizing output is Q_1, because the intersection of the MR_1 and MC now occurs at point U. Moving vertically up from that quantity on the new demand curve, the optimal price is at P_1.

As long as the firm is earning positive economic profits, new competitors will continue to enter the market, reducing the original firm's demand and marginal revenue curves. The long-run equilibrium is in the figure at point Y, where the firm's perceived demand curve touches the average cost curve. When price is equal to average cost, economic profits are zero. Thus, although a monopolistically competitive firm may earn positive economic profits in the short term, the process of new entry will drive down economic profits to zero in the long run. Remember that zero economic profit is not equivalent to zero accounting profit. A zero economic profit means the firm's accounting profit is equal to what its resources could earn in their next best use. **Figure 10.4** (b) shows the reverse situation, where a monopolistically competitive firm is originally losing money. The adjustment to long-run equilibrium is analogous to the previous example. The economic losses lead to firms exiting, which will result in increased demand for this particular firm, and consequently lower losses. Firms exit up to the point where there are no more losses in this market, for example when the demand curve touches the average cost curve, as in point Z.

Monopolistic competitors can make an economic profit or loss in the short run, but in the long run, entry and exit will drive these firms toward a zero economic profit outcome. However, the zero economic profit outcome in monopolistic competition looks different from the zero economic profit outcome in perfect competition in several ways relating both to efficiency and to variety in the market.

Monopolistic Competition and Efficiency

The long-term result of entry and exit in a perfectly competitive market is that all firms end up selling at the price level determined by the lowest point on the average cost curve. This outcome is why perfect competition displays productive efficiency: goods are produced at the lowest possible average cost. However, in monopolistic competition, the end result of entry and exit is that firms end up with a price that lies on the downward-sloping portion of the average cost curve, not at the very bottom of the AC curve. Thus, monopolistic competition will not be productively efficient.

In a perfectly competitive market, each firm produces at a quantity where price is set equal to marginal cost, both in the short and long run. This outcome is why perfect competition displays allocative efficiency: the social benefits of additional production, as measured by the marginal benefit, which is the same as the price, equal the marginal costs to society of that production. In a monopolistically competitive market, the rule for maximizing profit is to set MR = MC—and price is higher than marginal revenue, not equal to it because the demand curve is downward sloping. When P > MC, which is the outcome in a monopolistically competitive market, the benefits to society of providing additional quantity, as measured by the price that people are willing to pay, exceed the marginal costs to society of producing those units. A monopolistically competitive firm does not produce more, which means that society loses the net benefit of those extra units. This is the same argument we made about monopoly, but in this case the allocative inefficiency will be smaller. Thus, a monopolistically competitive industry will produce a lower quantity of a good and charge a higher price for it than would a perfectly competitive industry. See the following Clear It Up feature for more detail on the impact of demand shifts.

Why does a shift in perceived demand cause a shift in marginal revenue?

We use the combinations of price and quantity at each point on a firm's perceived demand curve to calculate total revenue for each combination of price and quantity. We then use this information on total revenue to calculate marginal revenue, which is the change in total revenue divided by the change in quantity. A change in perceived demand will change total revenue at every quantity of output and in turn, the change in total revenue will shift marginal revenue at each quantity of output. Thus, when entry occurs in a monopolistically competitive industry, the perceived demand curve for each firm will shift to the left, because a smaller quantity will be demanded at any given price. Another way of interpreting this shift in demand is to notice that, for each quantity sold, the firm will charge a lower price. Consequently, the marginal revenue will be lower for each quantity sold—and the marginal revenue curve will shift to the left as well. Conversely, exit causes the perceived demand curve for a monopolistically competitive firm to shift to the right and the corresponding marginal revenue curve to shift right, too.

A monopolistically competitive industry does not display productive or allocative efficiency in either the short run, when firms are making economic profits and losses, nor in the long run, when firms are earning zero profits.

The Benefits of Variety and Product Differentiation

Even though monopolistic competition does not provide productive efficiency or allocative efficiency, it does have benefits of its own. Product differentiation is based on variety and innovation. Most people would prefer to live in an economy with many kinds of clothes, foods, and car styles; not in a world of perfect competition where everyone will always wear blue jeans and white shirts, eat only spaghetti with plain red sauce, and drive an identical model of car. Most people would prefer to live in an economy where firms are struggling to figure out ways of attracting customers by methods like friendlier service, free delivery, guarantees of quality, variations on existing products, and a better shopping experience.

Economists have struggled, with only partial success, to address the question of whether a market-oriented economy produces the optimal amount of variety. Critics of market-oriented economies argue that society does not really need dozens of different athletic shoes or breakfast cereals or automobiles. They argue that much of the cost of creating such a high degree of product differentiation, and then of advertising and marketing this differentiation, is socially wasteful—that is, most people would be just as happy with a smaller range of differentiated products produced and sold at a lower price. Defenders of a market-oriented economy respond that if people do not want to buy differentiated products or highly advertised brand names, no one is forcing them to do so. Moreover, they argue that consumers benefit substantially when firms seek short-term profits by providing differentiated products. This controversy may never be fully resolved, in part because deciding on the optimal amount of variety is very difficult, and in part because the two sides often place different values on what variety means for consumers. Read the following Clear It Up feature for a discussion on the role that advertising plays in monopolistic competition.

How does advertising impact monopolistic competition?

The U.S. economy spent about $180.12 billion on advertising in 2014, according to eMarketer.com. Roughly one third of this was television advertising, and another third was divided roughly equally between internet, newspapers, and radio. The remaining third was divided between direct mail, magazines, telephone directory yellow pages, and billboards. Mobile devices are increasing the opportunities for advertisers.

Advertising is all about explaining to people, or making people believe, that the products of one firm are differentiated from another firm's products. In the framework of monopolistic competition, there are two ways to conceive of how advertising works: either advertising causes a firm's perceived demand curve to become more inelastic (that is, it causes the perceived demand curve to become steeper); or advertising causes demand for the firm's product to increase (that is, it causes the firm's perceived demand curve to shift to the right). In either case, a successful advertising campaign may allow a firm to sell either a greater quantity or to charge a higher price, or both, and thus increase its profits.

However, economists and business owners have also long suspected that much of the advertising may only offset other advertising. Economist A. C. Pigou wrote the following back in 1920 in his book, *The Economics of Welfare*:

> It may happen that expenditures on advertisement made by competing monopolists [that is, what we now call monopolistic competitors] will simply neutralise one another, and leave the industrial position exactly as it would have been if neither had expended anything. For, clearly, if each of two rivals makes equal efforts to attract the favour of the public away from the other, the total result is the same as it would have been if neither had made any effort at all.

10.2 | Oligopoly

By the end of this section, you will be able to:

- Explain why and how oligopolies exist
- Contrast collusion and competition
- Interpret and analyze the prisoner's dilemma diagram
- Evaluate the tradeoffs of imperfect competition

Many purchases that individuals make at the retail level are produced in markets that are neither perfectly competitive, monopolies, nor monopolistically competitive. Rather, they are oligopolies. Oligopoly arises when a small number of large firms have all or most of the sales in an industry. Examples of oligopoly abound and include the auto industry, cable television, and commercial air travel. Oligopolistic firms are like cats in a bag. They can either scratch each other to pieces or cuddle up and get comfortable with one another. If oligopolists compete hard, they may end up acting very much like perfect competitors, driving down costs and leading to zero profits for all. If oligopolists collude with each other, they may effectively act like a monopoly and succeed in pushing up prices and earning consistently high levels of profit. We typically characterize oligopolies by mutual interdependence where various decisions such as output, price, and advertising depend on other firm(s)' decisions. Analyzing the choices of oligopolistic firms about pricing and quantity produced involves considering the pros and cons of competition versus collusion at a given point in time.

Why Do Oligopolies Exist?

A combination of the barriers to entry that create monopolies and the product differentiation that characterizes monopolistic competition can create the setting for an oligopoly. For example, when a government grants a patent for an invention to one firm, it may create a monopoly. When the government grants patents to, for example, three different pharmaceutical companies that each has its own drug for reducing high blood pressure, those three firms may become an oligopoly.

Similarly, a natural monopoly will arise when the quantity demanded in a market is only large enough for a single firm to operate at the minimum of the long-run average cost curve. In such a setting, the market has room for only one firm, because no smaller firm can operate at a low enough average cost to compete, and no larger firm could sell what it produced given the quantity demanded in the market.

Quantity demanded in the market may also be two or three times the quantity needed to produce at the minimum of the average cost curve—which means that the market would have room for only two or three oligopoly firms (and they need not produce differentiated products). Again, smaller firms would have higher average costs and be unable to compete, while additional large firms would produce such a high quantity that they would not be able to sell it at a profitable price. This combination of economies of scale and market demand creates the barrier to entry, which led to the Boeing-Airbus oligopoly (also called a duopoly) for large passenger aircraft.

The product differentiation at the heart of monopolistic competition can also play a role in creating oligopoly. For example, firms may need to reach a certain minimum size before they are able to spend enough on advertising and marketing to create a recognizable brand name. The problem in competing with, say, Coca-Cola or Pepsi is not that producing fizzy drinks is technologically difficult, but rather that creating a brand name and marketing effort to equal Coke or Pepsi is an enormous task.

Collusion or Competition?

When oligopoly firms in a certain market decide what quantity to produce and what price to charge, they face a temptation to act as if they were a monopoly. By acting together, oligopolistic firms can hold down industry output, charge a higher price, and divide the profit among themselves. When firms act together in this way to reduce output and keep prices high, it is called **collusion**. A group of firms that have a formal agreement to collude to produce the monopoly output and sell at the monopoly price is called a **cartel**. See the following Clear It Up feature for a more in-depth analysis of the difference between the two.

This OpenStax book is available for free at http://cnx.org/content/col12122/1.4

Clear It Up

Collusion versus cartels: How to differentiate

In the United States, as well as many other countries, it is illegal for firms to collude since collusion is anti-competitive behavior, which is a violation of antitrust law. Both the Antitrust Division of the Justice Department and the Federal Trade Commission have responsibilities for preventing collusion in the United States.

The problem of enforcement is finding hard evidence of collusion. Cartels are formal agreements to collude. Because cartel agreements provide evidence of collusion, they are rare in the United States. Instead, most collusion is tacit, where firms implicitly reach an understanding that competition is bad for profits.

Economists have understood for a long time the desire of businesses to avoid competing so that they can instead raise the prices that they charge and earn higher profits. Adam Smith wrote in *Wealth of Nations* in 1776: "People of the same trade seldom meet together, even for merriment and diversion, but the conversation ends in a conspiracy against the public, or in some contrivance to raise prices."

Even when oligopolists recognize that they would benefit as a group by acting like a monopoly, each individual oligopoly faces a private temptation to produce just a slightly higher quantity and earn slightly higher profit—while still counting on the other oligopolists to hold down their production and keep prices high. If at least some oligopolists give in to this temptation and start producing more, then the market price will fall. A small handful of oligopoly firms may end up competing so fiercely that they all find themselves earning zero economic profits—as if they were perfect competitors.

The Prisoner's Dilemma

Because of the complexity of oligopoly, which is the result of mutual interdependence among firms, there is no single, generally-accepted theory of how oligopolies behave, in the same way that we have theories for all the other market structures. Instead, economists use **game theory**, a branch of mathematics that analyzes situations in which players must make decisions and then receive payoffs based on what other players decide to do. Game theory has found widespread applications in the social sciences, as well as in business, law, and military strategy.

The **prisoner's dilemma** is a scenario in which the gains from cooperation are larger than the rewards from pursuing self-interest. It applies well to oligopoly. The story behind the prisoner's dilemma goes like this:

> Two co-conspiratorial criminals are arrested. When they are taken to the police station, they refuse to say anything and are put in separate interrogation rooms. Eventually, a police officer enters the room where Prisoner A is being held and says: "You know what? Your partner in the other room is confessing. Your partner is going to get a light prison sentence of just one year, and because you're remaining silent, the judge is going to stick you with eight years in prison. Why don't you get smart? If you confess, too, we'll cut your jail time down to five years, and your partner will get five years, also." Over in the next room, another police officer is giving exactly the same speech to Prisoner B. What the police officers do not say is that if both prisoners remain silent, the evidence against them is not especially strong, and the prisoners will end up with only two years in jail each.

The game theory situation facing the two prisoners is in Table 10.2. To understand the dilemma, first consider the choices from Prisoner A's point of view. If A believes that B will confess, then A should confess, too, so as to not get stuck with the eight years in prison. However, if A believes that B will not confess, then A will be tempted to act selfishly and confess, so as to serve only one year. The key point is that A has an incentive to confess regardless of what choice B makes! B faces the same set of choices, and thus will have an incentive to confess regardless of what choice A makes. To confess is called the dominant strategy. It is the strategy an individual (or firm) will pursue regardless of the other individual's (or firm's) decision. The result is that if prisoners pursue their own self-interest, both are likely to confess, and end up doing a total of 10 years of jail time between them.

		Prisoner B	
		Remain Silent (cooperate with other prisoner)	Confess (do not cooperate with other prisoner)
Prisoner A	Remain Silent (cooperate with other prisoner)	A gets 2 years, B gets 2 years	A gets 8 years, B gets 1 year
	Confess (do not cooperate with other prisoner)	A gets 1 year, B gets 8 years	A gets 5 years B gets 5 years

Table 10.2 The Prisoner's Dilemma Problem

The game is called a dilemma because if the two prisoners had cooperated by both remaining silent, they would only have had to serve a total of four years of jail time between them. If the two prisoners can work out some way of cooperating so that neither one will confess, they will both be better off than if they each follow their own individual self-interest, which in this case leads straight into longer jail terms.

The Oligopoly Version of the Prisoner's Dilemma

The members of an oligopoly can face a prisoner's dilemma, also. If each of the oligopolists cooperates in holding down output, then high monopoly profits are possible. Each oligopolist, however, must worry that while it is holding down output, other firms are taking advantage of the high price by raising output and earning higher profits. **Table 10.3** shows the prisoner's dilemma for a two-firm oligopoly—known as a **duopoly**. If Firms A and B both agree to hold down output, they are acting together as a monopoly and will each earn $1,000 in profits. However, both firms' dominant strategy is to increase output, in which case each will earn $400 in profits.

		Firm B	
		Hold Down Output (cooperate with other firm)	Increase Output (do not cooperate with other firm)
Firm A	Hold Down Output (cooperate with other firm)	A gets $1,000, B gets $1,000	A gets $200, B gets $1,500
	Increase Output (do not cooperate with other firm)	A gets $1,500, B gets $200	A gets $400, B gets $400

Table 10.3 A Prisoner's Dilemma for Oligopolists

Can the two firms trust each other? Consider the situation of Firm A:

- If A thinks that B will cheat on their agreement and increase output, then A will increase output, too, because for A the profit of $400 when both firms increase output (the bottom right-hand choice in **Table 10.3**) is better than a profit of only $200 if A keeps output low and B raises output (the upper right-hand choice in the table).

- If A thinks that B will cooperate by holding down output, then A may seize the opportunity to earn higher profits by raising output. After all, if B is going to hold down output, then A can earn $1,500 in profits by expanding output (the bottom left-hand choice in the table) compared with only $1,000 by holding down output as well (the upper left-hand choice in the table).

Thus, firm A will reason that it makes sense to expand output if B holds down output and that it also makes sense to expand output if B raises output. Again, B faces a parallel set of decisions that will lead B also to expand output.

The result of this prisoner's dilemma is often that even though A and B could make the highest combined profits by cooperating in producing a lower level of output and acting like a monopolist, the two firms may well end up in

This OpenStax book is available for free at http://cnx.org/content/col12122/1.4

a situation where they each increase output and earn only $400 each in profits. The following Clear It Up feature discusses one cartel scandal in particular.

What is the Lysine cartel?

Lysine, a $600 million-a-year industry, is an amino acid that farmers use as a feed additive to ensure the proper growth of swine and poultry. The primary U.S. producer of lysine is Archer Daniels Midland (ADM), but several other large European and Japanese firms are also in this market. For a time in the first half of the 1990s, the world's major lysine producers met together in hotel conference rooms and decided exactly how much each firm would sell and what it would charge. The U.S. Federal Bureau of Investigation (FBI), however, had learned of the cartel and placed wire taps on a number of their phone calls and meetings.

From FBI surveillance tapes, following is a comment that Terry Wilson, president of the corn processing division at ADM, made to the other lysine producers at a 1994 meeting in Mona, Hawaii:

> I wanna go back and I wanna say something very simple. If we're going to trust each other, okay, and if I'm assured that I'm gonna get 67,000 tons by the year's end, we're gonna sell it at the prices we agreed to . . . The only thing we need to talk about there because we are gonna get manipulated by these [expletive] buyers—they can be smarter than us if we let them be smarter. . . . They [the customers] are not your friend. They are not my friend. And we gotta have 'em, but they are not my friends. You are my friend. I wanna be closer to you than I am to any customer. Cause you can make us ... money. ... And all I wanna tell you again is let's—let's put the prices on the board. Let's all agree that's what we're gonna do and then walk out of here and do it.

The price of lysine doubled while the cartel was in effect. Confronted by the FBI tapes, Archer Daniels Midland pled guilty in 1996 and paid a fine of $100 million. A number of top executives, both at ADM and other firms, later paid fines of up to $350,000 and were sentenced to 24–30 months in prison.

In another one of the FBI recordings, the president of Archer Daniels Midland told an executive from another competing firm that ADM had a slogan that, in his words, had "penetrated the whole company." The company president stated the slogan this way: "Our competitors are our friends. Our customers are the enemy." That slogan could stand as the motto of cartels everywhere.

How to Enforce Cooperation

How can parties who find themselves in a prisoner's dilemma situation avoid the undesired outcome and cooperate with each other? The way out of a prisoner's dilemma is to find a way to penalize those who do not cooperate.

Perhaps the easiest approach for colluding oligopolists, as you might imagine, would be to sign a contract with each other that they will hold output low and keep prices high. If a group of U.S. companies signed such a contract, however, it would be illegal. Certain international organizations, like the nations that are members of the Organization of Petroleum Exporting Countries (OPEC), have signed international agreements to act like a monopoly, hold down output, and keep prices high so that all of the countries can make high profits from oil exports. Such agreements, however, because they fall in a gray area of international law, are not legally enforceable. If Nigeria, for example, decides to start cutting prices and selling more oil, Saudi Arabia cannot sue Nigeria in court and force it to stop.

Link It Up

Visit the Organization of the Petroleum Exporting Countries website (http://openstaxcollege.org/l/OPEC) and learn more about its history and how it defines itself.

Because oligopolists cannot sign a legally enforceable contract to act like a monopoly, the firms may instead keep close tabs on what other firms are producing and charging. Alternatively, oligopolists may choose to act in a way that generates pressure on each firm to stick to its agreed quantity of output.

One example of the pressure these firms can exert on one another is the **kinked demand curve**, in which competing oligopoly firms commit to match price cuts, but not price increases. **Figure 10.5** shows this situation. Say that an oligopoly airline has agreed with the rest of a cartel to provide a quantity of 10,000 seats on the New York to Los Angeles route, at a price of $500. This choice defines the kink in the firm's perceived demand curve. The reason that the firm faces a kink in its demand curve is because of how the other oligopolists react to changes in the firm's price. If the oligopoly decides to produce more and cut its price, the other members of the cartel will immediately match any price cuts—and therefore, a lower price brings very little increase in quantity sold.

If one firm cuts its price to $300, it will be able to sell only 11,000 seats. However, if the airline seeks to raise prices, the other oligopolists will not raise their prices, and so the firm that raised prices will lose a considerable share of sales. For example, if the firm raises its price to $550, its sales drop to 5,000 seats sold. Thus, if oligopolists always match price cuts by other firms in the cartel, but do not match price increases, then none of the oligopolists will have a strong incentive to change prices, since the potential gains are minimal. This strategy can work like a silent form of cooperation, in which the cartel successfully manages to hold down output, increase price, and share a monopoly level of profits even without any legally enforceable agreement.

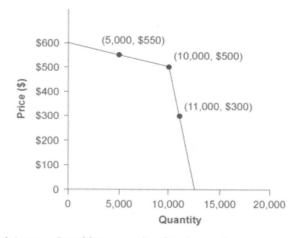

Figure 10.5 A Kinked Demand Curve Consider a member firm in an oligopoly cartel that is supposed to produce a quantity of 10,000 and sell at a price of $500. The other members of the cartel can encourage this firm to honor its commitments by acting so that the firm faces a kinked demand curve. If the oligopolist attempts to expand output and reduce price slightly, other firms also cut prices immediately—so if the firm expands output to 11,000, the price per unit falls dramatically, to $300. On the other side, if the oligopoly attempts to raise its price, other firms will not do so, so if the firm raises its price to $550, its sales decline sharply to 5,000. Thus, the members of a cartel can discipline each other to stick to the pre-agreed levels of quantity and price through a strategy of matching all price cuts but not matching any price increases.

Many real-world oligopolies, prodded by economic changes, legal and political pressures, and the egos of their top executives, go through episodes of cooperation and competition. If oligopolies could sustain cooperation with each

This OpenStax book is available for free at http://cnx.org/content/col12122/1.4

other on output and pricing, they could earn profits as if they were a single monopoly. However, each firm in an oligopoly has an incentive to produce more and grab a bigger share of the overall market; when firms start behaving in this way, the market outcome in terms of prices and quantity can be similar to that of a highly competitive market.

Tradeoffs of Imperfect Competition

Monopolistic competition is probably the single most common market structure in the U.S. economy. It provides powerful incentives for innovation, as firms seek to earn profits in the short run, while entry assures that firms do not earn economic profits in the long run. However, monopolistically competitive firms do not produce at the lowest point on their average cost curves. In addition, the endless search to impress consumers through product differentiation may lead to excessive social expenses on advertising and marketing.

Oligopoly is probably the second most common market structure. When oligopolies result from patented innovations or from taking advantage of economies of scale to produce at low average cost, they may provide considerable benefit to consumers. Oligopolies are often buffered by significant barriers to entry, which enable the oligopolists to earn sustained profits over long periods of time. Oligopolists also do not typically produce at the minimum of their average cost curves. When they lack vibrant competition, they may lack incentives to provide innovative products and high-quality service.

The task of public policy with regard to competition is to sort through these multiple realities, attempting to encourage behavior that is beneficial to the broader society and to discourage behavior that only adds to the profits of a few large companies, with no corresponding benefit to consumers. **Monopoly and Antitrust Policy** discusses the delicate judgments that go into this task.

Bring it Home

The Temptation to Defy the Law

Oligopolistic firms have been called "cats in a bag," as this chapter mentioned. The French detergent makers chose to "cozy up" with each other. The result? An uneasy and tenuous relationship. When the *Wall Street Journal* reported on the matter, it wrote: "According to a statement a Henkel manager made to the [French anti-trust] commission, the detergent makers wanted 'to limit the intensity of the competition between them and clean up the market.' Nevertheless, by the early 1990s, a price war had broken out among them." During the soap executives' meetings, sometimes lasting more than four hours, the companies established complex pricing structures. "One [soap] executive recalled 'chaotic' meetings as each side tried to work out how the other had bent the rules." Like many cartels, the soap cartel disintegrated due to the very strong temptation for each member to maximize its own individual profits.

How did this soap opera end? After an investigation, French antitrust authorities fined Colgate-Palmolive, Henkel, and Proctor & Gamble a total of €361 million ($484 million). A similar fate befell the icemakers. Bagged ice is a commodity, a perfect substitute, generally sold in 7- or 22-pound bags. No one cares what label is on the bag. By agreeing to carve up the ice market, control broad geographic swaths of territory, and set prices, the icemakers moved from perfect competition to a monopoly model. After the agreements, each firm was the sole supplier of bagged ice to a region. There were profits in both the long run and the short run. According to the courts: "These companies illegally conspired to manipulate the marketplace." Fines totaled about $600,000—a steep fine considering a bag of ice sells for under $3 in most parts of the United States.

Even though it is illegal in many parts of the world for firms to set prices and carve up a market, the temptation to earn higher profits makes it extremely tempting to defy the law.

KEY TERMS

cartel a group of firms that collude to produce the monopoly output and sell at the monopoly price

collusion when firms act together to reduce output and keep prices high

differentiated product a product that is consumers perceive as distinctive in some way

duopoly an oligopoly with only two firms

game theory a branch of mathematics that economists use to analyze situations in which players must make decisions and then receive payoffs based on what decisions the other players make

imperfectly competitive firms and organizations that fall between the extremes of monopoly and perfect competition

kinked demand curve a perceived demand curve that arises when competing oligopoly firms commit to match price cuts, but not price increases

monopolistic competition many firms competing to sell similar but differentiated products

oligopoly when a few large firms have all or most of the sales in an industry

prisoner's dilemma a game in which the gains from cooperation are larger than the rewards from pursuing self-interest

product differentiation any action that firms do to make consumers think their products are different from their competitors'

KEY CONCEPTS AND SUMMARY

10.1 Monopolistic Competition

Monopolistic competition refers to a market where many firms sell differentiated products. Differentiated products can arise from characteristics of the good or service, location from which the firm sells the product, intangible aspects of the product, and perceptions of the product.

The perceived demand curve for a monopolistically competitive firm is downward-sloping, which shows that it is a price maker and chooses a combination of price and quantity. However, the perceived demand curve for a monopolistic competitor is more elastic than the perceived demand curve for a monopolist, because the monopolistic competitor has direct competition, unlike the pure monopolist. A profit-maximizing monopolistic competitor will seek out the quantity where marginal revenue is equal to marginal cost. The monopolistic competitor will produce that level of output and charge the price that the firm's demand curve indicates.

If the firms in a monopolistically competitive industry are earning economic profits, the industry will attract entry until profits are driven down to zero in the long run. If the firms in a monopolistically competitive industry are suffering economic losses, then the industry will experience exit of firms until economic losses are driven up to zero in the long run.

A monopolistically competitive firm is not productively efficient because it does not produce at the minimum of its average cost curve. A monopolistically competitive firm is not allocatively efficient because it does not produce where P = MC, but instead produces where P > MC. Thus, a monopolistically competitive firm will tend to produce a lower quantity at a higher cost and to charge a higher price than a perfectly competitive firm.

Monopolistically competitive industries do offer benefits to consumers in the form of greater variety and incentives for improved products and services. There is some controversy over whether a market-oriented economy generates too much variety.

10.2 Oligopoly

An oligopoly is a situation where a few firms sell most or all of the goods in a market. Oligopolists earn their highest profits if they can band together as a cartel and act like a monopolist by reducing output and raising price. Since each member of the oligopoly can benefit individually from expanding output, such collusion often breaks down—especially since explicit collusion is illegal.

The prisoner's dilemma is an example of the application of game theory to analysis of oligopoly. It shows how, in certain situations, all sides can benefit from cooperative behavior rather than self-interested behavior. However, the challenge for the parties is to find ways to encourage cooperative behavior.

SELF-CHECK QUESTIONS

1. Suppose that, due to a successful advertising campaign, a monopolistic competitor experiences an increase in demand for its product. How will that affect the price it charges and the quantity it supplies?

2. Continuing with the scenario in question 1, in the long run, the positive economic profits that the monopolistic competitor earns will attract a response either from existing firms in the industry or firms outside. As those firms capture the original firm's profit, what will happen to the original firm's profit-maximizing price and output levels?

3. Consider the curve in the figure below, which shows the market demand, marginal cost, and marginal revenue curve for firms in an oligopolistic industry. In this example, we assume firms have zero fixed costs.

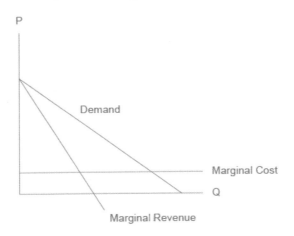

  a. Suppose the firms collude to form a cartel. What price will the cartel charge? What quantity will the cartel supply? How much profit will the cartel earn?
  b. Suppose now that the cartel breaks up and the oligopolistic firms compete as vigorously as possible by cutting the price and increasing sales. What will be the industry quantity and price? What will be the collective profits of all firms in the industry?
  c. Compare the equilibrium price, quantity, and profit for the cartel and cutthroat competition outcomes.

4. Sometimes oligopolies in the same industry are very different in size. Suppose we have a duopoly where one firm (Firm A) is large and the other firm (Firm B) is small, as the prisoner's dilemma box in **Table 10.4** shows.

	Firm B colludes with Firm A	Firm B cheats by selling more output
Firm A colludes with Firm B	A gets $1,000, B gets $100	A gets $800, B gets $200
Firm A cheats by selling more output	A gets $1,050, B gets $50	A gets $500, B gets $20

Table 10.4

Assuming that both firms know the payoffs, what is the likely outcome in this case?

REVIEW QUESTIONS

5. What is the relationship between product differentiation and monopolistic competition?

6. How is the perceived demand curve for a monopolistically competitive firm different from the perceived demand curve for a monopoly or a perfectly competitive firm?

7. How does a monopolistic competitor choose its profit-maximizing quantity of output and price?

8. How can a monopolistic competitor tell whether the price it is charging will cause the firm to earn profits or experience losses?

9. If the firms in a monopolistically competitive market are earning economic profits or losses in the short run, would you expect them to continue doing so in the long run? Why?

10. Is a monopolistically competitive firm productively efficient? Is it allocatively efficient? Why or why not?

11. Will the firms in an oligopoly act more like a monopoly or more like competitors? Briefly explain.

12. Does each individual in a prisoner's dilemma benefit more from cooperation or from pursuing self-interest? Explain briefly.

13. What stops oligopolists from acting together as a monopolist and earning the highest possible level of profits?

CRITICAL THINKING QUESTIONS

14. Aside from advertising, how can monopolistically competitive firms increase demand for their products?

15. Make a case for why monopolistically competitive industries never reach long-run equilibrium.

16. Would you rather have efficiency or variety? That is, one opportunity cost of the variety of products we have is that each product costs more per unit than if there were only one kind of product of a given type, like shoes. Perhaps a better question is, "What is the right amount of variety? Can there be too many varieties of shoes, for example?"

17. Would you expect the kinked demand curve to be more extreme (like a right angle) or less extreme (like a normal demand curve) if each firm in the cartel produces a near-identical product like OPEC and petroleum? What if each firm produces a somewhat different product? Explain your reasoning.

This OpenStax book is available for free at http://cnx.org/content/col12122/1.4

18. When OPEC raised the price of oil dramatically in the mid-1970s, experts said it was unlikely that the cartel could stay together over the long term—that the incentives for individual members to cheat would become too strong. More than forty years later, OPEC still exists. Why do you think OPEC has been able to beat the odds and continue to collude? *Hint:* You may wish to consider non-economic reasons.

PROBLEMS

19. Andrea's Day Spa began to offer a relaxing aromatherapy treatment. The firm asks you how much to charge to maximize profits. The first two columns in **Table 10.5** provide the price and quantity for the demand curve for treatments. The third column shows its total costs. For each level of output, calculate total revenue, marginal revenue, average cost, and marginal cost. What is the profit-maximizing level of output for the treatments and how much will the firm earn in profits?

Price	Quantity	TC
$25.00	0	$130
$24.00	10	$275
$23.00	20	$435
$22.50	30	$610
$22.00	40	$800
$21.60	50	$1,005
$21.20	60	$1,225

Table 10.5

20. Mary and Raj are the only two growers who provide organically grown corn to a local grocery store. They know that if they cooperated and produced less corn, they could raise the price of the corn. If they work independently, they will each earn $100. If they decide to work together and both lower their output, they can each earn $150. If one person lowers output and the other does not, the person who lowers output will earn $0 and the other person will capture the entire market and will earn $200. **Table 10.6** represents the choices available to Mary and Raj. What is the best choice for Raj if he is sure that Mary will cooperate? If Mary thinks Raj will cheat, what should Mary do and why? What is the prisoner's dilemma result? What is the preferred choice if they could ensure cooperation? A = Work independently; B = Cooperate and Lower Output. (Each results entry lists Raj's earnings first, and Mary's earnings second.)

		Mary	
		A	B
Raj	A	($100, $100)	($200, $0)
	B	($0, $200)	($150, $150)

Table 10.6

21. Jane and Bill are apprehended for a bank robbery. They are taken into separate rooms and questioned by the police about their involvement in the crime. The police tell them each that if they confess and turn the other person in, they will receive a lighter sentence. If they both confess, they will be each be sentenced to 30 years. If neither confesses, they will each receive a 20-year sentence. If only one confesses, the confessor will receive 15 years and the one who stayed silent will receive 35 years. Table 10.7 below represents the choices available to Jane and Bill. If Jane trusts Bill to stay silent, what should she do? If Jane thinks that Bill will confess, what should she do? Does Jane have a dominant strategy? Does Bill have a dominant strategy? A = Confess; B = Stay Silent. (Each results entry lists Jane's sentence first (in years), and Bill's sentence second.)

		Jane	
		A	B
Bill	A	(30, 30)	(15, 35)
	B	(35, 15)	(20, 20)

Table 10.7

This OpenStax book is available for free at http://cnx.org/content/col12122/1.4

11 | Monopoly and Antitrust Policy

Figure 11.1 Oligopoly versus Competitors in the Marketplace Large corporations, such as the natural gas producer Kinder Morgan, can bring economies of scale to the marketplace. Will that benefit consumers, or is more competition better? (Credit: modification of work by Derrick Coetzee/Flickr Creative Commons)

Bring it Home

More than Cooking, Heating, and Cooling

If you live in the United States, there is a slightly better than 50–50 chance your home is heated and cooled using natural gas. You may even use natural gas for cooking. However, those uses are not the primary uses of natural gas in the U.S. In 2016, according to the U.S. Energy Information Administration, home heating, cooling, and cooking accounted for just 16% of natural gas usage. What accounts for the rest? The greatest uses for natural gas are the generation of electric power (36%) and in industry (28%). Together these three uses for natural gas touch many areas of our lives, so why would there be any opposition to a merger of two natural gas firms? After all, a merger could mean increased efficiencies and reduced costs to people like you and me.

In October 2011, Kinder Morgan and El Paso Corporation, two natural gas firms, announced they were merging. The announcement stated the combined firm would link "nearly every major production region with markets," cut costs by "eliminating duplication in pipelines and other assets," and that "the savings could be passed on to consumers."

The objection? The $21.1 billion deal would give Kinder Morgan control of more than 80,000 miles of pipeline, making the new firm the third largest energy producer in North America. Policymakers and the public wondered whether the new conglomerate really would pass on cost savings to consumers, or would the merger give Kinder Morgan a strong oligopoly position in the natural gas marketplace?

That brings us to the central questions this chapter poses: What should the balance be between corporate size and a larger number of competitors in a marketplace, and what role should the government play in this balancing act?

Introduction to Monopoly and Antitrust Policy

In this chapter, you will learn about:

- Corporate Mergers
- Regulating Anticompetitive Behavior
- Regulating Natural Monopolies
- The Great Deregulation Experiment

The previous chapters on the theory of the firm identified three important lessons: First, that competition, by providing consumers with lower prices and a variety of innovative products, is a good thing; second, that large-scale production can dramatically lower average costs; and third, that markets in the real world are rarely perfectly competitive. As a consequence, government policymakers must determine how much to intervene to balance the potential benefits of large-scale production against the potential loss of competition that can occur when businesses grow in size, especially through mergers.

For example, in 2006, AT&T and BellSouth proposed a merger. At the time, there were very few mobile phone service providers. Both the Justice Department and the FCC blocked the proposal.

The two companies argued that the merger would benefit consumers, who would be able to purchase better telecommunications services at a cheaper price because the newly created firm would take advantage of economies of scale and eliminate duplicate investments. However, a number of activist groups like the Consumer Federation of America and Public Knowledge expressed fears that the merger would reduce competition and lead to higher prices for consumers for decades to come. In December 2006, the federal government allowed the merger to proceed. By 2009, the new post-merger AT&T was the eighth largest company by revenues in the United States, and by that measure the largest telecommunications company in the world. Economists have spent – and will still spend – years trying to determine whether the merger of AT&T and BellSouth, as well as other smaller mergers of telecommunications companies at about this same time, helped consumers, hurt them, or did not make much difference.

This chapter discusses public policy issues about competition. How can economists and governments determine when mergers of large companies like AT&T and BellSouth should be allowed and when they should be blocked? The government also plays a role in policing anticompetitive behavior other than mergers, like prohibiting certain kinds of contracts that might restrict competition. In the case of natural monopoly, however, trying to preserve competition probably will not work very well, and so government will often resort to regulation of price and/or quantity of output. In recent decades, there has been a global trend toward less government intervention in the price and output decisions of businesses.

11.1 | Corporate Mergers

By the end of this section, you will be able to:
- Explain antitrust law and its significance
- Calculate concentration ratios
- Calculate the Herfindahl-Herschman Index (HHI)
- Evaluate methods of antitrust regulation

A corporate **merger** occurs when two formerly separate firms combine to become a single firm. When one firm purchases another, it is called an **acquisition**. An acquisition may not look just like a merger, since the newly purchased firm may continue to operate under its former company name. Mergers can also be lateral, where two firms of similar sizes combine to become one. However, both mergers and acquisitions lead to two formerly separate firms operating under common ownership, and so they are commonly grouped together.

Regulations for Approving Mergers

Since a merger combines two firms into one, it can reduce the extent of competition between firms. Therefore, when two U.S. firms announce a merger or acquisition where at least one of the firms is above a minimum size of sales (a threshold that moves up gradually over time, and was at $76.3 million in 2015), or certain other conditions are met, they are required under law to notify the U.S. Federal Trade Commission (FTC). The left-hand panel of **Figure 11.2** (a) shows the number of mergers submitted for review to the FTC each year from 2002 to 2015. Mergers follow the business cycle, falling after the 2001 recession, peaking in 2007 as the Great Recession struck, and then rising since 2009. The right-hand panel of **Figure 11.2** (b) shows the distribution of those mergers submitted for review in 2015 as measured by the size of the transaction. It is important to remember that this total leaves out many small mergers under $50 million, which companies only need to report in certain limited circumstances. About a third of all reported merger and acquisition transactions in 2015 exceeded $500 million, while about 15 percent exceeded $1 billion.

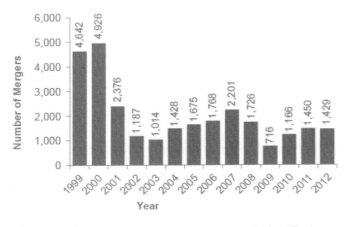

(a) Number of mergers submitted for review by the Federal Trade Commission, 1999-2012

(b) Size of transaction for mergers submitted for review in 2012 (in millions of dollars)

Figure 11.2 Number and Size of Mergers (a) The number of mergers grew from 2003 to 2007, then fell dramatically during the 2008-2009 Great Recession, before recovering since. (b) In 2015, the greatest number of mergers submitted for review by the Federal Trade Commission was for transactions between $500 million and $1 billion.

The laws that give government the power to block certain mergers, and even in some cases to break up large firms into smaller ones, are called **antitrust laws**. Before a large merger happens, the antitrust regulators at the FTC and the U.S. Department of Justice can allow the merger, prohibit it, or allow it if certain conditions are met. One common condition is that the merger will be allowed if the firm agrees to sell off certain parts. For example, in 2006, Johnson & Johnson bought the Pfizer's "consumer health" division, which included well-known brands like Listerine mouthwash and Sudafed cold medicine. As a condition of allowing the merger, Johnson & Johnson was required to sell off six brands to other firms, including Zantac® heartburn relief medication, Cortizone anti-itch cream, and Balmex diaper rash medication, to preserve a greater degree of competition in these markets.

The U.S. government approves most proposed mergers. In a market-oriented economy, firms have the freedom to make their own choices. Private firms generally have the freedom to:

- expand or reduce production

- set the price they choose

- open new factories or sales facilities or close them

- hire workers or to lay them off

- start selling new products or stop selling existing ones

If the owners want to acquire a firm or be acquired, or to merge with another firm, this decision is just one of many that firms are free to make. In these conditions, the managers of private firms will sometimes make mistakes. They may close down a factory which, it later turns out, would have been profitable. They may start selling a product that ends up losing money. A merger between two companies can sometimes lead to a clash of corporate personalities that makes both firms worse off. However, the fundamental belief behind a market-oriented economy is that firms, not governments, are in the best position to know if their actions will lead to attracting more customers or producing more efficiently.

Government regulators agree that most mergers are beneficial to consumers. As the Federal Trade Commission has noted on its website (as of November, 2013): "Most mergers actually benefit competition and consumers by allowing firms to operate more efficiently." At the same time, the FTC recognizes, "Some [mergers] are likely to lessen competition. That, in turn, can lead to higher prices, reduced availability of goods or services, lower quality of products, and less innovation. Some mergers create a concentrated market, while others enable a single firm to raise prices." The challenge for the antitrust regulators at the FTC and the U.S. Department of Justice is to figure out when a merger may hinder competition. This decision involves both numerical tools and some judgments that are difficult to quantify. The following Clear It Up explains the origins of U.S. antitrust law.

What is U.S. antitrust law?

In the closing decades of the 1800s, many industries in the U.S. economy were dominated by a single firm that had most of the sales for the entire country. Supporters of these large firms argued that they could take advantage of economies of scale and careful planning to provide consumers with products at low prices. However, critics pointed out that when competition was reduced, these firms were free to charge more and make permanently higher profits, and that without the goading of competition, it was not clear that they were as efficient or innovative as they could be.

In many cases, these large firms were organized in the legal form of a "trust," in which a group of formerly independent firms were consolidated by mergers and purchases, and a group of "trustees" then ran the companies as if they were a single firm. Thus, when the U.S. government sought to limit the power of these trusts, it passed the **Sherman Antitrust Act** in 1890 - the nation's first antitrust law. In an early demonstration of the law's power, the U.S. Supreme Court in 1911 upheld the government's right to break up Standard Oil, which had controlled about 90% of the country's oil refining, into 34 independent firms, including Exxon, Mobil, Amoco, and Chevron. In 1914, the **Clayton Antitrust Act** outlawed mergers and acquisitions (where the outcome would be to "substantially lessen competition" in an industry), price discrimination (where different customers are charged different prices for the same product), and tied sales (where purchase of one product commits the buyer to purchase some other product). Also in 1914, the Federal Trade Commission (FTC) was created to define more specifically what competition was unfair. In 1950, the **Celler-Kefauver Act** extended the Clayton Act by restricting vertical and conglomerate mergers. A vertical merger occurs when two or more firms, operating at different levels within an industry's supply chain, merge operations. A conglomerate merger is a merger between firms that are involved in totally unrelated business activities. In the twenty-first century, the FTC and the U.S. Department of Justice continue to enforce antitrust laws.

The Four-Firm Concentration Ratio

Regulators have struggled for decades to measure the degree of monopoly power in an industry. An early tool was the **concentration ratio**, which measures the combined market share (or percent of total industry sales) which account for the largest firms (typically the top four to eight). For an explanation of how high market concentrations can create inefficiencies in an economy, refer to **Monopoly**.

Say that the market for replacing broken automobile windshields in a certain city has 18 firms with the market shares in **Table 11.1**, where the **market share** is each firm's proportion of total sales in that market. We calculate the four-firm concentration ratio by adding the market shares of the four largest firms: in this case, 16 + 10 + 8 + 6 = 40. We do not consider this concentration ratio especially high, because the largest four firms have less than half the market.

If the market shares for replacing automobile windshields are:	
Smooth as Glass Repair Company	16% of the market

Table 11.1 Calculating Concentration Ratios from Market Shares

If the market shares for replacing automobile windshields are:	
The Auto Glass Doctor Company	10% of the market
Your Car Shield Company	8% of the market
Seven firms that each have 6% of the market	42% of the market, combined
Eight firms that each have 3% of the market	24% of the market, combined
Then the four-firm concentration ratio is 16 + 10 + 8 + 6 = 40.	

Table 11.1 Calculating Concentration Ratios from Market Shares

The concentration ratio approach can help to clarify some of the fuzziness over deciding when a merger might affect competition. For instance, if two of the smallest firms in the hypothetical market for repairing automobile windshields merged, the four-firm concentration ratio would not change—which implies that there is not much worry that the degree of competition in the market has notably diminished. However, if the top two firms merged, then the four-firm concentration ratio would become 46 (that is, 26 + 8 + 6 + 6). While this concentration ratio is modestly higher, the four-firm concentration ratio would still be less than half, so such a proposed merger might barely raise an eyebrow among antitrust regulators.

Link It Up

Visit this website (http://openstaxcollege.org/l/Google_FTC) to read an article about Google's run-in with the FTC.

The Herfindahl-Hirshman Index

A four-firm concentration ratio is a simple tool, which may reveal only part of the story. For example, consider two industries that both have a four-firm concentration ratio of 80. However, in one industry five firms each control 20% of the market, while in the other industry, the top firm holds 77% of the market and all the other firms have 1% each. Although the four-firm concentration ratios are identical, it would be reasonable to worry more about the extent of competition in the second case—where the largest firm is nearly a monopoly—than in the first.

Another approach to measuring industry concentration that can distinguish between these two cases is called the **Herfindahl-Hirschman Index (HHI)**. We calculate HHI by summing the squares of the market share of each firm in the industry, as the following Work It Out shows.

Work It Out ⊶⊙⊶⊙⊶⊙

Calculating HHI

Step 1. Calculate the HHI for a monopoly with a market share of 100%. Because there is only one firm, it has 100% market share. The HHI is $100^2 = 10,000$.

Step 2. For an extremely competitive industry, with dozens or hundreds of extremely small competitors, the HHI value might drop as low as 100 or even less. Calculate the HHI for an industry with 100 firms that each have 1% of the market. In this case, the HHI is $100(1^2) = 100$.

Step 3. Calculate the HHI for the industry in Table 11.1. In this case, the HHI is $16^2 + 10^2 + 8^2 + 7(6^2) + 8(3^2) = 744$.

Step 4. Note that the HHI gives greater weight to large firms.

Step 5. Consider the earlier example, comparing one industry where five firms each have 20% of the market with an industry where one firm has 77% and the other 23 firms have 1% each. The two industries have the same four-firm concentration ratio of 80. However, the HHI for the first industry is $5(20^2) = 2,000$, while the HHI for the second industry is much higher at $77^2 + 23(1^2) = 5,952$.

Step 6. Note that the near-monopolist in the second industry drives up the HHI measure of industrial concentration.

Step 7. Review Table 11.2 which gives some examples of the four-firm concentration ratio and the HHI in various U.S. industries in 2016. (You can find market share data from multiple industry sources. Data in the table are from: Statista.com (for wireless), *The Wall Street Journal* (for automobiles), Gartner.com (for computers) and the U.S. Bureau of Transportation Statistics (for airlines).)

U.S. Industry	Four-Firm Ratio	HHI
Wireless	98	2,736
Largest five: Verizon, AT&T, Sprint, T-Mobile, US Cellular		
Personal Computers	76	1,234
Largest five: HP, Lenovo, Dell, Asus, Apple, Acer		
Airlines	69	1,382
Largest five: American, Southwest, Delta, United, JetBlue		
Automobiles	58	1,099
Largest five: Ford, GM, Toyota, Chrysler, Nissan		

Table 11.2 Examples of Concentration Ratios and HHIs in the U.S. Economy, 2016

In the 1980s, the FTC followed these guidelines: If a merger would result in an HHI of less than 1,000, the FTC would probably approve it. If a merger would result in an HHI of more than 1,800, the FTC would probably challenge it. If a merger would result in an HHI between 1,000 and 1,800, then the FTC would scrutinize the plan and make a case-by-case decision. However, in the last several decades, the antitrust enforcement authorities have moved away from relying as heavily on measures of concentration ratios and HHIs to determine whether they will allow a merger, and instead they carry out more case-by-case analysis on the extent of competition in different industries.

New Directions for Antitrust

Both the four-firm concentration ratio and the Herfindahl-Hirschman index share some weaknesses. First, they begin from the assumption that the "market" under discussion is well-defined, and the only question is measuring how sales are divided in that market. Second, they are based on an implicit assumption that competitive conditions across industries are similar enough that a broad measure of concentration in the market is enough to make a decision about the effects of a merger. These assumptions, however, are not always correct. In response to these two problems, the antitrust regulators have been changing their approach in the last decade or two.

Defining a **market** is often controversial. For example, Microsoft in the early 2000s had a dominant share of the software for computer operating systems. However, in the total market for all computer software and services, including everything from games to scientific programs, the Microsoft share was only about 14% in 2014. A narrowly defined market will tend to make concentration appear higher, while a broadly defined market will tend to make it appear smaller.

In recent decades, there have been two especially important shifts affecting how we define markets: one centers on technology and the other centers on globalization. In addition, these two shifts are interconnected. With the vast improvement in communications technologies, including the development of the internet, a consumer can order books or pet supplies from all over the country or the world. As a result, the degree of competition many local retail businesses face has increased. The same effect may operate even more strongly in markets for business supplies, where so-called "business-to-business" websites can allow buyers and suppliers from anywhere in the world to find each other.

Globalization has changed the market boundaries. As recently as the 1970s, it was common for measurements of concentration ratios and HHIs to stop at national borders. Now, many industries find that their competition comes from the global market. A few decades ago, three companies, General Motors, Ford, and Chrysler, dominated the U.S. auto market. By 2014, however, production of these three firms accounted for less than half of U.S. auto sales, and they were facing competition from well-known car manufacturers such as Toyota, Honda, Nissan, Volkswagen, Mitsubishi, and Mazda. When analysts calculate HHIs with a global perspective, concentration in most major industries—including cars—is lower than in a purely domestic context.

Because attempting to define a particular market can be difficult and controversial, the Federal Trade Commission has begun to look less at market share and more at the data on actual competition between businesses. For example, in February 2007, Whole Foods Market and Wild Oats Market announced that they wished to merge. These were the two largest companies in the market that the government defined as "premium natural and organic supermarket chains." However, one could also argue that they were two relatively small companies in the broader market for all stores that sell groceries or specialty food products.

Rather than relying on a market definition, the government antitrust regulators looked at detailed evidence on profits and prices for specific stores in different cities, both before and after other competitive stores entered or exited. Based on that evidence, the Federal Trade Commission decided to block the merger. After two years of legal battles, the FTC eventually allowed the merger in 2009 under the conditions that Whole Foods sell off the Wild Oats brand name and a number of individual stores, to preserve competition in certain local markets. For more on the difficulties of defining markets, refer to **Monopoly**.

This new approach to antitrust regulation involves detailed analysis of specific markets and companies, instead of defining a market and counting up total sales. A common starting point is for antitrust regulators to use statistical tools and real-world evidence to estimate the **demand curves** and **supply curves** the firms proposing a merger face. A second step is to specify how competition occurs in this specific industry. Some possibilities include competing to cut prices, to raise output, to build a brand name through advertising, and to build a reputation for good service or high quality. With these pieces of the puzzle in place, it is then possible to build a statistical model that estimates the likely outcome for consumers if the two firms are allowed to merge. These models do require some degree of subjective judgment, and so they can become the subject of legal disputes between the antitrust authorities and the companies that wish to merge.

11.2 | Regulating Anticompetitive Behavior

By the end of this section, you will be able to:
- Analyze restrictive practices
- Explain tying sales, bundling, and predatory pricing
- Evaluate a real-world situation of possible anticompetitive and restrictive practices

The U.S. antitrust laws reach beyond blocking mergers that would reduce competition to include a wide array of anticompetitive practices. For example, it is illegal for competitors to form a cartel to collude to make pricing and output decisions, as if they were a monopoly firm. The Federal Trade Commission and the U.S. Department of Justice prohibit firms from agreeing to fix prices or output, rigging bids, or sharing or dividing markets by allocating customers, suppliers, territories, or lines of commerce.

In the late 1990s, for example, the antitrust regulators prosecuted an international cartel of vitamin manufacturers, including the Swiss firm Hoffman-La Roche, the German firm BASF, and the French firm Rhone-Poulenc. These firms reached agreements on how much to produce, how much to charge, and which firm would sell to which customers. Firms bought the high-priced vitamins like General Mills, Kellogg, Purina-Mills, and Proctor and Gamble which pushed up the prices more. Hoffman-La Roche pleaded guilty in May 1999 and agreed both to pay a fine of $500 million and to have at least one top executive serve four months of jail time.

Under U.S. antitrust laws, monopoly itself is not illegal. If a firm has a monopoly because of a newly patented invention, for example, the law explicitly allows a firm to earn higher-than-normal profits for a time as a reward for innovation. If a firm achieves a large share of the market by producing a better product at a lower price, such behavior is not prohibited by antitrust law.

Restrictive Practices

Antitrust law includes rules against **restrictive practices**—practices that do not involve outright agreements to raise price or to reduce the quantity produced, but that might have the effect of reducing competition. Antitrust cases involving restrictive practices are often controversial, because they delve into specific contracts or agreements between firms that are allowed in some cases but not in others.

For example, if a product manufacturer is selling to a group of dealers who then sell to the general public it is illegal for the manufacturer to demand a **minimum resale price maintenance agreement**, which would require the dealers to sell for at least a certain minimum price. A minimum price contract is illegal because it would restrict competition among dealers. However, the manufacturer is legally allowed to "suggest" minimum prices and to stop selling to dealers who regularly undercut the suggested price. If you think this rule sounds like a fairly subtle distinction, you are right.

An **exclusive dealing** agreement between a manufacturer and a dealer can be legal or illegal. It is legal if the purpose of the contract is to encourage competition between dealers. For example, it is legal for the Ford Motor Company to sell its cars to only Ford dealers, and for General Motors to sell to only GM dealers, and so on. However, exclusive deals may also limit competition. If one large retailer obtained the exclusive rights to be the sole distributor of televisions, computers, and audio equipment made by a number of companies, then this exclusive contract would have an anticompetitive effect on other retailers.

Tying sales happen when a customer is required to buy one product only if the customer also buys a second product. Tying sales are controversial because they force consumers to purchase a product that they may not actually want or need. Further, the additional, required products are not necessarily advantageous to the customer. Suppose that to purchase a popular DVD, the store required that you also purchase a certain portable TV model. These products are only loosely related, thus there is no reason to make the purchase of one contingent on the other. Even if a customer were interested in a portable TV, the tying to a particular model prevents the customer from having the option of selecting one from the numerous types available in the market.

A related, but not identical, concept is **bundling**, where a firm sells two or more products as one. Bundling typically offers an advantage for consumers by allowing them to acquire multiple products or services for a better price. For example, several cable companies allow customers to buy products like cable, internet, and a phone line through a special price available through bundling. Customers are also welcome to purchase these products separately, but the price of bundling is usually more appealing.

In some cases, we can view tying sales and bundling as anticompetitive. However, in other cases they may be legal and even common. It is common for people to purchase season tickets to a sports team or a set of concerts so to guarantee tickets to the few contests or shows that are most popular and likely to sell out. Computer software manufacturers may often bundle a number of different programs, even when the buyer wants only a few. Think about the software that is included in a new computer purchase, for example.

Recall from the chapter on **Monopoly** that predatory pricing occurs when the existing firm (or firms) reacts to a new firm by dropping prices very low, until the new firm is driven out of the market, at which point the existing firm raises prices again. This pattern of pricing is aimed at deterring new firms from entering the market. However, in practice, it can be hard to figure out when pricing is predatory. Say that American Airlines is flying between two cities, and a new airline starts flying between the same two cities, at a lower price. If American Airlines cuts its price to match the new entrant, is this predatory pricing or is it just market competition at work? A commonly proposed rule is that if a firm is selling for less than its average variable cost—that is, at a price where it should be shutting down—then there is evidence for predatory pricing. However, calculating in the real world what costs are variable and what costs are fixed is often not obvious, either.

The Microsoft antitrust case embodies many of these gray areas in restrictive practices, as the next Clear It Up shows.

Did Microsoft® engage in anticompetitive and restrictive practices?

The most famous restrictive practices case of recent years was a series of lawsuits by the U.S. government against Microsoft—lawsuits that some of Microsoft's competitors encouraged. All sides admitted that Microsoft's Windows program had a near-monopoly position in the market for the software used in general computer operating systems. All sides agreed that the software had many satisfied customers and that the computer software capabilities were compatible with Windows. Software that Microsoft and other companies produced had expanded dramatically in the 1990s. Having a **monopoly** or a near-monopoly is not necessarily illegal in and of itself, but in cases where one company controls a great deal of the market, antitrust regulators look at any allegations of restrictive practices with special care.

The antitrust regulators argued that Microsoft had gone beyond profiting from its software innovations and its dominant position in the software market for operating systems, and had tried to use its market power in operating systems software to take over other parts of the software industry. For example, the government argued that Microsoft had engaged in an anticompetitive form of exclusive dealing by threatening computer makers that, if they did not leave another firm's software off their machines (specifically, Netscape's Internet browser), then Microsoft would not sell them its operating system software. Government antitrust regulators accused Microsoft of tying together its Windows operating system software, where it had a monopoly, with its Internet Explorer browser software, where it did not have a monopoly, and thus using this bundling as an anticompetitive tool. The government also accused Microsoft of a form of predatory pricing; namely, giving away certain additional software products for free as part of Windows, as a way of driving out the competition from other software makers.

In April 2000, a federal court held that Microsoft's behavior had crossed the line into unfair competition, and recommended that the company be split into two competing firms. However, the court overturned that penalty on appeal, and in November 2002 Microsoft reached a settlement with the government that it would end its restrictive practices.

The concept of restrictive practices is continually evolving, as firms seek new ways to earn profits and government regulators define what is permissible. A situation where the law is evolving and changing is always somewhat troublesome, since laws are most useful and fair when firms know what they are in advance. In addition, since the law is open to interpretation, competitors who are losing out in the market can accuse successful firms of anticompetitive restrictive practices, and try to win through government regulation what they have failed to accomplish in the market.

Officials at the Federal Trade Commission and the Department of Justice are, of course, aware of these issues, but there is no easy way to resolve them.

11.3 | Regulating Natural Monopolies

By the end of this section, you will be able to:
- Evaluate the appropriate competition policy for a natural monopoly
- Interpret a graph of regulatory choices
- Contrast cost-plus and price cap regulation

Most true monopolies today in the U.S. are regulated, natural monopolies. A natural monopoly poses a difficult challenge for competition policy, because the structure of costs and demand makes competition unlikely or costly. A **natural monopoly** arises when average costs are declining over the range of production that satisfies market demand. This typically happens when fixed costs are large relative to variable costs. As a result, one firm is able to supply the total quantity demanded in the market at lower cost than two or more firms—so splitting up the natural monopoly would raise the average cost of production and force customers to pay more.

Public utilities, the companies that have traditionally provided water and electrical service across much of the United States, are leading examples of natural monopoly. It would make little sense to argue that a local water company should be divided into several competing companies, each with its own separate set of pipes and water supplies. Installing four or five identical sets of pipes under a city, one for each water company, so that each household could choose its own water provider, would be terribly costly. The same argument applies to the idea of having many competing companies for delivering electricity to homes, each with its own set of wires. Before the advent of wireless phones, the argument also applied to the idea of many different phone companies, each with its own set of phone wires running through the neighborhood.

The Choices in Regulating a Natural Monopoly

What then is the appropriate competition policy for a natural monopoly? **Figure 11.3** illustrates the case of natural monopoly, with a market demand curve that cuts through the downward-sloping portion of the **average cost curve**. Points A, B, C, and F illustrate four of the main choices for regulation. **Table 11.3** outlines the regulatory choices for dealing with a natural monopoly.

This OpenStax book is available for free at http://cnx.org/content/col12122/1.4

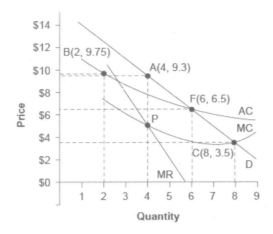

Figure 11.3 Regulatory Choices in Dealing with Natural Monopoly A natural monopoly will maximize profits by producing at the quantity where marginal revenue (MR) equals marginal costs (MC) and by then looking to the market demand curve to see what price to charge for this quantity. This monopoly will produce at point A, with a quantity of 4 and a price of 9.3. If antitrust regulators split this company exactly in half, then each half would produce at point B, with average costs of 9.75 and output of 2. The regulators might require the firm to produce where marginal cost crosses the market demand curve at point C. However, if the firm is required to produce at a quantity of 8 and sell at a price of 3.5, the firm will suffer from losses. The most likely choice is point F, where the firm is required to produce a quantity of 6 and charge a price of 6.5.

Quantity	Price	Total Revenue*	Marginal Revenue	Total Cost	Marginal Cost	Average Cost
1	14.7	14.7	14.7	11.0	-	11.00
2	12.4	24.7	10.0	19.5	8.5	9.75
3	10.6	31.7	7.0	25.5	6.0	8.50
4	9.3	37.2	5.5	31.0	5.5	7.75
5	8.0	40.0	2.8	35.0	4.0	7.00
6	6.5	39.0	−1.0	39.0	4.0	6.50
7	5.0	35.0	−4.0	42.0	3.0	6.00
8	3.5	28.0	−7.0	45.5	3.5	5.70
9	2.0	18.0	−10.0	49.5	4.0	5.5

Table 11.3 Regulatory Choices in Dealing with Natural Monopoly (*We obtain total revenue by multiplying price and quantity. However, we have rounded some of the price values in this table for ease of presentation.)

The first possibility is to leave the natural monopoly alone. In this case, the monopoly will follow its normal approach to maximizing profits. It determines the quantity where MR = MC, which happens at point P at a quantity of 4. The firm then looks to point A on the demand curve to find that it can charge a price of 9.3 for that profit-maximizing quantity. Since the price is above the average cost curve, the natural monopoly would earn economic profits.

A second outcome arises if antitrust authorities decide to divide the company, so that the new firms can compete. As a simple example, imagine that the company is cut in half. Thus, instead of one large firm producing a quantity of 4, two half-size firms each produce a quantity of 2. Because of the declining average cost curve (AC), the average cost of production for each of the half-size companies each producing 2, as point B shows, would be 9.75, while the average cost of production for a larger firm producing 4 would only be 7.75. Thus, the economy would become less productively efficient, since the good is produced at a higher average cost. In a situation with a downward-sloping average cost curve, two smaller firms will always have higher average costs of production than one larger firm for any quantity of total output. In addition, the antitrust authorities must worry that splitting the natural monopoly into pieces may be only the start of their problems. If one of the two firms grows larger than the other, it will have lower average costs and may be able to drive its competitor out of the market. Alternatively, two firms in a market may discover subtle ways of coordinating their behavior and keeping prices high. Either way, the result will not be the greater competition that was desired.

A third alternative is that regulators may decide to set prices and quantities produced for this industry. The regulators will try to choose a point along the market demand curve that benefits both consumers and the broader social interest. Point C illustrates one tempting choice: the regulator requires that the firm produce the quantity of output where marginal cost crosses the demand curve at an output of 8, and charge the price of 3.5, which is equal to **marginal cost** at that point. This rule is appealing because it requires price to be set equal to marginal cost, which is what would occur in a perfectly competitive market, and it would assure consumers a higher quantity and lower price than at the monopoly choice A. In fact, efficient allocation of resources would occur at point C, since the value to the consumers of the last unit bought and sold in this market is equal to the marginal cost of producing it.

Attempting to bring about point C through force of regulation, however, runs into a severe difficulty. At point C, with an output of 8, a price of 3.5 is below the average cost of production, which is 5.7, so if the firm charges a price of 3.5, it will be suffering losses. Unless the regulators or the government offer the firm an ongoing public subsidy (and there are numerous political problems with that option), the firm will lose money and go out of business.

Perhaps the most plausible option for the regulator is point F; that is, to set the price where AC crosses the demand curve at an output of 6 and a price of 6.5. This plan makes some sense at an intuitive level: let the natural monopoly charge enough to cover its average costs and earn a normal rate of profit, so that it can continue operating, but prevent the firm from raising prices and earning abnormally high monopoly profits, as it would at the monopoly choice A. Determining this level of output and price with the political pressures, time constraints, and limited information of the real world is much harder than identifying the point on a graph. For more on the problems that can arise from a centrally determined price, see the discussion of price floors and price ceilings in **Demand and Supply**.

Cost-Plus versus Price Cap Regulation

Regulators of public utilities for many decades followed the general approach of attempting to choose a point like F in **Figure 11.3**. They calculated the average cost of production for the water or electricity companies, added in an amount for the normal rate of profit the firm should expect to earn, and set the price for consumers accordingly. This method was known as **cost-plus regulation**.

Cost-plus regulation raises difficulties of its own. If producers receive reimbursement for their costs, plus a bit more, then at a minimum, producers have less reason to be concerned with high costs—because they can just pass them along in higher prices. Worse, firms under cost-plus regulation even have an incentive to generate high costs by building huge factories or employing many staff, because what they can charge is linked to the costs they incur.

Thus, in the 1980s and 1990s, some public utility regulators began to use **price cap regulation**, where the regulator sets a price that the firm can charge over the next few years. A common pattern was to require a price that declined slightly over time. If the firm can find ways of reducing its costs more quickly than the price caps, it can make a high level of profits. However, if the firm cannot keep up with the price caps or suffers bad luck in the market, it may suffer losses. A few years down the road, the regulators will then set a new series of price caps based on the firm's performance.

Price cap regulation requires delicacy. It will not work if the price regulators set the price cap unrealistically low. It may not work if the market changes dramatically so that the firm is doomed to incurring losses no matter what it does—say, if energy prices rise dramatically on world markets, then the company selling natural gas or heating oil to homes may not be able to meet price caps that seemed reasonable a year or two ago. However, if the regulators compare the prices with producers of the same good in other areas, they can, in effect, pressure a natural monopoly in one area to compete with the prices charged in other areas. Moreover, the possibility of earning greater profits or experiencing losses—instead of having an average rate of profit locked in every year by cost-plus regulation—can provide the natural monopoly with incentives for efficiency and innovation.

With natural monopoly, market competition is unlikely to take root, so if consumers are not to suffer the high prices

This OpenStax book is available for free at http://cnx.org/content/col12122/1.4

and restricted output of an unrestricted monopoly, government regulation will need to play a role. In attempting to design a system of price cap regulation with flexibility and incentive, government regulators do not have an easy task.

11.4 | The Great Deregulation Experiment

By the end of this section, you will be able to:

- Evaluate the effectiveness of price regulation and antitrust policy
- Explain regulatory capture and its significance

Governments at all levels across the United States have regulated prices in a wide range of industries. In some cases, like water and electricity that have natural monopoly characteristics, there is some room in economic theory for such regulation. However, once politicians are given a basis to intervene in markets and to choose prices and quantities, it is hard to know where to stop.

Doubts about Regulation of Prices and Quantities

Beginning in the 1970s, it became clear to policymakers of all political leanings that the existing price regulation was not working well. The United States carried out a great policy experiment—the **deregulation** that we discussed in **Monopoly**—removing government controls over prices and quantities produced in airlines, railroads, trucking, intercity bus travel, natural gas, and bank interest rates. The Clear It Up discusses the outcome of deregulation in one industry in particular—airlines.

What are the results of airline deregulation?

Why did the pendulum swing in favor of deregulation? Consider the airline industry. In the early days of air travel, no airline could make a profit just by flying passengers. Airlines needed something else to carry and the Postal Service provided that something with airmail. Thus, the first U.S. government regulation of the airline industry happened through the Postal Service, when in 1926 the Postmaster General began giving airlines permission to fly certain routes based on mail delivery needs—and the airlines took some passengers along for the ride. In 1934, the antitrust authorities charged the Postmaster General with colluding with the major airlines of that day to monopolize the nation's airways. In 1938, the U.S. government created the Civil Aeronautics Board (CAB) to regulate airfares and routes instead. For 40 years, from 1938 to 1978, the CAB approved all fares, controlled all entry and exit, and specified which airlines could fly which routes. There was zero entry of new airlines on the main routes across the country for 40 years, because the CAB did not think it was necessary.

In 1978, the Airline Deregulation Act took the government out of the business of determining airfares and schedules. The new law shook up the industry. Famous old airlines like Pan American, Eastern, and Braniff went bankrupt and disappeared. Some new airlines like People Express were created—and then vanished.

The greater competition from deregulation reduced airfares by about one-third over the next two decades, saving consumers billions of dollars a year. The average flight used to take off with just half its seats full; now it is two-thirds full, which is far more efficient. Airlines have also developed hub-and-spoke systems, where planes all fly into a central hub city at a certain time and then depart. As a result, one can fly between any of the spoke cities with just one connection—and there is greater service to more cities than before deregulation. With lower fares and more service, the number of air passengers doubled from the late 1970s to the start of the 2000s—an increase that, in turn, doubled the number of jobs in the airline industry. Meanwhile, with the watchful oversight of government safety inspectors, commercial air travel has continued to get safer over time.

The U.S. airline industry is far from perfect. For example, a string of mergers in recent years has raised concerns over how competition might be compromised.

One difficulty with government price regulation is what economists call **regulatory capture**, in which the firms that are supposedly regulated end up playing a large role in setting the regulations that they will follow. When the airline industry was regulated, for example, it suggested appointees to the regulatory board, sent lobbyists to argue with the board, provided most of the information on which the board made decisions, and offered well-paid jobs to at least some of the people leaving the board. In this situation, it is easy for regulators to poorly represent consumers. The result of regulatory capture is that government price regulation can often become a way for existing competitors to work together to reduce output, keep prices high, and limit competition.

The Effects of Deregulation

Deregulation, both of airlines and of other industries, has its negatives. The greater pressure of competition led to entry and exit. When firms went bankrupt or contracted substantially in size, they laid off workers who had to find other jobs. Market competition is, after all, a full-contact sport.

A number of major accounting scandals involving prominent corporations such as Enron, Tyco International, and WorldCom led to the **Sarbanes-Oxley Act** in 2002. The government designed Sarbanes-Oxley to increase confidence in financial information provided by public corporations to protect investors from accounting fraud.

The Great Recession, which began in late 2007, was caused at least in part by a global financial crisis, which began in the United States. The key component of the crisis was the creation and subsequent failure of several types of unregulated financial assets, such as collateralized mortgage obligations (CMOs, a type of mortgage-backed security), and credit default swaps (CDSs, insurance contracts on assets like CMOs that provided a payoff even if the holder of the CDS did not own the CMO). Private credit rating agencies such as Standard & Poors, Moody's, and Fitch rated many of these assets very safe.

The collapse of the markets for these assets precipitated the financial crisis and led to the failure of Lehman Brothers, a major investment bank, numerous large commercial banks, such as Wachovia, and even the Federal National Mortgage Corporation (Fannie Mae), which had to be nationalized—that is, taken over by the federal government. One response to the financial crisis was the **Dodd-Frank Act**, which majorly attempted to reform the financial system. The legislation's purpose, as noted on dodd-frank.com is:

> To promote the financial stability of the United States by improving accountability and transparency in the financial system, to end "too big to fail," to protect the American taxpayer by ending bailouts, [and] to protect consumers from abusive financial services practices. . .

All market-based economies operate against a background of laws and regulations, including laws about enforcing contracts, collecting taxes, and protecting health and the environment. The government policies that we discussed in this chapter—like blocking certain anticompetitive mergers, ending restrictive practices, imposing price cap regulation on natural monopolies, and deregulation—demonstrate the role of government to strengthen the incentives that come with a greater degree of competition.

Bring it Home

More than Cooking, Heating, and Cooling

What did the Federal Trade Commission (FTC) decide on the Kinder Morgan / El Paso Corporation merger? After careful examination, federal officials decided there was only one area of significant overlap that might provide the merged firm with strong market power. The FTC approved the merger, provided Kinder Morgan divest itself of the overlap area. Tallgrass purchased Kinder Morgan Interstate Gas Transmission, Trailblazer Pipeline Co. LLC, two processing facilities in Wyoming, and Kinder Morgan's 50 percent interest in the Rockies Express Pipeline to meet the FTC requirements. The FTC was attempting to strike a balance between potential cost reductions resulting from economies of scale and concentration of market power.

Did the price of natural gas decrease? Yes, rather significantly. In 2010, the wellhead price of natural gas was $4.48 per thousand cubic foot. In 2012 the price had fallen to just $2.66. Was the merger responsible for the large drop in price? The answer is uncertain. The larger contributor to the sharp drop in price was the overall increase in the supply of natural gas. Increasingly, more natural gas was able to be recovered by fracturing shale deposits, a process called fracking. Fracking, which is controversial for environmental reasons, enabled

This OpenStax book is available for free at http://cnx.org/content/col12122/1.4

the recovery of known reserves of natural gas that previously were not economically feasible to tap. Kinder Morgan's control of 80,000-plus miles of pipeline likely made moving the gas from wellheads to end users smoother and allowed for an even greater benefit from the increased supply.

KEY TERMS

acquisition when one firm purchases another

antitrust laws laws that give government the power to block certain mergers, and even in some cases to break up large firms into smaller ones

bundling a situation in which multiple products are sold as one

concentration ratio an early tool to measure the degree of monopoly power in an industry; measures what share of the total sales in the industry are accounted for by the largest firms, typically the top four to eight firms

cost-plus regulation when regulators permit a regulated firm to cover its costs and to make a normal level of profit

exclusive dealing an agreement that a dealer will sell only products from one manufacturer

four-firm concentration ratio the percentage of the total sales in the industry that are accounted for by the largest four firms

Herfindahl-Hirschman Index (HHI) approach to measuring market concentration by adding the square of the market share of each firm in the industry

market share the percentage of total sales in the market

merger when two formerly separate firms combine to become a single firm

minimum resale price maintenance agreement an agreement that requires a dealer who buys from a manufacturer to sell for at least a certain minimum price

price cap regulation when the regulator sets a price that a firm cannot exceed over the next few years

regulatory capture when the supposedly regulated firms end up playing a large role in setting the regulations that they will follow and as a result, they "capture" the people usually through the promise of a job in that "regulated" industry once their term in government has ended

restrictive practices practices that reduce competition but that do not involve outright agreements between firms to raise prices or to reduce the quantity produced

tying sales a situation where a customer is allowed to buy one product only if the customer also buys another product

KEY CONCEPTS AND SUMMARY

11.1 Corporate Mergers

A corporate merger involves two private firms joining together. An acquisition refers to one firm buying another firm. In either case, two formerly independent firms become one firm. Antitrust laws seek to ensure active competition in markets, sometimes by preventing large firms from forming through mergers and acquisitions, sometimes by regulating business practices that might restrict competition, and sometimes by breaking up large firms into smaller competitors.

A four-firm concentration ratio is one way of measuring the extent of competition in a market. We calculate it by adding the market shares—that is, the percentage of total sales—of the four largest firms in the market. A Herfindahl-Hirschman Index (HHI) is another way of measuring the extent of competition in a market. We calculate it by taking the market shares of all firms in the market, squaring them, and then summing the total.

The forces of globalization and new communications and information technology have increased the level of competition that many firms face by increasing the amount of competition from other regions and countries.

This OpenStax book is available for free at http://cnx.org/content/col12122/1.4

11.2 Regulating Anticompetitive Behavior

Antitrust firms block authorities from openly colluding to form a cartel that will reduce output and raise prices. Companies sometimes attempt to find other ways around these restrictions and, consequently, many antitrust cases involve restrictive practices that can reduce competition in certain circumstances, like tie-in sales, bundling, and predatory pricing.

11.3 Regulating Natural Monopolies

In the case of a natural monopoly, market competition will not work well and so, rather than allowing an unregulated monopoly to raise price and reduce output, the government may wish to regulate price and/or output. Common examples of regulation are public utilities, the regulated firms that often provide electricity and water service.

Cost-plus regulation refers to government regulating a firm which sets the price that a firm can charge over a period of time by looking at the firm's accounting costs and then adding a normal rate of profit. Price cap regulation refers to government regulation of a firm where the government sets a price level several years in advance. In this case, the firm can either earn high profits if it manages to produce at lower costs or sell a higher quantity than expected or suffer low profits or losses if costs are high or it sells less than expected.

11.4 The Great Deregulation Experiment

The U.S. economy experienced a wave of deregulation in the late 1970s and early 1980s, when the government eliminated a number of regulations that had set prices and quantities produced in a number of industries. Major accounting scandals in the early 2000s and, more recently, the Great Recession have spurred new regulation to prevent similar occurrences in the future. Regulatory capture occurs when the regulated industries end up having a strong influence over what regulations exist.

SELF-CHECK QUESTIONS

1. Is it true that a merger between two firms that are not already in the top four by size can affect both the four-firm concentration ratio and the Herfindahl-Hirshman Index? Explain briefly.

2. Is it true that the four-firm concentration ratio puts more emphasis on one or two very large firms, while the Herfindahl-Hirshman Index puts more emphasis on all the firms in the entire market? Explain briefly.

3. Some years ago, two intercity bus companies, Greyhound Lines, Inc. and Trailways Transportation System, wanted to merge. One possible definition of the market in this case was "the market for intercity bus service." Another possible definition was "the market for intercity transportation, including personal cars, car rentals, passenger trains, and commuter air flights." Which definition do you think the bus companies preferred, and why?

4. As a result of globalization and new information and communications technology, would you expect that the definitions of markets that antitrust authorities use will become broader or narrower?

5. Why would a firm choose to use one or more of the anticompetitive practices described in Regulating Anticompetitive Behavior?

6. Urban transit systems, especially those with rail systems, typically experience significant economies of scale in operation. Consider the transit system data in **Table 11.4**. Note that the quantity is in millions of riders.

Demand:	Quantity	1	2	3	4	5	6	7	8	9	10
	Price	10	9	8	7	6	5	4	3	2	1
	Marginal Revenue	10	8	6	4	2	0	–2	–4	–6	–8
Costs:	Marginal Cost	9	6	5	3	2	3	4	5	7	10
	Average Cost	9	7.5	6.7	5.8	5	4.7	4.6	4.6	4.9	5.4

Table 11.4

Draw the demand, marginal revenue, marginal cost, and average cost curves. Do they have the normal shapes?

7. From the graph you drew to answer **Exercise 11.6**, would you say this transit system is a natural monopoly? Justify.

Use the following information to answer the next three questions. In the years before wireless phones, when telephone technology required having a wire running to every home, it seemed plausible that telephone service had diminishing average costs and might require regulation like a natural monopoly. For most of the twentieth century, the national U.S. phone company was AT&T, and the company functioned as a regulated monopoly. Think about the deregulation of the U.S. telecommunications industry that has occurred over the last few decades. (This is not a research assignment, but a thought assignment based on what you have learned in this chapter.)

8. What real world changes made the deregulation possible?

9. What are some of the benefits of the deregulation?

10. What might some of the negatives of deregulation be?

REVIEW QUESTIONS

11. What is a corporate merger? What is an acquisition?

12. What is the goal of antitrust policies?

13. How do we measure a four-firm concentration ratio? What does a high measure mean about the extent of competition?

14. How do we measure a Herfindahl-Hirshman Index? What does a low measure mean about the extent of competition?

15. Why can it be difficult to decide what a "market" is for purposes of measuring competition?

16. What is a minimum resale price maintenance agreement? How might it reduce competition and when might it be acceptable?

17. What is exclusive dealing? How might it reduce competition and when might it be acceptable?

18. What is a tie-in sale? How might it reduce competition and when might it be acceptable?

19. What is predatory pricing? How might it reduce competition, and why might it be difficult to tell when it should be illegal?

20. If public utilities are a natural monopoly, what would be the danger in deregulating them?

21. If public utilities are a natural monopoly, what would be the danger in splitting them into a number of separate competing firms?

22. What is cost-plus regulation?

23. What is price cap regulation?

24. What is deregulation? Name some industries that have been deregulated in the United States.

25. What is regulatory capture?

This OpenStax book is available for free at http://cnx.org/content/col12122/1.4

26. Why does regulatory capture reduce the persuasiveness of the case for regulating industries for the benefit of consumers?

CRITICAL THINKING QUESTIONS

27. Does either the four-firm concentration ratio or the HHI directly measure the amount of competition in an industry? Why or why not?

28. What would be evidence of serious competition between firms in an industry? Can you identify two highly competitive industries?

29. Can you think of any examples of successful predatory pricing in the real world?

30. If you were developing a product (like a web browser) for a market with significant barriers to entry, how would you try to get your product into the market successfully?

31. In the middle of the twentieth century, major U.S. cities had multiple competing city bus companies. Today, there is usually only one and it runs as a subsidized, regulated monopoly. What do you suppose caused the change?

32. Why are urban areas willing to subsidize urban transit systems? Does the argument for subsidies make sense to you?

33. Deregulation, like all changes in government policy, always has pluses and minuses. What do you think some of the minuses might be for airline deregulation?

34. Do you think it is possible for government to outlaw everything that businesses could do wrong? If so, why does government not do that? If not, how can regulation stay ahead of rogue businesses that push the limits of the system until it breaks?

PROBLEMS

35. Use **Table 11.5** to calculate the four-firm concentration ratio for the U.S. auto market. Does this indicate a concentrated market or not?

GM	19%
Ford	17%
Toyota	14%
Chrysler	11%

Table 11.5 Global Auto Manufacturers with Top Four U.S. Market Share, June 2013 (Source: http://www.zacks.com/commentary/27690/auto-industry-stock-outlook-june-2013)

36. Use **Table 11.5** and **Table 11.6** to calculate the Herfindal-Hirschman Index for the U.S. auto market. Would the FTC approve a merger between GM and Ford?

Honda	10%
Nissan	7%
Hyundai	5%
Kia	4%
Subaru	3%
Volkswagen	3%

Table 11.6 Global Auto Manufacturers with additional U.S. Market Share, June 2013 (Source: http://www.zacks.com/commentary/27690/auto-industry-stock-outlook-june-2013)

Use **Table 11.4** to answer the following questions.

37. If the transit system were allowed to operate as an unregulated monopoly, what output would it supply and what price would it charge?

38. If the transit system were regulated to operate with no subsidy (i.e., at zero economic profit), what approximate output would it supply and what approximate price would it charge?

39. If the transit system were regulated to provide the most allocatively efficient quantity of output, what output would it supply and what price would it charge? What subsidy would be necessary to insure this efficient provision of transit services?

This OpenStax book is available for free at http://cnx.org/content/col12122/1.4

12 | Environmental Protection and Negative Externalities

Figure 12.1 Environmental Debate Across the country, countless people have protested, even risking arrest, against the Keystone XL Pipeline. (Credit: modification of image by "NoKXL"/Flickr Creative Commons)

Bring it Home

Keystone XL

You might have heard about Keystone XL in the news. It is a pipeline system designed to bring oil from Canada to the refineries near the Gulf of Mexico, as well as to boost crude oil production in the United States. While a private company, TransCanada, will own the pipeline, U.S. government approval is required because of its size and location. There are four phases in building the pipeline, with the first two currently in operation, bringing oil from Alberta, Canada, east across Canada, south through the United States into Nebraska and Oklahoma, and northeast again to Illinois. The project's third and fourth phases, known as Keystone XL, would create a pipeline southeast from Alberta straight to Nebraska, and then from Oklahoma to the Gulf of Mexico.

Sounds like a great idea, right? A pipeline that would move much needed crude oil to the Gulf refineries would increase oil production for manufacturing needs, reduce price pressure at the gas pump, and increase overall economic growth. Supporters argue that the pipeline is one of the safest pipelines built yet, and would reduce America's dependence on politically vulnerable Middle Eastern oil imports.

Not so fast, say its critics. The Keystone XL would be constructed over an enormous aquifer (one of the largest in the world) in the Midwest, and through an environmentally fragile area in Nebraska, causing great concern among environmentalists about possible destruction to the natural surroundings. They argue that leaks could taint valuable water sources and pipeline construction could disrupt and even harm indigenous species. Environmentalist groups have fought government approval of the proposed pipeline construction, and as of press time the pipeline projects remain stalled.

Environmental concerns matter when discussing issues related to economic growth. However, how much should economists factor in these issues when deciding policy? In the case of the pipeline, how do we know how much damage it would cause when we do not know how to put a value on the environment? Would the pipeline's benefits outweigh the opportunity cost? The issue of how to balance economic progress with unintended effects on our planet is the subject of this chapter.

Introduction to Environmental Protection and Negative Externalities

In this chapter, you will learn about:

- The Economics of Pollution

- Command-and-Control Regulation

- Market-Oriented Environmental Tools

- The Benefits and Costs of U.S. Environmental Laws

- International Environmental Issues

- The Tradeoff between Economic Output and Environmental Protection

In 1969, the Cuyahoga River in Ohio was so polluted that it spontaneously burst into flame. Air pollution was so bad at that time that Chattanooga, Tennessee was a city where, as an article from *Sports Illustrated* put it: "the death rate from tuberculosis was double that of the rest of Tennessee and triple that of the rest of the United States, a city in which the filth in the air was so bad it melted nylon stockings off women's legs, in which executives kept supplies of clean white shirts in their offices so they could change when a shirt became too gray to be presentable, in which headlights were turned on at high noon because the sun was eclipsed by the gunk in the sky."

The problem of pollution arises for every economy in the world, whether high-income or low-income, and whether market-oriented or command-oriented. Every country needs to strike some balance between production and environmental quality. This chapter begins by discussing how firms may fail to take certain social costs, like pollution, into their planning if they do not need to pay these costs. Traditionally, policies for environmental protection have focused on governmental limits on how much of each pollutant could be emitted. While this approach has had some success, economists have suggested a range of more flexible, market-oriented policies that reduce pollution at a lower cost. We will consider both approaches, but first let's see how economists frame and analyze these issues.

12.1 | The Economics of Pollution

By the end of this section, you will be able to:
- Explain and give examples of positive and negative externalities
- Identify equilibrium price and quantity
- Evaluate how firms can contribute to market failure

From 1970 to 2012, the U.S. population increased by one-third and the size of the U.S. economy more than doubled. Since the 1970s, however, the United States, using a variety of anti-pollution policies, has made genuine progress against a number of pollutants. **Table 12.1** lists the change in carbon dioxide emissions by energy users (from residential to industrial) according to the U.S. Energy Information Administration (EIA). The table shows that emissions of certain key air pollutants declined substantially from 2007 to 2012. They dropped 740 million metric tons (MMT) a year—a 12% reduction. This seems to indicate that there has been progress made in the United States in reducing overall carbon dioxide emissions, which contribute to the greenhouse effect.

This OpenStax book is available for free at http://cnx.org/content/col12122/1.4

End-use Sector	Primary Fossil Fuels			Purchased Electric Power	Total Primary Fossil Fuels
	Coal	Petroleum	Natural Gas		
Residential	0	(16)	3	(182)	(202)
Commercial	(4)	16	(13)	(168)	(145)
Industrial	(40)	(77)	(65)	(161)	(222)
Transportation	0	(174)	4	(1)	(171)
Power	(637)	(31)	(154)	-	-
Change 2007–2015	(686)	(282)	(232)	(−521)	(740)

Table 12.1 U.S. Carbon Dioxide (CO_2) Emissions from Fossil Fuels Consumed 2007–2012, Million Metric Tons (MMT) per Year (Source: EIA Monthly Energy Review)

Despite the gradual reduction in emissions from fossil fuels, many important environmental issues remain. Along with the still high levels of air and water pollution, other issues include hazardous waste disposal, destruction of wetlands and other wildlife habitats, and the impact on human health from pollution.

Externalities

Private markets, such as the cell phone industry, offer an efficient way to put buyers and sellers together and determine what goods they produce, how they produce them and who gets them. The principle that voluntary exchange benefits both buyers and sellers is a fundamental building block of the economic way of thinking. However, what happens when a voluntary exchange affects a third party who is neither the buyer nor the seller?

As an example, consider a concert producer who wants to build an outdoor arena that will host country music concerts a half-mile from your neighborhood. You will be able to hear these outdoor concerts while sitting on your back porch—or perhaps even in your dining room. In this case, the sellers and buyers of concert tickets may both be quite satisfied with their voluntary exchange, but you have no voice in their market transaction. The effect of a market exchange on a third party who is outside or "external" to the exchange is called an **externality**. Because externalities that occur in market transactions affect other parties beyond those involved, they are sometimes called **spillovers**.

Externalities can be negative or positive. If you hate country music, then having it waft into your house every night would be a **negative externality**. If you love country music, then what amounts to a series of free concerts would be a **positive externality**.

Pollution as a Negative Externality

Pollution is a negative externality. Economists illustrate the **social costs** of production with a demand and supply diagram. The social costs include the private costs of production that a company incurs and the external costs of pollution that pass on to society. **Figure 12.2** shows the demand and supply for manufacturing refrigerators. The demand curve (D) shows the quantity demanded at each price. The supply curve ($S_{private}$) shows the quantity of refrigerators that all firms in the industry supply at each price assuming they are taking only their private costs into account and they are allowed to emit pollution at zero cost. The market equilibrium (E_0), where quantity supplied equals quantity demanded, is at a price of $650 per refrigerator and a quantity of 45,000 refrigerators. **Table 12.2** reflects this information in the first three columns.

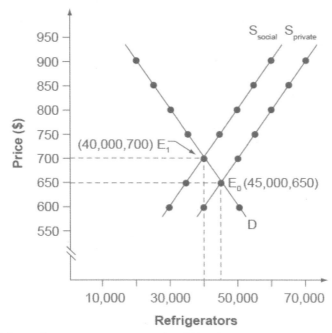

Figure 12.2 Taking Social Costs into Account: A Supply Shift If the firm takes only its own costs of production into account, then its supply curve will be $S_{private}$, and the market equilibrium will occur at E_0. Accounting for additional external costs of $100 for every unit produced, the firm's supply curve will be S_{social}. The new equilibrium will occur at E_1.

Price	Quantity Demanded	Quantity Supplied before Considering Pollution Cost	Quantity Supplied after Considering Pollution Cost
$600	50,000	40,000	30,000
$650	45,000	45,000	35,000
$700	40,000	50,000	40,000
$750	35,000	55,000	45,000
$800	30,000	60,000	50,000
$850	25,000	65,000	55,000
$900	20,000	70,000	60,000

Table 12.2 A Supply Shift Caused by Pollution Costs

However, as a by-product of the metals, plastics, chemicals and energy that refrigerator manufacturers use, some pollution is created. Let's say that, if these pollutants were emitted into the air and water, they would create costs of $100 per refrigerator produced. These costs might occur because of adverse effects on human health, property values, or wildlife habitat, reduction of recreation possibilities, or because of other negative impacts. In a market with no anti-pollution restrictions, firms can dispose of certain wastes absolutely free. Now imagine that firms which produce refrigerators must factor in these external costs of pollution—that is, the firms have to consider not only labor and material costs, but also the broader costs to society of harm to health and other costs caused by pollution. If the firm is required to pay $100 for the **additional external costs** of pollution each time it produces a refrigerator, production becomes more costly and the entire supply curve shifts up by $100.

As **Table 12.2** and **Figure 12.2** illustrate, the firm will need to receive a price of $700 per refrigerator and produce

This OpenStax book is available for free at http://cnx.org/content/col12122/1.4

a quantity of 40,000—and the firm's new supply curve will be S_{social}. The new equilibrium will occur at E_1. In short, taking the additional external costs of pollution into account results in a higher price, a lower quantity of production, and a lower quantity of pollution. The following Work It Out feature will walk you through an example, this time with musical accompaniment.

Work It Out ⊢O—O—O

Identifying the Equilibrium Price and Quantity

Table 12.3 shows the supply and demand conditions for a firm that will play trumpets on the streets when requested. We measure output is measured as the number of songs played.

Price	Quantity Demanded	Quantity Supplied without paying the costs of the externality	Quantity Supplied after paying the costs of the externality
$20	0	10	8
$18	1	9	7
$15	2.5	7.5	5.5
$12	4	6	4
$10	5	5	3
$5	7.5	2.5	0.5

Table 12.3 Supply and Demand Conditions for a Trumpet-Playing Firm

Step 1. Determine the negative externality in this situation. To do this, you must think about the situation and consider all parties that might be impacted. A negative externality might be the increase in noise pollution in the area where the firm is playing.

Step 2. Identify the initial equilibrium price and quantity only taking private costs into account. Next, identify the new equilibrium taking into account social costs as well as private costs. Remember that equilibrium is where the quantity demanded is equal to the quantity supplied.

Step 3. Look down the columns to where the quantity demanded (the second column) is equal to the "quantity supplied without paying the costs of the externality" (the third column). Then refer to the first column of that row to determine the equilibrium price. In this case, the equilibrium price and quantity would be at a price of $10 and a quantity of five when we only take into account private costs.

Step 4. Identify the equilibrium price and quantity when we take into account the additional external costs. Look down the columns of quantity demanded (the second column) and the "quantity supplied after paying the costs of the externality" (the fourth column) then refer to the first column of that row to determine the equilibrium price. In this case, the equilibrium will be at a price of $12 and a quantity of four.

Step 5. Consider how taking into account the externality affects the equilibrium price and quantity. Do this by comparing the two equilibrium situations. If the firm is forced to pay its additional external costs, then production of trumpet songs becomes more costly, and the supply curve will shift up.

Remember that the supply curve is based on choices about production that firms make while looking at their marginal costs, while the demand curve is based on the benefits that individuals perceive while maximizing utility. If no externalities existed, private costs would be the same as the costs to society as a whole, and private benefits would be the same as the benefits to society as a whole. Thus, if no externalities existed, the interaction of demand and supply will coordinate social costs and benefits.

However, when the externality of pollution exists, the supply curve no longer represents all social costs. Because externalities represent a case where markets no longer consider all social costs, but only some of them, economists commonly refer to externalities as an example of **market failure**. When there is market failure, the private market fails to achieve efficient output, because either firms do not account for all costs incurred in the production of output and/or consumers do not account for all benefits obtained (a positive externality). In the case of pollution, at the market output, social costs of production exceed social benefits to consumers, and the market produces too much of the product.

We can see a general lesson here. If firms were required to pay the social costs of pollution, they would create less pollution but produce less of the product and charge a higher price. In the next module, we will explore how governments require firms to account for the social costs of pollution.

12.2 | Command-and-Control Regulation

By the end of this section, you will be able to:
- Explain command-and-control regulation
- Evaluate the effectiveness of command-and-control regulation

When the United States started passing comprehensive environmental laws in the late 1960s and early 1970s, a typical law specified to companies how much pollution their smokestacks or drainpipes could emit and imposed penalties if companies exceeded the limit. Other laws required that companies install certain equipment—for example, on automobile tailpipes or on smokestacks—to reduce pollution. These types of laws, which specify allowable quantities of pollution and which also may detail which pollution-control technologies companies must use, fall under the category of **command-and-control regulation**. In effect, command-and-control regulation requires that firms increase their costs by installing anti-pollution equipment. Thus, firms are required to account for the social costs of pollution in deciding how much output to produce.

Command-and-control regulation has been highly successful in protecting and cleaning up the U.S. environment. In 1970, the Federal government created Environmental Protection Agency (EPA) to oversee all environmental laws. In the same year, Congress enacted the Clean Air Act to address air pollution. Just two years later, in 1972, Congress passed and the president signed the far-reaching Clean Water Act. These command-and-control environmental laws, and their amendments and updates, have been largely responsible for America's cleaner air and water in recent decades. However, economists have pointed out three difficulties with command-and-control environmental regulation.

First, command-and-control regulation offers no incentive to improve the quality of the environment beyond the standard set by a particular law. Once firms meet the standard, polluters have zero incentive to do better.

Second, command-and-control regulation is inflexible. It usually requires the same standard for all polluters, and often the same pollution-control technology as well. This means that command-and-control regulation draws no distinctions between firms that would find it easy and inexpensive to meet the pollution standard—or to reduce pollution even further—and firms that might find it difficult and costly to meet the standard. Firms have no reason to rethink their production methods in fundamental ways that might reduce pollution even more and at lower cost.

Third, legislators and EPA analysts write the command-and-control regulations, and so they are subject to compromises in the political process. Existing firms often argue (and lobby) that stricter environmental standards should not apply to them, only to new firms that wish to start production. Consequently, real-world environmental laws are full of fine print, loopholes, and exceptions.

Although critics accept the goal of reducing pollution, they question whether command-and-control regulation is the best way to design policy tools for accomplishing that goal. A different approach is the use of market-oriented tools, which we discussed in the next section.

12.3 | Market-Oriented Environmental Tools

By the end of this section, you will be able to:

- Show how pollution charges impact firm decisions
- Suggest other laws and regulations that could fall under pollution charges
- Explain the significance of marketable permits and property rights
- Evaluate which policies are most appropriate for various situations

Market-oriented environmental policies create incentives to allow firms some flexibility in reducing pollution. The three main categories of market-oriented approaches to pollution control are pollution charges, marketable permits, and better-defined property rights. All of these policy tools which we discuss, below, address the shortcomings of command-and-control regulation—albeit in different ways.

Pollution Charges

A **pollution charge** is a tax imposed on the quantity of pollution that a firm emits. A pollution charge gives a profit-maximizing firm an incentive to determine ways to reduce its emissions—as long as the marginal cost of reducing the emissions is less than the tax.

For example, consider a small firm that emits 50 pounds per year of small particles, such as soot, into the air. This particulate matter causes respiratory illnesses and also imposes costs on firms and individuals.

Figure 12.3 illustrates the marginal costs that a firm faces in reducing pollution. The marginal cost of pollution reduction, like most most marginal cost curves increases with output, at least in the short run. Reducing the first 10 pounds of particulate emissions costs the firm $300. Reducing the second 10 pounds would cost $500; reducing the third ten pounds would cost $900; reducing the fourth 10 pounds would cost $1,500; and the fifth 10 pounds would cost $2,500. This pattern for the costs of reducing pollution is common, because the firm can use the cheapest and easiest method to make initial reductions in pollution, but additional reductions in pollution become more expensive.

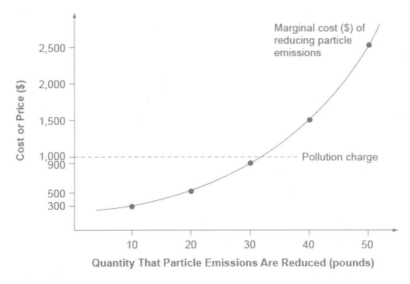

Figure 12.3 A Pollution Charge   If a pollution charge is set equal to $1,000, then the firm will have an incentive to reduce pollution by 30 pounds because the $900 cost of these reductions would be less than the cost of paying the pollution charge.

Imagine the firm now faces a pollution tax of $1,000 for every 10 pounds of particulates it emits. The firm has the choice of either polluting and paying the tax, or reducing the amount of particulates it emits and paying the cost of abatement as the figure shows. How much will the firm pollute and how much will the firm abate? The first 10 pounds would cost the firm $300 to abate. This is substantially less than the $1,000 tax, so the firm will choose to abate. The second 10 pounds would cost $500 to abate, which is still less than the tax, so it will choose to abate. The third 10 pounds would cost $900 to abate, which is slightly less than the $1,000 tax. The fourth 10 pounds would cost $1,500, which is much more costly than paying the tax. As a result, the firm will decide to reduce pollutants by 30 pounds, because the marginal cost of reducing pollution by this amount is less than the pollution tax. With a tax of $1,000, the firm has no incentive to reduce pollution more than 30 pounds.

A firm that has to pay a pollution tax will have an incentive to figure out the least expensive technologies for reducing pollution. Firms that can reduce pollution cheaply and easily will do so to minimize their pollution taxes; whereas firms that will incur high costs for reducing pollution will end up paying the pollution tax instead. If the pollution tax applies to every source of pollution, then there are no special favoritism or loopholes for politically well-connected producers.

For an example of a pollution charge at the household level, consider two ways of charging for garbage collection. One method is to have a flat fee per household, no matter how much garbage a household produces. An alternative approach is to have several levels of fees, depending on how much garbage the household produces—and to offer lower or free charges for recyclable materials. As of 2006 (latest statistics available), the EPA had recorded over 7,000 communities that have implemented "pay as you throw" programs. When people have a financial incentive to put out less garbage and to increase recycling, they find ways to make it happen.

Link It Up

Visit this website (http://openstaxcollege.org/l/payasyouthrow) to learn more about pay-as-you-throw programs, including viewing a map and a table that shows the number of communities using this program in each state.

A number of environmental policies are really pollution charges, although they often do not travel under that name. For example, the federal government and many state governments impose taxes on gasoline. We can view this tax as a charge on the air pollution that cars generate as well as a source of funding for maintaining roads. Gasoline taxes are far higher in most other countries than in the United States.

Similarly, the refundable charge of five or 10 cents that only 10 states have for returning recyclable cans and bottles works like a pollution tax that provides an incentive to avoid littering or throwing bottles in the trash. Compared with command-and-control regulation, a pollution tax reduces pollution in a more flexible and cost-effective way.

Link It Up

Visit this website (http://openstaxcollege.org/l/bottlebill) to see the current U.S. states with bottle bills and the states that have active campaigns for new bottle bills. You can also view current and proposed bills in Canada and other countries around the world.

Marketable Permits

When a city or state government sets up a **marketable permit program** (e.g. cap-and-trade), it must start by determining the overall quantity of pollution it will allow as it tries to meet national pollution standards. Then, it divides a number of permits allowing only this quantity of pollution among the firms that emit that pollutant. The government can sell or provide these permits to pollute free to firms.

Now, add two more conditions. Imagine that these permits are designed to reduce total emissions over time. For example, a permit may allow emission of 10 units of pollution one year, but only nine units the next year, then eight units the year after that, and so on down to some lower level. In addition, imagine that these are marketable permits, meaning that firms can buy and sell them.

To see how marketable permits can work to reduce pollution, consider the four firms in **Table 12.4**. The table shows current emissions of lead from each firm. At the start of the marketable permit program, each firm receives permits to allow this level of pollution. However, these permits are shrinkable, and next year the permits allow the firms to emit only half as much pollution. Let's say that in a year, Firm Gamma finds it easy and cheap to reduce emissions from 600 tons of lead to 200 tons, which means that it has permits that it is not using that allow emitting 100 tons of lead. Firm Beta reduces its lead pollution from 400 tons to 200 tons, so it does not need to buy any permits, and it does not have any extra permits to sell. However, although Firm Alpha can easily reduce pollution from 200 tons to 150 tons, it finds that it is cheaper to purchase permits from Gamma rather than to reduce its own emissions to 100. Meanwhile, Firm Delta did not even exist in the first period, so the only way it can start production is to purchase permits to emit 50 tons of lead.

The total quantity of pollution will decline. However, buying and selling the marketable permits will determine exactly which firms reduce pollution and by how much. With a system of marketable permits, the firms that find it least expensive to do so will reduce pollution the most.

	Firm Alpha	Firm Beta	Firm Gamma	Firm Delta
Current emissions—permits distributed free for this amount	200 tons	400 tons	600 tons	0 tons
How much pollution will these permits allow in one year?	100 tons	200 tons	300 tons	0 tons
Actual emissions one year in the future	150 tons	200 tons	200 tons	50 tons
Buyer or seller of marketable permit?	Buys permits for 50 tons	Doesn't buy or sell permits	Sells permits for 100 tons	Buys permits for 50 tons

Table 12.4 How Marketable Permits Work

Another application of marketable permits occurred when the U.S. government amended the Clean Air Act in 1990. The revised law sought to reduce sulfur dioxide emissions from electric power plants to half of the 1980 levels out of concern that sulfur dioxide was causing acid rain, which harms forests as well as buildings. In this case, the marketable permits the federal government issued were free of charge (no pun intended) to electricity-generating plants across the country, especially those that were burning coal (which produces sulfur dioxide). These permits were of the "shrinkable" type; that is, the amount of pollution allowed by a given permit declined with time.

Better-Defined Property Rights

A clarified and strengthened idea of property rights can also strike a balance between economic activity and pollution. Ronald Coase (1910–2013), who won the 1991 Nobel Prize in economics, offered a vivid illustration of an externality: a railroad track running beside a farmer's field where the railroad locomotive sometimes emits sparks and sets the field ablaze. Coase asked whose responsibility it was to address this spillover. Should the farmer be required to build a tall fence alongside the field to block the sparks, or should the railroad be required to place a gadget on the locomotive's smokestack to reduce the number of sparks?

Coase pointed out that one cannot resolve this issue until one clearly defines **property rights**—that is, the legal rights of ownership on which others are not allowed to infringe without paying compensation. Does the farmer have a property right not to have a field burned? Does the railroad have a property right to run its own trains on its own tracks? If neither party has a property right, then the two sides may squabble endlessly, doing nothing, and sparks will continue to set the field aflame. However, if either the farmer or the railroad has a well-defined legal responsibility, then that party will seek out and pay for the least costly method of reducing the risk that sparks will hit the field. The property right determines whether the farmer or the railroad pays the bills.

The property rights approach is highly relevant in cases involving endangered species. The U.S. government's endangered species list includes about 1,000 plants and animals, and about 90% of these species live on privately owned land. The protection of these endangered species requires careful thinking about incentives and property rights. The discovery of an endangered species on private land has often triggered an automatic reaction from the government to prohibit the landowner from using that land for any purpose that might disturb the imperiled creatures. Consider the incentives of that policy: If you admit to the government that you have an endangered species, the government effectively prohibits you from using your land. As a result, rumors abounded of landowners who followed a policy of "shoot, shovel, and shut up" when they found an endangered animal on their land. Other landowners have deliberately cut trees or managed land in a way that they knew would discourage endangered animals from locating there.

How effective are market-oriented environmental policy tools?

Environmentalists sometimes fear that market-oriented environmental tools are an excuse to weaken or eliminate strict limits on pollution emissions and instead to allow more pollution. It is true that if pollution charges are set very low or if marketable permits do not reduce pollution by very much then market-oriented tools will not work well. However, command-and-control environmental laws can also be full of loopholes or have exemptions that do not reduce pollution by much, either. The advantage of market-oriented environmental tools is not that they reduce pollution by more or less, but because of their incentives and flexibility, they can achieve any desired reduction in pollution at a lower cost to society.

A more productive policy would consider how to provide private landowners with an incentive to protect the endangered species that they find and to provide a habitat for additional endangered species. For example, the government might pay landowners who provide and maintain suitable habitats for endangered species or who restrict the use of their land to protect an endangered species. Again, an environmental law built on incentives and flexibility offers greater promise than a command-and-control approach when trying to oversee millions of acres of privately owned land.

Applying Market-Oriented Environmental Tools

Market-oriented environmental policies are a tool kit. Specific policy tools will work better in some situations than in others. For example, marketable permits work best when a few dozen or a few hundred parties are highly interested in trading, as in the cases of oil refineries that trade lead permits or electrical utilities that trade sulfur dioxide permits. However, for cases in which millions of users emit small amounts of pollution—such as emissions from car engines or unrecycled soda cans—and have no strong interest in trading, pollution charges will typically offer a better choice. We can also combine market-oriented environmental tools. We can view marketable permits as a form of improved property rights. Alternatively, the government could combine marketable permits with a pollution tax on any emissions not covered by a permit.

12.4 | The Benefits and Costs of U.S. Environmental Laws

By the end of this section, you will be able to:
- Evaluate the benefits and costs of environmental protection
- Explain the effects of ecotourism
- Apply marginal analysis to illustrate the marginal costs and marginal benefits of reducing pollution

Government economists have estimated that U.S. firms may pay more than $200 billion per year to comply with federal environmental laws. That is a sizable amount of money. Is the money well spent?

Benefits and Costs of Clean Air and Clean Water

We can divide the benefits of a cleaner environment into four areas: (1) people may stay healthier and live longer; (2) certain industries that rely on clean air and water, such as farming, fishing, and tourism, may benefit; (3) property values may be higher; and (4) people may simply enjoy a cleaner environment in a way that does not need to involve a market transaction. Some of these benefits, such as gains to tourism or farming, are relatively easy to value in economic terms. It is harder to assign a monetary value to others, such as the value of clean air for someone with asthma. It seems impossible to put a clear-cut monetary value on still others, such as the satisfaction you might feel from knowing that the air is clear over the Grand Canyon, even if you have never visited the Grand Canyon.

Although estimates of environmental benefits are not precise, they can still be revealing. For example, a study by the Environmental Protection Agency looked at the costs and benefits of the Clean Air Act from 1970 to 1990. It found that total costs over that time period were roughly $500 billion—a huge amount. However, it also found that a middle-range estimate of the health and other benefits from cleaner air was $22 trillion—about 44 times higher than the costs. A more recent EPA study estimated that the environmental benefits to Americans from the Clean Air Act will exceed their costs by a margin of four to one. The EPA estimated that "in 2010 the benefits of Clean Air Act programs will total about $110 billion. This estimate represents the value of avoiding increases in illness and premature death which would have prevailed." Saying that overall benefits of environmental regulation have exceeded costs in the past, however, is very different from saying that every environmental regulation makes sense. For example, studies suggest that when breaking down emission reductions by type of contaminants, the benefits of air pollution control outweigh the costs primarily for particulates and lead, but when looking at other air pollutants, the costs of reducing them may be comparable to or greater than the benefits. Just because some environmental regulations have had benefits much higher than costs does not prove that every individual regulation is a sensible idea.

Ecotourism: Making Environmentalism Pay

The definition of ecotourism is a little vague. Does it mean sleeping on the ground, eating roots, and getting close to wild animals? Does it mean flying in a helicopter to shoot anesthetic darts at African wildlife, or a little of both? The definition may be fuzzy, but tourists who hope to appreciate the ecology of their destination—"eco tourists"—are the impetus to a big and growing business. The International Ecotourism Society estimates that international tourists interested in seeing nature or wildlife will take 1.56 billion trips by 2020.

Link It Up

Visit The International Ecotourism Society's website (http://openstaxcollege.org/l/ecotourism) to learn more about The International Ecotourism Society, its programs, and tourism's role in sustainable community development.

Realizing the attraction of ecotourism, the residents of low-income countries may come to see that preserving wildlife habitats is more lucrative than, say, cutting down forests or grazing livestock to survive. In South Africa, Namibia, and Zimbabwe, for example, a substantial expansion of both rhinoceros and elephant populations is broadly credited to ecotourism, which has given local communities an economic interest in protecting them. Some of the leading ecotourism destinations include: Costa Rica and Panama in Central America; the Caribbean; Malaysia, and other South Pacific destinations; New Zealand; the Serengeti in Tanzania; the Amazon rain forests; and the Galapagos Islands. In many of these countries and regions, governments have enacted policies whereby they share revenues from ecotourism with local communities, to give people in those local communities a kind of property right that encourages them to conserve their local environment.

Ecotourism needs careful management, so that the combination of eager tourists and local entrepreneurs does not destroy what the visitors are coming to see. However, whatever one's qualms are about certain kinds of ecotourism—such as the occasional practice of rich tourists shooting elderly lions with high-powered rifles—it is worth remembering that the alternative is often that low-income people in poor countries will damage their local environment in their effort to survive.

Marginal Benefits and Marginal Costs

We can use the tools of marginal analysis to illustrate the marginal costs and the marginal benefits of reducing pollution. **Figure 12.4** illustrates a theoretical model of this situation. When the quantity of environmental protection is low so that pollution is extensive—for example, at quantity Qa—there are usually numerous relatively cheap and easy ways to reduce pollution, and the marginal benefits of doing so are quite high. At Qa, it makes sense to allocate more resources to fight pollution. However, as the extent of environmental protection increases, the cheap and easy ways of reducing pollution begin to decrease, and one must use more costly methods. The marginal cost curve rises. Also, as environmental protection increases, one achieves the largest marginal benefits first, followed by reduced marginal benefits. As the quantity of environmental protection increases to, say, Qb, the gap between marginal benefits and marginal costs narrows. At point Qc the marginal costs will exceed the marginal benefits. At this level of environmental protection, society is not allocating resources efficiently, because it is forfeiting too many resources to reduce pollution.

This OpenStax book is available for free at http://cnx.org/content/col12122/1.4

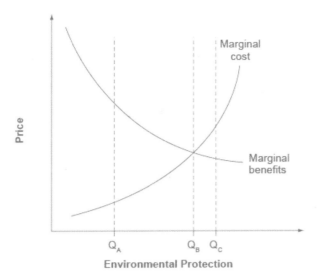

Figure 12.4 Marginal Costs and Marginal Benefits of Environmental Protection Reducing pollution is costly—one must sacrifice resources. The marginal costs of reducing pollution are generally increasing, because one can make the least expensive and easiest reductions, leaving the more expensive methods for later. The marginal benefits of reducing pollution are generally declining, because one can take the steps that provide the greatest benefit first, and steps that provide less benefit can wait until later.

As society draws closer to Qb, some might argue that it becomes more important to use market-oriented environmental tools to hold down the costs of reducing pollution. Their objective would be to avoid environmental rules that would provide the quantity of environmental protection at Qc, where marginal costs exceed marginal benefits. The following Clear It Up feature delves into how the EPA measures its policies – and the monetary value of our lives.

What's a life worth?

The U.S. Environmental Protection Agency (EPA) must estimate the value of saving lives by reducing pollution against the additional costs. In measuring the benefits of government environmental policies, the EPA's National Center for Environmental Economics (NCEE) values a statistical human life at $7.4 million (in 2006 U.S. dollars).

Economists value a human life on the basis of studies of the value that people actually place on human lives in their own decisions. For example, some jobs have a higher probability of death than others, and these jobs typically pay more to compensate for the risk. Examples are ocean fishery as opposed to fish farming, and ice trucking in Alaska as opposed to truck driving in the "lower forty-eight" states.

Government regulators use estimates such as these when deciding what proposed regulations are "reasonable," which means deciding which proposals have high enough benefits to justify their cost. For example, when the U.S. Department of Transportation makes decisions about what safety systems should be required in cars or airplanes, it will approve rules only where the estimated cost per life saved is $3 million or less.

Resources that we spend on life-saving regulations create tradeoff. A study by W. Kip Viscusi of Vanderbilt University estimated that when a regulation costs $50 million, it diverts enough spending in the rest of the economy from health care and safety expenditures that it costs a life. This finding suggests that any regulation that costs more than $50 million per life saved actually costs lives, rather than saving them.

12.5 | International Environmental Issues

By the end of this section, you will be able to:
- Explain biodiversity
- Analyze the partnership of high-income and low-income countries in efforts to address international externalities

Many countries around the world have become more aware of the benefits of environmental protection. Yet even if most nations individually took steps to address their environmental issues, no nation acting alone can solve certain environmental problems which spill over national borders. No nation by itself can reduce emissions of carbon dioxide and other gases by enough to solve the problem of global warming—not without the cooperation of other nations. Another issue is the challenge of preserving **biodiversity**, which includes the full spectrum of animal and plant genetic material. Although a nation can protect biodiversity within its own borders, no nation acting alone can protect biodiversity around the world. Global warming and biodiversity are examples of **international externalities**.

Bringing the nations of the world together to address environmental issues requires a difficult set of negotiations between countries with different income levels and different sets of priorities. If nations such as China, India, Brazil, Mexico, and others are developing their economies by burning vast amounts of fossil fuels or by stripping their forest and wildlife habitats, then the world's high-income countries acting alone will not be able to reduce greenhouse gases. However, low-income countries, with some understandable exasperation, point out that high-income countries do not have much moral standing to lecture them on the necessities of putting environmental protection ahead of economic growth. After all, high-income countries have historically been the primary contributors to greenhouse warming by burning **fossil fuels**—and still are today. It is hard to tell people who are living in a low-income country, where adequate diet, health care, and education are lacking, that they should sacrifice an improved quality of life for a cleaner environment.

Can rich and poor countries come together to address global environmental spillovers? At the initiative of the European Union and the most vulnerable developing nations, the Durban climate conference in December 2011 launched negotiations to develop a new international climate change agreement that covers all countries. The outcome of these negotiations was the Paris Climate Agreement, passed in 2016. The Paris Agreement committed participating countries to significant limits on CO_2 emissions. To date, 129 nations have signed on, including the two biggest emitters of greenhouse gases—China and the United States. The U.S. contribution to the agreement was the Clean Power Plan, which planned to reduce power plant CO_2 emissions across the U.S. by 17% to pre-2005 levels by 2020, and to further reduce emissions by a cumulative 32% by 2030. In early 2017, the Trump Administration announced plans to back out of the Paris Climate Agreement. Trump opposes the Clean Power plan, opting instead to shift focus to the use of natural gas. This represents a significant blow to the success of the Paris Agreement.

Visit this website (http://openstaxcollege.org/l/EC) to learn more about the European Commission.

If high-income countries want low-income countries to reduce their greenhouse emission gases, then the high-income countries may need to pay some of the costs. Perhaps some of these payments will happen through private markets. For example, some tourists from rich countries will pay handsomely to vacation near the natural treasures of low-income countries. Perhaps some of the transfer of resources can happen through making modern pollution-control technology available to poorer countries.

The practical details of what such an international system might look like and how it would operate across international borders are forbiddingly complex. However, it seems highly unlikely that some form of world government will impose a detailed system of environmental command-and-control regulation around the world. As a result, a decentralized and market-oriented approach may be the only practical way to address international issues such as global warming and biodiversity.

12.6 | The Tradeoff between Economic Output and Environmental Protection

By the end of this section, you will be able to:
- Apply the production possibility frontier to evaluate the tradeoff between economic output and the environment
- Interpret a graphic representation of the tradeoff between economic output and environmental protection

We can analyze the tradeoff between economic output and the environment with a production possibility frontier (PPF) such as the one in **Figure 12.5**. At one extreme, at a choice like P, a country would be selecting a high level of economic output but very little environmental protection. At the other extreme, at a choice like T, a country would be selecting a high level of environmental protection but little economic output. According to the graph, an increase in environmental protection involves an opportunity cost of less economic output. No matter what their preferences, all societies should wish to avoid choices like M, which are productively inefficient. Efficiency requires that the choice should be on the production possibility frontier.

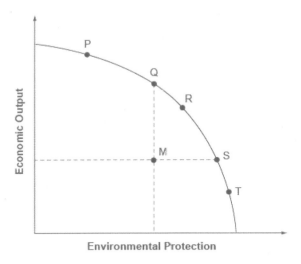

Figure 12.5 The Tradeoff between Economic Output and Environmental Protection Each society will have to weigh its own values and decide whether it prefers a choice like P with more economic output and less environmental protection, or a choice like T with more environmental protection and less economic output.

Economists do not have a great deal to say about the choice between P, Q, R, S and T in **Figure 12.5**, all of which lie along the production possibility frontier. Countries with low per capita gross domestic product (GDP), such as China, place a greater emphasis on economic output—which in turn helps to produce nutrition, shelter, health, education, and desirable consumer goods. Countries with higher income levels, where a greater share of people have access to the basic necessities of life, may be willing to place a relatively greater emphasis on environmental protection.

However, economists are united in their belief that an inefficient choice such as M is undesirable. Rather than choosing M, a nation could achieve either greater economic output with the same environmental protection, as at point Q, or greater environmental protection with the same level of output, as at point S. The problem with command-and-control environmental laws is that they sometimes involve a choice like M. Market-oriented environmental tools offer a mechanism for providing either the same environmental protection at lower cost, or providing a greater degree of environmental protection for the same cost.

Bring it Home

Keystone XL

How would an economist respond to claims of environmental damage caused by the Keystone XL project? Clearly, we can consider the environmental cost of oil spills a negative externality, but how large would these external costs be? Furthermore, are these costs "too high" when we measure them against any potential for economic benefit?

As this chapter indicates, in deciding whether pipeline construction is a good idea, an economist would want to know not only about the marginal benefits resulting from the additional pipeline construction, but also the potential marginal costs—and especially the pipeline's marginal external costs. Typically these come in the form of environmental impact statements, which are usually required for such projects. The most recent impact statement, released in March 2013 by the Nebraska Department of State, considered the possibility of fewer pipeline miles going over the aquifer system and avoiding completely environmentally fragile areas. It indicated that pipeline construction would not harm "most resources".

The Obama Administration declined to approve construction of the Keystone XL project. However, the Trump administration has already announced its willingness to do so. While we may fairly easily quantify the economic benefits of additional oil in the United States, the social costs are more challenging to measure. It seems that, in a period of less than robust economic growth, people are giving the benefit of the doubt that the marginal costs of additional oil generation will be less than the marginal benefits.

This OpenStax book is available for free at http://cnx.org/content/col12122/1.4

KEY TERMS

additional external cost additional costs incurred by third parties outside the production process when a unit of output
    is produced

biodiversity the full spectrum of animal and plant genetic material

command-and-control regulation laws that specify allowable quantities of pollution and that also may detail which
    pollution-control technologies one must use

externality a market exchange that affects a third party who is outside or "external" to the exchange; sometimes called a
    "spillover"

international externalities externalities that cross national borders and that a single nation acting alone cannot resolve

market failure When the market on its own does not allocate resources efficiently in a way that balances social costs
    and benefits; externalities are one example of a market failure

marketable permit program a permit that allows a firm to emit a certain amount of pollution; firms with more
    permits than pollution can sell the remaining permits to other firms

negative externality a situation where a third party, outside the transaction, suffers from a market transaction by others

pollution charge a tax imposed on the quantity of pollution that a firm emits; also called a pollution tax

positive externality a situation where a third party, outside the transaction, benefits from a market transaction by others

property rights the legal rights of ownership on which others are not allowed to infringe without paying compensation

social costs costs that include both the private costs incurred by firms and also additional costs incurred by third parties
    outside the production process, like costs of pollution

spillover see externality

KEY CONCEPTS AND SUMMARY

12.1 The Economics of Pollution
Economic production can cause environmental damage. This tradeoff arises for all countries, whether high-income or
low-income, and whether their economies are market-oriented or command-oriented.

An externality occurs when an exchange between a buyer and seller has an impact on a third party who is not part
of the exchange. An externality, which is sometimes also called a spillover, can have a negative or a positive impact
on the third party. If those parties imposing a negative externality on others had to account for the broader social
cost of their behavior, they would have an incentive to reduce the production of whatever is causing the negative
externality. In the case of a positive externality, the third party obtains benefits from the exchange between a buyer
and a seller, but they are not paying for these benefits. If this is the case, then markets would tend to under produce
output because suppliers are not aware of the additional demand from others. If the parties generating benefits to
others would somehow receive compensation for these external benefits, they would have an incentive to increase
production of whatever is causing the positive externality.

12.2 Command-and-Control Regulation
Command-and-control regulation sets specific limits for pollution emissions and/or specific pollution-control
technologies that firms must use. Although such regulations have helped to protect the environment, they have three
shortcomings: they provide no incentive for going beyond the limits they set; they offer limited flexibility on where
and how to reduce pollution; and they often have politically-motivated loopholes.

12.3 Market-Oriented Environmental Tools

Examples of market-oriented environmental policies, also called cap and trade programs, include pollution charges, marketable permits, and better-defined property rights. Market-oriented environmental policies include taxes, markets, and property rights so that those who impose negative externalities must face the social cost.

12.4 The Benefits and Costs of U.S. Environmental Laws

We can make a strong case, taken as a whole, that the benefits of U.S. environmental regulation have outweighed the costs. As the extent of environment regulation increases, additional expenditures on environmental protection will probably have increasing marginal costs and decreasing marginal benefits. This pattern suggests that the flexibility and cost savings of market-oriented environmental policies will become more important.

12.5 International Environmental Issues

Certain global environmental issues, such as global warming and biodiversity, spill over national borders and require addressing with some form of international agreement.

12.6 The Tradeoff between Economic Output and Environmental Protection

Depending on their different income levels and political preferences, countries are likely to make different choices about allocative efficiency—that is, the choice between economic output and environmental protection along the production possibility frontier. However, all countries should prefer to make a choice that shows productive efficiency—that is, the choice is somewhere on the production possibility frontier rather than inside it. Revisit **Choice in a World of Scarcity** for more on these terms.

SELF-CHECK QUESTIONS

1. Identify the following situations as an example of a negative or a positive externality:

    a. You are a birder (bird watcher), and your neighbor has put up several birdhouses in the yard as well as planting trees and flowers that attract birds.

    b. Your neighbor paints his house a hideous color.

    c. Investments in private education raise your country's standard of living.

    d. Trash dumped upstream flows downstream right past your home.

    e. Your roommate is a smoker, but you are a nonsmoker.

2. Identify whether the market supply curve will shift right or left or will stay the same for the following:

    a. Firms in an industry are required to pay a fine for their carbon dioxide emissions.

    b. Companies are sued for polluting the water in a river.

    c. Power plants in a specific city are not required to address the impact of their air quality emissions.

    d. Companies that use fracking to remove oil and gas from rock are required to clean up the damage.

3. For each of your answers to **Exercise 12.2**, will equilibrium price rise or fall or stay the same?

This OpenStax book is available for free at http://cnx.org/content/col12122/1.4

4. Table 12.5 provides the supply and demand conditions for a manufacturing firm. The third column represents a supply curve without accounting for the social cost of pollution. The fourth column represents the supply curve when the firm is required to account for the social cost of pollution. Identify the equilibrium before the social cost of production is included and after the social cost of production is included.

Price	Quantity Demanded	Quantity Supplied without paying the cost of the pollution	Quantity Supplied after paying the cost of the pollution
$10	450	400	250
$15	440	440	290
$20	430	480	330
$25	420	520	370
$30	410	560	410

Table 12.5

5. Consider two approaches to reducing emissions of CO_2 into the environment from manufacturing industries in the United States. In the first approach, the U.S. government makes it a policy to use only predetermined technologies. In the second approach, the U.S. government determines which technologies are cleaner and subsidizes their use. Of the two approaches, which is the command-and-control policy?

6. Classify the following pollution-control policies as command-and-control or market incentive based.
   a. A state emissions tax on the quantity of carbon emitted by each firm.
   b. The federal government requires domestic auto companies to improve car emissions by 2020.
   c. The EPA sets national standards for water quality.
   d. A city sells permits to firms that allow them to emit a specified quantity of pollution.
   e. The federal government pays fishermen to preserve salmon.

7. An emissions tax on a quantity of emissions from a firm is not a command-and-control approach to reducing pollution. Why?

8. Four firms called Elm, Maple, Oak, and Cherry, produce wooden chairs. However, they also produce a great deal of garbage (a mixture of glue, varnish, sandpaper, and wood scraps). The first row of **Table 12.6** shows the total amount of garbage (in tons) that each firm currently produces. The other rows of the table show the cost of reducing garbage produced by the first five tons, the second five tons, and so on. First, calculate the cost of requiring each firm to reduce the weight of its garbage by one-fourth. Now, imagine that the government issues marketable permits for the current level of garbage, but the permits will shrink the weight of allowable garbage for each firm by one-fourth. What will be the result of this alternative approach to reducing pollution?

	Elm	Maple	Oak	Cherry
Current production of garbage (in tons)	20	40	60	80
Cost of reducing garbage by first five tons	$5,500	$6,300	$7,200	$3,000
Cost of reducing garbage by second five tons	$6,000	$7,200	$7,500	$4,000
Cost of reducing garbage by third five tons	$6,500	$8,100	$7,800	$5,000
Cost of reducing garbage by fouth five tons	$7,000	$9,000	$8,100	$6,000
Cost of reducing garbage by fifth five tons	$0	$9,900	$8,400	$7,000

Table 12.6

9. The rows in **Table 12.7** show three market-oriented tools for reducing pollution. The columns of the table show three complaints about command-and-control regulation. Fill in the table by stating briefly how each market-oriented tool addresses each of the three concerns.

	Incentives to Go Beyond	Flexibility about Where and How Pollution Will Be Reduced	Political Process Creates Loopholes and Exceptions
Pollution Charges			
Marketable Permits			
Property Rights			

Table 12.7

This OpenStax book is available for free at http://cnx.org/content/col12122/1.4

10. Suppose a city releases 16 million gallons of raw sewage into a nearby lake. **Table 12.8** shows the total costs of cleaning up the sewage to different levels, together with the total benefits of doing so. (Benefits include environmental, recreational, health, and industrial benefits.)

	Total Cost (in thousands of dollars)	Total Benefits (in thousands of dollars)
16 million gallons	Current situation	Current situation
12 million gallons	50	800
8 million gallons	150	1300
4 million gallons	500	1650
0 gallons	1200	1900

Table 12.8

  a. Using the information in **Table 12.8**, calculate the marginal costs and marginal benefits of reducing sewage emissions for this city. See **Production, Costs and Industry Structure** if you need a refresher on how to calculate marginal costs.
  b. What is the optimal level of sewage for this city?
  c. Why not just pass a law that firms can emit zero sewage? After all, the total benefits of zero emissions exceed the total costs.

11. The state of Colorado requires oil and gas companies who use fracking techniques to return the land to its original condition after the oil and gas extractions. **Table 12.9** shows the total cost and total benefits (in dollars) of this policy.

Land Restored (in acres)	Total Cost	Total Benefit
0	$0	$0
100	$20	$140
200	$80	$240
300	$160	$320
400	$280	$380

Table 12.9

  a. Calculate the marginal cost and the marginal benefit at each quantity (acre) of land restored. See **Production, Costs and Industry Structure** if you need a refresher on how to calculate marginal costs and benefits.
  b. If we apply marginal analysis, what is the optimal amount of land to be restored?

12. Consider the case of global environmental problems that spill across international borders as a prisoner's dilemma of the sort studied in **Monopolistic Competition and Oligopoly**. Say that there are two countries, A and B. Each country can choose whether to protect the environment, at a cost of 10, or not to protect it, at a cost of zero. If one country decides to protect the environment, there is a benefit of 16, but the benefit is divided equally between the two countries. If both countries decide to protect the environment, there is a benefit of 32, which is divided equally between the two countries.

a. In **Table 12.10**, fill in the costs, benefits, and total payoffs to the countries of the following decisions. Explain why, without some international agreement, they are likely to end up with neither country acting to protect the environment.

		Country B	
		Protect	Not Protect
Country A	Protect		
	Not Protect		

Table 12.10

13. A country called Sherwood is very heavily covered with a forest of 50,000 trees. There are proposals to clear some of Sherwood's forest and grow corn, but obtaining this additional economic output will have an environmental cost from reducing the number of trees. **Table 12.11** shows possible combinations of economic output and environmental protection.

Combos	Corn Bushels (thousands)	Number of Trees (thousands)
P	9	5
Q	2	30
R	7	20
S	2	40
T	6	10

Table 12.11

a. Sketch a graph of a production possibility frontier with environmental quality on the horizontal axis, measured by the number of trees, and the quantity of economic output, measured in corn, on the vertical axis.
b. Which choices display productive efficiency? How can you tell?
c. Which choices show allocative efficiency? How can you tell?
d. In the choice between T and R, decide which one is better. Why?
e. In the choice between T and S, can you say which one is better, and why?
f. If you had to guess, which choice would you think is more likely to represent a command-and-control environmental policy and which choice is more likely to represent a market-oriented environmental policy, choice Q or S? Why?

REVIEW QUESTIONS

14. What is an externality?

15. Give an example of a positive externality and an example of a negative externality.

16. What is the difference between private costs and social costs?

17. In a market without environmental regulations, will the supply curve for a firm account for private costs, external costs, both, or neither? Explain.

18. What is command-and-control environmental regulation?

19. What are the three problems that economists have noted with regard to command-and-control regulation?

20. What is a pollution charge and what incentive does it provide for a firm to take external costs into account?

21. What is a marketable permit and what incentive does it provide for a firm to account for external costs?

22. What are better-defined property rights and what incentive do they provide to account for external costs?

23. As the extent of environmental protection expands, would you expect marginal costs of environmental protection to rise or fall? Why or why not?

24. As the extent of environmental protection expands, would you expect the marginal benefits of environmental protection to rise or fall? Why or why not?

25. What are the economic tradeoffs between low-income and high-income countries in international conferences on global environmental damage?

26. What arguments do low-income countries make in international discussions of global environmental clean-up?

27. In the tradeoff between economic output and environmental protection, what do the combinations on the protection possibility curve represent?

28. What does a point inside the production possibility frontier represent?

CRITICAL THINKING QUESTIONS

29. Suppose you want to put a dollar value on the external costs of carbon emissions from a power plant. What information or data would you obtain to measure the external [not social] cost?

30. Would environmentalists favor command-and-control policies as a way to reduce pollution? Why or why not?

31. Consider two ways of protecting elephants from poachers in African countries. In one approach, the government sets up enormous national parks that have sufficient habitat for elephants to thrive and forbids all local people to enter the parks or to injure either the elephants or their habitat in any way. In a second approach, the government sets up national parks and designates 10 villages around the edges of the park as official tourist centers that become places where tourists can stay and bases for guided tours inside the national park. Consider the different incentives of local villagers—who often are very poor—in each of these plans. Which plan seems more likely to help the elephant population?

32. Will a system of marketable permits work with thousands of firms? Why or why not?

33. Is zero pollution possible under a marketable permits system? Why or why not?

34. Is zero pollution an optimal goal? Why or why not?

35. From an economic perspective, is it sound policy to pursue a goal of zero pollution? Why or why not?

36. Recycling is a relatively inexpensive solution to much of the environmental contamination from plastics, glass, and other waste materials. Is it a sound policy to make it mandatory for everybody to recycle?

37. Can extreme levels of pollution hurt the economic development of a high-income country? Why or why not?

38. How can high-income countries benefit from covering much of the cost of reducing pollution created by low-income countries?

39. Technological innovations shift the production possibility curve. Look at graph you sketched for Exercise 12.13 Which types of technologies should a country promote? Should "clean" technologies be promoted over other technologies? Why or why not?

PROBLEMS

40. Show the market for cigarettes in equilibrium, assuming that there are no laws banning smoking in public. Label the equilibrium private market price and quantity as Pm and Qm. Add whatever is needed to the model to show the impact of the negative externality from second-hand smoking. (Hint: In this case it is the consumers, not the sellers, who are creating the negative externality.) Label the social optimal output and price as Pe and Qe. On the graph, shade in the deadweight loss at the market output.

41. Refer to Table 12.2. The externality created by the refrigerator production was $100. However, once we accounted for both the private and additional external costs, the market price increased by only $50. If the external costs were $100 why did the price only increase by $50 when we accounted for all costs?

42. Table 12.12, shows the supply and demand conditions for a firm that will play trumpets on the streets when requested. Qs_1 is the quantity supplied without social costs. Qs_2 is the quantity supplied with social costs. What is the negative externality in this situation? Identify the equilibrium price and quantity when we account only for private costs, and then when we account for social costs. How does accounting for the externality affect the equilibrium price and quantity?

P	Qd	Qs_1	Qs_2
$20	0	10	8
$18	1	9	7
$15	2.5	7.5	5.5
$12	4	6	4
$10	5	5	3
$5	7.5	2.5	0.5

Table 12.12

43. A city currently emits 16 million gallons (MG) of raw sewage into a lake that is beside the city. Table 12.13 shows the total costs (TC) in thousands of dollars of cleaning up the sewage to different levels, together with the total benefits (TB) of doing so. Benefits include environmental, recreational, health, and industrial benefits.

	TC	TB
16 MG	Current	Current
12 MG	50	800
8 MG	150	1300
4 MG	500	1850
0 MG	1200	2000

Table 12.13

a. Using the information in Table 12.13 calculate the marginal costs and marginal benefits of reducing sewage emissions for this city.

b. What is the optimal level of sewage for this city? How can you tell?

44. In the Land of Purity, there is only one form of pollution, called "gunk." Table 12.14 shows possible combinations of economic output and reduction of gunk, depending on what kinds of environmental regulations you choose.

Combos	Eco Output	Gunk Cleaned Up
J	800	10%
K	500	30%
L	600	40%
M	400	40%
N	100	90%

Table 12.14

a. Sketch a graph of a production possibility frontier with environmental quality on the horizontal axis, measured by the percentage reduction of gunk, and with the quantity of economic output on the vertical axis.

b. Which choices display productive efficiency? How can you tell?

c. Which choices show allocative efficiency? How can you tell?

d. In the choice between K and L, can you say which one is better and why?

e. In the choice between K and N, can you say which one is better, and why?

f. If you had to guess, which choice would you think is more likely to represent a command-and-control environmental policy and which choice is more likely to represent a market-oriented environmental policy, choice L or M? Why?

13 | Positive Externalities and Public Goods

Figure 13.1 View from Voyager I Launched by NASA on September 5, 1977, Voyager 1's primary mission was to provide detailed images of Jupiter, Saturn, and their moons. It took this photograph of Jupiter on its journey. In August of 2012, Voyager I entered interstellar space—the first human-made object to do so—and it is expected to send data and images back to earth until 2025. Such a technological feat entails many economic principles. (Credit: modification of work by NASA/JPL)

Bring it Home

The Benefits of Voyager I Endure

The rapid growth of technology has increased our ability to access and process data, to navigate through a busy city, and to communicate with friends on the other side of the globe. The research and development efforts of citizens, scientists, firms, universities, and governments have truly revolutionized the modern economy. To get a sense of how far we have come in a short period of time, let's compare one of humankind's greatest achievements to the smartphone most of us have in our coat pocket.

In 1977 the United States launched Voyager I, a spacecraft originally intended to reach Jupiter and Saturn, to send back photographs and other cosmic measurements. Voyager I, however, kept going, and going—past Jupiter and Saturn—right out of our solar system. At the time of its launch, Voyager had some of the most sophisticated computing processing power NASA could engineer (8,000 instructions per second), but today, we Earthlings use handheld devices that can process 14 billion instructions per second.

Still, the technology of today is a spillover product of the incredible feats NASA accomplished forty years ago. NASA research, for instance, is responsible for the kidney dialysis and mammogram machines that we use today. Research in new technologies not only produces private benefits to the investing firm, or in this case to NASA, but it also creates benefits for the broader society. In this way, new knowledge often becomes what economists refer to as a public good. This leads us to the topic of this chapter—technology, positive externalities, public goods, and the role of government in encouraging innovation and the social benefits that it provides.

Introduction to Positive Externalities and Public Goods

In this chapter, you will learn about:

- Why the Private Sector Underinvests in Technologies

- How Governments Can Encourage Innovation

- Public Goods

Can you imagine a world in which you did not own a cellular phone or use Wikipedia? New technology changes how people live and work and what they buy. Technology includes the invention of new products, new ways of producing goods and services, and even new ways of managing a company more efficiently. Research and development of technology is the difference between horses and automobiles, between candles and electric lights, between fetching water in buckets and indoor plumbing, and between infection and good health from antibiotics.

In December 2009, ABC News compiled a list of some of the technological breakthroughs that have revolutionized consumer products in the past 10 years:

- GPS tracking devices, originally developed by the defense department and available to consumers in 2000, give users up-to-date information on location and time through satellite technology.

- In 2000, Toyota introduced the Prius hybrid car, which greatly improved fuel efficiency.

- Also in 2000, AT&T offered its customers the ability to text on a mobile phone.

- In 2001, Wikipedia launched a user-generated encyclopedia on the Web.

- Even though Napster died in 2001, the company launched music downloading and file sharing, which revolutionized how consumers obtain their music and videos.

- Friendster kicked off the social networking business in 2003, and Twitter and Facebook followed.

- In 2003, international scientists completed the Human Genome project. It helps to fight disease and launch new pharmaceutical innovations.

- Also in 2003, the search engine became a way of life for obtaining information quickly. The search engine companies also became innovators in the digital software that dominates mobile devices.

- In 2006, Nintendo launched Wii and changed the way we play video games. Players can now be drawn into the action and use their bodies to respond rather than a handheld device.

- Apple introduced the iPhone in 2007 and launched an entire smartphone industry. In 2015, cell phones now recognize human voices via artificial intelligence.

With all new technologies, however, there are new challenges. This chapter deals with some of these issues: Will private companies be willing to invest in new technology? In what ways does new technology have positive externalities? What motivates inventors? Does government have a role to play in encouraging research and technology? Are there certain types of goods that markets fail to provide efficiently, and that only government can produce? What happens when consumption or production of a product creates positive externalities? Why is it unsurprising when we overuse a common resource, like marine fisheries?

This OpenStax book is available for free at http://cnx.org/content/col12122/1.4

13.1 | Why the Private Sector Underinvests in Innovation

By the end of this section, you will be able to:
- Identify the positive externalities of new technology.
- Explain the difference between private benefits and social benefits and give examples of each.
- Calculate and analyze rates of return

Market competition can provide an incentive for discovering new technology because a firm can earn higher profits by finding a way to produce products more cheaply or to create products with characteristics consumers want. As Gregory Lee, CEO of Samsung said, "Relentless pursuit of new innovation is the key principle of our business and enables consumers to discover a world of possibilities with technology." An innovative firm knows that it will usually have a temporary edge over its competitors and thus an ability to earn above-normal profits before competitors can catch up.

In certain cases, however, competition can discourage new technology, especially when other firms can quickly copy a new idea. Consider a pharmaceutical firm deciding to develop a new drug. On average, it can cost $800 million and take more than a decade to discover a new drug, perform the necessary safety tests, and bring the drug to market. If the research and development (R&D) effort fails—and every R&D project has some chance of failure—then the firm will suffer losses and could even be driven out of business. If the project succeeds, then the firm's competitors may figure out ways of adapting and copying the underlying idea, but without having to pay the costs themselves. As a result, the innovative company will bear the much higher costs of the R&D and will enjoy at best only a small, temporary advantage over the competition.

Many inventors over the years have discovered that their inventions brought them less profit than they might have reasonably expected.

- Eli Whitney (1765–1825) invented the cotton gin, but then southern cotton planters built their own seed-separating devices with a few minor changes in Whitney's design. When Whitney sued, he found that the courts in southern states would not uphold his patent rights.

- Thomas Edison (1847–1931) still holds the record for most patents granted to an individual. His first invention was an automatic vote counter, and despite the social benefits, he could not find a government that wanted to buy it.

- Gordon Gould came up with the idea behind the laser in 1957. He put off applying for a patent and, by the time he did apply, other scientists had laser inventions of their own. A lengthy legal battle resulted, in which Gould spent $100,000 on lawyers, before he eventually received a patent for the laser in 1977. Compared to the enormous social benefits of the laser, Gould received relatively little financial reward.

- In 1936, Alan Turing delivered a paper titled, "On Computable Numbers, with an Application to the Entscheidungsproblem," in which he presented the notion of a universal machine (later called the "Universal Turing Machine," and then the "Turing machine") capable of computing anything that is computable. The central concept of the modern computer was based on Turing's paper. Today scholars widely consider Turing as the father of theoretical computer science and artificial intelligence; however, the UK government prosecuted Turing in 1952 for homosexual acts and gave him the choice of chemical castration or prison. Turing chose castration and died in 1954 from cyanide poisoning.

A variety of studies by economists have found that the original inventor receives one-third to one-half of the total economic benefits from innovations, while other businesses and new product users receive the rest.

The Positive Externalities of New Technology

Will private firms in a market economy underinvest in research and technology? If a firm builds a factory or buys a piece of equipment, the firm receives all the economic benefits that result from the investments. However, when a firm invests in new technology, the **private benefits**, or profits, that the firm receives are only a portion of the overall social benefits. The **social benefits** of an innovation account for the value of all the positive externalities of the new idea or product, whether enjoyed by other companies or society as a whole, as well as the private benefits the firm that developed the new technology receives. As you learned in **Environmental Protection and Negative Externalities**, **positive externalities** are beneficial spillovers to a third party, or parties.

Consider the example of the Big Drug Company, which is planning its R&D budget for the next year. Economists and scientists working for Big Drug have compiled a list of potential research and development projects and estimated rates of return. (The rate of return is the estimated payoff from the project.) **Figure 13.2** shows how the calculations work. The downward-sloping $D_{Private}$ curve represents the firm's demand for financial capital and reflects the company's willingness to borrow to finance research and development projects at various interest rates. Suppose that this firm's investment in research and development creates a spillover benefit to other firms and households. After all, new innovations often spark other creative endeavors that society also values. If we add the spillover benefits society enjoys to the firm's private demand for financial capital, we can draw D_{Social} that lies above $D_{Private}$.

If there were a way for the firm to fully monopolize those social benefits by somehow making them unavailable to the rest of us, the firm's private demand curve would be the same as society's demand curve. According to **Figure 13.2** and **Table 13.1**, if the going rate of interest on borrowing is 8%, and the company can receive the private benefits of innovation only, then the company would finance $30 million. Society, at the same rate of 8%, would find it optimal to have $52 million of borrowing. Unless there is a way for the company to fully enjoy the total benefits, then it will borrow less than the socially optimal level of $52 million.

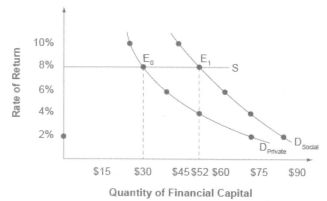

Figure 13.2 Positive Externalities and Technology Big Drug faces a cost of borrowing of 8%. If the firm receives only the private benefits of investing in R&D, then we show its demand curve for financial capital by $D_{Private}$, and the equilibrium will occur at $30 million. Because there are spillover benefits, society would find it optimal to have $52 million of investment. If the firm could keep the social benefits of its investment for itself, its demand curve for financial capital would be D_{Social} and it would be willing to borrow $52 million.

Rate of Return	$D_{Private}$ (in millions)	D_{Social} (in millions)
2%	$72	$84
4%	$52	$72
6%	$38	$62
8%	$30	$52
10%	$26	$44

Table 13.1 Return and Demand for Capital

Big Drug's original demand for financial capital ($D_{Private}$) is based on the profits received the firm receives. However, other pharmaceutical firms and health care companies may learn new lessons about how to treat certain medical conditions and are then able to create their own competing products. The social benefit of the drug takes into account the value of all the drug's positive externalities. If Big Drug were able to gain this social return instead of other companies, its demand for financial capital would shift to the demand curve D_{Social}, and it would be willing to borrow and invest $52 million. However, if Big Drug is receiving only 50 cents of each dollar of social benefits, the firm will not spend as much on creating new products. The amount it would be willing to spend would fall somewhere in between $D_{Private}$ and D_{Social}.

This OpenStax book is available for free at http://cnx.org/content/col12122/1.4

Why Invest in Human Capital?

The investment in anything, whether it is the construction of a new power plant or research in a new cancer treatment, usually requires a certain upfront cost with an uncertain future benefit. The investment in education, or human capital, is no different. Over the span of many years, a student and her family invest significant amounts of time and money into that student's education. The idea is that higher levels of educational attainment will eventually serve to increase the student's future productivity and subsequent ability to earn. Once the student crunches the numbers, does this investment pay off for her?

Almost universally, economists have found that the answer to this question is a clear "Yes." For example, several studies of the return to education in the United States estimate that the rate of return to a college education is approximately 10-15%. Data in **Table 13.2**, from the U.S. Bureau of Labor Statistics' *Usual Weekly Earnings of Wage and Salary Workers, Third Quarter 2014*, demonstrate that median weekly earnings are higher for workers who have completed more education. While these rates of return will beat equivalent investments in Treasury bonds or savings accounts, the estimated returns to education go primarily to the individual worker, so these returns are **private rates of return** to education.

	Less than a High School Degree	High School Degree, No College	Bachelor's Degree
Median Weekly Earnings (full-time workers over the age of 25)	$519	$698	$1,270

Table 13.2 Usual Weekly Earnings of Wage and Salary Workers, Fourth Quarter 2016   (Source: http://www.bls.gov/news.release/pdf/wkyeng.pdf)

What does society gain from investing in the education of another student? After all, if the government is spending taxpayer dollars to subsidize public education, society should expect some kind of return on that spending. Economists like George Psacharopoulos have found that, across a variety of nations, the **social rate of return** on schooling is also positive. After all, positive externalities exist from investment in education. While not always easy to measure, according to Walter McMahon, the positive externalities to education typically include better health outcomes for the population, lower levels of crime, a cleaner environment and a more stable, democratic government. For these reasons, many nations have chosen to use taxpayer dollars to subsidize primary, secondary, and higher education. Education clearly benefits the person who receives it, but a society where most people have a good level of education provides positive externalities for all.

Other Examples of Positive Externalities

Although technology may be the most prominent example of a positive externality, it is not the only one. For example, vaccinations against disease are not only a protection for the individual, but they have the positive spillover of protecting others who may become infected. When a number of homes in a neighborhood are modernized, updated, and restored, not only does it increase the homes' value, but other property values in the neighborhood may increase as well.

The appropriate public policy response to a positive externality, like a new technology, is to help the party creating the positive externality receive a greater share of the social benefits. In the case of vaccines, like flu shots, an effective policy might be to provide a subsidy to those who choose to get vaccinated.

Figure 13.3 shows the market for flu shots. The market demand curve D_{Market} for flu shots reflects only the marginal private benefits (MPB) that the vaccinated individuals receive from the shots. Assuming that there are no spillover costs in the production of flu shots, the market supply curve is given by the marginal private cost (MPC) of producing the vaccinations.

The equilibrium quantity of flu shots produced in the market, where MPB is equal to MPC, is Q_{Market} and the price of flu shots is P_{Market}. However, spillover benefits exist in this market because others, those who chose not to purchase a flu shot, receive a positive externality in a reduced chance of contracting the flu. When we add the spillover benefits to the marginal private benefit of flu shots, the marginal social benefit (MSB) of flu shots is given by D_{Social}. Because the MSB is greater than MPB, we see that the socially optimal level of flu shots is greater than the market quantity

(Q_{Social} exceeds Q_{Market}) and the corresponding price of flu shots, if the market were to produce Q_{Social}, would be at P_{Social}. Unfortunately, the marketplace does not recognize the positive externality and flu shots will go under produced and under consumed.

How can government try to move the market level of output closer to the socially desirable level of output? One policy would be to provide a subsidy, like a voucher, to any citizen who wishes to get vaccinated. This voucher would act as "income" that one could use purchase only a flu shot and, if the voucher were exactly equal to the per-unit spillover benefits, would increase market equilibrium to a quantity of Q_{Social} and a price of P_{Social} where MSB equals MSC. Suppliers of the flu shots would receive payment of P_{Social} per vaccination, while consumers of flu shots would redeem the voucher and only pay a price of $P_{Subsidy}$. When the government uses a subsidy in this way, it produces the socially optimal quantity of vaccinations.

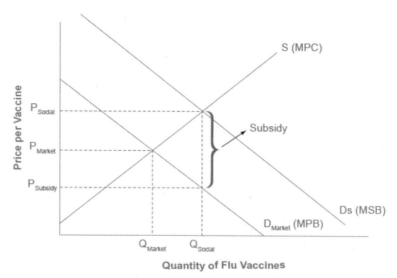

Figure 13.3 The Market for Flu Shots with Spillover Benefits (A Positive Externality) The market demand curve does not reflect the positive externality of flu vaccinations, so only Q_{Market} will be exchanged. This outcome is inefficient because the marginal social benefit exceeds the marginal social cost. If the government provides a subsidy to consumers of flu shots, equal to the marginal social benefit minus the marginal private benefit, the level of vaccinations can increase to the socially optimal quantity of Q_{Social}.

13.2 | How Governments Can Encourage Innovation

By the end of this section, you will be able to:
- Explain the effects of intellectual property rights on social and private rates of return.
- Identify three U.S. Government policies and explain how they encourage innovation

A number of different government policies can increase the incentives to innovate, including: guaranteeing intellectual property rights, government assistance with the costs of research and development, and cooperative research ventures between universities and companies.

Intellectual Property Rights

One way to increase new technology is to guarantee the innovator an exclusive right to that new product or process. **Intellectual property** rights include patents, which give the inventor the exclusive legal right to make, use, or sell the invention for a limited time, and copyright laws, which give the author an exclusive legal right over works of literature, music, film/video, and pictures. For example, if a pharmaceutical firm has a patent on a new drug, then no other firm can manufacture or sell that drug for 21 years, unless the firm with the patent grants permission. Without a patent, the pharmaceutical firm would have to face competition for any successful products, and could earn no more than a normal rate of profit. With a patent, a firm is able to earn monopoly profits on its product for a period of time—which offers an incentive for research and development. In general, how long can "a period of time" be? The

This OpenStax book is available for free at http://cnx.org/content/col12122/1.4

Clear It Up discusses patent and copyright protection timeframes for some works you might know.

How long is Mickey Mouse protected from being copied?

All patents and copyrights are scheduled to end someday. In 2003, copyright protection for Mickey Mouse was scheduled to run out. Once the copyright had expired, anyone would be able to copy Mickey Mouse cartoons or draw and sell new ones. In 1998, however, Congress passed the Sonny Bono Copyright Term Extension Act. For copyrights owned by companies or other entities, it increased or extended the copyright from 75 years to 95 years after publication. For copyrights owned by individuals, it increased or extended the copyright coverage from 50 years to 70 years after death. Along with protecting Mickey for another 20 years, the copyright extension affected about 400,000 books, movies, and songs.

Figure 13.4 illustrates how the total number of patent applications filed with the U.S. Patent and Trademark Office, as well as the total number of patents granted, surged in the mid-1990s with the invention of the internet, and is still going strong today.

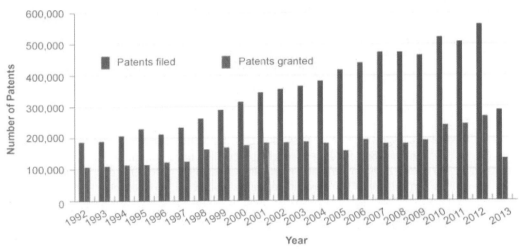

Figure 13.4 Patents Filed and Granted, 1981–2012 The number of applications filed for patents increased substantially beginning in the 1990s, due in part to the invention of the internet, which has led to many other inventions and to the 1998 Copyright Term Extension Act. (Source: http://www.uspto.gov/web/offices/ac/ido/oeip/taf/us_stat.htm)

While patents provide an incentive to innovate by protecting the innovator, they are not perfect. For example:

- In countries that already have patents, economic studies show that inventors receive only one-third to one-half of the total economic value of their inventions.

- In a fast-moving high-technology industry like biotechnology or semiconductor design, patents may be almost irrelevant because technology is advancing so quickly.

- Not every new idea can be protected with a patent or a copyright—for example, a new way of organizing a factory or a new way of training employees.

- Patents may sometimes cover too much or be granted too easily. In the early 1970s, Xerox had received over 1,700 patents on various elements of the photocopy machine. Every time Xerox improved the photocopier, it received a patent on the improvement.

- The 21-year time period for a patent is somewhat arbitrary. Ideally, a patent should cover a long enough period of time for the inventor to earn a good return, but not so long that it allows the inventor to charge a monopoly price permanently.

Because patents are imperfect and do not apply well to all situations, alternative methods of improving the rate of return for inventors of new technology are desirable. The following sections describe some of these possible alternative policies.

Policy #1: Government Spending on Research and Development

If the private sector does not have sufficient incentive to carry out research and development, one possibility is for the government to fund such work directly. Government spending can provide direct financial support for research and development (R&D) conducted at colleges and universities, nonprofit research entities, and sometimes by private firms, as well as at government-run laboratories. While government spending on research and development produces technology that is broadly available for firms to use, it costs taxpayers money and can sometimes be directed more for political than for scientific or economic reasons.

Visit the NASA website (http://openstaxcollege.org/l/NASA) and the USDA website (http://openstaxcollege.org/l/USDA) to read about government research that would not take place were it left to firms due to the externalities.

The first column of **Table 13.3** shows the sources of total U.S. spending on research and development. The second column shows the total dollars of R&D funding by each source. The third column shows that, relative to the total amount of funding, 22.7% comes from the federal government, about 69% of R&D is done by industry, and less than 4% is done by universities and colleges. (The percentages below do not add up to exactly 100% due to rounding.)

Sources of R&D Funding	Amount ($ billions)	Percent of the Total
Federal government	**$113.1**	**22.7%**
Industry	$344.9	69.0%
Universities and colleges	$17.1	3.4%
Nonprofits	$19.9	4.0%
Nonfederal government	$4.0	0.8%
Total	*$499*	

Table 13.3 U.S. Research and Development Expenditures, 2015 (Source: https://www.nsf.gov/statistics/2016/nsf16316/)

In the 1960s the federal government paid for about two-thirds of the nation's R&D. Over time, the U.S. economy has come to rely much more heavily on industry-funded R&D. The federal government has tried to focus its direct R&D spending on areas where private firms are not as active. One difficulty with direct government support of R&D is that it inevitably involves political decisions about which projects are worthy. The scientific question of whether research is worthwhile can easily become entangled with considerations like the location of the congressional district in which

This OpenStax book is available for free at http://cnx.org/content/col12122/1.4

the research funding is spent.

Policy #2: Tax Breaks for Research and Development

A complementary approach to supporting R&D that does not involve the government's close scrutiny of specific projects is to give firms a reduction in taxes depending on how much research and development they do. The federal government refers to this policy as the research and experimentation (R&E) tax credit. According to the Treasury Department: ". . . the R&E Credit is also a cost-effective policy for stimulating additional private sector investment. Most recent studies find that each dollar of foregone tax revenue through the R&E Tax Credit causes firms to invest at least a dollar in R&D, with some studies finding a benefit to cost ratio of 2 or 2.96."

Link It Up 👓

Visit this website (http://openstaxcollege.org/l/REtaxcredit) for more information on how the R&E Tax Credit encourages investment.

Policy #3 Cooperative Research

State and federal governments support research in a variety of ways. For example, United for Medical Research, a coalition of groups that seek funding for the National Institutes of Health, (which is supported by federal grants), states: "NIH-supported research added $69 billion to our GDP and supported seven million jobs in 2011 alone." The United States remains the leading sponsor of medical-related research spending $117 billion in 2011. Other institutions, such as the National Academy of Scientists and the National Academy of Engineers, receive federal grants for innovative projects. The Agriculture and Food Research Initiative (AFRI) at the United States Department of Agriculture awards federal grants to projects that apply the best science to the most important agricultural problems, from food safety to childhood obesity. Cooperation between government-funded universities, academies, and the private sector can spur product innovation and create whole new industries.

13.3 | Public Goods

By the end of this section, you will be able to:

- Identify a public good using nonexcludable and non-rival as criteria
- Explain the free rider problem
- Identify several sources of public goods

Even though new technology creates positive externalities so that perhaps one-third or one-half of the social benefit of new inventions spills over to others, the inventor still receives some private return. What about a situation where the positive externalities are so extensive that private firms could not expect to receive any of the social benefit? We call this kind of good a **public good**. Spending on national defense is a good example of a public good. Let's begin by defining the characteristics of a public good and discussing why these characteristics make it difficult for private firms to supply public goods. Then we will see how government may step in to address the issue.

The Definition of a Public Good

Economists have a strict definition of a public good, and it does not necessarily include all goods financed through taxes. To understand the defining characteristics of a public good, first consider an ordinary private good, like a piece of pizza. We can buy and sell a piece of pizza fairly easily because it is a separate and identifiable item. However, public goods are not separate and identifiable in this way.

Instead, public goods have two defining characteristics: they are nonexcludable and non-rival. The first characteristic, that a public good is **nonexcludable**, means that it is costly or impossible to exclude someone from using the good. If Larry buys a private good like a piece of pizza, then he can exclude others, like Lorna, from eating that pizza. However, if national defense is provided, then it includes everyone. Even if you strongly disagree with America's defense policies or with the level of defense spending, the national defense still protects you. You cannot choose to be unprotected, and national defense cannot protect everyone else and exclude you.

The second main characteristic of a public good, that it is **non-rival**, means that when one person uses the public good, another can also use it. With a private good like pizza, if Max is eating the pizza then Michelle cannot also eat it; that is, the two people are rivals in consumption. With a public good like national defense, Max's consumption of national defense does not reduce the amount left for Michelle, so they are non-rival in this area.

A number of government services are examples of public goods. For instance, it would not be easy to provide fire and police service so that some people in a neighborhood would be protected from the burning and burglary of their property, while others would not be protected at all. Protecting some necessarily means protecting others, too.

Positive externalities and public goods are closely related concepts. Public goods have positive externalities, like police protection or public health funding. Not all goods and services with positive externalities, however, are public goods. Investments in education have huge positive spillovers but can be provided by a private company. Private companies can invest in new inventions such as the Apple iPad and reap profits that may not capture all of the social benefits. We can also describe patents as an attempt to make new inventions into private goods, which are excludable and rivalrous, so that no one but the inventor can use them during the length of the patent.

The Free Rider Problem of Public Goods

Private companies find it difficult to produce public goods. If a good or service is nonexcludable, like national defense, so that it is impossible or very costly to exclude people from using this good or service, then how can a firm charge people for it?

Link It Up @🔗

Visit this website (http://openstaxcollege.org/l/freerider) to read about a connection between free riders and "bad music."

When individuals make decisions about buying a public good, a **free rider** problem can arise, in which people have an incentive to let others pay for the public good and then to "free ride" on the purchases of others. We can express the free rider problem in terms of the prisoner's dilemma game, which we discuss as a representation of oligopoly in **Monopolistic Competition and Oligopoly**. When individuals make decisions about buying a public good, a **free rider** problem can arise, in which people have an incentive to let others pay for the public good and then, since once there is a provided public good it is available to all, to "free ride" on the purchases of others.

There is a dilemma with the Prisoner's Dilemma, though. See the Work It Out feature.

Work It Out ⊸○—○—○

The Problem with the Prisoner's Dilemma

Suppose two people, Rachel and Samuel, are considering purchasing a public good. The difficulty with the prisoner's dilemma arises as each person thinks through his or her strategic choices.

Step 1. Rachel reasons in this way: If Samuel does not contribute, then I would be a fool to contribute. However, if Samuel does contribute, then I can come out ahead by not contributing.

Step 2. Either way, I should choose not to contribute, and instead hope that I can be a free rider who uses the public good paid for by Samuel.

Step 3. Samuel reasons the same way about Rachel

Step 4. When both people reason in that way, the public good never gets built, and there is no movement to the option where everyone cooperates—which is actually best for all parties.

The Role of Government in Paying for Public Goods

The key insight in paying for public goods is to find a way of assuring that everyone will make a contribution and to prevent free riders. For example, if people come together through the political process and agree to pay taxes and make group decisions about the quantity of public goods, they can defeat the free rider problem by requiring, through the law, that everyone contributes.

However, government spending and taxes are not the only way to provide public goods. In some cases, markets can produce public goods. For example, think about radio. It is nonexcludable, since once the radio signal is broadcast, it would be very difficult to stop someone from receiving it. It is non-rival, since one person listening to the signal does not prevent others from listening as well. Because of these features, it is practically impossible to charge listeners directly for listening to conventional radio broadcasts.

Radio has found a way to collect revenue by selling advertising, which is an indirect way of "charging" listeners by taking up some of their time. Ultimately, consumers who purchase the goods advertised are also paying for the radio service, since the station builds in the cost of advertising into the product cost. In a more recent development, satellite radio companies, such as SirusXM, charge a regular subscription fee for streaming music without commercials. In this case, however, the product is excludable—only those who pay for the subscription will receive the broadcast.

Some public goods will also have a mixture of public provision at no charge along with fees for some purposes, like a public city park that is free to use, but the government charges a fee for parking your car, for reserving certain picnic grounds, and for food sold at a refreshment stand.

Link It Up ⚭

Read this article (http://openstaxcollege.org/l/governmentpay) to find out what economists say the government should pay for.

In other cases, we can use social pressures and personal appeals, rather than the force of law, to reduce the number of free riders and to collect resources for the public good. For example, neighbors sometimes form an association to carry out beautification projects or to patrol their area after dark to discourage crime. In low-income countries, where social pressure strongly encourages all farmers to participate, farmers in a region may come together to work on a large irrigation project that will benefit all. We can view many fundraising efforts, including raising money for local charities and for the endowments of colleges and universities, as an attempt to use social pressure to discourage free riding and to generate the outcome that will produce a public benefit.

Common Resources and the "Tragedy of the Commons"

There are some goods that do not fall neatly into the categories of private good or public good. While it is easy to classify a pizza as a private good and a city park as a public good, what about an item that is nonexcludable and rivalrous, such as the queen conch?

In the Caribbean, the queen conch is a large marine mollusk that lives in shallow waters of sea grass. These waters are so shallow, and so clear, that a single diver may harvest many conch in a single day. Not only is conch meat a local delicacy and an important part of the local diet, but artists use the large ornate shells and craftsmen transform them. Because almost anyone with a small boat, snorkel, and mask, can participate in the conch harvest, it is essentially nonexcludable. At the same time, fishing for conch is rivalrous. Once a diver catches one conch another diver cannot catch it.

We call goods that are nonexcludable and rivalrous common resources. Because the waters of the Caribbean are open to all conch fishermen, and because any conch that *you* catch is conch that *I* cannot catch, fishermen tend to overharvest common resources like the conch.

The problem of overharvesting common resources is not a new one, but ecologist Garret Hardin put the tag "Tragedy of the Commons" to the problem in a 1968 article in the magazine *Science*. Economists view this as a problem of property rights. Since nobody owns the ocean, or the conch that crawl on the sand beneath it, no one individual has an incentive to protect that resource and responsibly harvest it. To address the issue of overharvesting conch and other marine fisheries, economists typically advocate simple devices like fishing licenses, harvest limits, and shorter fishing seasons. When the population of a species drops to critically low numbers, governments have even banned the harvest until biologists determine that the population has returned to sustainable levels. In fact, such is the case with the conch, the harvesting of which the government has effectively banned in the United States since 1986.

Visit this website (http://openstaxcollege.org/l/queenconch) for more on the queen conch industry.

Positive Externalities in Public Health Programs

One of the most remarkable changes in the standard of living in the last several centuries is that people are living longer. Thousands of years ago, scientists believe that human life expectancy ranged between 20 to 30 years. By 1900, average life expectancy in the United States was 47 years. By 2015, life expectancy was 79 years. Most of the gains in life expectancy in the history of the human race happened in the twentieth century.

The rise in life expectancy seems to stem from three primary factors. First, systems for providing clean water and disposing of human waste helped to prevent the transmission of many diseases. Second, changes in public behavior have advanced health. Early in the twentieth century, for example, people learned the importance of boiling bottles before using them for food storage and baby's milk, washing their hands, and protecting food from flies. More recent behavioral changes include reducing the number of people who smoke tobacco and precautions to limit sexually transmitted diseases. Third, medicine has played a large role. Scientists developed immunizations for diphtheria, cholera, pertussis, tuberculosis, tetanus, and yellow fever between 1890 and 1930. Penicillin, discovered in 1941, led to a series of other antibiotic drugs for bringing infectious diseases under control. In recent decades, drugs that reduce the risks of high blood pressure have had a dramatic effect in extending lives.

These advances in public health have all been closely linked to positive externalities and public goods. Public health officials taught hygienic practices to mothers in the early 1900s and encouraged less smoking in the late 1900s. Government funded many public sanitation systems and storm sewers because they have the key traits of public goods. In the twentieth century, many medical discoveries emerged from government or university-funded research. Patents and intellectual property rights provided an additional incentive for private inventors. The reason for requiring immunizations, phrased in economic terms, is that it prevents spillovers of illness to others—as well as helping the person immunized.

Bring it Home

The Benefits of Voyager I Endure

While we applaud the technology spillovers of NASA's space projects, we should also acknowledge that those benefits are not shared equally. Economists like Tyler Cowen, a professor at George Mason University, are seeing increasing evidence of a widening gap between those who have access to rapidly improving technology, and those who do not. According to Cowen, author of the recent book, *Average Is Over: Powering America Beyond the Age of the Great Stagnation*, this inequality in access to technology and information is going to deepen the inequality in skills, and ultimately, in wages and global standards of living.

KEY TERMS

external benefits (or positive externalities) beneficial spillovers to a third party of parties, who did not purchase the good or service that provided the externalities

free rider those who want others to pay for the public good and then plan to use the good themselves; if many people act as free riders, the public good may never be provided

intellectual property the body of law including patents, trademarks, copyrights, and trade secret law that protect the right of inventors to produce and sell their inventions

nonexcludable when it is costly or impossible to exclude someone from using the good, and thus hard to charge for it

nonrivalrous even when one person uses the good, others can also use it

positive externalities beneficial spillovers to a third party or parties

private benefits the benefits a person who consumes a good or service receives, or a new product's benefits or process that a company invents that the company captures

private rates of return when the estimated rates of return go primarily to an individual; for example, earning interest on a savings account

public good good that is nonexcludable and non-rival, and thus is difficult for market producers to sell to individual consumers

social benefits the sum of private benefits and external benefits

social rate of return when the estimated rates of return go primarily to society; for example, providing free education

KEY CONCEPTS AND SUMMARY

13.1 Why the Private Sector Underinvests in Innovation

Competition creates pressure to innovate. However, if one can easily copy new inventions, then the original inventor loses the incentive to invest further in research and development. New technology often has positive externalities; that is, there are often spillovers from the invention of new technology that benefit firms other than the innovator. The social benefit of an invention, once the firm accounts for these spillovers, typically exceeds the private benefit to the inventor. If inventors could receive a greater share of the broader social benefits for their work, they would have a greater incentive to seek out new inventions.

13.2 How Governments Can Encourage Innovation

Public policy with regard to technology must often strike a balance. For example, patents provide an incentive for inventors, but they should be limited to genuinely new inventions and not extend forever.

Government has a variety of policy tools for increasing the rate of return for new technology and encouraging its development, including: direct government funding of R&D, tax incentives for R&D, protection of intellectual property, and forming cooperative relationships between universities and the private sector.

13.3 Public Goods

A public good has two key characteristics: it is nonexcludable and non-rival. Nonexcludable means that it is costly or impossible for one user to exclude others from using the good. Non-rival means that when one person uses the good, it does not prevent others from using it. Markets often have a difficult time producing public goods because free riders will attempt to use the public good without paying for it. One can overcome the free rider problem through measures to assure that users of the public good pay for it. Such measures include government actions, social pressures, and specific situations where markets have discovered a way to collect payments.

This OpenStax book is available for free at http://cnx.org/content/col12122/1.4

SELF-CHECK QUESTIONS

1. Do market demand curves reflect positive externalities? Why or why not?

2. Suppose that Sony's R&D investment in digital devices has increased profits by 20%. Is this a private or social benefit?

3. The Gizmo Company is planning to develop new household gadgets. **Table 13.4** shows the company's demand for financial capital for research and development of these gadgets, based on expected rates of return from sales. Now, say that every investment would have an additional 5% social benefit—that is, an investment that pays at least a 6% return to the Gizmo Company will pay at least an 11% return for society as a whole; an investment that pays at least 7% for the Gizmo Company will pay at least 12% for society as a whole, and so on. Answer the questions that follow based on this information.

Estimated Rate of Return	Private profits of the firm from an R&D project (in $ millions)
10%	$100
9%	$102
8%	$108
7%	$118
6%	$133
5%	$153
4%	$183
3%	$223

Table 13.4

a. If the going interest rate is 9%, how much will Gizmo invest in R&D if it receives only the private benefits of this investment?

b. Assume that the interest rate is still 9%. How much will the firm invest if it also receives the social benefits of its investment? (Add an additional 5% return on all levels of investment.)

4. The Junkbuyers Company travels from home to home, looking for opportunities to buy items that would otherwise end up with the garbage, but which the company can resell or recycle. Which will be larger, the private or the social benefits?

5. When residents in a neighborhood tidy it and keep it neat, there are a number of positive spillovers: higher property values, less crime, happier residents. What types of government policies can encourage neighborhoods to clean up?

6. Education provides both private benefits to those who receive it and broader social benefits for the economy as a whole. Think about the types of policies a government can follow to address the issue of positive spillovers in technology and then suggest a parallel set of policies that governments could follow for addressing positive externalities in education.

7. Which of the following goods or services are nonexcludable?
   a. police protection
   b. streaming music from satellite transmission programs
   c. roads
   d. primary education
   e. cell phone service

8. Are the following goods non-rival in consumption?
   a. slice of pizza
   b. laptop computer
   c. public radio
   d. ice cream cone

REVIEW QUESTIONS

9. In what ways do company investments in research and development create positive externalities?

10. Will the demand for borrowing and investing in R&D be higher or lower if there are no external benefits?

11. Why might private markets tend to provide too few incentives for the development of new technology?

12. What can government do to encourage the development of new technology?

13. What are the two key characteristics of public goods?

14. Name two public goods and explain why they are public goods.

15. What is the free rider problem?

16. Explain why the federal government funds national defense.

CRITICAL THINKING QUESTIONS

17. Can a company be guaranteed all of the social benefits of a new invention? Why or why not?

18. Is it inevitable that government must become involved in supporting investments in new technology?

19. How do public television stations, like PBS, try to overcome the free rider problem?

20. Why is a football game on ESPN a quasi-public good but a game on the NBC, CBS, or ABC is a public good?

21. Provide two examples of goods/services that are classified as private goods/services even though they are provided by a federal government.

22. Radio stations, tornado sirens, light houses, and street lights are all public goods in that all are nonrivalrous and nonexclusionary. Therefore why does the government provide tornado sirens, street lights and light houses but not radio stations (other than PBS stations)?

This OpenStax book is available for free at http://cnx.org/content/col12122/1.4

PROBLEMS

23. HighFlyer Airlines wants to build new airplanes with greatly increased cabin space. This will allow HighFlyer Airlines to give passengers more comfort and sell more tickets at a higher price. However, redesigning the cabin means rethinking many other elements of the airplane as well, like engine and luggage placement, and the most efficient shape of the plane for moving through the air. HighFlyer Airlines has developed a list of possible methods to increase cabin space, along with estimates of how these approaches would affect the plane's operating costs and ticket sales. Based on these estimates, **Table 13.5** shows the value of R&D projects that provide at least a certain private rate of return. Column 1 = Private Rate of Return. Column 2 = Value of R&D Projects that Return at Least the Private Rate of Return to HighFlyer Airlines. Use the data to answer the following questions.

Private Rate of Return	Value of R&D
12%	$100
10%	$200
8%	$300
6%	$400
4%	$500

Table 13.5

a. If the opportunity cost of financial capital for HighFlyer Airlines is 6%, how much should the firm invest in R&D?

b. Assume that the social rate of return for R&D is an additional 2% on top of the private return; that is, an R&D investment that had a 7% private return to HighFlyer Airlines would have a 9% social return. How much investment is socially optimal at the 6% interest rate?

24. Assume that the marginal private costs of a firm producing fuel-efficient cars is greater than the marginal social costs. Assume that the marginal private benefits of a firm producing fuel-efficient cars is the same as the marginal social benefits. Discuss one way that the government can try to increase production and sales of fuel efficient cars to the socially desirable amount. *Hint*: the government is trying to affect production through costs, not benefits.

25. Becky and Sarah are sisters who share a room. Their room can easily get messy, and their parents are always telling them to tidy it. Here are the costs and benefits to both Becky and Sarah, of taking the time to clean their room: If both Becky and Sarah clean, they each spends two hours and get a clean room. If Becky decides not to clean and Sarah does all the cleaning, then Sarah spends 10 hours cleaning (Becky spends 0) but Sarah is exhausted. The same would occur for Becky if Sarah decided not to clean—Becky spends 10 hours and becomes exhausted. If both girls decide not to clean, they both have a dirty room.

a. What is the best outcome for Becky and Sarah? What is the worst outcome? (It would help you to construct a prisoner's dilemma table.)

b. Unfortunately, we know that the optimal outcome will most likely not happen, and that the sisters probably will choose the worst one instead. Explain what it is about Becky's and Sarah's reasoning that will lead them both to choose the worst outcome.

This OpenStax book is available for free at http://cnx.org/content/col12122/1.4

14 | Labor Markets and Income

Figure 14.1 What determines incomes? In the U.S., income is based on one's value to an employer, which depends in part on education. (Credit: modification of work by AFL-CIO America's Unions/Flickr Creative Commons and COD Newsroom/Flickr Creative Commons)

Bring it Home

The Increasing Value of a College Degree

Working your way through college used to be fairly common in the United States. According to a 2015 study by the Georgetown Center on Education and the Workforce, 40% of college students work 30 hours or more per week.

At the same time, the cost of college seems to rise every year. The data show that the cost of tuition, fees, room and board has more than doubled since 1984. Thus, even full time employment may not be enough to cover college expenses anymore. Working full time at minimum wage--40 hours per week, 52 weeks per year—earns $15,080 before taxes, which is less than the $19,548 the College Board estimates it cost in 2016 for a year of college at a public university. The result of these costs is that student loan debt topped $1.3 trillion this year.

Despite these disheartening figures, the value of a bachelor's degree has never been higher. How do we explain this? This chapter will tell us.

Introduction to Labor Markets and Income

In this chapter, you will learn about:

- The theory of labor markets

- How wages are determined in an imperfectly competitive labor market

- How unions affect wages and employment

- How labor market outcomes are determined under Bilateral Monopoly

- Theories of Employment Discrimination, and

- How Immigration affects labor market outcomes

In a market economy like the United States, income comes from ownership of the means of production: resources or assets. More precisely, one's income is a function of two things: the quantity of each resource one owns, and the value society places on those resources. Recall from the chapter on **Production, Costs, and Industry Structure**, each factor of production has an associated factor payment. For the majority of us, the most important resource we own is our labor. Thus, most of our income is wages, salaries, commissions, tips and other types of labor income. Your labor income depends on how many hours you have to work and the wage rate an employer will pay you for those hours. At the same time, some people own real estate, which they can either use themselves or rent out to other users. Some people have financial assets like bank accounts, stocks and bonds, for which they earn interest, dividends or some other form of income.

Each of these factor payments, like wages for labor and interest for financial capital, is determined in their respective factor markets. For the rest of this chapter, we will focus on labor markets, but other factor markets operate similarly. Later in Chapter 17 we will describe how this works for financial capital.

14.1 | The Theory of Labor Markets

By the end of this section, you will be able to:
- The Demand for Labor in Perfectly Competitive Output Markets
- The Demand for Labor in Imperfectly Competitive Output Markets
- What Determines the Going Market Wage Rate?

What is the labor market?

The labor market is the term that economists use for all the different markets for labor. There is no single labor market. Rather, there is a different market for every different type of labor. Labor differs by type of work (e.g. retail sales vs. scientist), skill level (entry level or more experienced), and location (the market for administrative assistants is probably more local or regional than the market for university presidents). While each labor market is different, they all tend to operate in similar ways. For example, when wages go up in one labor market, they tend to go up in others too. When economists talk about the labor market, they are describing these similarities.

The labor market, like all markets, has a demand and a supply. Why do firms demand labor? Why is an employer willing to pay you for your labor? It's not because the employer likes you or is socially conscious. Rather, it's because your labor is worth something to the employer--your work brings in revenues to the firm. How much is an employer willing to pay? That depends on the skills and experience you bring to the firm.

If a firm wants to maximize profits, it will never pay more (in terms of wages and benefits) for a worker than the value of his or her marginal productivity to the firm. We call this the **first rule of labor markets**.

Suppose a worker can produce two widgets per hour and the firm can sell each widget for $4 each. Then the worker is generating $8 per hour in revenues to the firm, and a profit-maximizing employer will pay the worker up to, but no

This OpenStax book is available for free at http://cnx.org/content/col12122/1.4

more than, $8 per hour, because that is what the worker is worth to the firm.

Recall the definition of marginal product. Marginal product is the additional output a firm can produce by adding one more worker to the production process. Since employers often hire labor by the hour, we'll define marginal product as the additional output the firm produces by adding one more worker hour to the production process. In this chapter, we assume that workers are homogeneous—they have the same background, experience and skills and they put in the same amount of effort. Thus, marginal product depends on the capital and technology with which workers have to work.

A typist can type more pages per hour with an electric typewriter than a manual typewriter, and he or she can type even more pages per hour with a personal computer and word processing software. A ditch digger can dig more cubic feet of dirt in an hour with a backhoe than with at shovel.

Thus, we can define the demand for labor as the marginal product of labor times the value of that output to the firm.

# Workers (L)	1	2	3	4
MP_L	4	3	2	1

Table 14.1 Marginal Product of Labor

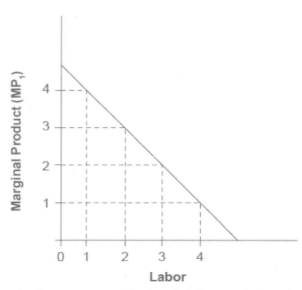

Figure 14.2 Marginal Product of Labor Because of fixed capital, the marginal product of labor declines as the employer hires additional workers.

On what does the value of each worker's marginal product depend? If we assume that the employer sells its output in a perfectly competitive market, the value of each worker's output will be the market price of the product. Thus,

Demand for Labor = MP_L x P = Value of the Marginal Product of Labor

We show this in **Table 14.2**, which is an expanded version of **Table 14.1**

# Workers (L)	1	2	3	4
MP_L	4	3	2	1
Price of Output	$4	$4	$4	$4

Table 14.2 Value of the Marginal Product of Labor

VMP$_L$	$16	$12	$8	$4

Table 14.2 Value of the Marginal Product of Labor

Note that the value of each additional worker is less than the ones who came before.

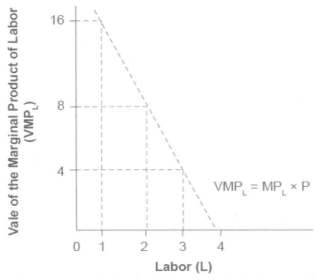

Figure 14.3 Value of the Marginal Product of Labor For firms operating in a competitive output market, the value of additional output sold is the price the firms receive for the output. Since MP$_L$ declines with additional labor employed, while that marginal product is worth the market price, the value of the marginal product declines as employment increases.

Demand for Labor in Perfectly Competitive Output Markets

The question for any firm is how much labor to hire.

We can define a **Perfectly Competitive Labor Market** as one where firms can hire all the labor they wish at the going market wage. Think about secretaries in a large city. Employers who need secretaries can probably hire as many as they need if they pay the going wage rate.

Graphically, this means that firms face a horizontal supply curve for labor, as Figure 14.3 shows.

Given the market wage, profit maximizing firms hire workers up to the point where: $W_{mkt} = VMP_L$

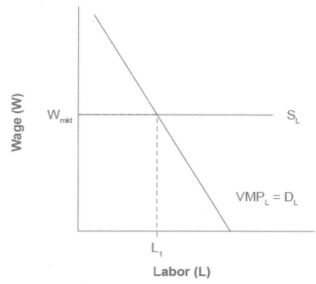

Figure 14.4 Equilibrium Employment for Firms in a Competitive Labor Market In a perfectly competitive labor market, firms can hire all the labor they want at the going market wage. Therefore, they hire workers up to the point L_1 where the going market wage equals the value of the marginal product of labor.

Derived Demand

Economists describe the demand for inputs like labor as a **derived demand**. Since the demand for labor is MPL*P, it is dependent on the demand for the product the firm is producing. We show this by the P term in the demand for labor. An increase in demand for the firm's product drives up the product's price, which increases the firm's demand for labor. Thus, we derive the demand for labor from the demand for the firm's output.

Demand for Labor in Imperfectly Competitive Output Markets

If the employer does not sell its output in a perfectly competitive industry, they face a downward sloping demand curve for output, which means that in order to sell additional output the firm must lower its price. This is true if the firm is a monopoly, but it's also true if the firm is an oligopoly or monopolistically competitive. In this situation, the value of a worker's marginal product is the marginal revenue, not the price. Thus, the demand for labor is the marginal product times the marginal revenue.

The Demand for Labor = MP_L x MR = Marginal Revenue Product

# Workers (L)	1	2	3	4
MP_L	4	3	2	1
Marginal Revenue	$4	$3	$2	$1
MRP_L	$16	$9	$4	$1

Table 14.3 Marginal Revenue Product

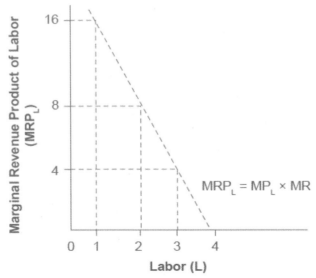

Figure 14.5 Marginal Revenue Product For firms with some market power in their output market, the value of additional output sold is the firm's marginal revenue. Since MP_L declines with additional labor employed and since MR declines with additional output sold, the firm's marginal revenue declines as employment increases.

Everything else remains the same as we described above in the discussion of the labor demand in perfectly competitive labor markets. Given the market wage, profit-maximizing firms will hire workers up to the point where the market wage equals the marginal revenue product, as **Figure 14.5** shows.

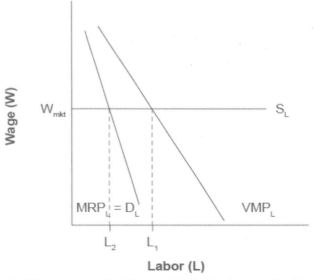

Figure 14.6 Equilibrium Level of Employment for Firms with Market Power For firms with market power in their output market, they choose the number of workers, L_2, where the going market wage equals the firm's marginal revenue product. Note that since marginal revenue is less than price, the demand for labor for a firm which has market power in its output market is less than the demand for labor (L_1) for a perfectly competitive firm. As a result, employment will be lower in an imperfectly competitive industry than in a perfectly competitive industry.

This OpenStax book is available for free at http://cnx.org/content/col12122/1.4

Do Profit Maximizing Employers Exploit Labor?

If you look back at Figure 14.4, you will see that only the firm pays the last worker it hires what they're worth to the firm. Every other worker brings in more revenue than the firm pays him or her. This has sometimes led to the claim that employers exploit workers because they do not pay workers what they are worth. Let's think about this claim. The first worker is worth $x to the firm, and the second worker is worth $y, but why are they worth that much? It is because of the capital and technology with which they work. The difference between workers' worth and their compensation goes to pay for the capital, technology, without which the workers wouldn't have a job. The difference also goes to the employer's profit, without which the firm would close and workers wouldn't have a job. The firm may be earning excessive profits, but that is a different topic of discussion.

What Determines the Going Market Wage Rate?

In the chapter on **Labor and Financial Markets**, we learned that the labor market has demand and supply curves like other markets. The demand for labor curve is a downward sloping function of the wage rate. The market demand for labor is the horizontal sum of all firms' demands for labor. The supply for labor curve is an upward sloping function of the wage rate. This is because if wages for a particular type of labor increase in a particular labor market, people with appropriate skills may change jobs, and vacancies will attract people from outside the geographic area. The market supply for labor is the horizontal summation of all individuals' supplies of labor.

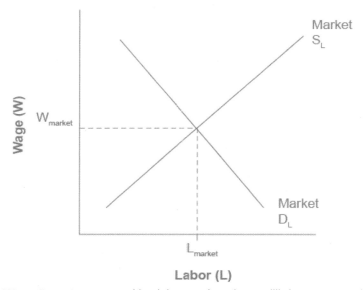

Figure 14.7 The Market Wage Rate In a competitive labor market, the equilibrium wage and employment level are determined where the market demand for labor equals the market supply of labor.

Like all equilibrium prices, the market wage rate is determined through the interaction of supply and demand in the labor market. Thus, we can see in **Figure 14.7** for competitive markets the wage rate and number of workers hired.

The FRED database has a great deal of data on labor markets, starting at **the wage rate and number of workers hired (https://openstax.org/l/cat10)** .

The United States Census Bureau for the Bureau of Labor Statistics publishes *The Current Population Survey*, which is a monthly survey of households (link is on that page), which provides data on labor supply, including numerous measures of the labor force size (disaggregated by age, gender and educational attainment), labor force participation rates for different demographic groups, and employment. It also includes more than 3,500 measures of earnings by different demographic groups.

The Current Employment Statistics, which is a survey of businesses, offers alternative estimates of employment across all sectors of the economy.

The link labeled "Productivity and Costs" has a wide range of data on productivity, labor costs and profits across the business sector.

14.2 | Wages and Employment in an Imperfectly Competitive Labor Market

By the end of this section, you will be able to:
- Define monopsony power
- Explain how imperfectly competitive labor markets determine wages and employment, where employers have market power

In the chapters on market structure, we observed that while economists use the theory of perfect competition as an ideal case of market structure, there are very few examples of perfectly competitive industries in the real world. What about labor markets? How many labor markets are perfectly competitive? There are probably more examples of perfectly competitive labor markets than perfectly competitive product markets, but that doesn't mean that all labor markets are competitive.

When a job applicant is bargaining with an employer for a position, the applicant is often at a disadvantage—needing the job more than the employer needs that particular applicant. John Bates Clark (1847–1938), often named as the first great American economist, wrote in 1907: "In the making of the wages contract the individual laborer is always at a disadvantage. He has something which he is obliged to sell and which his employer is not obliged to take, since he [that is, the employer] can reject single men with impunity."

To give workers more power, the U.S. government has passed, in response to years of labor protests, a number of laws to create a more equal balance of power between workers and employers. These laws include some of the following:

- Setting minimum hourly wages
- Setting maximum hours of work (at least before employers pay overtime rates)
- Prohibiting child labor
- Regulating health and safety conditions in the workplace
- Preventing discrimination on the basis of race, ethnicity, gender, sexual orientation, and age
- Requiring employers to provide family leave
- Requiring employers to give advance notice of layoffs
- Covering workers with unemployment insurance
- Setting a limit on the number of immigrant workers from other countries

Table 14.4 lists some prominent U.S. workplace protection laws. Many of the laws listed in the table were only the start of labor market regulations in these areas and have been followed, over time, by other related laws, regulations, and court rulings.

Law	Protection
National Labor-Management Relations Act of 1935 (the "Wagner Act")	Establishes procedures for establishing a union that firms are obligated to follow; sets up the National Labor Relations Board for deciding disputes
Social Security Act of 1935	Under Title III, establishes a state-run system of unemployment insurance, in which workers pay into a state fund when they are employed and received benefits for a time when they are unemployed
Fair Labor Standards Act of 1938	Establishes the minimum wage, limits on child labor, and rules requiring payment of overtime pay for those in jobs that are paid by the hour and exceed 40 hours per week
Taft-Hartley Act of 1947	Allows states to decide whether all workers at a firm can be required to join a union as a condition of employment; in the case of a disruptive union strike, permits the president to declare a "cooling-off period" during which workers have to return to work
Civil Rights Act of 1964	Title VII of the Act prohibits discrimination in employment on the basis of race, gender, national origin, religion, or sexual orientation
Occupational Health and Safety Act of 1970	Creates the Occupational Safety and Health Administration (OSHA), which protects workers from physical harm in the workplace
Employee Retirement and Income Security Act of 1974	Regulates employee pension rules and benefits
Pregnancy Discrimination Act of 1978	Prohibits discrimination against women in the workplace who are planning to get pregnant or who are returning to work after pregnancy
Immigration Reform and Control Act of 1986	Prohibits hiring of illegal immigrants; requires employers to ask for proof of citizenship; protects rights of legal immigrants
Worker Adjustment and Retraining Notification Act of 1988	Requires employers with more than 100 employees to provide written notice 60 days before plant closings or large layoffs
Americans with Disabilities Act of 1990	Prohibits discrimination against those with disabilities and requires reasonable accommodations for them on the job

Table 14.4 Prominent U.S. Workplace Protection Laws

Law	Protection
Family and Medical Leave Act of 1993	Allows employees to take up to 12 weeks of unpaid leave per year for family reasons, including birth or family illness
Pension Protection Act of 2006	Penalizes firms for underfunding their pension plans and gives employees more information about their pension accounts
Lilly Ledbetter Fair Pay Act of 2009	Restores protection for pay discrimination claims on the basis of sex, race, national origin, age, religion, or disability

Table 14.4 Prominent U.S. Workplace Protection Laws

There are two sources of imperfect competition in labor markets. These are demand side sources, that is, labor market power by employers, and supply side sources: labor market power by employees. In this section we will discuss the former. In the next section we will discuss the latter.

A competitive labor market is one where there are many potential employers for a given type of worker, say a secretary or an accountant. Suppose there is only one employer in a labor market. Because that employer has no direct competition in hiring, if they offer lower wages than would exist in a competitive market, employees will have few options. If they want a job, they must accept the offered wage rate. Since the employer is exploiting its market power, we call the firm a **monopsony**. The classical example of monopsony is the sole coal company in a West Virginia town. If coal miners want to work, they must accept what the coal company is paying. This is not the only example of monopsony. Think about surgical nurses in a town with only one hospital. Employers that have at least some market power over potential employees is not that unusual. After all, most firms have many employees while there is only one employer. Thus, even if there is some competition for workers, it may not feel that way to potential employees unless they do their research and find the opposite.

How does market power by an employer affect labor market outcomes? Intuitively, one might think that wages will be lower than in a competitive labor market. Let's prove it. We will tell the story for a monopsonist, but the results will be qualitatively similar, although less extreme for any firm with labor market power.

Think back to monopoly. The good news is that because the monopolist is the sole supplier in the market, it can charge any price it wishes. The bad news is that if it wants to sell a greater quantity of output, it must lower the price it charges. Monopsony is analogous. Because the monopsonist is the sole employer in a labor market, it can offer any wage that it wishes. However, because they face the market supply curve for labor, if they want to hire more workers, they must raise the wage they pay. This creates a quandary, which we can understand by introducing a new concept: the marginal cost of labor. The **marginal cost of labor** is the cost to the firm of hiring one more worker. However, here is the thing: we assume that the firm is determining how many workers to hire in total. They are not hiring sequentially. Let's look how this plays out with the example in Table 14.5.

Supply of Labor	1	2	3	4	5
Wage Rate	$1 per hour	$2 per hour	$3 per hour	$4 per hour	$5 per hour
Total Cost of Labor	$1	$4	$9	$16	$25
Marginal Cost of Labor	$1	$3	$5	$7	$9

Table 14.5 The Marginal Cost of Labor

There are a couple of things to notice from the table. First, the marginal cost increases faster than the wage rate. In fact, for any number of workers more than one, the marginal cost of labor is greater than the wage. This is because to hire one more worker requires paying a higher wage rate, not just for the new worker but for all the previous hires also. We can see this graphically in Figure 14.7.

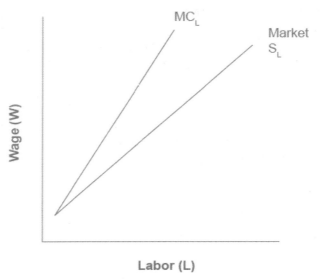

Figure 14.8 The Marginal Cost of Labor Since monopsonies are the sole demander for labor, they face the market supply curve for labor. In order to increase employment they must raise the wage they pay not just for new workers, but for all the existing workers they could have hired at the previous lower wage. As a result, the marginal cost of additional hiring labor is greater than the wage, and thus for any level of employment (above the first worker), MC_L is above the Market Supply of Labor.

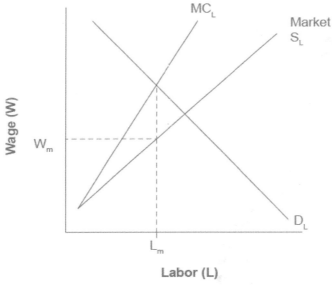

Figure 14.9 Labor Market Outcomes Under Monopsony A monopsony will hire workers up to the point Lm where its demand for labor equals the marginal cost of additional labor, paying the wage Wm given by the supply curve of labor necessary to obtain Lm workers.

If the firm wants to maximize profits, it will hire labor up to the point Lm where D_L = VMP (or MRP) = MC_L., as **Figure 14.9** shows. Then, the supply curve for labor shows the wage the firm will have to pay to attract Lm workers. Graphically, we can draw a vertical line up from Lm to the Supply Curve for label and then read the wage Wm off the vertical axis to the left.

How does this outcome compare to what would occur in a perfectly competitive market? A competitive market would operate where D_L = S_L, hiring Lc workers and paying Wc wage. In other words, under monopsony employers hire fewer workers and pay a lower wage. While pure monopsony may be rare, many employers have some degree of market power in labor markets. The outcomes for those employers will be qualitatively similar though not as extreme as monopsony.

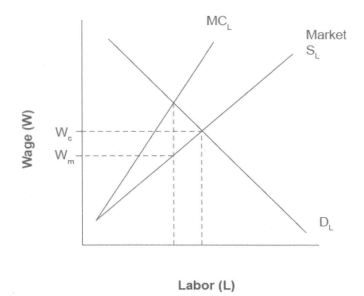

Labor (L)

Figure 14.10 Comparison of labor market outcomes: Monopsony vs. Perfect Competition A monopsony hires fewer workers Lm than would be hired in a competitive labor market Lc. In exploiting its market power, the monopsony can also pay a lower wage Wm than workers would earn in a competitive labor market Wc.

14.3 | Market Power on the Supply Side of Labor Markets: Unions

By the end of this section, you will be able to:
- Explain the concept of labor unions, including membership levels and wages
- Evaluate arguments for and against labor unions
- Analyze reasons for the decline in U.S. union membership

A labor union is an organization of workers that negotiates with employers over wages and working conditions. A labor union seeks to change the balance of power between employers and workers by requiring employers to deal with workers collectively, rather than as individuals. As such, a labor union operates like a monopoly in a labor market. We sometimes call negotiations between unions and firms **collective bargaining**.

The subject of labor unions can be controversial. Supporters of labor unions view them as the workers' primary line of defense against efforts by profit-seeking firms to hold down wages and benefits. Critics of labor unions view them as having a tendency to grab as much as they can in the short term, even if it means injuring workers in the long run by driving firms into bankruptcy or by blocking the new technologies and production methods that lead to economic growth. We will start with some facts about union membership in the United States.

Facts about Union Membership and Pay

According to the U.S. Bureau of Labor and Statistics, about 10.7% of all U.S. workers belong to unions. Following are some facts about unions for 2016:

- 11.2% of U.S. male workers belong to unions; 10.2% of female workers do
- 10.5% of white workers, 13% of black workers, and 8.8 % of Hispanic workers belong to unions
- 11.8% of full-time workers and 5.7% of part-time workers are union members
- 5.11% of workers ages 16–24 belong to unions, as do 13.9% of workers ages 45-54
- Occupations in which relatively high percentages of workers belong to unions are the federal government (27.4% belong to a union), state government (29.6%), local government (40.3%); transportation and utilities

(15.1%); natural resources, construction, and maintenance (16.3%); and production, transportation, and material moving (13.7%)

- Occupations that have relatively low percentages of unionized workers are agricultural workers (1.3%), financial services (2.4%), professional and business services (2.4%), leisure and hospitality (2.7%), and wholesale and retail trade (4.2%)

In summary, the percentage of workers belonging to a union is higher for men than women; higher for blacks than for whites or Hispanics; higher for the 45–64 age range; and higher among workers in government and manufacturing than workers in agriculture or service-oriented jobs. **Table 14.6** lists the largest U.S. labor unions and their membership.

Union	Membership
National Education Association (NEA)	2.9 million
Service Employees International Union (SEIU)	1.9 million
American Federation of Teachers (AFT)	1.5 million
International Brotherhood of Teamsters (IBT)	1.3 million
The American Federation of State, County, and Municipal Workers (AFSCME)	1.3 million
United Food and Commercial Workers International Union	1.3 million
International Brotherhood of Electrical Workers (IBEW)	662,000
United Steelworkers	591,000
International Association of Machinists and Aerospace Workers	569,000
International Union, United Automobile, Aerospace and Agricultural Implement Workers of America (UAW)	408,000

Table 14.6 The Largest American Unions in 2015   (Source: U.S. Department of Labor, Bureau of Labor Statistics)

In terms of pay, benefits, and hiring, U.S. unions offer a good news/bad news story. The good news for unions and their members is that their members earn about 20% more than nonunion workers, even after adjusting for factors such as years of work experience and education level. The bad news for unions is that the share of U.S. workers who belong to a labor union has been steadily declining for 50 years, as **Figure 14.11** shows. About one-quarter of all U.S. workers belonged to a union in the mid-1950s, but only 11.1% of U.S. workers are union members today. If you leave out government workers (which includes teachers in public schools), only 6.6% of the workers employed by private firms now work for a union.

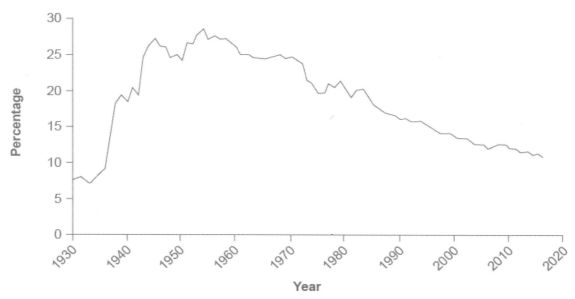

Figure 14.11 Percentage of Wage and Salary Workers Who Are Union Members The share of wage and salary workers who belong to unions rose sharply in the 1930s and 1940s, but has tailed off since then to 10.7% of all workers in 2016.

The following section analyzes the higher pay union workers receive compared the pay rates for nonunion workers. The section after that analyzes declining union membership levels. An overview of these two issues will allow us to discuss many aspects of how unions work.

Higher Wages for Union Workers

How does a union affect wages and employment? Because a union is the sole supplier of labor, it can act like a monopoly and ask for whatever wage rate it can obtain for its workers. If employers need workers, they have to meet the union's wage demand.

What are the limits on how much higher pay union workers can receive? To analyze these questions, let's consider a situation where all firms in an industry must negotiate with a single union, and no firm is allowed to hire nonunion labor. If no labor union existed in this market, then equilibrium (E) in the labor market would occur at the intersection of the demand for labor (D) and the supply of labor (S) as we see in **Figure 14.12**. This is the same result as we showed in Figure 14.6 above. The union can, however, threaten that, unless firms agree to the wages they demand, the workers will strike. As a result, the labor union manages to achieve, through negotiations with the firms, a union wage of Wu for its members, above what the equilibrium wage would otherwise have been.

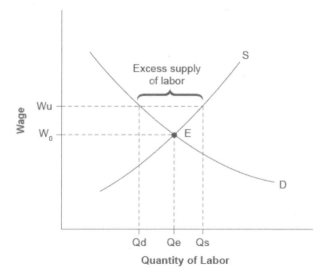

Figure 14.12 Union Wage Negotiations   Without a union, the equilibrium at E would have involved the wage We and the quantity of labor Qe. However, the union is able to use its bargaining power to raise the wage to Wu. The result is an excess supply of labor for union jobs. That is, a quantity of labor supplied, Qs is greater than firms' quantity demanded for labor, Qd.

This labor market situation resembles what a monopoly firm does in selling a product, but in this case a union is a monopoly selling labor to firms. At the higher union wage Wu, the firms in this industry will hire less labor than they would have hired in equilibrium. Moreover, an excess supply of workers want union jobs, but firms will not be hiring for such jobs.

From the union point of view, workers who receive higher wages are better off. However, notice that the quantity of workers (Qd) hired at the union wage Wu is smaller than the quantity Qe that the firm would have hired at the original equilibrium wage. A sensible union must recognize that when it pushes up the wage, it also reduces the firms' incentive to hire. This situation does not necessarily mean that union workers are fired. Instead, it may be that when union workers move on to other jobs or retire, they are not always replaced, or perhaps when a firm expands production, it expands employment somewhat less with a higher union wage than it would have done with the lower equilibrium wage. Other situations could be that a firm decides to purchase inputs from nonunion producers, rather than producing them with its own highly paid unionized workers, or perhaps the firm moves or opens a new facility in a state or country where unions are less powerful.

From the firm's point of view, the key question is whether union workers' higher wages are matched by higher productivity. If so, then the firm can afford to pay the higher union wages and, the demand curve for "unionized" labor could actually shift to the right. This could reduce the job losses as the equilibrium employment level shifts to the right and the difference between the equilibrium and the union wages will have been reduced. If worker unionization does not increase productivity, then the higher union wage will cause lower profits or losses for the firm.

Union workers might have higher productivity than nonunion workers for a number of reasons. First, higher wages may elicit higher productivity. Second, union workers tend to stay longer at a given job, a trend that reduces the employer's costs for training and hiring and results in workers with more years of experience. Many unions also offer job training and apprenticeship programs.

In addition, firms that are confronted with union demands for higher wages may choose production methods that involve more physical capital and less labor, resulting in increased labor productivity. **Table 14.7** provides an example. Assume that a firm can produce a home exercise cycle with three different combinations of labor and manufacturing equipment. Say that the firm pays labor $16 an hour (including benefits) and the machines for manufacturing cost $200 each. Under these circumstances, the total cost of producing a home exercise cycle will be lowest if the firm adopts the plan of 50 hours of labor and one machine, as the table shows. Now, suppose that a union negotiates a wage of $20 an hour including benefits. In this case, it makes no difference to the firm whether it uses more hours of labor and fewer machines or less labor and more machines, although it might prefer to use more machines and to hire fewer union workers. (After all, machines never threaten to strike—but they do not buy the final product or service either.)

In the final column of the table, the wage has risen to $24 an hour. In this case, the firm clearly has an incentive for using the plan that involves paying for fewer hours of labor and using three machines. If management responds to union demands for higher wages by investing more in machinery, then union workers can be more productive because they are working with more or better physical capital equipment than the typical nonunion worker. However, the firm will need to hire fewer workers.

Hours of Labor	Number of Machines	Cost of Labor + Cost of Machine $16/hour	Cost of Labor + Cost of Machine $20/hour	Cost of Labor + Cost of Machine $24/hour
30	3	$480 + $600 = $1,080	$600 + $600 = $1,200	$720 + $600 = $1,320
40	2	$640 + $400 = $1,040	$800 + $400 = $1,200	$960 + $400 = $1,360
50	1	$800 + $200 = $1,000	$1,000 + $200 = $1,200	$1,200 + $200 = $1,400

Table 14.7 Three Production Choices to Manufacture a Home Exercise Cycle

In some cases, unions have discouraged the use of labor-saving physical capital equipment—out of the reasonable fear that new machinery will reduce the number of union jobs. For example, in 2002, the union representing longshoremen who unload ships and the firms that operate shipping companies and port facilities staged a work stoppage that shut down the ports on the western coast of the United States. Two key issues in the dispute were the desire of the shipping companies and port operators to use handheld scanners for record-keeping and computer-operated cabs for loading and unloading ships—changes which the union opposed, along with overtime pay. President Obama threatened to use the Labor Management Relations Act of 1947—commonly known as the Taft-Hartley Act—where a court can impose an 80-day "cooling-off period" in order to allow time for negotiations to proceed without the threat of a work stoppage. Federal mediators were called in, and the two sides agreed to a deal in February 2015. The ultimate agreement allowed the new technologies, but also kept wages, health, and pension benefits high for workers. In the past, presidential use of the Taft-Hartley Act sometimes has made labor negotiations more bitter and argumentative but, in this case, it seems to have smoothed the road to an agreement.

In other instances, unions have proved quite willing to adopt new technologies. In one prominent example, during the 1950s and 1960s, the United Mineworkers union demanded that mining companies install labor-saving machinery in the mines. The mineworkers' union realized that over time, the new machines would reduce the number of jobs in the mines, but the union leaders also knew that the mine owners would have to pay higher wages if the workers became more productive, and mechanization was a necessary step toward greater productivity.

In fact, in some cases union workers may be more willing to accept new technology than nonunion workers, because the union workers believe that the union will negotiate to protect their jobs and wages, whereas nonunion workers may be more concerned that the new technology will replace their jobs. In addition, union workers, who typically have higher job market experience and training, are likely to suffer less and benefit more than non-union workers from the introduction of new technology. Overall, it is hard to make a definitive case that union workers as a group are always either more or less welcoming to new technology than are nonunion workers

The Decline in U.S. Union Membership

The proportion of U.S. workers belonging to unions has declined dramatically since the early 1950s. Economists have offered a number of possible explanations:

- The shift from manufacturing to service industries
- The force of globalization and increased competition from foreign producers
- A reduced desire for unions because of the workplace protection laws now in place
- U.S. legal environment that makes it relatively more difficult for unions to organize workers and expand their membership

This OpenStax book is available for free at http://cnx.org/content/col12122/1.4

Let's discuss each of these four explanations in more detail.

A first possible explanation for the decline in the share of U.S. workers belonging to unions involves the patterns of job growth in the manufacturing and service sectors of the economy as **Figure 14.13** shows. The U.S. economy had about 15 million manufacturing jobs in 1960. This total rose to 19 million by the late 1970s and then declined to 17 million in 2013. Meanwhile, the number of jobs in service industries and in government combined rose from 35 million in 1960 to over 118 million by 2013, according to the Bureau of Labor Statistics. Because over time unions were stronger in manufacturing than in service industries, the growth in jobs was not happening where the unions were. It is interesting to note that government workers comprise several of the biggest unions in the country, including the **American Federation of State, County and Municipal Employees (AFSCME)**; the **Service Employees International Union**; and the **National Education Association**. **Table 14.8** lists the membership of each of these unions. Outside of government employees, however, unions have not had great success in organizing the service sector.

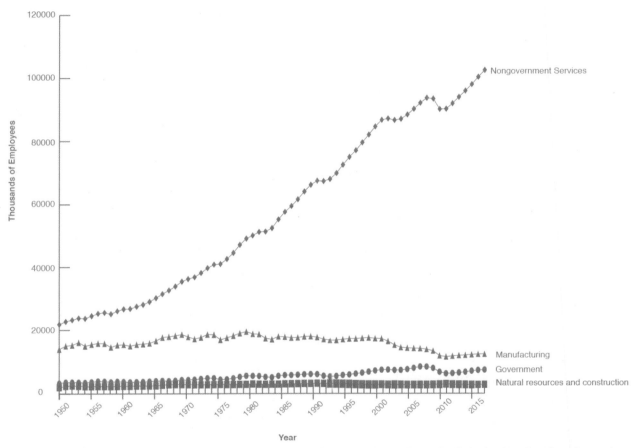

Figure 14.13 The Growth Service Jobs Jobs in services have increased dramatically in the last few decades. Jobs in government have increased modestly until 1990 and then declined slightly since then. Jobs in manufacturing peaked in the late 1970s and have declined more than a third since then.

A second explanation for the decline in the share of unionized workers looks at import competition. Starting in the 1960s, U.S. carmakers and steelmakers faced increasing competition from Japanese and European manufacturers. As sales of imported cars and steel rose, the number of jobs in U.S. auto manufacturing fell. This industry is heavily unionized. Not surprisingly, membership in the United Auto Workers, which was 975,000 in 1985, had fallen to roughly 390,000 by 2015. Import competition not only decreases the employment in sectors where unions were once strong, but also decreases the bargaining power of unions in those sectors. However, as we have seen, unions that organize public-sector workers, who are not threatened by import competition, have continued to see growth.

A third possible reason for the decline in the number of union workers is that citizens often call on their elected representatives to pass laws concerning work conditions, overtime, parental leave, regulation of pensions, and other issues. Unions offered strong political support for these laws aimed at protecting workers but, in an ironic twist, the passage of those laws then made many workers feel less need for unions.

These first three possible reasons for the decline of unions are all somewhat plausible, but they have a common problem. Most other developed economies have experienced similar economic and political trends, such as the shift from manufacturing to services, globalization, and increasing government social benefits and regulation of the workplace. Clearly there are cultural differences between countries as to their acceptance of unions in the workplace. The share of the population belonging to unions in other countries is very high compared with the share in the United States. **Table 14.8** shows the proportion of workers in a number of the world's high-income economies who belong to unions. The United States is near the bottom, along with France and Spain. The last column shows union coverage, defined as including those workers whose wages are determined by a union negotiation even if the workers do not officially belong to the union. In the United States, union membership is almost identical to union coverage. However, in many countries, the wages of many workers who do not officially belong to a union are still determined by collective bargaining between unions and firms.

Country	Union Density: Percentage of Workers Belonging to a Union	Union Coverage: Percentage of Workers Whose Wages Are Determined by Union Bargaining
Austria	37%	99%
France	9%	95%
Germany	26%	63%
Japan	22%	23%
Netherlands	25%	82%
Spain	11.3%	81%
Sweden	82%	92%
United Kingdom	29%	35%
United States	11.1%	12.5%

Table 14.8 International Comparisons of Union Membership and Coverage in 2012 (Source, CIA World Factbook, retrieved from www.cia.gov)

These international differences in union membership suggest a fourth reason for the decline of union membership in the United States: perhaps U.S. laws are less friendly to the formation of unions than such laws in other countries. The close connection between union membership and a friendly legal environment is apparent in the history of U.S. unions. The great rise in union membership in the 1930s followed the passage of the **National Labor-Management Relations Act** of 1935, which specified that workers had a right to organize unions and that management had to give them a fair chance to do so. The U.S. government strongly encouraged forming unions during the early 1940s in the belief that unions would help to coordinate the all-out production efforts needed during World War II. However, after World War II came the passage of the Taft-Hartley Act of 1947, which gave states the power to allow workers to opt out of the union in their workplace if they so desired. This law made the legal climate less encouraging to those seeking to form unions, and union membership levels soon started declining.

The procedures for forming a union differ substantially from country to country. For example, the procedures in the United States and those in Canada are strikingly different. When a group of workers wish to form a union in the United States, they announce this fact and set an election date when the firm's employees will vote in a secret ballot on whether to form a union. Supporters of the union lobby for a "yes" vote, and the firm's management lobbies for a "no" vote—often even hiring outside consultants for assistance in swaying workers to vote "no." In Canada, by contrast, a union is formed when a sufficient proportion of workers (usually about 60%) sign an official card saying

This OpenStax book is available for free at http://cnx.org/content/col12122/1.4

that they want a union. There is no separate "election date." The management of Canadian firms is limited by law in its ability to lobby against the union. In addition, although it is illegal to discriminate and fire workers based on their union activity in the United States, the penalties are slight, making this a not so costly way of deterring union activity. In short, forming unions is easier in Canada—and in many other countries—than in the United States.

In summary, union membership in the United States is lower than in many other high-income countries, a difference that may be due to different legal environments and cultural attitudes toward unions.

Link It Up ⌾

Visit this website (http://openstaxcollege.org/l/fastfoodwages) to read more about recent protests regarding minimum wage for fast food employees.

14.4 | Bilateral Monopoly

By the end of this section, you will be able to explain:

- How firms determine wages and employment when a specific labor market combines a union and a monopsony

What happens when there is market power on both sides of the labor market, in other words, when a union meets a monopsony? Economists call such a situation a **bilateral monopoly**.

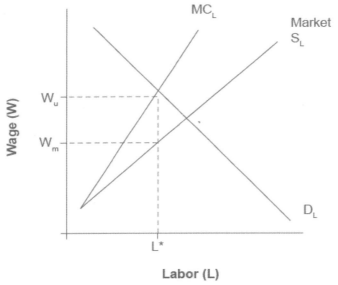

Figure 14.14 Bilateral Monopoly Employment, L*, will be lower in a bilateral monopoly than in a competitive labor market, but the equilibrium wage is indeterminate, somewhere in the range between Wu, what the union would choose, and Wm, what the monopsony would choose.

Figure 14.14 is a combination of Figure 14.6 and Figure 14.11. A monopsony wants to reduce wages as well as employment, Wm and L* in the figure. A union wants to increase wages, but at the cost of lower employment, Wu and L* in the figure. Since both sides want to reduce employment, we can be sure that the outcome will be lower employment compared to a competitive labor market. What happens to the wage, though, is based on the monopsonist's relative bargaining power compared to the union. The actual outcome is indeterminate in the graph, but it will be closer to Wu if the union has more power and closer to Wm if the monopsonist has more power.

14.5 | Employment Discrimination

By the end of this section, you will be able to:
- Analyze earnings gaps based on race and gender
- Explain the impact of discrimination in a competitive market
- Identify U.S. public policies designed to reduce discrimination

Discrimination involves acting on the belief that members of a certain group are inferior solely because of a factor such as race, gender, or religion. There are many types of discrimination but the focus here will be on discrimination in labor markets, which arises if workers with the same skill levels—as measured by education, experience, and expertise—receive different pay receive different pay or have different job opportunities because of their race or gender.

Earnings Gaps by Race and Gender

A possible signal of labor market discrimination is when an employer pays one group less than another. **Figure 14.15** shows the average wage of black workers as a ratio of the average wage of white workers and the average wage of female workers as a ratio of the average wage of male workers. Research by the economists Francine Blau and Laurence Kahn shows that the gap between the earnings of women and men did not move much in the 1970s, but has declined since the 1980s. According to the U.S. Census, the gap between the earnings of blacks and whites diminished in the 1970s, but has not changed in 50 years. In both gender and race, an earnings gap remains.

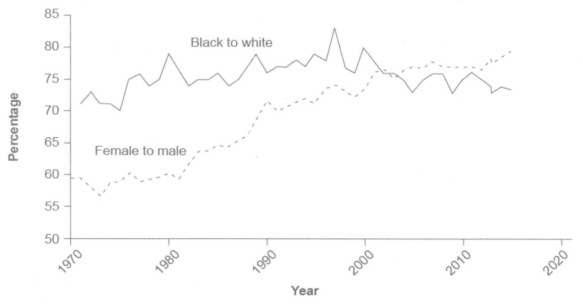

Figure 14.15 Wage Ratios by Sex and Race   The ratio of wages for black workers to white workers rose substantially in the late 1960s and through the 1970s, but has not changed much since then. The ratio of wages for female to male workers changed little through the 1970s, but has risen substantially since the 1980s. In both cases, a gap remains between the average wages of black and white workers and between the average wages of female and male workers. Source: U.S. Department of Labor, Bureau of Labor Statistics.

An earnings gap between average wages, in and of itself, does not prove that discrimination is occurring in the labor market. We need to apply the same productivity characteristics to all parties (employees) involved. Gender discrimination in the labor market occurs when employers pay women less than men despite having comparable levels of education, experience, and expertise. (Read the Clear It Up about the sex-discrimination suit brought against Wal-Mart.) Similarly, racial discrimination in the labor market exists when employers pay racially diverse employees less than their coworkers of the majority race despite having comparable levels of education, experience, and expertise. To bring a successful gender discrimination lawsuit, a female employee must prove the employer is paying her less than a male employee who holds a similar job, with similar educational attainment, and with similar expertise. Likewise,

This OpenStax book is available for free at http://cnx.org/content/col12122/1.4

someone who wants to sue on the grounds of racial discrimination must prove that the employer pays him or her less than an employee of another race who holds a similar job, with similar educational attainment, and with similar expertise.

The FRED database includes earnings by **earnings by age, gender and race/ethnicity (https://openstax.org/l/33501)** .

What was the sex-discrimination case against Wal-Mart?

In one of the largest class-action sex-discrimination cases in U.S. history, 1.2 million female employees of Wal-Mart claimed that the company engaged in wage and promotion discrimination. In 2011, the Supreme Court threw out the case on the grounds that the group was too large and too diverse to consider the case a class action suit. Lawyers for the women regrouped and are now suing in smaller groups. Part of the difficulty for the female employees is that the court said that local managers made pay and promotion decisions that were not necessarily the company's policies as a whole. Consequently, female Wal-Mart employees in Texas are arguing that their new suit will challenge the management of a "discrete group of regional district and store managers." They claim these managers made biased pay and promotion decisions. However, in 2013, a federal district court rejected a smaller California class action suit against the company.

On other issues, Wal-Mart made the news again in 2013 when the National Labor Relations Board found Wal-Mart guilty of illegally penalizing and firing workers who took part in labor protests and strikes. Wal-Mart has already paid $11.7 million in back wages and compensation damages to women in Kentucky who were denied jobs due to their sex.

Investigating the Female/Male Earnings Gap

As a result of changes in law and culture, women began to enter the paid workforce in substantial numbers in the mid- to late-twentieth century. By 2014, 58.1% of adult women held jobs while 72.0% of adult men did. Moreover, along with entering the workforce, women began to ratchet up their education levels. In 1971, 44% of undergraduate college degrees went to women. By 2014, women received 56% of bachelor's degrees. In 1970, women received 5.4% of the degrees from law schools and 8.4% of the degrees from medical schools. By 2014, women were receiving 47% of the law degrees and 48.0% of the medical degrees. These gains in education and experience have reduced the female/male wage gap over time. However, concerns remain about the extent to which women have not yet assumed a substantial share of the positions at the top of the largest companies or in the U.S. Congress.

There are factors that can lower women's average wages. Women are likely to bear a disproportionately large share of household responsibilities. A mother of young children is more likely to drop out of the labor force for several years or work on a reduced schedule than is the father. As a result, women in their 30s and 40s are likely, on average, to have less job experience than men. In the United States, childless women with the same education and experience levels as men are typically paid comparably. However, women with families and children are typically paid about 7% to 14% less than other women of similar education and work experience. (Meanwhile, married men earn about 10% to 15% more than single men with comparable education and work experience.)

We possibly could call the different patterns of family responsibilities discrimination, but it is primarily rooted in America's social patterns of discrimination, which involve the roles that fathers and mothers play in child-rearing, rather than discrimination by employers in hiring and salary decisions.

Link It Up

Visit this website (http://www.catalyst.org/) to read more about the persistently low numbers of women in executive roles in business and in the U.S. Congress.

Investigating the Black/White Earnings Gap

Blacks experienced blatant labor market discrimination during much of the twentieth century. Until the passage of the Civil Rights Act of 1964, it was legal in many states to refuse to hire a black worker, regardless of the credentials or experience of that worker. Moreover, blacks were often denied access to educational opportunities, which in turn meant that they had lower levels of qualifications for many jobs. At least one economic study has shown that the 1964 law is partially responsible for the narrowing of the gap in black–white earnings in the late 1960s and into the 1970s. For example, the ratio of total earnings of black male workers to white male workers rose from 62% in 1964 to 75.3% in 2013, according to the Bureau of Labor Statistics.

However, the earnings gap between black and white workers has not changed as much as the earnings gap between men and women has in the last half century. The remaining racial gap seems related both to continuing differences in education levels and to the presence of discrimination. Table 14.9 shows that the percentage of blacks who complete a four-year college degree remains substantially lower than the percentage of whites who complete college. According to the U.S. Census, both whites and blacks have higher levels of educational attainment than Hispanics and lower levels than Asians. The lower average levels of education for black workers surely explain part of the earnings gap. In fact, black women who have the same levels of education and experience as white women receive, on average, about the same level of pay. One study shows that white and black college graduates have identical salaries immediately after college; however, the racial wage gap widens over time, an outcome that suggests the possibility of continuing discrimination. Another study conducted a field experiment by responding to job advertisements with fictitious resumes with either very African American sounding names or very white sounding names and found out that white names received 50 percent more callbacks for interviews. This is suggestive of discrimination in job opportunities. Further, as the following Clear It Up feature explains, there is evidence to support that discrimination in the housing market is connected to employment discrimination.

	White	Hispanic	Black	Asian
Completed four years of high school or more	93.0%	66.7%	87.0%	89.1%
Completed four years of college or more	36.2%	15.5%	22.5%	53.9%

Table 14.9 Educational Attainment by Race and Ethnicity in 2015   (Source: http://www.census.gov/hhes/socdemo/education/data/cps/2014/tables.html)

How is discrimination in the housing market connected to employment discrimination?

In a recent study by the Housing and Urban Development (HUD) department, realtors show black homebuyers 18 percent fewer homes compared to white homebuyers. Realtors show Asians are shown 19 percent fewer properties. Additionally, Hispanics experience more discrimination in renting apartments and undergo stiffer credit checks than white renters. In a 2012 U.S. Department of Housing and Urban Development and the nonprofit Urban Institute study, Hispanic testers who contacted agents about advertised rental units received information about 12 percent fewer units available and were shown seven percent fewer units than white renters. The $9 million study, based on research in 28 metropolitan areas, concluded that blatant "door slamming" forms of discrimination are on the decline but that the discrimination that does exist is harder to detect, and as a result, more difficult to remedy. According to the *Chicago Tribune*, HUD Secretary Shaun Donovan, who served in his role from 2009-2014, told reporters, "Just because it's taken on a hidden form doesn't make it any less harmful. You might not be able to move into that community with the good schools."

The lower levels of education for black workers can also be a result of discrimination—although it may be pre-labor market discrimination, rather than direct discrimination by employers in the labor market. For example, if discrimination in housing markets causes black families to live clustered together in certain poorer neighborhoods, then the black children will continue to have lower educational attainment then their white counterparts and, consequently, not be able to obtain the higher paying jobs that require higher levels of education. Another element to consider is that in the past, when blacks were effectively barred from many high-paying jobs, obtaining additional education could have seemed somewhat pointless, because the educational degrees would not pay off. Even though the government has legally abolished labor market discrimination, it can take some time to establish a culture and a tradition of valuing education highly. Additionally, a legacy of past discrimination may contribute to an attitude that blacks will have a difficult time succeeding in academic subjects. In any case, the impact of social discrimination in labor markets is more complicated than seeking to punish a few bigoted employers.

Competitive Markets and Discrimination

Gary Becker (b. 1930), who won the Nobel Prize in economics in 1992, was one of the first to analyze discrimination in economic terms. Becker pointed out that while competitive markets can allow some employers to practice discrimination, it can also provide profit-seeking firms with incentives not to discriminate. Given these incentives, Becker explored the question of why discrimination persists.

If a business is located in an area with a large minority population and refuses to sell to minorities, it will cut into its own profits. If some businesses run by bigoted employers refuse to pay women and/or minorities a wage based on their productivity, then other profit-seeking employers can hire these workers. In a competitive market, if the business owners care more about the color of money than about the color of skin, they will have an incentive to make buying, selling, hiring, and promotion decisions strictly based on economic factors.

Do not underestimate the power of markets to offer at least a degree of freedom to oppressed groups. In many countries, cohesive minority groups like Jews and emigrant Chinese have managed to carve out a space for themselves through their economic activities, despite legal and social discrimination against them. Many immigrants, including those who come to the United States, have taken advantage of economic freedom to make new lives for themselves. However, history teaches that market forces alone are unlikely to eliminate discrimination. After all, discrimination against African Americans persisted in the market-oriented U.S. economy during the century between President Abraham Lincoln's Emancipation Proclamation, which freed the slaves in 1863, and the passage of the Civil Rights Act of 1964—and has continued since then, too.

Therefore, why does discrimination persist in competitive markets? Gary Becker sought to explain this persistence. Discriminatory impulses can emerge at a number of levels: among managers, among workers, and among customers. Consider the situation of a manager who is not personally prejudiced, but who has many workers or customers who are prejudiced. If that manager treats minority groups or women fairly, the manager may find it hurts the morale of prejudiced co-workers or drives away prejudiced customers. In such a situation, a policy of nondiscrimination could reduce the firm's profits. After all, a business firm is part of society, and a firm that does not follow the societal norms is likely to suffer. Market forces alone are unlikely to overwhelm strong social attitudes about discrimination.

Link It Up

Visit this website (http://openstaxcollege.org/l/censusincome) to read more about wage discrimination.

Public Policies to Reduce Discrimination

A first public policy step against discrimination in the labor market is to make it illegal. For example, the Equal Pay Act of 1963 said that employers must pay men and women who do equal work the same. The Civil Rights Act of 1964 prohibits employment discrimination based on race, color, religion, sex, or national origin. The Age Discrimination in Employment Act of 1967 prohibited discrimination on the basis of age against individuals who are 40 years of age or older. The Civil Rights Act of 1991 provides monetary damages in cases of intentional employment discrimination. The Pregnancy Discrimination Act of 1978 was aimed at prohibiting discrimination against women in the workplace who are planning to get pregnant, are pregnant, or are returning after pregnancy. Passing a law, however, is only part of the answer, since discrimination by prejudiced employers may be less important than broader social patterns.

These laws against discrimination have reduced the gender wage gap. A 2007 Department of Labor study compared salaries of men and women who have similar educational achievement, work experience, and occupation and found that the gender wage gap is only 5%.

In the case of the earnings gap between blacks and whites (and also between Hispanics and whites), probably the single largest step that could be taken at this point in U.S. history to close the earnings gap would be to reduce the gap in educational achievement. Part of the answer to this issue involves finding ways to improve the performance of schools, which is a highly controversial topic in itself. In addition, the education gap is unlikely to close unless black and Hispanic families and peer groups strengthen their culture of support for educational achievement.

Affirmative action is the name given to active efforts by government or businesses that give special rights to minorities in hiring and promotion to make up for past discrimination. Affirmative action, in its limited and not especially controversial form, means making an effort to reach out to a broader range of minority candidates for jobs. In its more aggressive and controversial form, affirmative action required government and companies to hire a specific number or percentage of minority employees. However, the U.S. Supreme Court has ruled against state affirmative action laws. Today, the government applies affirmative action policies only to federal contractors who have lost a discrimination lawsuit. The federal Equal Employment Opportunity Commission (EEOC) enforces this type of redress.

An Increasingly Diverse Workforce

Racial and ethnic diversity is on the rise in the U.S. population and work force. As **Figure 14.16** shows, while the white Americans comprised 78% of the population in 2012, the U.S. Bureau of the Census projects that whites will comprise 69% of the U.S. population by 2060. Forecasters predict that the proportion of U.S. citizens who are of Hispanic background to rise substantially. Moreover, in addition to expected changes in the population, workforce diversity is increasing as the women who entered the workforce in the 1970s and 1980s are now moving up the promotion ladders within their organizations.

This OpenStax book is available for free at http://cnx.org/content/col12122/1.4

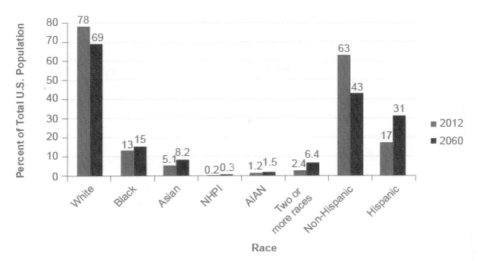

Figure 14.16 Projected Changes in America's Racial and Ethnic Diversity This figure shows projected changes in the ethnic makeup of the U.S. population by 2060. Note that "NHPI" stands for Native Hawaiian and Other Pacific Islander. "AIAN" stands for American Indian and Alaska Native. Source: US Department of Commerce

Regarding the future, optimists argue that the growing proportions of minority workers will break down remaining discriminatory barriers. The economy will benefit as an increasing proportion of workers from traditionally disadvantaged groups have a greater opportunity to fulfill their potential. Pessimists worry that the social tensions between men and women and between ethnic groups will rise and that workers will be less productive as a result. Anti-discrimination policy, at its best, seeks to help society move toward the more optimistic outcome.

The FRED database includes data on foreign and native born civilian **population (https://openstax.org/l/104)** and **labor force (https://openstax.org/l/32442)** .

14.6 | Immigration

Most Americans would be outraged if a law prevented them from moving to another city or another state. However, when the conversation turns to crossing national borders and are about other people arriving in the United States, laws preventing such movement often seem more reasonable. Some of the tensions over immigration stem from worries over how it might affect a country's culture, including differences in language, and patterns of family, authority, or gender relationships. Economics does not have much to say about such cultural issues. Some of the worries about immigration do, however, have to do with its effects on wages and income levels, and how it affects government taxes and spending. On those topics, economists have insights and research to offer.

Historical Patterns of Immigration

Supporters and opponents of immigration look at the same data and see different patterns. Those who express concern about immigration levels to the United States point to graphics like **Figure 14.17** which shows total inflows of immigrants decade by decade through the twentieth century. Clearly, the level of immigration has been high and rising in recent years, reaching and exceeding the towering levels of the early twentieth century. However, those who are less worried about immigration point out that the high immigration levels of the early twentieth century happened when total population was much lower. Since the U.S. population roughly tripled during the twentieth century, the seemingly high levels in immigration in the 1990s and 2000s look relatively smaller when they are divided by the population.

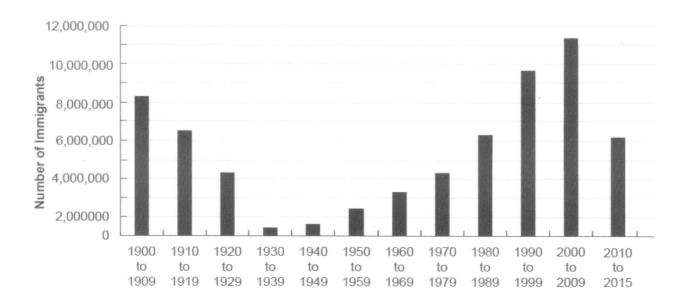

Figure 14.17 Immigration Since 1900 The number of immigrants in each decade declined between 1900 and the 1940s, rose sharply through 2009 and started to decline from 2010 to the present. (Source: U.S. Department of Homeland Security, *Yearbook of Immigration Statistics: 2011*, Table 1)

From where have the immigrants come? Immigrants from Europe were more than 90% of the total in the first decade of the twentieth century, but less than 20% of the total by the end of the century. By the 2000s, about half of U.S. immigration came from the rest of the Americas, especially Mexico, and about a quarter came from various countries in Asia.

Economic Effects of Immigration

A surge of immigration can affect the economy in a number of different ways. In this section, we will consider how immigrants might benefit the rest of the economy, how they might affect wage levels, and how they might affect government spending at the federal and local level.

To understand the economic consequences of immigration, consider the following scenario. Imagine that the immigrants entering the United States matched the existing U.S. population in age range, education, skill levels, family size, and occupations. How would immigration of this type affect the rest of the U.S. economy? Immigrants themselves would be much better off, because their standard of living would be higher in the United States. Immigrants would contribute to both increased production and increased consumption. Given enough time for adjustment, the range of jobs performed, income earned, taxes paid, and public services needed would not be much affected by this kind of immigration. It would be as if the population simply increased a little.

Now, consider the reality of recent immigration to the United States. Immigrants are not identical to the rest of the U.S. population. About one-third of immigrants over the age of 25 lack a high school diploma. As a result, many of the recent immigrants end up in jobs like restaurant and hotel work, lawn care, and janitorial work. This kind of immigration represents a shift to the right in the supply of unskilled labor for a number of jobs, which will lead to lower wages for these jobs. The middle- and upper-income households that purchase the services of these unskilled workers will benefit from these lower wages. However, low-skilled U.S. workers who must compete with low-skilled immigrants for jobs will tend to suffer from immigration.

The difficult policy questions about immigration are not so much about the overall gains to the rest of the economy, which seem to be real but small in the context of the U.S. economy, as they are about the disruptive effects of immigration in specific labor markets. One disruptive effect, as we noted, is that immigration weighted toward low-skill workers tends to reduce wages for domestic low-skill workers. A study by Michael S. Clune found that for each 10% rise in the number of employed immigrants with no more than a high school diploma in the labor market, high school students reduced their annual number of hours worked by 3%. The effects on wages of low-skill workers are

This OpenStax book is available for free at http://cnx.org/content/col12122/1.4

not large—perhaps in the range of decline of about 1%. These effects are likely kept low, in part, because of the legal floor of federal and state minimum wage laws. In addition, immigrants are also thought to contribute to increased demand for local goods and services which can stimulate the local low skilled labor market. It is also possible that employers, in the face of abundant low-skill workers may choose production processes which are more labor intensive than otherwise would have been. These various factors would explain the small negative wage effect that the native low-skill workers observed as a result of immigration.

Another potential disruptive effect is the impact on state and local government budgets. Many of the costs imposed by immigrants are costs that arise in state-run programs, like the cost of public schooling and of welfare benefits. However, many of the taxes that immigrants pay are federal taxes like income taxes and Social Security taxes. Many immigrants do not own property (such as homes and cars), so they do not pay property taxes, which are one of the main sources of state and local tax revenue. However, they do pay sales taxes, which are state and local, and the landlords of property they rent pay property taxes. According to the nonprofit Rand Corporation, the effects of immigration on taxes are generally positive at the federal level, but they are negative at the state and local levels in places where there are many low-skilled immigrants.

Link It Up

Visit this website (http://openstaxcollege.org/l/nber) to obtain more context regarding immigration.

Proposals for Immigration Reform

The Congressional Jordan Commission of the 1990s proposed reducing overall levels of immigration and refocusing U.S. immigration policy to give priority to immigrants with higher skill levels. In the labor market, focusing on high-skilled immigrants would help prevent any negative effects on low-skilled workers' wages. For government budgets, higher-skilled workers find jobs more quickly, earn higher wages, and pay more in taxes. Several other immigration-friendly countries, notably Canada and Australia, have immigration systems where those with high levels of education or job skills have a much better chance of obtaining permission to immigrate. For the United States, high tech companies regularly ask for a more lenient immigration policy to admit a greater quantity of highly skilled workers under the H1B visa program.

The Obama Administration proposed the so-called "DREAM Act" legislation, which would have offered a path to citizenship for illegal immigrants brought to the United States before the age of 16. Despite bipartisan support, the legislation failed to pass at the federal level. However, some state legislatures, such as California, have passed their own Dream Acts.

Between its plans for a border wall, increased deportation of undocumented immigrants, and even reductions in the number of highly skilled legal H1B immigrants, the Trump Administration has a much less positive approach to immigration. Most economists, whether conservative or liberal, believe that while immigration harms some domestic workers, the benefits to the nation exceed the costs. However, given the Trump Administration's opposition, any significant immigration reform is likely on hold.

The FRED database includes data on foreign and native born civilian population **(https://fred.stlouisfed.org/ categories/104) (https://fred.stlouisfed.org/categories/104)** and labor force **(https://fred.stlouisfed.org/ categories/32442) (https://fred.stlouisfed.org/categories/32442)** .

Bring it Home

The Increasing Value of a College Degree

The cost of college has increased dramatically in recent decades, causing many college students to take student loans to afford it. Despite this, the value of a college degree has never been higher. How can we explain this?

We can estimate the value of a bachelor's degree as the difference in lifetime earnings between the average holder of a bachelor's degree and the average high school graduate. This difference can be nearly $1 million. College graduates also have a significantly lower unemployment rate than those with lower educational attainments.

While a college degree holder's wages have increased somewhat, the major reason for the increase in value of a bachelor's degree has been the plummeting value of a high school diploma. In the twenty-first century, the majority of jobs require at least some post-secondary education. This includes manufacturing jobs that in the past would have afforded workers a middle class income with only a high school diploma. Those jobs are increasingly scarce. This phenomenon has also no doubt contributed to the increasing inequality of income that we observe in the U.S. today. We will discuss that topic next, in Chapter 15.

This OpenStax book is available for free at http://cnx.org/content/col12122/1.4

KEY TERMS

affirmative action active efforts by government or businesses that give special rights to minorities in hiring, promotion, or access to education to make up for past discrimination

bilateral monopoly a labor market with a monopsony on the demand side and a union on the supply side

collective bargaining negotiations between unions and a firm or firms

discrimination actions based on the belief that members of a certain group or groups are in some way inferior solely because of a factor such as race, gender, or religion

first rule of labor markets an employer will never pay a worker more than the value of the worker's marginal productivity to the firm

monopsony a labor market where there is only one employer

perfectly competitive labor market a labor market where neither suppliers of labor nor demanders of labor have any market power; thus, an employer can hire all the workers they would like at the going market wage

KEY CONCEPTS AND SUMMARY

14.1 The Theory of Labor Markets
A firm demands labor because of the value of the labor's marginal productivity. For a firm operating in a perfectly competitive output market, this will be the value of the marginal product, which we define as the marginal product of labor multiplied by the firm's output price. For a firm which is not perfectly competitive, the appropriate concept is the marginal revenue product, which we define as the marginal product of labor multiplied by the firm's marginal revenue. Profit maximizing firms employ labor up to the point where the market wage is equal to the firm's demand for labor. In a competitive labor market, we determine market wage through the interaction between the market supply and market demand for labor.

14.2 Wages and Employment in an Imperfectly Competitive Labor Market
A monopsony is the sole employer in a labor market. The monopsony can pay any wage it chooses, subject to the market supply of labor. This means that if the monopsony offers too low a wage, they may not find enough workers willing to work for them. Since to obtain more workers, they must offer a higher wage, the marginal cost of additional labor is greater than the wage. To maximize profits, a monopsonist will hire workers up to the point where the marginal cost of labor equals their labor demand. This results in a lower level of employment than a competitive labor market would provide, but also a lower equilibrium wage.

14.3 Market Power on the Supply Side of Labor Markets: Unions
A labor union is an organization of workers that negotiates as a group with employers over compensation and work conditions. Union workers in the United States are paid more on average than other workers with comparable education and experience. Thus, either union workers must be more productive to match this higher pay or the higher pay will lead employers to find ways of hiring fewer union workers than they otherwise would. American union membership has been falling for decades. Some possible reasons include the shift of jobs to service industries; greater competition from globalization; the passage of worker-friendly legislation; and U.S. laws that are less favorable to organizing unions.

14.4 Bilateral Monopoly
A bilateral monopoly is a labor market with a union on the supply side and a monopsony on the demand side. Since both sides have monopoly power, the equilibrium level of employment will be lower than that for a competitive labor market, but the equilibrium wage could be higher or lower depending on which side negotiates better. The union favors a higher wage, while the monopsony favors a lower wage, but the outcome is indeterminate in the model.

14.5 Employment Discrimination

Discrimination occurs in a labor market when employers pay workers with the same economic characteristics, such as education,experience, and skill, are paid different amounts because of race, gender, religion, age, or disability status. In the United States, female workers on average earn less than male workers, and black workers on average earn less than white workers. There is controversy over to which discrimination differences in factors like education and job experience can explain these earnings gaps. Free markets can allow discrimination to occur, but the threat of a loss of sales or a loss of productive workers can also create incentives for a firm not to discriminate. A range of public policies can be used to reduce earnings gaps between men and women or between white and other racial/ethnic groups: requiring equal pay for equal work, and attaining more equal educational outcomes.

14.6 Immigration

The recent level of U.S. immigration is at a historically high level if we measure it in absolute numbers, but not if we measure it as a share of population. The overall gains to the U.S. economy from immigration are real but relatively small. However, immigration also causes effects like slightly lower wages for low-skill workers and budget problems for certain state and local governments.

SELF-CHECK QUESTIONS

1. Table 14.10 shows levels of employment (Labor), the marginal product at each of those levels, and the price at which the firm can sell output in the perfectly competitive market where it operates.

Labor	Marginal Product of Labor	Price of the Product
1	10	$4
2	8	$4
3	7	$4
4	5	$4
5	3	$4
6	1	$4

Table 14.10

a. What is the value of the marginal product at each level of labor?
b. If the firm operates in a perfectly competitive labor market where the going market wage is $12, what is the firm's profit maximizing level of employment?

This OpenStax book is available for free at http://cnx.org/content/col12122/1.4

2. **Table 14.11** shows levels of employment (Labor), the marginal product at each of those levels, and a monopoly's marginal revenue.

Labor	Marginal Product of Labor	Price of the Product
1	10	$10
2	8	$7
3	7	$5
4	5	$4
5	3	$2
6	1	$1

Table 14.11

    a. What is the monopoly's marginal revenue product at each level of employment?

    b. If the monopoly operates in a perfectly competitive labor market where the going market wage is $20, what is the firm's profit maximizing level of employment?

3. **Table 14.12** shows the quantity demanded and supplied in the labor market for driving city buses in the town of Unionville, where all the bus drivers belong to a union.

Wage Per Hour	Quantity of Workers Demanded	Quantity of Workers Supplied
$14	12,000	6,000
$16	10,000	7,000
$18	8,000	8,000
$20	6,000	9,000
$22	4,000	10,000
$24	2,000	11,000

Table 14.12

    a. What would the equilibrium wage and quantity be in this market if no union existed?

    b. Assume that the union has enough negotiating power to raise the wage to $4 per hour higher than it would otherwise be. Is there now excess demand or excess supply of labor?

4. Do unions typically oppose new technology out of a fear that it will reduce the number of union jobs? Why or why not?

5. Compared with the share of workers in most other high-income countries, is the share of U.S. workers whose wages are determined by union bargaining higher or lower? Why or why not?

6. Are firms with a high percentage of union employees more likely to go bankrupt because of the higher wages that they pay? Why or why not?

7. Do countries with a higher percentage of unionized workers usually have less growth in productivity because of strikes and other disruptions caused by the unions? Why or why not?

8. **Table 14.13** shows information from the supply curve for labor for a monopsonist, that is, the wage rate required at each level of employment.

Labor	Wage
1	1
2	3
3	5
4	7
5	8
6	10

Table 14.13

    a. What is the monopsonist's marginal cost of labor at each level of employment?

    b. If each unit of labor's marginal revenue product is $13, what is the firm's profit maximizing level of employment and wage?

9. Explain in each of the following situations how market forces might give a business an incentive to act in a less discriminatory fashion.

    a. A local flower delivery business run by a bigoted white owner notices that many of its local customers are black.

    b. An assembly line has traditionally only hired men, but it is having a hard time hiring sufficiently qualified workers.

    c. A biased owner of a firm that provides home health care services would like to pay lower wages to Hispanic workers than to other employees.

10. Does the earnings gap between the average wages of females and the average wages of males prove labor market discrimination? Why or why not?

11. If immigration is reduced, what is the impact on the wage for low-skilled labor? Explain.

REVIEW QUESTIONS

12. What determines the demand for labor for a firm operating in a perfectly competitive output market?

13. What determines the demand for labor for a firm with market power in the output market?

14. What is a perfectly competitive labor market?

15. What is a labor union?

16. Why do employers have a natural advantage in bargaining with employees?

17. What are some of the most important laws that protect employee rights?

18. How does the presence of a labor union change negotiations between employers and workers?

19. What is the long-term trend in American union membership?

20. Would you expect the presence of labor unions to lead to higher or lower pay for worker-members? Would you expect a higher or lower quantity of workers hired by those employers? Explain briefly.

21. What are the main causes for the recent trends in union membership rates in the United States? Why are union rates lower in the United States than in many other developed countries?

22. What is a monopsony?

23. What is the marginal cost of labor?

24. How does monopsony affect the equilibrium wage and employment levels?

25. What is a bilateral monopoly?

26. How does a bilateral monopoly affect the equilibrium wage and employment levels compared to a perfectly competitive labor market?

27. Describe how the earnings gap between men and women has evolved in recent decades.

28. Describe how the earnings gap between blacks and whites has evolved in recent decades.

29. Does a gap between the average earnings of men and women, or between whites and blacks, prove that employers are discriminating in the labor market? Explain briefly.

30. Will a free market tend to encourage or discourage discrimination? Explain briefly.

31. What policies, when used together with antidiscrimination laws, might help to reduce the earnings gap between men and women or between white and black workers?

32. Describe how affirmative action is applied in the labor market.

33. What factors can explain the relatively small effect of low-skilled immigration on the wages of low-skilled workers?

34. Have levels of immigration to the United States been relatively high or low in recent years? Explain.

35. How would you expect immigration by primarily low-skill workers to affect American low-skilled workers?

CRITICAL THINKING QUESTIONS

36. What is the marginal cost of labor for a firm that operates in a competitive labor market? How does this compare with the MCL for a monopsony?

37. Given the decline in union membership over the past 50 years, what does the theory of bilateral monopoly suggest will have happened to the equilibrium level of wages over time? Why?

38. Are unions and technological improvements complementary? Why or why not?

39. Will union membership continue to decline? Why or why not?

40. If it is not profitable to discriminate, why does discrimination persist?

41. If a company has discriminated against minorities in the past, should it be required to give priority to minority applicants today? Why or why not?

42. If the United States allows a greater quantity of highly skilled workers, what will be the impact on the average wages of highly skilled employees?

43. If all countries eliminated all barriers to immigration, would global economic growth increase? Why or why not?

This OpenStax book is available for free at http://cnx.org/content/col12122/1.4

15 | Poverty and Economic Inequality

Figure 15.1 Occupying Wall Street On September 17, 2011, Occupy Wall Street began in New York City's Wall Street financial district. (Credit: modification of work by David Shankbone/Flickr Creative Commons)

Bring it Home

Occupy Wall Street

In September 2011, a group of protesters gathered in Zuccotti Park in New York City to decry what they perceived as increasing social and economic inequality in the United States. Calling their protest "Occupy Wall Street," they argued that the concentration of wealth among the richest 1% in the United States was both economically unsustainable and inequitable, and needed to be changed. The protest then spread to other major cities, and the Occupy movement was born.

Why were people so upset? How much wealth is concentrated among the top 1% in our society? How did they acquire so much wealth? These are very real, very important questions in the United States now, and this chapter on poverty and economic inequality will help us address the causes behind this sentiment.

Introduction to Poverty and Economic Inequality

In this chapter, you will learn about:

- Drawing the Poverty Line

- The Poverty Trap

- The Safety Net

- Income Inequality: Measurement and Causes

- Government Policies to Reduce Income Inequality

The labor markets that determine the pay that workers receive do not take into account how much income a family needs for food, shelter, clothing, and health care. Market forces do not worry about what happens to families when a major local employer goes out of business. Market forces do not take time to contemplate whether those who are earning higher incomes should pay an even higher share of taxes.

However, labor markets do create considerable income inequalities. In 2014, the median American family income was $57,939 (the median is the level where half of all families had more than that level and half had less). According to the U.S. Census Bureau, the federal government classified almost nine million U.S. families as below the poverty line in that year. Think about a family of three—perhaps a single mother with two children—attempting to pay for the basics of life on perhaps $17,916 per year. After paying for rent, healthcare, clothing, and transportation, such a family might have $6,000 to spend on food. Spread over 365 days, the food budget for the entire family would be about $17 per day. To put this in perspective, most cities have restaurants where $17 will buy you an appetizer for one.

This chapter explores how the U.S. government defines poverty, the balance between assisting the poor without discouraging work, and how federal antipoverty programs work. It also discusses income inequality—how economists measure inequality, why inequality has changed in recent decades, the range of possible government policies to reduce inequality, and the danger of a tradeoff that too great a reduction in inequality may reduce incentives for producing output.

15.1 | Drawing the Poverty Line

By the end of this section, you will be able to:
- Explain economic inequality and how the poverty line is determined
- Analyze the U.S. poverty rate over time, noting its prevalence among different groups of citizens

Comparisons of high and low incomes raise two different issues: economic inequality and **poverty**. Poverty is measured by the number of people who fall below a certain level of income—called the **poverty line**—that defines the income one needs for a basic standard of living. **Income inequality** compares the share of the total income (or wealth) in society that different groups receive. For example, compare the share of income that the top 10% receive to the share of income that the bottom 10% receive.

In the United States, the official definition of the poverty line traces back to a single person: Mollie Orshansky. In 1963, Orshansky, who was working for the Social Security Administration, published an article called "Children of the Poor" in a highly useful and dry-as-dust publication called the *Social Security Bulletin*. Orshansky's idea was to define a poverty line based on the cost of a healthy diet.

Her previous job had been at the U.S. Department of Agriculture, where she had worked in an agency called the Bureau of Home Economics and Human Nutrition. One task of this bureau had been to calculate how much it would cost to feed a nutritionally adequate diet to a family. Orshansky found that the average family spent one-third of its income on food. She then proposed that the poverty line be the amount one requires to buy a nutritionally adequate diet, given the size of the family, multiplied by three.

The current U.S. poverty line is essentially the same as the Orshansky poverty line, although the government adjusts the dollar amounts to represent the same buying power over time. The U.S. poverty line in 2015 ranged from $11,790 for a single individual to $25,240 for a household of four people.

Figure 15.2 shows the U.S. **poverty rate** over time; that is, the percentage of the population below the poverty line in any given year. The poverty rate declined through the 1960s, rose in the early 1980s and early 1990s, but seems to have been slightly lower since the mid-1990s. However, in no year in the last four decades has the poverty rate been less than 11% of the U.S. population—that is, at best about one American in nine is below the poverty line. In recent years, the poverty rate appears to have peaked at 15.9% in 2011 before dropping to 14.5% in 2013. **Table 15.1** compares poverty rates for different groups in 2011. As you will see when we delve further into these numbers, poverty rates are relatively low for whites, for the elderly, for the well-educated, and for male-headed households. Poverty rates for females, Hispanics, and African Americans are much higher than for whites. While Hispanics and

This OpenStax book is available for free at http://cnx.org/content/col12122/1.4

African Americans have a higher percentage of individuals living in poverty than others, most people in the United States living below the poverty line are white.

Link It Up

Visit this website (http://openstaxcollege.org/l/povertyprogram) for more information on U.S. poverty.

Figure 15.2 The U.S. Poverty Rate since 1960 The poverty rate fell dramatically during the 1960s, rose in the early 1980s and early 1990s, and, after declining in the 1990s through mid-2000s, rose to 15.9% in 2011, which is close to the 1960 levels. In 2013, the poverty dropped slightly to 14.5%. (Source: U.S. Census Bureau)

Group	Poverty Rate
Females	15.8%
Males	13.1%
White	9.6%
Black	27.1%
Hispanic	23.5%

Table 15.1 Poverty Rates by Group, 2013

Group	Poverty Rate
Under age 18	19.9%
Ages 18–24	20.6%
Ages 25–34	15.9%
Ages 35–44	12.2%
Ages 45–54	10.9%
Ages 55–59	10.7%
Ages 60–64	10.8%
Ages 65 and older	9.5%

Table 15.1 Poverty Rates by Group, 2013

The concept of a poverty line raises many tricky questions. In a vast country like the United States, should there be a national poverty line? After all, according to the Federal Register, the median household income for a family of four was $102,552 in New Jersey and $57,132 in Mississippi in 2013, and prices of some basic goods like housing are quite different between states. The poverty line is based on cash income, which means it does not account for government programs that provide assistance to the poor in a non-cash form, like Medicaid (health care for low-income individuals and families) and food aid. Also, low-income families can qualify for federal housing assistance. (We will discuss these and other government aid programs in detail later in this chapter.)

Should the government adjust the poverty line to account for the value of such programs? Many economists and policymakers wonder whether we should rethink the concept of what poverty means in the twenty-first century. The following Clear It Up feature explains the poverty lines set by the World Bank for low-income countries around the world.

How do economists measure poverty in low-income countries?

The World Bank sets two poverty lines for low-income countries around the world. One poverty line is set at an income of $1.25/day per person. The other is at $2/day. By comparison, the U.S. 2015 poverty line of $20,090 annually for a family of three works out to $18.35 per person per day.

Clearly, many people around the world are far poorer than Americans, as Table 15.2 shows. China and India both have more than a billion people; Nigeria is the most populous country in Africa; and Egypt is the most populous country in the Middle East. In all four of those countries, in the mid-2000s, a substantial share of the population subsisted on less than $2/day. About half the world lives on less than $2.50 a day, and 80 percent of the world lives on less than $10 per day. (Of course, the cost of food, clothing, and shelter in those countries can be very different from those costs in the United States, so the $2 and $2.50 figures may mean greater purchasing power than they would in the United States.)

Country	Share of Population below $1.25/Day	Share of Population below $2.00/Day
Brazil (in 2009)	6.1%	10.8%
China (in 2009)	11.8%	27.2%
Egypt (in 2008)	1.7%	15.4%
India (in 2010)	32.7%	68.8%
Mexico (in 2010)	0.7%	4.5%
Nigeria (in 2010)	68.0%	84.5%

Table 15.2 Poverty Lines for Low-Income Countries, mid-2000s (Source: http://data.worldbank.org/indicator/SI.POV.DDAY)

Any poverty line will be somewhat arbitrary, and it is useful to have a poverty line whose basic definition does not change much over time. If Congress voted every few years to redefine poverty, then it would be difficult to compare rates over time. After all, would a lower poverty rate change the definition, or that people were actually better off? Government statisticians at the U.S. Census Bureau have ongoing research programs to address questions like these.

15.2 | The Poverty Trap

By the end of this section, you will be able to:
- Explain the poverty trap, noting how government programs impact it
- Identify potential issues in government programs that seek to reduce poverty
- Calculate a budget constraint line that represents the poverty trap

Can you give people too much help, or the wrong kind of help? When people are provided with food, shelter, healthcare, income, and other necessities, assistance may reduce their incentive to work. Consider a program to fight poverty that works in this reasonable-sounding manner: the government provides assistance to the poor, but as the poor earn income to support themselves, the government reduces the level of assistance it provides. With such a program, every time a poor person earns $100, the person loses $100 in government support. As a result, the person experiences no net gain for working. Economists call this problem the **poverty trap**.

Consider the situation a single-parent family faces. **Figure 15.3** illustrates a single mother (earning $8 an hour) with two children. First, consider the labor-leisure budget constraint that this family faces in a situation without government assistance. On the horizontal axis is hours of leisure (or time spent with family responsibilities) increasing in quantity from right to left. Also on the horizontal axis is the number of hours at paid work, going from zero hours on the right to the maximum of 2,500 hours on the left. On the vertical axis is the amount of income per year rising from low to higher amounts of income. The budget constraint line shows that at zero hours of leisure and 2,500 hours of work, the maximum amount of income is $20,000 ($8 × 2,500 hours). At the other extreme of the budget constraint line, an individual would work zero hours, earn zero income, but enjoy 2,500 hours of leisure. At point A on the budget constraint line, by working 40 hours a week, 50 weeks a year, the utility-maximizing choice is to work a total of 2,000 hours per year and earn $16,000.

Now suppose that a government antipoverty program guarantees every family with a single mother and two children $18,000 in income. This is represented on the graph by a horizontal line at $18,000. With this program, each time the mother earns $1,000, the government will deduct $1,000 of its support. Table 15.3 shows what will happen at each combination of work and government support.

Figure 15.3 The Poverty Trap in Action The original choice is 500 hours of leisure, 2,000 hours of work at point A, and income of $16,000. With a guaranteed income of $18,000, this family would receive $18,000 whether it provides zero hours of work or 2,000 hours of work. Only if the family provides, say, 2,300 hours of work does its income rise above the guaranteed level of $18,000—and even then, the marginal gain to income from working many hours is small.

Amount Worked (hours)	Total Earnings	Government Support	Total Income
0	0	$18,000	$18,000
500	$4,000	$14,000	$18,000
1,000	$8,000	$10,000	$18,000
1,500	$12,000	$6,000	$18,000
2,000	$16,000	$2,000	$18,000
2,500	$20,000	0	$20,000

Table 15.3 Total Income at Various Combinations of Work and Support

The new budget line, with the antipoverty program in place, is the horizontal and heavy line that is flat at $18,000. If the mother does not work at all, she receives $18,000, all from the government. If she works full time, giving up 40 hours per week with her children, she still ends up with $18,000 at the end of the year. Only if she works 2,300 hours in the year—which is an average of 44 hours per week for 50 weeks a year—does household income rise to $18,400. Even in this case, all of her year's work means that household income rises by only $400 over the income she would receive if she did not work at all. She would need to work 50 hours a week to reach $20,000.

The poverty trap is even stronger than this simplified example shows, because a working mother will have extra expenses like clothing, transportation, and child care that a nonworking mother will not face, making the economic gains from working even smaller. Moreover, those who do not work fail to build up job experience and contacts, which makes working in the future even less likely.

To reduce the poverty trap the government could design an antipoverty program so that, instead of reducing

This OpenStax book is available for free at http://cnx.org/content/col12122/1.4

government payments by $1 for every $1 earned, the government would reduce payments by some smaller amount instead. Imposing requirements for work as a condition of receiving benefits and setting a time limit on benefits can also reduce the harshness of the poverty trap.

Figure 15.4 illustrates a government program that guarantees $18,000 in income, even for those who do not work at all, but then reduces this amount by 50 cents for each $1 earned. The new, higher budget line in Figure 15.4 shows that, with this program, additional hours of work will bring some economic gain. Because of the reduction in government income when an individual works, an individual earning $8.00 will really net only $4.00 per hour. The vertical intercept of this higher budget constraint line is at $28,000 ($18,000 + 2,500 hours × $4.00 = $28,000). The horizontal intercept is at the point on the graph where $18,000 and 2500 hours of leisure is set. Table 15.4 shows the total income differences with various choices of labor and leisure.

However, this type of program raises other issues. First, even if it does not eliminate the incentive to work by reducing government payments by $1 for every $1 earned, enacting such a program may still reduce the incentive to work. At least some people who would be working 2,000 hours each year without this program might decide to work fewer hours but still end up with more income—that is, their choice on the new budget line would be like S, above and to the right of the original choice P. Of course, others may choose a point like R, which involves the same amount of work as P, or even a point to the left of R that involves more work.

The second major issue is that when the government phases out its support payments more slowly, the antipoverty program costs more money. Still, it may be preferable in the long run to spend more money on a program that retains a greater incentive to work, rather than spending less money on a program that nearly eliminates any gains from working.

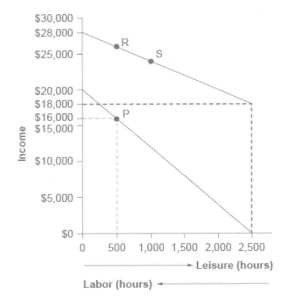

Figure 15.4 Loosening the Poverty Trap: Reducing Government Assistance by 50 Cents for Every $1 Earned On the original labor-leisure opportunity set, the lower budget set shown by the smaller dashed line in the figure, the preferred choice P is 500 hours of leisure and $16,000 of income. Then, the government created an antipoverty program that guarantees $18,000 in income even to those who work zero hours, shown by the larger dashed line. In addition, every $1 earned means phasing out 50 cents of benefits. This program leads to the higher budget set, which the diagram shows. The hope is that this program will provide incentives to work the same or more hours, despite receiving income assistance. However, it is possible that the recipients will choose a point on the new budget set like S, with less work, more leisure, and greater income, or a point like R, with the same work and greater income.

Amount Worked (hours)	Total Earnings	Government Support	Total Income
0	0	$18,000	$18,000
500	$4,000	$16,000	$20,000
1,000	$8,000	$14,000	$22,000
1,500	$12,000	$12,000	$24,000
2,000	$16,000	$10,000	$26,000
2,500	$20,000	$8,000	$28,000

Table 15.4 The Labor-Leisure Tradeoff with Assistance Reduced by 50 Cents for Every Dollar Earned

The next module will consider a variety of government support programs focused specifically on the poor, including welfare, SNAP (Supplemental Nutrition Assistance Program), Medicaid, and the earned income tax credit (EITC). Although these programs vary from state to state, it is generally a true statement that in many states from the 1960s into the 1980s, if poor people worked, their level of income barely rose—or did not rise at all—after factoring in the reduction in government support payments. The following Work It Out feature shows how this happens.

Calculating a Budget Constraint Line

Jason earns $9.00 an hour, and a government antipoverty program provides a floor of $10,000 guaranteed income. The government reduces government support by $0.50 for each $1.00 earned. What are the horizontal and vertical intercepts of the budget constraint line? Assume the maximum hours for work or leisure is 2,500 hours.

Step 1. Determine the amount of the government guaranteed income. In this case, it is $10,000.

Step 2. Plot that guaranteed income as a horizontal line on the budget constraint line.

Step 3. Determine what Jason earns if he has no income and enjoys 2,500 hours of leisure. In this case, he will receive the guaranteed $10,000 (the horizontal intercept).

Step 4. Calculate how much Jason's salary will be reduced due to the reduction in government income. In Jason's case, it will be reduced by one half. He will, in effect, net only $4.50 an hour.

Step 5. If Jason works 1,000 hours, at a maximum what income will Jason receive? Jason will receive $10,000 in government assistance. He will net only $4.50 for every hour he chooses to work. If he works 1,000 hours at $4.50, his earned income is $4,500 plus the $10,000 in government income. Thus, the total maximum income (the vertical intercept) is $10,000 + $4,500 = $14,500.

15.3 | The Safety Net

By the end of this section, you will be able to:
- Identify the antipoverty government programs that comprise the safety net
- Explain the the safety net programs' primary goals and how these programs have changed over time
- Discuss the complexities of these safety net programs and why they can be controversial

The U.S. government has implemented a number of programs to assist those below the poverty line and those who have incomes just above the poverty line, to whom we refer as the **near-poor**. Such programs are called the **safety**

net, to recognize that they offer some protection for those who find themselves without jobs or income.

Temporary Assistance for Needy Families

From the Great Depression until 1996, the United States' most visible antipoverty program was Aid to Families with Dependent Children (AFDC), which provided cash payments to mothers with children who were below the poverty line. Many just called this program "welfare." In 1996, Congress passed and President Bill Clinton signed into law the Personal Responsibility and Work Opportunity Reconciliation Act, more commonly called the "welfare reform act." The new law replaced AFDC with Temporary Assistance for Needy Families (TANF).

Link It Up 🔗

Visit this website (http://openstaxcollege.org/l/Clinton_speech) to watch a video of President Bill Clinton's Welfare Reform speech.

TANF brought several dramatic changes in how welfare operated. Under the old AFDC program, states set the level of welfare benefits that they would pay to the poor, and the federal government guaranteed it would chip in some of the money as well. The federal government's welfare spending would rise or fall depending on the number of poor people, and on how each state set its own welfare contribution.

Under TANF, however, the federal government gives a fixed amount of money to each state. The state can then use the money for almost any program with an antipoverty component: for example, the state might use the money to give cash to poor families, or to reduce teenage pregnancy, or even to raise the high school graduation rate. However, the federal government imposed two key requirements. First, if states are to keep receiving the TANF grants, they must impose work requirements so that most of those receiving TANF benefits are working (or attending school). Second, no one can receive TANF benefits with federal money for more than a total of five years over his or her lifetime. The old AFDC program had no such work requirements or time limits.

TANF attempts to avoid the poverty trap by requiring that welfare recipients work and by limiting the length of time they can receive benefits. In its first few years, the program was quite successful. The number of families receiving payments in 1995, the last year of AFDC, was 4.8 million. By 2012, according to the Congressional Research Service, the average number of families receiving payments under TANF was 1.8 million—a decline of more than half.

TANF benefits to poor families vary considerably across states. For example, again according to the Congressional Research Service, in 2011 the highest monthly payment in Alaska to a single mother with two children was $923, while in Mississippi the highest monthly payment to that family was $170. These payments reflect differences in states' cost of living. Total spending on TANF was approximately $16.6 billion in 1997. As of 2012, spending was at $12 billion, an almost 28% decrease, split about evenly between the federal and state governments. When you take into account the effects of inflation, the decline is even greater. Moreover, there seemed little evidence that poor families were suffering a reduced standard of living as a result of TANF—although, on the other side, there was not much evidence that poor families had greatly improved their total levels of income, either.

The Earned Income Tax Credit (EITC)

The **earned income tax credit (EITC)**, first passed in 1975, is a method of assisting the working poor through the tax system. The EITC is one of the largest assistance program for low-income groups, and projections for 2013 expected 26 million households to take advantage of it at an estimated cost of $50 billion. In 2013, for example, a single parent with two children would have received a tax credit of $5,372 up to an income level of $17,530. The amount of the tax break increases with the amount of income earned, up to a point. The earned income tax credit has often been popular with both economists and the general public because of the way it effectively increases the payment received for work.

What about the danger of the poverty trap that every additional $1 earned will reduce government support payments by close to $1? To minimize this problem, the earned income tax credit is phased out slowly. According to the Tax Policy Center, for a single-parent family with two children in 2013, the credit is not reduced at all (but neither is it increased) as earnings rise from $13,430 to $17,530. Then, for every $1 earned above $17,530, the amount received from the credit is reduced by 21.06 cents, until the credit phases out completely at an income level of $46,227.

Figure 15.5 illustrates that the earned income tax credits, child tax credits, and the TANF program all cost the federal government money—either in direct outlays or in loss of tax revenues. CTC stands for the government tax cuts for the child tax credit.

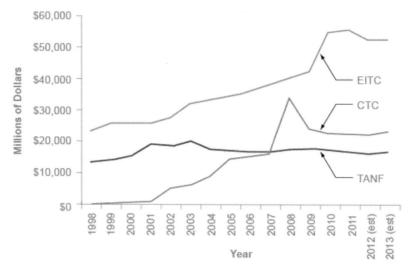

Figure 15.5 Real Federal Spending on CTC, EITC, and TANF, 1975-2013 EITC increased from more than $20 billion in 2000 to over an estimated $50 billion by 2013, far exceeding estimated 2013 outlays in the CTC (Child Tax Credits) and TANF of over $20 billion and $10 billion, respectively. (Source: Office of Management and Budget)

In recent years, the EITC has become a hugely expensive government program for providing income assistance to the poor and near-poor, costing about $60 billion in 2012. In that year, the EITC provided benefits to about 27 million families and individuals and, on average, is worth about $2,296 per family (with children), according to the Tax Policy Center. One reason that the TANF law worked as well as it did is that the government greatly expanded EITC in the late 1980s and again in the early 1990s, which increased the returns to work for low-income Americans.

Supplemental Nutrition Assistance Program (SNAP)

Often called "food stamps," **Supplemental Nutrition Assistance Program (SNAP)** is a federally funded program, started in 1964, in which each month poor people receive a card like a debit card that they can use to buy food. The amount of food aid for which a household is eligible varies by income, number of children, and other factors but, in general, households are expected to spend about 30% of their own net income on food, and if 30% of their net income is not enough to purchase a nutritionally adequate diet, then those households are eligible for SNAP.

SNAP can contribute to the poverty trap. For every $100 earned, the government assumes that a family can spend $30 more for food, and thus reduces its eligibility for food aid by $30. This decreased benefit is not a complete disincentive to work—but combined with how other programs reduce benefits as income increases, it adds to the problem. SNAP, however, does try to address the poverty trap with its own set of work requirements and time limits.

Why give debit cards and not just cash? Part of the political support for SNAP comes from a belief that since recipients must spend the the cards on food, they cannot "waste" them on other forms of consumption. From an economic point of view, however, the belief that cards must increase spending on food seems wrong-headed. After all, say that a poor family is spending $2,500 per year on food, and then it starts receiving $1,000 per year in SNAP aid. The family might react by spending $3,500 per year on food (income plus aid), or it might react by continuing to spend $2,500 per year on food, but use the $1,000 in food aid to free up $1,000 that it can now spend on other goods.

This OpenStax book is available for free at http://cnx.org/content/col12122/1.4

Thus, it is reasonable to think of SNAP cards as an alternative method, along with TANF and the earned income tax credit, of transferring income to the working poor.

Anyone eligible for TANF is also eligible for SNAP, although states can expand eligibility for food aid if they wish to do so. In some states, where TANF welfare spending is relatively low, a poor family may receive more in support from SNAP than from TANF. In 2014, about 40 million people received food aid at an annual cost of about $76 billion, with an average monthly benefit of about $287 per person per month. SNAP participation increased by 70% between 2007 and 2011, from 26.6 million participants to 45 million. According to the Congressional Budget Office, the 2008-2009 Great Recession and rising food prices caused this dramatic rise in participation.

The federal government deploys a range of income security programs that it funds through departments such as Health and Human Services, Agriculture, and Housing and Urban Development (HUD) (see **Figure 15.6**). According to the Office of Management and Budget, collectively, these three departments provided an estimated $62 billion of aid through programs such as supplemental feeding programs for women and children, subsidized housing, and energy assistance. The federal government also transfers funds to individual states through special grant programs.

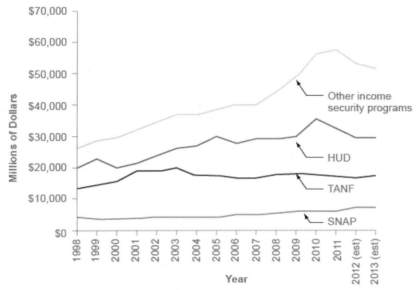

Figure 15.6 Expenditure Comparison of TANF, SNAP, HUD, and Other Income Security Programs, 1988–2013 (est.) Total expenditures on income security continued to rise between 1988 and 2010, while payments for TANF have increased from $13 billion in 1998 to an estimated $17.3 billion in 2013. SNAP has seen relatively small increments. These two programs comprise a relatively small portion of the estimated $106 billion dedicated to income security in 2013. Note that other programs and housing programs increased dramatically during the 2008 and 2010 time periods. (Source: Table 12.3 Section 600 Income Security, https://www.whitehouse.gov/sites/default/files/omb/budget/fy2013/assets/hist.pdf)

The safety net includes a number of other programs: government-subsidized school lunches and breakfasts for children from low-income families; the Special Supplemental Food Program for Women, Infants and Children (WIC), which provides food assistance for pregnant women and newborns; the Low Income Home Energy Assistance Program, which provides help with home heating bills; housing assistance, which helps pay the rent; and Supplemental Security Income, which provides cash support for the disabled and the elderly poor.

Medicaid

Congress created **Medicaid** in 1965. This is a joint health insurance program between both the states and the federal government. The federal government helps fund Medicaid, but each state is responsible for administering the program, determining the level of benefits, and determining eligibility. It provides medical insurance for certain low-income people, including those below the poverty line, with a focus on families with children, the elderly, and the disabled. About one-third of Medicaid spending is for low-income mothers with children. While an increasing share of the program funding in recent years has gone to pay for nursing home costs for the elderly poor. The program ensures that participants receive a basic level of benefits, but because each state sets eligibility requirements and provides varying levels of service, the program differs from state to state.

In the past, a common problem has been that many low-paying jobs pay enough to a breadwinner so that a family could lose its eligibility for Medicaid, yet the job does not offer health insurance benefits. A poor parent considering such a job might choose not to work rather than lose health insurance for his or her children. In this way, health insurance can become a part of the poverty trap. Many states recognized this problem in the 1980s and 1990s and expanded their Medicaid coverage to include not just the poor, but the near-poor earning up to 135% or even 185% of the poverty line. Some states also guaranteed that children would not lose coverage if their parents worked.

These expanded guarantees cost the government money, of course, but they also helped to encourage those on welfare to enter the labor force. As of 2014, approximately 69.7 million people participated in Medicaid. Of those enrolled, almost half are children. Healthcare expenditures, however, are highest for the elderly population, which comprises approximately 25% of participants. As **Figure 15.7** (a) indicates, the largest number of households that enroll in Medicaid are those with children. Lower-income adults are the next largest group enrolled in Medicaid at 28%. The blind and disabled are 16% of those enrolled, and seniors are 9% of those enrolled. **Figure 15.7** (b) shows how much actual Medicaid dollars the government spends for each group. Out of total Medicaid spending, the government spends more on seniors (20%) and the blind and disabled (44%). Thus, 64% of all Medicaid spending goes to seniors, the blind, and disabled. Children receive 21% of all Medicaid spending, followed by adults at 15%.

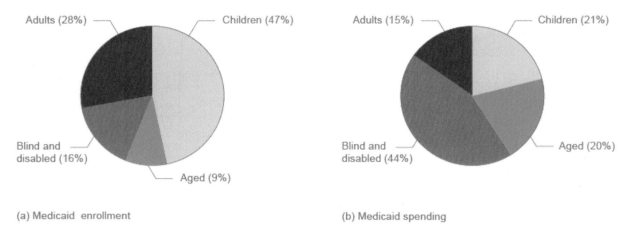

(a) Medicaid enrollment   (b) Medicaid spending

Figure 15.7 Medicaid Enrollment and Spending Part (a) shows the Medicaid enrollment by different populations, with children comprising the largest percentage at 47%, followed by adults at 28%, and the blind and disabled at 16%. Part (b) shows that Medicaid spending is principally for the blind and disabled, followed by the elderly. Although children are the largest population that Medicaid covers, expenditures on children are only at 21%.

15.4 | Income Inequality: Measurement and Causes

By the end of this section, you will be able to:

- Explain the distribution of income, and analyze the sources of income inequality in a market economy
- Measure income distribution in quintiles
- Calculate and graph a Lorenz curve
- Show income inequality through demand and supply diagrams

Poverty levels can be subjective based on the overall income levels of a country. Typically a government measures poverty based on a percentage of the median income. Income inequality, however, has to do with the distribution of that income, in terms of which group receives the most or the least income. Income inequality involves comparing those with high incomes, middle incomes, and low incomes—not just looking at those below or near the poverty line. In turn, measuring income inequality means dividing the population into various groups and then comparing the groups, a task that we can be carry out in several ways, as the next Clear It Up feature shows.

How do you separate poverty and income inequality?

Poverty can change even when inequality does not move at all. Imagine a situation in which income for everyone in the population declines by 10%. Poverty would rise, since a greater share of the population would now fall below the poverty line. However, inequality would be the same, because everyone suffered the same proportional loss. Conversely, a general rise in income levels over time would keep inequality the same, but reduce poverty.

It is also possible for income inequality to change without affecting the poverty rate. Imagine a situation in which a large number of people who already have high incomes increase their incomes by even more. Inequality would rise as a result—but the number of people below the poverty line would remain unchanged.

Why did inequality of household income increase in the United States in recent decades? A trend toward greater income inequality has occurred in many countries around the world, although the effect has been more powerful in the U.S. economy. Economists have focused their explanations for the increasing inequality on two factors that changed more or less continually from the 1970s into the 2000s. One set of explanations focuses on the changing shape of American households. The other focuses on greater inequality of wages, what some economists call "winner take all" labor markets. We will begin with how we measure inequality, and then consider the explanations for growing inequality in the United States.

Measuring Income Distribution by Quintiles

One common way of measuring income inequality is to rank all households by income, from lowest to highest, and then to divide all households into five groups with equal numbers of people, known as **quintiles**. This calculation allows for measuring the distribution of income among the five groups compared to the total. The first quintile is the lowest fifth or 20%, the second quintile is the next lowest, and so on. We can measure income inequality by comparing what share of the total income each quintile earns.

U.S. income distribution by quintile appears in **Table 15.5**. In 2011, for example, the bottom quintile of the income distribution received 3.2% of income; the second quintile received 8.4%; the third quintile, 14.3%; the fourth quintile, 23.0%; and the top quintile, 51.14%. The final column of **Table 15.5** shows what share of income went to households in the top 5% of the income distribution: 22.3% in 2011. Over time, from the late 1960s to the early 1980s, the top fifth of the income distribution typically received between about 43% to 44% of all income. The share of income that the top fifth received then begins to rise. Census Bureau researchers trace, much of this increase in the share of income going to the top fifth to an increase in the share of income going to the top 5%. The quintile measure shows how income inequality has increased in recent decades.

Year	Lowest Quintile	Second Quintile	Third Quintile	Fourth Quintile	Highest Quintile	Top 5%
1967	4.0	10.8	17.3	24.2	43.6	17.2
1970	4.1	10.8	17.4	24.5	43.3	16.6
1975	4.3	10.4	17.0	24.7	43.6	16.5
1980	4.2	10.2	16.8	24.7	44.1	16.5
1985	3.9	9.8	16.2	24.4	45.6	17.6
1990	3.8	9.6	15.9	24.0	46.6	18.5

Table 15.5 Share of Aggregate Income Received by Each Fifth and Top 5% of Households, 1967–2013 (Source: U.S. Census Bureau, Table 2)

Year	Lowest Quintile	Second Quintile	Third Quintile	Fourth Quintile	Highest Quintile	Top 5%
1995	3.7	9.1	15.2	23.3	48.7	21.0
2000	3.6	8.9	14.8	23.0	49.8	22.1
2005	3.4	8.6	14.6	23.0	50.4	22.2
2010	3.3	8.5	14.6	23.4	50.3	21.3
2013	3.2	8.4	14.4	23.0	51	22.2

Table 15.5 Share of Aggregate Income Received by Each Fifth and Top 5% of Households, 1967–2013 (Source: U.S. Census Bureau, Table 2)

It can also be useful to divide the income distribution in ways other than quintiles; for example, into tenths or even into percentiles (that is, hundredths). A more detailed breakdown can provide additional insights. For example, the last column of **Table 15.5** shows the income received by the top 5% percent of the income distribution. Between 1980 and 2013, the share of income going to the top 5% increased by 5.7 percentage points (from 16.5% in 1980 to 22.2% in 2013). From 1980 to 2013 the share of income going to the top quintile increased by 7.0 percentage points (from 44.1% in 1980 to 51% in 2013). Thus, the top 20% of householders (the fifth quintile) received over half (51%) of all the income in the United States in 2013.

Lorenz Curve

We can present the data on income inequality in various ways. For example, you could draw a bar graph that showed the share of income going to each fifth of the income distribution. **Figure 15.8** presents an alternative way of showing inequality data in a **Lorenz curve**. This curve shows the cumulative share of population on the horizontal axis and the cumulative percentage of total income received on the vertical axis.

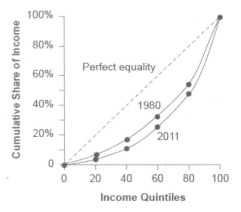

Figure 15.8 The Lorenz Curve A Lorenz curve graphs the cumulative shares of income received by everyone up to a certain quintile. The income distribution in 1980 was closer to the perfect equality line than the income distribution in 2011—that is, the U.S. income distribution became more unequal over time.

Every Lorenz curve diagram begins with a line sloping up at a 45-degree angle. We show it as a dashed line in **Figure 15.8**. The points along this line show what perfect equality of the income distribution looks like. It would mean, for example, that the bottom 20% of the income distribution receives 20% of the total income, the bottom 40% gets 40% of total income, and so on. The other lines reflect actual U.S. data on inequality for 1980 and 2011.

The trick in graphing a Lorenz curve is that you must change the shares of income for each specific quintile, which we show in the first column of numbers in **Table 15.6**, into cumulative income, which we show in the second column of numbers. For example, the bottom 40% of the cumulative income distribution will be the sum of the first and second quintiles; the bottom 60% of the cumulative income distribution will be the sum of the first, second, and third

This OpenStax book is available for free at http://cnx.org/content/col12122/1.4

quintiles, and so on. The final entry in the cumulative income column needs to be 100%, because by definition, 100% of the population receives 100% of the income.

Income Category	Share of Income in 1980 (%)	Cumulative Share of Income in 1980 (%)	Share of Income in 2013 (%)	Cumulative Share of Income in 2013 (%)
First quintile	4.2	4.2	3.2	3.2
Second quintile	10.2	14.4	8.4	11.6
Third quintile	16.8	31.2	14.4	26.0
Fourth quintile	24.7	55.9	23.0	49.0
Fifth quintile	44.1	100.0	51.0	100.0

Table 15.6 Calculating the Lorenz Curve

In a Lorenz curve diagram, a more unequal distribution of income will loop farther down and away from the 45-degree line, while a more equal distribution of income will move the line closer to the 45-degree line. Figure Figure 15.8 illustrates the greater inequality of the U.S. income distribution between 1980 and 2013 because the Lorenz curve for 2013 is farther from the 45-degree line than for 1980. The Lorenz curve is a useful way of presenting the quintile data that provides an image of all the quintile data at once. The next Clear It Up feature shows how income inequality differs in various countries compared to the United States.

Clear It Up

How does economic inequality vary around the world?

The U.S. economy has a relatively high degree of income inequality by global standards. As Table 15.7 shows, based on a variety of national surveys for a selection of years in the last five years of the 2000s (with the exception of Germany, and adjusted to make the measures more comparable), the U.S. economy has greater inequality than Germany (along with most Western European countries). The region of the world with the highest level of income inequality is Latin America, illustrated in the numbers for Brazil and Mexico. The level of inequality in the United States is lower than in some of the low-income countries of the world, like China and Nigeria, or some middle-income countries like the Russian Federation. However, not all poor countries have highly unequal income distributions. India provides a counterexample.

Country	Survey Year	First Quintile	Second Quintile	Third Quintile	Fourth Quintile	Fifth Quintile
United States	2013	3.2%	8.4%	14.4%	23.0%	51.0%
Germany	2000	8.5%	13.7%	17.8%	23.1%	36.9%
Brazil	2009	2.9%	7.1%	12.4%	19.0%	58.6%
Mexico	2010	4.9%	8.8%	13.3%	20.2%	52.8%
China	2009	4.7%	9.7%	15.3%	23.2%	47.1%
India	2010	8.5%	12.1%	15.7%	20.8%	42.8%
Russia	2009	6.1%	10.4%	14.8%	21.3%	47.1%
Nigeria	2010	4.4%	8.3%	13.0%	20.3%	54.0%

Table 15.7 Income Distribution in Select Countries (Source: U.S. data from U.S. Census Bureau Table 2. Other data from The World Bank Poverty and Inequality Data Base, http://databank.worldbank.org/data/views/reports/tableview.aspx#)

Link It Up

Visit this website (http://openstaxcollege.org/l/inequality/) to watch a video of wealth inequality across the world.

Causes of Growing Inequality: The Changing Composition of American Households

In 1970, 41% of married women were in the labor force, but by 2015, according to the Bureau of Labor Statistics, 56.7% of married women were in the labor force. One result of this trend is that more households have two earners. Moreover, it has become more common for one high earner to marry another high earner. A few decades ago, the common pattern featured a man with relatively high earnings, such as an executive or a doctor, marrying a woman who did not earn as much, like a secretary or a nurse. Often, the woman would leave paid employment, at least for a few years, to raise a family. However, now doctors are marrying doctors and executives are marrying executives, and mothers with high-powered careers are often returning to work while their children are quite young. This pattern of households with two high earners tends to increase the proportion of high-earning households.

According to data in the National Journal, even as two-earner couples have increased, so have single-parent households. Of all U.S. families, 13.1% were headed by single mothers. The poverty rate among single-parent households tends to be relatively high.

This OpenStax book is available for free at http://cnx.org/content/col12122/1.4

These changes in family structure, including the growth of single-parent families who tend to be at the lower end of the income distribution, and the growth of two-career high-earner couples near the top end of the income distribution, account for roughly half of the rise in income inequality across households in recent decades.

Link It Up @&

Visit this website (http://openstaxcollege.org/l/US_wealth) to watch a video that illustrates the distribution of wealth in the United States.

Causes of Growing Inequality: A Shift in the Distribution of Wages

Another factor behind the rise in U.S. income inequality is that earnings have become less equal since the late 1970s. In particular, the earnings of high-skilled labor relative to low-skilled labor have increased. Winner-take-all labor markets result from changes in technology, which have increased global demand for "stars,"—whether the best CEO, doctor, basketball player, or actor. This global demand pushes salaries far above productivity differences versus educational differences. One way to measure this change is to take workers' earnings with at least a four-year college bachelor's degree (including those who went on and completed an advanced degree) and divide them by workers' earnings with only a high school degree. The result is that those in the 25–34 age bracket with college degrees earned about 1.67 times as much as high school graduates in 2010, up from 1.59 times in 1995, according to U.S. Census data. Winner-take-all labor market theory argues that the salary gap between the median and the top 1 percent is not due to educational differences.

Economists use the demand and supply model to reason through the most likely causes of this shift. According to the National Center for Education Statistics, in recent decades, the supply of U.S. workers with college degrees has increased substantially. For example, 840,000 four-year bachelor's degrees were conferred on Americans in 1970. In 2013-2014, 1,894,934 such degrees were conferred—an increase of over 90%. In **Figure 15.9**, this shift in supply to the right, from S_0 to S_1, should result in a lower equilibrium wage for high-skilled labor. Thus, we can explain the increase in the price of high-skilled labor by a greater demand, like the movement from D_0 to D_1. Evidently, combining both the increase in supply and in demand has resulted in a shift from E_0 to E_1, and a resulting higher wage.

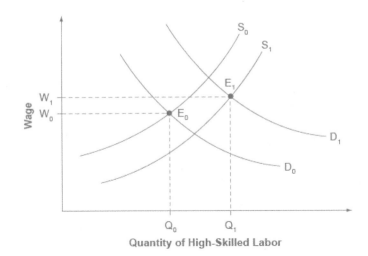

Figure 15.9 Why Would Wages Rise for High-Skilled Labor? The proportion of workers attending college has increased in recent decades, so the supply curve for high-skilled labor has shifted to the right, from S_0 to S_1. If the demand for high-skilled labor had remained at D_0, then this shift in supply would have led to lower wages for high-skilled labor. However, the wages for high-skilled labor, especially if there is a large global demand, have increased even with the shift in supply to the right. The explanation must lie in a shift to the right in demand for high-skilled labor, from D_0 to D_1. The figure shows how a combination of the shift in supply, from S_0 to S_1, and the shift in demand, from D_0 to D_1, led to both an increase in the quantity of high-skilled labor hired and also to a rise in the wage for such labor, from W_0 to W_1.

What factors would cause the demand for high-skilled labor to rise? The most plausible explanation is that while the explosion in new information and communications technologies over the last several decades has helped many workers to become more productive, the benefits have been especially great for high-skilled workers like top business managers, consultants, and design professionals. The new technologies have also helped to encourage globalization, the remarkable increase in international trade over the last few decades, by making it more possible to learn about and coordinate economic interactions all around the world. In turn, the rising impact of foreign trade in the U.S. economy has opened up greater opportunities for high-skilled workers to sell their services around the world, and lower-skilled workers have to compete with a larger supply of similarly skilled workers around the globe.

We can view the market for high-skilled labor as a race between forces of supply and demand. Additional education and on-the-job training will tend to increase the high-skilled labor supply and to hold down its relative wage. Conversely, new technology and other economic trends like globalization tend to increase the demand for high-skilled labor and push up its relative wage. We can view the greater inequality of wages as a sign that demand for skilled labor is increasing faster than supply. Alternatively, if the supply of lower skilled workers exceeds the demand, then average wages in the lower quintiles of the income distribution will decrease. The combination of forces in the high-skilled and low-skilled labor markets leads to increased income disparity.

15.5 | Government Policies to Reduce Income Inequality

By the end of this section, you will be able to:
- Explain the arguments for and against government intervention in a market economy
- Identify beneficial ways to reduce the economic inequality in a society
- Show the tradeoff between incentives and income equality

No society should expect or desire complete equality of income at a given point in time, for a number of reasons. First, most workers receive relatively low earnings in their first few jobs, higher earnings as they reach middle age, and then lower earnings after retirement. Thus, a society with people of varying ages will have a certain amount of income inequality. Second, people's preferences and desires differ. Some are willing to work long hours to have income for large houses, fast cars and computers, luxury vacations, and the ability to support children and grandchildren.

This OpenStax book is available for free at http://cnx.org/content/col12122/1.4

These factors all imply that a snapshot of inequality in a given year does not provide an accurate picture of how people's incomes rise and fall over time. Even if we expect some degree of economic inequality at any point in time, how much inequality should there be? There is also the difference between income and wealth, as the following Clear It Up feature explains.

How do you measure wealth versus income inequality?

Income is a flow of money received, often measured on a monthly or an annual basis. **Wealth** is the sum of the value of all assets, including money in bank accounts, financial investments, a pension fund, and the value of a home. In calculating wealth, one must subtract all debts, such as debt owed on a home mortgage and on credit cards. A retired person, for example, may have relatively little income in a given year, other than a pension or Social Security. However, if that person has saved and invested over time, the person's accumulated wealth can be quite substantial.

In the United States, the wealth distribution is more unequal than the income distribution, because differences in income can accumulate over time to make even larger differences in wealth. However, we can measure the degree of inequality in the wealth distribution with the same tools we use to measure the inequality in the income distribution, like quintile measurements. Once every three years the Federal Reserve Bank publishes the *Survey of Consumer Finance* which reports a collection of data on wealth.

Even if they cannot answer the question of how much inequality is too much, economists can still play an important role in spelling out policy options and tradeoffs. If a society decides to reduce the level of economic inequality, it has three main sets of tools: redistribution from those with high incomes to those with low incomes; trying to assure that a ladder of opportunity is widely available; and a tax on inheritance.

Redistribution

Redistribution means taking income from those with higher incomes and providing income to those with lower incomes. Earlier in this chapter, we considered some of the key government policies that provide support for the poor: the welfare program TANF, the earned income tax credit, SNAP, and Medicaid. If a reduction in inequality is desired, these programs could receive additional funding.

The federal income tax, which is a **progressive tax system** designed in such a way that the rich pay a higher percent in income taxes than the poor funds the programs. Data from household income tax returns in 2009 shows that the top 1% of households had an average income of $1,219,700 per year in pre-tax income and paid an average federal tax rate of 28.9%. The **effective income tax**, which is total taxes paid divided by total income (all sources of income such as wages, profits, interest, rental income, and government transfers such as veterans' benefits), was much lower. The effective tax paid by that top 1% of householders paid was 20.4%, while the bottom two quintiles actually paid negative effective income taxes, because of provisions like the earned income tax credit. News stories occasionally report on a high-income person who has managed to pay very little in taxes, but while such individual cases exist, according to the Congressional Budget Office, the typical pattern is that people with higher incomes pay a higher average share of their income in federal income taxes.

Of course, the fact that some degree of redistribution occurs now through the federal income tax and government antipoverty programs does not settle the questions of how much redistribution is appropriate, and whether more redistribution should occur.

The Ladder of Opportunity

Economic inequality is perhaps most troubling when it is not the result of effort or talent, but instead is determined by the circumstances under which a child grows up. One child attends a well-run grade school and high school and heads on to college, while parents help out by supporting education and other interests, paying for college, a first car, and a first house, and offering work connections that lead to internships and jobs. Another child attends a poorly run grade school, barely makes it through a low-quality high school, does not go to college, and lacks family and peer support. These two children may be similar in their underlying talents and in the effort they put forth, but their economic outcomes are likely to be quite different.

Public policy can attempt to build a ladder of opportunities so that, even though all children will never come from identical families and attend identical schools, each child has a reasonable opportunity to attain an economic niche in society based on their interests, desires, talents, and efforts. **Table 15.8** shows some of those initiatives.

Children	College Level	Adults
• Improved day care	• Widespread loans and grants for those in financial need	• Opportunities for retraining and acquiring new skills
• Enrichment programs for preschoolers	• Public support for a range of institutions from two-year community colleges to large research universities	• Prohibiting discrimination in job markets and housing on the basis of race, gender, age, and disability
• Improved public schools	-	-
• After school and community activities	-	-
• Internships and apprenticeships	-	-

Table 15.8 Public Policy Initiatives

Some have called the United States a land of opportunity. Although the general idea of a ladder of opportunity for all citizens continues to exert a powerful attraction, specifics are often quite controversial. Society can experiment with a wide variety of proposals for building a ladder of opportunity, especially for those who otherwise seem likely to start their lives in a disadvantaged position. The government needs to carry out such policy experiments in a spirit of open-mindedness, because some will succeed while others will not show positive results or will cost too much to enact on a widespread basis.

Inheritance Taxes

There is always a debate about inheritance taxes. It goes like this: Why should people who have worked hard all their lives and saved up a substantial nest egg not be able to give their money and possessions to their children and grandchildren? In particular, it would seem un-American if children were unable to inherit a family business or a family home. Alternatively, many Americans are far more comfortable with inequality resulting from high-income people who earned their money by starting innovative new companies than they are with inequality resulting from high-income people who have inherited money from rich parents.

The United States does have an **estate tax**—that is, a tax imposed on the value of an inheritance—which suggests a willingness to limit how much wealth one can pass on as an inheritance. However, according to the Center on Budget and Policy Priorities, in 2015 the estate tax applied only to those leaving inheritances of more than $5.43 million and thus applies to only a tiny percentage of those with high levels of wealth.

The Tradeoff between Incentives and Income Equality

Government policies to reduce poverty or to encourage economic equality, if carried to extremes, can injure incentives for economic output. The poverty trap, for example, defines a situation where guaranteeing a certain level of income can eliminate or reduce the incentive to work. An extremely high degree of redistribution, with very high taxes on the rich, would be likely to discourage work and entrepreneurship. Thus, it is common to draw the tradeoff between economic output and equality, as **Figure 15.10** (a) shows. In this formulation, if society wishes a high level of economic output, like point A, it must also accept a high degree of inequality. Conversely, if society wants a high level of equality, like point B, it must accept a lower level of economic output because of reduced incentives for production.

This view of the tradeoff between economic output and equality may be too pessimistic, and **Figure 15.10** (b) presents an alternate vision. Here, the tradeoff between economic output and equality first slopes up, in the vicinity of choice C, suggesting that certain programs might increase both output and economic equality. For example, the policy of providing free public education has an element of redistribution, since the value of the public schooling received by children of low-income families is clearly higher than what low-income families pay in taxes. A well-educated population, however, is also an enormously powerful factor in providing the skilled workers of tomorrow and helping the economy to grow and expand. In this case, equality and economic growth may complement each other.

Moreover, policies to diminish inequality and soften the hardship of poverty may sustain political support for a market economy. After all, if society does not make some effort toward reducing inequality and poverty, the alternative might be that people would rebel against market forces. Citizens might seek economic security by demanding that their legislators pass laws forbidding employers from ever laying off workers or reducing wages, or laws that would impose price floors and price ceilings and shut off international trade. From this viewpoint, policies to reduce inequality may help economic output by building social support for allowing markets to operate.

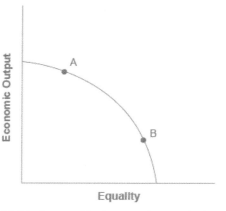 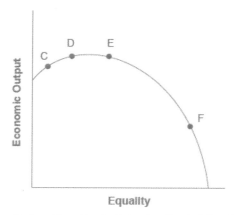

(a) Greater equality always reduces output   (b) Equality and output rise together but then face a tradeoff

Figure 15.10 The Tradeoff between Incentives and Economic Equality (a) Society faces a trade-off where any attempt to move toward greater equality, like moving from choice A to B, involves a reduction in economic output. (b) Situations can arise like point C, where it is possible both to increase equality and also to increase economic output, to a choice like D. It may also be possible to increase equality with little impact on economic output, like the movement from choice D to E. However, at some point, too aggressive a push for equality will tend to reduce economic output, as in the shift from E to F.

The tradeoff in **Figure 15.10** (b) then flattens out in the area between points D and E, which reflects the pattern that a number of countries that provide similar levels of income to their citizens—the United States, Canada, European Union nations, Japan, and Australia—have different levels of inequality. The pattern suggests that countries in this range could choose a greater or a lesser degree of inequality without much impact on economic output. Only if these countries push for a much higher level of equality, like at point F, will they experience the diminished incentives that lead to lower levels of economic output. In this view, while a danger always exists that an agenda to reduce poverty or inequality can be poorly designed or pushed too far, it is also possible to discover and design policies that improve equality and do not injure incentives for economic output by very much—or even improve such incentives.

Bring it Home

Occupy Wall Street

The Occupy movement took on a life of its own over the last few months of 2011, bringing to light issues that many people faced on the lower end of the income distribution. The contents of this chapter indicate that there is a significant amount of income inequality in the United States. The question is: What should be done about it?

The 2008-2009 Great Recession caused unemployment to rise and incomes to fall. Many people attribute the recession to mismanagement of the financial system by bankers and financial managers—those in the 1% of the income distribution—but those in lower quintiles bore the greater burden of the recession through unemployment. This seemed to present the picture of inequality in a different light: the group that seemed responsible for the recession was not the group that seemed to bear the burden of the decline in output. A burden shared can bring a society closer together. A burden pushed off onto others can polarize it.

On one level, the problem with trying to reduce income inequality comes down to whether you still believe in the American Dream. If you believe that one day you will have your American Dream—a large income, large house, happy family, or whatever else you would like to have in life—then you do not necessarily want to prevent anyone else from living out their dream. You certainly would not want to run the risk that someone would want to take part of your dream away from you. Thus, there is some reluctance to engage in a redistributive policy to reduce inequality.

However, when those for whom the likelihood of living the American Dream is very small are considered, there are sound arguments in favor of trying to create greater balance. As the text indicated, a little more income equality, gained through long-term programs like increased education and job training, can increase overall economic output. Then everyone is made better off, and the 1% will not seem like such a small group any more.

KEY TERMS

earned income tax credit (EITC) a method of assisting the working poor through the tax system

effective income tax percentage of total taxes paid divided by total income

estate tax a tax imposed on the value of an inheritance

income a flow of money received, often measured on a monthly or an annual basis

income inequality when one group receives a disproportionate share of total income or wealth than others

Lorenz curve a graph that compares the cumulative income actually received to a perfectly equal distribution of income; it shows the share of population on the horizontal axis and the cumulative percentage of total income received on the vertical axis

Medicaid a federal–state joint program enacted in 1965 that provides medical insurance for certain (not all) low-income people, including the near-poor as well as those below the poverty line, and focusing on low-income families with children, the low-income elderly, and the disabled

near-poor those who have incomes just above the poverty line

poverty the situation of being below a certain level of income one needs for a basic standard of living

poverty line the specific amount of income one requires for a basic standard of living

poverty rate percentage of the population living below the poverty line

poverty trap antipoverty programs set up so that government benefits decline substantially as people earn more income—as a result, working provides little financial gain

progressive tax system a tax system in which the rich pay a higher percentage of their income in taxes, rather than a higher absolute amount

quintile dividing a group into fifths, a method economists often use to look at distribution of income

redistribution taking income from those with higher incomes and providing income to those with lower incomes

safety net the group of government programs that provide assistance to the poor and the near-poor

Supplemental Nutrition Assistance Program (SNAP) a federally funded program, started in 1964, in which each month poor people receive SNAP cards they can use to buy food

wealth the sum of the value of all assets, including money in bank accounts, financial investments, a pension fund, and the value of a home

KEY CONCEPTS AND SUMMARY

15.1 Drawing the Poverty Line

Wages are influenced by Supply and demand in labor markets influence wages. This can lead to very low incomes for some people and very high incomes for others. Poverty and income inequality are not the same thing. Poverty applies to the condition of people who cannot afford the necessities of life. Income inequality refers to the disparity between those with higher and lower incomes. The poverty rate is what percentage of the population lives below the poverty line, which the amount of income that it takes to purchase the necessities of life determines. Choosing a poverty line will always be somewhat controversial.

15.2 The Poverty Trap

A poverty trap occurs when government-support payments for the poor decline as the poor earn more income. As a result, the poor do not end up with much more income when they work, because the loss of government support largely or completely offsets any income that one earns by working. Phasing out government benefits more slowly, as well as imposing requirements for work as a condition of receiving benefits and a time limit on benefits can reduce the harshness of the poverty trap.

15.3 The Safety Net

We call the group of government programs that assist the poor the safety net. In the United States, prominent safety net programs include Temporary Assistance to Needy Families (TANF), the Supplemental Nutrition Assistance Program (SNAP), the earned income tax credit (EITC), Medicaid, and the Special Supplemental Food Program for Women, Infants, and Children (WIC).

15.4 Income Inequality: Measurement and Causes

Measuring inequality involves making comparisons across the entire distribution of income, not just the poor. One way of doing this is to divide the population into groups, like quintiles, and then calculate what share of income each group receives. An alternative approach is to draw Lorenz curves, which compare the cumulative income actually received to a perfectly equal distribution of income. Income inequality in the United States increased substantially from the late 1970s and early 1980s into the 2000s. The two most common explanations that economists cite are changes in household structures that have led to more two-earner couples and single-parent families, and the effect of new information and communications technology on wages.

15.5 Government Policies to Reduce Income Inequality

Policies that can affect the level of economic inequality include redistribution between rich and poor, making it easier for people to climb the ladder of opportunity; and estate taxes, which are taxes on inheritances. Pushing too aggressively for economic equality can run the risk of decreasing economic incentives. However, a moderate push for economic equality can increase economic output, both through methods like improved education and by building a base of political support for market forces.

SELF-CHECK QUESTIONS

1. Describe how each of these changes is likely to affect poverty and inequality:
     a. Incomes rise for low-income and high-income workers, but rise more for the high-income earners.
     b. Incomes fall for low-income and high-income workers, but fall more for high-income earners.

2. Jonathon is a single father with one child. He can work as a server for $6 per hour for up to 1,500 hours per year. He is eligible for welfare, and so if he does not earn any income, he will receive a total of $10,000 per year. He can work and still receive government benefits, but for every $1 of income, his welfare stipend is $1 less. Create a table similar to **Table 15.4** that shows Jonathan's options. Use four columns, the first showing number of hours to work, the second showing his earnings from work, the third showing the government benefits he will receive, and the fourth column showing his total income (earnings + government support). Sketch a labor-leisure diagram of Jonathan's opportunity set with and without government support.

3. Imagine that the government reworks the welfare policy that was affecting Jonathan in question 1, so that for each dollar someone like Jonathan earns at work, his government benefits diminish by only 30 cents. Reconstruct the table from question 1 to account for this change in policy. Draw Jonathan's labor-leisure opportunity sets, both for before this welfare program is enacted and after it is enacted.

4. We have discovered that the welfare system discourages recipients from working because the more income they earn, the less welfare benefits they receive. How does the earned income tax credit attempt to loosen the poverty trap?

5. How does the TANF attempt to loosen the poverty trap?

This OpenStax book is available for free at http://cnx.org/content/col12122/1.4

6. A group of 10 people have the following annual incomes: $24,000, $18,000, $50,000, $100,000, $12,000, $36,000, $80,000, $10,000, $24,000, $16,000. Calculate the share of total income that each quintile receives from this income distribution. Do the top and bottom quintiles in this distribution have a greater or larger share of total income than the top and bottom quintiles of the U.S. income distribution?

7. **Table 15.9** shows the share of income going to each quintile of the income distribution for the United Kingdom in 1979 and 1991. Use this data to calculate what the points on a Lorenz curve would be, and sketch the Lorenz curve. How did inequality in the United Kingdom shift over this time period? How can you see the patterns in the quintiles in the Lorenz curves?

Share of Income	1979	1991
Top quintile	39.7%	42.9%
Fourth quintile	24.8%	22.7%
Middle quintile	17.0%	16.3%
Second quintile	11.5%	11.5%
Bottom quintile	7.0%	6.6%

Table 15.9 Income Distribution in the United Kingdom, 1979 and 1991

8. Using two demand and supply diagrams, one for the low-wage labor market and one for the high-wage labor market, explain how information technology can increase income inequality if it is a complement to high-income workers like salespeople and managers, but a substitute for low-income workers like file clerks and telephone receptionists.

9. Using two demand and supply diagrams, one for the low-wage labor market and one for the high-wage labor market, explain how a program that increased educational levels for a substantial number of low-skill workers could reduce income inequality.

10. Here is one hypothesis: A well-funded social safety net can increase economic equality but will reduce economic output. Explain why this might be so, and sketch a production possibility curve that shows this tradeoff.

11. Here is a second hypothesis: A well-funded social safety net may lead to less regulation of the market economy. Explain why this might be so, and sketch a production possibility curve that shows this tradeoff.

12. Which set of policies is more likely to cause a tradeoff between economic output and equality: policies of redistribution or policies aimed at the ladder of opportunity? Explain how the production possibility frontier tradeoff between economic equality and output might look in each case.

13. Why is there reluctance on the part of some in the United States to redistribute income so that greater equality can be achieved?

REVIEW QUESTIONS

14. How is the poverty rate calculated?

15. What is the poverty line?

16. What is the difference between poverty and income inequality?

17. How does the poverty trap discourage people from working?

18. How can the effect of the poverty trap be reduced?

19. Who are the near-poor?

20. What is the safety net?

21. Briefly explain the differences between TANF, the earned income tax credit, SNAP, and Medicaid.

22. Who is included in the top income quintile?

23. What is measured on the two axes of a Lorenz curve?

24. If a country had perfect income equality what would the Lorenz curve look like?

25. How has the inequality of income changed in the U.S. economy since the late 1970s?

26. What are some reasons why a certain degree of inequality of income would be expected in a market economy?

27. What are the main reasons economists give for the increase in inequality of incomes?

28. Identify some public policies that can reduce the level of economic inequality.

29. Describe how a push for economic equality might reduce incentives to work and produce output. Then describe how a push for economic inequality might not have such effects.

CRITICAL THINKING QUESTIONS

30. What goods and services would you include in an estimate of the basic necessities for a family of four?

31. If a family of three earned $20,000, would they be able to make ends meet given the official poverty threshold?

32. **Exercise 15.2** and **Exercise 15.3** asked you to describe the labor-leisure tradeoff for Jonathon. Since, in the first example, there is no monetary incentive for Jonathon to work, explain why he may choose to work anyway. Explain what the opportunity costs of working and not working might be for Jonathon in each example. Using your tables and graphs from **Exercise 15.2** and **Exercise 15.3**, analyze how the government welfare system affects Jonathan's incentive to work.

33. Explain how you would create a government program that would give an incentive for labor to increase hours and keep labor from falling into the poverty trap.

34. Many critics of government programs to help low-income individuals argue that these programs create a poverty trap. Explain how programs such as TANF, EITC, SNAP, and Medicaid will affect low-income individuals and whether or not you think these programs will benefit families and children.

35. Think about the business cycle: during a recession, unemployment increases; it decreases in an expansionary phase. Explain what happens to TANF, SNAP, and Medicaid programs at each phase of the business cycle (recession, trough, expansion, and peak).

36. Explain how a country may experience greater equality in the distribution of income, yet still experience high rates of poverty. *Hint*: Look at the **Clear It Up** "How do governments measure poverty in low-income countries?" and compare to **Table 15.5**.

37. The demand for skilled workers in the United States has been increasing. To increase the supply of skilled workers, many argue that immigration reform to allow more skilled labor into the United States is needed. Explain whether you agree or disagree.

38. Explain a situation using the supply and demand for skilled labor in which the increased number of college graduates leads to depressed wages. Given the rising cost of going to college, explain why a college education will or will not increase income inequality.

39. What do you think is more important to focus on when considering inequality: income inequality or wealth inequality?

40. To reduce income inequality, should the marginal tax rates on the top 1% be increased?

41. Redistribution of income occurs through the federal income tax and government antipoverty programs. Explain whether or not this level of redistribution is appropriate and whether more redistribution should occur.

42. How does a society or a country make the decision about the tradeoff between equality and economic output? *Hint*: Think about the political system.

43. Explain what the long- and short-term consequences are of not promoting equality or working to reduce poverty.

This OpenStax book is available for free at http://cnx.org/content/col12122/1.4

PROBLEMS

44. In country A, the population is 300 million and 50 million people are living below the poverty line. What is the poverty rate?

45. In country B, the population is 900 million and 100 million people are living below the poverty line. What is the poverty rate?

46. Susan is a single mother with three children. She can earn $8 per hour and works up to 2,000 hours per year. However, if she does not earn any income at all, she will receive government benefits totaling $16,000 per year. For every $1 of income she earns, her level of government support will be reduced by $1. Create a table, patterned after Table 15.8. The first column should show Susan's choices of how many hours to work per year, up to 2,000 hours. The second column should show her earnings from work. The third column should show her level of government support, given her earnings. The final column should show her total income, combining earnings and government support.

47. A group of 10 people have the following annual incomes: $55,000, $30,000, $15,000, $20,000, $35,000, $80,000, $40,000, $45,000, $30,000, $50,000. Calculate the share of total income each quintile of this income distribution received. Do the top and bottom quintiles in this distribution have a greater or larger share of total income than the top and bottom quintiles of the U.S. income distribution for 2005?

This OpenStax book is available for free at http://cnx.org/content/col12122/1.4

16 | Information, Risk, and Insurance

Figure 16.1 Former President Obama's Health Care Reform   The Patient Protection and Affordable Care Act has become a controversial topic—one which relates strongly to the topic of this chapter. (Credit: modification of work by Daniel Borman/Flickr Creative Commons)

Bring it Home

What's the Big Deal with Obamacare?

In August 2009, many members of the U.S. Congress used their summer recess to return to their home districts and hold town hall-style meetings to discuss President Obama's proposed changes to the U.S. healthcare system. This was officially known as the Patient Protection and Affordable Care Act (PPACA) or as the Affordable Care Act (ACA), but was more popularly known as Obamacare. The bill's opponents' claims ranged from the charge that the changes were unconstitutional and would add $750 billion to the deficit, to extreme claims about the inclusion of things like the implantation of microchips and so-called "death panels" that decide which critically-ill patients receive care and which do not.

Why did people react so strongly? After all, the intent of the law is to make healthcare insurance more affordable, to allow more people to obtain insurance, and to reduce the costs of healthcare. For each year from 2000 to 2011, these costs grew at least double the rate of inflation. In 2014, healthcare spending accounted for around 24% of all federal government spending. In the United States, we spend more for our healthcare than any other high-income nation, yet our health outcomes are worse than comparable high-income countries. In 2015, over 32 million people in the United States, about 12.8% of the non-elderly adult population, were without insurance. Even today, however, several years after the Act was signed into law and after the Supreme

Court mostly upheld it, a 2015 Kaiser Foundation poll found that 43% of likely voters viewed it unfavorably. Why is this?

The debate over the ACA and healthcare reform could take an entire textbook, but what this chapter will do is introduce the basics of insurance and the problems insurance companies face. It is these problems, and how insurance companies respond to them that, in part, explain the ACA.

Introduction to Information, Risk, and Insurance

In this chapter, you will learn about:

- The Problem of Imperfect Information and Asymmetric Information

- Insurance and Imperfect Information

Every purchase is based on a belief about the satisfaction that the good or service will provide. In turn, these beliefs are based on the information that the buyer has available. For many products, the information available to the buyer or the seller is imperfect or unclear, which can either make buyers regret past purchases or avoid making future ones.

This chapter discusses how imperfect and asymmetric information affect markets. The first module of the chapter discusses how asymmetric information affects markets for goods, labor, and financial capital. When buyers have less information about the quality of the good (for example, a gemstone) than sellers do, sellers may be tempted to mislead buyers. If a buyer cannot have at least some confidence in the quality of what he or she is purchasing, then he or she will be reluctant or unwilling to purchase the products. Thus, we require mechanisms to bridge this information gap, so buyers and sellers can engage in a transaction.

The second module of the chapter discusses insurance markets, which also face similar problems of imperfect information. For example, a car insurance company would prefer to sell insurance only to those who are unlikely to have auto accidents—but it is hard for the firm to identify those perfectly safe drivers. Conversely, car insurance buyers would like to persuade the auto insurance company that they are safe drivers and should pay only a low price for coverage. If insurance markets cannot find ways to grapple with these problems of imperfect information, then even people who have low or average risks of making claims may not be able to purchase insurance. The chapter on financial markets (markets for stocks and bonds) will show that the problems of imperfect information can be especially poignant. We cannot eliminate imperfect information, but we can often manage it.

16.1 | The Problem of Imperfect Information and Asymmetric Information

By the end of this section, you will be able to:
- Analyze the impact of both imperfect information and asymmetric information
- Evaluate the role of advertisements in creating imperfect information
- Identify ways to reduce the risk of imperfect information
- Explain how imperfect information can affect price, quantity, and quality

Consider a purchase that many people make at important times in their lives: buying expensive jewelry. In May 1994, celebrity psychologist Doree Lynn bought an expensive ring from a jeweler in Washington, D.C., which included an emerald that cost $14,500. Several years later, the emerald fractured. Lynn took it to another jeweler who found that cracks in the emerald had been filled with an epoxy resin. Lynn sued the original jeweler in 1997 for selling her a treated emerald without telling her, and won. The case publicized a number of little-known facts about precious stones. Most emeralds have internal flaws, and so they are soaked in clear oil or an epoxy resin to hide the flaws and make the color more deep and clear. Clear oil can leak out over time, and epoxy resin can discolor with age or heat. However, using clear oil or epoxy to "fill" emeralds is completely legal, as long as it is disclosed.

After Doree Lynn's lawsuit, the NBC news show "Dateline" bought emeralds at four prominent jewelry stores in New

York City in 1997. All the sales clerks at these stores, unaware that they were being recorded on a hidden camera, said the stones were untreated. When the emeralds were tested at a laboratory, however, technicians discovered they had all been treated with oil or epoxy. Emeralds are not the only gemstones that are treated. Diamonds, topaz, and tourmaline are also often irradiated to enhance colors. The general rule is that all treatments to gemstones should be revealed, but often sellers do not disclose this. As such, many buyers face a situation of **asymmetric information**, where two parties involved in an economic transaction have an unequal amount of information (one party knows much more than the other).

Many economic transactions occur in a situation of **imperfect information**, where either the buyer, the seller, or both, are less than 100% certain about the qualities of what they are buying and selling. Also, one may characterize the transaction as asymmetric information, in which one party has more information than the other regarding the economic transaction. Let's begin with some examples of how imperfect information complicates transactions in goods, labor, and financial capital markets. The presence of imperfect information can easily cause a decline in prices or quantities of products sold. However, buyers and sellers also have incentives to create mechanisms that will allow them to make mutually beneficial transactions even in the face of imperfect information.

If you are unclear about the difference between asymmetric information and imperfect information, read the following Clear It Up feature.

What is the difference between imperfect and asymmetric information?

For a market to reach equilibrium sellers and buyers must have full information about the product's price and quality. If there is limited information, then buyers and sellers may not be able to transact or will possibly make poor decisions.

Imperfect information refers to the situation where buyers and/or sellers do not have all of the necessary information to make an informed decision about the product's price or quality. The term imperfect information simply means that the buyers and/or sellers do not have all the information necessary to make an informed decision. Asymmetric information is the condition where one party, either the buyer or the seller, has more information about the product's quality or price than the other party. In either case (imperfect or asymmetric information) buyers or sellers need remedies to make more informed decisions.

"Lemons" and Other Examples of Imperfect Information

Consider Marvin, who is trying to decide whether to buy a used car. Let's assume that Marvin is truly clueless about what happens inside a car's engine. He is willing to do some background research, like reading *Consumer Reports* or checking websites that offer information about used cars makes and models and what they should cost. He might pay a mechanic to inspect the car. Even after devoting some money and time collecting information, however, Marvin still cannot be absolutely sure that he is buying a high-quality used car. He knows that he might buy the car, drive it home, and use it for a few weeks before discovering that car is a "lemon," which is slang for a defective product (especially a car).

Imagine that Marvin shops for a used car and finds two that look very similar in terms of mileage, exterior appearances, and age. One car costs $4,000, while the other car costs $4,600. Which car should Marvin buy?

If Marvin were choosing in a world of perfect information, the answer would be simple: he should buy the cheaper car. However, Marvin is operating in a world of imperfect information, where the sellers likely know more about the car's problems than he does, and have an incentive to hide the information. After all, the more problems the sellers disclose, the lower the car's selling price.

What should Marvin do? First, he needs to understand that even with imperfect information, prices still reflect information. Typically, used cars are more expensive on some dealer lots because the dealers have a trustworthy reputation to uphold. Those dealers try to fix problems that may not be obvious to their customers, in order to create good word of mouth about their vehicles' long term reliability. The short term benefits of selling their customers a "lemon" could cause a quick collapse in the dealer's reputation and a loss of long term profits. On other lots that are less well-established, one can find cheaper used cars, but the buyer takes on more risk when a dealer's reputation has little at stake. The cheapest cars of all often appear on Craigslist, where the individual seller has no reputation to defend. In sum, cheaper prices do carry more risk, so Marvin should balance his appetite for risk versus the potential headaches of many more unanticipated trips to the repair shop.

Similar problems with imperfect information arise in labor and financial capital markets. Consider Greta, who is applying for a job. Her potential employer, like the used car buyer, is concerned about ending up with a "lemon"—in this case a poor quality employee. The employer will collect information about Greta's academic and work history. In the end, however, a degree of uncertainty will inevitably remain regarding Greta's abilities, which are hard to demonstrate without actually observing her on the job. How can a potential employer screen for certain attributes, such as motivation, timeliness, and ability to get along with others? Employers often look to trade schools and colleges to pre-screen candidates. Employers may not even interview a candidate unless he has a degree and, sometimes, a degree from a particular school. Employers may also view awards, a high grade point average, and other accolades as a signal of hard work, perseverance, and ability. Employers may also seek references for insights into key attributes such as energy level and work ethic.

How Imperfect Information Can Affect Equilibrium Price and Quantity

The presence of imperfect information can discourage both buyers and sellers from participating in the market. Buyers may become reluctant to participate because they cannot determine the product's quality. Sellers of high-quality or medium-quality goods may be reluctant to participate, because it is difficult to demonstrate the quality of their goods to buyers—and since buyers cannot determine which goods have higher quality, they are likely to be unwilling to pay a higher price for such goods.

Economists sometimes refer to a market with few buyers and few sellers as a thin market. By contrast, they call a market with many buyers and sellers a thick market. When imperfect information is severe and buyers and sellers are discouraged from participating, markets may become extremely thin as a relatively small number of buyer and sellers attempt to communicate enough information that they can agree on a price.

When Price Mixes with Imperfect Information about Quality

A buyer confronted with imperfect information will often believe that the price reveals something about the product's quality. For example, a buyer may assume that a gemstone or a used car that costs more must be of higher quality, even though the buyer is not an expert on gemstones. Think of the expensive restaurant where the food must be good because it is so expensive or the shop where the clothes must be stylish because they cost so much, or the gallery where the art must be great, because the price tags are high. If you are hiring a lawyer, you might assume that a lawyer who charges $400 per hour must be better than a lawyer who charges $150 per hour. In these cases, price can act as a signal of quality.

When buyers use the market price to draw inferences about the products' quality, then markets may have trouble reaching an equilibrium price and quantity. Imagine a situation where a used car dealer has a lot full of used cars that do not seem to be selling, and so the dealer decides to cut the car prices to sell a greater quantity. In a market with imperfect information, many buyers may assume that the lower price implies low-quality cars. As a result, the lower price may not attract more customers. Conversely, a dealer who raises prices may find that customers assume that the higher price means that cars are of higher quality. As a result of raising prices, the dealer might sell more cars. (Whether or not consumers always behave rationally, as an economist would see it, is the subject of the following Clear It Up feature.)

The idea that higher prices might cause a greater quantity demanded and that lower prices might cause a lower quantity demanded runs exactly counter to the basic model of demand and supply (as we outlined in the **Demand and Supply** chapter). These contrary effects, however, will reach natural limits. At some point, if the price is high enough, the quantity demanded will decline. Conversely, when the price declines far enough, buyers will increasingly find value even if the quality is lower. In addition, information eventually becomes more widely known. An overpriced restaurant that charges more than the quality of its food is worth to many buyers will not last forever.

This OpenStax book is available for free at http://cnx.org/content/col12122/1.4

Is consumer behavior rational?

There is much human behavior that mainstream economists have tended to call "irrational" since it is consistently at odds with economists' utility maximizing models. The typical response is for economists to brush these behaviors aside and call them "anomalies" or unexplained quirks.

"If only you knew more economics, you would not be so irrational," is what many mainstream economists seem to be saying. A group known as behavioral economists has challenged this notion, because so much of this so-called "quirky" behavior is extremely common among us. For example, a conventional economist would say that if you lost a $10 bill today, and also received an extra $10 in your paycheck, you should feel perfectly neutral. After all, –$10 + $10 = $0. You are the same financially as you were before. However, behavioral economists have conducted research that shows many people will feel some negative emotion—anger or frustration—after those two things happen. We tend to focus more on the loss than the gain. Economists Daniel Kahneman and Amos Tversky in a famous 1979 *Econometrica* paper called this "loss aversion", where a $1 loss pains us 2.25 times more than a $1 gain helps us. This has implications for investing, as people tend to "overplay" the stock market by reacting more to losses than to gains.

Behavioral economics also tries to explain why people make seemingly irrational decisions in the presence of different situations, or how they "frame" the decision. We outline a popular example here: Imagine you have the opportunity to buy an alarm clock for $20 in Store A. Across the street, you learn, is the exact same clock at Store B for $10. You might say it is worth your time—a five-minute walk—to save $10. Now, take a different example: You are in Store A buying a $300 phone. Five minutes away, at Store B, the same phone is $290. You again save $10 by taking a five-minute walk. Do you do it?

Surprisingly, it is likely that you would not. Mainstream economists would say "$10 is $10" and that it would be irrational to make a five minute walk for $10 in one case and not the other. However, behavioral economists have pointed out that most of us evaluate outcomes relative to a reference point—here the cost of the product—and think of gains and losses as percentages rather than using actual savings.

Which view is right? Both have their advantages, but behavioral economists have at least shed a light on trying to describe and explain systematic behavior which some previously had dismissed as irrational. If most of us are engaged in some "irrational behavior," perhaps there are deeper underlying reasons for this behavior in the first place.

Mechanisms to Reduce the Risk of Imperfect Information

If you were selling a good like emeralds or used cars where imperfect information is likely to be a problem, how could you reassure possible buyers? If you were buying a good where imperfect information is a problem, what would it take to reassure you? Buyers and sellers in the goods market rely on reputation as well as guarantees, warrantees, and service contracts to assure product quality. The labor market uses occupational licenses and certifications to assure competency, while the financial capital market uses cosigners and collateral as insurance against unforeseen, detrimental events.

In the goods market, the seller might offer a **money-back guarantee**, an agreement that functions as a promise of quality. This strategy may be especially important for a company that sells goods through mail-order catalogs or over the web, whose customers cannot see the actual products, because it encourages people to buy something even if they are not certain they want to keep it.

L.L. Bean started using money-back-guarantees in 1911, when the founder stitched waterproof shoe rubbers together with leather shoe tops, and sold them as hunting shoes. He guaranteed satisfaction. However, the stitching came apart and, out of the first batch of 100 pairs that were sold, customers returned 90 pairs. L.L. Bean took out a bank loan, repaired all of the shoes, and replaced them. The L.L. Bean reputation for customer satisfaction began to spread. Many firms today offer money-back-guarantees for a few weeks or months, but L.L. Bean offers a complete money-back guarantee. Customers can always return anything they have bought from L.L. Bean, no matter how many years later or what condition the product is in, for a full money-back guarantee.

L.L. Bean has very few stores. Instead, most of its sales are made by mail, telephone, or, now, through their website. For this kind of firm, imperfect information may be an especially difficult problem, because customers cannot see and touch what they are buying. A combination of a money-back guarantee and a reputation for quality can help for a mail-order firm to flourish.

Link It Up ⌬

Visit this website (http://openstaxcollege.org/l/guarantee) to read about the origin of Eddie Bauer's 100% customer satisfaction guarantee.

Sellers may offer a **warranty**, which is a promise to fix or replace the good, at least for a certain time period. The seller may also offer a buyer a chance to buy a **service contract**, where the buyer pays an extra amount and the seller agrees to fix anything that goes wrong for a set time period. Service contracts are often an option for buyers of large purchases such as cars, appliances and even houses.

Guarantees, warranties, and service contracts are examples of explicit reassurance that sellers provide. In many cases, firms also offer unstated guarantees. For example, some movie theaters might refund the ticket cost to a customer who walks out complaining about the show. Likewise, while restaurants do not generally advertise a money-back guarantee or exchange policies, many restaurants allow customers to exchange one dish for another or reduce the price of the bill if the customer is not satisfied.

The rationale for these policies is that firms want repeat customers, who in turn will recommend the business to others. As such, establishing a good reputation is of paramount importance. When buyers know that a firm is concerned about its reputation, they are less likely to worry about receiving a poor-quality product. For example, a well-established grocery store with a good reputation can often charge a higher price than a temporary stand at a local farmer's market, where the buyer may never see the seller again.

Sellers of labor provide information through resumes, recommendations, school transcripts, and examples of their work. The labor market also uses **occupational licenses** to establish quality in the labor market. Occupational licenses, which government agencies typically issue, show that a worker has completed a certain type of education or passed a certain test. Some of the professionals who must hold a license are doctors, teachers, nurses, engineers, accountants, and lawyers. In addition, most states require a license to work as a barber, an embalmer, a dietitian, a massage therapist, a hearing aid dealer, a counselor, an insurance agent, and a real estate broker. Some other jobs require a license in only one state. Minnesota requires a state license to be a field archeologist. North Dakota has a state license for bait retailers. In Louisiana, one needs a state license to be a "stress analyst" and California requires a state license to be a furniture upholsterer. According to a 2013 study from the University of Chicago, about 29% of U.S. workers have jobs that require occupational licenses.

Occupational licenses have their downside as well, as they represent a barrier to entry to certain industries. This makes it more difficult for new entrants to compete with incumbents, which can lead to higher prices and less consumer choice. In occupations that require licenses, the government has decided that the additional information provided by licenses outweighs the negative effect on competition.

This OpenStax book is available for free at http://cnx.org/content/col12122/1.4

Are advertisers allowed to benefit from imperfect information?

Many advertisements seem full of imperfect information—at least by what they imply. Driving a certain car, drinking a particular soda, or wearing a certain shoe are all unlikely to bring fashionable friends and fun automatically, if at all. The government rules on advertising, enforced by the Federal Trade Commission (FTC), allow advertising to contain a certain amount of exaggeration about the general delight of using a product. They, however, also demand that if one presents a claim as a fact, it must be true.

Legally, deceptive advertising dates back to the 1950s when Colgate-Palmolive created a television advertisement that seemed to show Rapid Shave shaving cream being spread on sandpaper and then the sand was shaved off the sandpaper. What the television advertisement actually showed was sand sprinkled on Plexiglas—without glue—and then scraped aside by the razor.

In the 1960s, in magazine advertisements for Campbell's vegetable soup, the company was having problems getting an appetizing soup picture, because the vegetables kept sinking. To remedy this, they filled a bowl with marbles and poured the soup over the top, so that the bowl appeared to be crammed with vegetables.

In the late 1980s, the Volvo Company filmed a television advertisement that showed a monster truck driving over cars, crunching their roofs—all except for the Volvo, which did not crush. However, the FTC found in 1991 that the Volvo's roof from the filming had been reinforced with an extra steel framework, while they cut the roof supports on the other car brands.

The Wonder Bread Company ran television advertisements featuring "Professor Wonder," who said that because Wonder Bread contained extra calcium, it would help children's minds work better and improve their memory. The FTC objected, and in 2002 the company agreed to stop running the advertisements.

As we can see in each of these cases, the Federal Trade Commission (FTC) often checks factual claims about the product's performance, at least to some extent. Language and images that are exaggerated or ambiguous, but not actually false, are allowed in advertising. Untrue "facts" are not permitted. In any case, an old Latin saying applies when watching advertisements: *Caveat emptor*—that is, "let the buyer beware."

On the buyer's side of the labor market, a standard precaution against hiring a "lemon" of an employee is to specify that the first few months of employment are officially a trial or probationary period, and that the employer can dismiss the worker for any reason or no reason after that time. Sometimes workers also receive lower pay during this trial period.

In the financial capital market, before a bank makes a loan, it requires a prospective borrower to fill out forms regarding incomes sources. In addition, the bank conducts a credit check on the individual's past borrowing. Another approach is to require a **cosigner** on a loan; that is, another person or firm who legally pledges to repay some or all of the money if the original borrower does not do so. Another approach is to require **collateral**, often property or equipment that the bank would have a right to seize and sell if borrower does not repay the loan.

Buyers of goods and services cannot possibly become experts in evaluating the quality of gemstones, used cars, lawyers, and everything else they buy. Employers and lenders cannot be perfectly omniscient about whether possible workers will turn out well or potential borrowers will repay loans on time. However, the mechanisms that we mentioned above can reduce the risks associated with imperfect information so that the buyer and seller are willing to proceed.

16.2 | Insurance and Imperfect Information

By the end of this section, you will be able to:
- Explain how insurance works
- Identify and evaluate various forms of government and social insurance
- Discuss the problems caused by moral hazard and adverse selection
- Analyze the impact of government regulation of insurance

Insurance is a method that households and firms use to prevent any single event from having a significant detrimental financial effect. Generally, households or firms with insurance make regular payments, called **premiums**. The insurance company prices these premiums based on the probability of certain events occurring among a pool of people. Members of the group who then suffer a specified bad experience receive payments from this pool of money.

Many people have several kinds of insurance: health insurance that pays when they receive medical care; car insurance that pays if their car is in an automobile accident; house or renter's insurance that pays for stolen possessions or items damaged by fire; and life insurance, which pays for the family if the insured individual dies. **Table 16.1** lists a set of insurance markets.

Type of Insurance	Who Pays for It?	It Pays Out When . . .
Health insurance	Employers and individuals	Medical expenses are incurred
Life insurance	Employers and individuals	Policyholder dies
Automobile insurance	Individuals	Car is damaged, stolen, or causes damage to others
Property and homeowner's insurance	Homeowners and renters	Dwelling is damaged or burglarized
Liability insurance	Firms and individuals	An injury occurs for which you are partly responsible
Malpractice insurance	Doctors, lawyers, and other professionals	A poor quality of service is provided that causes harm to others

Table 16.1 Some Insurance Markets

All insurance involves imperfect information in both an obvious way and in a deeper way. At an obvious level, we cannot predict future events with certainty. For example, we cannot know with certainty who will have a car accident, become ill, die, or have his home robbed in the next year. Imperfect information also applies to estimating the risk that something will happen to any individual. It is difficult for an insurance company to estimate the risk that, say, a particular 20-year-old male driver from New York City will have an accident, because even within that group, some drivers will drive more safely than others. Thus, adverse events occur out of a combination of people's characteristics and choices that make the risks higher or lower and then the good or bad luck of what actually happens.

How Insurance Works

A simplified example of automobile insurance might work this way. Suppose we divide a group of 100 drivers into three groups. In a given year, 60 of those people have only a few door dings or chipped paint, which costs $100 each. Another 30 of the drivers have medium-sized accidents that cost an average of $1,000 in damages, and 10 of the drivers have large accidents that cost $15,000 in damages. For the moment, let's imagine that at the beginning of any year, there is no way of identifying the drivers who are low-risk, medium-risk, or high-risk. The total damage incurred by car accidents in this group of 100 drivers will be $186,000, that is:

This OpenStax book is available for free at http://cnx.org/content/col12122/1.4

$$\begin{aligned}
\text{Total damage} \; &= \; (60 \times \$100) + (30 \times \$1{,}000) + (10 \times \$15{,}000) \\
&= \; \$6{,}000 + \$30{,}000 + \$150{,}000 \\
&= \; \$186{,}000
\end{aligned}$$

If each of the 100 drivers pays a $1,860 premium each year, the insurance company will collect the $186,000 that is needed to cover the costs of the accidents that occur.

Since insurance companies have such a large number of clients, they are able to negotiate with health care and other service providers for lower rates than the individual would be able to get, thus increasing the benefit to consumers of becoming insured and saving the insurance company itself money when it pays out claims.

Insurance companies receive income, as **Figure 16.2** shows, from insurance premiums and investment income. The companies derive income from investing the funds that insurance companies received in the past but did not pay out as insurance claims in prior years. The insurance company receives a rate of return from investing these funds or reserves. The companies typically invest in fairly safe, liquid (easy to convert into cash) investments, as the insurance companies need to be able to readily access these funds when a major disaster strikes.

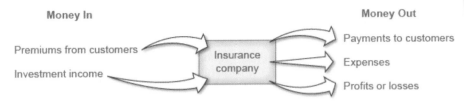

Figure 16.2 An Insurance Company: What Comes In, What Goes Out Money flows into an insurance company through premiums and investments and out through the payment of claims and operating expenses.

Government and Social Insurance

Federal and state governments run a number of insurance programs. Some of the programs look much like private insurance, in the sense that the members of a group make steady payments into a fund, and those in the group who suffer an adverse experience receive payments. Other programs protect against risk, but without an explicit fund set up. Following are some examples.

- Unemployment insurance: Employers in every state pay a small amount for unemployment insurance, which goes into a fund to pay benefits to workers who lose their jobs and do not find new jobs, for a period of time, usually up to six months.

- Pension insurance: Employers that offer pensions to their retired employees are required by law to pay a small fraction of what they are setting aside for pensions to the Pension Benefit Guarantee Corporation, which pays at least some pension benefits to workers if a company goes bankrupt and cannot pay the pensions it has promised.

- Deposit insurance: Banks are required by law to pay a small fraction of their deposits to the Federal Deposit Insurance Corporation, which goes into a fund that pays depositors the value of their bank deposits up to $250,000 (the amount was raised from $100,000 to $250,000 in 2008) if the bank should go bankrupt.

- Workman's compensation insurance: Employers are required by law to pay a small percentage of the salaries that they pay into funds, typically run at the state level, that pay benefits to workers who suffer an injury on the job.

- Retirement insurance: All workers pay a percentage of their income into Social Security and into Medicare, which then provides income and health care benefits to the elderly. Social Security and Medicare are not literally "insurance" in the sense that those currently contributing to the fund are not eligible for benefits. They function like insurance, however, in the sense that individuals make regular payments into the programs today in exchange for benefits they will receive in the case of a later event—either becoming old or becoming sick when old. A name for such programs is "social insurance."

The major additional costs to insurance companies, other than the payment of claims, are the costs of running a business: the administrative costs of hiring workers, administering accounts, and processing insurance claims. For most insurance companies, the insurance premiums coming in and the claims payments going out are much larger than the amounts earned by investing money or the administrative costs.

Thus, while factors like investment income earned on reserves, administrative costs, and groups with different risks complicate the overall picture, a fundamental law of insurance must hold true: The average person's payments into insurance over time must cover 1) the average person's claims, 2) the costs of running the company, and 3) leave room for the firm's profits.

Risk Groups and Actuarial Fairness

Not all of those who purchase insurance face the same risks. Some people may be more likely, because of genetics or personal habits, to fall sick with certain diseases. Some people may live in an area where car theft or home robbery is more likely than in other areas. Some drivers are safer than others. We can define a **risk group** can be defined as a group that shares roughly the same risks of an adverse event occurring.

Insurance companies often classify people into risk groups, and charge lower premiums to those with lower risks. If people are not separated into risk groups, then those with low risk must pay for those with high risks. In the simple example of how car insurance works, 60 drivers had very low damage of $100 each, 30 drivers had medium-sized accidents that cost $1,000 each, and 10 of the drivers had large accidents that cost $15,000. If all 100 of these drivers pay the same $1,860, then those with low damages are in effect paying for those with high damages.

If it is possible to classify drivers according to risk group, then the insurance company can charge each group according to its expected losses. For example, the insurance company might charge the 60 drivers who seem safest of all $100 apiece, which is the average value of the damages they cause. Then the intermediate group could pay $1,000 apiece and the high-cost group $15,000 each. When the level of insurance premiums that someone pays is equal to the amount that an average person in that risk group would collect in insurance payments, the level of insurance is said to be "actuarially fair."

Classifying people into risk groups can be controversial. For example, if someone had a major automobile accident last year, should the insurance company classify that person as a high-risk driver who is likely to have similar accidents in the future, or as a low-risk driver who was just extremely unlucky? The driver is likely to claim to be low-risk, and thus someone who should be in a risk group with those who pay low insurance premiums in the future. The insurance company is likely to believe that, on average, having a major accident is a signal of being a high-risk driver, and thus try to charge this driver higher insurance premiums. The next two sections discuss the two major problems of imperfect information in insurance markets—called moral hazard and adverse selection. Both problems arise from attempts to categorize those purchasing insurance into risk groups.

The Moral Hazard Problem

Moral hazard refers to the case when people engage in riskier behavior with insurance than they would if they did not have insurance. For example, if you have health insurance that covers the cost of visiting the doctor, you may be less likely to take precautions against catching an illness that might require a doctor's visit. If you have car insurance, you will worry less about driving or parking your car in ways that make it more likely to get dented. In another example, a business without insurance might install absolute top-level security and fire sprinkler systems to guard against theft and fire. If it is insured, that same business might only install a minimum level of security and fire sprinkler systems.

We cannot eliminate moral hazard, but insurance companies have some ways of reducing its effect. Investigations to prevent insurance fraud are one way of reducing the extreme cases of moral hazard. Insurance companies can also monitor certain kinds of behavior. To return to the example from above, they might offer a business a lower rate on property insurance if the business installs a top-level security and fire sprinkler system and has those systems inspected once a year.

Another method to reduce moral hazard is to require the injured party to pay a share of the costs. For example, insurance policies often have **deductibles**, which is an amount that the insurance policyholder must pay out of his or her own pocket before the insurance coverage starts paying. For example, auto insurance might pay for all losses greater than $500. Health insurance policies often have a **copayment**, in which the policyholder must pay a small amount. For example, a person might have to pay $20 for each doctor visit, and the insurance company would cover the rest. Another method of cost sharing is **coinsurance**, which means that the insurance company covers a certain percentage of the cost. For example, insurance might pay for 80% of the costs of repairing a home after a fire, but the homeowner would pay the other 20%.

All of these forms of cost sharing discourage moral hazard, because people know that they will have to pay something out of their own pocket when they make an insurance claim. The effect can be powerful. One prominent study found that when people face moderate deductibles and copayments for their health insurance, they consume about one-third less in medical care than people who have complete insurance and do not pay anything out of pocket, presumably because deductibles and copayments reduce the level of moral hazard. However, those who consumed less health care did not seem to have any difference in health status.

A final way of reducing moral hazard, which is especially applicable to health care, is to focus on healthcare provider incentives of providers rather than consumers. Traditionally, most health care in the United States has been provided on a **fee-for-service** basis, which means that medical care providers are paid for the services they provide and are paid more if they provide additional services. However, in the last decade or so, the structure of healthcare provision has shifted to an emphasis on health maintenance organizations (HMOs). A **health maintenance organization (HMO)** provides healthcare that receives a fixed amount per person enrolled in the plan—regardless of how many services are provided. In this case, a patient with insurance has an incentive to demand more care, but the healthcare provider, which is receiving only a fixed payment, has an incentive to reduce the moral hazard problem by limiting the quantity of care provided—as long as it will not lead to worse health problems and higher costs later. Today, many doctors are paid with some combination of managed care and fee-for-service; that is, a flat amount per patient, but with additional payments for the treatment of certain health conditions.

Imperfect information is the cause of the moral hazard problem. If an insurance company had perfect information on risk, it could simply raise its premiums every time an insured party engages in riskier behavior. However, an insurance company cannot monitor all the risks that people take all the time and so, even with various checks and cost sharing, moral hazard will remain a problem.

Link It Up @⚭⚭

Visit this website (http://openstaxcollege.org/l/healtheconomics) to read about the relationship between health care and behavioral economics.

The Adverse Selection Problem

Adverse selection refers to the problem in which insurance buyers have more information about whether they are high-risk or low-risk than the insurance company does. This creates an asymmetric information problem for the insurance company because buyers who are high-risk tend to want to buy more insurance, without letting the insurance company know about their higher risk. For example, someone purchasing health insurance or life insurance probably knows more about their family's health history than an insurer can reasonably find out even with a costly investigation. Someone purchasing car insurance may know that he or she are a high-risk driver who has not yet had a major accident—but it is hard for the insurance company to collect information about how people actually drive.

To understand how adverse selection can strangle an insurance market, recall the situation of 100 drivers who are buying automobile insurance, where 60 drivers had very low damages of $100 each, 30 drivers had medium-sized accidents that cost $1,000 each, and 10 of the drivers had large accidents that cost $15,000. That would equal $186,000 in total payouts by the insurance company. Imagine that, while the insurance company knows the overall size of the losses, it cannot identify the high-risk, medium-risk, and low-risk drivers. However, the drivers themselves know their risk groups. Since there is asymmetric information between the insurance company and the drivers, the insurance company would likely set the price of insurance at $1,860 per year, to cover the average loss (not including the cost of overhead and profit). The result is that those with low risks of only $100 will likely decide not to buy insurance; after all, it makes no sense for them to pay $1,860 per year when they are likely only to experience losses of $100. Those with medium risks of a $1,000 accident will not buy insurance either. Therefore, the insurance company ends up only selling insurance for $1,860 to high-risk drivers who will average $15,000 in claims apiece, and as a consequence, the insurance company ends up losing considerable money. If the insurance company tries to raise its premiums to cover the losses of those with high risks, then those with low or medium risks will be even more discouraged from buying insurance.

Rather than face such a situation of adverse selection, the insurance company may decide not to sell insurance in this market at all. If an insurance market is to exist, then one of two things must happen. First, the insurance company might find some way of separating insurance buyers into risk groups with some degree of accuracy and charging them accordingly, which in practice often means that the insurance company tries not to sell insurance to those who may pose high risks. Another scenario is that those with low risks must buy insurance, even if they have to pay more than the actuarially fair amount for their risk group. The notion that people can be required to purchase insurance raises the issue of government laws and regulations that influence the insurance industry.

U.S. Health Care in an International Context

The United States is the only high-income country in the world where private firms pay and provide for most health insurance. Greater government involvement in the provision of health insurance is one possible way of addressing moral hazard and adverse selection problems.

The moral hazard problem with health insurance is that when people have insurance, they will demand higher quantities of health care. In the United States, private healthcare insurance tends to encourage an ever-greater demand for healthcare services, which healthcare providers are happy to fulfill. **Table 16.2** shows that on a per-person basis, U.S. healthcare spending towers above healthcare spending of other countries. Note that while healthcare expenditures in the United States are far higher than healthcare expenditures in other countries, the health outcomes in the United States, as measured by life expectancy and lower rates of childhood mortality, tend to be lower. Health outcomes, however, may not be significantly affected by healthcare expenditures. Many studies have shown that a country's health is more closely related to diet, exercise, and genetic factors than to healthcare expenditure. This fact further emphasizes that the United States is spending very large amounts on medical care with little obvious health gain.

In the U.S. health insurance market, the main way of solving this adverse selection problem is that health insurance is often sold through groups based on place of employment, or, under The Affordable Care Act, from a state government sponsored health exchange market. From an insurance company's point of view, selling insurance through an employer mixes together a group of people—some with high risks of future health problems and some with lower risks—and thus reduces the insurance firm's fear of attracting only those who have high risks. However, many small companies do not provide health insurance to their employees, and many lower-paying jobs do not include health insurance. Even after we take into account all U.S. government programs that provide health insurance for the elderly and the poor, approximately 32 million Americans were without health insurance in 2015. While a government-controlled system can avoid the adverse selection problem entirely by providing at least basic health insurance for all, another option is to mandate that all Americans buy health insurance from some provider by preventing providers from denying individuals based on preexisting conditions. The Patient Protection and Affordable Care Act adopted this approach, which we will discuss later on in this chapter.

Country	Health Care Spending per Person (in 2008)	Male Life Expectancy at Birth, in Years (in 2012)	Female Life Expectancy at Birth, in Years (in 2012)	Male Chance of Dying before Age 5, per 1,000 (in 2012)	Female Chance of Dying before Age 5, per 1,000 (in 2012)
United States	$7,538	76	81	8	7
Germany	$3,737	78	83	4	4
France	$3,696	78	85	4	4

Table 16.2 A Comparison of Healthcare Spending Across Select Countries (Source: 2010 OECD study and World Fact Book)

Country	Health Care Spending per Person (in 2008)	Male Life Expectancy at Birth, in Years (in 2012)	Female Life Expectancy at Birth, in Years (in 2012)	Male Chance of Dying before Age 5, per 1,000 (in 2012)	Female Chance of Dying before Age 5, per 1,000 (in 2012)
Canada	$4,079	79	84	6	5
United Kingdom	$3,129	78	83	5	4

Table 16.2 A Comparison of Healthcare Spending Across Select Countries   (Source: 2010 OECD study and World Fact Book)

At its best, the largely private U.S. system of health insurance and healthcare delivery provides an extraordinarily high quality of care, along with generating a seemingly endless parade of life-saving innovations. However, the system also struggles to control its high costs and to provide basic medical care to all. Other countries have lower costs and more equal access, but they often struggle to provide rapid access to health care and to offer the near-miracles of the most up-to-date medical care. The challenge is a healthcare system that strikes the right balance between quality, access, and cost.

Government Regulation of Insurance

The U.S. insurance industry is primarily regulated at the state level. Since 1871 there has been a National Association of Insurance Commissioners that brings together these state regulators to exchange information and strategies. The state insurance regulators typically attempt to accomplish two things: to keep the price of insurance low and to ensure that everyone has insurance. These goals, however, can conflict with each other and also become easily entangled in politics.

If insurance premiums are set at actuarially fair levels, so that people end up paying an amount that accurately reflects their risk group, certain people will end up paying considerable amounts. For example, if health insurance companies were trying to cover people who already have a chronic disease like AIDS, or who were elderly, they would charge these groups very high premiums for health insurance, because their expected health care costs are quite high. Women in the age bracket 18–44 consume, on average, about 65% more in health care spending than men. Young male drivers have more car accidents than young female drivers. Thus, actuarially fair insurance would tend to charge young men much more for car insurance than young women. Because people in high-risk groups would find themselves charged so heavily for insurance, they might choose not to buy insurance at all.

State insurance regulators have sometimes reacted by passing rules that attempt to set low premiums for insurance. Over time, however, the fundamental law of insurance must hold: the average amount individuals receive cannot exceed the average amount paid in premiums. When rules are passed to keep premiums low, insurance companies try to avoid insuring any high-risk or even medium-risk parties. If a state legislature passes strict rules requiring insurance companies to sell to everyone at low prices, the insurance companies always have the option of withdrawing from doing business in that state. For example, the insurance regulators in New Jersey are well-known for attempting to keep auto insurance premiums low, and more than 20 different insurance companies stopped doing business in the state in the late 1990s and early 2000s. Similarly, in 2009, State Farm announced that it was withdrawing from selling property insurance in Florida.

In short, government regulators cannot force companies to charge low prices and provide high levels of insurance coverage—and thus take losses—for a sustained period of time. If insurance premiums are set below the actuarially fair level for a certain group, some other group will have to make up the difference. There are two other groups who can make up the difference: taxpayers or other insurance buyers.

In some industries, the U.S. government has decided free markets will not provide insurance at an affordable price, and so the government pays for it directly. For example, private health insurance is too expensive for many people whose incomes are too low. To combat this, the U.S. government, together with the states, runs the Medicaid program, which provides health care to those with low incomes. Private health insurance also does not work well for the elderly, because their average health care costs can be very high. Thus, the U.S. government started the Medicare program, which provides health insurance to all those over age 65. Other government-funded health-care programs are aimed at military veterans, as an added benefit, and children in families with relatively low incomes.

Another common government intervention in insurance markets is to require that everyone buy certain kinds of insurance. For example, most states legally require car owners to buy auto insurance. Likewise, when a bank loans someone money to buy a home, the person is typically required to have homeowner's insurance, which protects against fire and other physical damage (like hailstorms) to the home. A legal requirement that everyone must buy insurance means that insurance companies do not need to worry that those with low risks will avoid buying insurance. Since insurance companies do not need to fear adverse selection, they can set their prices based on an average for the market, and those with lower risks will, to some extent, end up subsidizing those with higher risks. However, even when laws are passed requiring people to purchase insurance, insurance companies cannot be compelled to sell insurance to everyone who asks—at least not at low cost. Thus, insurance companies will still try to avoid selling insurance to those with high risks whenever possible.

The government cannot pass laws that make the problems of moral hazard and adverse selection disappear, but the government can make political decisions that certain groups should have insurance, even though the private market would not otherwise provide that insurance. Also, the government can impose the costs of that decision on taxpayers or on other buyers of insurance.

The Patient Protection and Affordable Care Act

In March of 2010, President Obama signed into law the Patient Protection and Affordable Care Act (PPACA). The government started to phase in this highly contentious law over time starting in October of 2013. The goal of the act is to bring the United States closer to universal coverage. Some of the key features of the plan include:

- Individual mandate: All individuals, who do not receive health care through their employer or through a government program (for example, Medicare), are required to have health insurance or pay a fine. The individual mandate's goal was to reduce the adverse selection problem and keep prices down by requiring all consumers—even the healthiest ones—to have health insurance. Without the need to guard against adverse selection (whereby only the riskiest consumers buy insurance) by raising prices, health insurance companies could provide more reasonable plans to their customers.

- Each state is required to have health insurance exchanges, or utilize the federal exchange, whereby insurance companies compete for business. The goal of the exchanges is to improve competition in the market for health insurance.

- Employer mandate: All employers with more than 50 employees must offer health insurance to their employees.

The Affordable Care Act (ACA) is funded through additional taxes that include:

- Increasing the Medicare tax by 0.9 percent and adding a 3.8 percent tax on unearned income for high income taxpayers.

- Charging an annual fee on health insurance providers.

- Imposing other taxes such as a 2.3% tax on manufacturers and importers of certain medical devices.

Many people and politicians, including Donald Trump, have sought to overturn the bill. Those who oppose the bill believe it violates an individual's right to choose whether to have insurance or not. In 2012, a number of states challenged the law on the basis that the individual mandate provision is unconstitutional. In June 2012, the U.S. Supreme Court ruled in a 5–4 decision that the individual mandate is actually a tax, so it is constitutional as the federal government has the right to tax the populace.

Bring it Home

What's the Big Deal with Obamacare?

What is it that the Affordable Care Act (ACA) will actually do? To begin with, we should note that it is a massively complex law, with a large number of parts, some of which the Obama administration implemented immediately, and others that the government is supposed to phase in every year from 2013 through 2020.

This OpenStax book is available for free at http://cnx.org/content/col12122/1.4

Three of these parts are coverage for the uninsured—those without health insurance, coverage for individuals with preexisting conditions, and the so-called employer and individual mandates, which require employers to offer and people to purchase health insurance. However, with the new Trump administration, the ACA is under scrutiny and many components face repeal or drastic overhauling.

As we noted in the chapter, people face ever-increasing healthcare costs in the United States. Over the years, the ranks of the uninsured in the United States have grown as rising prices have pushed employers and individuals out of the market. Insurance companies have increasingly used pre-existing medical conditions to determine if someone is high risk, for whom insurance companies either charge higher prices, or they choose to deny insurance coverage to these individuals. Whatever the cause, we noted at the beginning of the chapter that prior to the ACA, more than 32 million Americans were uninsured. People who are uninsured tend to use emergency rooms for treatment—the most expensive form of healthcare, which has contributed significantly to rising costs.

The ACA introduced regulations designed to control increases in healthcare costs. One example is a cap on the amount healthcare providers can spend on administrative costs. Another is a requirement that healthcare providers switch to electronic medical records (EMRs), which will reduce administrative costs.

The ACA required that states establish health insurance exchanges, or markets, where people without health insurance, and businesses that do not provide it for their employees, can shop for different insurance plans. The purpose of these exchanges was to increase competition in insurance markets and thus reduce prices of policies.

Finally, the ACA mandated that people with preexisting conditions could no longer be denied health insurance. The U.S. Department of Health and Human Services estimates that the those without insurance in the US has fallen from 20.3% in 2012 to 11.5% in 2016. Accordingly, 20 million Americans gained coverage under the ACA.

What was the cost of this increased coverage and how was it paid? An insurance policy works by insuring against the possibility of needing healthcare. If there are high risk individuals in the insurance pool, the pool must be expanded to include enough low risk individuals to keep average premiums affordable. To that end, the ACA imposed the individual mandate, requiring all individuals to purchase insurance (or pay a penalty) whether they were high risk or not. Many young adults would choose to skip health insurance since the likelihood of their needing significant healthcare is small. The individual mandate brought in a significant amount of money to pay for the ACA. In addition, there were three other funding sources. The ACA took $716 billion which otherwise would have gone to Medicare spending. The ACA also increased the Medicare tax that wealthy Americans paid by an additional 0.9%. Furthermore, the government levied a 40% excess tax on high end (Cadillac) healthcare plans valued above a certain amount. Despite these funding sources, the Congressional Budget Office estimates that the ACA will increase the federal debt by $137 billion over the next decade.

The impact of the Patient Protection and Affordable Care Act has been a rise in Americans with health insurance. However, the increased costs for those buying Premium (Cadillac) health insurance plans, increased tax on the wealthy, and increased deficit spending, the ACA faces substantial opposition. The Trump administration vowed to repeal it on the campaign trail but no alternative bill has made its way before congress. Only time will tell if the Affordable Care Act will leave a legacy or will quickly be swept by the wayside, jeopardizing the 20 million newly insured Americans.

At the time of this writing, the final impact of the Patient Protection and Affordable Care Act is not clear. Millions of previously uninsured Americans now have coverage, but the increased cost of premium health insurance plans, increased Medicare tax on the wealthy and increased deficit spending have created significant political opposition. The Trump administration vowed to repeal the ACA, but his administration has not announced an alternative. Only time will tell.

KEY TERMS

adverse selection when groups with inherently higher risks than the average person seek out insurance, thus straining the insurance system

asymmetric information a situation where the seller or the buyer has more information than the other regarding the quality of the item for sale

coinsurance when an insurance policyholder pays a percentage of a loss, and the insurance company pays the remaining cost

collateral something valuable—often property or equipment—that a lender would have a right to seize and sell if the buyer does not repay the loan

copayment when an insurance policyholder must pay a small amount for each service, before insurance covers the rest

cosigner another person or firm who legally pledges to repay some or all of the money on a loan if the original borrower does not

deductible an amount that the insurance policyholders must pay out of their own pocket before the insurance coverage pays anything

fee-for-service when medical care providers are paid according to the services they provide

health maintenance organization (HMO) an organization that provides health care and is paid a fixed amount per person enrolled in the plan—regardless of how many services are provided

imperfect information a situation where either the buyer or the seller, or both, are uncertain about the qualities of what they are buying and selling

insurance method of protecting a person from financial loss, whereby policy holders make regular payments to an insurance entity; the insurance firm then remunerates a group member who suffers significant financial damage from an event covered by the policy

money-back guarantee a promise that the seller will refund the buyer's money under certain conditions

moral hazard when people have insurance against a certain event, they are less likely to guard against that event occurring

occupational license licenses issued by government agencies, which indicate that a worker has completed a certain type of education or passed a certain test

premium payment made to an insurance company

risk group a group that shares roughly the same risks of an adverse event occurring

service contract the buyer pays an extra amount and the seller agrees to fix anything specified in the contract that goes wrong for a set time period

warranty a promise to fix or replace the good for a certain period of time

KEY CONCEPTS AND SUMMARY

16.1 The Problem of Imperfect Information and Asymmetric Information

Many make economic transactions in a situation of imperfect information, where either the buyer, the seller, or both

This OpenStax book is available for free at http://cnx.org/content/col12122/1.4

are less than 100% certain about the qualities of what they are buying or selling. When information about the quality of products is highly imperfect, it may be difficult for a market to exist.

A "lemon" is a product that turns out, after the purchase, to have low quality. When the seller has more accurate information about the product's quality than the buyer, the buyer will be hesitant to buy, out of fear of purchasing a "lemon."

Markets have many ways to deal with imperfect information. In goods markets, buyers facing imperfect information about products may depend upon money-back guarantees, warranties, service contracts, and reputation. In labor markets, employers facing imperfect information about potential employees may turn to resumes, recommendations, occupational licenses for certain jobs, and employment for trial periods. In capital markets, lenders facing imperfect information about borrowers may require detailed loan applications and credit checks, cosigners, and collateral.

16.2 Insurance and Imperfect Information

Insurance is a way of sharing risk. People in a group pay premiums for insurance against some unpleasant event, and those in the group who actually experience the unpleasant event then receive some compensation. The fundamental law of insurance is that what the average person pays in over time cannot be less than what the average person gets out. In an actuarially fair insurance policy, the premiums that a person pays to the insurance company are the same as the average amount of benefits for a person in that risk group. Moral hazard arises in insurance markets because those who are insured against a risk will have less reason to take steps to avoid the costs from that risk.

Many insurance policies have deductibles, copayments, or coinsurance. A deductible is the maximum amount that the policyholder must pay out-of-pocket before the insurance company pays the rest of the bill. A copayment is a flat fee that an insurance policy-holder must pay before receiving services. Coinsurance requires the policyholder to pay a certain percentage of costs. Deductibles, copayments, and coinsurance reduce moral hazard by requiring the insured party to bear some of the costs before collecting insurance benefits.

In a fee-for-service health financing system, medical care providers receive reimbursement according to the cost of services they provide. An alternative method of organizing health care is through health maintenance organizations (HMOs), where medical care providers receive reimbursement according to the number of patients they handle, and it is up to the providers to allocate resources between patients who receive more or fewer health care services. Adverse selection arises in insurance markets when insurance buyers know more about the risks they face than does the insurance company. As a result, the insurance company runs the risk that low-risk parties will avoid its insurance because it is too costly for them, while high-risk parties will embrace it because it looks like a good deal to them.

SELF-CHECK QUESTIONS

1. For each of the following purchases, say whether you would expect the degree of imperfect information to be relatively high or relatively low:
   a. Buying apples at a roadside stand
   b. Buying dinner at the neighborhood restaurant around the corner
   c. Buying a used laptop computer at a garage sale
   d. Ordering flowers over the internet for your friend in a different city

2. Why is there asymmetric information in the labor market? What signals can an employer look for that might indicate the traits they are seeking in a new employee?

3. Why is it difficult to measure health outcomes?

REVIEW QUESTIONS

4. Why might it be difficult for a buyer and seller to agree on a price when imperfect information exists?

5. What do economists (and used-car dealers) mean by a "lemon"?

6. What are some ways a seller of goods might reassure a possible buyer who is faced with imperfect information?

7. What are some ways a seller of labor (that is, someone looking for a job) might reassure a possible employer who is faced with imperfect information?

8. What are some ways that someone looking for a loan might reassure a bank that is faced with imperfect information about whether the borrower will repay the loan?

9. What is an insurance premium?

10. In an insurance system, would you expect each person to receive in benefits pretty much what they pay in premiums or is it just that the average benefits paid will equal the average premiums paid?

11. What is an actuarially fair insurance policy?

12. What is the problem of moral hazard?

13. How can moral hazard lead to more costly insurance premiums than one was expected?

14. Define deductibles, copayments, and coinsurance.

15. How can deductibles, copayments, and coinsurance reduce moral hazard?

16. What is the key difference between a fee-for-service healthcare system and a system based on health maintenance organizations?

17. How might adverse selection make it difficult for an insurance market to operate?

18. What are some of the metrics economists use to measure health outcomes?

CRITICAL THINKING QUESTIONS

19. You are on the board of directors of a private high school, which is hiring new tenth-grade science teachers. As you think about hiring someone for a job, what are some mechanisms you might use to overcome the problem of imperfect information?

20. A website offers a place for people to buy and sell emeralds, but information about emeralds can be quite imperfect. The website then enacts a rule that all sellers in the market must pay for two independent examinations of their emerald, which are available to the customer for inspection.

    a. How would you expect this improved information to affect demand for emeralds on this website?

    b. How would you expect this improved information to affect the quantity of high-quality emeralds sold on the website?

21. How do you think the problem of moral hazard might have affected the safety of sports such as football and boxing when safety regulations started requiring that players wear more padding?

22. To what sorts of customers would an insurance company offer a policy with a high copay? What about a high premium with a lower copay?

PROBLEMS

23. Using Exercise 16.20, sketch the effects in parts (a) and (b) on a single supply and demand diagram. What prediction would you make about how the improved information alters the equilibrium quantity and price?

This OpenStax book is available for free at http://cnx.org/content/col12122/1.4

24. Imagine that you can divide 50-year-old men into two groups: those who have a family history of cancer and those who do not. For the purposes of this example, say that 20% of a group of 1,000 men have a family history of cancer, and these men have one chance in 50 of dying in the next year, while the other 80% of men have one chance in 200 of dying in the next year. The insurance company is selling a policy that will pay $100,000 to the estate of anyone who dies in the next year.

  a. If the insurance company were selling life insurance separately to each group, what would be the actuarially fair premium for each group?

  b. If an insurance company were offering life insurance to the entire group, but could not find out about family cancer histories, what would be the actuarially fair premium for the group as a whole?

  c. What will happen to the insurance company if it tries to charge the actuarially fair premium to the group as a whole rather than to each group separately?

This OpenStax book is available for free at http://cnx.org/content/col12122/1.4

17 | Financial Markets

Figure 17.1 Building Home Equity Many people choose to purchase their home rather than rent. This chapter explores how the global financial crisis has influenced home ownership. (Credit: modification of work by Diana Parkhouse/Flickr Creative Commones)

Bring it Home

The Housing Bubble and the 2007 Financial Crisis

In 2006, housing equity in the United States peaked at $13 trillion. That means that the market prices of homes, less what was still owed on the loans they used to buy these houses, equaled $13 trillion. This was a very good number, since the equity represented the value of the financial asset most U.S. citizens owned.

However, by 2008 this number declined to $8.8 trillion, and it plummeted further still in 2009. Combined with the decline in value of other financial assets held by U.S. citizens, by 2010, U.S. homeowners' wealth had shrunk $14 trillion! This is a staggering result, and it affected millions of lives: people had to alter their retirement, housing, and other important consumption decisions. Just about every other large economy in the world suffered a decline in the market value of financial assets, as a result of the 2008-2009 global financial crisis.

This chapter will explain why people purchase houses (other than as a place to live), why they buy other types of financial assets, and why businesses sell those financial assets in the first place. The chapter will also give us insight into why financial markets and assets go through boom and bust cycles like the one we described here.

Introduction to Financial Markets

In this chapter, you will learn about:

- How Businesses Raise Financial Capital

- How Households Supply Financial Capital

- How to Accumulate Personal Wealth

When a firm needs to buy new equipment or build a new facility, it often must go to the financial market to raise funds. Usually firms will add capacity during an economic expansion when profits are on the rise and consumer demand is high. Business investment is one of the critical ingredients needed to sustain economic growth. Even in the sluggish 2009 economy, U.S. firms invested $1.4 trillion in new equipment and structures, in the hope that these investments would generate profits in the years ahead.

Between the end of the recession in 2009 through the second quarter 2013, profits for the S&P 500 companies grew to 9.7 % despite the weak economy, with cost cutting and reductions in input costs driving much of that amount, according to the *Wall Street Journal*. **Figure 17.2** shows corporate profits after taxes (adjusted for inventory and capital consumption). Despite the steep decline in quarterly net profit in 2008, profits have recovered and surpassed pre-recession levels.

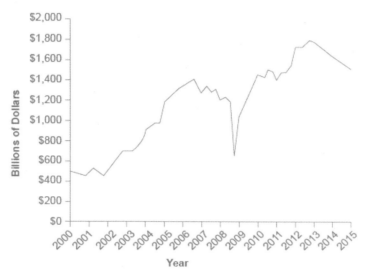

Figure 17.2 Corporate Profits After Tax (Adjusted for Inventory and Capital Consumption) Prior to 2008, corporate profits after tax more often than not increased each year. There was a significant drop in profits during 2008 and into 2009. The profit trend has since continued to increase each year, though at a less steady or consistent rate. (Source: Federal Reserve Economic Data (FRED) https://research.stlouisfed.org/fred2/series/CPATAX)

Many firms, from huge companies like General Motors to startup firms writing computer software, do not have the financial resources within the firm to make all the desired investments. These firms need financial capital from outside investors, and they are willing to pay interest for the opportunity to obtain a rate of return on the investment for that financial capital.

On the other side of the financial capital market, financial capital suppliers, like households, wish to use their savings in a way that will provide a return. Individuals cannot, however, take the few thousand dollars that they save in any given year, write a letter to General Motors or some other firm, and negotiate to invest their money with that firm. Financial capital markets bridge this gap: that is, they find ways to take the inflow of funds from many separate financial capital suppliers and transform it into the funds of financial capital demanders desire. Such financial markets include stocks, bonds, bank loans, and other financial investments.

Visit this website (http://openstaxcollege.org/l/marketoverview) to read more about financial markets.

Our perspective then shifts to consider how these financial investments appear to capital suppliers such as the households that are saving funds. Households have a range of investment options: bank accounts, certificates of deposit, money market mutual funds, bonds, stocks, stock and bond mutual funds, housing, and even tangible assets like gold. Finally, the chapter investigates two methods for becoming rich: a quick and easy method that does not work very well at all, and a slow, reliable method that can work very well over a lifetime.

17.1 | How Businesses Raise Financial Capital

By the end of this section, you will be able to:

- Describe financial capital and how it relates to profits
- Discuss the purpose and process of borrowing, bonds, and corporate stock
- Explain how firms choose between sources of financial capital

Firms often make decisions that involve spending money in the present and expecting to earn profits in the future. Examples include when a firm buys a machine that will last 10 years, or builds a new plant that will last for 30 years, or starts a research and development project. Firms can raise the financial capital they need to pay for such projects in four main ways: (1) from early-stage investors; (2) by reinvesting profits; (3) by borrowing through banks or bonds; and (4) by selling stock. When business owners choose financial capital sources, they also choose how to pay for them.

Early-Stage Financial Capital

Firms that are just beginning often have an idea or a prototype for a product or service to sell, but few customers, or even no customers at all, and thus are not earning profits. Such firms face a difficult problem when it comes to raising financial capital: How can a firm that has not yet demonstrated any ability to earn profits pay a rate of return to financial investors?

For many small businesses, the original source of money is the business owner. Someone who decides to start a restaurant or a gas station, for instance, might cover the startup costs by dipping into his or her own bank account, or by borrowing money (perhaps using a home as collateral). Alternatively, many cities have a network of well-to-do individuals, known as "angel investors," who will put their own money into small new companies at an early development stage, in exchange for owning some portion of the firm.

Venture capital firms make financial investments in new companies that are still relatively small in size, but that have potential to grow substantially. These firms gather money from a variety of individual or institutional investors, including banks, institutions like college endowments, insurance companies that hold financial reserves, and corporate pension funds. Venture capital firms do more than just supply money to small startups. They also provide advice on potential products, customers, and key employees. Typically, a venture capital fund invests in a number of firms, and then investors in that fund receive returns according to how the fund as a whole performs.

The amount of money invested in venture capital fluctuates substantially from year to year: as one example, venture capital firms invested more than $48.3 billion in 2014, according to the National Venture Capital Association. All early-stage investors realize that the majority of small startup businesses will never hit it big; many of them will go out of business within a few months or years. They also know that getting in on the ground floor of a few huge successes like a Netflix or an Amazon.com can make up for multiple failures. Therefore, early-stage investors are willing to take large risks in order to position themselves to gain substantial returns on their investment.

Profits as a Source of Financial Capital

If firms are earning profits (their revenues are greater than costs), they can choose to reinvest some of these profits in equipment, structures, and research and development. For many established companies, reinvesting their own profits is one primary source of financial capital. Companies and firms just getting started may have numerous attractive investment opportunities, but few current profits to invest. Even large firms can experience a year or two of earning low profits or even suffering losses, but unless the firm can find a steady and reliable financial capital source so that it can continue making real investments in tough times, the firm may not survive until better times arrive. Firms often need to find financial capital sources other than profits.

Borrowing: Banks and Bonds

When a firm has a record of at least earning significant revenues, and better still of earning profits, the firm can make a credible promise to pay interest, and so it becomes possible for the firm to borrow money. Firms have two main borrowing methods: banks and bonds.

A bank loan for a firm works in much the same way as a loan for an individual who is buying a car or a house. The firm borrows an amount of money and then promises to repay it, including some rate of interest, over a predetermined period of time. If the firm fails to make its loan payments, the bank (or banks) can often take the firm to court and require it to sell its buildings or equipment to make the loan payments.

Another source of financial capital is a bond. A **bond** is a financial contract: a borrower agrees to repay the amount that it borrowed and also an interest rate over a period of time in the future. A **corporate bond** is issued by firms, but bonds are also issued by various levels of government. For example, a **municipal bond** is issued by cities, a state bond by U.S. states, and a **Treasury bond** by the federal government through the U.S. Department of the Treasury. A bond specifies an amount that one will borrow, the interest rate that one will pay, and the time until repayment.

A large company, for example, might issue bonds for $10 million. The firm promises to make interest payments at an annual rate of 8%, or $800,000 per year and then, after 10 years, will repay the $10 million it originally borrowed. When a firm issues bonds, the total amount it divides. A firm seeks to borrow $50 million by issuing bonds, might actually issue 10,000 bonds of $5,000 each. In this way, an individual investor could, in effect, loan the firm $5,000, or any multiple of that amount. Anyone who owns a bond and receives the interest payments is called a **bondholder**. If a firm issues bonds and fails to make the promised interest payments, the bondholders can take the firm to court and require it to pay, even if the firm needs to raise the money by selling buildings or equipment. However, there is no guarantee the firm will have sufficient assets to pay off the bonds. The bondholders may recoup only a portion of what it loaned the firm.

Bank borrowing is more customized than issuing bonds, so it often works better for relatively small firms. The bank can get to know the firm extremely well—often because the bank can monitor sales and expenses quite accurately by looking at deposits and withdrawals. Relatively large and well-known firms often issue bonds instead. They use bonds to raise new financial capital that pays for investments, or to raise capital to pay off old bonds, or to buy other firms. However, the idea that firms or individuals use banks for relatively smaller loans and bonds for larger loans is not an ironclad rule: sometimes groups of banks make large loans and sometimes relatively small and lesser-known firms issue bonds.

Corporate Stock and Public Firms

A **corporation** is a business that "incorporates"—that is owned by shareholders that have limited liability for the company's debt but share in its profits (and losses). Corporations may be private or public, and may or may not have publicly traded stock. They may raise funds to finance their operations or new investments by raising capital through selling stock or issuing bonds.

Those who buy the stock become the firm's owners, or **shareholders**. **Stock** represents firm ownership; that is, a person who owns 100% of a company's stock, by definition, owns the entire company. The company's stock is divided into **shares**. Corporate giants like IBM, AT&T, Ford, General Electric, Microsoft, Merck, and Exxon all have millions of stock shares. In most large and well-known firms, no individual owns a majority of the stock shares. Instead, large numbers of shareholders—even those who hold thousands of shares—each have only a small slice of the firm's overall ownership.

When a large number of shareholders own a company, there are three questions to ask:

1. How and when does the company obtain money from its sale?

2. What rate of return does the company promise to pay when it sells stock?

3. Who makes decisions in a company owned by a large number of shareholders?

First, a firm receives money from the stock sale only when the company sells its own stock to the public (the public includes individuals, mutual funds, insurance companies, and pension funds). We call a firm's first stock sale to the public an **initial public offering (IPO)**. The IPO is important for two reasons. For one, the IPO, and any stock issued thereafter, such as stock held as treasury stock (shares that a company keeps in their own treasury) or new stock issued later as a secondary offering, provides the funds to repay the early-stage investors, like the angel investors and the venture capital firms. A venture capital firm may have a 40% ownership in the firm. When the firm sells stock, the venture capital firm sells its part ownership of the firm to the public. A second reason for the importance of the IPO is that it provides the established company with financial capital for substantially expanding its operations.

However, most of the time when one buys and sells corporate stock the firm receives no financial return at all. If you buy General Motors stock, you almost certainly buy them from the current share owner, and General Motors does not receive any of your money. This pattern should not seem particularly odd. After all, if you buy a house, the current owner receives your money, not the original house builder. Similarly, when you buy stock shares, you are buying a small slice of the firm's ownership from the existing owner—and the firm that originally issued the stock is not a part of this transaction.

Second, when a firm decides to issue stock, it must recognize that investors will expect to receive a rate of return. That rate of return can come in two forms. A firm can make a direct payment to its shareholders, called a **dividend**. Alternatively, a financial investor might buy a share of stock in Wal-Mart for $45 and then later sell it to someone else for $60, for $15 gain. We call the increase in the stock value (or of any asset) between when one buys and sells it a **capital gain**.

Third: Who makes the decisions about when a firm will issue stock, or pay dividends, or re-invest profits? To understand the answers to these questions, it is useful to separate firms into two groups: private and public.

A **private company** is owned by the people who run it on a day-to-day basis. Individuals can run a private company. We call this a **sole proprietorship**. If a group runs it, we call it a **partnership**. A private company can also be a corporation, but with no publicly issued stock. A small law firm run by one person, even if it employs some other lawyers, would be a sole proprietorship. Partners may jointly own a larger law firm. Most private companies are relatively small, but there are some large private corporations, with tens of billions of dollars in annual sales, that do not have publicly issued stock, such as farm products dealer Cargill, the Mars candy company, and the Bechtel engineering and construction firm.

When a firm decides to sell stock, which financial investors can buy and sell, we call it a **public company**. Shareholders own a public company. Since the shareholders are a very broad group, often consisting of thousands or even millions of investors, the shareholders vote for a board of directors, who in turn hire top executives to run the firm on a day-to-day basis. The more stock a shareholder owns, the more votes that shareholder is entitled to cast for the company's board of directors.

In theory, the board of directors helps to ensure that the firm runs in the interests of the true owners—the shareholders. However, the top executives who run the firm have a strong voice in choosing the candidates who will serve on their board of directors. After all, few shareholders are knowledgeable enough or have enough personal incentive to spend energy and money nominating alternative board members.

How Firms Choose between Financial Capital Sources

There are clear patterns in how businesses raise financial capital. We can explain these patterns in terms of imperfect information, which as we discussed in Information, Risk, and Insurance, is a situation where buyers and sellers in a market do not both have full and equal information. Those who are actually running a firm will almost always have more information about whether the firm is likely to earn profits in the future than outside investors who provide financial capital.

Any young startup firm is a risk. Some startup firms are only a little more than an idea on paper. The firm's founders inevitably have better information about how hard they are willing to work, and whether the firm is likely to succeed, than anyone else. When the founders invested their own money into the firm, they demonstrate a belief in its prospects. At this early stage, angel investors and venture capitalists try to overcome the imperfect information, at least in part, by knowing the managers and their business plan personally and by giving them advice.

Accurate information is sometimes not available because **corporate governance**, the name economists give to the institutions that are supposed to watch over top executives, fails, as the following Clear It Up feature on Lehman Brothers shows.

How did lack of corporate governance lead to the Lehman Brothers failure?

In 2008, Lehman Brothers was the fourth largest U.S. investment bank, with 25,000 employees. The firm had been in business for 164 years. On September 15, 2008, Lehman Brothers filed for Chapter 11 bankruptcy protection. There are many causes of the Lehman Brothers failure. One area of apparent failure was the lack of oversight by the Board of Directors to keep managers from undertaking excessive risk. We can attribute part of the oversight failure, according to Tim Geithner's April 10, 2010, testimony to Congress, to the Executive Compensation Committee's emphasis on short-term gains without enough consideration of the risks. In addition, according to the court examiner's report, the Lehman Brother's Board of Directors paid too little attention to the details of the operations of Lehman Brothers and also had limited financial service experience.

The board of directors, elected by the shareholders, is supposed to be the first line of corporate governance and oversight for top executives. A second institution of corporate governance is the auditing firm the company hires to review the company's financial records and certify that everything looks reasonable. A third institution of corporate governance is outside investors, especially large shareholders like those who invest large mutual funds or pension funds. In the case of Lehman Brothers, corporate governance failed to provide investors with accurate financial information about the firm's operations.

As a firm becomes at least somewhat established and its strategy appears likely to lead to profits in the near future, knowing the individual managers and their business plans on a personal basis becomes less important, because information has become more widely available regarding the company's products, revenues, costs, and profits. As a result, other outside investors who do not know the managers personally, like bondholders and shareholders, are more willing to provide financial capital to the firm.

At this point, a firm must often choose how to access financial capital. It may choose to borrow from a bank, issue bonds, or issue stock. The great disadvantage of borrowing money from a bank or issuing bonds is that the firm commits to scheduled interest payments, whether or not it has sufficient income. The great advantage of borrowing money is that the firm maintains control of its operations and is not subject to shareholders. Issuing stock involves selling off company ownership to the public and becoming responsible to a board of directors and the shareholders.

The benefit of issuing stock is that a small and growing firm increases its visibility in the financial markets and can access large amounts of financial capital for expansion, without worrying about repaying this money. If the firm is successful and profitable, the board of directors will need to decide upon a dividend payout or how to reinvest profits to further grow the company. Issuing and placing stock is expensive, requires the expertise of investment bankers and attorneys, and entails compliance with reporting requirements to shareholders and government agencies, such as the federal Securities and Exchange Commission (SEC).

17.2 | How Households Supply Financial Capital

By the end of this section, you will be able to:
- Show the relationship between savers, banks, and borrowers
- Calculate bond yield
- Contrast bonds, stocks, mutual funds, and assets
- Explain the tradeoffs between return and risk

This OpenStax book is available for free at http://cnx.org/content/col12122/1.4

The ways in which firms would prefer to raise funds are only half the story of financial markets. The other half is what those households and individuals who supply funds desire, and how they perceive the available choices. The focus of our discussion now shifts from firms on the demand side of financial capital markets to households on the supply side of those markets. We can divide the mechanisms for savings available to households into several categories: deposits in bank accounts; bonds; stocks; money market mutual funds; stock and bond mutual funds; and housing and other tangible assets like owning gold. We need to analyze each of these investments in terms of three factors: (1) the expected rate of return it will pay; (2) the risk that the return will be much lower or higher than expected; and (3) the investment's **liquidity**, which refers to how easily one can exchange money or financial assets for a good or service. We will do this analysis as we discuss each of these investments in the sections below. First, however, we need to understand the difference between expected rate of return, risk, and actual rate of return.

Expected Rate of Return, Risk, and Actual Rate of Return

The **expected rate of return** refers to how much a project or an investment is expected to return to the investor, either in future interest payments, capital gains, or increased profitability. It is usually the average return over a period of time, usually in years or even decades. We normally measure it as a percentage rate. **Risk** measures the uncertainty of that project's profitability. There are several types of risk, including default risk and interest rate risk. Default risk, as its name suggests, is the risk that the borrower fails to pay back the bond or loan. Interest rate risk is the danger that you might buy a long term bond at a 6% interest rate right before market rates suddenly rise, so had you waited, you could have received a similar bond that paid 9%. A high-risk investment is one for which a wide range of potential payoffs is reasonably probable. A low-risk investment may have actual returns that are fairly close to its expected rate of return year after year. A high-risk investment will have actual returns that are much higher than the expected rate of return in some months or years and much lower in other months or years. The **actual rate of return** refers to the total rate of return, including capital gains and interest paid on an investment at the end of a time period.

Bank Accounts

An intermediary is one who stands between two other parties. For example, a person who arranges a blind date between two other people is one kind of intermediary. In financial capital markets, banks are an example of a **financial intermediary**—that is, an institution that operates between a saver who deposits funds in a bank and a borrower who receives a loan from that bank. When a bank serves as a financial intermediary, unlike the situation with a couple on a blind date, the saver and the borrower never meet. In fact, it is not even possible to make direct connections between those who deposit funds in banks and those who borrow from banks, because all deposited funds end up in one big pool, which the financial institution then lends out.

Figure 17.3 illustrates the position of banks as a financial intermediary, with a pattern of deposits flowing into a bank and loans flowing out, and then repayment of the loans flowing back to the bank, with interest payments for the original savers.

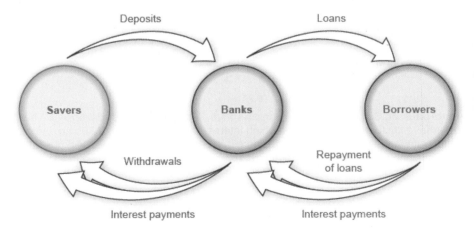

Figure 17.3 Banks as Financial Intermediaries Banks are a financial intermediary because they stand between savers and borrowers. Savers place deposits with banks, and then receive interest payments and withdraw money. Borrowers receive loans from banks, and repay the loans with interest.

Banks offer a range of accounts to serve different needs. A **checking account** typically pays little or no interest, but it facilitates transactions by giving you easy access to your money, either by writing a check or by using a **debit card** (that is, a card which works like a credit card, except that purchases are immediately deducted from your checking account rather than billed separately through a credit card company). A **savings account** typically pays some interest rate, but getting the money typically requires you to make a trip to the bank or an automatic teller machine (or you can access the funds electronically). The lines between checking and savings accounts have blurred in the last couple of decades, as many banks offer checking accounts that will pay an interest rate similar to a savings account if you keep a certain minimum amount in the account, or conversely, offer savings accounts that allow you to write at least a few checks per month.

Another way to deposit savings at a bank is to use a **certificate of deposit (CD)**. With a CD, you agree to deposit a certain amount of money, often measured in thousands of dollars, in the account for a stated period of time, typically ranging from a few months to several years. In exchange, the bank agrees to pay a higher interest rate than for a regular savings account. While you can withdraw the money before the allotted time, as the advertisements for CDs always warn, there is "a substantial penalty for early withdrawal."

Figure 17.4 shows the annual rate of interest paid on a six-month, one-year, and five-year CD since 1984, as reported by Bankrate.com. The interest rates that savings accounts pay are typically a little lower than the CD rate, because financial investors need to receive a slightly higher rate of interest as compensation for promising to leave deposits untouched for a period of time in a CD, and thus forfeiting some liquidity.

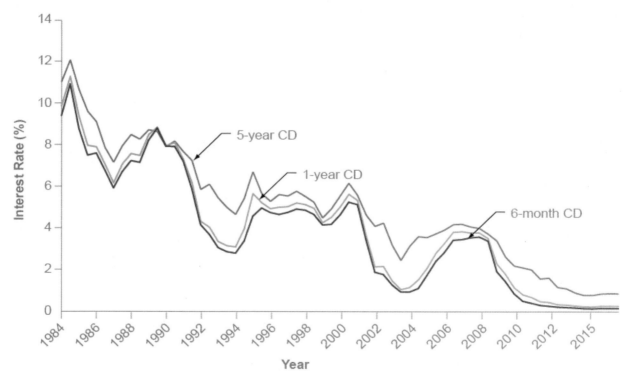

Figure 17.4 Interest Rates on Six-Month, One-Year, and Five-Year Certificates of Deposit The interest rates on certificates of deposit have fluctuated over time. The high interest rates of the early 1980s are indicative of the relatively high inflation rate in the United States at that time. Interest rates fluctuate with the business cycle, typically increasing during expansions and decreasing during a recession. Note the steep decline in CD rates since 2008, the beginning of the Great Recession.

The great advantages of bank accounts are that financial investors have very easy access to their money, and also money in bank accounts is extremely safe. In part, this safety arises because a bank account offers more security than keeping a few thousand dollars in the toe of a sock in your underwear drawer. In addition, the Federal Deposit Insurance Corporation (FDIC) protects the savings of the average person. Every bank is required by law to pay a fee to the FDIC, based on the size of its deposits. Then, if a bank should go bankrupt and not be able to repay depositors, the FDIC guarantees that all customers will receive their deposits back up to $250,000.

The bottom line on bank accounts looks like this: low risk means low rate of return but high liquidity.

This OpenStax book is available for free at http://cnx.org/content/col12122/1.4

Bonds

An investor who buys a bond expects to receive a rate of return. However, bonds vary in the rates of return that they offer, according to the riskiness of the borrower. We always can divide an interest rate into three components (as we explained in **Choice in a World of Scarcity**): compensation for delaying consumption, an adjustment for an inflationary rise in the overall level of prices, and a risk premium that takes the borrower's riskiness into account.

The U.S. government is an extremely safe borrower, so when the U.S. government issues Treasury bonds, it can pay a relatively low interest rate. Firms that appear to be safe borrowers, perhaps because of their sheer size or because they have consistently earned profits over time, will still pay a higher interest rate than the U.S. government. Firms that appear to be riskier borrowers, perhaps because they are still growing or their businesses appear shaky, will pay the highest interest rates when they issue bonds. We call bonds that offer high interest rates to compensate for their relatively high chance of default **high yield bonds** or **junk bonds**. A number of today's well-known firms issued junk bonds in the 1980s when they were starting to grow, including Turner Broadcasting and Microsoft.

Link It Up

Visit this website (http://openstaxcollege.org/l/bondsecurities) to read about Treasury bonds.

A bond issued by the U.S. government or a large corporation may seem to be relatively low risk: after all, the bond issuer has promised to make certain payments over time, and except for rare bankruptcy cases, these payments will occur. If a corporate bond issuer fails to make the payments that it owes to its bondholders, the bondholders can require that the company declare bankruptcy, sell off its assets, and pay them as much as it can. Even in the case of junk bonds, a wise investor can reduce the risk by purchasing bonds from a wide range of different companies since, even if a few firms go broke and do not pay, they are not all likely to go bankrupt.

As we noted before, bonds carry an interest rate risk. For example, imagine you decide to buy a 10-year bond that would pay an annual interest rate of 8%. Soon after you buy the bond, interest rates on bonds rise, so that now similar companies are paying an annual rate of 12%. Anyone who buys a bond now can receive annual payments of $120 per year, but since your bond was issued at an interest rate of 8%, you have tied up $1,000 and receive payments of only $80 per year. In the meaningful sense of opportunity cost, you are missing out on the higher payments that you could have received. Furthermore, you can calculate the amount you should be willing to pay now for future payments. To place a present discounted value on a future payment, decide what you would need in the present to equal a certain amount in the future. This calculation will require an interest rate. For example, if the interest rate is 25%, then a payment of $125 a year from now will have a present discounted value of $100—that is, you could take $100 in the present and have $125 in the future. (We discuss this further in the appendix on **Present Discounted Value**.)

In financial terms, a bond has several parts. A bond is basically an "I owe you" note that an investor receives in exchange for capital (money). The bond has a **face value**. This is the amount the borrower agrees to pay the investor at maturity. The bond has a **coupon rate** or interest rate, which is usually semi-annual, but can be paid at different times throughout the year. (Bonds used to be paper documents with coupons that investors clipped and turned in to the bank to receive interest.) The bond has a **maturity date** when the borrower will pay back its face value as well as its last interest payment. Combining the bond's face value, interest rate, and maturity date, and market interest rates, allows a buyer to compute a bond's **present value**, which is the most that a buyer would be willing to pay for a given bond. This may or may not be the same as the face value.

The **bond yield** measures the rate of return a bond is expected to pay over time. Investors can buy bonds when they are issued and they can buy and sell them during their lifetimes. When buying a bond that has been around for a few years, investors should know that the interest rate printed on a bond is often not the same as the bond yield, even on new bonds. Read the next Work It Out feature to see how this happens.

Calculating the Bond Yield

You have bought a $1,000 bond whose coupon rate is 8%. To calculate your return or yield, follow these steps:

1. Assume the following:
   Face value of a bond: $1,000
   Coupon rate: 8 %
   Annual payment: $80 per year

2. Consider the risk of the bond. If this bond carries no risk, then it would be safe to assume that the bond will sell for $1,000 when it is issued and pay the purchaser $80 per year until its maturity, at which time the final interest payment will be made and the original $1,000 will be repaid. Now, assume that over time the interest rates prevailing in the economy rise to 12% and that there is now only one year left to this bond's maturity. This makes the bond an unattractive investment, since an investor can find another bond that perhaps pays 12%. To induce the investor to buy the 8% bond, the bond seller will lower its price below its face value of $1,000.

3. Calculate the bond's price when its interest rate is less than the market interest rate. The expected payments from the bond one year from now are $1,080, because in the bond's last year the bond's issuer will make the final interest payment and then also repay the original $1,000. Given that interest rates are now 12%, you know that you could invest $964 in an alternative investment and receive $1,080 a year from now; that is, $964(1 + 0.12) = $1080. Therefore, you will not pay more than $964 for the original $1,000 bond.

4. Consider that the investor will receive the $1,000 face value, plus $80 for the last year's interest payment. The yield on the bond will be ($1080 − $964)/$964 = 12%. The yield, or total return, means interest payments, plus capital gains. Note that the interest or coupon rate of 8% did not change. When interest rates rise, bonds previously issued at lower interest rates will sell for less than face value. Conversely, when interest rates fall, bonds previously issued at higher interest rates will sell for more than face value.

Figure 17.5 shows bond yield for two kinds of bonds: 10-year Treasury bonds (which are officially called "notes") and corporate bonds issued by firms that have been given an AAA rating as relatively safe borrowers by Moody's, an independent firm that publishes such ratings. Even though corporate bonds pay a higher interest rate, because firms are riskier borrowers than the federal government, the rates tend to rise and fall together. Treasury bonds typically pay more than bank accounts, and corporate bonds typically pay a higher interest rate than Treasury bonds.

This OpenStax book is available for free at http://cnx.org/content/col12122/1.4

Figure 17.5 Interest Rates for Corporate Bonds and Ten-Year U.S. Treasury Bonds The interest rates for corporate bonds and U.S. Treasury bonds (officially "notes") rise and fall together, depending on conditions for borrowers and lenders in financial markets for borrowing. The corporate bonds always pay a higher interest rate, to make up for the higher risk they have of defaulting compared with the U.S. government.

The bottom line for bonds: rate of return—low to moderate, depending on the borrower's risk; risk—low to moderate, depending on whether interest rates in the economy change substantially after the bond is issued; liquidity—moderate, because the investor needs to sell the bond before the investor regains the cash.

Stocks

As we stated earlier, the rate of return on a financial investment in a share of stock can come in two forms: as dividends paid by the firm and as a capital gain achieved by selling the stock for more than you paid. The range of possible returns from buying stock is mind-bending. Firms can decide to pay dividends or not. A stock price can rise to a multiple of its original price or sink all the way to zero. Even in short periods of time, well-established companies can see large movements in their stock prices. For example, in July 1, 2011, Netflix stock peaked at $295 per share; one year later, on July 30, 2012, it was at $53.91 per share; in 2015, it had recovered to $414. When Facebook went public, its shares of stock sold for around $40 per share, but in 2015, they were selling for slightly over $83.

We will discuss the reasons why stock prices fall and rise so abruptly below, but first you need to know how we measure stock market performance. There are a number of different ways to measure the overall performance of the stock market, based on averaging different subsets of companies' stock prices. Perhaps the best-known stock market measure is the Dow Jones Industrial Average, which is based on 30 large U.S. companies' stock prices. Another stock market performance gauge, the Standard & Poor's 500, follows the stock prices of the 500 largest U.S. companies. The Wilshire 5000 tracks the stock prices of essentially all U.S. companies that have stock the public can buy and sell.

Other stock market measures focus on where stocks are traded. For example, the New York Stock Exchange monitors the performance of stocks that are traded on that exchange in New York City. The Nasdaq stock market includes about 3,600 stocks, with a concentration of technology stocks. Table 17.1 lists some of the most commonly cited measures of U.S. and international stock markets.

Measure of the Stock Market	Comments
Dow Jones Industrial Average (DJIA): http://indexes.dowjones.com	Based on 30 large companies from a diverse set of representative industries, chosen by analysts at Dow Jones and Company. The index was started in 1896.

Table 17.1 Some Stock Market Measures

Measure of the Stock Market	Comments
Standard & Poor's 500: http://www.standardandpoors.com	Based on 500 large U.S. firms, chosen by analysts at Standard & Poor's to represent the economy as a whole.
Wilshire 5000: http://www.wilshire.com	Includes essentially all U.S. companies with stock ownership. Despite the name, this index includes about 7,000 firms.
New York Stock Exchange: http://www.nyse.com	The oldest and largest U.S. stock market, dating back to 1792. It trades stocks for 2,800 companies of all sizes. It is located at 18 Broad St. in New York City.
NASDAQ: http://www.nasdaq.com	Founded in 1971 as an electronic stock market, allowing people to buy or sell from many physical locations. It has about 3,600 companies.
FTSE: http://www.ftse.com	Includes the 100 largest companies on the London Stock Exchange. Pronounced "footsie." Originally stood for Financial Times Stock Exchange.
Nikkei: http://www.nikkei.co.jp/nikkeiinfo/en/	Nikkei stands for *Nihon Keizai Shimbun*, which translates as the Japan Economic Journal, a major business newspaper in Japan. Index includes the 225 largest and most actively traded stocks on the Tokyo Stock Exchange.
DAX: http://www.exchange.de	Tracks 30 of the largest companies on the Frankfurt, Germany, stock exchange. DAX is an abbreviation for *Deutscher Aktien Index* (German Stock Index).

Table 17.1 Some Stock Market Measures

The trend in the stock market is generally up over time, but with some large dips along the way. **Figure 17.6** shows the path of the Standard & Poor's 500 index (which is measured on the left-hand vertical axis) and the Dow Jones Index (which is measured on the right-hand vertical axis). Broad stock market measures, like the ones we list here, tend to move together. The S&P 500 Index is the weighted average market capitalization of the firms selected to be in the index. The Dow Jones Industrial Average is the price weighted average of 30 industrial stocks tracked on the New York Stock Exchange.

When the Dow Jones average rises from 5,000 to 10,000, you know that the average price of the stocks in that index has roughly doubled. **Figure 17.6** shows that stock prices did not rise much in the 1970s, but then started a steady climb in the 1980s. From 2000 to 2013, stock prices bounced up and down, but ended up at about the same level.

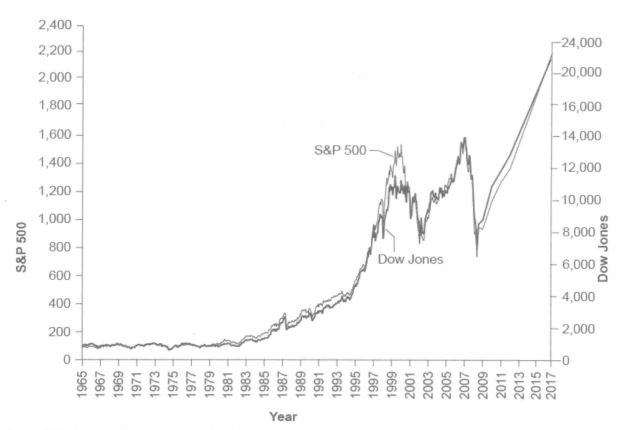

Figure 17.6 The Dow Jones Industrial Index and the Standard & Poor's 500, 1965–2017 Stock prices rose dramatically from the 1980s up to about 2000. From 2000 to 2013, stock prices bounced up and down, but ended up at about the same level.

Table 17.2 shows the total annual rate of return an investor would have received from buying the stocks in the S&P 500 index over recent decades. The total return here includes both dividends paid by these companies and also capital gains arising from increases in the stock value. (For technical reasons related to how we calculate the numbers, the dividends and capital gains do not add exactly to the total return.) From the 1950s to the 1980s, the average firm paid annual dividends equal to about 4% of its stock value. Since the 1990s, dividends have dropped and now often provide a return closer to 1% to 2%. In the 1960s and 1970s, the gap between percent earned on capital gains and dividends was much closer than it has been since the 1980s. In the 1980s and 1990s, capital gains were far higher than dividends. In the 2000s, dividends remained low and, while stock prices fluctuated, they ended the decade roughly where they had started.

Period	Total Annual Return	Capital Gains	Dividends
1950–1959	19.25%	13.58%	4.99%
1960–1969	7.78%	4.39%	3.25%
1970–1979	5.88%	1.60%	4.20%
1980–1989	17.55%	12.59%	4.40%
1990–1999	18.21%	15.31%	2.51%
2000–2009	−1.00%	−2.70%	1.70%

Table 17.2 Annual Returns on S&P 500 Stocks, 1950–2012

Period	Total Annual Return	Capital Gains	Dividends
2010	15.06%	13.22%	1.84%
2011	2.11%	0.04%	2.07%
2012	16.00%	13.87%	2.13%

Table 17.2 Annual Returns on S&P 500 Stocks, 1950–2012

The overall pattern is that stocks as a group have provided a high rate of return over extended periods of time, but this return comes with risks. The market value of individual companies can rise and fall substantially, both over short time periods and over the long run. During extended periods of time like the 1970s or the first decade of the 2000s, the overall stock market return can be quite modest. The stock market can sometimes fall sharply, as it did in 2008.

The bottom line on investing in stocks is that the rate of return over time will be high, but the risks are also high, especially in the short run. Liquidity is also high since one can sell stock in publicly held companies readily for spendable money.

Mutual Funds

Buying stocks or bonds issued by a single company is always somewhat risky. An individual firm may find itself buffeted by unfavorable supply and demand conditions or hurt by unlucky or unwise managerial decisions. Thus, a standard recommendation from financial investors is **diversification**, which means buying stocks or bonds from a wide range of companies. A saver who diversifies is following the old proverb: "Don't put all your eggs in one basket." In any broad group of companies, some firms will do better than expected and some will do worse—but the diversification has a tendency to cancel out extreme increases and decreases in value.

Purchasing a diversified group of stocks or bonds has become easier in the internet age, but it remains something of a task. To simplify the process, companies offer **mutual funds**, which consist of a variety of stocks or bonds from different companies. The financial investor buys mutual fund shares, and then receives a return based on how the fund as a whole performs. In 2012, according to the Investment Company Factbook, about 44% of U.S. households had a financial investment in a mutual fund—including many people who have their retirement savings or pension money invested in this way.

Mutual funds can focus in certain areas: one mutual fund might invest only in company stocks based in Indonesia, or only in bonds issued by large manufacturing companies, or only in biotechnology companies' stock. At the other end of the spectrum, a mutual fund might be quite broad. At the extreme, some mutual funds own a tiny share of every firm in the stock market, and thus the mutual fund's value will fluctuate with the overall stock market's average. We call a mutual fund that seeks only to mimic the market's overall performance an **index fund**.

Diversification can offset some of the risks of individual stocks rising or falling. Even investors who buy an indexed mutual fund designed to mimic some measure of the broad stock market, like the Standard & Poor's 500, had better prepare against some ups and downs, like those the stock market experienced in the first decade of the 2000s. In 2008 average U.S. stock funds declined 38%, reducing individual and household wealth. This steep drop in value hit hardest those who were close to retirement and were counting on their stock funds to supplement retirement income.

The bottom line on investing in mutual funds is that the rate of return over time will be high. The risks are also high, but the risks and returns for an individual mutual fund will be lower than those for an individual stock. As with stocks, liquidity is also high provided the mutual fund or stock index fund is readily traded.

Housing and Other Tangible Assets

Households can also seek a rate of return by purchasing tangible assets, especially housing. About two-thirds of U.S. households own their own home. An owner's **equity** in a house is the monetary value the owner would have after selling the house and repaying any outstanding bank loans he or she used to buy the house. For example, imagine that you buy a house for $200,000, paying 10% of the price as a down payment and taking out a bank loan for the remaining $180,000. Over time, you pay off some of your bank loan, so that only $100,000 remains, and the house's value on the market rises to $250,000. At that point, your equity in the home is the value of the home minus the value of the loan outstanding, which is $150,000. For many middle-class Americans, home equity is their single greatest

This OpenStax book is available for free at http://cnx.org/content/col12122/1.4

financial asset. The total value of all home equity held by U.S. households was $11.3 trillion at the end of 2015, according to Federal Reserve data.

Investment in a house is tangibly different from bank accounts, stocks, and bonds because a house offers both a financial and a nonfinancial return. If you buy a house to live in, part of the return on your investment occurs from your consumption of "housing services"—that is, having a place to live. (Of course, if you buy a home and rent it out, you receive rental payments for the housing services you provide, which would offer a financial return.) Buying a house to live in also offers the possibility of a capital gain from selling the house in the future for more than you paid for it. There can, however, be different outcomes, as the Clear It Up on the housing market shows.

Housing prices have usually risen steadily over time. For example, the median sales price for an existing one-family home was $122,900 in 1990, but 232,000 at the end of December 2016, according to FRED® Economic Data. Over these 24 years, home prices increased an average of 3.1% per year, which is an average financial return over this time. **Figure 17.7** shows U.S. Census data for the median average sales price of a house in the United States over this time period.

Link It Up @

Go to this website (http://openstaxcollege.org/l/investopedia) to experiment with a compound annual growth rate calculator.

However, the possible capital gains from rising housing prices are riskier than these national price averages. Certain regions of the country or metropolitan areas have seen drops in housing prices over time. The median housing price for the United States as a whole fell almost 7% in 2008 and again in 2009, dropping the median price from $247,900 to $216,700. As of 2016, home values had recovered and even exceeded their pre-recession levels.

Link It Up @

Visit this website (http://openstaxcollege.org/l/insidejob) to watch the trailer for *Inside Job*, a movie that explores the modern financial crisis.

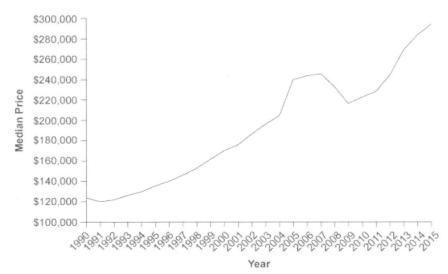

Figure 17.7 The Median Average Sales Price for New Single-Family Homes, 1990–2015 The median price is the price where half of sales prices are higher and half are lower. The median sales price for a new one-family home was $122,900 in 1990. It rose as high as $248,000 in 2007, before falling to $232,000 in 2008. In 2015, the median sales price was $294,000. Of course, this national figure conceals many local differences, like the areas where housing prices are higher or lower, or how housing prices have risen or fallen at certain times. (Source: U.S. Census)

Investors can also put money into other tangible assets such as gold, silver, and other precious metals, or in duller commodities like sugar, cocoa, coffee, orange juice, oil, and natural gas. The return on these investments derives from the saver's hope of buying low, selling high, and receiving a capital gain. Investing in, say, gold or coffee offers relatively little in the way of nonfinancial benefits to the user (unless the investor likes to caress gold or gaze upon a warehouse full of coffee). Typically, investors in these commodities never even see the physical good. Instead, they sign a contract that takes ownership of a certain quantity of these commodities, which are stored in a warehouse, and later they sell the ownership to someone else. As one example, from 1981 to 2005, the gold prices generally fluctuated between about $300 and $500 per ounce, but then rose sharply to over $1,100 per ounce by early 2010. In January 2017, prices were hovering around $1,191 per ounce.

A final area of tangible assets consists of "collectibles" like paintings, fine wine, jewelry, antiques, or even baseball cards. Most collectibles provide returns both in the form of services or of a potentially higher selling price in the future. You can use paintings by hanging them on the wall; jewelry by wearing it; baseball cards by displaying them. You can also hope to sell them someday for more than you paid for them. However, the evidence on prices of collectibles, while scanty, is that while they may go through periods where prices skyrocket for a time, you should not expect to make a higher-than-average rate of return over a sustained period of time from investing in this way.

The bottom line on investing in tangible assets: rate of return—moderate, especially if you can receive nonfinancial benefits from, for example, living in the house; risk—moderate for housing or high if you buy gold or baseball cards; liquidity—low, because it often takes considerable time and energy to sell a house or a piece of fine art and turn your capital gain into cash. The next Clear It Up feature explains the issues in the recent U.S. housing market crisis.

What was all the commotion in the recent U.S. housing market?

The cumulative average annual growth rate in housing prices from 1981 to 2000 was 5.1%. The price of an average U.S. home then took off from 2003 to 2005, rising more than 10% per year. No serious analyst believed this rate of growth was sustainable; after all, if housing prices grew at, say, 11% per year over time, the average price of a home would more than double every seven years. However, at the time many serious analysts saw no reason for deep concern. After all, housing prices often change in fits and starts, like all

This OpenStax book is available for free at http://cnx.org/content/col12122/1.4

prices, and a price surge for a few years is often followed by prices that are flat or even declining a bit as local markets adjust.

The sharp rise in housing prices was driven by a high level of demand for housing. Interest rates were low, so financial institutions encouraged people to borrow money to buy a house. Banks became much more flexible in their lending, making what were called "subprime" loans. Banks loaned money with low, or sometimes no down payment. They offered loans with very low payments for the first two years, but then much higher payments after that. The idea was that housing prices would keep rising, so the borrower would just refinance the mortgage two years in the future, and thus would not ever have to make the higher payments. Some banks even offered so-called NINJA loans, which meant a financial institution issued loan even though the borrower had no income, no job, nor assets.

In retrospect, these loans seem nearly crazy. Many borrowers figured, however, that as long as housing prices kept rising, it made sense to buy. Many lenders used a process called "securitizing," in which they sold their mortgages to financial companies, which put all the mortgages into a big pool, creating large financial securities, and then re-sold these mortgage-backed securities to investors. In this way, the lenders off-loaded the mortgage risks to investors. Investors were interested in mortgage-backed securities as they appeared to offer a steady stream of income, provided the borrowers repaid them. Investors relied on the ratings agencies to assess the credit risk associated with the mortgage-backed securities. In hindsight, it appears that the credit agencies were far too lenient in their ratings of many of the securitized loans. Bank and financial regulators watched the steady rise in the market for mortgage-backed securities, but saw no reason at the time to intervene.

When housing prices turned down, many households that had borrowed when prices were high found that what they owed the bank was more than what their home was worth. Many banks believed that they had diversified by selling their individual loans and instead buying securities based on mortgage loans from all over the country. After all, banks thought back in 2005, the average house price had not declined at any time since the Great Depression in the 1930s. These securities based on mortgage loans, however, turned out to be far riskier than expected. The bust in housing prices weakened both bank and household finances, and thus helped bring on the 2008-2009 Great Recession.

The Tradeoffs between Return and Risk

The discussion of financial investments has emphasized the expected rate of return, the risk, and the liquidity of each investment. Table 17.3 summarizes these characteristics.

Financial Investment	Return	Risk	Liquidity
Checking account	Very low	Very little	Very high
Savings account	Low	Very little	High
Certificate of deposit	Low to medium	Very little	Medium
Stocks	High	Medium to high	Medium
Bonds	Medium	Low to medium	Medium
Mutual funds	Medium to high	Medium to high	Medium to high
Housing	Medium	Medium	Low
Gold	Medium	High	Low
Collectibles	Low to medium	High	Low

Table 17.3 Key Characteristics for Financial Investments

The household investment choices listed here display a tradeoff between the expected return and the degree of risk involved. Bank accounts have very low risk and very low returns; bonds have higher risk but higher returns; and stocks are riskiest of all but have the potential for still higher returns. In effect, the higher average return compensates for the higher degree of risk. If risky assets like stocks did not also offer a higher average return, then few investors would want them.

This tradeoff between return and risk complicates the task of any financial investor: Is it better to invest safely or to take a risk and go for the high return? Ultimately, choices about risk and return will be based on personal preferences. However, it is often useful to examine risk and return in the context of different time frames.

The high returns of stock market investments refer to a high average return that we can expect over a period of several years or decades. The high risk of such investments refers to the fact that in shorter time frames, from months to a few years, the rate of return may fluctuate a great deal. Thus, a person near retirement age, who already owns a house, may prefer reduced risk and certainty about retirement income. For young workers, just starting to make a reasonably profitable living, it may make sense to put most of their savings for retirement in mutual funds. Mutual funds are able to take advantage of their buying and selling size and thereby reduce transaction costs for investors. Stocks are risky in the short term, to be sure, but when the worker can look forward to several decades during which stock market ups and downs can even out, stocks will typically pay a much higher return over that extended period than will bonds or bank accounts. Thus, one must consider tradeoffs between risk and return in the context of where the investor is in life.

17.3 | How to Accumulate Personal Wealth

By the end of this section, you will be able to:
- Explain the random walk theory
- Calculate simple and compound interest
- Evaluate how capital markets transform financial capital

Getting rich may seem straightforward enough. Figure out what companies are going to grow and earn high profits in the future, or figure out what companies are going to become popular for everyone else to buy. Those companies are the ones that will pay high dividends or whose stock price will climb in the future. Then, buy stock in those companies. Presto! Multiply your money!

Why is this path to riches not as easy as it sounds? This module first discusses the problems with picking stocks, and then discusses a more reliable but undeniably duller method of accumulating personal wealth.

Why It Is Hard to Get Rich Quick: The Random Walk Theory

The chief problem with attempting to buy stock in companies that will have higher prices in the future is that many other financial investors are trying to do the same thing. Thus, in attempting to get rich in the stock market, it is no help to identify a company that is going to earn high profits if many other investors have already reached the same conclusion, because the stock price will already be high, based on the expected high level of future profits.

The idea that stock prices are based on expectations about the future has a powerful and unexpected implication. If expectations determine stock price, then shifts in expectations will determine shifts in the stock price. Thus, what matters for predicting whether the stock price of a company will do well is not whether the company will actually earn profits in the future. Instead, you must find a company that analysts widely believe at present to have poor prospects, but that will actually turn out to be a shining star. Brigades of stock market analysts and individual investors are carrying out such research 24 hours a day.

The fundamental problem with predicting future stock winners is that, by definition, no one can predict the future news that alters expectations about profits. Because stock prices will shift in response to unpredictable future news, these prices will tend to follow what mathematicians call a "random walk with a trend." The "random walk" part means that, on any given day, stock prices are just as likely to rise as to fall. "With a trend" means that over time, the upward steps tend to be larger than the downward steps, so stocks do gradually climb.

If stocks follow a random walk, then not even financial professionals will be able to choose those that will beat the average consistently. While some investment advisers are better than average in any given year, and some even succeed for a number of years in a row, the majority of financial investors do not outguess the market. If we look back over time, it is typically true that half or two-thirds of the mutual funds that attempted to pick stocks which would rise more than the market average actually ended up performing worse than the market average. For the average investor who reads the newspaper business pages over a cup of coffee in the morning, the odds of doing better than full-time professionals is not very good at all. Trying to pick the stocks that will gain a great deal in the future is a risky and unlikely way to become rich.

Getting Rich the Slow, Boring Way

Many U.S. citizens can accumulate a large amount of wealth during their lifetimes, if they make two key choices. The first is to complete additional education and training. In 2014, the U.S. Census Bureau reported median earnings for households where the main earner had only a high school degree of $33,124; for those with a two-year associate degree, median earnings were $40,560 and for those with a four-year bachelor's degree, median income was $54,340. Learning is not only good for you, but it pays off financially, too.

The second key choice is to start saving money early in life, and to give the power of compound interest a chance. Imagine that at age 25, you save $3,000 and place that money into an account that you do not touch. In the long run, it is not unreasonable to assume a 7% real annual rate of return (that is, 7% above the rate of inflation) on money invested in a well-diversified stock portfolio. After 40 years, using the formula for compound interest, the original $3,000 investment will have multiplied nearly fifteen fold:

$$3,000(1 + .07)^{40} = \$44,923$$

Having $45,000 does not make you a millionaire. Notice, however, that this tidy sum is the result of saving $3,000 exactly once. Saving that amount every year for several decades—or saving more as income rises—will multiply the total considerably. This type of wealth will not rival the riches of Microsoft CEO Bill Gates, but remember that only half of Americans have any money in mutual funds at all. Accumulating hundreds of thousands of dollars by retirement is a perfectly achievable goal for a well-educated person who starts saving early in life—and that amount of accumulated wealth will put you at or near the top 10% of all American households. The following Work It Out feature shows the difference between simple and compound interest, and the power of compound interest.

Work It Out ⊢O─O─O

Simple and Compound Interest

Simple interest is an interest rate calculation only on the principal amount.

Step 1. Learn the formula for simple interest:

Principal × Rate × Time = Interest

Step 2. Practice using the simple interest formula.

Example 1: $100 Deposit at a simple interest rate of 5% held for one year is:

$100 × 0.05 × 1 = $5

Simple interest in this example is $15.

Example 2: $100 Deposit at a simple interest rate of 5% held for three years is:

$100 × 0.05 × 3 = $15

Simple interest in this example is $5.

Step 3. Calculate the total future amount using this formula:

Total future amount = principal + interest

Step 4. Put the two simple interest formulas together.

Total future amount (with simple interest) = Principal + (Principal × Rate × Time)

Step 5. Apply the simple interest formula to our three year example.

Total future amount (with simple interest) = $100 + ($100 × 0.05 × 3) = $115

Compound interest is an interest rate calculation on the principal plus the accumulated interest.

Step 6. To find the compound interest, we determine the difference between the future value and the present value of the principal. This is accomplished as follows:

$$\text{Future Value} = \text{Principal} \times (1 + \text{interest rate})^{\text{time}}$$

Compound interest = Future Value – Present Valve

Step 7. Apply this formula to our three-year scenario. Follow the calculations in

Table 17.4

Year 1	
Amount in Bank	$100
Bank Interest Rate	5%
Total	$105
	$100 + ($100 × 0.5)
Year 2	
Amount in Bank	$105
Bank Interest Rate	5%
Total	$110.25
	$105 + ($105 × .05)
Year 3	
Amount in Bank	$110.25
Bank Interest Rate	5%
Total	$115.75
	$110.25 + ($110.25 × .05)
Compound interest	$115.75 – $100 = $15.75

Table 17.4

Step 8. Note that, after three years, the total is $115.76. Therefore the total compound interest is $15.76. This is $0.76 more than we obtained with simple interest. While this may not seem like much, keep in mind that we were only working with $100 and over a relatively short time period. Compound interest can make a huge difference with larger sums of money and over longer periods of time.

Obtaining additional education and saving money early in life obviously will not make you rich overnight. Additional education typically means deferring earning income and living as a student for more years. Saving money often requires choices like driving an older or less expensive car, living in a smaller apartment or buying a smaller house, and making other day-to-day sacrifices. For most people, the tradeoffs for achieving substantial personal wealth will require effort, patience, and sacrifice.

How Capital Markets Transform Financial Flows

Financial capital markets have the power to repackage money as it moves from those who supply financial capital

This OpenStax book is available for free at http://cnx.org/content/col12122/1.4

to those who demand it. Banks accept checking account deposits and turn them into long-term loans to companies. Individual firms sell shares of stock and issue bonds to raise capital. Firms make and sell an astonishing array of goods and services, but an investor can receive a return on the company's decisions by buying stock in that company. Financial investors sell and resell stocks and bonds to one another. Venture capitalists and angel investors search for promising small companies. Mutual funds combine the stocks and bonds—and thus, indirectly, the products and investments—of many different companies.

Link It Up

Visit this website (http://openstaxcollege.org/l/austerebaltic/) to read an article about how austerity can work.

In this chapter, we discussed the basic mechanisms of financial markets. (A more advanced course in economics or finance will consider more sophisticated tools.) The fundamentals of those financial capital markets remain the same: Firms are trying to raise financial capital and households are looking for a desirable combination of rate of return, risk, and liquidity. Financial markets are society's mechanisms for bringing together these forces of demand and supply.

Bring it Home

The Housing Bubble and the Financial Crisis of 2007

The housing boom and bust in the United States, and the resulting multi-trillion-dollar decline in home equity, began with the fall of home prices starting in 2007. As home values dipped, many home prices fell below the amount the borrower owed on the mortgage and owners stopped paying and defaulted on their loan. Banks found that their assets (loans) became worthless. Many financial institutions around the world had invested in mortgage-backed securities, or had purchased insurance on mortgage-backed securities. When housing prices collapsed, the value of those financial assets collapsed as well. The asset side of the banks' balance sheets dropped, causing bank failures and bank runs. Around the globe, financial institutions were bankrupted or nearly so. The result was a large decrease in lending and borrowing, or a freezing up of available credit. When credit dries up, the economy is on its knees. The crisis was not limited to the United States. Iceland, Ireland, the United Kingdom, Spain, Portugal, and Greece all had similar housing boom and bust cycles, and similar credit freezes.

If businesses cannot access financial capital, they cannot make physical capital investments. Those investments ultimately lead to job creation. When credit dried up, businesses invested less, and they ultimately laid off millions of workers. This caused incomes to drop, which caused demand to drop. In turn businesses sold less, so they laid off more workers. Compounding these events, as economic conditions worsened, financial institutions were even less likely to make loans.

To make matters even worse, as businesses sold less, their expected future profit decreased, and this led to a drop in stock prices. Combining all these effects led to major decreases in incomes, demand, consumption, and employment, and to the Great Recession, which in the United States officially lasted from December 2007 to June 2009. During this time, the unemployment rate rose from 5% to a peak of 10.1%. Four years after the recession officially ended, unemployment was still stubbornly high, at 7.6%, and 11.8 million people were still unemployed.

As the world's leading consumer, if the United States goes into recession, it usually drags other countries down with it. The Great Recession was no exception. With few exceptions, U.S. trading partners also entered into recessions of their own, of varying lengths, or suffered slower economic growth. Like the United States, many European countries also gave direct financial assistance, so-called bailouts, to the institutions that make up their financial markets. There was good reason to do this. Financial markets bridge the gap between demanders and suppliers of financial capital. These institutions and markets need to function in order for an economy to invest in new financial capital.

However, much of this bailout money was borrowed, and this borrowed money contributed to another crisis in Europe. Because of the impact on their budgets of the financial crisis and the resulting bailouts, many countries found themselves with unsustainably high deficits. They chose to undertake austerity measures, large decreases in government spending and large tax increases, in order to reduce their deficits. Greece, Ireland, Spain, and Portugal have all had to undertake relatively severe austerity measures. The ramifications of this crisis have spread. Economists have even call into question the euro's viability into question.

KEY TERMS

actual rate of return the total rate of return, including capital gains and interest paid on an investment at the end of a time period

bond a financial contract through which a borrower like a corporation, a city or state, or the federal government agrees to repay the amount that it borrowed and also a rate of interest over a period of time in the future

bond yield the rate of return a bond is expected to pay at the time of purchase

bondholder someone who owns bonds and receives the interest payments

capital gain a financial gain from buying an asset, like a share of stock or a house, and later selling it at a higher price

certificate of deposit (CD) a mechanism for a saver to deposit funds at a bank and promise to leave them at the bank for a time, in exchange for a higher interest rate

checking account a bank account that typically pays little or no interest, but that gives easy access to money, either by writing a check or by using a "debit card"

compound interest an interest rate calculation on the principal plus the accumulated interest

corporate bond a bond issued by firms that wish to borrow

corporate governance the name economists give to the institutions that are supposed to watch over top executives in companies that shareholders own

corporation a business owned by shareholders who have limited liability for the company's debt yet a share of the company's profits; may be private or public and may or may not have publicly-traded stock

coupon rate the interest rate paid on a bond; can be annual or semi-annual

debit card a card that lets the person make purchases, and the financial insitution immediately deducts cost from that person's checking account

diversification investing in a wide range of companies to reduce the level of risk

dividend a direct payment from a firm to its shareholders

equity the monetary value a homeowner would have after selling the house and repaying any outstanding bank loans used to buy the house

expected rate of return how much a project or an investment is expected to return to the investor, either in future interest payments, capital gains, or increased profitability

face value the amount that the bond issuer or borrower agrees to pay the investor

financial intermediary an institution, like a bank, that receives money from savers and provides funds to borrowers

high yield bonds bonds that offer relatively high interest rates to compensate for their relatively high chance of default

index fund a mutual fund that seeks only to mimic the market's overall performance

initial public offering (IPO) the first sale of shares of stock by a firm to outside investors

junk bonds see high yield bonds

liquidity refers to how easily one can exchange money or financial assets for a good or service

maturity date the date that a borrower must repay a bond

municipal bonds a bond issued by cities that wish to borrow

mutual funds funds that buy a range of stocks or bonds from different companies, thus allowing an investor an easy way to diversify

partnership a company run by a group as opposed to an individual

present value a bond's current price at a given time

private company a firm owned by the people who run it on a day-to-day basis

public company a firm that has sold stock to the public, which in turn investors then can buy and sell

risk a measure of the uncertainty of that project's profitability

savings account a bank account that pays an interest rate, but withdrawing money typically requires a trip to the bank or an automatic teller machine

shareholders people who own at least some shares of stock in a firm

shares a firm's stock, divided into individual portions

simple interest an interest rate calculation only on the principal amount

sole proprietorship a company run by an individual as opposed to a group

stock a specific firm's claim on partial ownership

Treasury bond a bond issued by the federal government through the U.S. Department of the Treasury

venture capital financial investments in new companies that are still relatively small in size, but that have potential to grow substantially

KEY CONCEPTS AND SUMMARY

17.1 How Businesses Raise Financial Capital

Companies can raise early-stage financial capital in several ways: from their owners' or managers' personal savings, or credit cards and from private investors like angel investors and venture capital firms.

A bond is a financial contract through which a borrower agrees to repay the amount that it borrowed. A bond specifies an amount that one will borrow, the amounts that one will repay over time based on the interest rate when the bond is issued, and the time until repayment. Corporate bonds are issued by firms; municipal bonds are issued by cities, state bonds by U.S. states, and Treasury bonds by the federal government through the U.S. Department of the Treasury.

Stock represents firm ownership. A company's stock is divided into shares. A firm receives financial capital when it sells stock to the public. We call a company's first stock sale to the public the initial public offering (IPO). However, a firm does not receive any funds when one shareholder sells stock in the firm to another investor. One receives the rate of return on stock in two forms: dividends and capital gains.

A private company is usually owned by the people who run it on a day-to-day basis, although hired managers can run it. We call a private company owned and run by an individual a sole proprietorship, while a firm owned and run by a group is a partnership. When a firm decides to sell stock that financial investors can buy and sell, then the firm is owned by its shareholders—who in turn elect a board of directors to hire top day-to-day management. We call this a public company. Corporate governance is the name economists give to the institutions that are supposed to watch over top executives, though it does not always work.

This OpenStax book is available for free at http://cnx.org/content/col12122/1.4

17.2 How Households Supply Financial Capital

We can categorize all investments according to three key characteristics: average expected return, degree of risk, and liquidity. To obtain a higher rate of return, an investor must typically accept either more risk or less liquidity. Banks are an example of a financial intermediary, an institution that operates to coordinate supply and demand in the financial capital market. Banks offer a range of accounts, including checking accounts, savings accounts, and certificates of deposit. Under the Federal Deposit Insurance Corporation (FDIC), banks purchase insurance against the risk of a bank failure.

A typical bond promises the financial investor a series of payments over time, based on the interest rate at the time the financial institution issues the bond, and when the borrower repays it. Bonds that offer a high rate of return but also a relatively high chance of defaulting on the payments are called high-yield or junk bonds. The bond yield is the rate of return that a bond promises to pay at the time of purchase. Even when bonds make payments based on a fixed interest rate, they are somewhat risky, because if interest rates rise for the economy as a whole, an investor who owns bonds issued at lower interest rates is now locked into the low rate and suffers a loss.

Changes in the stock price depend on changes in expectations about future profits. Investing in any individual firm is somewhat risky, so investors are wise to practice diversification, which means investing in a range of companies. A mutual fund purchases an array of stocks and/or bonds. An investor in the mutual fund then receives a return depending on the fund's overall performance as a whole. A mutual fund that seeks to imitate the overall behavior of the stock market is called an index fund.

We can also regard housing and other tangible assets as forms of financial investment, which pay a rate of return in the form of capital gains. Housing can also offer a nonfinancial return—specifically, you can live in it.

17.3 How to Accumulate Personal Wealth

It is extremely difficult, even for financial professionals, to predict changes in future expectations and thus to choose the stocks whose price will rise in the future. Most Americans can accumulate considerable financial wealth if they follow two rules: complete significant additional education and training after graduating from high school and start saving money early in life.

SELF-CHECK QUESTIONS

1. Answer these three questions about early-stage corporate finance:
   a. Why do very small companies tend to raise money from private investors instead of through an IPO?
   b. Why do small, young companies often prefer an IPO to borrowing from a bank or issuing bonds?
   c. Who has better information about whether a small firm is likely to earn profits, a venture capitalist or a potential bondholder, and why?

2. From a firm's point of view, how is a bond similar to a bank loan? How are they different?

3. Calculate the equity each of these people has in his or her home:
   a. Fred just bought a house for $200,000 by putting 10% as a down payment and borrowing the rest from the bank.
   b. Freda bought a house for $150,000 in cash, but if she were to sell it now, it would sell for $250,000.
   c. Frank bought a house for $100,000. He put 20% down and borrowed the rest from the bank. However, the value of the house has now increased to $160,000 and he has paid off $20,000 of the bank loan.

4. Which has a higher average return over time: stocks, bonds, or a savings account? Explain your answer.

5. Investors sometimes fear that a high-risk investment is especially likely to have low returns. Is this fear true? Does a high risk mean the return must be low?

6. What is the total amount of interest from a $5,000 loan after three years with a simple interest rate of 6%?

7. If you receive $500 in simple interest on a loan that you made for $10,000 for five years, what was the interest rate you charged?

8. You open a 5-year CD for $1,000 that pays 2% interest, compounded annually. What is the value of that CD at the end of the five years?

REVIEW QUESTIONS

9. What are the most common ways for start-up firms to raise financial capital?

10. Why can firms not just use their own profits for financial capital, with no need for outside investors?

11. Why are banks more willing to lend to well-established firms?

12. What is a bond?

13. What does a share of stock represent?

14. When do firms receive money from a stock sale in their firm and when do they not receive money?

15. What is a dividend?

16. What is a capital gain?

17. What is the difference between a private company and a public company?

18. How do the shareholders who own a company choose the actual company managers?

19. Why are banks called "financial intermediaries"?

20. Name several different kinds of bank account. How are they different?

21. Why are bonds somewhat risky to buy, even though they make predetermined payments based on a fixed rate of interest?

22. Why should a financial investor care about diversification?

23. What is a mutual fund?

24. What is an index fund?

25. How is buying a house to live in a type of financial investment?

26. Why is it hard to forecast future movements in stock prices?

27. What are the two key choices U.S. citizens need to make that determines their relative wealth?

28. Is investing in housing always a very safe investment?

CRITICAL THINKING QUESTIONS

29. If you owned a small firm that had become somewhat established, but you needed a surge of financial capital to carry out a major expansion, would you prefer to raise the funds through borrowing or by issuing stock? Explain your choice.

30. Explain how a company can fail when the safeguards that should be in place fail.

31. What are some reasons why the investment strategy of a 30-year-old might differ from the investment strategy of a 65-year-old?

32. Explain why a financial investor in stocks cannot earn high capital gains simply by buying companies with a demonstrated record of high profits.

33. Explain what happens in an economy when the financial markets limit access to capital. How does this affect economic growth and employment?

34. You and your friend have opened an account on E-Trade and have each decided to select five similar companies in which to invest. You are diligent in monitoring your selections, tracking prices, current events, and actions the company has taken. Your friend chooses his companies randomly, pays no attention to the financial news, and spends his leisure time focused on everything besides his investments. Explain what might be the performance for each of your portfolios at the end of the year.

35. How do bank failures cause the economy to go into recession?

PROBLEMS

36. The Darkroom Windowshade Company has 100,000 shares of stock outstanding. The investors in the firm own the following numbers of shares: investor 1 has 20,000 shares; investor 2 has 18,000 shares; investor 3 has 15,000 shares; investor 4 has 10,000 shares; investor 5 has 7,000 shares; and investors 6 through 11 have 5,000 shares each. What is the minimum number of investors it would take to vote to change the company's top management? If investors 1 and 2 agree to vote together, can they be certain of always getting their way in how the company will be run?

37. Imagine that a local water company issued $10,000 ten-year bond at an interest rate of 6%. You are thinking about buying this bond one year before the end of the ten years, but interest rates are now 9%.

    a. Given the change in interest rates, would you expect to pay more or less than $10,000 for the bond?

    b. Calculate what you would actually be willing to pay for this bond.

38. Suppose Ford Motor Company issues a five year bond with a face value of $5,000 that pays an annual coupon payment of $150.

    a. What is the interest rate Ford is paying on the borrowed funds?

    b. Suppose the market interest rate rises from 3% to 4% a year after Ford issues the bonds. Will the value of the bond increase or decrease?

39. How much money do you have to put into a bank account that pays 10% interest compounded annually to have $10,000 in ten years?

40. Many retirement funds charge an administrative fee each year equal to 0.25% on managed assets. Suppose that Alexx and Spenser each invest $5,000 in the same stock this year. Alexx invests directly and earns 5% a year. Spenser uses a retirement fund and earns 4.75%. After 30 years, how much more will Alexx have than Spenser?

This OpenStax book is available for free at http://cnx.org/content/col12122/1.4

18 | Public Economy

Figure 18.1 Domestic Tires?   While these tires may all appear similar, some are made in the United States and others are not. Those that are not could be subject to a tariff that could cause the cost of all tires to be higher. (Credit: modification of work by Jayme del Rosario/Flickr Creative Commons)

Bring it Home

Chinese Tire Tariffs

Do you know where the tires on your car are made? If they were imported, they may be subject to a tariff (a tax on imported goods) that could raise the price of your car. What do you think about that tariff? Would you write to your representative or your senator about it? Would you start a Facebook or Twitter campaign?

Most people are unlikely to fight this kind of tax or even inform themselves about the issue in the first place. In *The Logic of Collective Action* (1965), economist Mancur Olson challenged the popular idea that, in a democracy, the majority view will prevail, and in doing so launched the modern study of public economy, sometimes referred to as public choice, a subtopic of microeconomics. In this chapter, we will look at the economics of government policy, why smaller, more organized groups have an incentive to work hard to enact certain policies, and why lawmakers ultimately make decisions that may result in bad economic policy.

Introduction to Public Economy

In this chapter, you will learn about:

- Voter Participation and Costs of Elections

- Special Interest Politics

- Flaws in the Democratic System of Government

As President Abraham Lincoln famously said in his 1863 *Gettysburg Address*, democratic governments are supposed to be "of the people, by the people, and for the people." Can we rely on democratic governments to enact sensible economic policies? After all, they react to voters, not to analyses of demand and supply curves. The main focus of an economics course is, naturally enough, to analyze the characteristics of markets and purely economic institutions. However, political institutions also play a role in allocating society's scarce resources, and economists have played an active role, along with other social scientists, in analyzing how such political institutions work.

Other chapters of this book discuss situations in which market forces can sometimes lead to undesirable results: monopoly, imperfect competition, and antitrust policy; negative and positive externalities; poverty and inequality of incomes; failures to provide insurance; and financial markets that may go from boom to bust. Many of these chapters suggest that the government's economic policies could address these issues.

However, just as markets can face issues and problems that lead to undesirable outcomes, a democratic system of government can also make mistakes, either by enacting policies that do not benefit society as a whole or by failing to enact policies that would have benefited society as a whole. This chapter discusses some practical difficulties of democracy from an economic point of view: we presume the actors in the political system follow their own self-interest, which is not necessarily the same as the public good. For example, many of those who are eligible to vote do not, which obviously raises questions about whether a democratic system will reflect everyone's interests. Benefits or costs of government action are sometimes concentrated on small groups, which in some cases may organize and have a disproportionately large impact on politics and in other cases may fail to organize and end up neglected. A legislator who worries about support from voters in his or her district may focus on spending projects specific to the district without sufficient concern for whether this spending is in the nation's interest.

When more than two choices exist, the principle that the majority of voters should decide may not always make logical sense, because situations can arise where it becomes literally impossible to decide what the "majority" prefers. Government may also be slower than private firms to correct its mistakes, because government agencies do not face competition or the threat of new entry.

18.1 | Voter Participation and Costs of Elections

By the end of this section, you will be able to:
- Explain the significance of rational ignorance
- Evaluate the impact of election expenses

In U.S. presidential elections over the last few decades, about 55% to 65% of voting-age citizens actually voted, according to the U.S. Census. In congressional elections when there is no presidential race, or in local elections, the turnout is typically lower, often less than half the eligible voters. In other countries, the share of adults who vote is often higher. For example, in national elections since the 1980s in Germany, Spain, and France, about 75% to 80% of those of voting age cast ballots. Even this total falls well short of 100%. Some countries have laws that require voting, among them Australia, Belgium, Italy, Greece, Turkey, Singapore, and most Latin American nations. At the time the United States was founded, voting was mandatory in Virginia, Maryland, Delaware, and Georgia. Even if the law can require people to vote, however, no law can require that each voter cast an informed or a thoughtful vote. Moreover, in the United States and in most countries around the world, the freedom to vote has also typically meant the freedom *not* to vote.

Why do people not vote? Perhaps they do not care too much about who wins, or they are uninformed about who is running, or they do not believe their vote will matter or change their lives in any way. These reasons are probably tied together, since people who do not believe their vote matters will not bother to become informed or care who wins. Economists have suggested why a utility-maximizing person might rationally decide not to vote or not to become informed about the election. While a single vote may decide a few elections in very small towns, in most elections of any size, the Board of Elections measures the margin of victory in hundreds, thousands, or even millions of votes. A rational voter will recognize that one vote is extremely unlikely to make a difference. This theory of **rational ignorance** holds that people will not vote if the costs of becoming informed and voting are too high, or they feel their vote will not be decisive in the election.

In a 1957 work, *An Economic Theory of Democracy,* the economist Anthony Downs stated the problem this way: "It seems probable that for a great many citizens in a democracy, rational behavior excludes any investment whatever in political information per se. No matter how significant a difference between parties is revealed to the rational citizen by his free information, or how uncertain he is about which party to support, he realizes that his vote has almost no chance of influencing the outcome… He will not even utilize all the free information available, since assimilating it takes time." In his classic 1948 novel *Walden Two,* the psychologist B. F. Skinner puts the issue even more succinctly via one of his characters, who states: "The chance that one man's vote will decide the issue in a national election…is less than the chance that he will be killed on his way to the polls." The following Clear It Up feature explores another aspect of the election process: spending.

How much is too much to spend on an election?

According to a report from *CBS News,* the 2016 elections for president, Congress, and state and local offices, saw a total of about $6.8 billion spent. The money raised went to the campaigns, including advertising, fundraising, travel, and staff. Many people worry that politicians spend too much time raising money and end up entangled with special interest groups that make major donations. Critics would prefer a system that restricts what candidates can spend, perhaps in exchange for limited public campaign financing or free television advertising time.

How much spending on campaigns is too much? Five billion dollars will buy many potato chips, but in the U.S. economy, which exceeded $18 trillion in 2016, the $6.8 billion spent on political campaigns was about 1/25 of 1% of the overall economy. Here is another way to think about campaign spending. *Total* government spending programs in 2016, including federal and state governments, was about $7 trillion, so the cost of choosing the people who would determine how to spend this money was less than 1/10 of 1% of that. In the context of the enormous U.S. economy, $6.8 billion is not as much money as it sounds. U.S. consumers spend about $2 billion per year on toothpaste and $7 billion on hair care products. In 2016, Proctor and Gamble spent $7.2 billion on advertising. It may not be sensible to believe the United States is going to decide its presidential elections for much less than Proctor and Gamble spends on advertisements.

Whatever we believe about whether candidates and their parties spend too much or too little on elections, the U.S. Supreme Court has placed limits on how government can limit campaign spending. In a 1976 decision, *Buckley v. Valeo,* the Supreme Court emphasized that the First Amendment to the U.S. Constitution specifies freedom of speech. The federal government and states can offer candidates a voluntary deal in which government makes some public financing available to candidates, but only if the candidates agree to abide by certain spending limits. Of course, candidates can also voluntarily agree to set certain spending limits if they wish. However, government cannot forbid people or organizations to raise and spend money above these limits if they choose.

In 2002, Congress passed and President George W. Bush signed into law the Bipartisan Campaign Reform Act (BCRA). The relatively noncontroversial portions of the act strengthen the rules requiring full and speedy disclosure of who contributes money to campaigns. However, some controversial portions of the Act limit the ability of individuals and groups to make certain kinds of political donations and they ban certain kinds of advertising in the months leading up to an election. Some called these bans into question after the release of two films: Michael Moore's *Fahrenheit 9/11* and Citizens United's *Hillary: The Movie.* At question was whether each film sought to discredit political candidates for office too close to an election, in violation of the BCRA. The lower courts found that Moore's film did not violate the Act, while Citizens United's did. The fight reached the Supreme Court, as *Citizens United v. Federal Election Commission,* saying that the First Amendment protects the rights of corporations as well as individuals to donate to political campaigns. The Court ruled, in a 5–4 decision, that the spending limits were unconstitutional. This controversial decision, which essentially allows unlimited contributions by corporations to political action committees, overruled several previous decisions and will likely be revisited in the future, due to the strength of the public reaction. For now, it has resulted in a sharp increase in election spending.

While many U.S. adults do not bother to vote in presidential elections, more than half do. What motivates them? Research on voting behavior has indicated that people who are more settled or more "connected" to society tend to vote more frequently. According to the *Washington Post*, more married people vote than single people. Those with a job vote more than the unemployed. Those who have lived longer in a neighborhood are more likely to vote than newcomers. Those who report that they know their neighbors and talk to them are more likely to vote than socially isolated people. Those with a higher income and level of education are also more likely to vote. These factors suggest that politicians are likely to focus more on the interests of married, employed, well-educated people with at least a middle-class level of income than on the interests of other groups. For example, those who vote may tend to be more supportive of financial assistance for the two-year and four-year colleges they expect their children to attend than they are of medical care or public school education aimed at families of the poor and unemployed.

Link It Up

Visit this website (http://openstaxcollege.org/l/votergroups) to see a breakdown of how different groups voted in 2012.

There have been many proposals to encourage greater voter turnout: making it easier to register to vote, keeping the polls open for more hours, or even moving Election Day to the weekend, when fewer people need to worry about jobs or school commitments. However, such changes do not seem to have caused a long-term upward trend in the number of people voting. After all, casting an informed vote will always impose some costs of time and energy. It is not clear how to strengthen people's feeling of connectedness to society in a way that will lead to a substantial increase in voter turnout. Without greater voter turnout, however, politicians elected by the votes of 60% or fewer of the population may not enact economic policy in the best interests of 100% of the population. Meanwhile, countering a long trend toward making voting easier, many states have recently erected new voting laws that critics say are actually barriers to voting. States have passed laws reducing early voting, restricting groups who are organizing get-out-the-vote efforts, enacted strict photo ID laws, as well as laws that require showing proof of U.S. citizenship. The ACLU argues that while these laws profess to prevent voter fraud, they are in effect making it harder for individuals to cast their vote.

18.2 | Special Interest Politics

By the end of this section, you will be able to:
- Explain how special interest groups and lobbyists can influence campaigns and elections
- Describe pork-barrel spending and logrolling

Many political issues are of intense interest to a relatively small group, as we noted above. For example, many U.S. drivers do not much care where their car tires were made—they just want good quality as inexpensively as possible. In September 2009, President Obama and Congress enacted a tariff (taxes added on imported goods) on tires imported from China that would increase the price by 35 percent in its first year, 30 percent in its second year, and 25 percent in its third year. Interestingly, the U.S. companies that make tires did not favor this step, because most of them also import tires from China and other countries. (See **Globalization and Protectionism** for more on tariffs.) However, the United Steelworkers union, which had seen jobs in the tire industry fall by 5,000 over the previous five years, lobbied fiercely for the tariff. With this tariff, the cost of all tires increased significantly. (See the closing Bring It Home feature at the end of this chapter for more information on the tire tariff.)

Special interest groups are groups that are small in number relative to the nation, but quite well organized and focused on a specific issue. A special interest group can pressure legislators to enact public policies that do not benefit society as a whole. Imagine an environmental rule to reduce air pollution that will cost 10 large companies $8 million each, for a total cost of $80 million. The social benefits from enacting this rule provide an average benefit of $10 for every person in the United States, for a total of about $3 trillion. Even though the benefits are far higher than the costs for society as a whole, the 10 companies are likely to lobby much more fiercely to avoid $8 million in costs than the average person is to argue for $10 worth of benefits.

As this example suggests, we can relate the problem of special interests in politics to an issue we raised in **Environmental Protection and Negative Externalities** about economic policy with respect to negative externalities and pollution—the problem called regulatory capture (which we defined in **Monopoly and Antitrust Policy**). In legislative bodies and agencies that write laws and regulations about how much corporations will pay in taxes, or rules for safety in the workplace, or instructions on how to satisfy environmental regulations, you can be sure the specific industry affected has lobbyists who study every word and every comma. They talk with the legislators who are writing the legislation and suggest alternative wording. They contribute to the campaigns of legislators on the key committees—and may even offer those legislators high-paying jobs after they have left office. As a result, it often turns out that those regulated can exercise considerable influence over the regulators.

Link It Up ⚭

Visit this website (http://openstaxcollege.org/l/lobbying) to read about lobbying.

In the early 2000s, about 40 million people in the United States were eligible for Medicare, a government program that provides health insurance for those 65 and older. On some issues, the elderly are a powerful interest group. They donate money and time to political campaigns, and in the 2012 presidential election, 70% of those over age 65 voted, while just 49% of those aged 18 to 24 cast a ballot, according to the U.S. Census.

In 2003, Congress passed and President George Bush signed into law a substantial expansion of Medicare that helped the elderly to pay for prescription drugs. The prescription drug benefit cost the federal government about $40 billion in 2006, and the Medicare system projected that the annual cost would rise to $121 billion by 2016. The political pressure to pass a prescription drug benefit for Medicare was apparently quite high, while the political pressure to assist the 40 million with no health insurance at all was considerably lower. One reason might be that the American Association for Retired People AARP, a well-funded and well-organized lobbying group represents senior citizens, while there is no umbrella organization to lobby for those without health insurance.

In the battle over passage of the 2010 Affordable Care Act (ACA), which became known as "Obamacare," there was heavy lobbying on all sides by insurance companies and pharmaceutical companies. However, labor unions and community groups financed a lobby group, Health Care for America Now (HCAN), to offset corporate lobbying. HCAN, spending $60 million dollars, was successful in helping pass legislation which added new regulations on insurance companies and a mandate that all individuals will obtain health insurance by 2014. The following Work It Out feature further explains voter incentives and lobbyist influence.

Work It Out ──○──○──○

Paying To Get Your Way

Suppose Congress proposes a tax on carbon emissions for certain factories in a small town of 10,000 people. Congress estimates the tax will reduce pollution to such an extent that it will benefit each resident by an equivalent of $300. The tax will also reduce profits to the town's two large factories by $1 million each. How much should the factory owners be willing to spend to fight the tax passage, and how much should the townspeople be willing to pay to support it? Why is society unlikely to achieve the optimal outcome?

Step 1. The two factory owners each stand to lose $1 million if the tax passes, so each should be willing to spend up to that amount to prevent the passage, a combined sum of $2 million. Of course, in the real world, there is no guarantee that lobbying efforts will be successful, so the factory owners may choose to invest an amount that is substantially lower.

Step 2. There are 10,000 townspeople, each standing to benefit by $300 if the tax passes. Theoretically, then, they should be willing to spend up to $3 million (10,000 × $300) to ensure passage. (Again, in the real world with no guarantees of success, they may choose to spend less.)

Step 3. It is costly and difficult for 10,000 people to coordinate in such a way as to influence public policy. Since each person stands to gain only $300, many may feel lobbying is not worth the effort.

Step 4. The two factory owners, however, find it very easy and profitable to coordinate their activities, so they have a greater incentive to do so.

Special interests may develop a close relationship with one political party, so their ability to influence legislation rises and falls as that party moves in or out of power. A special interest may even hurt a political party if it appears to a number of voters that the relationship is too cozy. In a close election, a small group that has been under-represented in the past may find that it can tip the election one way or another—so that group will suddenly receive considerable attention. Democratic institutions produce an ebb and flow of political parties and interests and thus offer both opportunities for special interests and ways of counterbalancing those interests over time.

Identifiable Winners, Anonymous Losers

A number of economic policies produce gains whose beneficiaries are easily identifiable, but costs that are partly or entirely shared by a large number who remain anonymous. A democratic political system probably has a bias toward those who are identifiable.

For example, policies that impose price controls—like rent control—may look as if they benefit renters and impose costs only on landlords. However, when landlords then decide to reduce the number of rental units available in the area, a number of people who would have liked to rent an apartment end up living somewhere else because no units were available. These would-be renters have experienced a cost of rent control, but it is hard to identify who they are.

Similarly, policies that block imports will benefit the firms that would have competed with those imports—and workers at those firms—who are likely to be quite visible. Consumers who would have preferred to purchase the imported products, and who thus bear some costs of the protectionist policy, are much less visible.

Specific tax breaks and spending programs also have identifiable winners and impose costs on others who are hard to identify. Special interests are more likely to arise from a group that is easily identifiable, rather than from a group where some of those who suffer may not even recognize they are bearing costs.

Pork Barrels and Logrolling

Politicians have an incentive to ensure that they spend government money in their home state or district, where it will benefit their constituents in a direct and obvious way. Thus, when legislators are negotiating over whether to support a piece of legislation, they commonly ask each other to include **pork-barrel spending**, legislation that benefits mainly a single political district. Pork-barrel spending is another case in which concentrated benefits and widely dispersed costs challenge democracy: the benefits of pork-barrel spending are obvious and direct to local voters, while the costs are spread over the entire country. Read the following Clear It Up feature for more information on pork-barrel spending.

This OpenStax book is available for free at http://cnx.org/content/col12122/1.4

How much impact can pork-barrel spending have?

Many observers widely regard U.S. Senator Robert C. Byrd of West Virginia, who was originally elected to the Senate in 1958 and served until 2010, as one of the masters of pork-barrel politics, directing a steady stream of federal funds to his home state. A journalist once compiled a list of structures in West Virginia at least partly government funded and named after Byrd: "the Robert C. Byrd Highway; the Robert C. Byrd Locks and Dam; the Robert C. Byrd Institute; the Robert C. Byrd Life Long Learning Center; the Robert C. Byrd Honors Scholarship Program; the Robert C. Byrd Green Bank Telescope; the Robert C. Byrd Institute for Advanced Flexible Manufacturing; the Robert C. Byrd Federal Courthouse; the Robert C. Byrd Health Sciences Center; the Robert C. Byrd Academic and Technology Center; the Robert C. Byrd United Technical Center; the Robert C. Byrd Federal Building; the Robert C. Byrd Drive; the Robert C. Byrd Hilltop Office Complex; the Robert C. Byrd Library; and the Robert C. Byrd Learning Resource Center; the Robert C. Byrd Rural Health Center." This list does not include government-funded projects in West Virginia that were not named after Byrd. Of course, we would have to analyze each of these expenditures in detail to figure out whether we should treat them as pork-barrel spending or whether they provide widespread benefits that reach beyond West Virginia. At least some of them, or a portion of them, certainly would fall into that category. Because there are currently no term limits for Congressional representatives, those who have been in office longer generally have more power to enact pork-barrel projects.

The amount that government spends on individual pork-barrel projects is small, but many small projects can add up to a substantial total. A nonprofit watchdog organization, called Citizens against Government Waste, produces an annual report, the *Pig Book* that attempts to quantify the amount of pork-barrel spending, focusing on items that only one member of Congress requested, that were passed into law without any public hearings, or that serve only a local purpose. Whether any specific item qualifies as pork can be controversial. Interestingly, the 2016 Congressional Pig Book exposed 123 earmarks in FY 2016, an increase of 17.1 percent from the 105 in FY 2015. The cost of earmarks in FY 2016 was $5.1 billion, an increase of 21.4 percent from the $4.2 billion in FY 2015. While the increase in cost over one year is disconcerting, the two-year rise of 88.9 percent over the $2.7 billion in FY 2014 causes concern.

Logrolling, an action in which all members of a group of legislators agree to vote for a package of otherwise unrelated laws that they individually favor, can encourage pork barrel spending. For example, if one member of the U.S. Congress suggests building a new bridge or hospital in his or her own congressional district, the other members might oppose it. However, if 51% of the legislators come together, they can pass a bill that includes a bridge or hospital for every one of their districts.

As a reflection of this interest of legislators in their own districts, the U.S. government has typically spread out its spending on military bases and weapons programs to congressional districts all across the country. In part, the government does this to help create a situation that encourages members of Congress to vote in support of defense spending.

18.3 | Flaws in the Democratic System of Government

By the end of this section, you will be able to:
- Assess the median voter theory
- Explain the voting cycle
- Analyze the interrelationship between markets and government

Most developed countries today have a democratic system of government: citizens express their opinions through votes and those votes affect the direction of the country. The advantage of democracy over other systems is that it allows everyone in a society an equal say and therefore may reduce the possibility of a small group of wealthy oligarchs oppressing the masses. There is no such thing as a perfect system, and democracy, for all its popularity, is not without its problems, a few of which we will examine here.

We sometimes sum up and oversimplify democracy in two words: "Majority rule." When voters face three or more choices, however, then voting may not always be a useful way of determining what the majority prefers.

As one example, consider an election in a state where 60% of the population is liberal and 40% is conservative. If there are only two candidates, one from each side, and if liberals and conservatives vote in the same 60–40 proportions in which they are represented in the population, then the liberal will win. What if the election ends up including two liberal candidates and one conservative? It is possible that the liberal vote will split and victory will go to the minority party. In this case, the outcome does not reflect the majority's preference.

Does the majority view prevail in the case of sugar quotas? Clearly there are more sugar consumers in the United States than sugar producers, but the U.S. domestic sugar lobby (www.sugarcane.org) has successfully argued for protection against imports since 1789. By law, therefore, U.S. cookie and candy makers must use 85% domestic sugar in their products. Meanwhile quotas on imported sugar restrict supply and keep the domestic sugar price up—raising prices for companies that use sugar in producing their goods and for consumers. The European Union allows sugar imports, and prices there are 40% lower than U.S. sugar prices. Sugar-producing countries in the Caribbean repeatedly protest the U.S. quotas at the World Trade Organization meetings, but each bite of cookie, at present, costs you more than if there were no sugar lobby. This case goes against the theory of the "median" voter in a democracy. The **median voter theory** argues that politicians will try to match policies to what pleases the median voter preferences. If we think of political positions along a spectrum from left to right, the median voter is in the middle of the spectrum. This theory argues that actual policy will reflect "middle of the road." In the case of sugar lobby politics, the *minority*, not the median, dominates policy.

Sometimes it is not even clear how to define the majority opinion. Step aside from politics for a moment and think about a choice facing three families (the Ortegas, the Schmidts, and the Alexanders) who are planning to celebrate New Year's Day together. They agree to vote on the menu, choosing from three entrees, and they agree that the majority vote wins. With three families, it seems reasonable that one producing choice will get a 2–1 majority. What if, however, their vote ends up looking like **Table 18.1**?

Clearly, the three families disagree on their first choice. However, the problem goes even deeper. Instead of looking at all three choices at once, compare them two at a time. (See **Figure 18.2**) In a vote of turkey versus beef, turkey wins by 2–1. In a vote of beef versus lasagna, beef wins 2–1. If turkey beats beef, and beef beats lasagna, then it might seem only logical that turkey must also beat lasagna. However, with the preferences, lasagna is preferred to turkey by a 2–1 vote, as well. If lasagna is preferred to turkey, and turkey beats beef, then surely it must be that lasagna also beats beef? Actually, no. Beef beats lasagna. In other words, the majority view may not win. Clearly, as any car salesmen will tell you, the way one presents choices to us influences our decisions.

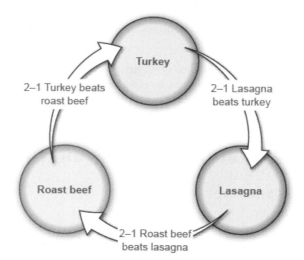

Figure 18.2 A Voting Cycle Given these choices, voting will struggle to produce a majority outcome. Turkey is favored over roast beef by 2–1 and roast beef is favored over lasagna by 2–1. If turkey beats roast beef and roast beef beats lasagna, then it might seem that turkey must beat lasagna, too. However, given these preferences, lasagna is favored over turkey by 2–1.

This OpenStax book is available for free at http://cnx.org/content/col12122/1.4

	The Ortega Family	The Schmidt Family	The Alexander Family
First Choice	Turkey	Roast beef	Lasagna
Second Choice	Roast beef	Lasagna	Turkey
Third Choice	Lasagna	Turkey	Roast beef

Table 18.1 Circular Preferences

We call the situation in which Choice A is preferred by a majority over Choice B, Choice B is preferred by a majority over Choice C, and Choice C is preferred by a majority over Choice A a **voting cycle**. It is easy to imagine sets of government choices—say, perhaps the choice between increased defense spending, increased government spending on health care, and a tax cut—in which a voting cycle could occur. The result will be determined by the order in which stakeholders present and vote on choices, not by majority rule, because every choice is both preferred to some alternative and also not preferred to another alternative.

Link It Up

Visit this website (http://www.fairvote.org/rcv#rcvbenefits) to read about instant runoff voting, a preferential voting system.

Where Is Government's Self-Correcting Mechanism?

When a firm produces a product no one wants to buy or produces at a higher cost than its competitors, the firm is likely to suffer losses. If it cannot change its ways, it will go out of business. This self-correcting mechanism in the marketplace can have harsh effects on workers or on local economies, but it also puts pressure on firms for good performance.

Government agencies, however, do not sell their products in a market. They receive tax dollars instead. They are not challenged by competitors as are private-sector firms. If the U.S. Department of Education or the U.S. Department of Defense is performing poorly, citizens cannot purchase their services from another provider and drive the existing government agencies into bankruptcy. If you are upset that the Internal Revenue Service is slow in sending you a tax refund or seems unable to answer your questions, you cannot decide to pay your income taxes through a different organization. Of course, elected politicians can assign new leaders to government agencies and instruct them to reorganize or to emphasize a different mission. The pressure government faces, however, to change its bureaucracy, to seek greater efficiency, and to improve customer responsiveness is much milder than the threat of being put out of business altogether.

This insight suggests that when government provides goods or services directly, we might expect it to do so with less efficiency than private firms—except in certain cases where the government agency may compete directly with private firms. At the local level, for example, government can provide directly services like garbage collection, using private firms under contract to the government, or by a mix of government employees competing with private firms.

A Balanced View of Markets and Government

The British statesman Sir Winston Churchill (1874–1965) once wrote: "No one pretends that democracy is perfect or all-wise. Indeed, it has been said that democracy is the worst form of government except for all of the other forms which have been tried from time to time." In that spirit, the theme of this discussion is certainly not that we should abandon democratic government. A practical student of public policy needs to recognize that in some cases, like the case of well-organized special interests or pork-barrel legislation, a democratic government may seek to enact economically unwise projects or programs. In other cases, by placing a low priority on the problems of those who are not well organized or who are less likely to vote, the government may fail to act when it could do some good. In these and other cases, there is no automatic reason to believe that government will necessarily make economically sensible choices.

"The true test of a first-rate mind is the ability to hold two contradictory ideas at the same time," wrote the American author F. Scott Fitzgerald (1896–1940). At this point in your study of microeconomics, you should be able to go one better than Fitzgerald and hold three somewhat contradictory ideas about the interrelationship between markets and government in your mind at the same time.

First, markets are extraordinarily useful and flexible institutions through which society can allocate its scarce resources. We introduced this idea with the subjects of international trade and demand and supply in other chapters and reinforced it in all the subsequent discussions of how households and firms make decisions.

Second, markets may sometimes produce unwanted results. A short list of the cases in which markets produce unwanted results includes monopoly and other cases of imperfect competition, pollution, poverty and inequality of incomes, discrimination, and failure to provide insurance.

Third, while government may play a useful role in addressing the problems of markets, government action is also imperfect and may not reflect majority views. Economists readily admit that, in settings like monopoly or negative externalities, a potential role exists for government intervention. However, in the real world, it is not enough to point out that government action might be a good idea. Instead, we must have some confidence that the government is likely to identify and carry out the appropriate public policy. To make sensible judgments about economic policy, we must see the strengths and weaknesses of both markets and government. We must not idealize or demonize either unregulated markets or government actions. Instead, consider the actual strengths and weaknesses of real-world markets and real-world governments.

These three insights seldom lead to simple or obvious political conclusions. As the famous British economist Joan Robinson wrote some decades ago: "[E]conomic theory, in itself, preaches no doctrines and cannot establish any universally valid laws. It is a method of ordering ideas and formulating questions." The study of economics is neither politically conservative, nor moderate, nor liberal. There are economists who are Democrats, Republicans, libertarians, socialists, and members of every other political group you can name. Of course, conservatives may tend to emphasize the virtues of markets and the limitations of government, while liberals may tend to emphasize the shortcomings of markets and the need for government programs. Such differences only illustrate that the language and terminology of economics is not limited to one set of political beliefs, but can be used by all.

Bring it Home

Chinese Tire Tariffs

In April 2009, the union representing U.S. tire manufacturing workers filed a request with the U.S. International Trade Commission (ITC), asking it to investigate tire imports from China. Under U.S. trade law, if imports from a country increase to the point that they cause market disruption in the United States, as determined by the ITC, then it can also recommend a remedy for this market disruption. In this case, the ITC determined that from 2004 to 2008, U.S. tire manufacturers suffered declines in production, financial health, and employment as a direct result of increases in tire imports from China. The ITC recommended placing an additional tax on tire imports from China. President Obama and Congress agreed with the ITC recommendation, and in June 2009 tariffs on Chinese tires increased from 4% to 39%.

Why would U.S. consumers buy imported tires from China in the first place? Most likely, because they are cheaper than tires produced domestically or in other countries. Therefore, this tariff increase should cause U.S. consumers to pay higher prices for tires, either because Chinese tires are now more expensive, or because U.S. consumers are pushed by the tariff to buy more expensive tires made by U.S. manufacturers or

This OpenStax book is available for free at http://cnx.org/content/col12122/1.4

those from other countries. In the end, this tariff made U.S. consumers pay more for tires.

Was this tariff met with outrage expressed via social media, traditional media, or mass protests? Were there "Occupy Wall Street-type" demonstrations? The answer is a resounding "No". Most U.S. tire consumers were likely unaware of the tariff increase, although they may have noticed the price increase, which was between $4 and $13 depending on the type of tire. Tire consumers are also potential voters. Conceivably, a tax increase, even a small one, might make voters unhappy. However, voters probably realized that it was not worth their time to learn anything about this issue or cast a vote based on it. They probably thought their vote would not matter in determining the outcome of an election or changing this policy.

Estimates of the impact of this tariff show it costs U.S. consumers around $1.11 billion annually. Of this amount, roughly $817 million ends up in the pockets of foreign tire manufacturers other than in China, and the remaining $294 million goes to U.S. tire manufacturers. In other words, the tariff increase on Chinese tires may have saved 1,200 jobs in the domestic tire sector, but it cost 3,700 jobs in other sectors, as consumers had to reduce their spending because they were paying more for tires. People actually lost their jobs as a result of this tariff. Workers in U.S. tire manufacturing firms earned about $40,000 in 2010. Given the number of jobs saved and the total cost to U.S. consumers, the cost of saving one job amounted to $926,500!

This tariff caused a net decline in U.S. social surplus. (We discuss total surplus in the **Demand and Supply** chapter, and tariffs in the **The International Trade and Capital Flows** chapter.) Instead of saving jobs, it cost jobs, and those jobs that it saved cost many times more than the people working in them could ever hope to earn. Why would the government do this?

The chapter answers this question by discussing the influence special interest groups have on economic policy. The steelworkers union, whose members make tires, saw increasingly more members lose their jobs as U.S. consumers consumed increasingly more cheap Chinese tires. By definition, this union is relatively small but well organized, especially compared to tire consumers. It stands to gain much for each of its members, compared to what each tire consumer may have to give up in terms of higher prices. Thus, the steelworkers union (joined by domestic tire manufacturers) has not only the means but the incentive to lobby economic policymakers and lawmakers. Given that U.S. tire consumers are a large and unorganized group, if they even are a group, it is unlikely they will lobby against higher tire tariffs. In the end, lawmakers tend to listen to those who lobby them, even though the results make for bad economic policy.

KEY TERMS

logrolling the situation in which groups of legislators all agree to vote for a package of otherwise unrelated laws that they individually favor

median voter theory theory that politicians will try to match policies to what pleases the median voter preferences

pork-barrel spending spending that benefits mainly a single political district

rational ignorance the theory that rational people will not vote if the costs of becoming informed and voting are too high or because they know their vote will not be decisive in the election

special interest groups groups that are small in number relative to the nation, but well organized and thus exert a disproportionate effect on political outcomes

voting cycle the situation in which a majority prefers A over B, B over C, and C over A

KEY CONCEPTS AND SUMMARY

18.1 Voter Participation and Costs of Elections
The theory of rational ignorance says voters will recognize that their single vote is extremely unlikely to influence the outcome of an election. As a consequence, they will choose to remain uninformed about issues and not vote. This theory helps explain why voter turnout is so low in the United States.

18.2 Special Interest Politics
Special interest politics arises when a relatively small group, called a special interest group, each of whose members has a large interest in a political outcome, devotes considerable time and energy to lobbying for the group's preferred choice. Meanwhile, the large majority, each of whose members has only a small interest in this issue, pays no attention.

We define pork--barrel spending as legislation whose benefits are concentrated on a single district while the costs are spread widely over the country. Logrolling refers to a situation in which two or more legislators agree to vote for each other's legislation, which can then encourage pork-barrel spending in many districts.

18.3 Flaws in the Democratic System of Government
Majority votes can run into difficulties when more than two choices exist. A voting cycle occurs when, in a situation with at least three choices, choice A is preferred by a majority vote to choice B, choice B is preferred by a majority vote to choice C, and choice C is preferred by a majority vote to choice A. In such a situation, it is impossible to identify what the majority prefers. Another difficulty arises when the vote is so divided that no choice receives a majority.

A practical approach to microeconomic policy will need to take a realistic view of the specific strengths and weaknesses of markets as well as government, rather than making the easy but wrong assumption that either the market or government is always beneficial or always harmful.

SELF-CHECK QUESTIONS

1. Based on the theory of rational ignorance, what should we expect to happen to voter turnout as the internet makes information easier to obtain?

2. What is the cost of voting in an election?

3. What is the main factor preventing a large community from influencing policy in the same way as a special interest group?

This OpenStax book is available for free at http://cnx.org/content/col12122/1.4

4. Why might legislators vote to impose a tariff on Egyptian cotton, when consumers in their districts would benefit from its availability?

5. True or false: Majority rule can fail to produce a single preferred outcome when there are more than two choices.

6. Anastasia, Emma, and Greta are deciding what to do on a weekend getaway. They each suggest a first, second, and third choice and then vote on the options. **Table 18.2** shows their first, second, and third choice preferences . Explain why they will have a hard time reaching a decision. Does the group prefer mountain biking to canoeing? What about canoeing compared to the beach? What about the beach compared to the original choice of mountain biking?

	Anastasia	Emma	Greta
First Choice	Beach	Mountain biking	Canoeing
Second Choice	Mountain biking	Canoeing	Beach
Third Choice	Canoeing	Beach	Mountain biking

Table 18.2

7. Suppose there is an election for Soft Drink Commissioner. The field consists of one candidate from the Pepsi party and four from the Coca-Cola party. This would seem to indicate a strong preference for Coca-Cola among the voting population, but the Pepsi candidate ends up winning in a landslide. Why does this happen?

REVIEW QUESTIONS

8. How does rational ignorance discourage voting?

9. How can a small special interest group win in a situation of majority voting when the benefits it seeks flow only to a small group?

10. How can pork-barrel spending occur in a situation of majority voting when it benefits only a small group?

11. Why do legislators vote for spending projects in districts that are not their own?

12. Why does a voting cycle make it impossible to decide on a majority-approved choice?

13. How does a government agency raise revenue differently from a private company, and how does that affect the way government makes decisions compared to business decisions?

CRITICAL THINKING QUESTIONS

14. What are some reasons people might find acquiring information about politics and voting rational, in contrast to rational ignorance theory?

15. What are some possible ways to encourage voter participation and overcome rational ignorance?

16. Given that rational ignorance discourages some people from becoming informed about elections, is it necessarily a good idea to encourage greater voter turnout? Why or why not?

17. When Microsoft was founded, the company devoted very few resources to lobbying activities. After a high-profile antitrust case against it, however, the company began to lobby heavily. Why does it make financial sense for companies to invest in lobbyists?

18. Representatives of competing firms often comprise special interest groups. Why are competitors sometimes willing to cooperate in order to form lobbying associations?

19. Special interests do not oppose regulations in all cases. The Marketplace Fairness Act of 2013 would require online merchants to collect sales taxes from their customers in other states. Why might a large online retailer like Amazon.com support such a measure?

20. To ensure safety and efficacy, the Food and Drug Administration regulates the medicines that pharmacies are allowed to sell in the United States. Sometimes this means a company must test a drug for years before it can reach the market. We can easily identify the winners in this system as those who are protected from unsafe drugs that might otherwise harm them. Who are the more anonymous losers who suffer from strict medical regulations?

21. How is it possible to bear a cost without realizing it? What are some examples of policies that affect people in ways of which they may not even be aware?

22. Is pork-barrel spending always a bad thing? Can you think of some examples of pork-barrel projects, perhaps from your own district, that have had positive results?

PROBLEMS

27. Say that the government is considering a ban on smoking in restaurants in Tobaccoville. There are 1 million people living there, and each would benefit by $200 from this smoking ban. However, there are two large tobacco companies in Tobaccoville and the ban would cost them $5 million each. What are the proposed policy's total costs and benefits? Do you think it will pass?

23. The United States currently uses a voting system called "first past the post" in elections, meaning that the candidate with the most votes wins. What are some of the problems with a "first past the post" system?

24. What are some alternatives to a "first past the post" system that might reduce the problem of voting cycles?

25. AT&T spent some $10 million dollars lobbying Congress to block entry of competitors into the telephone market in 1978. Why do you think it efforts failed?

26. Occupy Wall Street was a national (and later global) organized protest against the greed, bank profits, and financial corruption that led to the 2008–2009 recession. The group popularized slogans like "We are the 99%," meaning it represented the majority against the wealth of the top 1%. Does the fact that the protests had little to no effect on legislative changes support or contradict the chapter?

This OpenStax book is available for free at http://cnx.org/content/col12122/1.4

19 | The Macroeconomic Perspective

Figure 19.1 The Great Depression At times, such as when many people having trouble making ends meet, it is easy to tell how the economy is doing. This photograph shows people lined up during the Great Depression, waiting for relief checks. At other times, when some are doing well and others are not, it is more difficult to ascertain how the economy of a country is doing. (Credit: modification of work by the U.S. Library of Congress/Wikimedia Commons)

Bring it Home

How is the Economy Doing? How Does One Tell?

The 1990s were boom years for the U.S. economy. Beginning in the late 2000s, from 2007 to 2014 economic performance in in the U.S. was poor. What causes the economy to expand or contract? Why do businesses fail when they are making all the right decisions? Why do workers lose their jobs when they are hardworking and productive? Are bad economic times a failure of the market system? Are they a failure of the government? These are all questions of macroeconomics, which we will begin to address in this chapter. We will not be able to answer all of these questions here, but we will start with the basics: How is the economy doing? How can we tell?

The macro economy includes all buying and selling, all production and consumption; everything that goes on in every market in the economy. How can we get a handle on that? The answer begins more than 80 years ago, during the Great Depression. President Franklin D. Roosevelt and his economic advisers knew things were bad—but how could they express and measure just how bad it was? An economist named Simon Kuznets, who later won the Nobel Prize for his work, came up with a way to track what the entire economy is producing. In this chapter, you will learn how the government constructs GDP, how we use it, and why it is so important.

Introduction to the Macroeconomic Perspective

In this chapter, you will learn about:

- Measuring the Size of the Economy: Gross Domestic Product
- Adjusting Nominal Values to Real Values
- Tracking Real GDP over Time
- Comparing GDP among Countries
- How Well GDP Measures the Well-Being of Society

Macroeconomics focuses on the economy as a whole (or on whole economies as they interact). What causes recessions? What makes unemployment stay high when recessions are supposed to be over? Why do some countries grow faster than others? Why do some countries have higher standards of living than others? These are all questions that macroeconomics addresses. Macroeconomics involves adding up the economic activity of all households and all businesses in all markets to obtain the overall demand and supply in the economy. However, when we do that, something curious happens. It is not unusual that what results at the macro level is different from the sum of the microeconomic parts. What seems sensible from a microeconomic point of view can have unexpected or counterproductive results at the macroeconomic level. Imagine that you are sitting at an event with a large audience, like a live concert or a basketball game. A few people decide that they want a better view, and so they stand up. However, when these people stand up, they block the view for other people, and the others need to stand up as well if they wish to see. Eventually, nearly everyone is standing up, and as a result, no one can see much better than before. The rational decision of some individuals at the micro level—to stand up for a better view—ended up as self-defeating at the macro level. This is not macroeconomics, but it is an apt analogy.

Macroeconomics is a rather massive subject. How are we going to tackle it? **Figure 19.2** illustrates the structure we will use. We will study macroeconomics from three different perspectives:

1. What are the macroeconomic goals? (Macroeconomics as a discipline does not have goals, but we do have goals for the macro economy.)
2. What are the frameworks economists can use to analyze the macroeconomy?
3. Finally, what are the policy tools governments can use to manage the macroeconomy?

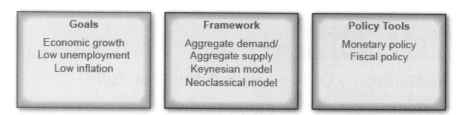

Figure 19.2 Macroeconomic Goals, Framework, and Policies   This chart shows what macroeconomics is about. The box on the left indicates a consensus of what are the most important goals for the macro economy, the middle box lists the frameworks economists use to analyze macroeconomic changes (such as inflation or recession), and the box on the right indicates the two tools the federal government uses to influence the macro economy.

Goals

In thinking about the macroeconomy's overall health, it is useful to consider three primary goals: economic growth, low unemployment, and low inflation.

- Economic growth ultimately determines the prevailing standard of living in a country. Economists measure growth by the percentage change in real (inflation-adjusted) gross domestic product. A growth rate of more than 3% is considered good.
- Unemployment, as measured by the unemployment rate, is the percentage of people in the labor force who do not have a job. When people lack jobs, the economy is wasting a precious resource-labor, and the result is

This OpenStax book is available for free at http://cnx.org/content/col12122/1.4

lower goods and services produced. Unemployment, however, is more than a statistic—it represents people's livelihoods. While measured unemployment is unlikely to ever be zero, economists consider a measured unemployment rate of 5% or less low (good).

- Inflation is a sustained increase in the overall level of prices, and is measured by the consumer price index. If many people face a situation where the prices that they pay for food, shelter, and healthcare are rising much faster than the wages they receive for their labor, there will be widespread unhappiness as their standard of living declines. For that reason, low inflation—an inflation rate of 1–2%—is a major goal.

Frameworks

As you learn in the micro part of this book, principal tools that economists use are theories and models (see **Welcome to Economics!** for more on this). In microeconomics, we used the theories of supply and demand. In macroeconomics, we use the theories of aggregate demand (AD) and aggregate supply (AS). This book presents two perspectives on macroeconomics: the Neoclassical perspective and the Keynesian perspective, each of which has its own version of AD and AS. Between the two perspectives, you will obtain a good understanding of what drives the macroeconomy.

Policy Tools

National governments have two tools for influencing the macroeconomy. The first is monetary policy, which involves managing the money supply and interest rates. The second is fiscal policy, which involves changes in government spending/purchases and taxes.

We will explain each of the items in **Figure 19.2** in detail in one or more other chapters. As you learn these things, you will discover that the goals and the policy tools are in the news almost every day.

19.1 | Measuring the Size of the Economy: Gross Domestic Product

By the end of this section, you will be able to:
- Identify the components of GDP on the demand side and on the supply side
- Evaluate how economists measure gross domestic product (GDP)
- Contrast and calculate GDP, net exports, and net national product

Macroeconomics is an empirical subject, so the first step toward understanding it is to measure the economy.

How large is the U.S. economy? Economists typically measure the size of a nation's overall economy by its **gross domestic product (GDP),** which is the value of all final goods and services produced within a country in a given year. Measuring GDP involves counting the production of millions of different goods and services—smart phones, cars, music downloads, computers, steel, bananas, college educations, and all other new goods and services that a country produced in the current year—and summing them into a total dollar value. This task is straightforward: take the quantity of everything produced, multiply it by the price at which each product sold, and add up the total. In 2016, the U.S. GDP totaled $18.6 trillion, the largest GDP in the world.

Each of the market transactions that enter into GDP must involve both a buyer and a seller. We can measure an economy's GDP either by the total dollar value of what consumers purchase in the economy, or by the total dollar value of what is the country produces. There is even a third way, as we will explain later.

GDP Measured by Components of Demand

Who buys all of this production? We can divide this demand into four main parts: consumer spending (consumption), business spending (investment), government spending on goods and services, and spending on net exports. (See the following Clear It Up feature to understand what we mean by investment.) **Table 19.1** shows how these four components added up to the GDP in 2016. **Figure 19.4** (a) shows the levels of consumption, investment, and government purchases over time, expressed as a percentage of GDP, while **Figure 19.4** (b) shows the levels of exports and imports as a percentage of GDP over time. A few patterns about each of these components are worth noticing. **Table 19.1** shows the components of GDP from the demand side.

Components of GDP on the Demand Side (in trillions of dollars)		Percentage of Total
Consumption	$12.8	68.8%
Investment	$3.0	16.1%
Government	$3.3	17.7%
Exports	$2.2	11.8%
Imports	−$2.7	−14.5%
Total GDP	**$18.6**	**100%**

Table 19.1 Components of U.S. GDP in 2016: From the Demand Side   (Source: http://bea.gov/iTable/index_nipa.cfm)

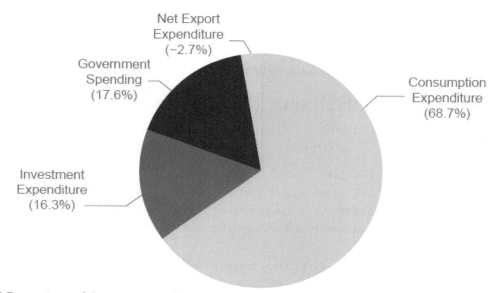

Figure 19.3 Percentage of Components of U.S. GDP on the Demand Side Consumption makes up over half of the demand side components of the GDP. (Source: http://bea.gov/iTable/index_nipa.cfm)

What does the word "investment" mean?

What do economists mean by investment, or business spending? In calculating GDP, investment does not refer to purchasing stocks and bonds or trading financial assets. It refers to purchasing new capital goods, that is, new commercial real estate (such as buildings, factories, and stores) and equipment, residential housing construction, and inventories. Inventories that manufacturers produce this year are included in this year's GDP—even if they are not yet sold. From the accountant's perspective, it is as if the firm invested in its own inventories. Business investment in 2016 was $3 trillion, according to the Bureau of Economic Analysis.

This OpenStax book is available for free at http://cnx.org/content/col12122/1.4

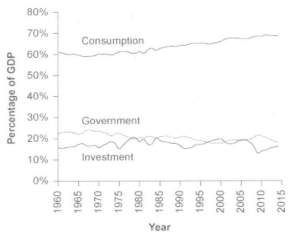

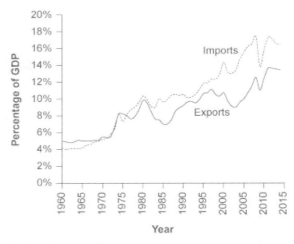

(a) Demand from consumption, investment, and government   (b) Imports and exports

Figure 19.4 Components of GDP on the Demand Side (a) Consumption is about two-thirds of GDP, and it has been on a slight upward trend over time. Business investment hovers around 15% of GDP, but it fluctuates more than consumption. Government spending on goods and services is slightly under 20% of GDP and has declined modestly over time. (b) Exports are added to total demand for goods and services, while imports are subtracted from total demand. If exports exceed imports, as in most of the 1960s and 1970s in the U.S. economy, a trade surplus exists. If imports exceed exports, as in recent years, then a trade deficit exists. (Source: http://bea.gov/iTable/index_nipa.cfm)

Consumption expenditure by households is the largest component of GDP, accounting for about two-thirds of the GDP in any year. This tells us that consumers' spending decisions are a major driver of the economy. However, consumer spending is a gentle elephant: when viewed over time, it does not jump around too much, and has increased modestly from about 60% of GDP in the 1960s and 1970s.

Investment expenditure refers to purchases of physical plant and equipment, primarily by businesses. If Starbucks builds a new store, or Amazon buys robots, they count these expenditures under business investment. Investment demand is far smaller than consumption demand, typically accounting for only about 15–18% of GDP, but it is very important for the economy because this is where jobs are created. However, it fluctuates more noticeably than consumption. Business investment is volatile. New technology or a new product can spur business investment, but then confidence can drop and business investment can pull back sharply.

If you have noticed any of the infrastructure projects (new bridges, highways, airports) launched during the 2009 recession, you have seen how important government spending can be for the economy. Government expenditure in the United States is close to 20% of GDP, and includes spending by all three levels of government: federal, state, and local. The only part of government spending counted in demand is government purchases of goods or services produced in the economy. Examples include the government buying a new fighter jet for the Air Force (federal government spending), building a new highway (state government spending), or a new school (local government spending). A significant portion of government budgets consists of transfer payments, like unemployment benefits, veteran's benefits, and Social Security payments to retirees. The government excludes these payments from GDP because it does not receive a new good or service in return or exchange. Instead they are transfers of income from taxpayers to others. If you are curious about the awesome undertaking of adding up GDP, read the following Clear It Up feature.

Clear It Up

How do statisticians measure GDP?

Government economists at the Bureau of Economic Analysis (BEA), within the U.S. Department of Commerce, piece together estimates of GDP from a variety of sources.

Once every five years, in the second and seventh year of each decade, the Bureau of the Census carries out a detailed census of businesses throughout the United States. In between, the Census Bureau carries out a monthly survey of retail sales. The government adjusts these figures with foreign trade data to account for exports that are produced in the United States and sold abroad and for imports that are produced abroad and sold here. Once every ten years, the Census Bureau conducts a comprehensive survey of housing and residential finance. Together, these sources provide the main basis for figuring out what is produced for consumers.

For investment, the Census Bureau carries out a monthly survey of construction and an annual survey of expenditures on physical capital equipment.

For what the federal government purchases, the statisticians rely on the U.S. Department of the Treasury. An annual Census of Governments gathers information on state and local governments. Because the government spends a considerable amount at all levels hiring people to provide services, it also tracks a large portion of spending through payroll records that state governments and the Social Security Administration collect.

With regard to foreign trade, the Census Bureau compiles a monthly record of all import and export documents. Additional surveys cover transportation and travel, and make adjustments for financial services that are produced in the United States for foreign customers.

Many other sources contribute to GDP estimates. Information on energy comes from the U.S. Department of Transportation and Department of Energy. The Agency for Health Care Research and Quality collects information on healthcare. Surveys of landlords find out about rental income. The Department of Agriculture collects statistics on farming.

All these bits and pieces of information arrive in different forms, at different time intervals. The BEA melds them together to produce GDP estimates on a quarterly basis (every three months). The BEA then "annualizes" these numbers by multiplying by four. As more information comes in, the BEA updates and revises these estimates. BEA releases the GDP "advance" estimate for a certain quarter one month after a quarter. The "preliminary" estimate comes out one month after that. The BEA publishes the "final" estimate one month later, but it is not actually final. In July, the BEA releases roughly updated estimates for the previous calendar year. Then, once every five years, after it has processed all the results of the latest detailed five-year business census, the BEA revises all of the past GDP estimates according to the newest methods and data, going all the way back to 1929.

Link It Up 🔗

Visit this website (http://openstaxcollege.org/l/beafaq) to read FAQs on the BEA site. You can even email your own questions!

When thinking about the demand for domestically produced goods in a global economy, it is important to count spending on exports—domestically produced goods that a country sells abroad. Similarly, we must also subtract spending on imports—goods that a country produces in other countries that residents of this country purchase. The GDP net export component is equal to the dollar value of exports (X) minus the dollar value of imports (M), (X − M). We call the gap between exports and imports the **trade balance**. If a country's exports are larger than its imports, then a country has a **trade surplus**. In the United States, exports typically exceeded imports in the 1960s and 1970s, as **Figure 19.4**(b) shows.

Since the early 1980s, imports have typically exceeded exports, and so the United States has experienced a **trade**

This OpenStax book is available for free at http://cnx.org/content/col12122/1.4

deficit in most years. The trade deficit grew quite large in the late 1990s and in the mid-2000s. **Figure 19.4** (b) also shows that imports and exports have both risen substantially in recent decades, even after the declines during the Great Recession between 2008 and 2009. As we noted before, if exports and imports are equal, foreign trade has no effect on total GDP. However, even if exports and imports are balanced overall, foreign trade might still have powerful effects on particular industries and workers by causing nations to shift workers and physical capital investment toward one industry rather than another.

Based on these four components of demand, we can measure GDP as:

$$\text{GDP} = \text{Consumption} + \text{Investment} + \text{Government} + \text{Trade balance}$$
$$\text{GDP} = \text{C} + \text{I} + \text{G} + (\text{X} - \text{M})$$

Understanding how to measure GDP is important for analyzing connections in the macro economy and for thinking about macroeconomic policy tools.

GDP Measured by What is Produced

Everything that we purchase somebody must first produce. **Table 19.2** breaks down what a country produces into five categories: **durable goods**, **nondurable goods**, **services**, **structures**, and the change in **inventories**. Before going into detail about these categories, notice that total GDP measured according to what is produced is exactly the same as the GDP measured by looking at the five components of demand. **Figure 19.5** provides a visual representation of this information.

	Components of GDP on the Supply Side (in trillions of dollars)	Percentage of Total
Goods		
Durable goods	$3.0	16.1%
Nondurable goods	$2.5	13.4%
Services	$11.6	62.4%
Structures	$1.5	8.1%
Change in inventories	$0.0	0.0%
Total GDP	**$18.6**	**100%**

Table 19.2 Components of U.S. GDP on the Production Side, 2016   (Source: http://bea.gov/iTable/index_nipa.cfm)

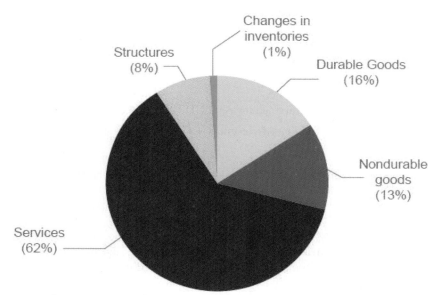

Figure 19.5 Percentage of Components of GDP on the Production Side Services make up over 60 percent of the production side components of GDP in the United States.

Since every market transaction must have both a buyer and a seller, GDP must be the same whether measured by what is demanded or by what is produced. **Figure 19.6** shows these components of what is produced, expressed as a percentage of GDP, since 1960.

This OpenStax book is available for free at http://cnx.org/content/col12122/1.4

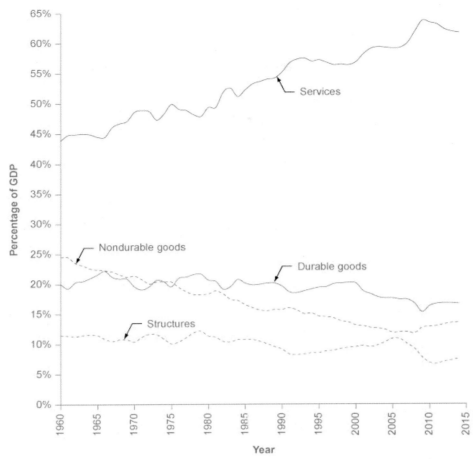

Figure 19.6 Types of Production   Services are the largest single component of total supply, representing over 60 percent of GDP, up from about 45 perent in the early 1960s. Durable and nondurable goods constitute the manufacturing sector, and they have declined from 45 percent of GDP in 1960 to about 30 percent in 2016. Nondurable goods used to be larger than durable goods, but in recent years, nondurable goods have been dropping to below the share of durable goods, which is less than 20% of GDP. Structures hover around 10% of GDP. We do not show here the change in inventories, the final component of aggregate supply. It is typically less than 1% of GDP.

In thinking about what is produced in the economy, many non-economists immediately focus on solid, long-lasting goods, like cars and computers. By far the largest part of GDP, however, is services. Moreover, services have been a growing share of GDP over time. A detailed breakdown of the leading service industries would include healthcare, education, and legal and financial services. It has been decades since most of the U.S. economy involved making solid objects. Instead, the most common jobs in a modern economy involve a worker looking at pieces of paper or a computer screen; meeting with co-workers, customers, or suppliers; or making phone calls.

Even within the overall category of goods, long-lasting durable goods like cars and refrigerators are about the same share of the economy as short-lived nondurable goods like food and clothing. The category of structures includes everything from homes, to office buildings, shopping malls, and factories. Inventories is a small category that refers to the goods that one business has produced but has not yet sold to consumers, and are still sitting in warehouses and on shelves. The amount of inventories sitting on shelves tends to decline if business is better than expected, or to rise if business is worse than expected.

Another Way to Measure GDP: The National Income Approach

GDP is a measure of what is produced in a nation. The primary way GDP is estimated is with the Expenditure Approach we discussed above, but there is another way. Everything a firm produces, when sold, becomes revenues to the firm. Businesses use revenues to pay their bills: Wages and salaries for labor, interest and dividends for capital, rent for land, profit to the entrepreneur, etc. So adding up all the income produced in a year provides a second way of measuring GDP. This is why the terms GDP and **national income** are sometimes used interchangeably. The total value of a nation's output is equal to the total value of a nation's income.

The Problem of Double Counting

We define GDP as the current value of all final goods and services produced in a nation in a year. What are final goods? They are goods at the furthest stage of production at the end of a year. Statisticians who calculate GDP must avoid the mistake of **double counting**, in which they count output more than once as it travels through the production stages. For example, imagine what would happen if government statisticians first counted the value of tires that a tire manufacturer produces, and then counted the value of a new truck that an automaker sold that contains those tires. In this example, the statisticians would have counted the value of the tires twice-because the truck's price includes the value of the tires.

To avoid this problem, which would overstate the size of the economy considerably, government statisticians count just the value of **final goods and services** in the chain of production that are sold for consumption, investment, government, and trade purposes. Statisticians exclude intermediate **intermediate goods**, which are goods that go into producing other goods, from GDP calculations. From the example above, they will only count the Ford truck's value. The value of what businesses provide to other businesses is captured in the final products at the end of the production chain.

The concept of GDP is fairly straightforward: it is just the dollar value of all final goods and services produced in the economy in a year. In our decentralized, market-oriented economy, actually calculating the more than $18 trillion-dollar U.S. GDP—along with how it is changing every few months—is a full-time job for a brigade of government statisticians.

What is Counted in GDP	What is not included in GDP
Consumption	Intermediate goods
Business investment	Transfer payments and non-market activities
Government spending on goods and services	Used goods
Net exports	Illegal goods

Table 19.3 Counting GDP

Notice the items that are not counted into GDP, as Table 19.3 outlines. The sales of used goods are not included because they were produced in a previous year and are part of that year's GDP. The entire underground economy of services paid "under the table" and illegal sales should be counted, but is not, because it is impossible to track these sales. In Friedrich Schneider's recent study of shadow economies, he estimated the underground economy in the United States to be 6.6% of GDP, or close to $2 trillion dollars in 2013 alone. Transfer payments, such as payment by the government to individuals, are not included, because they do not represent production. Also, production of some goods—such as home production as when you make your breakfast—is not counted because these goods are not sold in the marketplace.

Visit this website (http://openstaxcollege.org/l/undergroundecon) to read about the "New Underground Economy."

Other Ways to Measure the Economy

Besides GDP, there are several different but closely related ways of measuring the size of the economy. We mentioned above that we can think of GDP as total production and as total purchases. We can also think of it as total income since anything one produces and sells yields income.

One of the closest cousins of GDP is the **gross national product (GNP)**. GDP includes only what country produces within its borders. GNP adds what domestic businesses and labor abroad produces, and subtracts any payments that foreign labor and businesses located in the United States send home to other countries. In other words, GNP is based more on what a country's citizens and firms produce, wherever they are located, and GDP is based on what happens within a certain county's geographic boundaries. For the United States, the gap between GDP and GNP is relatively small; in recent years, only about 0.2%. For small nations, which may have a substantial share of their population working abroad and sending money back home, the difference can be substantial.

We calculate **net national product (NNP)** by taking GNP and then subtracting the value of how much physical capital is worn out, or reduced in value because of aging, over the course of a year. The process by which capital ages and loses value is called **depreciation**. We can further subdivide NNP into **national income**, which includes all income to businesses and individuals, and personal income, which includes only income to people.

For practical purposes, it is not vital to memorize these definitions. However, it is important to be aware that these differences exist and to know what statistic you are examining, so that you do not accidentally compare, say, GDP in one year or for one country with GNP or NNP in another year or another country. To get an idea of how these calculations work, follow the steps in the following Work It Out feature.

Work It Out ─O─O─O

Calculating GDP, Net Exports, and NNP

Based on the information in Table 19.4:

    a. What is the value of GDP?

    b. What is the value of net exports?

    c. What is the value of NNP?

Government purchases	$120 billion
Depreciation	$40 billion
Consumption	$400 billion
Business Investment	$60 billion
Exports	$100 billion

Table 19.4

Imports	$120 billion
Income receipts from rest of the world	$10 billion
Income payments to rest of the world	$8 billion

Table 19.4

Step 1. To calculate GDP use the following formula:

$$
\begin{aligned}
\text{GDP} &= \text{Consumption} + \text{Investment} + \text{Government spending} + (\text{Exports} - \text{Imports}) \\
&= \text{C} + \text{I} + \text{G} + (\text{X} - \text{M}) \\
&= \$400 + \$60 + \$120 + (\$100 - \$120) \\
&= \$560 \text{ billion}
\end{aligned}
$$

Step 2. To calculate net exports, subtract imports from exports.

$$
\begin{aligned}
\text{Net exports} &= \text{X} - \text{M} \\
&= \$100 - \$120 \\
&= -\$20 \text{ billion}
\end{aligned}
$$

Step 3. To calculate NNP, use the following formula:

$$
\begin{aligned}
\text{NNP} &= \text{GDP} + \text{Income receipts from the rest of the world} \\
&\quad - \text{Income payments to the rest of the world} - \text{Depreciation} \\
&= \$560 + \$10 - \$8 - \$40 \\
&= \$522 \text{ billion}
\end{aligned}
$$

19.2 | Adjusting Nominal Values to Real Values

By the end of this section, you will be able to:
- Contrast nominal GDP and real GDP
- Explain GDP deflator
- Calculate real GDP based on nominal GDP values

When examining economic statistics, there is a crucial distinction worth emphasizing. The distinction is between nominal and real measurements, which refer to whether or not inflation has distorted a given statistic. Looking at economic statistics without considering inflation is like looking through a pair of binoculars and trying to guess how close something is: unless you know how strong the lenses are, you cannot guess the distance very accurately. Similarly, if you do not know the inflation rate, it is difficult to figure out if a rise in GDP is due mainly to a rise in the overall level of prices or to a rise in quantities of goods produced. The **nominal value** of any economic statistic means that we measure the statistic in terms of actual prices that exist at the time. The **real value** refers to the same statistic after it has been adjusted for inflation. Generally, it is the real value that is more important.

Converting Nominal to Real GDP

Table 19.5 shows U.S. GDP at five-year intervals since 1960 in nominal dollars; that is, GDP measured using the actual market prices prevailing in each stated year. **Figure 19.7** also reflects this data in a graph.

Year	Nominal GDP (billions of dollars)	GDP Deflator (2005 = 100)
1960	543.3	19.0
1965	743.7	20.3
1970	1,075.9	24.8
1975	1,688.9	34.1
1980	2,862.5	48.3
1985	4,346.7	62.3
1990	5,979.6	72.7
1995	7,664.0	81.7
2000	10,289.7	89.0
2005	13,095.4	100.0
2010	14,958.3	110.0

Table 19.5 U.S. Nominal GDP and the GDP Deflator   (Source: www.bea.gov)

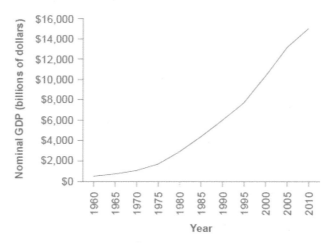

Figure 19.7 U.S. Nominal GDP, 1960–2010   Nominal GDP values have risen exponentially from 1960 through 2010, according to the BEA.

If an unwary analyst compared nominal GDP in 1960 to nominal GDP in 2010, it might appear that national output had risen by a factor of more than twenty-seven over this time (that is, GDP of $14,958 billion in 2010 divided by GDP of $543 billion in 1960 = 27.5). This conclusion would be highly misleading. Recall that we define nominal GDP as the quantity of every good or service produced multiplied by the price at which it was sold, summed up for all goods and services. In order to see how much production has actually increased, we need to extract the effects of higher prices on nominal GDP. We can easily accomplish this using the GDP deflator.

The GDP deflator is a price index measuring the average prices of all goods and services included in the economy. We explore price indices in detail and how we compute them in **Inflation**, but this definition will do in the context of this chapter. **Table 19.5** provides the GDP deflator data and **Figure 19.8** shows it graphically.

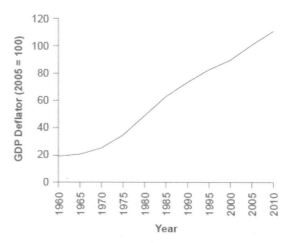

Figure 19.8 U.S. GDP Deflator, 1960–2010   Much like nominal GDP, the GDP deflator has risen exponentially from 1960 through 2010. (Source: BEA)

Figure 19.8 shows that the price level has risen dramatically since 1960. The price level in 2010 was almost six times higher than in 1960 (the deflator for 2010 was 110 versus a level of 19 in 1960). Clearly, much of the growth in nominal GDP was due to inflation, not an actual change in the quantity of goods and services produced, in other words, not in real GDP. Recall that nominal GDP can rise for two reasons: an increase in output, and/or an increase in prices. What is needed is to extract the increase in prices from nominal GDP so as to measure only changes in output. After all, the dollars used to measure nominal GDP in 1960 are worth more than the inflated dollars of 1990—and the price index tells exactly how much more. This adjustment is easy to do if you understand that nominal measurements are in value terms, where

$$\text{Value} \quad = \quad \text{Price} \times \text{Quantity}$$
$$\text{or}$$
$$\text{Nominal GDP} \quad = \quad \text{GDP Deflator} \times \text{Real GDP}$$

Let's look at an example at the micro level. Suppose the t-shirt company, Coolshirts, sells 10 t-shirts at a price of $9 each.

$$
\begin{aligned}
\text{Coolshirt's nominal revenue from sales} \quad &= \quad \text{Price} \times \text{Quantity} \\
&= \quad \$9 \times 10 \\
&= \quad \$90
\end{aligned}
$$

Then,

$$
\begin{aligned}
\text{Coolshirt's real income} \quad &= \quad \frac{\text{Nominal revenue}}{\text{Price}} \\
&= \quad \frac{\$90}{\$9} \\
&= \quad 10
\end{aligned}
$$

In other words, when we compute "real" measurements we are trying to obtain actual quantities, in this case, 10 t-shirts.

With GDP, it is just a tiny bit more complicated. We start with the same formula as above:

$$\text{Real GDP} \quad = \quad \frac{\text{Nominal GDP}}{\text{Price Index}}$$

For reasons that we will explain in more detail below, mathematically, a price index is a two-digit decimal number like 1.00 or 0.85 or 1.25. Because some people have trouble working with decimals, when the price index is published, it has traditionally been multiplied by 100 to get integer numbers like 100, 85, or 125. What this means is that when we "deflate" nominal figures to get real figures (by dividing the nominal by the price index). We also need to remember to divide the published price index by 100 to make the math work. Thus, the formula becomes:

This OpenStax book is available for free at http://cnx.org/content/col12122/1.4

$$\text{Real GDP} = \frac{\text{Nominal GDP}}{\text{Price Index} / 100}$$

Now read the following Work It Out feature for more practice calculating real GDP.

Work It Out ──○──○──○

Computing GDP

It is possible to use the data in Table 19.5 to compute real GDP.

Step 1. Look at Table 19.5, to see that, in 1960, nominal GDP was $543.3 billion and the price index (GDP deflator) was 19.0.

Step 2. To calculate the real GDP in 1960, use the formula:

$$\text{Real GDP} = \frac{\text{Nominal GDP}}{\text{Price Index} / 100}$$
$$= \frac{\$543.3 \text{ billion}}{19 / 100}$$
$$= \$2,859.5 \text{ billion}$$

We'll do this in two parts to make it clear. First adjust the price index: 19 divided by 100 = 0.19. Then divide into nominal GDP: $543.3 billion / 0.19 = $2,859.5 billion.

Step 3. Use the same formula to calculate the real GDP in 1965.

$$\text{Real GDP} = \frac{\text{Nominal GDP}}{\text{Price Index} / 100}$$
$$= \frac{\$743.7 \text{ billion}}{20.3 / 100}$$
$$= \$3,663.5 \text{ billion}$$

Step 4. Continue using this formula to calculate all of the real GDP values from 1960 through 2010. The calculations and the results are in Table 19.6.

Year	Nominal GDP (billions of dollars)	GDP Deflator (2005 = 100)	Calculations	Real GDP (billions of 2005 dollars)
1960	543.3	19.0	543.3 / (19.0/100)	2859.5
1965	743.7	20.3	743.7 / (20.3/100)	3663.5
1970	1075.9	24.8	1,075.9 / (24.8/100)	4338.3
1975	1688.9	34.1	1,688.9 / (34.1/100)	4952.8
1980	2862.5	48.3	2,862.5 / (48.3/100)	5926.5
1985	4346.7	62.3	4,346.7 / (62.3/100)	6977.0
1990	5979.6	72.7	5,979.6 / (72.7/100)	8225.0

Table 19.6 Converting Nominal to Real GDP   (Source: Bureau of Economic Analysis, www.bea.gov)

Year	Nominal GDP (billions of dollars)	GDP Deflator (2005 = 100)	Calculations	Real GDP (billions of 2005 dollars)
1995	7664.0	82.0	7,664 / (82.0/100)	9346.3
2000	10289.7	89.0	10,289.7 / (89.0/100)	11561.5
2005	13095.4	100.0	13,095.4 / (100.0/100)	13095.4
2010	14958.3	110.0	14,958.3 / (110.0/100)	13598.5

Table 19.6 Converting Nominal to Real GDP (Source: Bureau of Economic Analysis, www.bea.gov)

There are a couple things to notice here. Whenever you compute a real statistic, one year (or period) plays a special role. It is called the base year (or base period). The base year is the year whose prices we use to compute the real statistic. When we calculate real GDP, for example, we take the quantities of goods and services produced in each year (for example, 1960 or 1973) and multiply them by their prices in the base year (in this case, 2005), so we get a measure of GDP that uses prices that do not change from year to year. That is why real GDP is labeled "Constant Dollars" or, in this example, "2005 Dollars," which means that real GDP is constructed using prices that existed in 2005. While the example here uses 2005 as the base year, more generally, you can use any year as the base year. The formula is:

$$\text{GDP deflator} \ = \ \frac{\text{Nominal GDP}}{\text{Real GDP}} \times 100$$

Rearranging the formula and using the data from 2005:

$$
\begin{aligned}
\text{Real GDP} \ &= \ \frac{\text{Nominal GDP}}{\text{Price Index} \ / \ 100} \\
&= \ \frac{\$13{,}095.4 \text{ billion}}{100 \ / \ 100} \\
&= \ \$13{,}095.4 \text{ billion}
\end{aligned}
$$

Comparing real GDP and nominal GDP for 2005, you see they are the same. This is no accident. It is because we have chosen 2005 as the "base year" in this example. Since the price index in the base year always has a value of 100 (by definition), nominal and real GDP are always the same in the base year.

Look at the data for 2010.

$$
\begin{aligned}
\text{Real GDP} \ &= \ \frac{\text{Nominal GDP}}{\text{Price Index} \ / \ 100} \\
&= \ \frac{\$14{,}958.3 \text{ billion}}{110 \ / \ 100} \\
&= \ \$13{,}598.5 \text{ billion}
\end{aligned}
$$

Use this data to make another observation: As long as inflation is positive, meaning prices increase on average from year to year, real GDP should be less than nominal GDP in any year after the base year. The reason for this should be clear: The value of nominal GDP is "inflated" by inflation. Similarly, as long as inflation is positive, real GDP should be greater than nominal GDP in any year before the base year.

Figure 19.9 shows the U.S. nominal and real GDP since 1960. Because 2005 is the base year, the nominal and real values are exactly the same in that year. However, over time, the rise in nominal GDP looks much larger than the rise in real GDP (that is, the nominal GDP line rises more steeply than the real GDP line), because the presence of inflation, especially in the 1970s exaggerates the rise in nominal GDP.

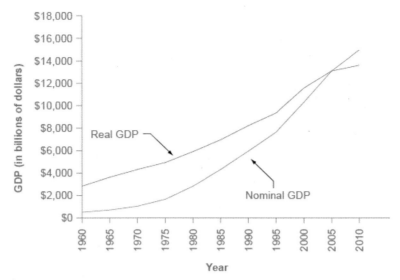

Figure 19.9 U.S. Nominal and Real GDP, 1960–2012 The red line measures U.S. GDP in nominal dollars. The black line measures U.S. GDP in real dollars, where all dollar values are converted to 2005 dollars. Since we express real GDP in 2005 dollars, the two lines cross in 2005. However, real GDP will appear higher than nominal GDP in the years before 2005, because dollars were worth less in 2005 than in previous years. Conversely, real GDP will appear lower in the years after 2005, because dollars were worth more in 2005 than in later years.

Let's return to the question that we posed originally: How much did GDP increase in real terms? What was the real GDP growth rate from 1960 to 2010? To find the real growth rate, we apply the formula for percentage change:

$$\frac{2010 \text{ real GDP} - 1960 \text{ real GDP}}{1960 \text{ real GDP}} \times 100 = \% \text{ change}$$

$$\frac{13{,}598.5 - 2{,}859.5}{2{,}859.5} \times 100 = 376\%$$

In other words, the U.S. economy has increased real production of goods and services by nearly a factor of four since 1960. Of course, that understates the material improvement since it fails to capture improvements in the quality of products and the invention of new products.

There is a quicker way to answer this question approximately, using another math trick. Because:

$$\text{Nominal} = \text{Price} \times \text{Quantity}$$
$$\% \text{ change in Nominal} = \% \text{ change in Price} + \% \text{ change in Quantity}$$
$$\text{OR}$$
$$\% \text{ change in Quantity} = \% \text{ change in Nominal} - \% \text{ change in Price}$$

Therefore, real GDP growth rate (% change in quantity) equals the growth rate in nominal GDP (% change in value) minus the inflation rate (% change in price).

Note that using this equation provides an approximation for small changes in the levels. For more accurate measures, one should use the first formula.

19.3 | Tracking Real GDP over Time

By the end of this section, you will be able to:
- Explain recessions, depressions, peaks, and troughs
- Evaluate the importance of tracking real GDP over time

This OpenStax book is available for free at http://cnx.org/content/col12122/1.4

When news reports indicate that "the economy grew 1.2% in the first quarter," the reports are referring to the percentage change in real GDP. By convention, governments report GDP growth is at an annualized rate: Whatever the calculated growth in real GDP was for the quarter, we multiply it by four when it is reported as if the economy were growing at that rate for a full year.

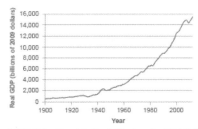

Figure 19.10 U.S. GDP, 1900–2016 Real GDP in the United States in 2016 (in 2009 dollars) was about $16.7 trillion. After adjusting to remove the effects of inflation, this represents a roughly 20-fold increase in the economy's production of goods and services since the start of the twentieth century. (Source: bea.gov)

Figure 19.10 shows the pattern of U.S. real GDP since 1900. Short term declines have regularly interrupted the generally upward long-term path of GDP. We call a significant decline in real GDP a **recession**. We call an especially lengthy and deep recession a **depression**. The severe drop in GDP that occurred during the 1930s Great Depression is clearly visible in the figure, as is the 2008–2009 Great Recession.

Real GDP is important because it is highly correlated with other measures of economic activity, like employment and unemployment. When real GDP rises, so does employment.

The most significant human problem associated with recessions (and their larger, uglier cousins, depressions) is that a slowdown in production means that firms need to lay off or fire some of their workers. Losing a job imposes painful financial and personal costs on workers, and often on their extended families as well. In addition, even those who keep their jobs are likely to find that wage raises are scanty at best—or their employers may ask them to take pay cuts.

Table 19.7 lists the pattern of recessions and expansions in the U.S. economy since 1900. We call the highest point of the economy, before the recession begins, the **peak**. Conversely, the lowest point of a recession, before a recovery begins, is the **trough**. Thus, a recession lasts from peak to trough, and an economic upswing runs from trough to peak. We call the economy's movement from peak to trough and trough to peak the **business cycle**. It is intriguing to notice that the three longest trough-to-peak expansions of the twentieth century have happened since 1960. The most recent recession started in December 2007 and ended formally in June 2009. This was the most severe recession since the 1930s Great Depression. The ongoing expansion since the June 2009 trough will also be quite long, comparatively, having already reached 90 months at the end of 2016.

Trough	Peak	Months of Contraction	Months of Expansion
December 1900	September 1902	18	21
August 1904	May 1907	23	33
June 1908	January 1910	13	19
January 1912	January 1913	24	12
December 1914	August 1918	23	44
March 1919	January 1920	7	10
July 1921	May 1923	18	22
July 1924	October 1926	14	27

Table 19.7 U.S. Business Cycles since 1900   (Source: http://www.nber.org/cycles/main.html)

Trough	Peak	Months of Contraction	Months of Expansion
November 1927	August 1929	23	21
March 1933	May 1937	43	50
June 1938	February 1945	13	80
October 1945	November 1948	8	37
October 1949	July 1953	11	45
May 1954	August 1957	10	39
April 1958	April 1960	8	24
February 1961	December 1969	10	106
November 1970	November 1973	11	36
March 1975	January 1980	16	58
July 1980	July 1981	6	12
November 1982	July 1990	16	92
March 1991	March 2001	8	120
November 2001	December 2007	8	73

Table 19.7 U.S. Business Cycles since 1900   (Source: http://www.nber.org/cycles/main.html)

A private think tank, the National Bureau of Economic Research (NBER), tracks business cycles for the U.S. economy. However, the effects of a severe recession often linger after the official ending date assigned by the NBER.

19.4 | Comparing GDP among Countries

By the end of this section, you will be able to:
- Explain how we can use GDP to compare the economic welfare of different nations
- Calculate the conversion of GDP to a common currency by using exchange rates
- Calculate GDP per capita using population data

It is common to use GDP as a measure of economic welfare or standard of living in a nation. When comparing the GDP of different nations for this purpose, two issues immediately arise. First, we measure a country's GDP in its own currency: the United States uses the U.S. dollar; Canada, the Canadian dollar; most countries of Western Europe, the euro; Japan, the yen; Mexico, the peso; and so on. Thus, comparing GDP between two countries requires converting to a common currency. A second issue is that countries have very different numbers of people. For instance, the United States has a much larger economy than Mexico or Canada, but it also has almost three times as many people as Mexico and nine times as many people as Canada. Thus, if we are trying to compare standards of living across countries, we need to divide GDP by population.

Converting Currencies with Exchange Rates

To compare the GDP of countries with different currencies, it is necessary to convert to a "common denominator" using an **exchange rate**, which is the value of one currency in terms of another currency. We express exchange rates either as the units of country A's currency that need to be traded for a single unit of country B's currency (for example, Japanese yen per British pound), or as the inverse (for example, British pounds per Japanese yen). We can use two types of exchange rates for this purpose, market exchange rates and purchasing power parity (PPP)

This OpenStax book is available for free at http://cnx.org/content/col12122/1.4

equivalent exchange rates. Market exchange rates vary on a day-to-day basis depending on supply and demand in foreign exchange markets. PPP-equivalent exchange rates provide a longer run measure of the exchange rate. For this reason, economists typically use PPP-equivalent exchange rates for GDP cross country comparisons. We will discuss exchange rates in more detail in **Exchange Rates and International Capital Flows**. The following Work It Out feature explains how to convert GDP to a common currency.

Work It Out ⊢O⊸O⊸O

Converting GDP to a Common Currency

Using the exchange rate to convert GDP from one currency to another is straightforward. Say that the task is to compare Brazil's GDP in 2013 of 4.8 trillion reals with the U.S. GDP of $16.6 trillion for the same year.

Step 1. Determine the exchange rate for the specified year. In 2013, the exchange rate was 2.230 reals = $1. (These numbers are realistic, but rounded off to simplify the calculations.)

Step 2. Convert Brazil's GDP into U.S. dollars:

$$\text{Brazil's GDP in \$ U.S.} = \frac{\text{Brazil's GDP in reals}}{\text{Exchange rate (reals/\$ U.S.)}}$$

$$= \frac{\text{4.8 trillion reals}}{\text{2.230 reals per \$ U.S.}}$$

$$= \text{\$2.2 trillion}$$

Step 3. Compare this value to the GDP in the United States in the same year. The U.S. GDP was $16.6 trillion in 2013, which is nearly eight times that of GDP in Brazil in 2012.

Step 4. View **Table 19.8** which shows the size of and variety of GDPs of different countries in 2013, all expressed in U.S. dollars. We calculate each using the process that we explained above.

Country	GDP in Billions of Domestic Currency		Domestic Currency/U.S. Dollars (PPP Equivalent)	GDP (in billions of U.S. dollars)
Brazil	4,844.80	reals	2.157	2,246.00
Canada	1,881.20	dollars	1.030	1,826.80
China	58,667.30	yuan	6.196	9,469.10
Egypt	1,753.30	pounds	6.460	271.40
Germany	2,737.60	euros	0.753	3,636.00
India	113,550.70	rupees	60.502	1,876.80
Japan	478,075.30	yen	97.596	4,898.50
Mexico	16,104.40	pesos	12.772	1,260.90
South Korea	1,428,294.70	won	1,094.925	1,304.467
United Kingdom	1,612.80	pounds	0.639	2,523.20

Table 19.8 Comparing GDPs Across Countries, 2013 (Source: http://www.imf.org/external/pubs/ft/weo/2013/01/weodata/index.aspx)

Country	GDP in Billions of Domestic Currency		Domestic Currency/U.S. Dollars (PPP Equivalent)	GDP (in billions of U.S. dollars)
United States	16,768.10	dollars	1.000	16,768.10

Table 19.8 Comparing GDPs Across Countries, 2013   (Source: http://www.imf.org/external/pubs/ft/weo/2013/01/weodata/index.aspx)

GDP Per Capita

The U.S. economy has the largest GDP in the world, by a considerable amount. The United States is also a populous country; in fact, it is the third largest country by population in the world, although well behind China and India. Is the U.S. economy larger than other countries just because the United States has more people than most other countries, or because the U.S. economy is actually larger on a per-person basis? We can answer this question by calculating a country's **GDP per capita**; that is, the GDP divided by the population.

$$\text{GDP per capita} \;=\; \text{GDP/population}$$

The second column of **Table 19.9** lists the GDP of the same selection of countries that appeared in the previous **Tracking Real GDP over Time** and **Table 19.8**, showing their GDP as converted into U.S. dollars (which is the same as the last column of the previous table). The third column gives the population for each country. The fourth column lists the GDP per capita. We obtain GDP per capita in two steps: First, by multiplying column two (GDP, in billions of dollars) by 1000 so it has the same units as column three (Population, in millions). Then divide the result (GDP in millions of dollars) by column three (Population, in millions).

Country	GDP (in billions of U.S. dollars)	Population (in millions)	Per Capita GDP (in U.S. dollars)
Brazil	2,246.00	199.20	11,275.10
Canada	1,826.80	35.10	52,045.58
China	9,469.10	1,360.80	6,958.48
Egypt	271.40	83.70	3,242.90
Germany	3,636.00	80.80	44,999.50
India	1,876.80	1,243.30	1,509.50
Japan	4,898.50	127.3	38,479.97
Mexico	1,260.90	118.40	10,649.90
South Korea	1,304.47	50.20	25,985.46
United Kingdom	2,523.20	64.10	39,363.50
United States	16,768.10	316.30	53,013.28

Table 19.9 GDP Per Capita, 2013   (Source: http://www.imf.org/external/pubs/ft/weo/2013/01/weodata/index.aspx)

This OpenStax book is available for free at http://cnx.org/content/col12122/1.4

Notice that the ranking by GDP is different from the ranking by GDP per capita. India has a somewhat larger GDP than Germany, but on a per capita basis, Germany has more than 10 times India's standard of living. Will China soon have a better standard of living than the U.S.? Read the following Clear It Up feature to find out.

Is China going to surpass the United States in terms of standard of living?

As Table 19.9 shows, China has the second largest GDP of the countries: $9.5 trillion compared to the United States' $16.8 trillion. Perhaps it will surpass the United States, but probably not any time soon. China has a much larger population so that in per capita terms, its GDP is less than one fifth that of the United States ($6,958.48 compared to $53,013). The Chinese people are still quite poor relative to the United States and other developed countries. One caveat: For reasons we will discuss shortly, GDP per capita can give us only a rough idea of the differences in living standards across countries.

The world's high-income nations—including the United States, Canada, the Western European countries, and Japan—typically have GDP per capita in the range of $20,000 to $50,000. Middle-income countries, which include much of Latin America, Eastern Europe, and some countries in East Asia, have GDP per capita in the range of $6,000 to $12,000. The world's low-income countries, many of them located in Africa and Asia, often have GDP per capita of less than $2,000 per year.

19.5 | How Well GDP Measures the Well-Being of Society

By the end of this section, you will be able to:
- Discuss how productivity influences the standard of living
- Explain the limitations of GDP as a measure of the standard of living
- Analyze the relationship between GDP data and fluctuations in the standard of living

The level of GDP per capita clearly captures some of what we mean by the phrase "standard of living." Most of the migration in the world, for example, involves people who are moving from countries with relatively low GDP per capita to countries with relatively high GDP per capita.

"Standard of living" is a broader term than GDP. While GDP focuses on production that is bought and sold in markets, **standard of living** includes all elements that affect people's well-being, whether they are bought and sold in the market or not. To illuminate the difference between GDP and standard of living, it is useful to spell out some things that GDP does not cover that are clearly relevant to standard of living.

Limitations of GDP as a Measure of the Standard of Living

While GDP includes spending on recreation and travel, it does not cover leisure time. Clearly, however, there is a substantial difference between an economy that is large because people work long hours, and an economy that is just as large because people are more productive with their time so they do not have to work as many hours. The GDP per capita of the U.S. economy is larger than the GDP per capita of Germany, as Table 19.9 showed, but does that prove that the standard of living in the United States is higher? Not necessarily, since it is also true that the average U.S. worker works several hundred hours more per year more than the average German worker. Calculating GDP does not account for the German worker's extra vacation weeks.

While GDP includes what a country spends on environmental protection, healthcare, and education, it does not include actual levels of environmental cleanliness, health, and learning. GDP includes the cost of buying pollution-control equipment, but it does not address whether the air and water are actually cleaner or dirtier. GDP includes spending on medical care, but does not address whether life expectancy or infant mortality have risen or fallen. Similarly, it counts spending on education, but does not address directly how much of the population can read, write, or do basic mathematics.

GDP includes production that is exchanged in the market, but it does not cover production that is not exchanged in the market. For example, hiring someone to mow your lawn or clean your house is part of GDP, but doing these tasks yourself is not part of GDP. One remarkable change in the U.S. economy in recent decades is the growth in women's participation in the labor force. As of 1970, only about 42% of women participated in the paid labor force. By the second decade of the 2000s, nearly 60% of women participated in the paid labor force according to the Bureau of Labor Statistics. As women are now in the labor force, many of the services they used to produce in the non-market economy like food preparation and child care have shifted to some extent into the market economy, which makes the GDP appear larger even if people actually are not consuming more services.

GDP has nothing to say about the level of inequality in society. GDP per capita is only an average. When GDP per capita rises by 5%, it could mean that GDP for everyone in the society has risen by 5%, or that GDP of some groups has risen by more while that of others has risen by less—or even declined. GDP also has nothing in particular to say about the amount of variety available. If a family buys 100 loaves of bread in a year, GDP does not care whether they are all white bread, or whether the family can choose from wheat, rye, pumpernickel, and many others—it just looks at the total amount the family spends on bread.

Likewise, GDP has nothing much to say about what technology and products are available. The standard of living in, for example, 1950 or 1900 was not affected only by how much money people had—it was also affected by what they could buy. No matter how much money you had in 1950, you could not buy an iPhone or a personal computer.

In certain cases, it is not clear that a rise in GDP is even a good thing. If a city is wrecked by a hurricane, and then experiences a surge of rebuilding construction activity, it would be peculiar to claim that the hurricane was therefore economically beneficial. If people are led by a rising fear of crime, to pay for installing bars and burglar alarms on all their windows, it is hard to believe that this increase in GDP has made them better off. Similarly, some people would argue that sales of certain goods, like pornography or extremely violent movies, do not represent a gain to society's standard of living.

Does a Rise in GDP Overstate or Understate the Rise in the Standard of Living?

The fact that GDP per capita does not fully capture the broader idea of standard of living has led to a concern that the increases in GDP over time are illusory. It is theoretically possible that while GDP is rising, the standard of living could be falling if human health, environmental cleanliness, and other factors that are not included in GDP are worsening. Fortunately, this fear appears to be overstated.

In some ways, the rise in GDP understates the actual rise in the standard of living. For example, the typical workweek for a U.S. worker has fallen over the last century from about 60 hours per week to less than 40 hours per week. Life expectancy and health have risen dramatically, and so has the average level of education. Since 1970, the air and water in the United States have generally been getting cleaner. Companies have developed new technologies for entertainment, travel, information, and health. A much wider variety of basic products like food and clothing is available today than several decades ago. Because GDP does not capture leisure, health, a cleaner environment, the possibilities that new technology creates, or an increase in variety, the actual rise in the standard of living for Americans in recent decades has exceeded the rise in GDP.

On the other side, crime rates, traffic congestion levels, and income inequality are higher in the United States now than they were in the 1960s. Moreover, a substantial number of services that women primarily provided in the non-market economy are now part of the market economy that GDP counts. By ignoring these factors, GDP would tend to overstate the true rise in the standard of living.

Visit this website (http://openstaxcollege.org/l/amdreamvalue) to read about the American Dream and standards of living.

GDP is Rough, but Useful

A high level of GDP should not be the only goal of macroeconomic policy, or government policy more broadly. Even though GDP does not measure the broader standard of living with any precision, it does measure production well and it does indicate when a country is materially better or worse off in terms of jobs and incomes. In most countries, a significantly higher GDP per capita occurs hand in hand with other improvements in everyday life along many dimensions, like education, health, and environmental protection.

No single number can capture all the elements of a term as broad as "standard of living." Nonetheless, GDP per capita is a reasonable, rough-and-ready measure of the standard of living.

Bring it Home

How is the Economy Doing? How Does One Tell?

To determine the state of the economy, one needs to examine economic indicators, such as GDP. To calculate GDP is quite an undertaking. It is the broadest measure of a nation's economic activity and we owe a debt to Simon Kuznets, the creator of the measurement, for that.

The sheer size of the U.S. economy as measured by GDP is huge—as of the fourth quarter of 2016, $18.9 trillion worth of goods and services were produced annually. Real GDP informed us that the 2008–2009 recession was severe and that the recovery from that recession has been slow, but the economy is improving. GDP per capita gives a rough estimate of a nation's standard of living. This chapter is the building block for other chapters that explore more economic indicators such as unemployment, inflation, or interest rates, and perhaps more importantly, will explain how they are related and what causes them to rise or fall.

KEY TERMS

business cycle the economy's relatively short-term movement in and out of recession

depreciation the process by which capital ages over time and therefore loses its value

depression an especially lengthy and deep decline in output

double counting a potential mistake to avoid in measuring GDP, in which output is counted more than once as it travels through the stages of production

durable good long-lasting good like a car or a refrigerator

exchange rate the price of one currency in terms of another currency

final good and service output used directly for consumption, investment, government, and trade purposes; contrast with "intermediate good"

GDP per capita GDP divided by the population

gross domestic product (GDP) the value of the output of all goods and services produced within a country in a year

gross national product (GNP) includes what is produced domestically and what is produced by domestic labor and business abroad in a year

intermediate good output provided to other businesses at an intermediate stage of production, not for final users; contrast with "final good and service"

inventory good that has been produced, but not yet been sold

national income includes all income earned: wages, profits, rent, and profit income

net national product (NNP) GDP minus depreciation

nominal value the economic statistic actually announced at that time, not adjusted for inflation; contrast with real value

nondurable good short-lived good like food and clothing

peak during the business cycle, the highest point of output before a recession begins

real value an economic statistic after it has been adjusted for inflation; contrast with nominal value

recession a significant decline in national output

service product which is intangible (in contrast to goods) such as entertainment, healthcare, or education

standard of living all elements that affect people's happiness, whether people buy or sell these elements in the market or not

structure building used as residence, factory, office building, retail store, or for other purposes

trade balance gap between exports and imports

trade deficit exists when a nation's imports exceed its exports and it calculates them as imports –exports

trade surplus exists when a nation's exports exceed its imports and it calculates them as exports – imports

trough during the business cycle, the lowest point of output in a recession, before a recovery begins

This OpenStax book is available for free at http://cnx.org/content/col12122/1.4

KEY CONCEPTS AND SUMMARY

19.1 Measuring the Size of the Economy: Gross Domestic Product

Economists generally express the size of a nation's economy as its gross domestic product (GDP), which measures the value of the output of all goods and services produced within the country in a year. Economists measure GDP by taking the quantities of all goods and services produced, multiplying them by their prices, and summing the total. Since GDP measures what is bought and sold in the economy, we can measure it either by the sum of what is purchased in the economy or what is produced.

We can divide demand into consumption, investment, government, exports, and imports. We can divide what is produced in the economy into durable goods, nondurable goods, services, structures, and inventories. To avoid double counting, GDP counts only final output of goods and services, not the production of intermediate goods or the value of labor in the chain of production.

19.2 Adjusting Nominal Values to Real Values

The nominal value of an economic statistic is the commonly announced value. The real value is the value after adjusting for changes in inflation. To convert nominal economic data from several different years into real, inflation-adjusted data, the starting point is to choose a base year arbitrarily and then use a price index to convert the measurements so that economists measure them in the money prevailing in the base year.

19.3 Tracking Real GDP over Time

Over the long term, U.S. real GDP have increased dramatically. At the same time, GDP has not increased the same amount each year. The speeding up and slowing down of GDP growth represents the business cycle. When GDP declines significantly, a recession occurs. A longer and deeper decline is a depression. Recessions begin at the business cycle's peak and end at the trough.

19.4 Comparing GDP among Countries

Since we measure GDP in a country's currency, in order to compare different countries' GDPs, we need to convert them to a common currency. One way to do that is with the exchange rate, which is the price of one country's currency in terms of another. Once we express GDPs in a common currency, we can compare each country's GDP per capita by dividing GDP by population. Countries with large populations often have large GDPs, but GDP alone can be a misleading indicator of a nation's wealth. A better measure is GDP per capita.

19.5 How Well GDP Measures the Well-Being of Society

GDP is an indicator of a society's standard of living, but it is only a rough indicator. GDP does not directly take account of leisure, environmental quality, levels of health and education, activities conducted outside the market, changes in inequality of income, increases in variety, increases in technology, or the (positive or negative) value that society may place on certain types of output.

SELF-CHECK QUESTIONS

1. Country A has export sales of $20 billion, government purchases of $1,000 billion, business investment is $50 billion, imports are $40 billion, and consumption spending is $2,000 billion. What is the dollar value of GDP?

2. Which of the following are included in GDP, and which are not?
   a. The cost of hospital stays
   b. The rise in life expectancy over time
   c. Child care provided by a licensed day care center
   d. Child care provided by a grandmother
   e. A used car sale
   f. A new car sale
   g. The greater variety of cheese available in supermarkets
   h. The iron that goes into the steel that goes into a refrigerator bought by a consumer.

3. Using data from **Table 19.5** how much of the nominal GDP growth from 1980 to 1990 was real GDP and how much was inflation?

4. Without looking at **Table 19.7**, return to **Figure 19.10**. If we define a recession as a significant decline in national output, can you identify any post-1960 recessions in addition to the 2008-2009 recession? (This requires a judgment call.)

5. According to **Table 19.7**, how often have recessions occurred since the end of World War II (1945)?

6. According to **Table 19.7**, how long has the average recession lasted since the end of World War II?

7. According to **Table 19.7**, how long has the average expansion lasted since the end of World War II?

8. Is it possible for GDP to rise while at the same time per capita GDP is falling? Is it possible for GDP to fall while per capita GDP is rising?

9. The Central African Republic has a GDP of 1,107,689 million CFA francs and a population of 4.862 million. The exchange rate is 284.681CFA francs per dollar. Calculate the GDP per capita of Central African Republic.

10. Explain briefly whether each of the following would cause GDP to overstate or understate the degree of change in the broad standard of living.
   a. The environment becomes dirtier
   b. The crime rate declines
   c. A greater variety of goods become available to consumers
   d. Infant mortality declines

REVIEW QUESTIONS

11. What are the main components of measuring GDP with what is demanded?

12. What are the main components of measuring GDP with what is produced?

13. Would you usually expect GDP as measured by what is demanded to be greater than GDP measured by what is supplied, or the reverse?

14. Why must you avoid double counting when measuring GDP?

15. What is the difference between a series of economic data over time measured in nominal terms versus the same data series over time measured in real terms?

16. How do you convert a series of nominal economic data over time to real terms?

17. What are typical GDP patterns for a high-income economy like the United States in the long run and the short run?

18. What are the two main difficulties that arise in comparing different countries's GDP?

19. List some of the reasons why economists should not consider GDP an effective measure of the standard of living in a country.

CRITICAL THINKING QUESTIONS

20. U.S. macroeconomic data are among the best in the world. Given what you learned in the **Clear It Up** "How do statisticians measure GDP?", does this surprise you, or does this simply reflect the complexity of a modern economy?

21. What does GDP not tell us about the economy?

22. Should people typically pay more attention to their real income or their nominal income? If you choose the latter, why would that make sense in today's world? Would your answer be the same for the 1970s?

23. Why do you suppose that U.S. GDP is so much higher today than 50 or 100 years ago?

24. Why do you think that GDP does not grow at a steady rate, but rather speeds up and slows down?

25. Cross country comparisons of GDP per capita typically use purchasing power parity equivalent exchange rates, which are a measure of the long run equilibrium value of an exchange rate. In fact, we used PPP equivalent exchange rates in this module. Why could using market exchange rates, which sometimes change dramatically in a short period of time, be misleading?

PROBLEMS

28. Last year, a small nation with abundant forests cut down $200 worth of trees. It then turned $100 worth of trees into $150 worth of lumber. It used $100 worth of that lumber to produce $250 worth of bookshelves. Assuming the country produces no other outputs, and there are no other inputs used in producing trees, lumber, and bookshelves, what is this nation's GDP? In other words, what is the value of the final goods the nation produced including trees, lumber and bookshelves?

29. The "prime" interest rate is the rate that banks charge their best customers. Based on the nominal interest rates and inflation rates in **Table 19.10**, in which of the years would it have been best to be a lender? Based on the nominal interest rates and inflation rates in **Table 19.10**, in which of the years given would it have been best to be a borrower?

Year	Prime Interest Rate	Inflation Rate
1970	7.9%	5.7%
1974	10.8%	11.0%
1978	9.1%	7.6%
1981	18.9%	10.3%

Table 19.10

26. Why might per capita GDP be only an imperfect measure of a country's standard of living?

27. How might you measure a "green" GDP?

30. A mortgage loan is a loan that a person makes to purchase a house. **Table 19.11** provides a list of the mortgage interest rate for several different years and the rate of inflation for each of those years. In which years would it have been better to be a person borrowing money from a bank to buy a home? In which years would it have been better to be a bank lending money?

Year	Mortgage Interest Rate	Inflation Rate
1984	12.4%	4.3%
1990	10%	5.4%
2001	7.0%	2.8%

Table 19.11

31. Ethiopia has a GDP of $8 billion (measured in U.S. dollars) and a population of 55 million. Costa Rica has a GDP of $9 billion (measured in U.S. dollars) and a population of 4 million. Calculate the per capita GDP for each country and identify which one is higher.

32. In 1980, Denmark had a GDP of $70 billion (measured in U.S. dollars) and a population of 5.1 million. In 2000, Denmark had a GDP of $160 billion (measured in U.S. dollars) and a population of 5.3 million. By what percentage did Denmark's GDP per capita rise between 1980 and 2000?

33. The Czech Republic has a GDP of 1,800 billion koruny. The exchange rate is 25 koruny/U.S. dollar. The Czech population is 20 million. What is the GDP per capita of the Czech Republic expressed in U.S. dollars?

This OpenStax book is available for free at http://cnx.org/content/col12122/1.4

20 | Economic Growth

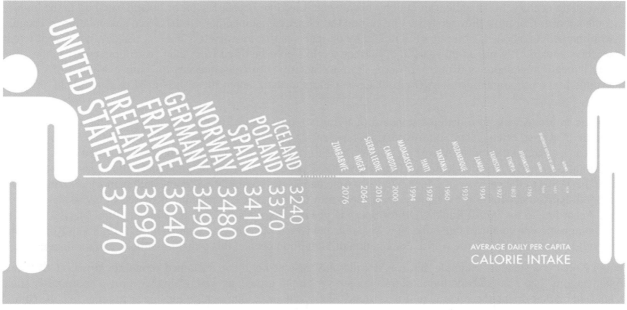

Figure 20.1 Average Daily Calorie Consumption Not only has the number of calories that people consume per day increased, so has the amount of food calories that people are able to afford based on their working wages. (Credit: modification of work by Lauren Manning/Flickr Creative Commons)

Bring it Home

Calories and Economic Growth

On average, humans need about 2,500 calories a day to survive, depending on height, weight, and gender. The economist Brad DeLong estimates that the average worker in the early 1600s earned wages that could afford him 2,500 food calories. This worker lived in Western Europe. Two hundred years later, that same worker could afford 3,000 food calories. However, between 1800 and 1875, just a time span of just 75 years, economic growth was so rapid that western European workers could purchase 5,000 food calories a day. By 2012, a low skilled worker in an affluent Western European/North American country could afford to purchase 2.4 million food calories per day.

What caused such a rapid rise in living standards between 1800 and 1875 and thereafter? Why is it that many countries, especially those in Western Europe, North America, and parts of East Asia, can feed their populations more than adequately, while others cannot? We will look at these and other questions as we examine long-run economic growth.

Introduction to Economic Growth

In this chapter, you will learn about:

- The Relatively Recent Arrival of Economic Growth
- Labor Productivity and Economic Growth
- Components of Economic Growth

- Economic Convergence

Every country worries about economic growth. In the United States and other high-income countries, the question is whether economic growth continues to provide the same remarkable gains in our standard of living as it did during the twentieth century. Meanwhile, can middle-income countries like Brazil, Egypt, or Poland catch up to the higher-income countries, or must they remain in the second tier of per capita income? Of the world's population of roughly 7.5 billion people, about 1.1 billion are scraping by on incomes that average less than $2 per day, not that different from the standard of living 2,000 years ago. Can the world's poor be lifted from their fearful poverty? As the 1995 Nobel laureate in economics, Robert E. Lucas Jr., once noted: "The consequences for human welfare involved in questions like these are simply staggering: Once one starts to think about them, it is hard to think about anything else."

Dramatic improvements in a nation's standard of living are possible. After the Korean War in the late 1950s, the Republic of Korea, often called South Korea, was one of the poorest economies in the world. Most South Koreans worked in peasant agriculture. According to the British economist Angus Maddison, who devoted life's work to measuring GDP and population in the world economy, GDP per capita in 1990 international dollars was $854 per year. From the 1960s to the early twenty-first century, a time period well within the lifetime and memory of many adults, the South Korean economy grew rapidly. Over these four decades, GDP per capita increased by more than 6% per year. According to the World Bank, GDP for South Korea now exceeds $30,000 in nominal terms, placing it firmly among high-income countries like Italy, New Zealand, and Israel. Measured by total GDP in 2015, South Korea is the eleventh-largest economy in the world. For a nation of 50 million people, this transformation is extraordinary.

South Korea is a standout example, but it is not the only case of rapid and sustained economic growth. Other East Asian nations, like Thailand and Indonesia, have seen very rapid growth as well. China has grown enormously since it enacted market-oriented economic reforms around 1980. GDP per capita in high-income economies like the United States also has grown dramatically albeit over a longer time frame. Since the Civil War, the U.S. economy has transformed from a primarily rural and agricultural economy to an economy based on services, manufacturing, and technology.

20.1 | The Relatively Recent Arrival of Economic Growth

By the end of this section, you will be able to:
- Explain the conditions that have allowed for modern economic growth in the last two centuries
- Analyze the influence of public policies on an economy's long-run economic growth

Let's begin with a brief overview of spectacular economic growth patterns around the world in the last two centuries. We commonly refer to this as the period of **modern economic growth**. (Later in the chapter we will discuss lower economic growth rates and some key ingredients for economic progress.) Rapid and sustained economic growth is a relatively recent experience for the human race. Before the last two centuries, although rulers, nobles, and conquerors could afford some extravagances and although economies rose above the subsistence level, the average person's standard of living had not changed much for centuries.

Progressive, powerful economic and institutional changes started to have a significant effect in the late eighteenth and early nineteenth centuries. According to the Dutch economic historian Jan Luiten van Zanden, slavery-based societies, favorable demographics, global trading routes, and standardized trading institutions that spread with different empires set the stage for the Industrial Revolution to succeed. The **Industrial Revolution** refers to the widespread use of power-driven machinery and the economic and social changes that resulted in the first half of the 1800s. Ingenious machines—the steam engine, the power loom, and the steam locomotive—performed tasks that otherwise would have taken vast numbers of workers to do. The Industrial Revolution began in Great Britain, and soon spread to the United States, Germany, and other countries.

The jobs for ordinary people working with these machines were often dirty and dangerous by modern standards, but the alternative jobs of that time in peasant agriculture and small-village industry were often dirty and dangerous, too. The new jobs of the Industrial Revolution typically offered higher pay and a chance for social mobility. A self-reinforcing cycle began: New inventions and investments generated profits, the profits provided funds for more new investment and inventions, and the investments and inventions provided opportunities for further profits. Slowly, a group of national economies in Europe and North America emerged from centuries of sluggishness into a period of rapid modern growth. During the last two centuries, the average GDP growth rate per capita in the leading industrialized countries has been about 2% per year. What were times like before then? Read the following Clear It Up feature for the answer.

What were economic conditions like before 1870?

Angus Maddison, a quantitative economic historian, led the most systematic inquiry into national incomes before 1870. Economists recently have refined and used his methods to compile GDP per capita estimates from year 1 C.E. to 1348. Table 20.1 is an important counterpoint to most of the narrative in this chapter. It shows that nations can decline as well as rise. A wide array of forces, such as epidemics, natural and weather-related disasters, the inability to govern large empires, and the remarkably slow pace of technological and institutional progress explain declines in income. Institutions are the traditions and laws by which people in a community agree to behave and govern themselves. Such institutions include marriage, religion, education, and laws of governance. Institutional progress is the development and codification of these institutions to reinforce social order, and thus, economic growth.

One example of such an institution is the Magna Carta (Great Charter), which the English nobles forced King John to sign in 1215. The Magna Carta codified the principles of due process, whereby a free man could not be penalized unless his peers had made a lawful judgment against him. The United States in its own constitution later adopted this concept. This social order may have contributed to England's GDP per capita in 1348, which was second to that of northern Italy.

In studying economic growth, a country's institutional framework plays a critical role. Table 20.1 also shows relative global equality for almost 1,300 years. After this, we begin to see significant divergence in income (not in the table).

Year	Northern Italy	Spain	England	Holland	Byzantium	Iraq	Egypt	Japan
1	$800	$600	$600	$600	$700	$700	$700	-
730	-	-	-	-	-	$920	$730	$402
1000	-	-	-	-	$600	$820	$600	-
1150	-	-	-	-	$580	$680	$660	$520
1280	-	-	-	-	-	-	$670	$527
1300	$1,588	$864	$892	-	-	-	$610	-
1348	$1,486	$907	$919	-	-	-	-	-

Table 20.1 GDP Per Capita Estimates in Current International Dollars from AD 1 to 1348 (Source: Bolt and van Zanden. "The First Update of the Maddison Project. Re-Estimating Growth Before 1820." 2013)

Another fascinating and underreported fact is the high levels of income, compared to others at that time, attained by the Islamic Empire Abbasid Caliphate—which was founded in present-day Iraq in 730 C.E. At its height, the empire spanned large regions of the Middle East, North Africa, and Spain until its gradual decline over 200 years.

The Industrial Revolution led to increasing inequality among nations. Some economies took off, whereas others, like many of those in Africa or Asia, remained close to a subsistence standard of living. General calculations show that the 17 countries of the world with the most-developed economies had, on average, 2.4 times the GDP per capita of the world's poorest economies in 1870. By 1960, the most developed economies had 4.2 times the GDP per capita of the poorest economies.

However, by the middle of the twentieth century, some countries had shown that catching up was possible. Japan's economic growth took off in the 1960s and 1970s, with a growth rate of real GDP per capita averaging 11% per year during those decades. Certain countries in Latin America experienced a boom in economic growth in the 1960s as well. In Brazil, for example, GDP per capita expanded by an average annual rate of 11.1% from 1968 to 1973. In the 1970s, some East Asian economies, including South Korea, Thailand, and Taiwan, saw rapid growth. In these countries, growth rates of 11% to 12% per year in GDP per capita were not uncommon. More recently, China, with its population of nearly 1.4 billion people, grew at a per capita rate 9% per year from 1984 into the 2000s. India, with a population of 1.3 billion, has shown promising signs of economic growth, with growth in GDP per capita of about 4% per year during the 1990s and climbing toward 7% to 8% per year in the 2000s.

Link It Up

Visit this website (http://openstaxcollege.org/l/asiadevbank) to read about the Asian Development Bank.

These waves of catch-up economic growth have not reached all shores. In certain African countries like Niger, Tanzania, and Sudan, for example, GDP per capita at the start of the 2000s was still less than $300, not much higher than it was in the nineteenth century and for centuries before that. In the context of the overall situation of low-income people around the world, the good economic news from China (population: 1.4 billion) and India (population: 1.3 billion) is, nonetheless, astounding and heartening.

Economic growth in the last two centuries has made a striking change in the human condition. Richard Easterlin, an economist at the University of Southern California, wrote in 2000:

> By many measures, a revolution in the human condition is sweeping the world. Most people today are better fed, clothed, and housed than their predecessors two centuries ago. They are healthier, live longer, and are better educated. Women's lives are less centered on reproduction and political democracy has gained a foothold. Although Western Europe and its offshoots have been the leaders of this advance, most of the less developed nations have joined in during the 20th century, with the newly emerging nations of sub-Saharan Africa the latest to participate. Although the picture is not one of universal progress, it is the greatest advance in the human condition of the world's population ever achieved in such a brief span of time.

Rule of Law and Economic Growth

Economic growth depends on many factors. Key among those factors is adherence to the **rule of law** and protection of property rights and **contractual rights** by a country's government so that markets can work effectively and efficiently. Laws must be clear, public, fair, enforced, and equally applicable to all members of society. Property rights, as you might recall from **Environmental Protection and Negative Externalities** are the rights of individuals and firms to own property and use it as they see fit. If you have $100, you have the right to use that money, whether you spend it, lend it, or keep it in a jar. It is your property. The definition of property includes physical property as well as the right to your training and experience, especially since your training is what determines your livelihood. Using this property includes the right to enter into contracts with other parties with your property. Individuals or firms must own the property to enter into a contract.

Contractual rights, then, are based on property rights and they allow individuals to enter into agreements with others regarding the use of their property providing recourse through the legal system in the event of noncompliance. One example is the employment agreement: a skilled surgeon operates on an ill person and expects payment. Failure to pay would constitute property theft by the patient. The theft is property the services that the surgeon provided. In a society with strong property rights and contractual rights, the terms of the patient–surgeon contract will be fulfilled, because the surgeon would have recourse through the court system to extract payment from that individual. Without a legal system that enforces contracts, people would not be likely to enter into contracts for current or future services because of the risk of non-payment. This would make it difficult to transact business and would slow economic growth.

The World Bank considers a country's legal system effective if it upholds property rights and contractual rights. The World Bank has developed a ranking system for countries' legal systems based on effective protection of property rights and rule-based governance using a scale from 1 to 6, with 1 being the lowest and 6 the highest rating. In 2013, the world average ranking was 2.9. The three countries with the lowest ranking of 1.5 were Afghanistan, the Central African Republic, and Zimbabwe. Their GDP per capita was $679, $333, and $1,007 respectively. The World Bank cites Afghanistan as having a low standard of living, weak government structure, and lack of adherence to the rule of law, which has stymied its economic growth. The landlocked Central African Republic has poor economic resources as well as political instability and is a source of children used in human trafficking. Zimbabwe has had declining and often negative growth for much of the period since 1998. Land redistribution and price controls have disrupted the economy, and corruption and violence have dominated the political process. Although global economic growth has increased, those countries lacking a clear system of property rights and an independent court system free from corruption have lagged far behind.

20.2 | Labor Productivity and Economic Growth

By the end of this section, you will be able to:
- Identify the role of labor productivity in promoting economic growth
- Analyze the sources of economic growth using the aggregate production function
- Measure an economy's rate of productivity growth
- Evaluate the power of sustained growth

Sustained long-term economic growth comes from increases in worker productivity, which essentially means how well we do things. In other words, how efficient is your nation with its time and workers? **Labor productivity** is the value that each employed person creates per unit of his or her input. The easiest way to comprehend labor productivity is to imagine a Canadian worker who can make 10 loaves of bread in an hour versus a U.S. worker who in the same hour can make only two loaves of bread. In this fictional example, the Canadians are more productive. More productivity essentially means you can do more in the same amount of time. This in turn frees up resources for workers to use elsewhere.

What determines how productive workers are? The answer is pretty intuitive. The first determinant of labor productivity is human capital. **Human capital** is the accumulated knowledge (from education and experience), skills, and expertise that the average worker in an economy possesses. Typically the higher the average level of education in an economy, the higher the accumulated human capital and the higher the labor productivity.

The second factor that determines labor productivity is technological change. **Technological change** is a combination of **invention**—advances in knowledge—and **innovation**, which is putting those advances to use in a new product or service. For example, the transistor was invented in 1947. It allowed us to miniaturize the footprint of electronic devices and use less power than the tube technology that came before it. Innovations since then have produced smaller and better transistors that are ubiquitous in products as varied as smart-phones, computers, and escalators. Developing the transistor has allowed workers to be anywhere with smaller devices. People can use these devices to communicate with other workers, measure product quality or do any other task in less time, improving worker productivity.

The third factor that determines labor productivity is economies of scale. Recall that economies of scale are the cost advantages that industries obtain due to size. (Read more about economies of scale in **Production, Cost and Industry Structure**.) Consider again the case of the fictional Canadian worker who could produce 10 loaves of bread in an hour. If this difference in productivity was due only to economies of scale, it could be that the Canadian worker had access to a large industrial-size oven while the U.S. worker was using a standard residential size oven.

Now that we have explored the determinants of worker productivity, let's turn to how economists measure economic growth and productivity.

Sources of Economic Growth: The Aggregate Production Function

To analyze the sources of economic growth, it is useful to think about a **production function**, which is the technical relationship by which economic inputs like labor, machinery, and raw materials are turned into outputs like goods and services that consumers use. A microeconomic production function describes a firm's or perhaps an industry's inputs and outputs. In macroeconomics, we call the connection from inputs to outputs for the entire economy an **aggregate production function**.

Components of the Aggregate Production Function

Economists construct different production functions depending on the focus of their studies. **Figure 20.2** presents two examples of aggregate production functions. In the first production function in **Figure 20.2** (a), the output is GDP. The inputs in this example are workforce, human capital, physical capital, and technology. We discuss these inputs further in the module, Components of Economic Growth.

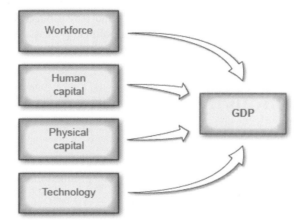

(a) Aggregate production function with GDP as its output

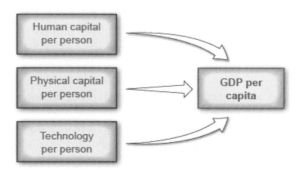

(b) Aggregate production function with GDP per capita as its output

Figure 20.2 Aggregate Production Functions   An aggregate production function shows what goes into producing the output for an overall economy. (a) This aggregate production function has GDP as its output. (b) This aggregate production function has GDP per capita as its output. Because we calculate it on a per-person basis, we already figure the labor input into the other factors and we do not need to list it separately.

Measuring Productivity

An economy's rate of productivity growth is closely linked to the growth rate of its GDP per capita, although the

This OpenStax book is available for free at http://cnx.org/content/col12122/1.4

two are not identical. For example, if the percentage of the population who holds jobs in an economy increases, GDP per capita will increase but the productivity of individual workers may not be affected. Over the long term, the only way that GDP per capita can grow continually is if the productivity of the average worker rises or if there are complementary increases in capital.

A common measure of U.S. productivity per worker is dollar value per hour the worker contributes to the employer's output. This measure excludes government workers, because their output is not sold in the market and so their productivity is hard to measure. It also excludes farming, which accounts for only a relatively small share of the U.S. economy. **Figure 20.3** shows an index of output per hour, with 2009 as the base year (when the index equals 100). The index equaled about 106 in 2014. In 1972, the index equaled 50, which shows that workers have more than doubled their productivity since then.

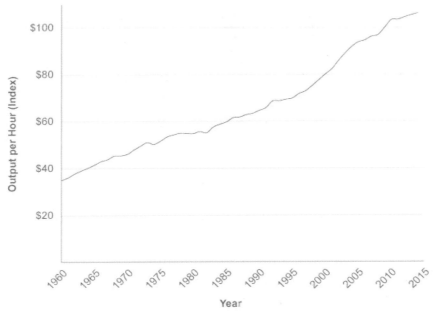

Figure 20.3 Output per Hour Worked in the U.S. Economy, 1947–2011 Output per hour worked is a measure of worker productivity. In the U.S. economy, worker productivity rose more quickly in the 1960s and the mid-1990s compared with the 1970s and 1980s. However, these growth-rate differences are only a few percentage points per year. Look carefully to see them in the changing slope of the line. The average U.S. worker produced over twice as much per hour in 2014 than he did in the early 1970s. (Source: U.S. Department of Labor, Bureau of Labor Statistics.)

According to the Department of Labor, U.S. productivity growth was fairly strong in the 1950s but then declined in the 1970s and 1980s before rising again in the second half of the 1990s and the first half of the 2000s. In fact, the rate of productivity measured by the change in output per hour worked averaged 3.2% per year from 1950 to 1970; dropped to 1.9% per year from 1970 to 1990; and then climbed back to over 2.3% from 1991 to the present, with another modest slowdown after 2001. **Figure 20.4** shows average annual rates of productivity growth averaged over time since 1950.

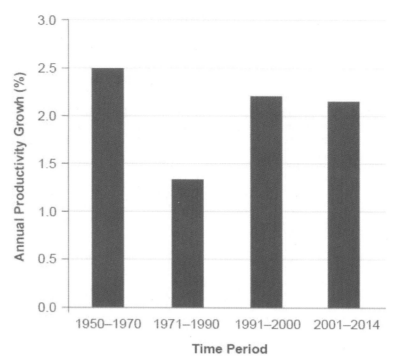

Figure 20.4 Productivity Growth Since 1950   U.S. growth in worker productivity was very high between 1950 and 1970. It then declined to lower levels in the 1970s and the 1980s. The late 1990s and early 2000s saw productivity rebound, but then productivity sagged a bit in the 2000s. Some think the productivity rebound of the late 1990s and early 2000s marks the start of a "new economy" built on higher productivity growth, but we cannot determine this until more time has passed. (Source: U.S. Department of Labor, Bureau of Labor Statistics.)

The "New Economy" Controversy

In recent years a controversy has been brewing among economists about the resurgence of U.S. productivity in the second half of the 1990s. One school of thought argues that the United States had developed a "new economy" based on the extraordinary advances in communications and information technology of the 1990s. The most optimistic proponents argue that it would generate higher average productivity growth for decades to come. The pessimists, alternatively, argue that even five or ten years of stronger productivity growth does not prove that higher productivity will last for the long term. It is hard to infer anything about long-term productivity trends during the later part of the 2000s, because the steep 2008-2009 recession, with its sharp but not completely synchronized declines in output and employment, complicates any interpretation. While productivity growth was high in 2009 and 2010 (around 3%), it has slowed down since then.

Productivity growth is also closely linked to the average level of wages. Over time, the amount that firms are willing to pay workers will depend on the value of the output those workers produce. If a few employers tried to pay their workers less than what those workers produced, then those workers would receive offers of higher wages from other profit-seeking employers. If a few employers mistakenly paid their workers more than what those workers produced, those employers would soon end up with losses. In the long run, productivity per hour is the most important determinant of the average wage level in any economy. To learn how to compare economies in this regard, follow the steps in the following Work It Out feature.

Work It Out ○—○—○

Comparing the Economies of Two Countries

The Organization for Economic Co-operation and Development (OECD) tracks data on the annual growth rate of real GDP per hour worked. You can find these data on the OECD data webpage "Growth in GDP per capita,

This OpenStax book is available for free at http://cnx.org/content/col12122/1.4

productivity and ULC" at this (http://stats.oecd.org/Index.aspx?DataSetCode=PDB_GR) website.

Step 1. Visit the OECD website given above and select two countries to compare.

Step 2. On the drop-down menu "Subject," select " GDP per capita, constant prices," and under "Measure," select "Annual growth/change." Then record the data for the countries you have chosen for the five most recent years.

Step 3. Go back to the drop-down "Subject" menu and select "GDP per hour worked, constant prices," and under "Measure" again select "Annual growth/change." Select data for the same years for which you selected GDP per capita data.

Step 4. Compare real GDP growth for both countries. Table 20.2 provides an example of a comparison between Belgium and Canada.

Australia	2011	2012	2013	2014	2015
Real GDP/Capita Growth (%)	2.3%	1.5%	1.3%	1.4	0.1%
Real GDP Growth/Hours Worked (%)	1.7%	−0.1%	1.4%	2.2%	−0.2%
Belgium	2011	2012	2013	2014	2015
Real GDP/Capita Growth (%)	0.9	−0.6	−0.5	1.2	1.0
Real GDP Growth/Hours Worked (%)	−0.5	−0.3	0.4	1.4	0.9

Table 20.2

Step 5. For both measures, growth in Canada is greater than growth in Belgium for the first four years. In addition, there are year-to-year fluctuations. Many factors can affect growth. For example, one factor that may have contributed to Canada's stronger growth may be its larger inflows of immigrants, who generally contribute to economic growth.

The Power of Sustained Economic Growth

Nothing is more important for people's standard of living than sustained economic growth. Even small changes in the rate of growth, when sustained and compounded over long periods of time, make an enormous difference in the standard of living. Consider Table 20.3, in which the rows of the table show several different rates of growth in GDP per capita and the columns show different periods of time. Assume for simplicity that an economy starts with a GDP per capita of 100. The table then applies the following formula to calculate what GDP will be at the given growth rate in the future:

$$\text{GDP at starting date} \times (1 + \text{growth rate of GDP})^{\text{years}} = \text{GDP at end date}$$

For example, an economy that starts with a GDP of 100 and grows at 3% per year will reach a GDP of 209 after 25 years; that is, $100\,(1.03)^{25} = 209$.

The slowest rate of GDP per capita growth in the table, just 1% per year, is similar to what the United States experienced during its weakest years of productivity growth. The second highest rate, 3% per year, is close to what the U.S. economy experienced during the strong economy of the late 1990s and into the 2000s. Higher rates of per capita growth, such as 5% or 8% per year, represent the experience of rapid growth in economies like Japan, Korea, and China.

Table 20.3 shows that even a few percentage points of difference in economic growth rates will have a profound effect if sustained and compounded over time. For example, an economy growing at a 1% annual rate over 50 years will see its GDP per capita rise by a total of 64%, from 100 to 164 in this example. However, a country growing at a 5% annual rate will see (almost) the same amount of growth—from 100 to 163—over just 10 years. Rapid rates of economic growth can bring profound transformation. (See the following Clear It Up feature on the relationship between compound growth rates and compound interest rates.) If the rate of growth is 8%, young adults starting at age 20 will see the average standard of living in their country more than double by the time they reach age 30, and grow nearly sixfold by the time they reach age 45.

Growth Rate	Value of an original 100 in 10 Years	Value of an original 100 in 25 Years	Value of an original 100 in 50 Years
1%	110	128	164
3%	134	209	438
5%	163	339	1,147
8%	216	685	4,690

Table 20.3 Growth of GDP over Different Time Horizons

This OpenStax book is available for free at http://cnx.org/content/col12122/1.4

How are compound growth rates and compound interest rates related?

The formula for GDP growth rates over different periods of time, as **Figure 20.3** shows, is exactly the same as the formula for how a given amount of financial savings grows at a certain interest rate over time, as presented in **Choice in a World of Scarcity**. Both formulas have the same ingredients:

- an original starting amount, in one case GDP and in the other case an amount of financial saving;
- a percentage increase over time, in one case the GDP growth rate and in the other case an interest rate;
- and an amount of time over which this effect happens.

Recall that compound interest is interest that is earned on past interest. It causes the total amount of financial savings to grow dramatically over time. Similarly, compound rates of economic growth, or the **compound growth rate**, means that we multiply the rate of growth by a base that includes past GDP growth, with dramatic effects over time.

For example, in 2013, the Central Intelligence Agency's World Fact Book reported that South Korea had a GDP of $1.67 trillion with a growth rate of 2.8%. We can estimate that at that growth rate, South Korea's GDP will be $1.92 trillion in five years. If we apply the growth rate to each year's ending GDP for the next five years, we will calculate that at the end of year one, GDP is $1.72 trillion. In year two, we start with the end-of-year one value of $1.72 and increase it by 2.8%. Year three starts with the end-of-year two GDP, and we increase it by 2.8% and so on, as **Table 20.4** depicts.

Year	Starting GDP	Growth Rate 2%	Year-End Amount
1	$1.67 Trillion ×	(1+0.028)	$1.72 Trillion
2	$1.72 Trillion ×	(1+0.028)	$1.76 Trillion
3	$1.76 Trillion ×	(1+0.028)	$1.81 Trillion
4	$1.81 Trillion ×	(1+0.028)	$1.87 Trillion
5	$1.87 Trillion ×	(1+0.028)	$1.92 Trillion

Table 20.4

Another way to calculate the growth rate is to apply the following formula:

$$\text{Future Value} = \text{Present Value} \times (1 + g)^n$$

Where "future value" is the value of GDP five years hence, "present value" is the starting GDP amount of $1.67 trillion, "g" is the growth rate of 2.8%, and "n" is the number of periods for which we are calculating growth.

$$\text{Future Value} = 1.67 \times (1+0.028)^5 = \$1.92 \text{ trillion}$$

20.3 | Components of Economic Growth

By the end of this section, you will be able to:
- Discuss the components of economic growth, including physical capital, human capital, and technology
- Explain capital deepening and its significance
- Analyze the methods employed in economic growth accounting studies
- Identify factors that contribute to a healthy climate for economic growth

Over decades and generations, seemingly small differences of a few percentage points in the annual rate of economic growth make an enormous difference in GDP per capita. In this module, we discuss some of the components of economic growth, including physical capital, human capital, and technology.

The category of **physical capital** includes the plant and equipment that firms use as well as things like roads (also called **infrastructure**). Again, greater physical capital implies more output. Physical capital can affect productivity in two ways: (1) an increase in the *quantity* of physical capital (for example, more computers of the same quality); and (2) an increase in the *quality* of physical capital (same number of computers but the computers are faster, and so on). **Human capital** refers to the skills and knowledge that make workers productive. Human capital and physical capital accumulation are similar: In both cases, investment now pays off in higher productivity in the future.

The category of **technology** is the "joker in the deck." Earlier we described it as the combination of invention and innovation. When most people think of new technology, the invention of new products like the laser, the smartphone, or some new wonder drug come to mind. In food production, developing more drought-resistant seeds is another example of technology. Technology, as economists use the term, however, includes still more. It includes new ways of organizing work, like the invention of the assembly line, new methods for ensuring better quality of output in factories, and innovative institutions that facilitate the process of converting inputs into output. In short, technology comprises all the advances that make the existing machines and other inputs produce more, and at higher quality, as well as altogether new products.

It may not make sense to compare the GDPs of China and say, Benin, simply because of the great difference in population size. To understand economic growth, which is really concerned with the growth in living standards of an average person, it is often useful to focus on GDP per capita. Using GDP per capita also makes it easier to compare countries with smaller numbers of people, like Belgium, Uruguay, or Zimbabwe, with countries that have larger populations, like the United States, the Russian Federation, or Nigeria.

To obtain a per capita production function, divide each input in **Figure 20.2**(a) by the population. This creates a second aggregate production function where the output is GDP per capita (that is, GDP divided by population). The inputs are the average level of human capital per person, the average level of physical capital per person, and the level of technology per person—see **Figure 20.2**(b). The result of having population in the denominator is mathematically appealing. Increases in population lower per capita income. However, increasing population is important for the average person only if the rate of income growth exceeds population growth. A more important reason for constructing a per capita production function is to understand the contribution of human and physical capital.

Capital Deepening

When society increases the level of capital per person, we call the result **capital deepening**. The idea of capital deepening can apply both to additional human capital per worker and to additional physical capital per worker.

Recall that one way to measure human capital is to look at the average levels of education in an economy. **Figure 20.5** illustrates the human capital deepening for U.S. workers by showing that the proportion of the U.S. population with a high school and a college degree is rising. As recently as 1970, for example, only about half of U.S. adults had at least a high school diploma. By the start of the twenty-first century, more than 80% of adults had graduated from high school. The idea of human capital deepening also applies to the years of experience that workers have, but the average experience level of U.S. workers has not changed much in recent decades. Thus, the key dimension for deepening human capital in the U.S. economy focuses more on additional education and training than on a higher average level of work experience.

This OpenStax book is available for free at http://cnx.org/content/col12122/1.4

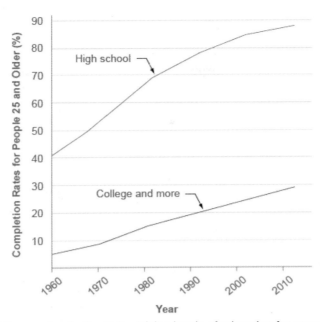

Figure 20.5 Human Capital Deepening in the U.S. Rising levels of education for persons 25 and older show the deepening of human capital in the U.S. economy. Even today, under one-third of U.S. adults have completed a four-year college degree. There is clearly room for additional deepening of human capital to occur. (Source: US Department of Education, National Center for Education Statistics)

Figure 20.6 shows physical capital deepening in the U.S. economy. The average U.S. worker in the late 2000s was working with physical capital worth almost three times as much as that of the average worker of the early 1950s.

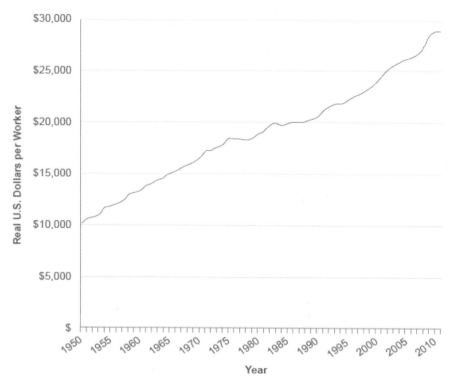

Figure 20.6 Physical Capital per Worker in the United States The value of the physical capital, measured by plant and equipment, used by the average worker in the U.S. economy has risen over the decades. The increase may have leveled off a bit in the 1970s and 1980s, which were, not coincidentally, times of slower-than-usual growth in worker productivity. We see a renewed increase in physical capital per worker in the late 1990s, followed by a flattening in the early 2000s. (Source: Center for International Comparisons of Production, Income and Prices, University of Pennsylvania)

Not only does the current U.S. economy have better-educated workers with more and improved physical capital than it did several decades ago, but these workers have access to more advanced technologies. Growth in technology is impossible to measure with a simple line on a graph, but evidence that we live in an age of technological marvels is all around us—discoveries in genetics and in the structure of particles, the wireless internet, and other inventions almost too numerous to count. The U.S. Patent and Trademark Office typically has issued more than 150,000 patents annually in recent years.

This recipe for economic growth—investing in labor productivity, with investments in human capital and technology, as well as increasing physical capital—also applies to other economies. South Korea, for example, already achieved universal enrollment in primary school (the equivalent of kindergarten through sixth grade in the United States) by 1965, when Korea's GDP per capita was still near its rock bottom low. By the late 1980s, Korea had achieved almost universal secondary school education (the equivalent of a high school education in the United States). With regard to physical capital, Korea's rates of investment had been about 15% of GDP at the start of the 1960s, but doubled to 30–35% of GDP by the late 1960s and early 1970s. With regard to technology, South Korean students went to universities and colleges around the world to obtain scientific and technical training, and South Korean firms reached out to study and form partnerships with firms that could offer them technological insights. These factors combined to foster South Korea's high rate of economic growth.

Growth Accounting Studies

Since the late 1950s, economists have conducted growth accounting studies to determine the extent to which physical and human capital deepening and technology have contributed to growth. The usual approach uses an aggregate production function to estimate how much of per capita economic growth can be attributed to growth in physical capital and human capital. We can measure these two inputs at least roughly. The part of growth that is unexplained by measured inputs, called the residual, is then attributed to growth in technology. The exact numerical estimates differ from study to study and from country to country, depending on how researchers measured these three main

This OpenStax book is available for free at http://cnx.org/content/col12122/1.4

factors and over what time horizons. For studies of the U.S. economy, three lessons commonly emerge from growth accounting studies.

First, technology is typically the most important contributor to U.S. economic growth. Growth in human capital and physical capital often explains only half or less than half of the economic growth that occurs. New ways of doing things are tremendously important.

Second, while investment in physical capital is essential to growth in labor productivity and GDP per capita, building human capital is at least as important. Economic growth is not just a matter of more machines and buildings. One vivid example of the power of human capital and technological knowledge occurred in Europe in the years after World War II (1939–1945). During the war, a large share of Europe's physical capital, such as factories, roads, and vehicles, was destroyed. Europe also lost an overwhelming amount of human capital in the form of millions of men, women, and children who died during the war. However, the powerful combination of skilled workers and technological knowledge, working within a market-oriented economic framework, rebuilt Europe's productive capacity to an even higher level within less than two decades.

A third lesson is that these three factors of human capital, physical capital, and technology work together. Workers with a higher level of education and skills are often better at coming up with new technological innovations. These technological innovations are often ideas that cannot increase production until they become a part of new investment in physical capital. New machines that embody technological innovations often require additional training, which builds worker skills further. If the recipe for economic growth is to succeed, an economy needs all the ingredients of the aggregate production function. See the following Clear It Up feature for an example of how human capital, physical capital, and technology can combine to significantly impact lives.

How do girls' education and economic growth relate in low-income countries?

In the early 2000s, according to the World Bank, about 110 million children between the ages of 6 and 11 were not in school—and about two-thirds of them were girls. In Afghanistan, for example, the literacy rate for those aged 15-24 for the period 2005-2014 was 62% for males and only 32% for females. In Benin, in West Africa, it was 55% for males and 31% for females. In Nigeria, Africa's most populous country, it was 76% for males and 58 percent for females.

Whenever any child does not receive a basic education, it is both a human and an economic loss. In low-income countries, wages typically increase by an average of 10 to 20% with each additional year of education. There is, however, some intriguing evidence that helping girls in low-income countries to close the education gap with boys may be especially important, because of the social role that many of the girls will play as mothers and homemakers.

Girls in low-income countries who receive more education tend to grow up to have fewer, healthier, better-educated children. Their children are more likely to be better nourished and to receive basic health care like immunizations. Economic research on women in low-income economies backs up these findings. When 20 women obtain one additional year of schooling, as a group they will, on average, have one less child. When 1,000 women obtain one additional year of schooling, on average one to two fewer women from that group will die in childbirth. When a woman stays in school an additional year, that factor alone means that, on average, each of her children will spend an additional half-year in school. Education for girls is a good investment because it is an investment in economic growth with benefits beyond the current generation.

A Healthy Climate for Economic Growth

While physical and human capital deepening and better technology are important, equally important to a nation's well-being is the climate or system within which these inputs are cultivated. Both the type of market economy and a legal system that governs and sustains property rights and contractual rights are important contributors to a healthy economic climate.

A healthy economic climate usually involves some sort of market orientation at the microeconomic, individual, or firm decision-making level. Markets that allow personal and business rewards and incentives for increasing human and physical capital encourage overall macroeconomic growth. For example, when workers participate in a competitive and well-functioning labor market, they have an incentive to acquire additional human capital, because additional education and skills will pay off in higher wages. Firms have an incentive to invest in physical capital and in training workers, because they expect to earn higher profits for their shareholders. Both individuals and firms look for new technologies, because even small inventions can make work easier or lead to product improvement. Collectively, such individual and business decisions made within a market structure add up to macroeconomic growth. Much of the rapid growth since the late nineteenth century has come from harnessing the power of competitive markets to allocate resources. This market orientation typically reaches beyond national borders and includes openness to international trade.

A general orientation toward markets does not rule out important roles for government. There are times when markets fail to allocate capital or technology in a manner that provides the greatest benefit for society as a whole. The government's role is to correct these failures. In addition, government can guide or influence markets toward certain outcomes. The following examples highlight some important areas that governments around the world have chosen to invest in to facilitate capital deepening and technology:

- Education. The Danish government requires all children under 16 to attend school. They can choose to attend a public school (*Folkeskole*) or a private school. Students do not pay tuition to attend *Folkeskole*. Thirteen percent of primary/secondary (elementary/high) school is private, and the government supplies vouchers to citizens who choose private school.

- Savings and Investment. In the United States, as in other countries, the government taxes gains from private investment. Low capital gains taxes encourage investment and so also economic growth.

- Infrastructure. The Japanese government in the mid-1990s undertook significant infrastructure projects to improve roads and public works. This in turn increased the stock of physical capital and ultimately economic growth.

- Special Economic Zones. The island of Mauritius is one of the few African nations to encourage international trade in government-supported **special economic zones (SEZ)**. These are areas of the country, usually with access to a port where, among other benefits, the government does not tax trade. As a result of its SEZ, Mauritius has enjoyed above-average economic growth since the 1980s. Free trade does not have to occur in an SEZ however. Governments can encourage international trade across the board, or surrender to protectionism.

- Scientific Research. The European Union has strong programs to invest in scientific research. The researchers Abraham García and Pierre Mohnen demonstrate that firms which received support from the Austrian government actually increased their research intensity and had more sales. Governments can support scientific research and technical training that helps to create and spread new technologies. Governments can also provide a legal environment that protects the ability of inventors to profit from their inventions.

There are many more ways in which the government can play an active role in promoting economic growth. We explore them in other chapters and in particular in **Macroeconomic Policy Around the World**. A healthy climate for growth in GDP per capita and labor productivity includes human capital deepening, physical capital deepening, and technological gains, operating in a market-oriented economy with supportive government policies.

20.4 | Economic Convergence

By the end of this section, you will be able to:
- Explain economic convergence
- Analyze various arguments for and against economic convergence
- Evaluate the speed of economic convergence between high-income countries and the rest of the world

Some low-income and middle-income economies around the world have shown a pattern of **convergence**, in which their economies grow faster than those of high-income countries. GDP increased by an average rate of 2.7% per year in the 1990s and 2.3% per year from 2000 to 2008 in the high-income countries of the world, which include the

United States, Canada, the European Union countries, Japan, Australia, and New Zealand.

Table 20.5 lists 10 countries that belong to an informal "fast growth club." These countries averaged GDP growth (after adjusting for inflation) of at least 5% per year in both the time periods from 1990 to 2000 and from 2000 to 2008. Since economic growth in these countries has exceeded the average of the world's high-income economies, these countries may converge with the high-income countries. The second part of Table 20.5 lists the "slow growth club," which consists of countries that averaged GDP growth of 2% per year or less (after adjusting for inflation) during the same time periods. The final portion of Table 20.5 shows GDP growth rates for the countries of the world divided by income.

Country	Average Growth Rate of Real GDP 1990–2000	Average Growth Rate of Real GDP 2000–2008
Fast Growth Club (5% or more per year in both time periods)		
Cambodia	7.1%	9.1%
China	10.6%	9.9%
India	6.0%	7.1%
Ireland	7.5%	5.1%
Jordan	5.0%	6.3%
Laos	6.5%	6.8 %
Mozambique	6.4%	7.3%
Sudan	5.4%	7.3%
Uganda	7.1%	7.3%
Vietnam	7.9%	7.3%
Slow Growth Club (2% or less per year in both time periods)		
Central African Republic	2.0%	0.8%
France	2.0%	1.8%
Germany	1.8%	1.3%
Guinea-Bissau	1.2%	0.2%
Haiti	−1.5%	0.3%
Italy	1.6%	1.2%
Jamaica	0.9%	1.4%
Japan	1.3%	1.3%
Switzerland	1.0%	2.0%
United States (for reference)	3.2%	2.2%

Table 20.5 Economic Growth around the World   (Source: http://databank.worldbank.org/data/views/variableSelection/selectvariables.aspx?source=world-development-indicators#c_u)

Country	Average Growth Rate of Real GDP 1990–2000	Average Growth Rate of Real GDP 2000–2008
World Overview		
High income	2.7%	2.3%
Low income	3.8%	5.6%
Middle income	4.7%	6.1%

Table 20.5 Economic Growth around the World   (Source: http://databank.worldbank.org/data/views/variableSelection/selectvariables.aspx?source=world-development-indicators#c_u)

Each of the countries in **Table 20.5** has its own unique story of investments in human and physical capital, technological gains, market forces, government policies, and even lucky events, but an overall pattern of convergence is clear. The low-income countries have GDP growth that is faster than that of the middle-income countries, which in turn have GDP growth that is faster than that of the high-income countries. Two prominent members of the fast-growth club are China and India, which between them have nearly 40% of the world's population. Some prominent members of the slow-growth club are high-income countries like France, Germany, Italy, and Japan.

Will this pattern of economic convergence persist into the future? This is a controversial question among economists that we will consider by looking at some of the main arguments on both sides.

Arguments Favoring Convergence

Several arguments suggest that low-income countries might have an advantage in achieving greater worker productivity and economic growth in the future.

A first argument is based on diminishing marginal returns. Even though deepening human and physical capital will tend to increase GDP per capita, the law of diminishing returns suggests that as an economy continues to increase its human and physical capital, the marginal gains to economic growth will diminish. For example, raising the average education level of the population by two years from a tenth-grade level to a high school diploma (while holding all other inputs constant) would produce a certain increase in output. An additional two-year increase, so that the average person had a two-year college degree, would increase output further, but the marginal gain would be smaller. Yet another additional two-year increase in the level of education, so that the average person would have a four-year-college bachelor's degree, would increase output still further, but the marginal increase would again be smaller. A similar lesson holds for physical capital. If the quantity of physical capital available to the average worker increases, by, say, $5,000 to $10,000 (again, while holding all other inputs constant), it will increase the level of output. An additional increase from $10,000 to $15,000 will increase output further, but the marginal increase will be smaller.

Low-income countries like China and India tend to have lower levels of human capital and physical capital, so an investment in capital deepening should have a larger marginal effect in these countries than in high-income countries, where levels of human and physical capital are already relatively high. Diminishing returns implies that low-income economies could converge to the levels that the high-income countries achieve.

A second argument is that low-income countries may find it easier to improve their technologies than high-income countries. High-income countries must continually invent new technologies, whereas low-income countries can often find ways of applying technology that has already been invented and is well understood. The economist Alexander Gerschenkron (1904–1978) gave this phenomenon a memorable name: "the advantages of backwardness." Of course, he did not literally mean that it is an advantage to have a lower standard of living. He was pointing out that a country that is behind has some extra potential for catching up.

Finally, optimists argue that many countries have observed the experience of those that have grown more quickly and have learned from it. Moreover, once the people of a country begin to enjoy the benefits of a higher standard of living, they may be more likely to build and support the market-friendly institutions that will help provide this standard of living.

Link It Up

View this video (http://openstaxcollege.org/l/tedhansrosling) to learn about economic growth across the world.

Arguments That Convergence Is neither Inevitable nor Likely

If the economy's growth depended only on the deepening of human capital and physical capital, then we would expect that economy's growth rate to slow down over the long run because of diminishing marginal returns. However, there is another crucial factor in the aggregate production function: technology.

Developing new technology can provide a way for an economy to sidestep the diminishing marginal returns of capital deepening. **Figure 20.7** shows how. The figure's horizontal axis measures the amount of capital deepening, which on this figure is an overall measure that includes deepening of both physical and human capital. The amount of human and physical capital per worker increases as you move from left to right, from C_1 to C_2 to C_3. The diagram's vertical axis measures per capita output. Start by considering the lowest line in this diagram, labeled Technology 1. Along this aggregate production function, the level of technology is held constant, so the line shows only the relationship between capital deepening and output. As capital deepens from C_1 to C_2 to C_3 and the economy moves from R to U to W, per capita output does increase—but the way in which the line starts out steeper on the left but then flattens as it moves to the right shows the diminishing marginal returns, as additional marginal amounts of capital deepening increase output by ever-smaller amounts. The shape of the aggregate production line (Technology 1) shows that the ability of capital deepening, by itself, to generate sustained economic growth is limited, since diminishing returns will eventually set in.

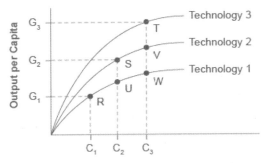

Figure 20.7 Capital Deepening and New Technology   Imagine that the economy starts at point R, with the level of physical and human capital C_1 and the output per capita at G_1. If the economy relies only on capital deepening, while remaining at the technology level shown by the Technology 1 line, then it would face diminishing marginal returns as it moved from point R to point U to point W. However, now imagine that capital deepening is combined with improvements in technology. Then, as capital deepens from C_1 to C_2, technology improves from Technology 1 to Technology 2, and the economy moves from R to S. Similarly, as capital deepens from C_2 to C_3, technology increases from Technology 2 to Technology 3, and the economy moves from S to T. With improvements in technology, there is no longer any reason that economic growth must necessarily slow down.

Now, bring improvements in technology into the picture. Improved technology means that with a given set of inputs, more output is possible. The production function labeled Technology 1 in the figure is based on one level of technology, but Technology 2 is based on an improved level of technology, so for every level of capital deepening on the horizontal axis, it produces a higher level of output on the vertical axis. In turn, production function Technology 3 represents a still higher level of technology, so that for every level of inputs on the horizontal axis, it produces a higher level of output on the vertical axis than either of the other two aggregate production functions.

Most healthy, growing economies are deepening their human and physical capital and increasing technology at the same time. As a result, the economy can move from a choice like point R on the Technology 1 aggregate production line to a point like S on Technology 2 and a point like T on the still higher aggregate production line (Technology 3). With the combination of technology and capital deepening, the rise in GDP per capita in high-income countries does not need to fade away because of diminishing returns. The gains from technology can offset the diminishing returns involved with capital deepening.

Will technological improvements themselves run into diminishing returns over time? That is, will it become continually harder and more costly to discover new technological improvements? Perhaps someday, but, at least over the last two centuries since the beginning of the Industrial Revolution, improvements in technology have not run into diminishing marginal returns. Modern inventions, like the internet or discoveries in genetics or materials science, do not seem to provide smaller gains to output than earlier inventions like the steam engine or the railroad. One reason that technological ideas do not seem to run into diminishing returns is that we often can apply widely the ideas of new technology at a marginal cost that is very low or even zero. A specific worker or group of workers must use a specific additional machine, or an additional year of education. Many workers across the economy can use a new technology or invention at very low marginal cost.

The argument that it is easier for a low-income country to copy and adapt existing technology than it is for a high-income country to invent new technology is not necessarily true, either. When it comes to adapting and using new technology, a society's performance is not necessarily guaranteed, but is the result of whether the country's economic, educational, and public policy institutions are supportive. In theory, perhaps, low-income countries have many opportunities to copy and adapt technology, but if they lack the appropriate supportive economic infrastructure and institutions, the theoretical possibility that backwardness might have certain advantages is of little practical relevance.

Link It Up 🔗

Visit this website (http://openstaxcollege.org/l/Indiapoverty) to read more about economic growth in India.

The Slowness of Convergence

Although economic convergence between the high-income countries and the rest of the world seems possible and even likely, it will proceed slowly. Consider, for example, a country that starts off with a GDP per capita of $40,000, which would roughly represent a typical high-income country today, and another country that starts out at $4,000, which is roughly the level in low-income but not impoverished countries like Indonesia, Guatemala, or Egypt. Say that the rich country chugs along at a 2% annual growth rate of GDP per capita, while the poorer country grows at the aggressive rate of 7% per year. After 30 years, GDP per capita in the rich country will be $72,450 (that is, $40,000 $(1 + 0.02)^{30}$) while in the poor country it will be $30,450 (that is, $4,000 $(1 + 0.07)^{30}$). Convergence has occurred. The rich country used to be 10 times as wealthy as the poor one, and now it is only about 2.4 times as wealthy. Even after 30 consecutive years of very rapid growth, however, people in the low-income country are still likely to feel quite poor compared to people in the rich country. Moreover, as the poor country catches up, its opportunities for catch-up growth are reduced, and its growth rate may slow down somewhat.

This OpenStax book is available for free at http://cnx.org/content/col12122/1.4

The slowness of convergence illustrates again that small differences in annual rates of economic growth become huge differences over time. The high-income countries have been building up their advantage in standard of living over decades—more than a century in some cases. Even in an optimistic scenario, it will take decades for the low-income countries of the world to catch up significantly.

Bring it Home

Calories and Economic Growth

We can tell the story of modern economic growth by looking at calorie consumption over time. The dramatic rise in incomes allowed the average person to eat better and consume more calories. How did these incomes increase? The neoclassical growth consensus uses the aggregate production function to suggest that the period of modern economic growth came about because of increases in inputs such as technology and physical and human capital. Also important was the way in which technological progress combined with physical and human capital deepening to create growth and convergence. The issue of distribution of income notwithstanding, it is clear that the average worker can afford more calories in 2017 than in 1875.

Aside from increases in income, there is another reason why the average person can afford more food. Modern agriculture has allowed many countries to produce more food than they need. Despite having more than enough food, however, many governments and multilateral agencies have not solved the food distribution problem. In fact, food shortages, famine, or general food insecurity are caused more often by the failure of government macroeconomic policy, according to the Nobel Prize-winning economist Amartya Sen. Sen has conducted extensive research into issues of inequality, poverty, and the role of government in improving standards of living. Macroeconomic policies that strive toward stable inflation, full employment, education of women, and preservation of property rights are more likely to eliminate starvation and provide for a more even distribution of food.

Because we have more food per capita, global food prices have decreased since 1875. The prices of some foods, however, have decreased more than the prices of others. For example, researchers from the University of Washington have shown that in the United States, calories from zucchini and lettuce are 100 times more expensive than calories from oil, butter, and sugar. Research from countries like India, China, and the United States suggests that as incomes rise, individuals want more calories from fats and protein and fewer from carbohydrates. This has very interesting implications for global food production, obesity, and environmental consequences. Affluent urban India has an obesity problem much like many parts of the United States. The forces of convergence are at work.

KEY TERMS

aggregate production function the process whereby an economy as a whole turns economic inputs such as human capital, physical capital, and technology into output measured as GDP per capita

capital deepening an increase by society in the average level of physical and/or human capital per person

compound growth rate the rate of growth when multiplied by a base that includes past GDP growth

contractual rights the rights of individuals to enter into agreements with others regarding the use of their property providing recourse through the legal system in the event of noncompliance

convergence pattern in which economies with low per capita incomes grow faster than economies with high per capita incomes

human capital the accumulated skills and education of workers

Industrial Revolution the widespread use of power-driven machinery and the economic and social changes that occurred in the first half of the 1800s

infrastructure a component of physical capital such as roads and rail systems

innovation putting advances in knowledge to use in a new product or service

invention advances in knowledge

labor productivity the value of what is produced per worker, or per hour worked (sometimes called worker productivity)

modern economic growth the period of rapid economic growth from 1870 onward

physical capital the plant and equipment that firms use in production; this includes infrastructure

production function the process whereby a firm turns economic inputs like labor, machinery, and raw materials into outputs like goods and services that consumers use

rule of law the process of enacting laws that protect individual and entity rights to use their property as they see fit. Laws must be clear, public, fair, and enforced, and applicable to all members of society

special economic zone (SEZ) area of a country, usually with access to a port where, among other benefits, the government does not tax trade

technological change a combination of invention—advances in knowledge—and innovation

technology all the ways in which existing inputs produce more or higher quality, as well as different and altogether new products

KEY CONCEPTS AND SUMMARY

20.1 The Relatively Recent Arrival of Economic Growth

Since the early nineteenth century, there has been a spectacular process of long-run economic growth during which the world's leading economies—mostly those in Western Europe and North America—expanded GDP per capita at an average rate of about 2% per year. In the last half-century, countries like Japan, South Korea, and China have shown the potential to catch up. The Industrial Revolution facilitated the extensive process of economic growth, that economists often refer to as modern economic growth. This increased worker productivity and trade, as well as the

This OpenStax book is available for free at http://cnx.org/content/col12122/1.4

development of governance and market institutions.

20.2 Labor Productivity and Economic Growth

We can measure productivity, the value of what is produced per worker, or per hour worked, as the level of GDP per worker or GDP per hour. The United States experienced a productivity slowdown between 1973 and 1989. Since then, U.S. productivity has rebounded for the most part, but annual growth in productivity in the nonfarm business sector has been less than one percent each year between 2011 and 2016. It is not clear what productivity growth will be in the coming years. The rate of productivity growth is the primary determinant of an economy's rate of long-term economic growth and higher wages. Over decades and generations, seemingly small differences of a few percentage points in the annual rate of economic growth make an enormous difference in GDP per capita. An aggregate production function specifies how certain inputs in the economy, like human capital, physical capital, and technology, lead to the output measured as GDP per capita.

Compound interest and compound growth rates behave in the same way as productivity rates. Seemingly small changes in percentage points can have big impacts on income over time.

20.3 Components of Economic Growth

Over decades and generations, seemingly small differences of a few percentage points in the annual rate of economic growth make an enormous difference in GDP per capita. Capital deepening refers to an increase in the amount of capital per worker, either human capital per worker, in the form of higher education or skills, or physical capital per worker. Technology, in its economic meaning, refers broadly to all new methods of production, which includes major scientific inventions but also small inventions and even better forms of management or other types of institutions. A healthy climate for growth in GDP per capita consists of improvements in human capital, physical capital, and technology, in a market-oriented environment with supportive public policies and institutions.

20.4 Economic Convergence

When countries with lower GDP levels per capita catch up to countries with higher GDP levels per capita, we call the process convergence. Convergence can occur even when both high- and low-income countries increase investment in physical and human capital with the objective of growing GDP. This is because the impact of new investment in physical and human capital on a low-income country may result in huge gains as new skills or equipment combine with the labor force. In higher-income countries, however, a level of investment equal to that of the low income country is not likely to have as big an impact, because the more developed country most likely already has high levels of capital investment. Therefore, the marginal gain from this additional investment tends to be successively less and less. Higher income countries are more likely to have diminishing returns to their investments and must continually invent new technologies. This allows lower-income economies to have a chance for convergent growth. However, many high-income economies have developed economic and political institutions that provide a healthy economic climate for an ongoing stream of technological innovations. Continuous technological innovation can counterbalance diminishing returns to investments in human and physical capital.

SELF-CHECK QUESTIONS

1. Explain what the Industrial Revolution was and where it began.

2. Explain the difference between property rights and contractual rights. Why do they matter to economic growth?

3. Are there other ways in which we can measure productivity besides the amount produced per hour of work?

4. Assume there are two countries: South Korea and the United States. South Korea grows at 4% and the United States grows at 1%. For the sake of simplicity, assume they both start from the same fictional income level, $10,000. What will the incomes of the United States and South Korea be in 20 years? By how many multiples will each country's income grow in 20 years?

5. What do the growth accounting studies conclude are the determinants of growth? Which is more important, the determinants or how they are combined?

6. What policies can the government of a free-market economy implement to stimulate economic growth?

7. List the areas where government policy can help economic growth.

8. Use an example to explain why, after periods of rapid growth, a low-income country that has not caught up to a high-income country may feel poor.

9. Would the following events usually lead to capital deepening? Why or why not?
   a. A weak economy in which businesses become reluctant to make long-term investments in physical capital.
   b. A rise in international trade.
   c. A trend in which many more adults participate in continuing education courses through their employers and at colleges and universities.

10. What are the "advantages of backwardness" for economic growth?

11. Would you expect capital deepening to result in diminished returns? Why or why not? Would you expect improvements in technology to result in diminished returns? Why or why not?

12. Why does productivity growth in high-income economies not slow down as it runs into diminishing returns from additional investments in physical capital and human capital? Does this show one area where the theory of diminishing returns fails to apply? Why or why not?

REVIEW QUESTIONS

13. How did the Industrial Revolution increase the economic growth rate and income levels in the United States?

14. How much should a nation be concerned if its rate of economic growth is just 2% slower than other nations?

15. How is GDP per capita calculated differently from labor productivity?

16. How do gains in labor productivity lead to gains in GDP per capita?

17. What is an aggregate production function?

18. What is capital deepening?

19. What do economists mean when they refer to improvements in technology?

20. For a high-income economy like the United States, what aggregate production function elements are most important in bringing about growth in GDP per capita? What about a middle-income country such as Brazil? A low-income country such as Niger?

21. List some arguments for and against the likelihood of convergence.

CRITICAL THINKING QUESTIONS

22. Over the past 50 years, many countries have experienced an annual growth rate in real GDP per capita greater than that of the United States. Some examples are China, Japan, South Korea, and Taiwan. Does that mean the United States is regressing relative to other countries? Does that mean these countries will eventually overtake the United States in terms of the growth rate of real GDP per capita? Explain.

23. **Labor Productivity and Economic Growth** outlined the logic of how increased productivity is associated with increased wages. Detail a situation where this is not the case and explain why it is not.

24. Change in labor productivity is one of the most watched international statistics of growth. Visit the St. Louis Federal Reserve website and find the data section (http://research.stlouisfed.org). Find international comparisons of labor productivity, listed under the FRED Economic database (Growth Rate of Total Labor Productivity), and compare two countries in the recent past. State what you think the reasons for differences in labor productivity could be.

25. Refer back to the **Work It Out** about Comparing the Economies of Two Countries and examine the data for the two countries you chose. How are they similar? How are they different?

This OpenStax book is available for free at http://cnx.org/content/col12122/1.4

26. Education seems to be important for human capital deepening. As people become better educated and more knowledgeable, are there limits to how much additional benefit more education can provide? Why or why not?

27. Describe some of the political and social tradeoffs that might occur when a less developed country adopts a strategy to promote labor force participation and economic growth via investment in girls' education.

28. Why is investing in girls' education beneficial for growth?

PROBLEMS

32. An economy starts off with a GDP per capita of $5,000. How large will the GDP per capita be if it grows at an annual rate of 2% for 20 years? 2% for 40 years? 4% for 40 years? 6% for 40 years?

33. An economy starts off with a GDP per capita of 12,000 euros. How large will the GDP per capita be if it grows at an annual rate of 3% for 10 years? 3% for 30 years? 6% for 30 years?

29. How is the concept of technology, as defined with the aggregate production function, different from our everyday use of the word?

30. What sorts of policies can governments implement to encourage convergence?

31. As technological change makes us more sedentary and food costs increase, obesity is likely. What factors do you think may limit obesity?

34. Say that the average worker in Canada has a productivity level of $30 per hour while the average worker in the United Kingdom has a productivity level of $25 per hour (both measured in U.S. dollars). Over the next five years, say that worker productivity in Canada grows at 1% per year while worker productivity in the UK grows 3% per year. After five years, who will have the higher productivity level, and by how much?

35. Say that the average worker in the U.S. economy is eight times as productive as an average worker in Mexico. If the productivity of U.S. workers grows at 2% for 25 years and the productivity of Mexico's workers grows at 6% for 25 years, which country will have higher worker productivity at that point?

This OpenStax book is available for free at http://cnx.org/content/col12122/1.4

21 | Unemployment

Figure 21.1 Out of Business Borders was one of the many companies unable to recover from the 2008-2009 economic recession. (Credit: modification of work by Luis Villa del Campo/Flickr Creative Commons)

Bring it Home

Unemployment and the Great Recession

Nearly eight million U.S. jobs were lost as a consequence of the Great Recession, which lasted from December 2007 to June 2009. At the outset of the recession, the unemployment rate was 5.0%. The rate began rising several months after the recession began, and it peaked at 10.0% in October 2009, several months after the recession ended, according to the Bureau of Labor Statistics (BLS). The job loss represented a huge number of positions gone. Subsequently, the recovery was tepid. Companies added some positions, but as of summer 2013, four years after the end of the recession, unemployment was about 7.5%, well above the pre-recession rate. Employment began increasing at the outset of 2010, and reached its pre-recession level in mid-2014. However, because of population and labor force growth, the unemployment rate at that point was still slightly above 6%. The economy only returned to an unemployment rate of 5.0% in September 2015, and it has remained at or slightly below that level since then, up through January 2017.

This brief overview of unemployment during and after the Great Recession highlights a few important points. First, unemployment is a lagging indicator of business activity. It didn't begin to increase until a few months after the onset of the recession, and it didn't begin to decline until several months after the recovery. Second, the decline in the unemployment rate was quite slow, with the pre-recession unemployment rate only reaching a higher level than six years after the recession ended. This reflects a combination of slow increase in the number of jobs and ongoing increases in the size of the population and the labor force.

It turns out that recent recessions, going back to the early 1990s, have been characterized by longer periods of recovery than their predecessors. We will return to this point at the end of the chapter. However, first we need to examine unemployment. What constitutes it, and how do we measure it?

Introduction to Unemployment

In this chapter, you will learn about:

- How Economists Define and Compute Unemployment Rate
- Patterns of Unemployment
- What Causes Changes in Unemployment over the Short Run
- What Causes Changes in Unemployment over the Long Run

Unemployment can be a terrible and wrenching life experience—like a serious automobile accident or a messy divorce—whose consequences only someone who has gone through it can fully understand. For unemployed individuals and their families, there is the day-to-day financial stress of not knowing from where the next paycheck is coming. There are painful adjustments, like watching your savings account dwindle, selling a car and buying a cheaper one, or moving to a less expensive place to live. Even when the unemployed person finds a new job, it may pay less than the previous one. For many people, their job is an important part of their self worth. When unemployment separates people from the workforce, it can affect family relationships as well as mental and physical health.

The human costs of unemployment alone would justify making a low level of unemployment an important public policy priority. However, unemployment also includes economic costs to the broader society. When millions of unemployed but willing workers cannot find jobs, economic resource are unused. An economy with high unemployment is like a company operating with a functional but unused factory. The opportunity cost of unemployment is the output that the unemployed workers could have produced.

This chapter will discuss how economists define and compute the unemployment rate. It will examine the patterns of unemployment over time, for the U.S. economy as a whole, for different demographic groups in the U.S. economy, and for other countries. It will then consider an economic explanation for unemployment, and how it explains the patterns of unemployment and suggests public policies for reducing it.

21.1 | How Economists Define and Compute Unemployment Rate

By the end of this section, you will be able to:
- Calculate the labor force participation rate and the unemployment rate
- Explain hidden unemployment and what it means to be in or out of the labor force
- Evaluate the collection and interpretation of unemployment data

Newspaper or television reports typically describe unemployment as a percentage or a rate. A recent report might have said, for example, *from August 2009 to November 2009, the U.S. unemployment rate rose from 9.7% to 10.0%, but by June 2010, it had fallen to 9.5%.* At a glance, the changes between the percentages may seem small. However, remember that the U.S. economy has about 160 million adults (as of the beginning of 2017) who either have jobs or are looking for them. A rise or fall of just 0.1% in the unemployment rate of 160 million potential workers translates into 160,000 people, which is roughly the total population of a city like Syracuse, New York, Brownsville, Texas, or Pasadena, California. Large rises in the unemployment rate mean large numbers of job losses. In November 2009, at the peak of the recession, about 15 million people were out of work. Even with the unemployment rate now at 4.8% as of January 2017, about 7.6 million people who would like to have jobs are out of work.

This OpenStax book is available for free at http://cnx.org/content/col12122/1.4

Link It Up

The Bureau of Labor Statistics (http://openstaxcollege.org/l/BLS1) tracks and reports all data related to unemployment.

Who's In or Out of the Labor Force?

Should we count everyone without a job as unemployed? Of course not. For example, we should not count children as unemployed. Surely, we should not count the retired as unemployed. Many full-time college students have only a part-time job, or no job at all, but it seems inappropriate to count them as suffering the pains of unemployment. Some people are not working because they are rearing children, ill, on vacation, or on parental leave.

The point is that we do not just divide the adult population into employed and unemployed. A third group exists: people who do not have a job, and for some reason—retirement, looking after children, taking a voluntary break before a new job—are not interested in having a job, either. It also includes those who do want a job but have quit looking, often due to discouragement due to their inability to find suitable employment. Economists refer to this third group of those who are not working and not looking for work as **out of the labor force** or not in the labor force.

The U.S. unemployment rate, which is based on a monthly survey carried out by the U.S. Bureau of the Census, asks a series of questions to divide the adult population into employed, unemployed, or not in the labor force. To be classified as unemployed, a person must be without a job, currently available to work, and actively looking for work in the previous four weeks. Thus, a person who does not have a job but who is not currently available to work or has not actively looked for work in the last four weeks is counted as out of the labor force.

Employed: currently working for pay

Unemployed: Out of work and actively looking for a job

Out of the labor force: Out of paid work and not actively looking for a job

Labor force: the number of employed plus the unemployed

Calculating the Unemployment Rate

Figure 21.2 shows the three-way division of the 16-and-over population. In January 2017, about 62.9% of the adult population was "in the labor force"; that is, people are either employed or without a job but looking for work. We can divide those in the labor force into the employed and the unemployed. **Table 21.1** shows those values. The **unemployment rate** is not the percentage of the total adult population without jobs, but rather the percentage of adults who are in the labor force but who do not have jobs:

$$\text{Unemployment rate} = \frac{\text{Unemployed people}}{\text{Total labor force}} \times 100$$

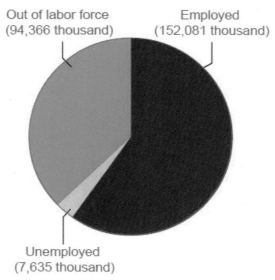

Figure 21.2 Employed, Unemployed, and Out of the Labor Force Distribution of Adult Population (age 16 and older), January 2017 The total adult, working-age population in January 2017 was 254.1 million. Out of this total population, 152.1 were classified as employed, and 7.6 million were classified as unemployed. The remaining 94.4 were classified as out of the labor force. As you will learn, however, this seemingly simple chart does not tell the whole story.

Total adult population over the age of 16	254.082 million
In the labor force	159.716 million (62.9%)
Employed	152.081 million
Unemployed	7.635 million
Out of the labor force	94.366 million (37.1%)

Table 21.1 U.S. Employment and Unemployment, January 2017 (Source: https://data.bls.gov)

In this example, we can calculate the unemployment rate as 7.635 million unemployed people divided by 159.716 million people in the labor force, which works out to a 4.8% rate of unemployment. The following Work It Out feature will walk you through the steps of this calculation.

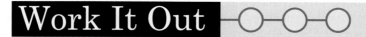

Calculating Labor Force Percentages

How do economists arrive at the percentages in and out of the labor force and the unemployment rate? We will use the values in Table 21.1 to illustrate the steps.

To determine the percentage in the labor force:

Step 1. Divide the number of people in the labor force (159.716 million) by the total adult (working-age) population (254.082 million).

Step 2. Multiply by 100 to obtain the percentage.

This OpenStax book is available for free at http://cnx.org/content/col12122/1.4

$$\text{Percentage in the labor force} = \frac{159.716}{254.082}$$
$$= 0.6286$$
$$= 62.9\%$$

To determine the percentage out of the labor force:

Step 1. Divide the number of people out the labor force (94.366 million) by the total adult (working-age) population (254.082 million).

Step 2. Multiply by 100 to obtain the percentage.

$$\text{Percentage in the labor force} = \frac{94.366}{254.082}$$
$$= 0.3714$$
$$= 37.1\%$$

To determine the unemployment rate:

Step 1. Divide the number of unemployed people (7.635 million) by the total labor force (157 million).

Step 2. Multiply by 100 to obtain the rate.

$$\text{Unemployment rate} = \frac{7.635}{159.716}$$
$$= 0.0478$$
$$= 4.8\%$$

Hidden Unemployment

Even with the "out of the labor force" category, there are still some people who are mislabeled in the categorization of employed, unemployed, or out of the labor force. There are some people who have only part time or temporary jobs, and they are looking for full time and permanent employment that are counted as employed, although they are not employed in the way they would like or need to be. Additionally, there are individuals who are **underemployed**. This includes those who are trained or skilled for one type or level of work but are working in a lower paying job or one that does not utilize their skills. For example, we would consider an individual with a college degree in finance who is working as a sales clerk underemployed. They are, however, also counted in the employed group. All of these individuals fall under the umbrella of the term "hidden unemployment." **Discouraged workers**, those who have stopped looking for employment and, hence, are no longer counted in the unemployed also fall into this group

Labor Force Participation Rate

Another important statistic is the **labor force participation rate**. This is the percentage of adults in an economy who are either employed or who are unemployed and looking for a job. Using the data in **Figure 21.2** and **Table 21.1**, those included in this calculation would be the 159.716 million individuals in the labor force. We calculate the rate by taking the number of people in the labor force, that is, the number employed and the number unemployed, divided by the total adult population and multiplying by 100 to get the percentage. For the data from January 2017, the labor force participation rate is 62.9%. Historically, the civilian labor force participation rate in the United States climbed beginning in the 1960s as women increasingly entered the workforce, and it peaked at just over 67% in late 1999 to early 2000. Since then, the labor force participation rate has steadily declined, slowly to about 66% in 2008, early in the Great Recession, and then more rapidly during and after that recession, reaching its present level, where it has remained stable, near the end of 2013.

The Establishment Payroll Survey

When the unemployment report comes out each month, the Bureau of Labor Statistics (BLS) also reports on the number of jobs created—which comes from the establishment payroll survey. The payroll survey is based on a survey of about 147,000 businesses and government agencies throughout the United States. It generates payroll employment estimates by the following criteria: all employees, average weekly hours worked, and average hourly, weekly, and overtime earnings. One of the criticisms of this survey is that it does not count the self-employed. It also does not make a distinction between new, minimum wage, part time or temporary jobs and full time jobs with "decent" pay.

How Does the U.S. Bureau of Labor Statistics Collect the U.S.

Unemployment Data?

The unemployment rate announced by the U.S. Bureau of Labor Statistics on the first Friday of each month for the previous month is based on the Current Population Survey (CPS), which the Bureau has carried out every month since 1940. The Bureau takes great care to make this survey representative of the country as a whole. The country is first divided into 3,137 areas. The U.S. Bureau of the Census then selects 729 of these areas to survey. It divides the 729 areas into districts of about 300 households each, and divides each district into clusters of about four dwelling units. Every month, Census Bureau employees call about 15,000 of the four-household clusters, for a total of 60,000 households. Employees interview households for four consecutive months, then rotate them out of the survey for eight months, and then interview them again for the same four months the following year, before leaving the sample permanently.

Based on this survey, state, industry, urban and rural areas, gender, age, race or ethnicity, and level of education statistics comprise components that contribute to unemployment rates. A wide variety of other information is available, too. For example, how long have people been unemployed? Did they become unemployed because they quit, or were laid off, or their employer went out of business? Is the unemployed person the only wage earner in the family? The Current Population Survey is a treasure trove of information about employment and unemployment. If you are wondering what the difference is between the CPS and EPS, read the following Clear it Up feature.

What is the difference between CPS and EPS?

The United States Census Bureau conducts the Current Population Survey (CPS), which measures the percentage of the labor force that is unemployed. The Bureau of Labor Statistics' establishment payroll survey (EPS) is a payroll survey that measures the net change in jobs created for the month.

Criticisms of Measuring Unemployment

There are always complications in measuring the number of unemployed. For example, what about people who do not have jobs and would be available to work, but are discouraged by the lack of available jobs in their area and stopped looking? Such people, and their families, may be suffering the pains of unemployment. However, the survey counts them as out of the labor force because they are not actively looking for work. Other people may tell the Census Bureau that they are ready to work and looking for a job but, truly, they are not that eager to work and are not looking very hard at all. They are counted as unemployed, although they might more accurately be classified as out of the labor force. Still other people may have a job, perhaps doing something like yard work, child care, or cleaning houses, but are not reporting the income earned to the tax authorities. They may report being unemployed, when they actually are working.

Although the unemployment rate gets most of the public and media attention, economic researchers at the Bureau of Labor Statistics publish a wide array of surveys and reports that try to measure these kinds of issues and to develop a more nuanced and complete view of the labor market. It is not exactly a hot news flash that economic statistics are imperfect. Even imperfect measures like the unemployment rate, however, can still be quite informative, when interpreted knowledgeably and sensibly.

Link It Up

Click here (http://openstaxcollege.org/l/BLS_CPS) to learn more about the CPS and to read frequently asked questions about employment and labor.

21.2 | Patterns of Unemployment

By the end of this section, you will be able to:

- Explain historical patterns of unemployment in the U.S.
- Identify trends of unemployment based on demographics
- Evaluate global unemployment rates

Let's look at how unemployment rates have changed over time and how various groups of people are affected by unemployment differently.

The Historical U.S. Unemployment Rate

Figure 21.3 shows the historical pattern of U.S. unemployment since 1955.

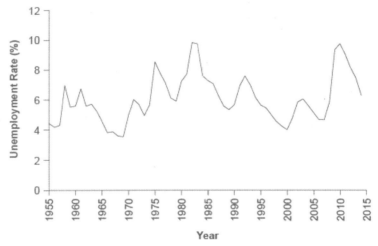

Figure 21.3 The U.S. Unemployment Rate, 1955–2015 The U.S. unemployment rate moves up and down as the economy moves in and out of recessions. However, over time, the unemployment rate seems to return to a range of 4% to 6%. There does not seem to be a long-term trend toward the rate moving generally higher or generally lower. (Source: Federal Reserve Economic Data (FRED) https://research.stlouisfed.org/fred2/series/LRUN64TTUSA156S0)

As we look at this data, several patterns stand out:

1. Unemployment rates do fluctuate over time. During the deep recessions of the early 1980s and of 2007–2009, unemployment reached roughly 10%. For comparison, during the 1930s Great Depression, the unemployment rate reached almost 25% of the labor force.

2. Unemployment rates in the late 1990s and into the mid-2000s were rather low by historical standards. The unemployment rate was below 5% from 1997 to 2000, and near 5% during almost all of 2006–2007, and 5% or slightly less from September 2015 through January 2017 (the latest date for which data are available as of this writing). The previous time unemployment had been less than 5% for three consecutive years was three

decades earlier, from 1968 to 1970.

3. The unemployment rate never falls all the way to zero. It almost never seems to get below 3%—and it stays that low only for very short periods. (We discuss reasons why this is the case later in this chapter.)

4. The timing of rises and falls in unemployment matches fairly well with the timing of upswings and downswings in the overall economy, except that unemployment tends to lag changes in economic activity, and especially so during upswings of the economy following a recession. During periods of recession and depression, unemployment is high. During periods of economic growth, unemployment tends to be lower.

5. No significant upward or downward trend in unemployment rates is apparent. This point is especially worth noting because the U.S. population more than quadrupled from 76 million in 1900 to over 324 million by 2017. Moreover, a higher proportion of U.S. adults are now in the paid workforce, because women have entered the paid labor force in significant numbers in recent decades. Women comprised 18% of the paid workforce in 1900 and nearly half of the paid workforce in 2017. However, despite the increased number of workers, as well as other economic events like globalization and the continuous invention of new technologies, the economy has provided jobs without causing any long-term upward or downward trend in unemployment rates.

Unemployment Rates by Group

Unemployment is not distributed evenly across the U.S. population. **Figure 21.4** shows unemployment rates broken down in various ways: by gender, age, and race/ethnicity.

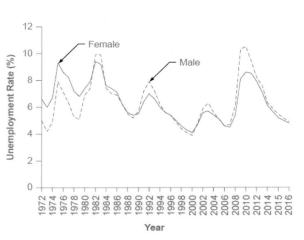

(a) Unemployment rates by gender

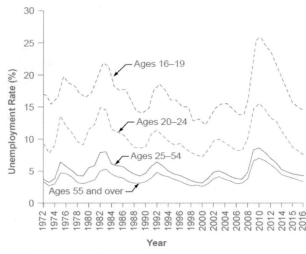

(b) Unemployment rates for women, by age

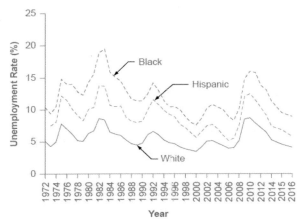

(c) Unemployment rates by race and ethnicity

Figure 21.4 Unemployment Rate by Demographic Group (a) By gender, 1972–2016. Unemployment rates for men used to be lower than unemployment rates for women, but in recent decades, the two rates have been very close, often– and especially during and soon after the Great Recession – with the unemployment rate for men somewhat higher. (b) By age, 1972–2016. Unemployment rates are highest for the very young and become lower with age. (c) By race and ethnicity, 1972–2016. Although unemployment rates for all groups tend to rise and fall together, the unemployment rate for blacks is typically about twice as high as that for whites, while the unemployment rate for Hispanics is in between. (Source: www.bls.gov)

The unemployment rate for women had historically tended to be higher than the unemployment rate for men, perhaps reflecting the historical pattern that women were seen as "secondary" earners. By about 1980, however, the unemployment rate for women was essentially the same as that for men, as **Figure 21.4** (a) shows. During the 2008-2009 recession and in the immediate aftermath, the unemployment rate for men exceeded the unemployment rate for women. Subsequently, however, the gap has narrowed.

Link It Up ⚭

Read this report (http://openstaxcollege.org/l/BLS_recession) for detailed information on the 2008–2009 recession. It also provides some very useful information on the statistics of unemployment.

Younger workers tend to have higher unemployment, while middle-aged workers tend to have lower unemployment, probably because the middle-aged workers feel the responsibility of needing to have a job more heavily. Younger workers move in and out of jobs more than middle-aged workers, as part of the process of matching of workers and jobs, and this contributes to their higher unemployment rates. In addition, middle-aged workers are more likely to feel the responsibility of needing to have a job more heavily. Elderly workers have extremely low rates of unemployment, because those who do not have jobs often exit the labor force by retiring, and thus are not counted in the unemployment statistics. **Figure 21.4** (b) shows unemployment rates for women divided by age. The pattern for men is similar.

The unemployment rate for African-Americans is substantially higher than the rate for other racial or ethnic groups, a fact that surely reflects, to some extent, a pattern of discrimination that has constrained blacks' labor market opportunities. However, the gaps between unemployment rates for whites and for blacks and Hispanics diminished in the 1990s, as **Figure 21.4** (c) shows. In fact, unemployment rates for blacks and Hispanics were at the lowest levels for several decades in the mid-2000s before rising during the recent Great Recession.

Finally, those with less education typically suffer higher unemployment. In January 2017, for example, the unemployment rate for those with a college degree was 2.5%; for those with some college but not a four year degree, the unemployment rate was 3.8%; for high school graduates with no additional degree, the unemployment rate was 5.3%; and for those without a high school diploma, the unemployment rate was 7.7%. This pattern arises because additional education typically offers better connections to the labor market and higher demand. With less attractive labor market opportunities for low-skilled workers compared to the opportunities for the more highly-skilled, including lower pay, low-skilled workers may be less motivated to find jobs.

Breaking Down Unemployment in Other Ways

The Bureau of Labor Statistics also gives information about the reasons for unemployment, as well as the length of time individuals have been unemployed. **Table 21.2**, for example, shows the four reasons for unemployment and the percentages of the currently unemployed that fall into each category. **Table 21.3** shows the length of unemployment. For both of these, the data is from January 2017.(bls.gov)

Reason	Percentage
New Entrants	10.8%
Re-entrants	28.7%
Job Leavers	11.4%
Job Losers: Temporary	14.0%
Job Losers: Non Temporary	35.1%

Table 21.2 Reasons for Unemployment, January 2017

This OpenStax book is available for free at http://cnx.org/content/col12122/1.4

Length of Time	Percentage
Under 5 weeks	32.5%
5 to 14 weeks	27.5%
15 to 26 weeks	15.7%
Over 27 weeks	27.4%

Table 21.3 Length of Unemployment, January 2017

Link It Up

Watch this speech (http://openstaxcollege.org/l/droids) on the impact of droids on the labor market.

International Unemployment Comparisons

From an international perspective, the U.S. unemployment rate typically has looked a little better than average. **Table 21.4** compares unemployment rates for 1991, 1996, 2001, 2006 (just before the recession), and 2012 (somewhat after the recession) from several other high-income countries.

Country	1991	1996	2001	2006	2012
United States	6.8%	5.4%	4.8%	4.4%	8.1%
Canada	9.8%	8.8%	6.4%	6.2%	6.3%
Japan	2.1%	3.4%	5.1%	4.5%	3.9%
France	9.5%	12.5%	8.7%	10.1%	10.0%
Germany	5.6%	9.0%	8.9%	9.8%	5.5%
Italy	6.9%	11.7%	9.6%	7.8%	10.8%
Sweden	3.1%	9.9%	5.0%	5.2%	7.9%
United Kingdom	8.8%	8.1%	5.1%	5.5%	8.0%

Table 21.4 International Comparisons of Unemployment Rates

However, we need to treat cross-country comparisons of unemployment rates with care, because each country has slightly different definitions of unemployment, survey tools for measuring unemployment, and also different labor markets. For example, Japan's unemployment rates appear quite low, but Japan's economy has been mired in slow growth and recession since the late 1980s, and Japan's unemployment rate probably paints too rosy a picture of its labor market. In Japan, workers who lose their jobs are often quick to exit the labor force and not look for a new job, in which case they are not counted as unemployed. In addition, Japanese firms are often quite reluctant to fire workers, and so firms have substantial numbers of workers who are on reduced hours or officially employed, but doing very little. We can view this Japanese pattern as an unusual method for society to provide support for the unemployed, rather than a sign of a healthy economy.

Link It Up

We hear about the Chinese economy in the news all the time. The value of the Chinese yuan in comparison to the U.S. dollar is likely to be part of the nightly business report, so why is the Chinese economy not included in this discussion of international unemployment? The lack of reliable statistics is the reason. This article (http://openstaxcollege.org/l/ChinaEmployment) explains why.

Comparing unemployment rates in the United States and other high-income economies with unemployment rates in Latin America, Africa, Eastern Europe, and Asia is very difficult. One reason is that the statistical agencies in many poorer countries lack the resources and technical capabilities of the U.S. Bureau of the Census. However, a more difficult problem with international comparisons is that in many low-income countries, most workers are not involved in the labor market through an employer who pays them regularly. Instead, workers in these countries are engaged in short-term work, subsistence activities, and barter. Moreover, the effect of unemployment is very different in high-income and low-income countries. Unemployed workers in the developed economies have access to various government programs like unemployment insurance, welfare, and food stamps. Such programs may barely exist in poorer countries. Although unemployment is a serious problem in many low-income countries, it manifests itself in a different way than in high-income countries.

21.3 | What Causes Changes in Unemployment over the Short Run

By the end of this section, you will be able to:
• Analyze cyclical unemployment
• Explain the relationship between sticky wages and employment using various economic arguments
• Apply supply and demand models to unemployment and wages

We have seen that unemployment varies across times and places. What causes changes in unemployment? There are different answers in the short run and in the long run. Let's look at the short run first.

Cyclical Unemployment

Let's make the plausible assumption that in the short run, from a few months to a few years, the quantity of hours that the average person is willing to work for a given wage does not change much, so the labor supply curve does not shift much. In addition, make the standard *ceteris paribus* assumption that there is no substantial short-term change in the age structure of the labor force, institutions and laws affecting the labor market, or other possibly relevant factors.

One primary determinant of the demand for labor from firms is how they perceive the state of the macro economy. If firms believe that business is expanding, then at any given wage they will desire to hire a greater quantity of labor, and the labor demand curve shifts to the right. Conversely, if firms perceive that the economy is slowing down or entering a recession, then they will wish to hire a lower quantity of labor at any given wage, and the labor demand curve will shift to the left. Economists call the variation in unemployment that the economy causes moving from expansion to recession or from recession to expansion (i.e. the business cycle) **cyclical unemployment**.

From the standpoint of the supply-and-demand model of competitive and flexible labor markets, unemployment represents something of a puzzle. In a supply-and-demand model of a labor market, as **Figure 21.5** illustrates, the labor market should move toward an equilibrium wage and quantity. At the equilibrium wage (We), the equilibrium quantity (Qe) of labor supplied by workers should be equal to the quantity of labor demanded by employers.

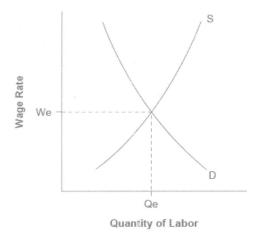

Figure 21.5 The Unemployment and Equilibrium in the Labor Market In a labor market with flexible wages, the equilibrium will occur at wage We and quantity Qe, where the number of people who want jobs (shown by S) equals the number of jobs available (shown by D).

One possibility for unemployment is that people who are unemployed are those who are not willing to work at the current equilibrium wage, say $10 an hour, but would be willing to work at a higher wage, like $20 per hour. The monthly Current Population Survey would count these people as unemployed, because they say they are ready and looking for work (at $20 per hour). However, from an economist's perspective, these people are choosing to be unemployed.

Probably a few people are unemployed because of unrealistic expectations about wages, but they do not represent the majority of the unemployed. Instead, unemployed people often have friends or acquaintances of similar skill levels who are employed, and the unemployed would be willing to work at the jobs and wages similar to what those people are receiving. However, the employers of their friends and acquaintances do not seem to be hiring. In other words, these people are involuntarily unemployed. What causes involuntary unemployment?

Why Wages Might Be Sticky Downward

If a labor market model with flexible wages does not describe unemployment very well—because it predicts that anyone willing to work at the going wage can always find a job—then it may prove useful to consider economic models in which wages are not flexible or adjust only very slowly. In particular, even though wage increases may occur with relative ease, wage decreases are few and far between.

One set of reasons why wages may be "sticky downward," as economists put it, involves economic laws and institutions. For low-skilled workers receiving minimum wage, it is illegal to reduce their wages. For union workers operating under a multiyear contract with a company, wage cuts might violate the contract and create a labor dispute or a strike. However, minimum wages and union contracts are not a sufficient reason why wages would be sticky downward for the U.S. economy as a whole. After all, out of the 150 million or so employed workers in the U.S. economy, only about 2.6 million—less than 2% of the total—do not receive compensation above the minimum wage. Similarly, labor unions represent only about 11% of American wage and salary workers. In other high-income countries, more workers may have their wages determined by unions or the minimum wage may be set at a level that applies to a larger share of workers. However, for the United States, these two factors combined affect only about 15% or less of the labor force.

Economists looking for reasons why wages might be sticky downwards have focused on factors that may characterize most labor relationships in the economy, not just a few. Many have proposed a number of different theories, but they share a common tone.

One argument is that even employees who are not union members often work under an **implicit contract**, which is that the employer will try to keep wages from falling when the economy is weak or the business is having trouble, and the employee will not expect huge salary increases when the economy or the business is strong. This wage-setting behavior acts like a form of insurance: the employee has some protection against wage declines in bad times, but pays for that protection with lower wages in good times. Clearly, this sort of implicit contract means that firms will be hesitant to cut wages, lest workers feel betrayed and work less hard or even leave the firm.

Efficiency wage theory argues that workers' productivity depends on their pay, and so employers will often find it worthwhile to pay their employees somewhat more than market conditions might dictate. One reason is that employees who receive better pay than others will be more productive because they recognize that if they were to lose their current jobs, they would suffer a decline in salary. As a result, they are motivated to work harder and to stay with the current employer. In addition, employers know that it is costly and time-consuming to hire and train new employees, so they would prefer to pay workers a little extra now rather than to lose them and have to hire and train new workers. Thus, by avoiding wage cuts, the employer minimizes costs of training and hiring new workers, and reaps the benefits of well-motivated employees.

The **adverse selection of wage cuts argument** points out that if an employer reacts to poor business conditions by reducing wages for all workers, then the best workers, those with the best employment alternatives at other firms, are the most likely to leave. The least attractive workers, with fewer employment alternatives, are more likely to stay. Consequently, firms are more likely to choose which workers should depart, through layoffs and firings, rather than trimming wages across the board. Sometimes companies that are experiencing difficult times can persuade workers to take a pay cut for the short term, and still retain most of the firm's workers. However, it is far more typical for companies to lay off some workers, rather than to cut wages for everyone.

The **insider-outsider model** of the labor force, in simple terms, argues that those already working for firms are "insiders," while new employees, at least for a time, are "outsiders." A firm depends on its insiders to keep the organization running smoothly, to be familiar with routine procedures, and to train new employees. However, cutting wages will alienate the insiders and damage the firm's productivity and prospects.

Finally, the **relative wage coordination argument** points out that even if most workers were hypothetically willing to see a decline in their own wages in bad economic times as long as everyone else also experiences such a decline, there is no obvious way for a decentralized economy to implement such a plan. Instead, workers confronted with the possibility of a wage cut will worry that other workers will not have such a wage cut, and so a wage cut means being worse off both in absolute terms and relative to others. As a result, workers fight hard against wage cuts.

These theories of why wages tend not to move downward differ in their logic and their implications, and figuring out the strengths and weaknesses of each theory is an ongoing subject of research and controversy among economists. All tend to imply that wages will decline only very slowly, if at all, even when the economy or a business is having tough times. When wages are inflexible and unlikely to fall, then either short-run or long-run unemployment can result. **Figure 21.6** illustrates this.

This OpenStax book is available for free at http://cnx.org/content/col12122/1.4

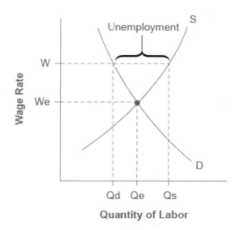

Figure 21.6 Sticky Wages in the Labor Market   Because the wage rate is stuck at W, above the equilibrium, the number of those who want jobs (Qs) is greater than the number of job openings (Qd). The result is unemployment, shown by the bracket in the figure.

Figure 21.7 shows the interaction between shifts in labor demand and wages that are sticky downward. **Figure 21.7** (a) illustrates the situation in which the demand for labor shifts to the right from D_0 to D_1. In this case, the equilibrium wage rises from W_0 to W_1 and the equilibrium quantity of labor hired increases from Q_0 to Q_1. It does not hurt employee morale at all for wages to rise.

Figure 21.7 (b) shows the situation in which the demand for labor shifts to the left, from D_0 to D_1, as it would tend to do in a recession. Because wages are sticky downward, they do not adjust toward what would have been the new equilibrium wage (W_1), at least not in the short run. Instead, after the shift in the labor demand curve, the same quantity of workers is willing to work at that wage as before; however, the quantity of workers demanded at that wage has declined from the original equilibrium (Q_0) to Q_2. The gap between the original equilibrium quantity (Q_0) and the new quantity demanded of labor (Q_2) represents workers who would be willing to work at the going wage but cannot find jobs. The gap represents the economic meaning of unemployment.

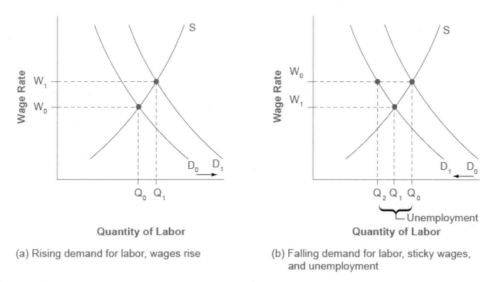

(a) Rising demand for labor, wages rise

(b) Falling demand for labor, sticky wages, and unemployment

Figure 21.7 Rising Wage and Low Unemployment: Where Is the Unemployment in Supply and Demand?   (a) In a labor market where wages are able to rise, an increase in the demand for labor from D_0 to D_1 leads to an increase in equilibrium quantity of labor hired from Q_0 to Q_1 and a rise in the equilibrium wage from W_0 to W_1. (b) In a labor market where wages do not decline, a fall in the demand for labor from D_0 to D_1 leads to a decline in the quantity of labor demanded at the original wage (W_0) from Q_0 to Q_2. These workers will want to work at the prevailing wage (W_0), but will not be able to find jobs.

This analysis helps to explain the connection that we noted earlier: that unemployment tends to rise in recessions and to decline during expansions. The overall state of the economy shifts the labor demand curve and, combined with wages that are sticky downwards, unemployment changes. The rise in unemployment that occurs because of a recession is cyclical unemployment.

Link It Up 🔗

The St. Louis Federal Reserve Bank is the best resource for macroeconomic time series data, known as the Federal Reserve Economic Data (FRED). FRED (http://openstaxcollege.org/l/FRED_employment) provides complete data sets on various measures of the unemployment rate as well as the monthly Bureau of Labor Statistics report on the results of the household and employment surveys.

21.4 | What Causes Changes in Unemployment over the Long Run

By the end of this section, you will be able to:

- Explain frictional and structural unemployment
- Assess relationships between the natural rate of employment and potential real GDP, productivity, and public policy
- Identify recent patterns in the natural rate of employment
- Propose ways to combat unemployment

Cyclical unemployment explains why unemployment rises during a recession and falls during an economic expansion, but what explains the remaining level of unemployment even in good economic times? Why is the unemployment rate never zero? Even when the U.S. economy is growing strongly, the unemployment rate only rarely dips as low as 4%. Moreover, the discussion earlier in this chapter pointed out that unemployment rates in many European countries like Italy, France, and Germany have often been remarkably high at various times in the last few decades. Why does some level of unemployment persist even when economies are growing strongly? Why are unemployment rates continually higher in certain economies, through good economic years and bad? Economists have a term to describe the remaining level of unemployment that occurs even when the economy is healthy: they call it the **natural rate of unemployment**.

The Long Run: The Natural Rate of Unemployment

The natural rate of unemployment is not "natural" in the sense that water freezes at 32 degrees Fahrenheit or boils at 212 degrees Fahrenheit. It is not a physical and unchanging law of nature. Instead, it is only the "natural" rate because it is the unemployment rate that would result from the combination of economic, social, and political factors that exist at a time—assuming the economy was neither booming nor in recession. These forces include the usual pattern of companies expanding and contracting their workforces in a dynamic economy, social and economic forces that affect the labor market, or public policies that affect either the eagerness of people to work or the willingness of businesses to hire. Let's discuss these factors in more detail.

Frictional Unemployment

In a market economy, some companies are always going broke for a variety of reasons: old technology; poor management; good management that happened to make bad decisions; shifts in tastes of consumers so that less of the firm's product is desired; a large customer who went broke; or tough domestic or foreign competitors. Conversely, other companies will be doing very well for just the opposite reasons and looking to hire more employees. In a perfect world, all of those who lost jobs would immediately find new ones. However, in the real world, even if the number of job seekers is equal to the number of job vacancies, it takes time to find out about new jobs, to interview and figure out if the new job is a good match, or perhaps to sell a house and buy another in proximity to a new job. Economists call the unemployment that occurs in the meantime, as workers move between jobs, **frictional unemployment**. Frictional unemployment is not inherently a bad thing. It takes time on part of both the employer and the individual to match those looking for employment with the correct job openings. For individuals and companies to be successful and productive, you want people to find the job for which they are best suited, not just the first job offered.

In the mid-2000s, before the 2008–2009 recession, it was true that about 7% of U.S. workers saw their jobs disappear in any three-month period. However, in periods of economic growth, these destroyed jobs are counterbalanced for the economy as a whole by a larger number of jobs created. In 2005, for example, there were typically about 7.5 million unemployed people at any given time in the U.S. economy. Even though about two-thirds of those unemployed people found a job in 14 weeks or fewer, the unemployment rate did not change much during the year, because those who found new jobs were largely offset by others who lost jobs.

Of course, it would be preferable if people who were losing jobs could immediately and easily move into newly created jobs, but in the real world, that is not possible. Someone who is laid off by a textile mill in South Carolina cannot turn around and immediately start working for a textile mill in California. Instead, the adjustment process happens in ripples. Some people find new jobs near their old ones, while others find that they must move to new locations. Some people can do a very similar job with a different company, while others must start new career paths. Some people may be near retirement and decide to look only for part-time work, while others want an employer that offers a long-term career path. The frictional unemployment that results from people moving between jobs in a dynamic economy may account for one to two percentage points of total unemployment.

The level of frictional unemployment will depend on how easy it is for workers to learn about alternative jobs, which may reflect the ease of communications about job prospects in the economy. The extent of frictional unemployment will also depend to some extent on how willing people are to move to new areas to find jobs—which in turn may depend on history and culture.

Frictional unemployment and the natural rate of unemployment also seem to depend on the age distribution of the population. **Figure 21.4** (b) showed that unemployment rates are typically lower for people between 25–54 years of age or aged 55 and over than they are for those who are younger. "Prime-age workers," as those in the 25–54 age bracket are sometimes called, are typically at a place in their lives when they want to have a job and income arriving at all times. In addition, older workers who lose jobs may prefer to opt for retirement. By contrast, it is likely that a relatively high proportion of those who are under 25 will be trying out jobs and life options, and this leads to greater job mobility and hence higher frictional unemployment. Thus, a society with a relatively high proportion of young workers, like the U.S. beginning in the mid-1960s when Baby Boomers began entering the labor market, will tend to have a higher unemployment rate than a society with a higher proportion of its workers in older ages.

Structural Unemployment

Another factor that influences the natural rate of unemployment is the amount of **structural unemployment**. The structurally unemployed are individuals who have no jobs because they lack skills valued by the labor market, either because demand has shifted away from the skills they do have, or because they never learned any skills. An example of the former would be the unemployment among aerospace engineers after the U.S. space program downsized in the 1970s. An example of the latter would be high school dropouts.

Some people worry that technology causes structural unemployment. In the past, new technologies have put lower skilled employees out of work, but at the same time they create demand for higher skilled workers to use the new technologies. Education seems to be the key in minimizing the amount of structural unemployment. Individuals who have degrees can be retrained if they become structurally unemployed. For people with no skills and little education, that option is more limited.

Natural Unemployment and Potential Real GDP

The natural unemployment rate is related to two other important concepts: full employment and potential real GDP. Economists consider the economy to be at full employment when the actual unemployment rate is equal to the natural unemployment rate. When the economy is at full employment, real GDP is equal to potential real GDP. By contrast, when the economy is below full employment, the unemployment rate is greater than the natural unemployment rate and real GDP is less than potential. Finally, when the economy is above full employment, then the unemployment rate is less than the natural unemployment rate and real GDP is greater than potential. Operating above potential is only possible for a short while, since it is analogous to all workers working overtime.

Productivity Shifts and the Natural Rate of Unemployment

Unexpected shifts in productivity can have a powerful effect on the natural rate of unemployment. Over time, workers' productivity determines the level of wages in an economy. After all, if a business paid workers more than could be justified by their productivity, the business will ultimately lose money and go bankrupt. Conversely, if a business tries to pay workers less than their productivity then, in a competitive labor market, other businesses will find it worthwhile to hire away those workers and pay them more.

However, adjustments of wages to productivity levels will not happen quickly or smoothly. Employers typically review wages only once or twice a year. In many modern jobs, it is difficult to measure productivity at the individual level. For example, how precisely would one measure the quantity produced by an accountant who is one of many people working in the tax department of a large corporation? Because productivity is difficult to observe, employers often determine wage increases based on recent experience with productivity. If productivity has been rising at, say, 2% per year, then wages rise at that level as well. However, when productivity changes unexpectedly, it can affect the natural rate of unemployment for a time.

The U.S. economy in the 1970s and 1990s provides two vivid examples of this process. In the 1970s, productivity growth slowed down unexpectedly (as we discussed in **Economic Growth**). For example, output per hour of U.S. workers in the business sector increased at an annual rate of 3.3% per year from 1960 to 1973, but only 0.8% from 1973 to 1982. **Figure 21.8** (a) illustrates the situation where the demand for labor—that is, the quantity of labor that business is willing to hire at any given wage—has been shifting out a little each year because of rising productivity, from D_0 to D_1 to D_2. As a result, equilibrium wages have been rising each year from W_0 to W_1 to W_2. However, when productivity unexpectedly slows down, the pattern of wage increases does not adjust right away. Wages keep rising each year from W_2 to W_3 to W_4, but the demand for labor is no longer shifting up. A gap opens where the quantity of labor supplied at wage level W_4 is greater than the quantity demanded. The natural rate of unemployment rises. In the aftermath of this unexpectedly low productivity in the 1970s, the national unemployment rate did not fall below 7% from May, 1980 until 1986. Over time, the rise in wages will adjust to match the slower gains in productivity, and the unemployment rate will ease back down, but this process may take years.

This OpenStax book is available for free at http://cnx.org/content/col12122/1.4

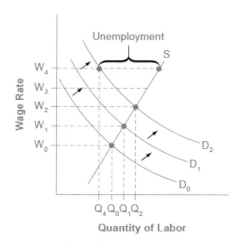
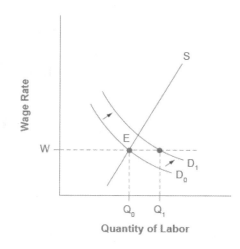

(a) Productivity rises, and then stops rising   (b) Productivity doesn't change, and then rises

Figure 21.8 Unexpected Productivity Changes and Unemployment (a) Productivity is rising, increasing the demand for labor. Employers and workers become used to the pattern of wage increases. Then productivity suddenly stops increasing. However, the expectations of employers and workers for wage increases do not shift immediately, so wages keep rising as before. However, the demand for labor has not increased, so at wage W_4, unemployment exists where the quantity supplied of labor exceeds the quantity demanded. (b) The rate of productivity increase has been zero for a time, so employers and workers have come to accept the equilibrium wage level (W). Then productivity increases unexpectedly, shifting demand for labor from D_0 to D_1. At the wage (W), this means that the quantity demanded of labor exceeds the quantity supplied, and with job offers plentiful, the unemployment rate will be low.

The late 1990s provide an opposite example: instead of the surprise decline in productivity that occurred in the 1970s, productivity unexpectedly rose in the mid-1990s. The annual growth rate of real output per hour of labor increased from 1.7% from 1980–1995, to an annual rate of 2.6% from 1995–2001. Let's simplify the situation a bit, so that the economic lesson of the story is easier to see graphically, and say that productivity had not been increasing at all in earlier years, so the intersection of the labor market was at point E in **Figure 21.8** (b), where the demand curve for labor (D_0) intersects the supply curve for labor. As a result, real wages were not increasing. Now, productivity jumps upward, which shifts the demand for labor out to the right, from D_0 to D_1. At least for a time, however, wages are still set according to the earlier expectations of no productivity growth, so wages do not rise. The result is that at the prevailing wage level (W), the quantity of labor demanded (Qd) will for a time exceed the quantity of labor supplied (Qs), and unemployment will be very low—actually below the natural level of unemployment for a time. This pattern of unexpectedly high productivity helps to explain why the unemployment rate stayed below 4.5%—quite a low level by historical standards—from 1998 until after the U.S. economy had entered a recession in 2001.

Levels of unemployment will tend to be somewhat higher on average when productivity is unexpectedly low, and conversely, will tend to be somewhat lower on average when productivity is unexpectedly high. However, over time, wages do eventually adjust to reflect productivity levels.

Public Policy and the Natural Rate of Unemployment

Public policy can also have a powerful effect on the natural rate of unemployment. On the supply side of the labor market, public policies to assist the unemployed can affect how eager people are to find work. For example, if a worker who loses a job is guaranteed a generous package of unemployment insurance, welfare benefits, food stamps, and government medical benefits, then the opportunity cost of unemployment is lower and that worker will be less eager to seek a new job.

What seems to matter most is not just the amount of these benefits, but how long they last. A society that provides generous help for the unemployed that cuts off after, say, six months, may provide less of an incentive for unemployment than a society that provides less generous help that lasts for several years. Conversely, government assistance for job search or retraining can in some cases encourage people back to work sooner. See the Clear it Up to learn how the U.S. handles unemployment insurance.

How does U.S. unemployment insurance work?

Unemployment insurance is a joint federal–state program that the federal government enacted in 1935. While the federal government sets minimum standards for the program, state governments conduct most of the administration.

The funding for the program is a federal tax collected from employers. The federal government requires tax collection on the first $7,000 in wages paid to each worker; however, states can choose to collect the tax on a higher amount if they wish, and 41 states have set a higher limit. States can choose the length of time that they pay benefits, although most states limit unemployment benefits to 26 weeks—with extensions possible in times of especially high unemployment. The states then use the fund to pay benefits to those who become unemployed. Average unemployment benefits are equal to about one-third of the wage that the person earned in his or her previous job, but the level of unemployment benefits varies considerably across states.

Bottom 10 States That Pay the Lowest Benefit per Week		Top 10 States That Pay the Highest Benefit per Week	
Delaware	$330	Massachusetts	$672
Georgia	$330	Minnesota	$683
South Carolina	$326	Washington	$681
Missouri	$320	New Jersey	$657
Florida	$275	North Dakota	$633
Tennessee	$275	Connecticut	$598
Alabama	$265	Oregon	$590
Louisiana	$247	Pennsylvania	$573
Arizona	$240	Colorado	$568
Mississippi	$235	Rhode Island	$566

Table 21.5 Maximum Weekly Unemployment Benefits by State in 2017   (Source: http://www.savingtoinvest.com/maximum-weekly-unemployment-benefits-by-state/)

One other interesting thing to note about the classifications of unemployment—an individual does not have to collect unemployment benefits to be classified as unemployed. While there are statistics kept and studied relating to how many people are collecting unemployment insurance, this is not the source of unemployment rate information.

Link It Up

View this article (http://openstaxcollege.org/l/NYT_Benefits) for an explanation of exactly who is eligible for unemployment benefits.

On the demand side of the labor market, government rules, social institutions, and the presence of unions can affect the willingness of firms to hire. For example, if a government makes it hard for businesses to start up or to expand, by wrapping new businesses in bureaucratic red tape, then businesses will become more discouraged about hiring. Government regulations can make it harder to start a business by requiring that a new business obtain many permits and pay many fees, or by restricting the types and quality of products that a company can sell. Other government regulations, like zoning laws, may limit where companies can conduct business, or whether businesses are allowed to be open during evenings or on Sunday.

Whatever defenses may be offered for such laws in terms of social value—like the value some Christians place on not working on Sunday, or Orthodox Jews or highly observant Muslims on Saturday—these kinds of restrictions impose a barrier between some willing workers and other willing employers, and thus contribute to a higher natural rate of unemployment. Similarly, if government makes it difficult to fire or lay off workers, businesses may react by trying not to hire more workers than strictly necessary—since laying these workers off would be costly and difficult. High minimum wages may discourage businesses from hiring low-skill workers. Government rules may encourage and support powerful unions, which can then push up wages for union workers, but at a cost of discouraging businesses from hiring those workers.

The Natural Rate of Unemployment in Recent Years

The underlying economic, social, and political factors that determine the natural rate of unemployment can change over time, which means that the natural rate of unemployment can change over time, too.

Estimates by economists of the natural rate of unemployment in the U.S. economy in the early 2000s run at about 4.5 to 5.5%. This is a lower estimate than earlier. We outline three of the common reasons that economists propose for this change below.

1. The internet has provided a remarkable new tool through which job seekers can find out about jobs at different companies and can make contact with relative ease. An internet search is far easier than trying to find a list of local employers and then hunting up phone numbers for all of their human resources departments, and requesting a list of jobs and application forms. Social networking sites such as LinkedIn have changed how people find work as well.

2. The growth of the temporary worker industry has probably helped to reduce the natural rate of unemployment. In the early 1980s, only about 0.5% of all workers held jobs through temp agencies. By the early 2000s, the figure had risen above 2%. Temp agencies can provide jobs for workers while they are looking for permanent work. They can also serve as a clearinghouse, helping workers find out about jobs with certain employers and getting a tryout with the employer. For many workers, a temp job is a stepping-stone to a permanent job that they might not have heard about or obtained any other way, so the growth of temp jobs will also tend to reduce frictional unemployment.

3. The aging of the "baby boom generation"—the especially large generation of Americans born between 1946 and 1964—meant that the proportion of young workers in the economy was relatively high in the 1970s, as the boomers entered the labor market, but is relatively low today. As we noted earlier, middle-aged and older workers are far more likely to experience low unemployment than younger workers, a factor that tends to reduce the natural rate of unemployment as the baby boomers age.

The combined result of these factors is that the natural rate of unemployment was on average lower in the 1990s and the early 2000s than in the 1980s. The 2008–2009 Great Recession pushed monthly unemployment rates up to 10% in late 2009. However, even at that time, the Congressional Budget Office was forecasting that by 2015, unemployment rates would fall back to about 5%. During the last four months of 2015 the unemployment rate held steady at 5.0%. Throughout 2016 and up through January 2017, the unemployment rate has remained at or slightly below 5%. As of the first quarter of 2017, the Congressional Budget Office estimates the natural rate to be 4.74%, and the measured unemployment rate for January 2017 is 4.8%.

The Natural Rate of Unemployment in Europe

By the standards of other high-income economies, the natural rate of unemployment in the U.S. economy appears relatively low. Through good economic years and bad, many European economies have had unemployment rates hovering near 10%, or even higher, since the 1970s. European rates of unemployment have been higher not because recessions in Europe have been deeper, but rather because the conditions underlying supply and demand for labor have been different in Europe, in a way that has created a much higher natural rate of unemployment.

Many European countries have a combination of generous welfare and unemployment benefits, together with nests of rules that impose additional costs on businesses when they hire. In addition, many countries have laws that require firms to give workers months of notice before laying them off and to provide substantial severance or retraining packages after laying them off. The legally required notice before laying off a worker can be more than three months in Spain, Germany, Denmark, and Belgium, and the legally required severance package can be as high as a year's salary or more in Austria, Spain, Portugal, Italy, and Greece. Such laws will surely discourage laying off or firing current workers. However, when companies know that it will be difficult to fire or lay off workers, they also become hesitant about hiring in the first place.

We can attribute the typically higher levels of unemployment in many European countries in recent years, which have prevailed even when economies are growing at a solid pace, to the fact that the sorts of laws and regulations that lead to a high natural rate of unemployment are much more prevalent in Europe than in the United States.

A Preview of Policies to Fight Unemployment

The **Government Budgets and Fiscal Policy** and **Macroeconomic Policy Around the World** chapters provide a detailed discussion of how to fight unemployment, when we can discuss these policies in the context of the full array of macroeconomic goals and frameworks for analysis. However, even at this preliminary stage, it is useful to preview the main issues concerning policies to fight unemployment.

The remedy for unemployment will depend on the diagnosis. Cyclical unemployment is a short-term problem, caused because the economy is in a recession. Thus, the preferred solution will be to avoid or minimize recessions. As **Government Budgets and Fiscal Policy** discusses, governments can enact this policy by stimulating the overall buying power in the economy, so that firms perceive that sales and profits are possible, which makes them eager to hire.

Dealing with the natural rate of unemployment is trickier. In a market-oriented economy, firms will hire and fire workers. Governments cannot control this. Furthermore, the evolving age structure of the economy's population, or unexpected shifts in productivity are beyond a government's control and, will affect the natural rate of unemployment for a time. However, as the example of high ongoing unemployment rates for many European countries illustrates, government policy clearly can affect the natural rate of unemployment that will persist even when GDP is growing.

When a government enacts policies that will affect workers or employers, it must examine how these policies will affect the information and incentives employees and employers have to find one another. For example, the government may have a role to play in helping some of the unemployed with job searches. Governments may need to rethink the design of their programs that offer assistance to unemployed workers and protections to employed workers so that they will not unduly discourage the supply of labor. Similarly, governments may need to reassess rules that make it difficult for businesses to begin or to expand so that they will not unduly discourage the demand for labor. The message is not that governments should repeal all laws affecting labor markets, but only that when they enact such laws, a society that cares about unemployment will need to consider the tradeoffs involved.

Bring it Home

Unemployment and the Great Recession

In the review of unemployment during and after the Great Recession at the outset of this chapter, we noted that unemployment tends to be a lagging indicator of business activity. This has historically been the case, and it is evident for all recessions that have taken place since the end of World War II. In brief, this results from the costs to employers of recruitment, hiring, and training workers. Those costs represent investments by firms in their work forces.

At the outset of a recession, when a firm realizes that demand for its product or service is not as strong as anticipated, it has an incentive to lay off workers. However, doing so runs the risk of losing those workers, and if the weak demand proves to be only temporary, the firm will be obliged to recruit, hire, and train new workers. Thus, firms tend to retain workers initially in a downturn. Similarly, as business begins to pick up when a recession is over, firms are not sure if the improvement will last. Rather than incur the costs of hiring and training new workers, they will wait, and perhaps resort to overtime work for existing workers, until they are confident that the recession is over.

Another point that we noted at the outset is that the duration of recoveries in employment following recessions has been longer following the last three recessions (going back to the early 1990s) than previously. Nir Jaimovich and Henry Siu have argued that these "jobless recoveries" are a consequence of job polarization – the disappearance of employment opportunities focused on "routine" tasks. Job polarization refers to the increasing concentration of employment in the highest- and lowest-wage occupations, as jobs in middle-skill occupations disappear. Job polarization is an outcome of technological progress in robotics, computing, and information and communication technology. The result of this progress is a decline in demand for labor in occupations that perform "routine" tasks – tasks that are limited in scope and can be performed by following a well-defined set of procedures – and hence a decline in the share of total employment that is composed of routine occupations. Jaimovich and Siu have shown that job polarization characterizes the aftermath of the last three recessions, and this appears to be responsible for the jobless recoveries.

KEY TERMS

adverse selection of wage cuts argument if employers reduce wages for all workers, the best will leave

cyclical unemployment unemployment closely tied to the business cycle, like higher unemployment during a recession

discouraged workers those who have stopped looking for employment due to the lack of suitable positions available

efficiency wage theory the theory that the productivity of workers, either individually or as a group, will increase if the employer pays them more

frictional unemployment unemployment that occurs as workers move between jobs

implicit contract an unwritten agreement in the labor market that the employer will try to keep wages from falling when the economy is weak or the business is having trouble, and the employee will not expect huge salary increases when the economy or the business is strong

insider-outsider model those already working for the firm are "insiders" who know the procedures; the other workers are "outsiders" who are recent or prospective hires

labor force participation rate this is the percentage of adults in an economy who are either employed or who are unemployed and looking for a job

natural rate of unemployment the unemployment rate that would exist in a growing and healthy economy from the combination of economic, social, and political factors that exist at a given time

out of the labor force those who are not working and not looking for work—whether they want employment or not; also termed "not in the labor force"

relative wage coordination argument across-the-board wage cuts are hard for an economy to implement, and workers fight against them

structural unemployment unemployment that occurs because individuals lack skills valued by employers

underemployed individuals who are employed in a job that is below their skills

unemployment rate the percentage of adults who are in the labor force and thus seeking jobs, but who do not have jobs

KEY CONCEPTS AND SUMMARY

21.1 How Economists Define and Compute Unemployment Rate

Unemployment imposes high costs. Unemployed individuals suffer from loss of income and from stress. An economy with high unemployment suffers an opportunity cost of unused resources. We can divide the adult population into those in the labor force and those out of the labor force. In turn, we divide those in the labor force into employed and unemployed. A person without a job must be willing and able to work and actively looking for work to be counted as unemployed; otherwise, a person without a job is counted as out of the labor force. Economists define the unemployment rate as the number of unemployed persons divided by the number of persons in the labor force (not the overall adult population). The Current Population Survey (CPS) conducted by the United States Census Bureau measures the percentage of the labor force that is unemployed. The establishment payroll survey by the Bureau of Labor Statistics measures the net change in jobs created for the month.

21.2 Patterns of Unemployment

The U.S. unemployment rate rises during periods of recession and depression, but falls back to the range of 4% to

6% when the economy is strong. The unemployment rate never falls to zero. Despite enormous growth in the size of the U.S. population and labor force in the twentieth century, along with other major trends like globalization and new technology, the unemployment rate shows no long-term rising trend.

Unemployment rates differ by group: higher for African-Americans and Hispanics than for whites; higher for less educated than more educated; higher for the young than the middle-aged. Women's unemployment rates used to be higher than men's, but in recent years men's and women's unemployment rates have been very similar. In recent years, unemployment rates in the United States have compared favorably with unemployment rates in most other high-income economies.

21.3 What Causes Changes in Unemployment over the Short Run

Cyclical unemployment rises and falls with the business cycle. In a labor market with flexible wages, wages will adjust in such a market so that quantity demanded of labor always equals the quantity supplied of labor at the equilibrium wage. Economists have proposed many theories for why wages might not be flexible, but instead may adjust only in a "sticky" way, especially when it comes to downward adjustments: implicit contracts, efficiency wage theory, adverse selection of wage cuts, insider-outsider model, and relative wage coordination.

21.4 What Causes Changes in Unemployment over the Long Run

The natural rate of unemployment is the rate of unemployment that the economic, social, and political forces in the economy would cause even when the economy is not in a recession. These factors include the frictional unemployment that occurs when people either choose to change jobs or are put out of work for a time by the shifts of a dynamic and changing economy. They also include any laws concerning conditions of hiring and firing that have the undesired side effect of discouraging job formation. They also include structural unemployment, which occurs when demand shifts permanently away from a certain type of job skill.

SELF-CHECK QUESTIONS

1. Suppose the adult population over the age of 16 is 237.8 million and the labor force is 153.9 million (of whom 139.1 million are employed). How many people are "not in the labor force?" What are the proportions of employed, unemployed and not in the labor force in the population? *Hint*: Proportions are percentages.

2. Using the above data, what is the unemployment rate? These data are U.S. statistics from 2010. How does it compare to the February 2015 unemployment rate computed earlier?

3. Over the long term, has the U.S. unemployment rate generally trended up, trended down, or remained at basically the same level?

4. Whose unemployment rates are commonly higher in the U.S. economy:
  a. Whites or nonwhites?
  b. The young or the middle-aged?
  c. College graduates or high school graduates?

5. Beginning in the 1970s and continuing for three decades, women entered the U.S. labor force in a big way. If we assume that wages are sticky in a downward direction, but that around 1970 the demand for labor equaled the supply of labor at the current wage rate, what do you imagine happened to the wage rate, employment, and unemployment as a result of increased labor force participation?

6. Is the increase in labor force participation rates among women better thought of as causing an increase in cyclical unemployment or an increase in the natural rate of unemployment? Why?

7. Many college students graduate from college before they have found a job. When graduates begin to look for a job, they are counted as what category of unemployed?

REVIEW QUESTIONS

8. What is the difference between being unemployed and being out of the labor force?

9. How do you calculate the unemployment rate? How do you calculate the labor force participation rate?

10. Are all adults who do not hold jobs counted as unemployed?

11. If you are out of school but working part time, are you considered employed or unemployed in U.S. labor statistics? If you are a full time student and working 12 hours a week at the college cafeteria are you considered employed or not in the labor force? If you are a senior citizen who is collecting social security and a pension and working as a greeter at Wal-Mart are you considered employed or not in the labor force?

12. What happens to the unemployment rate when unemployed workers are reclassified as discouraged workers?

13. What happens to the labor force participation rate when employed individuals are reclassified as unemployed? What happens when they are reclassified as discouraged workers?

14. What are some of the problems with using the unemployment rate as an accurate measure of overall joblessness?

15. What criteria do the BLS use to count someone as employed? As unemployed?

16. Assess whether the following would be counted as "unemployed" in the Current Employment Statistics survey.

    a. A husband willingly stays home with children while his wife works.

    b. A manufacturing worker whose factory just closed down.

    c. A college student doing an unpaid summer internship.

    d. A retiree.

    e. Someone who has been out of work for two years but keeps looking for a job.

    f. Someone who has been out of work for two months but isn't looking for a job.

    g. Someone who hates her present job and is actively looking for another one.

    h. Someone who decides to take a part time job because she could not find a full time position.

17. Are U.S. unemployment rates typically higher, lower, or about the same as unemployment rates in other high-income countries?

18. Are U.S. unemployment rates distributed evenly across the population?

19. When would you expect cyclical unemployment to be rising? Falling?

20. Why is there unemployment in a labor market with flexible wages?

21. Name and explain some of the reasons why wages are likely to be sticky, especially in downward adjustments.

22. What term describes the remaining level of unemployment that occurs even when the economy is healthy?

23. What forces create the natural rate of unemployment for an economy?

24. Would you expect the natural rate of unemployment to be roughly the same in different countries?

25. Would you expect the natural rate of unemployment to remain the same within one country over the long run of several decades?

26. What is frictional unemployment? Give examples of frictional unemployment.

27. What is structural unemployment? Give examples of structural unemployment.

28. After several years of economic growth, would you expect the unemployment in an economy to be mainly cyclical or mainly due to the natural rate of unemployment? Why?

29. What type of unemployment (cyclical, frictional, or structural) applies to each of the following:
   a. landscapers laid off in response to a drop in new housing construction during a recession.
   b. coal miners laid off due to EPA regulations that shut down coal fired power
   c. a financial analyst who quits his/her job in Chicago and is pursing similar work in Arizona
   d. printers laid off due to drop in demand for printed catalogues and flyers as firms go the internet to promote an advertise their products.
   e. factory workers in the U.S. laid off as the plants shut down and move to Mexico and Ireland.

CRITICAL THINKING QUESTIONS

30. Using the definition of the unemployment rate, is an increase in the unemployment rate necessarily a bad thing for a nation?

31. Is a decrease in the unemployment rate necessarily a good thing for a nation? Explain.

32. If many workers become discouraged from looking for jobs, explain how the number of jobs could decline but the unemployment rate could fall at the same time.

33. Would you expect hidden unemployment to be higher, lower, or about the same when the unemployment rate is high, say 10%, versus low, say 4%? Explain.

34. Is the higher unemployment rates for minority workers necessarily an indication of discrimination? What could be some other reasons for the higher unemployment rate?

35. While unemployment is highly negatively correlated with the level of economic activity, in the real world it responds with a lag. In other words, firms do not immediately lay off workers in response to a sales decline. They wait a while before responding. Similarly, firms do not immediately hire workers when sales pick up. What do you think accounts for the lag in response time?

36. Why do you think that unemployment rates are lower for individuals with more education?

37. Do you think it is rational for workers to prefer sticky wages to wage cuts, when the consequence of sticky wages is unemployment for some workers? Why or why not? How do the reasons for sticky wages explained in this section apply to your argument?

38. Under what condition would a decrease in unemployment be bad for the economy?

39. Under what condition would an increase in the unemployment rate be a positive sign?

40. As the baby boom generation retires, the ratio of retirees to workers will increase noticeably. How will this affect the Social Security program? How will this affect the standard of living of the average American?

41. Unemployment rates have been higher in many European countries in recent decades than in the United States. Is the main reason for this long-term difference in unemployment rates more likely to be cyclical unemployment or the natural rate of unemployment? Explain briefly.

42. Is it desirable to pursue a goal of zero unemployment? Why or why not?

43. Is it desirable to eliminate natural unemployment? Why or why not? *Hint*: Think about what our economy would look like today and what assumptions would have to be met to have a zero rate of natural unemployment.

44. The U.S. unemployment rate increased from 4.6% in July 2001 to 5.9% by June 2002. Without studying the subject in any detail, would you expect that a change of this kind is more likely to be due to cyclical unemployment or a change in the natural rate of unemployment? Why?

PROBLEMS

45. A country with a population of eight million adults has five million employed, 500,000 unemployed, and the rest of the adult population is out of the labor force. What's the unemployment rate? What share of population is in the labor force? Sketch a pie chart that divides the adult population into these three groups.

46. A government passes a family-friendly law that no companies can have evening, nighttime, or weekend hours, so that everyone can be home with their families during these times. Analyze the effect of this law using a demand and supply diagram for the labor market: first assuming that wages are flexible, and then assuming that wages are sticky downward.

47. As the baby boomer generation retires, what should happen to wages and employment? Can you show this graphically?

This OpenStax book is available for free at http://cnx.org/content/col12122/1.4

22 | Inflation

Figure 22.1 Big Bucks in Zimbabwe This bill was worth 100 billion Zimbabwean dollars when issued in 2008. There were even bills issued with a face value of 100 trillion Zimbabwean dollars. The bills had $100,000,000,000,000 written on them. Unfortunately, they were almost worthless. At one point, 621,984,228 Zimbabwean dollars were equal to one U.S. dollar. Eventually, the country abandoned its own currency and allowed people to use foreign currency for purchases. (Credit: modification of work by Samantha Marx/Flickr Creative Commons)

Bring it Home

A $550 Million Loaf of Bread?

If you were born within the last three decades in the United States, Canada, or many other countries in the developed world, you probably have no real experience with a high rate of inflation. Inflation is when most prices in an entire economy are rising. However, there is an extreme form of inflation called hyperinflation. This occurred in Germany between 1921 and 1928, and more recently in Zimbabwe between 2008 and 2009. In November 2008, Zimbabwe had an inflation rate of 79.6 billion percent. In contrast, in 2014, the United States had an average annual rate of inflation of 1.6%.

Zimbabwe's inflation rate was so high it is difficult to comprehend, so let's put it into context. It is equivalent to price increases of 98% per day. This means that, from one day to the next, prices essentially double. What is life like in an economy afflicted with hyperinflation? Most of you reading this will have never experienced this phenomenon. The government adjusted prices for commodities in Zimbabwean dollars several times *each day*. There was no desire to hold on to currency since it lost value by the minute. The people there spent a great deal of time getting rid of any cash they acquired by purchasing whatever food or other commodities they could find. At one point, a loaf of bread cost 550 million Zimbabwean dollars. Teachers' salaries were in the trillions a month; however, this was equivalent to only one U.S. dollar a day. At its height, it took 621,984,228 Zimbabwean dollars to purchase one U.S. dollar.

Government agencies had no money to pay their workers so they started printing money to pay their bills rather than raising taxes. Rising prices caused the government to enact price controls on private businesses, which led to shortages and the emergence of black markets. In 2009, the country abandoned its currency and allowed people to use foreign currencies for purchases.

How does this happen? How can both government and the economy fail to function at the most basic level? Before we consider these extreme cases of hyperinflation, let's first look at inflation itself.

Introduction to Inflation

In this chapter, you will learn about:

- Tracking Inflation
- How to Measure Changes in the Cost of Living
- How the U.S. and Other Countries Experience Inflation
- The Confusion Over Inflation
- Indexing and Its Limitations

Inflation is a general and ongoing rise in the level of prices in an entire economy. Inflation does not refer to a change in relative prices. A relative price change occurs when you see that the price of tuition has risen, but the price of laptops has fallen. Inflation, on the other hand, means that there is pressure for prices to rise in most markets in the economy. In addition, price increases in the supply-and-demand model were one-time events, representing a shift from a previous equilibrium to a new one. Inflation implies an ongoing rise in prices. If inflation happened for one year and then stopped, then it would not be inflation any more.

This chapter begins by showing how to combine prices of individual goods and services to create a measure of overall inflation. It discusses the historical and recent experience of inflation, both in the United States and in other countries around the world. Other chapters have sometimes included a note under an exhibit or a parenthetical reminder in the text saying that the numbers have been adjusted for inflation. In this chapter, it is time to show how to use inflation statistics to adjust other economic variables, so that you can tell how much of, for example, we can attribute the rise in GDP over different periods of time to an actual increase in the production of goods and services and how much we should attribute to the fact that prices for most items have risen.

Inflation has consequences for people and firms throughout the economy, in their roles as lenders and borrowers, wage-earners, taxpayers, and consumers. The chapter concludes with a discussion of some imperfections and biases in the inflation statistics, and a preview of policies for fighting inflation that we will discuss in other chapters.

22.1 | Tracking Inflation

By the end of this section, you will be able to:
- Calculate the annual rate of inflation
- Explain and use index numbers and base years when simplifying the total quantity spent over a year for products
- Calculate inflation rates using index numbers

Dinner table conversations where you might have heard about inflation usually entail reminiscing about when "everything seemed to cost so much less. You used to be able to buy three gallons of gasoline for a dollar and then go see an afternoon movie for another dollar." **Table 22.1** compares some prices of common goods in 1970 and 2017. Of course, the average prices in this table may not reflect the prices where you live. The cost of living in New York City is much higher than in Houston, Texas, for example. In addition, certain products have evolved over recent decades. A new car in 2017, loaded with antipollution equipment, safety gear, computerized engine controls, and many other technological advances, is a more advanced machine (and more fuel efficient) than your typical 1970s car. However, put details like these to one side for the moment, and look at the overall pattern. The primary reason behind the price rises in **Table 22.1**—and all the price increases for the other products in the economy—is not specific to the market for housing or cars or gasoline or movie tickets. Instead, it is part of a general rise in the level of all prices. At the

This OpenStax book is available for free at http://cnx.org/content/col12122/1.4

beginning of 2017, $1 had about the same purchasing power in overall terms of goods and services as 18 cents did in 1972, because of the amount of inflation that has occurred over that time period.

Items	1970	2017
Pound of ground beef	$0.66	$3.62
Pound of butter	$0.87	$2.03
Movie ticket	$1.55	$8.65
Sales price of new home (median)	$22,000	$312,900
New car	$3,000	$4,077
Gallon of gasoline	$0.36	$2.35
Average hourly wage for a manufacturing worker	$3.23	$20.65
Per capita GDP	$5,069	$57,294

Table 22.1 Price Comparisons, 1970 and 2017   (Sources: See chapter References at end of book.)

Moreover, the power of inflation does not affect just goods and services, but wages and income levels, too. The second-to-last row of **Table 22.1** shows that the average hourly wage for a manufacturing worker increased nearly six-fold from 1970 to 2017. The average worker in 2017 is better educated and more productive than the average worker in 1970—but not six times more productive. Per capita GDP increased substantially from 1970 to 2017, but is the average person in the U.S. economy really more than eleven times better off in just 47 years? Not likely.

A modern economy has millions of goods and services whose prices are continually quivering in the breezes of supply and demand. How can all of these shifts in price attribute to a single inflation rate? As with many problems in economic measurement, the conceptual answer is reasonably straightforward: Economists combine prices of a variety of goods and services into a single price level. The inflation rate is simply the percentage change in the price level. Applying the concept, however, involves some practical difficulties.

The Price of a Basket of Goods

To calculate the price level, economists begin with the concept of a **basket of goods and services**, consisting of the different items individuals, businesses, or organizations typically buy. The next step is to look at how the prices of those items change over time. In thinking about how to combine individual prices into an overall price level, many people find that their first impulse is to calculate the average of the prices. Such a calculation, however, could easily be misleading because some products matter more than others.

Changes in the prices of goods for which people spend a larger share of their incomes will matter more than changes in the prices of goods for which people spend a smaller share of their incomes. For example, an increase of 10% in the rental rate on housing matters more to most people than whether the price of carrots rises by 10%. To construct an overall measure of the price level, economists compute a weighted average of the prices of the items in the basket, where the weights are based on the actual quantities of goods and services people buy. The following Work It Out feature walks you through the steps of calculating the annual rate of inflation based on a few products.

Work It Out ─○─○─○

Calculating an Annual Rate of Inflation

Consider the simple basket of goods with only three items, represented in Table 22.2. Say that in any given month, a college student spends money on 20 hamburgers, one bottle of aspirin, and five movies. The table provides prices for these items over four years through each time period (Pd). Prices of some goods in the basket may rise while others fall. In this example, the price of aspirin does not change over the four years, while movies increase in price and hamburgers bounce up and down. The table shows the cost of buying the given basket of goods at the prices prevailing at that time.

Items	Hamburger	Aspirin	Movies	Total	Inflation Rate
Qty	20	1 bottle	5	-	-
(Pd 1) Price	$3.00	$10.00	$6.00	-	-
(Pd 1) Amount Spent	$60.00	$10.00	$30.00	$100.00	-
(Pd 2) Price	$3.20	$10.00	$6.50	-	-
(Pd 2) Amount Spent	$64.00	$10.00	$32.50	$106.50	6.5%
(Pd 3) Price	$3.10	$10.00	$7.00	-	-
(Pd 3) Amount Spent	$62.00	$10.00	$35.00	$107.00	0.5%
(Pd 4) Price	$3.50	$10.00	$7.50	-	-
(Pd 4) Amount Spent	$70.00	$10.00	$37.50	$117.50	9.8%

Table 22.2 A College Student's Basket of Goods

To calculate the annual rate of inflation in this example:

Step 1. Find the percentage change in the cost of purchasing the overall basket of goods between the time periods. The general equation for percentage changes between two years, whether in the context of inflation or in any other calculation, is:

$$\frac{(\text{Level in new year} - \text{Level in previous year})}{\text{Level in previous year}} \times 100 = \text{Percentage change}$$

Step 2. From period 1 to period 2, the total cost of purchasing the basket of goods in Table 22.2 rises from $100 to $106.50. Therefore, the percentage change over this time—the inflation rate—is:

$$\frac{(106.50 - 100)}{100.0} = 0.065 = 6.5\%$$

Step 3. From period 2 to period 3, the overall change in the cost of purchasing the basket rises from $106.50 to $107. Thus, the inflation rate over this time, again calculated by the percentage change, is approximately:

$$\frac{(107 - 106.50)}{106.50} = 0.0047 = 0.47\%$$

Step 4. From period 3 to period 4, the overall cost rises from $107 to $117.50. The inflation rate is thus:

$$\frac{(117.50 - 107)}{107} = 0.098 = 9.8\%$$

This calculation of the change in the total cost of purchasing a basket of goods accounts for how much a student spends on each good. Hamburgers are the lowest-priced good in this example, and aspirin is the highest-priced. If an individual buys a greater quantity of a low-price good, then it makes sense that changes in the price of that good should have a larger impact on the buying power of that person's money. The larger impact of hamburgers shows up in the "amount spent" row, where, in all time periods, hamburgers are the largest item within the amount spent row.

Index Numbers

The numerical results of a calculation based on a basket of goods can get a little messy. The simplified example in Table 22.2 has only three goods and the prices are in even dollars, not numbers like 79 cents or $124.99. If the list

This OpenStax book is available for free at http://cnx.org/content/col12122/1.4

of products were much longer, and we used more realistic prices, the total quantity spent over a year might be some messy-looking number like $17,147.51 or $27,654.92.

To simplify the task of interpreting the price levels for more realistic and complex baskets of goods, economists typically report the price level in each period as an **index number**, rather than as the dollar amount for buying the basket of goods. Economists create price indices to calculate an overall average change in relative prices over time. To convert the money spent on the basket to an index number, economists arbitrarily choose one year to be the **base year**, or starting point from which we measure changes in prices. The base year, by definition, has an index number equal to 100. This sounds complicated, but it is really a simple math trick. In the example above, say that we choose time period 3 as the base year. Since the total amount of spending in that year is $107, we divide that amount by itself ($107) and multiply by 100. Again, this is because the index number in the base year *always* has to have a value of 100. Then, to figure out the values of the index number for the other years, we divide the dollar amounts for the other years by 1.07 as well. Note also that the dollar signs cancel out so that index numbers have no units.

Table 22.3 shows calculations for the other values of the index number, based on the example in **Table 22.2**. Because we calculate the index numbers so that they are in exactly the same proportion as the total dollar cost of purchasing the basket of goods, we can calculate the inflation rate based on the index numbers, using the percentage change formula. Thus, the inflation rate from period 1 to period 2 would be

$$\frac{(99.5 - 93.4)}{93.4} = 0.065 = 6.5\%$$

This is the same answer that we derived when measuring inflation based on the dollar cost of the basket of goods for the same time period.

	Total Spending	Index Number	Inflation Rate Since Previous Period
Period 1	$100	$\frac{100}{1.07} = 93.4$	
Period 2	$106.50	$\frac{106.50}{1.07} = 99.5$	$\frac{(99.5 - 93.4)}{93.4} = 0.065 = 6.5\%$
Period 3	$107	$\frac{107}{1.07} = 100.0$	$\frac{100 - 99.5}{99.5} = 0.005 = 0.5\%$
Period 4	$117.50	$\frac{117.50}{1.07} = 109.8$	$\frac{109.8 - 100}{100} = 0.098 = 9.8\%$

Table 22.3 Calculating Index Numbers When Period 3 is the Base Year

If the inflation rate is the same whether it is based on dollar values or index numbers, then why bother with the index numbers? The advantage is that indexing allows easier eyeballing of the inflation numbers. If you glance at two index numbers like 107 and 110, you know automatically that the rate of inflation between the two years is about, but not quite exactly equal to, 3%. By contrast, imagine that we express the price levels in absolute dollars of a large basket of goods, so that when you looked at the data, the numbers were $19,493.62 and $20,040.17. Most people find it difficult to eyeball those kinds of numbers and say that it is a change of about 3%. However, the two numbers expressed in absolute dollars are exactly in the same proportion of 107 to 110 as the previous example. If you're wondering why simple subtraction of the index numbers wouldn't work, read the following Clear It Up feature.

Clear It Up

Why do you not just subtract index numbers?

A word of warning: When a price index moves from, say, 107 to 110, the rate of inflation is not *exactly* 3%. Remember, the inflation rate is not derived by subtracting the index numbers, but rather through the percentage-change calculation. We calculate the precise inflation rate as the price index moves from 107 to 110 as 100 x (110 − 107) / 107 = 100 x 0.028 = 2.8%. When the base year is fairly close to 100, a quick subtraction is not a terrible shortcut to calculating the inflation rate—but when precision matters down to tenths of a percent, subtracting will not give the right answer.

Two final points about index numbers are worth remembering. First, index numbers have no dollar signs or other units attached to them. Although we can use index numbers to calculate a percentage inflation rate, the index numbers themselves do not have percentage signs. Index numbers just mirror the proportions that we find in other data. They transform the other data so that it is easier to work with the data.

Second, the choice of a base year for the index number—that is, the year that is automatically set equal to 100—is arbitrary. We choose it as a starting point from which we can track changes in prices. In the official inflation statistics, it is common to use one base year for a few years, and then to update it, so that the base year of 100 is relatively close to the present. However, any base year that we choose for the index numbers will result in exactly the same inflation rate. To see this in the previous example, imagine that period 1 is the base year when total spending was $100, and we assign it an index number of 100. At a glance, you can see that the index numbers would now exactly match the dollar figures, and the inflation rate in the first period would be 6.5%.

Now that we see how indexes work to track inflation, the next module will show us how economists measure the cost of living.

Link It Up

Watch this video (http://openstaxcollege.org/l/Duck_Tales) from the cartoon *Duck Tales* to view a mini-lesson on inflation.

22.2 | How to Measure Changes in the Cost of Living

By the end of this section, you will be able to:
- Use the Consumer Price Index (CPI) to calculate U.S. inflation rates
- Identify several ways the Bureau of Labor Statistics avoids biases in the Consumer Price Index (CPI)
- Differentiate among the Consumer Price Index (CPI), the Producer Price Index (PPI), the International Price Index, the Employment Cost Index, and the GDP deflator.

The most commonly cited measure of inflation in the United States is the **Consumer Price Index (CPI)**. Government statisticians at the U.S. Bureau of Labor Statistics calculate the CPI based on the prices in a fixed basket of goods and services that represents the purchases of the average family of four. In recent years, the statisticians have paid considerable attention to a subtle problem: that the change in the total cost of buying a fixed basket of goods and services over time is conceptually not quite the same as the change in the cost of living, because the cost of living represents how much it costs for a person to feel that his or her consumption provides an equal level of satisfaction or utility.

To understand the distinction, imagine that over the past 10 years, the cost of purchasing a fixed basket of goods increased by 25% and your salary also increased by 25%. Has your personal standard of living held constant? If you do not necessarily purchase an identical fixed basket of goods every year, then an inflation calculation based on the cost of a fixed basket of goods may be a misleading measure of how your cost of living has changed. Two problems arise here: substitution bias and quality/new goods bias.

When the price of a good rises, consumers tend to purchase less of it and to seek out substitutes instead. Conversely, as the price of a good falls, people will tend to purchase more of it. This pattern implies that goods with generally rising prices should tend over time to become less important in the overall basket of goods used to calculate inflation, while goods with falling prices should tend to become more important. Consider, as an example, a rise in the price of peaches by $100 per pound. If consumers were utterly inflexible in their demand for peaches, this would lead to a big rise in the price of food for consumers. Alternatively, imagine that people are utterly indifferent to whether they have peaches or other types of fruit. Now, if peach prices rise, people completely switch to other fruit choices and the average price of food does not change at all. A fixed and unchanging basket of goods assumes that consumers are locked into buying exactly the same goods, regardless of price changes—not a very likely assumption. Thus, **substitution bias**—the rise in the price of a fixed basket of goods over time—tends to overstate the rise in a consumer's true cost of living, because it does not take into account that the person can substitute away from goods whose relative prices have risen.

The other major problem in using a fixed basket of goods as the basis for calculating inflation is how to deal with the arrival of improved versions of older goods or altogether new goods. Consider the problem that arises if a cereal is improved by adding 12 essential vitamins and minerals—and also if a box of the cereal costs 5% more. It would clearly be misleading to count the entire resulting higher price as inflation, because the new price reflects a higher quality (or at least different) product. Ideally, one would like to know how much of the higher price is due to the quality change, and how much of it is just a higher price. The Bureau of Labor Statistics, which is responsible for computing the Consumer Price Index, must deal with these difficulties in adjusting for quality changes.

Link It Up

Visit this website (http://openstax.org/l/Fords) to view a list of Ford car prices between 1909 and 1927. Consider how these prices compare to today's models. Is the product today of a different quality?

We can think of a new product as an extreme improvement in quality—from something that did not exist to something that does. However, the basket of goods that was fixed in the past obviously does not include new goods created since then. The basket of goods and services in the Consumer Price Index (CPI) is revised and updated over time, and so new products are gradually included. However, the process takes some time. For example, room air conditioners were widely sold in the early 1950s, but were not introduced into the basket of goods behind the Consumer Price Index until 1964. The VCR and personal computer were available in the late 1970s and widely sold by the early 1980s, but did not enter the CPI basket of goods until 1987. By 1996, there were more than 40 million cellular phone subscribers in the United States—but cell phones were not yet part of the CPI basket of goods. The parade of inventions has continued, with the CPI inevitably lagging a few years behind.

The arrival of new goods creates problems with respect to the accuracy of measuring inflation. The reason people buy new goods, presumably, is that the new goods offer better value for money than existing goods. Thus, if the price index leaves out new goods, it overlooks one of the ways in which the cost of living is improving. In addition, the price of a new good is often higher when it is first introduced and then declines over time. If the new good is not included in the CPI for some years, until its price is already lower, the CPI may miss counting this price decline altogether. Taking these arguments together, the **quality/new goods bias** means that the rise in the price of a fixed basket of goods over time tends to overstate the rise in a consumer's true cost of living, because it does not account for how improvements in the quality of existing goods or the invention of new goods improves the standard of living. The following Clear It Up feature is a must-read on how statisticians comprise and calculate the CPI.

How do U.S. government statisticians measure the Consumer Price Index?

When the U.S. Bureau of Labor Statistics (BLS) calculates the Consumer Price Index, the first task is to decide on a basket of goods that is representative of the purchases of the average household. We do this by using the Consumer Expenditure Survey, a national survey of about 7,000 households, which provides detailed information on spending habits. Statisticians divide consumer expenditures into eight major groups (seen below), which in turn they divide into more than 200 individual item categories. The BLS currently uses 1982–1984 as the base period.

For each of the 200 individual expenditure items, the BLS chooses several hundred very specific examples of that item and looks at the prices of those examples. In figuring out the "breakfast cereal" item under the overall category of "foods and beverages," the BLS picks several hundred examples of breakfast cereal. One example might be the price of a 24-oz. box of a particular brand of cereal sold at a particular store. The BLS statistically selects specific products and sizes and stores to reflect what people buy and where they shop. The basket of goods in the Consumer Price Index thus consists of about 80,000 products; that is, several hundred specific products in over 200 broad-item categories. Statisticians rotate about one-quarter of these 80,000 specific products of the sample each year, and replace them with a different set of products.

The next step is to collect data on prices. Data collectors visit or call about 23,000 stores in 87 urban areas all over the United States every month to collect prices on these 80,000 specific products. The BLS also conducts a survey of 50,000 landlords or tenants to collect information about rents.

Statisticians then calculate the Consumer Price Index by taking the 80,000 prices of individual products and combining them, using weights (see Figure 22.2) determined by the quantities of these products that people buy and allowing for factors like substitution between goods and quality improvements, into price indices for the 200 or so overall items. Then, the statisticians combine the price indices for the 200 items into an overall Consumer Price Index. According the Consumer Price Index website, there are eight categories that data collectors use:

The Eight Major Categories in the Consumer Price Index

1. Food and beverages (breakfast cereal, milk, coffee, chicken, wine, full-service meals, and snacks)

2. Housing (renter's cost of housing, homeowner's cost of housing, fuel oil, bedroom furniture)

3. Apparel (men's shirts and sweaters, women's dresses, jewelry)

4. Transportation (new vehicles, airline fares, gasoline, motor vehicle insurance)

5. Medical care (prescription drugs and medical supplies, physicians' services, eyeglasses and eye care, hospital services)

6. Recreation (televisions, cable television, pets and pet products, sports equipment, admissions)

7. Education and communication (college tuition, postage, telephone services, computer software and accessories)

8. Other goods and services (tobacco and smoking products, haircuts and other personal services, funeral expenses)

This OpenStax book is available for free at http://cnx.org/content/col12122/1.4

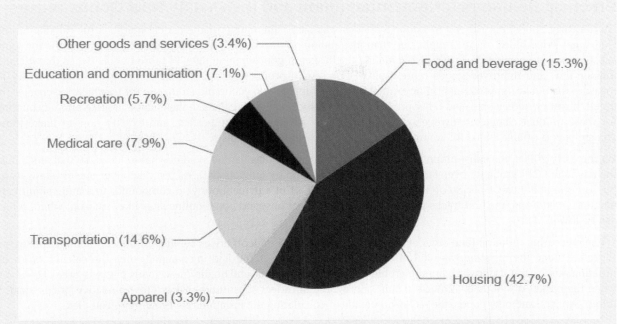

Figure 22.2 The Weighting of CPI Components Of the eight categories used to generate the Consumer Price Index, housing is the highest at 42.7%. The next highest category, food and beverage at 15.3%, is less than half the size of housing. Other goods and services, and apparel, are the lowest at 3.4% and 3.3%, respectively. (Source: www.bls.gov/cpi)

The CPI and Core Inflation Index

Imagine if you were driving a company truck across the country- you probably would care about things like the prices of available roadside food and motel rooms as well as the truck's operating condition. However, the manager of the firm might have different priorities. He would care mostly about the truck's on-time performance and much less so about the food you were eating and the places you were staying. In other words, the company manager would be paying attention to the firm's production, while ignoring transitory elements that impacted you, but did not affect the company's bottom line.

In a sense, a similar situation occurs with regard to measures of inflation. As we've learned, CPI measures prices as they affect everyday household spending. Economists typically calculate a **core inflation index** by taking the CPI and excluding volatile economic variables. In this way, economists have a better sense of the underlying trends in prices that affect the cost of living.

Examples of excluded variables include energy and food prices, which can jump around from month to month because of the weather. According to an article by Kent Bernhard, during Hurricane Katrina in 2005, a key supply point for the nation's gasoline was nearly knocked out. Gas prices quickly shot up across the nation, in some places by up to 40 cents a gallon in one day. This was not the cause of an economic policy but rather a short-lived event until the pumps were restored in the region. In this case, the CPI that month would register the change as a cost of living event to households, but the core inflation index would remain unchanged. As a result, the Federal Reserve's decisions on interest rates would not be influenced. Similarly, droughts can cause world-wide spikes in food prices that, if temporary, do not affect the nation's economic capability.

As former Chairman of the Federal Reserve Ben Bernanke noted in 1999 about the core inflation index, "It provide(s) a better guide to monetary policy than the other indices, since it measures the more persistent underlying inflation rather than transitory influences on the price level." Bernanke also noted that it helps communicate that the Federal Reserve does not need to respond to every inflationary shock since some price changes are transitory and not part of a structural change in the economy.

In sum, both the CPI and the core inflation index are important, but serve different audiences. The CPI helps households understand their overall cost of living from month to month, while the core inflation index is a preferred gauge from which to make important government policy changes.

Practical Solutions for the Substitution and the Quality/New Goods Biases

By the early 2000s, the Bureau of Labor Statistics was using alternative mathematical methods for calculating the Consumer Price Index, more complicated than just adding up the cost of a fixed basket of goods, to allow for some substitution between goods. It was also updating the basket of goods behind the CPI more frequently, so that it could include new and improved goods more rapidly. For certain products, the BLS was carrying out studies to try to measure the quality improvement. For example, with computers, an economic study can try to adjust for changes in speed, memory, screen size, and other product characteristics, and then calculate the change in price after accounting for these product changes. However, these adjustments are inevitably imperfect, and exactly how to make these adjustments is often a source of controversy among professional economists.

By the early 2000s, the substitution bias and quality/new goods bias had been somewhat reduced, so that since then the rise in the CPI probably overstates the true rise in inflation by only about 0.5% per year. Over one or a few years, this is not much. Over a period of a decade or two, even half of a percent per year compounds to a more significant amount. In addition, the CPI tracks prices from physical locations, and not at online sites like Amazon, where prices can be lower.

When measuring inflation (and other economic statistics, too), a tradeoff arises between simplicity and interpretation. If we calculate the inflation rate with a basket of goods that is fixed and unchanging, then the calculation of an inflation rate is straightforward, but the problems of substitution bias and quality/new goods bias will arise. However, when the basket of goods is allowed to shift and evolve to reflect substitution toward lower relative prices, quality improvements, and new goods, the technical details of calculating the inflation rate grow more complex.

Additional Price Indices: PPI, GDP Deflator, and More

The basket of goods behind the Consumer Price Index represents an average hypothetical U.S. household's consumption, which is to say that it does not exactly capture anyone's personal experience. When the task is to calculate an average level of inflation, this approach works fine. What if, however, you are concerned about inflation experienced by a certain group, like the elderly, or the poor, or single-parent families with children, or Hispanic-Americans? In specific situations, a price index based on the buying power of the average consumer may not feel quite right.

This problem has a straightforward solution. If the Consumer Price Index does not serve the desired purpose, then invent another index, based on a basket of goods appropriate for the group of interest. The Bureau of Labor Statistics publishes a number of experimental price indices: some for particular groups like the elderly or the poor, some for different geographic areas, and some for certain broad categories of goods like food or housing.

The BLS also calculates several price indices that are not based on baskets of consumer goods. For example, the **Producer Price Index (PPI)** is based on prices paid for supplies and inputs by producers of goods and services. We can break it down into price indices for different industries, commodities, and stages of processing (like finished goods, intermediate goods, or crude materials for further processing). There is an **International Price Index** based on the prices of merchandise that is exported or imported. An **Employment Cost Index** measures wage inflation in the labor market. The **GDP deflator**, which the Bureau of Economic Analysis measures, is a price index that includes all the GDP components (that is, consumption plus investment plus government plus exports minus imports). Unlike the CPI, its baskets are not fixed but re-calculate what that year's GDP would have been worth using the base-year's prices. MIT's Billion Prices Project is a more recent alternative attempt to measure prices: economists collect data online from retailers and then put them into an index that they compare to the CPI (Source: http://bpp.mit.edu/usa/).

What's the best measure of inflation? If one is concerned with the most accurate measure of inflation, one should use the GDP deflator as it picks up the prices of goods and services produced. However, it is not a good measure of the cost of living as it includes prices of many products not purchased by households (for example, aircraft, fire engines, factory buildings, office complexes, and bulldozers). If one wants the most accurate measure of inflation as it impacts households, one should use the CPI, as it only picks up prices of products purchased by households. That is why economists sometimes refer to the CPI as the cost-of-living index. As the Bureau of Labor Statistics states on its website: "The 'best' measure of inflation for a given application depends on the intended use of the data."

This OpenStax book is available for free at http://cnx.org/content/col12122/1.4

22.3 | How the U.S. and Other Countries Experience Inflation

By the end of this section, you will be able to:
- Identify patterns of inflation for the United States using data from the Consumer Price Index
- Identify patterns of inflation on an international level

In the last three decades, inflation has been relatively low in the U.S. economy, with the Consumer Price Index typically rising 2% to 4% per year. Looking back over the twentieth century, there have been several periods where inflation caused the price level to rise at double-digit rates, but nothing has come close to hyperinflation.

Historical Inflation in the U.S. Economy

Figure 22.3 (a) shows the level of prices in the Consumer Price Index stretching back to 1913. In this case, the base years (when the CPI is defined as 100) are set for the average level of prices that existed from 1982 to 1984. **Figure 22.3** (b) shows the annual percentage changes in the CPI over time, which is the inflation rate.

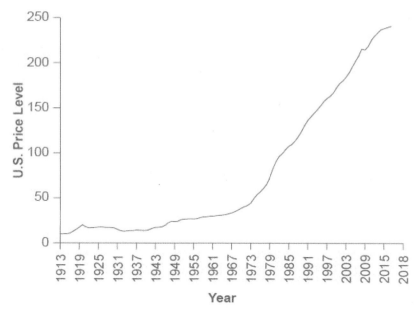

(a) U.S. price level 1913-2016

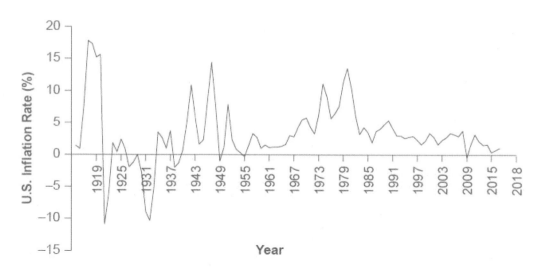

(b) U.S. inflation rate 1913-2016

Figure 22.3 U.S. Price Level and Inflation Rates since 1913   Graph a shows the trends in the U.S. price level from the year 1913 to 2016. In 1913, the graph starts out close to 10, rises to around 20 in 1920, stays around 16 or 17 until 1931, then falls to 13 or 14 until 1940. It gradually increases until about 1973, then increases more rapidly through the remainder of the 1970s and beyond, with periodic dips, until 2016, when it reached around 240. Graph b shows the trends in U.S. inflation rates from the year 1914 to 2016. In 1916, the graph starts out with inflation at almost 8%, jumps to about 17% in 1917, drops drastically to close to –11% in 1921, goes up and down periodically, with peaks in the 1940s and the 1970s, until settling to around 1.3% in 2016.

The first two waves of inflation are easy to characterize in historical terms: they are right after World War I and World War II. However, there are also two periods of severe negative inflation—called **deflation**—in the early decades of the twentieth century: one following the deep 1920-21 recession of and the other during the 1930s Great Depression of the 1930s. (Since inflation is a time when the buying power of money in terms of goods and services is reduced, deflation will be a time when the buying power of money in terms of goods and services increases.) For the period from 1900 to about 1960, the major inflations and deflations nearly balanced each other out, so the average annual rate of inflation over these years was only about 1% per year. A third wave of more severe inflation arrived in the

This OpenStax book is available for free at http://cnx.org/content/col12122/1.4

1970s and departed in the early 1980s.

Link It Up

Visit this website (http://openstax.org/l/CPI_calculator) to use an inflation calculator and discover how prices have changed in the last 100 years.

Times of recession or depression often seem to be times when the inflation rate is lower, as in the recession of 1920–1921, the Great Depression, the recession of 1980–1982, and the Great Recession in 2008–2009. There were a few months in 2009 that were deflationary, but not at an annual rate. High levels of unemployment typically accompany recessions, and the total demand for goods falls, pulling the price level down. Conversely, the rate of inflation often, but not always, seems to start moving up when the economy is growing very strongly, like right after wartime or during the 1960s. The frameworks for macroeconomic analysis, that we developed in other chapters, will explain why recession often accompanies higher unemployment and lower inflation, while rapid economic growth often brings lower unemployment but higher inflation.

Inflation around the World

Around the rest of the world, the pattern of inflation has been very mixed; **Figure 22.4** shows inflation rates over the last several decades. Many industrialized countries, not just the United States, had relatively high inflation rates in the 1970s. For example, in 1975, Japan's inflation rate was over 8% and the inflation rate for the United Kingdom was almost 25%. In the 1980s, inflation rates came down in the United States and in Europe and have largely stayed down.

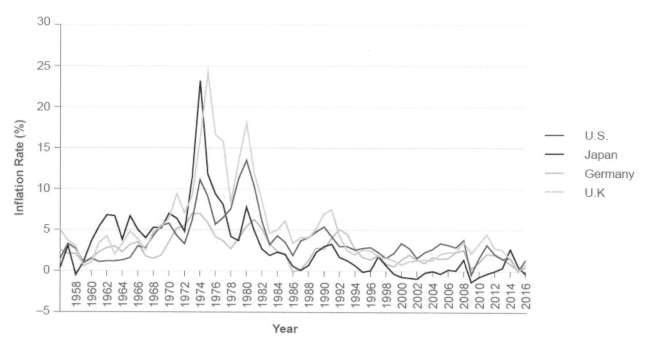

Figure 22.4 Countries with Relatively Low Inflation Rates, 1960–2016 This chart shows the annual percentage change in consumer prices compared with the previous year's consumer prices in the United States, the United Kingdom, Japan, and Germany.

Countries with controlled economies in the 1970s, like the Soviet Union and China, historically had very low rates of measured inflation—because prices were forbidden to rise by law, except for the cases where the government deemed a price increase to be due to quality improvements. However, these countries also had perpetual shortages of goods, since forbidding prices to rise acts like a price ceiling and creates a situation where quantity demanded often exceeds quantity supplied. As Russia and China made a transition toward more market-oriented economies, they also experienced outbursts of inflation, although we should regard the statistics for these economies as somewhat shakier. Inflation in China averaged about 10% per year for much of the 1980s and early 1990s, although it has dropped off since then. Russia experienced **hyperinflation**—an outburst of high inflation—of 2,500% per year in the early 1990s, although by 2006 Russia's consumer price inflation had dipped below 10% per year, as **Figure 22.5** shows. The closest the United States has ever reached hyperinflation was during the 1860–1865 Civil War, in the Confederate states.

This OpenStax book is available for free at http://cnx.org/content/col12122/1.4

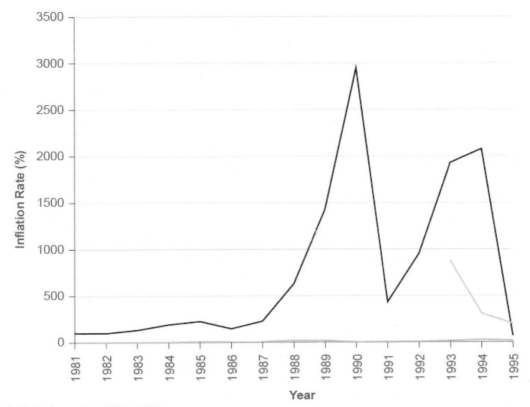

(a) Inflation rates 1980-1995

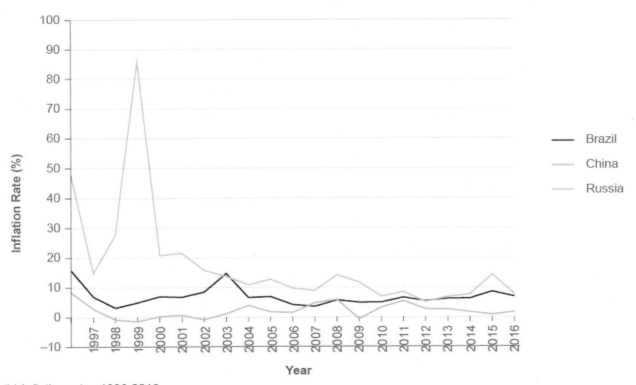

(b) Inflation rates 1996-2016

Figure 22.5 Countries with Relatively High Inflation Rates, 1980–2016 These charts show the percentage change in consumer prices compared with the previous year's consumer prices in Brazil, China, and Russia. (a) Of these, Brazil and Russia experienced very high inflation at some point between the late-1980s and late-1990s. (b) Though not as high, China also had high inflation rates in the mid-1990s. Even though their inflation rates have come down over the last two decades, several of these countries continue to see significant inflation rates. (Sources: http://www.inflation.eu/inflation-rates; http://research.stlouisfed.org/fred2/series/FPCPITOTLZGBRA; http://research.stlouisfed.org/fred2/series/CHNCPIALLMINMEI; http://research.stlouisfed.org/fred2/series/FPCPITOTLZGRUS)

Many countries in Latin America experienced raging inflation during the 1980s and early 1990s, with inflation rates often well above 100% per year. In 1990, for example, both Brazil and Argentina saw inflation climb above 2000%. Certain countries in Africa experienced extremely high rates of inflation, sometimes bordering on hyperinflation, in the 1990s. Nigeria, the most populous country in Africa, had an inflation rate of 75% in 1995.

In the early 2000s, the problem of inflation appears to have diminished for most countries, at least in comparison to the worst times of recent decades. As we noted in this earlier Bring it Home feature, in recent years, the world's worst example of hyperinflation was in Zimbabwe, where at one point the government was issuing bills with a face value of $100 trillion (in Zimbabwean dollars)—that is, the bills had $100,000,000,000,000 written on the front, but were almost worthless. In many countries, the memory of double-digit, triple-digit, and even quadruple-digit inflation is not very far in the past.

22.4 | The Confusion Over Inflation

By the end of this section, you will be able to:
- Explain how inflation can cause redistributions of purchasing power
- Identify ways inflation can blur the perception of supply and demand
- Explain the economic benefits and challenges of inflation

Economists usually oppose high inflation, but they oppose it in a milder way than many non-economists. Robert Shiller, one of 2013's Nobel Prize winners in economics, carried out several surveys during the 1990s about attitudes toward inflation. One of his questions asked, "Do you agree that preventing high inflation is an important national priority, as important as preventing drug abuse or preventing deterioration in the quality of our schools?" Answers were on a scale of 1–5, where 1 meant "Fully agree" and 5 meant "Completely disagree." For the U.S. population as a whole, 52% answered "Fully agree" that preventing high inflation was a highly important national priority and just 4% said "Completely disagree." However, among professional economists, only 18% answered "Fully agree," while the same percentage of 18% answered "Completely disagree."

The Land of Funny Money

What are the economic problems caused by inflation, and why do economists often regard them with less concern than the general public? Consider a very short story: "The Land of Funny Money."

One morning, everyone in the Land of Funny Money awakened to find that everything denominated in money had increased by 20%. The change was completely unexpected. Every price in every store was 20% higher. Paychecks were 20% higher. Interest rates were 20 % higher. The amount of money, everywhere from wallets to savings accounts, was 20% larger. This overnight inflation of prices made newspaper headlines everywhere in the Land of Funny Money. However, the headlines quickly disappeared, as people realized that in terms of what they could actually buy with their incomes, this inflation had no economic impact. Everyone's pay could still buy exactly the same set of goods as it did before. Everyone's savings were still sufficient to buy exactly the same car, vacation, or retirement that they could have bought before. Equal levels of inflation in all wages and prices ended up not mattering much at all.

When the people in Robert Shiller's surveys explained their concern about inflation, one typical reason was that they feared that as prices rose, they would not be able to afford to buy as much. In other words, people were worried because they did not live in a place like the Land of Funny Money, where all prices and wages rose simultaneously. Instead, people live here on Planet Earth, where prices might rise while wages do not rise at all, or where wages rise more slowly than prices.

This OpenStax book is available for free at http://cnx.org/content/col12122/1.4

Economists note that over most periods, the inflation level in prices is roughly similar to the inflation level in wages, and so they reason that, on average, over time, people's economic status is not greatly changed by inflation. If all prices, wages, and interest rates adjusted automatically and immediately with inflation, as in the Land of Funny Money, then no one's purchasing power, profits, or real loan payments would change. However, if other economic variables do not move exactly in sync with inflation, or if they adjust for inflation only after a time lag, then inflation can cause three types of problems: unintended redistributions of purchasing power, blurred price signals, and difficulties in long-term planning.

Unintended Redistributions of Purchasing Power

Inflation can cause redistributions of purchasing power that hurt some and help others. People who are hurt by inflation include those who are holding considerable cash, whether it is in a safe deposit box or in a cardboard box under the bed. When inflation happens, the buying power of cash diminishes. However, cash is only an example of a more general problem: anyone who has financial assets invested in a way that the nominal return does not keep up with inflation will tend to suffer from inflation. For example, if a person has money in a bank account that pays 4% interest, but inflation rises to 5%, then the real rate of return for the money invested in that bank account is negative 1%.

The problem of a good-looking nominal interest rate transforming into an ugly-looking real interest rate can be worsened by taxes. The U.S. income tax is charged on the nominal interest received in dollar terms, without an adjustment for inflation. Thus, the government taxes a person who invests $10,000 and receives a 5% nominal rate of interest on the $500 received—no matter whether the inflation rate is 0%, 5%, or 10%. If inflation is 0%, then the real interest rate is 5% and all $500 is a gain in buying power. However, if inflation is 5%, then the real interest rate is zero and the person had no real gain—but owes income tax on the nominal gain anyway. If inflation is 10%, then the real interest rate is *negative* 5% and the person is actually falling behind in buying power, but would still owe taxes on the $500 in nominal gains.

Inflation can cause unintended redistributions for wage earners, too. Wages do typically creep up with inflation over time, eventually. The last row of **Table 22.1** at the start of this chapter showed that the average hourly wage in manufacturing in the U.S. economy increased from $3.23 in 1970 to $20.65 in 2017, which is an increase by a factor of more than six. Over that time period, the Consumer Price Index increased by an almost identical amount. However, increases in wages may lag behind inflation for a year or two, since wage adjustments are often somewhat sticky and occur only once or twice a year. Moreover, the extent to which wages keep up with inflation creates insecurity for workers and may involve painful, prolonged conflicts between employers and employees. If the government adjusts minimum wage for inflation only infrequently, minimum wage workers are losing purchasing power from their nominal wages, as **Figure 22.6** shows.

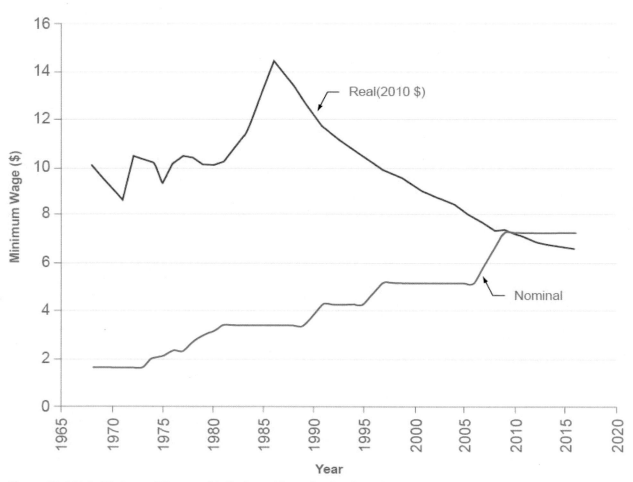

Figure 22.6 U.S. Minimum Wage and Inflation   After adjusting for inflation, the federal minimum wage dropped more than 30 percent from 1967 to 2010, even though the nominal figure climbed from $1.40 to $7.25 per hour. Increases in the minimum wage in between 2008 and 2010 kept the decline from being worse—as it would have been if the wage had remained the same as it did from 1997 through 2007. Since 2010, the real minimum wage has continued to decline. (Sources: http://www.dol.gov/whd/minwage/chart.htm; http://data.bls.gov/cgi-bin/surveymost?cu)

One sizable group of people has often received a large share of their income in a form that does not increase over time: retirees who receive a private company pension. Most pensions have traditionally been set as a fixed nominal dollar amount per year at retirement. For this reason, economists call pensions "defined benefits" plans. Even if inflation is low, the combination of inflation and a fixed income can create a substantial problem over time. A person who retires on a fixed income at age 65 will find that losing just 1% to 2% of buying power per year to inflation compounds to a considerable loss of buying power after a decade or two.

Fortunately, pensions and other defined benefits retirement plans are increasingly rare, replaced instead by "defined contribution" plans, such as 401(k)s and 403(b)s. In these plans, the employer contributes a fixed amount to the worker's retirement account on a regular basis (usually every pay check). The employee often contributes as well. The worker invests these funds in a wide range of investment vehicles. These plans are tax deferred, and they are portable so that if the individual takes a job with a different employer, their 401(k) comes with them. To the extent that the investments made generate real rates of return, retirees do not suffer from the inflation costs of traditional pensioners.

However, ordinary people can sometimes benefit from the unintended redistributions of inflation. Consider someone who borrows $10,000 to buy a car at a fixed interest rate of 9%. If inflation is 3% at the time the loan is made, then he or she must repay the loan at a real interest rate of 6%. However, if inflation rises to 9%, then the real interest rate on the loan is zero. In this case, the borrower's benefit from inflation is the lender's loss. A borrower paying a fixed interest rate, who benefits from inflation, is just the flip side of an investor receiving a fixed interest rate, who suffers

This OpenStax book is available for free at http://cnx.org/content/col12122/1.4

from inflation. The lesson is that when interest rates are fixed, rises in the rate of inflation tend to penalize suppliers of financial capital, who receive repayment in dollars that are worth less because of inflation, while demanders of financial capital end up better off, because they can repay their loans in dollars that are worth less than originally expected.

The unintended redistributions of buying power that inflation causes may have a broader effect on society. America's widespread acceptance of market forces rests on a perception that people's actions have a reasonable connection to market outcomes. When inflation causes a retiree who built up a pension or invested at a fixed interest rate to suffer, however, while someone who borrowed at a fixed interest rate benefits from inflation, it is hard to believe that this outcome was deserved in any way. Similarly, when homeowners benefit from inflation because the price of their homes rises, while renters suffer because they are paying higher rent, it is hard to see any useful incentive effects. One of the reasons that the general public dislikes inflation is a sense that it makes economic rewards and penalties more arbitrary—and therefore likely to be perceived as unfair – even dangerous, as the next Clear It Up feature shows.

Is there a connection between German hyperinflation and Hitler's rise to power?

Germany suffered an intense hyperinflation of its currency, the Mark, in the years after World War I, when the Weimar Republic in Germany resorted to printing money to pay its bills and the onset of the Great Depression created the social turmoil that Adolf Hitler was able to take advantage of in his rise to power. Shiller described the connection this way in a National Bureau of Economic Research 1996 Working Paper:

> A fact that is probably little known to young people today, even in Germany, is that the final collapse of the Mark in 1923, the time when the Mark's inflation reached astronomical levels (inflation of 35,974.9% in November 1923 alone, for an annual rate that month of 4.69×10^{28}%), came in the same month as did Hitler's Beer Hall Putsch, his Nazi Party's armed attempt to overthrow the German government. This failed putsch resulted in Hitler's imprisonment, at which time he wrote his book *Mein Kampf*, setting forth an inspirational plan for Germany's future, suggesting plans for world domination. . .

> . . . Most people in Germany today probably do not clearly remember these events; this lack of attention to it may be because its memory is blurred by the more dramatic events that succeeded it (the Nazi seizure of power and World War II). However, to someone living through these historical events in sequence . . . [the putsch] may have been remembered as vivid evidence of the potential effects of inflation.

Blurred Price Signals

Prices are the messengers in a market economy, conveying information about conditions of demand and supply. Inflation blurs those price messages. Inflation means that we perceive price signals more vaguely, like a radio program received with considerable static. If the static becomes severe, it is hard to tell what is happening.

In Israel, when inflation accelerated to an annual rate of 500% in 1985, some stores stopped posting prices directly on items, since they would have had to put new labels on the items or shelves every few days to reflect inflation. Instead, a shopper just took items from a shelf and went up to the checkout register to find out the price for that day. Obviously, this situation makes comparing prices and shopping for the best deal rather difficult. When the levels and changes of prices become uncertain, businesses and individuals find it harder to react to economic signals. In a world where inflation is at a high rate, but bouncing up and down to some extent, does a higher price of a good mean that inflation has risen, or that supply of that good has decreased, or that demand for that good has increased? Should a buyer of the good take the higher prices as an economic hint to start substituting other products—or have the prices of the substitutes risen by an equal amount? Should a seller of the good take a higher price as a reason to increase production—or is the higher price only a sign of a general inflation in which the prices of all inputs to production are rising as well? The true story will presumably become clear over time, but at a given moment, who can say?

High and variable inflation means that the incentives in the economy to adjust in response to changes in prices are weaker. Markets will adjust toward their equilibrium prices and quantities more erratically and slowly, and many individual markets will experience a greater chance of surpluses and shortages.

Problems of Long-Term Planning

Inflation can make long-term planning difficult. In discussing unintended redistributions, we considered the case of someone trying to plan for retirement with a pension that is fixed in nominal terms and a high rate of inflation. Similar problems arise for all people trying to save for retirement, because they must consider what their money will really buy several decades in the future when we cannot know the rate of future inflation.

Inflation, especially at moderate or high levels, will pose substantial planning problems for businesses, too. A firm can make money from inflation—for example, by paying bills and wages as late as possible so that it can pay in inflated dollars, while collecting revenues as soon as possible. A firm can also suffer losses from inflation, as in the case of a retail business that gets stuck holding too much cash, only to see inflation eroding the value of that cash. However, when a business spends its time focusing on how to profit by inflation, or at least how to avoid suffering from it, an inevitable tradeoff strikes: less time is spent on improving products and services or on figuring out how to make existing products and services more cheaply. An economy with high inflation rewards businesses that have found clever ways of profiting from inflation, which are not necessarily the businesses that excel at productivity, innovation, or quality of service.

In the short term, low or moderate levels of inflation may not pose an overwhelming difficulty for business planning, because costs of doing business and sales revenues may rise at similar rates. If, however, inflation varies substantially over the short or medium term, then it may make sense for businesses to stick to shorter-term strategies. The evidence as to whether relatively low rates of inflation reduce productivity is controversial among economists. There is some evidence that if inflation can be held to moderate levels of less than 3% per year, it need not prevent a nation's real economy from growing at a healthy pace. For some countries that have experienced hyperinflation of several thousand percent per year, an annual inflation rate of 20–30% may feel basically the same as zero. However, several economists have pointed to the suggestive fact that when U.S. inflation heated up in the early 1970s—to 10%—U.S. growth in productivity slowed down, and when inflation slowed down in the 1980s, productivity edged up again not long thereafter, as **Figure 22.7** shows.

Figure 22.7 U.S. Inflation Rate and U.S. Labor Productivity, 1961–2014 Over the last several decades in the United States, there have been times when rising inflation rates have been closely followed by lower productivity rates and lower inflation rates have corresponded to increasing productivity rates. As the graph shows, however, this correlation does not always exist.

Any Benefits of Inflation?

Although the economic effects of inflation are primarily negative, two countervailing points are worth noting. First,

This OpenStax book is available for free at http://cnx.org/content/col12122/1.4

the impact of inflation will differ considerably according to whether it is creeping up slowly at 0% to 2% per year, galloping along at 10% to 20% per year, or racing to the point of hyperinflation at, say, 40% per month. Hyperinflation can rip an economy and a society apart. An annual inflation rate of 2%, 3%, or 4%, however, is a long way from a national crisis. Low inflation is also better than deflation which occurs with severe recessions.

Second, economists sometimes argue that moderate inflation may help the economy by making wages in labor markets more flexible. The discussion in **Unemployment** pointed out that wages tend to be sticky in their downward movements and that unemployment can result. A little inflation could nibble away at real wages, and thus help real wages to decline if necessary. In this way, even if a moderate or high rate of inflation may act as sand in the gears of the economy, perhaps a low rate of inflation serves as oil for the gears of the labor market. This argument is controversial. A full analysis would have to account for all the effects of inflation. It does, however, offer another reason to believe that, all things considered, very low rates of inflation may not be especially harmful.

22.5 | Indexing and Its Limitations

By the end of this section, you will be able to:
- Explain the relationship between indexing and inflation
- Identify three ways the government can control inflation through macroeconomic policy

When a price, wage, or interest rate is adjusted automatically with inflation, economists use the term **indexed**. An indexed payment increases according to the index number that measures inflation. Those in private markets and government programs observe a wide range of indexing arrangements. Since the negative effects of inflation depend in large part on having inflation unexpectedly affect one part of the economy but not another—say, increasing the prices that people pay but not the wages that workers receive—indexing will take some of the sting out of inflation.

Indexing in Private Markets

In the 1970s and 1980s, labor unions commonly negotiated wage contracts that had **cost-of-living adjustments (COLAs)** which guaranteed that their wages would keep up with inflation. These contracts were sometimes written as, for example, COLA plus 3%. Thus, if inflation was 5%, the wage increase would automatically be 8%, but if inflation rose to 9%, the wage increase would automatically be 12%. COLAs are a form of indexing applied to wages.

Loans often have built-in inflation adjustments, too, so that if the inflation rate rises by two percentage points, then the interest rate that a financial institution charges on the loan rises by two percentage points as well. An **adjustable-rate mortgage (ARM)** is a type of loan that one can use to purchase a home in which the interest rate varies with the rate of inflation. Often, a borrower will be able receive a lower interest rate if borrowing with an ARM, compared to a fixed-rate loan. The reason is that with an ARM, the lender is protected against the risk that higher inflation will reduce the real loan payments, and so the risk premium part of the interest rate can be correspondingly lower.

A number of ongoing or long-term business contracts also have provisions that prices will adjust automatically according to inflation. Sellers like such contracts because they are not locked into a low nominal selling price if inflation turns out higher than expected. Buyers like such contracts because they are not locked into a high buying price if inflation turns out to be lower than expected. A contract with automatic adjustments for inflation in effect agrees on a real price for the borrower to pay, rather than a nominal price.

Indexing in Government Programs

Many government programs are indexed to inflation. The U.S. income tax code is designed so that as a person's income rises above certain levels, the tax rate on the marginal income earned rises as well. That is what the expression "move into a higher tax bracket" means. For example, according to the basic tax tables from the Internal Revenue Service, in 2017 a single person owed 10% of all taxable income from $0 to $9,325; 15% of all income from $9,326 to $37,950; 25% of all taxable income from $37,951 to $91,900; 28% of all taxable income from $91,901 to $191,650; 33% of all taxable income from $191,651 to $416,700; 35% of all taxable income from $416,701 to $418,400; and 39.6% of all income from $418,401 and above.

Because of the many complex provisions in the rest of the tax code, it is difficult to determine exactly the taxes an individual owes the government based on these numbers, but the numbers illustrate the basic theme that tax rates rise as the marginal dollar of income rises. Until the late 1970s, if nominal wages increased along with inflation, people were moved into higher tax brackets and owed a higher proportion of their income in taxes, even though their real income had not risen. In 1981, the government eliminated this "bracket creep". Now, the income levels where higher tax rates kick in are indexed to rise automatically with inflation.

The Social Security program offers two examples of indexing. Since the passage of the Social Security Indexing Act of 1972, the level of Social Security benefits increases each year along with the Consumer Price Index. Also, Social Security is funded by payroll taxes, which the government imposes on the income earned up to a certain amount—$117,000 in 2014. The government adjusts this level of income upward each year according to the rate of inflation, so that an indexed increase in the Social Security tax base accompanies the indexed rise in the benefit level.

As yet another example of a government program affected by indexing, in 1996 the U.S., government began offering indexed bonds. Bonds are means by which the U.S. government (and many private-sector companies as well) borrows money; that is, investors buy the bonds, and then the government repays the money with interest. Traditionally, government bonds have paid a fixed rate of interest. This policy gave a government that had borrowed an incentive to encourage inflation, because it could then repay its past borrowing in inflated dollars at a lower real interest rate. However, indexed bonds promise to pay a certain real rate of interest above whatever inflation rate occurs. In the case of a retiree trying to plan for the long term and worried about the risk of inflation, for example, indexed bonds that guarantee a rate of return higher than inflation—no matter the level of inflation—can be a very comforting investment.

Might Indexing Reduce Concern over Inflation?

Indexing may seem like an obviously useful step. After all, when individuals, firms, and government programs are indexed against inflation, then people can worry less about arbitrary redistributions and other effects of inflation.

However, some of the fiercest opponents of inflation express grave concern about indexing. They point out that indexing is always partial. Not every employer will provide COLAs for workers. Not all companies can assume that costs and revenues will rise in lockstep with the general rates of inflation. Not all interest rates for borrowers and savers will change to match inflation exactly. However, as partial inflation indexing spreads, the political opposition to inflation may diminish. After all, older people whose Social Security benefits are protected against inflation, or banks that have loaned their money with adjustable-rate loans, no longer have as much reason to care whether inflation heats up. In a world where some people are indexed against inflation and some are not, financially savvy businesses and investors may seek out ways to be protected against inflation, while the financially unsophisticated and small businesses may suffer from it most.

A Preview of Policy Discussions of Inflation

This chapter has focused on how economists measure inflation, historical experience with inflation, how to adjust nominal variables into real ones, how inflation affects the economy, and how indexing works. We have barely hinted at the causes of inflation, and we have not addressed government policies to deal with inflation. We will examine these issues in depth in other chapters. However, it is useful to offer a preview here.

We can sum up the cause of inflation in one phrase: Too many dollars chasing too few goods. The great surges of inflation early in the twentieth century came after wars, which are a time when government spending is very high, but consumers have little to buy, because production is going to the war effort. Governments also commonly impose price controls during wartime. After the war, the price controls end and pent-up buying power surges forth, driving up inflation. Otherwise, if too few dollars are chasing too many goods, then inflation will decline or even turn into deflation. Therefore, we typically associate slowdowns in economic activity, as in major recessions and the Great Depression, with a reduction in inflation or even outright deflation.

The policy implications are clear. If we are to avoid inflation, the amount of purchasing power in the economy must grow at roughly the same rate as the production of goods. Macroeconomic policies that the government can use to affect the amount of purchasing power—through taxes, spending, and regulation of interest rates and credit—can thus cause inflation to rise or reduce inflation to lower levels.

This OpenStax book is available for free at http://cnx.org/content/col12122/1.4

Bring it Home

A $550 Million Loaf of Bread?

As we will learn in **Money and Banking**, the existence of money provides enormous benefits to an economy. In a real sense, money is the lubrication that enhances the workings of markets. Money makes transactions easier. It allows people to find employment producing one product, then use the money earned to purchase the other products they need to live. However, too much money in circulation can lead to inflation. Extreme cases of governments recklessly printing money lead to hyperinflation. Inflation reduces the value of money. Hyperinflation, because money loses value so quickly, ultimately results in people no longer using money. The economy reverts to barter, or it adopts another country's more stable currency, like U.S. dollars. In the meantime, the economy literally falls apart as people leave jobs and fend for themselves because it is not worth the time to work for money that will be worthless in a few days.

Only national governments have the power to cause hyperinflation. Hyperinflation typically happens when government faces extraordinary demands for spending, which it cannot finance by taxes or borrowing. The only option is to print money—more and more of it. With more money in circulation chasing the same amount (or even fewer) goods and services, the only result is increasingly higher prices until the economy and/or the government collapses. This is why economists are generally wary of letting inflation spiral out of control.

KEY TERMS

adjustable-rate mortgage (ARM) a loan a borrower uses to purchase a home in which the interest rate varies with market interest rates

base year arbitrary year whose value as an index number economists define as 100; inflation from the base year to other years can easily be seen by comparing the index number in the other year to the index number in the base year—for example, 100; so, if the index number for a year is 105, then there has been exactly 5% inflation between that year and the base year

basket of goods and services a hypothetical group of different items, with specified quantities of each one meant to represent a "typical" set of consumer purchases, used as a basis for calculating how the price level changes over time

Consumer Price Index (CPI) a measure of inflation that U.S. government statisticians calculate based on the price level from a fixed basket of goods and services that represents the average consumer's purchases

core inflation index a measure of inflation typically calculated by taking the CPI and excluding volatile economic variables such as food and energy prices to better measure the underlying and persistent trend in long-term prices

cost-of-living adjustments (COLAs) a contractual provision that wage increases will keep up with inflation

deflation negative inflation; most prices in the economy are falling

Employment Cost Index a measure of inflation based on wages paid in the labor market

GDP deflator a measure of inflation based on the prices of all the GDP components

hyperinflation an outburst of high inflation that often occurs (although not exclusively) when economies shift from a controlled economy to a market-oriented economy

index number a unit-free number derived from the price level over a number of years, which makes computing inflation rates easier, since the index number has values around 100

indexed a price, wage, or interest rate is adjusted automatically for inflation

inflation a general and ongoing rise in price levels in an economy

International Price Index a measure of inflation based on the prices of merchandise that is exported or imported

Producer Price Index (PPI) a measure of inflation based on prices paid for supplies and inputs by producers of goods and services

quality/new goods bias inflation calculated using a fixed basket of goods over time tends to overstate the true rise in cost of living, because it does not account for improvements in the quality of existing goods or the invention of new goods

substitution bias an inflation rate calculated using a fixed basket of goods over time tends to overstate the true rise in the cost of living, because it does not take into account that the person can substitute away from goods whose prices rise considerably

KEY CONCEPTS AND SUMMARY

22.1 Tracking Inflation

Economists measure the price level by using a basket of goods and services and calculating how the total cost of buying that basket of goods will increase over time. Economists often express the price level in terms of index numbers, which transform the cost of buying the basket of goods and services into a series of numbers in the same proportion to each other, but with an arbitrary base year of 100. We measure the inflation rate as the percentage change between price levels or index numbers over time.

22.2 How to Measure Changes in the Cost of Living

Measuring price levels with a fixed basket of goods will always have two problems: the substitution bias, by which a fixed basket of goods does not allow for buying more of what becomes relatively less expensive and less of what becomes relatively more expensive; and the quality/new goods bias, by which a fixed basket cannot account for improvements in quality and the advent of new goods. These problems can be reduced in degree—for example, by allowing the basket of goods to evolve over time—but we cannot totally eliminate them. The most commonly cited measure of inflation is the Consumer Price Index (CPI), which is based on a basket of goods representing what the typical consumer buys. The Core Inflation Index further breaks down the CPI by excluding volatile economic commodities. Several price indices are not based on baskets of consumer goods. The GDP deflator is based on all GDP components. The Producer Price Index is based on prices of supplies and inputs bought by producers of goods and services. An Employment Cost Index measures wage inflation in the labor market. An International Price Index is based on the prices of merchandise that is exported or imported.

22.3 How the U.S. and Other Countries Experience Inflation

In the U.S. economy, the annual inflation rate in the last two decades has typically been around 2% to 4%. The periods of highest inflation in the United States in the twentieth century occurred during the years after World Wars I and II, and in the 1970s. The period of lowest inflation—actually, with deflation—was the 1930s Great Depression.

22.4 The Confusion Over Inflation

Unexpected inflation will tend to hurt those whose money received, in terms of wages and interest payments, does not rise with inflation. In contrast, inflation can help those who owe money that they can pay in less valuable, inflated dollars. Low rates of inflation have relatively little economic impact over the short term. Over the medium and the long term, even low rates of inflation can complicate future planning. High rates of inflation can muddle price signals in the short term and prevent market forces from operating efficiently, and can vastly complicate long-term savings and investment decisions.

22.5 Indexing and Its Limitations

A payment is indexed if it is automatically adjusted for inflation. Examples of indexing in the private sector include wage contracts with cost-of-living adjustments (COLAs) and loan agreements like adjustable-rate mortgages (ARMs). Examples of indexing in the public sector include tax brackets and Social Security payments.

SELF-CHECK QUESTIONS

1. Table **22.4** shows the fruit prices that the typical college student purchased from 2001 to 2004. What is the amount spent each year on the "basket" of fruit with the quantities shown in column 2?

Items	Qty	(2001) Price	(2001) Amount Spent	(2002) Price	(2002) Amount Spent	(2003) Price	(2003) Amount Spent	(2004) Price	(2004) Amount Spent
Apples	10	$0.50		$0.75		$0.85		$0.88	
Bananas	12	$0.20		$0.25		$0.25		$0.29	
Grapes	2	$0.65		$0.70		$0.90		$0.95	
Raspberries	1	$2.00		$1.90		$2.05		$2.13	$2.13
Total									

Table 22.4

2. Construct the price index for a "fruit basket" in each year using 2003 as the base year.

3. Compute the inflation rate for fruit prices from 2001 to 2004.

4. Edna is living in a retirement home where most of her needs are taken care of, but she has some discretionary spending. Based on the basket of goods in **Table 22.5**, by what percentage does Edna's cost of living increase between time 1 and time 2?

Items	Quantity	(Time 1) Price	(Time 2) Price
Gifts for grandchildren	12	$50	$60
Pizza delivery	24	$15	$16
Blouses	6	$60	$50
Vacation trips	2	$400	$420

Table 22.5

5. **How to Measure Changes in the Cost of Living** introduced a number of different price indices. Which price index would be best to use to adjust your paycheck for inflation?

6. The Consumer Price Index is subject to the substitution bias and the quality/new goods bias. Are the Producer Price Index and the GDP Deflator also subject to these biases? Why or why not?

7. Go to this **website (http://www.measuringworth.com/ppowerus/)** for the Purchasing Power Calculator at MeasuringWorth.com. How much money would it take today to purchase what one dollar would have bought in the year of your birth?

8. If inflation rises unexpectedly by 5%, would a state government that had recently borrowed money to pay for a new highway benefit or lose?

9. How should an increase in inflation affect the interest rate on an adjustable-rate mortgage?

10. A fixed-rate mortgage has the same interest rate over the life of the loan, whether the mortgage is for 15 or 30 years. By contrast, an adjustable-rate mortgage changes with market interest rates over the life of the mortgage. If inflation falls unexpectedly by 3%, what would likely happen to a homeowner with an adjustable-rate mortgage?

REVIEW QUESTIONS

11. How do economists use a basket of goods and services to measure the price level?

12. Why do economists use index numbers to measure the price level rather than dollar value of goods?

13. What is the difference between the price level and the rate of inflation?

14. Why does "substitution bias" arise if we calculate the inflation rate based on a fixed basket of goods?

15. Why does the "quality/new goods bias" arise if we calculate the inflation rate based on a fixed basket of goods?

16. What has been a typical range of inflation in the U.S. economy in the last decade or so?

17. Over the last century, during what periods was the U.S. inflation rate highest and lowest?

18. What is deflation?

19. Identify several parties likely to be helped and hurt by inflation.

20. What is indexing?

21. Name several forms of indexing in the private and public sector.

CRITICAL THINKING QUESTIONS

22. Inflation rates, like most statistics, are imperfect measures. Can you identify some ways that the inflation rate for fruit does not perfectly capture the rising price of fruit?

23. Given the federal budget deficit in recent years, some economists have argued that by adjusting Social Security payments for inflation using the CPI, Social Security is overpaying recipients. What is their argument, and do you agree or disagree with it?

24. Why is the GDP deflator not an accurate measure of inflation as it impacts a household?

25. Imagine that the government statisticians who calculate the inflation rate have been updating the basic basket of goods once every 10 years, but now they decide to update it every five years. How will this change affect the amount of substitution bias and quality/new goods bias?

26. Describe a situation, either a government policy situation, an economic problem, or a private sector situation, where using the CPI to convert from nominal to real would be more appropriate than using the GDP deflator.

27. Describe a situation, either a government policy situation, an economic problem, or a private sector situation, where using the GDP deflator to convert from nominal to real would be more appropriate than using the CPI.

28. Why do you think the U.S. experience with inflation over the last 50 years has been so much milder than in many other countries?

29. If, over time, wages and salaries on average rise at least as fast as inflation, why do people worry about how inflation affects incomes?

30. Who in an economy is the big winner from inflation?

31. If a government gains from unexpected inflation when it borrows, why would it choose to offer indexed bonds?

32. Do you think perfect indexing is possible? Why or why not?

PROBLEMS

33. The index number representing the price level changes from 110 to 115 in one year, and then from 115 to 120 the next year. Since the index number increases by five each year, is five the inflation rate each year? Is the inflation rate the same each year? Explain your answer.

34. The total price of purchasing a basket of goods in the United Kingdom over four years is: year 1=£940, year 2=£970, year 3=£1000, and year 4=£1070. Calculate two price indices, one using year 1 as the base year (set equal to 100) and the other using year 4 as the base year (set equal to 100). Then, calculate the inflation rate based on the first price index. If you had used the other price index, would you get a different inflation rate? If you are unsure, do the calculation and find out.

35. Within 1 or 2 percentage points, what has the U.S. inflation rate been during the last 20 years? Draw a graph to show the data.

36. If inflation rises unexpectedly by 5%, indicate for each of the following whether the economic actor is helped, hurt, or unaffected:
 a. A union member with a COLA wage contract
 b. Someone with a large stash of cash in a safe deposit box
 c. A bank lending money at a fixed rate of interest
 d. A person who is not due to receive a pay raise for another 11 months

37. Rosalie the Retiree knows that when she retires in 16 years, her company will give her a one-time payment of $20,000. However, if the inflation rate is 6% per year, how much buying power will that $20,000 have when measured in today's dollars? *Hint*: Start by calculating the rise in the price level over the 16 years.

23 | The International Trade and Capital Flows

Figure 23.1 A World of Money   We are all part of the global financial system, which includes many different currencies. (Credit: modification of work by epSos.de/Flickr Creative Commons)

Bring it Home

More than Meets the Eye in the Congo

How much do you interact with the global financial system? Do you think not much? Think again. Suppose you take out a student loan, or you deposit money into your bank account. You just affected domestic savings and borrowing. Now say you are at the mall and buy two T-shirts "made in China," and later contribute to a charity that helps refugees. What is the impact? You affected how much money flows into and out of the United States. If you open an IRA savings account and put money in an international mutual fund, you are involved in the flow of money overseas. While your involvement may not seem as influential as that of someone like the president, who can increase or decrease foreign aid and, thereby, have a huge impact on money flows in and out of the country, you do interact with the global financial system on a daily basis.

The balance of payments—a term you will meet soon—seems like a huge topic, but once you learn the specific components of trade and money, it all makes sense. Along the way, you may have to give up some common misunderstandings about trade and answer some questions: If a country is running a trade deficit, is that bad? Is a trade surplus good? For example, look at the Democratic Republic of the Congo (often referred to as "Congo"), a large country in Central Africa. In 2013, it ran a trade surplus of $1 billion, so it must be doing well, right? In contrast, the trade deficit in the United States was $508 billion in 2013. Do these figures suggest that the United States economy is performing worse than the Congolese economy? Not necessarily. The U.S. trade deficit tends to worsen as the economy strengthens. In contrast, high poverty rates in the Congo persist, and these rates are not going down even with the positive trade balance. Clearly, it is more complicated than simply asserting that running a trade deficit is bad for the economy. You will learn more about these issues and others in this chapter.

Introduction to International Trade and Capital Flows

In this chapter, you will learn about:

- Measuring Trade Balances
- Trade Balances in Historical and International Context
- Trade Balances and Flows of Financial Capital
- The National Saving and Investment Identity
- The Pros and Cons of Trade Deficits and Surpluses
- The Difference between Level of Trade and the Trade Balance

The **balance of trade** (or trade balance) is any gap between a nation's dollar value of its exports, or what its producers sell abroad, and a nation's dollar value of imports, or the foreign-made products and services that households and businesses purchase. Recall from **The Macroeconomic Perspective** that if exports exceed imports, the economy has a trade surplus. If imports exceed exports, the economy has a trade deficit. If exports and imports are equal, then trade is balanced, but what happens when trade is out of balance and large trade surpluses or deficits exist?

Germany, for example, has had substantial trade surpluses in recent decades, in which exports have greatly exceeded imports. According to the Central Intelligence Agency's The World Factbook, in 2016, Germany ran a trade surplus of $295 billion. In contrast, the U.S. economy in recent decades has experienced large trade deficits, in which imports have considerably exceeded exports. In 2016, for example, U.S. imports exceeded exports by $502 billion.

A series of financial crises triggered by unbalanced trade can lead economies into deep recessions. These crises begin with large trade deficits. At some point, foreign investors become pessimistic about the economy and move their money to other countries. The economy then drops into deep recession, with real GDP often falling up to 10% or more in a single year. This happened to Mexico in 1995 when their GDP fell 8.1%. A number of countries in East Asia—Thailand, South Korea, Malaysia, and Indonesia—succumbed to the same economic illness in 1997–1998 (called the Asian Financial Crisis). In the late 1990s and into the early 2000s, Russia and Argentina had the identical experience. What are the connections between imbalances of trade in goods and services and the flows of international financial capital that set off these economic avalanches?

We will start by examining the balance of trade in more detail, by looking at some patterns of trade balances in the United States and around the world. Then we will examine the intimate connection between international flows of goods and services and international flows of financial capital, which to economists are really just two sides of the same coin. People often assume that trade surpluses like those in Germany must be a positive sign for an economy, while trade deficits like those in the United States must be harmful. As it turns out, both trade surpluses and deficits can be either good or bad. We will see why in this chapter.

23.1 | Measuring Trade Balances

By the end of this section, you will be able to:

- Explain merchandise trade balance, current account balance, and unilateral transfers
- Identify components of the U.S. current account balance
- Calculate the merchandise trade balance and current account balance using import and export data for a country

A few decades ago, it was common to track the solid or physical items that planes, trains, and trucks transported between countries as a way of measuring the balance of trade. Economists call this measurement is called the

merchandise trade balance. In most high-income economies, including the United States, goods comprise less than half of a country's total production, while services comprise more than half. The last two decades have seen a surge in international trade in services, powered by technological advances in telecommunications and computers that have made it possible to export or import customer services, finance, law, advertising, management consulting, software, construction engineering, and product design. Most global trade still takes the form of goods rather than services, and the government announces and the media prominently report the merchandise trade balance. Old habits are hard to break. Economists, however, typically rely on broader measures such as the balance of trade or the **current account balance** which includes other international flows of income and foreign aid.

Components of the U.S. Current Account Balance

Table 23.1 breaks down the four main components of the U.S. current account balance for the last quarter of 2015 (seasonally adjusted). The first line shows the merchandise trade balance; that is, exports and imports of goods. Because imports exceed exports, the trade balance in the final column is negative, showing a merchandise trade deficit. We can explain how the government collects this trade information in the following Clear It Up feature.

	Value of Exports (money flowing into the United States)	Value of Imports (money flowing out of the United States)	Balance
Goods	$410.0	$595.5	–$185.3
Services	$180.4	$122.3	$58.1
Income receipts and payments	$203.0	$152.4	$50.6
Unilateral transfers	$27.3	$64.4	–$37.1
Current account balance	$820.7	$934.4	–$113.7

Table 23.1 Components of the U.S. Current Account Balance for 2015 (in billions)

How does the U.S. government collect trade statistics?

Do not confuse the balance of trade (which tracks imports and exports), with the current account balance, which includes not just exports and imports, but also income from investment and transfers.

The Bureau of Economic Analysis (BEA) within the U.S. Department of Commerce compiles statistics on the balance of trade using a variety of different sources. Merchandise importers and exporters must file monthly documents with the Census Bureau, which provides the basic data for tracking trade. To measure international trade in services—which can happen over a telephone line or computer network without shipping any physical goods—the BEA carries out a set of surveys. Another set of BEA surveys tracks investment flows, and there are even specific surveys to collect travel information from U.S. residents visiting Canada and Mexico. For measuring unilateral transfers, the BEA has access to official U.S. government spending on aid, and then also carries out a survey of charitable organizations that make foreign donations.

The BEA then cross-checks this information on international flows of goods and capital against other available data. For example, the Census Bureau also collects data from the shipping industry, which it can use to check the data on trade in goods. All companies involved in international flows of capital—including banks and companies making financial investments like stocks—must file reports, which the U.S. Department of the Treasury ultimately checks. The BEA also can cross check information on foreign trade by looking at data collected by other countries on their foreign trade with the United States, and also at the data collected by various international organizations. Take these data sources, stir carefully, and you have the U.S. balance of trade statistics. Much of the statistics that we cite in this chapter come from these sources.

The second row of **Table 23.1** provides data on trade in services. Here, the U.S. economy is running a surplus. Although the level of trade in services is still relatively small compared to trade in goods, the importance of services has expanded substantially over the last few decades. For example, U.S. exports of services were equal to about one-half of U.S. exports of goods in 2015, compared to one-fifth in 1980.

The third component of the current account balance, labeled "income payments," refers to money that U.S. financial investors received on their foreign investments (money flowing into the United States) and payments to foreign investors who had invested their funds here (money flowing out of the United States). The reason for including this money on foreign investment in the overall measure of trade, along with goods and services, is that, from an economic perspective, income is just as much an economic transaction as car, wheat, or oil shipments: it is just trade that is happening in the financial capital market.

The final category of the current account balance is **unilateral transfers**, which are payments that government, private charities, or individuals make in which they send money abroad without receiving any direct good or service. Economic or military assistance from the U.S. government to other countries fits into this category, as does spending abroad by charities to address poverty or social inequalities. When an individual in the United States sends money overseas, as is the case with some immigrants, it is also counted in this category. The current account balance treats these unilateral payments like imports, because they also involve a stream of payments leaving the country. For the U.S. economy, unilateral transfers are almost always negative. This pattern, however, does not always hold. In 1991, for example, when the United States led an international coalition against Saddam Hussein's Iraq in the Gulf War, many other nations agreed that they would make payments to the United States to offset the U.S. war expenses. These payments were large enough that, in 1991, the overall U.S. balance on unilateral transfers was a positive $10 billion.

The following Work It Out feature steps you through the process of using the values for goods, services, and income payments to calculate the merchandise balance and the current account balance.

Work It Out ─○─○─○

Calculating the Merchandise Balance and the Current Account Balance

	Exports (in $ billions)	Imports (in $ billions)	Balance
Goods			
Services			
Income payments			
Unilateral transfers			
Current account balance			

Table 23.2 Calculating Merchandise Balance and Current Account Balance

Use the information given below to fill in **Table 23.2**, and then calculate:

- The merchandise balance
- The current account balance

Known information:

- Unilateral transfers: $130
- Exports in goods: $1,046
- Exports in services: $509
- Imports in goods: $1,562
- Imports in services: $371
- Income received by U.S. investors on foreign stocks and bonds: $561
- Income received by foreign investors on U.S. assets: $472

Step 1. Focus on goods and services first. Enter the dollar amount of exports of both goods and services under the Export column.

Step 2. Enter imports of goods and services under the Import column.

Step 3. Under the Export column and in the row for Income payments, enter the financial flows of money coming back to the United States. U.S. investors are earning this income from abroad.

Step 4. Under the Import column and in the row for Income payments, enter the financial flows of money going out of the United States to foreign investors. Foreign investors are earning this money on U.S. assets, like stocks.

Step 5. Unilateral transfers are money flowing out of the United States in the form of, for example, military aid, foreign aid, and global charities. Because the money leaves the country, enter it under Imports and in the final column as well, as a negative.

Step 6. Calculate the trade balance by subtracting imports from exports in both goods and services. Enter this in the final Balance column. This can be positive or negative.

Step 7. Subtract the income payments flowing out of the country (under Imports) from the money coming back to the United States (under Exports) and enter this amount under the Balance column.

Step 8. Enter unilateral transfers as a negative amount under the Balance column.

Step 9. The merchandise trade balance is the difference between exports of goods and imports of goods—the first number under Balance.

Step 10. Now sum up your columns for Exports, Imports, and Balance. The final balance number is the current account balance.

The merchandise balance of trade is the difference between exports and imports. In this case, it is equal to $1,046 – $1,562, a trade deficit of –$516 billion. The current account balance is –$419 billion. See the completed Table 23.3.

	Value of Exports (money flowing into the United States)	Value of Imports (money flowing out of the United States)	Balance
Goods	$1,510.3	$2,272.9	–$762.6
Services	$750.9	$488.7	$262.2
Income receipts and payments	$782.9	$600.5	$182.4
Unilateral transfers	$128.6	$273.6	–$145.0

	Value of Exports (money flowing into the United States)	Value of Imports (money flowing out of the United States)	Balance
Current account balance	$3,172.7	$3,635.7	−$463.0

Table 23.3 Completed Merchandise Balance and Current Account Balance

23.2 | Trade Balances in Historical and International Context

By the end of this section, you will be able to:
- Analyze graphs of the current account balance and the merchandise trade balance
- Identify patterns in U.S. trade surpluses and deficits
- Compare the U.S. trade surpluses and deficits to other countries' trade surpluses and deficits

We present the history of the U.S. current account balance in recent decades in several different ways. **Figure 23.2** (a) shows the current account balance and the merchandise trade balance in dollar terms. **Figure 23.2** (b) shows the current account balance and merchandise account balance yet again, this time as a share of the GDP for that year. By dividing the trade deficit in each year by GDP in that year, **Figure 23.2** (b) factors out both inflation and growth in the real economy.

This OpenStax book is available for free at http://cnx.org/content/col12122/1.4

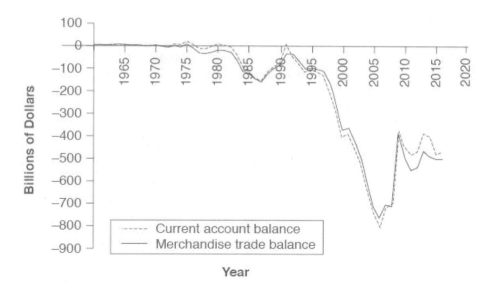

(a) The current account and merchandise trade balance in nominal dollars

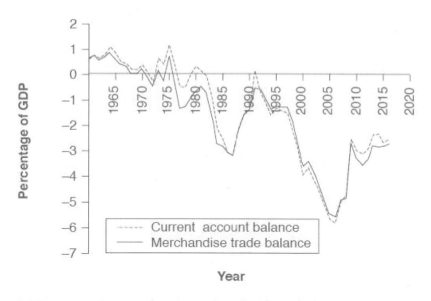

(b) The current account and merchandise trade balance as a percentage of GDP

Figure 23.2 Current Account Balance and Merchandise Trade Balance, 1960–2015 (a) The current account balance and the merchandise trade balance in billions of dollars from 1960 to 2015. If the lines are above zero dollars, the United States was running a positive trade balance and current account balance. If the lines fall below zero dollars, the United States is running a trade deficit and a deficit in its current account balance. (b) This shows the same items—trade balance and current account balance—in relationship to the size of the U.S. economy, or GDP, from 1960 to 2015.

By either measure, the U.S. balance of trade pattern is clear. From the 1960s into the 1970s, the U.S. economy had mostly small trade surpluses—that is, the graphs in **Figure 23.2** show positive numbers. However, starting in the 1980s, the trade deficit increased rapidly, and after a tiny surplus in 1991, the current account trade deficit became even larger in the late 1990s and into the mid-2000s. However, the trade deficit declined in 2009 after the recession had taken hold, then rebounded partially in 2010 and has remained stable up through 2016.

Table 23.4 shows the U.S. trade picture in 2013 compared with some other economies from around the world. While the U.S. economy has consistently run trade deficits in recent years, Japan and many European nations, among them France and Germany, have consistently run trade surpluses. Some of the other countries listed include Brazil, the largest economy in Latin America; Nigeria, along with South Africa competing to be the largest economy in Africa; and China, India, and Korea. The first column offers one measure of an economy's globalization: **exports of goods and services as a percentage of GDP**. The second column shows the trade balance. Usually, most countries have trade surpluses or deficits that are less than 5% of GDP. As you can see, the U.S. current account balance is –2.6% of GDP, while Germany's is 8.4% of GDP.

	Exports of Goods and Services	**Current Account Balance**
United States	17.6%	–2.6%
Japan	16.2%	3.1%
Germany	46.8%	8.4%
United Kingdom	27.2%	–5.4%
Canada	31.5%	–3.2%
Sweden	45.6%	5.2%
Korea	45.9%	7.7%
Mexico	35.4%	–2.9%
Brazil	13.0%	–3.3%
China	22.1%	3.0%
India	19.9%	–1.1%
Nigeria	10.7%	-3.3%
World	-	0.0%

Table 23.4 Level and Balance of Trade in 2015 (figures as a percentage of GDP, Source: http://data.worldbank.org/indicator/BN.CAB.XOKA.GD.ZS)

23.3 | Trade Balances and Flows of Financial Capital

By the end of this section, you will be able to:
- Explain the connection between trade balances and financial capital flows
- Calculate comparative advantage
- Explain balanced trade in terms of investment and capital flows

As economists see it, trade surpluses can be either good or bad, depending on circumstances, and trade deficits can be good or bad, too. The challenge is to understand how the international flows of goods and services are connected with international flows of **financial capital**. In this module we will illustrate the intimate connection between trade balances and flows of financial capital in two ways: a parable of trade between Robinson Crusoe and Friday, and a circular flow diagram representing flows of trade and payments.

A Two-Person Economy: Robinson Crusoe and Friday

To understand how economists view trade deficits and surpluses, consider a parable based on the story of Robinson Crusoe. Crusoe, as you may remember from the classic novel by Daniel Defoe first published in 1719, was

This OpenStax book is available for free at http://cnx.org/content/col12122/1.4

shipwrecked on a desert island. After living alone for some time, he is joined by a second person, whom he names Friday. Think about the balance of trade in a two-person economy like that of Robinson and Friday.

Robinson and Friday trade goods and services. Perhaps Robinson catches fish and trades them to Friday for coconuts, or Friday weaves a hat out of tree fronds and trades it to Robinson for help in carrying water. For a period of time, each individual trade is self-contained and complete. Because each trade is voluntary, both Robinson and Friday must feel that they are receiving fair value for what they are giving. As a result, each person's exports are always equal to his imports, and trade is always in balance between the two. Neither person experiences either a trade deficit or a trade surplus.

However, one day Robinson approaches Friday with a proposition. Robinson wants to dig ditches for an irrigation system for his garden, but he knows that if he starts this project, he will not have much time left to fish and gather coconuts to feed himself each day. He proposes that Friday supply him with a certain number of fish and coconuts for several months, and then after that time, he promises to repay Friday out of the extra produce that he will be able to grow in his irrigated garden. If Friday accepts this offer, then a trade imbalance comes into being. For several months, Friday will have a trade surplus: that is, he is exporting to Robinson more than he is importing. More precisely, he is giving Robinson fish and coconuts, and at least for the moment, he is receiving nothing in return. Conversely, Robinson will have a trade deficit, because he is importing more from Friday than he is exporting.

This parable raises several useful issues in thinking about what a trade deficit and a trade surplus really mean in economic terms. The first issue that this story of Robinson and Friday raises is this: Is it better to have a trade surplus or a trade deficit? The answer, as in any voluntary market interaction, is that if both parties agree to the transaction, then they may both be better off. Over time, if Robinson's irrigated garden is a success, it is certainly possible that both Robinson and Friday can benefit from this agreement.

The parable raises a second issue: What can go wrong? Robinson's proposal to Friday introduces an element of uncertainty. Friday is, in effect, making a loan of fish and coconuts to Robinson, and Friday's happiness with this arrangement will depend on whether Robinson repays that loan as planned, in full and on time. Perhaps Robinson spends several months loafing and never builds the irrigation system, or perhaps Robinson has been too optimistic about how much he will be able to grow with the new irrigation system, which turns out not to be very productive. Perhaps, after building the irrigation system, Robinson decides that he does not want to repay Friday as much as he previously agreed. Any of these developments will prompt a new round of negotiations between Friday and Robinson. Why the repayment failed is likely to shape Friday's attitude toward these renegotiations. If Robinson worked very hard and the irrigation system just did not increase production as intended, Friday may have some sympathy. If Robinson loafed or if he just refuses to pay, Friday may become irritated.

A third issue that the parable raises is that an intimate relationship exists between a trade deficit and international borrowing, and between a trade surplus and international lending. The size of Friday's trade surplus is exactly how much he is lending to Robinson. The size of Robinson's trade deficit is exactly how much he is borrowing from Friday. To economists, a trade surplus literally means the same thing as an outflow of financial capital, and a trade deficit literally means the same thing as an inflow of financial capital. This last insight is worth exploring in greater detail, which we will do in the following section.

The story of Robinson and Friday also provides a good opportunity to consider the law of comparative advantage, which you learn more about in the **International Trade** chapter. The following Work It Out feature steps you through calculating comparative advantage for the wheat and cloth traded between the United States and Great Britain in the 1800s.

Work It Out ⊢O─O─O

Calculating Comparative Advantage

In the 1800s, the United States and Britain traded wheat and cloth. **Table 23.5** shows the varying hours of labor per unit of output.

	Wheat (in bushels)	Cloth (in yards)	Relative labor cost of wheat (Pw/Pc)	Relative labor cost of cloth (Pc/Pw)
United States	8	9	8/9	9/8
Britain	4	3	4/3	3/4

Table 23.5

Step 1. Observe from Table 23.5 that, in the United States, it takes eight hours to supply a bushel of wheat and nine hours to supply a yard of cloth. In contrast, it takes four hours to supply a bushel of wheat and three hours to supply a yard of cloth in Britain.

Step 2. Recognize the difference between absolute advantage and comparative advantage. Britain has an absolute advantage (lowest cost) in each good, since it takes a lower amount of labor to make each good in Britain. Britain also has a comparative advantage in the production of cloth (lower opportunity cost in cloth (3/4 versus 9/8)). The United States has a comparative advantage in wheat production (lower opportunity cost of 8/9 versus 4/3).

Step 3. Determine the relative price of one good in terms of the other good. The price of wheat, in this example, is the amount of cloth you have to give up. To find this price, convert the hours per unit of wheat and cloth into units per hour. To do so, observe that in the United States it takes eight hours to make a bushel of wheat, so workers can process 1/8 of a bushel of wheat in an hour. It takes nine hours to make a yard of cloth in the United States, so workers can produce 1/9 of a yard of cloth in an hour. If you divide the amount of cloth (1/9 of a yard) by the amount of wheat you give up (1/8 of a bushel) in an hour, you find the price (8/9) of one good (wheat) in terms of the other (cloth).

The Balance of Trade as the Balance of Payments

The connection between trade balances and international flows of financial capital is so close that economists sometimes describe the balance of trade as the balance of payments. Each category of the current account balance involves a corresponding flow of payments between a given country and the rest of the world economy.

Figure 23.3 shows the flow of goods and services and payments between one country—the United States in this example—and the rest of the world. The top line shows U.S. exports of goods and services, while the second line shows financial payments from purchasers in other countries back to the U.S. economy. The third line then shows U.S. imports of goods, services, and investment, and the fourth line shows payments from the home economy to the rest of the world. Flow of goods and services (lines one and three) show up in the current account, while we find flow of funds (lines two and four) in the financial account.

The bottom four lines in Figure 23.3 show the flows of investment income. In the first of the bottom lines, we see investments made abroad with funds flowing from the home country to the rest of the world. Investment income stemming from an investment abroad then runs in the other direction from the rest of the world to the home country. Similarly, we see on the bottom third line, an investment from the rest of the world into the home country and investment income (bottom fourth line) flowing from the home country to the rest of the world. We find the investment income (bottom lines two and four) in the current account, while investment to the rest of the world or into the home country (lines one and three) is in the financial account. This figure does not show unilateral transfers, the fourth item in the current account.

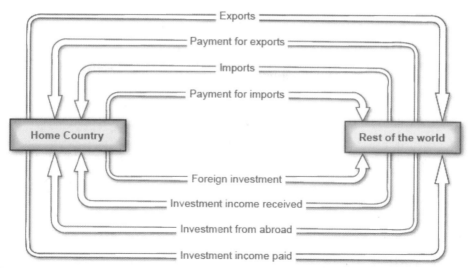

Figure 23.3 Flow of Investment Goods and Capital   Each element of the current account balance involves a flow of financial payments between countries. The top line shows exports of goods and services leaving the home country; the second line shows the money that the home country receives for those exports. The third line shows imports that the home country receives; the fourth line shows the payments that the home country sent abroad in exchange for these imports.

A current account deficit means that, the country is a net borrower from abroad. Conversely, a positive current account balance means a country is a net lender to the rest of the world. Just like the parable of Robinson and Friday, the lesson is that a trade surplus means an overall outflow of financial investment capital, as domestic investors put their funds abroad, while a deficit in the current account balance is exactly equal to the overall or net inflow of foreign investment capital from abroad.

It is important to recognize that an inflow and outflow of foreign capital does not necessarily refer to a debt that governments owe to other governments, although government debt may be part of the picture. Instead, these international flows of financial capital refer to all of the ways in which private investors in one country may invest in another country—by buying real estate, companies, and financial investments like stocks and bonds.

23.4 | The National Saving and Investment Identity

By the end of this section, you will be able to:
- Explain the determinants of trade and current account balance
- Identify and calculate supply and demand for financial capital
- Explain how a nation's own level of domestic saving and investment determines a nation's balance of trade
- Predict the rising and falling of trade deficits based on a nation's saving and investment identity

The close connection between trade balances and international flows of savings and investments leads to a macroeconomic analysis. This approach views trade balances—and their associated flows of financial capital—in the context of the overall levels of savings and financial investment in the economy.

Understanding the Determinants of the Trade and Current Account Balance

The **national saving and investment identity** provides a useful way to understand the determinants of the trade and current account balance. In a nation's financial capital market, the quantity of financial capital supplied at any given time must equal the quantity of financial capital demanded for purposes of making investments. What is on the supply and demand sides of financial capital? See the following Clear It Up feature for the answer to this question.

What comprises the supply and demand of financial capital?

A country's national savings is the total of its domestic savings by household and companies (private savings) as well as the government (public savings). If a country is running a trade deficit, it means money from abroad is entering the country and the government considers it part of the supply of financial capital.

The demand for financial capital (money) represents groups that are borrowing the money. Businesses need to borrow to finance their investments in factories, materials, and personnel. When the federal government runs a budget deficit, it is also borrowing money from investors by selling Treasury bonds. Therefore, both business investment and the federal government can demand (or borrow) the supply of savings.

There are two main sources for the supply of financial capital in the U.S. economy: saving by individuals and firms, called S, and the inflow of financial capital from foreign investors, which is equal to the trade deficit (M − X), or imports minus exports. There are also two main sources of demand for financial capital in the U.S. economy: private sector investment, I, and government borrowing, where the government needs to borrow when government spending, G, is higher than the taxes collected, T. We can express this national savings and investment identity in algebraic terms:

$$\text{Supply of financial capital} = \text{Demand for financial capital}$$
$$S + (M - X) = I + (G - T)$$

Again, in this equation, S is private savings, T is taxes, G is government spending, M is imports, X is exports, and I is investment. This relationship is true as a matter of definition because, for the macro economy, the quantity supplied of financial capital must be equal to the quantity demanded.

However, certain components of the national savings and investment identity can switch between the supply side and the demand side. Some countries, like the United States in most years since the 1970s, have budget deficits, which mean the government is spending more than it collects in taxes, and so the government needs to borrow funds. In this case, the government term would be G − T > 0, showing that spending is larger than taxes, and the government would be a demander of financial capital on the left-hand side of the equation (that is, a borrower), not a supplier of financial capital on the right-hand side. However, if the government runs a budget surplus so that the taxes exceed spending, as the U.S. government did from 1998 to 2001, then the government in that year was contributing to the supply of financial capital (T − G > 0), and would appear on the left (saving) side of the national savings and investment identity.

Similarly, if a national economy runs a trade surplus, the trade sector will involve an outflow of financial capital to other countries. A trade surplus means that the domestic financial capital is in surplus within a country and can be invested in other countries.

The fundamental notion that total quantity of financial capital demanded equals total quantity of financial capital supplied must always remain true. Domestic savings will always appear as part of the supply of financial capital and domestic investment will always appear as part of the demand for financial capital. However, the government and trade balance elements of the equation can move back and forth as either suppliers or demanders of financial capital, depending on whether government budgets and the trade balance are in surplus or deficit.

Domestic Saving and Investment Determine the Trade Balance

One insight from the national saving and investment identity is that a nation's own levels of domestic saving and investment determine a nation's balance of trade. To understand this point, rearrange the identity to put the balance of trade all by itself on one side of the equation. Consider first the situation with a trade deficit, and then the situation with a trade surplus.

In the case of a trade deficit, the national saving and investment identity can be rewritten as:

$$\text{Trade deficit} = \text{Domestic investment} - \text{Private domestic saving} - \text{Government (or public) savings}$$
$$(M - X) = I - S - (T - G)$$

In this case, domestic investment is higher than domestic saving, including both private and government saving. The only way that domestic investment can exceed domestic saving is if capital is flowing into a country from abroad. After all, that extra financial capital for investment has to come from someplace.

Now consider a trade *surplus* from the standpoint of the national saving and investment identity:

$$\text{Trade surplus} = \text{Private domestic saving} + \text{Public saving} - \text{Domestic investment}$$
$$(X - M) = S + (T - G) - I$$

In this case, domestic savings (both private and public) is higher than domestic investment. That extra financial capital will be invested abroad.

This connection of domestic saving and investment to the trade balance explains why economists view the balance of trade as a fundamentally macroeconomic phenomenon. As the national saving and investment identity shows, the performance of certain sectors of an economy, like cars or steel, do not determine the trade balance. Further, whether the nation's trade laws and regulations encourage free trade or protectionism also does not determine the trade balance (see **Globalization and Protectionism**).

Exploring Trade Balances One Factor at a Time

The national saving and investment identity also provides a framework for thinking about what will cause trade deficits to rise or fall. Begin with the version of the identity that has domestic savings and investment on the left and the trade deficit on the right:

$$\text{Domestic investment} - \text{Private domestic savings} - \text{Public domestic savings} = \text{Trade deficit}$$
$$I - S - (T - G) = (M - X)$$

Now, consider the factors on the left-hand side of the equation one at a time, while holding the other factors constant.

As a first example, assume that the level of domestic investment in a country rises, while the level of private and public saving remains unchanged. **Table 23.6** shows the result in the first row under the equation. Since the equality of the national savings and investment identity must continue to hold—it is, after all, an identity that must be true by definition—the rise in domestic investment will mean a higher trade deficit. This situation occurred in the U.S. economy in the late 1990s. Because of the surge of new information and communications technologies that became available, business investment increased substantially. A fall in private saving during this time and a rise in government saving more or less offset each other. As a result, the financial capital to fund that business investment came from abroad, which is one reason for the very high U.S. trade deficits of the late 1990s and early 2000s.

Domestic Investment	−	Private Domestic Savings	−	Public Domestic Savings	=	Trade Deficit
I	−	S	−	(T – G)	=	(M – X)
Up		No change		No change		Then M – X must rise
No change		Up		No change		Then M – X must fall
No change		No change		Down		Then M – X must rise

Table 23.6 Causes of a Changing Trade Balance

As a second scenario, assume that the level of domestic savings rises, while the level of domestic investment and public savings remain unchanged. In this case, the trade deficit would decline. As domestic savings rises, there would be less need for foreign financial capital to meet investment needs. For this reason, a policy proposal often made for reducing the U.S. trade deficit is to increase private saving—although exactly how to increase the overall rate of saving has proven controversial.

As a third scenario, imagine that the government budget deficit increased dramatically, while domestic investment and private savings remained unchanged. This scenario occurred in the U.S. economy in the mid-1980s. The federal budget deficit increased from $79 billion in 1981 to $221 billion in 1986—an increase in the demand for financial capital of $142 billion. The current account balance collapsed from a surplus of $5 billion in 1981 to a deficit of $147 billion in 1986—an increase in the supply of financial capital from abroad of $152 billion. The connection at that time is clear: a sharp increase in government borrowing increased the U.S. economy's demand for financial capital, and foreign investors through the trade deficit primarily supplied that increase. The following Work It Out feature walks you through a scenario in which private domestic savings has to rise by a certain amount to reduce a trade deficit.

Work It Out ⊢O⊣O⊣O

Solving Problems with the Saving and Investment Identity

Use the saving and investment identity to answer the following question: Country A has a trade deficit of $200 billion, private domestic savings of $500 billion, a government deficit of $200 billion, and private domestic investment of $500 billion. To reduce the $200 billion trade deficit by $100 billion, by how much does private domestic savings have to increase?

Step 1. Write out the savings investment formula solving for the trade deficit or surplus on the left:

$$(X - M) \ = \ S + (T - G) - I$$

Step 2. In the formula, put the amount for the trade deficit in as a negative number (X – M). The left side of your formula is now:

$$-200 \ = \ S + (T - G) - I$$

Step 3. Enter the private domestic savings (S) of $500 in the formula:

$$-200 \ = \ 500 + (T - G) - I$$

Step 4. Enter the private domestic investment (I) of $500 into the formula:

$$-200 \ = \ 500 + (T - G) - 500$$

Step 5. The government budget surplus or balance is represented by (T – G). Enter a budget deficit amount for (T – G) of –200:

$$-200 \ = \ 500 + (-200) - 500$$

Step 6. Your formula now is:

$$(X - M) \ = \ S + (T - G) - I$$
$$-200 \ = \ 500 + (-200) - 500$$

The question is: To reduce your trade deficit (X – M) of –200 to –100 (in billions of dollars), by how much will savings have to rise?

$$(X - M) \ = \ S + (T - G) - I$$
$$-100 \ = \ S + (-200) - 500$$
$$600 \ = \ S$$

Step 7. Summarize the answer: Private domestic savings needs to rise by $100 billion, to a total of $600 billion, for the two sides of the equation to remain equal (–100 = –100).

Short-Term Movements in the Business Cycle and the Trade Balance

In the short run, whether an economy is in a recession or on the upswing can affect trade imbalances. A recession tends to make a trade deficit smaller, or a trade surplus larger, while a period of strong economic growth tends to make a trade deficit larger, or a trade surplus smaller.

As an example, note in **Figure 23.2** that the U.S. trade deficit declined by almost half from 2006 to 2009. One primary reason for this change is that during the recession, as the U.S. economy slowed down, it purchased fewer of all goods, including fewer imports from abroad. However, buying power abroad fell less, and so U.S. exports did not

This OpenStax book is available for free at http://cnx.org/content/col12122/1.4

fall by as much.

Conversely, in the mid-2000s, when the U.S. trade deficit became very large, a contributing short-term reason is that the U.S. economy was growing. As a result, there was considerable aggressive buying in the U.S. economy, including the buying of imports. Thus, a trade deficit (or a much lower trade surplus) often accompanies a rapidly growing domestic economy, while a trade surplus (or a much lower trade deficit) accompanies a slowing or recessionary domestic economy.

When the trade deficit rises, it necessarily means a greater net inflow of foreign financial capital. The national saving and investment identity teaches that the rest of the economy can absorb this inflow of foreign financial capital in several different ways. For example, reduced private savings could offset the additional inflow of financial capital from abroad, leaving domestic investment and public saving unchanged. Alternatively, the inflow of foreign financial capital could result in higher domestic investment, leaving private and public saving unchanged. Yet another possibility is that greater government borrowing could absorb the inflow of foreign financial capital, leaving domestic saving and investment unchanged. The national saving and investment identity does not specify which of these scenarios, alone or in combination, will occur—only that one of them must occur.

23.5 | The Pros and Cons of Trade Deficits and Surpluses

By the end of this section, you will be able to:
- Identify three ways in which borrowing money or running a trade deficit can result in a healthy economy
- Identify three ways in which borrowing money or running a trade deficit can result in a weaker economy

Because flows of trade always involve flows of financial payments, flows of international trade are actually the same as flows of international financial capital. The question of whether trade deficits or surpluses are good or bad for an economy is, in economic terms, exactly the same question as whether it is a good idea for an economy to rely on net inflows of financial capital from abroad or to make net investments of financial capital abroad. Conventional wisdom often holds that borrowing money is foolhardy, and that a prudent country, like a prudent person, should always rely on its own resources. While it is certainly possible to borrow too much—as anyone with an overloaded credit card can testify—borrowing at certain times can also make sound economic sense. For both individuals and countries, there is no economic merit in a policy of abstaining from participation in financial capital markets.

It makes economic sense to borrow when you are buying something with a long-run payoff; that is, when you are making an investment. For this reason, it can make economic sense to borrow for a college education, because the education will typically allow you to earn higher wages, and so to repay the loan and still come out ahead. It can also make sense for a business to borrow in order to purchase a machine that will last 10 years, as long as the machine will increase output and profits by more than enough to repay the loan. Similarly, it can make economic sense for a national economy to borrow from abroad, as long as it wisely invests the money in ways that will tend to raise the nation's economic growth over time. Then, it will be possible for the national economy to repay the borrowed money over time and still end up better off than before.

One vivid example of a country that borrowed heavily from abroad, invested wisely, and did perfectly well is the United States during the nineteenth century. The United States ran a trade deficit in 40 of the 45 years from 1831 to 1875, which meant that it was importing capital from abroad over that time. However, that financial capital was mostly invested in projects like railroads that brought a substantial economic payoff. (See the following Clear It Up feature for more on this.)

A more recent example along these lines is the experience of South Korea, which had trade deficits during much of the 1970s—and so was an importer of capital over that time. However, South Korea also had high rates of investment in physical plant and equipment, and its economy grew rapidly. From the mid-1980s into the mid-1990s, South Korea often had trade surpluses—that is, it was repaying its past borrowing by sending capital abroad.

In contrast, some countries have run large trade deficits, borrowed heavily in global capital markets, and ended up in all kinds of trouble. Two specific sorts of trouble are worth examining. First, a borrower nation can find itself in a bind if it does not invest the incoming funds from abroad in a way that leads to increased productivity. Several of

Latin America's large economies, including Mexico and Brazil, ran large trade deficits and borrowed heavily from abroad in the 1970s, but the inflow of financial capital did not boost productivity sufficiently, which meant that these countries faced enormous troubles repaying the money borrowed when economic conditions shifted during the 1980s. Similarly, it appears that a number of African nations that borrowed foreign funds in the 1970s and 1980s did not invest in productive economic assets. As a result, several of those countries later faced large interest payments, with no economic growth to show for the borrowed funds.

Clear It Up

Are trade deficits always harmful?

For most years of the nineteenth century, U.S. imports exceeded exports and the U.S. economy had a trade deficit. Yet the string of trade deficits did not hold back the economy at all. Instead, the trade deficits contributed to the strong economic growth that gave the U.S. economy the highest per capita GDP in the world by around 1900.

The U.S. trade deficits meant that the U.S. economy was receiving a net inflow of foreign capital from abroad. Much of that foreign capital flowed into two areas of investment—railroads and public infrastructure like roads, water systems, and schools—which were important to helping the U.S. economy grow.

We should not overstate the effect of foreign investment capital on U.S. economic growth. In most years the foreign financial capital represented no more than 6–10% of the funds that the government used for overall physical investment in the economy. Nonetheless, the trade deficit and the accompanying investment funds from abroad were clearly a help, not a hindrance, to the U.S. economy in the nineteenth century.

A second "trouble" is: What happens if the foreign money flows in, and then suddenly flows out again? We raised this scenario at the start of the chapter. In the mid-1990s, a number of countries in East Asia—Thailand, Indonesia, Malaysia, and South Korea—ran large trade deficits and imported capital from abroad. However, in 1997 and 1998 many foreign investors became concerned about the health of these economies, and quickly pulled their money out of stock and bond markets, real estate, and banks. The extremely rapid departure of that foreign capital staggered the banking systems and economies of these countries, plunging them into deep recession. We investigate and discuss the links between international capital flows, banks, and recession in **The Impacts of Government Borrowing**.

While a trade deficit is not always harmful, there is no guarantee that running a trade surplus will bring robust economic health. For example, Germany and Japan ran substantial trade surpluses for most of the last three decades. Regardless of their persistent trade surpluses, both countries have experienced occasional recessions and neither country has had especially robust annual growth in recent years. Read more about Japan's trade surplus in the next Clear It Up feature.

Link It Up

Watch this video (http://openstaxcollege.org/l/tradedeficit) on whether or not trade deficit is good for the economy.

The sheer size and persistence of the U.S. trade deficits and inflows of foreign capital since the 1980s are a legitimate cause for concern. The huge U.S. economy will not be destabilized by an outflow of international capital as easily as, say, the comparatively tiny economies of Thailand and Indonesia were in 1997–1998. Even an economy that is not knocked down, however, can still be shaken. American policymakers should certainly be paying attention to those cases where a pattern of extensive and sustained current account deficits and foreign borrowing has gone badly—if only as a cautionary tale.

Are trade surpluses always beneficial? Considering Japan since the 1990s.

Perhaps no economy around the world is better known for its trade surpluses than Japan. Since 1990, the size of these surpluses has often been near $100 billion per year. When Japan's economy was growing vigorously in the 1960s and 1970s, many, especially non-economists, described its large trade surpluses either a cause or a result of its robust economic health. However, from a standpoint of economic growth, Japan's economy has been teetering in and out of recession since 1990, with real GDP growth averaging only about 1% per year, and an unemployment rate that has been creeping higher. Clearly, a whopping trade surplus is no guarantee of economic good health.

Instead, Japan's trade surplus reflects that Japan has a very high rate of domestic savings, more than the Japanese economy can invest domestically, and so it invests the extra funds abroad. In Japan's slow economy, consumption of imports is relatively low, and the growth of consumption is relatively slow. Thus, Japan's exports continually exceed its imports, leaving the trade surplus continually high. Recently, Japan's trade surpluses began to deteriorate. In 2013, Japan ran a trade deficit due to the high cost of imported oil. By 2015, Japan again had a surplus.

23.6 | The Difference between Level of Trade and the Trade Balance

By the end of this section, you will be able to:
- Identify three factors that influence a country's level of trade
- Differentiate between balance of trade and level of trade

A nation's *level* of trade may at first sound like much the same issue as the *balance* of trade, but these two are actually quite separate. It is perfectly possible for a country to have a very high level of trade—measured by its exports of goods and services as a share of its GDP—while it also has a near-balance between exports and imports. A high level of trade indicates that the nation exports a good portion of its production. It is also possible for a country's trade to be a relatively low share of GDP, relative to global averages, but for the imbalance between its exports and its imports to be quite large. We emphasized this general theme earlier in **Measuring Trade Balances**, which offered some illustrative figures on trade levels and balances.

A country's level of trade tells how much of its production it exports. We measure this by the percent of exports out of GDP. It indicates the degree of an economy's globalization. Some countries, such as Germany, have a high level of trade—they export almost 50% of their total production. The balance of trade tells us if the country is running a trade surplus or trade deficit. A country can have a low level of trade but a high trade deficit. (For example, the United States only exports 13% of GDP, but it has a trade deficit of over $500 billion.)

Three factors strongly influence a nation's level of trade: the size of its economy, its geographic location, and its history of trade. Large economies like the United States can do much of their trading internally, while small economies like Sweden have less ability to provide what they want internally and tend to have higher ratios of exports and imports to GDP. Nations that are neighbors tend to trade more, since costs of transportation and communication are lower. Moreover, some nations have long and established patterns of international trade, while others do not.

Consequently, a relatively small economy like Sweden, with many nearby trading partners across Europe and a long history of foreign trade, has a high level of trade. Brazil and India, which are fairly large economies that have often sought to inhibit trade in recent decades, have lower levels of trade; whereas, the United States and Japan are extremely large economies that have comparatively few nearby trading partners. Both countries actually have quite low levels of trade by world standards. The ratio of exports to GDP in either the United States or in Japan is about half of the world average.

The balance of trade is a separate issue from the level of trade. The United States has a low level of trade, but had enormous trade deficits for most years from the mid-1980s into the 2000s. Japan has a low level of trade by world standards, but has typically shown large trade surpluses in recent decades. Nations like Germany and the United Kingdom have medium to high levels of trade by world standards, but Germany had a moderate trade surplus in 2015, while the United Kingdom had a moderate trade deficit. Their trade picture was roughly in balance in the late 1990s. Sweden had a high level of trade and a moderate trade surplus in 2015, while Mexico had a high level of trade and a moderate trade deficit that same year.

In short, it is quite possible for nations with a relatively low level of trade, expressed as a percentage of GDP, to have relatively large trade deficits. It is also quite possible for nations with a near balance between exports and imports to worry about the consequences of high levels of trade for the economy. It is not inconsistent to believe that a high level of trade is potentially beneficial to an economy, because of the way it allows nations to play to their comparative advantages, and to also be concerned about any macroeconomic instability caused by a long-term pattern of large trade deficits. The following Clear It Up feature discusses how this sort of dynamic played out in Colonial India.

Are trade surpluses always beneficial? Considering Colonial India.

India was formally under British rule from 1858 to 1947. During that time, India consistently had trade surpluses with Great Britain. Anyone who believes that trade surpluses are a sign of economic strength and dominance while trade deficits are a sign of economic weakness must find this pattern odd, since it would mean that colonial India was successfully dominating and exploiting Great Britain for almost a century—which was not true.

Instead, India's trade surpluses with Great Britain meant that each year there was an overall flow of financial capital from India to Great Britain. In India, many heavily criticized this financial capital flow as the "drain," and they viewed eliminating the financial capital drain as one of the many reasons why India would benefit from achieving independence.

Final Thoughts about Trade Balances

Trade deficits can be a good or a bad sign for an economy, and trade surpluses can be a good or a bad sign. Even a trade balance of zero—which just means that a nation is neither a net borrower nor lender in the international economy—can be either a good or bad sign. The fundamental economic question is not whether a nation's economy is borrowing or lending at all, but whether the particular borrowing or lending in the particular economic conditions of that country makes sense.

It is interesting to reflect on how public attitudes toward trade deficits and surpluses might change if we could somehow change the labels that people and the news media affix to them. If we called a trade deficit "attracting foreign financial capital"—which accurately describes what a trade deficit means—then trade deficits might look more attractive. Conversely, if we called a trade surplus "shipping financial capital abroad"—which accurately captures what a trade surplus does—then trade surpluses might look less attractive. Either way, the key to understanding trade balances is to understand the relationships between flows of trade and flows of international payments, and what these relationships imply about the causes, benefits, and risks of different kinds of trade balances. The first step along this journey of understanding is to move beyond knee-jerk reactions to terms like "trade surplus,"

This OpenStax book is available for free at http://cnx.org/content/col12122/1.4

"trade balance," and "trade deficit."

Bring it Home

More than Meets the Eye in the Congo

Now that you see the big picture, you undoubtedly realize that all of the economic choices you make, such as depositing savings or investing in an international mutual fund, do influence the flow of goods and services as well as the flows of money around the world.

You now know that a trade surplus does not necessarily tell us whether an economy is performing well or not. The Democratic Republic of the Congo ran a trade surplus in 2013, as we learned in the beginning of the chapter. Yet its current account balance was –$2.8 billion. However, the return of political stability and the rebuilding in the aftermath of the civil war there has meant a flow of investment and financial capital into the country. In this case, a negative current account balance means the country is being rebuilt—and that is a good thing.

KEY TERMS

balance of trade (trade balance) the gap, if any, between a nation's exports and imports

current account balance a broad measure of the balance of trade that includes trade in goods and services, as well as international flows of income and foreign aid

exports of goods and services as a percentage of GDP the dollar value of exports divided by the dollar value of a country's GDP

financial capital the international flows of money that facilitates trade and investment

merchandise trade balance the balance of trade looking only at goods

national savings and investment identity the total of private savings and public savings (a government budget surplus)

unilateral transfers "one-way payments" that governments, private entities, or individuals make that they sent abroad with nothing received in return

KEY CONCEPTS AND SUMMARY

23.1 Measuring Trade Balances
The trade balance measures the gap between a country's exports and its imports. In most high-income economies, goods comprise less than half of a country's total production, while services comprise more than half. The last two decades have seen a surge in international trade in services; however, most global trade still takes the form of goods rather than services. The current account balance includes the trade in goods, services, and money flowing into and out of a country from investments and unilateral transfers.

23.2 Trade Balances in Historical and International Context
The United States developed large trade surpluses in the early 1980s, swung back to a tiny trade surplus in 1991, and then had even larger trade deficits in the late 1990s and early 2000s. As we will see below, a trade deficit necessarily means a net inflow of financial capital from abroad, while a trade surplus necessarily means a net outflow of financial capital from an economy to other countries.

23.3 Trade Balances and Flows of Financial Capital
International flows of goods and services are closely connected to the international flows of financial capital. A current account deficit means that, after taking all the flows of payments from goods, services, and income together, the country is a net borrower from the rest of the world. A current account surplus is the opposite and means the country is a net lender to the rest of the world.

23.4 The National Saving and Investment Identity
The national saving and investment identity is based on the relationship that the total quantity of financial capital supplied from all sources must equal the total quantity of financial capital demanded from all sources. If S is private saving, T is taxes, G is government spending, M is imports, X is exports, and I is investment, then for an economy with a current account deficit and a budget deficit:

$$\text{Supply of financial capital} = \text{Demand for financial capital}$$
$$S + (M - X) = I + (G - T)$$

A recession tends to increase the trade balance (meaning a higher trade surplus or lower trade deficit), while economic boom will tend to decrease the trade balance (meaning a lower trade surplus or a larger trade deficit).

This OpenStax book is available for free at http://cnx.org/content/col12122/1.4

23.5 The Pros and Cons of Trade Deficits and Surpluses

Trade surpluses are no guarantee of economic health, and trade deficits are no guarantee of economic weakness. Either trade deficits or trade surpluses can work out well or poorly, depending on whether a government wisely invests the corresponding flows of financial capital.

23.6 The Difference between Level of Trade and the Trade Balance

There is a difference between the level of a country's trade and the balance of trade. The government measures its level of trade by the percentage of exports out of GDP, or the size of the economy. Small economies that have nearby trading partners and a history of international trade will tend to have higher levels of trade. Larger economies with few nearby trading partners and a limited history of international trade will tend to have lower levels of trade. The level of trade is different from the trade balance. The level of trade depends on a country's history of trade, its geography, and the size of its economy. A country's balance of trade is the dollar difference between its exports and imports.

Trade deficits and trade surpluses are not necessarily good or bad—it depends on the circumstances. Even if a country is borrowing, if it invests that money in productivity-boosting investments it can lead to an improvement in long-term economic growth.

SELF-CHECK QUESTIONS

1. If foreign investors buy more U.S. stocks and bonds, how would that show up in the current account balance?

2. If the trade deficit of the United States increases, how is the current account balance affected?

3. State whether each of the following events involves a financial flow to the Mexican economy or a financial flow out of the Mexican economy:
- a. Mexico imports services from Japan
- b. Mexico exports goods to Canada
- c. U.S. investors receive a return from past financial investments in Mexico

4. In what way does comparing a country's exports to GDP reflect its degree of globalization?

5. At one point Canada's GDP was $1,800 billion and its exports were $542 billion. What was Canada's export ratio at this time?

6. The GDP for the United States is $18,036 billion and its current account balance is –$484 billion. What percent of GDP is the current account balance?

7. Why does the trade balance and the current account balance track so closely together over time?

8. State whether each of the following events involves a financial flow to the U.S. economy or away from the U.S. economy:
- a. Export sales to Germany
- b. Returns paid on past U.S. financial investments in Brazil
- c. Foreign aid from the U.S. government to Egypt
- d. Imported oil from the Russian Federation
- e. Japanese investors buying U.S. real estate

9. How does the bottom portion of **Figure 23.3**, showing the international flow of investments and capital, differ from the upper portion?

10. Explain the relationship between a current account deficit or surplus and the flow of funds.

11. Using the national savings and investment identity, explain how each of the following changes (*ceteris paribus*) will increase or decrease the trade balance:
- a. A lower domestic savings rate
- b. The government changes from running a budget surplus to running a budget deficit
- c. The rate of domestic investment surges

12. If a country is running a government budget surplus, why is (T – G) on the left side of the saving-investment identity?

13. What determines the size of a country's trade deficit?

14. If domestic investment increases, and there is no change in the amount of private and public saving, what must happen to the size of the trade deficit?

15. Why does a recession cause a trade deficit to increase?

16. Both the United States and global economies are booming. Will U.S. imports and/or exports increase?

17. For each of the following, indicate which type of government spending would justify a budget deficit and which would not.
  a. Increased federal spending on Medicare
  b. Increased spending on education
  c. Increased spending on the space program
  d. Increased spending on airports and air traffic control

18. How did large trade deficits hurt the East Asian countries in the mid 1980s? (Recall that trade deficits are equivalent to inflows of financial capital from abroad.)

19. Describe a scenario in which a trade surplus benefits an economy and one in which a trade surplus is occurring in an economy that performs poorly. What key factor or factors are making the difference in the outcome that results from a trade surplus?

20. The United States exports 14% of GDP while Germany exports about 50% of its GDP. Explain what that means.

21. Explain briefly whether each of the following would be more likely to lead to a higher level of trade for an economy, or a greater imbalance of trade for an economy.
  a. Living in an especially large country
  b. Having a domestic investment rate much higher than the domestic savings rate
  c. Having many other large economies geographically nearby
  d. Having an especially large budget deficit
  e. Having countries with a tradition of strong protectionist legislation shutting out imports

REVIEW QUESTIONS

22. If imports exceed exports, is it a trade deficit or a trade surplus? What about if exports exceed imports?

23. What is included in the current account balance?

24. In recent decades, has the U.S. trade balance usually been in deficit, surplus, or balanced?

25. Does a trade surplus mean an overall inflow of financial capital to an economy, or an overall outflow of financial capital? What about a trade deficit?

26. What are the two main sides of the national savings and investment identity?

27. What are the main components of the national savings and investment identity?

28. When is a trade deficit likely to work out well for an economy? When is it likely to work out poorly?

29. Does a trade surplus help to guarantee strong economic growth?

30. What three factors will determine whether a nation has a higher or lower share of trade relative to its GDP?

31. What is the difference between trade deficits and balance of trade?

This OpenStax book is available for free at http://cnx.org/content/col12122/1.4

CRITICAL THINKING QUESTIONS

32. Occasionally, a government official will argue that a country should strive for both a trade surplus and a healthy inflow of capital from abroad. Explain why such a statement is economically impossible.

33. A government official announces a new policy. The country wishes to eliminate its trade deficit, but will strongly encourage financial investment from foreign firms. Explain why such a statement is contradictory.

34. If a country is a big exporter, is it more exposed to global financial crises?

35. If countries reduced trade barriers, would the international flows of money increase?

36. Is it better for your country to be an international lender or borrower?

37. Many think that the size of a trade deficit is due to a lack of competitiveness of domestic sectors, such as autos. Explain why this is not true.

38. If you observed a country with a rapidly growing trade surplus over a period of a year or so, would you be more likely to believe that the country's economy was in a period of recession or of rapid growth? Explain.

39. Occasionally, a government official will argue that a country should strive for both a trade surplus and a healthy inflow of capital from abroad. Is this possible?

40. What is more important, a country's current account balance or GDP growth? Why?

41. Will nations that are more involved in foreign trade tend to have higher trade imbalances, lower trade imbalances, or is the pattern unpredictable?

42. Some economists warn that the persistent trade deficits and a negative current account balance that the United States has run will be a problem in the long run. Do you agree or not? Explain your answer.

PROBLEMS

43. In 2001, the United Kingdom's economy exported goods worth £192 billion and services worth another £77 billion. It imported goods worth £225 billion and services worth £66 billion. Receipts of income from abroad were £140 billion while income payments going abroad were £131 billion. Government transfers from the United Kingdom to the rest of the world were £23 billion, while various U.K government agencies received payments of £16 billion from the rest of the world.

   a. Calculate the U.K. merchandise trade deficit for 2001.

   b. Calculate the current account balance for 2001.

   c. Explain how you decided whether payments on foreign investment and government transfers counted on the positive or the negative side of the current account balance for the United Kingdom in 2001.

44. Imagine that the U.S. economy finds itself in the following situation: a government budget deficit of $100 billion, total domestic savings of $1,500 billion, and total domestic physical capital investment of $1,600 billion. According to the national saving and investment identity, what will be the current account balance? What will be the current account balance if investment rises by $50 billion, while the budget deficit and national savings remain the same?

45. **Table 23.7** provides some hypothetical data on macroeconomic accounts for three countries represented by A, B, and C and measured in billions of currency units. In **Table 23.7**, private household saving is SH, tax revenue is T, government spending is G, and investment spending is I.

	A	B	C
SH	700	500	600
T	00	500	500
G	600	350	650
I	800	400	450

Table 23.7 Macroeconomic Accounts

a. Calculate the trade balance and the net inflow of foreign saving for each country.
b. State whether each one has a trade surplus or deficit (or balanced trade).
c. State whether each is a net lender or borrower internationally and explain.

46. Imagine that the economy of Germany finds itself in the following situation: the government budget has a surplus of 1% of Germany's GDP; private savings is 20% of GDP; and physical investment is 18% of GDP.

a. Based on the national saving and investment identity, what is the current account balance?
b. If the government budget surplus falls to zero, how will this affect the current account balance?

This OpenStax book is available for free at http://cnx.org/content/col12122/1.4

24 | The Aggregate Demand/ Aggregate Supply Model

Figure 24.1 New Home Construction At the peak of the housing bubble, many people across the country were able to secure the loans necessary to build new houses. (Credit: modification of work by Tim Pierce/Flickr Creative Commons)

Bring it Home

From Housing Bubble to Housing Bust

The United States experienced rising home ownership rates for most of the last two decades. Between 1990 and 2006, the U.S. housing market grew. Homeownership rates grew from 64% to a high of over 69% between 2004 and 2005. For many people, this was a period in which they could either buy first homes or buy a larger and more expensive home. During this time mortgage values tripled. Housing became more accessible to Americans and was considered to be a safe financial investment. Figure 24.2 shows how new single family home sales peaked in 2005 at 107,000 units.

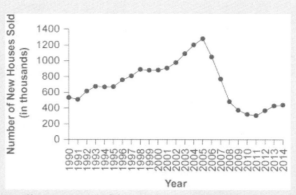

Figure 24.2 New Single Family Houses Sold From the early 1990s up through 2005, the number of new single family houses sold rose steadily. In 2006, the number dropped dramatically and this dramatic decline continued through 2011. By 2014, the number of new houses sold had begun to climb back up, but the levels are still lower than those of 1990. (Source: U.S. Census Bureau)

The housing bubble began to show signs of bursting in 2005, as delinquency and late payments began to grow and an oversupply of new homes on the market became apparent. Dropping home values contributed to a decrease in the overall wealth of the household sector and caused homeowners to pull back on spending. Several mortgage lenders were forced to file for bankruptcy because homeowners were not making their payments, and by 2008 the problem had spread throughout the financial markets. Lenders clamped down on credit and the housing bubble burst. Financial markets were now in crisis and unable or unwilling to even extend credit to credit-worthy customers.

The housing bubble and the crisis in the financial markets were major contributors to the Great Recession that led to unemployment rates over 10% and falling GDP. While the United States is still recovering from the impact of the Great Recession, it has made substantial progress in restoring financial market stability through implementing aggressive fiscal and monetary policy.

The economic history of the United States is cyclical in nature with recessions and expansions. Some of these fluctuations are severe, such as the economic downturn that occurred during the Great Depression in the 1930s which lasted several years. Why does the economy grow at different rates in different years? What are the causes of the cyclical behavior of the economy? This chapter will introduce an important model, the aggregate demand–aggregate supply model, to begin our understanding of why economies expand and contract over time.

Introduction to the Aggregate Supply–Aggregate Demand Model

In this chapter, you will learn about:

- Macroeconomic Perspectives on Demand and Supply

- Building a Model of Aggregate Supply and Aggregate Demand

- Shifts in Aggregate Supply

- Shifts in Aggregate Demand

- How the AS–AD Model Incorporates Growth, Unemployment, and Inflation

- Keynes' Law and Say's Law in the AS–AD Model

A key part of macroeconomics is the use of models to analyze macro issues and problems. How is the rate of economic growth connected to changes in the unemployment rate? Is there a reason why unemployment and inflation seem to move in opposite directions: lower unemployment and higher inflation from 1997 to 2000, higher unemployment and lower inflation in the early 2000s, lower unemployment and higher inflation in the mid-2000s,

This OpenStax book is available for free at http://cnx.org/content/col12122/1.4

and then higher unemployment and lower inflation in 2009? Why did the current account deficit rise so high, but then decline in 2009?

To analyze questions like these, we must move beyond discussing macroeconomic issues one at a time, and begin building economic models that will capture the relationships and interconnections between them. The next three chapters take up this task. This chapter introduces the macroeconomic model of aggregate supply and aggregate demand, how the two interact to reach a macroeconomic equilibrium, and how shifts in aggregate demand or aggregate supply will affect that equilibrium. This chapter also relates the model of aggregate supply and aggregate demand to the three goals of economic policy (growth, unemployment, and inflation), and provides a framework for thinking about many of the connections and tradeoffs between these goals. The chapter on **The Keynesian Perspective** focuses on the macroeconomy in the short run, where aggregate demand plays a crucial role. The chapter on **The Neoclassical Perspective** explores the macroeconomy in the long run, where aggregate supply plays a crucial role.

24.1 | Macroeconomic Perspectives on Demand and Supply

By the end of this section, you will be able to:
- Explain Say's Law and understand why it primarily applies in the long run
- Explain Keynes' Law and understand why it primarily applies in the short run

Macroeconomists over the last two centuries have often divided into two groups: those who argue that supply is the most important determinant of the size of the macroeconomy while demand just tags along, and those who argue that demand is the most important factor in the size of the macroeconomy while supply just tags along.

Say's Law and the Macroeconomics of Supply

Those economists who emphasize the role of supply in the macroeconomy often refer to the work of a famous early nineteenth century French economist named Jean-Baptiste Say (1767–1832). **Say's law** is: "Supply creates its own demand." As a matter of historical accuracy, it seems clear that Say never actually wrote down this law and that it oversimplifies his beliefs, but the law lives on as useful shorthand for summarizing a point of view.

The intuition behind Say's law is that each time a good or service is produced and sold, it generates income that is earned for someone: a worker, a manager, an owner, or those who are workers, managers, and owners at firms that supply inputs along the chain of production. We alluded to this earlier in our discussion of the National Income approach to measuring GDP. The forces of supply and demand in individual markets will cause prices to rise and fall. The bottom line remains, however, that every sale represents income to someone, and so, Say's law argues, a given value of supply must create an equivalent value of demand somewhere else in the economy. Because Jean-Baptiste Say, Adam Smith, and other economists writing around the turn of the nineteenth century who discussed this view were known as "classical" economists, modern economists who generally subscribe to the Say's law view on the importance of supply for determining the size of the macroeconomy are called **neoclassical economists**.

If supply always creates exactly enough demand at the macroeconomic level, then (as Say himself recognized) it is hard to understand why periods of recession and high unemployment should ever occur. To be sure, even if total supply always creates an equal amount of total demand, the economy could still experience a situation of some firms earning profits while other firms suffer losses. Nevertheless, a recession is not a situation where all business failures are exactly counterbalanced by an offsetting number of successes. A recession is a situation in which the economy as a whole is shrinking in size, business failures outnumber the remaining success stories, and many firms end up suffering losses and laying off workers.

Say's law that supply creates its own demand does seem a good approximation for the long run. Over periods of some years or decades, as the productive power of an economy to supply goods and services increases, total demand in the economy grows at roughly the same pace. However, over shorter time horizons of a few months or even years, recessions or even depressions occur in which firms, as a group, seem to face a lack of demand for their products.

Keynes' Law and the Macroeconomics of Demand

The alternative to Say's law, with its emphasis on supply, is **Keynes' law**: "Demand creates its own supply." As a matter of historical accuracy, just as Jean-Baptiste Say never wrote down anything as simpleminded as Say's law, John Maynard Keynes never wrote down Keynes' law, but the law is a useful simplification that conveys a certain point of view.

When Keynes wrote his influential work *The General Theory of Employment, Interest, and Money* during the 1930s Great Depression, he pointed out that during the Depression, the economy's capacity to supply goods and services had not changed much. U.S. unemployment rates soared higher than 20% from 1933 to 1935, but the number of possible workers had not increased or decreased much. Factories closed, but machinery and equipment had not disappeared. Technologies that had been invented in the 1920s were not un-invented and forgotten in the 1930s. Thus, Keynes argued that the Great Depression—and many ordinary recessions as well—were not caused by a drop in the ability of the economy to supply goods as measured by labor, physical capital, or technology. He argued the economy often produced less than its full potential, not because it was technically impossible to produce more with the existing workers and machines, but because a lack of demand in the economy as a whole led to inadequate incentives for firms to produce. In such cases, he argued, the level of GDP in the economy was not primarily determined by the potential of what the economy could supply, but rather by the amount of total demand.

Keynes' law seems to apply fairly well in the short run of a few months to a few years, when many firms experience either a drop in demand for their output during a recession or so much demand that they have trouble producing enough during an economic boom. However, demand cannot tell the whole macroeconomic story, either. After all, if demand was all that mattered at the macroeconomic level, then the government could make the economy as large as it wanted just by pumping up total demand through a large increase in the government spending component or by legislating large tax cuts to push up the consumption component. Economies do, however, face genuine limits to how much they can produce, limits determined by the quantity of labor, physical capital, technology, and the institutional and market structures that bring these factors of production together. These constraints on what an economy can supply at the macroeconomic level do not disappear just because of an increase in demand.

Combining Supply and Demand in Macroeconomics

Two insights emerge from this overview of Say's law with its emphasis on macroeconomic supply and Keynes' law with its emphasis on macroeconomic demand. The first conclusion, which is not exactly a hot news flash, is that an economic approach focused only on the supply side or only on the demand side can be only a partial success. We need to take into account both supply and demand. The second conclusion is that since Keynes' law applies more accurately in the short run and Say's law applies more accurately in the long run, the tradeoffs and connections between the three goals of macroeconomics may be different in the short run and the long run.

24.2 | Building a Model of Aggregate Demand and Aggregate Supply

By the end of this section, you will be able to:
- Explain the aggregate supply curve and how it relates to real GDP and potential GDP
- Explain the aggregate demand curve and how it is influenced by price levels
- Interpret the aggregate demand/aggregate supply model
- Identify the point of equilibrium in the aggregate demand/aggregate supply model
- Define short run aggregate supply and long run aggregate supply

To build a useful macroeconomic model, we need a model that shows what determines total supply or total demand for the economy, and how total demand and total supply interact at the macroeconomic level. We call this the **aggregate demand/aggregate supply model**. This module will explain aggregate supply, aggregate demand, and the equilibrium between them. The following modules will discuss the causes of shifts in aggregate supply and aggregate demand.

The Aggregate Supply Curve and Potential GDP

Firms make decisions about what quantity to supply based on the profits they expect to earn. They determine profits, in turn, by the price of the outputs they sell and by the prices of the inputs, like labor or raw materials, that they need to buy. **Aggregate supply (AS)** refers to the total quantity of output (i.e. real GDP) firms will produce and sell. The

aggregate supply (AS) curve shows the total quantity of output (i.e. real GDP) that firms will produce and sell at each price level.

Figure 24.3 shows an aggregate supply curve. In the following paragraphs, we will walk through the elements of the diagram one at a time: the horizontal and vertical axes, the aggregate supply curve itself, and the meaning of the potential GDP vertical line.

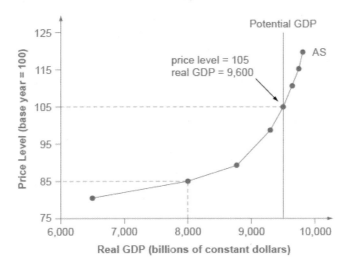

Figure 24.3 The Aggregate Supply Curve Aggregate supply (AS) slopes up, because as the price level for outputs rises, with the price of inputs remaining fixed, firms have an incentive to produce more to earn higher profits. The potential GDP line shows the maximum that the economy can produce with full employment of workers and physical capital.

The diagram's horizontal axis shows real GDP—that is, the level of GDP adjusted for inflation. The vertical axis shows the price level, which measures the average price of all goods and services produced in the economy. In other words, the price level in the AD-AS model is what we called the GDP Deflator in **The Macroeconomic Perspective**. Remember that the price level is different from the inflation rate. Visualize the price level as an index number, like the Consumer Price Index, while the inflation rate is the percentage change in the price level over time.

As the price level rises, real GDP rises as well. Why? The price level on the vertical axis represents prices for final goods or outputs bought in the economy—i.e. the GDP deflator—not the price level for intermediate goods and services that are inputs to production. Thus, the AS curve describes how suppliers will react to a higher price level for final outputs of goods and services, while holding the prices of inputs like labor and energy constant. If firms across the economy face a situation where the price level of what they produce and sell is rising, but their costs of production are not rising, then the lure of higher profits will induce them to expand production. In other words, an aggregate supply curve shows how producers as a group will respond to an increase in aggregate demand.

An AS curve's slope changes from nearly flat at its far left to nearly vertical at its far right. At the far left of the aggregate supply curve, the level of output in the economy is far below **potential GDP**, which we define as the amount of real GDP an economy can produce by fully employing its existing levels of labor, physical capital, and technology, in the context of its existing market and legal institutions. At these relatively low levels of output, levels of unemployment are high, and many factories are running only part-time, or have closed their doors. In this situation, a relatively small increase in the prices of the outputs that businesses sell—while assuming no rise in input prices—can encourage a considerable surge in the quantity of aggregate supply because so many workers and factories are ready to swing into production.

As the GDP increases, however, some firms and industries will start running into limits: perhaps nearly all of the expert workers in a certain industry will have jobs or factories in certain geographic areas or industries will be running at full speed. In the AS curve's intermediate area, a higher price level for outputs continues to encourage a greater quantity of output—but as the increasingly steep upward slope of the aggregate supply curve shows, the increase in real GDP in response to a given rise in the price level will not be as large. (Read the following Clear It Up feature to learn why the AS curve crosses potential GDP.)

Why does AS cross potential GDP?

Economists typically draw the aggregate supply curve to cross the potential GDP line. This shape may seem puzzling: How can an economy produce at an output level which is higher than its "potential" or "full employment" GDP? The economic intuition here is that if prices for outputs were high enough, producers would make fanatical efforts to produce: all workers would be on double-overtime, all machines would run 24 hours a day, seven days a week. Such hyper-intense production would go beyond using potential labor and physical capital resources fully, to using them in a way that is not sustainable in the long term. Thus, it is possible for production to sprint above potential GDP, but only in the short run.

At the far right, the aggregate supply curve becomes nearly vertical. At this quantity, higher prices for outputs cannot encourage additional output, because even if firms want to expand output, the inputs of labor and machinery in the economy are fully employed. In this example, the vertical line in the exhibit shows that potential GDP occurs at a total output of 9,500. When an economy is operating at its potential GDP, machines and factories are running at capacity, and the unemployment rate is relatively low—at the natural rate of unemployment. For this reason, potential GDP is sometimes also called **full-employment GDP**.

The Aggregate Demand Curve

Aggregate demand (AD) refers to the amount of total spending on domestic goods and services in an economy. (Strictly speaking, AD is what economists call total planned expenditure. We will further explain this distinction in the appendix **The Expenditure-Output Model** . For now, just think of aggregate demand as total spending.) It includes all four components of demand: consumption, investment, government spending, and net exports (exports minus imports). This demand is determined by a number of factors, but one of them is the price level—recall though, that the price level is an index number such as the GDP deflator that measures the average price of the things we buy. The **aggregate demand (AD) curve** shows the total spending on domestic goods and services at each price level.

Figure 24.4 presents an aggregate demand (AD) curve. Just like the aggregate supply curve, the horizontal axis shows real GDP and the vertical axis shows the price level. The AD curve slopes down, which means that increases in the price level of outputs lead to a lower quantity of total spending. The reasons behind this shape are related to how changes in the price level affect the different components of aggregate demand. The following components comprise aggregate demand: consumption spending (C), investment spending (I), government spending (G), and spending on exports (X) minus imports (M): C + I + G + X – M.

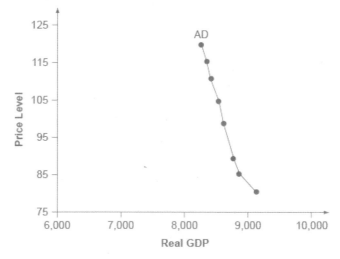

Figure 24.4 The Aggregate Demand Curve Aggregate demand (AD) slopes down, showing that, as the price level rises, the amount of total spending on domestic goods and services declines.

This OpenStax book is available for free at http://cnx.org/content/col12122/1.4

The wealth effect holds that as the price level increases, the buying power of savings that people have stored up in bank accounts and other assets will diminish, eaten away to some extent by inflation. Because a rise in the price level reduces people's wealth, consumption spending will fall as the price level rises.

The interest rate effect is that as prices for outputs rise, the same purchases will take more money or credit to accomplish. This additional demand for money and credit will push interest rates higher. In turn, higher interest rates will reduce borrowing by businesses for investment purposes and reduce borrowing by households for homes and cars—thus reducing consumption and investment spending.

The foreign price effect points out that if prices rise in the United States while remaining fixed in other countries, then goods in the United States will be relatively more expensive compared to goods in the rest of the world. U.S. exports will be relatively more expensive, and the quantity of exports sold will fall. U.S. imports from abroad will be relatively cheaper, so the quantity of imports will rise. Thus, a higher domestic price level, relative to price levels in other countries, will reduce net export expenditures.

Among economists all three of these effects are controversial, in part because they do not seem to be very large. For this reason, the aggregate demand curve in **Figure 24.4** slopes downward fairly steeply. The steep slope indicates that a higher price level for final outputs reduces aggregate demand for all three of these reasons, but that the change in the quantity of aggregate demand as a result of changes in price level is not very large.

Read the following Work It Out feature to learn how to interpret the AD/AS model. In this example, aggregate supply, aggregate demand, and the price level are given for the imaginary country of Xurbia.

Work It Out

Interpreting the AD/AS Model

Table 24.1 shows information on aggregate supply, aggregate demand, and the price level for the imaginary country of Xurbia. What information does **Table 24.1** tell you about the state of the Xurbia's economy? Where is the equilibrium price level and output level (this is the SR macroequilibrium)? Is Xurbia risking inflationary pressures or facing high unemployment? How can you tell?

Price Level	Aggregate Demand	Aggregate Supply
110	$700	$600
120	$690	$640
130	$680	$680
140	$670	$720
150	$660	$740
160	$650	$760
170	$640	$770

Table 24.1 Price Level: Aggregate Demand/Aggregate Supply

To begin to use the AD/AS model, it is important to plot the AS and AD curves from the data provided. What is the equilibrium?

Step 1. Draw your x- and y-axis. Label the x-axis Real GDP and the y-axis Price Level.

Step 2. Plot AD on your graph.

Step 3. Plot AS on your graph.

Step 4. Look at **Figure 24.5** which provides a visual to aid in your analysis.

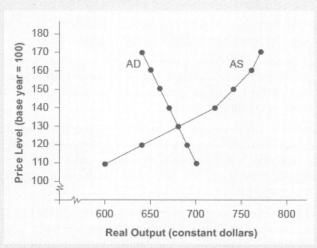

Figure 24.5 The AD/AS Curves AD and AS curves created from the data in **Table 24.1**.

Step 5. Determine where AD and AS intersect. This is the equilibrium with price level at 130 and real GDP at $680.

Step 6. Look at the graph to determine where equilibrium is located. We can see that this equilibrium is fairly far from where the AS curve becomes near-vertical (or at least quite steep) which seems to start at about $750 of real output. This implies that the economy is not close to potential GDP. Thus, unemployment will be high. In the relatively flat part of the AS curve, where the equilibrium occurs, changes in the price level will not be a major concern, since such changes are likely to be small.

Step 7. Determine what the steep portion of the AS curve indicates. Where the AS curve is steep, the economy is at or close to potential GDP.

Step 8. Draw conclusions from the given information:

- If equilibrium occurs in the flat range of AS, then economy is not close to potential GDP and will be experiencing unemployment, but stable price level.

- If equilibrium occurs in the steep range of AS, then the economy is close or at potential GDP and will be experiencing rising price levels or inflationary pressures, but will have a low unemployment rate.

Equilibrium in the Aggregate Demand/Aggregate Supply Model

The intersection of the aggregate supply and aggregate demand curves shows the equilibrium level of real GDP and the equilibrium price level in the economy. At a relatively low price level for output, firms have little incentive to produce, although consumers would be willing to purchase a large quantity of output. As the price level rises, aggregate supply rises and aggregate demand falls until the equilibrium point is reached.

Figure 24.6 combines the AS curve from **Figure 24.3** and the AD curve from **Figure 24.4** and places them both on a single diagram. In this example, the equilibrium point occurs at point E, at a price level of 90 and an output level of 8,800.

This OpenStax book is available for free at http://cnx.org/content/col12122/1.4

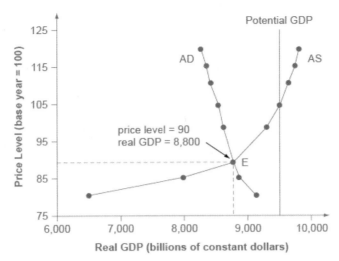

Figure 24.6 Aggregate Supply and Aggregate Demand The equilibrium, where aggregate supply (AS) equals aggregate demand (AD), occurs at a price level of 90 and an output level of 8,800.

Confusion sometimes arises between the aggregate supply and aggregate demand model and the microeconomic analysis of demand and supply in particular markets for goods, services, labor, and capital. Read the following Clear It Up feature to gain an understanding of whether AS and AD are macro or micro.

Are AS and AD macro or micro?

These aggregate supply and demand models and the microeconomic analysis of demand and supply in particular markets for goods, services, labor, and capital have a superficial resemblance, but they also have many underlying differences.

For example, the vertical and horizontal axes have distinctly different meanings in macroeconomic and microeconomic diagrams. The vertical axis of a microeconomic demand and supply diagram expresses a price (or wage or rate of return) for an individual good or service. This price is implicitly relative: it is intended to be compared with the prices of other products (for example, the price of pizza relative to the price of fried chicken). In contrast, the vertical axis of an aggregate supply and aggregate demand diagram expresses the level of a price index like the Consumer Price Index or the GDP deflator—combining a wide array of prices from across the economy. The price level is absolute: it is not intended to be compared to any other prices since it is essentially the average price of all products in an economy. The horizontal axis of a microeconomic supply and demand curve measures the quantity of a particular good or service. In contrast, the horizontal axis of the aggregate demand and aggregate supply diagram measures GDP, which is the sum of all the final goods and services produced in the economy, not the quantity in a specific market.

In addition, the economic reasons for the shapes of the curves in the macroeconomic model are different from the reasons behind the shapes of the curves in microeconomic models. Demand curves for individual goods or services slope down primarily because of the existence of substitute goods, not the wealth effects, interest rate, and foreign price effects associated with aggregate demand curves. The slopes of individual supply and demand curves can have a variety of different slopes, depending on the extent to which quantity demanded and quantity supplied react to price in that specific market, but the slopes of the AS and AD curves are much the same in every diagram (although as we shall see in later chapters, short-run and long-run perspectives will emphasize different parts of the AS curve).

In short, just because the AD/AS diagram has two lines that cross, do not assume that it is the same as every other diagram where two lines cross. The intuitions and meanings of the macro and micro diagrams are only distant cousins from different branches of the economics family tree.

Defining SRAS and LRAS

In the Clear It Up feature titled "Why does AS cross potential GDP?" we differentiated between short run changes in aggregate supply which the AS curve shows and long run changes in aggregate supply which the vertical line at potential GDP defines. In the short run, if demand is too low (or too high), it is possible for producers to supply less GDP (or more GDP) than potential. In the long run, however, producers are limited to producing at potential GDP. For this reason, we may also refer to what we have been calling the AS curve as the **short run aggregate supply (SRAS) curve**. We may also refer to the vertical line at potential GDP as the **long run aggregate supply (LRAS) curve**.

24.3 | Shifts in Aggregate Supply

By the end of this section, you will be able to:
- Explain how productivity growth changes the aggregate supply curve
- Explain how changes in input prices change the aggregate supply curve

The original equilibrium in the AD/AS diagram will shift to a new equilibrium if the AS or AD curve shifts. When the aggregate supply curve shifts to the right, then at every price level, producers supply a greater quantity of real GDP. When the AS curve shifts to the left, then at every price level, producers supply a lower quantity of real GDP. This module discusses two of the most important factors that can lead to shifts in the AS curve: productivity growth and changes in input prices.

How Productivity Growth Shifts the AS Curve

In the long run, the most important factor shifting the AS curve is productivity growth. Productivity means how much output can be produced with a given quantity of labor. One measure of this is output per worker or GDP per capita. Over time, productivity grows so that the same quantity of labor can produce more output. Historically, the real growth in GDP per capita in an advanced economy like the United States has averaged about 2% to 3% per year, but productivity growth has been faster during certain extended periods like the 1960s and the late 1990s through the early 2000s, or slower during periods like the 1970s. A higher level of productivity shifts the AS curve to the right, because with improved productivity, firms can produce a greater quantity of output at every price level. **Figure 24.7** (a) shows an outward shift in productivity over two time periods. The AS curve shifts out from $SRAS_0$ to $SRAS_1$ to $SRAS_2$, and the equilibrium shifts from E_0 to E_1 to E_2. Note that with increased productivity, workers can produce more GDP. Thus, full employment corresponds to a higher level of potential GDP, which we show as a rightward shift in LRAS from $LRAS_0$ to $LRAS_1$ to $LRAS_2$.

This OpenStax book is available for free at http://cnx.org/content/col12122/1.4

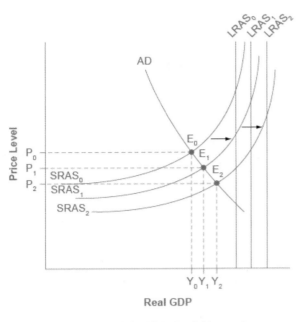

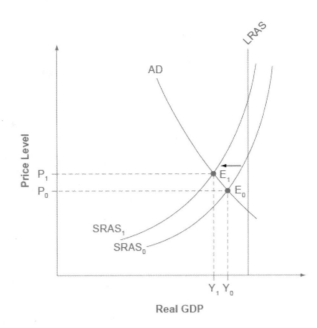

(a) Productivity growth shifts AS to the right

(b) Higher prices for key inputs shifts AS to the left

Figure 24.7 Shifts in Aggregate Supply (a) The rise in productivity causes the SRAS curve to shift to the right. The original equilibrium E_0 is at the intersection of AD and $SRAS_0$. When SRAS shifts right, then the new equilibrium E_1 is at the intersection of AD and $SRAS_1$, and then yet another equilibrium, E_2, is at the intersection of AD and $SRAS_2$. Shifts in SRAS to the right, lead to a greater level of output and to downward pressure on the price level. (b) A higher price for inputs means that at any given price level for outputs, a lower real GDP will be produced so aggregate supply will shift to the left from $SRAS_0$ to $SRAS_1$. The new equilibrium, E_1, has a reduced quantity of output and a higher price level than the original equilibrium (E_0).

A shift in the SRAS curve to the right will result in a greater real GDP and downward pressure on the price level, if aggregate demand remains unchanged. However, if this shift in SRAS results from gains in productivity growth, which we typically measure in terms of a few percentage points per year, the effect will be relatively small over a few months or even a couple of years. Recall how in **Choice in a World of Scarcity**, we said that a nation's production possibilities frontier is fixed in the short run, but shifts out in the long run? This is the same phenomenon using a different model.

How Changes in Input Prices Shift the AS Curve

Higher prices for inputs that are widely used across the entire economy can have a macroeconomic impact on aggregate supply. Examples of such widely used inputs include labor and energy products. Increases in the price of such inputs will cause the SRAS curve to shift to the left, which means that at each given price level for outputs, a higher price for inputs will discourage production because it will reduce the possibilities for earning profits. **Figure 24.7** (b) shows the aggregate supply curve shifting to the left, from $SRAS_0$ to $SRAS_1$, causing the equilibrium to move from E_0 to E_1. The movement from the original equilibrium of E_0 to the new equilibrium of E_1 will bring a nasty set of effects: reduced GDP or recession, higher unemployment because the economy is now further away from potential GDP, and an inflationary higher price level as well. For example, the U.S. economy experienced recessions in 1974–1975, 1980–1982, 1990–91, 2001, and 2007–2009 that were each preceded or accompanied by a rise in the key input of oil prices. In the 1970s, this pattern of a shift to the left in SRAS leading to a stagnant economy with high unemployment and inflation was nicknamed **stagflation**.

Conversely, a decline in the price of a key input like oil will shift the SRAS curve to the right, providing an incentive for more to be produced at every given price level for outputs. From 1985 to 1986, for example, the average price of crude oil fell by almost half, from $24 a barrel to $12 a barrel. Similarly, from 1997 to 1998, the price of a barrel of crude oil dropped from $17 per barrel to $11 per barrel. In both cases, the plummeting oil price led to a situation like that which we presented earlier in **Figure 24.7** (a), where the outward shift of SRAS to the right allowed the economy to expand, unemployment to fall, and inflation to decline.

Along with energy prices, two other key inputs that may shift the SRAS curve are the cost of labor, or wages, and the cost of imported goods that we use as inputs for other products. In these cases as well, the lesson is that lower prices for inputs cause SRAS to shift to the right, while higher prices cause it to shift back to the left. Note that, unlike changes in productivity, changes in input prices do not generally cause LRAS to shift, only SRAS.

Other Supply Shocks

The aggregate supply curve can also shift due to shocks to input goods or labor. For example, an unexpected early freeze could destroy a large number of agricultural crops, a shock that would shift the AS curve to the left since there would be fewer agricultural products available at any given price.

Similarly, shocks to the labor market can affect aggregate supply. An extreme example might be an overseas war that required a large number of workers to cease their ordinary production in order to go fight for their country. In this case, SRAS and LRAS would both shift to the left because there would be fewer workers available to produce goods at any given price.

24.4 | Shifts in Aggregate Demand

By the end of this section, you will be able to:
- Explain how imports influence aggregate demand
- Identify ways in which business confidence and consumer confidence can affect aggregate demand
- Explain how government policy can change aggregate demand
- Evaluate why economists disagree on the topic of tax cuts

As we mentioned previously, the components of aggregate demand are consumption spending (C), investment spending (I), government spending (G), and spending on exports (X) minus imports (M). (Read the following Clear It Up feature for explanation of why imports are subtracted from exports and what this means for aggregate demand.) A shift of the AD curve to the right means that at least one of these components increased so that a greater amount of total spending would occur at every price level. A shift of the AD curve to the left means that at least one of these components decreased so that a lesser amount of total spending would occur at every price level. **The Keynesian Perspective** will discuss the components of aggregate demand and the factors that affect them. Here, the discussion will sketch two broad categories that could cause AD curves to shift: changes in consumer or firm behavior and changes in government tax or spending policy.

Do imports diminish aggregate demand?

We have seen that the formula for aggregate demand is AD = C + I + G + X - M, where M is the total value of imported goods. Why is there a minus sign in front of imports? Does this mean that more imports will result in a lower level of aggregate demand? The short answer is yes, because aggregate demand is defined as total demand for domestically produced goods and services.

When an American buys a foreign product, for example, it gets counted along with all the other consumption. Thus, the income generated does not go to American producers, but rather to producers in another country. It would be wrong to count this as part of domestic demand. Therefore, imports added in consumption are subtracted back out in the M term of the equation.

Because of the way in which we write the demand equation, it is easy to make the mistake of thinking that imports are bad for the economy. Just keep in mind that every negative number in the M term has a corresponding positive number in the C or I or G term, and they always cancel out.

How Changes by Consumers and Firms Can Affect AD

When consumers feel more confident about the future of the economy, they tend to consume more. If business confidence is high, then firms tend to spend more on investment, believing that the future payoff from that investment will be substantial. Conversely, if consumer or business confidence drops, then consumption and investment spending decline.

The University of Michigan publishes a survey of consumer confidence and constructs an index of consumer confidence each month. The survey results are then reported at **http://www.sca.isr.umich.edu (http://www.sca.isr.umich.edu/)** , which break down the change in consumer confidence among different income levels. According to that index, consumer confidence averaged around 90 prior to the Great Recession, and then it fell to below 60 in late 2008, which was the lowest it had been since 1980. Since then, confidence has climbed from a 2011 low of 55.8 back to a level in the low 80s, which economists consider close to a healthy state.

The Organization for Economic Development and Cooperation (OECD) publishes one measure of business confidence: the "business tendency surveys". The OECD collects business opinion survey data for 21 countries on future selling prices and employment, among other business climate elements. After sharply declining during the Great Recession, the measure has risen above zero again and is back to long-term averages (the indicator dips below zero when business outlook is weaker than usual). Of course, either of these survey measures is not very precise. They can however, suggest when confidence is rising or falling, as well as when it is relatively high or low compared to the past.

Because economists associate a rise in confidence with higher consumption and investment demand, it will lead to an outward shift in the AD curve, and a move of the equilibrium, from E_0 to E_1, to a higher quantity of output and a higher price level, as **Figure 24.8** (a) shows.

Consumer and business confidence often reflect macroeconomic realities; for example, confidence is usually high when the economy is growing briskly and low during a recession. However, economic confidence can sometimes rise or fall for reasons that do not have a close connection to the immediate economy, like a risk of war, election results, foreign policy events, or a pessimistic prediction about the future by a prominent public figure. U.S. presidents, for example, must be careful in their public pronouncements about the economy. If they offer economic pessimism, they risk provoking a decline in confidence that reduces consumption and investment and shifts AD to the left, and in a self-fulfilling prophecy, contributes to causing the recession that the president warned against in the first place. **Figure 24.8** (b) shows a shift of AD to the left, and the corresponding movement of the equilibrium, from E_0 to E_1, to a lower quantity of output and a lower price level.

Link It Up 🔗

Visit this website (http://openstaxcollege.org/l/consumerconfid) for data on consumer confidence.

Link It Up 🔗

Visit this website (http://openstaxcollege.org/l/businessconfid) for data on business confidence.

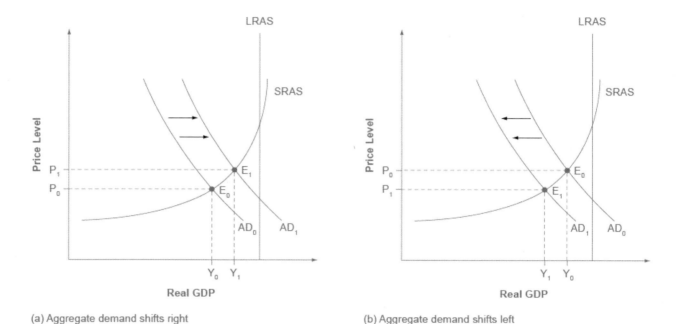

(a) Aggregate demand shifts right   (b) Aggregate demand shifts left

Figure 24.8 Shifts in Aggregate Demand (a) An increase in consumer confidence or business confidence can shift AD to the right, from AD_0 to AD_1. When AD shifts to the right, the new equilibrium (E_1) will have a higher quantity of output and also a higher price level compared with the original equilibrium (E_0). In this example, the new equilibrium (E_1) is also closer to potential GDP. An increase in government spending or a cut in taxes that leads to a rise in consumer spending can also shift AD to the right. (b) A decrease in consumer confidence or business confidence can shift AD to the left, from AD_0 to AD_1. When AD shifts to the left, the new equilibrium (E_1) will have a lower quantity of output and also a lower price level compared with the original equilibrium (E_0). In this example, the new equilibrium (E_1) is also farther below potential GDP. A decrease in government spending or higher taxes that leads to a fall in consumer spending can also shift AD to the left.

How Government Macroeconomic Policy Choices Can Shift AD

Government spending is one component of AD. Thus, higher government spending will cause AD to shift to the right, as in **Figure 24.8** (a), while lower government spending will cause AD to shift to the left, as in **Figure 24.8** (b). For example, in the United States, government spending declined by 3.2% of GDP during the 1990s, from 21% of GDP in 1991, and to 17.8% of GDP in 1998. However, from 2005 to 2009, the peak of the Great Recession, government spending increased from 19% of GDP to 21.4% of GDP. If changes of a few percentage points of GDP seem small to you, remember that since GDP was about $14.4 trillion in 2009, a seemingly small change of 2% of GDP is equal to close to $300 billion.

Tax policy can affect consumption and investment spending, too. Tax cuts for individuals will tend to increase consumption demand, while tax increases will tend to diminish it. Tax policy can also pump up investment demand by offering lower tax rates for corporations or tax reductions that benefit specific kinds of investment. Shifting C or I will shift the AD curve as a whole.

This OpenStax book is available for free at http://cnx.org/content/col12122/1.4

During a recession, when unemployment is high and many businesses are suffering low profits or even losses, the U.S. Congress often passes tax cuts. During the 2001 recession, for example, the U.S. Congress enacted a tax cut into law. At such times, the political rhetoric often focuses on how people experiencing hard times need relief from taxes. The aggregate supply and aggregate demand framework, however, offers a complementary rationale, as **Figure 24.9** illustrates. The original equilibrium during a recession is at point E_0, relatively far from the full employment level of output. The tax cut, by increasing consumption, shifts the AD curve to the right. At the new equilibrium (E_1), real GDP rises and unemployment falls and, because in this diagram the economy has not yet reached its potential or full employment level of GDP, any rise in the price level remains muted. Read the following Clear It Up feature to consider the question of whether economists favor tax cuts or oppose them.

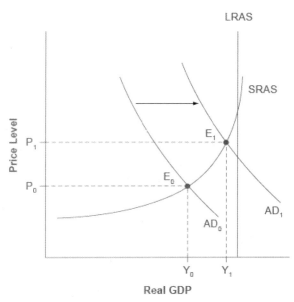

Figure 24.9 Recession and Full Employment in the AD/AS Model Whether the economy is in a recession is illustrated in the AD/AS model by how close the equilibrium is to the potential GDP line as indicated by the vertical LRAS line. In this example, the level of output Y_0 at the equilibrium E_0 is relatively far from the potential GDP line, so it can represent an economy in recession, well below the full employment level of GDP. In contrast, the level of output Y_1 at the equilibrium E_1 is relatively close to potential GDP, and so it would represent an economy with a lower unemployment rate.

Do economists favor tax cuts or oppose them?

One of the most fundamental divisions in American politics over the last few decades has been between those who believe that the government should cut taxes substantially and those who disagree. Ronald Reagan rode into the presidency in 1980 partly because of his promise, soon carried out, to enact a substantial tax cut. George Bush lost his bid for reelection against Bill Clinton in 1992 partly because he had broken his 1988 promise: "Read my lips! No new taxes!" In the 2000 presidential election, both George W. Bush and Al Gore advocated substantial tax cuts and Bush succeeded in pushing a tax cut package through Congress early in 2001. More recently in 2017, Donald Trump has pushed for tax cuts to stimulate the economy. Disputes over tax cuts often ignite at the state and local level as well.

What side do economists take? Do they support broad tax cuts or oppose them? The answer, unsatisfying to zealots on both sides, is that it depends. One issue is whether equally large government spending cuts accompany the tax cuts. Economists differ, as does any broad cross-section of the public, on how large government spending should be and what programs the government might cut back. A second issue, more relevant to the discussion in this chapter, concerns how close the economy is to the full employment output level. In a recession, when the AD and AS curves intersect far below the full employment level, tax cuts can make sense as a way of shifting AD to the right. However, when the economy is already performing extremely well, tax cuts may shift AD so far to the right as to generate inflationary pressures, with little gain to GDP.

With the AD/AS framework in mind, many economists might readily believe that the 1981 Reagan tax cuts, which took effect just after two serious recessions, were beneficial economic policy. Similarly, Congress enacted the 2001 Bush tax cuts and the 2009 Obama tax cuts during recessions. However, some of the same economists who favor tax cuts during recession would be much more dubious about identical tax cuts at a time the economy is performing well and cyclical unemployment is low.

Government spending and tax rate changes can be useful tools to affect aggregate demand. We will discuss these in greater detail in the **Government Budgets and Fiscal Policy** chapter and **The Impacts of Government Borrowing**. Other policy tools can shift the aggregate demand curve as well. For example, as we will discus in the **Monetary Policy and Bank Regulation** chapter, the Federal Reserve can affect interest rates and credit availability. Higher interest rates tend to discourage borrowing and thus reduce both household spending on big-ticket items like houses and cars and investment spending by business. Conversely, lower interest rates will stimulate consumption and investment demand. Interest rates can also affect exchange rates, which in turn will have effects on the export and import components of aggregate demand.

Clarifying the details of these alternative policies and how they affect the components of aggregate demand can wait for **The Keynesian Perspective** chapter. Here, the key lesson is that a shift of the aggregate demand curve to the right leads to a greater real GDP and to upward pressure on the price level. Conversely, a shift of aggregate demand to the left leads to a lower real GDP and a lower price level. Whether these changes in output and price level are relatively large or relatively small, and how the change in equilibrium relates to potential GDP, depends on whether the shift in the AD curve is happening in the AS curve's relatively flat or relatively steep portion.

24.5 | How the AD/AS Model Incorporates Growth, Unemployment, and Inflation

By the end of this section, you will be able to:
- Use the aggregate demand/aggregate supply model to show periods of economic growth and recession
- Explain how unemployment and inflation impact the aggregate demand/aggregate supply model
- Evaluate the importance of the aggregate demand/aggregate supply model

The AD/AS model can convey a number of interlocking relationships between the three macroeconomic goals of growth, unemployment, and low inflation. Moreover, the AD/AS framework is flexible enough to accommodate both the Keynes' law approach that focuses on aggregate demand and the short run, while also including the Say's law approach that focuses on aggregate supply and the long run. These advantages are considerable. Every model is a simplified version of the deeper reality and, in the context of the AD/AS model, the three macroeconomic goals arise in ways that are sometimes indirect or incomplete. In this module, we consider how the AD/AS model illustrates the three macroeconomic goals of economic growth, low unemployment, and low inflation.

Growth and Recession in the AD/AS Diagram

In the AD/AS diagram, long-run economic growth due to productivity increases over time will be represented by a gradual shift to the right of aggregate supply. The vertical line representing potential GDP (or the "full employment level of GDP") will gradually shift to the right over time as well. Earlier **Figure 24.7** (a) showed a pattern of economic growth over three years, with the AS curve shifting slightly out to the right each year. However, the factors that determine the speed of this long-term economic growth rate—like investment in physical and human capital, technology, and whether an economy can take advantage of catch-up growth—do not appear directly in the AD/AS diagram.

In the short run, GDP falls and rises in every economy, as the economy dips into recession or expands out of recession.

The AD/AS diagram illustrates recessions when the equilibrium level of real GDP is substantially below potential GDP, as we see at the equilibrium point E_0 in **Figure 24.9**. From another standpoint, in years of resurgent economic growth the equilibrium will typically be close to potential GDP, as equilibrium point E_1 in that earlier figure shows.

Unemployment in the AD/AS Diagram

We described two types of unemployment in the **Unemployment** chapter. Short run variations in unemployment (cyclical unemployment) are caused by the business cycle as the economy expands and contracts. Over the long run, in the United States, the unemployment rate typically hovers around 5% (give or take one percentage point or so), when the economy is healthy. In many of the national economies across Europe, the unemployment rate in recent decades has only dropped to about 10% or a bit lower, even in good economic years. We call this baseline level of unemployment that occurs year-in and year-out the natural rate of unemployment and we determine it by how well the structures of market and government institutions in the economy lead to a matching of workers and employers in the labor market. Potential GDP can imply different unemployment rates in different economies, depending on the natural rate of unemployment for that economy.

The AD/AS diagram shows cyclical unemployment by how close the economy is to the potential or full GDP employment level. Returning to **Figure 24.9**, relatively low cyclical unemployment for an economy occurs when the level of output is close to potential GDP, as in the equilibrium point E_1. Conversely, high cyclical unemployment arises when the output is substantially to the left of potential GDP on the AD/AS diagram, as at the equilibrium point E_0. Although we do not show the factors that determine the natural rate of unemployment separately in the AD/AS model, they are implicitly part of what determines potential GDP or full employment GDP in a given economy.

Inflationary Pressures in the AD/AS Diagram

Inflation fluctuates in the short run. Higher inflation rates have typically occurred either during or just after economic booms: for example, the biggest spurts of inflation in the U.S. economy during the twentieth century followed the wartime booms of World War I and World War II. Conversely, rates of inflation generally decline during recessions. As an extreme example, inflation actually became negative—a situation called "deflation"—during the Great Depression. Even during the relatively short 1991-1992 recession, the inflation rate declined from 5.4% in 1990 to 3.0% in 1992. During the relatively short 2001 recession, the rate of inflation declined from 3.4% in 2000 to 1.6% in 2002. During the deep recession of 2007–2009, the inflation rate declined from 3.8% in 2008 to –0.4% in 2009. Some countries have experienced bouts of high inflation that lasted for years. In the U.S. economy since the mid–1980s, inflation does not seem to have had any long-term trend to be substantially higher. Instead, it has stayed in the 1–5% range annually.

The AD/AS framework implies two ways that inflationary pressures may arise. One possible trigger is if aggregate demand continues to shift to the right when the economy is already at or near potential GDP and full employment, thus pushing the macroeconomic equilibrium into the AS curve's steep portion. In **Figure 24.10** (a), there is a shift of aggregate demand to the right. The new equilibrium E_1 is clearly at a higher price level than the original equilibrium E_0. In this situation, the aggregate demand in the economy has soared so high that firms in the economy are not capable of producing additional goods, because labor and physical capital are fully employed, and so additional increases in aggregate demand can only result in a rise in the price level.

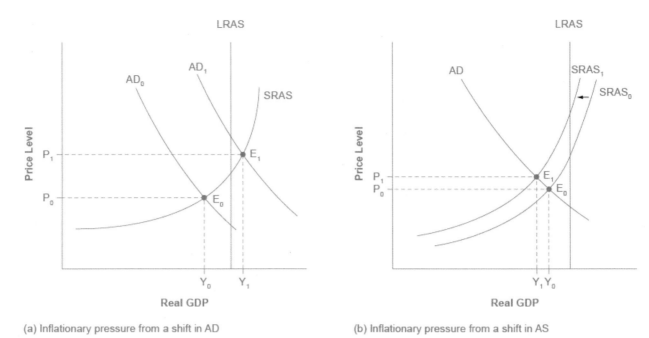

(a) Inflationary pressure from a shift in AD   (b) Inflationary pressure from a shift in AS

Figure 24.10 Sources of Inflationary Pressure in the AD/AS Model (a) A shift in aggregate demand, from AD_0 to AD_1, when it happens in the area of the SRAS curve that is near potential GDP, will lead to a higher price level and to pressure for a higher price level and inflation. The new equilibrium (E1) is at a higher price level (P1) than the original equilibrium. (b) A shift in aggregate supply, from $SRAS_0$ to $SRAS_1$, will lead to a lower real GDP and to pressure for a higher price level and inflation. The new equilibrium (E_1) is at a higher price level (P_1), while the original equilibrium (E_0) is at the lower price level (P_0).

An alternative source of inflationary pressures can occur due to a rise in input prices that affects many or most firms across the economy—perhaps an important input to production like oil or labor—and causes the aggregate supply curve to shift back to the left. In **Figure 24.10** (b), the SRAS curve's shift to the left also increases the price level from P_0 at the original equilibrium (E_0) to a higher price level of P_1 at the new equilibrium (E_1). In effect, the rise in input prices ends up, after the final output is produced and sold, passing along in the form of a higher price level for outputs.

The AD/AS diagram shows only a one-time shift in the price level. It does not address the question of what would cause inflation either to vanish after a year, or to sustain itself for several years. There are two explanations for why inflation may persist over time. One way that continual inflationary price increases can occur is if the government continually attempts to stimulate aggregate demand in a way that keeps pushing the AD curve when it is already in the SRAS curve's steep portion. A second possibility is that, if inflation has been occurring for several years, people might begin to expect a certain level of inflation. If they do, then these expectations will cause prices, wages and interest rates to increase annually by the amount of the inflation expected. These two reasons are interrelated, because if a government fosters a macroeconomic environment with inflationary pressures, then people will grow to expect inflation. However, the AD/AS diagram does not show these patterns of ongoing or expected inflation in a direct way.

Importance of the Aggregate Demand/Aggregate Supply Model

Macroeconomics takes an overall view of the economy, which means that it needs to juggle many different concepts. For example, start with the three macroeconomic goals of growth, low inflation, and low unemployment. Aggregate demand has four elements: consumption, investment, government spending, and exports less imports. Aggregate supply reveals how businesses throughout the economy will react to a higher price level for outputs. Finally, a wide array of economic events and policy decisions can affect aggregate demand and aggregate supply, including government tax and spending decisions; consumer and business confidence; changes in prices of key inputs like oil; and technology that brings higher levels of productivity.

The aggregate demand/aggregate supply model is one of the fundamental diagrams in this course (like the budget constraint diagram that we introduced in the **Choice in a World of Scarcity** chapter and the supply and demand diagram in the **Demand and Supply** chapter) because it provides an overall framework for bringing these factors together in one diagram. Some version of the AD/AS model will appear in every chapter in the rest of this book.

24.6 | Keynes' Law and Say's Law in the AD/AS Model

By the end of this section, you will be able to:
- Identify the neoclassical zone, the intermediate zone, and the Keynesian zone in the aggregate demand/aggregate supply model
- Use an aggregate demand/aggregate supply model as a diagnostic test to understand the current state of the economy

We can use the AD/AS model to illustrate both Say's law that supply creates its own demand and Keynes' law that demand creates its own supply. Consider the SRAS curve's three zones which **Figure 24.11** identifies: the Keynesian zone, the neoclassical zone, and the intermediate zone.

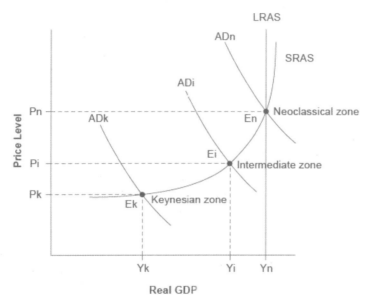

Figure 24.11 Keynes, Neoclassical, and Intermediate Zones in the Aggregate Supply Curve Near the equilibrium Ek, in the Keynesian zone at the far left of the SRAS curve, small shifts in AD, either to the right or the left, will affect the output level Yk, but will not much affect the price level. In the Keynesian zone, AD largely determines the quantity of output. Near the equilibrium En, in the neoclassical zone at the SRAS curve's far right, small shifts in AD, either to the right or the left, will have relatively little effect on the output level Yn, but instead will have a greater effect on the price level. In the neoclassical zone, the near-vertical SRAS curve close to the level of potential GDP largely determines the quantity of output. In the intermediate zone around equilibrium Ei, movement in AD to the right will increase both the output level and the price level, while a movement in AD to the left would decrease both the output level and the price level.

Focus first on the **Keynesian zone**, that portion of the SRAS curve on the far left which is relatively flat. If the AD curve crosses this portion of the SRAS curve at an equilibrium point like Ek, then certain statements about the economic situation will follow. In the Keynesian zone, the equilibrium level of real GDP is far below potential GDP, the economy is in recession, and cyclical unemployment is high. If aggregate demand shifted to the right or left in the Keynesian zone, it will determine the resulting level of output (and thus unemployment). However, inflationary price pressure is not much of a worry in the Keynesian zone, since the price level does not vary much in this zone.

Now, focus your attention on the **neoclassical zone** of the SRAS curve, which is the near-vertical portion on the right-hand side. If the AD curve crosses this portion of the SRAS curve at an equilibrium point like En where output is at or near potential GDP, then the size of potential GDP pretty much determines the level of output in the economy.

Since the equilibrium is near potential GDP, cyclical unemployment is low in this economy, although structural unemployment may remain an issue. In the neoclassical zone, shifts of aggregate demand to the right or the left have little effect on the level of output or employment. The only way to increase the size of the real GDP in the neoclassical zone is for AS to shift to the right. However, shifts in AD in the neoclassical zone will create pressures to change the price level.

Finally, consider the SRAS curve's **intermediate zone** in Figure 24.11. If the AD curve crosses this portion of the SRAS curve at an equilibrium point like Ei, then we might expect unemployment and inflation to move in opposing directions. For instance, a shift of AD to the right will move output closer to potential GDP and thus reduce unemployment, but will also lead to a higher price level and upward pressure on inflation. Conversely, a shift of AD to the left will move output further from potential GDP and raise unemployment, but will also lead to a lower price level and downward pressure on inflation.

This approach of dividing the SRAS curve into different zones works as a diagnostic test that we can apply to an economy, like a doctor checking a patient for symptoms. First, figure out in what zone the economy is. This will clarify the economic issues, tradeoffs, and policy choices. Some economists believe that the economy is strongly predisposed to be in one zone or another. Thus, hard-line Keynesian economists believe that the economies are in the Keynesian zone most of the time, and so they view the neoclassical zone as a theoretical abstraction. Conversely, hard-line neoclassical economists argue that economies are in the neoclassical zone most of the time and that the Keynesian zone is a distraction. The Keynesian Perspective and The Neoclassical Perspective should help to clarify the underpinnings and consequences of these contrasting views of the macroeconomy.

Bring it Home

From Housing Bubble to Housing Bust

We can explain economic fluctuations, whether those experienced during the 1930s Great Depression, the 1970s stagflation, or the 2008-2009 Great Recession, can be explained using the AD/AS diagram. Short-run fluctuations in output occur due to shifts of the SRAS curve, the AD curve, or both. In the case of the housing bubble, rising home values caused the AD curve to shift to the right as more people felt that rising home values increased their overall wealth. Many homeowners took on mortgages that exceeded their ability to pay because, as home values continued to rise, the increased value would pay off any debt outstanding. Increased wealth due to rising home values lead to increased home equity loans and increased spending. All these activities pushed AD to the right, contributing to low unemployment rates and economic growth in the United States. When the housing bubble burst, overall wealth dropped dramatically, wiping out the recent gains. This drop in home values was a demand shock to the U.S. economy because of its impact directly on the wealth of the household sector, and its contagion into the financial that essentially locked up new credit. The AD curve shifted to the left as evidenced by the Great Recession's rising unemployment.

Understanding the source of these macroeconomic fluctuations provided monetary and fiscal policy makers with insight about what policy actions to take to mitigate the impact of the housing crisis. From a monetary policy perspective, the Federal Reserve lowered short-term interest rates to between 0% and 0.25 %, to loosen up credit throughout the financial system. Discretionary fiscal policy measures included the passage of the Emergency Economic Stabilization Act of 2008 that allowed for the purchase of troubled assets, such as mortgages, from financial institutions and the American Recovery and Reinvestment Act of 2009 that increased government spending on infrastructure, provided for tax cuts, and increased transfer payments. In combination, both monetary and fiscal policy measures were designed to help stimulate aggregate demand in the U.S. economy, pushing the AD curve to the right.

While most economists agree on the usefulness of the AD/AS diagram in analyzing the sources of these fluctuations, there is still some disagreement about the effectiveness of policy decisions that are useful in stabilizing these fluctuations. We discuss the possible policy actions and the differences among economists about their effectiveness in more detail in The Keynesian Perspective, Monetary Policy and Bank Regulation, and Government Budgets and Fiscal Policy.

KEY TERMS

aggregate demand (AD) the amount of total spending on domestic goods and services in an economy

aggregate demand (AD) curve the total spending on domestic goods and services at each price level

aggregate demand/aggregate supply model a model that shows what determines total supply or total demand for the economy, and how total demand and total supply interact at the macroeconomic level

aggregate supply (AS) the total quantity of output (i.e. real GDP) firms will produce and sell

aggregate supply (AS) curve the total quantity of output (i.e. real GDP) that firms will produce and sell at each price level

full-employment GDP another name for potential GDP, when the economy is producing at its potential and unemployment is at the natural rate of unemployment

intermediate zone portion of the SRAS curve where GDP is below potential but not so far below as in the Keynesian zone; the SRAS curve is upward-sloping, but not vertical in the intermediate zone

Keynesian zone portion of the SRAS curve where GDP is far below potential and the SRAS curve is flat

Keynes' law "demand creates its own supply"

long run aggregate supply (LRAS) curve vertical line at potential GDP showing no relationship between the price level for output and real GDP in the long run

neoclassical economists economists who generally emphasize the importance of aggregate supply in determining the size of the macroeconomy over the long run

neoclassical zone portion of the SRAS curve where GDP is at or near potential output where the SRAS curve is steep

potential GDP the maximum quantity that an economy can produce given full employment of its existing levels of labor, physical capital, technology, and institutions

Say's law "supply creates its own demand"

short run aggregate supply (SRAS) curve positive short run relationship between the price level for output and real GDP, holding the prices of inputs fixed

stagflation an economy experiences stagnant growth and high inflation at the same time

KEY CONCEPTS AND SUMMARY

24.1 Macroeconomic Perspectives on Demand and Supply

Neoclassical economists emphasize Say's law, which holds that supply creates its own demand. Keynesian economists emphasize Keynes' law, which holds that demand creates its own supply. Many mainstream economists take a Keynesian perspective, emphasizing the importance of aggregate demand, for the short run, and a neoclassical perspective, emphasizing the importance of aggregate supply, for the long run.

24.2 Building a Model of Aggregate Demand and Aggregate Supply

The upward-sloping short run aggregate supply (SRAS) curve shows the positive relationship between the price level and the level of real GDP in the short run. Aggregate supply slopes up because when the price level for outputs increases, while the price level of inputs remains fixed, the opportunity for additional profits encourages more production. The aggregate supply curve is near-horizontal on the left and near-vertical on the right. In the long run, we show the aggregate supply by a vertical line at the level of potential output, which is the maximum level of output the economy can produce with its existing levels of workers, physical capital, technology, and economic institutions.

The downward-sloping aggregate demand (AD) curve shows the relationship between the price level for outputs and the quantity of total spending in the economy. It slopes down because of: (a) the wealth effect, which means that a higher price level leads to lower real wealth, which reduces the level of consumption; (b) the interest rate effect, which holds that a higher price level will mean a greater demand for money, which will tend to drive up interest rates and reduce investment spending; and (c) the foreign price effect, which holds that a rise in the price level will make domestic goods relatively more expensive, discouraging exports and encouraging imports.

24.3 Shifts in Aggregate Supply

The aggregate demand/aggregate supply (AD/AS) diagram shows how AD and AS interact. The intersection of the AD and AS curves shows the equilibrium output and price level in the economy. Movements of either AS or AD will result in a different equilibrium output and price level. The aggregate supply curve will shift out to the right as productivity increases. It will shift back to the left as the price of key inputs rises, and will shift out to the right if the price of key inputs falls. If the AS curve shifts back to the left, the combination of lower output, higher unemployment, and higher inflation, called stagflation, occurs. If AS shifts out to the right, a combination of lower inflation, higher output, and lower unemployment is possible.

24.4 Shifts in Aggregate Demand

The AD curve will shift out as the components of aggregate demand—C, I, G, and X–M—rise. It will shift back to the left as these components fall. These factors can change because of different personal choices, like those resulting from consumer or business confidence, or from policy choices like changes in government spending and taxes. If the AD curve shifts to the right, then the equilibrium quantity of output and the price level will rise. If the AD curve shifts to the left, then the equilibrium quantity of output and the price level will fall. Whether equilibrium output changes relatively more than the price level or whether the price level changes relatively more than output is determined by where the AD curve intersects with the AS curve.

The AD/AS diagram superficially resembles the microeconomic supply and demand diagram on the surface, but in reality, what is on the horizontal and vertical axes and the underlying economic reasons for the shapes of the curves are very different. We can illustrate long-term economic growth in the AD/AS framework by a gradual shift of the aggregate supply curve to the right. We illustrate a recession when the intersection of AD and AS is substantially below potential GDP, while we illustrate an expanding economy when the intersection of AS and AD is near potential GDP.

24.5 How the AD/AS Model Incorporates Growth, Unemployment, and Inflation

Cyclical unemployment is relatively large in the AD/AS framework when the equilibrium is substantially below potential GDP. Cyclical unemployment is small in the AD/AS framework when the equilibrium is near potential GDP. The natural rate of unemployment, as determined by the labor market institutions of the economy, is built into what economists mean by potential GDP, but does not otherwise appear in an AD/AS diagram. The AD/AS framework shows pressures for inflation to rise or fall when the movement from one equilibrium to another causes the price level to rise or to fall. The balance of trade does not appear directly in the AD/AS diagram, but it appears indirectly in several ways. Increases in exports or declines in imports can cause shifts in AD. Changes in the price of key imported inputs to production, like oil, can cause shifts in AS. The AD/AS model is the key model we use in this book to understand macroeconomic issues.

24.6 Keynes' Law and Say's Law in the AD/AS Model

We can divide the SRAS curve into three zones. Keynes' law says demand creates its own supply, so that changes in aggregate demand cause changes in real GDP and employment. We can show Keynes' law on the horizontal Keynesian zone of the aggregate supply curve. The Keynesian zone occurs at the left of the SRAS curve where it is fairly flat, so movements in AD will affect output, but have little effect on the price level. Say's law says supply creates its own demand. Changes in aggregate demand have no effect on real GDP and employment, only on the price level. We can show Say's law on the vertical neoclassical zone of the aggregate supply curve. The neoclassical zone occurs at the right of the SRAS curve where it is fairly vertical, and so movements in AD will affect the price level, but have little impact on output. The intermediate zone in the middle of the SRAS curve is upward-sloping, so a rise in AD will cause higher output and price level, while a fall in AD will lead to a lower output and price level.

SELF-CHECK QUESTIONS

1. Describe the mechanism by which supply creates its own demand.

2. Describe the mechanism by which demand creates its own supply.

3. The short run aggregate supply curve was constructed assuming that as the price of outputs increases, the price of inputs stays the same. How would an increase in the prices of important inputs, like energy, affect aggregate supply?

4. In the AD/AS model, what prevents the economy from achieving equilibrium at potential output?

5. Suppose the U.S. Congress passes significant immigration reform that makes it more difficult for foreigners to come to the United States to work. Use the AD/AS model to explain how this would affect the equilibrium level of GDP and the price level.

6. Suppose concerns about the size of the federal budget deficit lead the U.S. Congress to cut all funding for research and development for ten years. Assuming this has an impact on technology growth, what does the AD/AS model predict would be the likely effect on equilibrium GDP and the price level?

7. How would a dramatic increase in the value of the stock market shift the AD curve? What effect would the shift have on the equilibrium level of GDP and the price level?

8. Suppose Mexico, one of our largest trading partners and purchaser of a large quantity of our exports, goes into a recession. Use the AD/AS model to determine the likely impact on our equilibrium GDP and price level.

9. A policymaker claims that tax cuts led the economy out of a recession. Can we use the AD/AS diagram to show this?

10. Many financial analysts and economists eagerly await the press releases for the reports on the home price index and consumer confidence index. What would be the effects of a negative report on both of these? What about a positive report?

11. What impact would a decrease in the size of the labor force have on GDP and the price level according to the AD/AS model?

12. Suppose, after five years of sluggish growth, the European Union's economy picks up speed. What would be the likely impact on the U.S. trade balance, GDP, and employment?

13. Suppose the Federal Reserve begins to increase the supply of money at an increasing rate. What impact would that have on GDP, unemployment, and inflation?

14. If the economy is operating in the neoclassical zone of the SRAS curve and aggregate demand falls, what is likely to happen to real GDP?

15. If the economy is operating in the Keynesian zone of the SRAS curve and aggregate demand falls, what is likely to happen to real GDP?

REVIEW QUESTIONS

16. What is Say's law?

17. What is Keynes' law?

18. Do neoclassical economists believe in Keynes' law or Say's law?

19. Does Say's law apply more accurately in the long run or the short run? What about Keynes' law?

20. What is on the horizontal axis of the AD/AS diagram? What is on the vertical axis?

21. What is the economic reason why the SRAS curve slopes up?

22. What are the components of the aggregate demand (AD) curve?

23. What are the economic reasons why the AD curve slopes down?

24. Briefly explain the reason for the near-horizontal shape of the SRAS curve on its far left.

25. Briefly explain the reason for the near-vertical shape of the SRAS curve on its far right.

26. What is potential GDP?

27. Name some factors that could cause the SRAS curve to shift, and say whether they would shift SRAS to the right or to the left.

28. Will the shift of SRAS to the right tend to make the equilibrium quantity and price level higher or lower? What about a shift of SRAS to the left?

29. What is stagflation?

30. Name some factors that could cause AD to shift, and say whether they would shift AD to the right or to the left.

31. Would a shift of AD to the right tend to make the equilibrium quantity and price level higher or lower? What about a shift of AD to the left?

32. How is long-term growth illustrated in an AD/AS model?

33. How is recession illustrated in an AD/AS model?

34. How is cyclical unemployment illustrated in an AD/AS model?

35. How is the natural rate of unemployment illustrated in an AD/AS model?

36. How is pressure for inflationary price increases shown in an AD/AS model?

37. What are some of the ways in which exports and imports can affect the AD/AS model?

38. What is the Keynesian zone of the SRAS curve? How much is the price level likely to change in the Keynesian zone?

39. What is the neoclassical zone of the SRAS curve? How much is the output level likely to change in the neoclassical zone?

40. What is the intermediate zone of the SRAS curve? Will a rise in output be accompanied by a rise or a fall in the price level in this zone?

CRITICAL THINKING QUESTIONS

41. Why would an economist choose either the neoclassical perspective or the Keynesian perspective, but not both?

42. On a microeconomic demand curve, a decrease in price causes an increase in quantity demanded because the product in question is now relatively less expensive than substitute products. Explain why aggregate demand does not increase for the same reason in response to a decrease in the aggregate price level. In other words, what causes total spending to increase if it is not because goods are now cheaper?

43. Economists expect that as the labor market continues to tighten going into the latter part of 2015 that workers should begin to expect wage increases in 2015 and 2016. Assuming this occurs and it was the only development in the labor market that year, how would this affect the AS curve? What if it was also accompanied by an increase in worker productivity?

44. If new government regulations require firms to use a cleaner technology that is also less efficient than what they previously used, what would the effect be on output, the price level, and employment using the AD/AS diagram?

45. During spring 2016 the Midwestern United States, which has a large agricultural base, experiences above-average rainfall. Using the AD/AS diagram, what is the effect on output, the price level, and employment?

46. Hydraulic fracturing (fracking) has the potential to significantly increase the amount of natural gas produced in the United States. If a large percentage of factories and utility companies use natural gas, what will happen to output, the price level, and employment as fracking becomes more widely used?

47. Some politicians have suggested tying the minimum wage to the consumer price index (CPI). Using the AD/AS diagram, what effects would this policy most likely have on output, the price level, and employment?

This OpenStax book is available for free at http://cnx.org/content/col12122/1.4

48. If households decide to save a larger portion of their income, what effect would this have on the output, employment, and price level in the short run? What about the long run?

49. If firms become more optimistic about the future of the economy and, at the same time, innovation in 3-D printing makes most workers more productive, what is the combined effect on output, employment, and the price-level?

50. If Congress cuts taxes at the same time that businesses become more pessimistic about the economy, what is the combined effect on output, the price level, and employment using the AD/AS diagram?

51. Suppose the level of structural unemployment increases. How would you illustrate the increase in structural unemployment in the AD/AS model? *Hint*: How does structural unemployment affect potential GDP?

52. If foreign wealth-holders decide that the United States is the safest place to invest their savings, what would the effect be on the economy here? Show graphically using the AD/AS model.

53. The AD/AS model is static. It shows a snapshot of the economy at a given point in time. Both economic growth and inflation are dynamic phenomena. Suppose economic growth is 3% per year and aggregate demand is growing at the same rate. What does the AD/AS model say the inflation rate should be?

54. Explain why the short-run aggregate supply curve might be fairly flat in the Keynesian zone of the SRAS curve. How might we tell if we are in the Keynesian zone of the AS?

55. Explain why the short-run aggregate supply curve might be vertical in the neoclassical zone of the SRAS curve. How might we tell if we are in the neoclassical zone of the AS?

56. Why might it be important for policymakers to know which in zone of the SRAS curve the economy is?

57. In your view, is the economy currently operating in the Keynesian, intermediate or neoclassical portion of the economy's aggregate supply curve?

58. Are Say's law and Keynes' law necessarily mutually exclusive?

PROBLEMS

59. Review the problem in the **Work It Out** titled "Interpreting the AD/AS Model." Like the information provided in that feature, **Table 24.2** shows information on aggregate supply, aggregate demand, and the price level for the imaginary country of Xurbia.

Price Level	AD	AS
110	700	600
120	690	640
130	680	680
140	670	720
150	660	740
160	650	760
170	640	770

Table 24.2 Price Level: AD/AS

a. Plot the AD/AS diagram from the data. Identify the equilibrium.
b. Imagine that, as a result of a government tax cut, aggregate demand becomes higher by 50 at every price level. Identify the new equilibrium.
c. How will the new equilibrium alter output? How will it alter the price level? What do you think will happen to employment?

60. The imaginary country of Harris Island has the aggregate supply and aggregate demand curves as **Table 24.3** shows.

Price Level	AD	AS
100	700	200
120	600	325
140	500	500
160	400	570
180	300	620

Table 24.3 Price Level: AD/AS

a. Plot the AD/AS diagram. Identify the equilibrium.
b. Would you expect unemployment in this economy to be relatively high or low?
c. Would you expect concern about inflation in this economy to be relatively high or low?
d. Imagine that consumers begin to lose confidence about the state of the economy, and so AD becomes lower by 275 at every price level. Identify the new aggregate equilibrium.
e. How will the shift in AD affect the original output, price level, and employment?

61. Table 24.4 describes Santher's economy.

Price Level	AD	AS
50	1,000	250
60	950	580
70	900	750
80	850	850
90	800	900

Table 24.4 Price Level: AD/AS

a. Plot the AD/AS curves and identify the equilibrium.
b. Would you expect unemployment in this economy to be relatively high or low?
c. Would you expect prices to be a relatively large or small concern for this economy?
d. Imagine that input prices fall and so AS shifts to the right by 150 units. Identify the new equilibrium.
e. How will the shift in AS affect the original output, price level, and employment?

This OpenStax book is available for free at http://cnx.org/content/col12122/1.4

25 | The Keynesian Perspective

Figure 25.1 Signs of a Recession Home foreclosures were just one of the many signs and symptoms of the recent Great Recession. During that time, many businesses closed and many people lost their jobs. (Credit: modification of work by Taber Andrew Bain/Flickr Creative Commons)

Bring it Home

The Great Recession

The 2008-2009 Great Recession hit the U.S. economy hard. According to the Bureau of Labor Statistics (BLS), the number of unemployed Americans rose from 6.8 million in May 2007 to 15.4 million in October 2009. During that time, the U.S. Census Bureau estimated that approximately 170,000 small businesses closed. Mass layoffs peaked in February 2009 when employers gave 326,392 workers notice. U.S. productivity and output fell as well. Job losses, declining home values, declining incomes, and uncertainty about the future caused consumption expenditures to decrease. According to the BLS, household spending dropped by 7.8%.

Home foreclosures and the meltdown in U.S. financial markets called for immediate action by Congress, the President, and the Federal Reserve Bank. For example, the government implemented programs such as the American Restoration and Recovery Act to help millions of people by providing tax credits for homebuyers, paying "cash for clunkers," and extending unemployment benefits. From cutting back on spending, filing for unemployment, and losing homes, millions of people were affected by the recession. While the United States is now on the path to recovery, people will feel the impact for many years to come.

What caused this recession and what prevented the economy from spiraling further into another depression? Policymakers looked to the lessons learned from the 1930s Great Depression and to John Maynard Keynes' models to analyze the causes and find solutions to the country's economic woes. The Keynesian perspective is the subject of this chapter.

Introduction to the Keynesian Perspective

In this chapter, you will learn about:

- Aggregate Demand in Keynesian Analysis

- The Building Blocks of Keynesian Analysis

- The Phillips Curve

- The Keynesian Perspective on Market Forces

We have learned that the level of economic activity, for example output, employment, and spending, tends to grow over time. In **The Keynesian Perspective** we learned the reasons for this trend. **The Macroeconomic Perspective** pointed out that the economy tends to cycle around the long-run trend. In other words, the economy does not always grow at its average growth rate. Sometimes economic activity grows at the trend rate, sometimes it grows more than the trend, sometimes it grows less than the trend, and sometimes it actually declines. You can see this cyclical behavior in **Figure 25.2**.

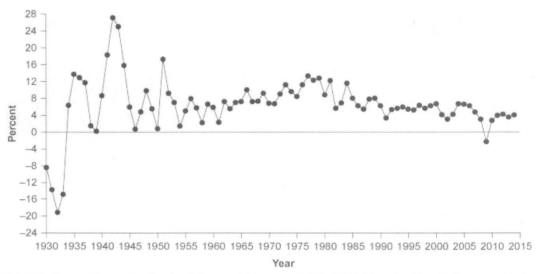

Figure 25.2 U.S. Gross Domestic Product, Percent Changes 1930–2014 The chart tracks the percent change in GDP since 1930. The magnitude of both recessions and peaks was quite large between 1930 and 1945. (Source: Bureau of Economic Analysis, "National Economic Accounts")

This empirical reality raises two important questions: How can we explain the cycles, and to what extent can we moderate them? This chapter (on the Keynesian perspective) and **The Neoclassical Perspective** explore those questions from two different points of view, building on what we learned in **The Aggregate Demand/Aggregate Supply Model**.

25.1 | Aggregate Demand in Keynesian Analysis

By the end of this section, you will be able to:
- Explain real GDP, recessionary gaps, and inflationary gaps
- Recognize the Keynesian AD/AS model
- Identify the determining factors of both consumption expenditure and investment expenditure
- Analyze the factors that determine government spending and net exports

The Keynesian perspective focuses on aggregate demand. The idea is simple: firms produce output only if they expect it to sell. Thus, while the availability of the factors of production determines a nation's potential GDP, the amount of

This OpenStax book is available for free at http://cnx.org/content/col12122/1.4

goods and services that actually sell, known as **real GDP**, depends on how much demand exists across the economy. **Figure 25.3** illustrates this point.

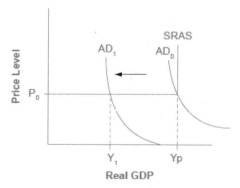

Figure 25.3 The Keynesian AD/AS Model The Keynesian View of the AD/AS Model uses an SRAS curve, which is horizontal at levels of output below potential and vertical at potential output. Thus, when beginning from potential output, any decrease in AD affects only output, but not prices. Any increase in AD affects only prices, not output.

Keynes argued that, for reasons we explain shortly, aggregate demand is not stable—that it can change unexpectedly. Suppose the economy starts where AD intersects SRAS at P_0 and Yp. Because Yp is potential output, the economy is at full employment. Because AD is volatile, it can easily fall. Thus, even if we start at Yp, if AD falls, then we find ourselves in what Keynes termed a **recessionary gap**. The economy is in equilibrium but with less than full employment, as Y_1 in **Figure 25.3** shows. Keynes believed that the economy would tend to stay in a recessionary gap, with its attendant unemployment, for a significant period of time.

In the same way (although we do not show it in the figure), if AD increases, the economy could experience an **inflationary gap**, where demand is attempting to push the economy past potential output. Consequently, the economy experiences inflation. The key policy implication for either situation is that government needs to step in and close the gap, increasing spending during recessions and decreasing spending during booms to return aggregate demand to match potential output.

Recall from **The Aggregate Supply-Aggregate Demand Model** that aggregate demand is total spending, economy-wide, on domestic goods and services. (Aggregate demand (AD) is actually what economists call total planned expenditure. Read the appendix on **The Expenditure-Output Model** for more on this.) You may also remember that aggregate demand is the sum of four components: consumption expenditure, investment expenditure, government spending, and spending on net exports (exports minus imports). In the following sections, we will examine each component through the Keynesian perspective.

What Determines Consumption Expenditure?

Consumption expenditure is spending by households and individuals on durable goods, nondurable goods, and services. Durable goods are items that last and provide value over time, such as automobiles. Nondurable goods are things like groceries—once you consume them, they are gone. Recall from **The Macroeconomic Perspective** that services are intangible things consumers buy, like healthcare or entertainment.

Keynes identified three factors that affect consumption:

- Disposable income: For most people, the single most powerful determinant of how much they consume is how much income they have in their take-home pay, also known as **disposable income**, which is income after taxes.

- Expected future income: Consumer expectations about future income also are important in determining consumption. If consumers feel optimistic about the future, they are more likely to spend and increase overall aggregate demand. News of recession and troubles in the economy will make them pull back on consumption.

- Wealth or credit: When households experience a rise in wealth, they may be willing to consume a higher share of their income and to save less. When the U.S. stock market rose dramatically in the late 1990s, for example, U.S. savings rates declined, probably in part because people felt that their wealth had increased and there was less need to save. How do people spend beyond their income, when they perceive their wealth increasing? The answer is borrowing. On the other side, when the U.S. stock market declined about 40% from March 2008 to

March 2009, people felt far greater uncertainty about their economic future, so savings rates increased while consumption declined.

Finally, Keynes noted that a variety of other factors combine to determine how much people save and spend. If household preferences about saving shift in a way that encourages consumption rather than saving, then AD will shift out to the right.

Link It Up

Visit this website (http://openstaxcollege.org/l/Diane_Rehm) for more information about how the recession affected various groups of people.

What Determines Investment Expenditure?

We call spending on new capital goods investment expenditure. Investment falls into four categories: producer's durable equipment and software, nonresidential structures (such as factories, offices, and retail locations), changes in inventories, and residential structures (such as single-family homes, townhouses, and apartment buildings). Businesses conduct the first three types of investment, while households conduct the last.

Keynes's treatment of investment focuses on the key role of expectations about the future in influencing business decisions. When a business decides to make an investment in physical assets, like plants or equipment, or in intangible assets, like skills or a research and development project, that firm considers both the expected investment benefits (future profit expectations) and the investment costs (interest rates).

- Expectations of future profits: The clearest driver of investment benefits is expectations for future profits. When we expect an economy to grow, businesses perceive a growing market for their products. Their higher degree of business confidence will encourage new investment. For example, in the second half of the 1990s, U.S. investment levels surged from 18% of GDP in 1994 to 21% in 2000. However, when a recession started in 2001, U.S. investment levels quickly sank back to 18% of GDP by 2002.

- Interest rates also play a significant role in determining how much investment a firm will make. Just as individuals need to borrow money to purchase homes, so businesses need financing when they purchase big ticket items. The cost of investment thus includes the interest rate. Even if the firm has the funds, the interest rate measures the opportunity cost of purchasing business capital. Lower interest rates stimulate investment spending and higher interest rates reduce it.

Many factors can affect the expected profitability on investment. For example, if the energy prices decline, then investments that use energy as an input will yield higher profits. If government offers special incentives for investment (for example, through the tax code), then investment will look more attractive; conversely, if government removes special investment incentives from the tax code, or increases other business taxes, then investment will look less attractive. As Keynes noted, business investment is the most variable of all the components of aggregate demand.

What Determines Government Spending?

The third component of aggregate demand is federal, state, and local government spending. Although we usually view the United States as a market economy, government still plays a significant role in the economy. As we discuss in **Environmental Protection and Negative Externalities** and **Positive Externalitites and Public Goods**, government provides important public services such as national defense, transportation infrastructure, and education.

Keynes recognized that the government budget offered a powerful tool for influencing aggregate demand. Not only

This OpenStax book is available for free at http://cnx.org/content/col12122/1.4

could more government spending stimulate AD (or less government spending reduce it), but lowering or raising tax rates could influence consumption and investment spending. Keynes concluded that during extreme times like deep recessions, only the government had the power and resources to move aggregate demand.

What Determines Net Exports?

Recall that exports are domestically produced products that sell abroad while imports are foreign produced products that consumers purchase domestically. Since we define aggregate demand as spending on domestic goods and services, export expenditures add to AD, while import expenditures subtract from AD.

Two sets of factors can cause shifts in export and import demand: changes in relative growth rates between countries and changes in relative prices between countries. What is happening in the countries' economies that would be purchasing those exports heavily affects the level of demand for a nation's exports. For example, if major importers of American-made products like Canada, Japan, and Germany have recessions, exports of U.S. products to those countries are likely to decline. Conversely, the amount of income in the domestic economy directly affects the quantity of a nation's imports: more income will bring a higher level of imports.

Relative prices of goods in domestic and international markets can also affect exports and imports. If U.S. goods are relatively cheaper compared with goods made in other places, perhaps because a group of U.S. producers has mastered certain productivity breakthroughs, then U.S. exports are likely to rise. If U.S. goods become relatively more expensive, perhaps because a change in the exchange rate between the U.S. dollar and other currencies has pushed up the price of inputs to production in the United States, then exports from U.S. producers are likely to decline.

Table 25.1 summarizes the reasons we have explained for changes in aggregate demand.

Reasons for a Decrease in Aggregate Demand	Reasons for an Increase in Aggregate Demand
Consumption • Rise in taxes • Fall in income • Rise in interest rates • Desire to save more • Decrease in wealth • Fall in future expected income	**Consumption** • Decrease in taxes • Increase in income • Fall in interest rates • Desire to save less • Rise in wealth • Rise in future expected income
Investment • Fall in expected rate of return • Rise in interest rates • Drop in business confidence	**Investment** • Rise in expected rate of return • Drop in interest rates • Rise in business confidence
Government • Reduction in government spending • Increase in taxes	**Government** • Increase in government spending • Decrease in taxes
Net Exports • Decrease in foreign demand • Relative price increase of U.S. goods	**Net Exports** • Increase in foreign demand • Relative price drop of U.S. goods

Table 25.1 Determinants of Aggregate Demand

25.2 | The Building Blocks of Keynesian Analysis

By the end of this section, you will be able to:
- Evaluate the Keynesian view of recessions through an understanding of sticky wages and prices and the importance of aggregate demand
- Explain the coordination argument, menu costs, and macroeconomic externality
- Analyze the impact of the expenditure multiplier

Now that we have a clear understanding of what constitutes aggregate demand, we return to the Keynesian argument using the model of aggregate demand/aggregate supply (AD/AS). (For a similar treatment using Keynes' income-expenditure model, see the appendix on **The Expenditure-Output Model**.)

Keynesian economics focuses on explaining why recessions and depressions occur and offering a policy prescription for minimizing their effects. The Keynesian view of recession is based on two key building blocks. First, aggregate demand is not always automatically high enough to provide firms with an incentive to hire enough workers to reach full employment. Second, the macroeconomy may adjust only slowly to shifts in aggregate demand because of **sticky wages and prices**, which are wages and prices that do not respond to decreases or increases in demand. We will consider these two claims in turn, and then see how they are represented in the AD/AS model.

The first building block of the Keynesian diagnosis is that recessions occur when the level of demand for goods and services is less than what is produced when labor is fully employed. In other words, the intersection of aggregate supply and aggregate demand occurs at a level of output less than the level of GDP consistent with full employment. Suppose the stock market crashes, as in 1929, or suppose the housing market collapses, as in 2008. In either case, household wealth will decline, and consumption expenditure will follow. Suppose businesses see that consumer spending is falling. That will reduce expectations of the profitability of investment, so businesses will decrease investment expenditure.

This seemed to be the case during the Great Depression, since the physical capacity of the economy to supply goods did not alter much. No flood or earthquake or other natural disaster ruined factories in 1929 or 1930. No outbreak of disease decimated the ranks of workers. No key input price, like the price of oil, soared on world markets. The U.S. economy in 1933 had just about the same factories, workers, and state of technology as it had had four years earlier in 1929—and yet the economy had shrunk dramatically. This also seems to be what happened in 2008.

As Keynes recognized, the events of the Depression contradicted Say's law that "supply creates its own demand." Although production capacity existed, the markets were not able to sell their products. As a result, real GDP was less than potential GDP.

Visit this website (http://openstaxcollege.org/l/expenditures) for raw data used to calculate GDP.

Wage and Price Stickiness

Keynes also pointed out that although AD fluctuated, prices and wages did not immediately respond as economists often expected. Instead, prices and wages are "sticky," making it difficult to restore the economy to full employment and potential GDP. Keynes emphasized one particular reason why wages were sticky: the **coordination argument**. This argument points out that, even if most people would be willing—at least hypothetically—to see a decline in their own wages in bad economic times as long as everyone else also experienced such a decline, a market-oriented economy has no obvious way to implement a plan of coordinated wage reductions. **Unemployment** proposed a number of reasons why wages might be sticky downward, most of which center on the argument that businesses avoid wage cuts because they may in one way or another depress morale and hurt the productivity of the existing workers.

Some modern economists have argued in a Keynesian spirit that, along with wages, other prices may be sticky, too. Many firms do not change their prices every day or even every month. When a firm considers changing prices, it must consider two sets of costs. First, changing prices uses company resources: managers must analyze the competition and market demand and decide the new prices, they must update sales materials, change billing records, and redo product and price labels. Second, frequent price changes may leave customers confused or angry—especially if they discover that a product now costs more than they expected. These costs of changing prices are called **menu costs**—like the costs of printing a new set of menus with different prices in a restaurant. Prices do respond to forces of supply and demand, but from a macroeconomic perspective, the process of changing all prices throughout the economy takes time.

To understand the effect of sticky wages and prices in the economy, consider **Figure 25.4** (a) illustrating the overall labor market, while **Figure 25.4** (b) illustrates a market for a specific good or service. The original equilibrium (E_0) in each market occurs at the intersection of the demand curve (D_0) and supply curve (S_0). When aggregate demand declines, the demand for labor shifts to the left (to D_1) in **Figure 25.4** (a) and the demand for goods shifts to the left (to D_1) in **Figure 25.4** (b). However, because of sticky wages and prices, the wage remains at its original level (W_0) for a period of time and the price remains at its original level (P_0).

As a result, a situation of excess supply—where the quantity supplied exceeds the quantity demanded at the existing wage or price—exists in markets for both labor and goods, and Q_1 is less than Q_0 in both **Figure 25.4** (a) and **Figure 25.4** (b). When many labor markets and many goods markets all across the economy find themselves in this position, the economy is in a recession; that is, firms cannot sell what they wish to produce at the existing market price and do not wish to hire all who are willing to work at the existing market wage. The Clear It Up feature discusses this problem in more detail.

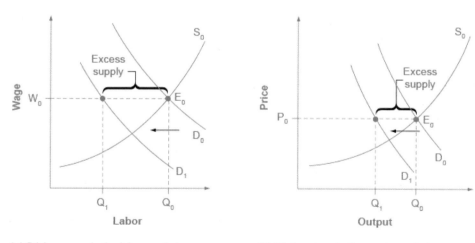

(a) Sticky wages in the labor market   (b) Sticky prices in the goods market

Figure 25.4 Sticky Prices and Falling Demand in the Labor and Goods Market In both (a) and (b), demand shifts left from D_0 to D_1. However, the wage in (a) and the price in (b) do not immediately decline. In (a), the quantity demanded of labor at the original wage (W_0) is Q_0, but with the new demand curve for labor (D_1), it will be Q_1. Similarly, in (b), the quantity demanded of goods at the original price (P_0) is Q_0, but at the new demand curve (D_1) it will be Q_1. An excess supply of labor will exist, which we call unemployment. An excess supply of goods will also exist, where the quantity demanded is substantially less than the quantity supplied. Thus, sticky wages and sticky prices, combined with a drop in demand, bring about unemployment and recession.

Why Is the Pace of Wage Adjustments Slow?

The recovery after the Great Recession in the United States has been slow, with wages stagnant, if not declining. In fact, many low-wage workers at McDonalds, Dominos, and Walmart have threatened to strike for higher wages. Their plight is part of a larger trend in job growth and pay in the post–recession recovery.

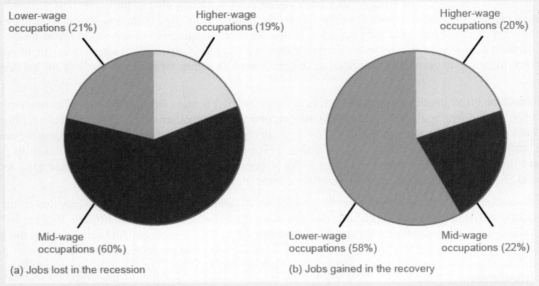

Figure 25.5 Jobs Lost/Gained in the Recession/Recovery Data in the aftermath of the Great Recession suggests that jobs lost were in mid-wage occupations, while jobs gained were in low-wage occupations.

The National Employment Law Project compiled data from the Bureau of Labor Statistics and found that, during the Great Recession, 60% of job losses were in medium-wage occupations. Most of them were replaced during the recovery period with lower-wage jobs in the service, retail, and food industries. **Figure 25.5** illustrates this data.

Wages in the service, retail, and food industries are at or near minimum wage and tend to be both downwardly and upwardly "sticky." Wages are downwardly sticky due to minimum wage laws. They may be upwardly sticky if insufficient competition in low-skilled labor markets enables employers to avoid raising wages that would reduce their profits. At the same time, however, the Consumer Price Index increased 11% between 2007 and 2012, pushing real wages down.

The Two Keynesian Assumptions in the AD/AS Model

Figure 25.6 is the AD/AS diagram which illustrates these two Keynesian assumptions—the importance of aggregate demand in causing recession and the stickiness of wages and prices. Note that because of the stickiness of wages and prices, the aggregate supply curve is flatter than either supply curve (labor or specific good). In fact, if wages and prices were so sticky that they did not fall at all, the aggregate supply curve would be completely flat below potential GDP, as **Figure 25.6** shows. This outcome is an important example of a **macroeconomic externality**, where what happens at the macro level is different from and inferior to what happens at the micro level. For example, a firm should respond to a decrease in demand for its product by cutting its price to increase sales. However, if all firms experience a decrease in demand for their products, sticky prices in the aggregate prevent aggregate demand from rebounding (which we would show as a movement along the AD curve in response to a lower price level).

The original equilibrium of this economy occurs where the aggregate demand function (AD_0) intersects with AS. Since this intersection occurs at potential GDP (Yp), the economy is operating at full employment. When aggregate demand shifts to the left, all the adjustment occurs through decreased real GDP. There is no decrease in the price level. Since the equilibrium occurs at Y_1, the economy experiences substantial unemployment.

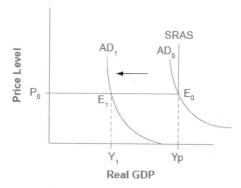

Figure 25.6 A Keynesian Perspective of Recession This figure illustrates the two key assumptions behind Keynesian economics. A recession begins when aggregate demand declines from AD_0 to AD_1. The recession persists because of the assumption of fixed wages and prices, which makes the SRAS flat below potential GDP. If that were not the case, the price level would fall also, raising GDP and limiting the recession. Instead the intersection E_1 occurs in the flat portion of the SRAS curve where GDP is less than potential.

The Expenditure Multiplier

A key concept in Keynesian economics is the **expenditure multiplier**. The expenditure multiplier is the idea that not only does spending affect the equilibrium level of GDP, but that spending is powerful. More precisely, it means that a change in spending causes a more than proportionate change in GDP.

$$\frac{\Delta Y}{\Delta \text{Spending}} > 1$$

The reason for the expenditure multiplier is that one person's spending becomes another person's income, which leads to additional spending and additional income so that the cumulative impact on GDP is larger than the initial increase in spending. The appendix on **The Expenditure-Output Model** provides the details of the multiplier process, but the concept is important enough for us to summarize here. While the multiplier is important for understanding the effectiveness of fiscal policy, it occurs whenever any autonomous increase in spending occurs. Additionally, the multiplier operates in a negative as well as a positive direction. Thus, when investment spending collapsed during the Great Depression, it caused a much larger decrease in real GDP. The size of the multiplier is critical and was a key element in discussions of the effectiveness of the Obama administration's fiscal stimulus package, officially titled the American Recovery and Reinvestment Act of 2009.

25.3 | The Phillips Curve

By the end of this section, you will be able to:
- Explain the Phillips curve, noting its impact on the theories of Keynesian economics
- Graph a Phillips curve
- Identify factors that cause the instability of the Phillips curve
- Analyze the Keynesian policy for reducing unemployment and inflation

The simplified AD/AS model that we have used so far is fully consistent with Keynes's original model. More recent research, though, has indicated that in the real world, an aggregate supply curve is more curved than the right angle that we used in this chapter. Rather, the real-world AS curve is very flat at levels of output far below potential ("the Keynesian zone"), very steep at levels of output above potential ("the neoclassical zone") and curved in between ("the intermediate zone"). **Figure 25.7** illustrates this. The typical aggregate supply curve leads to the concept of the Phillips curve.

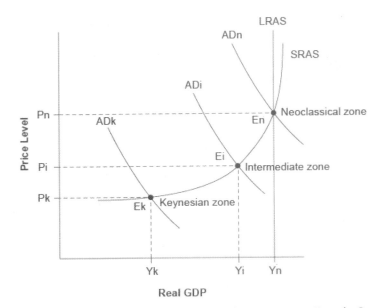

Figure 25.7 Keynes, Neoclassical, and Intermediate Zones in the Aggregate Supply Curve Near the equilibrium Ek, in the Keynesian zone at the SRAS curve's far left, small shifts in AD, either to the right or the left, will affect the output level Yk, but will not much affect the price level. In the Keynesian zone, AD largely determines the quantity of output. Near the equilibrium En, in the neoclassical zone, at the SRAS curve's far right, small shifts in AD, either to the right or the left, will have relatively little effect on the output level Yn, but instead will have a greater effect on the price level. In the neoclassical zone, the near-vertical SRAS curve close to the level of potential GDP (as represented by the LRAS line) largely determines the quantity of output. In the intermediate zone around equilibrium Ei, movement in AD to the right will increase both the output level and the price level, while a movement in AD to the left would decrease both the output level and the price level.

The Discovery of the Phillips Curve

In the 1950s, A.W. Phillips, an economist at the London School of Economics, was studying the Keynesian analytical framework. The Keynesian theory implied that during a recession inflationary pressures are low, but when the level of output is at or even pushing beyond potential GDP, the economy is at greater risk for inflation. Phillips analyzed 60 years of British data and did find that tradeoff between unemployment and inflation, which became known as the **Phillips curve**. **Figure 25.8** shows a theoretical Phillips curve, and the following Work It Out feature shows how the pattern appears for the United States.

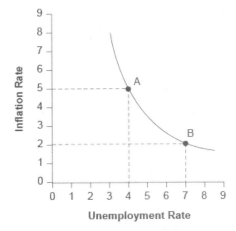

Figure 25.8 A Keynesian Phillips Curve Tradeoff between Unemployment and Inflation A Phillips curve illustrates a tradeoff between the unemployment rate and the inflation rate. If one is higher, the other must be lower. For example, point A illustrates a 5% inflation rate and a 4% unemployment. If the government attempts to reduce inflation to 2%, then it will experience a rise in unemployment to 7%, as point B shows.

This OpenStax book is available for free at http://cnx.org/content/col12122/1.4

Work It Out ⊸⊸⊸⊸

The Phillips Curve for the United States

Step 1. Go to this website (http://1.usa.gov/1c3psdL) to see the 2005 *Economic Report of the President.*

Step 2. Scroll down and locate Table B-63 in the Appendices. This table is titled "Changes in special consumer price indexes, 1960–2004."

Step 3. Download the table in Excel by selecting the XLS option and then selecting the location in which to save the file.

Step 4. Open the downloaded Excel file.

Step 5. View the third column (labeled "Year to year"). This is the inflation rate, measured by the percentage change in the Consumer Price Index.

Step 6. Return to the website and scroll to locate the Appendix Table B-42 "Civilian unemployment rate, 1959–2004.

Step 7. Download the table in Excel.

Step 8. Open the downloaded Excel file and view the second column. This is the overall unemployment rate.

Step 9. Using the data available from these two tables, plot the Phillips curve for 1960–69, with unemployment rate on the x-axis and the inflation rate on the y-axis. Your graph should look like **Figure 25.9**.

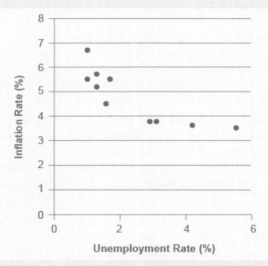

Figure 25.9 The Phillips Curve from 1960–1969 This chart shows the negative relationship between unemployment and inflation.

Step 10. Plot the Phillips curve for 1960–1979. What does the graph look like? Do you still see the tradeoff between inflation and unemployment? Your graph should look like **Figure 25.10**.

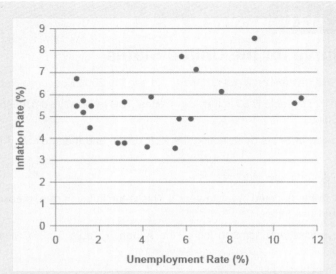

Figure 25.10 U.S. Phillips Curve, 1960–1979 The tradeoff between unemployment and inflation appeared to break down during the 1970s as the Phillips Curve shifted out to the right.

Over this longer period of time, the Phillips curve appears to have shifted out. There is no tradeoff any more.

The Instability of the Phillips Curve

During the 1960s, economists viewed the Phillips curve as a policy menu. A nation could choose low inflation and high unemployment, or high inflation and low unemployment, or anywhere in between. Economies could use fiscal and monetary policy to move up or down the Phillips curve as desired. Then a curious thing happened. When policymakers tried to exploit the tradeoff between inflation and unemployment, the result was an increase in both inflation and unemployment. What had happened? The Phillips curve shifted.

The U.S. economy experienced this pattern in the deep recession from 1973 to 1975, and again in back-to-back recessions from 1980 to 1982. Many nations around the world saw similar increases in unemployment and inflation. This pattern became known as stagflation. (Recall from **The Aggregate Demand/Aggregate Supply Model** that stagflation is an unhealthy combination of high unemployment and high inflation.) Perhaps most important, stagflation was a phenomenon that traditional Keynesian economics could not explain.

Economists have concluded that two factors cause the Phillips curve to shift. The first is supply shocks, like the mid-1970s oil crisis, which first brought stagflation into our vocabulary. The second is changes in people's expectations about inflation. In other words, there may be a tradeoff between inflation and unemployment when people expect no inflation, but when they realize inflation is occurring, the tradeoff disappears. Both factors (supply shocks and changes in inflationary expectations) cause the aggregate supply curve, and thus the Phillips curve, to shift.

In short, we should interpret a downward-sloping Phillips curve as valid for short-run periods of several years, but over longer periods, when aggregate supply shifts, the downward-sloping Phillips curve can shift so that unemployment and inflation are both higher (as in the 1970s and early 1980s) or both lower (as in the early 1990s or first decade of the 2000s).

Keynesian Policy for Fighting Unemployment and Inflation

Keynesian macroeconomics argues that the solution to a recession is **expansionary fiscal policy**, such as tax cuts to stimulate consumption and investment, or direct increases in government spending that would shift the aggregate demand curve to the right. For example, if aggregate demand was originally at ADr in **Figure 25.11**, so that the economy was in recession, the appropriate policy would be for government to shift aggregate demand to the right from ADr to ADf, where the economy would be at potential GDP and full employment.

Keynes noted that while it would be nice if the government could spend additional money on housing, roads, and other amenities, he also argued that if the government could not agree on how to spend money in practical ways, then it could spend in impractical ways. For example, Keynes suggested building monuments, like a modern

This OpenStax book is available for free at http://cnx.org/content/col12122/1.4

equivalent of the Egyptian pyramids. He proposed that the government could bury money underground, and let mining companies start digging up the money again. These suggestions were slightly tongue-in-cheek, but their purpose was to emphasize that a Great Depression is no time to quibble over the specifics of government spending programs and tax cuts when the goal should be to pump up aggregate demand by enough to lift the economy to potential GDP.

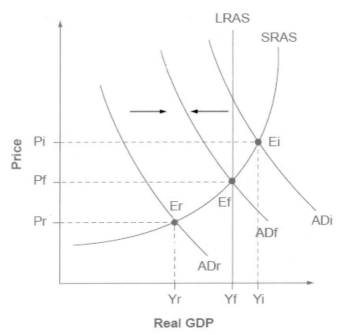

Figure 25.11 Fighting Recession and Inflation with Keynesian Policy If an economy is in recession, with an equilibrium at Er, then the Keynesian response would be to enact a policy to shift aggregate demand to the right from ADr toward ADf. If an economy is experiencing inflationary pressures with an equilibrium at Ei, then the Keynesian response would be to enact a policy response to shift aggregate demand to the left, from ADi toward ADf.

The other side of Keynesian policy occurs when the economy is operating above potential GDP. In this situation, unemployment is low, but inflationary rises in the price level are a concern. The Keynesian response would be **contractionary fiscal policy**, using tax increases or government spending cuts to shift AD to the left. The result would be downward pressure on the price level, but very little reduction in output or very little rise in unemployment. If aggregate demand was originally at ADi in **Figure 25.11**, so that the economy was experiencing inflationary rises in the price level, the appropriate policy would be for government to shift aggregate demand to the left, from ADi toward ADf, which reduces the pressure for a higher price level while the economy remains at full employment.

In the Keynesian economic model, too little aggregate demand brings unemployment and too much brings inflation. Thus, you can think of Keynesian economics as pursuing a "Goldilocks" level of aggregate demand: not too much, not too little, but looking for what is just right.

25.4 | The Keynesian Perspective on Market Forces

By the end of this section, you will be able to:
- Explain the Keynesian perspective on market forces
- Analyze the role of government policy in economic management

Ever since the birth of Keynesian economics in the 1930s, controversy has simmered over the extent to which government should play an active role in managing the economy. In the aftermath of the human devastation and misery of the Great Depression, many people—including many economists—became more aware of vulnerabilities within the market-oriented economic system. Some supporters of Keynesian economics advocated a high degree of government planning in all parts of the economy.

However, Keynes himself was careful to separate the issue of aggregate demand from the issue of how well individual markets worked. He argued that individual markets for goods and services were appropriate and useful, but that sometimes that level of aggregate demand was just too low. When 10 million people are willing and able to work, but one million of them are unemployed, he argued, individual markets may be doing a perfectly good job of allocating the efforts of the nine million workers—the problem is that insufficient aggregate demand exists to support jobs for all 10 million. Thus, he believed that, while government should ensure that overall level of aggregate demand is sufficient for an economy to reach full employment, this task did not imply that the government should attempt to set prices and wages throughout the economy, nor to take over and manage large corporations or entire industries directly.

Even if one accepts the Keynesian economic theory, a number of practical questions remain. In the real world, can government economists identify potential GDP accurately? Is a desired increase in aggregate demand better accomplished by a tax cut or by an increase in government spending? Given the inevitable delays and uncertainties as governments enact policies into law, is it reasonable to expect that the government can implement Keynesian economics? Can fixing a recession really be just as simple as pumping up aggregate demand? **Government Budgets and Fiscal Policy** will probe these issues. The Keynesian approach, with its focus on aggregate demand and sticky prices, has proved useful in understanding how the economy fluctuates in the short run and why recessions and cyclical unemployment occur. In **The Neoclassical Perspective**, we will consider some of the shortcomings of the Keynesian approach and why it is not especially well-suited for long-run macroeconomic analysis.

Bring it Home

The Great Recession

The lessons learned during the 1930s Great Depression and the aggregate expenditure model that John Maynard Keynes proposed gave the modern economists and policymakers of today the tools to effectively navigate the treacherous economy in the latter half of the 2000s. In "How the Great Recession Was Brought to an End", Alan S. Blinder and Mark Zandi wrote that the actions taken by today's policymakers stand in sharp contrast to those of the early years of the Great Depression. Today's economists and policymakers were not content to let the markets recover from recession without taking proactive measures to support consumption and investment. The Federal Reserve actively lowered short-term interest rates and developed innovative ways to pump money into the economy so that credit and investment would not dry up. Both Presidents Bush and Obama and Congress implemented a variety of programs ranging from tax rebates to "Cash for Clunkers" to the Troubled Asset Relief Program to stimulate and stabilize household consumption and encourage investment. Although these policies came under harsh criticism from the public and many politicians, they lessened the impact of the economic downturn and may have saved the country from a second Great Depression.

KEY TERMS

contractionary fiscal policy tax increases or cuts in government spending designed to decrease aggregate demand and reduce inflationary pressures

coordination argument downward wage and price flexibility requires perfect information about the level of lower compensation acceptable to other laborers and market participants

disposable income income after taxes

expansionary fiscal policy tax cuts or increases in government spending designed to stimulate aggregate demand and move the economy out of recession

expenditure multiplier Keynesian concept that asserts that a change in autonomous spending causes a more than proportionate change in real GDP

inflationary gap equilibrium at a level of output above potential GDP

macroeconomic externality occurs when what happens at the macro level is different from and inferior to what happens at the micro level; an example would be where upward sloping supply curves for firms become a flat aggregate supply curve, illustrating that the price level cannot fall to stimulate aggregate demand

menu costs costs firms face in changing prices

Phillips curve the tradeoff between unemployment and inflation

real GDP the amount of goods and services actually sold in a nation

recessionary gap equilibrium at a level of output below potential GDP

sticky wages and prices a situation where wages and prices do not fall in response to a decrease in demand, or do not rise in response to an increase in demand

KEY CONCEPTS AND SUMMARY

25.1 Aggregate Demand in Keynesian Analysis

Aggregate demand is the sum of four components: consumption, investment, government spending, and net exports. Consumption will change for a number of reasons, including movements in income, taxes, expectations about future income, and changes in wealth levels. Investment will change in response to its expected profitability, which in turn is shaped by expectations about future economic growth, the creation of new technologies, the price of key inputs, and tax incentives for investment. Investment will also change when interest rates rise or fall. Political considerations determine government spending and taxes. Exports and imports change according to relative growth rates and prices between two economies.

25.2 The Building Blocks of Keynesian Analysis

Keynesian economics is based on two main ideas: (1) aggregate demand is more likely than aggregate supply to be the primary cause of a short-run economic event like a recession; (2) wages and prices can be sticky, and so, in an economic downturn, unemployment can result. The latter is an example of a macroeconomic externality. While surpluses cause prices to fall at the micro level, they do not necessarily at the macro level. Instead the adjustment to a decrease in demand occurs only through decreased quantities. One reason why prices may be sticky is menu costs, the costs of changing prices. These include internal costs a business faces in changing prices in terms of labeling, recordkeeping, and accounting, and also the costs of communicating the price change to (possibly unhappy) customers. Keynesians also believe in the existence of the expenditure multiplier—the notion that a change in autonomous expenditure causes a more than proportionate change in GDP.

25.3 The Phillips Curve

A Phillips curve shows the tradeoff between unemployment and inflation in an economy. From a Keynesian viewpoint, the Phillips curve should slope down so that higher unemployment means lower inflation, and vice versa. However, a downward-sloping Phillips curve is a short-term relationship that may shift after a few years.

Keynesian macroeconomics argues that the solution to a recession is expansionary fiscal policy, such as tax cuts to stimulate consumption and investment, or direct increases in government spending that would shift the aggregate demand curve to the right. The other side of Keynesian policy occurs when the economy is operating above potential GDP. In this situation, unemployment is low, but inflationary rises in the price level are a concern. The Keynesian response would be contractionary fiscal policy, using tax increases or government spending cuts to shift AD to the left.

25.4 The Keynesian Perspective on Market Forces

The Keynesian prescription for stabilizing the economy implies government intervention at the macroeconomic level—increasing aggregate demand when private demand falls and decreasing aggregate demand when private demand rises. This does not imply that the government should be passing laws or regulations that set prices and quantities in microeconomic markets.

SELF-CHECK QUESTIONS

1. In the Keynesian framework, which of the following events might cause a recession? Which might cause inflation? Sketch AD/AS diagrams to illustrate your answers.
  a. A large increase in the price of the homes people own.
  b. Rapid growth in the economy of a major trading partner.
  c. The development of a major new technology offers profitable opportunities for business.
  d. The interest rate rises.
  e. The good imported from a major trading partner become much less expensive.

2. In a Keynesian framework, using an AD/AS diagram, which of the following government policy choices offer a possible solution to recession? Which offer a possible solution to inflation?
  a. A tax increase on consumer income.
  b. A surge in military spending.
  c. A reduction in taxes for businesses that increase investment.
  d. A major increase in what the U.S. government spends on healthcare.

3. Use the AD/AS model to explain how an inflationary gap occurs, beginning from the initial equilibrium in **Figure 25.6**.

4. Suppose the U.S. Congress cuts federal government spending in order to balance the Federal budget. Use the AD/AS model to analyze the likely impact on output and employment. *Hint*: revisit **Figure 25.6**.

5. How would a decrease in energy prices affect the Phillips curve?

6. Does Keynesian economics require government to set controls on prices, wages, or interest rates?

7. List three practical problems with the Keynesian perspective.

REVIEW QUESTIONS

8. Name some economic events not related to government policy that could cause aggregate demand to shift.

9. Name some government policies that could cause aggregate demand to shift.

10. From a Keynesian point of view, which is more likely to cause a recession: aggregate demand or aggregate supply, and why?

This OpenStax book is available for free at http://cnx.org/content/col12122/1.4

11. Why do sticky wages and prices increase the impact of an economic downturn on unemployment and recession?

12. Explain what economists mean by "menu costs."

13. What tradeoff does a Phillips curve show?

14. Would you expect to see long-run data trace out a stable downward-sloping Phillips curve?

15. What is the Keynesian prescription for recession? For inflation?

16. How did the Keynesian perspective address the economic market failure of the Great Depression?

CRITICAL THINKING QUESTIONS

17. In its recent report, The Conference Board's *Global Economic Outlook 2015*, updated November 2014 (http://www.conference-board.org/data/ globaloutlook.cfm), projects China's growth between 2015 and 2019 to be about 5.5%. *International Business Times* (http://www.ibtimes.com/us-exports-china-have-grown-294-over-past-decade-1338693) reports that China is the United States' third largest export market, with exports to China growing 294% over the last ten years. Explain what impact China has on the U.S. economy.

18. What may happen if growth in China continues or contracts?

19. Does it make sense that wages would be sticky downwards but not upwards? Why or why not?

20. Suppose the economy is operating at potential GDP when it experiences an increase in export demand. How might the economy increase production of exports to meet this demand, given that the economy is already at full employment?

21. Do you think the Phillips curve is a useful tool for analyzing the economy today? Why or why not?

22. Return to the table from the *Economic Report of the President* in the earlier **Work It Out** feature titled "The Phillips Curve for the United States." How would you expect government spending to have changed over the last six years?

23. Explain what types of policies the federal government may have implemented to restore aggregate demand and the potential obstacles policymakers may have encountered.

This OpenStax book is available for free at http://cnx.org/content/col12122/1.4

26 | The Neoclassical Perspective

Figure 26.1 Impact of the Great Recession We can see the impact of the Great Recession in many areas of the economy that impact our daily lives. One of the most visible signs was in the housing market where many people were forced to abandon their homes and other buildings, including ones midway through construction. (Credit: modification of work by A McLin/Flickr Creative Commons)

Bring it Home

Navigating Unchartered Waters

The Great Recession ended in June 2009 after 18 months, according to the National Bureau of Economic Research (NBER). The NBER examines a variety of measures of economic activity to gauge the economy's overall health. These measures include real income, wholesale and retail sales, employment, and industrial production. In the years since the official end of this historic economic downturn, it has become clear that the Great Recession was two-pronged, hitting the U.S. economy with the collapse of the housing market and the failure of the financial system's credit institutions, further contaminating global economies. While the stock market rapidly lost trillions of dollars of value, consumer spending dried up, and companies began cutting jobs, economic policymakers were struggling with how to best combat and prevent a national, and even global economic collapse. In the end, policymakers used a number of controversial monetary and fiscal policies to support the housing market and domestic industries as well as to stabilize the financial sector. Some of these initiatives included:

- Federal Reserve Bank purchase of both traditional and nontraditional assets off banks' balance sheets. By doing this, the Fed injected money into the banking system and increased the amounts of funds available to lend to the business sector and consumers. This also dropped short-term interest rates to as low as zero percent, which had the effect of devaluing U.S. dollars in the global market and boosting exports.

- The Congress and the President also passed several pieces of legislation that would stabilize the financial market. The Troubled Asset Relief Program (TARP), passed in late 2008, allowed the government to inject cash into troubled banks and other financial institutions and help support General Motors and Chrysler as they faced bankruptcy and threatened job losses throughout their supply chain. The American Recovery and Reinvestment Act in early 2009 provided tax rebates to low- and middle-income households to encourage consumer spending.

Four years after the end of the Great Recession, the economy has yet to return to its pre-recession levels of productivity and growth. Annual productivity increased only 1.9% between 2009 and 2012 compared to its 2.7% annual growth rate between 2000 and 2007, unemployment remains above the natural rate, and real GDP continues to lag behind potential growth. The actions the government has taken to stabilize the economy are still under scrutiny and debate about their effectiveness continues. In this chapter, we will discuss the neoclassical perspective on economics and compare it to the Keynesian perspective. At the end of the chapter, we will use the neoclassical perspective to analyze the actions the government has taken in the Great Recession.

Introduction to the Neoclassical Perspective

In this chapter, you will learn about:

- The Building Blocks of Neoclassical Analysis

- The Policy Implications of the Neoclassical Perspective

- Balancing Keynesian and Neoclassical Models

In Chicago, Illinois, the highest recorded temperature was 105° in July 1995, while the lowest recorded temperature was 27° below zero in January 1958. Understanding why these extreme weather patterns occurred would be interesting. However, if you wanted to understand the typical weather pattern in Chicago, instead of focusing on one-time extremes, you would need to look at the entire pattern of data over time.

A similar lesson applies to the study of macroeconomics. It is interesting to study extreme situations, like the 1930s Great Depression or what many have called the 2008-2009 Great Recession. If you want to understand the whole picture, however, you need to look at the long term. Consider the unemployment rate. The unemployment rate has fluctuated from as low as 3.5% in 1969 to as high as 9.7% in 1982 and 9.6% in 2009. Even as the U.S. unemployment rate rose during recessions and declined during expansions, it kept returning to the general neighborhood of 5.0–5.5%. When the nonpartisan Congressional Budget Office carried out its long-range economic forecasts in 2010, it assumed that from 2015 to 2020, after the recession has passed, the unemployment rate would be 5.0%. From a long-run perspective, the economy seems to keep adjusting back to this rate of unemployment.

As the name "neoclassical" implies, this perspective of how the macroeconomy works is a "new" view of the "old" classical model of the economy. The classical view, the predominant economic philosophy until the Great Depression, was that short-term fluctuations in economic activity would rather quickly, with flexible prices, adjust back to full employment. This view of the economy implied a vertical aggregate supply curve at full employment GDP, and prescribed a "hands off" policy approach. For example, if the economy were to slip into recession (a leftward shift of the aggregate demand curve), it would temporarily exhibit a surplus of goods. Falling prices would eliminate this surplus, and the economy would return to full employment level of GDP. No active fiscal or monetary policy was needed. In fact, the classical view was that expansionary fiscal or monetary policy would only cause inflation, rather than increase GDP. The deep and lasting impact of the Great Depression changed this thinking and Keynesian economics, which prescribed active fiscal policy to alleviate weak aggregate demand, became the more mainstream perspective.

This OpenStax book is available for free at http://cnx.org/content/col12122/1.4

26.1 | The Building Blocks of Neoclassical Analysis

By the end of this section, you will be able to:
- Explain the importance of potential GDP in the long run
- Analyze the role of flexible prices
- Interpret a neoclassical model of aggregate demand and aggregate supply
- Evaluate different ways for measuring the speed of macroeconomic adjustment

The **neoclassical perspective** on macroeconomics holds that, in the long run, the economy will fluctuate around its potential GDP and its natural rate of unemployment. This chapter begins with two building blocks of neoclassical economics: (1) potential GDP determines the economy's the size and (2) wages and prices will adjust in a flexible manner so that the economy will adjust back to its potential GDP level of output. The key policy implication is this: The government should focus more on long-term growth and on controlling inflation than on worrying about recession or cyclical unemployment. This focus on long-run growth rather than the short-run fluctuations in the business cycle means that neoclassical economics is more useful for long-run macroeconomic analysis and Keynesian economics is more useful for analyzing the macroeconomic short run. Let's consider the two neoclassical building blocks in turn, and how we can embody them in the aggregate demand/aggregate supply model.

The Importance of Potential GDP in the Long Run

Over the long run, the level of potential GDP determines the size of real GDP. When economists refer to "potential GDP" they are referring to that level of output that an economy can achieve when all resources (land, labor, capital, and entrepreneurial ability) are fully employed. While the unemployment rate in labor markets will never be zero, full employment in the labor market refers to zero cyclical unemployment. There will still be some level of unemployment due to frictional or structural unemployment, but when the economy is operating with zero cyclical unemployment, economists say that the economy is at the natural rate of unemployment or at full employment.

Economists benchmark actual or real GDP against the potential GDP to determine how well the economy is performing. As explained in **Economic Growth**, we can explain GDP growth by increases and investment in physical capital and human capital per person as well as advances in technology. **Physical capital per person** refers to the amount and kind of machinery and equipment available to help people get work done. Compare, for example, your productivity in typing a term paper on a typewriter to working on your laptop with word processing software. Clearly, you will be able to be more productive using word processing software. The technology and level of capital of your laptop and software has increased your productivity. More broadly, the development of GPS technology and Universal Product Codes (those barcodes on every product we buy) has made it much easier for firms to track shipments, tabulate inventories, and sell and distribute products. These two technological innovations, and many others, have increased a nation's ability to produce goods and services for a given population. Likewise, increasing human capital involves increasing levels of knowledge, education, and skill sets per person through vocational or higher education. Physical and human capital improvements with technological advances will increase overall productivity and, thus, GDP.

To see how these improvements have increased productivity and output at the national level, we should examine evidence from the United States. The United States experienced significant growth in the twentieth century due to phenomenal changes in infrastructure, equipment, and technological improvements in physical capital and human capital. The population more than tripled in the twentieth century, from 76 million in 1900 to over 300 million in 2016. The human capital of modern workers is far higher today because the education and skills of workers have risen dramatically. In 1900, only about one-eighth of the U.S. population had completed high school and just one person in 40 had completed a four-year college degree. By 2010, more than 87% of Americans had a high school degree and over 29% had a four-year college degree as well. In 2014, 40% of working-age Americans had a four-year college degree. The average amount of physical capital per worker has grown dramatically. The technology available to modern workers is extraordinarily better than a century ago: cars, airplanes, electrical machinery, smartphones, computers, chemical and biological advances, materials science, health care—the list of technological advances could run on and on. More workers, higher skill levels, larger amounts of physical capital per worker, and amazingly better technology, and potential GDP for the U.S. economy has clearly increased a great deal since 1900.

This growth has fallen below its potential GDP and, at times, has exceeded its potential. For example from 2008 to

2009, the U.S. economy tumbled into recession and remains below its potential. At other times, like in the late 1990s, the economy ran at potential GDP—or even slightly ahead. **Figure 26.2** shows the actual data for the increase in real GDP since 1960. The slightly smoother line shows the potential GDP since 1960 as estimated by the nonpartisan Congressional Budget Office. Most economic recessions and upswings are times when the economy is 1–3% below or above potential GDP in a given year. Clearly, short-run fluctuations around potential GDP do exist, but over the long run, the upward trend of potential GDP determines the size of the economy.

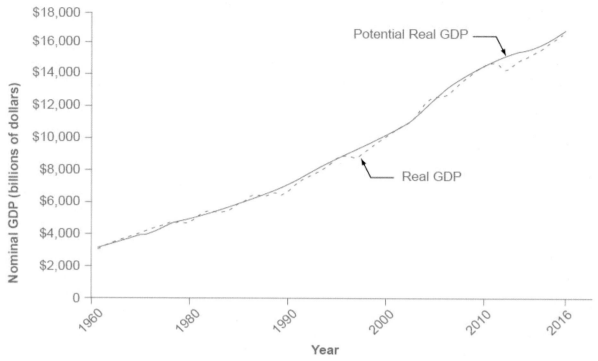

Figure 26.2 Potential and Actual GDP (in 2009 Dollars) Actual GDP falls below potential GDP during and after recessions, like the recessions of 1980 and 1981–82, 1990–91, 2001, and 2008–2009 and continues below potential GDP through 2016. In other cases, actual GDP can be above potential GDP for a time, as in the late 1990s.

In the aggregate demand/aggregate supply model, we show potential GDP as a vertical line. Neoclassical economists who focus on potential GDP as the primary determinant of real GDP argue that the long-run aggregate supply curve is located at potential GDP—that is, we draw the long-run aggregate supply curve as a vertical line at the level of potential GDP, as **Figure 26.3** shows. A vertical LRAS curve means that the level of aggregate supply (or potential GDP) will determine the economy's real GDP, regardless of the level of aggregate demand. Over time, increases in the quantity and quality of physical capital, increases in human capital, and technological advancements shift potential GDP and the vertical LRAS curve gradually to the right. Economists often describe this gradual increase in an economy's potential GDP as a nation's long-term economic growth.

This OpenStax book is available for free at http://cnx.org/content/col12122/1.4

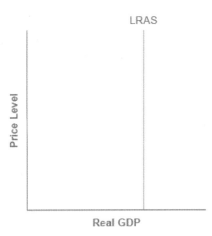

Figure 26.3 A Vertical AS Curve In the neoclassical model, we draw the aggregate supply curve as a vertical line at the level of potential GDP. If AS is vertical, then it determines the level of real output, no matter where we draw the aggregate demand curve. Over time, the LRAS curve shifts to the right as productivity increases and potential GDP expands.

The Role of Flexible Prices

How does the macroeconomy adjust back to its level of potential GDP in the long run? What if aggregate demand increases or decreases? Economists base the neoclassical view of how the macroeconomy adjusts on the insight that even if wages and prices are "sticky", or slow to change, in the short run, they are flexible over time. To understand this better, let's follow the connections from the short-run to the long-run macroeconomic equilibrium.

The aggregate demand and aggregate supply diagram in **Figure 26.4** shows two aggregate supply curves. We draw the original upward sloping aggregate supply curve ($SRAS_0$) is a short-run or Keynesian AS curve. The vertical aggregate supply curve ($LRASn$) is the long-run or neoclassical AS curve, which is located at potential GDP. The original aggregate demand curve, labeled AD_0, so that the original equilibrium occurs at point E_0, at which point the economy is producing at its potential GDP.

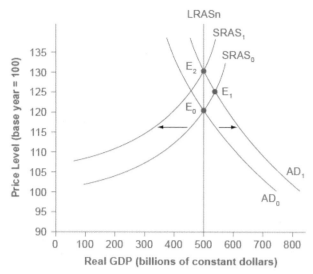

Figure 26.4 The Rebound to Potential GDP after AD Increases The original equilibrium (E_0), at an output level of 500 and a price level of 120, happens at the intersection of the aggregate demand curve (AD_0) and the short-run aggregate supply curve ($SRAS_0$). The output at E_0 is equal to potential GDP. Aggregate demand shifts right from AD_0 to AD_1. The new equilibrium is E_1, with a higher output level of 550 and an increase in the price level to 125. With unemployment rates unsustainably low, eager employers bid up wages, which shifts short-run aggregate supply to the left, from $SRAS_0$ to $SRAS_1$. The new equilibrium (E_2) is at the same original level of output, 500, but at a higher price level of 130. Thus, the long-run aggregate supply curve (LRASn), which is vertical at the level of potential GDP, determines the level of real GDP in this economy in the long run.

Now, imagine that some economic event boosts aggregate demand: perhaps a surge of export sales or a rise in business confidence that leads to more investment, perhaps a policy decision like higher government spending, or perhaps a tax cut that leads to additional aggregate demand. The short-run Keynesian analysis is that the rise in aggregate demand will shift the aggregate demand curve out to the right, from AD_0 to AD_1, leading to a new equilibrium at point E_1 with higher output, lower unemployment, and pressure for an inflationary rise in the price level.

In the long-run neoclassical analysis, however, the chain of economic events is just beginning. As economic output rises above potential GDP, the level of unemployment falls. The economy is now above full employment and there is a labor shortage. Eager employers are trying to bid workers away from other companies and to encourage their current workers to exert more effort and to work longer hours. This high demand for labor will drive up wages. Most employers review their workers salaries only once or twice a year, and so it will take time before the higher wages filter through the economy. As wages do rise, it will mean a leftward shift in the short-run Keynesian aggregate supply curve back to $SRAS_1$, because the price of a major input to production has increased. The economy moves to a new equilibrium (E_2). The new equilibrium has the same level of real GDP as did the original equilibrium (E_0), but there has been an inflationary increase in the price level.

This description of the short-run shift from E_0 to E_1 and the long-run shift from E_1 to E_2 is a step-by-step way of making a simple point: the economy cannot sustain production above its potential GDP in the long run. An economy may produce above its level of potential GDP in the short run, under pressure from a surge in aggregate demand. Over the long run, however, that surge in aggregate demand ends up as an increase in the price level, not as a rise in output.

The rebound of the economy back to potential GDP also works in response to a shift to the left in aggregate demand. **Figure 26.5** again starts with two aggregate supply curves, with $SRAS_0$ showing the original upward sloping short-run Keynesian AS curve and LRASn showing the vertical long-run neoclassical aggregate supply curve. A decrease in aggregate demand—for example, because of a decline in consumer confidence that leads to less consumption and more saving—causes the original aggregate demand curve AD_0 to shift back to AD_1. The shift from the original equilibrium (E_0) to the new equilibrium (E_1) results in a decline in output. The economy is now below full employment and there is a surplus of labor. As output falls below potential GDP, unemployment rises. While a lower price level (i.e., deflation) is rare in the United States, it does happen occasionally during very weak periods of economic activity. For practical purposes, we might consider a lower price level in the AD–AS model as indicative of disinflation, which is a decline in the inflation rate. Thus, the long-run aggregate supply curve LRASn, which is

This OpenStax book is available for free at http://cnx.org/content/col12122/1.4

vertical at the level of potential GDP, ultimately determines this economy's real GDP.

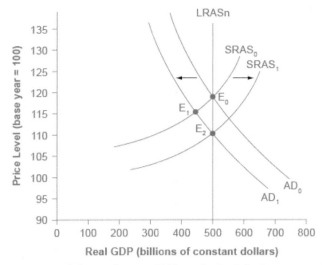

Figure 26.5 A Rebound Back to Potential GDP from a Shift to the Left in Aggregate Demand The original equilibrium (E_0), at an output level of 500 and a price level of 120, happens at the intersection of the aggregate demand curve (AD_0) and the short-run aggregate supply curve ($SRAS_0$). The output at E_0 is equal to potential GDP. Aggregate demand shifts left, from AD_0 to AD_1. The new equilibrium is at E_1, with a lower output level of 450 and downward pressure on the price level of 115. With high unemployment rates, wages are held down. Lower wages are an economy-wide decrease in the price of a key input, which shifts short-run aggregate supply to the right, from $SRAS_0$ to $SRAS_1$. The new equilibrium (E_2) is at the same original level of output, 500, but at a lower price level of 110.

Again, from the neoclassical perspective, this short-run scenario is only the beginning of the chain of events. The higher level of unemployment means more workers looking for jobs. As a result, employers can hold down on pay increases—or perhaps even replace some of their higher-paid workers with unemployed people willing to accept a lower wage. As wages stagnate or fall, this decline in the price of a key input means that the short-run Keynesian aggregate supply curve shifts to the right from its original ($SRAS_0$ to $SRAS_1$). The overall impact in the long run, as the macroeconomic equilibrium shifts from E_0 to E_1 to E_2, is that the level of output returns to potential GDP, where it started. There is, however, downward pressure on the price level. Thus, in the neoclassical view, changes in aggregate demand can have a short-run impact on output and on unemployment—but only a short-run impact. In the long run, when wages and prices are flexible, potential GDP and aggregate supply determine real GDP's size.

How Fast Is the Speed of Macroeconomic Adjustment?

How long does it take for wages and prices to adjust, and for the economy to rebound to its potential GDP? This subject is highly contentious. Keynesian economists argue that if the adjustment from recession to potential GDP takes a very long time, then neoclassical theory may be more hypothetical than practical. In response to John Maynard Keynes' immortal words, "In the long run we are all dead," neoclassical economists respond that even if the adjustment takes as long as, say, ten years the neoclassical perspective remains of central importance in understanding the economy.

One subset of neoclassical economists holds that wage and price adjustment in the macroeconomy might be quite rapid. The theory of **rational expectations** holds that people form the most accurate possible expectations about the future that they can, using all information available to them. In an economy where most people have rational expectations, economic adjustments may happen very quickly.

To understand how rational expectations may affect the speed of price adjustments, think about a situation in the real estate market. Imagine that several events seem likely to push up home values in the neighborhood. Perhaps a local employer announces that it plans to hire many more people or the city announces that it will build a local park or a library in that neighborhood. The theory of rational expectations points out that even though none of the changes will happen immediately, home prices in the neighborhood will rise immediately, because the expectation that homes will be worth more in the future will lead buyers to be willing to pay more in the present. The amount of the immediate increase in home prices will depend on how likely it seems that the announcements about the future will actually happen and on how distant the local jobs and neighborhood improvements are in the future. The key point is that, because of rational expectations, prices do not wait on events, but adjust immediately.

At a macroeconomic level, the theory of rational expectations points out that if the aggregate supply curve is vertical over time, then people should rationally expect this pattern. When a shift in aggregate demand occurs, people and businesses with rational expectations will know that its impact on output and employment will be temporary, while its impact on the price level will be permanent. If firms and workers perceive the outcome of the process in advance, and if all firms and workers know that everyone else is perceiving the process in the same way, then they have no incentive to go through an extended series of short-run scenarios, like a firm first hiring more people when aggregate demand shifts out and then firing those same people when aggregate supply shifts back. Instead, everyone will recognize where this process is heading—toward a change in the price level—and then will act on that expectation. In this scenario, the expected long-run change in the price level may happen very quickly, without a drawn-out zigzag of output and employment first moving one way and then the other.

The theory that people and firms have rational expectations can be a useful simplification, but as a statement about how people and businesses actually behave, the assumption seems too strong. After all, many people and firms are not especially well informed, either about what is happening in the economy or about how the economy works. An alternate assumption is that people and firms act with **adaptive expectations**: they look at past experience and gradually adapt their beliefs and behavior as circumstances change, but are not perfect synthesizers of information and accurate predictors of the future in the sense of rational expectations theory. If most people and businesses have some form of adaptive expectations, then the adjustment from the short run and long run will be traced out in incremental steps that occur over time.

The empirical evidence on the speed of macroeconomic adjustment of prices and wages is not clear-cut. The speed of macroeconomic adjustment probably varies among different countries and time periods. A reasonable guess is that the initial short-run effect of a shift in aggregate demand might last two to five years, before the adjustments in wages and prices cause the economy to adjust back to potential GDP. Thus, one might think of the short run for applying Keynesian analysis as time periods less than two to five years, and the long run for applying neoclassical analysis as longer than five years. For practical purposes, this guideline is frustratingly imprecise, but when analyzing a complex social mechanism like an economy as it evolves over time, some imprecision seems unavoidable.

26.2 | The Policy Implications of the Neoclassical Perspective

By the end of this section, you will be able to:
- Discuss why and how economists measure inflation expectations
- Analyze the impacts of fiscal and monetary policy on aggregate supply and aggregate demand
- Explain the neoclassical Phillips curve, noting its tradeoff between inflation and unemployment
- Identify clear distinctions between neoclassical economics and Keynesian economics

To understand the policy recommendations of the neoclassical economists, it helps to start with the Keynesian perspective. Suppose a decrease in aggregate demand causes the economy to go into recession with high unemployment. The Keynesian response would be to use government policy to stimulate aggregate demand and eliminate the recessionary gap. The neoclassical economists believe that the Keynesian response, while perhaps well intentioned, will not have a good outcome for reasons we will discuss shortly. Since the neoclassical economists believe that the economy will correct itself over time, the only advantage of a Keynesian stabilization policy would be to accelerate the process and minimize the time that the unemployed are out of work. Is that the likely outcome?

Keynesian macroeconomic policy requires some optimism about the government's ability to recognize a situation of too little or too much aggregate demand, and to adjust aggregate demand accordingly with the right level of changes in taxes or spending, all enacted in a timely fashion. After all, neoclassical economists argue, it takes government statisticians months to produce even preliminary estimates of GDP so that politicians know whether a recession is occurring—and those preliminary estimates may be revised substantially later. Moreover, there is the question of timely action. The political process can take more months to enact a tax cut or a spending increase. Political or economic considerations may determine the amount of tax or spending changes. Then the economy will take still more months to put into effect changes in aggregate demand through spending and production. When economists and policy makers consider all of these time lags and political realities, active fiscal policy may fail to address the current problem, and could even make the future economy worse. The average U.S. post-World War II recession has lasted only about a year. By the time government policy activates, the recession will likely be over. As a consequence, the only result of government fine-tuning will be to stimulate the economy when it is already recovering (or to contract the economy when it is already falling). In other words, an active macroeconomic policy is likely to exacerbate the cycles rather than dampen them. Some neoclassical economists believe a large part of the business cycles we observe are due to flawed government policy. To learn about this issue further, read the following Clear It Up feature.

Clear It Up

Why and how do economists measure inflation expectations?

People take expectations about inflation into consideration every time they make a major purchase, such as a house or a car. As inflation fluctuates, so too does the nominal interest rate on loans to buy these goods. The nominal interest rate is comprised of the real rate, plus an **expected inflation** factor. Expected inflation also tells economists about how the public views the economy's direction. Suppose the public expects inflation to increase. This could be the result of positive demand shock due to an expanding economy and increasing aggregate demand. It could also be the result of a negative supply shock, perhaps from rising energy prices, and decreasing aggregate supply. In either case, the public may expect the central bank to engage in contractionary monetary policy to reduce inflation, and this policy results in higher interest rates. If, however economists expect inflation to decrease, the public may anticipate a recession. In turn, the public may expect expansionary monetary policy, and lower interest rates, in the short run. By monitoring expected inflation, economists garner information about the effectiveness of macroeconomic policies. Additionally, monitoring expected inflation allows for projecting the direction of real interest rates that isolate for the effect of inflation. This information is necessary for making decisions about financing investments.

Expectations about inflation may seem like a highly theoretical concept, but, in fact the Federal Reserve Bank measures, inflation expectations based upon early research conducted by Joseph Livingston, a financial journalist for the *Philadelphia Inquirer*. In 1946, he started a twice-a-year survey of economists about their expectations of inflation. After Livingston's death in 1969, the Federal Reserve Bank and other economic research agencies such as the Survey Research Center at the University of Michigan, the American Statistical Association, and the National Bureau of Economic Research continued the survey.

Current Federal Reserve research compares these expectations to actual inflation that has occurred, and the results, so far, are mixed. Economists' forecasts, however, have become notably more accurate in the last few decades. Economists are actively researching how inflation expectations and other economic variables form and change.

Link It Up

Visit this website (https://www.clevelandfed.org/newsroom-and-events/publications/economic-commentary/economic-commentary-archives/2009-economic-commentaries/ec-20090809-a-new-approach-to-gauging-inflation-expectations.aspx) to read "The Federal Reserve Bank of Cleveland's Economic Commentary: A New Approach to Gauging Inflation Expectations" by Joseph G. Haubrich for more information about how economists forecast expected inflation.

The Neoclassical Phillips Curve Tradeoff

The Keynesian Perspective introduced the Phillips curve and explained how it is derived from the aggregate supply curve. The short run upward sloping aggregate supply curve implies a downward sloping Phillips curve; thus, there is a tradeoff between inflation and unemployment in the short run. By contrast, a neoclassical long-run aggregate supply curve will imply a vertical shape for the Phillips curve, indicating no long run tradeoff between inflation and unemployment. **Figure 26.6** (a) shows the vertical AS curve, with three different levels of aggregate demand, resulting in three different equilibria, at three different price levels. At every point along that vertical AS curve, potential GDP and the rate of unemployment remains the same. Assume that for this economy, the natural rate of unemployment is 5%. As a result, the long-run Phillips curve relationship, in **Figure 26.6** (b), is a vertical line, rising up from 5% unemployment, at any level of inflation. Read the following Work It Out feature for additional information on how to interpret inflation and unemployment rates.

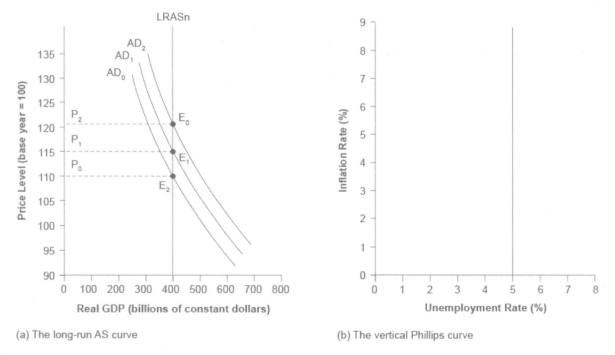

(a) The long-run AS curve   (b) The vertical Phillips curve

Figure 26.6 From a Long-Run AS Curve to a Long-Run Phillips Curve (a) With a vertical LRAS curve, shifts in aggregate demand do not alter the level of output but do lead to changes in the price level. Because output is unchanged between the equilibria E_0, E_1, and E_2, all unemployment in this economy will be due to the natural rate of unemployment. (b) If the natural rate of unemployment is 5%, then the Phillips curve will be vertical. That is, regardless of changes in the price level, the unemployment rate remains at 5%.

This OpenStax book is available for free at http://cnx.org/content/col12122/1.4

Work It Out ⊸○─○─○

Tracking Inflation and Unemployment Rates

Suppose that you have collected data for years on inflation and unemployment rates and recorded them in a table, such as Table 26.1. How do you interpret that information?

Year	Inflation Rate	Unemployment Rate
1970	2%	4%
1975	3%	3%
1980	2%	4%
1985	1%	6%
1990	1%	4%
1995	4%	2%
2000	5%	4%

Table 26.1

Step 1. Plot the data points in a graph with inflation rate on the vertical axis and unemployment rate on the horizontal axis. Your graph will appear similar to Figure 26.7.

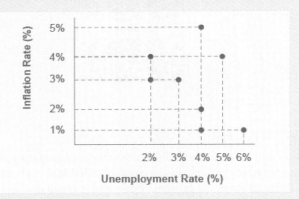

Figure 26.7 Inflation Rates

Step 2. What patterns do you see in the data? You should notice that there are years when unemployment falls but inflation rises, and other years where unemployment rises and inflation falls.

Step 3. Can you determine the natural rate of unemployment from the data or from the graph? As you analyze the graph, it appears that the natural rate of unemployment lies at 4%. This is the rate that the economy appears to adjust back to after an apparent change in the economy. For example, in 1975 the economy appeared to have an increase in aggregate demand. The unemployment rate fell to 3% but inflation increased from 2% to 3%. By 1980, the economy had adjusted back to 4% unemployment and the inflation rate had returned to 2%. In 1985, the economy looks to have suffered a recession as unemployment rose to 6% and inflation fell to 1%. This would be consistent with a decrease in aggregate demand. By 1990, the economy recovered back to 4% unemployment, but at a lower inflation rate of 1%. In 1995 the economy again rebounded and unemployment fell to 2%, but inflation increased to 4%, which is consistent with a large increase in aggregate demand. The economy adjusted back to 4% unemployment but at a higher rate of inflation of 5%. Then in 2000, both unemployment and inflation increased to 5% and 4%, respectively.

Step 4. Do you see the Phillips curve(s) in the data? If we trace the downward sloping trend of data points, we could see a short-run Phillips curve that exhibits the inverse tradeoff between higher unemployment and lower inflation rates. If we trace the vertical line of data points, we could see a long-run Phillips curve at the 4% natural rate of unemployment.

The unemployment rate on the long-run Phillips curve will be the natural rate of unemployment. A small inflationary increase in the price level from AD_0 to AD_1 will have the same natural rate of unemployment as a larger inflationary increase in the price level from AD_0 to AD_2. The macroeconomic equilibrium along the vertical aggregate supply curve can occur at a variety of different price levels, and the natural rate of unemployment can be consistent with all different rates of inflation. The great economist Milton Friedman (1912–2006) summed up the neoclassical view of the long-term Phillips curve tradeoff in a 1967 speech: "[T]here is always a temporary trade-off between inflation and unemployment; there is no permanent trade-off."

In the Keynesian perspective, the primary focus is on getting the level of aggregate demand right in relationship to an upward-sloping aggregate supply curve. That is, the government should adjust AD so that the economy produces at its potential GDP, not so low that cyclical unemployment results and not so high that inflation results. In the neoclassical perspective, aggregate supply will determine output at potential GDP, the natural rate of unemployment determines unemployment, and shifts in aggregate demand are the primary determinant of changes in the price level.

Link It Up 🔗

Visit this website (http://openstaxcollege.org/l/modeledbehavior) to read about the effects of economic intervention.

Fighting Unemployment or Inflation?

As we explained in **Unemployment**, economists divide unemployment into two categories: cyclical unemployment and the natural rate of unemployment, which is the sum of frictional and structural unemployment. Cyclical unemployment results from fluctuations in the business cycle and is created when the economy is producing below potential GDP—giving potential employers less incentive to hire. When the economy is producing at potential GDP, cyclical unemployment will be zero. Because of labor market dynamics, in which people are always entering or exiting the labor force, the unemployment rate never falls to 0%, not even when the economy is producing at or even slightly above potential GDP. Probably the best we can hope for is for the number of job vacancies to equal the number of job seekers. We know that it takes time for job seekers and employers to find each other, and this time is the cause of frictional unemployment. Most economists do not consider frictional unemployment to be a "bad" thing. After all, there will always be workers who are unemployed while looking for a job that is a better match for their skills. There will always be employers that have an open position, while looking for a worker that is a better match for the job. Ideally, these matches happen quickly, but even when the economy is very strong there will be some natural unemployment and this is what the natural rate of unemployment measures.

The neoclassical view of unemployment tends to focus attention away from the cyclical unemployment problem—that is, unemployment caused by recession—while putting more attention on the unemployment rate issue that prevails even when the economy is operating at potential GDP. To put it another way, the neoclassical view of unemployment tends to focus on how the government can adjust public policy to reduce the natural rate of unemployment. Such policy changes might involve redesigning unemployment and welfare programs so that they support those in need, but also offer greater encouragement for job-hunting. It might involve redesigning business rules with an eye to whether they are unintentionally discouraging businesses from taking on new employees. It might involve building institutions to improve the flow of information about jobs and the mobility of workers, to help bring workers and employers together more quickly. For those workers who find that their skills are permanently no longer in demand (for example, the structurally unemployed), economists can design policy to provide opportunities for retraining so that these workers can reenter the labor force and seek employment.

Neoclassical economists will not tend to see aggregate demand as a useful tool for reducing unemployment; after all, with a vertical aggregate supply curve determining economic output, then aggregate demand has no long-run effect on unemployment. Instead, neoclassical economists believe that aggregate demand should be allowed to expand only to match the gradual shifts of aggregate supply to the right—keeping the price level much the same and inflationary pressures low.

If aggregate demand rises rapidly in the neoclassical model, in the long run it leads only to inflationary pressures. **Figure 26.8** shows a vertical LRAS curve and three different levels of aggregate demand, rising from AD_0 to AD_1 to AD_2. As the macroeconomic equilibrium rises from E_0 to E_1 to E_2, the price level rises, but real GDP does not budge; nor does the rate of unemployment, which adjusts to its natural rate. Conversely, reducing inflation has no long-term costs, either. Think about **Figure 26.8** in reverse, as the aggregate demand curve shifts from AD_2 to AD_1 to AD_0, and the equilibrium moves from E_2 to E_1 to E_0. During this process, the price level falls, but, in the long run, neither real GDP nor the natural unemployment rate changes.

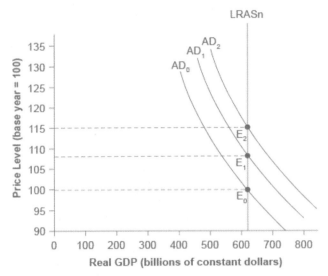

Figure 26.8 How Aggregate Demand Determines the Price Level in the Long Run As aggregate demand shifts to the right, from AD_0 to AD_1 to AD_2, real GDP in this economy and the level of unemployment do not change. However, there is inflationary pressure for a higher price level as the equilibrium changes from E_0 to E_1 to E_2.

Link It Up ☜☞

Visit this website (http://openstaxcollege.org/l/inflatemploy) to read about how inflation and unemployment are related.

Fighting Recession or Encouraging Long-Term Growth?

Neoclassical economists believe that the economy will rebound out of a recession or eventually contract during an expansion because prices and wage rates are flexible and will adjust either upward or downward to restore the economy to its potential GDP. Thus, the key policy question for neoclassicals is how to promote growth of potential GDP. We know that economic growth ultimately depends on the growth rate of long-term productivity. Productivity measures how effective inputs are at producing outputs. We know that U.S. productivity has grown on average about 2% per year. That means that the same amount of inputs produce 2% more output than the year before. We also know that productivity growth varies a great deal in the short term due to cyclical factors. It also varies somewhat in the long term. From 1953–1972, U.S. labor productivity (as measured by output per hour in the business sector) grew at 3.2% per year. From 1973–1992, productivity growth declined significantly to 1.8% per year. Then, from 1993–2014, productivity growth increased slightly to 2% per year. The neoclassical economists believe the underpinnings of long-run productivity growth to be an economy's investments in human capital, physical capital, and technology, operating together in a market-oriented environment that rewards innovation. Government policy should focus on promoting these factors.

Summary of Neoclassical Macroeconomic Policy Recommendations

Let's summarize what neoclassical economists recommend for macroeconomic policy. Neoclassical economists do not believe in "fine-tuning" the economy. They believe that a stable economic environment with a low rate of inflation fosters economic growth. Similarly, tax rates should be low and unchanging. In this environment, private economic agents can make the best possible investment decisions, which will lead to optimal investment in physical and human capital as well as research and development to promote improvements in technology.

Summary of Neoclassical Economics versus Keynesian Economics

Table 26.2 summarizes the key differences between the two schools of thought.

Summary	Neoclassical Economics	Keynesian Economics
Focus: long-term or short term	Long-term	Short-term
Prices and wages: sticky or flexible?	Flexible	Sticky
Economic output: Primarily determined by aggregate demand or aggregate supply?	Aggregate supply	Aggregate demand
Aggregate supply: vertical or upward-sloping?	Vertical	Upward-sloping
Phillips curve vertical or downward-sloping	Vertical	Downward sloping

Table 26.2 Neoclassical versus Keynesian Economics

This OpenStax book is available for free at http://cnx.org/content/col12122/1.4

Summary	Neoclassical Economics	Keynesian Economics
Is aggregate demand a useful tool for controlling inflation?	Yes	Yes
What should be the primary area of policy emphasis for reducing unemployment?	Reform labor market institutions to reduce natural rate of unemployment	Increase aggregate demand to eliminate cyclical unemployment
Is aggregate demand a useful tool for ending recession?	At best, only in the short-run temporary sense, but may just increase inflation instead	Yes

Table 26.2 Neoclassical versus Keynesian Economics

26.3 | Balancing Keynesian and Neoclassical Models

By the end of this section, you will be able to:
- Evaluate how neoclassical economists and Keynesian economists react to recessions
- Analyze the interrelationship between the neoclassical and Keynesian economic models

We can compare finding the balance between Keynesian and Neoclassical models to the challenge of riding two horses simultaneously. When a circus performer stands on two horses, with a foot on each one, much of the excitement for the viewer lies in contemplating the gap between the two. As modern macroeconomists ride into the future on two horses—with one foot on the short-term Keynesian perspective and one foot on the long-term neoclassical perspective—the balancing act may look uncomfortable, but there does not seem to be any way to avoid it. Each approach, Keynesian and neoclassical, has its strengths and weaknesses.

The short-term Keynesian model, built on the importance of aggregate demand as a cause of business cycles and a degree of wage and price rigidity, does a sound job of explaining many recessions and why cyclical unemployment rises and falls. By focusing on the short-run aggregate demand adjustments, Keynesian economics risks overlooking the long-term causes of economic growth or the natural rate of unemployment that exist even when the economy is producing at potential GDP.

The neoclassical model, with its emphasis on aggregate supply, focuses on the underlying determinants of output and employment in markets, and thus tends to put more emphasis on economic growth and how labor markets work. However, the neoclassical view is not especially helpful in explaining why unemployment moves up and down over short time horizons of a few years. Nor is the neoclassical model especially helpful when the economy is mired in an especially deep and long-lasting recession, like the 1930s Great Depression. Keynesian economics tends to view inflation as a price that might sometimes be paid for lower unemployment; neoclassical economics tends to view inflation as a cost that offers no offsetting gains in terms of lower unemployment.

Macroeconomics cannot, however, be summed up as an argument between one group of economists who are pure Keynesians and another group who are pure neoclassicists. Instead, many mainstream economists believe both the Keynesian and neoclassical perspectives. Robert Solow, the Nobel laureate in economics in 1987, described the dual approach in this way:

> At short time scales, I think, something sort of 'Keynesian' is a good approximation, and surely better than anything straight 'neoclassical.' At very long time scales, the interesting questions are best studied in a neoclassical framework, and attention to the Keynesian side of things would be a minor distraction. At the five-to-ten-year time scale, we have to piece things together as best we can, and look for a hybrid model that will do the job.

Many modern macroeconomists spend considerable time and energy trying to construct models that blend the most attractive aspects of the Keynesian and neoclassical approaches. It is possible to construct a somewhat complex mathematical model where aggregate demand and sticky wages and prices matter in the short run, but wages, prices, and aggregate supply adjust in the long run. However, creating an overall model that encompasses both short-term Keynesian and long-term neoclassical models is not easy.

Bring it Home

Navigating Unchartered Waters

Were the policies that the government implemented to stabilize the economy and financial markets during the Great Recession effective? Many economists from both the Keynesian and neoclassical schools have found that they were, although to varying degrees. Alan Blinder of Princeton University and Mark Zandi for Moody's Analytics found that, without fiscal policy, GDP decline would have been significantly more than its 3.3% in 2008 followed by its 0.1% decline in 2009. They also estimated that there would have been 8.5 million more job losses had the government not intervened in the market with the TARP to support the financial industry and key automakers General Motors and Chrysler. Federal Reserve Bank economists Carlos Carvalho, Stefano Eusip, and Christian Grisse found in their study, *Policy Initiatives in the Global Recession: What Did Forecasters Expect?* that once the government implemented policies, forecasters adapted their expectations to these policies. They were more likely to anticipate increases in investment due to lower interest rates brought on by monetary policy and increased economic growth resulting from fiscal policy.

The difficulty with evaluating the effectiveness of the stabilization policies that the government took in response to the Great Recession is that we will never know what would have happened had the government not implemented those policies. Surely some of the programs were more effective at creating and saving jobs, while other programs were less so. The final conclusion on the effectiveness of macroeconomic policies is still up for debate, and further study will no doubt consider the impact of these policies on the U.S. budget and deficit, as well as the U.S. dollar's value in the financial market.

KEY TERMS

adaptive expectations the theory that people look at past experience and gradually adapt their beliefs and behavior as circumstances change

expected inflation a future rate of inflation that consumers and firms build into current decision making

neoclassical perspective the philosophy that, in the long run, the business cycle will fluctuate around the potential, or full-employment, level of output

physical capital per person the amount and kind of machinery and equipment available to help a person produce a good or service

rational expectations the theory that people form the most accurate possible expectations about the future that they can, using all information available to them

KEY CONCEPTS AND SUMMARY

26.1 The Building Blocks of Neoclassical Analysis

The neoclassical perspective argues that, in the long run, the economy will adjust back to its potential GDP level of output through flexible price levels. Thus, the neoclassical perspective views the long-run AS curve as vertical. A rational expectations perspective argues that people have excellent information about economic events and how the economy works and that, as a result, price and other economic adjustments will happen very quickly. In adaptive expectations theory, people have limited information about economic information and how the economy works, and so price and other economic adjustments can be slow.

26.2 The Policy Implications of the Neoclassical Perspective

Neoclassical economists tend to put relatively more emphasis on long-term growth than on fighting recession, because they believe that recessions will fade in a few years and long-term growth will ultimately determine the standard of living. They tend to focus more on reducing the natural rate of unemployment caused by economic institutions and government policies than the cyclical unemployment caused by recession.

Neoclassical economists also see no social benefit to inflation. With an upward-sloping Keynesian AS curve, inflation can arise because an economy is approaching full employment. With a vertical long-run neoclassical AS curve, inflation does not accompany any rise in output. If aggregate supply is vertical, then aggregate demand does not affect the quantity of output. Instead, aggregate demand can only cause inflationary changes in the price level. A vertical aggregate supply curve, where the quantity of output is consistent with many different price levels, also implies a vertical Phillips curve.

26.3 Balancing Keynesian and Neoclassical Models

The Keynesian perspective considers changes to aggregate demand to be the cause of business cycle fluctuations. Keynesians are likely to advocate that policy makers actively attempt to reverse recessionary and inflationary periods because they are not convinced that the self-correcting economy can easily return to full employment.

The neoclassical perspective places more emphasis on aggregate supply. Neoclassical economists believe that long term productivity growth determines the potential GDP level and that the economy typically will return to full employment after a change in aggregate demand. Skeptical of the effectiveness and timeliness of Keynesian policy, neoclassical economists are more likely to advocate a hands-off, or fairly limited, role for active stabilization policy.

While Keynesians would tend to advocate an acceptable tradeoff between inflation and unemployment when counteracting a recession, neoclassical economists argue that no such tradeoff exists. Any short-term gains in lower unemployment will eventually vanish and the result of active policy will only be inflation.

SELF-CHECK QUESTIONS

1. Do rational expectations tend to look back at past experience while adaptive expectations look ahead to the future? Explain your answer.

2. Legislation proposes that the government should use macroeconomic policy to achieve an unemployment rate of zero percent, by increasing aggregate demand for as much and as long as necessary to accomplish this goal. From a neoclassical perspective, how will this policy affect output and the price level in the short run and in the long run? Sketch an aggregate demand/aggregate supply diagram to illustrate your answer. *Hint*: revisit **Figure 26.4**.

3. Would it make sense to argue that rational expectations economics is an extreme version of neoclassical economics? Explain.

4. Summarize the Keynesian and Neoclassical models.

REVIEW QUESTIONS

5. Does neoclassical economics focus on the long term or the short term? Explain your answer.

6. Does neoclassical economics view prices and wages as sticky or flexible? Why?

7. What shape is the long-run aggregate supply curve? Why does it have this shape?

8. What is the difference between rational expectations and adaptive expectations?

9. A neoclassical economist and a Keynesian economist are studying the economy of Vineland. It appears that Vineland is beginning to experience a mild recession with a decrease in aggregate demand. Which of these two economists would likely advocate that the government of Vineland take active measures to reverse this decline in aggregate demand? Why?

10. Do neoclassical economists tend to focus more on long term economic growth or on recessions? Explain briefly.

11. Do neoclassical economists tend to focus more on cyclical unemployment or on inflation? Explain briefly.

12. Do neoclassical economists see a value in tolerating a little more inflation if it brings additional economic output? Explain your answer.

13. If aggregate supply is vertical, what role does aggregate demand play in determining output? In determining the price level?

14. What is the shape of the neoclassical long-run Phillips curve? What assumptions do economists make that lead to this shape?

15. When the economy is experiencing a recession, why would a neoclassical economist be unlikely to argue for aggressive policy to stimulate aggregate demand and return the economy to full employment? Explain your answer.

16. If the economy is suffering through a rampant inflationary period, would a Keynesian economist advocate for stabilization policy that involves higher taxes and higher interest rates? Explain your answer.

CRITICAL THINKING QUESTIONS

17. If most people have rational expectations, how long will recessions last?

18. Explain why the neoclassical economists believe that the government does not need to do much about unemployment. Do you agree or disagree? Explain.

19. Economists from all theoretical persuasions criticized the American Recovery and Reinvestment Act. The "Stimulus Package" was arguably a Keynesian measure so why would a Keynesian economist be critical of it? Why would neoclassical economists be critical?

20. Is it a logical contradiction to be a neoclassical Keynesian? Explain.

This OpenStax book is available for free at http://cnx.org/content/col12122/1.4

PROBLEMS

21. Use **Table 26.3** to answer the following questions.

Price Level	Aggregate Supply	Aggregate Demand
90	3,000	3,500
95	3,000	3,000
100	3,000	2,500
105	3,000	2,200
110	3,000	2,100

Table 26.3

a. Sketch an aggregate supply and aggregate demand diagram.
b. What is the equilibrium output and price level?
c. If aggregate demand shifts right, what is equilibrium output?
d. If aggregate demand shifts left, what is equilibrium output?
e. In this scenario, would you suggest using aggregate demand to alter the level of output or to control any inflationary increases in the price level?

27 | Money and Banking

Figure 27.1 Cowrie Shell or Money? Is this an image of a cowrie shell or money? The answer is: Both. For centuries, people used the extremely durable cowrie shell as a medium of exchange in various parts of the world. (Credit: modification of work by "prilfish"/Flickr Creative Commons)

Bring it Home

The Many Disguises of Money: From Cowries to Bitcoins

Here is a trivia question: In the history of the world, what item did people use for money over the broadest geographic area and for the longest period of time? The answer is not gold, silver, or any precious metal. It is the cowrie, a mollusk shell found mainly off the Maldives Islands in the Indian Ocean. Cowries served as money as early as 700 B.C. in China. By the 1500s, they were in widespread use across India and Africa. For several centuries after that, cowries were the means for exchange in markets including southern Europe, western Africa, India, and China: everything from buying lunch or a ferry ride to paying for a shipload of silk or rice. Cowries were still acceptable as a way of paying taxes in certain African nations in the early twentieth century.

What made cowries work so well as money? First, they are extremely durable—lasting a century or more. As the late economic historian Karl Polyani put it, they can be "poured, sacked, shoveled, hoarded in heaps" while remaining "clean, dainty, stainless, polished, and milk-white." Second, parties could use cowries either by counting shells of a certain size, or—for large purchases—by measuring the weight or volume of the total shells they would exchange. Third, it was impossible to counterfeit a cowrie shell, but dishonest people could counterfeit gold or silver coins by making copies with cheaper metals. Finally, in the heyday of cowrie money, from the 1500s into the 1800s, governments, first the Portuguese, then the Dutch and English, tightly controlled collecting cowries. As a result, the supply of cowries grew quickly enough to serve the needs of commerce, but not so quickly that they were no longer scarce. Money throughout the ages has taken many different forms and continues to evolve even today. What do you think money is?

Introduction to Money and Banking

In this chapter, you will learn about:

- Defining Money by Its Functions
- Measuring Money: Currency, M1, and M2
- The Role of Banks
- How Banks Create Money

The discussion of money and banking is a central component in studying macroeconomics. At this point, you should have firmly in mind the main goals of macroeconomics from **Welcome to Economics!**: economic growth, low unemployment, and low inflation. We have yet to discuss money and its role in helping to achieve our macroeconomic goals.

You should also understand Keynesian and neoclassical frameworks for macroeconomic analysis and how we can embody these frameworks in the aggregate demand/aggregate supply (AD/AS) model. With the goals and frameworks for macroeconomic analysis in mind, the final step is to discuss the two main categories of macroeconomic policy: monetary policy, which focuses on money, banking and interest rates; and fiscal policy, which focuses on government spending, taxes, and borrowing. This chapter discusses what economists mean by money, and how money is closely interrelated with the banking system. **Monetary Policy and Bank Regulation** furthers this discussion.

27.1 | Defining Money by Its Functions

By the end of this section, you will be able to:
- Explain the various functions of money
- Contrast commodity money and fiat money

Money for the sake of money is not an end in itself. You cannot eat dollar bills or wear your bank account. Ultimately, the usefulness of money rests in exchanging it for goods or services. As the American writer and humorist Ambrose Bierce (1842–1914) wrote in 1911, money is a "blessing that is of no advantage to us excepting when we part with it." Money is what people regularly use when purchasing or selling goods and services, and thus both buyers and sellers must widely accept money. This concept of money is intentionally flexible, because money has taken a wide variety of forms in different cultures.

Barter and the Double Coincidence of Wants

To understand the usefulness of money, we must consider what the world would be like without money. How would people exchange goods and services? Economies without money typically engage in the barter system. **Barter**—literally trading one good or service for another—is highly inefficient for trying to coordinate the trades in a modern advanced economy. In an economy without money, an exchange between two people would involve a **double coincidence of wants**, a situation in which two people each want some good or service that the other person can provide. For example, if an accountant wants a pair of shoes, this accountant must find someone who has a pair of shoes in the correct size and who is willing to exchange the shoes for some hours of accounting services. Such a trade is likely to be difficult to arrange. Think about the complexity of such trades in a modern economy, with its extensive division of labor that involves thousands upon thousands of different jobs and goods.

Another problem with the barter system is that it does not allow us to easily enter into future contracts for purchasing many goods and services. For example, if the goods are perishable it may be difficult to exchange them for other goods in the future. Imagine a farmer wanting to buy a tractor in six months using a fresh crop of strawberries. Additionally, while the barter system might work adequately in small economies, it will keep these economies from growing. The time that individuals would otherwise spend producing goods and services and enjoying leisure time they spend bartering.

Functions for Money

Money solves the problems that the barter system creates. (We will get to its definition soon.) First, money serves as a **medium of exchange**, which means that money acts as an intermediary between the buyer and the seller. Instead of exchanging accounting services for shoes, the accountant now exchanges accounting services for money. The accountant then uses this money to buy shoes. To serve as a medium of exchange, people must widely accept money as a method of payment in the markets for goods, labor, and financial capital.

Second, money must serve as a **store of value**. In a barter system, we saw the example of the shoemaker trading shoes for accounting services. However, she risks having her shoes go out of style, especially if she keeps them in a warehouse for future use—their value will decrease with each season. Shoes are not a good store of value. Holding money is a much easier way of storing value. You know that you do not need to spend it immediately because it will still hold its value the next day, or the next year. This function of money does not require that money is a *perfect* store of value. In an economy with inflation, money loses some buying power each year, but it remains money.

Third, money serves as a **unit of account**, which means that it is the ruler by which we measure values. For example, an accountant may charge $100 to file your tax return. That $100 can purchase two pair of shoes at $50 a pair. Money acts as a common denominator, an accounting method that simplifies thinking about trade-offs.

Finally, another function of money is that it must serve as a **standard of deferred payment**. This means that if money is usable today to make purchases, it must also be acceptable to make purchases today that the purchaser will pay in the *future*. Loans and future agreements are stated in monetary terms and the standard of deferred payment is what allows us to buy goods and services today and pay in the future. Thus, **money** serves all of these functions— it is a medium of exchange, store of value, unit of account, and standard of deferred payment.

Commodity versus Fiat Money

Money has taken a wide variety of forms in different cultures. People have used gold, silver, cowrie shells, cigarettes, and even cocoa beans as money. Although we use these items as **commodity money**, they also have a value from use as something other than money. For example, people have used gold throughout the ages as money although today we do not use it as money but rather value it for its other attributes. Gold is a good conductor of electricity and the electronics and aerospace industry use it. Other industries use gold too, such as to manufacture energy efficient reflective glass for skyscrapers and is used in the medical industry as well. Of course, gold also has value because of its beauty and malleability in creating jewelry.

As commodity money, gold has historically served its purpose as a medium of exchange, a store of value, and as a unit of account. **Commodity-backed currencies** are dollar bills or other currencies with values backed up by gold or other commodities held at a bank. During much of its history, gold and silver backed the money supply in the United States. Interestingly, antique dollars dated as late as 1957, have "Silver Certificate" printed over the portrait of George Washington, as **Figure 27.2** shows. This meant that the holder could take the bill to the appropriate bank and exchange it for a dollar's worth of silver.

Figure 27.2 A Silver Certificate and a Modern U.S. Bill Until 1958, silver certificates were commodity-backed money—backed by silver, as indicated by the words "Silver Certificate" printed on the bill. Today, The Federal Reserve backs U.S. bills, but as fiat money (inconvertible paper money made legal tender by a government decree). (Credit: "The.Comedian"/Flickr Creative Commons)

As economies grew and became more global in nature, the use of commodity monies became more cumbersome. Countries moved towards the use of **fiat money**. Fiat money has no intrinsic value, but is declared by a government to be a country's legal tender. The United States' paper money, for example, carries the statement: "THIS NOTE IS LEGAL TENDER FOR ALL DEBTS, PUBLIC AND PRIVATE." In other words, by government decree, if you owe a debt, then legally speaking, you can pay that debt with the U.S. currency, even though it is not backed by a commodity. The only backing of our money is universal faith and trust that the currency has value, and nothing more.

Link It Up

Watch this video (http://openstaxcollege.org/l/moneyhistory) on the "History of Money."

27.2 | Measuring Money: Currency, M1, and M2

By the end of this section, you will be able to:
- Contrast M1 money supply and M2 money supply
- Classify monies as M1 money supply or M2 money supply

Cash in your pocket certainly serves as money; however, what about checks or credit cards? Are they money, too? Rather than trying to state a single way of measuring money, economists offer broader definitions of money based on liquidity. Liquidity refers to how quickly you can use a financial asset to buy a good or service. For example, cash is very liquid. You can use your $10 bill easily to buy a hamburger at lunchtime. However, $10 that you have in your savings account is not so easy to use. You must go to the bank or ATM machine and withdraw that cash to buy your lunch. Thus, $10 in your savings account is *less* liquid.

The Federal Reserve Bank, which is the central bank of the United States, is a bank regulator and is responsible for monetary policy and defines money according to its liquidity. There are two definitions of money: M1 and M2 money supply. **M1 money supply** includes those monies that are very liquid such as cash, checkable (demand) deposits, and traveler's checks **M2 money supply** is less liquid in nature and includes M1 plus savings and time deposits, certificates of deposits, and money market funds.

M1 money supply includes **coins and currency in circulation**—the coins and bills that circulate in an economy that the U.S. Treasury does not hold at the Federal Reserve Bank, or in bank vaults. Closely related to currency are checkable deposits, also known as **demand deposits**. These are the amounts held in checking accounts. They are called demand deposits or checkable deposits because the banking institution must give the deposit holder his money "on demand" when the customer writes a check or uses a debit card. These items together—currency, and checking accounts in banks—comprise the definition of money known as M1, which the Federal Reserve System measures daily.

A broader definition of money, M2 includes everything in M1 but also adds other types of deposits. For example, M2 includes **savings deposits** in banks, which are bank accounts on which you cannot write a check directly, but from which you can easily withdraw the money at an automatic teller machine or bank. Many banks and other financial institutions also offer a chance to invest in **money market funds**, where they pool together the deposits of many individual investors and invest them in a safe way, such as short-term government bonds. Another ingredient of M2 are the relatively small (that is, less than about $100,000) certificates of deposit (CDs) or **time deposits**, which are accounts that the depositor has committed to leaving in the bank for a certain period of time, ranging from a few months to a few years, in exchange for a higher interest rate. In short, all these types of M2 are money that you can withdraw and spend, but which require a greater effort to do so than the items in M1. **Figure 27.3** should help in visualizing the relationship between M1 and M2. Note that M1 is included in the M2 calculation.

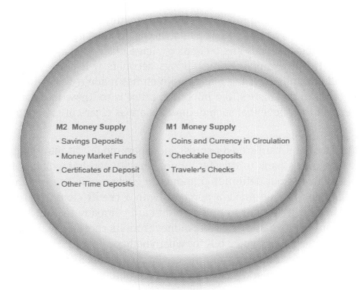

Figure 27.3 The Relationship between M1 and M2 Money M1 and M2 money have several definitions, ranging from narrow to broad. M1 = coins and currency in circulation + checkable (demand) deposit + traveler's checks. M2 = M1 + savings deposits + money market funds + certificates of deposit + other time deposits.

The Federal Reserve System is responsible for tracking the amounts of M1 and M2 and prepares a weekly release of information about the money supply. To provide an idea of what these amounts sound like, according to the Federal Reserve Bank's measure of the U.S. money stock, at the end of February 2015, M1 in the United States was $3 trillion, while M2 was $11.8 trillion. **Table 27.1** provides a breakdown of the portion of each type of money that comprised M1 and M2 in February 2015, as provided by the Federal Reserve Bank.

Components of M1 in the U.S. (February 2015, Seasonally Adjusted)	$ billions
Currency	$1,271.8
Traveler's checks	$2.9
Demand deposits and other checking accounts	$1,713.5
Total M1	$2,988.2 (or $3 trillion)
Components of M2 in the U.S. (February 2015, Seasonally Adjusted)	$ billions
M1 money supply	$2,988.2
Savings accounts	$7,712.1
Time deposits	$509.2
Individual money market mutual fund balances	$610.8
Total M2	$11,820.3 (or $11.8 trillion)

Table 27.1 M1 and M2 Federal Reserve Statistical Release, Money Stock Measures (Source: Federal Reserve Statistical Release, http://www.federalreserve.gov/RELEASES/h6/current/default.htm#t2tg1link)

The lines separating M1 and M2 can become a little blurry. Sometimes businesses do not treat elements of M1 alike. For example, some businesses will not accept personal checks for large amounts, but will accept traveler's checks or cash. Changes in banking practices and technology have made the savings accounts in M2 more similar to the checking accounts in M1. For example, some savings accounts will allow depositors to write checks, use automatic teller machines, and pay bills over the internet, which has made it easier to access savings accounts. As with many other economic terms and statistics, the important point is to know the strengths and limitations of the various definitions of money, not to believe that such definitions are as clear-cut to economists as, say, the definition of nitrogen is to chemists.

Where does "plastic money" like debit cards, credit cards, and smart money fit into this picture? A **debit card**, like a check, is an instruction to the user's bank to transfer money directly and immediately from your bank account to the seller. It is important to note that in our definition of money, it is *checkable deposits* that are money, not the paper check or the debit card. Although you can make a purchase with a **credit card**, the financial institution does not consider it money but rather a short term loan from the credit card company to you. When you make a credit card purchase, the credit card company immediately transfers money from its checking account to the seller, and at the end of the month, the credit card company sends you a bill for what you have charged that month. Until you pay the credit card bill, you have effectively borrowed money from the credit card company. With a **smart card**, you can store a certain value of money on the card and then use the card to make purchases. Some "smart cards" used for specific purposes, like long-distance phone calls or making purchases at a campus bookstore and cafeteria, are not really all that smart, because you can only use them for certain purchases or in certain places.

In short, credit cards, debit cards, and smart cards are different ways to move money when you make a purchase. However, having more credit cards or debit cards does not change the quantity of money in the economy, any more than printing more checks increases the amount of money in your checking account.

One key message underlying this discussion of M1 and M2 is that money in a modern economy is not just paper bills and coins. Instead, money is closely linked to bank accounts. The banking system largely conducts macroeconomic policies concerning money. The next section explains how banks function and how a nation's banking system has the power to create money.

This OpenStax book is available for free at http://cnx.org/content/col12122/1.4

Link It Up 🔗

Read a brief article (http://openstaxcollege.org/l/Sweden) on the current monetary challenges in Sweden.

27.3 | The Role of Banks

By the end of this section, you will be able to:

- Explain how banks act as intermediaries between savers and borrowers
- Evaluate the relationship between banks, savings and loans, and credit unions
- Analyze the causes of bankruptcy and recessions

Somebody once asked the late bank robber named Willie Sutton why he robbed banks. He answered: "That's where the money is." While this may have been true at one time, from the perspective of modern economists, Sutton is both right and wrong. He is wrong because the overwhelming majority of money in the economy is not in the form of currency sitting in vaults or drawers at banks, waiting for a robber to appear. Most money is in the form of bank accounts, which exist only as electronic records on computers. From a broader perspective, however, the bank robber was more right than he may have known. Banking is intimately interconnected with money and consequently, with the broader economy.

Banks make it far easier for a complex economy to carry out the extraordinary range of transactions that occur in goods, labor, and financial capital markets. Imagine for a moment what the economy would be like if everybody had to make all payments in cash. When shopping for a large purchase or going on vacation you might need to carry hundreds of dollars in a pocket or purse. Even small businesses would need stockpiles of cash to pay workers and to purchase supplies. A bank allows people and businesses to store this money in either a checking account or savings account, for example, and then withdraw this money as needed through the use of a direct withdrawal, writing a check, or using a debit card.

Banks are a critical intermediary in what we call the **payment system**, which helps an economy exchange goods and services for money or other financial assets. Also, those with extra money that they would like to save can store their money in a bank rather than look for an individual who is willing to borrow it from them and then repay them at a later date. Those who want to borrow money can go directly to a bank rather than trying to find someone to lend them cash. **Transaction costs** are the costs associated with finding a lender or a borrower for this money. Thus, banks lower transactions costs and act as financial intermediaries—they bring savers and borrowers together. Along with making transactions much safer and easier, banks also play a key role in creating money.

Banks as Financial Intermediaries

An "intermediary" is one who stands between two other parties. Banks are a **financial intermediary**—that is, an institution that operates between a saver who deposits money in a bank and a borrower who receives a loan from that bank. Financial intermediaries include other institutions in the financial market such as insurance companies and pension funds, but we will not include them in this discussion because they are not **depository institutions**, which are institutions that accept money *deposits* and then use these to make loans. All the deposited funds mingle in one big pool, which the financial institution then lends. **Figure 27.4** illustrates the position of banks as financial intermediaries, with deposits flowing into a bank and loans flowing out. Of course, when banks make loans to firms, the banks will try to funnel financial capital to healthy businesses that have good prospects for repaying the loans, not to firms that are suffering losses and may be unable to repay.

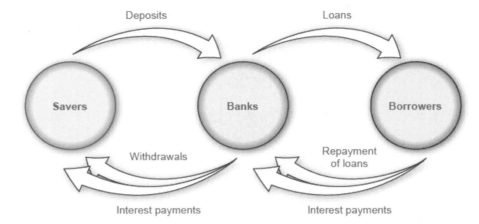

Figure 27.4 Banks as Financial Intermediaries Banks act as financial intermediaries because they stand between savers and borrowers. Savers place deposits with banks, and then receive interest payments and withdraw money. Borrowers receive loans from banks and repay the loans with interest. In turn, banks return money to savers in the form of withdrawals, which also include interest payments from banks to savers.

How are banks, savings and loans, and credit unions related?

Banks have a couple of close cousins: savings institutions and credit unions. Banks, as we explained, receive deposits from individuals and businesses and make loans with the money. Savings institutions are also sometimes called "savings and loans" or "thrifts." They also take loans and make deposits. However, from the 1930s until the 1980s, federal law limited how much interest savings institutions were allowed to pay to depositors. They were also required to make most of their loans in the form of housing-related loans, either to homebuyers or to real-estate developers and builders.

A credit union is a nonprofit financial institution that its members own and run. Members of each credit union decide who is eligible to be a member. Usually, potential members would be everyone in a certain community, or groups of employees, or members of a certain organization. The credit union accepts deposits from members and focuses on making loans back to its members. While there are more credit unions than banks and more banks than savings and loans, the total assets of credit unions are growing.

In 2008, there were 7,085 banks. Due to the bank failures of 2007–2009 and bank mergers, there were 5,571 banks in the United States at the end of the fourth quarter in 2014. According to the Credit Union National Association, as of December 2014 there were 6,535 credit unions with assets totaling $1.1 billion. A day of "Transfer Your Money" took place in 2009 out of general public disgust with big bank bailouts. People were encouraged to transfer their deposits to credit unions. This has grown into the ongoing Move Your Money Project. Consequently, some now hold deposits as large as $50 billion. However, as of 2013, the 12 largest banks (0.2%) controlled 69 percent of all banking assets, according to the Dallas Federal Reserve.

A Bank's Balance Sheet

A **balance sheet** is an accounting tool that lists assets and liabilities. An **asset** is something of value that you own and you can use to produce something. For example, you can use the cash you own to pay your tuition. If you own a home, this is also an asset. A **liability** is a debt or something you owe. Many people borrow money to buy homes. In this case, a home is the asset, but the mortgage is the liability. The **net worth** is the asset value minus how much is owed (the liability). A bank's balance sheet operates in much the same way. A bank's net worth as **bank capital**. We also refer to a bank has assets such as cash held in its vaults, monies that the bank holds at the Federal Reserve bank (called "reserves"), loans that it makes to customers, and bonds.

Figure 27.5 illustrates a hypothetical and simplified balance sheet for the Safe and Secure Bank. Because of the two-column format of the balance sheet, with the T-shape formed by the vertical line down the middle and the horizontal line under "Assets" and "Liabilities," we sometimes call it a **T-account**.

Assets		Liabilities + Net Worth	
Loans	$5 million	Deposits	$10 million
U.S. Government Securities (USGS)	$4 million		
Reserves	$2 million	Net Worth	$1 million

Figure 27.5 A Balance Sheet for the Safe and Secure Bank

The "T" in a T-account separates the assets of a firm, on the left, from its liabilities, on the right. All firms use T-accounts, though most are much more complex. For a bank, the assets are the financial instruments that either the bank is holding (its reserves) or those instruments where other parties owe money to the bank—like loans made by the bank and U.S. Government Securities, such as U.S. treasury bonds purchased by the bank. Liabilities are what the bank owes to others. Specifically, the bank owes any deposits made in the bank to those who have made them. The net worth of the bank is the total assets minus total liabilities. Net worth is included on the liabilities side to have the T account balance to zero. For a healthy business, net worth will be positive. For a bankrupt firm, net worth will be negative. In either case, on a bank's T-account, assets will always equal liabilities plus net worth.

When bank customers deposit money into a checking account, savings account, or a certificate of deposit, the bank views these deposits as liabilities. After all, the bank owes these deposits to its customers, when the customers wish to withdraw their money. In the example in **Figure 27.5**, the Safe and Secure Bank holds $10 million in deposits.

Loans are the first category of bank assets in **Figure 27.5**. Say that a family takes out a 30-year mortgage loan to purchase a house, which means that the borrower will repay the loan over the next 30 years. This loan is clearly an asset from the bank's perspective, because the borrower has a legal obligation to make payments to the bank over time. However, in practical terms, how can we measure the value of the mortgage loan that the borrower is paying over 30 years in the present? One way of measuring the value of something—whether a loan or anything else—is by estimating what another party in the market is willing to pay for it. Many banks issue home loans, and charge various handling and processing fees for doing so, but then sell the loans to other banks or financial institutions who collect the loan payments. We call the market where financial institutions make loans to borrowers the primary loan market, while the market in which financial institutions buy and sell these loans is the secondary loan market.

One key factor that affects what financial institutions are willing to pay for a loan, when they buy it in the secondary loan market, is the perceived riskiness of the loan: that is, given the borrower's characteristics, such as income level and whether the local economy is performing strongly, what proportion of loans of this type will the borrower repay? The greater the risk that a borrower will not repay loan, the less that any financial institution will pay to acquire the loan. Another key factor is to compare the interest rate the financial institution charged on the original loan with the current interest rate in the economy. If the original loan requires the borrower to pay a low interest rate, but current interest rates are relatively high, then a financial institution will pay less to acquire the loan. In contrast, if the original loan requires the borrower to pay a high interest rate, while current interest rates are relatively low, then a financial institution will pay more to acquire the loan. For the Safe and Secure Bank in this example, the total value of its loans if they sold them to other financial institutions in the secondary market is $5 million.

The second category of bank asset is bonds, which are a common mechanism for borrowing, used by the federal and local government, and also private companies, and nonprofit organizations. A bank takes some of the money it has received in deposits and uses the money to buy bonds—typically bonds issued that the U.S. government issues. Government bonds are low-risk because the government is virtually certain to pay off the bond, albeit at a low rate of interest. These bonds are an asset for banks in the same way that loans are an asset: The bank will receive a stream of payments in the future. In our example, the Safe and Secure Bank holds bonds worth a total value of $4 million.

The final entry under assets is **reserves**, which is money that the bank keeps on hand, and that it does not lend or invest in bonds—and thus does not lead to interest payments. The Federal Reserve requires that banks keep a certain percentage of depositors' money on "reserve," which means either in their vaults or at the Federal Reserve Bank. We call this a reserve requirement. (**Monetary Policy and Bank Regulation** will explain how the level of these required reserves are one policy tool that governments have to influence bank behavior.) Additionally, banks may also want to keep a certain amount of reserves on hand in excess of what is required. The Safe and Secure Bank is holding

$2 million in reserves.

We define net worth of a bank as its total assets minus its total liabilities. For the Safe and Secure Bank in **Figure 27.5**, net worth is equal to $1 million; that is, $11 million in assets minus $10 million in liabilities. For a financially healthy bank, the net worth will be positive. If a bank has negative net worth and depositors tried to withdraw their money, the bank would not be able to give all depositors their money.

Link It Up

For some concrete examples of what banks do, watch this video (http://openstaxcollege.org/l/makingsense) from Paul Solman's "Making Sense of Financial News."

How Banks Go Bankrupt

A bank that is bankrupt will have a negative net worth, meaning its assets will be worth less than its liabilities. How can this happen? Again, looking at the balance sheet helps to explain.

A well-run bank will assume that a small percentage of borrowers will not repay their loans on time, or at all, and factor these missing payments into its planning. Remember, the calculations of the banks' expenses every year include a factor for loans that borrowers do not repay, and the value of a bank's loans on its balance sheet assumes a certain level of riskiness because some customers will not repay loans. Even if a bank expects a certain number of loan defaults, it will suffer if the number of loan defaults is much greater than expected, as can happen during a recession. For example, if the Safe and Secure Bank in **Figure 27.5** experienced a wave of unexpected defaults, so that its loans declined in value from $5 million to $3 million, then the assets of the Safe and Secure Bank would decline so that the bank had negative net worth.

Clear It Up

What led to the 2008–2009 financial crisis?

Many banks make mortgage loans so that people can buy a home, but then do not keep the loans on their books as an asset. Instead, the bank sells the loan. These loans are "securitized," which means that they are bundled together into a financial security that a financial institution sells to investors. Investors in these mortgage-backed securities receive a rate of return based on the level of payments that people make on all the mortgages that stand behind the security.

Securitization offers certain advantages. If a bank makes most of its loans in a local area, then the bank may be financially vulnerable if the local economy declines, so that many people are unable to make their payments. However, if a bank sells its local loans, and then buys a mortgage-backed security based on home loans in many parts of the country, it can avoid exposure to local financial risks. (In the simple example in the text, banks just own "bonds." In reality, banks can own a number of financial instruments, as long as these financial investments are safe enough to satisfy the government bank regulators.) From the standpoint of a local homebuyer, securitization offers the benefit that a local bank does not need to have significant extra funds to make a loan, because the bank is only planning to hold that loan for a short time, before selling the loan so that it can pool it into a financial security.

This OpenStax book is available for free at http://cnx.org/content/col12122/1.4

However, securitization also offers one potentially large disadvantage. If a bank plans to hold a mortgage loan as an asset, the bank has an incentive to scrutinize the borrower carefully to ensure that the customer is likely to repay the loan. However, a bank that plans to sell the loan may be less careful in making the loan in the first place. The bank will be more willing to make what we call "subprime loans," which are loans that have characteristics like low or zero down-payment, little scrutiny of whether the borrower has a reliable income, and sometimes low payments for the first year or two that will be followed by much higher payments. Economists dubbed some financial institutions that made subprime loans in the mid-2000s NINJA loans: loans that financial institutions made even though the borrower had demonstrated No Income, No Job, or Assets.

Financial institutions typically sold these subprime loans and turned them into financial securities—but with a twist. The idea was that if losses occurred on these mortgage-backed securities, certain investors would agree to take the first, say, 5% of such losses. Other investors would agree to take, say, the next 5% of losses. By this approach, still other investors would not need to take any losses unless these mortgage-backed financial securities lost 25% or 30% or more of their total value. These complex securities, along with other economic factors, encouraged a large expansion of subprime loans in the mid-2000s.

The economic stage was now set for a banking crisis. Banks thought they were buying only ultra-safe securities, because even though the securities were ultimately backed by risky subprime mortgages, the banks only invested in the part of those securities where they were protected from small or moderate levels of losses. However, as housing prices fell after 2007, and the deepening recession made it harder for many people to make their mortgage payments, many banks found that their mortgage-backed financial assets could be worth much less than they had expected—and so the banks were faced with staring bankruptcy. In the 2008–2011 period, 318 banks failed in the United States.

The risk of an unexpectedly high level of loan defaults can be especially difficult for banks because a bank's liabilities, namely it customers' deposits. Customers can withdraw funds quickly but many of the bank's assets like loans and bonds will only be repaid over years or even decades. This **asset-liability time mismatch**—the ability for customers to withdraw bank's liabilities in the short term while customers repay its assets in the long term—can cause severe problems for a bank. For example, imagine a bank that has loaned a substantial amount of money at a certain interest rate, but then sees interest rates rise substantially. The bank can find itself in a precarious situation. If it does not raise the interest rate it pays to depositors, then deposits will flow to other institutions that offer the higher interest rates that are now prevailing. However, if the bank raises the interest rates that it pays to depositors, it may end up in a situation where it is paying a higher interest rate to depositors than it is collecting from those past loans that it at lower interest rates. Clearly, the bank cannot survive in the long term if it is paying out more in interest to depositors than it is receiving from borrowers.

How can banks protect themselves against an unexpectedly high rate of loan defaults and against the risk of an asset-liability time mismatch? One strategy is for a bank to **diversify** its loans, which means lending to a variety of customers. For example, suppose a bank specialized in lending to a niche market—say, making a high proportion of its loans to construction companies that build offices in one downtown area. If that one area suffers an unexpected economic downturn, the bank will suffer large losses. However, if a bank loans both to consumers who are buying homes and cars and also to a wide range of firms in many industries and geographic areas, the bank is less exposed to risk. When a bank diversifies its loans, those categories of borrowers who have an unexpectedly large number of defaults will tend to be balanced out, according to random chance, by other borrowers who have an unexpectedly low number of defaults. Thus, diversification of loans can help banks to keep a positive net worth. However, if a widespread recession occurs that touches many industries and geographic areas, diversification will not help.

Along with diversifying their loans, banks have several other strategies to reduce the risk of an unexpectedly large number of loan defaults. For example, banks can sell some of the loans they make in the secondary loan market, as we described earlier, and instead hold a greater share of assets in the form of government bonds or reserves. Nevertheless, in a lengthy recession, most banks will see their net worth decline because customers will not repay a higher share of loans in tough economic times.

27.4 | How Banks Create Money

By the end of this section, you will be able to:
- Utilize the money multiplier formulate to determine how banks create money
- Analyze and create T-account balance sheets
- Evaluate the risks and benefits of money and banks

Banks and money are intertwined. It is not just that most money is in the form of bank accounts. The banking system can literally create money through the process of making loans. Let's see how.

Money Creation by a Single Bank

Start with a hypothetical bank called Singleton Bank. The bank has $10 million in deposits. The T-account balance sheet for Singleton Bank, when it holds all of the deposits in its vaults, is in **Figure 27.6**. At this stage, Singleton Bank is simply storing money for depositors and is using these deposits to make loans. In this simplified example, Singleton Bank cannot earn any interest income from these loans and cannot pay its depositors an interest rate either.

Assets		Liabilities + Net Worth	
Reserves	$10 million	Deposits	$10 million

Figure 27.6 Singleton Bank's Balance Sheet: Receives $10 million in Deposits

The Federal Reserve requires Singleton Bank to keep $1 million on reserve (10% of total deposits). It will loan out the remaining $9 million. By loaning out the $9 million and charging interest, it will be able to make interest payments to depositors and earn interest income for Singleton Bank (for now, we will keep it simple and not put interest income on the balance sheet). Instead of becoming just a storage place for deposits, Singleton Bank can become a financial intermediary between savers and borrowers.

This change in business plan alters Singleton Bank's balance sheet, as **Figure 27.7** shows. Singleton's assets have changed. It now has $1 million in reserves and a loan to Hank's Auto Supply of $9 million. The bank still has $10 million in deposits.

Assets		Liabilities + Net Worth	
Reserves	$1 million	Deposits	$10 million
Loan to Hank's Auto Supply	$9 million		

Figure 27.7 Singleton Bank's Balance Sheet: 10% Reserves, One Round of Loans

Singleton Bank lends $9 million to Hank's Auto Supply. The bank records this loan by making an entry on the balance sheet to indicate that it has made a loan. This loan is an asset, because it will generate interest income for the bank. Of course, the loan officer will not allow let Hank to walk out of the bank with $9 million in cash. The bank issues Hank's Auto Supply a cashier's check for the $9 million. Hank deposits the loan in his regular checking account with First National. The deposits at First National rise by $9 million and its reserves also rise by $9 million, as **Figure 27.8** shows. First National must hold 10% of additional deposits as required reserves but is free to loan out the rest

Assets		Liabilities + Net Worth	
Reserves	+ $9 million	Deposits	+ $9 million

Figure 27.8 First National Balance Sheet

Making loans that are deposited into a demand deposit account increases the M1 money supply. Remember the definition of M1 includes checkable (demand) deposits, which one can easily use as a medium of exchange to buy goods and services. Notice that the money supply is now $19 million: $10 million in deposits in Singleton bank and $9 million in deposits at First National. Obviously as Hank's Auto Supply writes checks to pay its bills the deposits will draw down. However, the bigger picture is that a bank must hold enough money in reserves to meet its liabilities.

This OpenStax book is available for free at http://cnx.org/content/col12122/1.4

The rest the bank loans out. In this example so far, bank lending has expanded the money supply by $9 million.

Now, First National must hold only 10% as required reserves ($900,000) but can lend out the other 90% ($8.1 million) in a loan to Jack's Chevy Dealership as **Figure 27.9** shows.

Assets		Liabilities + Net Worth	
Reserves	$900,000	Deposits	+ $9 million
Loans	$8.1 million		

Figure 27.9 First National Balance Sheet

If Jack's deposits the loan in its checking account at Second National, the money supply just increased by an additional $8.1 million, as **Figure 27.10** shows.

Assets		Liabilities + Net Worth	
Reserves	+ $8.1 million	Deposits	+ $8.1 million

Figure 27.10 Second National Bank's Balance Sheet

How is this money creation possible? It is possible because there are multiple banks in the financial system, they are required to hold only a fraction of their deposits, and loans end up deposited in other banks, which increases deposits and, in essence, the money supply.

Link It Up

Watch this video (http://openstaxcollege.org/l/createmoney) to learn more about how banks create money.

The Money Multiplier and a Multi-Bank System

In a system with multiple banks, Singleton Bank deposited the initial excess reserve amount that it decided to lend to Hank's Auto Supply into First National Bank, which is free to loan out $8.1 million. If all banks loan out their excess reserves, the money supply will expand. In a multi-bank system, institutions determine the amount of money that the system can create by using the money multiplier. This tells us by how many times a loan will be "multiplied" as it is spent in the economy and then re-deposited in other banks.

Fortunately, a formula exists for calculating the total of these many rounds of lending in a banking system. The **money multiplier formula** is:

$$\frac{1}{\text{Reserve Requirement}}$$

We then multiply the money multiplier by the change in excess reserves to determine the total amount of M1 money supply created in the banking system. See the Work it Out feature to walk through the multiplier calculation.

Work It Out ○—○—○

Using the Money Multiplier Formula

Using the money multiplier for the example in this text:

Step 1. In the case of Singleton Bank, for whom the reserve requirement is 10% (or 0.10), the money multiplier is 1 divided by .10, which is equal to 10.

Step 2. We have identified that the excess reserves are $9 million, so, using the formula we can determine the total change in the M1 money supply:

$$\text{Total Change in the M1 Money Supply} = \frac{1}{\text{Reserve Requirement}} \times \text{Excess Requirement}$$
$$= \frac{1}{0.10} \times \$9 \text{ million}$$
$$= 10 \times \$9 \text{ million}$$
$$= \$90 \text{ million}$$

Step 3. Thus, we can say that, in this example, the total quantity of money generated in this economy after all rounds of lending are completed will be $90 million.

Cautions about the Money Multiplier

The money multiplier will depend on the proportion of reserves that the Federal Reserve Band requires banks to hold. Additionally, a bank can also choose to hold extra reserves. Banks may decide to vary how much they hold in reserves for two reasons: macroeconomic conditions and government rules. When an economy is in recession, banks are likely to hold a higher proportion of reserves because they fear that customers are less likely to repay loans when the economy is slow. The Federal Reserve may also raise or lower the required reserves held by banks as a policy move to affect the quantity of money in an economy, as **Monetary Policy and Bank Regulation** will discuss.

The process of how banks create money shows how the quantity of money in an economy is closely linked to the quantity of lending or credit in the economy. All the money in the economy, except for the original reserves, is a result of bank loans that institutions repeatedly re-deposit and loan.

Finally, the money multiplier depends on people re-depositing the money that they receive in the banking system. If people instead store their cash in safe-deposit boxes or in shoeboxes hidden in their closets, then banks cannot recirculate the money in the form of loans. Central banks have an incentive to assure that bank deposits are safe because if people worry that they may lose their bank deposits, they may start holding more money in cash, instead of depositing it in banks, and the quantity of loans in an economy will decline. Low-income countries have what economists sometimes refer to as "mattress savings," or money that people are hiding in their homes because they do not trust banks. When mattress savings in an economy are substantial, banks cannot lend out those funds and the money multiplier cannot operate as effectively. The overall quantity of money and loans in such an economy will decline.

Link It Up 🔗

Watch a video (http://openstaxcollege.org/l/moneymyth) of Jem Bendell discussing "The Money Myth."

Money and Banks—Benefits and Dangers

Money and banks are marvelous social inventions that help a modern economy to function. Compared with the alternative of barter, money makes market exchanges vastly easier in goods, labor, and financial markets. Banking makes money still more effective in facilitating exchanges in goods and labor markets. Moreover, the process of banks making loans in financial capital markets is intimately tied to the creation of money.

However, the extraordinary economic gains that are possible through money and banking also suggest some possible corresponding dangers. If banks are not working well, it sets off a decline in convenience and safety of transactions throughout the economy. If the banks are under financial stress, because of a widespread decline in the value of their assets, loans may become far less available, which can deal a crushing blow to sectors of the economy that depend on borrowed money like business investment, home construction, and car manufacturing. The 2008–2009 Great Recession illustrated this pattern.

Bring it Home

The Many Disguises of Money: From Cowries to Bit Coins

The global economy has come a long way since it started using cowrie shells as currency. We have moved away from commodity and commodity-backed paper money to fiat currency. As technology and global integration increases, the need for paper currency is diminishing, too. Every day, we witness the increased use of debit and credit cards.

The latest creation and perhaps one of the purest forms of fiat money is the Bitcoin. Bitcoins are a digital currency that allows users to buy goods and services online. Customers can purchase products and services such as videos and books using Bitcoins. This currency is not backed by any commodity nor has any government decreed as legal tender, yet customers use it as a medium of exchange and can store its value (online at least). It is also unregulated by any central bank, but is created online through people solving very complicated mathematics problems and receiving payment afterward. Bitcoin.org is an information source if you are curious. Bitcoins are a relatively new type of money. At present, because it is not sanctioned as a legal currency by any country nor regulated by any central bank, it lends itself for use in illegal as well as legal trading activities. As technology increases and the need to reduce transactions costs associated with using traditional forms of money increases, Bitcoins or some sort of digital currency may replace our dollar bill, just as man replaced the cowrie shell.

KEY TERMS

asset item of value that a firm or an individual owns

asset–liability time mismatch customers can withdraw a bank's liabilities in the short term while customers repay its assets in the long term

balance sheet an accounting tool that lists assets and liabilities

bank capital a bank's net worth

barter literally, trading one good or service for another, without using money

coins and currency in circulation the coins and bills that circulate in an economy that are not held by the U.S Treasury, at the Federal Reserve Bank, or in bank vaults

commodity money an item that is used as money, but which also has value from its use as something other than money

commodity-backed currencies dollar bills or other currencies with values backed up by gold or another commodity

credit card immediately transfers money from the credit card company's checking account to the seller, and at the end of the month the user owes the money to the credit card company; a credit card is a short-term loan

debit card like a check, is an instruction to the user's bank to transfer money directly and immediately from your bank account to the seller

demand deposit checkable deposit in banks that is available by making a cash withdrawal or writing a check

depository institution institution that accepts money deposits and then uses these to make loans

diversify making loans or investments with a variety of firms, to reduce the risk of being adversely affected by events at one or a few firms

double coincidence of wants a situation in which two people each want some good or service that the other person can provide

fiat money has no intrinsic value, but is declared by a government to be the country's legal tender

financial intermediary an institution that operates between a saver with financial assets to invest and an entity who will borrow those assets and pay a rate of return

liability any amount or debt that a firm or an individual owes

M1 money supply a narrow definition of the money supply that includes currency and checking accounts in banks, and to a lesser degree, traveler's checks.

M2 money supply a definition of the money supply that includes everything in M1, but also adds savings deposits, money market funds, and certificates of deposit

medium of exchange whatever is widely accepted as a method of payment

money whatever serves society in four functions: as a medium of exchange, a store of value, a unit of account, and a standard of deferred payment.

money market fund the deposits of many investors are pooled together and invested in a safe way like short-term government bonds

money multiplier formula total money in the economy divided by the original quantity of money, or change in the

This OpenStax book is available for free at http://cnx.org/content/col12122/1.4

total money in the economy divided by a change in the original quantity of money

net worth the excess of the asset value over and above the amount of the liability; total assets minus total liabilities

payment system helps an economy exchange goods and services for money or other financial assets

reserves funds that a bank keeps on hand and that it does not loan out or invest in bonds

savings deposit bank account where you cannot withdraw money by writing a check, but can withdraw the money at a bank—or can transfer it easily to a checking account

smart card stores a certain value of money on a card and then one can use the card to make purchases

standard of deferred payment money must also be acceptable to make purchases today that will be paid in the future

store of value something that serves as a way of preserving economic value that one can spend or consume in the future

T-account a balance sheet with a two-column format, with the T-shape formed by the vertical line down the middle and the horizontal line under the column headings for "Assets" and "Liabilities"

time deposit account that the depositor has committed to leaving in the bank for a certain period of time, in exchange for a higher rate of interest; also called certificate of deposit

transaction costs the costs associated with finding a lender or a borrower for money

unit of account the common way in which we measure market values in an economy

KEY CONCEPTS AND SUMMARY

27.1 Defining Money by Its Functions
Money is what people in a society regularly use when purchasing or selling goods and services. If money were not available, people would need to barter with each other, meaning that each person would need to identify others with whom they have a double coincidence of wants—that is, each party has a specific good or service that the other desires. Money serves several functions: a medium of exchange, a unit of account, a store of value, and a standard of deferred payment. There are two types of money: commodity money, which is an item used as money, but which also has value from its use as something other than money; and fiat money, which has no intrinsic value, but is declared by a government to be the country's legal tender.

27.2 Measuring Money: Currency, M1, and M2
We measure money with several definitions: M1 includes currency and money in checking accounts (demand deposits). Traveler's checks are also a component of M1, but are declining in use. M2 includes all of M1, plus savings deposits, time deposits like certificates of deposit, and money market funds.

27.3 The Role of Banks
Banks facilitate using money for transactions in the economy because people and firms can use bank accounts when selling or buying goods and services, when paying a worker or receiving payment, and when saving money or receiving a loan. In the financial capital market, banks are financial intermediaries; that is, they operate between savers who supply financial capital and borrowers who demand loans. A balance sheet (sometimes called a T-account) is an accounting tool which lists assets in one column and liabilities in another. The bank's liabilities are its deposits. The bank's assets include its loans, its ownership of bonds, and its reserves (which it does not loan out). We calculate a bank's net worth by subtracting its liabilities from its assets. Banks run a risk of negative net worth if the value of their assets declines. The value of assets can decline because of an unexpectedly high number of defaults on loans, or if interest rates rise and the bank suffers an asset-liability time mismatch in which the bank is receiving a low interest rate on its long-term loans but must pay the currently higher market interest rate to attract depositors. Banks

can protect themselves against these risks by choosing to diversify their loans or to hold a greater proportion of their assets in bonds and reserves. If banks hold only a fraction of their deposits as reserves, then the process of banks' lending money, re-depositing those loans in banks, and the banks making additional loans will create money in the economy.

27.4 How Banks Create Money

We define the money multiplier as the quantity of money that the banking system can generate from each $1 of bank reserves. The formula for calculating the multiplier is 1/reserve ratio, where the reserve ratio is the fraction of deposits that the bank wishes to hold as reserves. The quantity of money in an economy and the quantity of credit for loans are inextricably intertwined. The network of banks making loans, people making deposits, and banks making more loans creates much of the money in an economy.

Given the macroeconomic dangers of a malfunctioning banking system, **Monetary Policy and Bank Regulation** will discuss government policies for controlling the money supply and for keeping the banking system safe.

SELF-CHECK QUESTIONS

1. In many casinos, a person buys chips to use for gambling. Within the casino's walls, customers often can use these chips to buy food and drink or even a hotel room. Do chips in a gambling casino serve all three functions of money?

2. Can you name some item that is a store of value, but does not serve the other functions of money?

3. If you are out shopping for clothes and books, what is easiest and most convenient for you to spend: M1 or M2? Explain your answer.

4. For the following list of items, indicate if they are in M1, M2, or neither:
  a. Your $5,000 line of credit on your Bank of America card
  b. $50 dollars' worth of traveler's checks you have not used yet
  c. $1 in quarters in your pocket
  d. $1200 in your checking account
  e. $2000 you have in a money market account

5. Explain why the money listed under assets on a bank balance sheet may not actually be in the bank?

6. Imagine that you are in the position of buying loans in the secondary market (that is, buying the right to collect the payments on loans) for a bank or other financial services company. Explain why you would be willing to pay more or less for a given loan if:
  a. The borrower has been late on a number of loan payments
  b. Interest rates in the economy as a whole have risen since the bank made the loan
  c. The borrower is a firm that has just declared a high level of profits
  d. Interest rates in the economy as a whole have fallen since the bank made the loan

REVIEW QUESTIONS

7. What are the four functions that money serves?

8. How does the existence of money simplify the process of buying and selling?

9. What is the double-coincidence of wants?

10. What components of money do we count as part of M1?

11. What components of money do we count in M2?

12. Why do we call a bank a financial intermediary?

13. What does a balance sheet show?

14. What are a bank's assets? What are its liabilities?

15. How do you calculate a bank's net worth?

16. How can a bank end up with negative net worth?

17. What is the asset-liability time mismatch that all banks face?

This OpenStax book is available for free at http://cnx.org/content/col12122/1.4

18. What is the risk if a bank does not diversify its loans?

19. How do banks create money?

20. What is the formula for the money multiplier?

CRITICAL THINKING QUESTIONS

21. The Bring it Home Feature discusses the use of cowrie shells as money. Although we no longer use cowrie shells as money, do you think other forms of commodity monies are possible? What role might technology play in our definition of money?

22. Imagine that you are a barber in a world without money. Explain why it would be tricky to obtain groceries, clothing, and a place to live.

23. Explain why you think the Federal Reserve Bank tracks M1 and M2.

24. The total amount of U.S. currency in circulation divided by the U.S. population comes out to about $3,500 per person. That is more than most of us carry. Where is all the cash?

25. Explain the difference between how you would characterize bank deposits and loans as assets and liabilities on your own personal balance sheet and how a bank would characterize deposits and loans as assets and liabilities on its balance sheet.

26. Should banks have to hold 100% of their deposits? Why or why not?

27. Explain what will happen to the money multiplier process if there is an increase in the reserve requirement?

28. What do you think the Federal Reserve Bank did to the reserve requirement during the 2008–2009 Great Recession?

PROBLEMS

29. If you take $100 out of your piggy bank and deposit it in your checking account, how did M1 change? Did M2 change?

30. A bank has deposits of $400. It holds reserves of $50. It has purchased government bonds worth $70. It has made loans of $500. Set up a T-account balance sheet for the bank, with assets and liabilities, and calculate the bank's net worth.

31. Humongous Bank is the only bank in the economy. The people in this economy have $20 million in money, and they deposit all their money in Humongous Bank.

a. Humongous Bank decides on a policy of holding 100% reserves. Draw a T-account for the bank.

b. Humongous Bank is required to hold 5% of its existing $20 million as reserves, and to loan out the rest. Draw a T-account for the bank after it has made its first round of loans.

c. Assume that Humongous bank is part of a multibank system. How much will money supply increase with that original $19 million loan?

28 | Monetary Policy and Bank Regulation

Figure 28.1 Marriner S. Eccles Federal Reserve Headquarters, Washington D.C.   Some of the most influential decisions regarding monetary policy in the United States are made behind these doors. (Credit: modification of work by "squirrel83"/Flickr Creative Commons)

Bring it Home

The Problem of the Zero Percent Interest Rate Lower Bound

Most economists believe that monetary policy (the manipulation of interest rates and credit conditions by a nation's central bank) has a powerful influence on a nation's economy. Monetary policy works when the central bank reduces interest rates and makes credit more available. As a result, business investment and other types of spending increase, causing GDP and employment to grow.

However, what if the interest rates banks pay are close to zero already? They cannot be made negative, can they? That would mean that lenders pay borrowers for the privilege of taking their money. Yet, this was the situation the U.S. Federal Reserve found itself in at the end of the 2008–2009 recession. The federal funds rate, which is the interest rate for banks that the Federal Reserve targets with its monetary policy, was slightly above 5% in 2007. By 2009, it had fallen to 0.16%.

The Federal Reserve's situation was further complicated because fiscal policy, the other major tool for managing the economy, was constrained by fears that the federal budget deficit and the public debt were already too high. What were the Federal Reserve's options? How could the Federal Reserve use monetary policy to stimulate the economy? The answer, as we will see in this chapter, was to change the rules of the game.

Introduction to Monetary Policy and Bank Regulation

In this chapter, you will learn about:

- The Federal Reserve Banking System and Central Banks
- Bank Regulation
- How a Central Bank Executes Monetary Policy
- Monetary Policy and Economic Outcomes
- Pitfalls for Monetary Policy

Money, loans, and banks are all interconnected. Money is deposited in bank accounts, which is then loaned to businesses, individuals, and other banks. When the interlocking system of money, loans, and banks works well, economic transactions smoothly occur in goods and labor markets and savers are connected with borrowers. If the money and banking system does not operate smoothly, the economy can either fall into recession or suffer prolonged inflation.

The government of every country has public policies that support the system of money, loans, and banking. However, these policies do not always work perfectly. This chapter discusses how monetary policy works and what may prevent it from working perfectly.

28.1 | The Federal Reserve Banking System and Central Banks

By the end of this section, you will be able to:
- Explain the structure and organization of the U.S. Federal Reserve
- Discuss how central banks impact monetary policy, promote financial stability, and provide banking services

In making decisions about the money supply, a central bank decides whether to raise or lower interest rates and, in this way, to influence macroeconomic policy, whose goal is low unemployment and low inflation. The central bank is also responsible for regulating all or part of the nation's banking system to protect bank depositors and insure the health of the bank's balance sheet.

We call the organization responsible for conducting monetary policy and ensuring that a nation's financial system operates smoothly the **central bank**. Most nations have central banks or currency boards. Some prominent central banks around the world include the European Central Bank, the Bank of Japan, and the Bank of England. In the United States, we call the central bank the Federal Reserve—often abbreviated as just "the Fed." This section explains the U.S. Federal Reserve's organization and identifies the major central bank's responsibilities.

Structure/Organization of the Federal Reserve

Unlike most central banks, the Federal Reserve is semi-decentralized, mixing government appointees with representation from private-sector banks. At the national level, it is run by a Board of Governors, consisting of seven members appointed by the President of the United States and confirmed by the Senate. Appointments are for 14-year terms and they are arranged so that one term expires January 31 of every even-numbered year. The purpose of the long and staggered terms is to insulate the Board of Governors as much as possible from political pressure so that governors can make policy decisions based only on their economic merits. Additionally, except when filling an unfinished term, each member only serves one term, further insulating decision-making from politics. The Fed's policy decisions do not require congressional approval, and the President cannot ask for a Federal Reserve Governor to resign as the President can with cabinet positions.

One member of the Board of Governors is designated as the Chair. For example, from 1987 until early 2006, the Chair was Alan Greenspan. From 2006 until 2014, Ben Bernanke held the post. The current Chair, Janet Yellen, has made

This OpenStax book is available for free at http://cnx.org/content/col12122/1.4

many headlines already. Why? See the following Clear It Up feature to find out.

Who has the most immediate economic power in the world?

Figure 28.2 Chair of the Federal Reserve Board   Janet L. Yellen is the first woman to hold the position of Chair of the Federal Reserve Board of Governors. (Credit: Board of Governors of the Federal Reserve System)

What individual can make financial market crash or soar just by making a public statement? It is not Bill Gates or Warren Buffett. It is not even the President of the United States. The answer is the Chair of the Federal Reserve Board of Governors. In early 2014, Janet L. Yellen, (**Figure 28.2**) became the first woman to hold this post. The media had described Yellen as "perhaps the most qualified Fed chair in history." With a Ph.D. in economics from Yale University, Yellen has taught macroeconomics at Harvard, the London School of Economics, and most recently at the University of California at Berkeley. From 2004–2010, Yellen was President of the Federal Reserve Bank of San Francisco. Not an ivory tower economist, Yellen became one of the few economists who warned about a possible bubble in the housing market, more than two years before the financial crisis occurred. Yellen served on the Board of Governors of the Federal Reserve twice, most recently as Vice Chair. She also spent two years as Chair of the President's Council of Economic Advisors. If experience and credentials mean anything, Yellen is likely to be an effective Fed chair.

The Fed Chair is first among equals on the Board of Governors. While he or she has only one vote, the Chair controls the agenda, and is the Fed's public voice, so he or she has more power and influence than one might expect.

Link It Up

Visit this website (http://openstaxcollege.org/l/Governors) to see who the current members of the Federal Reserve Board of Governors are. You can follow the links provided for each board member to learn more about their backgrounds, experiences, and when their terms on the board will end.

The Federal Reserve is more than the Board of Governors. The Fed also includes 12 regional Federal Reserve banks, each of which is responsible for supporting the commercial banks and economy generally in its district. **Figure 28.3** shows the Federal Reserve districts and the cities where their regional headquarters are located. The commercial banks in each district elect a Board of Directors for each regional Federal Reserve bank, and that board chooses a president for each regional Federal Reserve district. Thus, the Federal Reserve System includes both federally and private-sector appointed leaders.

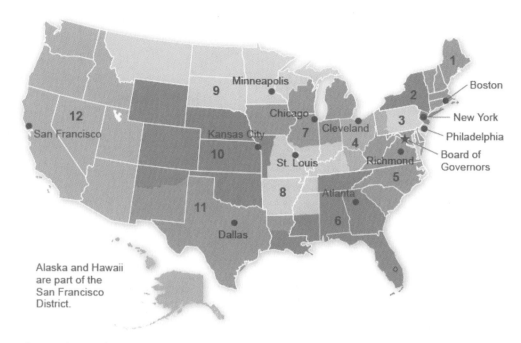

Figure 28.3 The Twelve Federal Reserve Districts   There are twelve regional Federal Reserve banks, each with its district.

What Does a Central Bank Do?

The Federal Reserve, like most central banks, is designed to perform three important functions:

1. To conduct monetary policy

2. To promote stability of the financial system

3. To provide banking services to commercial banks and other depository institutions, and to provide banking services to the federal government.

The first two functions are sufficiently important that we will discuss them in their own modules. The third function we will discuss here.

The Federal Reserve provides many of the same services to banks as banks provide to their customers. For example, all commercial banks have an account at the Fed where they deposit reserves. Similarly, banks can obtain loans from the Fed through the "discount window" facility, which we will discuss in more detail later. The Fed is also responsible for check processing. When you write a check, for example, to buy groceries, the grocery store deposits the check in its bank account. Then, the grocery store's bank returns the physical check (or an image of that actual check) to your bank, after which it transfers funds from your bank account to the grocery store's account. The Fed is responsible for each of these actions.

On a more mundane level, the Federal Reserve ensures that enough currency and coins are circulating through the financial system to meet public demands. For example, each year the Fed increases the amount of currency available in banks around the Christmas shopping season and reduces it again in January.

Finally, the Fed is responsible for assuring that banks are in compliance with a wide variety of consumer protection laws. For example, banks are forbidden from discriminating on the basis of age, race, sex, or marital status. Banks are also required to disclose publicly information about the loans they make for buying houses and how they distribute

This OpenStax book is available for free at http://cnx.org/content/col12122/1.4

the loans geographically, as well as by sex and race of the loan applicants.

28.2 | Bank Regulation

By the end of this section, you will be able to:
- Discuss the relationship between bank regulation and monetary policy
- Explain bank supervision
- Explain how deposit insurance and lender of last resort are two strategies to protect against bank runs

A safe and stable national financial system is a critical concern of the Federal Reserve. The goal is not only to protect individuals' savings, but to protect the integrity of the financial system itself. This esoteric task is usually behind the scenes, but came into view during the 2008–2009 financial crisis, when for a brief period of time, critical parts of the financial system failed and firms became unable to obtain financing for ordinary parts of their business. Imagine if suddenly you were unable to access the money in your bank accounts because your checks were not accepted for payment and your debit cards were declined. This gives an idea of a failure of the payments/financial system.

Bank regulation is intended to maintain banks' solvency by avoiding excessive risk. Regulation falls into a number of categories, including reserve requirements, capital requirements, and restrictions on the types of investments banks may make. In **Money and Banking**, we learned that banks are required to hold a minimum percentage of their deposits on hand as reserves. "On hand" is a bit of a misnomer because, while a portion of bank reserves are held as cash in the bank, the majority are held in the bank's account at the Federal Reserve, and their purpose is to cover desired withdrawals by depositors. Another part of bank regulation is restrictions on the types of investments banks are allowed to make. Banks are permitted to make loans to businesses, individuals, and other banks. They can purchase U.S. Treasury securities but, to protect depositors, they are not permitted to invest in the stock market or other assets that are perceived as too risky.

Bank capital is the difference between a bank's assets and its liabilities. In other words, it is a bank's net worth. A bank must have positive net worth; otherwise it is insolvent or bankrupt, meaning it would not have enough assets to pay back its liabilities. Regulation requires that banks maintain a minimum net worth, usually expressed as a percent of their assets, to protect their depositors and other creditors.

Link It Up

Visit this website (http://openstaxcollege.org/l/bankregulation) to read the brief article, "Stop Confusing Monetary Policy and Bank Regulation."

Bank Supervision

Several government agencies monitor banks' balance sheets to make sure they have positive net worth and are not taking too high a level of risk. Within the U.S. Department of the Treasury, the Office of the Comptroller of the Currency has a national staff of bank examiners who conduct on-site reviews of the 1,500 or so of the largest national banks. The bank examiners also review any foreign banks that have branches in the United States. The Office of the Comptroller of the Currency also monitors and regulates about 800 savings and loan institutions.

The National Credit Union Administration (NCUA) supervises credit unions, which are nonprofit banks that their members run and own. There are over 6,000 credit unions in the U.S. economy, although the typical credit union is small compared to most banks.

The Federal Reserve also has some responsibility for supervising financial institutions. For example, we call conglomerate firms that own banks and other businesses "bank holding companies." While other regulators like the Office of the Comptroller of the Currency supervises the banks, the Federal Reserve supervises the holding companies.

When bank supervision (and bank-like institutions such as savings and loans and credit unions) works well, most banks will remain financially healthy most of the time. If the bank supervisors find that a bank has low or negative net worth, or is making too high a proportion of risky loans, they can require that the bank change its behavior—or, in extreme cases, even force the bank to close or be sold to a financially healthy bank.

Bank supervision can run into both practical and political questions. The practical question is that measuring the value of a bank's assets is not always straightforward. As we discussed in **Money and Banking**, a bank's assets are its loans, and the value of these assets depends on estimates about the risk that customers will not repay these loans. These issues can become even more complex when a bank makes loans to banks or firms in other countries, or arranges financial deals that are much more complex than a basic loan.

The political question arises because a bank supervisor's decision to require a bank to close or to change its financial investments is often controversial, and the bank supervisor often comes under political pressure from the bank's owners and the local politicians to keep quiet and back off.

For example, many observers have pointed out that Japan's banks were in deep financial trouble through most of the 1990s; however, nothing substantial had been done about it by the early 2000s. A similar unwillingness to confront problems with struggling banks is visible across the rest of the world, in East Asia, Latin America, Eastern Europe, Russia, and elsewhere.

In the United States, the government passed laws in the 1990s requiring that bank supervisors make their findings open and public, and that they act as soon as they identify a problem. However, as many U.S. banks were staggered by the 2008-2009 recession, critics of the bank regulators asked pointed questions about why the regulators had not foreseen the banks' financial shakiness earlier, before such large losses had a chance to accumulate.

Bank Runs

Back in the nineteenth century and during the first few decades of the twentieth century (around and during the Great Depression), putting your money in a bank could be nerve-wracking. Imagine that the net worth of your bank became negative, so that the bank's assets were not enough to cover its liabilities. In this situation, whoever withdrew their deposits first received all of their money, and those who did not rush to the bank quickly enough, lost their money. We call depositors racing to the bank to withdraw their deposits, as **Figure 28.4** shows a **bank run**. In the movie *It's a Wonderful Life*, the bank manager, played by Jimmy Stewart, faces a mob of worried bank depositors who want to withdraw their money, but manages to allay their fears by allowing some of them to withdraw a portion of their deposits—using the money from his own pocket that was supposed to pay for his honeymoon.

This OpenStax book is available for free at http://cnx.org/content/col12122/1.4

Figure 28.4 A Run on the Bank Bank runs during the Great Depression only served to worsen the economic situation. (Credit: National Archives and Records Administration)

The risk of bank runs created instability in the banking system. Even a rumor that a bank might experience negative net worth could trigger a bank run and, in a bank run, even healthy banks could be destroyed. Because a bank loans out most of the money it receives, and because it keeps only limited reserves on hand, a bank run of any size would quickly drain any of the bank's available cash. When the bank had no cash remaining, it only intensified the fears of remaining depositors that they could lose their money. Moreover, a bank run at one bank often triggered a chain reaction of runs on other banks. In the late nineteenth and early twentieth century, bank runs were typically not the original cause of a recession—but they could make a recession much worse.

Deposit Insurance

To protect against bank runs, Congress has put two strategies into place: **deposit insurance** and the lender of last resort. Deposit insurance is an insurance system that makes sure depositors in a bank do not lose their money, even if the bank goes bankrupt. About 70 countries around the world, including all of the major economies, have deposit insurance programs. In the United States, the Federal Deposit Insurance Corporation (FDIC) is responsible for deposit insurance. Banks pay an insurance premium to the FDIC. The insurance premium is based on the bank's level of deposits, and then adjusted according to the riskiness of a bank's financial situation. In 2009, for example, a fairly safe bank with a high net worth might have paid 10–20 cents in insurance premiums for every $100 in bank deposits, while a risky bank with very low net worth might have paid 50–60 cents for every $100 in bank deposits.

Bank examiners from the FDIC evaluate the banks' balance sheets, looking at the asset and liability values to determine the risk level. The FDIC provides deposit insurance for about 5,898 banks (as of the end of February 2017). Even if a bank fails, the government guarantees that depositors will receive up to $250,000 of their money in each account, which is enough for almost all individuals, although not sufficient for many businesses. Since the United States enacted deposit insurance in the 1930s, no one has lost any of their insured deposits. Bank runs no longer happen at insured banks.

Lender of Last Resort

The problem with bank runs is not that insolvent banks will fail; they are, after all, bankrupt and need to be shut down. The problem is that bank runs can cause solvent banks to fail and spread to the rest of the financial system. To prevent this, the Fed stands ready to lend to banks and other financial institutions when they cannot obtain funds from anywhere else. This is known as the **lender of last resort** role. For banks, the central bank acting as a lender of last resort helps to reinforce the effect of deposit insurance and to reassure bank customers that they will not lose their money.

The lender of last resort task can arise in other financial crises, as well. During the 1987 stock market crash panic, when U.S. stock values fell by 25% in a single day, the Federal Reserve made a number of short-term emergency loans so that the financial system could keep functioning. During the 2008-2009 recession, we can interpret the Fed's "quantitative easing" policies (discussed below) as a willingness to make short-term credit available as needed in a time when the banking and financial system was under stress.

28.3 | How a Central Bank Executes Monetary Policy

By the end of this section, you will be able to:
- Explain the reason for open market operations
- Evaluate reserve requirements and discount rates
- Interpret and show bank activity through balance sheets

The Federal Reserve's most important function is to conduct the nation's monetary policy. Article I, Section 8 of the U.S. Constitution gives Congress the power "to coin money" and "to regulate the value thereof." As part of the 1913 legislation that created the Federal Reserve, Congress delegated these powers to the Fed. Monetary policy involves managing interest rates and credit conditions, which influences the level of economic activity, as we describe in more detail below.

A central bank has three traditional tools to implement monetary policy in the economy:
- Open market operations
- Changing reserve requirements
- Changing the discount rate

In discussing how these three tools work, it is useful to think of the central bank as a "bank for banks"—that is, each private-sector bank has its own account at the central bank. We will discuss each of these monetary policy tools in the sections below.

Open Market Operations

The most common monetary policy tool in the U.S. is **open market operations**. These take place when the central bank sells or buys U.S. Treasury bonds in order to influence the quantity of bank reserves and the level of interest rates. The specific interest rate targeted in open market operations is the federal funds rate. The name is a bit of a misnomer since the federal funds rate is the interest rate that commercial banks charge making overnight loans to other banks. As such, it is a very short term interest rate, but one that reflects credit conditions in financial markets very well.

The **Federal Open Market Committee (FOMC)** makes the decisions regarding these open market operations. The FOMC comprises seven members of the Federal Reserve's Board of Governors. It also includes five voting members who the Board draws, on a rotating basis, from the regional Federal Reserve Banks. The New York district president is a permanent FOMC voting member and the Board fills other four spots on a rotating, annual basis, from the other 11 districts. The FOMC typically meets every six weeks, but it can meet more frequently if necessary. The FOMC tries to act by consensus; however, the Federal Reserve's chairman has traditionally played a very powerful role in defining and shaping that consensus. For the Federal Reserve, and for most central banks, open market operations have, over the last few decades, been the most commonly used tool of monetary policy.

Link It Up

Visit this website (http://openstaxcollege.org/l/monetarypolicy) for the Federal Reserve to learn more about current monetary policy.

To understand how open market operations affect the money supply, consider the balance sheet of Happy Bank, displayed in **Figure 28.5**. **Figure 28.5** (a) shows that Happy Bank starts with $460 million in assets, divided among reserves, bonds and loans, and $400 million in liabilities in the form of deposits, with a net worth of $60 million. When the central bank purchases $20 million in bonds from Happy Bank, the bond holdings of Happy Bank fall by $20 million and the bank's reserves rise by $20 million, as **Figure 28.5** (b) shows. However, Happy Bank only wants to hold $40 million in reserves (the quantity of reserves with which it started in **Figure 28.5**) (a), so the bank decides to loan out the extra $20 million in reserves and its loans rise by $20 million, as **Figure 28.5**(c) shows. The central bank's open market operation causes Happy Bank to make loans instead of holding its assets in the form of government bonds, which expands the money supply. As the new loans are deposited in banks throughout the economy, these banks will, in turn, loan out some of the deposits they receive, triggering the money multiplier that we discussed in **Money and Banking**.

Assets		Liabilities + Net Worth	
Reserves	40	Deposits	400
Bonds	120		
Loans	300	Net Worth	60

(a) The original balance sheet

Assets		Liabilities + Net Worth	
Reserves	40 + 20 = 60	Deposits	400
Bonds	120 – 20 = 100		
Loans	300	Net Worth	60

(b) The central bank buys bonds

Assets		Liabilities + Net Worth	
Reserves	60 – 20 = 40	Deposits	400
Bonds	100		
Loans	300 + 20 = 320	Net Worth	60

(c) The bank makes additional loans

Figure 28.5

Where did the Federal Reserve get the $20 million that it used to purchase the bonds? A central bank has the power to create money. In practical terms, the Federal Reserve would write a check to Happy Bank, so that Happy Bank can have that money credited to its bank account at the Federal Reserve. In truth, the Federal Reserve created the money to purchase the bonds out of thin air—or with a few clicks on some computer keys.

Open market operations can also reduce the quantity of money and loans in an economy. **Figure 28.6** (a) shows the balance sheet of Happy Bank before the central bank sells bonds in the open market. When Happy Bank purchases $30 million in bonds, Happy Bank sends $30 million of its reserves to the central bank, but now holds an additional $30 million in bonds, as **Figure 28.6** (b) shows. However, Happy Bank wants to hold $40 million in reserves, as in **Figure 28.6** (a), so it will adjust down the quantity of its loans by $30 million, to bring its reserves back to the desired level, as **Figure 28.6** (c) shows. In practical terms, a bank can easily reduce its quantity of loans. At any given time, a bank is receiving payments on loans that it made previously and also making new loans. If the bank just slows down or briefly halts making new loans, and instead adds those funds to its reserves, then its overall quantity of loans will decrease. A decrease in the quantity of loans also means fewer deposits in other banks, and other banks reducing their lending as well, as the money multiplier that we discussed in **Money and Banking** takes effect. What about all those bonds? How do they affect the money supply? Read the following Clear It Up feature for the answer.

Assets		Liabilities + Net Worth	
Reserves	40	Deposits	400
Bonds	120		
Loans	300	Net Worth	60

(a) The original balance sheet

Assets		Liabilities + Net Worth	
Reserves	40 - 30 = 10	Deposits	400
Bonds	120 + 30 = 150		
Loans	300	Net Worth	60

(b) The central bank sells bonds to the bank

Assets		Liabilities + Net Worth	
Reserves	10 + 30 = 40	Deposits	400
Bonds	150		
Loans	300 – 30 = 270	Net Worth	60

(c) The bank makes fewer loans

Figure 28.6

Clear It Up

Does selling or buying bonds increase the money supply?

Is it a sale of bonds by the central bank which increases bank reserves and lowers interest rates or is it a purchase of bonds by the central bank? The easy way to keep track of this is to treat the central bank as being *outside* the banking system. When a central bank buys bonds, money is flowing from the central bank to individual banks in the economy, increasing the money supply in circulation. When a central bank sells bonds, then money from individual banks in the economy is flowing into the central bank—reducing the quantity of money in the economy.

Changing Reserve Requirements

A second method of conducting monetary policy is for the central bank to raise or lower the **reserve requirement**, which, as we noted earlier, is the percentage of each bank's deposits that it is legally required to hold either as cash in their vault or on deposit with the central bank. If banks are required to hold a greater amount in reserves, they have less money available to lend out. If banks are allowed to hold a smaller amount in reserves, they will have a greater amount of money available to lend out.

In early 2015, the Federal Reserve required banks to hold reserves equal to 0% of the first $14.5 million in deposits, then to hold reserves equal to 3% of the deposits up to $103.6 million, and 10% of any amount above $103.6 million. The Fed makes small changes in the reserve requirements almost every year. For example, the $103.6 million dividing line is sometimes bumped up or down by a few million dollars. In practice, the Fed rarely uses large changes in reserve requirements to execute monetary policy. A sudden demand that all banks increase their reserves would be extremely disruptive and difficult for them to comply, while loosening requirements too much would create a danger of banks inability to meet withdrawal demands.

Changing the Discount Rate

The Federal Reserve was founded in the aftermath of the 1907 Financial Panic when many banks failed as a result of bank runs. As mentioned earlier, since banks make profits by lending out their deposits, no bank, even those that are not bankrupt, can withstand a bank run. As a result of the Panic, the Federal Reserve was founded to be the "lender of last resort." In the event of a bank run, sound banks, (banks that were not bankrupt) could borrow as much cash as they needed from the Fed's discount "window" to quell the bank run. We call the interest rate banks pay for such loans the **discount rate**. (They are so named because the bank makes loans against its outstanding loans "at a discount" of their face value.) Once depositors became convinced that the bank would be able to honor their withdrawals, they no longer had a reason to make a run on the bank. In short, the Federal Reserve was originally intended to provide credit passively, but in the years since its founding, the Fed has taken on a more active role with monetary policy.

The third traditional method for conducting monetary policy is to raise or lower the discount rate. If the central bank raises the discount rate, then commercial banks will reduce their borrowing of reserves from the Fed, and instead call in loans to replace those reserves. Since fewer loans are available, the money supply falls and market interest rates rise. If the central bank lowers the discount rate it charges to banks, the process works in reverse.

In recent decades, the Federal Reserve has made relatively few discount loans. Before a bank borrows from the Federal Reserve to fill out its required reserves, the bank is expected to first borrow from other available sources, like other banks. This is encouraged by the Fed charging a higher discount rate than the federal funds rate. Given that most banks borrow little at the discount rate, changing the discount rate up or down has little impact on their behavior. More importantly, the Fed has found from experience that open market operations are a more precise and powerful means of executing any desired monetary policy.

In the Federal Reserve Act, the phrase "...to afford means of rediscounting commercial paper" is contained in its long title. This was the main tool for monetary policy when the Fed was initially created. This illustrates how monetary policy has evolved and how it continues to do so.

28.4 | Monetary Policy and Economic Outcomes

By the end of this section, you will be able to:
- Contrast expansionary monetary policy and contractionary monetary policy
- Explain how monetary policy impacts interest rates and aggregate demand
- Evaluate Federal Reserve decisions over the last forty years
- Explain the significance of quantitative easing (QE)

A monetary policy that lowers interest rates and stimulates borrowing is an **expansionary monetary policy** or **loose monetary policy**. Conversely, a monetary policy that raises interest rates and reduces borrowing in the economy is a **contractionary monetary policy** or **tight monetary policy**. This module will discuss how expansionary and contractionary monetary policies affect interest rates and aggregate demand, and how such policies will affect macroeconomic goals like unemployment and inflation. We will conclude with a look at the Fed's monetary policy practice in recent decades.

The Effect of Monetary Policy on Interest Rates

Consider the market for loanable bank funds in **Figure 28.7**. The original equilibrium (E_0) occurs at an 8% interest rate and a quantity of funds loaned and borrowed of $10 billion. An expansionary monetary policy will shift the supply of loanable funds to the right from the original supply curve (S_0) to S_1, leading to an equilibrium (E_1) with a lower 6% interest rate and a quantity $14 billion in loaned funds. Conversely, a contractionary monetary policy will shift the supply of loanable funds to the left from the original supply curve (S_0) to S_2, leading to an equilibrium (E_2) with a higher 10% interest rate and a quantity of $8 billion in loaned funds.

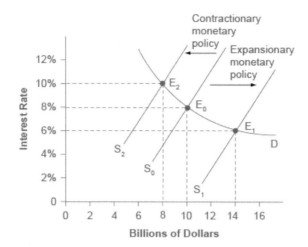

Figure 28.7 Monetary Policy and Interest Rates The original equilibrium occurs at E_0. An expansionary monetary policy will shift the supply of loanable funds to the right from the original supply curve (S_0) to the new supply curve (S_1) and to a new equilibrium of E_1, reducing the interest rate from 8% to 6%. A contractionary monetary policy will shift the supply of loanable funds to the left from the original supply curve (S_0) to the new supply (S_2), and raise the interest rate from 8% to 10%.

How does a central bank "raise" interest rates? When describing the central bank's monetary policy actions, it is common to hear that the central bank "raised interest rates" or "lowered interest rates." We need to be clear about this: more precisely, through open market operations the central bank changes bank reserves in a way which affects the supply curve of loanable funds. As a result, **Figure 28.7** shows that interest rates change. If they do not meet the Fed's target, the Fed can supply more or less reserves until interest rates do.

Recall that the specific interest rate the Fed targets is the **federal funds rate**. The Federal Reserve has, since 1995, established its target federal funds rate in advance of any open market operations.

Of course, financial markets display a wide range of interest rates, representing borrowers with different risk premiums and loans that they must repay over different periods of time. In general, when the federal funds rate drops substantially, other interest rates drop, too, and when the federal funds rate rises, other interest rates rise. However, a fall or rise of one percentage point in the federal funds rate—which remember is for borrowing overnight—will typically have an effect of less than one percentage point on a 30-year loan to purchase a house or a three-year loan to purchase a car. Monetary policy can push the entire spectrum of interest rates higher or lower, but the forces of supply and demand in those specific markets for lending and borrowing set the specific interest rates.

The Effect of Monetary Policy on Aggregate Demand

Monetary policy affects interest rates and the available quantity of loanable funds, which in turn affects several components of aggregate demand. Tight or contractionary monetary policy that leads to higher interest rates and a reduced quantity of loanable funds will reduce two components of aggregate demand. Business investment will decline because it is less attractive for firms to borrow money, and even firms that have money will notice that, with higher interest rates, it is relatively more attractive to put those funds in a financial investment than to make an investment in physical capital. In addition, higher interest rates will discourage consumer borrowing for big-ticket items like houses and cars. Conversely, loose or expansionary monetary policy that leads to lower interest rates and a higher quantity of loanable funds will tend to increase business investment and consumer borrowing for big-ticket items.

If the economy is suffering a recession and high unemployment, with output below potential GDP, expansionary monetary policy can help the economy return to potential GDP. **Figure 28.8** (a) illustrates this situation. This example uses a short-run upward-sloping Keynesian aggregate supply curve (SRAS). The original equilibrium during a recession of E_0 occurs at an output level of 600. An expansionary monetary policy will reduce interest rates and stimulate investment and consumption spending, causing the original aggregate demand curve (AD_0) to shift right to AD_1, so that the new equilibrium (E_1) occurs at the potential GDP level of 700.

This OpenStax book is available for free at http://cnx.org/content/col12122/1.4

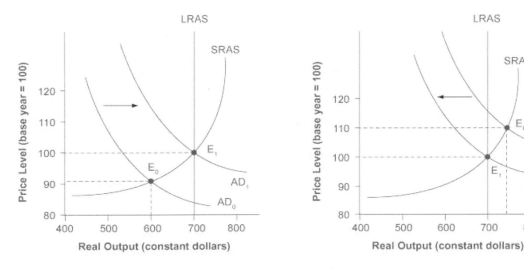

(a) Expansionary monetary policy   (b) Contractionary monetary policy

Figure 28.8 Expansionary or Contractionary Monetary Policy (a) The economy is originally in a recession with the equilibrium output and price shown at E_0. Expansionary monetary policy will reduce interest rates and shift aggregate demand to the right from AD_0 to AD_1, leading to the new equilibrium (E_1) at the potential GDP level of output with a relatively small rise in the price level. (b) The economy is originally producing above the potential GDP level of output at the equilibrium E_0 and is experiencing pressures for an inflationary rise in the price level. Contractionary monetary policy will shift aggregate demand to the left from AD_0 to AD_1, thus leading to a new equilibrium (E_1) at the potential GDP level of output.

Conversely, if an economy is producing at a quantity of output above its potential GDP, a contractionary monetary policy can reduce the inflationary pressures for a rising price level. In **Figure 28.8** (b), the original equilibrium (E_0) occurs at an output of 750, which is above potential GDP. A contractionary monetary policy will raise interest rates, discourage borrowing for investment and consumption spending, and cause the original demand curve (AD_0) to shift left to AD_1, so that the new equilibrium (E_1) occurs at the potential GDP level of 700.

These examples suggest that monetary policy should be **countercyclical**; that is, it should act to counterbalance the business cycles of economic downturns and upswings. The Fed should loosen monetary policy when a recession has caused unemployment to increase and tighten it when inflation threatens. Of course, countercyclical policy does pose a danger of overreaction. If loose monetary policy seeking to end a recession goes too far, it may push aggregate demand so far to the right that it triggers inflation. If tight monetary policy seeking to reduce inflation goes too far, it may push aggregate demand so far to the left that a recession begins. **Figure 28.9** (a) summarizes the chain of effects that connect loose and tight monetary policy to changes in output and the price level.

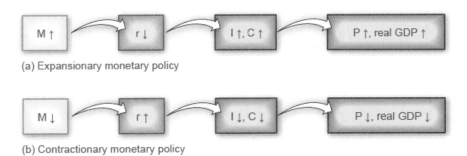

(a) Expansionary monetary policy

(b) Contractionary monetary policy

Figure 28.9 The Pathways of Monetary Policy (a) In expansionary monetary policy the central bank causes the supply of money and loanable funds to increase, which lowers the interest rate, stimulating additional borrowing for investment and consumption, and shifting aggregate demand right. The result is a higher price level and, at least in the short run, higher real GDP. (b) In contractionary monetary policy, the central bank causes the supply of money and credit in the economy to decrease, which raises the interest rate, discouraging borrowing for investment and consumption, and shifting aggregate demand left. The result is a lower price level and, at least in the short run, lower real GDP.

Federal Reserve Actions Over Last Four Decades

For the period from the mid-1970s up through the end of 2007, we can summarize Federal Reserve monetary policy by looking at how it targeted the federal funds interest rate using open market operations.

Of course, telling the story of the U.S. economy since 1975 in terms of Federal Reserve actions leaves out many other macroeconomic factors that were influencing unemployment, recession, economic growth, and inflation over this time. The nine episodes of Federal Reserve action outlined in the sections below also demonstrate that we should consider the central bank as one of the leading actors influencing the macro economy. As we noted earlier, the single person with the greatest power to influence the U.S. economy is probably the Federal Reserve chairperson.

Figure 28.10 shows how the Federal Reserve has carried out monetary policy by targeting the federal funds interest rate in the last few decades. The graph shows the federal funds interest rate (remember, this interest rate is set through open market operations), the unemployment rate, and the inflation rate since 1975. Different episodes of monetary policy during this period are indicated in the figure.

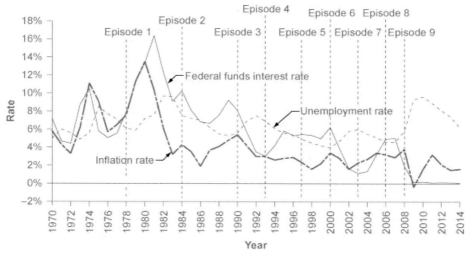

Figure 28.10 Monetary Policy, Unemployment, and Inflation   Through the episodes here, the Federal Reserve typically reacted to higher inflation with a contractionary monetary policy and a higher interest rate, and reacted to higher unemployment with an expansionary monetary policy and a lower interest rate.

Episode 1

Consider Episode 1 in the late 1970s. The rate of inflation was very high, exceeding 10% in 1979 and 1980, so the Federal Reserve used tight monetary policy to raise interest rates, with the federal funds rate rising from 5.5% in 1977 to 16.4% in 1981. By 1983, inflation was down to 3.2%, but aggregate demand contracted sharply enough that back-to-back recessions occurred in 1980 and in 1981–1982, and the unemployment rate rose from 5.8% in 1979 to 9.7% in 1982.

Episode 2

In Episode 2, when economists persuaded the Federal Reserve in the early 1980s that inflation was declining, the Fed began slashing interest rates to reduce unemployment. The federal funds interest rate fell from 16.4% in 1981 to 6.8% in 1986. By 1986 or so, inflation had fallen to about 2% and the unemployment rate had come down to 7%, and was still falling.

Episode 3

However, in Episode 3 in the late 1980s, inflation appeared to be creeping up again, rising from 2% in 1986 up toward 5% by 1989. In response, the Federal Reserve used contractionary monetary policy to raise the federal funds rates from 6.6% in 1987 to 9.2% in 1989. The tighter monetary policy stopped inflation, which fell from above 5% in 1990 to under 3% in 1992, but it also helped to cause the 1990-1991 recession, and the unemployment rate rose from 5.3% in 1989 to 7.5% by 1992.

Episode 4

This OpenStax book is available for free at http://cnx.org/content/col12122/1.4

In Episode 4, in the early 1990s, when the Federal Reserve was confident that inflation was back under control, it reduced interest rates, with the federal funds interest rate falling from 8.1% in 1990 to 3.5% in 1992. As the economy expanded, the unemployment rate declined from 7.5% in 1992 to less than 5% by 1997.

Episodes 5 and 6

In Episodes 5 and 6, the Federal Reserve perceived a risk of inflation and raised the federal funds rate from 3% to 5.8% from 1993 to 1995. Inflation did not rise, and the period of economic growth during the 1990s continued. Then in 1999 and 2000, the Fed was concerned that inflation seemed to be creeping up so it raised the federal funds interest rate from 4.6% in December 1998 to 6.5% in June 2000. By early 2001, inflation was declining again, but a recession occurred in 2001. Between 2000 and 2002, the unemployment rate rose from 4.0% to 5.8%.

Episodes 7 and 8

In Episodes 7 and 8, the Federal Reserve conducted a loose monetary policy and slashed the federal funds rate from 6.2% in 2000 to just 1.7% in 2002, and then again to 1% in 2003. They actually did this because of fear of Japan-style deflation. This persuaded them to lower the Fed funds further than they otherwise would have. The recession ended, but, unemployment rates were slow to decline in the early 2000s. Finally, in 2004, the unemployment rate declined and the Federal Reserve began to raise the federal funds rate until it reached 5% by 2007.

Episode 9

In Episode 9, as the Great Recession took hold in 2008, the Federal Reserve was quick to slash interest rates, taking them down to 2% in 2008 and to nearly 0% in 2009. When the Fed had taken interest rates down to near-zero by December 2008, the economy was still deep in recession. Open market operations could not make the interest rate turn negative. The Federal Reserve had to think "outside the box."

Quantitative Easing

The most powerful and commonly used of the three traditional tools of monetary policy—open market operations—works by expanding or contracting the money supply in a way that influences the interest rate. In late 2008, as the U.S. economy struggled with recession, the Federal Reserve had already reduced the interest rate to near-zero. With the recession still ongoing, the Fed decided to adopt an innovative and nontraditional policy known as **quantitative easing (QE)**. This is the purchase of long-term government and private mortgage-backed securities by central banks to make credit available so as to stimulate aggregate demand.

Quantitative easing differed from traditional monetary policy in several key ways. First, it involved the Fed purchasing long term Treasury bonds, rather than short term Treasury bills. In 2008, however, it was impossible to stimulate the economy any further by lowering short term rates because they were already as low as they could get. (Read the closing Bring it Home feature for more on this.) Therefore, Chairman Bernanke sought to lower long-term rates utilizing quantitative easing.

This leads to a second way QE is different from traditional monetary policy. Instead of purchasing Treasury securities, the Fed also began purchasing private mortgage-backed securities, something it had never done before. During the financial crisis, which precipitated the recession, mortgage-backed securities were termed "toxic assets," because when the housing market collapsed, no one knew what these securities were worth, which put the financial institutions which were holding those securities on very shaky ground. By offering to purchase mortgage-backed securities, the Fed was both pushing long term interest rates down and also removing possibly "toxic assets" from the balance sheets of private financial firms, which would strengthen the financial system.

Quantitative easing (QE) occurred in three episodes:

1. During QE$_1$, which began in November 2008, the Fed purchased $600 billion in mortgage-backed securities from government enterprises Fannie Mae and Freddie Mac.

2. In November 2010, the Fed began QE$_2$, in which it purchased $600 billion in U.S. Treasury bonds.

3. QE$_3$, began in September 2012 when the Fed commenced purchasing $40 billion of additional mortgage-backed securities per month. This amount was increased in December 2012 to $85 billion per month. The Fed stated that, when economic conditions permit, it will begin tapering (or reducing the monthly purchases). By October 2014, the Fed had announced the final $15 billion bond purchase, ending Quantitative Easing.

We usually think of the quantitative easing policies that the Federal Reserve adopted (as did other central banks around the world) as temporary emergency measures. If these steps are to be temporary, then the Federal Reserve will need to stop making these additional loans and sell off the financial securities it has accumulated. The concern is that the process of quantitative easing may prove more difficult to reverse than it was to enact. The evidence suggests that QE_1 was somewhat successful, but that QE_2 and QE_3 have been less so.

28.5 | Pitfalls for Monetary Policy

By the end of this section, you will be able to:
- Analyze whether monetary policy decisions should be made more democratically
- Calculate the velocity of money
- Evaluate the central bank's influence on inflation, unemployment, asset bubbles, and leverage cycles
- Calculate the effects of monetary stimulus

In the real world, effective monetary policy faces a number of significant hurdles. Monetary policy affects the economy only after a time lag that is typically long and of variable length. Remember, monetary policy involves a chain of events: the central bank must perceive a situation in the economy, hold a meeting, and make a decision to react by tightening or loosening monetary policy. The change in monetary policy must percolate through the banking system, changing the quantity of loans and affecting interest rates. When interest rates change, businesses must change their investment levels and consumers must change their borrowing patterns when purchasing homes or cars. Then it takes time for these changes to filter through the rest of the economy.

As a result of this chain of events, monetary policy has little effect in the immediate future. Instead, its primary effects are felt perhaps one to three years in the future. The reality of long and variable time lags does not mean that a central bank should refuse to make decisions. It does mean that central banks should be humble about taking action, because of the risk that their actions can create as much or more economic instability as they resolve.

Excess Reserves

Banks are legally required to hold a minimum level of reserves, but no rule prohibits them from holding additional **excess reserves** above the legally mandated limit. For example, during a recession banks may be hesitant to lend, because they fear that when the economy is contracting, a high proportion of loan applicants become less likely to repay their loans.

When many banks are choosing to hold excess reserves, expansionary monetary policy may not work well. This may occur because the banks are concerned about a deteriorating economy, while the central bank is trying to expand the money supply. If the banks prefer to hold excess reserves above the legally required level, the central bank cannot force individual banks to make loans. Similarly, sensible businesses and consumers may be reluctant to borrow substantial amounts of money in a recession, because they recognize that firms' sales and employees' jobs are more insecure in a recession, and they do not want to face the need to make interest payments. The result is that during an especially deep recession, an expansionary monetary policy may have little effect on either the price level or the real GDP.

Japan experienced this situation in the 1990s and early 2000s. Japan's economy entered a period of very slow growth, dipping in and out of recession, in the early 1990s. By February 1999, the Bank of Japan had lowered the equivalent of its federal funds rate to 0%. It kept it there most of the time through 2003. Moreover, in the two years from March 2001 to March 2003, the Bank of Japan also expanded the country's money supply by about 50%—an enormous increase. Even this highly expansionary monetary policy, however, had no substantial effect on stimulating aggregate demand. Japan's economy continued to experience extremely slow growth into the mid-2000s.

Should monetary policy decisions be made more democratically?

Should a nation's Congress or legislature comprised of elected representatives conduct monetary policy or should a politically appointed central bank that is more independent of voters take charge? Here are some of the arguments.

The Case for Greater Democratic Control of Monetary Policy

Elected representatives pass taxes and spending bills to conduct fiscal policy by passing tax and spending bills. They could handle monetary policy in the same way. They will sometimes make mistakes, but in a democracy, it is better to have elected officials who are accountable to voters make mistakes instead of political appointees. After all, the people appointed to the top governing positions at the Federal Reserve—and to most central banks around the world—are typically bankers and economists. They are not representatives of borrowers like small businesses or farmers nor are they representatives of labor unions. Central banks might not be so quick to raise interest rates if they had to pay more attention to firms and people in the real economy.

The Case for an Independent Central Bank

Because the central bank has some insulation from day-to-day politics, its members can take a nonpartisan look at specific economic situations and make tough, immediate decisions when necessary. The idea of giving a legislature the ability to create money and hand out loans is likely to end up badly, sooner or later. It is simply too tempting for lawmakers to expand the money supply to fund their projects. The long term result will be rampant inflation. Also, a central bank, acting according to the laws passed by elected officials, can respond far more quickly than a legislature. For example, the U.S. budget takes months to debate, pass, and sign into law, but monetary policy decisions happen much more rapidly. Day-to-day democratic control of monetary policy is impractical and seems likely to lead to an overly expansionary monetary policy and higher inflation.

The problem of excess reserves does not affect contractionary policy. Central bankers have an old saying that monetary policy can be like pulling and pushing on a string: when the central bank pulls on the string and uses contractionary monetary policy, it can definitely raise interest rates and reduce aggregate demand. However, when the central bank tries to push on the string of expansionary monetary policy, the string may sometimes just fold up limp and have little effect, because banks decide not to loan out their excess reserves. Do not take this analogy too literally—expansionary monetary policy usually does have real effects, after that inconveniently long and variable lag. There are also times, like Japan's economy in the late 1990s and early 2000s, when expansionary monetary policy has been insufficient to lift a recession-prone economy.

Unpredictable Movements of Velocity

Velocity is a term that economists use to describe how quickly money circulates through the economy. We define the **velocity** of money in a year as:

$$\text{Velocity} = \frac{\text{nominal GDP}}{\text{money supply}}$$

Specific measurements of velocity depend on the definition of the money supply used. Consider the velocity of M1, the total amount of currency in circulation and checking account balances. In 2009, for example, M1 was $1.7 trillion and nominal GDP was $14.3 trillion, so the velocity of M1 was 8.4 ($14.3 trillion/$1.7 trillion). A higher velocity of money means that the average dollar circulates more times in a year. A lower velocity means that the average dollar circulates fewer times in a year.

See the following Clear It Up feature for a discussion of how deflation could affect monetary policy.

What happens during episodes of deflation?

Deflation occurs when the rate of inflation is negative; that is, instead of money having less purchasing power over time, as occurs with inflation, money is worth more. Deflation can make it very difficult for monetary policy to address a recession.

Remember that the real interest rate is the nominal interest rate minus the rate of inflation. If the nominal interest rate is 7% and the rate of inflation is 3%, then the borrower is effectively paying a 4% real interest rate. If the nominal interest rate is 7% and there is *deflation* of 2%, then the real interest rate is actually 9%. In this way, an unexpected deflation raises the real interest payments for borrowers. It can lead to a situation where borrowers do not repay an unexpectedly high number of loans, and banks find that their net worth is decreasing or negative. When banks are suffering losses, they become less able and eager to make new loans. Aggregate demand declines, which can lead to recession.

Then the double-whammy: After causing a recession, deflation can make it difficult for monetary policy to work. Say that the central bank uses expansionary monetary policy to reduce the nominal interest rate all the way to zero—but the economy has 5% deflation. As a result, the real interest rate is 5%, and because a central bank cannot make the nominal interest rate negative, expansionary policy cannot reduce the real interest rate further.

In the U.S. economy during the early 1930s, deflation was 6.7% per year from 1930–1933, which caused many borrowers to default on their loans and many banks to end up bankrupt, which in turn contributed substantially to the Great Depression. Not all episodes of deflation, however, end in economic depression. Japan, for example, experienced deflation of slightly less than 1% per year from 1999–2002, which hurt the Japanese economy, but it still grew by about 0.9% per year over this period. There is at least one historical example of deflation coexisting with rapid growth. The U.S. economy experienced deflation of about 1.1% per year over the quarter-century from 1876–1900, but real GDP also expanded at a rapid clip of 4% per year over this time, despite some occasional severe recessions.

The central bank should be on guard against deflation and, if necessary, use expansionary monetary policy to prevent any long-lasting or extreme deflation from occurring. Except in severe cases like the Great Depression, deflation does not guarantee economic disaster.

Changes in velocity can cause problems for monetary policy. To understand why, rewrite the definition of velocity so that the money supply is on the left-hand side of the equation. That is:

$$\text{Money supply} \times \text{velocity} = \text{Nominal GDP}$$

Recall from **The Macroeconomic Perspective** that

$$\text{Nominal GDP} = \text{Price Level (or GDP Deflator)} \times \text{Real GDP}.$$

Therefore,

$$\text{Money Supply} \times \text{velocity} = \text{Nominal GDP} = \text{Price Level} \times \text{Real GDP}.$$

We sometimes call this equation the **basic quantity equation of money** but, as you can see, it is just the definition of velocity written in a different form. This equation must hold true, by definition.

If velocity is constant over time, then a certain percentage rise in the money supply on the left-hand side of the basic quantity equation of money will inevitably lead to the same percentage rise in nominal GDP—although this change could happen through an increase in inflation, or an increase in real GDP, or some combination of the two. If velocity is changing over time but in a constant and predictable way, then changes in the money supply will continue to have a predictable effect on nominal GDP. If velocity changes unpredictably over time, however, then the effect of changes in the money supply on nominal GDP becomes unpredictable.

Figure 28.11 illustrates the actual velocity of money in the U.S. economy as measured by using M1, the most common definition of the money supply. From 1960 up to about 1980, velocity appears fairly predictable; that is, it is increasing at a fairly constant rate. In the early 1980s, however, velocity as calculated with M1 becomes more variable. The reasons for these sharp changes in velocity remain a puzzle. Economists suspect that the changes in velocity are related to innovations in banking and finance which have changed how we are using money in making economic transactions: for example, the growth of electronic payments; a rise in personal borrowing and credit card usage; and accounts that make it easier for people to hold money in savings accounts, where it is counted as M2, right up to the moment that they want to write a check on the money and transfer it to M1. So far at least, it has proven difficult to draw clear links between these kinds of factors and the specific up-and-down fluctuations in M1. Given many changes in banking and the prevalence of electronic banking, economists now favor M2 as a measure of money rather than the narrower M1.

This OpenStax book is available for free at http://cnx.org/content/col12122/1.4

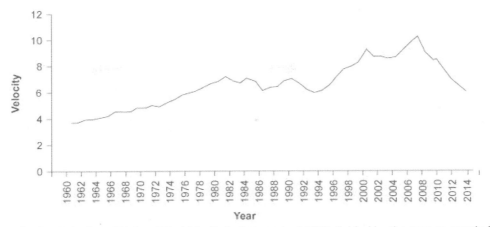

Figure 28.11 Velocity Calculated Using M1 Velocity is the nominal GDP divided by the money supply for a given year. We can calculate different measures of velocity by using different measures of the money supply. Velocity, as calculated by using M1, has lacked a steady trend since the 1980s, instead bouncing up and down. (credit: Federal Reserve Bank of St. Louis)

In the 1970s, when velocity as measured by M1 seemed predictable, a number of economists, led by Nobel laureate Milton Friedman (1912–2006), argued that the best monetary policy was for the central bank to increase the money supply at a constant growth rate. These economists argued that with the long and variable lags of monetary policy, and the political pressures on central bankers, central bank monetary policies were as likely to have undesirable as to have desirable effects. Thus, these economists believed that the monetary policy should seek steady growth in the money supply of 3% per year. They argued that a steady monetary growth rate would be correct over longer time periods, since it would roughly match the growth of the real economy. In addition, they argued that giving the central bank less discretion to conduct monetary policy would prevent an overly activist central bank from becoming a source of economic instability and uncertainty. In this spirit, Friedman wrote in 1967: "The first and most important lesson that history teaches about what monetary policy can do—and it is a lesson of the most profound importance—is that monetary policy can prevent money itself from being a major source of economic disturbance."

As the velocity of M1 began to fluctuate in the 1980s, having the money supply grow at a predetermined and unchanging rate seemed less desirable, because as the quantity theory of money shows, the combination of constant growth in the money supply and fluctuating velocity would cause nominal GDP to rise and fall in unpredictable ways. The jumpiness of velocity in the 1980s caused many central banks to focus less on the rate at which the quantity of money in the economy was increasing, and instead to set monetary policy by reacting to whether the economy was experiencing or in danger of higher inflation or unemployment.

Unemployment and Inflation

If you were to survey central bankers around the world and ask them what they believe should be the primary task of monetary policy, the most popular answer by far would be fighting inflation. Most central bankers believe that the neoclassical model of economics accurately represents the economy over the medium to long term. Remember that in the neoclassical model of the economy, we draw the aggregate supply curve as a vertical line at the level of potential GDP, as **Figure 28.12** shows. In the neoclassical model, economists determine the level of potential GDP (and the natural rate of unemployment that exists when the economy is producing at potential GDP) by real economic factors. If the original level of aggregate demand is AD_0, then an expansionary monetary policy that shifts aggregate demand to AD_1 only creates an inflationary increase in the price level, but it does not alter GDP or unemployment. From this perspective, all that monetary policy can do is to lead to low inflation or high inflation—and low inflation provides a better climate for a healthy and growing economy. After all, low inflation means that businesses making investments can focus on real economic issues, not on figuring out ways to protect themselves from the costs and risks of inflation. In this way, a consistent pattern of low inflation can contribute to long-term growth.

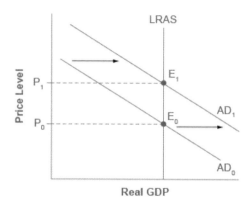

Figure 28.12 Monetary Policy in a Neoclassical Model In a neoclassical view, monetary policy affects only the price level, not the level of output in the economy. For example, an expansionary monetary policy causes aggregate demand to shift from the original AD_0 to AD_1. However, the adjustment of the economy from the original equilibrium (E_0) to the new equilibrium (E_1) represents an inflationary increase in the price level from P_0 to P_1, but has no effect in the long run on output or the unemployment rate. In fact, no shift in AD will affect the equilibrium quantity of output in this model.

This vision of focusing monetary policy on a low rate of inflation is so attractive that many countries have rewritten their central banking laws since in the 1990s to have their bank practice **inflation targeting**, which means that the central bank is legally required to focus primarily on keeping inflation low. By 2014, central banks in 28 countries, including Austria, Brazil, Canada, Israel, Korea, Mexico, New Zealand, Spain, Sweden, Thailand, and the United Kingdom faced a legal requirement to target the inflation rate. A notable exception is the Federal Reserve in the United States, which does not practice inflation-targeting. Instead, the law governing the Federal Reserve requires it to take both unemployment and inflation into account.

Economists have no final consensus on whether a central bank should be required to focus only on inflation or should have greater discretion. For those who subscribe to the inflation targeting philosophy, the fear is that politicians who are worried about slow economic growth and unemployment will constantly pressure the central bank to conduct a loose monetary policy—even if the economy is already producing at potential GDP. In some countries, the central bank may lack the political power to resist such pressures, with the result of higher inflation, but no long-term reduction in unemployment. The U.S. Federal Reserve has a tradition of independence, but central banks in other countries may be under greater political pressure. For all of these reasons—long and variable lags, excess reserves, unstable velocity, and controversy over economic goals—monetary policy in the real world is often difficult. The basic message remains, however, that central banks can affect aggregate demand through the conduct of monetary policy and in that way influence macroeconomic outcomes.

Asset Bubbles and Leverage Cycles

One long-standing concern about having the central bank focus on inflation and unemployment is that it may be overlooking certain other economic problems that are coming in the future. For example, from 1994 to 2000 during what was known as the "dot-com" boom, the U.S. stock market, which the Dow Jones Industrial Index measures (which includes 30 very large companies from across the U.S. economy), nearly tripled in value. The Nasdaq index, which includes many smaller technology companies, increased in value by a multiple of five from 1994 to 2000. These rates of increase were clearly not sustainable. Stock values as measured by the Dow Jones were almost 20% lower in 2009 than they had been in 2000. Stock values in the Nasdaq index were 50% lower in 2009 than they had been in 2000. The drop-off in stock market values contributed to the 2001 recession and the higher unemployment that followed.

We can tell a similar story about housing prices in the mid-2000s. During the 1970s, 1980s, and 1990s, housing prices increased at about 6% per year on average. During what came to be known as the "housing bubble" from 2003 to 2005, housing prices increased at almost double this annual rate. These rates of increase were clearly not sustainable. When housing prices fell in 2007 and 2008, many banks and households found that their assets were worth less than they expected, which contributed to the recession that started in 2007.

At a broader level, some economists worry about a leverage cycle, where "leverage" is a term financial economists

This OpenStax book is available for free at http://cnx.org/content/col12122/1.4

use to mean "borrowing." When economic times are good, banks and the financial sector are eager to lend, and people and firms are eager to borrow. Remember that a money multiplier determines the amount of money and credit in an economy —a process of loans made, money deposited, and more loans made. In good economic times, this surge of lending exaggerates the episode of economic growth. It can even be part of what lead prices of certain assets—like stock prices or housing prices—to rise at unsustainably high annual rates. At some point, when economic times turn bad, banks and the financial sector become much less willing to lend, and credit becomes expensive or unavailable to many potential borrowers. The sharp reduction in credit, perhaps combined with the deflating prices of a dot-com stock price bubble or a housing bubble, makes the economic downturn worse than it would otherwise be.

Thus, some economists have suggested that the central bank should not just look at economic growth, inflation, and unemployment rates, but should also keep an eye on asset prices and leverage cycles. Such proposals are quite controversial. If a central bank had announced in 1997 that stock prices were rising "too fast" or in 2004 that housing prices were rising "too fast," and then taken action to hold down price increases, many people and their elected political representatives would have been outraged. Neither the Federal Reserve nor any other central banks want to take the responsibility of deciding when stock prices and housing prices are too high, too low, or just right. As further research explores how asset price bubbles and leverage cycles can affect an economy, central banks may need to think about whether they should conduct monetary policy in a way that would seek to moderate these effects.

Let's end this chapter with a Work it Out exercise in how the Fed—or any central bank—would stir up the economy by increasing the money supply.

Work It Out ⊸○⊸○⊸○

Calculating the Effects of Monetary Stimulus

Suppose that the central bank wants to stimulate the economy by increasing the money supply. The bankers estimate that the velocity of money is 3, and that the price level will increase from 100 to 110 due to the stimulus. Using the quantity equation of money, what will be the impact of an $800 billion dollar increase in the money supply on the quantity of goods and services in the economy given an initial money supply of $4 trillion?

Step 1. We begin by writing the quantity equation of money: $MV = PQ$. We know that initially $V = 3$, $M = 4{,}000$ (billion) and $P = 100$. Substituting these numbers in, we can solve for Q:

$$\begin{aligned} MV &= PQ \\ 4{,}000 \times 3 &= 100 \times Q \\ Q &= 120 \end{aligned}$$

Step 2. Now we want to find the effect of the addition $800 billion in the money supply, together with the increase in the price level. The new equation is:

$$\begin{aligned} MV &= PQ \\ 4{,}800 \times 3 &= 110 \times Q \\ Q &= 130.9 \end{aligned}$$

Step 3. If we take the difference between the two quantities, we find that the monetary stimulus increased the quantity of goods and services in the economy by 10.9 billion.

The discussion in this chapter has focused on domestic monetary policy; that is, the view of monetary policy within an economy. **Exchange Rates and International Capital Flows** explores the international dimension of monetary policy, and how monetary policy becomes involved with exchange rates and international flows of financial capital.

Bring it Home

The Problem of the Zero Percent Interest Rate Lower Bound

In 2008, the U.S. Federal Reserve found itself in a difficult position. The federal funds rate was on its way to near zero, which meant that traditional open market operations, by which the Fed purchases U.S. Treasury Bills to lower short term interest rates, was no longer viable. This so called "zero bound problem," prompted the Fed, under then Chair Ben Bernanke, to attempt some unconventional policies, collectively called quantitative easing. By early 2014, quantitative easing nearly quintupled the amount of bank reserves. This likely contributed to the U.S. economy's recovery, but the impact was muted, probably due to some of the hurdles mentioned in the last section of this module. The unprecedented increase in bank reserves also led to fears of inflation. As of early 2015, however, there have been no serious signs of a boom, with core inflation around a stable 1.7%.

This OpenStax book is available for free at http://cnx.org/content/col12122/1.4

KEY TERMS

bank run when depositors race to the bank to withdraw their deposits for fear that otherwise they would be lost

basic quantity equation of money money supply × velocity = nominal GDP

central bank institution which conducts a nation's monetary policy and regulates its banking system

contractionary monetary policy a monetary policy that reduces the supply of money and loans

countercyclical moving in the opposite direction of the business cycle of economic downturns and upswings

deposit insurance an insurance system that makes sure depositors in a bank do not lose their money, even if the bank goes bankrupt

discount rate the interest rate charged by the central bank on the loans that it gives to other commercial banks

excess reserves reserves banks hold that exceed the legally mandated limit

expansionary monetary policy a monetary policy that increases the supply of money and the quantity of loans

federal funds rate the interest rate at which one bank lends funds to another bank overnight

inflation targeting a rule that the central bank is required to focus only on keeping inflation low

lender of last resort an institution that provides short-term emergency loans in conditions of financial crisis

loose monetary policy see expansionary monetary policy

open market operations the central bank selling or buying Treasury bonds to influence the quantity of money and the level of interest rates

quantitative easing (QE) the purchase of long term government and private mortgage-backed securities by central banks to make credit available in hopes of stimulating aggregate demand

reserve requirement the percentage amount of its total deposits that a bank is legally obligated to to either hold as cash in their vault or deposit with the central bank

tight monetary policy see contractionary monetary policy

velocity the speed with which money circulates through the economy; calculated as the nominal GDP divided by the money supply

KEY CONCEPTS AND SUMMARY

28.1 The Federal Reserve Banking System and Central Banks
The most prominent task of a central bank is to conduct monetary policy, which involves changes to interest rates and credit conditions, affecting the amount of borrowing and spending in an economy. Some prominent central banks around the world include the U.S. Federal Reserve, the European Central Bank, the Bank of Japan, and the Bank of England.

28.2 Bank Regulation
A bank run occurs when there are rumors (possibly true, possibly false) that a bank is at financial risk of having negative net worth. As a result, depositors rush to the bank to withdraw their money and put it someplace safer. Even false rumors, if they cause a bank run, can force a healthy bank to lose its deposits and be forced to close. Deposit insurance guarantees bank depositors that, even if the bank has negative net worth, their deposits will be protected. In

the United States, the Federal Deposit Insurance Corporation (FDIC) collects deposit insurance premiums from banks and guarantees bank deposits up to $250,000. Bank supervision involves inspecting the balance sheets of banks to make sure that they have positive net worth and that their assets are not too risky. In the United States, the Office of the Comptroller of the Currency (OCC) is responsible for supervising banks and inspecting savings and loans and the National Credit Union Administration (NCUA) is responsible for inspecting credit unions. The FDIC and the Federal Reserve also play a role in bank supervision.

When a central bank acts as a lender of last resort, it makes short-term loans available in situations of severe financial panic or stress. The failure of a single bank can be treated like any other business failure. Yet if many banks fail, it can reduce aggregate demand in a way that can bring on or deepen a recession. The combination of deposit insurance, bank supervision, and lender of last resort policies help to prevent weaknesses in the banking system from causing recessions.

28.3 How a Central Bank Executes Monetary Policy

A central bank has three traditional tools to conduct monetary policy: open market operations, which involves buying and selling government bonds with banks; reserve requirements, which determine what level of reserves a bank is legally required to hold; and discount rates, which is the interest rate charged by the central bank on the loans that it gives to other commercial banks. The most commonly used tool is open market operations.

28.4 Monetary Policy and Economic Outcomes

An expansionary (or loose) monetary policy raises the quantity of money and credit above what it otherwise would have been and reduces interest rates, boosting aggregate demand, and thus countering recession. A contractionary monetary policy, also called a tight monetary policy, reduces the quantity of money and credit below what it otherwise would have been and raises interest rates, seeking to hold down inflation. During the 2008–2009 recession, central banks around the world also used quantitative easing to expand the supply of credit.

28.5 Pitfalls for Monetary Policy

Monetary policy is inevitably imprecise, for a number of reasons: (a) the effects occur only after long and variable lags; (b) if banks decide to hold excess reserves, monetary policy cannot force them to lend; and (c) velocity may shift in unpredictable ways. The basic quantity equation of money is $MV = PQ$, where M is the money supply, V is the velocity of money, P is the price level, and Q is the real output of the economy. Some central banks, like the European Central Bank, practice inflation targeting, which means that the only goal of the central bank is to keep inflation within a low target range. Other central banks, such as the U.S. Federal Reserve, are free to focus on either reducing inflation or stimulating an economy that is in recession, whichever goal seems most important at the time.

SELF-CHECK QUESTIONS

1. Why is it important for the members of the Board of Governors of the Federal Reserve to have longer terms in office than elected officials, like the President?

2. Given the danger of bank runs, why do banks not keep the majority of deposits on hand to meet the demands of depositors?

3. Bank runs are often described as "self-fulfilling prophecies." Why is this phrase appropriate to bank runs?

4. If the central bank sells $500 in bonds to a bank that has issued $10,000 in loans and is exactly meeting the reserve requirement of 10%, what will happen to the amount of loans and to the money supply in general?

5. What would be the effect of increasing the banks' reserve requirements on the money supply?

6. Why does contractionary monetary policy cause interest rates to rise?

7. Why does expansionary monetary policy causes interest rates to drop?

8. Why might banks want to hold excess reserves in time of recession?

9. Why might the velocity of money change unexpectedly?

This OpenStax book is available for free at http://cnx.org/content/col12122/1.4

REVIEW QUESTIONS

10. How is a central bank different from a typical commercial bank?

11. List the three traditional tools that a central bank has for controlling the money supply.

12. How is bank regulation linked to the conduct of monetary policy?

13. What is a bank run?

14. In a program of deposit insurance as it is operated in the United States, what is being insured and who pays the insurance premiums?

15. In government programs of bank supervision, what is being supervised?

16. What is the lender of last resort?

17. Name and briefly describe the responsibilities of each of the following agencies: FDIC, NCUA, and OCC.

18. Explain how to use an open market operation to expand the money supply.

19. Explain how to use the reserve requirement to expand the money supply.

20. Explain how to use the discount rate to expand the money supply.

21. How do the expansionary and contractionary monetary policy affect the quantity of money?

22. How do tight and loose monetary policy affect interest rates?

23. How do expansionary, tight, contractionary, and loose monetary policy affect aggregate demand?

24. Which kind of monetary policy would you expect in response to high inflation: expansionary or contractionary? Why?

25. Explain how to use quantitative easing to stimulate aggregate demand.

26. Which kind of monetary policy would you expect in response to recession: expansionary or contractionary? Why?

27. How might each of the following factors complicate the implementation of monetary policy: long and variable lags, excess reserves, and movements in velocity?

28. Define the velocity of the money supply.

29. What is the basic quantity equation of money?

30. How does a monetary policy of inflation target work?

CRITICAL THINKING QUESTIONS

31. Why do presidents typically reappoint Chairs of the Federal Reserve Board even when they were originally appointed by a president of a different political party?

32. In what ways might monetary policy be superior to fiscal policy? In what ways might it be inferior?

33. The term "moral hazard" describes increases in risky behavior resulting from efforts to make that behavior safer. How does the concept of moral hazard apply to deposit insurance and other bank regulations?

34. Explain what would happen if banks were notified they had to increase their required reserves by one percentage point from, say, 9% to10% of deposits. What would their options be to come up with the cash?

35. A well-known economic model called the Phillips Curve (discussed in **The Keynesian Perspective** chapter) describes the short run tradeoff typically observed between inflation and unemployment. Based on the discussion of expansionary and contractionary monetary policy, explain why one of these variables usually falls when the other rises.

36. How does rule-based monetary policy differ from discretionary monetary policy (that is, monetary policy not based on a rule)? What are some of the arguments for each?

37. Is it preferable for central banks to primarily target inflation or unemployment? Why?

PROBLEMS

38. Suppose the Fed conducts an open market purchase by buying $10 million in Treasury bonds from Acme Bank. Sketch out the balance sheet changes that will occur as Acme converts the bond sale proceeds to new loans. The initial Acme bank balance sheet contains the following information: Assets – reserves 30, bonds 50, and loans 50; Liabilities – deposits 300 and equity 30.

39. Suppose the Fed conducts an open market sale by selling $10 million in Treasury bonds to Acme Bank. Sketch out the balance sheet changes that will occur as Acme restores its required reserves (10% of deposits) by reducing its loans. The initial balance sheet for Acme Bank contains the following information: Assets – reserves 30, bonds 50, and loans 250; Liabilities – deposits 300 and equity 30.

40. All other things being equal, by how much will nominal GDP expand if the central bank increases the money supply by $100 billion, and the velocity of money is 3? (Use this information as necessary to answer the following 4 questions.)

41. Suppose now that economists expect the velocity of money to increase by 50% as a result of the monetary stimulus. What will be the total increase in nominal GDP?

42. If GDP is 1,500 and the money supply is 400, what is velocity?

43. If GDP now rises to 1,600, but the money supply does not change, how has velocity changed?

44. If GDP now falls back to 1,500 and the money supply falls to 350, what is velocity?

29 | Exchange Rates and International Capital Flows

Figure 29.1 Trade Around the World   Is a trade deficit between the United States and the European Union good or bad for the U.S. economy? (Credit: modification of work by Milad Mosapoor/Wikimedia Commons)

Bring it Home

Is a Stronger Dollar Good for the U.S. Economy?

From 2002 to 2008, the U.S. dollar lost more than a quarter of its value in foreign currency markets. On January 1, 2002, one dollar was worth 1.11 euros. On April 24, 2008 it hit its lowest point with a dollar being worth 0.64 euros. During this period, the trade deficit between the United States and the European Union grew from a yearly total of approximately –85.7 billion dollars in 2002 to 95.8 billion dollars in 2008. Was this a good thing or a bad thing for the U.S. economy?

We live in a global world. U.S. consumers buy trillions of dollars worth of imported goods and services each year, not just from the European Union, but from all over the world. U.S. businesses sell trillions of dollars' worth of exports. U.S. citizens, businesses, and governments invest trillions of dollars abroad every year. Foreign investors, businesses, and governments invest trillions of dollars in the United States each year. Indeed, foreigners are a major buyer of U.S. federal debt

Many people feel that a weaker dollar is bad for America, that it's an indication of a weak economy, but is it? This chapter will help answer that question.

Introduction to Exchange Rates and International Capital

Flows

In this chapter, you will learn about:

- How the Foreign Exchange Market Works

- Demand and Supply Shifts in Foreign Exchange Markets

- Macroeconomic Effects of Exchange Rates

- Exchange Rate Policies

The world has over 150 different currencies, from the Afghanistan afghani and the Albanian lek all the way through the alphabet to the Zambian kwacha and the Zimbabwean dollar. For international economic transactions, households or firms will wish to exchange one currency for another. Perhaps the need for exchanging currencies will come from a German firm that exports products to Russia, but then wishes to exchange the Russian rubles it has earned for euros, so that the firm can pay its workers and suppliers in Germany. Perhaps it will be a South African firm that wishes to purchase a mining operation in Angola, but to make the purchase it must convert South African rand to Angolan kwanza. Perhaps it will be an American tourist visiting China, who wishes to convert U.S. dollars to Chinese yuan to pay the hotel bill.

Exchange rates can sometimes change very swiftly. For example, in the United Kingdom the pound was worth about $1.50 just before the nation voted to leave the European Union (also known as the Brexit vote), but fell to $1.37 just after the vote and continued falling to reach 30-year lows a few months later. For firms engaged in international buying, selling, lending, and borrowing, these swings in exchange rates can have an enormous effect on profits.

This chapter discusses the international dimension of money, which involves conversions from one currency to another at an exchange rate. An exchange rate is nothing more than a price—that is, the price of one currency in terms of another currency—and so we can analyze it with the tools of supply and demand. The first module of this chapter begins with an overview of foreign exchange markets: their size, their main participants, and the vocabulary for discussing movements of exchange rates. The following module uses demand and supply graphs to analyze some of the main factors that cause shifts in exchange rates. A final module then brings the central bank and monetary policy back into the picture. Each country must decide whether to allow the market to determine its exchange rate, or have the central bank intervene. All the choices for exchange rate policy involve distinctive tradeoffs and risks.

29.1 | How the Foreign Exchange Market Works

By the end of this section, you will be able to:
- Define "foreign exchange market"
- Describe different types of investments like foreign direct investments (FDI), portfolio investments, and hedging
- Explain how appreciating or depreciating currency affects exchange rates
- Identify who benefits from a stronger currency and benefits from a weaker currency

Most countries have different currencies, but not all. Sometimes small economies use an economically larger neighbor's currency. For example, Ecuador, El Salvador, and Panama have decided to **dollarize**—that is, to use the U.S. dollar as their currency. Sometimes nations share a common currency. A large-scale example of a common currency is the decision by 17 European nations—including some very large economies such as France, Germany, and Italy—to replace their former currencies with the euro. With these exceptions, most of the international economy takes place in a situation of multiple national currencies in which both people and firms need to convert from one currency to another when selling, buying, hiring, borrowing, traveling, or investing across national borders. We call the market in which people or firms use one currency to purchase another currency the **foreign exchange market**.

You have encountered the basic concept of exchange rates in earlier chapters. In **The International Trade and Capital Flows**, for example, we discussed how economists use exchange rates to compare GDP statistics from countries where they measure GDP in different currencies. These earlier examples, however, took the actual exchange rate as given, as if it were a fact of nature. In reality, the exchange rate is a price—the price of one currency expressed in terms of units of another currency. The key framework for analyzing prices, whether in this course, any other economics course, in public policy, or business examples, is the operation of supply and demand in markets.

Link It Up

Visit this website (http://openstax.org/l/exratecalc) for an exchange rate calculator.

The Extraordinary Size of the Foreign Exchange Markets

The quantities traded in foreign exchange markets are breathtaking. A 2013 Bank of International Settlements survey found that $5.3 trillion *per day* was traded on foreign exchange markets, which makes the foreign exchange market the largest market in the world economy. In contrast, 2013 U.S. real GDP was $15.8 trillion *per year*.

Table 29.1 shows the currencies most commonly traded on foreign exchange markets. The U.S. dollar dominates the foreign exchange market, followed by the euro, the British pound, the Australian dollar, and the Japanese yen.

Currency	% Daily Share
U.S. dollar	87.6%
Euro	31.3%
Japanese yen	21.6%
British pound	12.8%
Australian dollar	6.9%
Canadian dollar	5.1%
Swiss franc	4.8%
Chinese yuan	2.6%

Table 29.1 Currencies Traded Most on Foreign Exchange Markets as of April, 2016 (Source: http://www.bis.org/publ/rpfx16fx.pdf)

Demanders and Suppliers of Currency in Foreign Exchange Markets

In foreign exchange markets, demand and supply become closely interrelated, because a person or firm who demands one currency must at the same time supply another currency—and vice versa. To get a sense of this, it is useful to consider four groups of people or firms who participate in the market: (1) firms that are involved in international trade of goods and services; (2) tourists visiting other countries; (3) international investors buying ownership (or part-ownership) of a foreign firm; (4) international investors making financial investments that do not involve ownership. Let's consider these categories in turn.

Firms that buy and sell on international markets find that their costs for workers, suppliers, and investors are measured in the currency of the nation where their production occurs, but their revenues from sales are measured in the currency of the different nation where their sales happened. Thus, a Chinese firm exporting abroad will earn some other currency—say, U.S. dollars—but will need Chinese yuan to pay the workers, suppliers, and investors who are based in China. In the foreign exchange markets, this firm will be a supplier of U.S. dollars and a demander of Chinese yuan.

International tourists will supply their home currency to receive the currency of the country they are visiting. For example, an American tourist who is visiting China will supply U.S. dollars into the foreign exchange market and demand Chinese yuan.

We often divide financial investments that cross international boundaries, and require exchanging currency into two categories. **Foreign direct investment (FDI)** refers to purchasing a firm (at least ten percent) in another country or starting up a new enterprise in a foreign country For example, in 2008 the Belgian beer-brewing company InBev bought the U.S. beer-maker Anheuser-Busch for $52 billion. To make this purchase, InBev would have to supply euros (the currency of Belgium) to the foreign exchange market and demand U.S. dollars.

The other kind of international financial investment, **portfolio investment**, involves a purely financial investment that does not entail any management responsibility. An example would be a U.S. financial investor who purchased U.K. government bonds, or deposited money in a British bank. To make such investments, the American investor would supply U.S. dollars in the foreign exchange market and demand British pounds.

Business people often link portfolio investment to expectations about how exchange rates will shift. Look at a U.S. financial investor who is considering purchasing U.K. issued bonds. For simplicity, ignore any bond interest payment (which will be small in the short run anyway) and focus on exchange rates. Say that a British pound is currently worth $1.50 in U.S. currency. However, the investor believes that in a month, the British pound will be worth $1.60 in U.S. currency. Thus, as **Figure 29.2** (a) shows, this investor would change $24,000 for 16,000 British pounds. In a month, if the pound is worth $1.60, then the portfolio investor can trade back to U.S. dollars at the new exchange rate, and have $25,600—a nice profit. A portfolio investor who believes that the foreign exchange rate for the pound will work in the opposite direction can also invest accordingly. Say that an investor expects that the pound, now worth $1.50 in U.S. currency, will decline to $1.40. Then, as **Figure 29.2** (b) shows, that investor could start off with £20,000 in British currency (borrowing the money if necessary), convert it to $30,000 in U.S. currency, wait a month, and then convert back to approximately £21,429 in British currency—again making a nice profit. Of course, this kind of investing comes without guarantees, and an investor will suffer losses if the exchange rates do not move as predicted.

(a) An international investor who expects that, in the future, a British pound(£) will buy $1.60 in U.S. currency instead of its current exchange rate of $1.50 may hope for the following chain of events to occur:

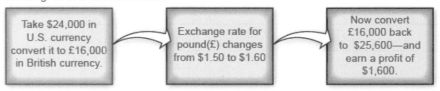

(b) An international investor who expects that, in the future, a British pound(£) will buy only $1.40 in U.S. currency instead of its current exchange rate of $1.50 may hope for the following chain of events to occur:

Figure 29.2 A Portfolio Investor Trying to Benefit from Exchange Rate Movements Expectations of a currency's future value can drive its demand and supply in foreign exchange markets.

This OpenStax book is available for free at http://cnx.org/content/col12122/1.4

Many portfolio investment decisions are not as simple as betting that the currency's value will change in one direction or the other. Instead, they involve firms trying to protect themselves from movements in exchange rates. Imagine you are running a U.S. firm that is exporting to France. You have signed a contract to deliver certain products and will receive 1 million euros a year from now. However, you do not know how much this contract will be worth in U.S. dollars, because the dollar/euro exchange rate can fluctuate in the next year. Let's say you want to know for sure what the contract will be worth, and not take a risk that the euro will be worth less in U.S. dollars than it currently is. You can **hedge**, which means using a financial transaction to protect yourself against a risk from one of your investments (in this case, currency risk from the contract). Specifically, you can sign a financial contract and pay a fee that guarantees you a certain exchange rate one year from now—regardless of what the market exchange rate is at that time. Now, it is possible that the euro will be worth more in dollars a year from now, so your hedging contract will be unnecessary, and you will have paid a fee for nothing. However, if the value of the euro in dollars declines, then you are protected by the hedge. When parties wish to enter financial contracts like hedging, they normally rely on a financial institution or brokerage company to handle the hedging. These companies either take a fee or create a spread in the exchange rate in order to earn money through the service they provide.

Both foreign direct investment and portfolio investment involve an investor who supplies domestic currency and demands a foreign currency. With portfolio investment, the client purchases less than ten percent of a company. As such, business players often get involved with portfolio investment with a short term focus. With foreign direct investment the investor purchases more than ten percent of a company and the investor typically assumes some managerial responsibility. Thus, foreign direct investment tends to have a more long-run focus. As a practical matter, an investor can withdraw portfolio investments from a country much more quickly than foreign direct investments. A U.S. portfolio investor who wants to buy or sell U.K. government bonds can do so with a phone call or a few computer keyboard clicks. However, a U.S. firm that wants to buy or sell a company, such as one that manufactures automobile parts in the United Kingdom, will find that planning and carrying out the transaction takes a few weeks, even months. **Table 29.2** summarizes the main categories of currency demanders and suppliers.

Demand for the U.S. Dollar Comes from...	Supply of the U.S. Dollar Comes from...
A U.S. exporting firm that earned foreign currency and is trying to pay U.S.-based expenses	A foreign firm that has sold imported goods in the United States, earned U.S. dollars, and is trying to pay expenses incurred in its home country
Foreign tourists visiting the United States	U.S. tourists leaving to visit other countries
Foreign investors who wish to make direct investments in the U.S. economy	U.S. investors who want to make foreign direct investments in other countries
Foreign investors who wish to make portfolio investments in the U.S. economy	U.S. investors who want to make portfolio investments in other countries

Table 29.2 The Demand and Supply Line-ups in Foreign Exchange Markets

Participants in the Exchange Rate Market

The foreign exchange market does not involve the ultimate suppliers and demanders of foreign exchange literally seeking each other. If Martina decides to leave her home in Venezuela and take a trip in the United States, she does not need to find a U.S. citizen who is planning to take a vacation in Venezuela and arrange a person-to-person currency trade. Instead, the foreign exchange market works through financial institutions, and it operates on several levels.

Most people and firms who are exchanging a substantial quantity of currency go to a bank, and most banks provide foreign exchange as a service to customers. These banks (and a few other firms), known as dealers, then trade the foreign exchange. This is called the interbank market.

In the world economy, roughly 2,000 firms are foreign exchange dealers. The U.S. economy has less than 100 foreign exchange dealers, but the largest 12 or so dealers carry out more than half the total transactions. The foreign exchange market has no central location, but the major dealers keep a close watch on each other at all times.

The foreign exchange market is huge not because of the demands of tourists, firms, or even foreign direct investment, but instead because of portfolio investment and the actions of interlocking foreign exchange dealers. International tourism is a very large industry, involving about $1 trillion per year. Global exports are about 23% of global GDP; which is about $18 trillion per year. Foreign direct investment totaled about $1.5 trillion in the end of 2013. These quantities are dwarfed, however, by the $5.3 trillion *per day* traded in foreign exchange markets. Most transactions in the foreign exchange market are for portfolio investment—relatively short-term movements of financial capital between currencies—and because of the large foreign exchange dealers' actions as they constantly buy and sell with each other.

Strengthening and Weakening Currency

When the prices of most goods and services change, the price "rises or "falls". For exchange rates, the terminology is different. When the exchange rate for a currency rises, so that the currency exchanges for more of other currencies, we refer to it as **appreciating** or "strengthening." When the exchange rate for a currency falls, so that a currency trades for less of other currencies, we refer to it as **depreciating** or "weakening."

To illustrate the use of these terms, consider the exchange rate between the U.S. dollar and the Canadian dollar since 1980, in **Figure 29.3** (a). The vertical axis in **Figure 29.3** (a) shows the price of $1 in U.S. currency, measured in terms of Canadian currency. Clearly, exchange rates can move up and down substantially. A U.S. dollar traded for $1.17 Canadian in 1980. The U.S. dollar appreciated or strengthened to $1.39 Canadian in 1986, depreciated or weakened to $1.15 Canadian in 1991, and then appreciated or strengthened to $1.60 Canadian by early in 2002, fell to roughly $1.20 Canadian in 2009, and then had a sharp spike up and decline in 2009 and 2010. In May of 2017, the U.S. dollar stood at $1.36 Canadian. The units in which we measure exchange rates can be confusing, because we measure the exchange rate of the U.S. dollar exchange using a different currency—the Canadian dollar. However, exchange rates always measure the price of one unit of currency by using a different currency.

This OpenStax book is available for free at http://cnx.org/content/col12122/1.4

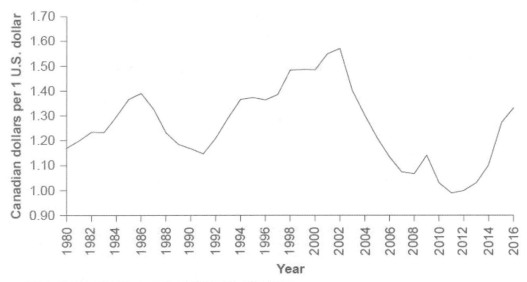

(a) U.S. dollar exchange rate in Canadian dollars

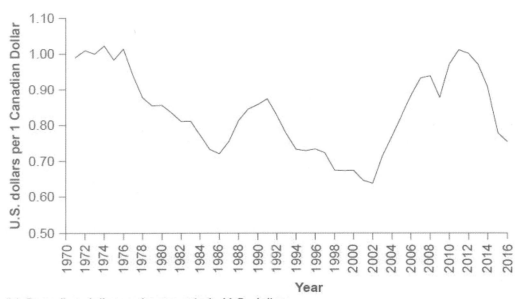

(b) Canadian dollar exchange rate in U.S. dollars

Figure 29.3 Strengthen or Appreciate vs. Weaken or Depreciate Exchange rates tend to fluctuate substantially, even between bordering companies such as the United States and Canada. By looking closely at the time values (the years vary slightly on these graphs), it is clear that the values in part (a) are a mirror image of part (b), which demonstrates that the depreciation of one currency correlates to the appreciation of the other and vice versa. This means that when comparing the exchange rates between two countries (in this case, the United States and Canada), the depreciation (or weakening) of one country (the U.S. dollar for this example) indicates the appreciation (or strengthening) of the other currency (which in this example is the Canadian dollar). (Source: Federal Reserve Economic Data (FRED) https://research.stlouisfed.org/fred2/series/EXCAUS)

In looking at the exchange rate between two currencies, the appreciation or strengthening of one currency must mean the depreciation or weakening of the other. **Figure 29.3** (b) shows the exchange rate for the Canadian dollar, measured in terms of U.S. dollars. The exchange rate of the U.S. dollar measured in Canadian dollars, in **Figure 29.3** (a), is a perfect mirror image with the Canadian dollar exchange rate measured in U.S. dollars, in **Figure 29.3** (b). A fall in the Canada $/U.S. $ ratio means a rise in the U.S. $/Canada $ ratio, and vice versa.

With the price of a typical good or service, it is clear that higher prices benefit sellers and hurt buyers, while lower prices benefit buyers and hurt sellers. In the case of exchange rates, where the buyers and sellers are not always intuitively obvious, it is useful to trace how a stronger or weaker currency will affect different market participants. Consider, for example, the impact of a stronger U.S. dollar on six different groups of economic actors, as **Figure 29.4** shows: (1) U.S. exporters selling abroad; (2) foreign exporters (that is, firms selling imports in the U.S. economy); (3) U.S. tourists abroad; (4) foreign tourists visiting the United States; (5) U.S. investors (either foreign direct investment or portfolio investment) considering opportunities in other countries; (6) and foreign investors considering opportunities in the U.S. economy.

Figure 29.4 How Do Exchange Rate Movements Affect Each Group? Exchange rate movements affect exporters, tourists, and international investors in different ways.

For a U.S. firm selling abroad, a stronger U.S. dollar is a curse. A strong U.S. dollar means that foreign currencies are correspondingly weak. When this exporting firm earns foreign currencies through its export sales, and then converts them back to U.S. dollars to pay workers, suppliers, and investors, the stronger dollar means that the foreign currency buys fewer U.S. dollars than if the currency had not strengthened, and that the firm's profits (as measured in dollars) fall. As a result, the firm may choose to reduce its exports, or it may raise its selling price, which will also tend to reduce its exports. In this way, a stronger currency reduces a country's exports.

Conversely, for a foreign firm selling in the U.S. economy, a stronger dollar is a blessing. Each dollar earned through export sales, when traded back into the exporting firm's home currency, will now buy more home currency than expected before the dollar had strengthened. As a result, the stronger dollar means that the importing firm will earn higher profits than expected. The firm will seek to expand its sales in the U.S. economy, or it may reduce prices, which will also lead to expanded sales. In this way, a stronger U.S. dollar means that consumers will purchase more from foreign producers, expanding the country's level of imports.

For a U.S. tourist abroad, who is exchanging U.S. dollars for foreign currency as necessary, a stronger U.S. dollar is a benefit. The tourist receives more foreign currency for each U.S. dollar, and consequently the cost of the trip in U.S. dollars is lower. When a country's currency is strong, it is a good time for citizens of that country to tour abroad. Imagine a U.S. tourist who has saved up $5,000 for a trip to South Africa. In 2010, $1 bought 7.3 South African rand, so the tourist had 36,500 rand to spend. In 2012, $1 bought 8.2 rand, so the tourist had 41,000 rand to spend. By 2015, $1 bought nearly 13 rand. Clearly, more recent years have been better for U.S. tourists to visit South Africa. For foreign visitors to the United States, the opposite pattern holds true. A relatively stronger U.S. dollar means that their own currencies are relatively weaker, so that as they shift from their own currency to U.S. dollars, they have fewer U.S. dollars than previously. When a country's currency is strong, it is not an especially good time for foreign tourists to visit.

A stronger dollar injures the prospects of a U.S. financial investor who has already invested money in another country. A U.S. financial investor abroad must first convert U.S. dollars to a foreign currency, invest in a foreign country, and then later convert that foreign currency back to U.S. dollars. If in the meantime the U.S. dollar becomes stronger and

This OpenStax book is available for free at http://cnx.org/content/col12122/1.4

the foreign currency becomes weaker, then when the investor converts back to U.S. dollars, the rate of return on that investment will be less than originally expected at the time it was made.

However, a stronger U.S. dollar boosts the returns of a foreign investor putting money into a U.S. investment. That foreign investor converts from the home currency to U.S. dollars and seeks a U.S. investment, while later planning to switch back to the home currency. If, in the meantime, the dollar grows stronger, then when the time comes to convert from U.S. dollars back to the foreign currency, the investor will receive more foreign currency than expected at the time the original investment was made.

The preceding paragraphs all focus on the case where the U.S. dollar becomes stronger. The first column in **Figure 29.4** illustrates the corresponding happy or unhappy economic reactions. The following Work It Out feature centers the analysis on the opposite: a weaker dollar.

Work It Out ─○─○─○

Effects of a Weaker Dollar

Let's work through the effects of a weaker dollar on a U.S. exporter, a foreign exporter into the United States, a U.S. tourist going abroad, a foreign tourist coming to the United States, a U.S. investor abroad, and a foreign investor in the United States.

Step 1. Note that the demand for U.S. exports is a function of the price of those exports, which depends on the dollar price of those goods and the exchange rate of the dollar in terms of foreign currency. For example, a Ford pickup truck costs $25,000 in the United States. When it is sold in the United Kingdom, the price is $25,000 / $1.30 per British pound, or £19,231. The dollar affects the price foreigners face who may purchase U.S. exports.

Step 2. Consider that, if the dollar weakens, the pound rises in value. If the pound rises to $2.00 per pound, then the price of a Ford pickup is now $25,000 / $2.00 = £12,500. A weaker dollar means the foreign currency buys more dollars, which means that U.S. exports appear less expensive.

Step 3. Summarize that a weaker U.S. dollar leads to an increase in U.S. exports. For a foreign exporter, the outcome is just the opposite.

Step 4. Suppose a brewery in England is interested in selling its Bass Ale to a grocery store in the United States. If the price of a six pack of Bass Ale is £6.00 and the exchange rate is $1.30 per British pound, the price for the grocery store is 6.00 × $1.30 = $7.80 per six pack. If the dollar weakens to $2.00 per pound, the price of Bass Ale is now 6.00 × $2.00 = $12.

Step 5. Summarize that, from the perspective of U.S. purchasers, a weaker dollar means that foreign currency is more expensive, which means that foreign goods are more expensive also. This leads to a decrease in U.S. imports, which is bad for the foreign exporter.

Step 6. Consider U.S. tourists going abroad. They face the same situation as a U.S. importer—they are purchasing a foreign trip. A weaker dollar means that their trip will cost more, since a given expenditure of foreign currency (e.g., hotel bill) will take more dollars. The result is that the tourist may not stay as long abroad, and some may choose not to travel at all.

Step 7. Consider that, for the foreign tourist to the United States, a weaker dollar is a boon. It means their currency goes further, so the cost of a trip to the United States will be less. Foreigners may choose to take longer trips to the United States, and more foreign tourists may decide to take U.S. trips.

Step 8. Note that a U.S. investor abroad faces the same situation as a U.S. importer—they are purchasing a foreign asset. A U.S. investor will see a weaker dollar as an increase in the "price" of investment, since the same number of dollars will buy less foreign currency and thus less foreign assets. This should decrease the amount of U.S. investment abroad.

Step 9. Note also that foreign investors in the Unites States will have the opposite experience. Since foreign currency buys more dollars, they will likely invest in more U.S. assets.

At this point, you should have a good sense of the major players in the foreign exchange market: firms involved in international trade, tourists, international financial investors, banks, and foreign exchange dealers. The next module shows how players can use the tools of demand and supply in foreign exchange markets to explain the underlying causes of stronger and weaker currencies (we address "stronger" and "weaker" more in the following Clear It Up feature).

Why is a stronger currency not necessarily better?

One common misunderstanding about exchange rates is that a "stronger" or "appreciating" currency must be better than a "weaker" or "depreciating" currency. After all, is it not obvious that "strong" is better than "weak"? Do not let the terminology confuse you. When a currency becomes stronger, so that it purchases more of other currencies, it benefits some in the economy and injures others. Stronger currency is not necessarily better, it is just different.

29.2 | Demand and Supply Shifts in Foreign Exchange Markets

By the end of this section, you will be able to:
- Explain supply and demand for exchange rates
- Define arbitrage
- Explain purchasing power parity's importance when comparing countries.

The foreign exchange market involves firms, households, and investors who demand and supply currencies coming together through their banks and the key foreign exchange dealers. **Figure 29.5** (a) offers an example for the exchange rate between the U.S. dollar and the Mexican peso. The vertical axis shows the exchange rate for U.S. dollars, which in this case is measured in pesos. The horizontal axis shows the quantity of U.S. dollars traded in the foreign exchange market each day. The demand curve (D) for U.S. dollars intersects with the supply curve (S) of U.S. dollars at the equilibrium point (E), which is an exchange rate of 10 pesos per dollar and a total volume of $8.5 billion.

This OpenStax book is available for free at http://cnx.org/content/col12122/1.4

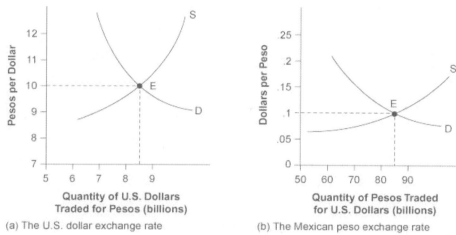

Figure 29.5 Demand and Supply for the U.S. Dollar and Mexican Peso Exchange Rate (a) The quantity measured on the horizontal axis is in U.S. dollars, and the exchange rate on the vertical axis is the price of U.S. dollars measured in Mexican pesos. (b) The quantity measured on the horizontal axis is in Mexican pesos, while the price on the vertical axis is the price of pesos measured in U.S. dollars. In both graphs, the equilibrium exchange rate occurs at point E, at the intersection of the demand curve (D) and the supply curve (S).

Figure 29.5 (b) presents the same demand and supply information from the perspective of the Mexican peso. The vertical axis shows the exchange rate for Mexican pesos, which is measured in U.S. dollars. The horizontal axis shows the quantity of Mexican pesos traded in the foreign exchange market. The demand curve (D) for Mexican pesos intersects with the supply curve (S) of Mexican pesos at the equilibrium point (E), which is an exchange rate of 10 cents in U.S. currency for each Mexican peso and a total volume of 85 billion pesos. Note that the two exchange rates are inverses: 10 pesos per dollar is the same as 10 cents per peso (or $0.10 per peso). In the actual foreign exchange market, almost all of the trading for Mexican pesos is for U.S. dollars. What factors would cause the demand or supply to shift, thus leading to a change in the equilibrium exchange rate? We discuss the answer to this question in the following section.

Expectations about Future Exchange Rates

One reason to demand a currency on the foreign exchange market is the belief that the currency's value is about to increase. One reason to supply a currency—that is, sell it on the foreign exchange market—is the expectation that the currency's value is about to decline. For example, imagine that a leading business newspaper, like the *Wall Street Journal* or the *Financial Times*, runs an article predicting that the Mexican peso will appreciate in value. **Figure 29.6** illustrates the likely effects of such an article. Demand for the Mexican peso shifts to the right, from D_0 to D_1, as investors become eager to purchase pesos. Conversely, the supply of pesos shifts to the left, from S_0 to S_1, because investors will be less willing to give them up. The result is that the equilibrium exchange rate rises from 10 cents/peso to 12 cents/peso and the equilibrium exchange rate rises from 85 billion to 90 billion pesos as the equilibrium moves from E_0 to E_1.

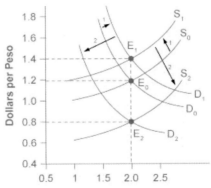

Figure 29.6 Exchange Rate Market for Mexican Peso Reacts to Expectations about Future Exchange Rates
An announcement that the peso exchange rate is likely to strengthen in the future will lead to greater demand for the peso in the present from investors who wish to benefit from the appreciation. Similarly, it will make investors less likely to supply pesos to the foreign exchange market. Both the shift of demand to the right and the shift of supply to the left cause an immediate appreciation in the exchange rate.

Figure 29.6 also illustrates some peculiar traits of supply and demand diagrams in the foreign exchange market. In contrast to all the other cases of supply and demand you have considered, in the foreign exchange market, supply and demand typically both move at the same time. Groups of participants in the foreign exchange market like firms and investors include some who are buyers and some who are sellers. An expectation of a future shift in the exchange rate affects both buyers and sellers—that is, it affects both demand and supply for a currency.

The shifts in demand and supply curves both cause the exchange rate to shift in the same direction. In this example, they both make the peso exchange rate stronger. However, the shifts in demand and supply work in opposing directions on the quantity traded. In this example, the rising demand for pesos is causing the quantity to rise while the falling supply of pesos is causing quantity to fall. In this specific example, the result is a higher quantity. However, in other cases, the result could be that quantity remains unchanged or declines.

This example also helps to explain why exchange rates often move quite substantially in a short period of a few weeks or months. When investors expect a country's currency to strengthen in the future, they buy the currency and cause it to appreciate immediately. The currency's appreciation can lead other investors to believe that future appreciation is likely—and thus lead to even further appreciation. Similarly, a fear that a currency *might* weaken quickly leads to an *actual* weakening of the currency, which often reinforces the belief that the currency will weaken further. Thus, beliefs about the future path of exchange rates can be self-reinforcing, at least for a time, and a large share of the trading in foreign exchange markets involves dealers trying to outguess each other on what direction exchange rates will move next.

Differences across Countries in Rates of Return

The motivation for investment, whether domestic or foreign, is to earn a return. If rates of return in a country look relatively high, then that country will tend to attract funds from abroad. Conversely, if rates of return in a country look relatively low, then funds will tend to flee to other economies. Changes in the expected rate of return will shift demand and supply for a currency. For example, imagine that interest rates rise in the United States as compared with Mexico. Thus, financial investments in the United States promise a higher return than previously. As a result, more investors will demand U.S. dollars so that they can buy interest-bearing assets and fewer investors will be willing to supply U.S. dollars to foreign exchange markets. Demand for the U.S. dollar will shift to the right, from D_0 to D_1, and supply will shift to the left, from S_0 to S_1, as **Figure 29.7** shows. The new equilibrium (E_1), will occur at an exchange rate of nine pesos/dollar and the same quantity of $8.5 billion. Thus, a higher interest rate or rate of return relative to other countries leads a nation's currency to appreciate or strengthen, and a lower interest rate relative to other countries leads a nation's currency to depreciate or weaken. Since a nation's central bank can use monetary policy to affect its interest rates, a central bank can also cause changes in exchange rates—a connection that we will discuss in more detail later in this chapter.

This OpenStax book is available for free at http://cnx.org/content/col12122/1.4

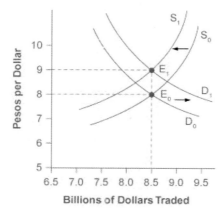

Figure 29.7 Exchange Rate Market for U.S. Dollars Reacts to Higher Interest Rates   A higher rate of return for U.S. dollars makes holding dollars more attractive. Thus, the demand for dollars in the foreign exchange market shifts to the right, from D_0 to D_1, while the supply of dollars shifts to the left, from S_0 to S_1. The new equilibrium (E_1) has a stronger exchange rate than the original equilibrium (E_0), but in this example, the equilibrium quantity traded does not change.

Relative Inflation

If a country experiences a relatively high inflation rate compared with other economies, then the buying power of its currency is eroding, which will tend to discourage anyone from wanting to acquire or to hold the currency. **Figure 29.8** shows an example based on an actual episode concerning the Mexican peso. In 1986–87, Mexico experienced an inflation rate of over 200%. Not surprisingly, as inflation dramatically decreased the peso's purchasing power in Mexico. The peso's exchange rate value declined as well. **Figure 29.8** shows that the demand for the peso on foreign exchange markets decreased from D_0 to D_1, while the peso's supply increased from S_0 to S_1. The equilibrium exchange rate fell from $2.50 per peso at the original equilibrium (E_0) to $0.50 per peso at the new equilibrium (E_1). In this example, the quantity of pesos traded on foreign exchange markets remained the same, even as the exchange rate shifted.

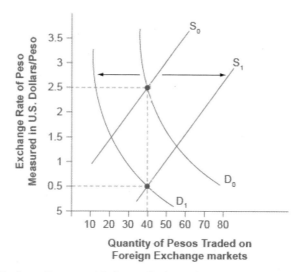

Figure 29.8 Exchange Rate Markets React to Higher Inflation   If a currency is experiencing relatively high inflation, then its buying power is decreasing and international investors will be less eager to hold it. Thus, a rise in inflation in the Mexican peso would lead demand to shift from D_0 to D_1, and supply to increase from S_0 to S_1. Both movements in demand and supply would cause the currency to depreciate. Here, we draw the effect on the quantity traded as a decrease, but in truth it could be an increase or no change, depending on the actual movements of demand and supply.

Link It Up

Visit this website (http://openstaxcollege.org/l/bigmac) to learn about the Big Mac index.

Purchasing Power Parity

Over the long term, exchange rates must bear some relationship to the currency's buying power in terms of internationally traded goods. If at a certain exchange rate it was much cheaper to buy internationally traded goods—such as oil, steel, computers, and cars—in one country than in another country, businesses would start buying in the cheap country, selling in other countries, and pocketing the profits.

For example, if a U.S. dollar is worth $1.30 in Canadian currency, then a car that sells for $20,000 in the United States should sell for $26,000 in Canada. If the price of cars in Canada were much lower than $26,000, then at least some U.S. car-buyers would convert their U.S. dollars to Canadian dollars and buy their cars in Canada. If the price of cars were much higher than $26,000 in this example, then at least some Canadian buyers would convert their Canadian dollars to U.S. dollars and go to the United States to purchase their cars. This is known as **arbitrage**, the process of buying and selling goods or currencies across international borders at a profit. It may occur slowly, but over time, it will force prices and exchange rates to align so that the price of internationally traded goods is similar in all countries.

We call the exchange rate that equalizes the prices of internationally traded goods across countries the **purchasing power parity (PPP)** exchange rate. A group of economists at the International Comparison Program, run by the World Bank, have calculated the PPP exchange rate for all countries, based on detailed studies of the prices and quantities of internationally tradable goods.

The purchasing power parity exchange rate has two functions. First, economists often use PPP exchange rates for international comparison of GDP and other economic statistics. Imagine that you are preparing a table showing the size of GDP in many countries in several recent years, and for ease of comparison, you are converting all the values into U.S. dollars. When you insert the value for Japan, you need to use a yen/dollar exchange rate. However, should you use the market exchange rate or the PPP exchange rate? Market exchange rates bounce around. In 2014, the exchange rate was 105 yen/dollar, but in late 2015 the U.S. dollar exchange rate versus the yen was 121 yen/dollar. For simplicity, say that Japan's GDP was ¥500 trillion in both 2014 and 2015. If you use the market exchange rates, then Japan's GDP will be $4.8 trillion in 2014 (that is, ¥500 trillion /(¥105/dollar)) and $4.1 trillion in 2015 (that is, ¥500 trillion /(¥121/dollar)).

The misleading appearance of a changing Japanese economy occurs only because we used the market exchange rate, which often has short-run rises and falls. However, PPP exchange rates stay fairly constant and change only modestly, if at all, from year to year.

The second function of PPP is that exchanges rates will often get closer to it as time passes. It is true that in the short and medium run, as exchange rates adjust to relative inflation rates, rates of return, and to expectations about how interest rates and inflation will shift, the exchange rates will often move away from the PPP exchange rate for a time. However, knowing the PPP will allow you to track and predict exchange rate relationships.

29.3 | Macroeconomic Effects of Exchange Rates

By the end of this section you will be able to:
- Explain how exchange rate shifting influences aggregate demand and supply
- Explain how shifting exchange rates also can influence loans and banks

A central bank will be concerned about the exchange rate for multiple reasons: (1) Movements in the exchange rate will affect the quantity of aggregate demand in an economy; (2) frequent substantial fluctuations in the exchange rate can disrupt international trade and cause problems in a nation's banking system–this may contribute to an unsustainable balance of trade and large inflows of international financial capital, which can set up the economy for a deep recession if international investors decide to move their money to another country. Let's discuss these scenarios in turn.

Exchange Rates, Aggregate Demand, and Aggregate Supply

Foreign trade in goods and services typically involves incurring the costs of production in one currency while receiving revenues from sales in another currency. As a result, movements in exchange rates can have a powerful effect on incentives to export and import, and thus on aggregate demand in the economy as a whole.

For example, in 1999, when the euro first became a currency, its value measured in U.S. currency was $1.06/euro. By the end of 2013, the euro had risen (and the U.S. dollar had correspondingly weakened) to $1.37/euro. However, by the end of February, 2017, the exchange rate was once again $1.06/euro. Consider the situation of a French firm that each year incurs €10 million in costs, and sells its products in the United States for $10 million. In 1999, when this firm converted $10 million back to euros at the exchange rate of $1.06/euro (that is, $10 million × [€1/$1.06]), it received €9.4 million, and suffered a loss. In 2013, when this same firm converted $10 million back to euros at the exchange rate of $1.37/euro (that is, $10 million × [€1 euro/$1.37]), it received approximately €7.3 million and an even larger loss. In the beginning of 2017, with the exchange rate back at $1.06/euro the firm would suffer a loss once again. This example shows how a stronger euro discourages exports by the French firm, because it makes the costs of production in the domestic currency higher relative to the sales revenues earned in another country. From the point of view of the U.S. economy, the example also shows how a weaker U.S. dollar encourages exports.

Since an increase in exports results in more dollars flowing into the economy, and an increase in imports means more dollars are flowing out, it is easy to conclude that exports are "good" for the economy and imports are "bad," but this overlooks the role of exchange rates. If an American consumer buys a Japanese car for $20,000 instead of an American car for $30,000, it may be tempting to argue that the American economy has lost out. However, the Japanese company will have to convert those dollars to yen to pay its workers and operate its factories. Whoever buys those dollars will have to use them to purchase American goods and services, so the money comes right back into the American economy. At the same time, the consumer saves money by buying a less expensive import, and can use the extra money for other purposes.

Fluctuations in Exchange Rates

Exchange rates can fluctuate a great deal in the short run. As yet one more example, the Indian rupee moved from 39 rupees/dollar in February 2008 to 51 rupees/dollar in March 2009, a decline of more than one-fourth in the value of the rupee on foreign exchange markets. **Figure 29.9** earlier showed that even two economically developed neighboring economies like the United States and Canada can see significant movements in exchange rates over a few years. For firms that depend on export sales, or firms that rely on imported inputs to production, or even purely domestic firms that compete with firms tied into international trade—which in many countries adds up to half or more of a nation's GDP—sharp movements in exchange rates can lead to dramatic changes in profits and losses. A central bank may desire to keep exchange rates from moving too much as part of providing a stable business climate, where firms can focus on productivity and innovation, not on reacting to exchange rate fluctuations.

One of the most economically destructive effects of exchange rate fluctuations can happen through the banking system. Financial institutions measure most international loans are measured in a few large currencies, like U.S. dollars, European euros, and Japanese yen. In countries that do not use these currencies, banks often borrow funds in the currencies of other countries, like U.S. dollars, but then lend in their own domestic currency. The left-hand chain of events in **Figure 29.9** shows how this pattern of international borrowing can work. A bank in Thailand borrows one million in U.S. dollars. Then the bank converts the dollars to its domestic currency—in the case of Thailand, the currency is the baht—at a rate of 40 baht/dollar. The bank then lends the baht to a firm in Thailand. The business repays the loan in baht, and the bank converts it back to U.S. dollars to pay off its original U.S. dollar loan.

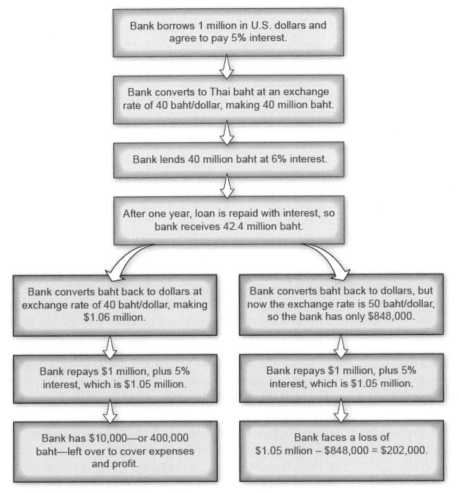

Figure 29.9 International Borrowing   The scenario of international borrowing that ends on the left is a success story, but the scenario that ends on the right shows what happens when the exchange rate weakens.

This process of borrowing in a foreign currency and lending in a domestic currency can work just fine, as long as the exchange rate does not shift. In the scenario outlined, if the dollar strengthens and the baht weakens, a problem arises. The right-hand chain of events in **Figure 29.9** illustrates what happens when the baht unexpectedly weakens from 40 baht/dollar to 50 baht/dollar. The Thai firm still repays the loan in full to the bank. However, because of the shift in the exchange rate, the bank cannot repay its loan in U.S. dollars. (Of course, if the exchange rate had changed in the other direction, making the Thai currency stronger, the bank could have realized an unexpectedly large profit.)

In 1997–1998, countries across eastern Asia, like Thailand, Korea, Malaysia, and Indonesia, experienced a sharp depreciation of their currencies, in some cases 50% or more. These countries had been experiencing substantial inflows of foreign investment capital, with bank lending increasing by 20% to 30% per year through the mid-1990s. When their exchange rates depreciated, the banking systems in these countries were bankrupt. Argentina experienced a similar chain of events in 2002. When the Argentine peso depreciated, Argentina's banks found themselves unable to pay back what they had borrowed in U.S. dollars.

Banks play a vital role in any economy in facilitating transactions and in making loans to firms and consumers. When most of a country's largest banks become bankrupt simultaneously, a sharp decline in aggregate demand and a deep recession results. Since the main responsibilities of a central bank are to control the money supply and to ensure that the banking system is stable, a central bank must be concerned about whether large and unexpected exchange rate depreciation will drive most of the country's existing banks into bankruptcy. For more on this concern, return to the

This OpenStax book is available for free at http://cnx.org/content/col12122/1.4

chapter on **The International Trade and Capital Flows**.

Summing Up Public Policy and Exchange Rates

Every nation would prefer a stable exchange rate to facilitate international trade and reduce the degree of risk and uncertainty in the economy. However, a nation may sometimes want a weaker exchange rate to stimulate aggregate demand and reduce a recession, or a stronger exchange rate to fight inflation. The country must also be concerned that rapid movements from a weak to a strong exchange rate may cripple its export industries, while rapid movements from a strong to a weak exchange rate can cripple its banking sector. In short, every choice of an exchange rate—whether it should be stronger or weaker, or fixed or changing—represents potential tradeoffs.

29.4 | Exchange Rate Policies

By the end of this section, you will be able to:

- Differentiate among a floating exchange rate, a soft peg, a hard peg, and a merged currency
- Identify the tradeoffs that come with a floating exchange rate, a soft peg, a hard peg, and a merged currency

Exchange rate policies come in a range of different forms listed in **Figure 29.10**: let the foreign exchange market determine the exchange rate; let the market set the value of the exchange rate most of the time, but have the central bank sometimes intervene to prevent fluctuations that seem too large; have the central bank guarantee a specific exchange rate; or share a currency with other countries. Let's discuss each type of exchange rate policy and its tradeoffs.

Figure 29.10 A Spectrum of Exchange Rate Policies A nation may adopt one of a variety of exchange rate regimes, from floating rates in which the foreign exchange market determines the rates to pegged rates where governments intervene to manage the exchange rate's value, to a common currency where the nation adopts another country or group of countries' currency.

Floating Exchange Rates

We refer to a policy which allows the foreign exchange market to set exchange rates as a **floating exchange rate**. The U.S. dollar is a floating exchange rate, as are the currencies of about 40% of the countries in the world economy. The major concern with this policy is that exchange rates can move a great deal in a short time.

Consider the U.S. exchange rate expressed in terms of another fairly stable currency, the Japanese yen, as **Figure 29.11** shows. On January 1, 2002, the exchange rate was 133 yen/dollar. On January 1, 2005, it was 103 yen/dollar. On June 1, 2007, it was 122 yen/dollar, on January 1, 2012, it was 77 yen per dollar, and on March 1, 2015, it was 120 yen per dollar. As investor sentiment swings back and forth, driving exchange rates up and down, exporters, importers, and banks involved in international lending are all affected. At worst, large movements in exchange rates can drive companies into bankruptcy or trigger a nationwide banking collapse. However, even in the moderate case of the yen/dollar exchange rate, these movements of roughly 30 percent back and forth impose stress on both economies as firms must alter their export and import plans to take the new exchange rates into account. Especially in smaller countries where international trade is a relatively large share of GDP, exchange rate movements can rattle their economies.

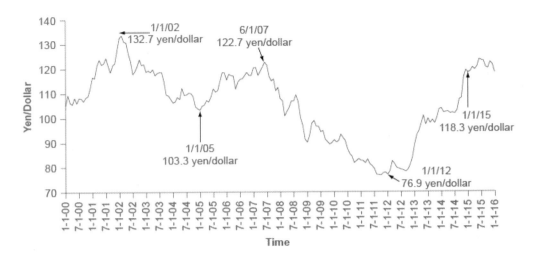

Figure 29.11 U.S. Dollar Exchange Rate in Japanese Yen Even seemingly stable exchange rates such as the Japanese Yen to the U.S. Dollar can vary when closely examined over time. This figure shows a relatively stable rate between 2011 and 2013. In 2013, there was a drastic depreciation of the Yen (relative to the U.S. Dollar) by about 14% and again at the end of the year in 2014 also by about 14%. (Source: Federal Reserve Economic Data (FRED) https://research.stlouisfed.org/fred2/series/DEXJPUS)

However, movements of floating exchange rates have advantages, too. After all, prices of goods and services rise and fall throughout a market economy, as demand and supply shift. If an economy experiences strong inflows or outflows of international financial capital, or has relatively high inflation, or if it experiences strong productivity growth so that purchasing power changes relative to other economies, then it makes economic sense for the exchange rate to shift as well.

Floating exchange rate advocates often argue that if government policies were more predictable and stable, then inflation rates and interest rates would be more predictable and stable. Exchange rates would bounce around less, too. The economist Milton Friedman (1912–2006), for example, wrote a defense of floating exchange rates in 1962 in his book *Capitalism and Freedom*:

> Being in favor of floating exchange rates does not mean being in favor of unstable exchange rates. When we support a free price system [for goods and services] at home, this does not imply that we favor a system in which prices fluctuate wildly up and down. What we want is a system in which prices are free to fluctuate but in which the forces determining them are sufficiently stable so that in fact prices move within moderate ranges. This is equally true in a system of floating exchange rates. The ultimate objective is a world in which exchange rates, while free to vary, are, in fact, highly stable because basic economic policies and conditions are stable.

Advocates of floating exchange rates admit that, yes, exchange rates may sometimes fluctuate. They point out, however, that if a central bank focuses on preventing either high inflation or deep recession, with low and reasonably steady interest rates, then exchange rates will have less reason to vary.

Using Soft Pegs and Hard Pegs

When a government intervenes in the foreign exchange market so that the currency's exchange rate is different from what the market would have produced, it establishes a "peg" for its currency. A **soft peg** is the name for an exchange rate policy where the government usually allows the market to set exchange rate, but in some cases, especially if the exchange rate seems to be moving rapidly in one direction, the central bank will intervene in the market. With a **hard peg** exchange rate policy, the central bank sets a fixed and unchanging value for the exchange rate. A central bank can implement soft peg and hard peg policies.

Suppose the market exchange rate for the Brazilian currency, the real, would be 35 cents/real with a daily quantity of 15 billion real traded in the market, as the equilibrium E_0 in **Figure 29.12** (a) and **Figure 29.12** (b) show. However, Brazil's government decides that the exchange rate should be 30 cents/real, as **Figure 29.12** (a) shows. Perhaps

This OpenStax book is available for free at http://cnx.org/content/col12122/1.4

Brazil sets this lower exchange rate to benefit its export industries. Perhaps it is an attempt to stimulate aggregate demand by stimulating exports. Perhaps Brazil believes that the current market exchange rate is higher than the long-term purchasing power parity value of the real, so it is minimizing fluctuations in the real by keeping it at this lower rate. Perhaps the government set the target exchange rate sometime in the past, and it is now maintaining it for the sake of stability. Whatever the reason, if Brazil's central bank wishes to keep the exchange rate below the market level, it must face the reality that at this weaker exchange rate of 30 cents/real, the quantity demanded of its currency at 17 billion reals is greater than the quantity supplied of 13 billion reals in the foreign exchange market.

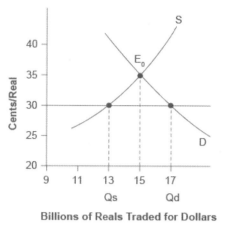 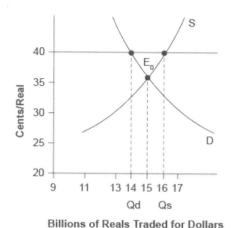

(a) Pegging an exchange rate below equilibrium   (b) Pegging an exchange rate above equilibrium

Figure 29.12 Pegging an Exchange Rate (a) If an exchange rate is pegged below what would otherwise be the equilibrium, then the currency's quantity demanded will exceed the quantity supplied. (b) If an exchange rate is pegged above what would otherwise be the equilibrium, then the currency's quantity supplied exceeds the quantity demanded.

The Brazilian central bank could weaken its exchange rate in two ways. One approach is to use an expansionary monetary policy that leads to lower interest rates. In foreign exchange markets, the lower interest rates will reduce demand and increase supply of the real and lead to depreciation. Central banks do not use this technique often because lowering interest rates to weaken the currency may be in conflict with the country's monetary policy goals. Alternatively, Brazil's central bank could trade directly in the foreign exchange market. The central bank can expand the money supply by creating reals, use the reals to purchase foreign currencies, and avoid selling any of its own currency. In this way, it can fill the gap between quantity demanded and quantity supplied of its currency.

Figure 29.12 (b) shows the opposite situation. Here, the Brazilian government desires a stronger exchange rate of 40 cents/real than the market rate of 35 cents/real. Perhaps Brazil desires the stronger currency to reduce aggregate demand and to fight inflation, or perhaps Brazil believes that that current market exchange rate is temporarily lower than the long-term rate. Whatever the reason, at the higher desired exchange rate, the quantity supplied of 16 billion reals exceeds the quantity demanded of 14 billion reals.

Brazil's central bank can use a contractionary monetary policy to raise interest rates, which will increase demand and reduce currency supply on foreign exchange markets, and lead to an appreciation. Alternatively, Brazil's central bank can trade directly in the foreign exchange market. In this case, with an excess supply of its own currency in foreign exchange markets, the central bank must use reserves of foreign currency, like U.S. dollars, to demand its own currency and thus cause an appreciation of its exchange rate.

Both a soft peg and a hard peg policy require that the central bank intervene in the foreign exchange market. However, a hard peg policy attempts to preserve a fixed exchange rate at all times. A soft peg policy typically allows the exchange rate to move up and down by relatively small amounts in the short run of several months or a year, and to move by larger amounts over time, but seeks to avoid extreme short-term fluctuations.

Tradeoffs of Soft Pegs and Hard Pegs

When a country decides to alter the market exchange rate, it faces a number of tradeoffs. If it uses monetary policy to alter the exchange rate, it then cannot at the same time use monetary policy to address issues of inflation or recession. If it uses direct purchases and sales of foreign currencies in exchange rates, then it must face the issue of how it will handle its reserves of foreign currency. Finally, a pegged exchange rate can even create additional movements of the exchange rate. For example, even the possibility of government intervention in exchange rate markets will lead to rumors about whether and when the government will intervene, and dealers in the foreign exchange market will react to those rumors. Let's consider these issues in turn.

One concern with pegged exchange rate policies is that they imply a country's monetary policy is no longer focused on controlling inflation or shortening recessions, but now must also take the exchange rate into account. For example, when a country pegs its exchange rate, it will sometimes face economic situations where it would like to have an expansionary monetary policy to fight recession—but it cannot do so because that policy would depreciate its exchange rate and break its hard peg. With a soft peg exchange rate policy, the central bank can sometimes ignore the exchange rate and focus on domestic inflation or recession—but in other cases the central bank may ignore inflation or recession and instead focus on its soft peg exchange rate. With a hard peg policy, domestic monetary policy is effectively no longer determined by domestic inflation or unemployment, but only by what monetary policy is needed to keep the exchange rate at the hard peg.

Another issue arises when a central bank intervenes directly in the exchange rate market. If a central bank ends up in a situation where it is perpetually creating and selling its own currency on foreign exchange markets, it will be buying the currency of other countries, like U.S. dollars or euros, to hold as reserves. Holding large reserves of other currencies has an opportunity cost, and central banks will not wish to boost such reserves without limit.

In addition, a central bank that causes a large increase in the supply of money is also risking an inflationary surge in aggregate demand. Conversely, when a central bank wishes to buy its own currency, it can do so by using its reserves of international currency like the U.S. dollar or the euro. However, if the central bank runs out of such reserves, it can no longer use this method to strengthen its currency. Thus, buying foreign currencies in exchange rate markets can be expensive and inflationary, while selling foreign currencies can work only until a central bank runs out of reserves.

Yet another issue is that when a government pegs its exchange rate, it may unintentionally create another reason for additional fluctuation. With a soft peg policy, foreign exchange dealers and international investors react to every rumor about how or when the central bank is likely to intervene to influence the exchange rate, and as they react to rumors the exchange rate will shift up and down. Thus, even though the goal of a soft peg policy is to reduce short-term fluctuations of the exchange rate, the existence of the policy—when anticipated in the foreign exchange market—may sometimes increase short-term fluctuations as international investors try to anticipate how and when the central bank will act. The following Clear It Up feature discusses the effects of **international capital flows**—capital that flows across national boundaries as either portfolio investment or direct investment.

How do Tobin taxes control the flow of capital?

Some countries like Chile and Malaysia have sought to reduce movements in exchange rates by limiting international financial capital inflows and outflows. The government can enact this policy either through targeted taxes or by regulations.

Taxes on international capital flows are sometimes known as **Tobin taxes**, named after James Tobin, the 1981 Nobel laureate in economics who proposed such a tax in a 1972 lecture. For example, a government might tax all foreign exchange transactions, or attempt to tax short-term portfolio investment while exempting long-term foreign direct investment. Countries can also use regulation to forbid certain kinds of foreign investment in the first place or to make it difficult for international financial investors to withdraw their funds from a country.

The goal of such policies is to reduce international capital flows, especially short-term portfolio flows, in the hope that doing so will reduce the chance of large movements in exchange rates that can bring macroeconomic disaster.

However, proposals to limit international financial flows have severe practical difficulties. National governments impose taxes, not international ones. If one government imposes a Tobin tax on exchange rate transactions carried out within its territory, a firm based someplace like the Grand Caymans, an island nation in the Caribbean well-known for allowing some financial wheeling and dealing might easily operate the exchange rate market. In an interconnected global economy, if goods and services are allowed to flow across national borders, then payments need to flow across borders, too. It is very difficult—in fact close to impossible—for a nation to allow only the flows of payments that relate to goods and services, while clamping down or taxing other flows of financial capital. If a nation participates in international trade, it must also participate in international capital movements.

Finally, countries all over the world, especially low-income countries, are crying out for foreign investment to help develop their economies. Policies that discourage international financial investment may prevent some possible harm, but they rule out potentially substantial economic benefits as well.

A hard peg exchange rate policy will not allow short-term fluctuations in the exchange rate. If the government first announces a hard peg and then later changes its mind—perhaps the government becomes unwilling to keep interest rates high or to hold high levels of foreign exchange reserves—then the result of abandoning a hard peg could be a dramatic shift in the exchange rate.

In the mid-2000s, about one-third of the countries in the world used a soft peg approach and about one-quarter used a hard peg approach. The general trend in the 1990s was to shift away from a soft peg approach in favor of either floating rates or a hard peg. The concern is that a successful soft peg policy may, for a time, lead to very little variation in exchange rates, so that firms and banks in the economy begin to act as if a hard peg exists. When the exchange rate does move, the effects are especially painful because firms and banks have not planned and hedged against a possible change. Thus, the argument went, it is better either to be clear that the exchange rate is always flexible, or that it is fixed, but choosing an in-between soft peg option may end up being worst of all.

A Merged Currency

A final approach to exchange rate policy is for a nation to choose a common currency shared with one or more nations is also called a **merged currency**. A merged currency approach eliminates foreign exchange risk altogether. Just as no one worries about exchange rate movements when buying and selling between New York and California, Europeans know that the value of the euro will be the same in Germany and France and other European nations that have adopted the euro.

However, a merged currency also poses problems. Like a hard peg, a merged currency means that a nation has given up altogether on domestic monetary policy, and instead has put its interest rate policies in other hands. When Ecuador uses the U.S. dollar as its currency, it has no voice in whether the Federal Reserve raises or lowers interest rates. The European Central Bank that determines monetary policy for the euro has representatives from all the euro nations. However, from the standpoint of, say, Portugal, there will be times when the decisions of the European Central Bank about monetary policy do not match the decisions that a Portuguese central bank would have made.

The lines between these four different exchange rate policies can blend into each other. For example, a soft peg exchange rate policy in which the government almost never acts to intervene in the exchange rate market will look a great deal like a floating exchange rate. Conversely, a soft peg policy in which the government intervenes often to keep the exchange rate near a specific level will look a lot like a hard peg. A decision to merge currencies with another country is, in effect, a decision to have a permanently fixed exchange rate with those countries, which is like a very hard exchange rate peg. **Table 29.3** summarizes the range of exchange rates policy choices, with their advantages and disadvantages.

Situation	Floating Exchange Rates	Soft Peg	Hard Peg	Merged Currency
Large short-run fluctuations in exchange rates?	Often considerable in the short term	Maybe less in the short run, but still large changes over time	None, unless a change in the fixed rate	None

Table 29.3 Tradeoffs of Exchange Rate Policies

Situation	Floating Exchange Rates	Soft Peg	Hard Peg	Merged Currency
Large long-term fluctuations in exchange rates?	Can often happen	Can often happen	Cannot happen unless hard peg changes, in which case substantial volatility can occur	Cannot happen
Power of central bank to conduct countercyclical monetary policy?	Flexible exchange rates make monetary policy stronger	Some power, although conflicts may arise between exchange rate policy and countercyclical policy	Very little; central bank must keep exchange rate fixed	None; nation does not have its own currency
Costs of holding foreign exchange reserves?	Do not need to hold reserves	Hold moderate reserves that rise and fall over time	Hold large reserves	No need to hold reserves
Risk of ending up with an exchange rate that causes a large trade imbalance and very high inflows or outflows of financial capital?	Adjusts often	Adjusts over the medium term, if not the short term	May end up over time either far above or below the market level	Cannot adjust

Table 29.3 Tradeoffs of Exchange Rate Policies

Global macroeconomics would be easier if the whole world had one currency and one central bank. The exchange rates between different currencies complicate the picture. If financial markets solely set exchange rates, they fluctuate substantially as short-term portfolio investors try to anticipate tomorrow's news. If the government attempts to intervene in exchange rate markets through soft pegs or hard pegs, it gives up at least some of the power to use monetary policy to focus on domestic inflations and recessions, and it risks causing even greater fluctuations in foreign exchange markets.

There is no consensus among economists about which exchange rate policies are best: floating, soft peg, hard peg, or merged currencies. The choice depends both on how well a nation's central bank can implement a specific exchange rate policy and on how well a nation's firms and banks can adapt to different exchange rate policies. A national economy that does a fairly good job at achieving the four main economic goals of growth, low inflation, low unemployment, and a sustainable balance of trade will probably do just fine most of the time with any exchange rate policy. Conversely, no exchange rate policy is likely to save an economy that consistently fails at achieving these goals. Alternatively, a merged currency applied across wide geographic and cultural areas carries with it its own set of problems, such as the ability for countries to conduct their own independent monetary policies.

Bring it Home

Is a Stronger Dollar Good for the U.S. Economy?

The foreign exchange value of the dollar is a price and whether a higher price is good or bad depends on where you are standing: sellers benefit from higher prices and buyers are harmed. A stronger dollar is good for U.S. imports (and people working for U.S. importers) and U.S. investment abroad. It is also good for U.S. tourists going to other countries, since their dollar goes further. However, a stronger dollar is bad for U.S. exports (and people working in U.S. export industries); it is bad for foreign investment in the United States (leading, for example, to higher U.S. interest rates); and it is bad for foreign tourists (as well as U.S hotels, restaurants, and others in the tourist industry). In short, whether the U.S. dollar is good or bad is a more complex question than you may have thought. The economic answer is "it depends."

KEY TERMS

appreciating when a currency is worth more in terms of other currencies; also called "strengthening"

arbitrage the process of buying a good and selling goods across borders to take advantage of international price differences

depreciating when a currency is worth less in terms of other currencies; also called "weakening"

dollarize a country that is not the United States uses the U.S. dollar as its currency

floating exchange rate a country lets the exchange rate market determine its currency's value

foreign direct investment (FDI) purchasing more than ten percent of a firm or starting a new enterprise in another country

foreign exchange market the market in which people use one currency to buy another currency

hard peg an exchange rate policy in which the central bank sets a fixed and unchanging value for the exchange rate

hedge using a financial transaction as protection against risk

international capital flows flow of financial capital across national boundaries either as portfolio investment or direct investment

merged currency when a nation chooses to use another nation's currency

portfolio investment an investment in another country that is purely financial and does not involve any management responsibility

purchasing power parity (PPP) the exchange rate that equalizes the prices of internationally traded goods across countries

soft peg an exchange rate policy in which the government usually allows the market to set the exchange rate, but in some cases, especially if the exchange rate seems to be moving rapidly in one direction, the central bank will intervene

Tobin taxes see international capital flows

KEY CONCEPTS AND SUMMARY

29.1 How the Foreign Exchange Market Works

In the foreign exchange market, people and firms exchange one currency to purchase another currency. The demand for dollars comes from those U.S. export firms seeking to convert their earnings in foreign currency back into U.S. dollars; foreign tourists converting their earnings in a foreign currency back into U.S. dollars; and foreign investors seeking to make financial investments in the U.S. economy. On the supply side of the foreign exchange market for the trading of U.S. dollars are foreign firms that have sold imports in the U.S. economy and are seeking to convert their earnings back to their home currency; U.S. tourists abroad; and U.S. investors seeking to make financial investments in foreign economies. When currency A can buy more of currency B, then currency A has strengthened or appreciated relative to B. When currency A can buy less of currency B, then currency A has weakened or depreciated relative to B. If currency A strengthens or appreciates relative to currency B, then currency B must necessarily weaken or depreciate with regard to currency A. A stronger currency benefits those who are buying with that currency and injures those who are selling. A weaker currency injures those, like importers, who are buying with that currency and benefits those who are selling with it, like exporters.

This OpenStax book is available for free at http://cnx.org/content/col12122/1.4

29.2 Demand and Supply Shifts in Foreign Exchange Markets

In the extreme short run, ranging from a few minutes to a few weeks, speculators who are trying to invest in currencies that will grow stronger, and to sell currencies that will grow weaker influence exchange rates. Such speculation can create a self-fulfilling prophecy, at least for a time, where an expected appreciation leads to a stronger currency and vice versa. In the relatively short run, differences in rates of return influence exchange rate markets. Countries with relatively high real rates of return (for example, high interest rates) will tend to experience stronger currencies as they attract money from abroad, while countries with relatively low rates of return will tend to experience weaker exchange rates as investors convert to other currencies.

In the medium run of a few months or a few years, inflation rates influence exchange rate markets. Countries with relatively high inflation will tend to experience less demand for their currency than countries with lower inflation, and thus currency depreciation. Over long periods of many years, exchange rates tend to adjust toward the purchasing power parity (PPP) rate, which is the exchange rate such that the prices of internationally tradable goods in different countries, when converted at the PPP exchange rate to a common currency, are similar in all economies.

29.3 Macroeconomic Effects of Exchange Rates

A central bank will be concerned about the exchange rate for several reasons. Exchange rates will affect imports and exports, and thus affect aggregate demand in the economy. Fluctuations in exchange rates may cause difficulties for many firms, but especially banks. The exchange rate may accompany unsustainable flows of international financial capital.

29.4 Exchange Rate Policies

In a floating exchange rate policy, a government determines its country's exchange rate in the foreign exchange market. In a soft peg exchange rate policy, the foreign exchange market usually determines a country's exchange rate, but the government sometimes intervenes to strengthen or weaken it. In a hard peg exchange rate policy, the government chooses an exchange rate. A central bank can intervene in exchange markets in two ways. It can raise or lower interest rates to make the currency stronger or weaker. It also can directly purchase or sell its currency in foreign exchange markets. All exchange rates policies face tradeoffs. A hard peg exchange rate policy will reduce exchange rate fluctuations, but means that a country must focus its monetary policy on the exchange rate, not on fighting recession or controlling inflation. When a nation merges its currency with another nation, it gives up on nationally oriented monetary policy altogether.

A soft peg exchange rate may create additional volatility as exchange rate markets try to anticipate when and how the government will intervene. A flexible exchange rate policy allows monetary policy to focus on inflation and unemployment, and allows the exchange rate to change with inflation and rates of return, but also raises a risk that exchange rates may sometimes make large and abrupt movements. The spectrum of exchange rate policies includes: (a) a floating exchange rate, (b) a pegged exchange rate, soft or hard, and (c) a merged currency. Monetary policy can focus on a variety of goals: (a) inflation; (b) inflation or unemployment, depending on which is the most dangerous obstacle; and (c) a long-term rule based policy designed to keep the money supply stable and predictable.

SELF-CHECK QUESTIONS

1. How will a stronger euro affect the following economic agents?
   a. A British exporter to Germany.
   b. A Dutch tourist visiting Chile.
   c. A Greek bank investing in a Canadian government bond.
   d. A French exporter to Germany.

2. Suppose that political unrest in Egypt leads financial markets to anticipate a depreciation in the Egyptian pound. How will that affect the demand for pounds, supply of pounds, and exchange rate for pounds compared to, say, U.S. dollars?

3. Suppose U.S. interest rates decline compared to the rest of the world. What would be the likely impact on the demand for dollars, supply of dollars, and exchange rate for dollars compared to, say, euros?

4. Suppose Argentina gets inflation under control and the Argentine inflation rate decreases substantially. What would likely happen to the demand for Argentine pesos, the supply of Argentine pesos, and the peso/U.S. dollar exchange rate?

5. This chapter has explained that "one of the most economically destructive effects of exchange rate fluctuations can happen through the banking system," if banks borrow from abroad to lend domestically. Why is this less likely to be a problem for the U.S. banking system?

6. A booming economy can attract financial capital inflows, which promote further growth. However, capital can just as easily flow out of the country, leading to economic recession. Is a country whose economy is booming because it decided to stimulate consumer spending more or less likely to experience capital flight than an economy whose boom is caused by economic investment expenditure?

7. How would a contractionary monetary policy affect the exchange rate, net exports, aggregate demand, and aggregate supply?

8. A central bank can allow its currency to fall indefinitely, but it cannot allow its currency to rise indefinitely. Why not?

9. Is a country for which imports and exports comprise a large fraction of the GDP more likely to adopt a flexible exchange rate or a fixed (hard peg) exchange rate?

REVIEW QUESTIONS

10. What is the foreign exchange market?

11. Describe some buyers and some sellers in the market for U.S. dollars.

12. What is the difference between foreign direct investment and portfolio investment?

13. What does it mean to hedge a financial transaction?

14. What does it mean to say that a currency appreciates? Depreciates? Becomes stronger? Becomes weaker?

15. Does an expectation of a stronger exchange rate in the future affect the exchange rate in the present? If so, how?

16. Does a higher rate of return in a nation's economy, all other things being equal, affect the exchange rate of its currency? If so, how?

17. Does a higher inflation rate in an economy, other things being equal, affect the exchange rate of its currency? If so, how?

18. What is the purchasing power parity exchange rate?

19. What are some of the reasons a central bank is likely to care, at least to some extent, about the exchange rate?

20. How can an unexpected fall in exchange rates injure the financial health of a nation's banks?

21. What is the difference between a floating exchange rate, a soft peg, a hard peg, and dollarization?

22. List some advantages and disadvantages of the different exchange rate policies.

CRITICAL THINKING QUESTIONS

23. Why would a nation "dollarize"—that is, adopt another country's currency instead of having its own?

24. Can you think of any major disadvantages to dollarization? How would a central bank work in a country that has dollarized?

25. If a country's currency is expected to appreciate in value, what would you think will be the impact of expected exchange rates on yields (e.g., the interest rate paid on government bonds) in that country? *Hint*: Think about how expected exchange rate changes and interest rates affect a currency's demand and supply.

26. Do you think that a country experiencing hyperinflation is more or less likely to have an exchange rate equal to its purchasing power parity value when compared to a country with a low inflation rate?

27. Suppose a country has an overall balance of trade so that exports of goods and services equal imports of goods and services. Does that imply that the country has balanced trade with *each* of its trading partners?

28. We learned that changes in exchange rates and the corresponding changes in the balance of trade amplify monetary policy. From the perspective of a nation's central bank, is this a good thing or a bad thing?

29. If a developing country needs foreign capital inflows, management expertise, and technology, how can it encourage foreign investors while at the same time protect itself against capital flight and banking system collapse, as happened during the Asian financial crisis?

30. Many developing countries, like Mexico, have moderate to high rates of inflation. At the same time, international trade plays an important role in their economies. What type of exchange rate regime would be best for such a country's currency *vis à vis* the U.S. dollar?

31. What would make a country decide to change from a common currency, like the euro, back to its own currency?

PROBLEMS

32. A British pound cost $2.00 in U.S. dollars in 2008, but $1.27 in U.S. dollars in 2017. Was the pound weaker or stronger against the dollar? Did the dollar appreciate or depreciate versus the pound?

This OpenStax book is available for free at http://cnx.org/content/col12122/1.4

30 | Government Budgets and Fiscal Policy

Figure 30.1 Shut Downs and Parks Yellowstone National Park is one of the many national parks forced to close down during the government shut down in October 2013. (Credit: modification of work by "daveynin"/flickr Creative Commons)

Bring it Home

No Yellowstone Park?

You had trekked all the way to see Yellowstone National Park in the beautiful month of October 2013, only to find it... closed. Closed! Why?

For two weeks in October 2013, the U.S. federal government shut down. Many federal services, like the national parks, closed and 800,000 federal employees were furloughed. Tourists were shocked and so was the rest of the world: Congress and the President could not agree on a budget. Inside the Capitol, Republicans and Democrats argued about spending priorities and whether to increase the national debt limit. Each year's budget, which is over $3 trillion of spending, must be approved by Congress and signed by the President. Two thirds of the budget are entitlements and other mandatory spending which occur without congressional or presidential action once the programs are established. Tied to the budget debate was the issue of increasing the debt ceiling—how high the U.S. government's national debt can be. The House of Representatives refused to sign on to the bills to fund the government unless they included provisions to stop or change the Affordable Health Care Act (more colloquially known as Obamacare). As the days progressed, the United States came very close to defaulting on its debt.

Why does the federal budget create such intense debates? What would happen if the United States actually defaulted on its debt? In this chapter, we will examine the federal budget, taxation, and fiscal policy. We will also look at the annual federal budget deficits and the national debt.

Introduction to Government Budgets and Fiscal Policy

In this chapter, you will learn about:

- Government Spending

- Taxation

- Federal Deficits and the National Debt

- Using Fiscal Policy to Fight Recessions, Unemployment, and Inflation

- Automatic Stabilizers

- Practical Problems with Discretionary Fiscal Policy

- The Question of a Balanced Budget

All levels of government—federal, state, and local—have budgets that show how much revenue the government expects to receive in taxes and other income and how the government plans to spend it. Budgets, however, can shift dramatically within a few years, as policy decisions and unexpected events disrupt earlier tax and spending plans.

In this chapter, we revisit fiscal policy, which we first covered in **Welcome to Economics!** Fiscal policy is one of two policy tools for fine tuning the economy (the other is monetary policy). While policymakers at the Federal Reserve make monetary policy, Congress and the President make fiscal policy.

The discussion of fiscal policy focuses on how federal government taxing and spending affects aggregate demand. All government spending and taxes affect the economy, but fiscal policy focuses strictly on federal government policies. We begin with an overview of U.S. government spending and taxes. We then discuss fiscal policy from a short-run perspective; that is, how government uses tax and spending policies to address recession, unemployment, and inflation; how periods of recession and growth affect government budgets; and the merits of balanced budget proposals.

30.1 | Government Spending

By the end of this section, you will be able to:
- Identify U.S. budget deficit and surplus trends over the past five decades
- Explain the differences between the U.S. federal budget, and state and local budgets

Government spending covers a range of services that the federal, state, and local governments provide. When the federal government spends more money than it receives in taxes in a given year, it runs a **budget deficit**. Conversely, when the government receives more money in taxes than it spends in a year, it runs a **budget surplus**. If government spending and taxes are equal, it has a **balanced budget**. For example, in 2009, the U.S. government experienced its largest budget deficit ever, as the federal government spent $1.4 trillion more than it collected in taxes. This deficit was about 10% of the size of the U.S. GDP in 2009, making it by far the largest budget deficit relative to GDP since the mammoth borrowing the government used to finance World War II.

This section presents an overview of government spending in the United States.

Total U.S. Government Spending

Federal spending in nominal dollars (that is, dollars not adjusted for inflation) has grown by a multiple of more than 38 over the last four decades, from $93.4 billion in 1960 to $3.9 trillion in 2014. Comparing spending over time in nominal dollars is misleading because it does not take into account inflation or growth in population and the real economy. A more useful method of comparison is to examine government spending as a percent of GDP over time.

The top line in **Figure 30.2** shows the federal spending level since 1960, expressed as a share of GDP. Despite a widespread sense among many Americans that the federal government has been growing steadily larger, the graph shows that federal spending has hovered in a range from 18% to 22% of GDP most of the time since 1960. The other lines in **Figure 30.2** show the major federal spending categories: national defense, Social Security, health programs, and interest payments. From the graph, we see that national defense spending as a share of GDP has generally declined since the 1960s, although there were some upward bumps in the 1980s buildup under President Ronald Reagan and in the aftermath of the terrorist attacks on September 11, 2001. In contrast, Social Security and healthcare have grown steadily as a percent of GDP. Healthcare expenditures include both payments for senior citizens (Medicare), and payments for low-income Americans (Medicaid). State governments also partially fund Medicaid. Interest payments are the final main category of government spending in Figure 30.2.

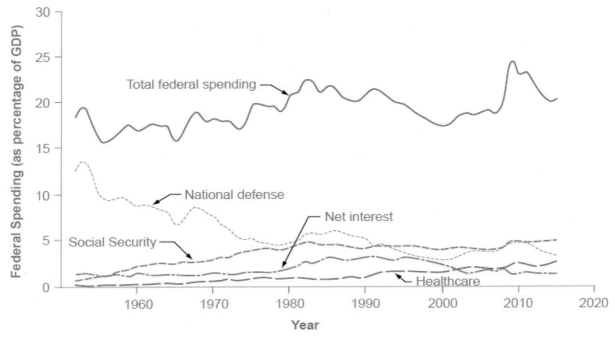

Figure 30.2 Federal Spending, 1960–2014 Since 1960, total federal spending has ranged from about 18% to 22% of GDP, although it climbed above that level in 2009, but quickly dropped back down to that level by 2013. The share that the government has spent on national defense has generally declined, while the share it has spent on Social Security and on healthcare expenses (mainly Medicare and Medicaid) has increased. (Source: *Economic Report of the President,* Tables B-2 and B-22, http://www.gpo.gov/fdsys/pkg/ERP-2014/content-detail.html)

Each year, the government borrows funds from U.S. citizens and foreigners to cover its budget deficits. It does this by selling securities (Treasury bonds, notes, and bills)—in essence borrowing from the public and promising to repay with interest in the future. From 1961 to 1997, the U.S. government has run budget deficits, and thus borrowed funds, in almost every year. It had budget surpluses from 1998 to 2001, and then returned to deficits.

The interest payments on past federal government borrowing were typically 1–2% of GDP in the 1960s and 1970s but then climbed above 3% of GDP in the 1980s and stayed there until the late 1990s. The government was able to repay some of its past borrowing by running surpluses from 1998 to 2001 and, with help from low interest rates, the interest payments on past federal government borrowing had fallen back to 1.4% of GDP by 2012.

We investigate the government borrowing and debt patterns in more detail later in this chapter, but first we need to clarify the difference between the deficit and the debt. *The deficit is not the debt.* The difference between the deficit and the debt lies in the time frame. The government deficit (or surplus) refers to what happens with the federal government budget each year. The government debt is accumulated over time. It is the sum of all past deficits and surpluses. If you borrow $10,000 per year for each of the four years of college, you might say that your annual deficit was $10,000, but your accumulated debt over the four years is $40,000.

These four categories—national defense, Social Security, healthcare, and interest payments—account for roughly 73% of all federal spending, as **Figure 30.3** shows. The remaining 27% wedge of the pie chart covers all other categories of federal government spending: international affairs; science and technology; natural resources and the environment; transportation; housing; education; income support for the poor; community and regional development; law enforcement and the judicial system; and the administrative costs of running the government.

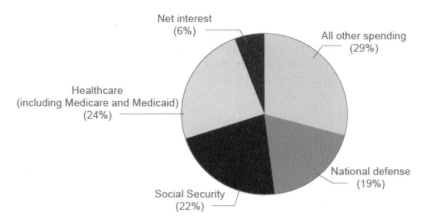

Figure 30.3 Slices of Federal Spending, 2014 About 73% of government spending goes to four major areas: national defense, Social Security, healthcare, and interest payments on past borrowing. This leaves about 29% of federal spending for all other functions of the U.S. government. (Source: https://www.whitehouse.gov/omb/budget/ Historicals/)

State and Local Government Spending

Although federal government spending often gets most of the media attention, state and local government spending is also substantial—at about $3.1 trillion in 2014. **Figure 30.4** shows that state and local government spending has increased during the last four decades from around 8% to around 14% today. The single biggest item is education, which accounts for about one-third of the total. The rest covers programs like highways, libraries, hospitals and healthcare, parks, and police and fire protection. Unlike the federal government, all states (except Vermont) have balanced budget laws, which means any gaps between revenues and spending must be closed by higher taxes, lower spending, drawing down their previous savings, or some combination of all of these.

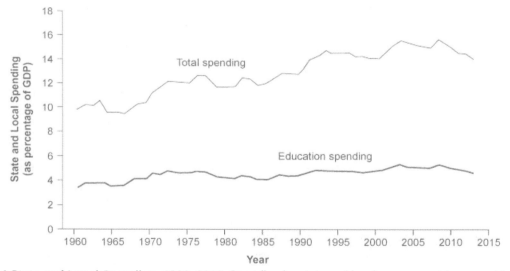

Figure 30.4 State and Local Spending, 1960–2013 Spending by state and local government increased from about 10% of GDP in the early 1960s to 14–16% by the mid-1970s. It has remained at roughly that level since. The single biggest spending item is education, including both K–12 spending and support for public colleges and universities, which has been about 4–5% of GDP in recent decades. Source: (Source: Bureau of Economic Analysis.)

U.S. presidential candidates often run for office pledging to improve the public schools or to get tough on crime. However, in the U.S. government system, these tasks are primarily state and local government responsibilities. In fiscal year 2014 state and local governments spent about $840 billion per year on education (including K–12 and college and university education), compared to only $100 billion by the federal government, according to usgovernmentspending.com. In other words, about 90 cents of every dollar spent on education happens at the state and local level. A politician who really wants hands-on responsibility for reforming education or reducing crime might do better to run for mayor of a large city or for state governor rather than for president of the United States.

30.2 | Taxation

By the end of this section, you will be able to:
- Differentiate among a regressive tax, a proportional tax, and a progressive tax
- Identify major revenue sources for the U.S. federal budget

There are two main categories of taxes: those that the federal government collects and those that the state and local governments collect. What percentage the government collects and for what it uses that revenue varies greatly. The following sections will briefly explain the taxation system in the United States.

Federal Taxes

Just as many Americans erroneously think that federal spending has grown considerably, many also believe that taxes have increased substantially. The top line of **Figure 30.5** shows total federal taxes as a share of GDP since 1960. Although the line rises and falls, it typically remains within the range of 17% to 20% of GDP, except for 2009, when taxes fell substantially below this level, due to recession.

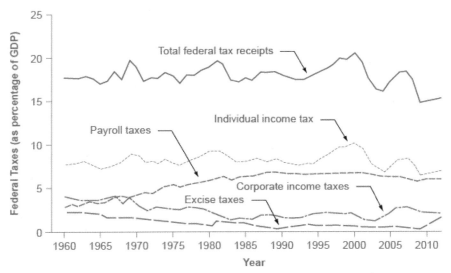

Figure 30.5 Federal Taxes, 1960–2014 Federal tax revenues have been about 17–20% of GDP during most periods in recent decades. The primary sources of federal taxes are individual income taxes and the payroll taxes that finance Social Security and Medicare. Corporate income taxes and social insurance taxes provide smaller shares of revenue. (Source: *Economic Report of the President, 2015.* Table B-21, https://www.whitehouse.gov/administration/eop/cea/economic-report-of-the-President/2015)

Figure 30.5 also shows the taxation patterns for the main categories that the federal government taxes: individual income taxes, corporate income taxes, and social insurance and retirement receipts. When most people think of federal government taxes, the first tax that comes to mind is the **individual income tax** that is due every year on April 15 (or the first business day after). The personal income tax is the largest single source of federal government revenue, but it still represents less than half of federal tax revenue.

The second largest source of federal revenue is the **payroll tax** (captured in social insurance and retirement receipts), which provides funds for Social Security and Medicare. Payroll taxes have increased steadily over time. Together, the personal income tax and the payroll tax accounted for about 80% of federal tax revenues in 2014. Although personal income tax revenues account for more total revenue than the payroll tax, nearly three-quarters of households pay more in payroll taxes than in income taxes.

The income tax is a **progressive tax**, which means that the tax rates increase as a household's income increases. Taxes also vary with marital status, family size, and other factors. The **marginal tax rates** (the tax due on all yearly income) for a single taxpayer range from 10% to 35%, depending on income, as the following Clear It Up feature explains.

How does the marginal rate work?

Suppose that a single taxpayer's income is $35,000 per year. Also suppose that income from $0 to $9,075 is taxed at 10%, income from $9,075 to $36,900 is taxed at 15%, and, finally, income from $36,900 and beyond is taxed at 25%. Since this person earns $35,000, their marginal tax rate is 15%.

The key fact here is that the federal income tax is designed so that tax rates increase as income increases, up to a certain level. The payroll taxes that support Social Security and Medicare are designed in a different way. First, the payroll taxes for Social Security are imposed at a rate of 12.4% up to a certain wage limit, set at $118,500 in 2015. Medicare, on the other hand, pays for elderly healthcare, and is fixed at 2.9%, with no upper ceiling.

In both cases, the employer and the employee split the payroll taxes. An employee only sees 6.2% deducted from his or her paycheck for Social Security, and 1.45% from Medicare. However, as economists are quick to point out, the employer's half of the taxes are probably passed along to the employees in the form of lower wages, so in reality, the worker pays all of the payroll taxes.

We also call the Medicare payroll tax a **proportional tax**; that is, a flat percentage of all wages earned. The Social Security payroll tax is proportional up to the wage limit, but above that level it becomes a **regressive tax**, meaning that people with higher incomes pay a smaller share of their income in tax.

The third-largest source of federal tax revenue, as **Figure 30.5** shows is the **corporate income tax**. The common name for corporate income is "profits." Over time, corporate income tax receipts have declined as a share of GDP, from about 4% in the 1960s to an average of 1% to 2% of GDP in the first decade of the 2000s.

The federal government has a few other, smaller sources of revenue. It imposes an **excise tax**—that is, a tax on a particular good—on gasoline, tobacco, and alcohol. As a share of GDP, the amount the government collects from these taxes has stayed nearly constant over time, from about 2% of GDP in the 1960s to roughly 3% by 2014, according to the nonpartisan Congressional Budget Office. The government also imposes an **estate and gift tax** on people who pass large amounts of assets to the next generation—either after death or during life in the form of gifts. These estate and gift taxes collected about 0.2% of GDP in the first decade of the 2000s. By a quirk of legislation, the government repealed the estate and gift tax in 2010, but reinstated it in 2011. Other federal taxes, which are also relatively small in magnitude, include tariffs the government collects on imported goods and charges for inspections of goods entering the country.

State and Local Taxes

At the state and local level, taxes have been rising as a share of GDP over the last few decades to match the gradual rise in spending, as **Figure 30.6** illustrates. The main revenue sources for state and local governments are sales taxes, property taxes, and revenue passed along from the federal government, but many state and local governments also levy personal and corporate income taxes, as well as impose a wide variety of fees and charges. The specific sources of tax revenue vary widely across state and local governments. Some states rely more on property taxes, some on sales taxes, some on income taxes, and some more on revenues from the federal government.

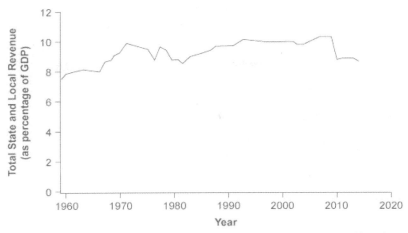

Figure 30.6 State and Local Tax Revenue as a Share of GDP, 1960–2014 State and local tax revenues have increased to match the rise in state and local spending. (Source: *Economic Report of the President, 2015.* Table B-21, https://www.whitehouse.gov/administration/eop/cea/economic-report-of-the-President/2015)

30.3 | Federal Deficits and the National Debt

By the end of this section, you will be able to:
- Explain the U.S. federal budget in terms of annual debt and accumulated debt
- Understand how economic growth or decline can influence a budget surplus or budget deficit

Having discussed the revenue (taxes) and expense (spending) side of the budget, we now turn to the annual budget deficit or surplus, which is the difference between the tax revenue collected and spending over a fiscal year, which starts October 1 and ends September 30 of the next year.

Figure 30.7 shows the pattern of annual federal budget deficits and surpluses, back to 1930, as a share of GDP. When the line is above the horizontal axis, the budget is in surplus. When the line is below the horizontal axis, a budget deficit occurred. Clearly, the biggest deficits as a share of GDP during this time were incurred to finance World War II. Deficits were also large during the 1930s, the 1980s, the early 1990s, and most recently during the 2008-2009 recession.

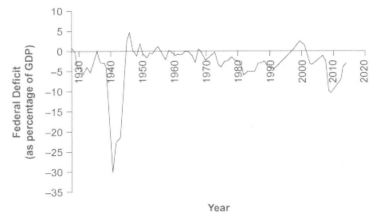

Figure 30.7 Pattern of Federal Budget Deficits and Surpluses, 1929–2014 The federal government has run budget deficits for decades. The budget was briefly in surplus in the late 1990s, before heading into deficit again in the first decade of the 2000s—and especially deep deficits in the 2008-2009 recession. (Source: Federal Reserve Bank of St. Louis (FRED). http://research.stlouisfed.org/fred2/series/FYFSGDA188S)

Debt/GDP Ratio

Another useful way to view the budget deficit is through the prism of accumulated debt rather than annual deficits. The **national debt** refers to the total amount that the government has borrowed over time. In contrast, the budget deficit refers to how much the government has borrowed in one particular year. **Figure 30.8** shows the ratio of debt/GDP since 1940. Until the 1970s, the debt/GDP ratio revealed a fairly clear pattern of federal borrowing. The government ran up large deficits and raised the debt/GDP ratio in World War II, but from the 1950s to the 1970s the government ran either surpluses or relatively small deficits, and so the debt/GDP ratio drifted down. Large deficits in the 1980s and early 1990s caused the ratio to rise sharply. When budget surpluses arrived from 1998 to 2001, the debt/GDP ratio declined substantially. The budget deficits starting in 2002 then tugged the debt/GDP ratio higher—with a big jump when the recession took hold in 2008–2009.

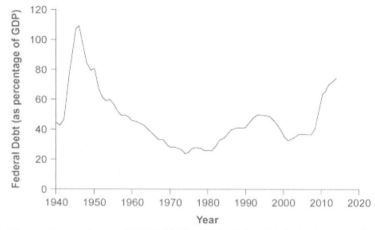

Figure 30.8 Federal Debt as a Percentage of GDP, 1942–2014 Federal debt is the sum of annual budget deficits and surpluses. Annual deficits do not always mean that the debt/GDP ratio is rising. During the 1960s and 1970s, the government often ran small deficits, but since the debt was growing more slowly than the economy, the debt/GDP ratio was declining over this time. In the 2008–2009 recession, the debt/GDP ratio rose sharply. (Source: *Economic Report of the President, Table B-20,* http://www.gpo.gov/fdsys/pkg/ERP-2015/content-detail.html)

The next Clear it Up feature discusses how the government handles the national debt.

What is the national debt?

One year's federal budget deficit causes the federal government to sell Treasury bonds to make up the difference between spending programs and tax revenues. The dollar value of all the outstanding Treasury bonds on which the federal government owes money is equal to the national debt.

The Path from Deficits to Surpluses to Deficits

Why did the budget deficits suddenly turn to surpluses from 1998 to 2001 and why did the surpluses return to deficits in 2002? Why did the deficit become so large after 2007? **Figure 30.9** suggests some answers. The graph combines the earlier information on total federal spending and taxes in a single graph, but focuses on the federal budget since 1990.

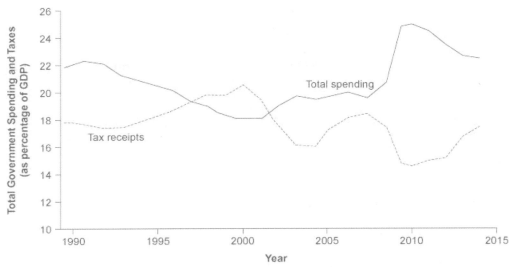

Figure 30.9 Total Government Spending and Taxes as a Share of GDP, 1990–2014   When government spending exceeds taxes, the gap is the budget deficit. When taxes exceed spending, the gap is a budget surplus. The recessionary period starting in late 2007 saw higher spending and lower taxes, combining to create a large deficit in 2009. (Source: *Economic Report of the President, Tables B-21 and B-1*,"http://www.gpo.gov/fdsys/pkg/ERP-2015/ content-detail.html)

Government spending as a share of GDP declined steadily through the 1990s. The biggest single reason was that defense spending declined from 5.2% of GDP in 1990 to 3.0% in 2000, but interest payments by the federal government also fell by about 1.0% of GDP. However, federal tax collections increased substantially in the later 1990s, jumping from 18.1% of GDP in 1994 to 20.8% in 2000. Powerful economic growth in the late 1990s fueled the boom in taxes. Personal income taxes rise as income goes up; payroll taxes rise as jobs and payrolls go up; corporate income taxes rise as profits go up. At the same time, government spending on transfer payments such as unemployment benefits, foods stamps, and welfare declined with more people working.

This sharp increase in tax revenues and decrease in expenditures on transfer payments was largely unexpected even by experienced budget analysts, and so budget surpluses came as a surprise. However, in the early 2000s, many of these factors started running in reverse. Tax revenues sagged, due largely to the recession that started in March 2001, which reduced revenues. Congress enacted a series of tax cuts and President George W. Bush signed them into law, starting in 2001. In addition, government spending swelled due to increases in defense, healthcare, education, Social Security, and support programs for those who were hurt by the recession and the slow growth that followed. Deficits returned. When the severe recession hit in late 2007, spending climbed and tax collections fell to historically unusual levels, resulting in enormous deficits.

Longer-term U.S. budget forecasts, a decade or more into the future, predict enormous deficits. The higher deficits during the 2008-2009 recession have repercussions, and the demographics will be challenging. The primary reason is the "baby boom"—the exceptionally high birthrates that began in 1946, right after World War II, and lasted for about two decades. Starting in 2010, the front edge of the baby boom generation began to reach age 65, and in the next two decades, the proportion of Americans over the age of 65 will increase substantially. The current level of the payroll taxes that support Social Security and Medicare will fall well short of the projected expenses of these programs, as the following Clear It Up feature shows; thus, the forecast is for large budget deficits. A decision to collect more revenue to support these programs or to decrease benefit levels would alter this long-term forecast.

What is the long-term budget outlook for Social Security and Medicare?

In 1946, just one American in 13 was over age 65. By 2000, it was one in eight. By 2030, one American in five will be over age 65. Two enormous U.S. federal programs focus on the elderly—Social Security and Medicare. The growing numbers of elderly Americans will increase spending on these programs, as well as on Medicaid. The current payroll tax levied on workers, which supports all of Social Security and the hospitalization insurance part of Medicare, will not be enough to cover the expected costs, so what are the options?

Long-term projections from the Congressional Budget Office in 2009 are that Medicare and Social Security spending combined will rise from 8.3% of GDP in 2009 to about 13% by 2035 and about 20% in 2080. If this rise in spending occurs, without any corresponding rise in tax collections, then some mix of changes must occur: (1) taxes will need to increase dramatically; (2) other spending will need to be cut dramatically; (3) the retirement age and/or age receiving Medicare benefits will need to increase, or (4) the federal government will need to run extremely large budget deficits.

Some proposals suggest removing the cap on wages subject to the payroll tax, so that those with very high incomes would have to pay the tax on the entire amount of their wages. Other proposals suggest moving Social Security and Medicare from systems in which workers pay for retirees toward programs that set up accounts where workers save funds over their lifetimes and then draw out after retirement to pay for healthcare.

The United States is not alone in this problem. Providing the promised level of retirement and health benefits to a growing proportion of elderly with a falling proportion of workers is an even more severe problem in many European nations and in Japan. How to pay promised levels of benefits to the elderly will be a difficult public policy decision.

In the next module we shift to the use of fiscal policy to counteract business cycle fluctuations. In addition, we will explore proposals requiring a balanced budget—that is, for government spending and taxes to be equal each year. **The Impacts of Government Borrowing** will also cover how fiscal policy and government borrowing will affect national saving—and thus affect economic growth and trade imbalances.

30.4 | Using Fiscal Policy to Fight Recession, Unemployment, and Inflation

By the end of this section, you will be able to:
- Explain how expansionary fiscal policy can shift aggregate demand and influence the economy
- Explain how contractionary fiscal policy can shift aggregate demand and influence the economy

Fiscal policy is the use of government spending and tax policy to influence the path of the economy over time. Graphically, we see that fiscal policy, whether through changes in spending or taxes, shifts the aggregate demand outward in the case of **expansionary fiscal policy** and inward in the case of **contractionary fiscal policy**. We know from the chapter on economic growth that over time the quantity and quality of our resources grow as the population and thus the labor force get larger, as businesses invest in new capital, and as technology improves. The result of this is regular shifts to the right of the aggregate supply curves, as **Figure 30.10** illustrates.

The original equilibrium occurs at E_0, the intersection of aggregate demand curve AD_0 and aggregate supply curve $SRAS_0$, at an output level of 200 and a price level of 90. One year later, aggregate supply has shifted to the right to $SRAS_1$ in the process of long-term economic growth, and aggregate demand has also shifted to the right to AD_1, keeping the economy operating at the new level of potential GDP. The new equilibrium (E_1) is an output level of

This OpenStax book is available for free at http://cnx.org/content/col12122/1.4

206 and a price level of 92. One more year later, aggregate supply has again shifted to the right, now to SRAS$_2$, and aggregate demand shifts right as well to AD$_2$. Now the equilibrium is E$_2$, with an output level of 212 and a price level of 94. In short, the figure shows an economy that is growing steadily year to year, producing at its potential GDP each year, with only small inflationary increases in the price level.

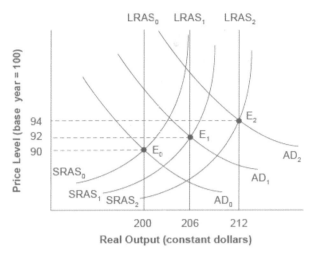

Figure 30.10 A Healthy, Growing Economy   In this well-functioning economy, each year aggregate supply and aggregate demand shift to the right so that the economy proceeds from equilibrium E$_0$ to E$_1$ to E$_2$. Each year, the economy produces at potential GDP with only a small inflationary increase in the price level. However, if aggregate demand does not smoothly shift to the right and match increases in aggregate supply, growth with deflation can develop.

Aggregate demand and aggregate supply do not always move neatly together. Think about what causes shifts in aggregate demand over time. As aggregate supply increases, incomes tend to go up. This tends to increase consumer and investment spending, shifting the aggregate demand curve to the right, but in any given period it may not shift the same amount as aggregate supply. What happens to government spending and taxes? Government spends to pay for the ordinary business of government- items such as national defense, social security, and healthcare, as **Figure 30.10** shows. Tax revenues, in part, pay for these expenditures. The result may be an increase in aggregate demand more than or less than the increase in aggregate supply. Aggregate demand may fail to increase along with aggregate supply, or aggregate demand may even shift left, for a number of possible reasons: households become hesitant about consuming; firms decide against investing as much; or perhaps the demand from other countries for exports diminishes.

For example, investment by private firms in physical capital in the U.S. economy boomed during the late 1990s, rising from 14.1% of GDP in 1993 to 17.2% in 2000, before falling back to 15.2% by 2002. Conversely, if shifts in aggregate demand run ahead of increases in aggregate supply, inflationary increases in the price level will result. Business cycles of recession and recovery are the consequence of shifts in aggregate supply and aggregate demand. As these occur, the government may choose to use fiscal policy to address the difference.

Monetary Policy and Bank Regulation shows us that a central bank can use its powers over the banking system to engage in countercyclical—or "against the business cycle"—actions. If recession threatens, the central bank uses an expansionary monetary policy to increase the money supply, increase the quantity of loans, reduce interest rates, and shift aggregate demand to the right. If inflation threatens, the central bank uses contractionary monetary policy to reduce the money supply, reduce the quantity of loans, raise interest rates, and shift aggregate demand to the left. Fiscal policy is another macroeconomic policy tool for adjusting aggregate demand by using either government spending or taxation policy.

Expansionary Fiscal Policy

Expansionary fiscal policy increases the level of aggregate demand, through either increases in government spending or reductions in tax rates. Expansionary policy can do this by (1) increasing consumption by raising disposable income through cuts in personal income taxes or payroll taxes; (2) increasing investment spending by raising after-tax profits through cuts in business taxes; and (3) increasing government purchases through increased federal government spending on final goods and services and raising federal grants to state and local governments to increase their expenditures on final goods and services. Contractionary fiscal policy does the reverse: it decreases the level of aggregate demand by decreasing consumption, decreasing investment, and decreasing government spending, either through cuts in government spending or increases in taxes. The aggregate demand/aggregate supply model is useful in judging whether expansionary or contractionary fiscal policy is appropriate.

Consider first the situation in **Figure 30.11**, which is similar to the U.S. economy during the 2008-2009 recession. The intersection of aggregate demand (AD_0) and aggregate supply ($SRAS_0$) is occurring below the level of potential GDP as the LRAS curve indicates. At the equilibrium (E_0), a recession occurs and unemployment rises. In this case, expansionary fiscal policy using tax cuts or increases in government spending can shift aggregate demand to AD_1, closer to the full-employment level of output. In addition, the price level would rise back to the level P_1 associated with potential GDP.

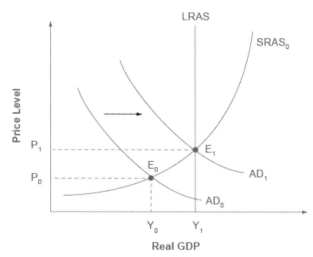

Figure 30.11 Expansionary Fiscal Policy The original equilibrium (E_0) represents a recession, occurring at a quantity of output (Y_0) below potential GDP. However, a shift of aggregate demand from AD_0 to AD_1, enacted through an expansionary fiscal policy, can move the economy to a new equilibrium output of E_1 at the level of potential GDP which the LRAS curve shows. Since the economy was originally producing below potential GDP, any inflationary increase in the price level from P_0 to P_1 that results should be relatively small.

Should the government use tax cuts or spending increases, or a mix of the two, to carry out expansionary fiscal policy? During the 2008-2009 Great Recession (which started, actually, in late 2007), the U.S. economy suffered a 3.1% cumulative loss of GDP. That may not sound like much, but it's more than one year's average growth rate of GDP. Over that time frame, the unemployment rate doubled from 5% to 10%. The consensus view is that this was possibly the worst economic downturn in U.S. history since the 1930's Great Depression. The choice between whether to use tax or spending tools often has a political tinge. As a general statement, conservatives and Republicans prefer to see expansionary fiscal policy carried out by tax cuts, while liberals and Democrats prefer that the government implement expansionary fiscal policy through spending increases. In a bipartisan effort to address the extreme situation, the Obama administration and Congress passed an $830 billion expansionary policy in early 2009 involving both tax cuts and increases in government spending. At the same time, however, the federal stimulus was partially offset when state and local governments, whose budgets were hard hit by the recession, began cutting their spending.

The conflict over which policy tool to use can be frustrating to those who want to categorize economics as "liberal" or "conservative," or who want to use economic models to argue against their political opponents. However, advocates of smaller government, who seek to reduce taxes and government spending can use the AD AS model, as well as advocates of bigger government, who seek to raise taxes and government spending. Economic studies of specific taxing and spending programs can help inform decisions about whether the government should change taxes or spending, and in what ways. Ultimately, decisions about whether to use tax or spending mechanisms to implement macroeconomic policy is a political decision rather than a purely economic one.

Contractionary Fiscal Policy

Fiscal policy can also contribute to pushing aggregate demand beyond potential GDP in a way that leads to inflation.

This OpenStax book is available for free at http://cnx.org/content/col12122/1.4

As **Figure 30.12** shows, a very large budget deficit pushes up aggregate demand, so that the intersection of aggregate demand (AD_0) and aggregate supply ($SRAS_0$) occurs at equilibrium E_0, which is an output level above potential GDP. Economists sometimes call this an "overheating economy" where demand is so high that there is upward pressure on wages and prices, causing inflation. In this situation, contractionary fiscal policy involving federal spending cuts or tax increases can help to reduce the upward pressure on the price level by shifting aggregate demand to the left, to AD_1, and causing the new equilibrium E_1 to be at potential GDP, where aggregate demand intersects the LRAS curve.

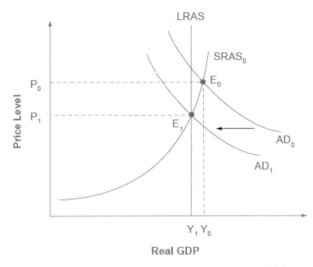

Figure 30.12 A Contractionary Fiscal Policy The economy starts at the equilibrium quantity of output Y_0, which is above potential GDP. The extremely high level of aggregate demand will generate inflationary increases in the price level. A contractionary fiscal policy can shift aggregate demand down from AD_0 to AD_1, leading to a new equilibrium output E_1, which occurs at potential GDP, where AD1 intersects the LRAS curve.

Again, the AD–AS model does not dictate how the government should carry out this contractionary fiscal policy. Some may prefer spending cuts; others may prefer tax increases; still others may say that it depends on the specific situation. The model only argues that, in this situation, the government needs to reduce aggregate demand.

30.5 | Automatic Stabilizers

By the end of this section, you will be able to:
- Describe how the federal government can use discretionary fiscal policy to stabilize the economy
- Identify examples of automatic stabilizers
- Understand how a government can use standardized employment budget to identify automatic stabilizers

The millions of unemployed in 2008–2009 could collect unemployment insurance benefits to replace some of their salaries. Federal fiscal policies include **discretionary fiscal policy**, when the government passes a new law that explicitly changes tax or spending levels. The 2009 stimulus package is an example. Changes in tax and spending levels can also occur automatically, due to **automatic stabilizers**, such as unemployment insurance and food stamps, which are programs that are already laws that stimulate aggregate demand in a recession and hold down aggregate demand in a potentially inflationary boom.

Counterbalancing Recession and Boom

Consider first the situation where aggregate demand has risen sharply, causing the equilibrium to occur at a level of output above potential GDP. This situation will increase inflationary pressure in the economy. The policy prescription in this setting would be a dose of contractionary fiscal policy, implemented through some combination of higher taxes and lower spending. To some extent, *both* changes happen automatically. On the tax side, a rise in aggregate demand means that workers and firms throughout the economy earn more. Because taxes are based on personal income and corporate profits, a rise in aggregate demand automatically increases tax payments. On the spending side, stronger aggregate demand typically means lower unemployment and fewer layoffs, and so there is less need for government spending on unemployment benefits, welfare, Medicaid, and other programs in the social safety net.

The process works in reverse, too. If aggregate demand were to fall sharply so that a recession occurs, then the prescription would be for expansionary fiscal policy—some mix of tax cuts and spending increases. The lower level of aggregate demand and higher unemployment will tend to pull down personal incomes and corporate profits, an effect that will reduce the amount of taxes owed automatically. Higher unemployment and a weaker economy should lead to increased government spending on unemployment benefits, welfare, and other similar domestic programs. In 2009, the stimulus package included an extension in the time allowed to collect unemployment insurance. In addition, the automatic stabilizers react to a weakening of aggregate demand with expansionary fiscal policy and react to a strengthening of aggregate demand with contractionary fiscal policy, just as the AD/AS analysis suggests.

A combination of automatic stabilizers and discretionary fiscal policy produced the very large budget deficit in 2009. The Great Recession, starting in late 2007, meant less tax-generating economic activity, which triggered the automatic stabilizers that reduce taxes. Most economists, even those who are concerned about a possible pattern of persistently large budget deficits, are much less concerned or even quite supportive of larger budget deficits in the short run of a few years during and immediately after a severe recession.

A glance back at economic history provides a second illustration of the power of automatic stabilizers. Remember that the length of economic upswings between recessions has become longer in the U.S. economy in recent decades (as we discussed in **Unemployment**). The three longest economic booms of the twentieth century happened in the 1960s, the 1980s, and the 1991–2001 time period. One reason why the economy has tipped into recession less frequently in recent decades is that the size of government spending and taxes has increased in the second half of the twentieth century. Thus, the automatic stabilizing effects from spending and taxes are now larger than they were in the first half of the twentieth century. Around 1900, for example, federal spending was only about 2% of GDP. In 1929, just before the Great Depression hit, government spending was still just 4% of GDP. In those earlier times, the smaller size of government made automatic stabilizers far less powerful than in the last few decades, when government spending often hovers at 20% of GDP or more.

The Standardized Employment Deficit or Surplus

Each year, the nonpartisan Congressional Budget Office (CBO) calculates the **standardized employment budget**—that is, what the budget deficit or surplus would be if the economy were producing at potential GDP, where people who look for work were finding jobs in a reasonable period of time and businesses were making normal profits, with the result that both workers and businesses would be earning more and paying more taxes. In effect, the standardized employment deficit eliminates the impact of the automatic stabilizers. **Figure 30.13** compares the actual budget deficits of recent decades with the CBO's standardized deficit.

Link It Up

Visit this website (http://openstaxcollege.org/l/CBO) to learn more from the Congressional Budget Office.

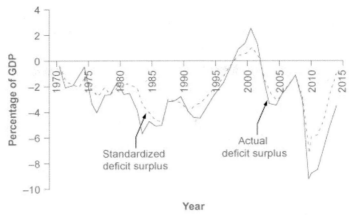

Figure 30.13 Comparison of Actual Budget Deficits with the Standardized Employment Deficit When the economy is in recession, the standardized employment budget deficit is less than the actual budget deficit because the economy is below potential GDP, and the automatic stabilizers are reducing taxes and increasing spending. When the economy is performing extremely well, the standardized employment deficit (or surplus) is higher than the actual budget deficit (or surplus) because the economy is producing about potential GDP, so the automatic stabilizers are increasing taxes and reducing the need for government spending. (Sources: *Actual and Cyclically Adjusted Budget Surpluses/Deficits*, http://www.cbo.gov/publication/43977; and *Economic Report of the President, Table B-1*, http://www.gpo.gov/fdsys/pkg/ERP-2013/content-detail.html)

Notice that in recession years, like the early 1990s, 2001, or 2009, the standardized employment deficit is smaller than the actual deficit. During recessions, the automatic stabilizers tend to increase the budget deficit, so if the economy was instead at full employment, the deficit would be reduced. However, in the late 1990s the standardized employment budget surplus was lower than the actual budget surplus. The gap between the standardized budget deficit or surplus and the actual budget deficit or surplus shows the impact of the automatic stabilizers. More generally, the standardized budget figures allow you to see what the budget deficit would look like with the economy held constant—at its potential GDP level of output.

Automatic stabilizers occur quickly. Lower wages means that a lower amount of taxes is withheld from paychecks right away. Higher unemployment or poverty means that government spending in those areas rises as quickly as people apply for benefits. However, while the automatic stabilizers offset part of the shifts in aggregate demand, they do not offset all or even most of it. Historically, automatic stabilizers on the tax and spending side offset about 10% of any initial movement in the level of output. This offset may not seem enormous, but it is still useful. Automatic stabilizers, like shock absorbers in a car, can be useful if they reduce the impact of the worst bumps, even if they do not eliminate the bumps altogether.

30.6 | Practical Problems with Discretionary Fiscal Policy

By the end of this section, you will be able to:
- Understand how fiscal policy and monetary policy are interconnected
- Explain the three lag times that often occur when solving economic problems
- Identify the legal and political challenges of responding to an economic problem

In the early 1960s, many leading economists believed that the problem of the business cycle, and the swings between cyclical unemployment and inflation, were a thing of the past. On the cover of its December 31, 1965, issue, *Time* magazine, then the premier news magazine in the United States, ran a picture of John Maynard Keynes, and the story inside identified Keynesian theories as "the prime influence on the world's economies." The article reported that policymakers have "used Keynesian principles not only to avoid the violent [business] cycles of prewar days but to produce phenomenal economic growth and to achieve remarkably stable prices."

This happy consensus, however, did not last. The U.S. economy suffered one recession from December 1969 to November 1970, a deeper recession from November 1973 to March 1975, and then double-dip recessions from

January to June 1980 and from July 1981 to November 1982. At various times, inflation and unemployment both soared. Clearly, the problems of macroeconomic policy had not been completely solved. As economists began to consider what had gone wrong, they identified a number of issues that make discretionary fiscal policy more difficult than it had seemed in the rosy optimism of the mid-1960s.

Fiscal Policy and Interest Rates

Because fiscal policy affects the quantity that the government borrows in financial capital markets, it not only affects aggregate demand—it can also affect interest rates. In **Figure 30.14**, the original equilibrium (E_0) in the financial capital market occurs at a quantity of $800 billion and an interest rate of 6%. However, an increase in government budget deficits shifts the demand for financial capital from D_0 to D_1. The new equilibrium (E_1) occurs at a quantity of $900 billion and an interest rate of 7%.

A consensus estimate based on a number of studies is that an increase in budget deficits (or a fall in budget surplus) by 1% of GDP will cause an increase of 0.5–1.0% in the long-term interest rate.

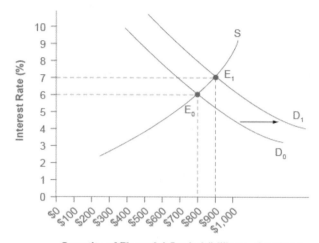

Figure 30.14 Fiscal Policy and Interest Rates When a government borrows money in the financial capital market, it causes a shift in the demand for financial capital from D_0 to D_1. As the equilibrium moves from E_0 to E_1, the equilibrium interest rate rises from 6% to 7% in this example. In this way, an expansionary fiscal policy intended to shift aggregate demand to the right can also lead to a higher interest rate, which has the effect of shifting aggregate demand back to the left.

A problem arises here. An expansionary fiscal policy, with tax cuts or spending increases, is intended to increase aggregate demand. If an expansionary fiscal policy also causes higher interest rates, then firms and households are discouraged from borrowing and spending (as occurs with tight monetary policy), thus reducing aggregate demand. Even if the direct effect of expansionary fiscal policy on increasing demand is not totally offset by lower aggregate demand from higher interest rates, fiscal policy can end up less powerful than was originally expected. We refer to this as **crowding out**, where government borrowing and spending results in higher interest rates, which reduces business investment and household consumption.

The broader lesson is that the government must coordinate fiscal and monetary policy. If expansionary fiscal policy is to work well, then the central bank can also reduce or keep short-term interest rates low. Conversely, monetary policy can also help to ensure that contractionary fiscal policy does not lead to a recession.

Long and Variable Time Lags

The government can change monetary policy several times each year, but it takes much longer to enact fiscal policy. Imagine that the economy starts to slow down. It often takes some months before the economic statistics signal clearly that a downturn has started, and a few months more to confirm that it is truly a recession and not just a one- or two-month blip. Economists often call the time it takes to determine that a recession has occurred the **recognition lag**. After this lag, policymakers become aware of the problem and propose fiscal policy bills. The bills go into various congressional committees for hearings, negotiations, votes, and then, if passed, eventually for the president's

This OpenStax book is available for free at http://cnx.org/content/col12122/1.4

signature. Many fiscal policy bills about spending or taxes propose changes that would start in the next budget year or would be phased in gradually over time. Economists often refer to the time it takes to pass a bill as the **legislative lag**. Finally, once the government passes the bill it takes some time to disperse the funds to the appropriate agencies to implement the programs. Economists call the time it takes to start the projects the **implementation lag**.

Moreover, the exact level of fiscal policy that the government should implement is never completely clear. Should it increase the budget deficit by 0.5% of GDP? By 1% of GDP? By 2% of GDP? In an AD/AS diagram, it is straightforward to sketch an aggregate demand curve shifting to the potential GDP level of output. In the real world, we only know roughly, not precisely, the actual level of potential output, and exactly how a spending cut or tax increase will affect aggregate demand is always somewhat controversial. Also unknown is the state of the economy at any point in time. During the early days of the Obama administration, for example, no one knew the true extent of the economy's deficit. During the 2008-2009 financial crisis, the rapid collapse of the banking system and automotive sector made it difficult to assess how quickly the economy was collapsing.

Thus, it can take many months or even more than a year to begin an expansionary fiscal policy after a recession has started—and even then, uncertainty will remain over exactly how much to expand or contract taxes and spending. When politicians attempt to use countercyclical fiscal policy to fight recession or inflation, they run the risk of responding to the macroeconomic situation of two or three years ago, in a way that may be exactly wrong for the economy at that time. George P. Schultz, a professor of economics, former Secretary of the Treasury, and Director of the Office of Management and Budget, once wrote: "While the economist is accustomed to the concept of lags, the politician likes instant results. The tension comes because, as I have seen on many occasions, the economist's lag is the politician's nightmare."

Temporary and Permanent Fiscal Policy

A temporary tax cut or spending increase will explicitly last only for a year or two, and then revert to its original level. A permanent tax cut or spending increase is expected to stay in place for the foreseeable future. The effect of temporary and permanent fiscal policies on aggregate demand can be very different. Consider how you would react if the government announced a tax cut that would last one year and then be repealed, in comparison with how you would react if the government announced a permanent tax cut. Most people and firms will react more strongly to a permanent policy change than a temporary one.

This fact creates an unavoidable difficulty for countercyclical fiscal policy. The appropriate policy may be to have an expansionary fiscal policy with large budget deficits during a recession, and then a contractionary fiscal policy with budget surpluses when the economy is growing well. However, if both policies are explicitly temporary ones, they will have a less powerful effect than a permanent policy.

Structural Economic Change Takes Time

When an economy recovers from a recession, it does not usually revert to its exact earlier shape. Instead, the economy's internal structure evolves and changes and this process can take time. For example, much of the economic growth of the mid-2000s was in the construction sector (especially of housing) and finance. However, when housing prices started falling in 2007 and the resulting financial crunch led into recession (as we discussed in **Monetary Policy and Bank Regulation**), both sectors contracted. The manufacturing sector of the U.S. economy has been losing jobs in recent years as well, under pressure from technological change and foreign competition. Many of the people who lost work from these sectors in the 2008-2009 Great Recession will never return to the same jobs in the same sectors of the economy. Instead, the economy will need to grow in new and different directions, as the following Clear It Up feature shows. Fiscal policy can increase overall demand, but the process of structural economic change—the expansion of a new set of industries and the movement of workers to those industries—inevitably takes time.

Why do jobs vanish?

People can lose jobs for a variety of reasons: because of a recession, but also because of longer-run changes in the economy, such as new technology. Productivity improvements in auto manufacturing, for example, can reduce the number of workers needed, and eliminate these jobs in the long run. The internet has created jobs but also caused job loss, from travel agents to book store clerks. Many of these jobs may never come back. Short-run fiscal policy to reduce unemployment can create jobs, but it cannot replace jobs that will never return.

The Limitations of Fiscal Policy

Fiscal policy can help an economy that is producing below its potential GDP to expand aggregate demand so that it produces closer to potential GDP, thus lowering unemployment. However, fiscal policy cannot help an economy produce at an output level above potential GDP without causing inflation At this point, unemployment becomes so low that workers become scarce and wages rise rapidly.

Link It Up

Visit this website (http://openstaxcollege.org/l/fiscalpolicy) to read about how fiscal policies are affecting the recovery.

Political Realties and Discretionary Fiscal Policy

A final problem for discretionary fiscal policy arises out of the difficulties of explaining to politicians how countercyclical fiscal policy that runs against the tide of the business cycle should work. Some politicians have a gut-level belief that when the economy and tax revenues slow down, it is time to hunker down, pinch pennies, and trim expenses. Countercyclical policy, however, says that when the economy has slowed, it is time for the government to stimulate the economy, raising spending, and cutting taxes. This offsets the drop in the economy in the other sectors. Conversely, when economic times are good and tax revenues are rolling in, politicians often feel that it is time for tax cuts and new spending. However, countercyclical policy says that this economic boom should be an appropriate time for keeping taxes high and restraining spending.

Politicians tend to prefer expansionary fiscal policy over contractionary policy. There is rarely a shortage of proposals for tax cuts and spending increases, especially during recessions. However, politicians are less willing to hear the message that in good economic times, they should propose tax increases and spending limits. In the economic upswing of the late 1990s and early 2000s, for example, the U.S. GDP grew rapidly. Estimates from respected government economic forecasters like the nonpartisan Congressional Budget Office and the Office of Management and Budget stated that the GDP was above potential GDP, and that unemployment rates were unsustainably low. However, no mainstream politician took the lead in saying that the booming economic times might be an appropriate time for spending cuts or tax increases. As of February 2017, President Trump has expressed plans to increase spending on national defense by 10% or $54 billion, increase infrastructure investment by $1 trillion, cut corporate and personal income taxes, all while maintaining the existing spending on Social Security and Medicare. The only way this math adds up is with a sizeable increase in the Federal budget deficit.

Discretionary Fiscal Policy: Summing Up

Expansionary fiscal policy can help to end recessions and contractionary fiscal policy can help to reduce inflation. Given the uncertainties over interest rate effects, time lags, temporary and permanent policies, and unpredictable political behavior, many economists and knowledgeable policymakers had concluded by the mid-1990s that discretionary fiscal policy was a blunt instrument, more like a club than a scalpel. It might still make sense to use

This OpenStax book is available for free at http://cnx.org/content/col12122/1.4

it in extreme economic situations, like an especially deep or long recession. For less extreme situations, it was often preferable to let fiscal policy work through the automatic stabilizers and focus on monetary policy to steer short-term countercyclical efforts.

30.7 | The Question of a Balanced Budget

By the end of this section, you will be able to:
- Understand the arguments for and against requiring the U.S. federal budget to be balanced
- Consider the long-run and short-run effects of a federal budget deficit

For many decades, going back to the 1930s, various legislators have put forward proposals to require that the U.S. government balance its budget every year. In 1995, a proposed constitutional amendment that would require a balanced budget passed the U.S. House of Representatives by a wide margin, and failed in the U.S. Senate by only a single vote. (For the balanced budget to have become an amendment to the Constitution would have required a two-thirds vote by Congress and passage by three-quarters of the state legislatures.)

Most economists view the proposals for a perpetually balanced budget with bemusement. After all, in the short term, economists would expect the budget deficits and surpluses to fluctuate up and down with the economy and the automatic stabilizers. Economic recessions should automatically lead to larger budget deficits or smaller budget surpluses, while economic booms lead to smaller deficits or larger surpluses. A requirement that the budget be balanced each and every year would prevent these automatic stabilizers from working and would worsen the severity of economic fluctuations.

Some supporters of the balanced budget amendment like to argue that, since households must balance their own budgets, the government should too. However, this analogy between household and government behavior is severely flawed. Most households do not balance their budgets every year. Some years households borrow to buy houses or cars or to pay for medical expenses or college tuition. Other years they repay loans and save funds in retirement accounts. After retirement, they withdraw and spend those savings. Also, the government is not a household for many reasons, one of which is that the government has macroeconomic responsibilities. The argument of Keynesian macroeconomic policy is that the government needs to lean against the wind, spending when times are hard and saving when times are good, for the sake of the overall economy.

There is also no particular reason to expect a government budget to be balanced in the medium term of a few years. For example, a government may decide that by running large budget deficits, it can make crucial long-term investments in human capital and physical infrastructure that will build the country's long-term productivity. These decisions may work out well or poorly, but they are not always irrational. Such policies of ongoing government budget deficits may persist for decades. As the U.S. experience from the end of World War II up to about 1980 shows, it is perfectly possible to run budget deficits almost every year for decades, but as long as the percentage increases in debt are smaller than the percentage growth of GDP, the debt/GDP ratio will decline at the same time.

Nothing in this argument is a claim that budget deficits are always a wise policy. In the short run, a government that runs a very large budget deficit can shift aggregate demand to the right and trigger severe inflation. Additionally, governments may borrow for foolish or impractical reasons. **The Impacts of Government Borrowing** will discuss how large budget deficits, by reducing national saving, can in certain cases reduce economic growth and even contribute to international financial crises. A requirement that the budget be balanced in each calendar year, however, is a misguided overreaction to the fear that in some cases, budget deficits can become too large.

Bring it Home

No Yellowstone Park?

The 2013 federal budget shutdown illustrated the many sides to fiscal policy and the federal budget. In 2013, Republicans and Democrats could not agree on which spending policies to fund and how large the government debt should be. Due to the severity of the 2008-2009 recession, the fiscal stimulus, and previous policies, the federal budget deficit and debt was historically high. One way to try to cut federal spending and borrowing was to refuse to raise the legal federal debt limit, or tie on conditions to appropriation bills to stop the Affordable Health Care Act. This disagreement led to a two-week federal government shutdown and got close to the deadline where the federal government would default on its Treasury bonds. Finally, however, a compromise emerged and the government avoided default. This shows clearly how closely fiscal policies are tied to politics.

This OpenStax book is available for free at http://cnx.org/content/col12122/1.4

KEY TERMS

automatic stabilizers tax and spending rules that have the effect of slowing down the rate of decrease in aggregate demand when the economy slows down and restraining aggregate demand when the economy speeds up, without any additional change in legislation

balanced budget when government spending and taxes are equal

budget deficit when the federal government spends more money than it receives in taxes in a given year

budget surplus when the government receives more money in taxes than it spends in a year

contractionary fiscal policy fiscal policy that decreases the level of aggregate demand, either through cuts in government spending or increases in taxes

corporate income tax a tax imposed on corporate profits

crowding out federal spending and borrowing causes interest rates to rise and business investment to fall

discretionary fiscal policy the government passes a new law that explicitly changes overall tax or spending levels with the intent of influencing the level or overall economic activity

estate and gift tax a tax on people who pass assets to the next generation—either after death or during life in the form of gifts

excise tax a tax on a specific good—on gasoline, tobacco, and alcohol

expansionary fiscal policy fiscal policy that increases the level of aggregate demand, either through increases in government spending or cuts in taxes

implementation lag the time it takes for the funds relating to fiscal policy to be dispersed to the appropriate agencies to implement the programs

individual income tax a tax based on the income, of all forms, received by individuals

legislative lag the time it takes to get a fiscal policy bill passed

marginal tax rates or the tax that must be paid on all yearly income

national debt the total accumulated amount the government has borrowed, over time, and not yet paid back

payroll tax a tax based on the pay received from employers; the taxes provide funds for Social Security and Medicare

progressive tax a tax that collects a greater share of income from those with high incomes than from those with lower incomes

proportional tax a tax that is a flat percentage of income earned, regardless of level of income

recognition lag the time it takes to determine that a recession has occurred

regressive tax a tax in which people with higher incomes pay a smaller share of their income in tax

standardized employment budget the budget deficit or surplus in any given year adjusted for what it would have been if the economy were producing at potential GDP

KEY CONCEPTS AND SUMMARY

30.1 Government Spending

Fiscal policy is the set of policies that relate to federal government spending, taxation, and borrowing. In recent decades, the level of federal government spending and taxes, expressed as a share of GDP, has not changed much, typically fluctuating between about 18% to 22% of GDP. However, the level of state spending and taxes, as a share of GDP, has risen from about 12–13% to about 20% of GDP over the last four decades. The four main areas of federal spending are national defense, Social Security, healthcare, and interest payments, which together account for about 70% of all federal spending. When a government spends more than it collects in taxes, it is said to have a budget deficit. When a government collects more in taxes than it spends, it is said to have a budget surplus. If government spending and taxes are equal, it is said to have a balanced budget. The sum of all past deficits and surpluses make up the government debt.

30.2 Taxation

The two main federal taxes are individual income taxes and payroll taxes that provide funds for Social Security and Medicare; these taxes together account for more than 80% of federal revenues. Other federal taxes include the corporate income tax, excise taxes on alcohol, gasoline and tobacco, and the estate and gift tax. A progressive tax is one, like the federal income tax, where those with higher incomes pay a higher share of taxes out of their income than those with lower incomes. A proportional tax is one, like the payroll tax for Medicare, where everyone pays the same share of taxes regardless of income level. A regressive tax is one, like the payroll tax (above a certain threshold) that supports Social Security, where those with high income pay a lower share of income in taxes than those with lower incomes.

30.3 Federal Deficits and the National Debt

For most of the twentieth century, the U.S. government took on debt during wartime and then paid down that debt slowly in peacetime. However, it took on quite substantial debts in peacetime in the 1980s and early 1990s, before a brief period of budget surpluses from 1998 to 2001, followed by a return to annual budget deficits since 2002, with very large deficits in the recession of 2008 and 2009. A budget deficit or budget surplus is measured annually. Total government debt or national debt is the sum of budget deficits and budget surpluses over time.

30.4 Using Fiscal Policy to Fight Recession, Unemployment, and Inflation

Expansionary fiscal policy increases the level of aggregate demand, either through increases in government spending or through reductions in taxes. Expansionary fiscal policy is most appropriate when an economy is in recession and producing below its potential GDP. Contractionary fiscal policy decreases the level of aggregate demand, either through cuts in government spending or increases in taxes. Contractionary fiscal policy is most appropriate when an economy is producing above its potential GDP.

30.5 Automatic Stabilizers

Fiscal policy is conducted both through discretionary fiscal policy, which occurs when the government enacts taxation or spending changes in response to economic events, or through automatic stabilizers, which are taxing and spending mechanisms that, by their design, shift in response to economic events without any further legislation. The standardized employment budget is the calculation of what the budget deficit or budget surplus would have been in a given year if the economy had been producing at its potential GDP in that year. Many economists and politicians criticize the use of fiscal policy for a variety of reasons, including concerns over time lags, the impact on interest rates, and the inherently political nature of fiscal policy. We cover the critique of fiscal policy in the next module.

30.6 Practical Problems with Discretionary Fiscal Policy

Because fiscal policy affects the quantity of money that the government borrows in financial capital markets, it not only affects aggregate demand—it can also affect interest rates. If an expansionary fiscal policy also causes higher interest rates, then firms and households are discouraged from borrowing and spending, reducing aggregate demand in a situation called crowding out. Given the uncertainties over interest rate effects, time lags (implementation lag, legislative lag, and recognition lag), temporary and permanent policies, and unpredictable political behavior, many economists and knowledgeable policymakers have concluded that discretionary fiscal policy is a blunt instrument and better used only in extreme situations.

This OpenStax book is available for free at http://cnx.org/content/col12122/1.4

30.7 The Question of a Balanced Budget

Balanced budget amendments are a popular political idea, but the economic merits behind such proposals are questionable. Most economists accept that fiscal policy needs to be flexible enough to accommodate unforeseen expenditures, such as wars or recessions. While persistent, large budget deficits can indeed be a problem, a balanced budget amendment prevents even small, temporary deficits that might, in some cases, be necessary.

SELF-CHECK QUESTIONS

1. When governments run budget deficits, how do they make up the differences between tax revenue and spending?

2. When governments run budget surpluses, what is done with the extra funds?

3. Is it possible for a nation to run budget deficits and still have its debt/GDP ratio fall? Explain your answer. Is it possible for a nation to run budget surpluses and still have its debt/GDP ratio rise? Explain your answer.

4. Suppose that gifts were taxed at a rate of 10% for amounts up to $100,000 and 20% for anything over that amount. Would this tax be regressive or progressive?

5. If an individual owns a corporation for which he is the only employee, which different types of federal tax will he have to pay?

6. What taxes would an individual pay if he were self-employed and the business is not incorporated?

7. The social security tax is 6.2% on employees' income earned below $113,000. Is this tax progressive, regressive or proportional?

8. Debt has a certain self-reinforcing quality to it. There is one category of government spending that automatically increases along with the federal debt. What is it?

9. True or False:
  a. Federal spending has grown substantially in recent decades.
  b. By world standards, the U.S. government controls a relatively large share of the U.S. economy.
  c. A majority of the federal government's revenue is collected through personal income taxes.
  d. Education spending is slightly larger at the federal level than at the state and local level.
  e. State and local government spending has not risen much in recent decades.
  f. Defense spending is higher now than ever.
  g. The share of the economy going to federal taxes has increased substantially over time.
  h. Foreign aid is a large portion, although less than half, of federal spending.
  i. Federal deficits have been very large for the last two decades.
  j. The accumulated federal debt as a share of GDP is near an all-time high.

10. What is the main reason for employing contractionary fiscal policy in a time of strong economic growth?

11. What is the main reason for employing expansionary fiscal policy during a recession?

12. In a recession, does the actual budget surplus or deficit fall above or below the standardized employment budget?

13. What is the main advantage of automatic stabilizers over discretionary fiscal policy?

14. Explain how automatic stabilizers work, both on the taxation side and on the spending side, first in a situation where the economy is producing less than potential GDP and then in a situation where the economy is producing more than potential GDP.

15. What would happen if expansionary fiscal policy was implemented in a recession but, due to lag, did not actually take effect until after the economy was back to potential GDP?

16. What would happen if contractionary fiscal policy were implemented during an economic boom but, due to lag, it did not take effect until the economy slipped into recession?

17. Do you think the typical time lag for fiscal policy is likely to be longer or shorter than the time lag for monetary policy? Explain your answer?

18. How would a balanced budget amendment affect a decision by Congress to grant a tax cut during a recession?

19. How would a balanced budget amendment change the effect of automatic stabilizer programs?

REVIEW QUESTIONS

20. Give some examples of changes in federal spending and taxes by the government that would be fiscal policy and some that would not.

21. Have the spending and taxes of the U.S. federal government generally had an upward or a downward trend in the last few decades?

22. What are the main categories of U.S. federal government spending?

23. What is the difference between a budget deficit, a balanced budget, and a budget surplus?

24. Have spending and taxes by state and local governments in the United States had a generally upward or downward trend in the last few decades?

25. What are the main categories of U.S. federal government taxes?

26. What is the difference between a progressive tax, a proportional tax, and a regressive tax?

27. What has been the general pattern of U.S. budget deficits in recent decades?

28. What is the difference between a budget deficit and the national debt?

29. What is the difference between expansionary fiscal policy and contractionary fiscal policy?

30. Under what general macroeconomic circumstances might a government use expansionary fiscal policy? When might it use contractionary fiscal policy?

31. What is the difference between discretionary fiscal policy and automatic stabilizers?

32. Why do automatic stabilizers function "automatically?"

33. What is the standardized employment budget?

34. What are some practical weaknesses of discretionary fiscal policy?

35. What are some of the arguments for and against a requirement that the federal government budget be balanced every year?

CRITICAL THINKING QUESTIONS

36. Why is government spending typically measured as a percentage of GDP rather than in nominal dollars?

37. Why are expenditures such as crime prevention and education typically done at the state and local level rather than at the federal level?

38. Why is spending by the U.S. government on scientific research at NASA fiscal policy while spending by the University of Illinois is not fiscal policy? Why is a cut in the payroll tax fiscal policy whereas a cut in a state income tax is not fiscal policy?

39. Excise taxes on tobacco and alcohol and state sales taxes are often criticized for being regressive. Although everyone pays the same rate regardless of income, why might this be so?

40. What is the benefit of having state and local taxes on income instead of collecting all such taxes at the federal level?

41. In a booming economy, is the federal government more likely to run surpluses or deficits? What are the various factors at play?

This OpenStax book is available for free at http://cnx.org/content/col12122/1.4

42. Economist Arthur Laffer famously pointed out that, in some cases, income tax revenue can actually go up when tax rates go down. Why might this be the case?

43. Is it possible for a nation to run budget deficits and still have its debt/GDP ratio fall? Explain your answer. Is it possible for a nation to run budget surpluses and still have its debt/GDP ratio rise? Explain your answer.

44. How will cuts in state budget spending affect federal expansionary policy?

45. Is expansionary fiscal policy more attractive to politicians who believe in larger government or to politicians who believe in smaller government? Explain your answer.

46. Is Medicaid (federal government aid to low-income families and individuals) an automatic stabilizer?

47. What is a potential problem with a temporary tax increase designed to increase aggregate demand if people know that it is temporary?

48. If the government gives a $300 tax cut to everyone in the country, explain the mechanism by which this will cause interest rates to rise.

49. Do you agree or disagree with this statement: "It is in the best interest of our economy for Congress and the President to run a balanced budget each year." Explain your answer.

50. During the Great Recession of 2008–2009, what actions would have been required of Congress and the President had a balanced budget amendment to the Constitution been ratified? What impact would that have had on the unemployment rate?

PROBLEMS

51. A government starts off with a total debt of $3.5 billion. In year one, the government runs a deficit of $400 million. In year two, the government runs a deficit of $1 billion. In year three, the government runs a surplus of $200 million. What is the total debt of the government at the end of year three?

52. If a government runs a budget deficit of $10 billion dollars each year for ten years, then a surplus of $1 billion for five years, and then a balanced budget for another ten years, what is the government debt?

53. Specify whether expansionary or contractionary fiscal policy would seem to be most appropriate in response to each of the situations below and sketch a diagram using aggregate demand and aggregate supply curves to illustrate your answer:
   a. A recession.
   b. A stock market collapse that hurts consumer and business confidence.
   c. Extremely rapid growth of exports.
   d. Rising inflation.
   e. A rise in the natural rate of unemployment.
   f. A rise in oil prices.

This OpenStax book is available for free at http://cnx.org/content/col12122/1.4

31 | The Impacts of Government Borrowing

Figure 31.1 President Lyndon B. Johnson President Lyndon Johnson played a pivotal role in financing higher education. (Credit: modification of image by LBJ Museum & Library)

Bring it Home

Financing Higher Education

On November 8, 1965, President Lyndon B. Johnson signed The Higher Education Act of 1965 into law. With a stroke of the pen, he implemented what we know as the financial aid, work study, and student loan programs to help Americans pay for a college education. In his remarks, the President said:

> Here the seeds were planted from which grew my firm conviction that for the individual, education is the path to achievement and fulfillment; for the Nation, it is a path to a society that is not only free but civilized; and for the world, it is the path to peace—for it is education that places reason over force.

This Act, he said, "is responsible for funding higher education for millions of Americans. It is the embodiment of the United States' investment in 'human capital'." Since Johnson signed the Act into law, the government has renewed it several times.

The purpose of The Higher Education Act of 1965 was to build the country's human capital by creating educational opportunity for millions of Americans. The three criteria that the government uses to judge eligibility are income, full-time or part-time attendance, and the cost of the institution. According to the 2011–2012 National Postsecondary Student Aid Study (NPSAS:12), in the 2011–2012 school year, over 70% of all full-time college students received some form of federal financial aid; 47% received grants; and another 55% received federal government student loans. The budget to support financial aid has increased not only because of more enrollment, but also because of increased tuition and fees for higher education.

The current Trump administration is currently questioning these increases and the entire notion of how the government should deal with higher education. The President and Congress are charged with balancing fiscal responsibility and important government-financed expenditures like investing in human capital.

Introduction to the Impacts of Government Borrowing

In this chapter, you will learn about:

- How Government Borrowing Affects Investment and the Trade Balance
- Fiscal Policy, Investment, and Economic Growth
- How Government Borrowing Affects Private Saving
- Fiscal Policy and the Trade Balance

Governments have many competing demands for financial support. Any spending should be tempered by fiscal responsibility and by looking carefully at the spending's impact. When a government spends more than it collects in taxes, it runs a budget deficit. It then needs to borrow. When government borrowing becomes especially large and sustained, it can substantially reduce the financial capital available to private sector firms, as well as lead to trade imbalances and even financial crises.

The **Government Budgets and Fiscal Policy** chapter introduced the concepts of deficits and debt, as well as how a government could use fiscal policy to address recession or inflation. This chapter begins by building on the national savings and investment identity, which we first first introduced in **The International Trade and Capital Flows** chapter, to show how government borrowing affects firms' physical capital investment levels and trade balances. A prolonged period of budget deficits may lead to lower economic growth, in part because the funds that the government borrows to fund its budget deficits are typically no longer available for private investment. Moreover, a sustained pattern of large budget deficits can lead to disruptive economic patterns of high inflation, substantial inflows of financial capital from abroad, plummeting exchange rates, and heavy strains on a country's banking and financial system.

31.1 | How Government Borrowing Affects Investment and the Trade Balance

By the end of this section, you will be able to:
- Explain the national saving and investment identity in terms of demand and supply
- Evaluate the role of budget surpluses and trade surpluses in national saving and investment identity

When governments are borrowers in financial markets, there are three possible sources for the funds from a macroeconomic point of view: (1) households might save more; (2) private firms might borrow less; and (3) the additional funds for government borrowing might come from outside the country, from foreign financial investors. Let's begin with a review of why one of these three options must occur, and then explore how interest rates and exchange rates adjust to these connections.

The National Saving and Investment Identity

The national saving and investment identity, which we first introduced in **The International Trade and Capital Flows** chapter, provides a framework for showing the relationships between the sources of demand and supply in financial capital markets. The identity begins with a statement that must always hold true: the quantity of financial capital supplied in the market must equal the quantity of financial capital demanded.

The U.S. economy has two main sources for financial capital: private savings from inside the U.S. economy and public savings.

$$\text{Total savings} = \text{Private savings (S)} + \text{Public savings (T} - \text{G)}$$

This OpenStax book is available for free at http://cnx.org/content/col12122/1.4

These include the inflow of foreign financial capital from abroad. The inflow of savings from abroad is, by definition, equal to the trade deficit, as we explained in **The International Trade and Capital Flows** chapter. We can write this inflow of foreign investment capital as imports (M) minus exports (X). There are also two main sources of demand for financial capital: private sector investment (I) and government borrowing. Government borrowing in any given year is equal to the budget deficit, which we can write as the difference between government spending (G) and net taxes (T). Let's call this equation 1.

$$\text{Quantity supplied of financial capital} = \text{Quantity demanded of financial capital}$$
$$\text{Private savings} + \text{Inflow of foreign savings} = \text{Private investment} + \text{Government budget deficit}$$
$$S + (M - X) = I + (G - T)$$

Governments often spend more than they receive in taxes and, therefore, public savings (T – G) is negative. This causes a need to borrow money in the amount of (G – T) instead of adding to the nation's savings. If this is the case, we can view governments as demanders of financial capital instead of suppliers. In algebraic terms, we can rewrite the national savings and investment identity like this:

$$\text{Private investment} = \text{Private savings} + \text{Public savings} + \text{Trade deficit}$$
$$I = S + (T - G) + (M - X)$$

Let's call this equation 2. We must accompany a change in any part of the national saving and investment identity by offsetting changes in at least one other part of the equation because we assume that the equality of quantity supplied and quantity demanded always holds. If the government budget deficit changes, then either private saving or investment or the trade balance—or some combination of the three—must change as well. **Figure 31.2** shows the possible effects.

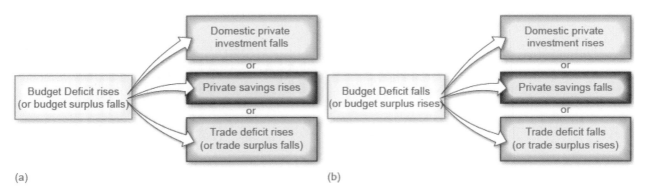

Figure 31.2 Effects of Change in Budget Surplus or Deficit on Investment, Savings, and The Trade Balance Chart (a) shows the potential results when the budget deficit rises (or budget surplus falls). Chart (b) shows the potential results when the budget deficit falls (or budget surplus rises).

What about Budget Surpluses and Trade Surpluses?

The national saving and investment identity must always hold true because, by definition, the quantity supplied and quantity demanded in the financial capital market must always be equal. However, the formula will look somewhat different if the government budget is in deficit rather than surplus or if the balance of trade is in surplus rather than deficit. For example, in 1999 and 2000, the U.S. government had budget surpluses, although the economy was still experiencing trade deficits. When the government was running budget surpluses, it was acting as a saver rather than a borrower, and supplying rather than demanding financial capital. As a result, we would write the national saving and investment identity during this time as:

$$\text{Quantity supplied of financial capital} = \text{Quantity demanded of financial capital}$$
$$\text{Private savings} + \text{Trade deficit} + \text{Government surplus} = \text{Private investment}$$
$$S + (M - X) + (T - G) = I$$

Let's call this equation 3. Notice that this expression is mathematically the same as equation 2 except the savings and investment sides of the identity have simply flipped sides.

During the 1960s, the U.S. government was often running a budget deficit, but the economy was typically running trade surpluses. Since a trade surplus means that an economy is experiencing a net outflow of financial capital, we would write the national saving and investment identity as:

$$\text{Quantity supplied of financial capital} = \text{Quantity demanded of financial capital}$$
$$\text{Private savings} = \text{Private investment} + \text{Outflow of foreign savings} + \text{Government budget deficit}$$
$$S = I + (X - M) + (G - T)$$

Instead of the balance of trade representing part of the supply of financial capital, which occurs with a trade deficit, a trade surplus represents an outflow of financial capital leaving the domestic economy and invested elsewhere in the world.

$$\text{Quantity supplied of financial capital} = \text{Quantity demanded of financial capital demand}$$
$$\text{Private savings} = \text{Private investment} + \text{Government budget deficit} + \text{Trade surplus}$$
$$S = I + (G - T) + (X - M)$$

We assume that the point to these equations is that the national saving and investment identity always hold. When you write these relationships, it is important to engage your brain and think about what is on the supply and demand side of the financial capital market before you start your calculations.

As you can see in **Figure 31.3**, the Office of Management and Budget shows that the United States has consistently run budget deficits since 1977, with the exception of 1999 and 2000. What is alarming is the dramatic increase in budget deficits that has occurred since 2008, which in part reflects declining tax revenues and increased safety net expenditures due to the Great Recession. (Recall that T is net taxes. When the government must transfer funds back to individuals for safety net expenditures like Social Security and unemployment benefits, budget deficits rise.) These deficits have implications for the future health of the U.S. economy.

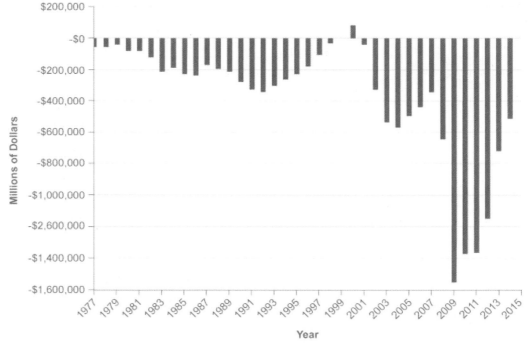

Figure 31.3 United States On-Budget, Surplus, and Deficit, 1977–2014 ($ millions)   The United States has run a budget deficit for over 30 years, with the exception of 1999 and 2000. Military expenditures, entitlement programs, and the decrease in tax revenue coupled with increased safety net support during the Great Recession are major contributors to the dramatic increases in the deficit after 2008. (Source: Table 1.1, "Summary of Receipts, Outlays, and Surpluses or Deficits," https://www.whitehouse.gov/omb/budget/Historicals)

A rising budget deficit may result in a fall in domestic investment, a rise in private savings, or a rise in the trade deficit. The following modules discuss each of these possible effects in more detail.

This OpenStax book is available for free at http://cnx.org/content/col12122/1.4

31.2 | Fiscal Policy and the Trade Balance

By the end of this section, you will be able to:
- Discuss twin deficits as they related to budget and trade deficit
- Explain the relationship between budget deficits and exchange rates
- Explain the relationship between budget deficits and inflation
- Identify causes of recessions

Government budget balances can affect the trade balance. As **The Keynesian Perspective** chapter discusses, a net inflow of foreign financial investment always accompanies a trade deficit, while a net outflow of financial investment always accompanies a trade surplus. One way to understand the connection from budget deficits to trade deficits is that when government creates a budget deficit with some combination of tax cuts or spending increases, it will increase aggregate demand in the economy, and some of that increase in aggregate demand will result in a higher level of imports. A higher level of imports, with exports remaining fixed, will cause a larger trade deficit. That means foreigners' holdings of dollars increase as Americans purchase more imported goods. Foreigners use those dollars to invest in the United States, which leads to an inflow of foreign investment. One possible source of funding our budget deficit is foreigners buying Treasury securities that the U.S. government sells, thus a trade deficit often accompanies a budget deficit.

Twin Deficits?

In the mid-1980s, it was common to hear economists and even newspaper articles refer to the twin deficits, as the budget deficit and trade deficit both grew substantially. **Figure 31.4** shows the pattern. The federal budget deficit went from 2.6% of GDP in 1981 to 5.1% of GDP in 1985—a drop of 2.5% of GDP. Over that time, the trade deficit moved from 0.5% in 1981 to 2.9% in 1985—a drop of 2.4% of GDP. In the mid-1980s an inflow of foreign investment capital matched, the considerable increase in government borrowing, so the government budget deficit and the trade deficit moved together.

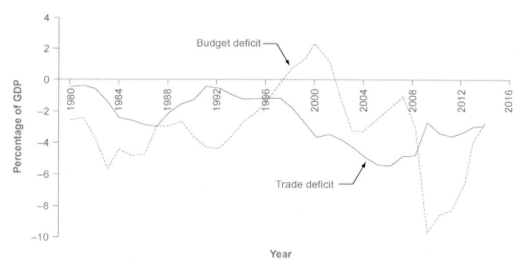

Figure 31.4 U.S. Budget Deficits and Trade Deficits In the 1980s, the budget deficit and the trade deficit declined at the same time. However, since then, the deficits have stopped being twins. The trade deficit grew smaller in the early 1990s as the budget deficit increased, and then the trade deficit grew larger in the late 1990s as the budget deficit turned into a surplus. In the first half of the 2000s, both budget and trade deficits increased. However, in 2009, the trade deficit declined as the budget deficit increased.

Of course, no one should expect the budget deficit and trade deficit to move in lockstep, because the other parts of the national saving and investment identity—investment and private savings—will often change as well. In the late 1990s, for example, the government budget balance turned from deficit to surplus, but the trade deficit remained large and growing. During this time, the inflow of foreign financial investment was supporting a surge of physical capital investment by U.S. firms. In the first half of the 2000s, the budget and trade deficits again increased together, but in

2009, the budget deficit increased while the trade deficit declined. The budget deficit and the trade deficits are related to each other, but they are more like cousins than twins.

Budget Deficits and Exchange Rates

Exchange rates can also help to explain why budget deficits are linked to trade deficits. **Figure 31.5** shows a situation using the exchange rate for the U.S. dollar, measured in euros. At the original equilibrium (E_0), where the demand for U.S. dollars (D_0) intersects with the supply of U.S. dollars (S_0) on the foreign exchange market, the exchange rate is 0.9 euros per U.S. dollar and the equilibrium quantity traded in the market is \$100 billion per day (which was roughly the quantity of dollar–euro trading in exchange rate markets in the mid-2000s). Then the U.S. budget deficit rises and foreign financial investment provides the source of funds for that budget deficit.

International financial investors, as a group, will demand more U.S. dollars on foreign exchange markets to purchase the U.S. government bonds, and they will supply fewer of the U.S. dollars that they already hold in these markets. Demand for U.S. dollars on the foreign exchange market shifts from D_0 to D_1 and the supply of U.S. dollars falls from S_0 to S_1. At the new equilibrium (E_1), the exchange rate has appreciated to 1.05 euros per dollar while, in this example, the quantity of dollars traded remains the same.

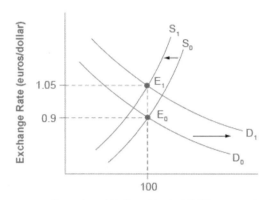

Figure 31.5 Budget Deficits and Exchange Rates   Imagine that the U.S. government increases its borrowing and the funds come from European financial investors. To purchase U.S. government bonds, those European investors will need to demand more U.S. dollars on foreign exchange markets, causing the demand for U.S. dollars to shift to the right from D_0 to D_1. European financial investors as a group will also be less likely to supply U.S. dollars to the foreign exchange markets, causing the supply of U.S. dollars to shift from S_0 to S_1. The equilibrium exchange rate strengthens from 0.9 euro/ dollar at E_0 to 1.05 euros/dollar at E_1.

A stronger exchange rate, of course, makes it more difficult for exporters to sell their goods abroad while making imports cheaper, so a trade deficit (or a reduced trade surplus) results. Thus, a budget deficit can easily result in an inflow of foreign financial capital, a stronger exchange rate, and a trade deficit.

You can also imagine interest rates are driving the exchange rate appreciation. As we explained earlier in **Figure 31.8**, a budget deficit increases demand in markets for domestic financial capital, raising the domestic interest rate. A higher interest rate will attract an inflow of foreign financial capital, and appreciate the exchange rate in response to the increase in demand for U.S. dollars by foreign investors and a decrease in supply of U. S. dollars. Because of higher interest rates in the United States, Americans find U.S. bonds more attractive than foreign bonds. When Americans are buying fewer foreign bonds, they are supplying fewer U.S. dollars. U.S. dollar depreciation leads to a larger trade deficit (or reduced surplus). The connections between inflows of foreign investment capital, interest rates, and exchange rates are all just different ways of drawing the same economic connections: a larger budget deficit can result in a larger trade deficit, although do not expect the connection to be one-to-one.

From Budget Deficits to International Economic Crisis

We lay out step-by-step the economic story of how an outflow of international financial capital can cause a deep recession in the **Exchange Rates and International Capital Flows** chapter. When international financial investors decide to withdraw their funds from a country like Turkey, they increase the supply of the Turkish lira and reduce the demand for lira, depreciating the lira exchange rate. When firms and the government in a country like

Turkey borrow money in international financial markets, they typically do so in stages. First, banks in Turkey borrow in a widely used currency like U.S. dollars or euros, then convert those U.S. dollars to lira, and then lend the money to borrowers in Turkey. If the lira's exchange rate value depreciates, then Turkey's banks will find it impossible to repay the international loans that are in U.S. dollars or euros.

The combination of less foreign investment capital and banks that are bankrupt can sharply reduce aggregate demand, which causes a deep recession. Many countries around the world have experienced this kind of recession in recent years: along with Turkey in 2002, Mexico followed this general pattern in 1995, Thailand and countries across East Asia in 1997–1998, Russia in 1998, and Argentina in 2002. In many of these countries, large government budget deficits played a role in setting the stage for the financial crisis. A moderate increase in a budget deficit that leads to a moderate increase in a trade deficit and a moderate appreciation of the exchange rate is not necessarily a cause for concern. However, beyond some point that is hard to define in advance, a series of large budget deficits can become a cause for concern among international investors.

One reason for concern is that extremely large budget deficits mean that aggregate demand may shift so far to the right as to cause high inflation. The example of Turkey is a situation where very large budget deficits brought inflation rates well into double digits. In addition, very large budget deficits at some point begin to raise a fear that the government would not repay the borrowing. In the last 175 years, the government of Turkey has been unable to pay its debts and defaulted on its loans six times. Brazil's government has been unable to pay its debts and defaulted on its loans seven times; Venezuela, nine times; and Argentina, five times. The risk of high inflation or a default on repaying international loans will worry international investors, since both factors imply that the rate of return on their investments in that country may end up lower than expected. If international investors start withdrawing the funds from a country rapidly, the scenario of less investment, a depreciated exchange rate, widespread bank failure, and deep recession can occur. The following Clear It Up feature explains other impacts of large deficits.

What are the risks of chronic large deficits in the United States?

If a government runs large budget deficits for a sustained period of time, what can go wrong? According to a recent Brookings Institution report, a key risk of a large budget deficit is that government debt may grow too high compared to the country's GDP growth. As debt grows, the national savings rate will decline, leaving less available in financial capital for private investment. The impact of chronically large budget deficits is as follows:

- As the population ages, there will be an increasing demand for government services that may cause higher government deficits. Government borrowing and its interest payments will pull resources away from domestic investment in human capital and physical capital that is essential to economic growth.

- Interest rates may start to rise so that the cost of financing government debt will rise as well, creating pressure on the government to reduce its budget deficits through spending cuts and tax increases. These steps will be politically painful, and they will also have a contractionary effect on aggregate demand in the economy.

- Rising percentage of debt to GDP will create uncertainty in the financial and global markets that might cause a country to resort to inflationary tactics to reduce the real value of the debt outstanding. This will decrease real wealth and damage confidence in the country's ability to manage its spending. After all, if the government has borrowed at a fixed interest rate of, say, 5%, and it lets inflation rise above that 5%, then it will effectively be able to repay its debt at a negative real interest rate.

The conventional reasoning suggests that the relationship between sustained deficits that lead to high levels of government debt and long-term growth is negative. How significant this relationship is, how big an issue it is compared to other macroeconomic issues, and the direction of causality, is less clear.

What remains important to acknowledge is that the relationship between debt and growth is negative and that for some countries, the relationship may be stronger than in others. It is also important to acknowledge the direction of causality: does high debt cause slow growth, slow growth cause high debt, or are both high debt and slow growth the result of third factors? In our analysis, we have argued simply that high debt causes slow growth. There may be more to this debate than we have space to discuss here.

Using Fiscal Policy to Address Trade Imbalances

If a nation is experiencing the inflow of foreign investment capital associated with a trade deficit because foreign investors are making long-term direct investments in firms, there may be no substantial reason for concern. After all, many low-income nations around the world would welcome direct investment by multinational firms that ties them more closely into the global networks of production and distribution of goods and services. In this case, the inflows of foreign investment capital and the trade deficit are attracted by the opportunities for a good rate of return on private sector investment in an economy.

However, governments should beware of a sustained pattern of high budget deficits and high trade deficits. The danger arises in particular when the inflow of foreign investment capital is not funding long-term physical capital investment by firms, but instead is short-term portfolio investment in government bonds. When inflows of foreign financial investment reach high levels, foreign financial investors will be on the alert for any reason to fear that the country's exchange rate may decline or the government may be unable to repay what it has borrowed on time. Just as a few falling rocks can trigger an avalanche; a relatively small piece of bad news about an economy can trigger an enormous outflow of short-term financial capital.

Reducing a nation's budget deficit will not always be a successful method of reducing its trade deficit, because other elements of the national saving and investment identity, like private saving or investment, may change instead. In those cases when the budget deficit is the main cause of the trade deficit, governments should take steps to reduce their budget deficits, lest they make their economy vulnerable to a rapid outflow of international financial capital that could bring a deep recession.

Bring it Home

Financing Higher Education

Between 1982 and 2012, the increases in the cost of a college education had far outpaced that of the income of the typical American family. According to President Obama's research staff, the cost of education at a four-year public college increased by 257% compared to an increase in family incomes of only 16% over the prior 30 years. The ongoing debate over a balanced budget and proposed cutbacks accentuated the need to increase investment in human capital to grow the economy versus deepening the already significant debt levels of the U.S. government. In summer 2013, President Obama presented a plan to make college more affordable that included increasing Pell Grant awards and the number of recipients, caps on interest rates for student loans, and providing education tax credits. In addition, the plan includes an accountability method for institutions of higher education that focuses on completion rates and creates a College Scorecard. Whether or not all these initiatives come to fruition remains to be seen, but they are indicative of creative approaches that government can take to meet its obligation from both a public and fiscal policy perspective.

31.3 | How Government Borrowing Affects Private Saving

By the end of this section, you will be able to:
- Apply Ricardian equivalence to evaluate how government borrowing affects private saving
- Interpret a graphic representation of Ricardian equivalence

A change in government budgets may impact private saving. Imagine that people watch government budgets and adjust their savings accordingly. For example, whenever the government runs a budget deficit, people might reason: "Well, a higher budget deficit means that I'm just going to owe more taxes in the future to pay off all that government borrowing, so I'll start saving now." If the government runs budget surpluses, people might reason: "With these budget surpluses (or lower budget deficits), interest rates are falling, so that saving is less attractive. Moreover, with a budget surplus the country will be able to afford a tax cut sometime in the future. I won't bother saving as much now."

The theory that rational private households might shift their saving to offset government saving or borrowing is known as **Ricardian equivalence** because the idea has intellectual roots in the writings of the early nineteenth-century economist David Ricardo (1772–1823). If Ricardian equivalence holds completely true, then in the national saving and investment identity, any change in budget deficits or budget surpluses would be completely offset by a corresponding change in private saving. As a result, changes in government borrowing would have no effect at all on either physical capital investment or trade balances.

In practice, the private sector only sometimes and partially adjusts its savings behavior to offset government budget deficits and surpluses. **Figure 31.6** shows the patterns of U.S. government budget deficits and surpluses and the rate of private saving—which includes saving by both households and firms—since 1980. The connection between the two is not at all obvious. In the mid-1980s, for example, government budget deficits were quite large, but there is no corresponding surge of private saving. However, when budget deficits turn to surpluses in the late 1990s, there is a simultaneous decline in private saving. When budget deficits get very large in 2008 and 2009, there is some sign of a rise in saving. A variety of statistical studies based on the U.S. experience suggests that when government borrowing increases by $1, private saving rises by about 30 cents. A World Bank study from the late 1990s, looking at government budgets and private saving behavior in countries around the world, found a similar result.

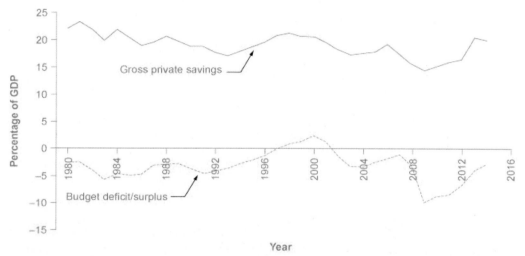

Figure 31.6 U.S. Budget Deficits and Private Savings The theory of Ricardian equivalence suggests that additional private saving will offset any increase in government borrowing, while reduced private saving will offset any decrease in government borrowing. Sometimes this theory holds true, and sometimes it does not. (Source: Bureau of Economic Analysis and Federal Reserve Economic Data)

Private saving does increase to some extent when governments run large budget deficits, and private saving falls when governments reduce deficits or run large budget surpluses. However, the offsetting effects of private saving compared to government borrowing are much less than one-to-one. In addition, this effect can vary a great deal from country to country, from time to time, and over the short and the long run.

If the funding for a larger budget deficit comes from international financial investors, then a trade deficit may accompany a budget deficit. In some countries, this pattern of **twin deficits** has set the stage for international financial investors first to send their funds to a country and cause an appreciation of its exchange rate and then to pull their funds out and cause a depreciation of the exchange rate and a financial crisis as well. It depends on whether funding comes from international financial investors.

31.4 | Fiscal Policy, Investment, and Economic Growth

By the end of this section, you will be able to:
- Explain crowding out and its effect on physical capital investment
- Explain the relationship between budget deficits and interest rates
- Identify why economic growth is tied to investments in physical capital, human capital, and technology

The underpinnings of economic growth are investments in physical capital, human capital, and technology, all set in an economic environment where firms and individuals can react to the incentives provided by well-functioning markets and flexible prices. Government borrowing can reduce the financial capital available for private firms to invest in physical capital. However, government spending can also encourage certain elements of long-term growth, such as spending on roads or water systems, on education, or on research and development that creates new technology.

Crowding Out Physical Capital Investment

A larger budget deficit will increase demand for financial capital. If private saving and the trade balance remain the same, then less financial capital will be available for private investment in physical capital. When government borrowing soaks up available financial capital and leaves less for private investment in physical capital, economists call the result crowding out.

To understand the potential impact of crowding out, consider the U.S. economy's situation before the exceptional circumstances of the recession that started in late 2007. In 2005, for example, the budget deficit was roughly 4% of GDP. Private investment by firms in the U.S. economy has hovered in the range of 14% to 18% of GDP in recent decades. However, in any given year, roughly half of U.S. investment in physical capital just replaces machinery and equipment that has worn out or become technologically obsolete. Only about half represents an increase in the total quantity of physical capital in the economy. Investment in new physical capital in any year is about 7% to 9% of GDP. In this situation, even U.S. budget deficits in the range of 4% of GDP can potentially crowd out a substantial share of new investment spending. Conversely, a smaller budget deficit (or an increased budget surplus) increases the pool of financial capital available for private investment.

Visit this website (http://openstaxcollege.org/l/debtclock) to view the "U.S. Debt Clock."

Figure 31.7 shows the patterns of U.S. budget deficits and private investment since 1980. If greater government deficits lead to less private investment in physical capital, and reduced government deficits or budget surpluses lead to more investment in physical capital, these two lines should move up and down simultaneously. This pattern occurred in the late 1990s and early 2000s. The U.S. federal budget went from a deficit of 2.2% of GDP in 1995 to a budget surplus of 2.4% of GDP in 2000—a swing of 4.6% of GDP. From 1995 to 2000, private investment in physical capital rose from 15% to 18% of GDP—a rise of 3% of GDP. Then, when the U.S. government again started running budget deficits in the early 2000s, less financial capital became available for private investment, and the rate of private investment fell back to about 15% of GDP by 2003.

This OpenStax book is available for free at http://cnx.org/content/col12122/1.4

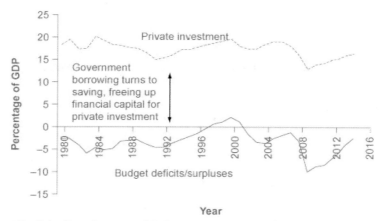

Figure 31.7 U.S. Budget Deficits/Surpluses and Private Investment The connection between private savings and flows of international capital plays a role in budget deficits and surpluses. Consequently, government borrowing and private investment sometimes rise and fall together. For example, the 1990s show a pattern in which reduced government borrowing helped to reduce crowding out so that more funds were available for private investment.

This argument does not claim that a government's budget deficits will exactly shadow its national rate of private investment; after all, we must account for private saving and inflows of foreign financial investment. In the mid-1980s, for example, government budget deficits increased substantially without a corresponding drop off in private investment. In 2009, nonresidential private fixed investment dropped by $300 billion from its previous level of $1,941 billion in 2008, primarily because, during a recession, firms lack both the funds and the incentive to invest. Investment growth between 2009 and 2014 averaged approximately 5.9% to $2,210.5 billion—only slightly above its 2008 level, according to the Bureau of Economic Analysis. During that same period, interest rates dropped from 3.94% to less than a quarter percent as the Federal Reserve took dramatic action to prevent a depression by increasing the money supply through lowering short-term interest rates. The "crowding out" of private investment due to government borrowing to finance expenditures appears to have been suspended during the Great Recession. However, as the economy improves and interest rates rise, government borrowing may potentially create pressure on interest rates.

The Interest Rate Connection

Assume that government borrowing of substantial amounts will have an effect on the quantity of private investment. How will this affect interest rates in financial markets? In **Figure 31.8**, the original equilibrium (E_0) where the demand curve (D_0) for financial capital intersects with the supply curve (S_0) occurs at an interest rate of 5% and an equilibrium quantity equal to 20% of GDP. However, as the government budget deficit increases, the demand curve for financial capital shifts from D_0 to D_1. The new equilibrium (E_1) occurs at an interest rate of 6% and an equilibrium quantity of 21% of GDP.

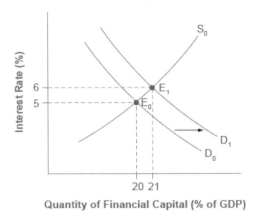

Figure 31.8 Budget Deficits and Interest Rates   In the financial market, an increase in government borrowing can shift the demand curve for financial capital to the right from D_0 to D_1. As the equilibrium interest rate shifts from E_0 to E_1, the interest rate rises from 5% to 6% in this example. The higher interest rate is one economic mechanism by which government borrowing can crowd out private investment.

A survey of economic studies on the connection between government borrowing and interest rates in the U.S. economy suggests that an increase of 1% in the budget deficit will lead to a rise in interest rates of between 0.5 and 1.0%, other factors held equal. In turn, a higher interest rate tends to discourage firms from making physical capital investments. One reason government budget deficits crowd out private investment, therefore, is the increase in interest rates. There are, however, economic studies that show a limited connection between the two (at least in the United States), but as the budget deficit grows, the dangers of rising interest rates become more real.

At this point, you may wonder about the Federal Reserve. After all, can the Federal Reserve not use expansionary monetary policy to reduce interest rates, or in this case, to prevent interest rates from rising? This useful question emphasizes the importance of considering how fiscal and monetary policies work in relation to each other. Imagine a central bank faced with a government that is running large budget deficits, causing a rise in interest rates and crowding out private investment. If the budget deficits are increasing aggregate demand when the economy is already producing near potential GDP, threatening an inflationary increase in price levels, the central bank may react with a contractionary monetary policy. In this situation, the higher interest rates from the government borrowing would be made even higher by contractionary monetary policy, and the government borrowing might crowd out a great deal of private investment.

Alternatively, if the budget deficits are increasing aggregate demand when the economy is producing substantially less than potential GDP, an inflationary increase in the price level is not much of a danger and the central bank might react with expansionary monetary policy. In this situation, higher interest rates from government borrowing would be largely offset by lower interest rates from expansionary monetary policy, and there would be little crowding out of private investment.

However, even a central bank cannot erase the overall message of the national savings and investment identity. If government borrowing rises, then private investment must fall, or private saving must rise, or the trade deficit must fall. By reacting with contractionary or expansionary monetary policy, the central bank can only help to determine which of these outcomes is likely.

Public Investment in Physical Capital

Government can invest in physical capital directly: roads and bridges; water supply and sewers; seaports and airports; schools and hospitals; plants that generate electricity, like hydroelectric dams or windmills; telecommunications facilities; and military weapons. In 2014, the U.S. federal government budget for Fiscal Year 2014 shows that the United States spent about $92 billion on transportation, including highways, mass transit, and airports. **Table 31.1** shows the federal government's total outlay for 2014 for major public physical capital investment in the United States. We have omitted physical capital related to the military or to residences where people live from this table, because the focus here is on public investments that have a direct effect on raising output in the private sector.

This OpenStax book is available for free at http://cnx.org/content/col12122/1.4

Type of Public Physical Capital	Federal Outlays 2014 ($ millions)
Transportation	$91,915
Community and regional development	$20,670
Natural resources and the environment	$36,171
Education, training, employment, and social services	$90,615
Other	$37,282
Total	$276,653

Table 31.1 Grants for Major Physical Capital Investment, 2014

Public physical capital investment of this sort can increase the economy's output and productivity. An economy with reliable roads and electricity will be able to produce more. However, it is hard to quantify how much government investment in physical capital will benefit the economy, because government responds to political as well as economic incentives. When a firm makes an investment in physical capital, it is subject to the discipline of the market: If it does not receive a positive return on investment, the firm may lose money or even go out of business.

In some cases, lawmakers make investments in physical capital as a way of spending money in key politicians' districts. The result may be unnecessary roads or office buildings. Even if a project is useful and necessary, it might be done in a way that is excessively costly, because local contractors who make campaign contributions to politicians appreciate the extra business. Alternatively, governments sometimes do not make the investments they should because a decision to spend on infrastructure does not need to just make economic sense. It must be politically popular as well. Managing public investment cost-effectively can be difficult.

If a government decides to finance an investment in public physical capital with higher taxes or lower government spending in other areas, it need not worry that it is directly crowding out private investment. Indirectly however, higher household taxes could cut down on the level of private savings available and have a similar effect. If a government decides to finance an investment in public physical capital by borrowing, it may end up increasing the quantity of public physical capital at the cost of crowding out investment in private physical capital, which could be more beneficial to the economy.

Public Investment in Human Capital

In most countries, the government plays a large role in society's investment in human capital through the education system. A highly educated and skilled workforce contributes to a higher rate of economic growth. For the low-income nations of the world, additional investment in human capital seems likely to increase productivity and growth. For the United States, critics have raised tough questions about how much increases in government spending on education will improve the actual level of education.

Among economists, discussions of education reform often begin with some uncomfortable facts. As **Figure 31.9** shows, spending per student for kindergarten through grade 12 (K–12) increased substantially in real dollars through 2010. The U.S. Census Bureau reports that current spending per pupil for elementary and secondary education rose from $5,001 in 1998 to $10,608 in 2012. However, as measured by standardized tests like the SAT, the level of student academic achievement has barely budged in recent decades. On international tests, U.S. students lag behind students from many other countries. (Of course, test scores are an imperfect measure of education for a variety of reasons. It would be difficult, however, to argue that there are not real problems in the U.S. education system and that the tests are just inaccurate.)

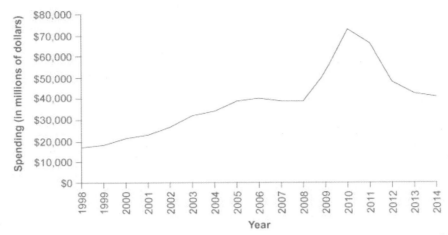

Figure 31.9 Total Spending for Elementary, Secondary, and Vocational Education (1998–2014) in the United States The graph shows that government spending on education was continually increasing up until 2006 where it leveled off until 2008 when it increased dramatically. Since 2010, spending has steadily decreased. (Source: Office of Management and Budget)

The fact that increased financial resources have not brought greater measurable gains in student performance has led some education experts to question whether the problems may be due to structure, not just to the resources spent.

Other government programs seek to increase human capital either before or after the K–12 education system. Programs for early childhood education, like the federal **Head Start program**, are directed at families where the parents may have limited educational and financial resources. Government also offers substantial support for universities and colleges. For example, in the United States about 60% of students take at least a few college or university classes beyond the high school level. In Germany and Japan, about half of all students take classes beyond the comparable high school level. In the countries of Latin America, only about one student in four takes classes beyond the high school level, and in the nations of sub-Saharan Africa, only about one student in 20.

Not all spending on educational human capital needs to happen through the government: many college students in the United States pay a substantial share of the cost of their education. If low-income countries of the world are going to experience a widespread increase in their education levels for grade-school children, government spending seems likely to play a substantial role. For the U.S. economy, and for other high-income countries, the primary focus at this time is more on how to get a bigger return from existing spending on education and how to improve the performance of the average high school graduate, rather than dramatic increases in education spending.

How Fiscal Policy Can Improve Technology

Research and development (R&D) efforts are the lifeblood of new technology. According to the National Science Foundation, federal outlays for research, development, and physical plant improvements to various governmental agencies have remained at an average of 8.8% of GDP. About one-fifth of U.S. R&D spending goes to defense and space-oriented research. Although defense-oriented R&D spending may sometimes produce consumer-oriented spinoffs, R&D that is aimed at producing new weapons is less likely to benefit the civilian economy than direct civilian R&D spending.

Fiscal policy can encourage R&D using either direct spending or tax policy. Government could spend more on the R&D that it carries out in government laboratories, as well as expanding federal R&D grants to universities and colleges, nonprofit organizations, and the private sector. By 2014, the federal share of R&D outlays totaled $135.5 billion, or about 4% of the federal government's total budget outlays, according to data from the National Science Foundation. Fiscal policy can also support R&D through tax incentives, which allow firms to reduce their tax bill as they increase spending on research and development.

Summary of Fiscal Policy, Investment, and Economic Growth

Investment in physical capital, human capital, and new technology is essential for long-term economic growth, as **Table 31.2** summarizes. In a market-oriented economy, private firms will undertake most of the investment in physical capital, and fiscal policy should seek to avoid a long series of outsized budget deficits that might crowd out

This OpenStax book is available for free at http://cnx.org/content/col12122/1.4

such investment. We will see the effects of many growth-oriented policies very gradually over time, as students are better educated, we make physical capital investments, and man invents and implements new technologies.

	Physical Capital	Human Capital	New Technology
Private Sector	New investment in property and equipment	On-the-job training	Research and development
Public Sector	Public infrastructure	Public education Job training	Research and development encouraged through private sector incentives and direct spending.

Table 31.2 Investment Role of Public and Private Sector in a Market Economy

KEY TERMS

Head Start program a program for early childhood education directed at families with limited educational and financial resources.

Ricardian equivalence the theory that rational private households might shift their saving to offset government saving or borrowing

twin deficits deficits that occur when a country is running both a trade and a budget deficit

KEY CONCEPTS AND SUMMARY

31.1 How Government Borrowing Affects Investment and the Trade Balance
A change in any part of the national saving and investment identity suggests that if the government budget deficit changes, then either private savings, private investment in physical capital, or the trade balance—or some combination of the three—must change as well.

31.2 Fiscal Policy and the Trade Balance
The government need not balance its budget every year. However, a sustained pattern of large budget deficits over time risks causing several negative macroeconomic outcomes: a shift to the right in aggregate demand that causes an inflationary increase in the price level; crowding out private investment in physical capital in a way that slows down economic growth; and creating a dependence on inflows of international portfolio investment which can sometimes turn into outflows of foreign financial investment that can be injurious to a macroeconomy.

31.3 How Government Borrowing Affects Private Saving
The theory of Ricardian equivalence holds that changes in private saving will offset changes in government borrowing or saving. Thus, greater private saving will offset higher budget deficits, while greater private borrowing will offset larger budget surpluses. If the theory holds true, then changes in government borrowing or saving would have no effect on private investment in physical capital or on the trade balance. However, empirical evidence suggests that the theory holds true only partially.

31.4 Fiscal Policy, Investment, and Economic Growth
Economic growth comes from a combination of investment in physical capital, human capital, and technology. Government borrowing can crowd out private sector investment in physical capital, but fiscal policy can also increase investment in publicly owned physical capital, human capital (education), and research and development. Possible methods for improving education and society's investment in human capital include spending more money on teachers and other educational resources, and reorganizing the education system to provide greater incentives for success. Methods for increasing research and development spending to generate new technology include direct government spending on R&D and tax incentives for businesses to conduct additional R&D.

SELF-CHECK QUESTIONS

1. In a country, private savings equals 600, the government budget surplus equals 200, and the trade surplus equals 100. What is the level of private investment in this economy?

2. Assume an economy has a budget surplus of 1,000, private savings of 4,000, and investment of 5,000.
  a. Write out a national saving and investment identity for this economy.
  b. What will be the balance of trade in this economy?
  c. If the budget surplus changes to a budget deficit of 1000, with private saving and investment unchanged, what is the new balance of trade in this economy?

This OpenStax book is available for free at http://cnx.org/content/col12122/1.4

3. In the late 1990s, the U.S. government moved from a budget deficit to a budget surplus and the trade deficit in the U.S. economy grew substantially. Using the national saving and investment identity, what can you say about the direction in which saving and/or investment must have changed in this economy?

4. Imagine an economy in which Ricardian equivalence holds. This economy has a budget deficit of 50, a trade deficit of 20, private savings of 130, and investment of 100. If the budget deficit rises to 70, how are the other terms in the national saving and investment identity affected?

5. Why have many education experts recently placed an emphasis on altering the incentives that U.S. schools face rather than on increasing their budgets? Without endorsing any of these proposals as especially good or bad, list some of the ways in which incentives for schools might be altered.

6. What are some steps the government can take to encourage research and development?

REVIEW QUESTIONS

7. Based on the national saving and investment identity, what are the three ways the macroeconomy might react to greater government budget deficits?

8. How would you expect larger budget deficits to affect private sector investment in physical capital? Why?

9. Under what conditions will a larger budget deficit cause a trade deficit?

10. What is the theory of Ricardian equivalence?

11. What does the concept of rationality have to do with Ricardian equivalence?

12. What are some of the ways fiscal policy might encourage economic growth?

13. What are some fiscal policies for improving a society's human capital?

14. What are some fiscal policies for improving the technologies that the economy will have to draw upon in the future?

15. Explain how cuts in funding for programs such as Head Start might affect the development of human capital in the United States.

CRITICAL THINKING QUESTIONS

16. Assume there is no discretionary increase in government spending. Explain how an improving economy will affect the budget balance and, in turn, investment and the trade balance.

17. Explain how decreased domestic investments that occur due to a budget deficit will affect future economic growth.

18. The U.S. government has shut down a number of times in recent history. Explain how a government shutdown will affect the variables in the national investment and savings identity. Could the shutdown affect the government budget deficit?

19. Explain how a shift from a government budget deficit to a budget surplus might affect the exchange rate.

20. Describe how a plan for reducing the government deficit might affect a college student, a young professional, and a middle-income family.

21. Explain whether or not you agree with the premise of the Ricardian equivalence theory that rational people might reason: "Well, a higher budget deficit (surplus) means that I'm just going to owe more (less) taxes in the future to pay off all that government borrowing, so I'll start saving (spending) now." Why or why not?

22. Explain why the government might prefer to provide incentives to private firms to do investment or research and development, rather than simply doing the spending itself?

23. Under what condition would crowding out not inhibit long-run economic growth? Under what condition would crowding out impede long-run economic growth?

24. What must take place for the government to run deficits without any crowding out?

PROBLEMS

25. Sketch a diagram of how a budget deficit causes a trade deficit. (*Hint*: Begin with what will happen to the exchange rate when foreigners demand more U.S. government debt.)

26. Sketch a diagram of how sustained budget deficits cause low economic growth.

27. Assume that the newly independent government of Tanzania employed you in 1964. Now free from British rule, the Tanzanian parliament has decided that it will spend 10 million shillings on schools, roads, and healthcare for the year. You estimate that the net taxes for the year are eight million shillings. The government will finance the difference by selling 10-year government bonds at 12% interest per year. Parliament must add the interest on outstanding bonds to government expenditure each year. Assume that Parliament places additional taxes to finance this increase in government expenditure so the gap between government spending is always two million. If the school, road, and healthcare budget are unchanged, compute the value of the accumulated debt in 10 years.

28. Illustrate the concept of Ricardian equivalence using the demand and supply of financial capital graph.

29. During the most recent recession, some economists argued that the change in the interest rates that comes about due to deficit spending implied in the demand and supply of financial capital graph would not occur. A simple reason was that the government was stepping in to invest when private firms were not. Using a graph, explain how the use by government in investment offsets the deficit demand.

This OpenStax book is available for free at http://cnx.org/content/col12122/1.4

32 | Macroeconomic Policy Around the World

Figure 32.1 Looking for Work Job fairs and job centers are often available to help match people to jobs. This fair took place in the U.S. (Hawaii), a high-income country with policies to keep unemployment levels in check. Unemployment is an issue that has different causes in different countries, and is especially severe in the low- and middle-income economies around the world. (Credit: modification of work by Daniel Ramirez/Flickr Creative Commons)

Bring it Home

Youth Unemployment: Three Cases

Chad Harding, a young man from Cape Town, South Africa, completed school having done well on his exams. He had high hopes for the future. Like many young South Africans, however, he had difficulty finding a job. "I was just stuck at home waiting, waiting for something to come up," he said in a BBC interview in 2012. In South Africa 54.6% of young females and 47.2% of males are unemployed. In fact, the problem is not limited to South Africa. Seventy-three million of the world's youth aged 15 to 24 are currently unemployed, according to the International Labour Organization.

According to the *Wall Street Journal,* in India, 60% of the labor force is self-employed, largely because of labor market regulation. A recent World Bank World Development Report says that India's unemployed youth accounted for 9.9% of the youth work force in 2010. In Spain (a far richer country) in the same year, the female/male youth unemployment rate was 39.8% and 43.2% respectively.

Youth unemployment is a significant issue in many parts of the world. However, despite the apparent similarities in rates between South Africa, Spain, and India, macroeconomic policy solutions to decrease youth unemployment in these three countries are different. This chapter will look at macroeconomic policies around the world, specifically those related to reducing unemployment, promoting economic growth, and stable inflation and exchange rates. Then we will look again at the three cases of South Africa, Spain, and India.

Introduction to Macroeconomic Policy around the World

In this chapter, you will learn about:

- The Diversity of Countries and Economies across the World

- Improving Countries' Standards of Living

- Causes of Unemployment around the World

- Causes of Inflation in Various Countries and Regions

- Balance of Trade Concerns

There are extraordinary differences in the composition and performance of economies across the world. What explains these differences? Are countries motivated by similar goals when it comes to macroeconomic policy? Can we apply the same macroeconomic framework that we developed in this text to understand the performance of these countries? Let's take each of these questions in turn.

Explaining differences: Recall from **Unemployment** that we explained the difference in composition and performance of economies by appealing to an aggregate production function. We argued that differences in productivity explain the diversity of average incomes across the world, which in turn were affected by inputs such as capital deepening, human capital, and "technology." Every economy has its own distinctive economic characteristics, institutions, history, and political realities, which imply that access to these "ingredients" will vary by country and so will economic performance.

For example, South Korea invested heavily in education and technology to increase agricultural productivity in the early 1950s. Some of this investment came from its historical relationship with the United States. As a result of these and many other institutions, its economy has managed to converge to the levels of income in leading economies like Japan and the United States.

Similar goals and frameworks: Many economies that have performed well in terms of per capita income have—for better or worse—been motivated by a similar goal: to maintain the quality of life of their citizens. Quality of life is a broad term, but as you can imagine it includes but is not limited to such things as low level of unemployment, price stability (low levels of inflation), and the ability to trade. These seem to be universal macroeconomic goals as we discussed in **The Macroeconomic Perspective**. No country would argue against them. To study macroeconomic policy around the world, we begin by comparing standards of living. In keeping with these goals, we also look at indicators such as unemployment, inflation, and the balance of trade policies across countries. Remember that every country has had a diverse set of experiences; therefore although our goals may be similar, each country may well require macroeconomic policies tailored to its circumstances.

Link It Up ⚭

For more reading on the topic of youth unemployment, visit this website (http://openstaxcollege.org/l/genjobless) to read "Generation Jobless" in the *Economist*.

This OpenStax book is available for free at http://cnx.org/content/col12122/1.4

32.1 | The Diversity of Countries and Economies across the World

By the end of this section, you will be able to:
- Analyze GDP per capita as a measure of the diversity of international standards of living
- Identify what classifies a country as low-income, middle-income, or high-income
- Explain how geography, demographics, industry structure, and economic institutions influence standards of living

The national economies that comprise the global economy are remarkably diverse. Let us use one key indicator of the standard of living, GDP per capita, to quantify this diversity. You will quickly see that quantifying this diversity is fraught with challenges and limitations. As we explained in **The Macroeconomic Perspective**, we must consider using purchasing power parity or "international dollars" to convert average incomes into comparable units. Purchasing power parity, as we formally defined in **Exchange Rates and International Capital Flows**, takes into account that prices of the same good are different across countries.

The Macroeconomic Perspective explained how to measure GDP, the challenges of using GDP to compare standards of living, and the difficulty of confusing economic size with distribution. In China's case, for example, China ranks as the second largest global economy, second to only the United States, with Japan ranking third. However, when we take China's GDP of $9.2 trillion and divide it by its population of 1.4 billion, then the per capita GDP is only $6,900, which is significantly lower than that of Japan, at $38,500, and that of the United States, at $52,800. Measurement issues aside, it's worth repeating that the goal, then, is to not only increase GDP, but to strive toward increased GDP per capita to increase overall living standards for individuals. As we have learned from **Economic Growth**, countries can achieve this at the national level by designing policies that increase worker productivity, deepen capital, and advance technology.

GDP per capita also allows us to rank countries into high-, middle-, or low-income groups. Low-income countries are those with $1,025 per capita GDP per year; middle-income countries have a per capita GDP between $1,025 and $12,475; while high-income countries have over $12,475 per year per capita income. As **Table 32.1** and **Figure 32.2** show, high-income countries earn 68% of world income, but represent just 12% of the global population. Low-income countries earn 1% of total world income, but represent 18.5% of global population.

Ranking based on GDP/capita	GDP (in billions)	% of Global GDP	Population	% of Global Population
Low income ($1,025 or less)	$612.7	0.8%	848,700,000	11.8%
Middle income ($1,025 - $12,475)	$23,930	31.7%	4,970,000,000	69.4%

Table 32.1 World Income versus Global Population (Source:http://databank.worldbank.org/data/views/reports/tableview.aspx?isshared=true&ispopular=series&pid=20)

Ranking based on GDP/capita	GDP (in billions)	% of Global GDP	Population	% of Global Population
High income (more than $12,475)	$51,090,000,000	67.5%	1,306,000,000	18.8%
World Total income	*$75,592,941*		*7,162,119,434*	

Table 32.1 World Income versus Global Population　(Source:http://databank.worldbank.org/data/ views/reports/tableview.aspx?isshared=true&ispopular=series&pid=20)

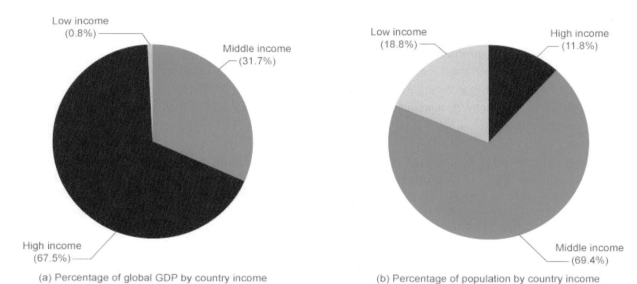

(a) Percentage of global GDP by country income　　　(b) Percentage of population by country income

Figure 32.2 Percent of Global GDP and Percent of Population　The pie charts show the GDP (from 2011) for countries categorized into low, middle, or high income. Low-income are those earning less than $1,025 (less than 1% of global income). They represent 18.5% of the world population. Middle-income countries are those with per capita income of $1,025–$12,475 (31.1% of global income). They represent 69.5% of world population. High-income countries have 68.3% of global income and 12% of the world's population. (Source: http://databank.worldbank.org/ data/views/reports/tableview.aspx?isshared=true&ispopular=series&pid=20)

An overview of the regional averages of GDP per person for developing countries, measured in comparable international dollars as well as population in 2008 (**Figure 32.3**), shows that the differences across these regions are stark. As **Table 32.2** shows, nominal GDP per capita in 2012 for the 581.4 million people living in Latin America and the Caribbean region was $9,190, which far exceeds that of South Asia and sub-Saharan Africa. In turn, people in the world's high-income nations, such as those who live in the European Union nations or North America, have a per capita GDP three to four times that of the people of Latin America. To put things in perspective, North America and the European Union have slightly more than 9% of the world's population, but they produce and consume close to 70% of the world's GDP.

This OpenStax book is available for free at http://cnx.org/content/col12122/1.4

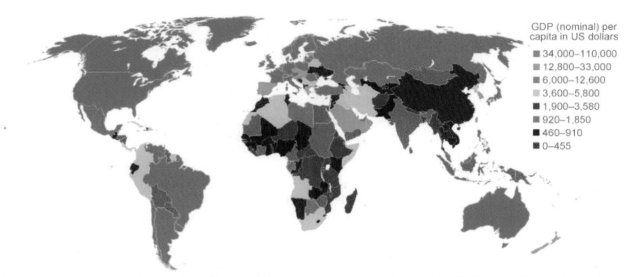

Figure 32.3 GDP Per Capita in U.S. Dollars (2008) There is a clear imbalance in the GDP across the world. North America, Australia, and Western Europe have the highest GDPs while large areas of the world have dramatically lower GDPs. (Credit: modification of work by Bsrboy/Wikimedia Commons)

	Population (in millions)	**GDP Per Capita**
East Asia and Pacific	2,006	$5,536
South Asia	1,671	$1,482
Sub-Saharan Africa	936.1	$1,657
Latin America and Caribbean	588	$9,536
Middle East and North Africa	345.4	$3,456
Europe and Central Asia	272.2	$7,118

Table 32.2 Regional Comparisons of Nominal GDP per Capita and Population in 2013 (Source: http://databank.worldbank.org/data/home.aspx)

Such comparisons between regions are admittedly rough. After all, per capita GDP cannot fully capture the quality of life. Many other factors have a large impact on the standard of living, like health, education, human rights, crime and personal safety, and environmental quality. These measures also reveal very wide differences in the standard of living across the regions of the world. Much of this is correlated with per capita income, but there are exceptions. For example, life expectancy at birth in many low-income regions approximates those who are more affluent. The data also illustrate that nobody can claim to have perfect standards of living. For instance, despite very high income levels, there is still undernourishment in Europe and North America.

Link It Up

Economists know that there are many factors that contribute to your standard of living. People in high-income countries may have very little time due to heavy workloads and may feel disconnected from their community. Lower-income countries may be more community centered, but have little in the way of material wealth. It is hard to measure these characteristics of standard of living. The Organization for Economic Co-Operation and Development has developed the "OECD Better Life Index." Visit this website (http://openstaxcollege.org/l/standofliving) to see how countries measure up to your expected standard of living.

The differences in economic statistics and other measures of well-being, substantial though they are, do not fully capture the reasons for the enormous differences between countries. Aside from the neoclassical determinants of growth, four additional determinants are significant in a wide range of statistical studies and are worth mentioning: geography, demography, industrial structure, and institutions.

Geographic and Demographic Differences

Countries have geographic differences: some have extensive coastlines, some are landlocked. Some have large rivers that have been a path of commerce for centuries, or mountains that have been a barrier to trade. Some have deserts, some have rain forests. These differences create different positive and negative opportunities for commerce, health, and the environment.

Countries also have considerable differences in the age distribution of the population. Many high-income nations are approaching a situation by 2020 or so in which the elderly will form a much larger share of the population. Most low-income countries still have a higher proportion of youth and young adults, but by about 2050, the elderly populations in these low-income countries are expected to boom as well. These demographic changes will have considerable impact on the standard of living of the young and the old.

Differences in Industry Structure and Economic Institutions

Countries have differences in industry structure. In the world's high-income economies, only about 2% of GDP comes from agriculture; the average for the rest of the world is 12%. Countries have strong differences in degree of urbanization.

Countries also have strong differences in economic institutions: some nations have economies that are extremely market-oriented, while other nations have command economies. Some nations are open to international trade, while others use tariffs and import quotas to limit the impact of trade. Some nations are torn by long-standing armed conflicts; other nations are largely at peace. There are also differences in political, religious, and social institutions.

No nation intentionally aims for a low standard of living, high rates of unemployment and inflation, or an unsustainable trade imbalance. However, nations will differ in their priorities and in the situations in which they find themselves, and so their policy choices can reasonably vary, too. The next modules will discuss how nations around the world, from high income to low income, approach the four macroeconomic goals of economic growth, low unemployment, low inflation, and a sustainable balance of trade.

32.2 | Improving Countries' Standards of Living

By the end of this section, you will be able to:
- Analyze the growth policies of low-income countries seeking to improve standards of living
- Analyze the growth policies of middle-income countries, particularly the East Asian Tigers with their focus on technology and market-oriented incentives
- Analyze the struggles facing economically-challenged countries wishing to enact growth policies
- Evaluate the success of sending aid to low-income countries

Jobs are created in economies that grow. What is the origin of economic growth? According to most economists who believe in the **growth consensus**, economic growth (as we discussed in **Economic Growth**) is built on a foundation of productivity improvements. In turn, productivity increases are the result of greater human and physical capital and technology, all interacting in a market-driven economy. In the pursuit of economic growth, however, some countries and regions start from different levels, as the differences in per capita GDP presented earlier in **Table 32.2** illustrate.

Growth Policies for the High-Income Countries

For the high-income countries, the challenge of economic growth is to push continually for a more educated workforce that can create, invest in, and apply new technologies. In effect, the goal of their growth-oriented public policy is to shift their aggregate supply curves to the right (refer to **The Aggregate Demand/Aggregate Supply Model**). The main public policies targeted at achieving this goal are fiscal policies focused on investment, including investment in human capital, in technology, and in physical plant and equipment. These countries also recognize that economic growth works best in a stable and market-oriented economic climate. For this reason, they use monetary policy to keep inflation low and stable, and to minimize the risk of exchange rate fluctuations, while also encouraging domestic and international competition.

However, early in the second decade of the 2000s, many high-income countries found themselves more focused on the short term than on the long term. The United States, Western Europe, and Japan all experienced a combination of financial crisis and deep recession, and the after-effects of the recession—like high unemployment rates—seemed likely to linger for several years. Most of these governments took aggressive, and in some cases controversial, steps to jump-start their economies by running very large budget deficits as part of expansionary fiscal policy. These countries must adopt a course that combines lower government spending and higher taxes.

Similarly, many central banks ran highly expansionary monetary policies, with both near-zero interest rates and unconventional loans and investments. For example, in 2012, Shinzo Abe (see **Figure 32.4**), then newly-elected Prime Minister of Japan, unveiled a plan to pull his country out of its two-decade-long slump in economic growth. It included both fiscal stimulus and an increase in the money supply. The plan was quite successful in the short run. However, according to the *Economist*, with public debt "expected to approach 240% of GDP," (as of 2012 it was 226% of GDP) printing money and public-works spending were only short-term solutions.

Figure 32.4 Japan's Prime Minister, Shinzo Abe Japan's Prime Minister used fiscal and monetary policies to stimulate his country's economy, which has worked in only the short run. (Credit: modification of work by Chatham House/Flickr Creative Commons)

As we discussed in other chapters, macroeconomics needs to have both a short-run and a long-run focus. The challenge for many of the developed countries in the next few years will be to exit from the short-term policies that they used to correct the 2008–2009 recession. Since the return to growth has been sluggish, it has been politically challenging for these governments to refocus their efforts on new technology, education, and physical capital investment.

Growth Policies for the Middle-Income Economies

The world's great economic success stories in the last few decades began in the 1970s with that group of nations sometimes known as the **East Asian Tigers**: South Korea, Thailand, Malaysia, Indonesia, and Singapore. The list sometimes includes Hong Kong and Taiwan, although often under international law they are treated as part of China, rather than as separate countries. The economic growth of the Tigers has been phenomenal, typically averaging 5.5% real per capita growth for several decades. In the 1980s, other countries began to show signs of convergence. China began growing rapidly, often at annual rates of 8% to 10% per year. India began growing rapidly, first at rates of about 5% per year in the 1990s, but then higher still in the first decade of the 2000s.

We know the underlying causes of these rapid growth rates:

- China and the East Asian Tigers, in particular, have been among the highest savers in the world, often saving one-third or more of GDP as compared to the roughly one-fifth of GDP, which would be a more typical saving rate in Latin America and Africa. These countries harnessed higher savings for domestic investment to build physical capital.

- These countries had policies that supported heavy investments in human capital, first building up primary-level education and then expanding secondary-level education. Many focused on encouraging math and science education, which is useful in engineering and business.

- Governments made a concerted effort to seek out applicable technology, by sending students and government commissions abroad to look at the most efficient industrial operations elsewhere. They also created policies to support innovative companies that wished to build production facilities to take advantage of the abundant and inexpensive human capital.

- China and India in particular also allowed far greater freedom for market forces, both within their own domestic economies and also in encouraging their firms to participate in world markets.

This combination of technology, human capital, and physical capital, combined with the incentives of a market-oriented economic context, proved an extremely powerful stimulant to growth. Challenges that these middle-income countries faced are a legacy of government economic controls that for political reasons can be dismantled only slowly over time. In many of them, the government heavily regulates the banking and financial sector. Governments have also sometimes selected certain industries to receive low-interest loans or government subsidies. These economies have found that an increased dose of market-oriented incentives for firms and workers has been a critical ingredient in the recipe for faster growth. To learn more about measuring economic growth, read the following Clear It Up feature.

What is the rule of 72?

It is worth pausing a moment to marvel at the East Asian Tigers' growth rates. If per capita GDP grows at, say, 6% per year, then you can apply the formula for compound growth rates—that is $(1 + 0.06)^{30}$—meaning a nation's level of per capita GDP will rise by a multiple of almost six over 30 years. Another strategy is to apply the rule of 72. The rule of 72 is an approximation to figure out doubling time. We divide the rule number, 72, by the annual growth rate to obtain the approximate number of years it will take for income to double. If we have a 6% growth rate, it will take 72/6, or 12 years, for incomes to double. Using this rule here suggests that a Tiger that grows at 6% will double its GDP every 12 years. In contrast, a technological leader, chugging along with per capita growth rates of about 2% per year, would double its income in 36 years.

Growth Policies for Economically-Challenged Countries

Many economically-challenged or low-income countries are geographically located in Sub-Saharan Africa. Other pockets of low income are in the former Soviet Bloc, and in parts of Central America and the Caribbean.

There are macroeconomic policies and prescriptions that might alleviate the extreme poverty and low standard of living. However, many of these countries lack the economic and legal stability, along with market-oriented institutions, needed to provide a fertile climate for domestic economic growth and to attract foreign investment. Thus, macroeconomic policies for low income economies are vastly different from those of the high income economies. The World Bank has made it a priority to combat poverty and raise overall income levels through 2030. One of the key obstacles to achieving this is the political instability that seems to be a common feature of low-income countries.

Figure 32.5 shows the ten lowest income countries as ranked by The World Bank in 2013. These countries share some common traits, the most significant of which is the recent failures of their governments to provide a legal framework for economic growth. Ethiopia and Eritrea recently ended a long-standing war in 2000. Civil and ethnic wars have plagued countries such as Burundi and Liberia. Command economies, corruption, as well as political factionalism and infighting are commonly adopted elements in these low-income countries. The Democratic Republic of the Congo (often referred to as "Congo") is a resource-wealthy country that has not been able to increase its subsistence standard of living due to the political environment.

This OpenStax book is available for free at http://cnx.org/content/col12122/1.4

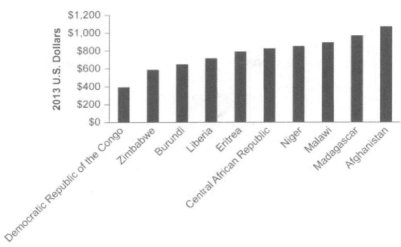

Figure 32.5 The Ten Lowest Income Countries This bar chart that shows ten low-income countries, which include, from lowest income to highest: Democratic Republic of the Congo, Zimbabwe, Burundi, Liberia, Eritrea, Central African Republic, Niger, Madagascar, and Afghanistan. (Source: http://databank.worldbank.org/data/views/reports/map.aspx#)

Low-income countries are at a disadvantage because any incomes that people receive are spent immediately on necessities such as food. People in these countries live on less than $1,035 per year, which is less than $100 per month. Lack of saving means a lack of capital accumulation and a lack of loanable funds for investment in physical and human capital. Recent research by two MIT economists, Abhijit Bannerjee and Esther Duflo, has confirmed that the households in these economies are trapped in low incomes because they cannot muster enough investment to push themselves out of poverty.

For example, the average citizen of Burundi, the lowest-income country, subsists on $150 per year (adjusted to 2005 dollars). According to Central Intelligence Agency data in its CIA Factbook, as of 2013, 90% of Burundi's population is agrarian, with coffee and tea as the main income producing crop. Only one in two children attends school and, as **Figure 32.6** shows, many are not in schools comparable to what occurs in developed countries. The CIA Factbook also estimates that 15% of Burundi's population suffers from HIV/AIDS. Political instability has made it difficult for Burundi to make significant headway toward growth, as verified by the electrification of only 2% of households and 42% of its national income coming from foreign aid.

Figure 32.6 Lack of Funds for Investing in Human Capital In low-income countries, people often spend all income on necessities for living and cannot accumulate or investe in physical or human capital. The students in this photograph learn in an outside "classroom" void of not only technology, but even chairs and desks. (Credit: Rafaela Printes/Flickr Creative Commons)

Link It Up

The World Factbook website (http://openstaxcollege.org/l/worldfactbook) is loaded with maps, flags, and other information about countries across the globe.

Other low-income countries share similar stories. These countries have found it difficult to generate investments for themselves or to find foreign investors willing to put up the money for more than the basic needs. Foreign aid and external investment comprise significant portions of the income in these economies, but are not sufficient to allow for the capital accumulation necessary to invest in physical and human capital. However, is foreign aid always a contributor to economic growth? It can be a controversial issue, as the next Clear it Up feature points out.

Clear It Up

Does foreign aid to low-income countries work?

According to the Organization of Economic Cooperation and Development (OECD), about $134 billion per year in foreign aid flows from the high-income countries of the world to the low-income ones. Relative to the size of their populations or economies, this is not a large amount for either donors or recipients. For low-income countries, aid averages about 1.3 percent of their GDP. However, even this relatively small amount has been highly controversial.

Supporters of additional foreign aid point to the extraordinary human suffering in the world's low-and middle-income countries. They see opportunities all across Africa, Asia, and Latin America to set up health clinics and schools. They want to help with the task of building economic infrastructure: clean water, plumbing, electricity, and roads. Supporters of this aid include formal state-sponsored institutions like the United Kingdom's Department for International Development (DFID) or independent non-governmental organizations (NGOs) like CARE International that also receive donor government funds. For example, because of an outbreak of meningitis in Ethiopia in 2010, DFID channeled significant funds to the Ethiopian Ministry of Health to train rural health care workers and also for vaccines. These monies helped the Ministry offset shortfalls in their budget.

Opponents of increased aid do not quarrel with the goal of reducing human suffering, but they suggest that foreign aid has often proved a poor tool for advancing that goal. For example, according to an article in the *Attaché Journal of International Affairs*, the Canadian foreign aid organization (CIDA) provided $100 million to Tanzania to grow wheat. The project did produce wheat, but nomadic pastoralists and other villagers who had lived on the land were driven off 100,000 acres of land to make way for the project. The damage in terms of human rights and lost livelihoods was significant. Villagers were beaten and killed because some refused to leave the land. At times, the unintended collateral damage from foreign aid can be significant.

William Easterly, professor of economics at New York University and author of *The White Man's Burden*, argues that countries often receive aid for political reasons and ends up doing more harm than good. If a country's government creates a reasonably stable and market-oriented macroeconomic climate, then foreign investors will be likely to provide funds for many profitable activities. For example, according to *The New York Times*, Facebook is partnering with multiple organizations in a project called Internet.org to provide access in remote and low-income areas of the world, and Google began its own initiative called Project Loon.

This OpenStax book is available for free at http://cnx.org/content/col12122/1.4

Facebook's first forays into providing internet access via mobile phones began in stable, market-oriented countries like India, Brazil, Indonesia, Turkey, and the Philippines.

Policymakers are now wiser about foreign aid limitations than they were a few decades ago. In targeted and specific cases, especially if foreign aid is channeled to long-term investment projects, foreign aid can have a modest role to play in reducing the extreme levels of deprivation that hundreds of millions of people around the world experience.

Link It Up 👓

Watch this video (http://openstaxcollege.org/l/foodafrica) on the complexities of providing economic aid in Africa.

32.3 | Causes of Unemployment around the World

By the end of this section, you will be able to:
- Explain the nature and causes of unemployment
- Analyze the natural rate of unemployment and the factors that affect it
- Identify how undeveloped labor markets can result in the same hardships as unemployment

We can categorize the causes of unemployment in the world's high-income countries in two ways: either cyclical unemployment caused by the economy when in a recession, or the natural rate of unemployment caused by factors in labor markets, such as government regulations regarding hiring and starting businesses.

Unemployment from a Recession

For unemployment caused by a recession, the Keynesian economic model points out that both monetary and fiscal policy tools are available. The monetary policy prescription for dealing with recession is straightforward: run an expansionary monetary policy to increase the quantity of money and loans, drive down interest rates, and increase aggregate demand. In a recession, there is usually relatively little danger of inflation taking off, and so even a central bank, with fighting inflation as its top priority, can usually justify some reduction in interest rates.

With regard to fiscal policy, the automatic stabilizers that we discussed in **Government Budgets and Fiscal Policy** should be allowed to work, even if this means larger budget deficits in times of recession. There is less agreement over whether, in addition to automatic stabilizers, governments in a recession should try to adopt discretionary fiscal policy of additional tax cuts or spending increases. In the case of the Great Recession, the case for this kind of extra-aggressive expansionary fiscal policy is stronger, but for a smaller recession, given the time lags of implementing fiscal policy, countries should use discretionary fiscal policy with caution.

However, the aftermath of the Recession emphasizes that expansionary fiscal and monetary policies do not turn off a recession like flipping a switch turns off a lamp. Even after a recession is officially over, and positive growth has returned, it can take some months—or even a couple of years—before private-sector firms believe the economic climate is healthy enough that they can expand their workforce.

The Natural Rate of Unemployment

Unemployment rates in European nations have typically been higher than in the United States. In 2006, before the start of the Great Recession, the U.S. unemployment rate was 4.6%, compared with 9% in France, 10.4% in Germany, and 7.1% in Sweden. We can attribute the pattern of generally higher unemployment rates in Europe, which dates back to the 1970s, to the fact that European economies have a higher natural rate of unemployment because they have a greater number of rules and restrictions that discourage firms from hiring and unemployed workers from taking jobs.

Addressing the natural rate of unemployment is straightforward in theory but difficult in practice. Government can play a useful role in providing unemployment and welfare payments, for example, by passing rules about where and when businesses can operate, and assuring that the workplace is safe. However, these well-intentioned laws can, in some cases, become so intrusive that businesses decide to place limits on their hiring.

For example, a law that imposes large costs on a business that tries to fire or lay off workers will mean that businesses try to avoid hiring in the first place, as is the case in France. According to *Business Week*, "France has 2.4 times as many companies with 49 employees as with 50 ... according to the French labor code, once a company has at least 50 employees inside France, management must create three worker councils, introduce profit sharing, and submit restructuring plans to the councils if the company decides to fire workers for economic reasons." This labor law essentially limits employment (or raises the natural rate of unemployment).

Undeveloped Labor Markets

Low-income and middle-income countries face employment issues that go beyond unemployment as it is understood in the high-income economies. A substantial number of workers in these economies provide many of their own needs by farming, fishing, or hunting. They barter and trade with others and may take a succession of short-term or one-day jobs, sometimes receiving pay with food or shelter, sometimes with money. They are not "unemployed" in the sense that we use the term in the United States and Europe, but neither are they employed in a regular wage-paying job.

The starting point of economic activity, as we discussed in **Welcome to Economics!**, is the division of labor, in which workers specialize in certain tasks and trade the fruits of their labor with others. Workers who are not connected to a labor market are often unable to specialize very much. Because these workers are not "officially" employed, they are often not eligible for social benefits like unemployment insurance or old-age payments—if such payments are even available in their country. Helping these workers to become more connected to the labor market and the economy is an important policy goal. Recent research by development economists suggests that one of the key factors in raising people in low-income countries out of the worst kind of poverty is whether they can make a connection to a somewhat regular wage-paying job.

32.4 | Causes of Inflation in Various Countries and Regions

By the end of this section, you will be able to:
- Identify the causes and effects of inflation in various economic markets
- Explain the significance of a converging economy

Policymakers of the high-income economies appear to have learned some lessons about fighting inflation. First, whatever happens with aggregate supply and aggregate demand in the short run, countries can use monetary policy to prevent inflation from becoming entrenched in the economy in the medium and long term. Second, there is no long-run gain to letting inflation become established. In fact, allowing inflation to become lasting and persistent poses undesirable risks and tradeoffs. When inflation is high, businesses and individuals need to spend time and effort worrying about protecting themselves against inflation, rather than seeking better ways to serve customers. In short, the high-income economies appear to have both a political consensus to hold inflation low and the economic tools to do so.

In a number of middle- and low-income economies around the world, inflation is far from a solved problem. In the early 2000s, Turkey experienced inflation of more than 50% per year for several years. Belarus had inflation of about 100% per year from 2000 to 2001. From 2008 to 2010, Venezuela and Myanmar had inflation rates of 20% to 30%

This OpenStax book is available for free at http://cnx.org/content/col12122/1.4

per year. Indonesia, Iran, Nigeria, the Russian Federation, and Ukraine all had double-digit inflation for most of the years from 2000 to 2010. Zimbabwe had hyperinflation, with inflation rates that went from more than 100% per year in the mid-2000s to a rate of several million percent in 2008.

In these countries, the problem of very high inflation generally arises from huge budget deficits, which the government finances by printing its domestic currency. This is a case of "too much money chasing too few goods." In the case of Zimbabwe, the government covered its widening deficits by printing ever higher currency notes, including a $100 trillion bill. By late 2008, the money was nearly worthless, which led Zimbabwe to adopt the U.S. dollar, immediately halting their hyperinflation. In some countries, the central bank makes loans to politically favored firms, essentially printing money to do so, and this too leads to higher inflation.

A number of countries have managed to sustain solid levels of economic growth for sustained periods of time with inflation levels that would sound high by recent U.S. standards, like 10% to 30% per year. In such economies, the governments index most contracts, wage levels, and interest rates to inflation. Indexing wage contracts and interest rates means that they will increase when inflation increases to retain purchasing power. When wages do not rise as price levels rise, this leads to a decline in the real wage rate and a decrease in the standard of living. Likewise, interest rates that are not indexed mean that money lenders will receive payment in devalued currency and will also lose purchasing power on monies that they lent. It is clearly possible—and perhaps sometimes necessary—for a **converging economy** (the economy of a country that demonstrates the ability to catch up to the technology leaders) to live with a degree of uncertainty over inflation that would be politically unacceptable in the high-income economies.

32.5 | Balance of Trade Concerns

By the end of this section, you will be able to:
- Explain the meaning of trade balance and its implications for the foreign exchange market
- Analyze concerns over international trade in goods and services and international flows of capital
- Identify and evaluate market-oriented economic reforms

In the 1950s and 1960s, and even into the 1970s, low- and middle-income countries often viewed openness to global flows of goods, services, and financial capital in a negative light. These countries feared that foreign trade would mean both economic losses as high-income trading partners "exploited" their economy and they lost domestic political control to powerful business interests and multinational corporations.

These negative feelings about international trade have evolved. After all, the great economic success stories of recent years like Japan, the East Asian Tiger economies, China, and India, all took advantage of opportunities to sell in global markets. European economies thrive with high levels of trade. In the North American Free Trade Agreement (NAFTA), the United States, Canada, and Mexico pledged themselves to reduce trade barriers. Many countries have clearly learned that reducing barriers to trade is at least potentially beneficial to the economy. Many smaller world economies have learned an even tougher lesson: if they do not participate actively in world trade, they are unlikely to join the success stories among the converging economies. There are no examples in world history of small economies that remained apart from the global economy but still attained a high standard of living.

Although almost every country now claims that its goal is to participate in global trade, the possible negative consequences have remained highly controversial. It is useful to divide these possible negative consequences into issues involving trade of goods and services and issues involving international capital flows. These issues are related, but not the same. An economy may have a high level of trade in goods and services relative to GDP, but if exports and imports are balanced, the net flow of foreign investment in and out of the economy will be zero. Conversely, an economy may have only a moderate level of trade relative to GDP, but find that it has a substantial current account trade imbalance. Thus, it is useful to consider the concerns over international trade of goods and services and international flows of financial capital separately.

Concerns over International Trade in Goods and Services

There is a long list of worries about foreign trade in goods and services: fear of job loss, environmental dangers, unfair labor practices, and many other concerns. We discuss these arguments at some length in the chapter on **The International Trade and Capital Flows**.

Of all of the arguments for limitations on trade, perhaps the most controversial one among economists is the infant industry argument; that is, subsidizing or protecting new industries for a time until they become established. (**Globalization and Protectionism** explains this concept in more detail.) Countries have used such policies with some success at certain points in time, but in the world as a whole, support for key industries is far more often directed at long-established industries with substantial political power that are suffering losses and laying off workers, rather than potentially vibrant new industries that are not yet established. If government intends to favor certain industries, it needs to do so in a way that is temporary and that orients them toward a future of market competition, rather than a future of unending government subsidies and trade protection.

Concerns over International Flows of Capital

Recall from **The Macroeconomic Perspective** that a trade deficit exists when a nation's imports exceed its exports. In order for a trade deficit to take place, foreign countries must provide loans or investments, which they are willing to do because they expect eventual repayment (that the deficit will become a surplus). A trade surplus, you may remember, exists when a nation's exports exceed its imports. Thus, in order for a trade deficit to switch to a trade surplus, a nation's exports must rise and its imports must fall. Sometimes this happens when the currency decreases in value. For example, if the U.S. had a trade deficit and the dollar depreciated, imports would become more expensive. This would, in turn, benefit the foreign countries that provided the loans or investments.

The expected pattern of trade imbalances in the world economy has been that high-income economies will run trade surpluses, which means they will experience a net outflow of capital to foreign destinations or export more than they import, while low- and middle-income economies will run trade deficits, which means that they will experience a net inflow of foreign capital.

This international investing pattern can benefit all sides. Investors in the high-income countries benefit because they can receive high returns on their investments, and also because they can diversify their investments so that they are at less risk of a downturn in their own domestic economy. The low-income economies that receive an inflow of capital presumably have potential for rapid catch-up economic growth, and they can use the international financial capital inflow to help spur their physical capital investment. In addition, financial capital inflows often come with management abilities, technological expertise, and training.

However, for the last couple of decades, this cheerful scenario has faced two "dark clouds." The first cloud is the very large trade or current account deficits in the U.S. economy. (See **The International Trade and Capital Flows.**) Instead of offering net financial investment abroad, the U.S. economy is soaking up savings from all over the world. These substantial U.S. trade deficits may not be sustainable according to Sebastian Edwards writing for the National Bureau of Economic Research. While trade deficits on their own are not bad, the question is whether governments will reduce them gradually or hastily. In the gradual scenario, U.S. exports could grow more rapidly than imports over a period of years, aided U.S. dollar depreciation. An unintended consequence of the slow growth since the Great Recession has been a decline in the U.S. current account deficit's from 6% pre-recession to 3% most recently.

The other option is that the government could reduce the U.S. trade deficit in a rush. Here is one scenario: if foreign investors became less willing to hold U.S. dollar assets, the dollar exchange rate could weaken. As speculators see this process happening, they might rush to unload their dollar assets, which would drive the dollar down still further.

A lower U.S. dollar would stimulate aggregate demand by making exports cheaper and imports more expensive. It would mean higher prices for imported inputs throughout the economy, shifting the short-term aggregate supply curve to the left. The result could be a burst of inflation and, if the Federal Reserve were to run a tight monetary policy to reduce the inflation, it could also lead to recession. People sometimes talk as if the U.S. economy, with its great size, is invulnerable to this sort of pressure from international markets. While it is difficult to rock, it is not impossible for the $17 trillion U.S. economy to face these international pressures.

The second "dark cloud" is how the smaller world economies should deal with the possibility of sudden foreign financial capital inflows and outflows. Perhaps the most vivid recent example of the potentially destructive forces of international capital movements occurred in the East Asian Tiger economies in 1997–1998. Thanks to their excellent growth performance over the previous few decades, these economies had attracted considerable interest from foreign investors. In the mid-1990s, however, foreign investment into these countries surged even further. Much of this money funneled through banks that borrowed in U.S. dollars and loaned in their national currencies. Bank lending surged at rates of 20% per year or more. This inflow of foreign capital meant that investment in these economies exceeded the level of domestic savings, so that current account deficits in these countries jumped into the 5–10% GDP range.

The surge in bank lending meant that many banks in these East Asian countries did not do an especially good job of screening out safe and unsafe borrowers. Many of the loans—as high as 10% to 15% of all loans in some of these countries—started to turn bad. Fearing losses, foreign investors started pulling out their money. As the foreign money left, the exchange rates of these countries crashed, often falling by 50% or more in a few months. The banks were stuck with a mismatch: even if the rest of their domestic loans were repaid, they could never pay back the U.S. dollars that they owed. The banking sector as a whole went bankrupt. The lack of credit and lending in the economy collapsed aggregate demand, bringing on a deep recession.

If the flow and ebb of international capital markets can flip even the economies of the East Asian Tigers, with their stellar growth records, into a recession, then it is no wonder that other middle- and low-income countries around the world are concerned. Moreover, similar episodes of an inflow and then an outflow of foreign financial capital have rocked a number of economies around the world: for example, in the last few years, economies like Ireland, Iceland, and Greece have all experienced severe shocks when foreign lenders decided to stop extending funds. Especially in Greece, this caused the government to enact austerity measures which led to protests throughout the country (**Figure 32.7**).

Figure 32.7 Protests in Greece The economic conditions in Greece have deteriorated from the Great Recession such that the government had to enact austerity measures, (strict rules) cutting wages and increasing taxes on its population. Massive protests are but one byproduct. (Credit: modification of work by Apostolos/Flickr Creative Commons)

Many nations are taking steps to reduce the risk that their economy will be injured if foreign financial capital takes flight, including having their central banks hold large reserves of foreign exchange and stepping up their regulation of domestic banks to avoid a wave of imprudent lending. The most controversial steps in this area involve whether countries should try to take steps to control or reduce the flows of foreign capital. If a country could discourage some speculative short-term capital inflow, and instead only encourage investment capital that it committed for the medium and the long term, then it could be at least somewhat less susceptible to swings in the sentiments of global investors.

If economies participate in the global trade of goods and services, they will also need to participate in international flows of financial payments and investments. These linkages can offer great benefits to an economy. However, any nation that is experiencing a substantial and sustained pattern of trade deficits, along with the corresponding net inflow of international financial capital, has some reason for concern. During the Asian Financial Crisis in the late 1990s, countries that grew dramatically in the years leading up to the crisis as international capital flowed in, saw their economies collapse when the capital very quickly flowed out.

Market-Oriented Economic Reforms

The standard of living has increased dramatically for billions of people around the world in the last half century. Such increases have occurred not only in the technological leaders like the United States, Canada, the nations of Europe, and Japan, but also in the East Asian Tigers and in many nations of Latin America and Eastern Europe. The challenge for most of these countries is to maintain these growth rates. The economically-challenged regions of the world have stagnated and become stuck in poverty traps. These countries need to focus on the basics: health and education, or human capital development. As **Figure 32.8** illustrates, modern technology allows for the investment in education and human capital development in ways that would have not been possible just a few short years ago.

Figure 32.8 Solar-powered Technology Modern technologies, such as solar-power and Wi-Fi, enable students to obtain education even in remote parts of a country without electricity. These students in Ghana are sharing a laptop provided by a van with solar-power. (Credit: EIFL/Flickr Creative Commons)

Other than the issue of economic growth, the other three main goals of macroeconomic policy—that is, low unemployment, low inflation, and a sustainable balance of trade—all involve situations in which, for some reason, the economy fails to coordinate the forces of supply and demand. In the case of cyclical unemployment, for example, the intersection of aggregate supply and aggregate demand occurs at a level of output below potential GDP. In the case of the natural rate of unemployment, government regulations create a situation where otherwise-willing employers become unwilling to hire otherwise-willing workers. Inflation is a situation in which aggregate demand outstrips aggregate supply, at least for a time, so that too much buying power is chasing too few goods. A trade imbalance is a situation where, because of a net inflow or outflow of foreign capital, domestic savings are not aligned with domestic investment. Each of these situations can create a range of easier or harder policy choices.

Bring it Home

Youth Unemployment: Three Cases

Spain and South Africa had the same high youth unemployment in 2011, but the reasons for this unemployment are different. Spain's youth unemployment surged due to the 2008-2009 Great Recession and heavy indebtedness on the part of its citizens and its government. Spain's current account balance is negative, which means it is borrowing heavily. To cure cyclical unemployment during a recession, the Keynesian model suggests increases in government spending—fiscal expansion or monetary expansion. Neither option is open to Spain. It currently can borrow at only high interest rates, which will be a real problem in terms of debt service. In addition, the rest of the European Union (EU) has dragged its feet when it comes to debt forgiveness. Monetary expansion is not possible because Spain uses the euro and cannot devalue its currency unless it convinces all of the EU to do so. What can be done? The *Economist*, summarizing some ideas of economists and policymakers, suggests that Spain's only realistic (although painful) option is to reduce government-mandated wages, which would allow it to reduce government spending. As a result, the government would be able to lower tax rates on the working population. With a lower wage or lower tax environment, firms will hire more workers. This will lower unemployment and stimulate the economy. Spain can also encourage greater foreign investment and try to promote policies that encourage domestic savings.

South Africa has more of a natural rate of unemployment problem. It is an interesting case because its youth unemployment is mostly because its young are not ready to work. Economists commonly refer to this as an employability problem. According to interviews of South African firms as reported in the *Economist*, the young are academically smart but lack practical skills for the workplace. Despite a big push to increase investment in human capital, the results have not yet borne fruit. Recently the government unveiled a plan to pay unemployed youth while they were "trained-up" or apprenticed in South African firms. The government has room to increase fiscal expenditure, encourage domestic savings, and continue to fund investment in education, vocational training, and apprentice programs. South Africa can also improve the climate for foreign investment from technology leaders, which would encourage economic growth.

India has a smaller youth employment problem in terms of percentages. However, bear in mind that since this is a populous country, it turns out to be a significant problem in raw numbers. According to Kaushik Basu, writing for the BBC, "there are 45 national laws governing the hiring and firing decisions of firms and close to four times that amount at the state level". These laws make it difficult for companies to fire workers. To stay nimble and responsive to markets, Indian companies respond to these laws by hiring fewer workers. The Indian government can do much to solve this problem by adjusting its labor laws. Essentially, the government has to remove itself from firms' hiring and firing decisions, so that growing Indian firms can freely employ more workers. Indian workers, like those in South Africa, do not have workforce skills. Again, the government can increase its spending on education, vocational training, and workforce readiness programs.

Finally, India has a significant current account deficit. This deficit is mainly a result of short- and long-term capital flows. To solve this deficit, India has experimented by lifting the limitation on domestic savers from investing abroad. This is a step in the right direction that may dampen the growth in the current account deficit. A final policy possibility is to improve domestic capital markets so many self-employed Indians can obtain access to capital to realize their business ideas. If more Indians can obtain access to capital to start businesses, employment might increase.

KEY TERMS

converging economy economy of a country that has demonstrated the ability to catch up to the technology leaders by
investing in both physical and human capital

East Asian Tigers the economies of Taiwan, Singapore, Hong Kong, and South Korea, which maintained high growth
rates and rapid export-led industrialization between the early 1960s and 1990 allowing them to converge with the
technological leaders in high-income countries

growth consensus a series of studies that show, statistically, that 70% of the differences in income per person across
the world is explained by differences in physical capital (savings/investment)

high-income country nation with a per capita income of $12,475 or more; typically has high levels of human and
physical capital

low-income country a nation that has a per capita income of less than $1,025; a third of the world's population

middle-income country a nation with per capita income between $1,025 and $12, 475 and that has shown some
ability, even if not always sustained, to catch up to the technology leaders in high-income countries

KEY CONCEPTS AND SUMMARY

32.1 The Diversity of Countries and Economies across the World
Macroeconomic policy goals for most countries strive toward low levels of unemployment and inflation, as well
as stable trade balances. Economists analyze countries based on their GDP per person and ranked as low-, middle-
, and high-income countries. Low-income are those earning less than $1,025 (less than 1%) of global income.
They currently have 18.5% of the world population. Middle-income countries are those with per capital income of
$1,025–$12,475 (31.1% of global income). They have 69.5% of world population. High-income countries are those
with per capita income greater than $12,475 (68.3% of global income). They have 12% of the world's population.
Regional comparisons tend to be inaccurate because even countries within those regions tend to differ from each
other.

32.2 Improving Countries' Standards of Living
The fundamentals of growth are the same in every country: improvements in human capital, physical capital, and
technology interacting in a market-oriented economy. Countries that are high-income tend to focus on developing
and using new technology. Countries that are middle-income focus on increasing human capital and becoming
more connected to technology and global markets. They have charted unconventional paths by relying more on
state-led support rather than relying solely on markets. Low-income, economically-challenged countries have many
health and human development needs, but they are also challenged by the lack of investment and foreign aid to
develop infrastructure like roads. There are some bright spots when it comes to financial development and mobile
communications, which suggest that low-income countries can become technology leaders in their own right, but it
is too early to claim victory. These countries must do more to connect to the rest of the global economy and find the
technologies that work best for them.

32.3 Causes of Unemployment around the World
We can address cyclical unemployment by expansionary fiscal and monetary policy. The natural rate of
unemployment can be harder to solve, because it involves thinking carefully about the tradeoffs involved in laws that
affect employment and hiring. Unemployment is understood differently in high-income countries compared to low-
and middle-income countries. People in these countries are not "unemployed" in the sense that we use the term in the
United States and Europe, but neither are they employed in a regular wage-paying job. While some may have regular
wage-paying jobs, others are part of a barter economy.

32.4 Causes of Inflation in Various Countries and Regions
Most high-income economies have learned that their central banks can control inflation in the medium and the long

This OpenStax book is available for free at http://cnx.org/content/col12122/1.4

term. In addition, they have learned that inflation has no long-term benefits but potentially substantial long-term costs if it distracts businesses from focusing on real productivity gains. However, smaller economies around the world may face more volatile inflation because their smaller economies can be unsettled by international movements of capital and goods.

32.5 Balance of Trade Concerns

There are many legitimate concerns over possible negative consequences of free trade. Perhaps the single strongest response to these concerns is that there are good ways to address them without restricting trade and thus losing its benefits. There are two major issues involving trade imbalances. One is what will happen with the large U.S. trade deficits, and whether they will come down gradually or with a rush. The other is whether smaller countries around the world should take some steps to limit flows of international capital, in the hope that they will not be quite so susceptible to economic whiplash from international financial capital flowing in and out of their economies.

SELF-CHECK QUESTIONS

1. Using the data in **Table 32.3**, rank the seven regions of the world according to GDP and then according to GDP per capita.

	Population (in millions)	GDP Per Capita	GDP = Population × Per Capita GDP (in millions)
East Asia and Pacific	2,006	$5,536	$10,450,032
South Asia	1,671	$1,482	$2,288,812
Sub-Saharan Africa	936.1	$1,657	$1,287,650
Latin America and Caribbean	588	$9,536	$5,339,390
Middle East and North Africa	345.4	$3,456	$1,541,900
Europe and Central Asia	272.2	$7,118	$1,862,384

Table 32.3 GDP and Population of Seven Regions of the World

2. What are the drawbacks to analyzing the global economy on a regional basis?

3. Create a table that identifies the macroeconomic policies for a high-income country, a middle-income country, and a low-income country.

4. Use the data in the text to contrast the policy prescriptions of the high-income, middle-income, and low-income countries.

5. What are the different policy tools for dealing with cyclical unemployment?

6. Explain how the natural rate of unemployment may be higher in low-income countries.

7. How does indexing wage contracts to inflation help workers?

8. Use the AD/AS model to show how increases in government spending can lead to more inflation.

9. Show, using the AD/AS model, how governments can use monetary policy to decrease the price level.

10. What do international flows of capital have to do with trade imbalances?

11. Use the demand-and-supply of foreign currency graph to determine what would happen to a small, open economy that experienced capital outflows.

REVIEW QUESTIONS

12. What is the primary way in which economists measure standards of living?

13. What are some of the other ways of comparing the standard of living in countries around the world?

14. What are the four other factors that determine the economic standard of living around the world?

15. What other factors, aside from labor productivity, capital investment, and technology, impact the economic growth of a country? How?

16. What strategies did the East Asian Tigers employ to stimulate economic growth?

17. What are the two types of unemployment problems?

18. In low-income countries, does it make sense to argue that most of the people without long-term jobs are unemployed?

19. Is inflation likely to be a severe problem for at least some high-income economies in the near future?

20. Is inflation likely to be a problem for at least some low- and middle-income economies in the near future?

21. What are the major issues with regard to trade imbalances for the U.S. economy?

22. What are the major issues with regard to trade imbalances for low- and middle-income countries?

CRITICAL THINKING QUESTIONS

23. Demography can have important economic effects. The United States has an aging population. Explain one economic benefit and one economic cost of an aging population as well as of a population that is very young.

24. Explain why is it difficult to set aside funds for investment when you are in poverty.

25. Why do you think it is difficult for high-income countries to achieve high growth rates?

26. Is it possible to protect workers from losing their jobs without distorting the labor market?

27. Explain what will happen in a nation that tries to solve a structural unemployment problem using expansionary monetary and fiscal policy. Draw one AD/AS diagram, based on the Keynesian model, for what the nation hopes will happen. Then draw a second AD/AS diagram, based on the neoclassical model, for what is more likely to happen.

28. Why are inflationary dangers lower in the high-income economies than in low-income and middle-income economies?

29. Explain why converging economies may present a strong argument for limiting flows of capital but not for limiting trade.

This OpenStax book is available for free at http://cnx.org/content/col12122/1.4

PROBLEMS

30. Retrieve the following data from The World Bank database (http://databank.worldbank.org/data/home.aspx) for India, Spain, and South Africa for the most recent year available:

- GDP in constant international dollars or PPP
- Population
- GDP per person in constant international dollars
- Mortality rate, infant (per 1,000 live births)
- Health expenditure per capita (current U.S. dollars)
- Life expectancy at birth, total (years)

31. Prepare a chart that compares India, Spain, and South Africa based on the data you find. Describe the key differences between the countries. Rank these as high-, medium-, and low-income countries, explain what is surprising or expected about this data.

32. Use the Rule of 72 to estimate how long it will take for India, Spain, and South Africa to double their standards of living.

33. Using the research skills you have acquired, retrieve the following data from The World Bank database (http://databank.worldbank.org/data/home.aspx) for India, Spain, and South Africa for 2010–2015, if available:

- Telephone lines
- Mobile cellular subscriptions
- Secure Internet servers (per one million people)
- Electricity production (kWh)

Prepare a chart that compares these three countries. Describe the key differences between the countries.

34. Retrieve the unemployment data from The World Bank database (http://databank.worldbank.org/data/home.aspx) for India, Spain, and South Africa for 2011-2015. Prepare a chart that compares India, Spain, and South Africa based on the data. Describe the key differences between the countries. Rank these countries as high-, medium-, and low-income countries. Explain what is surprising or expected about this data. How did the Great Recession impact these countries?

35. Retrieve inflation data from The World Bank data base (http://databank.worldbank.org/data/home.aspx) for India, Spain, and South Africa for 2011–2015. Prepare a chart that compares India, Spain, and South Africa based on the data. Describe the key differences between the countries. Rank these countries as high-, medium-, and low-income. Explain what is surprising or expected about the data.

This OpenStax book is available for free at http://cnx.org/content/col12122/1.4

33 | International Trade

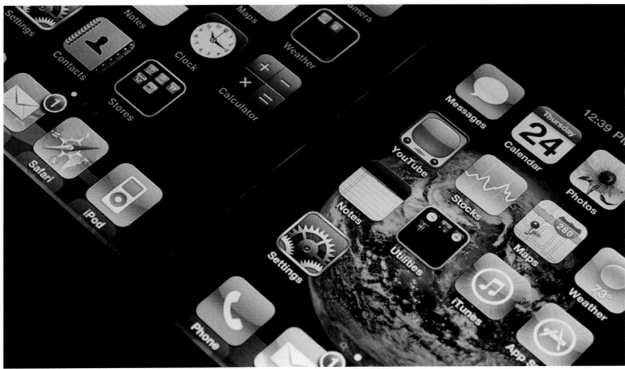

Figure 33.1 Apple or Samsung iPhone? While the iPhone is readily recognized as an Apple product, 26% of the component costs in it come from components made by rival phone-maker, Samsung. In international trade, there are often "conflicts" like this as each country or company focuses on what it does best. (Credit: modification of work by Yutaka Tsutano Creative Commons)

Bring it Home

Just Whose iPhone Is It?

The iPhone is a global product. Apple does not manufacture the iPhone components, nor does it assemble them. The assembly is done by Foxconn Corporation, a Taiwanese company, at its factory in Sengzhen, China. But, Samsung, the electronics firm and competitor to Apple, actually supplies many of the parts that make up an iPhone—representing about 26% of the costs of production. That means, that Samsung is both the biggest supplier and biggest competitor for Apple. Why do these two firms work together to produce the iPhone? To understand the economic logic behind international trade, you have to accept, as these firms do, that trade is about mutually beneficial exchange. Samsung is one of the world's largest electronics parts suppliers. Apple lets Samsung focus on making the best parts, which allows Apple to concentrate on its strength—designing elegant products that are easy to use. If each company (and by extension each country) focuses on what it does best, there will be gains for all through trade.

Introduction to International Trade

In this chapter, you will learn about:

- Absolute and Comparative Advantage

- What Happens When a Country Has an Absolute Advantage in All Goods

- Intra-industry Trade between Similar Economies

- The Benefits of Reducing Barriers to International Trade

We live in a global marketplace. The food on your table might include fresh fruit from Chile, cheese from France, and bottled water from Scotland. Your wireless phone might have been made in Taiwan or Korea. The clothes you wear might be designed in Italy and manufactured in China. The toys you give to a child might have come from India. The car you drive might come from Japan, Germany, or Korea. The gasoline in the tank might be refined from crude oil from Saudi Arabia, Mexico, or Nigeria. As a worker, if your job is involved with farming, machinery, airplanes, cars, scientific instruments, or many other technology-related industries, the odds are good that a hearty proportion of the sales of your employer—and hence the money that pays your salary—comes from export sales. We are all linked by international trade, and the volume of that trade has grown dramatically in the last few decades.

The first wave of globalization started in the nineteenth century and lasted up to the beginning of World War I. Over that time, global exports as a share of global GDP rose from less than 1% of GDP in 1820 to 9% of GDP in 1913. As the Nobel Prize-winning economist Paul Krugman of Princeton University wrote in 1995:

> It is a late-twentieth-century conceit that we invented the global economy just yesterday. In fact, world markets achieved an impressive degree of integration during the second half of the nineteenth century. Indeed, if one wants a specific date for the beginning of a truly global economy, one might well choose 1869, the year in which both the Suez Canal and the Union Pacific railroad were completed. By the eve of the First World War steamships and railroads had created markets for standardized commodities, like wheat and wool, that were fully global in their reach. Even the global flow of information was better than modern observers, focused on electronic technology, tend to realize: the first submarine telegraph cable was laid under the Atlantic in 1858, and by 1900 all of the world's major economic regions could effectively communicate instantaneously.

This first wave of globalization crashed to a halt early in the twentieth century. World War I severed many economic connections. During the Great Depression of the 1930s, many nations misguidedly tried to fix their own economies by reducing foreign trade with others. World War II further hindered international trade. Global flows of goods and financial capital were rebuilt only slowly after World War II. It was not until the early 1980s that global economic forces again became as important, relative to the size of the world economy, as they were before World War I.

33.1 | Absolute and Comparative Advantage

By the end of this section, you will be able to:
- Define absolute advantage, comparative advantage, and opportunity costs
- Explain the gains of trade created when a country specializes

The American statesman Benjamin Franklin (1706–1790) once wrote: "No nation was ever ruined by trade." Many economists would express their attitudes toward international trade in an even more positive manner. The evidence that international trade confers overall benefits on economies is pretty strong. Trade has accompanied economic growth in the United States and around the world. Many of the national economies that have shown the most rapid growth in the last several decades—for example, Japan, South Korea, China, and India—have done so by dramatically orienting their economies toward international trade. There is no modern example of a country that has shut itself off from world trade and yet prospered. To understand the benefits of trade, or why we trade in the first place, we need to understand the concepts of comparative and absolute advantage.

In 1817, David Ricardo, a businessman, economist, and member of the British Parliament, wrote a treatise called *On the Principles of Political Economy and Taxation*. In this treatise, Ricardo argued that specialization and free trade benefit all trading partners, even those that may be relatively inefficient. To see what he meant, we must be able to distinguish between absolute and comparative advantage.

A country has an **absolute advantage** over another country in producing a good if it uses fewer resources to produce that good. Absolute advantage can be the result of a country's natural endowment. For example, extracting oil in

Saudi Arabia is pretty much just a matter of "drilling a hole." Producing oil in other countries can require considerable exploration and costly technologies for drilling and extraction—if they have any oil at all. The United States has some of the richest farmland in the world, making it easier to grow corn and wheat than in many other countries. Guatemala and Colombia have climates especially suited for growing coffee. Chile and Zambia have some of the world's richest copper mines. As some have argued, "geography is destiny." Chile will provide copper and Guatemala will produce coffee, and they will trade. When each country has a product others need and it can produce it with fewer resources in one country than in another, then it is easy to imagine all parties benefitting from trade. However, thinking about trade just in terms of geography and absolute advantage is incomplete. Trade really occurs because of comparative advantage.

Recall from the chapter **Choice in a World of Scarcity** that a country has a comparative advantage when it can produce a good at a lower cost in terms of other goods. The question each country or company should be asking when it trades is this: "What do we give up to produce this good?" It should be no surprise that the concept of comparative advantage is based on this idea of opportunity cost from **Choice in a World of Scarcity**. For example, if Zambia focuses its resources on producing copper, it cannot use its labor, land and financial resources to produce other goods such as corn. As a result, Zambia gives up the opportunity to produce corn. How do we quantify the cost in terms of other goods? Simplify the problem and assume that Zambia just needs labor to produce copper and corn. The companies that produce either copper or corn tell you that it takes two hours to mine a ton of copper and one hour to harvest a bushel of corn. This means the opportunity cost of producing a ton of copper is two bushels of corn. The next section develops absolute and comparative advantage in greater detail and relates them to trade.

Visit this website (http://openstaxcollege.org/l/WTO) for a list of articles and podcasts pertaining to international trade topics.

A Numerical Example of Absolute and Comparative Advantage

Consider a hypothetical world with two countries, Saudi Arabia and the United States, and two products, oil and corn. Further assume that consumers in both countries desire both these goods. These goods are homogeneous, meaning that consumers/producers cannot differentiate between corn or oil from either country. There is only one resource available in both countries, labor hours. Saudi Arabia can produce oil with fewer resources, while the United States can produce corn with fewer resources. **Table 33.1** illustrates the advantages of the two countries, expressed in terms of how many hours it takes to produce one unit of each good.

Country	Oil (hours per barrel)	Corn (hours per bushel)
Saudi Arabia	1	4
United States	2	1

Table 33.1 How Many Hours It Takes to Produce Oil and Corn

In **Table 33.1**, Saudi Arabia has an absolute advantage in producing oil because it only takes an hour to produce a barrel of oil compared to two hours in the United States. The United States has an absolute advantage in producing corn.

To simplify, let's say that Saudi Arabia and the United States each have 100 worker hours (see **Table 33.2**). **Figure 33.2** illustrates what each country is capable of producing on its own using a production possibility frontier (PPF) graph. Recall from **Choice in a World of Scarcity** that the production possibilities frontier shows the maximum amount that each country can produce given its limited resources, in this case workers, and its level of technology.

Country	Oil Production using 100 worker hours (barrels)		Corn Production using 100 worker hours (bushels)
Saudi Arabia	100	or	25
United States	50	or	100

Table 33.2 Production Possibilities before Trade

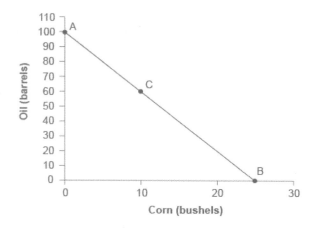

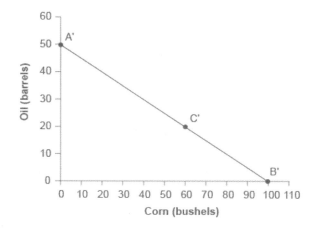

(a) Saudi Arabia

(b) The United States

Figure 33.2 Production Possibilities Frontiers   (a) Saudi Arabia can produce 100 barrels of oil at maximum and zero corn (point A), or 25 bushels of corn and zero oil (point B). It can also produce other combinations of oil and corn if it wants to consume both goods, such as at point C. Here it chooses to produce/consume 60 barrels of oil, leaving 40 work hours that to allocate to produce 10 bushels of corn, using the data in **Table 33.1**. (b) If the United States produces only oil, it can produce, at maximum, 50 barrels and zero corn (point A'), or at the other extreme, it can produce a maximum of 100 bushels of corn and no oil (point B'). Other combinations of both oil and corn are possible, such as point C'. All points above the frontiers are impossible to produce given the current level of resources and technology.

Arguably Saudi and U.S. consumers desire both oil and corn to live. Let's say that before trade occurs, both countries produce and consume at point C or C'. Thus, before trade, the Saudi Arabian economy will devote 60 worker hours to produce oil, as **Table 33.3** shows. Given the information in **Table 33.1**, this choice implies that it produces/consumes 60 barrels of oil. With the remaining 40 worker hours, since it needs four hours to produce a bushel of corn, it can produce only 10 bushels. To be at point C', the U.S. economy devotes 40 worker hours to produce 20 barrels of oil and it can allocate the remaining worker hours to produce 60 bushels of corn.

Country	Oil Production (barrels)	Corn Production (bushels)
Saudi Arabia (C)	60	10

Table 33.3 Production before Trade

This OpenStax book is available for free at http://cnx.org/content/col12122/1.4

Country	Oil Production (barrels)	Corn Production (bushels)
United States (C')	20	60
Total World Production	**80**	**70**

Table 33.3 Production before Trade

The slope of the production possibility frontier illustrates the opportunity cost of producing oil in terms of corn. Using all its resources, the United States can produce 50 barrels of oil *or* 100 bushels of corn; therefore, the opportunity cost of one barrel of oil is two bushels of corn—or the slope is 1/2. Thus, in the U.S. production possibility frontier graph, every increase in oil production of one barrel implies a decrease of two bushels of corn. Saudi Arabia can produce 100 barrels of oil *or* 25 bushels of corn. The opportunity cost of producing one barrel of oil is the loss of 1/4 of a bushel of corn that Saudi workers could otherwise have produced. In terms of corn, notice that Saudi Arabia gives up the least to produce a barrel of oil. **Table 33.4** summarizes these calculations.

Country	Opportunity cost of one unit — Oil (in terms of corn)	Opportunity cost of one unit — Corn (in terms of oil)
Saudi Arabia	¼	4
United States	2	½

Table 33.4 Opportunity Cost and Comparative Advantage

Again recall that we defined comparative advantage as the opportunity cost of producing goods. Since Saudi Arabia gives up the least to produce a barrel of oil, ($\frac{1}{4} < 2$ in **Table 33.4**) it has a comparative advantage in oil production.

The United States gives up the least to produce a bushel of corn, so it has a comparative advantage in corn production.

In this example, there is symmetry between absolute and comparative advantage. Saudi Arabia needs fewer worker hours to produce oil (absolute advantage, see **Table 33.1**), and also gives up the least in terms of other goods to produce oil (comparative advantage, see **Table 33.4**). Such symmetry is not always the case, as we will show after we have discussed gains from trade fully, but first, read the following Clear It Up feature to make sure you understand why the PPF line in the graphs is straight.

Can a production possibility frontier be straight?

When you first met the production possibility frontier (PPF) in the chapter on **Choice in a World of Scarcity** we drew it with an outward-bending shape. This shape illustrated that as we transferred inputs from producing one good to another—like from education to health services—there were increasing opportunity costs. In the examples in this chapter, we draw the PPFs as straight lines, which means that opportunity costs are constant. When we transfer a marginal unit of labor away from growing corn and toward producing oil, the decline in the quantity of corn and the increase in the quantity of oil is always the same. In reality this is possible only if the contribution of additional workers to output did not change as the scale of production changed. The linear production possibilities frontier is a less realistic model, but a straight line simplifies calculations. It also illustrates economic themes like absolute and comparative advantage just as clearly.

Gains from Trade

Consider the trading positions of the United States and Saudi Arabia after they have specialized and traded. Before trade, Saudi Arabia produces/consumes 60 barrels of oil and 10 bushels of corn. The United States produces/ consumes 20 barrels of oil and 60 bushels of corn. Given their current production levels, if the United States can trade an amount of corn fewer than 60 bushels and receives in exchange an amount of oil greater than 20 barrels, it will **gain from trade**. With trade, the United States can consume more of both goods than it did without specialization and trade. (Recall that the chapter **Welcome to Economics!** defined specialization as it applies to workers and firms. Economists also use specialization to describe the occurrence when a country shifts resources to focus on producing a good that offers comparative advantage.) Similarly, if Saudi Arabia can trade an amount of oil less than 60 barrels and receive in exchange an amount of corn greater than 10 bushels, it will have more of both goods than it did before specialization and trade. **Table 33.5** illustrates the range of trades that would benefit both sides.

The U.S. economy, after specialization, will benefit if it:	The Saudi Arabian economy, after specialization, will benefit if it:
Exports no more than 60 bushels of corn	Imports at least 10 bushels of corn
Imports at least 20 barrels of oil	Exports less than 60 barrels of oil

Table 33.5 The Range of Trades That Benefit Both the United States and Saudi Arabia

The underlying reason why trade benefits both sides is rooted in the concept of opportunity cost, as the following Clear It Up feature explains. If Saudi Arabia wishes to expand domestic production of corn in a world without international trade, then based on its opportunity costs it must give up four barrels of oil for every one additional bushel of corn. If Saudi Arabia could find a way to give up less than four barrels of oil for an additional bushel of corn (or equivalently, to receive more than one bushel of corn for four barrels of oil), it would be better off.

Clear It Up

What are the opportunity costs and gains from trade?

The range of trades that will benefit each country is based on the country's opportunity cost of producing each good. The United States can produce 100 bushels of corn or 50 barrels of oil. For the United States, the opportunity cost of producing one barrel of oil is two bushels of corn. If we divide the numbers above by 50, we get the same ratio: one barrel of oil is equivalent to two bushels of corn, or (100/50 = 2 and 50/50 = 1). In a trade with Saudi Arabia, if the United States is going to give up 100 bushels of corn in exports, it must import at least 50 barrels of oil to be just as well off. Clearly, to gain from trade it needs to be able to gain more than a half barrel of oil for its bushel of corn—or why trade at all?

Recall that David Ricardo argued that if each country specializes in its comparative advantage, it will benefit from trade, and total global output will increase. How can we show gains from trade as a result of comparative advantage and specialization? **Table 33.6** shows the output assuming that each country specializes in its comparative advantage and produces no other good. This is 100% specialization. Specialization leads to an increase in total world production. (Compare the total world production in **Table 33.3** to that in **Table 33.6**.)

Country	Quantity produced after 100% specialization — Oil (barrels)	Quantity produced after 100% specialization — Corn (bushels)
Saudi Arabia	100	0

Table 33.6 How Specialization Expands Output

This OpenStax book is available for free at http://cnx.org/content/col12122/1.4

Country	Quantity produced after 100% specialization — Oil (barrels)	Quantity produced after 100% specialization — Corn (bushels)
United States	0	100
Total World Production	100	100

Table 33.6 How Specialization Expands Output

What if we did not have complete specialization, as in **Table 33.6**? Would there still be gains from trade? Consider another example, such as when the United States and Saudi Arabia start at C and C', respectively, as **Figure 33.2** shows. Consider what occurs when trade is allowed and the United States exports 20 bushels of corn to Saudi Arabia in exchange for 20 barrels of oil.

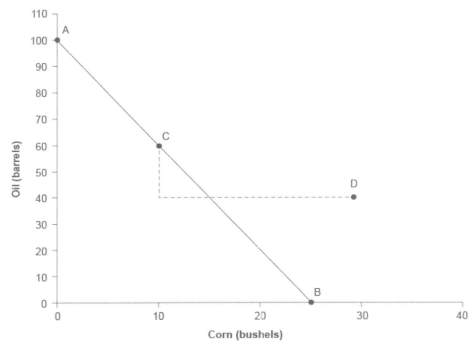

Figure 33.3 Production Possibilities Frontier in Saudi Arabia   Trade allows a country to go beyond its domestic production-possibility frontier

Starting at point C, which shows Saudi oil production of 60, reduce Saudi oil domestic oil consumption by 20, since 20 is exported to the United States and exchanged for 20 units of corn. This enables Saudi to reach point D, where oil consumption is now 40 barrels and corn consumption has increased to 30 (see **Figure 33.3**). Notice that even without 100% specialization, if the "trading price," in this case 20 barrels of oil for 20 bushels of corn, is greater than the country's opportunity cost, the Saudis will gain from trade. Since the post-trade consumption point D is beyond its production possibility frontier, Saudi Arabia has gained from trade.

Link It Up

Visit this website (http://wits.worldbank.org/trade-visualization.aspx) for trade-related data visualizations.

33.2 | What Happens When a Country Has an Absolute Advantage in All Goods

By the end of this section, you will be able to:
- Show the relationship between production costs and comparative advantage
- Identify situations of mutually beneficial trade
- Identify trade benefits by considering opportunity costs

What happens to the possibilities for trade if one country has an absolute advantage in everything? This is typical for high-income countries that often have well-educated workers, technologically advanced equipment, and the most up-to-date production processes. These high-income countries can produce all products with fewer resources than a low-income country. If the high-income country is more productive across the board, will there still be gains from trade? Good students of Ricardo understand that trade is about mutually beneficial exchange. Even when one country has an absolute advantage in all products, trade can still benefit both sides. This is because gains from trade come from specializing in one's comparative advantage.

Production Possibilities and Comparative Advantage

Consider the example of trade between the United States and Mexico described in **Table 33.7**. In this example, it takes four U.S. workers to produce 1,000 pairs of shoes, but it takes five Mexican workers to do so. It takes one U.S. worker to produce 1,000 refrigerators, but it takes four Mexican workers to do so. The United States has an absolute advantage in productivity with regard to both shoes and refrigerators; that is, it takes fewer workers in the United States than in Mexico to produce both a given number of shoes and a given number of refrigerators.

Country	Number of Workers needed to produce 1,000 units — Shoes	Number of Workers needed to produce 1,000 units — Refrigerators
United States	4 workers	1 worker
Mexico	5 workers	4 workers

Table 33.7 Resources Needed to Produce Shoes and Refrigerators

Absolute advantage simply compares the productivity of a worker between countries. It answers the question, "How many inputs do I need to produce shoes in Mexico?" Comparative advantage asks this same question slightly differently. Instead of comparing how many workers it takes to produce a good, it asks, "How much am I giving up to produce this good in this country?" Another way of looking at this is that comparative advantage identifies the good for which the producer's absolute advantage is relatively larger, or where the producer's absolute productivity disadvantage is relatively smaller. The United States can produce 1,000 shoes with four-fifths as many workers as Mexico (four versus five), but it can produce 1,000 refrigerators with only one-quarter as many workers (one versus four). So, the comparative advantage of the United States, where its absolute productivity advantage is relatively

This OpenStax book is available for free at http://cnx.org/content/col12122/1.4

greatest, lies with refrigerators, and Mexico's comparative advantage, where its absolute productivity disadvantage is least, is in the production of shoes.

Mutually Beneficial Trade with Comparative Advantage

When nations increase production in their area of comparative advantage and trade with each other, both countries can benefit. Again, the production possibility frontier is a useful tool to visualize this benefit.

Consider a situation where the United States and Mexico each have 40 workers. For example, as **Table 33.8** shows, if the United States divides its labor so that 40 workers are making shoes, then, since it takes four workers in the United States to make 1,000 shoes, a total of 10,000 shoes will be produced. (If four workers can make 1,000 shoes, then 40 workers will make 10,000 shoes). If the 40 workers in the United States are making refrigerators, and each worker can produce 1,000 refrigerators, then a total of 40,000 refrigerators will be produced.

Country	Shoe Production — using 40 workers		Refrigerator Production — using 40 workers
United States	10,000 shoes	or	40,000 refrigerators
Mexico	8,000 shoes	or	10,000 refrigerators

Table 33.8 Production Possibilities before Trade with Complete Specialization

As always, the slope of the production possibility frontier for each country is the opportunity cost of one refrigerator in terms of foregone shoe production–when labor is transferred from producing the latter to producing the former (see **Figure 33.4**).

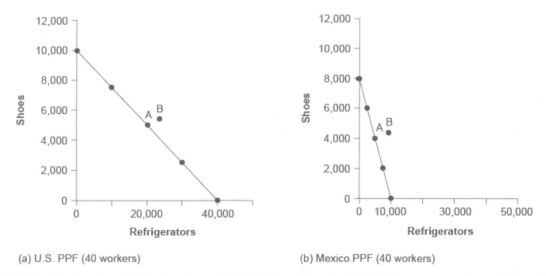

(a) U.S. PPF (40 workers)   (b) Mexico PPF (40 workers)

Figure 33.4 Production Possibility Frontiers (a) With 40 workers, the United States can produce either 10,000 shoes and zero refrigerators or 40,000 refrigerators and zero shoes. (b) With 40 workers, Mexico can produce a maximum of 8,000 shoes and zero refrigerators, or 10,000 refrigerators and zero shoes. All other points on the production possibility line are possible combinations of the two goods that can be produced given current resources. Point A on both graphs is where the countries start producing and consuming before trade. Point B is where they end up after trade.

Let's say that, in the situation before trade, each nation prefers to produce a combination of shoes and refrigerators that is shown at point A. **Table 33.9** shows the output of each good for each country and the total output for the two countries.

Country	Current Shoe Production	Current Refrigerator Production
United States	5,000	20,000
Mexico	4,000	5,000
Total	**9,000**	**25,000**

Table 33.9 Total Production at Point A before Trade

Continuing with this scenario, suppose that each country transfers some amount of labor toward its area of comparative advantage. For example, the United States transfers six workers away from shoes and toward producing refrigerators. As a result, U.S. production of shoes decreases by 1,500 units (6/4 × 1,000), while its production of refrigerators increases by 6,000 (that is, 6/1 × 1,000). Mexico also moves production toward its area of comparative advantage, transferring 10 workers away from refrigerators and toward production of shoes. As a result, production of refrigerators in Mexico falls by 2,500 (10/4 × 1,000), but production of shoes increases by 2,000 pairs (10/5 × 1,000). Notice that when both countries shift production toward each of their comparative advantages (what they are relatively better at), their combined production of both goods rises, as shown in **Table 33.10**. The reduction of shoe production by 1,500 pairs in the United States is more than offset by the gain of 2,000 pairs of shoes in Mexico, while the reduction of 2,500 refrigerators in Mexico is more than offset by the additional 6,000 refrigerators produced in the United States.

Country	Shoe Production	Refrigerator Production
United States	3,500	26,000
Mexico	6,000	2,500
Total	**9,500**	**28,500**

Table 33.10 Shifting Production Toward Comparative Advantage Raises Total Output

This numerical example illustrates the remarkable insight of comparative advantage: even when one country has an absolute advantage in all goods and another country has an absolute disadvantage in all goods, both countries can still benefit from trade. Even though the United States has an absolute advantage in producing both refrigerators and shoes, it makes economic sense for it to specialize in the good for which it has a comparative advantage. The United States will export refrigerators and in return import shoes.

How Opportunity Cost Sets the Boundaries of Trade

This example shows that both parties can benefit from specializing in their comparative advantages and trading. By using the opportunity costs in this example, it is possible to identify the range of possible trades that would benefit each country.

Mexico started out, before specialization and trade, producing 4,000 pairs of shoes and 5,000 refrigerators (see **Figure 33.4** and **Table 33.9**). Then, in the numerical example given, Mexico shifted production toward its comparative advantage and produced 6,000 pairs of shoes but only 2,500 refrigerators. Thus, if Mexico can export no more than 2,000 pairs of shoes (giving up 2,000 pairs of shoes) in exchange for imports of at least 2,500 refrigerators (a gain of 2,500 refrigerators), it will be able to consume more of both goods than before trade. Mexico will be unambiguously better off. Conversely, the United States started off, before specialization and trade, producing 5,000 pairs of shoes and 20,000 refrigerators. In the example, it then shifted production toward its comparative advantage, producing only 3,500 shoes but 26,000 refrigerators. If the United States can export no more than 6,000 refrigerators in exchange for imports of at least 1,500 pairs of shoes, it will be able to consume more of both goods and will be unambiguously better off.

The range of trades that can benefit both nations is shown in **Table 33.11**. For example, a trade where the U.S. exports 4,000 refrigerators to Mexico in exchange for 1,800 pairs of shoes would benefit both sides, in the sense that

This OpenStax book is available for free at http://cnx.org/content/col12122/1.4

both countries would be able to consume more of both goods than in a world without trade.

The U.S. economy, after specialization, will benefit if it:	The Mexican economy, after specialization, will benefit if it:
Exports fewer than 6,000 refrigerators	*Imports* at least 2,500 refrigerators
Imports at least 1,500 pairs of shoes	*Exports* no more than 2,000 pairs of shoes

Table 33.11 The Range of Trades That Benefit Both the United States and Mexico

Trade allows each country to take advantage of lower opportunity costs in the other country. If Mexico wants to produce more refrigerators without trade, it must face its domestic opportunity costs and reduce shoe production. If Mexico, instead, produces more shoes and then trades for refrigerators made in the United States, where the opportunity cost of producing refrigerators is lower, Mexico can in effect take advantage of the lower opportunity cost of refrigerators in the United States. Conversely, when the United States specializes in its comparative advantage of refrigerator production and trades for shoes produced in Mexico, international trade allows the United States to take advantage of the lower opportunity cost of shoe production in Mexico.

The theory of comparative advantage explains why countries trade: they have different comparative advantages. It shows that the gains from international trade result from pursuing comparative advantage and producing at a lower opportunity cost. The following Work It Out feature shows how to calculate absolute and comparative advantage and the way to apply them to a country's production.

Work It Out

Calculating Absolute and Comparative Advantage

In Canada a worker can produce 20 barrels of oil or 40 tons of lumber. In Venezuela, a worker can produce 60 barrels of oil or 30 tons of lumber.

Country	Oil (barrels)		Lumber (tons)
Canada	20	or	40
Venezuela	60	or	30

Table 33.12

a. Who has the absolute advantage in the production of oil or lumber? How can you tell?

b. Which country has a comparative advantage in the production of oil?

c. Which country has a comparative advantage in producing lumber?

d. In this example, is absolute advantage the same as comparative advantage, or not?

e. In what product should Canada specialize? In what product should Venezuela specialize?

Step 1. Make a table like Table 33.12.

Step 2. To calculate absolute advantage, look at the larger of the numbers for each product. One worker in Canada can produce more lumber (40 tons versus 30 tons), so Canada has the absolute advantage in lumber. One worker in Venezuela can produce 60 barrels of oil compared to a worker in Canada who can produce only 20.

Step 3. To calculate comparative advantage, find the opportunity cost of producing one barrel of oil in both countries. The country with the lowest opportunity cost has the comparative advantage. With the same labor time, Canada can produce either 20 barrels of oil or 40 tons of lumber. So in effect, 20 barrels of oil is equivalent to 40 tons of lumber: 20 oil = 40 lumber. Divide both sides of the equation by 20 to calculate the opportunity cost of one barrel of oil in Canada. 20/20 oil = 40/20 lumber. 1 oil = 2 lumber. To produce one additional barrel of oil in Canada has an opportunity cost of 2 lumber. Calculate the same way for Venezuela: 60 oil = 30 lumber. Divide both sides of the equation by 60. One oil in Venezuela has an opportunity cost of 1/2 lumber. Because 1/2 lumber < 2 lumber, Venezuela has the comparative advantage in producing oil.

Step 4. Calculate the opportunity cost of one lumber by reversing the numbers, with lumber on the left side of the equation. In Canada, 40 lumber is equivalent in labor time to 20 barrels of oil: 40 lumber = 20 oil. Divide each side of the equation by 40. The opportunity cost of one lumber is 1/2 oil. In Venezuela, the equivalent labor time will produce 30 lumber or 60 oil: 30 lumber = 60 oil. Divide each side by 30. One lumber has an opportunity cost of two oil. Canada has the lower opportunity cost in producing lumber.

Step 5. In this example, absolute advantage is the same as comparative advantage. Canada has the absolute and comparative advantage in lumber; Venezuela has the absolute and comparative advantage in oil.

Step 6. Canada should specialize in the commodity for which it has a relative lower opportunity cost, which is lumber, and Venezuela should specialize in oil. Canada will be exporting lumber and importing oil, and Venezuela will be exporting oil and importing lumber.

Comparative Advantage Goes Camping

To build an intuitive understanding of how comparative advantage can benefit all parties, set aside examples that involve national economies for a moment and consider the situation of a group of friends who decide to go camping together. The six friends have a wide range of skills and experiences, but one person in particular, Jethro, has done lots of camping before and is also a great athlete. Jethro has an absolute advantage in all aspects of camping: he is faster at carrying a backpack, gathering firewood, paddling a canoe, setting up tents, making a meal, and washing up. So here is the question: Because Jethro has an absolute productivity advantage in everything, should he do all the work?

Of course not! Even if Jethro is willing to work like a mule while everyone else sits around, he, like all mortals, only has 24 hours in a day. If everyone sits around and waits for Jethro to do everything, not only will Jethro be an unhappy camper, but there will not be much output for his group of six friends to consume. The theory of comparative advantage suggests that everyone will benefit if they figure out their areas of comparative advantage—that is, the area of camping where their productivity disadvantage is least, compared to Jethro. For example, it may be that Jethro is 80% faster at building fires and cooking meals than anyone else, but only 20% faster at gathering firewood and 10% faster at setting up tents. In that case, Jethro should focus on building fires and making meals, and others should attend to the other tasks, each according to where their productivity disadvantage is smallest. If the campers coordinate their efforts according to comparative advantage, they can all gain.

33.3 | Intra-industry Trade between Similar Economies

By the end of this section, you will be able to:
- Identify at least two advantages of intra-industry trading
- Explain the relationship between economies of scale and intra-industry trade

Absolute and comparative advantages explain a great deal about global trading patterns. For example, they help to explain the patterns that we noted at the start of this chapter, like why you may be eating fresh fruit from Chile or Mexico, or why lower productivity regions like Africa and Latin America are able to sell a substantial proportion of their exports to higher productivity regions like the European Union and North America. Comparative advantage, however, at least at first glance, does not seem especially well-suited to explain other common patterns of international trade.

The Prevalence of Intra-industry Trade between Similar Economies

The theory of comparative advantage suggests that trade should happen between economies with large differences in opportunity costs of production. Roughly half of all world trade involves shipping goods between the fairly similar

This OpenStax book is available for free at http://cnx.org/content/col12122/1.4

high-income economies of the United States, Canada, the European Union, Japan, Mexico, and China (see **Table 33.13**).

Country	U.S. Exports Go to ...	U.S. Imports Come from ...
European Union	19.0%	21.0%
Canada	22.0%	14.0%
Japan	4.0%	6.0%
Mexico	15.0%	13.0%
China	8.0%	20.0%

Table 33.13 Where U.S. Exports Go and U.S. Imports Originate (2015) (Source: https://www.census.gov/foreign-trade/Press-Release/current_press_release/ft900.pdf)

Moreover, the theory of comparative advantage suggests that each economy should specialize to a degree in certain products, and then exchange those products. A high proportion of trade, however, is **intra-industry trade**—that is, trade of goods within the same industry from one country to another. For example, the United States produces and exports autos and imports autos. **Table 33.14** shows some of the largest categories of U.S. exports and imports. In all of these categories, the United States is both a substantial exporter and a substantial importer of goods from the same industry. In 2014, according to the Bureau of Economic Analysis, the United States exported $146 billion worth of autos, and imported $327 billion worth of autos. About 60% of U.S. trade and 60% of European trade is intra-industry trade.

Some U.S. Exports	Quantity of Exports ($ billions)	Quantity of Imports ($ billions)
Autos	$146	$327
Food and beverages	$144	$126
Capital goods	$550	$551
Consumer goods	$199	$558
Industrial supplies	$507	$665
Other transportation	$45	$55

Table 33.14 Some Intra-Industry U.S. Exports and Imports in 2014 (Source: http://www.bea.gov/newsreleases/international/trade/tradnewsrelease.htm)

Why do similar high-income economies engage in intra-industry trade? What can be the economic benefit of having workers of fairly similar skills making cars, computers, machinery and other products which are then shipped across the oceans to and from the United States, the European Union, and Japan? There are two reasons: (1) The division of labor leads to learning, innovation, and unique skills; and (2) economies of scale.

Gains from Specialization and Learning

Consider the category of machinery, where the U.S. economy has considerable intra-industry trade. Machinery comes in many varieties, so the United States may be exporting machinery for manufacturing with wood, but importing machinery for photographic processing. The underlying reason why a country like the United States, Japan, or Germany produces one kind of machinery rather than another is usually not related to U.S., German, or Japanese firms and workers having generally higher or lower skills. It is just that, in working on very specific and particular products, firms in certain countries develop unique and different skills.

Specialization in the world economy can be very finely split. In fact, recent years have seen a trend in international trade, which economists call **splitting up the value chain**. The **value chain** describes how a good is produced in stages. As indicated in the beginning of the chapter, producing the iPhone involves designing and engineering the phone in the United States, supplying parts from Korea, assembling the parts in China, and advertising and marketing in the United States. Thanks in large part to improvements in communication technology, sharing information, and transportation, it has become easier to split up the value chain. Instead of production in a single large factory, different firms operating in various places and even different countries can divide the value chain. Because firms split up the value chain, international trade often does not involve nations trading whole finished products like automobiles or refrigerators. Instead, it involves shipping more specialized goods like, say, automobile dashboards or the shelving that fits inside refrigerators. Intra-industry trade between similar countries produces economic gains because it allows workers and firms to learn and innovate on particular products—and often to focus on very particular parts of the value chain.

Visit this website (http://openstaxcollege.org/l/iphoneassembly) for some interesting information about the assembly of the iPhone.

Economies of Scale, Competition, Variety

A second broad reason that intra-industry trade between similar nations produces economic gains involves economies of scale. The concept of economies of scale, as we introduced in **Production, Costs and Industry Structure**, means that as the scale of output goes up, average costs of production decline—at least up to a point. **Figure 33.5** illustrates economies of scale for a plant producing toaster ovens. The horizontal axis of the figure shows the quantity of production by a certain firm or at a certain manufacturing plant. The vertical axis measures the average cost of production. Production plant S produces a small level of output at 30 units and has an average cost of production of $30 per toaster oven. Plant M produces at a medium level of output at 50 units, and has an average cost of production of $20 per toaster oven. Plant L produces 150 units of output with an average cost of production of only $10 per toaster oven. Although plant V can produce 200 units of output, it still has the same unit cost as Plant L.

In this example, a small or medium plant, like S or M, will not be able to compete in the market with a large or a very large plant like L or V, because the firm that operates L or V will be able to produce and sell its output at a lower price. In this example, economies of scale operate up to point L, but beyond point L to V, the additional scale of production does not continue to reduce average costs of production.

This OpenStax book is available for free at http://cnx.org/content/col12122/1.4

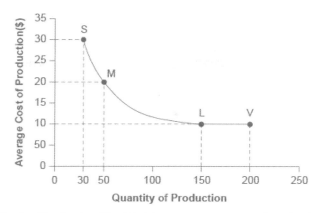

Figure 33.5 Economies of Scale Production Plant S, has an average cost of production of $30 per toaster oven. Production plant M has an average cost of production of $20 per toaster oven. Production plant L has an average cost of production of only $10 per toaster oven. Production plant V still has an average cost of production of $10 per toaster oven. Thus, production plant M can produce toaster ovens more cheaply than plant S because of economies of scale, and plants L or V can produce more cheaply than S or M because of economies of scale. However, the economies of scale end at an output level of 150. Plant V, despite being larger, cannot produce more cheaply on average than plant L.

The concept of economies of scale becomes especially relevant to international trade when it enables one or two large producers to supply the entire country. For example, a single large automobile factory could probably supply all the cars consumers purchase in a smaller economy like the United Kingdom or Belgium in a given year. However, if a country has only one or two large factories producing cars, and no international trade, then consumers in that country would have relatively little choice between kinds of cars (other than the color of the paint and other nonessential options). Little or no competition will exist between different car manufacturers.

International trade provides a way to combine the lower average production costs that come from economies of scale and still have competition and variety for consumers. Large automobile factories in different countries can make and sell their products around the world. If General Motors, Ford, and Chrysler were the only players in the U.S. automobile market, the level of competition and consumer choice would be considerably lower than when U.S. carmakers must face competition from Toyota, Honda, Suzuki, Fiat, Mitsubishi, Nissan, Volkswagen, Kia, Hyundai, BMW, Subaru, and others. Greater competition brings with it innovation and responsiveness to what consumers want. America's car producers make far better cars now than they did several decades ago, and much of the reason is competitive pressure, especially from East Asian and European carmakers.

Dynamic Comparative Advantage

The sources of gains from intra-industry trade between similar economies—namely, the learning that comes from a high degree of specialization and splitting up the value chain and from economies of scale—do not contradict the earlier theory of comparative advantage. Instead, they help to broaden the concept.

In intra-industry trade, climate or geography do not determine the level of worker productivity. Even the general level of education or skill does not determine it. Instead, how firms engage in specific learning about specialized products, including taking advantage of economies of scale determine the level of worker productivity. In this vision, comparative advantage can be dynamic—that is, it can evolve and change over time as one develops new skills and as manufacturers split the value chain in new ways. This line of thinking also suggests that countries are not destined to have the same comparative advantage forever, but must instead be flexible in response to ongoing changes in comparative advantage.

33.4 | The Benefits of Reducing Barriers to International Trade

By the end of this section, you will be able to:
- Explain tarrifs as barriers to trade
- Identify at least two benefits of reducing barriers to international trade

Tariffs are taxes that governments place on imported goods for a variety of reasons. Some of these reasons include protecting sensitive industries, for humanitarian reasons, and protecting against dumping. Traditionally, tariffs were used simply as a political tool to protect certain vested economic, social, and cultural interests. The World Trade Organization (WTO) is committed to lowering barriers to trade. The world's nations meet through the WTO to negotiate how they can reduce barriers to trade, such as tariffs. WTO negotiations happen in "rounds," where all countries negotiate one agreement to encourage trade, take a year or two off, and then start negotiating a new agreement. The current round of negotiations is called the Doha Round because it was officially launched in Doha, the capital city of Qatar, in November 2001. In 2009, economists from the World Bank summarized recent research and found that the Doha round of negotiations would increase the size of the world economy by $160 billion to $385 billion per year, depending on the precise deal that ended up being negotiated.

In the context of a global economy that currently produces more than $30 trillion of goods and services each year, this amount is not huge: it is an increase of 1% or less. But before dismissing the gains from trade too quickly, it is worth remembering two points.

- First, a gain of a few hundred billion dollars is enough money to deserve attention! Moreover, remember that this increase is not a one-time event; it would persist each year into the future.

- Second, the estimate of gains may be on the low side because some of the gains from trade are not measured especially well in economic statistics. For example, it is difficult to measure the potential advantages to consumers of having a variety of products available and a greater degree of competition among producers. Perhaps the most important unmeasured factor is that trade between countries, especially when firms are splitting up the value chain of production, often involves a transfer of knowledge that can involve skills in production, technology, management, finance, and law.

Low-income countries benefit more from trade than high-income countries do. In some ways, the giant U.S. economy has less need for international trade, because it can already take advantage of internal trade within its economy. However, many smaller national economies around the world, in regions like Latin America, Africa, the Middle East, and Asia, have much more limited possibilities for trade inside their countries or their immediate regions. Without international trade, they may have little ability to benefit from comparative advantage, slicing up the value chain, or economies of scale. Moreover, smaller economies often have fewer competitive firms making goods within their economy, and thus firms have less pressure from other firms to provide the goods and prices that consumers want.

The economic gains from expanding international trade are measured in hundreds of billions of dollars, and the gains from international trade as a whole probably reach well into the trillions of dollars. The potential for gains from trade may be especially high among the smaller and lower-income countries of the world.

Visit this website (http://openstaxcollege.org/l/tradebenefits) for a list of some benefits of trade.

This OpenStax book is available for free at http://cnx.org/content/col12122/1.4

From Interpersonal to International Trade

Most people find it easy to believe that they, personally, would not be better off if they tried to grow and process all of their own food, to make all of their own clothes, to build their own cars and houses from scratch, and so on. Instead, we all benefit from living in economies where people and firms can specialize and trade with each other.

The benefits of trade do not stop at national boundaries, either. Earlier we explained that the division of labor could increase output for three reasons: (1) workers with different characteristics can specialize in the types of production where they have a comparative advantage; (2) firms and workers who specialize in a certain product become more productive with learning and practice; and (3) economies of scale. These three reasons apply from the individual and community level right up to the international level. If it makes sense to you that interpersonal, intercommunity, and interstate trade offer economic gains, it should make sense that international trade offers gains, too.

International trade currently involves about $20 trillion worth of goods and services moving around the globe. Any economic force of that size, even if it confers overall benefits, is certain to cause disruption and controversy. This chapter has only made the case that trade brings economic benefits. Other chapters discuss, in detail, the public policy arguments over whether to restrict international trade.

Bring it Home

It's Apple's (Global) iPhone

Apple Corporation uses a global platform to produce the iPhone. Now that you understand the concept of comparative advantage, you can see why the engineering and design of the iPhone is done in the United States. The United States has built up a comparative advantage over the years in designing and marketing products, and sacrifices fewer resources to design high-tech devices relative to other countries. China has a comparative advantage in assembling the phone due to its large skilled labor force. Korea has a comparative advantage in producing components. Korea focuses its production by increasing its scale, learning better ways to produce screens and computer chips, and uses innovation to lower average costs of production. Apple, in turn, benefits because it can purchase these quality products at lower prices. Put the global assembly line together and you have the device with which we are all so familiar.

KEY TERMS

absolute advantage when one country can use fewer resources to produce a good compared to another country; when a country is more productive compared to another country

gain from trade a country that can consume more than it can produce as a result of specialization and trade

intra-industry trade international trade of goods within the same industry

splitting up the value chain many of the different stages of producing a good happen in different geographic locations

tariffs taxes that governments place on imported goods

value chain how a good is produced in stages

KEY CONCEPTS AND SUMMARY

33.1 Absolute and Comparative Advantage

A country has an absolute advantage in those products in which it has a productivity edge over other countries; it takes fewer resources to produce a product. A country has a comparative advantage when it can produce a good at a lower cost in terms of other goods. Countries that specialize based on comparative advantage gain from trade.

33.2 What Happens When a Country Has an Absolute Advantage in All Goods

Even when a country has high levels of productivity in all goods, it can still benefit from trade. Gains from trade come about as a result of comparative advantage. By specializing in a good that it gives up the least to produce, a country can produce more and offer that additional output for sale. If other countries specialize in the area of their comparative advantage as well and trade, the highly productive country is able to benefit from a lower opportunity cost of production in other countries.

33.3 Intra-industry Trade between Similar Economies

A large share of global trade happens between high-income economies that are quite similar in having well-educated workers and advanced technology. These countries practice intra-industry trade, in which they import and export the same products at the same time, like cars, machinery, and computers. In the case of intra-industry trade between economies with similar income levels, the gains from trade come from specialized learning in very particular tasks and from economies of scale. Splitting up the value chain means that several stages of producing a good take place in different countries around the world.

33.4 The Benefits of Reducing Barriers to International Trade

Tariffs are placed on imported goods as a way of protecting sensitive industries, for humanitarian reasons, and for protection against dumping. Traditionally, tariffs were used as a political tool to protect certain vested economic, social, and cultural interests. The WTO has been, and continues to be, a way for nations to meet and negotiate in order to reduce barriers to trade. The gains of international trade are very large, especially for smaller countries, but are beneficial to all.

SELF-CHECK QUESTIONS

1. True or False: The source of comparative advantage must be natural elements like climate and mineral deposits. Explain.

2. Brazil can produce 100 pounds of beef or 10 autos. In contrast the United States can produce 40 pounds of beef or 30 autos. Which country has the absolute advantage in beef? Which country has the absolute advantage in producing autos? What is the opportunity cost of producing one pound of beef in Brazil? What is the opportunity cost of producing one pound of beef in the United States?

3. In France it takes one worker to produce one sweater, and one worker to produce one bottle of wine. In Tunisia it takes two workers to produce one sweater, and three workers to produce one bottle of wine. Who has the absolute advantage in production of sweaters? Who has the absolute advantage in the production of wine? How can you tell?

4. In Germany it takes three workers to make one television and four workers to make one video camera. In Poland it takes six workers to make one television and 12 workers to make one video camera.
- a. Who has the absolute advantage in the production of televisions? Who has the absolute advantage in the production of video cameras? How can you tell?
- b. Calculate the opportunity cost of producing one additional television set in Germany and in Poland. (Your calculation may involve fractions, which is fine.) Which country has a comparative advantage in the production of televisions?
- c. Calculate the opportunity cost of producing one video camera in Germany and in Poland. Which country has a comparative advantage in the production of video cameras?
- d. In this example, is absolute advantage the same as comparative advantage, or not?
- e. In what product should Germany specialize? In what product should Poland specialize?

5. How can there be any economic gains for a country from both importing and exporting the same good, like cars?

6. Table 33.15 shows how the average costs of production for semiconductors (the "chips" in computer memories) change as the quantity of semiconductors built at that factory increases.
- a. Based on these data, sketch a curve with quantity produced on the horizontal axis and average cost of production on the vertical axis. How does the curve illustrate economies of scale?
- b. If the equilibrium quantity of semiconductors demanded is 90,000, can this economy take full advantage of economies of scale? What about if quantity demanded is 70,000 semiconductors? 50,000 semiconductors? 30,000 semiconductors?
- c. Explain how international trade could make it possible for even a small economy to take full advantage of economies of scale, while also benefiting from competition and the variety offered by several producers.

Quantity of Semiconductors	Average Total Cost
10,000	$8 each
20,000	$5 each
30,000	$3 each
40,000	$2 each
100,000	$2 each

Table 33.15

7. If the removal of trade barriers is so beneficial to international economic growth, why would a nation continue to restrict trade on some imported or exported products?

REVIEW QUESTIONS

8. What is absolute advantage? What is comparative advantage?

9. Under what conditions does comparative advantage lead to gains from trade?

10. What factors does Paul Krugman identify that supported expanding international trade in the 1800s?

11. Is it possible to have a comparative advantage in the production of a good but not to have an absolute advantage? Explain.

12. How does comparative advantage lead to gains from trade?

13. What is intra-industry trade?

14. What are the two main sources of economic gains from intra-industry trade?

15. What is splitting up the value chain?

CRITICAL THINKING QUESTIONS

17. Are differences in geography behind the differences in absolute advantages?

18. Why does the United States not have an absolute advantage in coffee?

19. Look at **Exercise 33.2**. Compute the opportunity costs of producing sweaters and wine in both France and Tunisia. Who has the lowest opportunity cost of producing sweaters and who has the lowest opportunity cost of producing wine? Explain what it means to have a lower opportunity cost.

20. You just overheard your friend say the following: "Poor countries like Malawi have no absolute advantages. They have poor soil, low investments in formal education and hence low-skill workers, no capital, and no natural resources to speak of. Because they have no advantage, they cannot benefit from trade." How would you respond?

21. Look at **Table 33.9**. Is there a range of trades for which there will be no gains?

16. Are the gains from international trade more likely to be relatively more important to large or small countries?

22. You just got a job in Washington, D.C. You move into an apartment with some acquaintances. All your roommates, however, are slackers and do not clean up after themselves. You, on the other hand, can clean faster than each of them. You determine that you are 70% faster at dishes and 10% faster with vacuuming. All of these tasks have to be done daily. Which jobs should you assign to your roommates to get the most free time overall? Assume you have the same number of hours to devote to cleaning. Now, since you are faster, you seem to get done quicker than your roommate. What sorts of problems may this create? Can you imagine a trade-related analogy to this problem?

23. Does intra-industry trade contradict the theory of comparative advantage?

24. Do consumers benefit from intra-industry trade?

25. Why might intra-industry trade seem surprising from the point of view of comparative advantage?

26. In World Trade Organization meetings, what do you think low-income countries lobby for?

27. Why might a low-income country put up barriers to trade, such as tariffs on imports?

28. Can a nation's comparative advantage change over time? What factors would make it change?

PROBLEMS

29. France and Tunisia both have Mediterranean climates that are excellent for producing/harvesting green beans and tomatoes. In France it takes two hours for each worker to harvest green beans and two hours to harvest a tomato. Tunisian workers need only one hour to harvest the tomatoes but four hours to harvest green beans. Assume there are only two workers, one in each country, and each works 40 hours a week.

    a. Draw a production possibilities frontier for each country. *Hint*: Remember the production possibility frontier is the maximum that all workers can produce at a unit of time which, in this problem, is a week.

    b. Identify which country has the absolute advantage in green beans and which country has the absolute advantage in tomatoes.

    c. Identify which country has the comparative advantage.

    d. How much would France have to give up in terms of tomatoes to gain from trade? How much would it have to give up in terms of green beans?

30. In Japan, one worker can make 5 tons of rubber or 80 radios. In Malaysia, one worker can make 10 tons of rubber or 40 radios.

    a. Who has the absolute advantage in the production of rubber or radios? How can you tell?

    b. Calculate the opportunity cost of producing 80 additional radios in Japan and in Malaysia. (Your calculation may involve fractions, which is fine.) Which country has a comparative advantage in the production of radios?

    c. Calculate the opportunity cost of producing 10 additional tons of rubber in Japan and in Malaysia. Which country has a comparative advantage in producing rubber?

    d. In this example, does each country have an absolute advantage and a comparative advantage in the same good?

    e. In what product should Japan specialize? In what product should Malaysia specialize?

31. Review the numbers for Canada and Venezuela from Table 33.12 which describes how many barrels of oil and tons of lumber the workers can produce. Use these numbers to answer the rest of this question.

    a. Draw a production possibilities frontier for each country. Assume there are 100 workers in each country. Canadians and Venezuelans desire both oil and lumber. Canadians want at least 2,000 tons of lumber. Mark a point on their production possibilities where they can get at least 3,000 tons.

    b. Assume that the Canadians specialize completely because they figured out they have a comparative advantage in lumber. They are willing to give up 1,000 tons of lumber. How much oil should they ask for in return for this lumber to be as well off as they were with no trade? How much should they ask for if they want to gain from trading with Venezuela? *Note*: We can think of this "ask" as the relative price or trade price of lumber.

    c. Is the Canadian "ask" you identified in (b) also beneficial for Venezuelans? Use the production possibilities frontier graph for Venezuela to show that Venezuelans can gain from trade.

32. In Exercise 33.31, is there an "ask" where Venezuelans may say "no thank you" to trading with Canada?

33. From earlier chapters you will recall that technological change shifts the average cost curves. Draw a graph showing how technological change could influence intra-industry trade.

34. Consider two countries: South Korea and Taiwan. Taiwan can produce one million mobile phones per day at the cost of $10 per phone and South Korea can produce 50 million mobile phones at $5 per phone. Assume these phones are the same type and quality and there is only one price. What is the minimum price at which both countries will engage in trade?

35. If trade increases world GDP by 1% per year, what is the global impact of this increase over 10 years? How does this increase compare to the annual GDP of a country like Sri Lanka? Discuss. *Hint*: To answer this question, here are steps you may want to consider. Go to the World Development Indicators (online) published by the World Bank. Find the current level of World GDP in constant international dollars. Also, find the GDP of Sri Lanka in constant international dollars. Once you have these two numbers, compute the amount the additional increase in global incomes due to trade and compare that number to Sri Lanka's GDP.

34 | Globalization and Protectionism

Figure 34.1 Flat Screen Competition The market for flat-panel displays in the United States is huge. The manufacturers of flat screens in the United States must compete against manufacturers from around the world. (Credit: modification of work by "Jemimus"/Flickr Creative Commons)

Bring it Home

What's the Downside of Protection?

Governments are motivated to limit and alter market outcomes for political or social ends. While governments can limit the rise in prices of some products, they cannot control how much people want to buy or how much firms are willing to sell. The laws of demand and supply still hold. Trade policy is an example where regulations can redirect economic forces, but it cannot stop them from manifesting themselves elsewhere.

Flat-panel displays, the displays for laptop computers, tablets, and flat screen televisions, are an example of such an enduring principle. In the early 1990s, the vast majority of flat-panel displays used in U.S.-manufactured laptops were imported, primarily from Japan. The small but politically powerful U.S. flat-panel-display industry filed a dumping complaint with the Commerce Department. They argued that Japanese firms were selling displays at "less than fair value," which made it difficult for U.S. firms to compete. This argument for trade protection is referred to as anti-dumping. Other arguments for protection in this complaint included national security. After a preliminary determination by the Commerce Department that the Japanese firms were dumping, the U.S. International Trade Commission imposed a 63% dumping margin (or tax) on the import of flat-panel displays. Was this a successful exercise of U.S. trade policy? See what you think after reading the chapter.

Introduction to Globalism and Protectionism

In this chapter, you will learn about:

- Protectionism: An Indirect Subsidy from Consumers to Producers

- International Trade and Its Effects on Jobs, Wages, and Working Conditions

- Arguments in Support of Restricting Imports

- How Trade Policy Is Enacted: Globally, Regionally, and Nationally

- The Tradeoffs of Trade Policy

The world has become more connected on multiple levels, especially economically. In 1970, imports and exports made up 11% of U.S. GDP, while now they make up 32%. However, the United States, due to its size, is less internationally connected than most countries. For example, according to the World Bank, 97% of Botswana's economic activity is connected to trade. This chapter explores trade policy—the laws and strategies a country uses to regulate international trade. This topic is not without controversy.

As the world has become more globally connected, firms and workers in high-income countries like the United States, Japan, or the nations of the European Union, perceive a competitive threat from firms in medium-income countries like Mexico, China, or South Africa, that have lower costs of living and therefore pay lower wages. Firms and workers in low-income countries fear that they will suffer if they must compete against more productive workers and advanced technology in high-income countries.

On a different tack, some environmentalists worry that multinational firms may evade environmental protection laws by moving their production to countries with loose or nonexistent pollution standards, trading a clean environment for jobs. Some politicians worry that their country may become overly dependent on key imported products, like oil, which in a time of war could threaten national security. All of these fears influence governments to reach the same basic policy conclusion: to protect national interests, whether businesses, jobs, or security, imports of foreign products should be restricted. This chapter analyzes such arguments. First, however, it is essential to learn a few key concepts and understand how the demand and supply model applies to international trade.

34.1 | Protectionism: An Indirect Subsidy from Consumers to Producers

By the end of this section, you will be able to:
- Explain protectionism and its three main forms
- Analyze protectionism through concepts of demand and supply, noting its effects on equilibrium
- Calculate the effects of trade barriers

When a government legislates policies to reduce or block international trade it is engaging in **protectionism**. Protectionist policies often seek to shield domestic producers and domestic workers from foreign competition. Protectionism takes three main forms: tariffs, import quotas, and nontariff barriers.

Recall from **International Trade** that tariffs are taxes that governments impose on imported goods and services. This makes imports more expensive for consumers, discouraging imports. For example, in recent years large, flat-screen televisions imported to the U.S. from China have faced a 5% tariff rate.

Another way to control trade is through **import quotas**, which are numerical limitations on the quantity of products that a country can import. For instance, during the early 1980s, the Reagan Administration imposed a quota on the import of Japanese automobiles. In the 1970s, many developed countries, including the United States, found themselves with declining textile industries. Textile production does not require highly skilled workers, so producers were able to set up lower-cost factories in developing countries. In order to "manage" this loss of jobs and income, the developed countries established an international Multifiber Agreement that essentially divided the market for textile exports between importers and the remaining domestic producers. The agreement, which ran from 1974 to 2004,

This OpenStax book is available for free at http://cnx.org/content/col12122/1.4

specified the exact quota of textile imports that each developed country would accept from each low-income country. A similar story exists for sugar imports into the United States, which are still governed by quotas.

Nontariff barriers are all the other ways that a nation can draw up rules, regulations, inspections, and paperwork to make it more costly or difficult to import products. A rule requiring certain safety standards can limit imports just as effectively as high tariffs or low import quotas, for instance. There are also nontariff barriers in the form of "rules-of-origin" regulations; these rules describe the "Made in Country X" label as the one in which the last substantial change in the product took place. A manufacturer wishing to evade import restrictions may try to change the production process so that the last big change in the product happens in his or her own country. For example, certain textiles are made in the United States, shipped to other countries, combined with textiles made in those other countries to make apparel—and then re-exported back to the United States for a final assembly, to escape paying tariffs or to obtain a "Made in the USA" label.

Despite import quotas, tariffs, and nontariff barriers, the share of apparel sold in the United States that is imported rose from about half in 1999 to about three-quarters today. The U.S. Bureau of Labor Statistics (BLS), estimated the number of U.S. jobs in textiles and apparel fell from 666,360 in 2007 to 385,240 in 2012, a 42% decline. Even more U.S. textile industry jobs would have been lost without tariffs. However, domestic jobs that are saved by import quotas come at a cost. Because textile and apparel protectionism adds to the costs of imports, consumers end up paying billions of dollars more for clothing each year.

When the United States eliminates trade barriers in one area, consumers spend the money they save on that product elsewhere in the economy. Thus, while eliminating trade barriers in one sector of the economy will likely result in some job loss in that sector, consumers will spend the resulting savings in other sectors of the economy and hence increase the number of jobs in those other sectors. Of course, workers in some of the poorest countries of the world who would otherwise have jobs producing textiles, would gain considerably if the United States reduced its barriers to trade in textiles. That said, there are good reasons to be wary about reducing barriers to trade. The 2012 and 2013 Bangladeshi fires in textile factories, which resulted in a horrific loss of life, present complications that our simplified analysis in the chapter will not capture.

Realizing the compromises between nations that come about due to trade policy, many countries came together in 1947 to form the General Agreement on Tariffs and Trade (GATT). (We'll cover the GATT in more detail later in the chapter.) This agreement has since been superseded by the **World Trade Organization (WTO)**, whose membership includes about 150 nations and most of the world's economies. It is the primary international mechanism through which nations negotiate their trade rules—including rules about tariffs, quotas, and nontariff barriers. The next section examines the results of such protectionism and develops a simple model to show the impact of trade policy.

Demand and Supply Analysis of Protectionism

To the non-economist, restricting imports may appear to be nothing more than taking sales from foreign producers and giving them to domestic producers. Other factors are at work, however, because firms do not operate in a vacuum. Instead, firms sell their products either to consumers or to other firms (if they are business suppliers), who are also affected by the trade barriers. A demand and supply analysis of protectionism shows that it is not just a matter of domestic gains and foreign losses, but a policy that imposes substantial domestic costs as well.

Consider two countries, Brazil and the United States, who produce sugar. Each country has a domestic supply and demand for sugar, as **Table 34.1** details and **Figure 34.2** illustrates. In Brazil, without trade, the equilibrium price of sugar is 12 cents per pound and the equilibrium output is 30 tons. When there is no trade in the United States, the equilibrium price of sugar is 24 cents per pound and the equilibrium quantity is 80 tons. We label these equilibrium points as point E in each part of the figure.

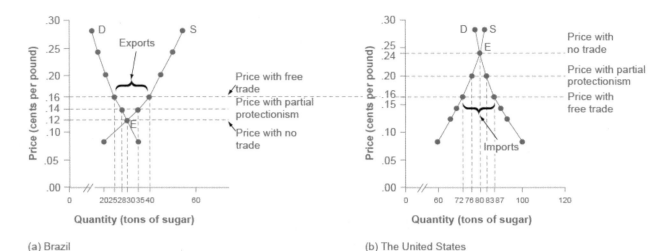

Figure 34.2 The Sugar Trade between Brazil and the United States Before trade, the equilibrium price of sugar in Brazil is 12 cents a pound and it is 24 cents per pound in the United States. When trade is allowed, businesses will buy cheap sugar in Brazil and sell it in the United States. This will result in higher prices in Brazil and lower prices in the United States. Ignoring transaction costs, prices should converge to 16 cents per pound, with Brazil exporting 15 tons of sugar and the United States importing 15 tons of sugar. If trade is only partly open between the countries, it will lead to an outcome between the free-trade and no-trade possibilities.

Price	Brazil: Quantity Supplied (tons)	Brazil: Quantity Demanded (tons)	U.S.: Quantity Supplied (tons)	U.S.: Quantity Demanded (tons)
8 cents	20	35	60	100
12 cents	30	30	66	93
14 cents	35	28	69	90
16 cents	40	25	72	87
20 cents	45	21	76	83
24 cents	50	18	80	80
28 cents	55	15	82	78

Table 34.1 The Sugar Trade between Brazil and the United States

If international trade between Brazil and the United States now becomes possible, profit-seeking firms will spot an opportunity: buy sugar cheaply in Brazil, and sell it at a higher price in the United States. As sugar is shipped from Brazil to the United States, the quantity of sugar produced in Brazil will be greater than Brazilian consumption (with the extra production exported), and the amount produced in the United States will be less than the amount of U.S. consumption (with the extra consumption imported). Exports to the United States will reduce the sugar supply in

This OpenStax book is available for free at http://cnx.org/content/col12122/1.4

Brazil, raising its price. Imports into the United States will increase the sugar supply, lowering its price. When the sugar price is the same in both countries, there is no incentive to trade further. As **Figure 34.2** shows, the equilibrium with trade occurs at a price of 16 cents per pound. At that price, the sugar farmers of Brazil supply a quantity of 40 tons, while the consumers of Brazil buy only 25 tons.

The extra 15 tons of sugar production, shown by the horizontal gap between the demand curve and the supply curve in Brazil, is exported to the United States. In the United States, at a price of 16 cents, the farmers produce a quantity of 72 tons and consumers demand a quantity of 87 tons. The excess demand of 15 tons by American consumers, shown by the horizontal gap between demand and domestic supply at the price of 16 cents, is supplied by imported sugar. Free trade typically results in income distribution effects, but the key is to recognize the overall gains from trade, as **Figure 34.3** shows. Building on the concepts that we outlined in **Demand and Supply** and **Demand, Supply, and Efficiency** in terms of consumer and producer surplus, **Figure 34.3** (a) shows that producers in Brazil gain by selling more sugar at a higher price, while **Figure 34.3** (b) shows consumers in the United States benefit from the lower price and greater availability of sugar. Consumers in Brazil are worse off (compare their no-trade consumer surplus with the free-trade consumer surplus) and U.S. producers of sugar are worse off. There are gains from trade—an increase in social surplus in each country. That is, both the United States and Brazil are better off than they would be without trade. The following Clear It Up feature explains how trade policy can influence low-income countries.

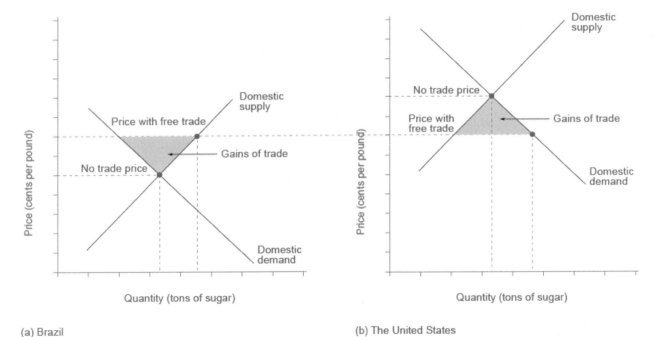

(a) Brazil   (b) The United States

Figure 34.3 Free Trade of Sugar   Free trade results in gains from trade. Total surplus increases in both countries, as the two blue-shaded areas show. However, there are clear income distribution effects. Producers gain in the exporting country, while consumers lose; and in the importing country, consumers gain and producers lose.

Link It Up ⌾

Visit this website (http://openstaxcollege.org/l/sugartrade) to read more about the global sugar trade.

Why are there low-income countries?

Why are the poor countries of the world poor? There are a number of reasons, but one of them will surprise you: the trade policies of the high-income countries. Following is a stark review of social priorities which the international aid organization, Oxfam International has widely publicized.

High-income countries of the world—primarily the United States, Canada, countries of the European Union, and Japan—subsidize their domestic farmers collectively by about $360 billion per year. By contrast, the total amount of foreign aid from these same high-income countries to the poor countries of the world is about $70 billion per year, or less than 20% of the farm subsidies. Why does this matter?

It matters because the support of farmers in high-income countries is devastating to the livelihoods of farmers in low-income countries. Even when their climate and land are well-suited to products like cotton, rice, sugar, or milk, farmers in low-income countries find it difficult to compete. Farm subsidies in the high-income countries cause farmers in those countries to increase the amount they produce. This increase in supply drives down world prices of farm products below the costs of production. As Michael Gerson of the *Washington Post* describes it: "[T]he effects in the cotton-growing regions of West Africa are dramatic . . . keep[ing] millions of Africans on the edge of malnutrition. In some of the poorest countries on Earth, cotton farmers are some of the poorest people, earning about a dollar a day. . . . Who benefits from the current system of subsidies? About 20,000 American cotton producers, with an average annual income of more than $125,000."

As if subsidies were not enough, often, the high-income countries block agricultural exports from low-income countries. In some cases, the situation gets even worse when the governments of high-income countries, having bought and paid for an excess supply of farm products, give away those products in poor countries and drive local farmers out of business altogether.

For example, shipments of excess milk from the European Union to Jamaica have caused great hardship for Jamaican dairy farmers. Shipments of excess rice from the United States to Haiti drove thousands of low-income rice farmers in Haiti out of business. The opportunity costs of protectionism are not paid just by domestic consumers, but also by foreign producers—and for many agricultural products, those foreign producers are the world's poor.

Now, let's look at what happens with protectionism. U.S. sugar farmers are likely to argue that, if only they could be protected from sugar imported from Brazil, the United States would have higher domestic sugar production, more jobs in the sugar industry, and American sugar farmers would receive a higher price. If the United States government sets a high-enough tariff on imported sugar, or sets an import quota at zero, the result will be that the quantity of sugar traded between countries could be reduced to zero, and the prices in each country will return to the levels before trade was allowed.

Blocking only some trade is also possible. Suppose that the United States passed a sugar import quota of seven tons. The United States will import no more than seven tons of sugar, which means that Brazil can export no more than seven tons of sugar to the United States. As a result, the price of sugar in the United States will be 20 cents, which is

This OpenStax book is available for free at http://cnx.org/content/col12122/1.4

the price where the quantity demanded is seven tons greater than the domestic quantity supplied. Conversely, if Brazil can export only seven tons of sugar, then the price of sugar in Brazil will be 14 cents per pound, which is the price where the domestic quantity supplied in Brazil is seven tons greater than domestic demand.

In general, when a country sets a low or medium tariff or import quota, the equilibrium price and quantity will be somewhere between those that prevail with no trade and those with completely free trade. The following Work It Out explores the impact of these trade barriers.

Work It Out ⊶⊸⊖

Effects of Trade Barriers

Let's look carefully at the effects of tariffs or quotas. If the U.S. government imposes a tariff or quota sufficient to eliminate trade with Brazil, two things occur: U.S. consumers pay a higher price and therefore buy a smaller quantity of sugar. U.S. producers obtain a higher price and they sell a larger quantity of sugar. We can measure the effects of a tariff on producers and consumers in the United States using two concepts that we developed in **Demand, Supply, and Efficiency**: consumer surplus and producer surplus.

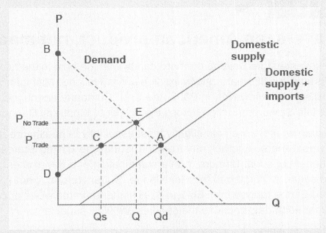

Figure 34.4 U.S. Sugar Supply and Demand   When there is free trade, the equilibrium is at point A. When there is no trade, the equilibrium is at point E.

Step 1. Look at **Figure 34.4**, which shows a hypothetical version of the demand and supply of sugar in the United States.

Step 2. Note that when there is free trade the sugar market is in equilibrium at point A where Domestic Quantity Demanded (Qd) = Quantity Supplied (Domestic Qs + Imports from Brazil) at a price of P_{Trade}.

Step 3. Note, also, that imports are equal to the distance between points C and A.

Step 4. Recall that consumer surplus is the value that consumers get beyond what they paid for when they buy a product. Graphically, it is the area under a demand curve but above the price. In this case, the consumer surplus in the United States is the area of the triangle formed by the points P_{Trade}, A, and B.

Step 5. Recall, also, that producer surplus is another name for profit—it is the income producers get above the cost of production, which is shown by the supply curve here. In this case, the producer surplus with trade is the area of the triangle formed by the points P_{trade}, C, and D.

Step 6. Suppose that the barriers to trade are imposed, imports are excluded, and the price rises to $P_{NoTrade}$. Look what happens to producer surplus and consumer surplus. At the higher price, the domestic quantity supplied increases from Qs to Q at point E. Because producers are selling more quantity at a higher price, the producer surplus increases to the area of the triangle $P_{NoTrade}$, E, and D.

Step 7. Compare the areas of the two triangles and you will see the increase in the producer surplus.

Step 8. Examine the consumer surplus. Consumers are now paying a higher price to get a lower quantity (Q instead of Qd). Their consumer surplus shrinks to the area of the triangle $P_{NoTrade}$, E, and B.

Step 9. Determine the net effect. The producer surplus increases by the area P_{trade}, C, E, $P_{NoTrade}$. The loss of consumer surplus, however, is larger. It is the area P_{trade}, A, E, $P_{NoTrade}$. In other words, consumers lose more than producers gain as a result of the trade barriers and the United States has a lower social surplus.

Who Benefits and Who Pays?

Using the demand and supply model, consider the impact of protectionism on producers and consumers in each of the two countries. For protected producers like U.S. sugar farmers, restricting imports is clearly positive. Without a need to face imported products, these producers are able to sell more, at a higher price. For consumers in the country with the protected good, in this case U.S. sugar consumers, restricting imports is clearly negative. They end up buying a lower quantity of the good and paying a higher price for what they do buy, compared to the equilibrium price and quantity with trade. The following Clear It Up feature considers why a country might outsource jobs even for a domestic product.

Why are Life Savers, an American product, not made in America?

In 1912, Clarence Crane invented Life Savers, the hard candy with the hole in the middle, in Cleveland, Ohio. Starting in the late 1960s and for 35 years afterward, a plant in Holland, Michigan produced 46 billion Life Savers a year, in 200 million rolls. However, in 2002, the Kraft Company announced that it would close the Michigan plant and move Life Saver production across the border to Montreal, Canada.

One reason is that Canadian workers are paid slightly less, especially in healthcare and insurance costs that are not linked to employment there. Another main reason is that the United States government keeps the sugar price high for the benefit of sugar farmers, with a combination of a government price floor program and strict quotas on imported sugar. According to the Coalition for Sugar Reform, from 2009 to 2012, the price of refined sugar in the United States ranged from 64% to 92% higher than the world price. Life Saver production uses over 100 tons of sugar each day, because the candies are 95% sugar.

A number of other candy companies have also reduced U.S. production and expanded foreign production. From 1997 to 2011, sugar-using industries eliminated some 127,000 jobs, or more than seven times the total employment in sugar production. While the candy industry is especially affected by the cost of sugar, the costs are spread more broadly. U.S. consumers pay roughly $1 billion per year in higher food prices because of elevated sugar costs. Meanwhile, sugar producers in low-income countries are driven out of business. Because of the sugar subsidies to domestic producers and the quotas on imports, they cannot sell their output profitably, or at all, in the United States market.

The fact that protectionism pushes up prices for consumers in the country enacting such protectionism is not always acknowledged openly, but it is not disputed. After all, if protectionism did not benefit domestic producers, there would not be much point in enacting such policies in the first place. Protectionism is simply a method of requiring consumers to subsidize producers. The subsidy is indirect, since consumers pay for it through higher prices, rather than a direct government subsidy paid with money collected from taxpayers. However, protectionism works like a subsidy, nonetheless. The American satirist Ambrose Bierce defined "tariff" this way in his 1911 book, *The Devil's Dictionary*: "Tariff, n. A scale of taxes on imports, designed to protect the domestic producer against the greed of his consumer."

The effect of protectionism on producers and consumers in the foreign country is complex. When a government uses an import quota to impose partial protectionism, Brazilian sugar producers receive a lower price for the sugar they sell in Brazil—but a higher price for the sugar they are allowed to export to the United States. Notice that some of the burden of protectionism, paid by domestic consumers, ends up in the hands of foreign producers in this case. Brazilian sugar consumers seem to benefit from U.S. protectionism, because it reduces the price of sugar that they pay (compared to the free-trade situation). On the other hand, at least some of these Brazilian sugar consumers also work as sugar farmers, so protectionism reduces their incomes and jobs. Moreover, if trade between the countries vanishes, Brazilian consumers would miss out on better prices for imported goods—which do not appear in our single-market example of sugar protectionism.

The effects of protectionism on foreign countries notwithstanding, protectionism requires domestic consumers of a product (consumers may include either households or other firms) to pay higher prices to benefit domestic producers of that product. In addition, when a country enacts protectionism, it loses the economic gains it would have been able to achieve through a combination of comparative advantage, specialized learning, and economies of scale, concepts that we discuss in **International Trade**.

34.2 | International Trade and Its Effects on Jobs, Wages, and Working Conditions

By the end of this section, you will be able to:
- Discuss how international trade influences the job market
- Analyze the opportunity cost of protectionism
- Explain how international trade impacts wages, labor standards, and working conditions

In theory at least, imports might injure workers in several different ways: fewer jobs, lower wages, or poor working conditions. Let's consider these in turn.

Fewer Jobs?

In the early 1990s, the United States was negotiating the North American Free Trade Agreement (NAFTA) with Mexico, an agreement that reduced tariffs, import quotas, and nontariff barriers to trade between the United States, Mexico, and Canada. H. Ross Perot, a 1992 candidate for U.S. president, claimed, in prominent campaign arguments, that if the United States expanded trade with Mexico, there would be a "giant sucking sound" as U.S. employers relocated to Mexico to take advantage of lower wages. After all, average wages in Mexico were, at that time, about one-eighth of those in the United States. NAFTA passed Congress, President Bill Clinton signed it into law, and it took effect in 1995. For the next six years, the United States economy had some of the most rapid job growth and low unemployment in its history. Those who feared that open trade with Mexico would lead to a dramatic decrease in jobs were proven wrong.

This result was no surprise to economists. After all, the trend toward globalization has been going on for decades, not just since NAFTA. If trade did reduce the number of available jobs, then the United States should have been seeing a steady loss of jobs for decades. While the United States economy does experience rises and falls in unemployment rates—according to the Bureau of Labor Statistics, from spring 2007 to late 2009, the unemployment rate rose from 4.4% to 10%. It has since fallen back to under 5% as of the end of 2016—the number of jobs is not falling over extended periods of time. The number of U.S. jobs rose from 71 million in 1970 to 145 million in 2014.

Protectionism certainly saves jobs in the specific industry being protected but, for two reasons, it costs jobs in other unprotected industries. First, if consumers are paying higher prices to the protected industry, they inevitably have less money to spend on goods from other industries, and so jobs are lost in those other industries. Second, if a firm sells the protected product to other firms, so that other firms must now pay a higher price for a key input, then those firms will lose sales to foreign producers who do not need to pay the higher price. Lost sales translate into lost jobs. The hidden opportunity cost of using protectionism to save jobs in one industry is jobs sacrificed in other industries. This is why the United States International Trade Commission, in its study of barriers to trade, predicts that reducing trade barriers would not lead to an overall loss of jobs. Protectionism reshuffles jobs from industries without import protections to industries that are protected from imports, but it does not create more jobs.

Moreover, the costs of saving jobs through protectionism can be very high. A number of different studies have attempted to estimate the cost to consumers in higher prices per job saved through protectionism. **Table 34.2** shows a sample of results, compiled by economists at the Federal Reserve Bank of Dallas. Saving a job through protectionism typically costs much more than the actual worker's salary. For example, a study published in 2002 compiled evidence that using protectionism to save an average job in the textile and apparel industry would cost $199,000 per job saved. In other words, those workers could have been paid $100,000 per year to be unemployed and the cost would only be half of what it is to keep them working in the textile and apparel industry. This result is not unique to textiles and apparel.

Industry Protected with Import Tariffs or Quotas	Annual Cost per Job Saved
Sugar	$826,000
Polyethylene resins	$812,000
Dairy products	$685,000
Frozen concentrated orange juice	$635,000
Ball bearings	$603,000
Machine tools	$479,000
Women's handbags	$263,000
Glassware	$247,000
Apparel and textiles	$199,000
Rubber footwear	$168,000
Women's nonathletic footwear	$139,000

Table 34.2 Cost to U.S. Consumers of Saving a Job through Protectionism   (Source: Federal Reserve Bank of Dallas)

Why does it cost so much to save jobs through protectionism? The basic reason is that not all of the extra money that consumers pay because of tariffs or quotas goes to save jobs. For example, if the government imposes tariffs on steel imports so that steel buyers pay a higher price, U.S. steel companies earn greater profits, buy more equipment, pay bigger bonuses to managers, give pay raises to existing employees—and also avoid firing some additional workers. Only part of the higher price of protected steel goes toward saving jobs. Also, when an industry is protected, the economy as a whole loses the benefits of playing to its comparative advantage—in other words, producing what it is best at. Therefore, part of the higher price that consumers pay for protected goods is lost economic efficiency, which we can measure as another deadweight loss, like what we discussed in **Labor and Financial Markets**.

There's a bumper sticker that speaks to the threat some U.S. workers feel from imported products: "Buy American—Save U.S. Jobs." If an economist were driving the car, the sticker might declare: "Block Imports—Save Jobs for Some Americans, Lose Jobs for Other Americans, and Also Pay High Prices."

Trade and Wages

Even if trade does not reduce the number of jobs, it could affect wages. Here, it is important to separate issues about the average level of wages from issues about whether the wages of certain workers may be helped or hurt by trade.

Because trade raises the amount that an economy can produce by letting firms and workers play to their comparative advantage, trade will also cause the average level of wages in an economy to rise. Workers who can produce more will be more desirable to employers, which will shift the demand for their labor out to the right, and increase wages in the labor market. By contrast, barriers to trade will reduce the average level of wages in an economy.

However, even if trade increases the overall wage level, it will still benefit some workers and hurt others. Workers in industries that are confronted by competition from imported products may find that demand for their labor decreases and shifts back to the left, so that their wages decline with a rise in international trade. Conversely, workers in industries that benefit from selling in global markets may find that demand for their labor shifts out to the right, so that trade raises their wages.

This OpenStax book is available for free at http://cnx.org/content/col12122/1.4

Link It Up

View this website (http://openstaxcollege.org/l/fairtradecoffee) to read an article on the issues surrounding fair trade coffee.

One concern is that while globalization may be benefiting high-skilled, high-wage workers in the United States, it may also impose costs on low-skilled, low-wage workers. After all, high-skilled U.S. workers presumably benefit from increased sales of sophisticated products like computers, machinery, and pharmaceuticals in which the United States has a comparative advantage. Meanwhile, low-skilled U.S. workers must now compete against extremely low-wage workers worldwide for making simpler products like toys and clothing. As a result, the wages of low-skilled U.S. workers are likely to fall. There are, however, a number of reasons to believe that while globalization has helped some U.S. industries and hurt others, it has not focused its negative impact on the wages of low-skilled Americans. First, about half of U.S. trade is intra-industry trade. That means the U.S. trades similar goods with other high-wage economies like Canada, Japan, Germany, and the United Kingdom. For instance, in 2014 the U.S. exported over 2 million cars, from all the major automakers, and also imported several million cars from other countries.

Most U.S. workers in these industries have above-average skills and wages—and many of them do quite well in the world of globalization. Some evidence suggested that intra-industry trade between similar countries had a small impact on domestic workers but later evidence indicates that it all depends on how flexible the labor market is. In other words, the key is how flexible workers are in finding jobs in different industries. The effect of trade on low-wage workers depends considerably on the structure of labor markets and indirect effects felt in other parts of the economy. For example, in the United States and the United Kingdom, because labor market frictions are low, the impact of trade on low income workers is small.

Second, many low-skilled U.S. workers hold service jobs that imports from low-wage countries cannot replace. For example, we cannot import lawn care services or moving and hauling services or hotel maids from countries long distances away like China or Bangladesh. Competition from imported products is not the primary determinant of their wages.

Finally, while the focus of the discussion here is on wages, it is worth pointing out that low-wage U.S. workers suffer due to protectionism in all the industries—even those in which they do not work. For example, food and clothing are protected industries. These low-wage workers therefore pay higher prices for these basic necessities and as such their dollar stretches over fewer goods.

The benefits and costs of increased trade in terms of its effect on wages are not distributed evenly across the economy. However, the growth of international trade has helped to raise the productivity of U.S. workers as a whole—and thus helped to raise the average level of wages.

Labor Standards and Working Conditions

Workers in many low-income countries around the world labor under conditions that would be illegal for a worker in the United States. Workers in countries like China, Thailand, Brazil, South Africa, and Poland are often paid less than the United States minimum wage. For example, in the United States, the minimum wage is $7.25 per hour. A typical wage in many low-income countries might be more like $7.25 per day, or often much less. Moreover, working conditions in low-income countries may be extremely unpleasant, or even unsafe. In the worst cases, production may involve the child labor or even workers who are treated nearly like slaves. These concerns over foreign labor standards do not affect most of U.S. trade, which is intra-industry and carried out with other high-income countries that have labor standards similar to the United States, but it is, nonetheless, morally and economically important.

In thinking about labor standards in other countries, it is important to draw some distinctions between what is truly unacceptable and what is painful to think about. Most people, economists included, have little difficulty with the idea that production by six-year-olds confined in factories or by slave labor is morally unacceptable. They would support aggressive efforts to eliminate such practices—including shutting out imported products made with such labor. Many cases, however, are less clear-cut. An opinion article in the *New York Times* several years ago described the case of Ahmed Zia, a 14-year-old boy from Pakistan. He earned $2 per day working in a carpet factory. He dropped out of school in second grade. Should the United States and other countries refuse to purchase rugs made by Ahmed and his co-workers? If the carpet factories were to close, the likely alternative job for Ahmed is farm work, and as Ahmed says of his carpet-weaving job: "This makes much more money and is more comfortable."

Other workers may have even less attractive alternative jobs, perhaps scavenging garbage or prostitution. The real problem for Ahmed and many others in low-income countries is not that globalization has made their lives worse, but rather that they have so few good life alternatives. The United States went through similar situations during the nineteenth and early twentieth centuries.

In closing, there is some irony when the United States government or U.S. citizens take issue with labor standards in low-income countries, because the United States is not a world leader in government laws to protect employees. According to a recent study by the Organization for Economic Cooperation and Development (OECD), the U.S. is the only one of 41 countries that does not provide mandated paid leave for new parents, and among the 40 countries that do mandate paid leave, the minimum duration is about two months. Many European workers receive six weeks or more of paid vacation per year. In the United States, vacations are often one to three weeks per year. If European countries accused the United States of using unfair labor standards to make U.S. products cheaply, and announced that they would shut out all U.S. imports until the United States adopted paid parental leave, added more national holidays, and doubled vacation time, Americans would be outraged. Yet when U.S. protectionists start talking about restricting imports from poor countries because of low wage levels and poor working conditions, they are making a very similar argument. This is not to say that labor conditions in low-income countries are not an important issue. They are. However, linking labor conditions in low-income countries to trade deflects the emphasis from the real question to ask: "What are acceptable and enforceable minimum labor standards and protections to have the world over?"

34.3 | Arguments in Support of Restricting Imports

By the end of this section, you will be able to:
- Explain and analyze various arguments that are in support of restricting imports, including the infant industry argument, the anti-dumping argument, the environmental protection argument, the unsafe consumer products argument, and the national interest argument
- Explain dumping and race to the bottom
- Evaluate the significance of countries' perceptions on the benefits of growing trade

As we previously noted, protectionism requires domestic consumers of a product to pay higher prices to benefit domestic producers of that product. Countries that institute protectionist policies lose the economic gains achieved through a combination of comparative advantage, specialized learning, and economies of scale. With these overall costs in mind, let us now consider, one by one, a number of arguments that support restricting imports.

The Infant Industry Argument

Imagine Bhutan wants to start its own computer industry, but it has no computer firms that can produce at a low enough price and high enough quality to compete in world markets. However, Bhutanese politicians, business leaders, and workers hope that if the local industry had a chance to get established, before it needed to face international competition, then a domestic company or group of companies could develop the skills, management, technology, and economies of scale that it needs to become a successful profit-earning domestic industry. Thus, the infant industry argument for protectionism is to block imports for a limited time, to give the infant industry time to mature, before it starts competing on equal terms in the global economy. (Revisit **Macroeconomic Policy Around the World** for more information on the infant industry argument.)

The infant industry argument is theoretically possible, even sensible: give an industry a short-term indirect subsidy through protection, and then reap the long-term economic benefits of having a vibrant, healthy industry. Implementation, however, is tricky. In many countries, infant industries have gone from babyhood to senility and obsolescence without ever having reached the profitable maturity stage. Meanwhile, the protectionism that was supposed to be short-term often took a very long time to be repealed.

As one example, Brazil treated its computer industry as an infant industry from the late 1970s until about 1990. In an attempt to establish its computer industry in the global economy, Brazil largely barred imports of computer products for several decades. This policy guaranteed increased sales for Brazilian computers. However, by the mid-1980s, due to lack of international competition, Brazil had a backward and out-of-date industry, typically lagging behind world standards for price and performance by three to five years—a long time in this fast-moving industry. After more than a decade, during which Brazilian consumers and industries that would have benefited from up-to-date computers paid the costs and Brazil's computer industry never competed effectively on world markets, Brazil phased out its infant industry policy for the computer industry.

Protectionism for infant industries always imposes costs on domestic users of the product, and typically has provided little benefit in the form of stronger, competitive industries. However, several countries in East Asia offer an exception. Japan, Korea, Thailand, and other countries in this region have sometimes provided a package of indirect and direct subsidies targeted at certain industries, including protection from foreign competition and government loans at interest rates below the market equilibrium. In Japan and Korea, for example, subsidies helped get their domestic steel and auto industries up and running.

Why did the infant industry policy of protectionism and other subsidies work fairly well in East Asia? An early 1990 World Bank study offered three guidelines to countries thinking about infant industry protection:

1. Do not hand out protectionism and other subsidies to all industries, but focus on a few industries where your country has a realistic chance to be a world-class producer.

2. Be very hesitant about using protectionism in areas like computers, where many other industries rely on having the best products available, because it is not useful to help one industry by imposing high costs on many other industries.

3. Have clear guidelines for when the infant industry policy will end.

In Korea in the 1970s and 1980s, a common practice was to link protectionism and subsidies to export sales in global markets. If export sales rose, then the infant industry had succeeded and the government could phase out protectionism. If export sales did not rise, then the infant industry policy had failed and the government could phase out protectionism. Either way, the protectionism would be temporary.

Following these rules is easier said than done. Politics often intrudes, both in choosing which industries will receive the benefits of treatment as "infants" and when to phase out import restrictions and other subsidies. Also, if the country's government wishes to impose costs on its citizens so that it can provide subsidies to a few key industries, it has many tools for doing such as direct government payments, loans, targeted tax reductions, and government support of research and development of new technologies. In other words, protectionism is not the only or even the best way to support key industries.

Link It Up ⚭

Visit this website (http://openstaxcollege.org/l/integration) to view a presentation by Pankaj Ghemawat questioning how integrated the world really is.

The Anti-Dumping Argument

Dumping refers to selling goods below their cost of production. **Anti-dumping laws** block imports that are sold below the cost of production by imposing tariffs that increase the price of these imports to reflect their cost of production. Since dumping is not allowed under World Trade Organization (WTO) rules, nations that believe they are on the receiving end of dumped goods can file a complaint with the WTO. Anti-dumping complaints have risen in recent years, from about 100 cases per year in the late 1980s to about 200 new cases each year by the late 2000s. Note that dumping cases are countercyclical. During recessions, case filings increase. During economic booms, case filings go down. Individual countries have also frequently started their own anti-dumping investigations. The U.S. government has dozens of anti-dumping orders in place from past investigations. In 2009, for example, some U.S. imports that were under anti-dumping orders included pasta from Turkey, steel pipe fittings from Thailand, pressure-sensitive plastic tape from Italy, preserved mushrooms and lined paper products from India, and cut-to-length carbon steel and non-frozen apple juice concentrate from China.

Why Might Dumping Occur?

Why would foreign firms export a product at less than its cost of production—which presumably means taking a loss? This question has two possible answers, one innocent and one more sinister.

The innocent explanation is that demand and supply set market prices, not the cost of production. Perhaps demand for a product shifts back to the left or supply shifts out to the right, which drives the market price to low levels—even below the cost of production. When a local store has a going-out-of-business sale, for example, it may sell goods at below the cost of production. If international companies find that there is excess supply of steel or computer chips or machine tools that is driving the market price down below their cost of production—this may be the market in action.

The sinister explanation is that dumping is part of a long-term strategy. Foreign firms sell goods at prices below the cost of production for a short period of time, and when they have driven out the domestic U.S. competition, they then raise prices. Economists sometimes call this scenario predatory pricing, which we discuss in the **Monopoly** chapter.

Should Anti-Dumping Cases Be Limited?

Anti-dumping cases pose two questions. How much sense do they make in economic theory? How much sense do they make as practical policy?

In terms of economic theory, the case for anti-dumping laws is weak. In a market governed by demand and supply, the government does not guarantee that firms will be able to make a profit. After all, low prices are difficult for producers, but benefit consumers. Moreover, although there are plenty of cases in which foreign producers have driven out domestic firms, there are zero documented cases in which the foreign producers then jacked up prices. Instead, foreign producers typically continue competing hard against each other and providing low prices to consumers. In short, it is difficult to find evidence of predatory pricing by foreign firms exporting to the United States.

Even if one could make a case that the government should sometimes enact anti-dumping rules in the short term, and then allow free trade to resume shortly thereafter, there is a growing concern that anti-dumping investigations often involve more politics than careful analysis. The U.S. Commerce Department is charged with calculating the appropriate "cost of production," which can be as much an art as a science.

For example, if a company built a new factory two years ago, should it count part of the factory's cost in this year's cost of production? When a company is in a country where the government controls prices, like China for example, how can one measure the true cost of production? When a domestic industry complains loudly enough, government regulators seem very likely to find that unfair dumping has occurred. A common pattern has arisen where a domestic industry files an anti-dumping complaint, the governments meet and negotiate a reduction in imports, and then the domestic producers drop the anti-dumping suit. In such cases, anti-dumping cases often appear to be little more than a cover story for imposing tariffs or import quotas.

In the 1980s, the United States, Canada, the European Union, Australia, and New Zealand implemented almost all the anti-dumping cases. By the 2000s, countries like Argentina, Brazil, South Korea, South Africa, Mexico, and India were filing the majority of the anti-dumping cases before the WTO. As the number of anti-dumping cases has increased, and as countries such as the United States and the European Union feel targeted by the anti-dumping actions of others, the WTO may well propose some additional guidelines to limit the reach of anti-dumping laws.

The Environmental Protection Argument

The potential for global trade to affect the environment has become controversial. A president of the Sierra Club, an environmental lobbying organization, once wrote: "The consequences of globalization for the environment are not good. ... Globalization, if we are lucky, will raise average incomes enough to pay for cleaning up some of the mess that we have made. But before we get there, globalization could also destroy enough of the planet's basic biological and physical systems that prospects for life itself will be radically compromised."

If free trade meant the destruction of life itself, then even economists would convert to protectionism! While globalization—and economic activity of all kinds—can pose environmental dangers, it seems quite possible that, with the appropriate safeguards in place, we can minimize the environmental impacts of trade. In some cases, trade may even bring environmental benefits.

In general, high-income countries such as the United States, Canada, Japan, and the nations of the European Union have relatively strict environmental standards. In contrast, middle- and low-income countries like Brazil, Nigeria, India, and China have lower environmental standards. The general view of the governments of such countries is that environmental protection is a luxury: as soon as their people have enough to eat, decent healthcare, and longer life expectancies, then they will spend more money on items such as sewage treatment plants, scrubbers to reduce air pollution from factory smokestacks, and national parks to protect wildlife.

This gap in environmental standards between high-income and low-income countries raises two worrisome possibilities in a world of increasing global trade: the "race to the bottom" scenario and the question of how quickly environmental standards will improve in low-income countries.

The Race to the Bottom Scenario

The **race to the bottom** scenario of global environmental degradation runs like this. Profit-seeking multinational companies shift their production from countries with strong environmental standards to countries with weak standards, thus reducing their costs and increasing their profits. Faced with such behavior, countries reduce their environmental standards to attract multinational firms, which, after all, provide jobs and economic clout. As a result, global production becomes concentrated in countries where firms can pollute the most and environmental laws everywhere "race to the bottom."

Although the race-to-the-bottom scenario sounds plausible, it does not appear to describe reality. In fact, the financial incentive for firms to shift production to poor countries to take advantage of their weaker environmental rules does not seem especially powerful. When firms decide where to locate a new factory, they look at many different factors: the costs of labor and financial capital; whether the location is close to a reliable suppliers of the inputs that they need; whether the location is close to customers; the quality of transportation, communications, and electrical power networks; the level of taxes; and the competence and honesty of the local government. The cost of environmental regulations is a factor, too, but typically environmental costs are no more than 1 to 2% of the costs that a large industrial plant faces. The other factors that determine location are much more important to these companies than trying to skimp on environmental protection costs.

When an international company does choose to build a plant in a low-income country with lax environmental laws, it typically builds a plant similar to those that it operates in high-income countries with stricter environmental standards. Part of the reason for this decision is that designing an industrial plant is a complex and costly task, and so if a plant works well in a high-income country, companies prefer to use the same design everywhere. Also, companies realize that if they create an environmental disaster in a low-income country, it is likely to cost them a substantial amount of money in paying for damages, lost trust, and reduced sales—by building up-to-date plants everywhere they minimize such risks. As a result of these factors, foreign-owned plants in low-income countries often have a better record of compliance with environmental laws than do locally-owned plants.

Pressuring Low-Income Countries for Higher Environmental Standards

In some cases, the issue is not so much whether globalization will pressure low-income countries to reduce their environmental standards, but instead whether the threat of blocking international trade can pressure these countries into adopting stronger standards. For example, restrictions on ivory imports in high-income countries, along with stronger government efforts to catch elephant poachers, have been credited with helping to reduce the illegal poaching of elephants in certain African countries.

However, it would be highly undemocratic for the well-fed citizens of high-income countries to attempt to dictate to the ill-fed citizens of low-income countries what domestic policies and priorities they must adopt, or how they should balance environmental goals against other priorities for their citizens. Furthermore, if high-income countries want stronger environmental standards in low-income countries, they have many options other than the threat of protectionism. For example, high-income countries could pay for anti-pollution equipment in low-income countries, or could help to pay for national parks. High-income countries could help pay for and carry out the scientific and economic studies that would help environmentalists in low-income countries to make a more persuasive case for the economic benefits of protecting the environment.

After all, environmental protection is vital to two industries of key importance in many low-income countries—agriculture and tourism. Environmental advocates can set up standards for labeling products, like "this tuna caught in a net that kept dolphins safe" or "this product made only with wood not taken from rainforests," so that consumer pressure can reinforce environmentalist values. The United Nations also reinforces these values, by sponsoring treaties to address issues such as climate change and global warming, the preservation of biodiversity, the spread of deserts, and the environmental health of the seabed. Countries that share a national border or are within a region often sign environmental agreements about air and water rights, too. The WTO is also becoming more aware of environmental issues and more careful about ensuring that increases in trade do not inflict environmental damage.

Finally, note that these concerns about the race to the bottom or pressuring low-income countries for more strict environmental standards do not apply very well to the roughly half of all U.S. trade that occurs with other high-income countries. Many European countries have stricter environmental standards in certain industries than the United States.

The Unsafe Consumer Products Argument

One argument for shutting out certain imported products is that they are unsafe for consumers. Consumer rights groups have sometimes warned that the World Trade Organization would require nations to reduce their health and safety standards for imported products. However, the WTO explains its current agreement on the subject in this way: "It allows countries to set their own standards." It also says "regulations must be based on science. . . . And they should not arbitrarily or unjustifiably discriminate between countries where identical or similar conditions prevail." Thus, for example, under WTO rules it is perfectly legitimate for the United States to pass laws requiring that *all* food products or cars sold in the United States meet certain safety standards approved by the United States government, whether or not other countries choose to pass similar standards. However, such standards must have some scientific basis. It is improper to impose one set of health and safety standards for domestically produced goods but a different set of standards for imports, or one set of standards for imports from Europe and a different set of standards for imports from Latin America.

In 2007, Mattel recalled nearly two million toys imported from China due to concerns about high levels of lead in the paint, as well as some loose parts. It is unclear if other toys were subject to similar standards. More recently, in 2013, Japan blocked imports of U.S. wheat because of concerns that genetically modified (GMO) wheat might be included in the shipments. The science on the impact of GMOs on health is still developing.

The National Interest Argument

Some argue that a nation should not depend too heavily on other countries for supplies of certain key products, such as oil, or for special materials or technologies that might have national security applications. On closer consideration, this argument for protectionism proves rather weak.

As an example, in the United States, oil provides about 36% of all the energy and 25% of the oil used in the United States economy is imported. Several times in the last few decades, when disruptions in the Middle East have shifted the supply curve of oil back to the left and sharply raised the price, the effects have been felt across the United States economy. This is not, however, a very convincing argument for restricting oil imports. If the United States needs to be protected from a possible cutoff of foreign oil, then a more reasonable strategy would be to import 100% of the petroleum supply now, and save U.S. domestic oil resources for when or if the foreign supply is cut off. It might also be useful to import extra oil and put it into a stockpile for use in an emergency, as the United States government did by starting a Strategic Petroleum Reserve in 1977. Moreover, it may be necessary to discourage people from using oil, and to start a high-powered program to seek out alternatives to oil. A straightforward way to do this would be to raise taxes on oil. Additionally, it makes no sense to argue that because oil is highly important to the United States economy, then the United States should shut out oil imports and use up its domestic supplies more quickly. U.S. domestic oil production is increasing. Shale oil is adding to domestic supply using fracking extraction techniques.

Whether or not to limit certain kinds of imports of key technologies or materials that might be important to national security and weapons systems is a slightly different issue. If weapons' builders are not confident that they can continue to obtain a key product in wartime, they might decide to avoid designing weapons that use this key product, or they can go ahead and design the weapons and stockpile enough of the key high-tech components or materials to last through an armed conflict. There is a U.S. Defense National Stockpile Center that has built up reserves of many

This OpenStax book is available for free at http://cnx.org/content/col12122/1.4

materials, from aluminum oxides, antimony, and bauxite to tungsten, vegetable tannin extracts, and zinc (although many of these stockpiles have been reduced and sold in recent years). Think every country is pro-trade? How about the U.S.? The following Clear It Up might surprise you.

Clear It Up

How does the United States really feel about expanding trade?

How do people around the world feel about expanding trade between nations? In summer 2007, the Pew Foundation surveyed 45,000 people in 47 countries. One of the questions asked about opinions on growing trade ties between countries. Table 34.3 shows the percentages who answered either "very good" or "somewhat good" for some of countries surveyed.

For those who think of the United States as the world's leading supporter of expanding trade, the survey results may be perplexing. When adding up the shares of those who say that growing trade ties between countries is "very good" or "somewhat good," Americans had the least favorable attitude toward increasing globalization, while the Chinese and South Africans ranked highest. In fact, among the 47 countries surveyed, the United States ranked by far the lowest on this measure, followed by Egypt, Italy, and Argentina.

Country	Very Good	Somewhat Good	Total
China	38%	53%	91%
South Africa	42%	43%	87%
South Korea	24%	62%	86%
Germany	30%	55%	85%
Canada	29%	53%	82%
United Kingdom	28%	50%	78%
Mexico	22%	55%	77%
Brazil	13%	59%	72%
Japan	17%	55%	72%
United States	14%	45%	59%

Table 34.3 The Status of Growing Trade Ties between Countries (Source: http://www.pewglobal.org/files/pdf/258.pdf)

One final reason why economists often treat the **national interest argument** skeptically is that lobbyists and politicians can tout almost any product as vital to national security. In 1954, the United States became worried that it was importing half of the wool required for military uniforms, so it declared wool and mohair to be "strategic materials" and began to give subsidies to wool and mohair farmers. Although the government removed wool from the official list of "strategic" materials in 1960, the subsidies for mohair continued for almost 40 years until the government repealed them in 1993, and then reinstated them in 2002. All too often, the national interest argument has become an excuse for handing out the indirect subsidy of protectionism to certain industries or companies. After all, politicians, not nonpartisan analysts make decisions about what constitutes a key strategic material.

34.4 | How Governments Enact Trade Policy: Globally,

Regionally, and Nationally

By the end of this section, you will be able to:
- Explain the origin and role of the World Trade Organization (WTO) and General Agreement on Tariffs and Trade (GATT)
- Discuss the significance and provide examples of regional trading agreements
- Analyze trade policy at the national level
- Evaluate long-term trends in barriers to trade

These public policy arguments about how nations should react to globalization and trade are fought out at several levels: at the global level through the World Trade Organization and through regional trade agreements between pairs or groups of countries.

The World Trade Organization

The World Trade Organization (WTO) was officially born in 1995, but its history is much longer. In the years after the Great Depression and World War II, there was a worldwide push to build institutions that would tie the nations of the world together. The United Nations officially came into existence in 1945. The World Bank, which assists the poorest people in the world, and the International Monetary Fund, which addresses issues raised by international financial transactions, were both created in 1946. The third planned organization was to be an International Trade Organization, which would manage international trade. The United Nations was unable to agree to this. Instead, 27 nations signed the **General Agreement on Tariffs and Trade (GATT)** in Geneva, Switzerland on October 30, 1947 to provide a forum in which nations could come together to negotiate reductions in tariffs and other barriers to trade. In 1995, the GATT transformed into the WTO.

The GATT process was to negotiate an agreement to reduce barriers to trade, sign that agreement, pause for a while, and then start negotiating the next agreement. **Table 34.4** shows rounds of talks in the GATT, and now the WTO. Notice that the early rounds of GATT talks took a relatively short time, included a small number of countries, and focused almost entirely on reducing tariffs. Since the mid-1960s, however, rounds of trade talks have taken years, included a large number of countries, and have included an ever-broadening range of issues.

Year	Place or Name of Round	Main Subjects	Number of Countries Involved
1947	Geneva	Tariff reduction	23
1949	Annecy	Tariff reduction	13
1951	Torquay	Tariff reduction	38
1956	Geneva	Tariff reduction	26
1960–61	Dillon round	Tariff reduction	26
1964–67	Kennedy round	Tariffs, anti-dumping measures	62
1973–79	Tokyo round	Tariffs, nontariff barriers	102

Table 34.4 The Negotiating Rounds of GATT and the World Trade Organization

This OpenStax book is available for free at http://cnx.org/content/col12122/1.4

Year	Place or Name of Round	Main Subjects	Number of Countries Involved
1986–94	Uruguay round	Tariffs, nontariff barriers, services, intellectual property, dispute settlement, textiles, agriculture, creation of WTO	123
2001–	Doha round	Agriculture, services, intellectual property, competition, investment, environment, dispute settlement	147

Table 34.4 The Negotiating Rounds of GATT and the World Trade Organization

The sluggish pace of GATT negotiations led to an old joke that GATT really stood for Gentleman's Agreement to Talk and Talk. The slow pace of international trade talks, however, is understandable, even sensible. Having dozens of nations agree to any treaty is a lengthy process. GATT often set up separate trading rules for certain industries, like agriculture, and separate trading rules for certain countries, like the low-income countries. There were rules, exceptions to rules, opportunities to opt out of rules, and precise wording to be fought over in every case. Like the GATT before it, the WTO is not a world government, with power to impose its decisions on others. The total staff of the WTO in 2014 is 640 people and its annual budget (as of 2014) is $197 million, which makes it smaller in size than many large universities.

Regional Trading Agreements

There are different types of economic integration across the globe, ranging from **free trade agreements**, in which participants allow each other's imports without tariffs or quotas, to **common markets**, in which participants have a common external trade policy as well as free trade within the group, to full **economic unions**, in which, in addition to a common market, monetary and fiscal policies are coordinated. Many nations belong both to the World Trade Organization and to regional trading agreements.

The best known of these regional trading agreements is the European Union. In the years after World War II, leaders of several European nations reasoned that if they could tie their economies together more closely, they might be more likely to avoid another devastating war. Their efforts began with a free trade association, evolved into a common market, and then transformed into what is now a full economic union, known as the European Union. The EU, as it is often called, has a number of goals. For example, in the early 2000s it introduced a common currency for Europe, the euro, and phased out most of the former national forms of money like the German mark and the French franc, though a few have retained their own currency. Another key element of the union is to eliminate barriers to the mobility of goods, labor, and capital across Europe.

For the United States, perhaps the best-known regional trading agreement is the North American Free Trade Agreement (NAFTA). The United States also participates in some less-prominent regional trading agreements, like the Caribbean Basin Initiative, which offers reduced tariffs for imports from these countries, and a free trade agreement with Israel.

The world has seen a flood of regional trading agreements in recent years. About 100 such agreements are now in place. **Table 34.5** lists a few of the more prominent ones. Some are just agreements to continue talking. Others set specific goals for reducing tariffs, import quotas, and nontariff barriers. One economist described the current trade treaties as a "spaghetti bowl," which is what a map with lines connecting all the countries with trade treaties looks like.

There is concern among economists who favor free trade that some of these regional agreements may promise free trade, but actually act as a way for the countries within the regional agreement to try to limit trade from anywhere else. In some cases, the regional trade agreements may even conflict with the broader agreements of the World Trade Organization.

Trade Agreements	Participating Countries
Asia Pacific Economic Cooperation (APEC)	Australia, Brunei, Canada, Chile, People's Republic of China, Hong Kong, China, Indonesia, Japan, Republic of Korea, Malaysia, Mexico, New Zealand, Papua New Guinea, Peru, Philippines, Russia, Singapore, Chinese Taipei, Thailand, United States, Vietnam
European Union (EU)	Austria, Belgium, Bulgaria, Cyprus, Czech Republic, Denmark, Estonia, Finland, France, Germany, Greece, Hungary, Ireland, Italy, Latvia, Lithuania, Luxembourg, Malta, Netherlands, Poland, Portugal, Romania, Slovakia, Slovenia, Spain, Sweden, United Kingdom*
North America Free Trade Agreement (NAFTA)	Canada, Mexico, United States
Latin American Integration Association (LAIA)	Argentina, Bolivia, Brazil, Chile, Columbia, Ecuador, Mexico, Paraguay, Peru, Uruguay, Venezuela
Association of Southeast Asian Nations (ASEAN)	Brunei, Cambodia, Indonesia, Laos, Malaysia, Myanmar, Philippines, Singapore, Thailand, Vietnam
Southern African Development Community (SADC)	Angola, Botswana, Congo, Lesotho, Madagascar, Malawi, Mauritius, Mozambique, Namibia, Seychelles, South Africa, Swaziland, Tanzania, Zambia, Zimbabwe

Table 34.5 Some Regional Trade Agreements * Following the 2016 referendum vote to leave the European Union, the UK government triggered the withdrawal process on March 29, 2017, setting the date for the UK to leave by April 2019.

Trade Policy at the National Level

Yet another dimension of trade policy, along with international and regional trade agreements, happens at the national level. The United States, for example, imposes import quotas on sugar, because of a fear that such imports would drive down the price of sugar and thus injure domestic sugar producers. One of the jobs of the United States Department of Commerce is to determine if there is import dumping from other countries. The United States International Trade Commission—a government agency—determines whether the dumping has substantially injured domestic industries, and if so, the president can impose tariffs that are intended to offset the unfairly low price.

In the arena of trade policy, the battle often seems to be between national laws that increase protectionism and international agreements that try to reduce protectionism, like the WTO. Why would a country pass laws or negotiate agreements to shut out certain foreign products, like sugar or textiles, while simultaneously negotiating to reduce trade barriers in general? One plausible answer is that international trade agreements offer a method for countries to restrain their own special interests. A member of Congress can say to an industry lobbying for tariffs or quotas on imports: "Sure would like to help you, but that pesky WTO agreement just won't let me."

Link It Up

If consumers are the biggest losers from trade, why do they not fight back? The quick answer is because it is easier to organize a small group of people around a narrow interest (producers) versus a large group that has diffuse interests (consumers). This is a question about trade policy theory. Visit this website (http://openstaxcollege.org/l/tradepolicy) and read the article by Jonathan Rauch.

Long-Term Trends in Barriers to Trade

In newspaper headlines, trade policy appears mostly as disputes and acrimony. Countries are almost constantly threatening to challenge other nations' "unfair" trading practices. Cases are brought to the dispute settlement procedures of the WTO, the European Union, NAFTA, and other regional trading agreements. Politicians in national legislatures, goaded on by lobbyists, often threaten to pass bills that will "establish a fair playing field" or "prevent unfair trade"—although most such bills seek to accomplish these high-sounding goals by placing more restrictions on trade. Protesters in the streets may object to specific trade rules or to the entire practice of international trade.

Through all the controversy, the general trend in the last 60 years is clearly toward lower barriers to trade. The average level of tariffs on imported products charged by industrialized countries was 40% in 1946. By 1990, after decades of GATT negotiations, it was down to less than 5%. One of the reasons that GATT negotiations shifted from focusing on tariff reduction in the early rounds to a broader agenda was that tariffs had been reduced so dramatically there was not much more to do in that area. U.S. tariffs have followed this general pattern: After rising sharply during the Great Depression, tariffs dropped off to less than 2% by the end of the century. Although measures of import quotas and nontariff barriers are less exact than those for tariffs, they generally appear to be at lower levels than they had been previously, too.

Thus, the last half-century has seen both a dramatic reduction in government-created barriers to trade, such as tariffs, import quotas, and nontariff barriers, and also a number of technological developments that have made international trade easier, like advances in transportation, communication, and information management. The result has been the powerful surge of international trade.

34.5 | The Tradeoffs of Trade Policy

By the end of this section, you will be able to:
- Asses the complexity of international trade
- Discuss why a market-oriented economy is so affected by international trade
- Explain disruptive market change

Economists readily acknowledge that international trade is not all sunshine, roses, and happy endings. Over time, the average person gains from international trade, both as a worker who has greater productivity and higher wages because of the benefits of specialization and comparative advantage, and as a consumer who can benefit from shopping all over the world for a greater variety of quality products at attractive prices. The "average person," however, is hypothetical, not real—representing a mix of those who have done very well, those who have done all right, and those who have done poorly. It is a legitimate concern of public policy to focus not just on the average or on the success stories, but also on those who have not been so fortunate. Workers in other countries, the environment, and prospects for new industries and materials that might be of key importance to the national economy are also all legitimate issues.

The common belief among economists is that it is better to embrace the gains from trade, and then deal with the costs and tradeoffs with other policy tools, than it is to cut off trade to avoid the costs and tradeoffs.

To gain a better intuitive understanding for this argument, consider a hypothetical American company called Technotron. Technotron invents a new scientific technology that allows the firm to increase the output and quality of its goods with a smaller number of workers at a lower cost. As a result of this technology, other U.S. firms in this industry will lose money and will also have to lay off workers—and some of the competing firms will even go bankrupt. Should the United States government protect the existing firms and their employees by making it illegal for Technotron to use its new technology? Most people who live in market-oriented economies would oppose trying to block better products that lower the cost of services. Certainly, there is a case for society providing temporary support and assistance for those who find themselves without work. Many would argue for government support of programs that encourage retraining and acquiring additional skills. Government might also support research and development efforts, so that other firms may find ways of outdoing Technotron. Blocking the new technology altogether, however, seems like a mistake. After all, few people would advocate giving up electricity because it caused so much disruption to the kerosene and candle business. Few would suggest holding back on improvements in medical technology because they might cause companies selling leeches and snake oil to lose money. In short, most people view disruptions due to technological change as a necessary cost that is worth bearing.

Now, imagine that Technotron's new "technology" is as simple as this: the company imports what it sells from another country. In other words, think of foreign trade as a type of innovative technology. The objective situation is now exactly the same as before. Because of Technotron's new technology—which in this case is importing goods from another county—other firms in this industry will lose money and lay off workers. Just as it would have been inappropriate and ultimately foolish to respond to the disruptions of new scientific technology by trying to shut it down, it would be inappropriate and ultimately foolish to respond to the disruptions of international trade by trying to restrict trade.

Some workers and firms will suffer because of international trade. In a living, breathing market-oriented economy, some workers and firms will always be experiencing disruptions, for a wide variety of reasons. Corporate management can be better or worse. Workers for a certain firm can be more or less productive. Tough domestic competitors can create just as much disruption as tough foreign competitors. Sometimes a new product is a hit with consumers; sometimes it is a flop. Sometimes a company is blessed by a run of good luck or stricken with a run of bad luck. For some firms, international trade will offer great opportunities for expanding productivity and jobs; for other firms, trade will impose stress and pain. The disruption caused by international trade is not fundamentally different from all the other disruptions caused by the other workings of a market economy.

In other words, the economic analysis of free trade does not rely on a belief that foreign trade is not disruptive or does not pose tradeoffs; indeed, the story of Technotron begins with a particular **disruptive market change**—a new technology—that causes real tradeoffs. In thinking about the disruptions of foreign trade, or any of the other possible costs and tradeoffs of foreign trade discussed in this chapter, the best public policy solutions typically do not involve protectionism, but instead involve finding ways for public policy to address the particular issues resulting from these disruptions, costs, and tradeoffs, while still allowing the benefits of international trade to occur.

Bring it Home

What's the Downside of Protection?

The domestic flat-panel display industry employed many workers before the ITC imposed the dumping margin tax. Flat-panel displays make up a significant portion of the cost of producing laptop computers—as much as 50%. Therefore, the antidumping tax would substantially increase the cost, and thus the price, of U.S.-manufactured laptops. As a result of the ITC's decision, Apple moved its domestic manufacturing plant for Macintosh computers to Ireland (where it had an existing plant). Toshiba shut down its U.S. manufacturing plant for laptops. And IBM cancelled plans to open a laptop manufacturing plant in North Carolina, instead deciding to expand production at its plant in Japan. In this case, rather than having the desired effect of protecting U.S. interests and giving domestic manufacturing an advantage over items manufactured elsewhere, it had the unintended effect of driving the manufacturing completely out of the country. Many people lost their jobs and most flat-panel display production now occurs in countries other than the United States.

KEY TERMS

anti-dumping laws laws that block imports sold below the cost of production and impose tariffs that would increase the price of these imports to reflect their cost of production

common market economic agreement between countries to allow free trade in goods, services, labor, and financial capital between members while having a common external trade policy

disruptive market change innovative new product or production technology which disrupts the status quo in a market, leading the innovators to earn more income and profits and the other firms to lose income and profits, unless they can come up with their own innovations

dumping selling internationally traded goods below their cost of production

economic union economic agreement between countries to allow free trade between members, a common external trade policy, and coordinated monetary and fiscal policies

free trade agreement economic agreement between countries to allow free trade between members

General Agreement on Tariffs and Trade (GATT) forum in which nations could come together to negotiate reductions in tariffs and other barriers to trade; the precursor to the World Trade Organization

import quotas numerical limits on the quantity of products that a country can import

national interest argument the argument that there are compelling national interests against depending on key imports from other nations

nontariff barriers ways a nation can draw up rules, regulations, inspections, and paperwork to make it more costly or difficult to import products

protectionism government policies to reduce or block imports

race to the bottom when production locates in countries with the lowest environmental (or other) standards, putting pressure on all countries to reduce their environmental standards

World Trade Organization (WTO) organization that seeks to negotiate reductions in barriers to trade and to adjudicate complaints about violations of international trade policy; successor to the General Agreement on Tariffs and Trade (GATT)

KEY CONCEPTS AND SUMMARY

34.1 Protectionism: An Indirect Subsidy from Consumers to Producers

There are three tools for restricting the flow of trade: tariffs, import quotas, and nontariff barriers. When a country places limitations on imports from abroad, regardless of whether it uses tariffs, quotas, or nontariff barriers, it is said to be practicing protectionism. Protectionism will raise the price of the protected good in the domestic market, which causes domestic consumers to pay more, but domestic producers to earn more.

34.2 International Trade and Its Effects on Jobs, Wages, and Working Conditions

As international trade increases, it contributes to a shift in jobs away from industries where that economy does not have a comparative advantage and toward industries where it does have a comparative advantage. The degree to which trade affects labor markets has much to do with the structure of the labor market in that country and the adjustment process in other industries. Global trade should raise the average level of wages by increasing productivity. However, this increase in average wages may include both gains to workers in certain jobs and industries and losses to others.

This OpenStax book is available for free at http://cnx.org/content/col12122/1.4

In thinking about labor practices in low-income countries, it is useful to draw a line between what is unpleasant to think about and what is morally objectionable. For example, low wages and long working hours in poor countries are unpleasant to think about, but for people in low-income parts of the world, it may well be the best option open to them. Practices like child labor and forced labor are morally objectionable and many countries refuse to import products made using these practices.

34.3 Arguments in Support of Restricting Imports

There are a number of arguments that support restricting imports. These arguments are based around industry and competition, environmental concerns, and issues of safety and security.

The infant industry argument for protectionism is that small domestic industries need to be temporarily nurtured and protected from foreign competition for a time so that they can grow into strong competitors. In some cases, notably in East Asia, this approach has worked. Often, however, the infant industries never grow up. On the other hand, arguments against dumping (which is setting prices below the cost of production to drive competitors out of the market), often simply seem to be a convenient excuse for imposing protectionism.

Low-income countries typically have lower environmental standards than high-income countries because they are more worried about immediate basics such as food, education, and healthcare. However, except for a small number of extreme cases, shutting off trade seems unlikely to be an effective method of pursuing a cleaner environment.

Finally, there are arguments involving safety and security. Under the rules of the World Trade Organization, countries are allowed to set whatever standards for product safety they wish, but the standards must be the same for domestic products as for imported products and there must be a scientific basis for the standard. The national interest argument for protectionism holds that it is unwise to import certain key products because if the nation becomes dependent on key imported supplies, it could be vulnerable to a cutoff. However, it is often wiser to stockpile resources and to use foreign supplies when available, rather than preemptively restricting foreign supplies so as not to become dependent on them.

34.4 How Governments Enact Trade Policy: Globally, Regionally, and Nationally

Governments determine trade policy at many different levels: administrative agencies within government, laws passed by the legislature, regional negotiations between a small group of nations (sometimes just two), and global negotiations through the World Trade Organization. During the second half of the twentieth century, trade barriers have, in general, declined quite substantially in the United States economy and in the global economy. One reason why countries sign international trade agreements to commit themselves to free trade is to give themselves protection against their own special interests. When an industry lobbies for protection from foreign producers, politicians can point out that, because of the trade treaty, their hands are tied.

34.5 The Tradeoffs of Trade Policy

International trade certainly has income distribution effects. This is hardly surprising. All domestic or international competitive market forces are disruptive. They cause companies and industries to rise and fall. Government has a role to play in cushioning workers against the disruptions of the market. However, just as it would be unwise in the long term to clamp down on new technology and other causes of disruption in domestic markets, it would be unwise to clamp down on foreign trade. In both cases, the disruption brings with it economic benefits.

SELF-CHECK QUESTIONS

1. Explain how a tariff reduction causes an increase in the equilibrium quantity of imports and a decrease in the equilibrium price. *Hint:* Consider the **Work It Out** "Effects of Trade Barriers."

2. Explain how a subsidy on agricultural goods like sugar adversely affects the income of foreign producers of imported sugar.

3. Explain how trade barriers save jobs in protected industries, but only by costing jobs in other industries.

4. Explain how trade barriers raise wages in protected industries by reducing average wages economy-wide.

5. How does international trade affect working conditions of low-income countries?

6. Do the jobs for workers in low-income countries that involve making products for export to high-income countries typically pay these workers more or less than their next-best alternative?

7. How do trade barriers affect the average income level in an economy?

8. How does the cost of "saving" jobs in protected industries compare to the workers' wages and salaries?

9. Explain how predatory pricing could be a motivation for dumping.

10. Why do low-income countries like Brazil, Egypt, or Vietnam have lower environmental standards than high-income countries like the Germany, Japan, or the United States?

11. Explain the logic behind the "race to the bottom" argument and the likely reason it has not occurred.

12. What are the conditions under which a country may use the unsafe products argument to block imports?

13. Why is the national security argument not convincing?

14. Assume a perfectly competitive market and the exporting country is small. Using a demand and supply diagram, show the impact of increasing standards on a low-income exporter of toys. Show the tariff's impact. Is the effect on toy prices the same or different? Why is a standards policy preferred to tariffs?

15. What is the difference between a free trade association, a common market, and an economic union?

16. Why would countries promote protectionist laws, while also negotiate for freer trade internationally?

17. What might account for the dramatic increase in international trade over the past 50 years?

18. How does competition, whether domestic or foreign, harm businesses?

19. What are the gains from competition?

REVIEW QUESTIONS

20. Who does protectionism protect? From what does it protect them?

21. Name and define three policy tools for enacting protectionism.

22. How does protectionism affect the price of the protected good in the domestic market?

23. Does international trade, taken as a whole, increase the total number of jobs, decrease the total number of jobs, or leave the total number of jobs about the same?

24. Is international trade likely to have roughly the same effect on the number of jobs in each individual industry?

25. How is international trade, taken as a whole, likely to affect the average level of wages?

26. Is international trade likely to have about the same effect on everyone's wages?

27. What are main reasons for protecting "infant industries"? Why is it difficult to stop protecting them?

28. What is dumping? Why does prohibiting it often work better in theory than in practice?

29. What is the "race to the bottom" scenario?

30. Do the rules of international trade require that all nations impose the same consumer safety standards?

31. What is the national interest argument for protectionism with regard to certain products?

32. Name several of the international treaties where countries negotiate with each other over trade policy.

33. What is the general trend of trade barriers over recent decades: higher, lower, or about the same?

34. If opening up to free trade would benefit a nation, then why do nations not just eliminate their trade barriers, and not bother with international trade negotiations?

35. Who gains and who loses from trade?

36. Why is trade a good thing if some people lose?

37. What are some ways that governments can help people who lose from trade?

CRITICAL THINKING QUESTIONS

38. Show graphically that for any tariff, there is an equivalent quota that would give the same result. What would be the difference, then, between the two types of trade barriers? *Hint*: It is not something you can see from the graph.

39. From the **Work It Out** "Effects of Trade Barriers," you can see that a tariff raises the price of imports. What is interesting is that the price rises by less than the amount of the tariff. Who pays the rest of the tariff amount? Can you show this graphically?

40. If trade barriers hurt the average worker in an economy (due to lower wages), why does government create trade barriers?

41. Why do you think labor standards and working conditions are lower in the low-income countries of the world than in countries like the United States?

42. How would direct subsidies to key industries be preferable to tariffs or quotas?

43. How can governments identify good candidates for infant industry protection? Can you suggest some key characteristics of good candidates? Why are industries like computers not good candidates for infant industry protection?

44. Microeconomic theory argues that it is economically rationale (and profitable) to sell additional output as long as the price covers the variable costs of production. How is this relevant to the determination of whether dumping has occurred?

45. How do you think Americans would feel if other countries began to urge the United States to increase environmental standards?

46. Is it legitimate to impose higher safety standards on imported goods that exist in the foreign country where the goods were produced?

47. Why might the unsafe consumer products argument be a more effective strategy (from the perspective of the importing country) than using tariffs or quotas to restrict imports?

48. Why might a tax on domestic consumption of resources critical for national security be a more efficient approach than barriers to imports?

49. Why do you think that the GATT rounds and, more recently, WTO negotiations have become longer and more difficult to resolve?

50. An economic union requires giving up some political autonomy to succeed. What are some examples of political power countries must give up to be members of an economic union?

51. What are some examples of innovative products that have disrupted their industries for the better?

52. In principle, the benefits of international trade to a country exceed the costs, no matter whether the country is importing or exporting. In practice, it is not always possible to compensate the losers in a country, for example, workers who lose their jobs due to foreign imports. In your opinion, does that mean that trade should be inhibited to prevent the losses?

53. Economists sometimes say that protectionism is the "second-best" choice for dealing with any particular problem. What they mean is that there is often a policy choice that is more direct or effective for dealing with the problem—a choice that would still allow the benefits of trade to occur. Explain why protectionism is a "second-best" choice for:
   a. helping workers as a group
   b. helping industries stay strong
   c. protecting the environment
   d. advancing national defense

54. Trade has income distribution effects. For example, suppose that because of a government-negotiated reduction in trade barriers, trade between Germany and the Czech Republic increases. Germany sells house paint to the Czech Republic. The Czech Republic sells alarm clocks to Germany. Would you expect this pattern of trade to increase or decrease jobs and wages in the paint industry in Germany? The alarm clock industry in Germany? The paint industry in Czech Republic? The alarm clock industry in Czech Republic? What has to happen for there to be no increase in total unemployment in both countries?

PROBLEMS

55. Assume two countries, Thailand (T) and Japan (J), have one good: cameras. The demand (d) and supply (s) for cameras in Thailand and Japan is described by the following functions: $Qd^T = 60 - P$

$$Qs^T = -5 + \frac{1}{4}P \qquad\qquad Qd^J = 80 - P$$

$$Qs^J = -10 + \frac{1}{2}P$$

P is the price measured in a common currency used in both countries, such as the Thai Baht.

    a. Compute the equilibrium price (P) and quantities (Q) in each country without trade.

    b. Now assume that free trade occurs. The free-trade price goes to 56.36 Baht. Who exports and imports cameras and in what quantities?

56. You have just been put in charge of trade policy for Malawi. Coffee is a recent crop that is growing well and the Malawian export market is developing. As such, Malawi coffee is an infant industry. Malawi coffee producers come to you and ask for tariff protection from cheap Tanzanian coffee. What sorts of policies will you enact? Explain.

57. The country of Pepperland exports steel to the Land of Submarines. Information for the quantity demanded (Qd) and quantity supplied (Qs) in each country, in a world without trade, are given in **Table 34.6** and **Table 34.7**.

Price ($)	Qd	Qs
60	230	180
70	200	200
80	170	220
90	150	240
100	140	250

Table 34.6 Pepperland

Price ($)	Qd	Qs
60	430	310
70	420	330
80	410	360
90	400	400
100	390	440

Table 34.7 Land of Submarines

    a. What would be the equilibrium price and quantity in each country in a world without trade? How can you tell?

    b. What would be the equilibrium price and quantity in each country if trade is allowed to occur? How can you tell?

    c. Sketch two supply and demand diagrams, one for each country, in the situation before trade.

    d. On those diagrams, show the equilibrium price and the levels of exports and imports in the world after trade.

    e. If the Land of Submarines imposes an anti-dumping import quota of 30, explain in general terms whether it will benefit or injure consumers and producers in each country.

    f. Does your general answer change if the Land of Submarines imposes an import quota of 70?

A | The Use of Mathematics in Principles of Economics

(This appendix should be consulted after first reading **Welcome to Economics!**) Economics is not math. There is no important concept in this course that cannot be explained without mathematics. That said, math is a tool that can be used to illustrate economic concepts. Remember the saying a picture is worth a thousand words? Instead of a picture, think of a graph. It is the same thing. Economists use models as the primary tool to derive insights about economic issues and problems. Math is one way of working with (or manipulating) economic models.

There are other ways of representing models, such as text or narrative. But why would you use your fist to bang a nail, if you had a hammer? Math has certain advantages over text. It disciplines your thinking by making you specify exactly what you mean. You can get away with fuzzy thinking in your head, but you cannot when you reduce a model to algebraic equations. At the same time, math also has disadvantages. Mathematical models are necessarily based on simplifying assumptions, so they are not likely to be perfectly realistic. Mathematical models also lack the nuances which can be found in narrative models. The point is that math is one tool, but it is not the only tool or even always the best tool economists can use. So what math will you need for this book? The answer is: little more than high school algebra and graphs. You will need to know:

- What a function is
- How to interpret the equation of a line (i.e., slope and intercept)
- How to manipulate a line (i.e., changing the slope or the intercept)
- How to compute and interpret a growth rate (i.e., percentage change)
- How to read and manipulate a graph

In this text, we will use the easiest math possible, and we will introduce it in this appendix. So if you find some math in the book that you cannot follow, come back to this appendix to review. Like most things, math has diminishing returns. A little math ability goes a long way; the more advanced math you bring in, the less additional knowledge that will get you. That said, if you are going to major in economics, you should consider learning a little calculus. It will be worth your while in terms of helping you learn advanced economics more quickly.

Algebraic Models

Often economic models (or parts of models) are expressed in terms of mathematical functions. What is a function? A function describes a relationship. Sometimes the relationship is a definition. For example (using words), your professor is Adam Smith. This could be expressed as Professor = Adam Smith. Or Friends = Bob + Shawn + Margaret.

Often in economics, functions describe cause and effect. The variable on the left-hand side is what is being explained ("the effect"). On the right-hand side is what is doing the explaining ("the causes"). For example, suppose your GPA was determined as follows:

$$GPA = 0.25 \times combined\_SAT + 0.25 \times class\_attendance + 0.50 \times hours\_spent\_studying$$

This equation states that your GPA depends on three things: your combined SAT score, your class attendance, and the number of hours you spend studying. It also says that study time is twice as important (0.50) as either combined_SAT score (0.25) or class_attendance (0.25). If this relationship is true, how could you raise your GPA? By not skipping class and studying more. Note that you cannot do anything about your SAT score, since if you are in college, you have (presumably) already taken the SATs.

Of course, economic models express relationships using economic variables, like Budget = money_spent_on_econ_books + money_spent_on_music, assuming that the only things you buy are economics books and music.

Most of the relationships we use in this course are expressed as linear equations of the form:

$$y = b + mx$$

Expressing Equations Graphically

Graphs are useful for two purposes. The first is to express equations visually, and the second is to display statistics or data. This section will discuss expressing equations visually.

To a mathematician or an economist, a variable is the name given to a quantity that may assume a range of values. In the equation of a line presented above, x and y are the variables, with x on the horizontal axis and y on the vertical axis, and b and m representing factors that determine the shape of the line. To see how this equation works, consider a numerical example:

$$y = 9 + 3x$$

In this equation for a specific line, the b term has been set equal to 9 and the m term has been set equal to 3. **Table A1** shows the values of x and y for this given equation. **Figure A1** shows this equation, and these values, in a graph. To construct the table, just plug in a series of different values for x, and then calculate what value of y results. In the figure, these points are plotted and a line is drawn through them.

x	y
0	9
1	12
2	15
3	18
4	21
5	24
6	27

Table A1 Values for the Slope Intercept Equation

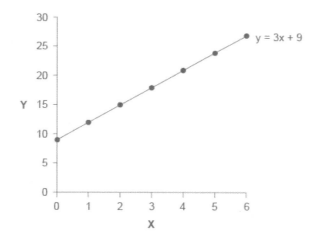

Figure A1 Slope and the Algebra of Straight Lines   This line graph has *x* on the horizontal axis and y on the vertical axis. The y-intercept—that is, the point where the line intersects the y-axis—is 9. The slope of the line is 3; that is, there is a rise of 3 on the vertical axis for every increase of 1 on the horizontal axis. The slope is the same all along a straight line.

This example illustrates how the b and m terms in an equation for a straight line determine the shape of the line. The

This OpenStax book is available for free at http://cnx.org/content/col12122/1.4

b term is called the y-intercept. The reason for this name is that, if x = 0, then the b term will reveal where the line intercepts, or crosses, the y-axis. In this example, the line hits the vertical axis at 9. The m term in the equation for the line is the slope. Remember that slope is defined as rise over run; more specifically, the slope of a line from one point to another is the change in the vertical axis divided by the change in the horizontal axis. In this example, each time the x term increases by one (the run), the y term rises by three. Thus, the slope of this line is three. Specifying a y-intercept and a slope—that is, specifying b and m in the equation for a line—will identify a specific line. Although it is rare for real-world data points to arrange themselves as an exact straight line, it often turns out that a straight line can offer a reasonable approximation of actual data.

Interpreting the Slope

The concept of slope is very useful in economics, because it measures the relationship between two variables. A positive slope means that two variables are positively related; that is, when x increases, so does y, or when x decreases, y decreases also. Graphically, a positive slope means that as a line on the line graph moves from left to right, the line rises. The length-weight relationship, shown in **Figure A3** later in this Appendix, has a positive slope. We will learn in other chapters that price and quantity supplied have a positive relationship; that is, firms will supply more when the price is higher.

A negative slope means that two variables are negatively related; that is, when x increases, y decreases, or when x decreases, y increases. Graphically, a negative slope means that, as the line on the line graph moves from left to right, the line falls. The altitude-air density relationship, shown in **Figure A4** later in this appendix, has a negative slope. We will learn that price and quantity demanded have a negative relationship; that is, consumers will purchase less when the price is higher.

A slope of zero means that there is no relationship between x and y. Graphically, the line is flat; that is, zero rise over the run. **Figure A5** of the unemployment rate, shown later in this appendix, illustrates a common pattern of many line graphs: some segments where the slope is positive, other segments where the slope is negative, and still other segments where the slope is close to zero.

The slope of a straight line between two points can be calculated in numerical terms. To calculate slope, begin by designating one point as the "starting point" and the other point as the "end point" and then calculating the rise over run between these two points. As an example, consider the slope of the air density graph between the points representing an altitude of 4,000 meters and an altitude of 6,000 meters:

Rise: Change in variable on vertical axis (end point minus original point)

$$= \ 0.100 - 0.307$$
$$= \ -0.207$$

Run: Change in variable on horizontal axis (end point minus original point)

$$= \ 6,000 - 4,000$$
$$= \ 2,000$$

Thus, the slope of a straight line between these two points would be that from the altitude of 4,000 meters up to 6,000 meters, the density of the air decreases by approximately 0.1 kilograms/cubic meter for each of the next 1,000 meters.

Suppose the slope of a line were to increase. Graphically, that means it would get steeper. Suppose the slope of a line were to decrease. Then it would get flatter. These conditions are true whether or not the slope was positive or negative to begin with. A higher positive slope means a steeper upward tilt to the line, while a smaller positive slope means a flatter upward tilt to the line. A negative slope that is larger in absolute value (that is, more negative) means a steeper downward tilt to the line. A slope of zero is a horizontal flat line. A vertical line has an infinite slope.

Suppose a line has a larger intercept. Graphically, that means it would shift out (or up) from the old origin, parallel to the old line. If a line has a smaller intercept, it would shift in (or down), parallel to the old line.

Solving Models with Algebra

Economists often use models to answer a specific question, like: What will the unemployment rate be if the economy grows at 3% per year? Answering specific questions requires solving the "system" of equations that represent the model.

Suppose the demand for personal pizzas is given by the following equation:

$$Qd = 16 - 2P$$

where Qd is the amount of personal pizzas consumers want to buy (i.e., quantity demanded), and P is the price of pizzas. Suppose the supply of personal pizzas is:

$$Qs = 2 + 5P$$

where Qs is the amount of pizza producers will supply (i.e., quantity supplied).

Finally, suppose that the personal pizza market operates where supply equals demand, or

$$Qd = Qs$$

We now have a system of three equations and three unknowns (Qd, Qs, and P), which we can solve with algebra:

Since Qd = Qs, we can set the demand and supply equation equal to each other:

$$Qd = Qs$$
$$16 - 2P = 2 + 5P$$

Subtracting 2 from both sides and adding 2P to both sides yields:

$$16 - 2P - 2 = 2 + 5P - 2$$
$$14 - 2P = 5P$$
$$14 - 2P + 2P = 5P + 2P$$
$$14 = 7P$$
$$\frac{14}{7} = \frac{7P}{7}$$
$$2 = P$$

In other words, the price of each personal pizza will be $2. How much will consumers buy?

Taking the price of $2, and plugging it into the demand equation, we get:

$$Qd = 16 - 2P$$
$$= 16 - 2(2)$$
$$= 16 - 4$$
$$= 12$$

So if the price is $2 each, consumers will purchase 12. How much will producers supply? Taking the price of $2, and plugging it into the supply equation, we get:

$$Qs = 2 + 5P$$
$$= 2 + 5(2)$$
$$= 2 + 10$$
$$= 12$$

So if the price is $2 each, producers will supply 12 personal pizzas. This means we did our math correctly, since Qd = Qs.

Solving Models with Graphs

If algebra is not your forte, you can get the same answer by using graphs. Take the equations for Qd and Qs and graph them on the same set of axes as shown in **Figure A2**. Since P is on the vertical axis, it is easiest if you solve each equation for P. The demand curve is then P = 8 − 0.5Qd and the supply curve is P = −0.4 + 0.2Qs. Note that the vertical intercepts are 8 and −0.4, and the slopes are −0.5 for demand and 0.2 for supply. If you draw the graphs carefully, you will see that where they cross (Qs = Qd), the price is $2 and the quantity is 12, just like the algebra predicted.

This OpenStax book is available for free at http://cnx.org/content/col12122/1.4

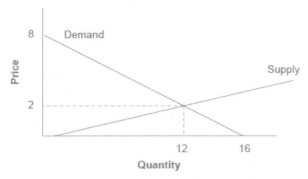

Figure A2 Supply and Demand Graph The equations for Qd and Qs are displayed graphically by the sloped lines.

We will use graphs more frequently in this book than algebra, but now you know the math behind the graphs.

Growth Rates

Growth rates are frequently encountered in real world economics. A growth rate is simply the percentage change in some quantity. It could be your income. It could be a business's sales. It could be a nation's GDP. The formula for computing a growth rate is straightforward:

$$\text{Percentage change} = \frac{\text{Change in quantity}}{\text{Quantity}}$$

Suppose your job pays $10 per hour. Your boss, however, is so impressed with your work that he gives you a $2 per hour raise. The percentage change (or growth rate) in your pay is $2/$10 = 0.20 or 20%.

To compute the growth rate for data over an extended period of time, for example, the average annual growth in GDP over a decade or more, the denominator is commonly defined a little differently. In the previous example, we defined the quantity as the initial quantity—or the quantity when we started. This is fine for a one-time calculation, but when we compute the growth over and over, it makes more sense to define the quantity as the average quantity over the period in question, which is defined as the quantity halfway between the initial quantity and the next quantity. This is harder to explain in words than to show with an example. Suppose a nation's GDP was $1 trillion in 2005 and $1.03 trillion in 2006. The growth rate between 2005 and 2006 would be the change in GDP ($1.03 trillion – $1.00 trillion) divided by the average GDP between 2005 and 2006 ($1.03 trillion + $1.00 trillion)/2. In other words:

$$= \frac{\$1.03 \text{ trillion} - \$1.00 \text{ trillion}}{(\$1.03 \text{ trillion} + \$1.00 \text{ trillion}) / 2}$$
$$= \frac{0.03}{1.015}$$
$$= 0.0296$$
$$= 2.96\% \text{ growth}$$

Note that if we used the first method, the calculation would be ($1.03 trillion – $1.00 trillion) / $1.00 trillion = 3% growth, which is approximately the same as the second, more complicated method. If you need a rough approximation, use the first method. If you need accuracy, use the second method.

A few things to remember: A positive growth rate means the quantity is growing. A smaller growth rate means the quantity is growing more slowly. A larger growth rate means the quantity is growing more quickly. A negative growth rate means the quantity is decreasing.

The same change over times yields a smaller growth rate. If you got a $2 raise each year, in the first year the growth rate would be $2/$10 = 20%, as shown above. But in the second year, the growth rate would be $2/$12 = 0.167 or 16.7% growth. In the third year, the same $2 raise would correspond to a $2/$14 = 14.2%. The moral of the story is this: To keep the growth rate the same, the change must increase each period.

Displaying Data Graphically and Interpreting the Graph

Graphs are also used to display data or evidence. Graphs are a method of presenting numerical patterns. They condense detailed numerical information into a visual form in which relationships and numerical patterns can be seen more easily. For example, which countries have larger or smaller populations? A careful reader could examine a long list of numbers representing the populations of many countries, but with over 200 nations in the world, searching through such a list would take concentration and time. Putting these same numbers on a graph can quickly reveal population patterns. Economists use graphs both for a compact and readable presentation of groups of numbers and for building an intuitive grasp of relationships and connections.

Three types of graphs are used in this book: line graphs, pie graphs, and bar graphs. Each is discussed below. We also provide warnings about how graphs can be manipulated to alter viewers' perceptions of the relationships in the data.

Line Graphs

The graphs we have discussed so far are called line graphs, because they show a relationship between two variables: one measured on the horizontal axis and the other measured on the vertical axis.

Sometimes it is useful to show more than one set of data on the same axes. The data in **Table A2** is displayed in **Figure A3** which shows the relationship between two variables: length and median weight for American baby boys and girls during the first three years of life. (The median means that half of all babies weigh more than this and half weigh less.) The line graph measures length in inches on the horizontal axis and weight in pounds on the vertical axis. For example, point A on the figure shows that a boy who is 28 inches long will have a median weight of about 19 pounds. One line on the graph shows the length-weight relationship for boys and the other line shows the relationship for girls. This kind of graph is widely used by healthcare providers to check whether a child's physical development is roughly on track.

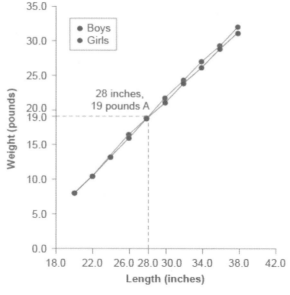

Figure A3 The Length-Weight Relationship for American Boys and Girls   The line graph shows the relationship between height and weight for boys and girls from birth to 3 years. Point A, for example, shows that a boy of 28 inches in height (measured on the horizontal axis) is typically 19 pounds in weight (measured on the vertical axis). These data apply only to children in the first three years of life.

Boys from Birth to 36 Months		Girls from Birth to 36 Months	
Length (inches)	Weight (pounds)	Length (inches)	Weight (pounds)
20.0	8.0	20.0	7.9
22.0	10.5	22.0	10.5

Table A2 Length to Weight Relationship for American Boys and Girls

This OpenStax book is available for free at http://cnx.org/content/col12122/1.4

Boys from Birth to 36 Months		Girls from Birth to 36 Months	
24.0	13.5	24.0	13.2
26.0	16.4	26.0	16.0
28.0	19.0	28.0	18.8
30.0	21.8	30.0	21.2
32.0	24.3	32.0	24.0
34.0	27.0	34.0	26.2
36.0	29.3	36.0	28.9
38.0	32.0	38.0	31.3

Table A2 Length to Weight Relationship for American Boys and Girls

Not all relationships in economics are linear. Sometimes they are curves. **Figure A4** presents another example of a line graph, representing the data from **Table A3**. In this case, the line graph shows how thin the air becomes when you climb a mountain. The horizontal axis of the figure shows altitude, measured in meters above sea level. The vertical axis measures the density of the air at each altitude. Air density is measured by the weight of the air in a cubic meter of space (that is, a box measuring one meter in height, width, and depth). As the graph shows, air pressure is heaviest at ground level and becomes lighter as you climb. **Figure A4** shows that a cubic meter of air at an altitude of 500 meters weighs approximately one kilogram (about 2.2 pounds). However, as the altitude increases, air density decreases. A cubic meter of air at the top of Mount Everest, at about 8,828 meters, would weigh only 0.023 kilograms. The thin air at high altitudes explains why many mountain climbers need to use oxygen tanks as they reach the top of a mountain.

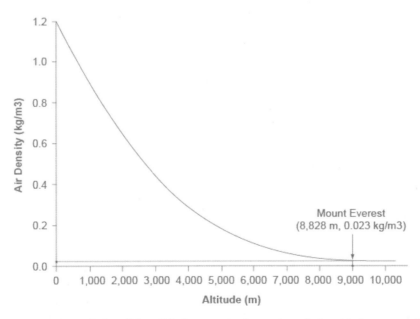

Figure A4 Altitude-Air Density Relationship   This line graph shows the relationship between altitude, measured in meters above sea level, and air density, measured in kilograms of air per cubic meter. As altitude rises, air density declines. The point at the top of Mount Everest has an altitude of approximately 8,828 meters above sea level (the horizontal axis) and air density of 0.023 kilograms per cubic meter (the vertical axis).

Altitude (meters)	Air Density (kg/cubic meters)
0	1.200
500	1.093
1,000	0.831
1,500	0.678
2,000	0.569
2,500	0.484
3,000	0.415
3,500	0.357
4,000	0.307
4,500	0.231
5,000	0.182
5,500	0.142
6,000	0.100
6,500	0.085
7,000	0.066
7,500	0.051
8,000	0.041
8,500	0.025
9,000	0.022
9,500	0.019
10,000	0.014

Table A3 Altitude to Air Density Relationship

The length-weight relationship and the altitude-air density relationships in these two figures represent averages. If you were to collect actual data on air pressure at different altitudes, the same altitude in different geographic locations will have slightly different air density, depending on factors like how far you are from the equator, local weather conditions, and the humidity in the air. Similarly, in measuring the height and weight of children for the previous line graph, children of a particular height would have a range of different weights, some above average and some below. In the real world, this sort of variation in data is common. The task of a researcher is to organize that data in a way that helps to understand typical patterns. The study of statistics, especially when combined with computer statistics and spreadsheet programs, is a great help in organizing this kind of data, plotting line graphs, and looking for typical underlying relationships. For most economics and social science majors, a statistics course will be required at some point.

One common line graph is called a time series, in which the horizontal axis shows time and the vertical axis displays another variable. Thus, a time series graph shows how a variable changes over time. **Figure A5** shows the unemployment rate in the United States since 1975, where unemployment is defined as the percentage of adults who want jobs and are looking for a job, but cannot find one. The points for the unemployment rate in each year are plotted

This OpenStax book is available for free at http://cnx.org/content/col12122/1.4

on the graph, and a line then connects the points, showing how the unemployment rate has moved up and down since 1975. The line graph makes it easy to see, for example, that the highest unemployment rate during this time period was slightly less than 10% in the early 1980s and 2010, while the unemployment rate declined from the early 1990s to the end of the 1990s, before rising and then falling back in the early 2000s, and then rising sharply during the recession from 2008–2009.

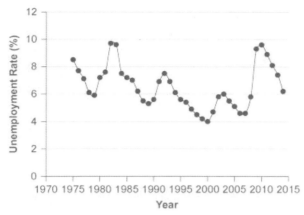

Figure A5 U.S. Unemployment Rate, 1975–2014 This graph provides a quick visual summary of unemployment data. With a graph like this, it is easy to spot the times of high unemployment and of low unemployment.

Pie Graphs

A pie graph (sometimes called a pie chart) is used to show how an overall total is divided into parts. A circle represents a group as a whole. The slices of this circular "pie" show the relative sizes of subgroups.

Figure A6 shows how the U.S. population was divided among children, working age adults, and the elderly in 1970, 2000, and what is projected for 2030. The information is first conveyed with numbers in **Table A4**, and then in three pie charts. The first column of **Table A4** shows the total U.S. population for each of the three years. Columns 2–4 categorize the total in terms of age groups—from birth to 18 years, from 19 to 64 years, and 65 years and above. In columns 2–4, the first number shows the actual number of people in each age category, while the number in parentheses shows the percentage of the total population comprised by that age group.

Year	Total Population	19 and Under	20–64 years	Over 65
1970	205.0 million	77.2 (37.6%)	107.7 (52.5%)	20.1 (9.8%)
2000	275.4 million	78.4 (28.5%)	162.2 (58.9%)	34.8 (12.6%)
2030	351.1 million	92.6 (26.4%)	188.2 (53.6%)	70.3 (20.0%)

Table A4 U.S. Age Distribution, 1970, 2000, and 2030 (projected)

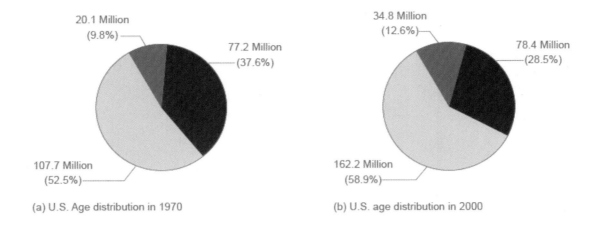

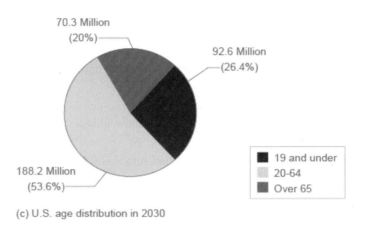

(c) U.S. age distribution in 2030

Figure A6 Pie Graphs of the U.S. Age Distribution (numbers in millions)   The three pie graphs illustrate the division of total population into three age groups for the three different years.

In a pie graph, each slice of the pie represents a share of the total, or a percentage. For example, 50% would be half of the pie and 20% would be one-fifth of the pie. The three pie graphs in **Figure A6** show that the share of the U.S. population 65 and over is growing. The pie graphs allow you to get a feel for the relative size of the different age groups from 1970 to 2000 to 2030, without requiring you to slog through the specific numbers and percentages in the table. Some common examples of how pie graphs are used include dividing the population into groups by age, income level, ethnicity, religion, occupation; dividing different firms into categories by size, industry, number of employees; and dividing up government spending or taxes into its main categories.

Bar Graphs

A bar graph uses the height of different bars to compare quantities. **Table A5** lists the 12 most populous countries in the world. **Figure A7** provides this same data in a bar graph. The height of the bars corresponds to the population of each country. Although you may know that China and India are the most populous countries in the world, seeing how the bars on the graph tower over the other countries helps illustrate the magnitude of the difference between the sizes of national populations.

This OpenStax book is available for free at http://cnx.org/content/col12122/1.4

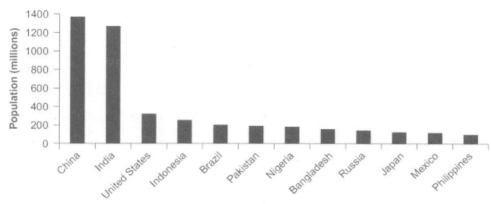

Figure A7 Leading Countries of the World by Population, 2015 (in millions) The graph shows the 12 countries of the world with the largest populations. The height of the bars in the bar graph shows the size of the population for each country.

Country	Population
China	1,369
India	1,270
United States	321
Indonesia	255
Brazil	204
Pakistan	190
Nigeria	184
Bangladesh	158
Russia	146
Japan	127
Mexico	121
Philippines	101

Table A5 Leading 12 Countries of the World by Population

Bar graphs can be subdivided in a way that reveals information similar to that we can get from pie charts. **Figure A8** offers three bar graphs based on the information from **Figure A6** about the U.S. age distribution in 1970, 2000, and 2030. **Figure A8** (a) shows three bars for each year, representing the total number of persons in each age bracket for each year. **Figure A8** (b) shows just one bar for each year, but the different age groups are now shaded inside the bar. In **Figure A8** (c), still based on the same data, the vertical axis measures percentages rather than the number of persons. In this case, all three bar graphs are the same height, representing 100% of the population, with each bar divided according to the percentage of population in each age group. It is sometimes easier for a reader to run his or her eyes across several bar graphs, comparing the shaded areas, rather than trying to compare several pie graphs.

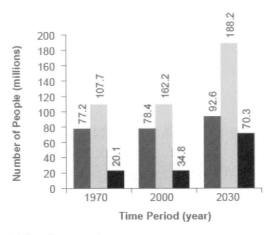

(a) Bars for separate age groups

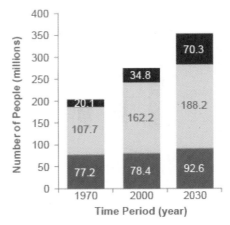

(b) Bars show total population divided into age groups

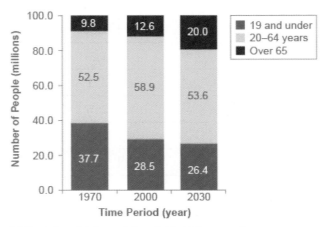

(c) Bars show total population divided into percentages

Figure A8 U.S. Population with Bar Graphs Population data can be represented in different ways. (a) Shows three bars for each year, representing the total number of persons in each age bracket for each year. (b) Shows just one bar for each year, but the different age groups are now shaded inside the bar. (c) Sets the vertical axis as a measure of percentages rather than the number of persons. All three bar graphs are the same height and each bar is divided according to the percentage of population in each age group.

Figure A7 and **Figure A8** show how the bars can represent countries or years, and how the vertical axis can represent a numerical or a percentage value. Bar graphs can also compare size, quantity, rates, distances, and other quantitative categories.

Comparing Line Graphs with Pie Charts and Bar Graphs

Now that you are familiar with pie graphs, bar graphs, and line graphs, how do you know which graph to use for your data? Pie graphs are often better than line graphs at showing how an overall group is divided. However, if a pie graph has too many slices, it can become difficult to interpret.

Bar graphs are especially useful when comparing quantities. For example, if you are studying the populations of different countries, as in **Figure A7**, bar graphs can show the relationships between the population sizes of multiple countries. Not only can it show these relationships, but it can also show breakdowns of different groups within the population.

A line graph is often the most effective format for illustrating a relationship between two variables that are both changing. For example, time series graphs can show patterns as time changes, like the unemployment rate over time.

This OpenStax book is available for free at http://cnx.org/content/col12122/1.4

Line graphs are widely used in economics to present continuous data about prices, wages, quantities bought and sold, the size of the economy.

How Graphs Can Be Misleading

Graphs not only reveal patterns; they can also alter how patterns are perceived. To see some of the ways this can be done, consider the line graphs of **Figure A9**, **Figure A10**, and **Figure A11**. These graphs all illustrate the unemployment rate—but from different perspectives.

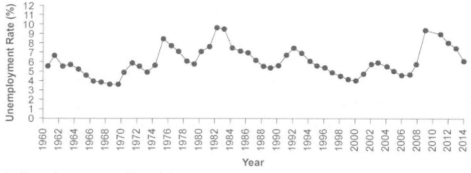

(a) Unemployment rate, wide and short

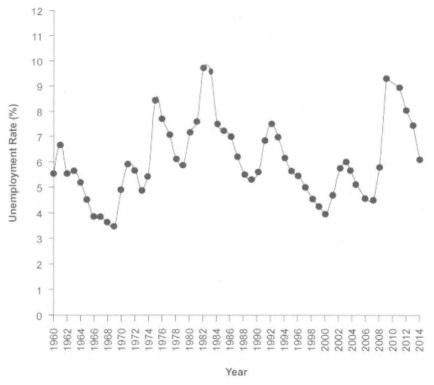

(b) Unemployment rate, narrow and tall

Figure A9

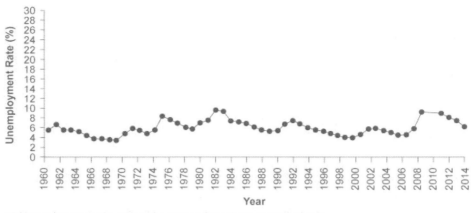

(c) Unemployment rate, with wider range of numbers on vertical axis

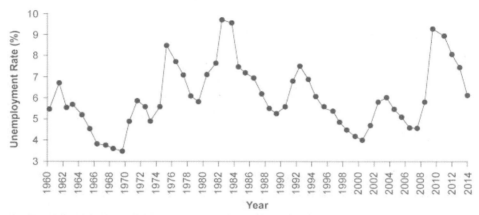

(d) Unemployment rate, with smaller range of numbers on vertical axis

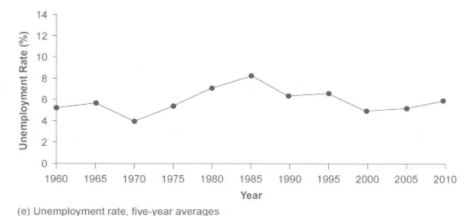

(e) Unemployment rate, five-year averages

Figure A10 Presenting Unemployment Rates in Different Ways, All of Them Accurate   Simply changing the width and height of the area in which data is displayed can alter the perception of the data.

This OpenStax book is available for free at http://cnx.org/content/col12122/1.4

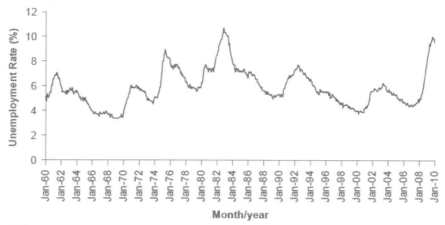

(f) Unemployment rate, monthly data

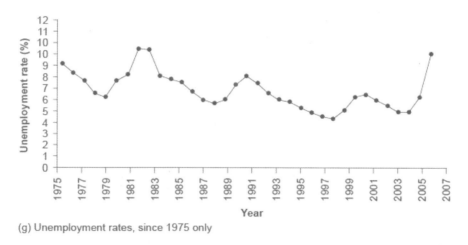

(g) Unemployment rates, since 1975 only

Figure A11 Presenting Unemployment Rates in Different Ways, All of Them Accurate Simply changing the width and height of the area in which data is displayed can alter the perception of the data.

Suppose you wanted a graph which gives the impression that the rise in unemployment in 2009 was not all that large, or all that extraordinary by historical standards. You might choose to present your data as in **Figure A9** (a). **Figure A9** (a) includes much of the same data presented earlier in **Figure A5**, but stretches the horizontal axis out longer relative to the vertical axis. By spreading the graph wide and flat, the visual appearance is that the rise in unemployment is not so large, and is similar to some past rises in unemployment. Now imagine you wanted to emphasize how unemployment spiked substantially higher in 2009. In this case, using the same data, you can stretch the vertical axis out relative to the horizontal axis, as in **Figure A9** (b), which makes all rises and falls in unemployment appear larger.

A similar effect can be accomplished without changing the length of the axes, but by changing the scale on the vertical axis. In **Figure A10** (c), the scale on the vertical axis runs from 0% to 30%, while in **Figure A10** (d), the vertical axis runs from 3% to 10%. Compared to **Figure A5**, where the vertical scale runs from 0% to 12%, **Figure A10** (c) makes the fluctuation in unemployment look smaller, while **Figure A10** (d) makes it look larger.

Another way to alter the perception of the graph is to reduce the amount of variation by changing the number of points plotted on the graph. **Figure A10** (e) shows the unemployment rate according to five-year averages. By averaging out some of the year-to-year changes, the line appears smoother and with fewer highs and lows. In reality, the unemployment rate is reported monthly, and **Figure A11** (f) shows the monthly figures since 1960, which fluctuate more than the five-year average. **Figure A11** (f) is also a vivid illustration of how graphs can compress lots of data. The graph includes monthly data since 1960, which over almost 50 years, works out to nearly 600 data points.

Reading that list of 600 data points in numerical form would be hypnotic. You can, however, get a good intuitive sense of these 600 data points very quickly from the graph.

A final trick in manipulating the perception of graphical information is that, by choosing the starting and ending points carefully, you can influence the perception of whether the variable is rising or falling. The original data show a general pattern with unemployment low in the 1960s, but spiking up in the mid-1970s, early 1980s, early 1990s, early 2000s, and late 2000s. **Figure A11** (g), however, shows a graph that goes back only to 1975, which gives an impression that unemployment was more-or-less gradually falling over time until the 2009 recession pushed it back up to its "original" level—which is a plausible interpretation if one starts at the high point around 1975.

These kinds of tricks—or shall we just call them "presentation choices"— are not limited to line graphs. In a pie chart with many small slices and one large slice, someone must decided what categories should be used to produce these slices in the first place, thus making some slices appear bigger than others. If you are making a bar graph, you can make the vertical axis either taller or shorter, which will tend to make variations in the height of the bars appear more or less.

Being able to read graphs is an essential skill, both in economics and in life. A graph is just one perspective or point of view, shaped by choices such as those discussed in this section. Do not always believe the first quick impression from a graph. View with caution.

Key Concepts and Summary

Math is a tool for understanding economics and economic relationships can be expressed mathematically using algebra or graphs. The algebraic equation for a line is $y = b + mx$, where x is the variable on the horizontal axis and y is the variable on the vertical axis, the b term is the y-intercept and the m term is the slope. The slope of a line is the same at any point on the line and it indicates the relationship (positive, negative, or zero) between two economic variables.

Economic models can be solved algebraically or graphically. Graphs allow you to illustrate data visually. They can illustrate patterns, comparisons, trends, and apportionment by condensing the numerical data and providing an intuitive sense of relationships in the data. A line graph shows the relationship between two variables: one is shown on the horizontal axis and one on the vertical axis. A pie graph shows how something is allotted, such as a sum of money or a group of people. The size of each slice of the pie is drawn to represent the corresponding percentage of the whole. A bar graph uses the height of bars to show a relationship, where each bar represents a certain entity, like a country or a group of people. The bars on a bar graph can also be divided into segments to show subgroups.

Any graph is a single visual perspective on a subject. The impression it leaves will be based on many choices, such as what data or time frame is included, how data or groups are divided up, the relative size of vertical and horizontal axes, whether the scale used on a vertical starts at zero. Thus, any graph should be regarded somewhat skeptically, remembering that the underlying relationship can be open to different interpretations.

Review Questions

Exercise A1

Name three kinds of graphs and briefly state when is most appropriate to use each type of graph.

Exercise A2

What is slope on a line graph?

Exercise A3

What do the slices of a pie chart represent?

Exercise A4

Why is a bar chart the best way to illustrate comparisons?

Exercise A5

How does the appearance of positive slope differ from negative slope and from zero slope?

This OpenStax book is available for free at http://cnx.org/content/col12122/1.4

B | Indifference Curves

Economists use a vocabulary of maximizing utility to describe people's preferences. In **Consumer Choices**, the level of utility that a person receives is described in numerical terms. This appendix presents an alternative approach to describing personal preferences, called indifference curves, which avoids any need for using numbers to measure utility. By setting aside the assumption of putting a numerical valuation on utility—an assumption that many students and economists find uncomfortably unrealistic—the indifference curve framework helps to clarify the logic of the underlying model.

What Is an Indifference Curve?

People cannot really put a numerical value on their level of satisfaction. However, they can, and do, identify what choices would give them more, or less, or the same amount of satisfaction. An indifference curve shows combinations of goods that provide an equal level of utility or satisfaction. For example, **Figure B1** presents three indifference curves that represent Lilly's preferences for the tradeoffs that she faces in her two main relaxation activities: eating doughnuts and reading paperback books. Each indifference curve (Ul, Um, and Uh) represents one level of utility. First we will explore the meaning of one particular indifference curve and then we will look at the indifference curves as a group.

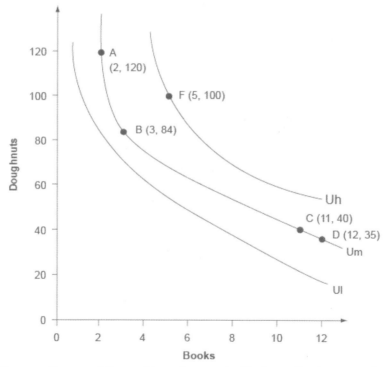

Figure B1 Lilly's Indifference Curves   Lilly would receive equal utility from all points on a given indifference curve. Any points on the highest indifference curve Uh, like F, provide greater utility than any points like A, B, C, and D on the middle indifference curve Um. Similarly, any points on the middle indifference curve Um provide greater utility than any points on the lowest indifference curve Ul.

The Shape of an Indifference Curve

The indifference curve Um has four points labeled on it: A, B, C, and D. Since an indifference curve represents a set of choices that have the same level of utility, Lilly must receive an equal amount of utility, judged according to her personal preferences, from two books and 120 doughnuts (point A), from three books and 84 doughnuts (point B) from 11 books and 40 doughnuts (point C) or from 12 books and 35 doughnuts (point D). She would also receive the same utility from any of the unlabeled intermediate points along this indifference curve.

Indifference curves have a roughly similar shape in two ways: 1) they are downward sloping from left to right; 2) they are convex with respect to the origin. In other words, they are steeper on the left and flatter on the right. The downward slope of the indifference curve means that Lilly must trade off less of one good to get more of the other, while holding utility constant. For example, points A and B sit on the same indifference curve Um, which means that they provide Lilly with the same level of utility. Thus, the marginal utility that Lilly would gain from, say, increasing her consumption of books from two to three must be equal to the marginal utility that she would lose if her consumption of doughnuts was cut from 120 to 84—so that her overall utility remains unchanged between points A and B. Indeed, the slope along an indifference curve as the marginal rate of substitution, which is the rate at which a person is willing to trade one good for another so that utility will remain the same.

Indifference curves like Um are steeper on the left and flatter on the right. The reason behind this shape involves diminishing marginal utility—the notion that as a person consumes more of a good, the marginal utility from each additional unit becomes lower. Compare two different choices between points that all provide Lilly an equal amount of utility along the indifference curve Um: the choice between A and B, and between C and D. In both choices, Lilly consumes one more book, but between A and B her consumption of doughnuts falls by 36 (from 120 to 84) and between C and D it falls by only five (from 40 to 35). The reason for this difference is that points A and C are different starting points, and thus have different implications for marginal utility. At point A, Lilly has few books and many doughnuts. Thus, her marginal utility from an extra book will be relatively high while the marginal utility of additional doughnuts is relatively low—so on the margin, it will take a relatively large number of doughnuts to offset the utility from the marginal book. At point C, however, Lilly has many books and few doughnuts. From this starting point, her marginal utility gained from extra books will be relatively low, while the marginal utility lost from additional doughnuts would be relatively high—so on the margin, it will take a relatively smaller number of doughnuts to offset the change of one marginal book. In short, the slope of the indifference curve changes because the marginal rate of substitution—that is, the quantity of one good that would be traded for the other good to keep utility constant—also changes, as a result of diminishing marginal utility of both goods.

The Field of Indifference Curves

Each indifference curve represents the choices that provide a single level of utility. Every level of utility will have its own indifference curve. Thus, Lilly's preferences will include an infinite number of indifference curves lying nestled together on the diagram—even though only three of the indifference curves, representing three levels of utility, appear on **Figure B1**. In other words, an infinite number of indifference curves are not drawn on this diagram—but you should remember that they exist.

Higher indifference curves represent a greater level of utility than lower ones. In **Figure B1**, indifference curve Ul can be thought of as a "low" level of utility, while Um is a "medium" level of utility and Uh is a "high" level of utility. All of the choices on indifference curve Uh are preferred to all of the choices on indifference curve Um, which in turn are preferred to all of the choices on Ul.

To understand why higher indifference curves are preferred to lower ones, compare point B on indifference curve Um to point F on indifference curve Uh. Point F has greater consumption of both books (five to three) and doughnuts (100 to 84), so point F is clearly preferable to point B. Given the definition of an indifference curve—that all the points on the curve have the same level of utility—if point F on indifference curve Uh is preferred to point B on indifference curve Um, then it must be true that all points on indifference curve Uh have a higher level of utility than all points on Um. More generally, for any point on a lower indifference curve, like Ul, you can identify a point on a higher indifference curve like Um or Uh that has a higher consumption of both goods. Since one point on the higher indifference curve is preferred to one point on the lower curve, and since all the points on a given indifference curve have the same level of utility, it must be true that all points on higher indifference curves have greater utility than all points on lower indifference curves.

These arguments about the shapes of indifference curves and about higher or lower levels of utility do not require any numerical estimates of utility, either by the individual or by anyone else. They are only based on the assumptions that when people have less of one good they need more of another good to make up for it, if they are keeping the same level of utility, and that as people have more of a good, the marginal utility they receive from additional units of that good will diminish. Given these gentle assumptions, a field of indifference curves can be mapped out to describe the preferences of any individual.

The Individuality of Indifference Curves

Each person determines his or her own preferences and utility. Thus, while indifference curves have the same general shape—they slope down, and the slope is steeper on the left and flatter on the right—the specific shape of indifference

This OpenStax book is available for free at http://cnx.org/content/col12122/1.4

curves can be different for every person. **Figure B1**, for example, applies only to Lilly's preferences. Indifference curves for other people would probably travel through different points.

Utility-Maximizing with Indifference Curves

People seek the highest level of utility, which means that they wish to be on the highest possible indifference curve. However, people are limited by their budget constraints, which show what tradeoffs are actually possible.

Maximizing Utility at the Highest Indifference Curve

Return to the situation of Lilly's choice between paperback books and doughnuts. Say that books cost $6, doughnuts are 50 cents each, and that Lilly has $60 to spend. This information provides the basis for the budget line shown in **Figure B2**. Along with the budget line are shown the three indifference curves from **Figure B1**. What is Lilly's utility-maximizing choice? Several possibilities are identified in the diagram.

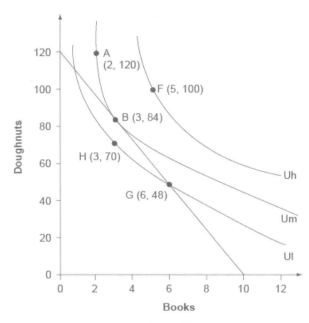

Figure B2 Indifference Curves and a Budget Constraint   Lilly's preferences are shown by the indifference curves. Lilly's budget constraint, given the prices of books and doughnuts and her income, is shown by the straight line. Lilly's optimal choice will be point B, where the budget line is tangent to the indifference curve Um. Lilly would have more utility at a point like F on the higher indifference curve Uh, but the budget line does not touch the higher indifference curve Uh at any point, so she cannot afford this choice. A choice like G is affordable to Lilly, but it lies on indifference curve Ul and thus provides less utility than choice B, which is on indifference curve Um.

The choice of F with five books and 100 doughnuts is highly desirable, since it is on the highest indifference curve Uh of those shown in the diagram. However, it is not affordable given Lilly's budget constraint. The choice of H with three books and 70 doughnuts on indifference curve Ul is a wasteful choice, since it is inside Lilly's budget set, and as a utility-maximizer, Lilly will always prefer a choice on the budget constraint itself. Choices B and G are both on the opportunity set. However, choice G of six books and 48 doughnuts is on lower indifference curve Ul than choice B of three books and 84 doughnuts, which is on the indifference curve Um. If Lilly were to start at choice G, and then thought about whether the marginal utility she was deriving from doughnuts and books, she would decide that some additional doughnuts and fewer books would make her happier—which would cause her to move toward her preferred choice B. Given the combination of Lilly's personal preferences, as identified by her indifference curves, and Lilly's opportunity set, which is determined by prices and income, B will be her utility-maximizing choice.

The highest achievable indifference curve touches the opportunity set at a single point of tangency. Since an infinite number of indifference curves exist, even if only a few of them are drawn on any given diagram, there will always exist one indifference curve that touches the budget line at a single point of tangency. All higher indifference curves, like Uh, will be completely above the budget line and, although the choices on that indifference curve would provide higher utility, they are not affordable given the budget set. All lower indifference curves, like Ul, will cross the budget line in two separate places. When one indifference curve crosses the budget line in two places, however, there will be another, higher, attainable indifference curve sitting above it that touches the budget line at only one point of tangency.

Changes in Income

A rise in income causes the budget constraint to shift to the right. In graphical terms, the new budget constraint will now be tangent to a higher indifference curve, representing a higher level of utility. A reduction in income will cause the budget constraint to shift to the left, which will cause it to be tangent to a lower indifference curve, representing a reduced level of utility. If income rises by, for example, 50%, exactly how much will a person alter consumption of books and doughnuts? Will consumption of both goods rise by 50%, or will the quantity of one good rise substantially, while the quantity of the other good rises only a little, or even declines?

Since personal preferences and the shape of indifference curves are different for each individual, the response to changes in income will be different, too. For example, consider the preferences of Manuel and Natasha in **Figure B3** (a) and **Figure B3** (b). They each start with an identical income of $40, which they spend on yogurts that cost $1 and rental movies that cost $4. Thus, they face identical budget constraints. However, based on Manuel's preferences, as revealed by his indifference curves, his utility-maximizing choice on the original budget set occurs where his opportunity set is tangent to the highest possible indifference curve at W, with three movies and 28 yogurts, while Natasha's utility-maximizing choice on the original budget set at Y will be seven movies and 12 yogurts.

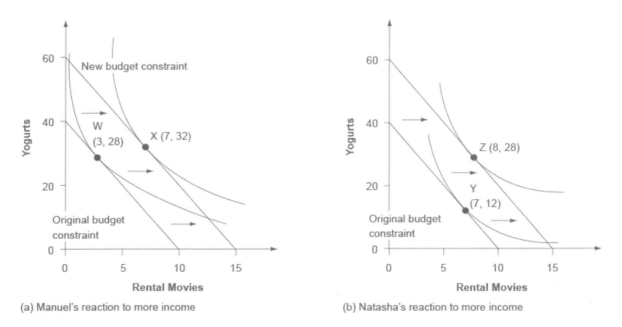

(a) Manuel's reaction to more income

(b) Natasha's reaction to more income

Figure B3 Manuel and Natasha's Indifference Curves Manuel and Natasha originally face the same budget constraints; that is, same prices and same income. However, the indifference curves that illustrate their preferences are not the same. (a) Manuel's original choice at W involves more yogurt and more movies, and he reacts to the higher income by mainly increasing consumption of movies at X. (b) Conversely, Natasha's original choice (Y) involves relatively more movies, but she reacts to the higher income by choosing relatively more yogurts. Even when budget constraints are the same, personal preferences lead to different original choices and to different reactions in response to a change in income.

Now, say that income rises to $60 for both Manuel and Natasha, so their budget constraints shift to the right. As shown in **Figure B3** (a), Manuel's new utility maximizing choice at X will be seven movies and 32 yogurts—that is, Manuel will choose to spend most of the extra income on movies. Natasha's new utility maximizing choice at Z will be eight movies and 28 yogurts—that is, she will choose to spend most of the extra income on yogurt. In this way, the indifference curve approach allows for a range of possible responses. However, if both goods are normal goods, then the typical response to a higher level of income will be to purchase more of them—although exactly how much more is a matter of personal preference. If one of the goods is an inferior good, the response to a higher level of income

This OpenStax book is available for free at http://cnx.org/content/col12122/1.4

will be to purchase less of it.

Responses to Price Changes: Substitution and Income Effects

A higher price for a good will cause the budget constraint to shift to the left, so that it is tangent to a lower indifference curve representing a reduced level of utility. Conversely, a lower price for a good will cause the opportunity set to shift to the right, so that it is tangent to a higher indifference curve representing an increased level of utility. Exactly how much a change in price will lead to the quantity demanded of each good will depend on personal preferences.

Anyone who faces a change in price will experience two interlinked motivations: a substitution effect and an income effect. The substitution effect is that when a good becomes more expensive, people seek out substitutes. If oranges become more expensive, fruit-lovers scale back on oranges and eat more apples, grapefruit, or raisins. Conversely, when a good becomes cheaper, people substitute toward consuming more. If oranges get cheaper, people fire up their juicing machines and ease off on other fruits and foods. The income effect refers to how a change in the price of a good alters the effective buying power of one's income. If the price of a good that you have been buying falls, then in effect your buying power has risen—you are able to purchase more goods. Conversely, if the price of a good that you have been buying rises, then the buying power of a given amount of income is diminished. (One common source of confusion is that the "income effect" does not refer to a change in actual income. Instead, it refers to the situation in which the price of a good changes, and thus the quantities of goods that can be purchased with a fixed amount of income change. It might be more accurate to call the "income effect" a "buying power effect," but the "income effect" terminology has been used for decades, and it is not going to change during this economics course.) Whenever a price changes, consumers feel the pull of both substitution and income effects at the same time.

Using indifference curves, you can illustrate the substitution and income effects on a graph. In **Figure B4**, Ogden faces a choice between two goods: haircuts or personal pizzas. Haircuts cost $20, personal pizzas cost $6, and he has $120 to spend.

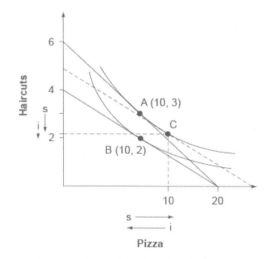

Figure B4 Substitution and Income Effects   The original choice is A, the point of tangency between the original budget constraint and indifference curve. The new choice is B, the point of tangency between the new budget constraint and the lower indifference curve. Point C is the tangency between the dashed line, where the slope shows the new higher price of haircuts, and the original indifference curve. The substitution effect is the shift from A to C, which means getting fewer haircuts and more pizza. The income effect is the shift from C to B; that is, the reduction in buying power that causes a shift from the higher indifference curve to the lower indifference curve, with relative prices remaining unchanged. The income effect results in less consumed of both goods. Both substitution and income effects cause fewer haircuts to be consumed. For pizza, in this case, the substitution effect and income effect cancel out, leading to the same amount of pizza consumed.

The price of haircuts rises to $30. Ogden starts at choice A on the higher opportunity set and the higher indifference curve. After the price of haircuts increases, he chooses B on the lower opportunity set and the lower indifference curve. Point B with two haircuts and 10 personal pizzas is immediately below point A with three haircuts and 10 personal pizzas, showing that Ogden reacted to a higher price of haircuts by cutting back only on haircuts, while leaving his consumption of pizza unchanged.

The dashed line in the diagram, and point C, are used to separate the substitution effect and the income effect. To understand their function, start by thinking about the substitution effect with this question: How would Ogden change his consumption if the relative prices of the two goods changed, but this change in relative prices did not affect his utility? The slope of the budget constraint is determined by the relative price of the two goods; thus, the slope of the original budget line is determined by the original relative prices, while the slope of the new budget line is determined by the new relative prices. With this thought in mind, the dashed line is a graphical tool inserted in a specific way: It is inserted so that it is parallel with the new budget constraint, so it reflects the new relative prices, but it is tangent to the original indifference curve, so it reflects the original level of utility or buying power.

Thus, the movement from the original choice (A) to point C is a substitution effect; it shows the choice that Ogden would make if relative prices shifted (as shown by the different slope between the original budget set and the dashed line) but if buying power did not shift (as shown by being tangent to the original indifference curve). The substitution effect will encourage people to shift away from the good which has become relatively more expensive—in Ogden's case, the haircuts on the vertical axis—and toward the good which has become relatively less expensive—in this case, the pizza on the vertical axis. The two arrows labeled with "s" for "substitution effect," one on each axis, show the direction of this movement.

The income effect is the movement from point C to B, which shows how Ogden reacts to a reduction in his buying power from the higher indifference curve to the lower indifference curve, but holding constant the relative prices (because the dashed line has the same slope as the new budget constraint). In this case, where the price of one good increases, buying power is reduced, so the income effect means that consumption of both goods should fall (if they are both normal goods, which it is reasonable to assume unless there is reason to believe otherwise). The two arrows labeled with "i" for "income effect," one on each axis, show the direction of this income effect movement.

Now, put the substitution and income effects together. When the price of pizza increased, Ogden consumed less of it, for two reasons shown in the exhibit: the substitution effect of the higher price led him to consume less and the income effect of the higher price also led him to consume less. However, when the price of pizza increased, Ogden consumed the same quantity of haircuts. The substitution effect of a higher price for pizza meant that haircuts became relatively less expensive (compared to pizza), and this factor, taken alone, would have encouraged Ogden to consume more haircuts. However, the income effect of a higher price for pizza meant that he wished to consume less of both goods, and this factor, taken alone, would have encouraged Ogden to consume fewer haircuts. As shown in **Figure B4**, in this particular example the substitution effect and income effect on Ogden's consumption of haircuts are offsetting—so he ends up consuming the same quantity of haircuts after the price increase for pizza as before.

The size of these income and substitution effects will differ from person to person, depending on individual preferences. For example, if Ogden's substitution effect away from pizza and toward haircuts is especially strong, and outweighs the income effect, then a higher price for pizza might lead to increased consumption of haircuts. This case would be drawn on the graph so that the point of tangency between the new budget constraint and the relevant indifference curve occurred below point B and to the right. Conversely, if the substitution effect away from pizza and toward haircuts is not as strong, and the income effect on is relatively stronger, then Ogden will be more likely to react to the higher price of pizza by consuming less of both goods. In this case, his optimal choice after the price change will be above and to the left of choice B on the new budget constraint.

Although the substitution and income effects are often discussed as a sequence of events, it should be remembered that they are twin components of a single cause—a change in price. Although you can analyze them separately, the two effects are always proceeding hand in hand, happening at the same time.

Indifference Curves with Labor-Leisure and Intertemporal Choices

The concept of an indifference curve applies to tradeoffs in any household choice, including the labor-leisure choice or the intertemporal choice between present and future consumption. In the labor-leisure choice, each indifference curve shows the combinations of leisure and income that provide a certain level of utility. In an intertemporal choice, each indifference curve shows the combinations of present and future consumption that provide a certain level of utility. The general shapes of the indifference curves—downward sloping, steeper on the left and flatter on the right—also remain the same.

A Labor-Leisure Example

Petunia is working at a job that pays $12 per hour but she gets a raise to $20 per hour. After family responsibilities and sleep, she has 80 hours per week available for work or leisure. As shown in **Figure B5**, the highest level of utility for Petunia, on her original budget constraint, is at choice A, where it is tangent to the lower indifference curve (Ul). Point A has 30 hours of leisure and thus 50 hours per week of work, with income of $600 per week (that is, 50 hours of work at $12 per hour). Petunia then gets a raise to $20 per hour, which shifts her budget constraint to the right. Her new utility-maximizing choice occurs where the new budget constraint is tangent to the higher indifference curve Uh. At B, Petunia has 40 hours of leisure per week and works 40 hours, with income of $800 per week (that is, 40 hours of work at $20 per hour).

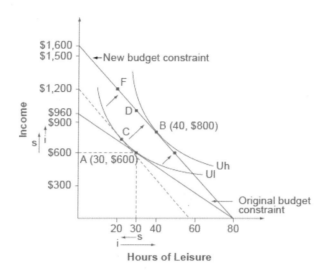

Figure B5 Effects of a Change in Petunia's Wage   Petunia starts at choice A, the tangency between her original budget constraint and the lower indifference curve Ul. The wage increase shifts her budget constraint to the right, so that she can now choose B on indifference curve Uh. The substitution effect is the movement from A to C. In this case, the substitution effect would lead Petunia to choose less leisure, which is relatively more expensive, and more income, which is relatively cheaper to earn. The income effect is the movement from C to B. The income effect in this example leads to greater consumption of both goods. Overall, in this example, income rises because of both substitution and income effects. However, leisure declines because of the substitution effect but increases because of the income effect—leading, in Petunia's case, to an overall increase in the quantity of leisure consumed.

Substitution and income effects provide a vocabulary for discussing how Petunia reacts to a higher hourly wage. The dashed line serves as the tool for separating the two effects on the graph.

The substitution effect tells how Petunia would have changed her hours of work if her wage had risen, so that income was relatively cheaper to earn and leisure was relatively more expensive, but if she had remained at the same level of utility. The slope of the budget constraint in a labor-leisure diagram is determined by the wage rate. Thus, the dashed line is carefully inserted with the slope of the new opportunity set, reflecting the labor-leisure tradeoff of the new wage rate, but tangent to the original indifference curve, showing the same level of utility or "buying power." The shift from original choice A to point C, which is the point of tangency between the original indifference curve and the dashed line, shows that because of the higher wage, Petunia will want to consume less leisure and more income. The "s" arrows on the horizontal and vertical axes of **Figure B5** show the substitution effect on leisure and on income.

The income effect is that the higher wage, by shifting the labor-leisure budget constraint to the right, makes it possible for Petunia to reach a higher level of utility. The income effect is the movement from point C to point B; that is, it shows how Petunia's behavior would change in response to a higher level of utility or "buying power," with the wage rate remaining the same (as shown by the dashed line being parallel to the new budget constraint). The income effect, encouraging Petunia to consume both more leisure and more income, is drawn with arrows on the horizontal and vertical axis of **Figure B5**.

Putting these effects together, Petunia responds to the higher wage by moving from choice A to choice B. This movement involves choosing more income, both because the substitution effect of higher wages has made income relatively cheaper or easier to earn, and because the income effect of higher wages has made it possible to have more income and more leisure. Her movement from A to B also involves choosing more leisure because, according to Petunia's preferences, the income effect that encourages choosing more leisure is stronger than the substitution effect that encourages choosing less leisure.

Figure B5 represents only Petunia's preferences. Other people might make other choices. For example, a person whose substitution and income effects on leisure exactly counterbalanced each other might react to a higher wage with a choice like D, exactly above the original choice A, which means taking all of the benefit of the higher wages in the form of income while working the same number of hours. Yet another person, whose substitution effect on leisure outweighed the income effect, might react to a higher wage by making a choice like F, where the response to higher wages is to work more hours and earn much more income. To represent these different preferences, you could easily draw the indifference curve Uh to be tangent to the new budget constraint at D or F, rather than at B.

An Intertemporal Choice Example

Quentin has saved up $10,000. He is thinking about spending some or all of it on a vacation in the present, and then will save the rest for another big vacation five years from now. Over those five years, he expects to earn a total 80% rate of return. **Figure B6** shows Quentin's budget constraint and his indifference curves between present consumption and future consumption. The highest level of utility that Quentin can achieve at his original intertemporal budget constraint occurs at point A, where he is consuming $6,000, saving $4,000 for the future, and expecting with the accumulated interest to have $7,200 for future consumption (that is, $4,000 in current financial savings plus the 80% rate of return).

However, Quentin has just realized that his expected rate of return was unrealistically high. A more realistic expectation is that over five years he can earn a total return of 30%. In effect, his intertemporal budget constraint has pivoted to the left, so that his original utility-maximizing choice is no longer available. Will Quentin react to the lower rate of return by saving more, or less, or the same amount? Again, the language of substitution and income effects provides a framework for thinking about the motivations behind various choices. The dashed line, which is a graphical tool to separate the substitution and income effect, is carefully inserted with the same slope as the new opportunity set, so that it reflects the changed rate of return, but it is tangent to the original indifference curve, so that it shows no change in utility or "buying power."

The substitution effect tells how Quentin would have altered his consumption because the lower rate of return makes future consumption relatively more expensive and present consumption relatively cheaper. The movement from the original choice A to point C shows how Quentin substitutes toward more present consumption and less future consumption in response to the lower interest rate, with no change in utility. The substitution arrows on the horizontal and vertical axes of **Figure B6** show the direction of the substitution effect motivation. The substitution effect suggests that, because of the lower interest rate, Quentin should consume more in the present and less in the future.

Quentin also has an income effect motivation. The lower rate of return shifts the budget constraint to the left, which means that Quentin's utility or "buying power" is reduced. The income effect (assuming normal goods) encourages less of both present and future consumption. The impact of the income effect on reducing present and future consumption in this example is shown with "i" arrows on the horizontal and vertical axis of **Figure B6**.

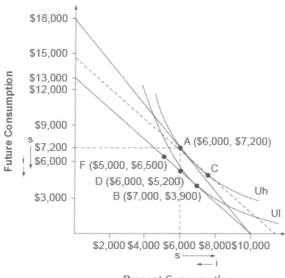

Figure B6 Indifference Curve and an Intertemporal Budget Constraint The original choice is A, at the tangency between the original budget constraint and the original indifference curve Uh. The dashed line is drawn parallel to the new budget set, so that its slope reflects the lower rate of return, but is tangent to the original indifference curve. The movement from A to C is the substitution effect: in this case, future consumption has become relatively more expensive, and present consumption has become relatively cheaper. The income effect is the shift from C to B; that is, the reduction in utility or "buying power" that causes a move to a lower indifference curve Ul, but with the relative price the same. It means less present and less future consumption. In the move from A to B, the substitution effect on present consumption is greater than the income effect, so the overall result is more present consumption. Notice that the lower indifference curve could have been drawn tangent to the lower budget constraint point D or point F, depending on personal preferences.

Taking both effects together, the substitution effect is encouraging Quentin toward more present and less future consumption, because present consumption is relatively cheaper, while the income effect is encouraging him to less present and less future consumption, because the lower interest rate is pushing him to a lower level of utility. For Quentin's personal preferences, the substitution effect is stronger so that, overall, he reacts to the lower rate of return with more present consumption and less savings at choice B. However, other people might have different preferences. They might react to a lower rate of return by choosing the same level of present consumption and savings at choice D, or by choosing less present consumption and more savings at a point like F. For these other sets of preferences, the income effect of a lower rate of return on present consumption would be relatively stronger, while the substitution effect would be relatively weaker.

Sketching Substitution and Income Effects

Indifference curves provide an analytical tool for looking at all the choices that provide a single level of utility. They eliminate any need for placing numerical values on utility and help to illuminate the process of making utility-maximizing decisions. They also provide the basis for a more detailed investigation of the complementary motivations that arise in response to a change in a price, wage or rate of return—namely, the substitution and income effects.

If you are finding it a little tricky to sketch diagrams that show substitution and income effects so that the points of tangency all come out correctly, it may be useful to follow this procedure.

Step 1. Begin with a budget constraint showing the choice between two goods, which this example will call "candy" and "movies." Choose a point A which will be the optimal choice, where the indifference curve will be tangent—but it is often easier not to draw in the indifference curve just yet. See **Figure B7**.

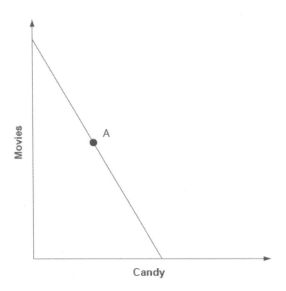

Figure B7

Step 2. Now the price of movies changes: let's say that it rises. That shifts the budget set inward. You know that the higher price will push the decision-maker down to a lower level of utility, represented by a lower indifference curve. But at this stage, draw only the new budget set. See **Figure B8**.

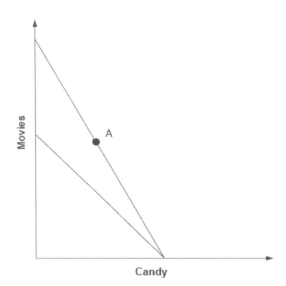

Figure B8

Step 3. The key tool in distinguishing between substitution and income effects is to insert a dashed line, parallel to the new budget line. This line is a graphical tool that allows you to distinguish between the two changes: (1) the effect on consumption of the two goods of the shift in prices—with the level of utility remaining unchanged—which is the substitution effect; and (2) the effect on consumption of the two goods of shifting from one indifference curve to the other—with relative prices staying unchanged—which is the income effect. The dashed line is inserted in this step. The trick is to have the dashed line travel close to the original choice A, but not directly through point A. See **Figure B9**.

This OpenStax book is available for free at http://cnx.org/content/col12122/1.4

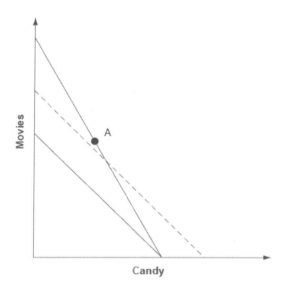

Figure B9

Step 4. Now, draw the original indifference curve, so that it is tangent to both point A on the original budget line and to a point C on the dashed line. Many students find it easiest to first select the tangency point C where the original indifference curve touches the dashed line, and then to draw the original indifference curve through A and C. The substitution effect is illustrated by the movement along the original indifference curve as prices change but the level of utility holds constant, from A to C. As expected, the substitution effect leads to less consumed of the good that is relatively more expensive, as shown by the "s" (substitution) arrow on the vertical axis, and more consumed of the good that is relatively less expensive, as shown by the "s" arrow on the horizontal axis. See **Figure B10**.

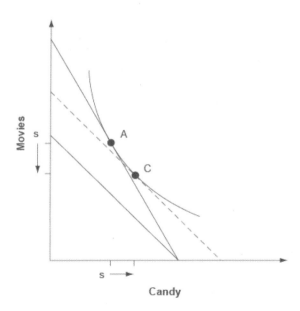

Figure B10

Step 5. With the substitution effect in place, now choose utility-maximizing point B on the new opportunity set. When you choose point B, think about whether you wish the substitution or the income effect to have a larger impact on the good (in this case, candy) on the horizontal axis. If you choose point B to be directly in a vertical line with point A (as is illustrated here), then the income effect will be exactly offsetting the substitution effect on the horizontal axis. If you insert point B so that it lies a little to right of the original point A, then the substitution effect will exceed income effect. If you insert point B so that it lies a little to the left of point A, then the income effect will exceed the substitution effect. The income effect is the movement from C to B, showing how choices shifted as a result of the decline in buying power and the movement between two levels of utility, with relative prices remaining the same. With normal goods, the negative income effect means less consumed of each good, as shown by the direction of the "i" (income effect) arrows on the vertical and horizontal axes. See **Figure B11**.

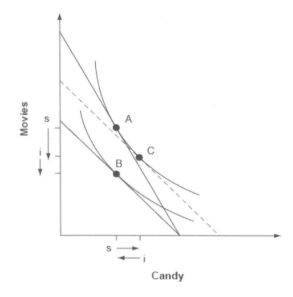

Figure B11

In sketching substitution and income effect diagrams, you may wish to practice some of the following variations: (1) Price falls instead of a rising; (2) The price change affects the good on either the vertical or the horizontal axis; (3) Sketch these diagrams so that the substitution effect exceeds the income effect; the income effect exceeds the substitution effect; and the two effects are equal.

One final note: The helpful dashed line can be drawn tangent to the new indifference curve, and parallel to the original budget line, rather than tangent to the original indifference curve and parallel to the new budget line. Some students find this approach more intuitively clear. The answers you get about the direction and relative sizes of the substitution and income effects, however, should be the same.

Key Concepts and Summary

An indifference curve is drawn on a budget constraint diagram that shows the tradeoffs between two goods. All points along a single indifference curve provide the same level of utility. Higher indifference curves represent higher levels of utility. Indifference curves slope downward because, if utility is to remain the same at all points along the curve, a reduction in the quantity of the good on the vertical axis must be counterbalanced by an increase in the quantity of the good on the horizontal axis (or vice versa). Indifference curves are steeper on the far left and flatter on the far right, because of diminishing marginal utility.

The utility-maximizing choice along a budget constraint will be the point of tangency where the budget constraint touches an indifference curve at a single point. A change in the price of any good has two effects: a substitution effect and an income effect. The substitution effect motivation encourages a utility-maximizer to buy less of what is relatively more expensive and more of what is relatively cheaper. The income effect motivation encourages a utility-maximizer to buy more of both goods if utility rises or less of both goods if utility falls (if they are both normal goods).

In a labor-leisure choice, every wage change has a substitution and an income effect. The substitution effect of a wage increase is to choose more income, since it is cheaper to earn, and less leisure, since its opportunity cost has increased. The income effect of a wage increase is to choose more of leisure and income, since they are both normal goods. The substitution and income effects of a wage decrease would reverse these directions.

In an intertemporal consumption choice, every interest rate change has a substitution and an income effect. The substitution effect of an interest rate increase is to choose more future consumption, since it is now cheaper to earn future consumption and less present consumption (more savings), since the opportunity cost of present consumption in terms of what is being given up in the future has increased. The income effect of an interest rate increase is to choose more of both present and future consumption, since they are both normal goods. The substitution and income effects of an interest rate decrease would reverse these directions.

Review Questions

Exercise B1

What point is preferred along an indifference curve?

Exercise B2

Why do indifference curves slope down?

Exercise B3

Why are indifference curves steep on the left and flatter on the right?

Exercise B4

How many indifference curves does a person have?

Exercise B5

How can you tell which indifference curves represent higher or lower levels of utility?

Exercise B6

What is a substitution effect?

Exercise B7

What is an income effect?

Exercise B8

Does the "income effect" involve a change in income? Explain.

Exercise B9

Does a change in price have both an income effect and a substitution effect? Does a change in income have both an income effect and a substitution effect?

Exercise B10

Would you expect, in some cases, to see only an income effect or only a substitution effect? Explain.

Exercise B11

Which is larger, the income effect or the substitution effect?

This OpenStax book is available for free at http://cnx.org/content/col12122/1.4

C | Present Discounted Value

As explained in **Financial Markets**, the prices of stocks and bonds depend on future events. The price of a bond depends on the future payments that the bond is expected to make, including both payments of interest and the repayment of the face value of the bond. The price of a stock depends on the expected future profits earned by the firm. The concept of a present discounted value (PDV), which is defined as the amount you should be willing to pay in the present for a stream of expected future payments, can be used to calculate appropriate prices for stocks and bonds. To place a present discounted value on a future payment, think about what amount of money you would need to have in the present to equal a certain amount in the future. This calculation will require an interest rate. For example, if the interest rate is 10%, then a payment of $110 a year from now will have a present discounted value of $100—that is, you could take $100 in the present and have $110 in the future. We will first shows how to apply the idea of present discounted value to a stock and then we will show how to apply it to a bond.

Applying Present Discounted Value to a Stock

Consider the case of Babble, Inc., a company that offers speaking lessons. For the sake of simplicity, say that the founder of Babble is 63 years old and plans to retire in two years, at which point the company will be disbanded. The company is selling 200 shares of stock and profits are expected to be $15 million right away, in the present, $20 million one year from now, and $25 million two years from now. All profits will be paid out as dividends to shareholders as they occur. Given this information, what will an investor pay for a share of stock in this company?

A financial investor, thinking about what future payments are worth in the present, will need to choose an interest rate. This interest rate will reflect the rate of return on other available financial investment opportunities, which is the opportunity cost of investing financial capital, and also a risk premium (that is, using a higher interest rate than the rates available elsewhere if this investment appears especially risky). In this example, say that the financial investor decides that appropriate interest rate to value these future payments is 15%.

Table C1 shows how to calculate the present discounted value of the future profits. For each time period, when a benefit is going to be received, apply the formula:

$$\text{Present discounted value} = \frac{\text{Future value received years in the future}}{(1 + \text{Interest rate})^{\text{numbers of years t}}}$$

Payments from Firm	Present Value
$15 million in present	$15 million
$20 million in one year	$20 million$/(1 + 0.15)^1$ = $17.4 million
$25 million in two years	$25 million$/(1 + 0.15)^2$ = $18.9 million
Total	*$51.3 million*

Table C1 Calculating Present Discounted Value of a Stock

Next, add up all the present values for the different time periods to get a final answer. The present value calculations ask what the amount in the future is worth in the present, given the 15% interest rate. Notice that a different PDV calculation needs to be done separately for amounts received at different times. Then, divide the PDV of total profits by the number of shares, 200 in this case: 51.3 million/200 = 0.2565 million. The price per share should be about $256,500 per share.

Of course, in the real world expected profits are a best guess, not a hard piece of data. Deciding which interest rate to apply for discounting to the present can be tricky. One needs to take into account both potential capital gains from the future sale of the stock and also dividends that might be paid. Differences of opinion on these issues are exactly why some financial investors want to buy a stock that other people want to sell: they are more optimistic about its future prospects. Conceptually, however, it all comes down to what you are willing to pay in the present for a stream of benefits to be received in the future.

Applying Present Discounted Value to a Bond

A similar calculation works in the case of bonds. **Financial Markets** explains that if the interest rate falls after a bond is issued, so that the investor has locked in a higher rate, then that bond will sell for more than its face value. Conversely, if the interest rate rises after a bond is issued, then the investor is locked into a lower rate, and the bond will sell for less than its face value. The present value calculation sharpens this intuition.

Think about a simple two-year bond. It was issued for $3,000 at an interest rate of 8%. Thus, after the first year, the bond pays interest of 240 (which is 3,000 × 8%). At the end of the second year, the bond pays $240 in interest, plus the $3,000 in principle. Calculate how much this bond is worth in the present if the discount rate is 8%. Then, recalculate if interest rates rise and the applicable discount rate is 11%. To carry out these calculations, look at the stream of payments being received from the bond in the future and figure out what they are worth in present discounted value terms. The calculations applying the present value formula are shown in **Table C2**.

Stream of Payments (for the 8% interest rate)	Present Value (for the 8% interest rate)	Stream of Payments (for the 11% interest rate)	Present Value (for the 11% interest rate)
$240 payment after one year	$240/(1 + 0.08)^1 =$ $222.20	$240 payment after one year	$240/(1 + 0.11)^1 =$ $216.20
$3,240 payment after second year	$3,240/(1 + 0.08)^2 =$ $2,777.80	$3,240 payment after second year	$3,240/(1 + 0.11)^2 =$ $2,629.60
Total	*$3,000*	*Total*	*$2,845.80*

Table C2 Computing the Present Discounted Value of a Bond

The first calculation shows that the present value of a $3,000 bond, issued at 8%, is just $3,000. After all, that is how much money the borrower is receiving. The calculation confirms that the present value is the same for the lender. The bond is moving money around in time, from those willing to save in the present to those who want to borrow in the present, but the present value of what is received by the borrower is identical to the present value of what will be repaid to the lender.

The second calculation shows what happens if the interest rate rises from 8% to 11%. The actual dollar payments in the first column, as determined by the 8% interest rate, do not change. However, the present value of those payments, now discounted at a higher interest rate, is lower. Even though the future dollar payments that the bond is receiving have not changed, a person who tries to sell the bond will find that the investment's value has fallen.

Again, real-world calculations are often more complex, in part because, not only the interest rate prevailing in the market, but also the riskiness of whether the borrower will repay the loan, will change. In any case, the price of a bond is always the present value of a stream of future expected payments.

Other Applications

Present discounted value is a widely used analytical tool outside the world of finance. Every time a business thinks about making a physical capital investment, it must compare a set of present costs of making that investment to the present discounted value of future benefits. When government thinks about a proposal to, for example, add safety features to a highway, it must compare costs incurred in the present to benefits received in the future. Some academic disputes over environmental policies, like how much to reduce carbon dioxide emissions because of the risk that they will lead to a warming of global temperatures several decades in the future, turn on how one compares present costs of pollution control with long-run future benefits. Someone who wins the lottery and is scheduled to receive a string of payments over 30 years might be interested in knowing what the present discounted value is of those payments. Whenever a string of costs and benefits stretches from the present into different times in the future, present discounted value becomes an indispensable tool of analysis.

D | The Expenditure-Output Model

(This appendix should be consulted after first reading **The Aggregate Demand/Aggregate Supply Model** and **The Keynesian Perspective**.) The fundamental ideas of Keynesian economics were developed before the AD/AS model was popularized. From the 1930s until the 1970s, Keynesian economics was usually explained with a different model, known as the expenditure-output approach. This approach is strongly rooted in the fundamental assumptions of Keynesian economics: it focuses on the total amount of spending in the economy, with no explicit mention of aggregate supply or of the price level (although as you will see, it is possible to draw some inferences about aggregate supply and price levels based on the diagram).

The Axes of the Expenditure-Output Diagram

The expenditure-output model, sometimes also called the Keynesian cross diagram, determines the equilibrium level of real GDP by the point where the total or aggregate expenditures in the economy are equal to the amount of output produced. The axes of the Keynesian cross diagram presented in **Figure D1** show real GDP on the horizontal axis as a measure of output and aggregate expenditures on the vertical axis as a measure of spending.

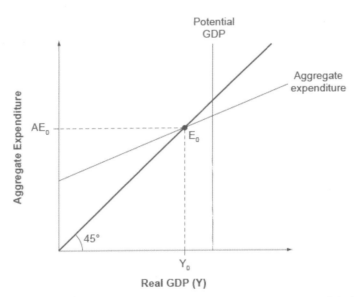

Figure D1 The Expenditure-Output Diagram   The aggregate expenditure-output model shows aggregate expenditures on the vertical axis and real GDP on the horizontal axis. A vertical line shows potential GDP where full employment occurs. The 45-degree line shows all points where aggregate expenditures and output are equal. The aggregate expenditure schedule shows how total spending or aggregate expenditure increases as output or real GDP rises. The intersection of the aggregate expenditure schedule and the 45-degree line will be the equilibrium. Equilibrium occurs at E_0, where aggregate expenditure AE_0 is equal to the output level Y_0.

Remember that GDP can be thought of in several equivalent ways: it measures both the value of spending on final goods and also the value of the production of final goods. All sales of the final goods and services that make up GDP will eventually end up as income for workers, for managers, and for investors and owners of firms. The sum of all the income received for contributing resources to GDP is called national income (Y). At some points in the discussion that follows, it will be useful to refer to real GDP as "national income." Both axes are measured in real (inflation-adjusted) terms.

The Potential GDP Line and the 45-degree Line

The Keynesian cross diagram contains two lines that serve as conceptual guideposts to orient the discussion. The first is a vertical line showing the level of potential GDP. Potential GDP means the same thing here that it means in the AD/AS diagrams: it refers to the quantity of output that the economy can produce with full employment of its labor and physical capital.

The second conceptual line on the Keynesian cross diagram is the 45-degree line, which starts at the origin and reaches up and to the right. A line that stretches up at a 45-degree angle represents the set of points (1, 1), (2, 2), (3, 3) and so on, where the measurement on the vertical axis is equal to the measurement on the horizontal axis. In this diagram, the 45-degree line shows the set of points where the level of aggregate expenditure in the economy, measured on the vertical axis, is equal to the level of output or national income in the economy, measured by GDP on the horizontal axis.

When the macroeconomy is in equilibrium, it must be true that the aggregate expenditures in the economy are equal to the real GDP—because by definition, GDP is the measure of what is spent on final sales of goods and services in the economy. Thus, the equilibrium calculated with a Keynesian cross diagram will always end up where aggregate expenditure and output are equal—which will only occur along the 45-degree line.

The Aggregate Expenditure Schedule

The final ingredient of the Keynesian cross or expenditure-output diagram is the aggregate expenditure schedule, which will show the total expenditures in the economy for each level of real GDP. The intersection of the aggregate expenditure line with the 45-degree line—at point E_0 in **Figure D1**—will show the equilibrium for the economy, because it is the point where aggregate expenditure is equal to output or real GDP. After developing an understanding of what the aggregate expenditures schedule means, we will return to this equilibrium and how to interpret it.

Building the Aggregate Expenditure Schedule

Aggregate expenditure is the key to the expenditure-income model. The aggregate expenditure schedule shows, either in the form of a table or a graph, how aggregate expenditures in the economy rise as real GDP or national income rises. Thus, in thinking about the components of the aggregate expenditure line—consumption, investment, government spending, exports and imports—the key question is how expenditures in each category will adjust as national income rises.

Consumption as a Function of National Income

How do consumption expenditures increase as national income rises? People can do two things with their income: consume it or save it (for the moment, let's ignore the need to pay taxes with some of it). Each person who receives an additional dollar faces this choice. The marginal propensity to consume (MPC), is the share of the additional dollar of income a person decides to devote to consumption expenditures. The marginal propensity to save (MPS) is the share of the additional dollar a person decides to save. It must always hold true that:

$$MPC + MPS = 1$$

For example, if the marginal propensity to consume out of the marginal amount of income earned is 0.9, then the marginal propensity to save is 0.1.

With this relationship in mind, consider the relationship among income, consumption, and savings shown in **Figure D2**. (Note that we use "Aggregate Expenditure" on the vertical axis in this and the following figures, because all consumption expenditures are parts of aggregate expenditures.)

An assumption commonly made in this model is that even if income were zero, people would have to consume something. In this example, consumption would be $600 even if income were zero. Then, the MPC is 0.8 and the MPS is 0.2. Thus, when income increases by $1,000, consumption rises by $800 and savings rises by $200. At an income of $4,000, total consumption will be the $600 that would be consumed even without any income, plus $4,000 multiplied by the marginal propensity to consume of 0.8, or $ 3,200, for a total of $ 3,800. The total amount of consumption and saving must always add up to the total amount of income. (Exactly how a situation of zero income and negative savings would work in practice is not important, because even low-income societies are not literally at zero income, so the point is hypothetical.) This relationship between income and consumption, illustrated in **Figure D2** and **Table D1**, is called the consumption function.

This OpenStax book is available for free at http://cnx.org/content/col12122/1.4

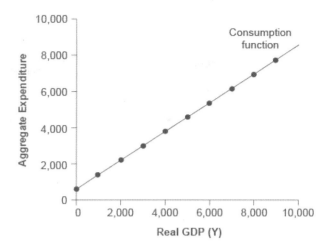

Figure D2 The Consumption Function   In the expenditure-output model, how does consumption increase with the level of national income? Output on the horizontal axis is conceptually the same as national income, since the value of all final output that is produced and sold must be income to someone, somewhere in the economy. At a national income level of zero, $600 is consumed. Then, each time income rises by $1,000, consumption rises by $800, because in this example, the marginal propensity to consume is 0.8.

The pattern of consumption shown in **Table D1** is plotted in **Figure D2**. To calculate consumption, multiply the income level by 0.8, for the marginal propensity to consume, and add $600, for the amount that would be consumed even if income was zero. Consumption plus savings must be equal to income.

Income	Consumption	Savings
$0	$600	–$600
$1,000	$1,400	–$400
$2,000	$2,200	–$200
$3,000	$3,000	$0
$4,000	$3,800	$200
$5,000	$4,600	$400
$6,000	$5,400	$600
$7,000	$6,200	$800
$8,000	$7,000	$1,000
$9,000	$7,800	$1,200

Table D1 The Consumption Function

However, a number of factors other than income can also cause the entire consumption function to shift. These factors were summarized in the earlier discussion of consumption, and listed in **Table D1**. When the consumption function moves, it can shift in two ways: either the entire consumption function can move up or down in a parallel manner, or the slope of the consumption function can shift so that it becomes steeper or flatter. For example, if a tax cut leads consumers to spend more, but does not affect their marginal propensity to consume, it would cause an upward shift to a new consumption function that is parallel to the original one. However, a change in household preferences for saving that reduced the marginal propensity to save would cause the slope of the consumption function to become steeper: that is, if the savings rate is lower, then every increase in income leads to a larger rise in consumption.

Investment as a Function of National Income

Investment decisions are forward-looking, based on expected rates of return. Precisely because investment decisions depend primarily on perceptions about future economic conditions, they do *not* depend primarily on the level of GDP in the current year. Thus, on a Keynesian cross diagram, the investment function can be drawn as a horizontal line, at a fixed level of expenditure. **Figure D3** shows an investment function where the level of investment is, for the sake of concreteness, set at the specific level of 500. Just as a consumption function shows the relationship between consumption levels and real GDP (or national income), the investment function shows the relationship between investment levels and real GDP.

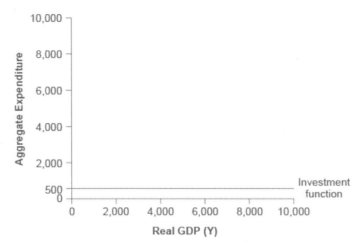

Figure D3 The Investment Function   The investment function is drawn as a flat line because investment is based on interest rates and expectations about the future, and so it does not change with the level of current national income. In this example, investment expenditures are at a level of 500. However, changes in factors like technological opportunities, expectations about near-term economic growth, and interest rates would all cause the investment function to shift up or down.

The appearance of the investment function as a horizontal line does not mean that the level of investment never moves. It means only that in the context of this two-dimensional diagram, the level of investment on the vertical aggregate expenditure axis does not vary according to the current level of real GDP on the horizontal axis. However, all the other factors that vary investment—new technological opportunities, expectations about near-term economic growth, interest rates, the price of key inputs, and tax incentives for investment—can cause the horizontal investment function to shift up or down.

Government Spending and Taxes as a Function of National Income

In the Keynesian cross diagram, government spending appears as a horizontal line, as in **Figure D4**, where government spending is set at a level of 1,300. As in the case of investment spending, this horizontal line does not mean that government spending is unchanging. It means only that government spending changes when Congress decides on a change in the budget, rather than shifting in a predictable way with the current size of the real GDP shown on the horizontal axis.

This OpenStax book is available for free at http://cnx.org/content/col12122/1.4

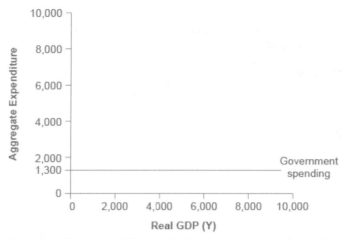

Figure D4 The Government Spending Function The level of government spending is determined by political factors, not by the level of real GDP in a given year. Thus, government spending is drawn as a horizontal line. In this example, government spending is at a level of 1,300. Congressional decisions to increase government spending will cause this horizontal line to shift up, while decisions to reduce spending would cause it to shift down.

The situation of taxes is different because taxes often rise or fall with the volume of economic activity. For example, income taxes are based on the level of income earned and sales taxes are based on the amount of sales made, and both income and sales tend to be higher when the economy is growing and lower when the economy is in a recession. For the purposes of constructing the basic Keynesian cross diagram, it is helpful to view taxes as a proportionate share of GDP. In the United States, for example, taking federal, state, and local taxes together, government typically collects about 30–35 % of income as taxes.

Table D2 revises the earlier table on the consumption function so that it takes taxes into account. The first column shows national income. The second column calculates taxes, which in this example are set at a rate of 30%, or 0.3. The third column shows after-tax income; that is, total income minus taxes. The fourth column then calculates consumption in the same manner as before: multiply after-tax income by 0.8, representing the marginal propensity to consume, and then add $600, for the amount that would be consumed even if income was zero. When taxes are included, the marginal propensity to consume is reduced by the amount of the tax rate, so each additional dollar of income results in a smaller increase in consumption than before taxes. For this reason, the consumption function, with taxes included, is flatter than the consumption function without taxes, as **Figure D5** shows.

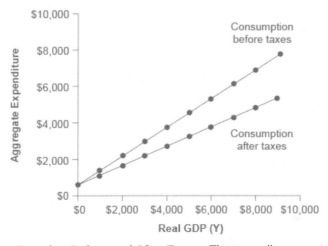

Figure D5 The Consumption Function Before and After Taxes The upper line repeats the consumption function from **Figure D2**. The lower line shows the consumption function if taxes must first be paid on income, and then consumption is based on after-tax income.

Income	Taxes	After-Tax Income	Consumption	Savings
$0	$0	$0	$600	–$600
$1,000	$300	$700	$1,160	–$460
$2,000	$600	$1,400	$1,720	–$320
$3,000	$900	$2,100	$2,280	–$180
$4,000	$1,200	$2,800	$2,840	–$40
$5,000	$1,500	$3,500	$3,400	$100
$6,000	$1,800	$4,200	$3,960	$240
$7,000	$2,100	$4,900	$4,520	$380
$8,000	$2,400	$5,600	$5,080	$520
$9,000	$2,700	$6,300	$5,640	$660

Table D2 The Consumption Function Before and After Taxes

Exports and Imports as a Function of National Income

The export function, which shows how exports change with the level of a country's own real GDP, is drawn as a horizontal line, as in the example in **Figure D6** (a) where exports are drawn at a level of $840. Again, as in the case of investment spending and government spending, drawing the export function as horizontal does not imply that exports never change. It just means that they do not change because of what is on the horizontal axis—that is, a country's own level of domestic production—and instead are shaped by the level of aggregate demand in other countries. More demand for exports from other countries would cause the export function to shift up; less demand for exports from other countries would cause it to shift down.

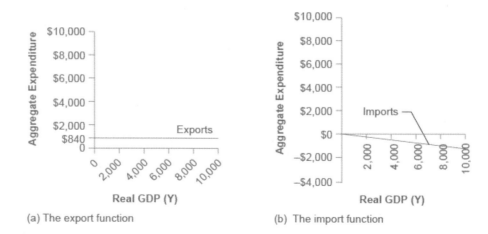

(a) The export function   (b) The import function

Figure D6 The Export and Import Functions   (a) The export function is drawn as a horizontal line because exports are determined by the buying power of other countries and thus do not change with the size of the domestic economy. In this example, exports are set at 840. However, exports can shift up or down, depending on buying patterns in other countries. (b) The import function is drawn in negative territory because expenditures on imported products are a subtraction from expenditures in the domestic economy. In this example, the marginal propensity to import is 0.1, so imports are calculated by multiplying the level of income by –0.1.

Imports are drawn in the Keynesian cross diagram as a downward-sloping line, with the downward slope determined

This OpenStax book is available for free at http://cnx.org/content/col12122/1.4

by the marginal propensity to import (MPI), out of national income. In **Figure D6** (b), the marginal propensity to import is 0.1. Thus, if real GDP is $5,000, imports are $500; if national income is $6,000, imports are $600, and so on. The import function is drawn as downward sloping and negative, because it represents a subtraction from the aggregate expenditures in the domestic economy. A change in the marginal propensity to import, perhaps as a result of changes in preferences, would alter the slope of the import function.

Work It Out ⊢○–○–○

Using an Algebraic Approach to the Expenditure-Output Model

In the expenditure-output or Keynesian cross model, the equilibrium occurs where the aggregate expenditure line (AE line) crosses the 45-degree line. Given algebraic equations for two lines, the point where they cross can be readily calculated. Imagine an economy with the following characteristics.

Y = Real GDP or national income

T = Taxes = $0.3Y$

C = Consumption = $140 + 0.9(Y - T)$

I = Investment = 400

G = Government spending = 800

X = Exports = 600

M = Imports = $0.15Y$

Step 1. Determine the aggregate expenditure function. In this case, it is:

$$AE = C + I + G + X - M$$
$$AE = 140 + 0.9(Y - T) + 400 + 800 + 600 - 0.15Y$$

Step 2. The equation for the 45-degree line is the set of points where GDP or national income on the horizontal axis is equal to aggregate expenditure on the vertical axis. Thus, the equation for the 45-degree line is: $AE = Y$.

Step 3. The next step is to solve these two equations for Y (or AE, since they will be equal to each other). Substitute Y for AE:

$$Y = 140 + 0.9(Y - T) + 400 + 800 + 600 - 0.15Y$$

Step 4. Insert the term 0.3Y for the tax rate T. This produces an equation with only one variable, Y.

Step 5. Work through the algebra and solve for Y.

$$\begin{aligned} Y &= 140 + 0.9(Y - 0.3Y) + 400 + 800 + 600 - 0.15Y \\ Y &= 140 + 0.9Y - 0.27Y + 1800 - 0.15Y \\ Y &= 1940 + 0.48Y \\ Y - 0.48Y &= 1940 \\ 0.52Y &= 1940 \\ \frac{0.52Y}{0.52} &= \frac{1940}{0.52} \\ Y &= 3730 \end{aligned}$$

This algebraic framework is flexible and useful in predicting how economic events and policy actions will affect real GDP.

Step 6. Say, for example, that because of changes in the relative prices of domestic and foreign goods, the marginal propensity to import falls to 0.1. Calculate the equilibrium output when the marginal propensity to import is changed to 0.1.

$$Y = 140 + 0.9(Y - 0.3Y) + 400 + 800 + 600 - 0.1Y$$
$$Y = 1940 - 0.53Y$$
$$0.47Y = 1940$$
$$Y = 4127$$

Step 7. Because of a surge of business confidence, investment rises to 500. Calculate the equilibrium output.

$$Y = 140 + 0.9(Y - 0.3Y) + 500 + 800 + 600 - 0.15Y$$
$$Y = 2040 + 0.48Y$$
$$Y - 0.48Y = 2040$$
$$0.52Y = 2040$$
$$Y = 3923$$

For issues of policy, the key questions would be how to adjust government spending levels or tax rates so that the equilibrium level of output is the full employment level. In this case, let the economic parameters be:

Y = National income

T = Taxes = 0.3Y

C = Consumption = 200 + 0.9(Y − T)

I = Investment = 600

G = Government spending = 1,000

X = Exports = 600

Y = Imports = 0.1(Y − T)

Step 8. Calculate the equilibrium for this economy (remember Y = AE).

$$Y = 200 + 0.9(Y - 0.3Y) + 600 + 1000 + 600 - 0.1(Y - 0.3Y)$$
$$Y - 0.63Y + 0.07Y = 2400$$
$$0.44Y = 2400$$
$$Y = 5454$$

Step 9. Assume that the full employment level of output is 6,000. What level of government spending would be necessary to reach that level? To answer this question, plug in 6,000 as equal to Y, but leave G as a variable, and solve for G. Thus:

$$6000 = 200 + 0.9(6000 - 0.3(6000)) + 600 + G + 600 - 0.1(6000 - 0.3(6000))$$

Step 10. Solve this problem arithmetically. The answer is: G = 1,240. In other words, increasing government spending by 240, from its original level of 1,000, to 1,240, would raise output to the full employment level of GDP.

Indeed, the question of how much to increase government spending so that equilibrium output will rise from 5,454 to 6,000 can be answered without working through the algebra, just by using the multiplier formula. The multiplier equation in this case is:

$$\frac{1}{1 - 0.56} = 2.27$$

Thus, to raise output by 546 would require an increase in government spending of 546/2.27=240, which is the same as the answer derived from the algebraic calculation.

This algebraic framework is highly flexible. For example, taxes can be treated as a total set by political considerations (like government spending) and not dependent on national income. Imports might be based on before-tax income, not after-tax income. For certain purposes, it may be helpful to analyze the economy without exports and imports. A more complicated approach could divide up consumption, investment, government, exports and imports into smaller categories, or to build in some variability in the rates of taxes, savings, and imports. A wise economist will shape the model

This OpenStax book is available for free at http://cnx.org/content/col12122/1.4

to fit the specific question under investigation.

Building the Combined Aggregate Expenditure Function

All the components of aggregate demand—consumption, investment, government spending, and the trade balance—are now in place to build the Keynesian cross diagram. **Figure D7** builds up an aggregate expenditure function, based on the numerical illustrations of C, I, G, X, and M that have been used throughout this text. The first three columns in **Table D3** are lifted from the earlier **Table D2**, which showed how to bring taxes into the consumption function. The first column is real GDP or national income, which is what appears on the horizontal axis of the income-expenditure diagram. The second column calculates after-tax income, based on the assumption, in this case, that 30% of real GDP is collected in taxes. The third column is based on an MPC of 0.8, so that as after-tax income rises by $700 from one row to the next, consumption rises by $560 (700 × 0.8) from one row to the next. Investment, government spending, and exports do not change with the level of current national income. In the previous discussion, investment was $500, government spending was $1,300, and exports were $840, for a total of $2,640. This total is shown in the fourth column. Imports are 0.1 of real GDP in this example, and the level of imports is calculated in the fifth column. The final column, aggregate expenditures, sums up C + I + G + X − M. This aggregate expenditure line is illustrated in **Figure D7**.

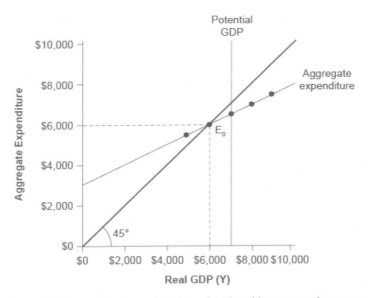

Figure D7 A Keynesian Cross Diagram Each combination of national income and aggregate expenditure (after-tax consumption, government spending, investment, exports, and imports) is graphed. The equilibrium occurs where aggregate expenditure is equal to national income; this occurs where the aggregate expenditure schedule crosses the 45-degree line, at a real GDP of $6,000. Potential GDP in this example is $7,000, so the equilibrium is occurring at a level of output or real GDP below the potential GDP level.

National Income	After-Tax Income	Consumption	Government Spending + Investment + Exports	Imports	Aggregate Expenditure
$3,000	$2,100	$2,280	$2,640	$300	$4,620
$4,000	$2,800	$2,840	$2,640	$400	$5,080
$5,000	$3,500	$3,400	$2,640	$500	$5,540
$6,000	$4,200	$3,960	$2,640	$600	$6,000

Table D3 National Income-Aggregate Expenditure Equilibrium

National Income	After-Tax Income	Consumption	Government Spending + Investment + Exports	Imports	Aggregate Expenditure
$7,000	$4,900	$4,520	$2,640	$700	$6,460
$8,000	$5,600	$5,080	$2,640	$800	$6,920
$9,000	$6,300	$5,640	$2,640	$900	$7,380

Table D3 National Income-Aggregate Expenditure Equilibrium

The aggregate expenditure function is formed by stacking on top of each other the consumption function (after taxes), the investment function, the government spending function, the export function, and the import function. The point at which the aggregate expenditure function intersects the vertical axis will be determined by the levels of investment, government, and export expenditures—which do not vary with national income. The upward slope of the aggregate expenditure function will be determined by the marginal propensity to save, the tax rate, and the marginal propensity to import. A higher marginal propensity to save, a higher tax rate, and a higher marginal propensity to import will all make the slope of the aggregate expenditure function flatter—because out of any extra income, more is going to savings or taxes or imports and less to spending on domestic goods and services.

The equilibrium occurs where national income is equal to aggregate expenditure, which is shown on the graph as the point where the aggregate expenditure schedule crosses the 45-degree line. In this example, the equilibrium occurs at 6,000. This equilibrium can also be read off the table under the figure; it is the level of national income where aggregate expenditure is equal to national income.

Equilibrium in the Keynesian Cross Model

With the aggregate expenditure line in place, the next step is to relate it to the two other elements of the Keynesian cross diagram. Thus, the first subsection interprets the intersection of the aggregate expenditure function and the 45-degree line, while the next subsection relates this point of intersection to the potential GDP line.

Where Equilibrium Occurs

The point where the aggregate expenditure line that is constructed from $C + I + G + X - M$ crosses the 45-degree line will be the equilibrium for the economy. It is the only point on the aggregate expenditure line where the total amount being spent on aggregate demand equals the total level of production. In **Figure D7**, this point of equilibrium (E_0) happens at 6,000, which can also be read off **Table D3**.

The meaning of "equilibrium" remains the same; that is, equilibrium is a point of balance where no incentive exists to shift away from that outcome. To understand why the point of intersection between the aggregate expenditure function and the 45-degree line is a macroeconomic equilibrium, consider what would happen if an economy found itself to the right of the equilibrium point E, say point H in **Figure D8**, where output is higher than the equilibrium. At point H, the level of aggregate expenditure is below the 45-degree line, so that the level of aggregate expenditure in the economy is less than the level of output. As a result, at point H, output is piling up unsold—not a sustainable state of affairs.

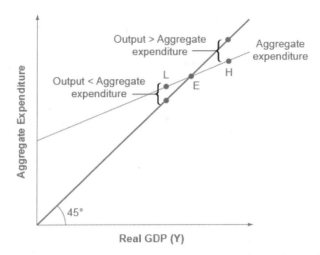

Figure D8 Equilibrium in the Keynesian Cross Diagram   If output was above the equilibrium level, at H, then the real output is greater than the aggregate expenditure in the economy. This pattern cannot hold, because it would mean that goods are produced but piling up unsold. If output was below the equilibrium level at L, then aggregate expenditure would be greater than output. This pattern cannot hold either, because it would mean that spending exceeds the number of goods being produced. Only point E can be at equilibrium, where output, or national income and aggregate expenditure, are equal. The equilibrium (E) must lie on the 45-degree line, which is the set of points where national income and aggregate expenditure are equal.

Conversely, consider the situation where the level of output is at point L—where real output is lower than the equilibrium. In that case, the level of aggregate demand in the economy is above the 45-degree line, indicating that the level of aggregate expenditure in the economy is greater than the level of output. When the level of aggregate demand has emptied the store shelves, it cannot be sustained, either. Firms will respond by increasing their level of production. Thus, the equilibrium must be the point where the amount produced and the amount spent are in balance, at the intersection of the aggregate expenditure function and the 45-degree line.

Work It Out ─○─○─○

Finding Equilibrium

Table D4 gives some information on an economy. The Keynesian model assumes that there is some level of consumption even without income. That amount is $236 − $216 = $20. $20 will be consumed when national income equals zero. Assume that taxes are 0.2 of real GDP. Let the marginal propensity to save of after-tax income be 0.1. The level of investment is $70, the level of government spending is $80, and the level of exports is $50. Imports are 0.2 of after-tax income. Given these values, you need to complete Table D4 and then answer these questions:

- What is the consumption function?
- What is the equilibrium?
- Why is a national income of $300 not at equilibrium?
- How do expenditures and output compare at this point?

National Income	Taxes	After-tax income	Consumption	I + G + X	Imports	Aggregate Expenditures
$300			$236			
$400						
$500						
$600						
$700						

Table D4

Step 1. Calculate the amount of taxes for each level of national income(reminder: GDP = national income) for each level of national income using the following as an example:

National Income (Y)	$300
Taxes = 0.2 or 20%	× 0.2
Tax amount (T)	$60

Step 2. Calculate after-tax income by subtracting the tax amount from national income for each level of national income using the following as an example:

National income minus taxes	$300
	−$60
After-tax income	$240

Step 3. Calculate consumption. The marginal propensity to save is given as 0.1. This means that the marginal propensity to consume is 0.9, since MPS + MPC = 1. Therefore, multiply 0.9 by the after-tax income amount using the following as an example:

After-tax Income	$240
MPC	× 0.9
Consumption	$216

Step 4. Consider why the table shows consumption of $236 in the first row. As mentioned earlier, the Keynesian model assumes that there is some level of consumption even without income. That amount is $236 − $216 = $20.

This OpenStax book is available for free at http://cnx.org/content/col12122/1.4

Step 5. There is now enough information to write the consumption function. The consumption function is found by figuring out the level of consumption that will happen when income is zero. Remember that:

$$C = \text{Consumption when national income is zero} + \text{MPC (after-tax income)}$$

Let C represent the consumption function, Y represent national income, and T represent taxes.

$$
\begin{aligned}
C &= \$20 + 0.9(Y - T) \\
&= \$20 + 0.9(\$300 - \$60) \\
&= \$236
\end{aligned}
$$

Step 6. Use the consumption function to find consumption at each level of national income.

Step 7. Add investment (I), government spending (G), and exports (X). Remember that these do not change as national income changes:

Step 8. Find imports, which are 0.2 of after-tax income at each level of national income. For example:

After-tax income	$240
Imports of 0.2 or 20% of Y – T	× 0.2
Imports	$48

Step 9. Find aggregate expenditure by adding C + I + G + X – I for each level of national income. Your completed table should look like **Table D5**.

National Income (Y)	Tax = 0.2 × Y (T)	After-tax income (Y – T)	Consumption C = $20 + 0.9(Y – T)	I + G + X	Minus Imports (M)	Aggregate Expenditures AE = C + I + G + X – M
$300	$60	$240	$236	$200	$48	$388
$400	$80	$320	$308	$200	$64	$444
$500	$100	$400	$380	$200	$80	$500
$600	$120	$480	$452	$200	$96	$556
$700	$140	$560	$524	$200	$112	$612

Table D5

Step 10. Answer the question: What is equilibrium? Equilibrium occurs where AE = Y. **Table D5** shows that equilibrium occurs where national income equals aggregate expenditure at $500.

Step 11. Find equilibrium mathematically, knowing that national income is equal to aggregate expenditure.

$$
\begin{aligned}
Y &= AE \\
&= C + I + G + X - M \\
&= \$20 + 0.9(Y - T) + \$70 + \$80 + \$50 - 0.2(Y - T) \\
&= \$220 + 0.9(Y - T) - 0.2(Y - T)
\end{aligned}
$$

Since T is 0.2 of national income, substitute T with 0.2 Y so that:

$$
\begin{aligned}
Y &= \$220 + 0.9(Y - 0.2Y) - 0.2(Y - 0.2Y) \\
&= \$220 + 0.9Y - 0.18Y - 0.2Y + 0.04Y \\
&= \$220 + 0.56Y
\end{aligned}
$$

Solve for Y.

$$Y = \$220 + 0.56Y$$
$$Y - 0.56Y = \$220$$
$$0.44Y = \$220$$
$$\frac{0.44Y}{0.44} = \frac{\$220}{0.44}$$
$$Y = \$500$$

Step 12. Answer this question: Why is a national income of $300 not an equilibrium? At national income of $300, aggregate expenditures are $388.

Step 13. Answer this question: How do expenditures and output compare at this point? Aggregate expenditures cannot exceed output (GDP) in the long run, since there would not be enough goods to be bought.

Recessionary and Inflationary Gaps

In the Keynesian cross diagram, if the aggregate expenditure line intersects the 45-degree line at the level of potential GDP, then the economy is in sound shape. There is no recession, and unemployment is low. But there is no guarantee that the equilibrium will occur at the potential GDP level of output. The equilibrium might be higher or lower.

For example, **Figure D9** (a) illustrates a situation where the aggregate expenditure line intersects the 45-degree line at point E_0, which is a real GDP of $6,000, and which is below the potential GDP of $7,000. In this situation, the level of aggregate expenditure is too low for GDP to reach its full employment level, and unemployment will occur. The distance between an output level like E_0 that is below potential GDP and the level of potential GDP is called a recessionary gap. Because the equilibrium level of real GDP is so low, firms will not wish to hire the full employment number of workers, and unemployment will be high.

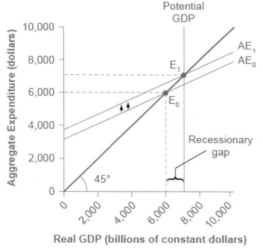

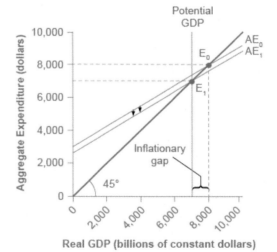

(a) Policy to address a recessionary gap.   (b) Policy to address an inflationary gap.

Figure D9 Addressing Recessionary and Inflationary Gaps (a) If the equilibrium occurs at an output below potential GDP, then a recessionary gap exists. The policy solution to a recessionary gap is to shift the aggregate expenditure schedule up from AE_0 to AE_1, using policies like tax cuts or government spending increases. Then the new equilibrium E_1 occurs at potential GDP. (b) If the equilibrium occurs at an output above potential GDP, then an inflationary gap exists. The policy solution to an inflationary gap is to shift the aggregate expenditure schedule down from AE_0 to AE_1, using policies like tax increases or spending cuts. Then, the new equilibrium E_1 occurs at potential GDP.

What might cause a recessionary gap? Anything that shifts the aggregate expenditure line down is a potential cause of recession, including a decline in consumption, a rise in savings, a fall in investment, a drop in government spending or a rise in taxes, or a fall in exports or a rise in imports. Moreover, an economy that is at equilibrium with a recessionary

This OpenStax book is available for free at http://cnx.org/content/col12122/1.4

gap may just stay there and suffer high unemployment for a long time; remember, the meaning of equilibrium is that there is no particular adjustment of prices or quantities in the economy to chase the recession away.

The appropriate response to a recessionary gap is for the government to reduce taxes or increase spending so that the aggregate expenditure function shifts up from AE_0 to AE_1. When this shift occurs, the new equilibrium E_1 now occurs at potential GDP as shown in **Figure D9** (a).

Conversely, **Figure D9** (b) shows a situation where the aggregate expenditure schedule (AE_0) intersects the 45-degree line above potential GDP. The gap between the level of real GDP at the equilibrium E_0 and potential GDP is called an inflationary gap. The inflationary gap also requires a bit of interpreting. After all, a naïve reading of the Keynesian cross diagram might suggest that if the aggregate expenditure function is just pushed up high enough, real GDP can be as large as desired—even doubling or tripling the potential GDP level of the economy. This implication is clearly wrong. An economy faces some supply-side limits on how much it can produce at a given time with its existing quantities of workers, physical and human capital, technology, and market institutions.

The inflationary gap should be interpreted, not as a literal prediction of how large real GDP will be, but as a statement of how much extra aggregate expenditure is in the economy beyond what is needed to reach potential GDP. An inflationary gap suggests that because the economy cannot produce enough goods and services to absorb this level of aggregate expenditures, the spending will instead cause an inflationary increase in the price level. In this way, even though changes in the price level do not appear explicitly in the Keynesian cross equation, the notion of inflation is implicit in the concept of the inflationary gap.

The appropriate Keynesian response to an inflationary gap is shown in **Figure D9** (b). The original intersection of aggregate expenditure line AE_0 and the 45-degree line occurs at $8,000, which is above the level of potential GDP at $7,000. If AE_0 shifts down to AE_1, so that the new equilibrium is at E_1, then the economy will be at potential GDP without pressures for inflationary price increases. The government can achieve a downward shift in aggregate expenditure by increasing taxes on consumers or firms, or by reducing government expenditures.

The Multiplier Effect

The Keynesian policy prescription has one final twist. Assume that for a certain economy, the intersection of the aggregate expenditure function and the 45-degree line is at a GDP of 700, while the level of potential GDP for this economy is $800. By how much does government spending need to be increased so that the economy reaches the full employment GDP? The obvious answer might seem to be $800 – $700 = $100; so raise government spending by $100. But that answer is incorrect. A change of, for example, $100 in government expenditures will have an effect of more than $100 on the equilibrium level of real GDP. The reason is that a change in aggregate expenditures circles through the economy: households buy from firms, firms pay workers and suppliers, workers and suppliers buy goods from other firms, those firms pay their workers and suppliers, and so on. In this way, the original change in aggregate expenditures is actually spent more than once. This is called the multiplier effect: An initial increase in spending, cycles repeatedly through the economy and has a larger impact than the initial dollar amount spent.

How Does the Multiplier Work?

To understand how the multiplier effect works, return to the example in which the current equilibrium in the Keynesian cross diagram is a real GDP of $700, or $100 short of the $800 needed to be at full employment, potential GDP. If the government spends $100 to close this gap, someone in the economy receives that spending and can treat it as income. Assume that those who receive this income pay 30% in taxes, save 10% of after-tax income, spend 10% of total income on imports, and then spend the rest on domestically produced goods and services.

As shown in the calculations in **Figure D10** and **Table D6**, out of the original $100 in government spending, $53 is left to spend on domestically produced goods and services. That $53 which was spent, becomes income to someone, somewhere in the economy. Those who receive that income also pay 30% in taxes, save 10% of after-tax income, and spend 10% of total income on imports, as shown in **Figure D10**, so that an additional $28.09 (that is, 0.53 × $53) is spent in the third round. The people who receive that income then pay taxes, save, and buy imports, and the amount spent in the fourth round is $14.89 (that is, 0.53 × $28.09).

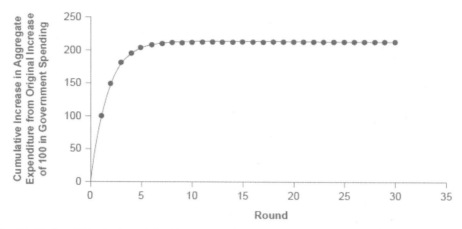

Figure D10 The Multiplier Effect An original increase of government spending of $100 causes a rise in aggregate expenditure of $100. But that $100 is income to others in the economy, and after they save, pay taxes, and buy imports, they spend $53 of that $100 in a second round. In turn, that $53 is income to others. Thus, the original government spending of $100 is multiplied by these cycles of spending, but the impact of each successive cycle gets smaller and smaller. Given the numbers in this example, the original government spending increase of $100 raises aggregate expenditure by $213; therefore, the multiplier in this example is $213/$100 = 2.13.

Original increase in aggregate expenditure from government spending	100
Which is income to people throughout the economy: Pay 30% in taxes. Save 10% of after-tax income. Spend 10% of income on imports. Second-round increase of…	70 − 7 − 10 = 53
Which is $53 of income to people through the economy: Pay 30% in taxes. Save 10% of after-tax income. Spend 10% of income on imports. Third-round increase of…	37.1 − 3.71 − 5.3 = 28.09
Which is $28.09 of income to people through the economy: Pay 30% in taxes. Save 10% of after-tax income. Spend 10% of income on imports. Fourth-round increase of…	19.663 − 1.96633 − 2.809 = 14.89

Table D6 Calculating the Multiplier Effect

Thus, over the first four rounds of aggregate expenditures, the impact of the original increase in government spending of $100 creates a rise in aggregate expenditures of $100 + $53 + $28.09 + $14.89 = $195.98. **Figure D10** shows these total aggregate expenditures after these first four rounds, and then the figure shows the total aggregate expenditures after 30 rounds. The additional boost to aggregate expenditures is shrinking in each round of consumption. After about 10 rounds, the additional increments are very small indeed—nearly invisible to the naked eye. After 30 rounds, the additional increments in each round are so small that they have no practical consequence. After 30 rounds, the cumulative value of the initial boost in aggregate expenditure is approximately $213. Thus, the government spending increase of $100 eventually, after many cycles, produced an increase of $213 in aggregate expenditure and real GDP. In this example, the multiplier is $213/$100 = 2.13.

Calculating the Multiplier

Fortunately for everyone who is not carrying around a computer with a spreadsheet program to project the impact of an original increase in expenditures over 20, 50, or 100 rounds of spending, there is a formula for calculating the multiplier.

$$\text{Spending Multiplier} = 1/(1 − \text{MPC} * (1 − \text{tax rate}) + \text{MPI})$$

The data from **Figure D10** and **Table D6** is:

This OpenStax book is available for free at http://cnx.org/content/col12122/1.4

- Marginal Propensity to Save (MPS) = 30%

- Tax rate = 10%

- Marginal Propensity to Import (MPI) = 10%

The MPC is equal to 1 – MPS, or 0.7. Therefore, the spending multiplier is:

$$\text{Spending Multiplier } = \frac{1}{1 - (0.7 - (0.10)(0.7) - 0.10)}$$
$$= \frac{1}{0.47}$$
$$= 2.13$$

A change in spending of $100 multiplied by the spending multiplier of 2.13 is equal to a change in GDP of $213. Not coincidentally, this result is exactly what was calculated in **Figure D10** after many rounds of expenditures cycling through the economy.

The size of the multiplier is determined by what proportion of the marginal dollar of income goes into taxes, saving, and imports. These three factors are known as "leakages," because they determine how much demand "leaks out" in each round of the multiplier effect. If the leakages are relatively small, then each successive round of the multiplier effect will have larger amounts of demand, and the multiplier will be high. Conversely, if the leakages are relatively large, then any initial change in demand will diminish more quickly in the second, third, and later rounds, and the multiplier will be small. Changes in the size of the leakages—a change in the marginal propensity to save, the tax rate, or the marginal propensity to import—will change the size of the multiplier.

Calculating Keynesian Policy Interventions

Returning to the original question: How much should government spending be increased to produce a total increase in real GDP of $100? If the goal is to increase aggregate demand by $100, and the multiplier is 2.13, then the increase in government spending to achieve that goal would be $100/2.13 = $47. Government spending of approximately $47, when combined with a multiplier of 2.13 (which is, remember, based on the specific assumptions about tax, saving, and import rates), produces an overall increase in real GDP of $100, restoring the economy to potential GDP of $800, as **Figure D11** shows.

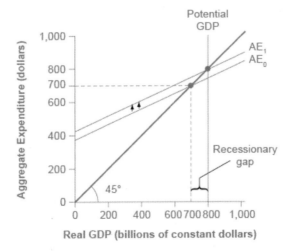

Figure D11 The Multiplier Effect in an Expenditure-Output Model   The power of the multiplier effect is that an increase in expenditure has a larger increase on the equilibrium output. The increase in expenditure is the vertical increase from AE_0 to AE_1. However, the increase in equilibrium output, shown on the horizontal axis, is clearly larger.

The multiplier effect is also visible on the Keynesian cross diagram. **Figure D11** shows the example we have been discussing: a recessionary gap with an equilibrium of $700, potential GDP of $800, the slope of the aggregate expenditure function (AE_0) determined by the assumptions that taxes are 30% of income, savings are 0.1 of after-tax income, and imports are 0.1 of before-tax income. At AE_1, the aggregate expenditure function is moved up to reach potential GDP.

Now, compare the vertical shift upward in the aggregate expenditure function, which is $47, with the horizontal shift outward in real GDP, which is $100 (as these numbers were calculated earlier). The rise in real GDP is more than double the rise in the aggregate expenditure function. (Similarly, if you look back at **Figure D9**, you will see that the vertical movements in the aggregate expenditure functions are smaller than the change in equilibrium output that is produced on the horizontal axis. Again, this is the multiplier effect at work.) In this way, the power of the multiplier is apparent in the income–expenditure graph, as well as in the arithmetic calculation.

The multiplier does not just affect government spending, but applies to any change in the economy. Say that business confidence declines and investment falls off, or that the economy of a leading trading partner slows down so that export sales decline. These changes will reduce aggregate expenditures, and then will have an even larger effect on real GDP because of the multiplier effect. Read the following Clear It Up feature to learn how the multiplier effect can be applied to analyze the economic impact of professional sports.

How can the multiplier be used to analyze the economic impact of professional sports?

Attracting professional sports teams and building sports stadiums to create jobs and stimulate business growth is an economic development strategy adopted by many communities throughout the United States. In his recent article, "Public Financing of Private Sports Stadiums," James Joyner of *Outside the Beltway* looked at public financing for NFL teams. Joyner's findings confirm the earlier work of John Siegfried of Vanderbilt University and Andrew Zimbalist of Smith College.

Siegfried and Zimbalist used the multiplier to analyze this issue. They considered the amount of taxes paid and dollars spent locally to see if there was a positive multiplier effect. Since most professional athletes and owners of sports teams are rich enough to owe a lot of taxes, let's say that 40% of any marginal income they earn is paid in taxes. Because athletes are often high earners with short careers, let's assume that they save one-third of their after-tax income.

However, many professional athletes do not live year-round in the city in which they play, so let's say that one-half of the money that they do spend is spent outside the local area. One can think of spending outside a local economy, in this example, as the equivalent of imported goods for the national economy.

Now, consider the impact of money spent at local entertainment venues other than professional sports. While the owners of these other businesses may be comfortably middle-income, few of them are in the economic stratosphere of professional athletes. Because their incomes are lower, so are their taxes; say that they pay only 35% of their marginal income in taxes. They do not have the same ability, or need, to save as much as professional athletes, so let's assume their MPC is just 0.8. Finally, because more of them live locally, they will spend a higher proportion of their income on local goods—say, 65%.

If these general assumptions hold true, then money spent on professional sports will have less local economic impact than money spent on other forms of entertainment. For professional athletes, out of a dollar earned, 40 cents goes to taxes, leaving 60 cents. Of that 60 cents, one-third is saved, leaving 40 cents, and half is spent outside the area, leaving 20 cents. Only 20 cents of each dollar is cycled into the local economy in the first round. For locally-owned entertainment, out of a dollar earned, 35 cents goes to taxes, leaving 65 cents. Of the rest, 20% is saved, leaving 52 cents, and of that amount, 65% is spent in the local area, so that 33.8 cents of each dollar of income is recycled into the local economy.

Siegfried and Zimbalist make the plausible argument that, within their household budgets, people have a fixed amount to spend on entertainment. If this assumption holds true, then money spent attending professional sports events is money that was not spent on other entertainment options in a given metropolitan area. Since the multiplier is lower for professional sports than for other local entertainment options, the arrival of professional sports to a city would reallocate entertainment spending in a way that causes the local economy to shrink, rather than to grow. Thus, their findings seem to confirm what Joyner reports and what newspapers across the country are reporting. A quick Internet search for "economic impact of sports" will yield numerous reports questioning this economic development strategy.

Multiplier Tradeoffs: Stability versus the Power of Macroeconomic Policy

Is an economy healthier with a high multiplier or a low one? With a high multiplier, any change in aggregate demand will tend to be substantially magnified, and so the economy will be more unstable. With a low multiplier, by contrast, changes in aggregate demand will not be multiplied much, so the economy will tend to be more stable.

However, with a low multiplier, government policy changes in taxes or spending will tend to have less impact on the equilibrium level of real output. With a higher multiplier, government policies to raise or reduce aggregate expenditures will have a larger effect. Thus, a low multiplier means a more stable economy, but also weaker government macroeconomic policy, while a high multiplier means a more volatile economy, but also an economy in which government macroeconomic policy is more powerful.

Key Concepts and Summary

The expenditure-output model or Keynesian cross diagram shows how the level of aggregate expenditure (on the vertical axis) varies with the level of economic output (shown on the horizontal axis). Since the value of all macroeconomic output also represents income to someone somewhere else in the economy, the horizontal axis can also be interpreted as national income. The equilibrium in the diagram will occur where the aggregate expenditure line crosses the 45-degree line, which represents the set of points where aggregate expenditure in the economy is equal to output (or national income). Equilibrium in a Keynesian cross diagram can happen at potential GDP, or below or above that level.

The consumption function shows the upward-sloping relationship between national income and consumption. The marginal propensity to consume (MPC) is the amount consumed out of an additional dollar of income. A higher marginal propensity to consume means a steeper consumption function; a lower marginal propensity to consume means a flatter consumption function. The marginal propensity to save (MPS) is the amount saved out of an additional dollar of income. It is necessarily true that MPC + MPS = 1. The investment function is drawn as a flat line, showing that investment in the current year does not change with regard to the current level of national income. However, the investment function will move up and down based on the expected rate of return in the future. Government spending is drawn as a horizontal line in the Keynesian cross diagram, because its level is determined by political considerations, not by the current level of income in the economy. Taxes in the basic Keynesian cross diagram are taken into account by adjusting the consumption function. The export function is drawn as a horizontal line in the Keynesian cross diagram, because exports do not change as a result of changes in domestic income, but they move as a result of changes in foreign income, as well as changes in exchange rates. The import function is drawn as a downward-sloping line, because imports rise with national income, but imports are a subtraction from aggregate demand. Thus, a higher level of imports means a lower level of expenditure on domestic goods.

In a Keynesian cross diagram, the equilibrium may be at a level below potential GDP, which is called a recessionary gap, or at a level above potential GDP, which is called an inflationary gap.

The multiplier effect describes how an initial change in aggregate demand generated several times as much as cumulative GDP. The size of the spending multiplier is determined by three leakages: spending on savings, taxes, and imports. The formula for the multiplier is:

$$\text{Multiplier} = \frac{1}{1 - (\text{MPC} \times (1 - \text{tax rate}) + \text{MPI})}$$

An economy with a lower multiplier is more stable—it is less affected either by economic events or by government policy than an economy with a higher multiplier.

Self-Check Questions

Exercise D1

Sketch the aggregate expenditure-output diagram with the recessionary gap.

Solution

The following figure shows the aggregate expenditure-output diagram with the recessionary gap.

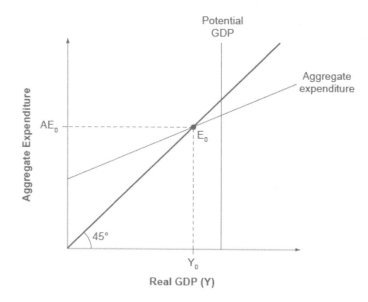

Figure D12

Exercise D2

Sketch the aggregate expenditure-output diagram with an inflationary gap.

Solution

The following figure shows the aggregate expenditure-output diagram with an inflationary gap.

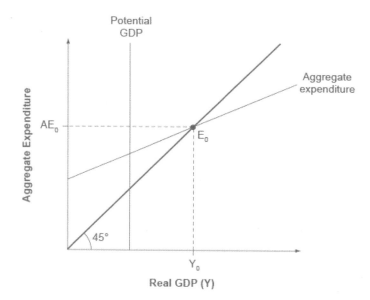

Figure D13

Exercise D3

An economy has the following characteristics:

Y = National income

This OpenStax book is available for free at http://cnx.org/content/col12122/1.4

Taxes = T = 0.25Y

C = Consumption = 400 + 0.85(Y − T)

I = 300

G = 200

X = 500

M = 0.1(Y − T)

Find the equilibrium for this economy. If potential GDP is 3,500, then what change in government spending is needed to achieve this level? Do this problem two ways. First, plug 3,500 into the equations and solve for G. Second, calculate the multiplier and figure it out that way.

Solution

First, set up the calculation.

$$AE = 400 + 0.85(Y − T) + 300 + 200 + 500 − 0.1(Y − T)$$
$$AE = Y$$

Then insert Y for AE and 0.25Y for T.

$$Y = 400 + 0.85(Y − 0.25Y) + 300 + 200 + 500 − 0.1(Y − 0.25Y)$$
$$Y = 1400 + 0.6375Y − 0.075Y$$
$$0.4375Y = 1400$$
$$Y = 3200$$

If full employment is 3,500, then one approach is to plug in 3,500 for Y throughout the equation, but to leave G as a separate variable.

$$Y = 400 + 0.85(Y − 0.25Y) + 300 + G + 500 + 0.1(Y − 0.25Y)$$
$$3500 = 400 + 0.85(3500 − 0.25(3500)) + 300 + G + 500 − 0.1(3500 − 0.25(3500))$$
$$G = 3500 − 400 − 2231.25 − 1300 − 500 + 262.5$$
$$G = 331.25$$

A G value of 331.25 is an increase of 131.25 from its original level of 200.

Alternatively, the multiplier is that, out of every dollar spent, 0.25 goes to taxes, leaving 0.75, and out of after-tax income, 0.15 goes to savings and 0.1 to imports. Because (0.75)(0.15) = 0.1125 and (0.75)(0.1) = 0.075, this means that out of every dollar spent: 1 −0.25 −0.1125 −0.075 = 0.5625.

Thus, using the formula, the multiplier is:

$$\frac{1}{1 − 0.5625} = 2.2837$$

To increase equilibrium GDP by 300, it will take a boost of 300/2.2837, which again works out to 131.25.

Exercise D4

Table D7 represents the data behind a Keynesian cross diagram. Assume that the tax rate is 0.4 of national income; the MPC out of the after-tax income is 0.8; investment is $2,000; government spending is $1,000; exports are $2,000 and imports are 0.05 of after-tax income. What is the equilibrium level of output for this economy?

National Income	After-tax Income	Consumption	I + G + X	Minus Imports	Aggregate Expenditures
$8,000		$4,340			
$9,000					

Table D7

National Income	After-tax Income	Consumption	I + G + X	Minus Imports	Aggregate Expenditures
$10,000					
$11,000					
$12,000					
$13,000					

Table D7

Solution

The following table illustrates the completed table. The equilibrium is level is italicized.

National Income	After-tax Income	Consumption	I + G + X	Minus Imports	Aggregate Expenditures
$8,000	$4,800	$4,340	$5,000	$240	$9,100
$9,000	$5,400	$4,820	$5,000	$270	$9,550
$10,000	*$6,000*	*$5,300*	*$5,000*	*$300*	*$10,000*
$11,000	$6,600	$5,780	$5,000	$330	$10,450
$12,000	$7,200	$6,260	$5,000	$360	$10,900
$13,000	$7,800	$46,740	$5,000	$4,390	$11,350

Table D8

The alternative way of determining equilibrium is to solve for Y, where Y = national income, using: $Y = AE = C + I + G + X – M$

$$Y = \$500 + 0.8(Y – T) + \$2,000 + \$1,000 + \$2,000 – 0.05(Y – T)$$

Solving for Y, we see that the equilibrium level of output is Y = $10,000.

Exercise D5

Explain how the multiplier works. Use an MPC of 80% in an example.

Solution

The multiplier refers to how many times a dollar will turnover in the economy. It is based on the Marginal Propensity to Consume (MPC) which tells how much of every dollar received will be spent. If the MPC is 80% then this means that out of every one dollar received by a consumer, $0.80 will be spent. This $0.80 is received by another person. In turn, 80% of the $0.80 received, or $0.64, will be spent, and so on. The impact of the multiplier is diluted when the effect of taxes and expenditure on imports is considered. To derive the multiplier, take the 1/1 – F; where F is equal to percent of savings, taxes, and expenditures on imports.

Review Questions

Exercise D6

What is on the axes of an expenditure-output diagram?

This OpenStax book is available for free at http://cnx.org/content/col12122/1.4

Exercise D7

What does the 45-degree line show?

Exercise D8

What determines the slope of a consumption function?

Exercise D9

What is the marginal propensity to consume, and how is it related to the marginal propensity to import?

Exercise D10

Why are the investment function, the government spending function, and the export function all drawn as flat lines?

Exercise D11

Why does the import function slope down? What is the marginal propensity to import?

Exercise D12

What are the components on which the aggregate expenditure function is based?

Exercise D13

Is the equilibrium in a Keynesian cross diagram usually expected to be at or near potential GDP?

Exercise D14

What is an inflationary gap? A recessionary gap?

Exercise D15

What is the multiplier effect?

Exercise D16

Why are savings, taxes, and imports referred to as "leakages" in calculating the multiplier effect?

Exercise D17

Will an economy with a high multiplier be more stable or less stable than an economy with a low multiplier in response to changes in the economy or in government policy?

Exercise D18

How do economists use the multiplier?

Critical Thinking Questions

Exercise D19

What does it mean when the aggregate expenditure line crosses the 45-degree line? In other words, how would you explain the intersection in words?

Exercise D20

Which model, the AD/AS or the AE model better explains the relationship between rising price levels and GDP? Why?

Exercise D21

What are some reasons that the economy might be in a recession, and what is the appropriate government action to alleviate the recession?

Exercise D22

What should the government do to relieve inflationary pressures if the aggregate expenditure is greater than potential GDP?

Exercise D23

Two countries are in a recession. Country A has an MPC of 0.8 and Country B has an MPC of 0.6. In which country will government spending have the greatest impact?

Exercise D24

Compare two policies: a tax cut on income or an increase in government spending on roads and bridges. What are both the short-term and long-term impacts of such policies on the economy?

Exercise D25

What role does government play in stabilizing the economy and what are the tradeoffs that must be considered?

Exercise D26

If there is a recessionary gap of $100 billion, should the government increase spending by $100 billion to close the gap? Why? Why not?

Exercise D27

What other changes in the economy can be evaluated by using the multiplier?

References

Joyner, James. Outside the Beltway. "Public Financing of Private Sports Stadiums." Last modified May 23, 2012. http://www.outsidethebeltway.com/public-financing-of-private-sports-stadiums/.

Siegfried, John J., and Andrew Zimbalist. "The Economics of Sports Facilities and Their Communities." *Journal of Economic Perspectives*. no. 3 (2000): 95-114. http://pubs.aeaweb.org/doi/pdfplus/10.1257/jep.14.3.95.

This OpenStax book is available for free at http://cnx.org/content/col12122/1.4

ANSWER KEY

Chapter 1

1. Scarcity means human wants for goods and services exceed the available supply. Supply is limited because resources are limited. Demand, however, is virtually unlimited. Whatever the supply, it seems human nature to want more.

2. 100 people / 10 people per ham = a maximum of 10 hams per month if all residents produce ham. Since consumption is limited by production, the maximum number of hams residents could consume per month is 10.

3. She is very productive at her consulting job, but not very productive growing vegetables. Time spent consulting would produce far more income than it what she could save growing her vegetables using the same amount of time. So on purely economic grounds, it makes more sense for her to maximize her income by applying her labor to what she does best (i.e. specialization of labor).

4. The engineer is better at computer science than at painting. Thus, his time is better spent working for pay at his job and paying a painter to paint his house. Of course, this assumes he does not paint his house for fun!

5. There are many physical systems that would work, for example, the study of planets (micro) in the solar system (macro), or solar systems (micro) in the galaxy (macro).

6. Draw a box outside the original circular flow to represent the foreign country. Draw an arrow from the foreign country to firms, to represents imports. Draw an arrow in the reverse direction representing payments for imports. Draw an arrow from firms to the foreign country to represent exports. Draw an arrow in the reverse direction to represent payments for imports.

7. There are many such problems. Consider the AIDS epidemic. Why are so few AIDS patients in Africa and Southeast Asia treated with the same drugs that are effective in the United States and Europe? It is because neither those patients nor the countries in which they live have the resources to purchase the same drugs.

8. Public enterprise means the factors of production (resources and businesses) are owned and operated by the government.

9. The United States is a large country economically speaking, so it has less need to trade internationally than the other countries mentioned. (This is the same reason that France and Italy have lower ratios than Belgium or Sweden.) One additional reason is that each of the other countries is a member of the European Union, where trade between members occurs without barriers to trade, like tariffs and quotas.

Chapter 2

1. The opportunity cost of bus tickets is the number of burgers that must be given up to obtain one more bus ticket. Originally, when the price of bus tickets was 50 cents per trip, this opportunity cost was 0.50/2 = .25 burgers. The reason for this is that at the original prices, one burger ($2) costs the same as four bus tickets ($0.50), so the opportunity cost of a burger is four bus tickets, and the opportunity cost of a bus ticket is .25 (the inverse of the opportunity cost of a burger). With the new, higher price of bus tickets, the opportunity cost rises to $1/$2 or 0.50. You can see this graphically since the slope of the new budget constraint is steeper than the original one. If Alphonso spends all of his budget on burgers, the higher price of bus tickets has no impact so the vertical intercept of the budget constraint is the same. If he spends all of his budget on bus tickets, he can now afford only half as many, so the vertical intercept is half as much. In short, the budget constraint rotates clockwise around the vertical intercept, steepening as it goes and the opportunity cost of bus tickets increases.

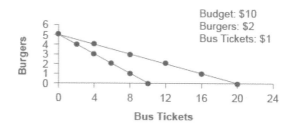

2. Because of the improvement in technology, the vertical intercept of the PPF would be at a higher level of healthcare. In other words, the PPF would rotate clockwise around the horizontal intercept. This would make the PPF steeper, corresponding to an increase in the opportunity cost of education, since resources devoted to education would now mean forgoing a greater quantity of healthcare.

3. No. Allocative efficiency requires productive efficiency, because it pertains to choices along the production possibilities frontier.

4. Both the budget constraint and the PPF show the constraint that each operates under. Both show a tradeoff between having more of one good but less of the other. Both show the opportunity cost graphically as the slope of the constraint (budget or PPF).

5. When individuals compare cost per unit in the grocery store, or characteristics of one product versus another, they are behaving approximately like the model describes.

6. Since an op-ed makes a case for what should be, it is considered normative.

7. Assuming that the study is not taking an explicit position about whether soft drink consumption is good or bad, but just reporting the science, it would be considered positive.

Chapter 3

1. Since $1.60 per gallon is above the equilibrium price, the quantity demanded would be lower at 550 gallons and the quantity supplied would be higher at 640 gallons. (These results are due to the laws of demand and supply, respectively.) The outcome of lower Qd and higher Qs would be a surplus in the gasoline market of 640 − 550 = 90 gallons.

2. To make it easier to analyze complex problems. *Ceteris paribus* allows you to look at the effect of one factor at a time on what it is you are trying to analyze. When you have analyzed all the factors individually, you add the results together to get the final answer.

3.
  a. An improvement in technology that reduces the cost of production will cause an increase in supply. Alternatively, you can think of this as a reduction in price necessary for firms to supply any quantity. Either way, this can be shown as a rightward (or downward) shift in the supply curve.
  b. An improvement in product quality is treated as an increase in tastes or preferences, meaning consumers demand more paint at any price level, so demand increases or shifts to the right. If this seems counterintuitive, note that demand in the future for the longer-lasting paint will fall, since consumers are essentially shifting demand from the future to the present.
  c. An increase in need causes an increase in demand or a rightward shift in the demand curve.
  d. Factory damage means that firms are unable to supply as much in the present. Technically, this is an increase in the cost of production. Either way you look at it, the supply curve shifts to the left.

4.
  a. More fuel-efficient cars means there is less need for gasoline. This causes a leftward shift in the demand for gasoline and thus oil. Since the demand curve is shifting down the supply curve, the equilibrium price and

This OpenStax book is available for free at http://cnx.org/content/col12122/1.4

quantity both fall.

b. Cold weather increases the need for heating oil. This causes a rightward shift in the demand for heating oil and thus oil. Since the demand curve is shifting up the supply curve, the equilibrium price and quantity both rise.

c. A discovery of new oil will make oil more abundant. This can be shown as a rightward shift in the supply curve, which will cause a decrease in the equilibrium price along with an increase in the equilibrium quantity. (The supply curve shifts down the demand curve so price and quantity follow the law of demand. If price goes down, then the quantity goes up.)

d. When an economy slows down, it produces less output and demands less input, including energy, which is used in the production of virtually everything. A decrease in demand for energy will be reflected as a decrease in the demand for oil, or a leftward shift in demand for oil. Since the demand curve is shifting down the supply curve, both the equilibrium price and quantity of oil will fall.

e. Disruption of oil pumping will reduce the supply of oil. This leftward shift in the supply curve will show a movement up the demand curve, resulting in an increase in the equilibrium price of oil and a decrease in the equilibrium quantity.

f. Increased insulation will decrease the demand for heating. This leftward shift in the demand for oil causes a movement down the supply curve, resulting in a decrease in the equilibrium price and quantity of oil.

g. Solar energy is a substitute for oil-based energy. So if solar energy becomes cheaper, the demand for oil will decrease as consumers switch from oil to solar. The decrease in demand for oil will be shown as a leftward shift in the demand curve. As the demand curve shifts down the supply curve, both equilibrium price and quantity for oil will fall.

h. A new, popular kind of plastic will increase the demand for oil. The increase in demand will be shown as a rightward shift in demand, raising the equilibrium price and quantity of oil.

5. Step 1. Draw the graph with the initial supply and demand curves. Label the initial equilibrium price and quantity. Step 2. Did the economic event affect supply or demand? Jet fuel is a cost of producing air travel, so an increase in jet fuel price affects supply. Step 3. An increase in the price of jet fuel caused a decrease in the cost of air travel. We show this as a downward or rightward shift in supply. Step 4. A rightward shift in supply causes a movement down the demand curve, lowering the equilibrium price of air travel and increasing the equilibrium quantity.

6. Step 1. Draw the graph with the initial supply and demand curves. Label the initial equilibrium price and quantity. Step 2. Did the economic event affect supply or demand? A tariff is treated like a cost of production, so this affects supply. Step 3. A tariff reduction is equivalent to a decrease in the cost of production, which we can show as a rightward (or downward) shift in supply. Step 4. A rightward shift in supply causes a movement down the demand curve, lowering the equilibrium price and raising the equilibrium quantity.

7. A price ceiling (which is below the equilibrium price) will cause the quantity demanded to rise and the quantity supplied to fall. This is why a price ceiling creates a shortage.

8. A price ceiling is just a legal restriction. Equilibrium is an economic condition. People may or may not obey the price ceiling, so the actual price may be at or above the price ceiling, but the price ceiling does not change the equilibrium price.

9. A price ceiling is a legal maximum price, but a price floor is a legal minimum price and, consequently, it would leave room for the price to rise to its equilibrium level. In other words, a price floor below equilibrium will not be binding and will have no effect.

10. Assuming that people obey the price ceiling, the market price will be below equilibrium, which means that Qd will be more than Qs. Buyers can only buy what is offered for sale, so the number of transactions will fall to Qs. This is easy to see graphically. By analogous reasoning, with a price floor the market price will be above the equilibrium price, so Qd will be less than Qs. Since the limit on transactions here is demand, the number of transactions will fall to Qd. Note that because both price floors and price ceilings reduce the number of transactions, social surplus is less.

11. Because the losses to consumers are greater than the benefits to producers, so the net effect is negative. Since the lost consumer surplus is greater than the additional producer surplus, social surplus falls.

Chapter 4

1. Changes in the wage rate (the price of labor) cause a movement along the demand curve. A change in anything else that affects demand for labor (e.g., changes in output, changes in the production process that use more or less labor, government regulation) causes a shift in the demand curve.

2. Changes in the wage rate (the price of labor) cause a movement along the supply curve. A change in anything else that affects supply of labor (e.g., changes in how desirable the job is perceived to be, government policy to promote training in the field) causes a shift in the supply curve.

3. Since a living wage is a suggested minimum wage, it acts like a price floor (assuming, of course, that it is followed). If the living wage is binding, it will cause an excess supply of labor at that wage rate.

4. Changes in the interest rate (i.e., the price of financial capital) cause a movement along the demand curve. A change in anything else (non-price variable) that affects demand for financial capital (e.g., changes in confidence about the future, changes in needs for borrowing) would shift the demand curve.

5. Changes in the interest rate (i.e., the price of financial capital) cause a movement along the supply curve. A change in anything else that affects the supply of financial capital (a non-price variable) such as income or future needs would shift the supply curve.

6. If market interest rates stay in their normal range, an interest rate limit of 35% would not be binding. If the equilibrium interest rate rose above 35%, the interest rate would be capped at that rate, and the quantity of loans would be lower than the equilibrium quantity, causing a shortage of loans.

7. b and c will lead to a fall in interest rates. At a lower demand, lenders will not be able to charge as much, and with more available lenders, competition for borrowers will drive rates down.

8. a and c will increase the quantity of loans. More people who want to borrow will result in more loans being given, as will more people who want to lend.

9. A price floor prevents a price from falling below a certain level, but has no effect on prices above that level. It will have its biggest effect in creating excess supply (as measured by the entire area inside the dotted lines on the graph, from D to S) if it is substantially above the equilibrium price. This is illustrated in the following figure.

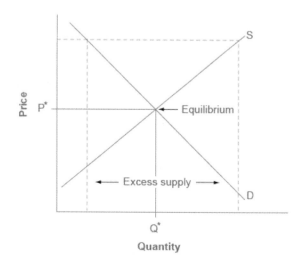

It will have a lesser effect if it is slightly above the equilibrium price. This is illustrated in the next figure.

This OpenStax book is available for free at http://cnx.org/content/col12122/1.4

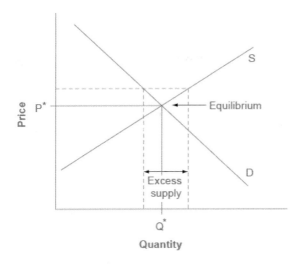

It will have no effect if it is set either slightly or substantially below the equilibrium price, since an equilibrium price above a price floor will not be affected by that price floor. The following figure illustrates these situations.

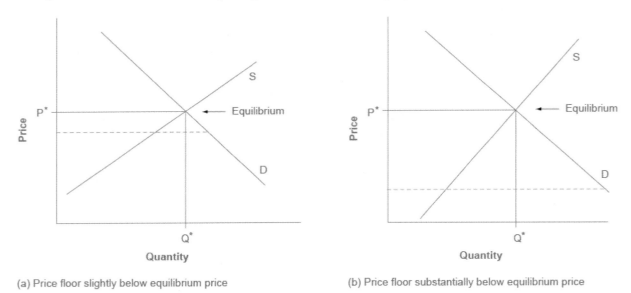

(a) Price floor slightly below equilibrium price   (b) Price floor substantially below equilibrium price

10. A price ceiling prevents a price from rising above a certain level, but has no effect on prices below that level. It will have its biggest effect in creating excess demand if it is substantially below the equilibrium price. The following figure illustrates these situations.

(a) Price ceiling substantially below equilibrium price

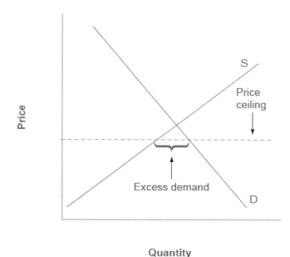

(b) Price ceiling slightly below equilibrium price

When the price ceiling is set substantially or slightly above the equilibrium price, it will have no effect on creating excess demand. The following figure illustrates these situations.

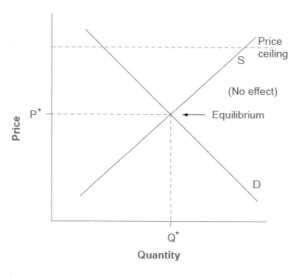

(a) Price ceiling substantially above equilibrium price

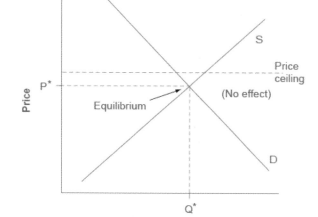

(b) Price ceiling slightly above equilibrium price

11. Neither. A shift in demand or supply means that at every price, either a greater or a lower quantity is demanded or supplied. A price floor does not shift a demand curve or a supply curve. However, if the price floor is set above the equilibrium, it will cause the quantity supplied on the supply curve to be greater than the quantity demanded on the demand curve, leading to excess supply.

12. Neither. A shift in demand or supply means that at every price, either a greater or a lower quantity is demanded or supplied. A price ceiling does not shift a demand curve or a supply curve. However, if the price ceiling is set below the equilibrium, it will cause the quantity demanded on the demand curve to be greater than the quantity supplied on the supply curve, leading to excess demand.

Chapter 5

1. From point B to point C, price rises from \$70 to \$80, and Qd decreases from 2,800 to 2,600. So:

$$\% \text{ change in quantity} = \frac{2600 - 2800}{(2600 + 2800) \div 2} \times 100$$

$$= \frac{-200}{2700} \times 100$$

$$= -7.41$$

$$\% \text{ change in price} = \frac{80 - 70}{(80 + 70) \div 2} \times 100$$

$$= \frac{10}{75} \times 100$$

$$= 13.33$$

$$\text{Elasticity of Demand} = \frac{-7.41\%}{13.33\%}$$

$$= 0.56$$

The demand curve is inelastic in this area; that is, its elasticity value is less than one. Answer from Point D to point E:

$$\% \text{ change in quantity} = \frac{2200 - 2400}{(2200 + 2400) \div 2} \times 100$$

$$= \frac{-200}{2300} \times 100$$

$$= -8.7$$

$$\% \quad \text{change in price} = \frac{100 - 90}{(100 + 90) \div 2} \times 100$$

$$= \frac{10}{95} \times 100$$

$$= 10.53$$

$$\text{Elasticity of Demand} = \frac{-8.7\%}{10.53\%}$$

$$= 0.83$$

The demand curve is inelastic in this area; that is, its elasticity value is less than one. Answer from Point G to point H:

$$\% \text{ change in quantity} = \frac{1600 - 1800}{1700} \times 100$$

$$= \frac{-200}{1700} \times 100$$

$$= -11.76$$

$$\% \text{ change in price} = \frac{130 - 120}{125} \times 100$$

$$= \frac{10}{125} \times 100$$

$$= 8.00$$

$$\text{Elasticity of Demand} = \frac{-11.76\%}{8.00\%}$$

$$= -1.47$$

The demand curve is elastic in this interval.

2. From point J to point K, price rises from \$8 to \$9, and quantity rises from 50 to 70. So:

$$\% \text{ change in quantity} = \frac{70 - 50}{(70 + 50) \div 2} \times 100$$

$$= \frac{20}{60} \times 100$$

$$= 33.33$$

$$\% \text{ change in price} = \frac{\$9 - \$8}{(\$9 + \$8) \div 2} \times 100$$

$$= \frac{1}{8.5} \times 100$$

$$= 11.76$$

$$\text{Elasticity of Supply} = \frac{33.33\%}{11.76\%}$$

$$= 2.83$$

The supply curve is elastic in this area; that is, its elasticity value is greater than one. From point L to point M, the price rises from $10 to $11, while the Qs rises from 80 to 88:

$$\% \text{ change in quantity} = \frac{88 - 80}{(88 + 80) \div 2} \times 100$$

$$= \frac{8}{84} \times 100$$

$$= 9.52$$

$$\% \text{change in price} = \frac{\$11 - \$10}{(\$11 + \$10) \div 2} \times 100$$

$$= \frac{1}{10.5} \times 100$$

$$= 9.52$$

$$\text{Elasticity of Demand} = \frac{9.52\%}{9.52\%}$$

$$= 1.0$$

The supply curve has unitary elasticity in this area. From point N to point P, the price rises from $12 to $13, and Qs rises from 95 to 100:

$$\% \text{ change in quantity} = \frac{100 - 95}{(100 + 95) \div 2} \times 100$$

$$= \frac{5}{97.5} \times 100$$

$$= 5.13$$

$$\% \text{ change in price} = \frac{\$13 - \$12}{(\$13 + \$12) \div 2} \times 100$$

$$= \frac{1}{12.5} \times 100$$

$$= 8.0$$

$$\text{Elasticity of Supply} = \frac{5.13\%}{8.0\%}$$

$$= 0.64$$

The supply curve is inelastic in this region of the supply curve.

3. The demand curve with constant unitary elasticity is concave because the absolute value of declines in price are not identical. The left side of the curve starts with high prices, and then price falls by smaller amounts as it goes down toward the right side. This results in a slope of demand that is steeper on the left but flatter on the right, creating a curved, concave shape.

4. The constant unitary elasticity is a straight line because the curve slopes upward and both price and quantity are increasing proportionally.

5. Carmakers can pass this cost along to consumers if the demand for these cars is inelastic. If the demand for these cars is elastic, then the manufacturer must pay for the equipment.

6. If the elasticity is 1.4 at current prices, you would advise the company to lower its price on the product, since a decrease in price will be offset by the increase in the amount of the drug sold. If the elasticity were 0.6, then you would advise the company to increase its price. Increases in price will offset the decrease in number of units sold, but increase your total revenue. If elasticity is 1, the total revenue is already maximized, and you would advise that the company maintain its current price level.

7. The percentage change in quantity supplied as a result of a given percentage change in the price of gasoline.

8.

$$
\begin{aligned}
\text{Percentage change in quantity demanded} &= [(\text{change in quantity})/(\text{original quantity})] \times 100 \\
&= [22 - 30]/[(22 + 30)/2] \times 100 \\
&= -8/26 \times 100 \\
&= -30.77 \\
\text{Percentage change in income} &= [(\text{change in income})/(\text{original income})] \times 100 \\
&= [38{,}000 - 25{,}000]/[(38{,}000 + 25{,}000)/2] \times 100 \\
&= 13/31.5 \times 100 \\
&= 41.27
\end{aligned}
$$

In this example, bread is an inferior good because its consumption falls as income rises.

9. The formula for cross-price elasticity is % change in Qd for apples / % change in P of oranges. Multiplying both sides by % change in P of oranges yields: % change in Qd for apples = cross-price elasticity X% change in P of oranges = 0.4 × (–3%) = –1.2%, or a 1.2 % decrease in demand for apples.

Chapter 6

1. The rows of the table in the problem do not represent the actual choices available on the budget set; that is, the combinations of round trips and phone minutes that Jeremy can afford with his budget. One of the choices listed in the problem, the six round trips, is not even available on the budget set. If Jeremy has only $10 to spend and a round trip costs $2 and phone calls cost $0.05 per minute, he could spend his entire budget on five round trips but no phone calls or 200 minutes of phone calls, but no round trips or any combination of the two in between. It is easy to see all of his budget options with a little algebra. The equation for a budget line is:

$$
\text{Budget} = P_{RT} \times Q_{RT} + P_{PC} \times Q_{PC}
$$

where P and Q are price and quantity of round trips ($_{RT}$) and phone calls ($_{PC}$) (per minute). In Jeremy's case the equation for the budget line is:

$$
\begin{aligned}
\$10 &= \$2 \times Q_{RT} + \$.05 \times Q_{PC} \\
\frac{\$10}{\$.05} &= \frac{\$2Q_{RT} + \$.05Q_{PC}}{\$.05} \\
200 &= 40Q_{RT} + Q_{PC} \\
Q_{PC} &= 200 - 40Q_{RT}
\end{aligned}
$$

If we choose zero through five round trips (column 1), the table below shows how many phone minutes can be afforded with the budget (column 3). The total utility figures are given in the table below.

Round Trips	Total Utility for Trips	Phone Minutes	Total Utility for Minutes	Total Utility
0	0	200	1100	1100
1	80	160	1040	1120
2	150	120	900	1050
3	210	80	680	890
4	260	40	380	640

Round Trips	Total Utility for Trips	Phone Minutes	Total Utility for Minutes	Total Utility
5	300	0	0	300

Adding up total utility for round trips and phone minutes at different points on the budget line gives total utility at each point on the budget line. The highest possible utility is at the combination of one trip and 160 minutes of phone time, with a total utility of 1120.

2. The first step is to use the total utility figures, shown in the table below, to calculate marginal utility, remembering that marginal utility is equal to the change in total utility divided by the change in trips or minutes.

Round Trips	Total Utility	Marginal Utility (per trip)	Phone Minutes	Total Utility	Marginal Utility (per minute)
0	0	-	200	1100	-
1	80	80	160	1040	60/40 = 1.5
2	150	70	120	900	140/40 = 3.5
3	210	60	80	680	220/40 = 5.5
4	260	50	40	380	300/40 = 7.5
5	300	40	0	0	380/40 = 9.5

Note that we cannot directly compare marginal utilities, since the units are trips versus phone minutes. We need a common denominator for comparison, which is price. Dividing MU by the price, yields columns 4 and 8 in the table below.

Round Trips	Total Utility	Marginal Utility (per trip)	MU/P	Phone Minutes	Total Utility	Marginal utility (per minute)	MU/P
0	0	-	-	200	1100	60/40 = 1.5	1.5/$0.05 = 30
1	80	80	80/$2 = 40	160	1040	140/40 = 3.5	3.5/$0.05 = 70
2	150	70	70/$2 = 35	120	900	220/40 = 5.5	5.5/$0.05 = 110
3	210	60	60/$2 = 30	80	680	300/40 =7.5	7.5/$0.05 = 150
4	260	50	50/$2 = 25	40	380	380/40 = 9.5	9.5/$0.05 = 190
5	300	40	40/$2 = 20	0	0	-	-

Start at the bottom of the table where the combination of round trips and phone minutes is (5, 0). This starting point is arbitrary, but the numbers in this example work best starting from the bottom. Suppose we consider moving to the next point up. At (4, 40), the marginal utility per dollar spent on a round trip is 25. The marginal utility per dollar spent on phone minutes is 190. Since 25 < 190, we are getting much more utility per dollar spent on phone minutes,

This OpenStax book is available for free at http://cnx.org/content/col12122/1.4

so let's choose more of those. At (3, 80), MU/P_{RT} is 30 < 150 (the MU/$_{PM}$), but notice that the difference is narrowing. We keep trading round trips for phone minutes until we get to (1, 160), which is the best we can do. The MU/P comparison is as close as it is going to get (40 vs. 70). Often in the real world, it is not possible to get MU/P exactly equal for both products, so you get as close as you can.

3. This is the opposite of the example explained in the text. A decrease in price has a substitution effect and an income effect. The substitution effect says that because the product is cheaper relative to other things the consumer purchases, he or she will tend to buy more of the product (and less of the other things). The income effect says that after the price decline, the consumer could purchase the same goods as before, and still have money left over to purchase more. For both reasons, a decrease in price causes an increase in quantity demanded.

4. This is a negative income effect. Because your parents' check failed to arrive, your monthly income is less than normal and your budget constraint shifts in toward the origin. If you only buy normal goods, the decrease in your income means you will buy less of every product.

Chapter 7

1. Accounting profit = total revenues minus explicit costs = $1,000,000 − ($600,000 + $150,000 + $200,000) = $50,000.

2. Economic profit = accounting profit minus implicit cost = $50,000 − $30,000 = $20,000.

3.

Quantity	Variable Cost	Fixed Cost	Total Cost	Average Variable Cost	Average Total Cost	Marginal Cost
0	0	$30	$30	-	-	
1	$10	$30	$40	$10.00	$40.00	$10
2	$25	$30	$55	$12.50	$27.50	$15
3	$45	$30	$75	$15.00	$25.00	$20
4	$70	$30	$100	$17.50	$25.00	$25
5	$100	$30	$130	$20.00	$26.00	$30
6	$135	$30	$165	$22.50	$27.50	$35

4.
   a. Total revenues in this example will be a quantity of five units multiplied by the price of $25/unit, which equals $125. Total costs when producing five units are $130. Thus, at this level of quantity and output the firm experiences losses (or negative profits) of $5.
   b. If price is less than average cost, the firm is not making a profit. At an output of five units, the average cost is $26/unit. Thus, at a glance you can see the firm is making losses. At a second glance, you can see that it must be losing $1 for each unit produced (that is, average cost of $26/unit minus the price of $25/unit). With five units produced, this observation implies total losses of $5.
   c. When producing five units, marginal costs are $30/unit. Price is $25/unit. Thus, the marginal unit is not adding to profits, but is actually subtracting from profits, which suggests that the firm should reduce its quantity produced.

6. The new table should look like this:

	Labor Cost	Machine Cost	Total Cost
Cost of technology 1	10 × $40 = $400	2 × $50 = $100	$500
Cost of technology 2	7 × $40 = $280	4 × $50 = $200	$480
Cost of technology 3	3 × $40 = $120	7 × $50 = $350	$470

The firm should choose production technology 3 since it has the lowest total cost. This makes sense since, with cheaper machine hours, one would expect a shift in the direction of more machines and less labor.

7.

	Labor Cost	Machine Cost	Total Cost
Cost of technology 1	10 × $40 = $400	2 × $55 = $110	$510
Cost of technology 2	7 × $40 = $280	4 × $55 = $220	$500
Cost of technology 3	3 × $40 = $120	7 × $55 = $385	$505

The firm should choose production technology 2 since it has the lowest total cost. Because the cost of machines increased (relative to the previous question), you would expect a shift toward less capital and more labor.

8. This is the situation that existed in the United States in the 1970s. Since there is only demand enough for 2.5 firms to reach the bottom of the average cost curve, you would expect one firm will not be around in the long run, and at least one firm will be struggling.

Chapter 8

1. No, you would not raise the price. Your product is exactly the same as the product of the many other firms in the market. If your price is greater than that of your competitors, then your customers would switch to them and stop buying from you. You would lose all your sales.

2. Possibly. Independent truckers are by definition small and numerous. All that is required to get into the business is a truck (not an inexpensive asset, though) and a commercial driver's license. To exit, one need only sell the truck. All trucks are essentially the same, providing transportation from point A to point B. (We're assuming we not talking about specialized trucks.) Independent truckers must take the going rate for their service, so independent trucking does seem to have most of the characteristics of perfect competition.

3. Holding total cost constant, profits at every output level would increase.

4. When the market price increases, marginal revenue increases. The firm would then increase production up to the point where the new price equals marginal cost, at a quantity of 90.

5. If marginal costs exceeds marginal revenue, then the firm will reduce its profits for every additional unit of output it produces. Profit would be greatest if it reduces output to where MR = MC.

6. The firm will be willing to supply fewer units at every price level. In other words, the firm's individual supply curve decreases and shifts to the left.

7. With a technological improvement that brings about a reduction in costs of production, an adjustment process will take place in the market. The technological improvement will result in an increase in supply curves, by individual firms and at the market level. The existing firms will experience higher profits for a while, which will attract other firms into the market. This entry process will stop whenever the market supply increases enough (both by existing and new firms) so profits are driven back to zero.

8. When wages increase, costs of production increase. Some firms would now be making economic losses and would shut down. The supply curve then starts shifting to the left, pushing the market price up. This process ends when all firms remaining in the market earn zero economic profits. The result is a contraction in the output produced in the market.

9. Perfect competition is considered to be "perfect" because both allocative and productive efficiency are met at the same time in a long-run equilibrium. If a market structure results in long-run equilibrium that does not minimize average total costs and/or does not charge a price equal to marginal cost, then either allocative or productive (or both) efficiencies are not met, and therefore the market cannot be labeled "perfect."

10. Think of the market price as representing the gain to society from a purchase, since it represents what someone is willing to pay. Think of the marginal cost as representing the cost to society from making the last unit of a good. If P > MC, then the benefits from producing more of a good exceed the costs, and society would gain from producing more of the good. If P < MC, then the social costs of producing the marginal good exceed the social benefits, and society should produce less of the good. Only if P = MC, the rule applied by a profit-maximizing perfectly competitive firm, will society's costs and benefits be in balance. This choice will be the option that brings the greatest overall benefit to society.

Chapter 9

1.
- a. A patent is a government-enforced barrier to entry.
- b. This is not a barrier to entry.
- c. This is not a barrier to entry.
- d. This is a barrier to entry, but it is not government-enforced.
- e. This is a barrier to entry, but it is not directly government enforced.

2.
- a. This is a government-enforced barrier to entry.
- b. This is an example of a government law, but perhaps it is not much of a barrier to entry if most people can pass the safety test and get insurance.
- c. Trademarks are enforced by government, and therefore are a barrier to entry.
- d. This is probably not a barrier to entry, since there are a number of different ways of getting pure water.
- e. This is a barrier to entry, but it is not government-enforced.

3. Because of economies of scale, each firm would produce at a higher average cost than before. (They would each have to build their own power lines.) As a result, they would each have to raise prices to cover their higher costs. The policy would fail.

4. Shorter patent protection would make innovation less lucrative, so the amount of research and development would likely decline.

5. If price falls below AVC, the firm will not be able to earn enough revenues even to cover its variable costs. In such a case, it will suffer a smaller loss if it shuts down and produces no output. By contrast, if it stayed in operation and produced the level of output where MR = MC, it would lose all of its fixed costs plus some variable costs. If it shuts down, it only loses its fixed costs.

6. This scenario is called "perfect price discrimination." The result would be that the monopolist would produce more output, the same amount in fact as would be produced by a perfectly competitive industry. However, there would be no consumer surplus since each buyer is paying exactly what they think the product is worth. Therefore, the monopolist would be earning the maximum possible profits.

Chapter 10

1. An increase in demand will manifest itself as a rightward shift in the demand curve, and a rightward shift in marginal revenue. The shift in marginal revenue will cause a movement up the marginal cost curve to the new intersection between MR and MC at a higher level of output. The new price can be read by drawing a line up from the new output level to the new demand curve, and then over to the vertical axis. The new price should be higher. The increase in quantity will cause a movement along the average cost curve to a possibly higher level of average cost. The price, though, will increase more, causing an increase in total profits.

2. As long as the original firm is earning positive economic profits, other firms will respond in ways that take away the original firm's profits. This will manifest itself as a decrease in demand for the original firm's product, a decrease in the firm's profit-maximizing price and a decrease in the firm's profit-maximizing level of output, essentially unwinding the process described in the answer to question 1. In the long-run equilibrium, all firms in monopolistically competitive markets will earn zero economic profits.

3.
   a. If the firms form a cartel, they will act like a monopoly, choosing the quantity of output where MR = MC. Drawing a line from the monopoly quantity up to the demand curve shows the monopoly price. Assuming that fixed costs are zero, and with an understanding of cost and profit, we can infer that when the marginal cost curve is horizontal, average cost is the same as marginal cost. Thus, the cartel will earn positive economic profits equal to the area of the rectangle, with a base equal to the monopoly quantity and a height equal to the difference between price (on the demand above the monopoly quantity) and average cost, as shown in the

following figure.
   b. The firms will expand output and cut price as long as there are profits remaining. The long-run equilibrium will occur at the point where average cost equals demand. As a result, the oligopoly will earn zero economic profits due to "cutthroat competition," as shown in the next figure.

   c. Pc > Pcc. Qc < Qcc. Profit for the cartel is positive and large. Profit for cutthroat competition is zero.

4. Firm B reasons that if it cheats and Firm A does not notice, it will double its money. Since Firm A's profits will

decline substantially, however, it is likely that Firm A will notice and if so, Firm A will cheat also, with the result that Firm B will lose 90% of what it gained by cheating. Firm A will reason that Firm B is unlikely to risk cheating. If neither firm cheats, Firm A earns $1000. If Firm A cheats, assuming Firm B does not cheat, A can boost its profits only a little, since Firm B is so small. If both firms cheat, then Firm A loses at least 50% of what it could have earned. The possibility of a small gain ($50) is probably not enough to induce Firm A to cheat, so in this case it is likely that both firms will collude.

Chapter 11

1. Yes, it is true. The HHI example is easy enough: since the market shares of all firms are included in the HHI calculation, a merger between two of the firms will change the HHI. For the four-firm concentration ratio, it is quite possible that a merger between, say, the fifth and sixth largest firms in the market could create a new firm that is then ranked in the top four in the market. In this case, a merger of two firms, neither in the top four, would still change the four-firm concentration ratio.

2. No, it is not true. The HHI includes the market shares of all firms in its calculation, but the squaring of the market shares has the effect of making the impact of the largest firms relatively bigger than in the 4-firm or 8-firm ratio.

3. The bus companies wanted the broader market definition (i.e., the second definition). If the narrow definition had been used, the combined bus companies would have had a near-monopoly on the market for intercity bus service. But they had only a sliver of the market for intercity transportation when everything else was included. The merger was allowed.

4. The common expectation is that the definition of markets will become broader because of greater competition from faraway places. However, this broadening doesn't necessarily mean that antitrust authorities can relax. There is also a fear that companies with a local or national monopoly may use the new opportunities to extend their reach across national borders, and that it will be difficult for national authorities to respond.

5. Because outright collusion to raise profits is illegal and because existing regulations include gray areas which firms may be able to exploit.

6. Yes, all curves have normal shapes.

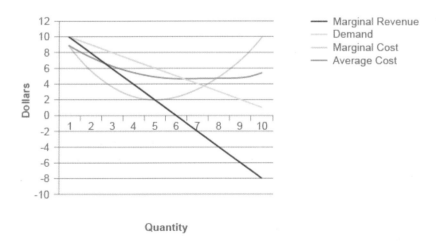

7. Yes it is a natural monopoly because average costs decline over the range that satisfies the market demand. For example, at the point where the demand curve and the average cost curve meet, there are economies of scale.

8. Improvements in technology that allowed phone calls to be made via microwave transmission, communications satellites, and other wireless technologies.

9. More consumer choice. Cheaper phone calls, especially long distance. Better-quality phone service in many cases.

Cheaper, faster, and better-quality data transmission. Spin-off technologies like free Internet-based calling and video calling.

10. More choice can sometimes make for difficult decisions—not knowing if you got the best plan for your situation, for example. Some phone service providers are less reliable than AT&T used to be.

Chapter 12

1.
    a. positive externality
    b. negative externality
    c. positive externality
    d. negative externality
    e. negative externality

2.
    a. supply shifts left
    b. supply shifts left
    c. supply stays the same
    d. supply shifts left

3.
    a. price will rise
    b. price will rise
    c. price stays the same
    d. price will rise.

4. The original equilibrium (before the external social cost of pollution is taken into account) is where the private supply curve crosses the demand curve. This original equilibrium is at a price of $15 and a quantity of 440. After taking into account the additional external cost of pollution, the production becomes more costly, and the supply curve shifts up. The new equilibrium will be at a price of $30 and a quantity of 410.

5. The first policy is command-and-control because it is a requirement that applies to all producers.

6.
    a. market-based
    b. command-and-control
    c. command-and-control
    d. market-based
    e. market-based

7. Even though state or local governments impose these taxes, a company has the flexibility to adopt technologies that will help it avoid the tax.

8. First, if each firm is required to reduce its garbage output by one-fourth, then Elm will reduce five tons at a cost of $5,500; Maple will reduce 10 tons at a cost of $13,500; Oak will reduce three tons at a cost of $22,500; and Cherry will reduce four tons at a cost of $18,000. Total cost of this approach: $59,500. If the system of marketable permits is put in place, and those permits shrink the weight of allowable garbage by one-quarter, then pollution must still be reduced by the same overall amount. However, now the reduction in pollution will take place where it is least expensive.

Reductions in Garbage	Who does the reducing?	At what cost?
First 5 tons	Cherry	$3,000

This OpenStax book is available for free at http://cnx.org/content/col12122/1.4

Reductions in Garbage	Who does the reducing?	At what cost?
Second 5 tons	Cherry	$4,000
Third 5 tons	Cherry	$5,000
Fourth 5 tons	Elm	$5,500
Fifth and sixth 5 tons	Elm and Cherry	$6,000 each
Seventh 5 tons	Maple	$6,300
Eighth 5 tons	Elm	$6,500
Ninth and tenth 5 tons	Elm and Cherry	$7,000 each

Thus, the overall pattern of reductions here will be that Elm reduces garbage by 20 tons and has 15 tons of permits to sell. Maple reduces by five tons and needs to buy five tons of permits. Oak does not reduce garbage at all, and needs to buy 15 tons of permits. Cherry reduces garbage by 25 tons, which leaves it with five tons of permits to sell. The total cost of these reductions would be $56,300, a definite reduction in costs from the $59,500 cost of the command-and-control option.

9.

	Incentives to Go Beyond	Flexibility about Where and How Pollution Will Be Reduced	Political Process Creates Loopholes and Exceptions
Pollution Charges	If you keep reducing pollution you reduce your charge	Reducing pollution by any method is fine	If charge applies to all emissions of pollution then no loopholes
Marketable Permits	If you reduce your pollution you can sell your extra pollution permits	Reductions of pollution will happen at firms where it is cheapest to do so, by the least expensive methods	If all polluters are required to have permits then there are no loopholes
Property Rights	The party that has to pay for the pollution has incentive to do so in a cost effect way	Reducing pollution by any method is fine	If the property rights are clearly defined, then it is not legally possible to avoid cleanup

10.

a. See the answers in the following table. The marginal cost is calculated as the change in total cost divided by the change in quantity.

	Total Cost (in thousands of dollars) [marginal cost]	Total Benefits (in thousands of dollars) [marginal benefit]
16 million gallons	Current situation	Current situation

	Total Cost (in thousands of dollars) [marginal cost]	Total Benefits (in thousands of dollars) [marginal benefit]
12 million gallons	50 [50]	800 [800]
8 million gallons	150 [100]	1,300 [500]
4 million gallons	500 [350]	1,850 [350]
0 gallons	1,200 [700]	2,000 [150]

   b. The "optimal" level of pollution is where the marginal benefits of reducing it are equal to the marginal cost. This is at four million gallons.

   c. Marginal analysis tells us if the marginal costs of cleanup are greater than the marginal benefit, society could use those resources more efficiently elsewhere in the economy.

11.

   a. See the next table for the answers, which were calculated using the traditional calculation of marginal cost equal to change in total cost divided by change in quantity.

Land Restored (in acres)	Total Cost [marginal cost]	Total Benefit [marginal benefit]
0	$0	$0
100	$20 [0.2]	$140 [1.4]
200	$80 [0.6]	$240 [1]
300	$160 [0.8]	$320 [0.8]
400	$280 [1.2]	$480 [0.6]

   b. The optimal amount of restored land is 300 acres. Beyond this quantity the marginal costs are greater than the marginal benefits.

12.

		Country B	
		Protect	Not Protect
Country A	Protect	Both A and B have a cost of 10 and a benefit of 16; each country has net = 6	A has a cost of 10 and a benefit of 8 (net = –2); B has a cost of 0 and a benefit of 8 (net = 8)
	Not Protect	A has a cost of 0 and a benefit of 8 (net = 8); B has a cost of 10 and a benefit of 8 (net = –2)	Both A and B have a zero cost and a zero benefit; each country has net = 0

Country B will reason this way: If A protects the environment, then we will have benefits of 6 if we act to protect the environment, but 8 if we do not, so we will not protect it. If A is not protecting the environment, we will have losses of 2 if we protect, but have zero if we do not protect, so again, we will not protect it. Country A will reason in a similar manner. The result is that both countries choose to not protect, even though they will achieve the largest social benefits—a combined benefit of 12 for the two countries—if they both choose to protect. Environmental treaties can be viewed as a way for countries to try to extricate themselves from this situation.

13.

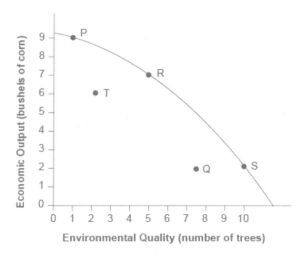

a.

b. Of the choices provided, P, R, and S demonstrate productive efficiency. These are the choices on the production possibility frontier.

c. Allocative efficiency is determined by the preferences—in this case by the preferences of society as expressed through government and other social institutions. Because you do not have information about these preferences, you really cannot say much about allocative efficiency.

d. In the choice between T and R, R should clearly be preferred, because it has both more corn and more trees. This answer illustrates why productive efficiency is beneficial. Compared with choices inside the PPF, it means more of one or both goods.

e. In the choice between T and S, it is not possible to say which choice is better. True, S is on the PPF and T is not—but that only addresses the issue of productive efficiency. If a society has a strong preference for economic output and places a lower value on trees, then allocative efficiency may lead to a choice of T over S. Of course, the reverse could also be true, leading to a choice of S. Without information on society's preferences to judge allocative efficiency, this question cannot be answered.

f. Compared with command-and-control policies, market-oriented policies allow either more output with the same environmental protection or more environmental protection with the same level of output—or more of both environmental protection and output. Thus, a choice like Q inside the PPF is more likely to represent a command-and-control policy demand than a choice like S on the frontier of the PPF.

Chapter 13

1. No. A market demand curve reflects only the private benefits of those who are consuming the product. Positive externalities are benefits that spill over to third parties, so they create social benefits, and are not captured by a market (or private benefit) demand curve.

2. Clearly Samsung is benefiting from the investment, so the 20% increase in profits is a private benefit. If Samsung is unable to capture all of the benefit, perhaps because other companies quickly copy and produce close substitutes, then Samsung's investment will produce social benefits.

3.

a. $102 million.

b. If the interest rate is 9%, the cost of financial capital, and the firm can capture the 5% return to society, the firm would invest as if its effective rate of return is 4%, so it will invest $183 million.

4. When the Junkbuyers Company purchases something for resale, presumably both the buyer and the seller benefit—otherwise, they would not need to make the transaction. However, the company also reduces the amount of garbage produced, which saves money for households and/or for the city that disposes of garbage. So the social benefits are larger than the private benefits.

5. Government programs that either pay for neighborhood clean-up directly or that provide reduced tax payments for those who clean up or fix up their own property could be enacted. It is also easy to imagine how a city might allow its businesses to form a group that would pay for and manage neighborhood cleanup.

6. Government programs that either pay for education directly or that provide loans or reduced tax payments for education could create positive spillovers. A city might allow its businesses to form a group that would coordinate business efforts with schools and local colleges and universities—allowing students to obtain real-world experience in their chosen fields and providing businesses with enthusiastic, trained workers.

7.
    a. Once citizens are protected from crime, it is difficult to exclude someone from this protection, so it is nonexcludable.
    b. Some satellite radio services, such as SiriusXM, are sold by subscription fee, so it is excludable.
    c. Once a road is built it is difficult to exclude people, although toll roads can exclude non-payers.
    d. Primary education can be provided by private companies and so it is excludable.
    e. Companies sell cell phone service and exclude those who do not pay.

8.
    a. Two people cannot enjoy the same slice of pizza at the same time, so private goods, such as a slice of pizza, are rivalrous.
    b. Two people cannot use one laptop at the same time, so they are rivalrous in consumption.
    c. Public radio can be heard by anyone with a radio, so many people can listen at the same time—the good is nonrivalrous.
    d. It is difficult for two people to simultaneously eat an ice cream cone, so it is rivalrous in consumption.

Chapter 14

3.
    a. With no union, the equilibrium wage rate would be $18 per hour and there would be 8,000 bus drivers.
    b. If the union has enough negotiating power to raise the wage to $4 per hour higher than under the original equilibrium, the new wage would be $22 per hour. At this wage, 4,000 workers would be demanded while 10,000 would be supplied, leading to an excess supply of 6,000 workers.

4. Unions have sometimes opposed new technology out of a fear of losing jobs, but in other cases unions have helped to facilitate the introduction of new technology because unionized workers felt that the union was looking after their interests or that their higher skills meant that their jobs were essentially protected. And the new technologies meant increased productivity.

5. In a few other countries (such as France and Spain), the percentage of workers belonging to a union is similar to that in the United States. Union membership rates, however, are generally lower in the United States. When the share of workers whose wages are determined by union negotiations is considered, the United States ranks by far the lowest (because in countries like France and Spain, union negotiations often determine pay even for nonunion employees).

6. No. While some unions may cause firms to go bankrupt, other unions help firms to become more competitive. No overall pattern exists.

7. From a social point of view, the benefits of unions and the costs seem to counterbalance. There is no evidence that in countries with a higher percentage of unionized workers, the economies grow more or less slowly.

9.
   a. Firms have a profit incentive to sell to everyone, regardless of race, ethnicity, religion, or gender.
   b. A business that needs to hire workers to expand may also find that if it draws only from its accustomed pool of workers—say, white men—it lacks the workers it needs to expand production. Such a business would have an incentive to hire more women and minorities.
   c. A discriminatory business that is underpaying its workers may find those workers leaving for jobs with another employer who offers better pay. This market pressure could cause the discriminatory business to behave better.

10. No. The earnings gap does not prove discrimination because it does not compare the wages of men and women in the same job who have the same amounts of education, experience, and productivity.

11. If a large share of immigrants have relatively low skills, then reducing the number of immigrants would shift the supply curve of low-skill labor back to the left, which would tend to raise the equilibrium wage for low-skill labor.

Chapter 15

1.
   a. Poverty falls, inequality rises.
   b. Poverty rises, inequality falls.

2. Jonathon's options for working and total income are shown in the following table. His labor-leisure diagram is shown in the figure following the table.

Number of Work Hours	Earnings from Work	Government Benefits	Total Income
1,500	$9,000	$1,000	$10,000
1,200	$7,200	$2,800	$10,000
900	$5,400	$4,600	$10,000
600	$3,600	$6,400	$10,000
300	$1,800	$8,200	$10,000
0	$0	$10,000	$10,000

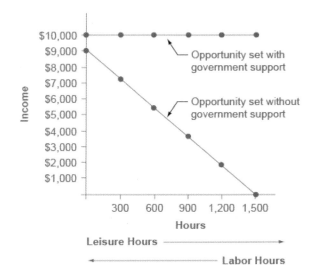

3. The following table shows a policy where only 30 cents in government support is pulled right back for every $1

of income earned. Jonathon's labor-leisure diagram is shown in the figure following the table. "Opportunity set after program" extends from (0, $16,300) to (1,500, $10,000). "Opportunity set before program" slopes downward from (0, $9,000) to (1,500, $0).

Number of Work Hours	Earnings from Work	Government Benefits	Total Income
1,500	$9,000	$7,300	$16,300
1,200	$7,200	$7,840	$15,040
900	$5,400	$8,380	$13,780
600	$3,600	$8,920	$12,520
300	$1,800	$9,460	$22,260
0	$0	$10,000	$10,000

4. The earned income tax credit works like this: a poor family receives a tax break that increases according to how much they work. Families that work more get more. In that sense it loosens the poverty trap by encouraging work. As families earn above the poverty level, the earned income tax credit is gradually reduced. For those near-poor families, the earned income tax credit is a partial disincentive to work.

5. TANF attempts to loosen the poverty trap by providing incentives to work in other ways. Specifically, it requires that people work (or complete their education) as a condition of receiving TANF benefits, and it places a time limit on benefits.

6. A useful first step is to rank the households by income, from lowest to highest. Then, since there are 10 households total, the bottom quintile will be the bottom two households, the second quintile will be the third and fourth households, and so on up to the top quintile. The quintiles and percentage of total income for the data provided are shown in the following table. Comparing this distribution to the U.S. income distribution for 2005, the top quintile in the example has a smaller share of total income than in the U.S. distribution and the bottom quintile has a larger share. This pattern usually means that the income distribution in the example is more equal than the U.S. distribution.

Income	Quintile	% of Total Income
$10,000	Total first quintile income: $22,000	6.0%

This OpenStax book is available for free at http://cnx.org/content/col12122/1.4

Income	Quintile	% of Total Income
$12,000		
$16,000	Total second quintile income: $34,000	9.2%
$18,000		
$24,000	Total third quintile income: $48,000	13.0%
$24,000		
$36,000	Total fourth quintile income: $86,000	23.2%
$50,000		
$80,000	Total top quintile income: $180,000	48.6%
$100,000		
$370,000	**Total Income**	

7. Just from glancing at the quintile information, it is fairly obvious that income inequality increased in the United Kingdom over this time: The top quintile is getting a lot more, and the lowest quintile is getting a bit less. Converting this information into a Lorenz curve, however, is a little trickier, because the Lorenz curve graphs the cumulative distribution, not the amount received by individual quintiles. Thus, as explained in the text, you have to add up the individual quintile data to convert the data to this form. The following table shows the actual calculations for the share of income in 1979 versus 1991. The figure following the table shows the perfect equality line and the Lorenz curves for 1979 and 1991. As shown, the income distribution in 1979 was closer to the perfect equality line than the income distribution in 1991—that is, the United Kingdom income distribution became more unequal over time.

Share of income received	1979	1991
Bottom 20%	7.0%	6.6%
Bottom 40%	18.5%	18.1%
Bottom 60%	35.5%	34.4%
Bottom 80%	60.3%	57.1%
All 100%	100.0%	100.0%

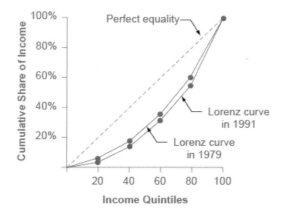

8. In the market for low-wage labor, information technology shifts the demand for low-wage labor to the left. One reason is that technology can often substitute for low-wage labor in certain kinds of telephone or bookkeeping jobs. In addition, information technology makes it easier for companies to manage connections with low-wage workers in other countries, thus reducing the demand for low-wage workers in the United States. In the market for high-wage labor, information technology shifts the demand for high-wage labor to the right. By using the new information and communications technologies, high-wage labor can become more productive and can oversee more tasks than before. The following figure illustrates these two labor markets. The combination of lower wages for low-wage labor and higher wages for high-wage labor means greater inequality.

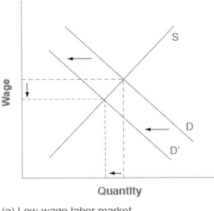
(a) Low-wage labor market

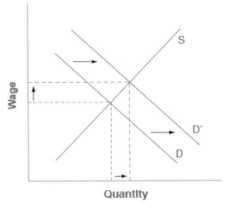
(b) High-wage labor market

9. In the market for low-wage labor, a skills program will shift supply to the left, which will tend to drive up wages for the remaining low-skill workers. In the market for high-wage labor, a skills program will shift supply to the right (because after the training program there are now more high-skilled workers at every wage), which will tend to drive down wages for high-skill workers. The combination of these two programs will result in a lesser degree of inequality. The following figure illustrates these two labor markets. In the market for high-wage labor, a skills program will shift supply to the right, which will tend to drive down wages for high-skill workers.

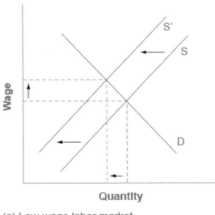
(a) Low-wage labor market

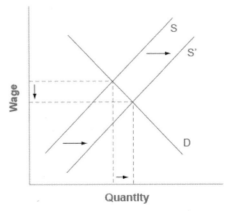
(b) High-wage labor market

10. A very strong push for economic equality might include extremely high taxes on high-wage earners to pay for extremely large government social payments for the poor. Such a policy could limit incentives for the high-wage workers, lock the poor into a poverty trap, and thus reduce output. The PPF in this case will have the standard appearance: it will be downward sloping.

11. For the second hypothesis, a well-funded social safety net might make people feel that even if their company goes bankrupt or they need to change jobs or industries, they will have some degree of protection. As a result, people may be more willing to allow markets to work without interference, and not to lobby as hard for rules that would prevent layoffs, set price controls, or block foreign trade. In this case, safety net programs that increase equality could also allow the market to work more freely in a way that could increase output. In this case, at least some portion of the PPF between equality and economic output would slope up.

12. Pure redistribution is more likely to cause a sharp tradeoff between economic output and equality than policies aimed at the ladder of opportunity. A production possibility frontier showing a strict tradeoff between economic output and equality will be downward sloping. A PPF showing that it is possible to increase equality, at least to some extent, while either increasing output or at least not diminishing it would have a PPF that first rises, perhaps has a flat area, and then falls.

13. Many view the redistribution of income to achieve greater equality as taking away from the rich to pay the poor, or as a "zero sum" game. By taking taxes from one group of people and redistributing them to another, the tax system is robbing some of the American Dream.

Chapter 16

1.
   a. Imperfect information is relatively low; after all, you can see the apples.
   b. Imperfect information is relatively low. The neighborhood restaurant probably has a certain local reputation.
   c. Imperfect information is relatively high. How can you tell whether the computer is really in good working order? Why are they selling it?
   d. Imperfect information is relatively high. What do those flowers really look like?

2. Asymmetric information often exists in the labor market because employers cannot observe many key employee attributes until after the person is hired. Employees, however, know whether they are energetic or detailed-oriented. Employers, therefore, often seek schools to pre-screen candidates. Employers may not even interview a candidate unless he has a degree and often a degree from a particular school. Employers may also view awards, a high grade point average, and other accolades as a signal of hard work, perseverance, and ability. Finally, employers seek references for insights into key attributes such as energy level, work ethic, and so on.

3. It is almost impossible to distinguish whether a health outcome such as life expectancy was the result of personal preferences that might affect health and longevity, such as diet, exercise, certain risky behavior, and consumption of certain items like tobacco, or the result of expenditures on health care (for example, annual check-ups).

Chapter 17

1.
   a. The management of small companies might rather do an IPO right away, but until they get the company up and running, most people would not pay very much for the stock because of the risks involved.
   b. A small company may be earning few or zero profits, and its owners want to reinvest their earnings in the future growth of the company. If this company issues bonds or borrows money, it is obligated to make interest payments, which can eat up the company's cash. If the company issues stock, it is not obligated to make payments to anyone (although it may choose to pay dividends).
   c. Venture capitalists are private investors who can keep close tabs on the management and strategy of the company—and thus reduce the problems of imperfect information about whether the firm is being well run. Venture capitalists often own a substantial portion of the firm and have much better information than a typical shareholder would.

2. From a firm's point of view, a bond is very similar to a bank loan. Both are ways of borrowing money. Both require paying interest. The major difference is who must be persuaded to lend money: a bank loan requires persuading the bank, while issuing bonds requires persuading a number of separate bondholders. Since a bank often knows a great deal about a firm (especially if the firm has its accounts with that bank), bank loans are more common where imperfect

information would otherwise be a problem.

3.

    a. Remember, equity is the market value of the house minus what is still owed to the bank. Thus: the value of the house is $200,000, Fred owes $180,000 to the bank, and his equity is $20,000.

    b. The value of Freda's house is $250,000. It does not matter what price she bought it for. She owes zero to the bank, so her equity is the whole $250,000.

    c. The value of Frank's house is $160,000. He owes $60,000 to the bank (the original $80,000 minus the $20,000 he has paid off the loan). His equity is $100,000.

4. Over a sustained period of time, stocks have an average return higher than bonds, and bonds have an average return higher than a savings account. This is because in any given year the value of a savings account changes very little. In contrast, stock values can grow or decline by a very large amount (for example, the S&P 500 increased 26% in 2009 after declining 37% in 2008. The value of a bond, which depends largely on interest rate fluctuations, varies far less than a stock, but more than a savings account.

5. When people believe that a high-risk investment must have a low return, they are getting confused between what risk and return mean. Yes, a high-risk investment might have a low return, but it might also have a high return. Risk refers to the fact that a wide range of outcomes is possible. However, a high-risk investment must, on average, expect a relatively high return or else no one would be willing to take the risk. Thus, it is quite possible—even likely—for an investment to have high risk and high return. Indeed, the reason that an investment has a high expected return is that it also has a high risk.

6. Principal + (principal × rate × time) $5,000 + ($5,000 × 0.06 × 3) = $5,900

7. Principal + (principal × rate × time); Interest = Principal × rate × time; $500 = $10,000 × rate × 5 years; $500 = $50,000 × rate; $500/$50,000 = rate; Rate = 1%

8. Principal$(1 + \text{interest rate})^{\text{time}} = \$1,000(1+0.02)^5 = \$1,104.08$

Chapter 18

1. All other things being equal, voter turnout should increase as the cost of casting an informed vote decreases.

2. The cost in time of voting, transportation costs to and from the polling place, and any additional time and effort spent becoming informed about the candidates.

3. The costs of organization and the small benefit to the individual.

4. Domestic cotton producers would lobby heavily to protect themselves from the competition, whereas the consumers have little incentive to organize.

5. True. This is exactly what occurs in a voting cycle. That is, the majority can prefer policy A to policy B, policy B to policy C, but also prefer policy C to policy A. Then, the majority will never reach a conclusive outcome.

6. The problem is an example of a voting cycle. The group will vote for mountain biking over canoeing by 2–1. It will vote for canoeing over the beach by 2–1. If mountain biking is preferred to canoeing and canoeing is preferred to the beach, it might seem that it must be true that mountain biking is the favorite. But in a vote of the beach versus mountain biking, the beach wins by a 2–1 vote. When a voting cycle occurs, choosing a single favorite that is always preferred by a majority becomes impossible.

7. The four Coca-Cola candidates compete with each other for Coca-Cola voters, whereas everyone who prefers Pepsi had only one candidate to vote for. Thus the will of the majority is not satisfied.

Chapter 19

1. GDP is C + I + G + (X – M). GDP = $2,000 billion + $50 billion + $1,000 billion + ($20 billion – $40 billion) =

This OpenStax book is available for free at http://cnx.org/content/col12122/1.4

$3,030

2.

    a. Hospital stays are part of GDP.

    b. Changes in life expectancy are not market transactions and not part of GDP.

    c. Child care that is paid for is part of GDP.

    d. If Grandma gets paid and reports this as income, it is part of GDP, otherwise not.

    e. A used car is not produced this year, so it is not part of GDP.

    f. A new car is part of GDP.

    g. Variety does not count in GDP, where the cheese could all be cheddar.

    h. The iron is not counted because it is an intermediate good.

3. From 1980 to 1990, real GDP grew by $(8,225.0 - 5,926.5) / (5,926.5) = 39\%$. Over the same period, prices increased by $(72.7 - 48.3) / (48.3/100) = 51\%$. So about 57% of the growth $51 / (51 + 39)$ was inflation, and the remainder: $39 / (51 + 39) = 43\%$ was growth in real GDP.

4. Two other major recessions are visible in the figure as slight dips: those of 1973–1975, and 1981–1982. Two other recessions appear in the figure as a flattening of the path of real GDP. These were in 1990–1991 and 2001.

5. 11 recessions in approximately 70 years averages about one recession every six years.

6. The table lists the "Months of Contraction" for each recession. Averaging these figures for the post-WWII recessions gives an average duration of 11 months, or slightly less than a year.

7. The table lists the "Months of Expansion." Averaging these figures for the post-WWII expansions gives an average expansion of 60.5 months, or more than five years.

8. Yes. The answer to both questions depends on whether GDP is growing faster or slower than population. If population grows faster than GDP, GDP increases, while GDP per capita decreases. If GDP falls, but population falls faster, then GDP decreases, while GDP per capita increases.

9. Start with Central African Republic's GDP measured in francs. Divide it by the exchange rate to convert to U.S. dollars, and then divide by population to obtain the per capita figure. That is, 1,107,689 million francs / 284.681 francs per dollar / 4.862 million people = $800.28 GDP per capita.

10.

    a. A dirtier environment would reduce the broad standard of living, but not be counted in GDP, so a rise in GDP would overstate the standard of living.

    b. A lower crime rate would raise the broad standard of living, but not be counted directly in GDP, and so a rise in GDP would understate the standard of living.

    c. A greater variety of goods would raise the broad standard of living, but not be counted directly in GDP, and so a rise in GDP would understate the rise in the standard of living.

    d. A decline in infant mortality would raise the broad standard of living, but not be counted directly in GDP, and so a rise in GDP would understate the rise in the standard of living.

Chapter 20

1. The Industrial Revolution refers to the widespread use of power-driven machinery and the economic and social changes that resulted in the first half of the 1800s. Ingenious machines—the steam engine, the power loom, and the steam locomotive—performed tasks that would have taken vast numbers of workers to do. The Industrial Revolution began in Great Britain, and soon spread to the United States, Germany, and other countries.

2. Property rights are the rights of individuals and firms to own property and use it as they see fit. Contractual rights are based on property rights and they allow individuals to enter into agreements with others regarding the use of their property providing recourse through the legal system in the event of noncompliance. Economic growth occurs when the standard of living increases in an economy, which occurs when output is increasing and incomes are rising. For this to happen, societies must create a legal environment that gives individuals the ability to use their property to their fullest and highest use, including the right to trade or sell that property. Without a legal system that enforces contracts, people would not be likely to enter into contracts for current or future services because of the risk of non-payment. This would make it difficult to transact business and would slow economic growth.

3. Yes. Since productivity is output per unit of input, we can measure productivity using GDP (output) per worker (input).

4. In 20 years the United States will have an income of $10,000 \times (1 + 0.01)^{20} = \$12,201.90$, and South Korea will have an income of $10,000 \times (1 + 0.04)^{20} = \$21,911.23$. South Korea has grown by a multiple of 2.1 and the United States by a multiple of 1.2.

5. Capital deepening and technology are important. What seems to be more important is how they are combined.

6. Government can contribute to economic growth by investing in human capital through the education system, building a strong physical infrastructure for transportation and commerce, increasing investment by lowering capital gains taxes, creating special economic zones that allow for reduced tariffs, and investing in research and development.

7. Public education, low investment taxes, funding for infrastructure projects, special economic zones

8. A good way to think about this is how a runner who has fallen behind in a race feels psychologically and physically as he catches up. Playing catch-up can be more taxing than maintaining one's position at the head of the pack.

9.
  a. No. Capital deepening refers to an increase in the amount of capital per person in an economy. A decrease in investment by firms will actually cause the opposite of capital deepening (since the population will grow over time).
  b. There is no direct connection between an increase in international trade and capital deepening. One could imagine particular scenarios where trade could lead to capital deepening (for example, if international capital inflows—which are the counterpart to increasing the trade deficit—lead to an increase in physical capital investment), but in general, no.
  c. Yes. Capital deepening refers to an increase in either physical capital or human capital per person. Continuing education or any time of lifelong learning adds to human capital and thus creates capital deepening.

10. The advantages of backwardness include faster growth rates because of the process of convergence, as well as the ability to adopt new technologies that were developed first in the "leader" countries. While being "backward" is not inherently a good thing, Gerschenkron stressed that there are certain advantages which aid countries trying to "catch up."

11. Capital deepening, by definition, should lead to diminished returns because you're investing more and more but using the same methods of production, leading to the marginal productivity declining. This is shown on a production function as a movement along the curve. Improvements in technology should not lead to diminished returns because you are finding new and more efficient ways of using the same amount of capital. This can be illustrated as a shift upward of the production function curve.

12. Productivity growth from new advances in technology will not slow because the new methods of production will be adopted relatively quickly and easily, at very low marginal cost. Also, countries that are seeing technology growth usually have a vast and powerful set of institutions for training workers and building better machines, which allows the maximum amount of people to benefit from the new technology. These factors have the added effect of making additional technological advances even easier for these countries.

Chapter 21

1. The population is divided into those "in the labor force" and those "not in the labor force." Thus, the number of adults not in the labor force is $237.8 - 153.9 = 83.9$ million. Since the labor force is divided into employed persons and

This OpenStax book is available for free at http://cnx.org/content/col12122/1.4

unemployed persons, the number of unemployed persons is 153.9 − 139.1 = 14.8 million. Thus, the adult population has the following proportions:

- 139.1/237.8 = 58.5% employed persons
- 14.8/237.8 = 6.2% unemployed persons
- 83.9/237.8 = 35.3% persons out of the labor force

2. The unemployment rate is defined as the number of unemployed persons as a percentage of the labor force or 14.8/153.9 = 9.6%. This is higher than the February 2015 unemployment rate, computed earlier, of 5.5%.

3. Over the long term, the U.S. unemployment rate has remained basically the same level.

4.

   a. Nonwhites

   b. The young

   c. High school graduates

5. Because of the influx of women into the labor market, the supply of labor shifts to the right. Since wages are sticky downward, the increased supply of labor causes an increase in people looking for jobs (Qs), but no change in the number of jobs available (Qe). As a result, unemployment increases by the amount of the increase in the labor supply. This can be seen in the following figure. Over time, as labor demand grows, the unemployment will decline and eventually wages will begin to increase again. But this increase in labor demand goes beyond the scope of this problem.

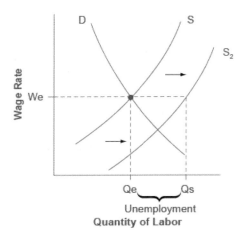

6. The increase in labor supply was a social demographic trend—it was not caused by the economy falling into a recession. Therefore, the influx of women into the work force increased the natural rate of unemployment.

7. New entrants to the labor force, whether from college or otherwise, are counted as frictionally unemployed until they find a job.

Chapter 22

1. To compute the amount spent on each fruit in each year, you multiply the quantity of each fruit by the price.

- 10 apples × 50 cents each = $5.00 spent on apples in 2001.
- 12 bananas × 20 cents each = $2.40 spent on bananas in 2001.
- 2 bunches of grapes at 65 cents each = $1.30 spent on grapes in 2001.
- 1 pint of raspberries at $2 each = $2.00 spent on raspberries in 2001.

Adding up the amounts gives you the total cost of the fruit basket. The total cost of the fruit basket in 2001 was $5.00 + $2.40 + $1.30 + $2.00 = $10.70. The total costs for all the years are shown in the following table.

2001	2002	2003	2004
$10.70	$13.80	$15.35	$16.31

2. If 2003 is the base year, then the index number has a value of 100 in 2003. To transform the cost of a fruit basket each year, we divide each year's value by $15.35, the value of the base year, and then multiply the result by 100. The price index is shown in the following table.

2001	2002	2003	2004
69.71	89.90	100.00	106.3

Note that the base year has a value of 100; years before the base year have values less than 100; and years after have values more than 100.

3. The inflation rate is calculated as the percentage change in the price index from year to year. For example, the inflation rate between 2001 and 2002 is (84.61 − 69.71) / 69.71 = 0.2137 = 21.37%. The inflation rates for all the years are shown in the last row of the following table, which includes the two previous answers.

Items	Qty	(2001) Price	(2001) Amount Spent	(2002) Price	(2002) Amount Spent	(2003) Price	(2003) Amount Spent	(2004) Price	(2004) Amount Spent
Apples	10	$0.50	$5.00	$0.75	$7.50	$0.85	$8.50	$0.88	$8.80
Bananas	12	$0.20	$2.40	$0.25	$3.00	$0.25	$3.00	$0.29	$3.48
Grapes	2	$0.65	$1.30	$0.70	$1.40	$0.90	$1.80	$0.95	$1.90
Raspberries	1	$2.00	$2.00	$1.90	$1.90	$2.05	$2.05	$2.13	$2.13
Total			$10.70		$13.80		$15.35		$16.31
Price Index			69.71		84.61		100.00		106.3
Inflation Rate					21.37%		18.19%		6.3%

4. Begin by calculating the total cost of buying the basket in each time period, as shown in the following table.

Items	Quantity	(Time 1) Price	(Time 1) Total Cost	(Time 2) Price	(Time 2) Total Cost
Gifts	12	$50	$600	$60	$720
Pizza	24	$15	$360	$16	$384
Blouses	6	$60	$360	$50	$300
Trips	2	$400	$800	$420	$840
Total Cost			$2,120		$2,244

The rise in cost of living is calculated as the percentage increase: $(2244 - 2120) / 2120 = 0.0585 = 5.85\%$.

5. Since the CPI measures the prices of the goods and services purchased by the typical urban consumer, it measures the prices of things that people buy with their paycheck. For that reason, the CPI would be the best price index to use for this purpose.

6. The PPI is subject to those biases for essentially the same reasons as the CPI is. The GDP deflator picks up prices of what is actually purchased that year, so there are no biases. That is the advantage of using the GDP deflator over the CPI.

7. The calculator requires you to input three numbers:
  - The first year, in this case the year of your birth
  - The amount of money you would want to translate in terms of its purchasing power
  - The last year—now or the most recent year the calculator will accept

My birth year is 1955. The amount is $1. The year 2012 is currently the latest year the calculator will accept. The simple purchasing power calculator shows that $1 of purchases in 1955 would cost $8.57 in 2012. The website also explains how the true answer is more complicated than that shown by the simple purchasing power calculator.

8. The state government would benefit because it would repay the loan in less valuable dollars than it borrowed. Plus, tax revenues for the state government would increase because of the inflation.

9. Higher inflation reduces real interest rates on fixed rate mortgages. Because ARMs can be adjusted, higher inflation leads to higher interest rates on ARMs.

10. Because the mortgage has an adjustable rate, the rate should fall by 3%, the same as inflation, to keep the real interest rate the same.

Chapter 23

1. The stock and bond values will not show up in the current account. However, the dividends from the stocks and the interest from the bonds show up as an import to income in the current account.

2. It becomes more negative as imports, which are a negative to the current account, are growing faster than exports, which are a positive.

3.
  a. Money flows out of the Mexican economy.
  b. Money flows into the Mexican economy.
  c. Money flows out of the Mexican economy.

4. GDP is a dollar value of all production of goods and services. Exports are produced domestically but shipped abroad. The percent ratio of exports to GDP gives us an idea of how important exports are to the national economy out of all goods and services produced. For example, exports represent only 14% of U.S. GDP, but 50% of Germany's GDP

5. Divide $542 billion by $1,800 billion.

6. Divide –$400 billion by $16,800 billion.

7. The trade balance is the difference between exports and imports. The current account balance includes this number (whether it is a trade balance or a trade surplus), but also includes international flows of money from global investments.

8.
  a. An export sale to Germany involves a financial flow from Germany to the U.S. economy.
  b. The issue here is not U.S. investments in Brazil, but the return paid on those investments, which involves a financial flow from the Brazilian economy to the U.S. economy.

    c. Foreign aid from the United States to Egypt is a financial flow from the United States to Egypt.

    d. Importing oil from the Russian Federation means a flow of financial payments from the U.S. economy to the Russian Federation.

    e. Japanese investors buying U.S. real estate is a financial flow from Japan to the U.S. economy.

9. The top portion tracks the flow of exports and imports and the payments for those. The bottom portion is looking at international financial investments and the outflow and inflow of monies from those investments. These investments can include investments in stocks and bonds or real estate abroad, as well as international borrowing and lending.

10. If more monies are flowing out of the country (for example, to pay for imports) it will make the current account more negative or less positive, and if more monies are flowing into the country, it will make the current account less negative or more positive.

11. Write out the national savings and investment identity for the situation of the economy implied by this question:

$$\text{Supply of capital} \;=\; \text{Demand for capital}$$
$$S + (M - X) + (T - G) \;=\; I \qquad\qquad \text{If domestic savings increases and}$$
$$\text{Savings} + (\text{trade deficit}) + (\text{government budget surplus}) \;=\; \text{Investment}$$

nothing else changes, then the trade deficit will fall. In effect, the economy would be relying more on domestic capital and less on foreign capital. If the government starts borrowing instead of saving, then the trade deficit must rise. In effect, the government is no longer providing savings and so, if nothing else is to change, more investment funds must arrive from abroad. If the rate of domestic investment surges, then, *ceteris paribus*, the trade deficit must also rise, to provide the extra capital. The *ceteris paribus*—or "other things being equal"—assumption is important here. In all of these situations, there is no reason to expect in the real world that the original change will affect only, or primarily, the trade deficit. The identity only says that something will adjust—it does not specify what.

12. The government is saving rather than borrowing. The supply of savings, whether private or public, is on the left side of the identity.

13. A trade deficit is determined by a country's level of private and public savings and the amount of domestic investment.

14. The trade deficit must increase. To put it another way, this increase in investment must be financed by an inflow of financial capital from abroad.

15. Incomes fall during a recession, and consumers buy fewer good, including imports.

16. A booming economy will increase the demand for goods in general, so import sales will increase. If our trading partners' economies are doing well, they will buy more of our products and so U.S. exports will increase.

17.

    a. Increased federal spending on Medicare may not increase productivity, so a budget deficit is not justified.

    b. Increased spending on education will increase productivity and foster greater economic growth, so a budget deficit is justified.

    c. Increased spending on the space program may not increase productivity, so a budget deficit is not justified.

    d. Increased spending on airports and air traffic control will increase productivity and foster greater economic growth, so a budget deficit is justified.

18. Foreign investors worried about repayment so they began to pull money out of these countries. The money can be pulled out of stock and bond markets, real estate, and banks.

19. A rapidly growing trade surplus could result from a number of factors, so you would not want to be too quick to assume a specific cause. However, if the choice is between whether the economy is in recession or growing rapidly, the answer would have to be recession. In a recession, demand for all goods, including imports, has declined; however, demand for exports from other countries has not necessarily altered much, so the result is a larger trade surplus.

This OpenStax book is available for free at http://cnx.org/content/col12122/1.4

20. Germany has a higher level of trade than the United States. The United States has a large domestic economy so it has a large volume of internal trade.

21.

a. A large economy tends to have lower levels of international trade, because it can do more of its trade internally, but this has little impact on its trade imbalance.

b. An imbalance between domestic physical investment and domestic saving (including government and private saving) will always lead to a trade imbalance, but has little to do with the level of trade.

c. Many large trading partners nearby geographically increases the level of trade, but has little impact one way or the other on a trade imbalance.

d. The answer here is not obvious. An especially large budget deficit means a large demand for financial capital which, according to the national saving and investment identity, makes it somewhat more likely that there will be a need for an inflow of foreign capital, which means a trade deficit.

e. A strong tradition of discouraging trade certainly reduces the level of trade. However, it does not necessarily say much about the balance of trade, since this is determined by both imports and exports, and by national levels of physical investment and savings.

Chapter 24

1. In order to supply goods, suppliers must employ workers, whose incomes increase as a result of their labor. They use this additional income to demand goods of an equivalent value to those they supply.

2. When consumers demand more goods than are available on the market, prices are driven higher and the additional opportunities for profit induce more suppliers to enter the market, producing an equivalent amount to that which is demanded.

3. Higher input prices make output less profitable, decreasing the desired supply. This is shown graphically as a leftward shift in the AS curve.

4. Equilibrium occurs at the level of GDP where AD = AS. Insufficient aggregate demand could explain why the equilibrium occurs at a level of GDP less than potential. A decrease (or leftward shift) in aggregate supply could be another reason.

5. Immigration reform as described should increase the labor supply, shifting SRAS to the right, leading to a higher equilibrium GDP and a lower price level.

6. Given the assumptions made here, the cuts in R&D funding should reduce productivity growth. The model would show this as a leftward shift in the SRAS curve, leading to a lower equilibrium GDP and a higher price level.

7. An increase in the value of the stock market would make individuals feel wealthier and thus more confident about their economic situation. This would likely cause an increase in consumer confidence leading to an increase in consumer spending, shifting the AD curve to the right. The result would be an increase in the equilibrium level of GDP and an increase in the price level.

8. Since imports depend on GDP, if Mexico goes into recession, its GDP declines and so do its imports. This decline in our exports can be shown as a leftward shift in AD, leading to a decrease in our GDP and price level.

9. Tax cuts increase consumer and investment spending, depending on where the tax cuts are targeted. This would shift AD to the right, so if the tax cuts occurred when the economy was in recession (and GDP was less than potential), the tax cuts would increase GDP and "lead the economy out of recession."

10. A negative report on home prices would make consumers feel like the value of their homes, which for most Americans is a major portion of their wealth, has declined. A negative report on consumer confidence would make consumers feel pessimistic about the future. Both of these would likely reduce consumer spending, shifting AD to the left, reducing GDP and the price level. A positive report on the home price index or consumer confidence would do the opposite.

11. A smaller labor force would be reflected in a leftward shift in AS, leading to a lower equilibrium level of GDP and higher price level.

12. Higher EU growth would increase demand for U.S. exports, reducing our trade deficit. The increased demand for exports would show up as a rightward shift in AD, causing GDP to rise (and the price level to rise as well). Higher GDP would require more jobs to fulfill, so U.S. employment would also rise.

13. Expansionary monetary policy shifts AD to the right. A continuing expansionary policy would cause larger and larger shifts (given the parameters of this problem). The result would be an increase in GDP and employment (a decrease in unemployment) and higher prices until potential output was reached. After that point, the expansionary policy would simply cause inflation.

14. Since the SRAS curve is vertical in the neoclassical zone, unless the economy is bordering the intermediate zone, a decrease in AS will cause a decrease in the price level, but no effect on real economic activity (for example, real GDP or employment).

15. Because the SRAS curve is horizontal in the Keynesian zone, a decrease in AD should depress real economic activity but have no effect on prices.

Chapter 25

1.

    a. An increase in home values will increase consumption spending (due to increased wealth). AD will shift to the right and may cause inflation if it goes beyond potential GDP.

    b. Rapid growth by a major trading partner will increase demand for exports. AD will shift to the right and may cause inflation if it goes beyond potential GDP.

    c. Increased profit opportunities will increase business investment. AD will shift to the right and may cause inflation if it goes beyond potential GDP.

    d. Higher interest rates reduce investment spending. AD will shift to the left and may cause recession if it falls below potential GDP.

    e. Demand for cheaper imports increases, reducing demand for domestic products. AD will shift to the left and may be recessionary.

2.

    a. A tax increase on consumer income will cause consumption to fall, pushing the AD curve left, and is a possible solution to inflation.

    b. A surge in military spending is an increase in government spending. This will cause the AD curve to shift to the right. If real GDP is less than potential GDP, then this spending would pull the economy out of a recession. If real GDP is to the right of potential GDP, then the AD curve will shift farther to the right and military spending will be inflationary.

    c. A tax cut focused on business investment will shift AD to the right. If the original macroeconomic equilibrium is below potential GDP, then this policy can help move an economy out of a recession.

    d. Government spending on healthcare will cause the AD curve to shift to the right. If real GDP is less than potential GDP, then this spending would pull the economy out of a recession. If real GDP is to th right of potential GDP, then the AD curve will shift farther to the right and healthcare spending will be inflationary.

3. An inflationary gap is the result of an increase in aggregate demand when the economy is at potential output. Since the AS curve is vertical at potential GDP, any increase in AD will lead to a higher price level (i.e. inflation) but no higher real GDP. This is easy to see if you draw AD_1 to the right of AD_0.

4. A decrease in government spending will shift AD to the left.

5. A decrease in energy prices, a positive supply shock, would cause the AS curve to shift out to the right, yielding more real GDP at a lower price level. This would shift the Phillips curve down toward the origin, meaning the economy would experience lower unemployment and a lower rate of inflation.

This OpenStax book is available for free at http://cnx.org/content/col12122/1.4

6. Keynesian economics does not require microeconomic price controls of any sort. It is true that many Keynesian economic prescriptions were for the government to influence the total amount of aggregate demand in the economy, often through government spending and tax cuts.

7. The three problems center on government's ability to estimate potential GDP, decide whether to influence aggregate demand through tax changes or changes in government spending, and the lag time that occurs as Congress and the President attempt to pass legislation.

Chapter 26

1. No, this statement is false. It would be more accurate to say that rational expectations seek to predict the future as accurately as possible, using all of past experience as a guide. Adaptive expectations are largely backward looking; that is, they adapt as experience accumulates, but without attempting to look forward.

2. An unemployment rate of zero percent is presumably well below the rate that is consistent with potential GDP and with the natural rate of unemployment. As a result, this policy would be attempting to push AD out to the right. In the short run, it is possible to have unemployment slightly below the natural rate for a time, at a price of higher inflation, as shown by the movement from E_0 to E_1 along the short-run AS curve. However, over time the extremely low unemployment rates will tend to cause wages to be bid up, and shift the short-run AS curve back to the left. The result would be a higher price level, but an economy still at potential GDP and the natural rate of unemployment, as determined by the long-run AS curve. If the government continues this policy, it will continually be pushing the price level higher and higher, but it will not be able to achieve its goal of zero percent unemployment, because that goal is inconsistent with market forces.

3. The statement is accurate. Rational expectations can be thought of as a version of neoclassical economics because it argues that potential GDP and the rate of unemployment are shaped by market forces as wages and prices adjust. However, it is an "extreme" version because it argues that this adjustment takes place very quickly. Other theories, like adaptive expectations, suggest that adjustment to the neoclassical outcome takes a few years.

4. The short-term Keynesian model is built on the importance of aggregate demand as a cause of business cycles and a degree of wage and price rigidity, and thus does a sound job of explaining many recessions and why cyclical unemployment rises and falls. The neoclassical model emphasizes aggregate supply by focusing on the underlying determinants of output and employment in markets, and thus tends to put more emphasis on economic growth and how labor markets work.

Chapter 27

1. As long as you remain within the walls of the casino, chips fit the definition of money; that is, they serve as a medium of exchange, a unit of account, and a store of value. Chips do not work very well as money once you leave the casino, but many kinds of money do not work well in other areas. For example, it is hard to spend money from Turkey or Brazil at your local supermarket or at the movie theater.

2. Many physical items that a person buys at one time but may sell at another time can serve as an answer to this question. Examples include a house, land, art, rare coins or stamps, and so on.

3. The currency and checks in M1 are easiest to spend. It is harder to spend M2 directly, although if there is an automatic teller machine in the shopping mall, you can turn M2 from your savings account into an M1 of currency quite quickly. If your answer is about "credit cards," then you are really talking about spending M1—although it is M1 from the account of the credit card company, which you will repay later when you credit card bill comes due.

4.
  a. Neither in M1 or M2
  b. That is part of M1, and because M2 includes M1 it is also part of M2
  c. Currency out in the public hands is part of M1 and M2
  d. Checking deposits are in M1 and M2

e. Money market accounts are in M2

5. A bank's assets include cash held in their vaults, but assets also include monies that the bank holds at the Federal Reserve Bank (called "reserves"), loans that are made to customers, and bonds.

6.

a. A borrower who has been late on a number of loan payments looks perhaps less likely to repay the loan, or to repay it on time, and so you would want to pay less for that loan.

b. If interest rates generally have risen, then this loan made at a time of relatively lower interest rates looks less attractive, and you would pay less for it.

c. If the borrower is a firm with a record of high profits, then it is likely to be able to repay the loan, and you would be willing to pay more for the loan.

d. If interest rates in the economy have fallen, then the loan is worth more.

Chapter 28

1. Longer terms insulate the Board from political forces. Since the presidency can potentially change every four years, the Federal Reserve's independence prevents drastic swings in monetary policy with every new administration and allows policy decisions to be made only on economic grounds.

2. Banks make their money from issuing loans and charging interest. The more money that is stored in the bank's vault, the less is available for lending and the less money the bank stands to make.

3. The fear and uncertainty created by the suggestion that a bank might fail can lead depositors to withdraw their money. If many depositors do this at the same time, the bank may not be able to meet their demands and will, indeed, fail.

4. The bank has to hold $1,000 in reserves, so when it buys the $500 in bonds, it will have to reduce its loans by $500 to make up the difference. The money supply decreases by the same amount.

5. An increase in reserve requirements would reduce the supply of money, since more money would be held in banks rather than circulating in the economy.

6. Contractionary policy reduces the amount of loanable funds in the economy. As with all goods, greater scarcity leads a greater price, so the interest rate, or the price of borrowing money, rises.

7. An increase in the amount of available loanable funds means that there are more people who want to lend. They, therefore, bid the price of borrowing (the interest rate) down.

8. In times of economic uncertainty, banks may worry that borrowers will lose the ability to repay their loans. They may also fear that a panic is more likely and they will need the excess reserves to meet their obligations.

9. If consumer optimism changes, spending can speed up or slow down. This could also happen in a case where consumers need to buy a large number of items quickly, such as in a situation of national emergency.

Chapter 29

1.

a. The British use the pound sterling, while Germans use the euro, so a British exporter will receive euros from export sales, which will need to be exchanged for pounds. A stronger euro will mean more pounds per euro, so the exporter will be better off. In addition, the lower price for German imports will stimulate demand for British exports. For both these reasons, a stronger euro benefits the British exporter.

b. The Dutch use euros while the Chileans use pesos, so the Dutch tourist needs to turn euros into Chilean pesos. An increase in the euro means that the tourist will get more pesos per euro. As a consequence, the Dutch tourist will have a less expensive vacation than he planned, so the tourist will be better off.

c. The Greek use euros while the Canadians use dollars. An increase in the euro means it will buy more Canadian dollars. As a result, the Greek bank will see a decrease in the cost of the Canadian bonds, so it may purchase more bonds. Either way, the Greek bank benefits.

d. Since both the French and Germans use the euro, an increase in the euro, in terms of other currencies, should have no impact on the French exporter.

2. Expected depreciation in a currency will lead people to divest themselves of the currency. We should expect to see an increase in the supply of pounds and a decrease in demand for pounds. The result should be a decrease in the value of the pound *vis à vis* the dollar.

3. Lower U.S. interest rates make U.S. assets less desirable compared to assets in the European Union. We should expect to see a decrease in demand for dollars and an increase in supply of dollars in foreign currency markets. As a result, we should expect to see the dollar depreciate compared to the euro.

4. A decrease in Argentine inflation relative to other countries should cause an increase in demand for pesos, a decrease in supply of pesos, and an appreciation of the peso in foreign currency markets.

5. The problem occurs when banks borrow foreign currency but lend in domestic currency. Since banks' assets (loans they made) are in domestic currency, while their debts (money they borrowed) are in foreign currency, when the domestic currency declines, their debts grow larger. If the domestic currency falls substantially in value, as happened during the Asian financial crisis, then the banking system could fail. This problem is unlikely to occur for U.S. banks because, even when they borrow from abroad, they tend to borrow dollars. Remember, there are trillions of dollars in circulation in the global economy. Since both assets and debts are in dollars, a change in the value of the dollar does not cause banking system failure the way it can when banks borrow in foreign currency.

6. While capital flight is possible in either case, if a country borrows to invest in real capital it is more likely to be able to generate the income to pay back its debts than a country that borrows to finance consumption. As a result, an investment-stimulated economy is less likely to provoke capital flight and economic recession.

7. A contractionary monetary policy, by driving up domestic interest rates, would cause the currency to appreciate. The higher value of the currency in foreign exchange markets would reduce exports, since from the perspective of foreign buyers, they are now more expensive. The higher value of the currency would similarly stimulate imports, since they would now be cheaper from the perspective of domestic buyers. Lower exports and higher imports cause net exports (EX – IM) to fall, which causes aggregate demand to fall. The result would be a decrease in GDP working through the exchange rate mechanism reinforcing the effect contractionary monetary policy has on domestic investment expenditure. However, cheaper imports would stimulate aggregate supply, bringing GDP back to potential, though at a lower price level.

8. For a currency to fall, a central bank need only supply more of its currency in foreign exchange markets. It can print as much domestic currency as it likes. For a currency to rise, a central bank needs to buy its currency in foreign exchange markets, paying with foreign currency. Since no central bank has an infinite amount of foreign currency reserves, it cannot buy its currency indefinitely.

9. Variations in exchange rates, because they change import and export prices, disturb international trade flows. When trade is a large part of a nation's economic activity, government will find it more advantageous to fix exchange rates to minimize disruptions of trade flows.

Chapter 30

1. The government borrows funds by selling Treasury bonds, notes, and bills.

2. The funds can be used to pay down the national debt or else be refunded to the taxpayers.

3. Yes, a nation can run budget deficits and see its debt/GDP ratio fall. In fact, this is not uncommon. If the deficit is small in a given year, than the addition to debt in the numerator of the debt/GDP ratio will be relatively small, while the growth in GDP is larger, and so the debt/GDP ratio declines. This was the experience of the U.S. economy for the period from the end of World War II to about 1980. It is also theoretically possible, although not likely, for a nation to have a budget surplus and see its debt/GDP ratio rise. Imagine the case of a nation with a small surplus, but in a recession year when the economy shrinks. It is possible that the decline in the nation's debt, in the numerator of the debt/GDP ratio, would be proportionally less than the fall in the size of GDP, so the debt/GDP ratio would rise.

4. Progressive. People who give larger gifts subject to the higher tax rate would typically have larger incomes as well.

5. Corporate income tax on his profits, individual income tax on his salary, and payroll tax taken out of the wages he pays himself.

6. individual income taxes

7. The tax is regressive because wealthy income earners are not taxed at all on income above $113,000. As a percent of total income, the social security tax hits lower income earners harder than wealthier individuals.

8. As debt increases, interest payments also rise, so that the deficit grows even if we keep other government spending constant.

9.

    a. As a share of GDP, this is false. In nominal dollars, it is true.

    b. False.

    c. False.

    d. False. Education spending is much higher at the state level.

    e. False. As a share of GDP, it is up about 50.

    f. As a share of GDP, this is false, and in real dollars, it is also false.

    g. False.

    h. False; it's about 1%.

    i. False. Although budget deficits were large in 2003 and 2004, and continued into the later 2000s, the federal government ran budget surpluses from 1998–2001.

    j. False.

10. To keep prices from rising too much or too rapidly.

11. To increase employment.

12. It falls below because less tax revenue than expected is collected.

13. Automatic stabilizers take effect very quickly, whereas discretionary policy can take a long time to implement.

14. In a recession, because of the decline in economic output, less income is earned, and so less in taxes is automatically collected. Many welfare and unemployment programs are designed so that those who fall into certain categories, like "unemployed" or "low income," are eligible for benefits. During a recession, more people fall into these categories and become eligible for benefits automatically. The combination of reduced taxes and higher spending is just what is needed for an economy in recession producing below potential GDP. With an economic boom, average income levels rise in the economy, so more in taxes is automatically collected. Fewer people meet the criteria for receiving government assistance to the unemployed or the needy, so government spending on unemployment assistance and welfare falls automatically. This combination of higher taxes and lower spending is just what is needed if an economy is producing above its potential GDP.

15. Prices would be pushed up as a result of too much spending.

16. Employment would suffer as a result of too little spending.

17. Monetary policy probably has shorter time lags than fiscal policy. Imagine that the data becomes fairly clear that an economy is in or near a recession. Expansionary monetary policy can be carried out through open market operations, which can be done fairly quickly, since the Federal Reserve's Open Market Committee meets six times a year. Also, monetary policy takes effect through interest rates, which can change fairly quickly. However, fiscal policy is carried out through acts of Congress that need to be signed into law by the president. Negotiating such laws often takes

This OpenStax book is available for free at http://cnx.org/content/col12122/1.4

months, and even after the laws are negotiated, it takes more months for spending programs or tax cuts to have an effect on the macroeconomy.

18. The government would have to make up the revenue either by raising taxes in a different area or cutting spending.

19. Programs where the amount of spending is not fixed, but rather determined by macroeconomic conditions, such as food stamps, would lose a great deal of flexibility if spending increases had to be met by corresponding tax increases or spending cuts.

Chapter 31

1. We use the national savings and investment identity to solve this question. In this case, the government has a budget surplus, so the government surplus appears as part of the supply of financial capital. Then:

$$\text{Quantity supplied of financial capital} = \text{Quantity demanded of financial capital}$$
$$S + (T - G) = I + (X - M)$$
$$600 + 200 = I + 100$$
$$I = 700$$

2.

a. Since the government has a budget surplus, the government budget term appears with the supply of capital. The following shows the national savings and investment identity for this economy.
$$\text{Quantity supplied of financial capital} = \text{Quantity demanded of financial capital}$$
$$S + (T - G) = I + (X - M)$$

b. Plugging the given values into the identity shown in part (a), we find that $(X - M) = 0$.

c. Since the government has a budget deficit, the government budget term appears with the demand for capital. You do not know in advance whether the economy has a trade deficit or a trade surplus. But when you see that the quantity demanded of financial capital exceeds the quantity supplied, you know that there must be an additional quantity of financial capital supplied by foreign investors, which means a trade deficit of 2000. This example shows that in this case there is a higher budget deficit, and a higher trade deficit.
$$\text{Quantity supplied of financial capital} = \text{Quantity demanded of financial capital}$$
$$S + (M - X) = I + (G - T)$$
$$4000 + 2000 = 5000 + 1000$$

3. In this case, the national saving and investment identity is written in this way:
$$\text{Quantity supplied of financial capital} = \text{Quantity demanded of financial capital}$$
$$(T - G) + (M - X) + S = I$$

The increase in the government budget surplus and the increase in the trade deficit both increased the supply of financial capital. If investment in physical capital remained unchanged, then private savings must go down, and if savings remained unchanged, then investment must go up. In fact, both effects happened; that is, in the late 1990s, in the U.S. economy, savings declined and investment rose.

4. Ricardian equivalence means that private saving changes to offset exactly any changes in the government budget. So, if the deficit increases by 20, private saving increases by 20 as well, and the trade deficit and the budget deficit will not change from their original levels. The original national saving and investment identity is written below. Notice that if any change in the $(G - T)$ term is offset by a change in the S term, then the other terms do not change. So if $(G - T)$ rises by 20, then S must also increase by 20.
$$\text{Quantity supplied of financial capital} = \text{Quantity demanded of financial capital}$$
$$S + (M - X) = I + (G - T)$$
$$130 + 20 = 100 + 50$$

5. In the last few decades, spending per student has climbed substantially. However, test scores have fallen over this time. This experience has led a number of experts to argue that the problem is not resources—or is not just resources by itself—but is also a problem of how schools are organized and managed and what incentives they have for success.

There are a number of proposals to alter the incentives that schools face, but relatively little hard evidence on what proposals work well. Without trying to evaluate whether these proposals are good or bad ideas, you can just list some of them: testing students regularly; rewarding teachers or schools that perform well on such tests; requiring additional teacher training; allowing students to choose between public schools; allowing teachers and parents to start new schools; giving student "vouchers" that they can use to pay tuition at either public or private schools.

6. The government can direct government spending to R&D. It can also create tax incentives for business to invest in R&D.

Chapter 32

1. The answers are shown in the following two tables.

Region	GDP (in millions)
East Asia	$10,450,032
Latin America	$5,339,390
South Asia	$2,288,812
Europe and Central Asia	$1,862,384
Middle East and North Africa	$1,541,900
Sub-Saharan Africa	$1,287,650

Region	GDP Per Capita (in millions)
East Asia	$5,246
Latin America	$1,388
South Asia	$1,415
Europe and Central Asia	$9,190
Middle East and North Africa	$4,535
Sub-Saharan Africa	$6,847

East Asia appears to be the largest economy on GDP basis, but on a per capita basis it drops to third, after Europe and Central Asia and Sub-Saharan Africa.

2. A region can have some of high-income countries and some of the low-income countries. Aggregating per capita real GDP will vary widely across countries within a region, so aggregating data for a region has little meaning. For example, if you were to compare per capital real GDP for the United States, Canada, Haiti, and Honduras, it looks much different than if you looked at the same data for North America as a whole. Thus, regional comparisons are broad-based and may not adequately capture an individual country's economic attributes.

3. The following table provides a summary of possible answers.

High-Income Countries	Middle-Income Countries	Low-Income Countries
• Foster a more educated workforce • Create, invest in, and apply new technologies • Adopt fiscal policies focused on investment, including investment in human capital, in technology, and in physical plant and equipment • Create stable and market-oriented economic climate • Use monetary policy to keep inflation low and stable • Minimize the risk of exchange rate fluctuations, while also encouraging domestic and international competition	• Invest in technology, human capital, and physical capital • Provide incentives of a market-oriented economic context • Work to reduce government economic controls on market activities • Deregulate the banking and financial sector • Reduce protectionist policies	• Eradicate poverty and extreme hunger • Achieve universal primary education • Promote gender equality • Reduce child mortality rates • Improve maternal health • Combat HIV/AIDS, malaria, and other diseases • Ensure environmental sustainability • Develop global partnerships for development

4. Low-income countries must adopt government policies that are market-oriented and that educate the workforce and population. After this is done, low-income countries should focus on eradicating other social ills that inhibit their growth. The economically challenged are stuck in poverty traps. They need to focus more on health and education and create a stable macroeconomic and political environment. This will attract foreign aid and foreign investment. Middle-income countries strive for increases in physical capital and innovation, while higher-income countries must work to maintain their economies through innovation and technology.

5. If there is a recession and unemployment increases, we can call on an expansionary fiscal policy (lower taxes or increased government spending) or an expansionary monetary policy (increase the money supply and lower interest rates). Both policies stimulate output and decrease unemployment.

6. Aside from a high natural rate of unemployment due to government regulations, subsistence households may be counted as not working.

7. Indexing wage contracts means wages rise when prices rise. This means what you can buy with your wages, your standard of living, remains the same. When wages are not indexed, or rise with inflation, your standard of living falls.

8. An increase in government spending shifts the AD curve to the right, raising both income and price levels.

9. A decrease in the money supply will shift the AD curve leftward and reduce income and price levels. Banks will have less money to lend. Interest rates will increase, affecting consumption and investment, which are both key determinants of aggregate demand.

10. Given the high level of activity in international financial markets, it is typically believed that financial flows across borders are the real reason for trade imbalances. For example, the United States had an enormous trade deficit in the late 1990s and early 2000s because it was attracting vast inflows of foreign capital. Smaller countries that have attracted such inflows of international capital worry that if the inflows suddenly turn to outflows, the resulting decline in their currency could collapse their banking system and bring on a deep recession.

11. The demand for the country's currency would decrease, lowering the exchange rate.

Chapter 33

1. False. Anything that leads to different levels of productivity between two economies can be a source of comparative advantage. For example, the education of workers, the knowledge base of engineers and scientists in a country, the part of a split-up value chain where they have their specialized learning, economies of scale, and other factors can all determine comparative advantage.

2. Brazil has the absolute advantage in producing beef and the United States has the absolute advantage in autos. The opportunity cost of producing one pound of beef is 1/10 of an auto; in the United States it is 3/4 of an auto.

3. In answering questions like these, it is often helpful to begin by organizing the information in a table, such as in the following table. Notice that, in this case, the productivity of the countries is expressed in terms of how many workers it takes to produce a unit of a product.

Country	One Sweater	One Bottle of wine
France	1 worker	1 worker
Tunisia	2 workers	3 workers

In this example, France has an absolute advantage in the production of both sweaters and wine. You can tell because it takes France less labor to produce a unit of the good.

4.
   a. In Germany, it takes fewer workers to make either a television or a video camera. Germany has an absolute advantage in the production of both goods.
   b. Producing an additional television in Germany requires three workers. Shifting those three German workers will reduce video camera production by 3/4 of a camera. Producing an additional television set in Poland requires six workers, and shifting those workers from the other good reduces output of video cameras by 6/12 of a camera, or 1/2. Thus, the opportunity cost of producing televisions is lower in Poland, so Poland has the comparative advantage in the production of televisions. *Note*: Do not let the fractions like 3/4 of a camera or 1/2 of a video camera bother you. If either country was to expand television production by a significant amount—that is, lots more than one unit—then we will be talking about whole cameras and not fractional ones. You can also spot this conclusion by noticing that Poland's absolute disadvantage is relatively lower in televisions, because Poland needs twice as many workers to produce a television but three times as many to produce a video camera, so the product with the relatively lower absolute disadvantage is Poland's comparative advantage.
   c. Producing a video camera in Germany requires four workers, and shifting those four workers away from television production has an opportunity cost of 4/3 television sets. Producing a video camera in Poland requires 12 workers, and shifting those 12 workers away from television production has an opportunity cost of two television sets. Thus, the opportunity cost of producing video cameras is lower in Germany, and video cameras will be Germany's comparative advantage.
   d. In this example, absolute advantage differs from comparative advantage. Germany has the absolute advantage in the production of both goods, but Poland has a comparative advantage in the production of televisions.
   e. Germany should specialize, at least to some extent, in the production of video cameras, export video cameras, and import televisions. Conversely, Poland should specialize, at least to some extent, in the production of televisions, export televisions, and import video cameras.

5. There are a number of possible advantages of intra-industry trade. Both nations can take advantage of extreme specialization and learning in certain kinds of cars with certain traits, like gas-efficient cars, luxury cars, sport-utility vehicles, higher- and lower-quality cars, and so on. Moreover, nations can take advantage of economies of scale, so that large companies will compete against each other across international borders, providing the benefits of competition and variety to customers. This same argument applies to trade between U.S. states, where people often buy products made by people of other states, even though a similar product is made within the boundaries of their own state. All states—and all countries—can benefit from this kind of competition and trade.

6.

a. Start by plotting the points on a sketch diagram and then drawing a line through them. The following figure illustrates the average costs of production of semiconductors.

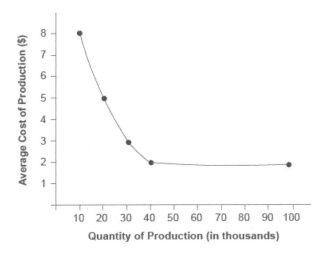

The curve illustrates economies of scale by showing that as the scale increases—that is, as production at this particular factory goes up—the average cost of production declines. The economies of scale exist up to an output of 40,000 semiconductors; at higher outputs, the average cost of production does not seem to decline any further.

b. At any quantity demanded above 40,000, this economy can take full advantage of economies of scale; that is, it can produce at the lowest cost per unit. Indeed, if the quantity demanded was quite high, like 500,000, then there could be a number of different factories all taking full advantage of economies of scale and competing with each other. If the quantity demanded falls below 40,000, then the economy by itself, without foreign trade, cannot take full advantage of economies of scale.

c. The simplest answer to this question is that the small country could have a large enough factory to take full advantage of economies of scale, but then export most of the output. For semiconductors, countries like Taiwan and Korea have recently fit this description. Moreover, this country could also import semiconductors from other countries which also have large factories, thus getting the benefits of competition and variety. A slightly more complex answer is that the country can get these benefits of economies of scale without producing semiconductors, but simply by buying semiconductors made at low cost around the world. An economy, especially a smaller country, may well end up specializing and producing a few items on a large scale, but then trading those items for other items produced on a large scale, and thus gaining the benefits of economies of scale by trade, as well as by direct production.

7. A nation might restrict trade on imported products to protect an industry that is important for national security. For example, nation X and nation Y may be geopolitical rivals, each with ambitions of increased political and economic strength. Even if nation Y has comparative advantage in the production of missile defense systems, it is unlikely that nation Y would seek to export those goods to nation X. It is also the case that, for some nations, the production of a particular good is a key component of national identity. In Japan, the production of rice is culturally very important.

It may be difficult for Japan to import rice from a nation like Vietnam, even if Vietnam has a comparative advantage in rice production.

Chapter 34

1. This is the opposite case of the Work It Out feature. A reduced tariff is like a decrease in the cost of production, which is shown by a downward (or rightward) shift in the supply curve.

2. A subsidy is like a reduction in cost. This shifts the supply curve down (or to the right), driving the price of sugar down. If the subsidy is large enough, the price of sugar can fall below the cost of production faced by foreign producers, which means they will lose money on any sugar they produce and sell.

3. Trade barriers raise the price of goods in protected industries. If those products are inputs in other industries, it raises their production costs and then prices, so sales fall in those other industries. Lower sales lead to lower employment. Additionally, if the protected industries are consumer goods, their customers pay higher prices, which reduce demand for other consumer products and thus employment in those industries.

4. Trade based on comparative advantage raises the average wage rate economy-wide, though it can reduce the incomes of import-substituting industries. By moving away from a country's comparative advantage, trade barriers do the opposite: they give workers in protected industries an advantage, while reducing the average wage economy-wide.

5. By raising incomes, trade tends to raise working conditions also, even though those conditions may not (yet) be equivalent to those in high-income countries.

6. They typically pay more than the next-best alternative. If a Nike firm did not pay workers at least as much as they would earn, for example, in a subsistence rural lifestyle, they many never come to work for Nike.

7. Since trade barriers raise prices, real incomes fall. The average worker would also earn less.

8. Workers working in other sectors and the protected sector see a decrease in their real wage.

9. If imports can be sold at extremely low prices, domestic firms would have to match those prices to be competitive. By definition, matching prices would imply selling under cost and, therefore, losing money. Firms cannot sustain losses forever. When they leave the industry, importers can "take over," raising prices to monopoly levels to cover their short-term losses and earn long-term profits.

10. Because low-income countries need to provide necessities—food, clothing, and shelter—to their people. In other words, they consider environmental quality a luxury.

11. Low-income countries can compete for jobs by reducing their environmental standards to attract business to their countries. This could lead to a competitive reduction in regulations, which would lead to greater environmental damage. While pollution management is a cost for businesses, it is tiny relative to other costs, like labor and adequate infrastructure. It is also costly for firms to locate far away from their customers, which many low-income countries are.

12. The decision should not be arbitrary or unnecessarily discriminatory. It should treat foreign companies the same way as domestic companies. It should be based on science.

13. Restricting imports today does not solve the problem. If anything, it makes it worse since it implies using up domestic sources of the products faster than if they are imported. Also, the national security argument can be used to support protection of nearly any product, not just things critical to our national security.

14. The effect of increasing standards may increase costs to the small exporting country. The supply curve of toys will shift to the left. Exports will decrease and toy prices will rise. Tariffs also raise prices. So the effect on the price of toys is the same. A tariff is a "second best" policy and also affects other sectors. However, a common standard across countries is a "first best" policy that attacks the problem at its root.

15. A free trade association offers free trade between its members, but each country can determine its own trade policy outside the association. A common market requires a common external trade policy in addition to free trade within the group. An economic union is a common market with coordinated fiscal and monetary policy.

16. International agreements can serve as a political counterweight to domestic special interests, thereby preventing stronger protectionist measures.

17. Reductions in tariffs, quotas, and other trade barriers, improved transportation, and communication media have made people more aware of what is available in the rest of the world.

18. Competition from firms with better or cheaper products can reduce a business's profits, and may drive it out of business. Workers would similarly lose income or even their jobs.

19. Consumers get better or less expensive products. Businesses with the better or cheaper products increase their profits. Employees of those businesses earn more income. On balance, the gains outweigh the losses to a nation.

This OpenStax book is available for free at http://cnx.org/content/col12122/1.4

REFERENCES

Welcome to Economics!

Bureau of Labor Statistics, U.S. Department of Labor. 2015. "The Employment Situation—February 2015." Accessed March 27, 2015. http://www.bls.gov/news.release/pdf/empsit.pdf.

Williamson, Lisa. "US Labor Market in 2012." *Bureau of Labor Statistics*. Accessed December 1, 2013. http://www.bls.gov/opub/mlr/2013/03/art1full.pdf.

The Heritage Foundation. 2015. "2015 Index of Economic Freedom." Accessed March 11, 2015. http://www.heritage.org/index/ranking.

Garling, Caleb. "S.F. plane crash: Reporting, emotions on social media," *The San Francisco Chronicle*. July 7, 2013. http://www.sfgate.com/news/article/S-F-plane-crash-Reporting-emotions-on-social-4651639.php.

Irvine, Jessica. "Social Networking Sites are Factories of Modern Ideas." *The Sydney Morning Herald*. November 25, 2011.http://www.smh.com.au/federal-politics/society-and-culture/social-networking-sites-are-factories-of-modern-ideas-20111124-1nwy3.html#ixzz2YZhPYeME.

Pew Research Center. 2015. "Social Networking Fact Sheet." Accessed March 11, 2015. http://www.pewinternet.org/fact-sheets/social-networking-fact-sheet/.

The World Bank Group. 2015. "World Data Bank." Accessed March 30, 2014. http://databank.worldbank.org/data/.

Choice in a World of Scarcity

Bureau of Labor Statistics, U.S. Department of Labor. 2015. "Median Weekly Earnings by Educational Attainment in 2014." Accessed March 27, 2015. http://www.bls.gov/opub/ted/2015/median-weekly-earnings-by-education-gender-race-and-ethnicity-in-2014.htm.

Robbins, Lionel. *An Essay on the Nature and Significance of Economic Science*. London: Macmillan. 1932.

United States Department of Transportation. "Total Passengers on U.S Airlines and Foreign Airlines U.S. Flights Increased 1.3% in 2012 from 2011." Accessed October 2013. http://www.rita.dot.gov/bts/press_releases/bts016_13

Smith, Adam. "Of Restraints upon the Importation from Foreign Countries." In *The Wealth of Nations*. London: Methuen & Co., 1904, first pub 1776), I.V. 2.9.

Smith, Adam. "Of the Propriety of Action." In *The Theory of Moral Sentiments*. London: A. Millar, 1759, 1.

Demand and Supply

Costanza, Robert, and Lisa Wainger. "No Accounting For Nature: How Conventional Economics Distorts the Value of Things." *The Washington Post*. September 2, 1990.

European Commission: Agriculture and Rural Development. 2013. "Overview of the CAP Reform: 2014-2024." Accessed April 13, 205. http://ec.europa.eu/agriculture/cap-post-2013/.

Radford, R. A. "The Economic Organisation of a P.O.W. Camp." *Economica*. no. 48 (1945): 189-201. http://www.jstor.org/stable/2550133.

Landsburg, Steven E. *The Armchair Economist: Economics and Everyday Life*. New York: The Free Press. 2012. specifically Section IV: How Markets Work.

National Chicken Council. 2015. "Per Capita Consumption of Poultry and Livestock, 1965 to Estimated 2015, in Pounds." Accessed April 13, 2015. http://www.nationalchickencouncil.org/about-the-industry/statistics/per-capita-consumption-of-poultry-and-livestock-1965-to-estimated-2012-in-pounds/.

Wessel, David. "Saudi Arabia Fears $40-a-Barrel Oil, Too." *The Wall Street Journal*. May 27, 2004, p. 42. http://online.wsj.com/news/articles/SB108561000087822300.

Pew Research Center. "Pew Research: Center for the People & the Press." http://www.people-press.org/.

Labor and Financial Markets

American Community Survey. 2012. "School Enrollment and Work Status: 2011." Accessed April 13, 2015. http://www.census.gov/prod/2013pubs/acsbr11-14.pdf.

National Center for Educational Statistics. "Digest of Education Statistics." (2008 and 2010). Accessed December 11, 2013. nces.ed.gov.

CreditCards.com. 2013. http://www.creditcards.com/credit-card-news/credit-card-industry-facts-personal-debt-statistics-1276.php.

Elasticity

Abkowitz, A. "How Netflix got started: Netflix founder and CEO Reed Hastings tells Fortune how he got the idea for the DVD-by-mail service that now has more than eight million customers." *CNN Money*. Last Modified January 28, 2009. http://archive.fortune.com/2009/01/27/news/newsmakers/hastings_netflix.fortune/index.htm.

Associated Press (a). "Analyst: Coinstar gains from Netflix pricing moves." *Boston Globe Media Partners, LLC*. Accessed June 24, 2013. http://www.boston.com/business/articles/2011/10/12/analyst_coinstar_gains_from_netflix_pricing_moves/.

Associated Press (b). "Netflix loses 800,000 US subscribers in tough 3Q." *ABC Inc*. Accessed June 24, 2013. http://abclocal.go.com/wpvi/story?section=news/business&id=8403368

Baumgardner, James. 2014. "Presentation on Raising the Excise Tax on Cigarettes: Effects on Health and the Federal Budget." Congressional Budget Office. Accessed March 27, 2015. http://www.cbo.gov/sites/default/files/45214-ICA_Presentation.pdf.

Funding Universe. 2015. "Netflix, Inc. History." Accessed March 11, 2015. http://www.fundinguniverse.com/company-histories/netflix-inc-history/.

Laporte, Nicole. "A tale of two Netflix." *Fast Company* 177 (July 2013) 31-32. Accessed December 3 2013. http://www.fastcompany-digital.com/fastcompany/20130708?pg=33#pg33

Liedtke, Michael, The Associated Press. "Investors bash Netflix stock after slower growth forecast - fee hikes expected to take toll on subscribers most likely to shun costly bundled Net, DVD service." *The Seattle Times*. Accessed June 24, 2013 from NewsBank on-line database (Access World News).

Netflix, Inc. 2013. "A Quick Update On Our Streaming Plans And Prices." Netflix (blog). Accessed March 11, 2015. http://blog.netflix.com/2014/05/a-quick-update-on-our-streaming-plans.html.

Organization for Economic Co-Operation and Development (OECC). n.d. "Average annual hours actually worked per worker." Accessed March 11, 2015. https://stats.oecd.org/Index.aspx?DataSetCode=ANHRS.

Savitz, Eric. "Netflix Warns DVD Subs Eroding; Q4 View Weak; Losses Ahead; Shrs Plunge." *Forbes.com*, 2011. Accessed December 3, 2013. http://www.forbes.com/sites/ericsavitz/2011/10/24/netflix-q3-top-ests-but-shares-hit-by-weak-q4-outlook/.

Statistica.com. 2014. "Coffee Export Volumes Worldwide in November 2014, by Leading Countries (in 60-kilo sacks)." Accessed March 27, 2015. http://www.statista.com/statistics/268135/ranking-of-coffee-exporting-countries/.

Stone, Marcie. "Netflix responds to customers angry with price hike; Netflix stock falls 9%." *News & Politics Examiner*, 2011. Clarity Digital Group. Accessed June 24, 2013. http://www.examiner.com/article/netflix-responds-to-customers-angry-with-price-hike-netflix-stock-falls-9.

Weinman, J. (2012). Die hard, hardly dying. Maclean's, 125(18), 44.

The World Bank Group. 2015. "Gross Savings (% of GDP)." Accessed March 11, 2015. http://data.worldbank.org/indicator/NY.GNS.ICTR.ZS.

Yahoo Finance. Retrieved from http://finance.yahoo.com/q?s=NFLX

Consumer Choices

U.S. Bureau of Labor Statistics. 2015. "Consumer Expenditures in 2013." Accessed March 11, 2015. http://www.bls.gov/cex/csxann13.pdf.

U.S. Bureau of Labor Statistics. 2015. "Employer Costs for Employee Compensation—December 2014." Accessed

March 11, 2015. http://www.bls.gov/news.release/pdf/ecec.pdf.

U.S. Bureau of Labor Statistics. 2015. "Labor Force Statistics from the Current Population Survey." Accessed March 11, 2015. http://www.bls.gov/cps/cpsaat22.htm.

Holden, Sarah, and Daniel Schrass. 2012. "The rose of IRAs in U.S Households' Saving for Retirement, 2012." *ICI Research Perspective* 18.8 (2012). http://www.ici.org/pdf/per18-08.pdf.

Kahneman, Daniel and Amos Tversky. "Prospect Theory: An Analysis of Decision under Risk." *Econometrica* 47.2 (March 1979) 263-291.

Thaler, Richard H. "Shifting Our Retirement Savings into Automatic." *The New York Times*, April 6, 2013. http://www.nytimes.com/2013/04/07/business/an-automatic-solution-for-the-retirement-savings-problem.html?pagewanted=all.

UNESCO Institute for Statistics. "Statistics in Brief / Profiles" Accessed August 2013. http://stats.uis.unesco.org/unesco/TableViewer/document.aspx?ReportId=121 &IF_Language=en&BR_Country=5580.

Production, Costs, and Industry Structure

2010 U.S. Census. www.census.gov.

Perfect Competition

Index Mundi. n.d. "Wheat Monthly Price—U.S. Dollars per Metric Ton." Accessed March 11, 2015. http://www.indexmundi.com/commodities/?commodity=wheat.

Knutson, J. "Wheat on the Defensive in the Northern Plains." *Agweek, Associated Press State Wire: North Dakota (ND)*. April 14, 2013.

SBA Office of Advocacy. 2014. "Frequently Asked Questions: Advocacy: the voice of small business in government." Accessed March 11, 2015. https://www.sba.gov/sites/default/files/advocacy/FAQ_March_2014_0.pdf.

Monopoly

Aboukhadijeh, Feross. "Chapter 20: Girding for War - The North and the South, 1861-1865." *StudyNotes, Inc.* Accessed July 7, 2013. http://www.apstudynotes.org/us-history/outlines/chapter-20-girding-for-war-the-north-and-the-south-1861-1865/.

British Parliament. "(28 August 1833). Slavery Abolition Act 1833; Section LXIV." Accessed July 2013. http://www.pdavis.nl/Legis_07.htm.

Dattel, E. (nd). "Cotton and the Civil War." *Mississippi Historical Society*. Accessed July 2013. http://mshistorynow.mdah.state.ms.us/articles/291/cotton-and-the-civil-war.

Gartner. 2015. "Gartner Says Tablet Sales Continue to Be Slow in 2015." Accessed March 12, 2015. http://www.gartner.com/newsroom/id/2954317.

Grogan, David. 2015. "Federal Judge Finds AmEx's Anti-Steering Rule Violates Antitrust Law." American Booksellers Association. Accessed March 12, 2015. http://www.bookweb.org/news/federal-judge-finds-amex%E2%80%99s-anti-steering-rule-violates-antitrust-law.

Massachusetts Historical Society. "The Coming of the American Revolution 1764-1776: The Boston Tea Party." Retrieved from http://www.masshist.org/revolution/teaparty.php.

Massachusetts Historical Society. "Whereas our Nation." *The Massachusetts Gazette*, p. 2. Accessed July 2013 http://www.masshist.org/revolution/image-viewer.php?old=1&item_id=457&img_step=1&nmask=1&mode=large.

Pelegrin, William. 2015. "Judge Overrules Antitrust Case Against Google , Says Setting Default Search Engines Is Fair." Digital Trends. Accessed March 12, 2015. http://www.digitaltrends.com/mobile/judge-tosses-out-google-antitrust-lawsuit/.

Monopolistic Competition and Oligopoly

Kantar Media. "Our Insights: Infographic—U.S. Advertising Year End Trends Report 2012." Accessed October 17,

2013. http://kantarmedia.us/insight-center/reports/infographic-us-advertising-year-end-trends-report-2012.

Statistica.com. 2015. "Number of Restaurants in the United States from 2011 to 2014." Accessed March 27, 2015. http://www.statista.com/statistics/244616/number-of-qsr-fsr-chain-independent-restaurants-in-the-us/.

The United States Department of Justice. "Antitrust Division." Accessed October 17, 2013. http://www.justice.gov/atr/.

eMarketer.com. 2014. "Total US Ad Spending to See Largest Increase Since 2004: Mobile advertising leads growth; will surpass radio, magazines and newspapers this year. Accessed March 12, 2015. http://www.emarketer.com/Article/Total-US-Ad-Spending-See-Largest-Increase-Since-2004/1010982.

Federal Trade Commission. "About the Federal Trade Commission." Accessed October 17, 2013. http://www.ftc.gov/ftc/about.shtm.

Monopoly and Antitrust Policy

Bishop, Todd. 2014. "Microsoft Exec Admits New Reality: Market Share No Longer 90% — It's 14%."GeekWire. Accessed March 27, 2015. http://www.geekwire.com/2014/microsoft-exec-admits-new-reality-market-share-longer-90-14/.

Catan, T., & Dezember, R. "Kinder-El Paso Merger to Face Antitrust Scrutiny," *Wall Street Journal*. October 19, 2011.

Collins, A. "Tallgrass Energy to Acquire Kinder Morgan Assets for $1.8B." *The Middle Market*, Accessed August 2013. http://www.themiddlemarket.com/news/tallgrass-energy-to-acquire-kinder-morgan-assets-for-1-point-8-billion-232862-1.html.

Conoco Phillips. "Why Natural Gas." Accessed August 2013. http://www.powerincooperation.com/en/pages/useful.html?gclid=COXg7rH3hrgCFWlp7AodtkgA3g.

De la Merced, M. (2012, August 20). "Kinder Morgan to Sell Assets to Tallgrass for $1.8 Billion." *The New York Times*. August 20, 2012.

The Federal Trade Commission. n.d. "The Federal Trade Commission's (FTC) Mission." Accessed March 27, 2015. https://www.ftc.gov/system/files/documents/reports/2014-one-page-ftc-performance-snapshot/150218fy14snapshot.pdf.

Kahn, C. "Kinder Morgan to Buy El Paso Corp. for $20.7B." *USA Today*. October 17, 2011.

Kinder Morgan. (2013). "Investor Information." Accessed August 2013. http://www.kindermorgan.com/investor/.

Rogowsky, Mark. 2014. "There'd Be No Wireless Wars Without The Blocked T-Mobile Merger, So Where Does That Leave Comcast-TWC?" Forbes.com. Accessed March 12, 2015. http://www.forbes.com/sites/markrogowsky/2014/08/27/t-mobile-and-sprint-continue-to-battle-thanks-to-the-government/.

U.S. Energy Information Administration (a). "Natural Gas Consumption by End User." Accessed May 31, 2013. http://www.eia.gov/dnav/ng/ng_cons_sum_dcu_nus_a.htm.

U.S. Energy Information Administration (b). "Natural Gas Prices." Accessed June 28, 2013. http://www.eia.gov/dnav/ng/ng_pri_sum_dcu_nus_a.htm.

The Wall Street Journal. 2015. "Auto Sales." Accessed April 10, 2015. http://online.wsj.com/mdc/public/page/2_3022-autosales.html.

Environmental Protection and Negative Externalities

Johnson, Oscar William. "Back on Track: Earth Day Success Story; The Chattanooga Choo-Choo No Longer Spews Foul Air." *Sports Illustrated*. April 30, 1990. http://www.si.com/vault/1990/04/30/121923/back-on-track-earth-day-success-story-the-chattanooga-choo-choo-no-longer-spews-foul-air.

U.S. Energy Information Administration. "Total Energy: Monthly Energy Review." *U.S. Department of Energy*. Accessed December 19, 2013. http://www.eia.gov/totalenergy/data/monthly/.

Environmental Protection Agency. "2006 Pay-As-You-Throw Programs." Accessed December 20, 2013. http://www.epa.gov/epawaste/conserve/tools/payt/states/06comm.htm.

European Union. "Durban Conference Delivers Breakthrough for Climate." Press release. December 11, 2012.

This OpenStax book is available for free at http://cnx.org/content/col12122/1.4

Accessed December 19, 2013. http://europa.eu/rapid/press-release_MEMO-11-895_en.htm?locale=en.

Positive Externalities and Public Goods

Arias, Omar and Walter W. McMahon. "Dynamic Rates of Return to Education in the U.S." *Economics of Education Review*. 20, 2001. 121–138.

Biography.com. 2015. "Alan Turing." Accessed April 1, 2015. http://www.biography.com/people/alan-turing-9512017.

Canty Media. 2015. "The World: Life Expectancy (2015) - Top 100+." Accessed April 1, 2015. http://www.geoba.se/population.php?pc=world&type=15.

Hyclak, Thomas, Geraint Johnes, and Robert Thornton. *Fundamentals of Labor Economics*. Boston: Houghton Mifflin Company, 2005.

McMahon, Walter. *Education and Development: Measuring the Social Benefits*. Oxford: Oxford University Press, 2000.

National Institute of Health. 2015. "Global Competitiveness—The Importance of U.S. Leadership in Science and Innovation for the Future of Our Economy and Our Health." Accessed April 1, 2015. http://www.nih.gov/about/impact/impact_global.pdf.

National Science Foundation. 2013. "U.S. R&D Spending Resumes Growth in 2010 and 2011 but Still Lags Behind the Pace of Expansion of the National Economy." Accessed April 1, 2015. http://www.nsf.gov/statistics/infbrief/nsf13313/.

Psacharopoulos, George. "Returns to Investment in Education: A Global Update." *World Development* 22, 1994. 1325–1343.

Salientes-Narisma, Corrie. "Samsung Shift to Innovative Devices Pay Off." *Inquirer Technology*. Accessed May 15, 2013. http://technology.inquirer.net/23831/samsungs-shift-to-innovative-devices-pays-off.

United States Department of the Treasury. "Research and Experimentation Tax Credit." Accessed November 2013. http://www.treasury.gov/press-center/news/Pages/investing-in-us-competitiveness.aspx.

U.S. Patent and Trademark Office. 2015. "U.S. Patent Statistics: Calendar Years 1963–2014." Accessed April 10, 2015. http://www.uspto.gov/web/offices/ac/ido/oeip/taf/us_stat.pdf.

United for Medical Research. "Profiles of Prosperity: How NIH-Supported Research Is Fueling Private Sector Growth and Innovation." Introduction. Accessed January 2014. http://www.unitedformedicalresearch.com/wp-content/uploads/2013/07/UMR_ProsperityReport_071913a.pdf.

Cowen, Tyler. *Average Is Over: Powering America Beyond the Age of the Great Stagnation*. Dutton Adult, 2013.

Hardin, Garret. "The Tragedy of the Commons." *Science* 162 (3859): 1243–48 (1968).

Labor Markets and Income

AFL-CIO. "Training and Apprenticeships." http://www.aflcio.org/Learn-About-Unions/Training-and-Apprenticeships.

Central Intelligence Agency. "The World Factbook." https://www.cia.gov/library/publications/the-world-factbook/index.html.

Clark, John Bates. *Essentials of Economic Theory: As Applied to Modern Problems of Industry and Public Policy*. New York: A. M. Kelley, 1907, 501.

United Auto Workers (UAW). "About: Who We Are." http://www.uaw.org/page/who-we-are.

United States Department of Labor: Bureau of Labor Statistics. "Economic News Release: Union Members Summary." Last modified January 23, 2013. http://www.bls.gov/news.release/union2.nr0.htm.

United States Department of Labor, Bureau of Labor Statistics. 2015. "Economic News; Union Members Summary." Accessed April 13, 2015. http://www.bls.gov/news.release/union2.nr0.htm.

Clune, Michael S. "The Fiscal Impacts of Immigrants: A California Case Study." In *The Immigration Debate: Studies on the Economic, Demographic, and Fiscal Effects of Immigration*, edited by James P. Smith and Barry Edmonston. Washington, DC: National Academy Press, 1998, 120–182. http://www.nap.edu/

openbook.php?record_id=5985&page=120.

Smith, James P. "Immigration Reform." *Rand Corporation: Rand Review.* http://www.rand.org/pubs/periodicals/rand-review/issues/2012/fall/leadership/immigration-reform.html.

U.S. Department of Homeland Security: Office of Immigration Statistics. "2011 Yearbook of Immigration Statistics." September 2012. http://www.dhs.gov/sites/default/files/publications/immigration-statistics/yearbook/2011/ois_yb_2011.pdf.

Anderson, Deborah J., Melissa Binder, and Kate Krause. "The Motherhood Wage Penalty Revisited: Experience, Heterogeneity, Work Effort, and Work-Schedule Flexibility." *Industrial and Labor Relations Review.* no. 2 (2003): 273–294. http://www2.econ.iastate.edu/classes/econ321/orazem/anderson_motherhood-penalty.pdf.

Turner, Margery Austin, Rob Santos, Diane K. Levy, Doug Wissoker, Claudia Aranda, Rob Pitingolo, and The Urban Institute. "Housing Discrimination Against Racial and Ethnic Minorities 2012." *U.S. Department of Housing and Urban Development.* Last modified June 2013. http://www.huduser.org/Publications/pdf/HUD-514_HDS2012.pdf.

Austin, Algernon. "The Unfinished March: An Overview." *Economic Policy Institute.* Last modified June 18, 2013. http://www.epi.org/publication/unfinished-march-overview/.

Bertrand, Marianne, and Sendhil Mullainathan. "Are Emily and Greg More Employable Than Lakisha and Jamal? A Field Experiment on Labor Market Discrimination." *American Economic Review.* no. 4 (2004): 991-1013. https://www.aeaweb.org/articles.php?doi=10.1257/0002828042002561&fnd=s.

Blau, Francine D., and Laurence M. Kahn. "The Gender Pay Gap: Have Women Gone as Far as They Can?" *Academy of Management Perspectives.* no. 1 (2007): 7–23. 10.5465/AMP.2007.24286161.

Card, David, and Alan B. Kruger. "Trends in Relative Black–White Earnings Revisited (Working Paper #310)." *Princeton University and the National Bureau of Economic Research.* December 1992. http://harris.princeton.edu/pubs/pdfs/310.pdf.

Donovan, Theresa. Jurist. "Federal Judge Rejects Class Status in Wal-Mart Discrimination Suit." Last modified August 5, 2013. http://jurist.org/paperchase/2013/08/federal-judge-rejects-class-status-in-wal-mart-discrimination-suit.php.

Harris, Elizabeth A. "Labor Panel Finds Illegal Punishments at Walmart." *The New York Times,* November 18, 2013. http://www.nytimes.com/2013/11/19/business/labor-panel-finds-illegal-punishments-at-walmart.html?_r=1&.

Kolesnikova, Natalia A., and Yang Liu. Federal Reserve Bank of St. Louis: The Regional Economist. "Gender Wage Gap May Be Much Smaller Than Most Think." Last modified October 2011. http://www.stlouisfed.org/publications/re/articles/?id=2160.

Podmolik, Mary Ellen. "HUD Finds Housing Discrimination 'Hidden' But Prevalent." *Chicago Tribune: Business,* June 12, 2013. http://articles.chicagotribune.com/2013-06-12/business/ct-biz-0612-housing-discrimination-20130612_1_renters-testers-chicago-area.

Spreen, Thomas Luke. United States Department of Labor: Bureau of Labor Statistics. "Recent College Graduates in the U.S. Labor Force: Data from the Current Population Survey." *Monthly Labor Review* (February, 2013). http://www.bls.gov/opub/mlr/2013/02/art1full.pdf .

U.S. Bureau of Labor Statistics: BLS Reports. 2014. "Women in the Labor Force: A Databook (Report 1052)." Accessed April 13, 2015. http://www.bls.gov/opub/reports/cps/women-in-the-labor-force-a-databook-2014.pdf.

U.S. Equal Employment Opportunity Commission, "Walmart to Pay More than $11.7 Million to Settle EEOC Sex Discrimination Suit." Last modified March 1, 2010. http://www.eeoc.gov/eeoc/newsroom/release/3-1-10.cfm.

United States Census Bureau. 2014. "Table 1. Educational Attainment of the Population 18 Years and Over, by Age, Sex, Race, and Hispanic Origin: 2014." Accessed April 13, 2015. http://www.census.gov/hhes/socdemo/education/data/cps/2014/tables.html.

United States Department of Labor: Bureau of Labor Statistics. "News Release: Usual Weekly Earnings of Wage and Salary Workers (Third Quarter 2013)." November 1, 2013. http://www.bls.gov/news.release/pdf/wkyeng.pdf.

Warner, Judith. 2014. "Fact Sheet: The Women's Leadership Gap: Women's Leadership by the Numbers." Center for American Progress. Accessed March 16, 2015. https://www.americanprogress.org/issues/women/report/2014/

This OpenStax book is available for free at http://cnx.org/content/col12122/1.4

03/07/85457/fact-sheet-the-womens-leadership-gap/.

Weinberger, Catherine J., and Lois Joy. "The Relative Earnings of Black College Graduates, 1980–2001." In *Race and Economic Opportunity in the 21st Century*, edited by Marlene Kim. New York: Routledge, 2007. http://www.econ.ucsb.edu/~weinberg/grads.pdf.

Poverty and Economic Inequality

Ebeling, Ashlea. 2014. "IRS Announces 2015 Estate And Gift Tax Limits." Forbes. Accessed March 16, 2015. http://www.forbes.com/sites/ashleaebeling/2014/10/30/irs-announces-2015-estate-and-gift-tax-limits/.

Federal Register: The Daily Journal of the United States Government. "State Median Income Estimates for a Four-Person Household: Notice of the Federal Fiscal Year (FFY) 2013 State Median Income Estimates for Use Under the Low Income Home Energy Assistance Program (LIHEAP)." Last modified March 15, 2012. https://www.federalregister.gov/articles/2012/03/15/2012-6220/state-median-income-estimates-for-a-four-person-household-notice-of-the-federal-fiscal-year-ffy-2013#t-1.

Luhby, Tami. 2014. "Income is on the rise . . . finally!" Accessed April 10, 2015. http://money.cnn.com/2014/08/20/news/economy/median-income/.

Meyer, Ali. 2015. "56,023,000: Record Number of Women Not in Labor Force." CNSNews.com. Accessed March 16, 2015. http://cnsnews.com/news/article/ali-meyer/56023000-record-number-women-not-labor-force.

Orshansky, Mollie. "Children of the Poor." *Social Security Bulletin*. 26 no. 7 (1963): 3–13. http://www.ssa.gov/policy/docs/ssb/v26n7/v26n7p3.pdf.

The World Bank. "Data: Poverty Headcount Ratio at $1.25 a Day (PPP) (% of Population)." http://data.worldbank.org/indicator/SI.POV.DDAY.

U.S. Department of Commerce: United States Census Bureau. "American FactFinder." http://factfinder2.census.gov/faces/nav/jsf/pages/index.xhtml.

U.S. Department of Commerce: United States Census Bureau. "Current Population Survey (CPS): CPS Table Creator." http://www.census.gov/cps/data/cpstablecreator.html.

U.S. Department of Commerce: United States Census Bureau. "Income: Table F-6. Regions—Families (All Races) by Median and Mean Income." http://www.census.gov/hhes/www/income/data/historical/families/.

U.S. Department of Commerce: United States Census Bureau. "Poverty: Poverty Thresholds." Last modified 2012. http://www.census.gov/hhes/www/poverty/data/threshld/.

U.S. Department of Health & Human Services. 2015. "2015 Poverty Guidelines." Accessed April 10, 2015. http://www.medicaid.gov/medicaid-chip-program-information/by-topics/eligibility/downloads/2015-federal-poverty-level-charts.pdf.

U.S. Department of Health & Human Services. 2015. "Information on Poverty and Income Statistics: A Summary of 2014 Current Population Survey Data." Accessed April 13, 2015. http://aspe.hhs.gov/hsp/14/povertyandincomeest/ib_poverty2014.pdf.

Congressional Budget Office. 2015. "The Effects of Potential Cuts in SNAP Spending on Households With Different Amounts of Income." Accessed April 13, 2015. https://www.cbo.gov/publication/49978.

Falk, Gene. Congressional Research Service. "The Temporary Assistance for Needy Families (TANF) Block Grant: Responses to Frequently Asked Questions." Last modified October 17, 2013. http://www.fas.org/sgp/crs/misc/RL32760.pdf.

Library of Congress. "Congressional Research Service." http://www.loc.gov/crsinfo/about/.

Office of Management and Budget. "Fiscal Year 2013 Historical Tables: Budget of the U.S. Government." http://www.whitehouse.gov/sites/default/files/omb/budget/fy2013/assets/hist.pdf.

Tax Policy Center: Urban Institute and Brookings Institution. "The Tax Policy Briefing Book: Taxation and the Family: What is the Earned Income Tax Credit?" http://www.taxpolicycenter.org/briefing-book/key-elements/family/eitc.cfm.

Frank, Robert H., and Philip J. Cook. *The Winner-Take-All Society*. New York: Martin Kessler Books at The Free Press, 1995.

Institute of Education Sciences: National Center for Education Statistics. "Fast Facts: Degrees Conferred by Sex and Race." http://nces.ed.gov/fastfacts/display.asp?id=72.

Nhan, Doris. "Census: More in U.S. Report Nontraditional Households." *National Journal.* Last modified May 1, 2012. http://www.nationaljournal.com/thenextamerica/demographics/census-more-in-u-s-report-nontraditional-households-20120430.

U.S. Bureau of Labor Statistics: BLS Reports. "Report 1040: Women in the Labor Force: A Databook." Last modified March 26, 2013. http://www.bls.gov/cps/wlf-databook-2012.pdf.

U.S. Department of Commerce: United States Census Bureau. "Income: Table H-2. Share of Aggregate Income Received by Each Fifth and Top 5 Percent of Households." http://www.census.gov/hhes/www/income/data/historical/household/.

United States Census Bureau. 2014. "2013 Highlights." Accessed April 13, 2015. http://www.census.gov/hhes/www/poverty/about/overview/.

United States Census Bureau. 2014. "Historical Income Tables: Households: Table H-2 Share of Aggregate Income Received by Each Fifth and Top 5% of Income. All Races." Accessed April 13, 2015. http://www.census.gov/hhes/www/income/data/historical/household/.

Board of Governors of the Federal Reserve System. "Research Resources: Survey of Consumer Finances." Last modified December 13, 2013. http://www.federalreserve.gov/econresdata/scf/scfindex.htm.

Congressional Budget Office. "The Distribution of Household Income and Federal Taxes, 2008 and 2009." Last modified July 10, 2012. http://www.cbo.gov/publication/43373.

Huang, Chye-Ching, and Nathaniel Frentz. "Myths and Realities About the Estate Tax." *Center on Budget and Policy Priorities.* Last modified August 29, 2013. http://www.cbpp.org/files/estatetaxmyths.pdf.

Information, Risk, and Insurance

Center on Budget and Policy Priorities. 2015. "Policy Basics: Where Do Our Federal Tax Dollars Go?" Accessed April 1, 2015. http://www.cbpp.org/cms/?fa=view&id=1258.

Consumer Reports. "Consumer Reports.org." http://www.consumerreports.org/cro/index.htm.

Federal Trade Commission. "About the Federal Trade Commission." Last modified October 17, 2013. http://www.ftc.gov/ftc/about.shtm.

Huffington Post. 2015. "HUFFPOLLSTER: Poll Shows Uptick In Obamacare Favorable Rating." Accessed April 1, 2015. http://www.huffingtonpost.com/2015/03/19/affordable-care-act-fav_n_6900938.html.

Kahneman, Daniel, and Amos Tversky. "Prospect Theory: An Analysis of Decision under Risk." *Econometrica.* 47, no. 2 (1979): 263-291. http://www.princeton.edu/~kahneman/docs/Publications/prospect_theory.pdf.

Rasmussen Reports, LLC. "Rasmussen Reports." http://www.rasmussenreports.com/.

Central Intelligence Agency. "The World Factbook." https://www.cia.gov/library/publications/the-world-factbook/index.html.

National Association of Insurance Commissioners. "National Association of Insurance Commissioners & The Center for Insurance Policy and Research." http://www.naic.org/.

OECD. "The Organisation for Economic Co-operation and Development (OECD)." http://www.oecd.org/about/.

USA Today. 2015. "Uninsured Rates Drop Dramatically under Obamacare." Accessed April 1, 2015. http://www.usatoday.com/story/news/nation/2015/03/16/uninsured-rates-drop-sharply-under-obamacare/24852325/.

Thaler, Richard H., and Sendhil Mullainathan. "The Concise Encyclopedia of Economics: Behavioral Economics." *Library of Economics and Liberty.* http://www.econlib.org/library/Enc/BehavioralEconomics.html.

Henry J. Kaiser Family Foundation, The. "Health Reform: Summary of the Affordable care Act." Last modified April 25, 2013. http://kff.org/health-reform/fact-sheet/summary-of-new-health-reform-law/.

Financial Markets

National Venture Capital Association. "Recent Stats & Studies." http://www.nvca.org/

index.php?option=com_content&view=article&id=344&Itemid=103Update.

Freddie Mac. 2015. "Freddie Mac Update: March 2015." Accessed April 13, 2015. http://www.freddiemac.com/investors/pdffiles/investor-presentation.pdf.

Former, Jamie D. "Should Your Small Business Go Public? Consider the Benefits and Risks of Becoming a Publicly Traded Company." *U.S. Small Business Administration: Community Blog (blog)*. Publication date March 23, 2010. http://www.sba.gov/community/blogs/community-blogs/business-law-advisor/should-your-small-business-go-public-consider-0.

Howley, Kathleen M. Bloomberg. "Home Value Highest Since '07 as U.S. Houses Make Cash." Last modified March 26, 2013. http://www.bloomberg.com/news/2013-03-26/home-value-highest-since-07-as-u-s-houses-make-cash-mortgages.html.

NASDAQ.com. 2015. "Facebook, Inc. Historical Stock Prices." Accessed March 28, 2015. http://www.nasdaq.com/symbol/fb/historical.

National Association of Realtors. 2015. "Existing-Home Sales: Latest News." Accessed April 1, 2015. http://www.realtor.org/topics/existing-home-sales/data.

PricewaterhouseCoopers LLP. 2015. "Annual Venture Capital Investment Tops $48 Billion in 2014, Reaching Hightest Level in Over a Decade, According to the Moneytree Report." Accessed April 1, 2015. http://www.pwc.com/us/en/press-releases/2015/annual-venture-capital-investment-tops-48-billion.jhtml.

Rooney, Ben. "Trading Program Sparked May 'Flash Crash'." *CNN Money*. Last modified October 1, 2010. http://money.cnn.com/2010/10/01/markets/SEC_CFTC_flash_crash/index.htm.

Investment Company Institute. "2013 Investment Company Fact Book, Chapter 6: Characteristics of Mutual Fund Owners." http://icifactbook.org/fb_ch6.html.

U.S. Department of Commerce: United States Census Bureau. "Income: Table H-13. Educational Attainment of Householder—Households with Householder 25 Years Old and Over by Median and Mean Income." http://www.census.gov/hhes/www/income/data/historical/household/.

United States Department of Labor. Bureau of Labor Statistics. 2015. "Table 9. Quartiles and Selected Deciles of Usual Weekly Earnings of Full-Time Wage and Salary Workers by Selected Characteristics, 2014 Annual Averages." Accessed April 1, 2015. http://www.bls.gov/news.release/wkyeng.t09.htm.

Public Economy

Olson, Mancur. *The Logic of Collective Action: Public Goods and the Theory of Groups*, (Boston: Harvard University Press, 1965).

Downs, Anthony. *An Economic Theory of Democracy*. New York: Harper, 1957.

Skinner, B.F. *Walden Two*. Indianapolis: Hackett Publishing Company, Inc., 1948.

American Civil Liberties Union (ACLU). "Voting Rights." https://www.aclu.org/voting-rights.

The New York Times. "The 2012 Money Race: Compare the Candidates." http://elections.nytimes.com/2012/campaign-finance.

The Washington Post. "Exit Polls 2012: Where Americans Stood this Election." Last modified November 7, 2012. http://www.washingtonpost.com/wp-srv/special/politics/2012-exit-polls/national-breakdown/.

Cornell University Law School: Legal Information Institute. "Citizens United v. Federal Election Committee (No. 08-205)." Last modified January 21, 2010. http://www.law.cornell.edu/supct/html/08-205.ZS.html.

U.S. Department of Commerce: United States Census Bureau. "Voting and Registration: Historical Time Series Tables; Table A-9: Reported Voting Rates in Presidential Election Years, by Selected Characteristics: November 1964 to 2012." http://www.census.gov/hhes/www/socdemo/voting/publications/historical/index.html

Roper Center Public Opinion Archives. "A Brief History of Public Opinion on the Government's Role in Providing Health Care." Last modified September 23, 2013.

U.S. Department of Commerce: United States Census Bureau. "Voting and Registration: Historical Time Series Tables; Table A-10: Reported Registration Rates in Presidential Election Years, by Selected Characteristics: November 1968 to 2012." http://www.census.gov/hhes/www/socdemo/voting/publications/historical/index.html

Nixon, Ron. "American Candy Makers. Pinched by Inflated Sugar Prices. Look Abroad." *The New York Times*. Last modified October 30, 2013. http://www.nytimes.com/2013/10/31/us/american-candy-makers-pinched-by-inflated-sugar-prices-look-abroad.html?_r=0.

Hufbauer, Gary Clyde, and Sean Lowry. "U.S. Tire Tariffs: Saving Few Jobs at High Cost (Policy Brief 12-9)." *Peterson Institute for International Economics*. Last modified April 2012.

The Macroeconomic Perspective

U.S. Department of Commerce: Bureau of Economic Analysis. "National data: National Income and Product Accounts Tables." http://bea.gov/iTable/iTable.cfm?ReqID=9&step=1.

U.S. Department of Commerce: United States Census Bureau. "Census of Governments: 2012 Census of Governments." http://www.census.gov/govs/cog/.

United States Department of Transportation. "About DOT." Last modified March 2, 2012. http://www.dot.gov/about.

U.S. Department of Energy. "Energy.gov." http://energy.gov/.

U.S. Department of Health & Human Services. "Agency for Healthcare Research and Quality." http://www.ahrq.gov/.

United States Department of Agriculture. "USDA." http://www.usda.gov/wps/portal/usda/usdahome.

Schneider, Friedrich. Department of Economics. "Size and Development of the Shadow Economy of 31 European and 5 other OECD Countries from 2003 to 2013: A Further Decline." *Johannes Kepler University*. Last modified April 5, 2013. http://www.econ.jku.at/members/Schneider/files/publications/2013/ShadEcEurope31_Jan2013.pdf.

The National Bureau of Economic Research. "Information on Recessions and Recoveries, the NBER Business Cycle Dating Committee, and related topics." http://www.nber.org/cycles/main.html.

Economic Growth

Bolt, Jutta, and Jan Luiten van Zanden. "The Maddison Project: The First Update of the Maddison Project Re-Estimating Growth Before 1820 (Maddison-Project Working Paper WP-4)." *University of Groningen: Groningen Growth and Development Centre*. Last modified January 2013. http://www.ggdc.net/maddison/publications/pdf/wp4.pdf.

Central Intelligence Agency. "The World Factbook: Country Comparison GDP (Purchasing Power Parity)." https://www.cia.gov/library/publications/the-world-factbook/rankorder/2001rank.html.

DeLong, Brad. "Lighting the Rocket of Growth and Lightening the Toil of Work: Another Outtake from My 'Slouching Towards Utopia' MS...." *This is Brad DeLong's Grasping Reality* (blog). September 3, 2013. http://delong.typepad.com/sdj/2013/09/lighting-the-rocket-of-growth-and-lightening-the-toil-of-work-another-outtake-from-my-slouching-towards-utopia-ms.html.

Easterlin, Richard A. "The Worldwide Standard of Living since 1800." *The Journal of Economic Perspectives*. no. 1 (2000): 7–26. http://pubs.aeaweb.org/doi/pdfplus/10.1257/jep.14.1.7.

Maddison, Angus. *Contours of the World Economy 1-2030 AD: Essays in Macro-Economic History*. Oxford: Oxford University Press, 2007.

British Library. "Treasures in Full: Magna Carta." http://www.bl.uk/treasures/magnacarta/.

Rothbard, Murray N. Ludwig von Mises Institute. "Property Rights and the Theory of Contracts." *The Ethics of Liberty*. Last modified June 22, 2007. http://mises.org/daily/2580.

Salois, Matthew J., J. Richard Tiffin, and Kelvin George Balcombe. IDEAS: Research Division of the Federal Reserve Bank of St. Louis. "Impact of Income on Calorie and Nutrient Intakes: A Cross-Country Analysis." Presention at the annual meeting of the Agricultural and Applied Economics Association, Pittsburg, PA, July 24–26, 2011. http://ideas.repec.org/p/ags/aaea11/103647.html.

van Zanden, Jan Luiten. *The Long Road to the Industrial Revolution: The European Economy in a Global Perspective, 1000–1800 (Global Economic History Series)*. Boston: Brill, 2009.

The World Bank. "CPIA Property Rights and Rule-based Governance Rating (1=low to 6=high)." http://data.worldbank.org/indicator/IQ.CPA.PROP.XQ.

This OpenStax book is available for free at http://cnx.org/content/col12122/1.4

Rex A. Hudson, ed. *Brazil: A Country Study.* "Spectacular Growth, 1968–73." Washington: GPO for the Library of Congress, 1997. http://countrystudies.us/brazil/64.htm.

"Women and the World Economy: A Guide to Womenomics." *The Economist,* April 12, 2006. http://www.economist.com/node/6802551.

Farole, Thomas, and Gokhan Akinci, eds. *Special Economic Zones: Progress, Emerging Challenges, and Future Directions.* Washington: The World Bank, 2011. http://publications.worldbank.org/index.php?main_page=product_info&products_id=24138.

Garcia, Abraham, and Pierre Mohnen. United Nations University, Maastricht Economic and Social Research and Training Centre on Innovation and Technology: UNU-MERIT. "Impact of Government Support on R&D and Innovation (Working Paper Series #2010-034)." http://www.merit.unu.edu/publications/wppdf/2010/wp2010-034.pdf.

Heston, Alan, Robert Summers, and Bettina Aten. "Penn World Table Version 7.1." *Center for International Comparisons of Production, Income and Prices at the University of Pennsylvania.* Last modified July 2012. https://pwt.sas.upenn.edu/php_site/pwt71/pwt71_form.php.

United States Department of Labor: Bureau of Labor Statistics. "Women at Work: A Visual Essay." *Monthly Labor Review,* October 2003, 45–50. http://www.bls.gov/opub/mlr/2003/10/ressum3.pdf.

Central Intelligence Agency. "The World Factbook: Country Comparison: GDP–Real Growth Rate." https://www.cia.gov/library/publications/the-world-factbook/rankorder/2003rank.html.

Sen, Amartya. "Hunger in the Contemporary World (Discussion Paper DEDPS/8)." *The Suntory Centre: London School of Economics and Political Science.* Last modified November 1997. http://sticerd.lse.ac.uk/dps/de/dedps8.pdf.

Unemployment

Bureau of Labor Statistics. Labor Force Statistics from the Current Population Survey. *Accessed March 6, 2015* http://data.bls.gov/timeseries/LNS14000000.

Cappelli, P. (20 June 2012). "Why Good People Can't Get Jobs: Chasing After the Purple Squirrel." http://knowledge.wharton.upenn.edu/article.cfm?articleid=3027.

Inflation

Sources for **Table 22.1**:
> http://www.eia.gov/dnav/pet/pet_pri_gnd_a_epmr_pte_dpgal_w.htm
> http://data.bls.gov/cgi-bin/surveymost?ap
> http://www.bls.gov/ro3/apmw.htm
> http://www.autoblog.com/2014/03/12/who-can-afford-the-average-car-price-only-folks-in-washington/
> https://www.census.gov/construction/nrs/pdf/uspricemon.pdf
> http://www.bls.gov/news.release/empsit.t24.htm
> http://variety.com/2015/film/news/movie-ticket-prices-increased-in-2014-1201409670/

US Inflation Calculator. "Historical Inflation Rates: 1914-2013." Accessed March 4, 2015. http://www.usinflationcalculator.com/inflation/historical-inflation-rates/.

Bernhard, Kent. "Pump Prices Jump Across U.S. after Katrina." *NBC News,* September 1, 2005. http://www.nbcnews.com/id/9146363/ns/business-local_business/t/pump-prices-jump-across-us-after-katrina/#.U00kRfk7um4.

Wynne, Mark A. "Core Inflation, A Review of Some Conceptual Issues." *Federal Reserve Bank of St. Louis.* p. 209. Accessed April 14, 2014. http://research.stlouisfed.org/publications/review/08/05/part2/Wynne.pdf

Shiller, Robert. "Why Do People Dislike Inflation?" *NBER Working Paper Series, National Bureau of Economic Research,* p. 52. 1996.

Wines, Michael. "How Bad is Inflation in Zimbabwe?" *The New York Times,* May 2, 2006. http://www.nytimes.com/2006/05/02/world/africa/02zimbabwe.html?pagewanted=all&_r=0.

Hanke, Steve H. "R.I.P. Zimbabwe Dollar." *CATO Institute.* Accessed December 31, 2013. http://www.cato.org/zimbabwe.

Massachusetts Institute of Technology. 2015. "Billion Prices Project." Accessed March 4, 2015. http://bpp.mit.edu/usa/.

The International Trade and Capital Flows

Central Intelligence Agency. "The World Factbook." Last modified October 31, 2013. https://www.cia.gov/library/publications/the-world-factbook/geos/gm.html.

U.S. Department of Commerce. "Bureau of Economic Analysis." Last modified December 1, 2013. http://www.bea.gov/.

U.S. Department of Commerce. "United States Census Bureau." http://www.census.gov/.

Tabuchi, Hiroko. "Japan Reports a $78 Billion Trade Deficit for 2012." *The New York Times*, January 23, 2013. http://www.nytimes.com/2013/01/24/business/global/japan-reports-a-78-billion-trade-deficit-for-2012.html?_r=0.

World Bank. 2014. "Exports of Goods and Services (% of GDP)." Accesed April 13, 2015. http://data.worldbank.org/indicator/NE.EXP.GNFS.ZS/countries.

The Aggregate Demand/Aggregate Supply Model

Keynes, John Maynard. *The General Theory of Employment, Interest and Money*. London: Palgrave Macmillan, 1936.

U.S. Department of Commerce: United States Census Bureau. "New Residential Sales: Historical Data." http://www.census.gov/construction/nrs/historical_data/.

Library of Economics and Liberty. "The Concise Encyclopedia of Economics: Jean-Baptiste Say." http://www.econlib.org/library/Enc/bios/Say.html.

Library of Economics and Liberty. "The Concise Encyclopedia of Economics: John Maynard Keynes." http://www.econlib.org/library/Enc/bios/Keynes.html.

Organization for Economic Cooperation and Development. 2015. "Business Tendency Surveys: Construction." Accessed March 4, 2015. http://stats.oecd.org/mei/default.asp?lang=e&subject=6.

University of Michigan. 2015. "Surveys of Consumers." Accessed March 4, 2015. http://www.sca.isr.umich.edu/tables.html.

The Keynesian Perspective

Mahapatra, Lisa. "US Exports To China Have Grown 294% Over The Past Decade." *International Business Times*. Last modified July 09, 2013. http://www.ibtimes.com/us-exports-china-have-grown-294-over-past-decade-1338693.

The Conference Board, Inc. "Global Economic Outlook 2014, November 2013." http://www.conference-board.org/data/globaloutlook.cfm.

Thomas, G. Scott. "Recession claimed 170,000 small businesses in two years." *The Business Journals*. Last modified July 24, 2012. http://www.bizjournals.com/bizjournals/on-numbers/scott-thomas/2012/07/recession-claimed-170000-small.html.

United States Department of Labor: Bureau of Labor Statistics. "Top Picks." http://data.bls.gov/cgi-bin/surveymost?bls.

Harford, Tim. "What Price Supply and Demand?" http://timharford.com/2014/01/what-price-supply-and-demand/?utm_source=dlvr.it&utm_medium=twitter.

National Employment Law Project. "Job Creation and Economic Recovery." http://www.nelp.org/index.php/content/content_issues/category/job_creation_and_economic_recovery/.

Hoover, Kevin. "Phillips Curve." *The Concise Encyclopedia of Economics*. http://www.econlib.org/library/Enc/PhillipsCurve.html.

U.S. Government Printing Office. "Economic Report of the President." http://1.usa.gov/1c3psdL.

Blinder, Alan S., and Mark Zandi. "How the Great Recession Was Brought to an End." Last modified July 27, 2010. http://www.princeton.edu/~blinder/End-of-Great-Recession.pdf.

The Neoclassical Perspective

Lumina Foundation. 2014. "A Stronger Nation Through Higher Education." Accessed March 4, 2015. http://www.luminafoundation.org/publications/A_stronger_nation_through_higher_education-2014.pdf.

The National Bureau of Economic Research. http://www.nber.org/.

U.S. Department of Commerce: United States Census Bureau. "The 2012 Statistical Abstract." http://www.census.gov/compendia/statab/cats/education.html.

U.S. Department of the Treasury. "TARP Programs." Last modified December 12, 2013. http://www.treasury.gov/initiatives/financial-stability/TARP-Programs/Pages/default.aspx.

United States Government. "Recovery.gov: Track the Money." Last modified October 30, 2013. http://www.recovery.gov/Pages/default.aspx.

American Statistical Association. "ASA Headlines." http://www.amstat.org/.

Haubrich, Joseph G., George Pennacchi, and Peter Ritchken. "Working Paper 11-07: Inflation Expectations, Real Rates, and Risk Premia: Evidence from Inflation Swaps." *Federal Reserve Bank of Cleveland*. Last modified March 2011. http://www.clevelandfed.org/research/workpaper/2011/wp1107.pdf.

University of Michigan: Institute for Social Research. "Survey Research Center." http://www.src.isr.umich.edu/.

Carvalho, Carlos, Stefano Eusepi, and Christian Grisse. "Policy Initiatives in the Global Recession: What Did Forecasters Expect?" *Federal Reserve Bank of New York: Current Issues in Economics and Finance*, 18, no. 2 (2012). http://www.newyorkfed.org/research/current_issues/ci18-2.pdf.

Money and Banking

Hogendorn, Jan and Marion Johnson. *The Shell Money of the Slave Trade*. Cambridge University Press, 2003. 6.

Federal Reserve Statistical Release. November 23, 2013. http://www.federalreserve.gov/RELEASES/h6/current/default.htm#t2tg1link.

Credit Union National Association. 2014. "Monthly Credit Union Estimates." Last accessed March 4, 2015. http://www.cuna.org/Research-And-Strategy/Credit-Union-Data-And-Statistics/.

Dallas Federal Reserve. 2013. "Ending `Too Big To Fail': A Proposal for Reform Before It's Too Late". Accessed March 4, 2015. http://www.dallasfed.org/news/speeches/fisher/2013/fs130116.cfm.

Richard W. Fisher. "Ending 'Too Big to Fail': A Proposal for Reform Before It's Too Late (With Reference to Patrick Henry, Complexity and Reality) Remarks before the Committee for the Republic, Washington, D.C. Dallas Federal Reserve. January 16, 2013.

"Commercial Banks in the U.S." Federal Reserve Bank of St. Louis. Accessed November 2013. http://research.stlouisfed.org/fred2/series/USNUM.

Bitcoin. 2013. www.bitcoin.org.

National Public Radio. *Lawmakers and Regulators Take Closer Look at Bitcoin*. November 19, 2013. http://thedianerehmshow.org/shows/2013-11-19/lawmakers-and-regulators-take-closer-look-bitcoin.

Monetary Policy and Bank Regulation

Matthews, Dylan. "Nine amazing facts about Janet Yellen, our next Fed chair." Wonkblog. *The Washington Post*. Posted October 09, 2013. http://www.washingtonpost.com/blogs/wonkblog/wp/2013/10/09/nine-amazing-facts-about-janet-yellen-our-next-fed-chair/.

Appelbaum, Binyamin. "Divining the Regulatory Goals of Fed Rivals." *The New York Times*. Posted August 14, 2013. http://www.nytimes.com/2013/08/14/business/economy/careers-of-2-fed-contenders-reveal-little-on-regulatory-approach.html?pagewanted=3.

U.S. Department of the Treasury. "Office of the Comptroller of the Currency." Accessed November 2013. http://www.occ.gov/.

National Credit Union Administration. "About NCUA." Accessed November 2013. http://www.ncua.gov/about/Pages/default.aspx.

Board of Governors of the Federal Reserve System. "Federal Open Market Committee." Accessed September 3, 2013. http://www.federalreserve.gov/monetarypolicy/fomc.htm.

Board of Governors of the Federal Reserve System. "Reserve Requirements." Accessed November 5, 2013. http://www.federalreserve.gov/monetarypolicy/reservereq.htm.

Cox, Jeff. 2014. "Fed Completes the Taper." Accessed March 31, 2015. http://www.cnbc.com/id/102132961.

Jahan, Sarwat. n.d. "Inflation Targeting: Holding the Line." International Monetary Fund. Accessed March 31, 2015. http://www.imf.org/external/pubs/ft/fandd/basics/target.htm.

Tobin, James. "The Concise Encyclopedia of Economics: Monetary Policy." *Library of Economics and Liberty*. Accessed November 2013. http://www.econlib.org/library/Enc/MonetaryPolicy.html.

Federal Reserve Bank of New York. "The Founding of the Fed." Accessed November 2013. http://www.newyorkfed.org/aboutthefed/history_article.html.

Exchange Rates and International Capital Flows

Friedman, Milton. *Capitalism and Freedom*. Chicago: University of Chicago Press, 1962.

Government Budgets and Fiscal Policy

Kramer, Mattea, et. al. *A People's Guide to the Federal Budget*. National Priorities Project. Northampton: Interlink Books, 2012.

Kurtzleben, Danielle. "10 States With The Largest Budget Shortfalls." *U.S. News & World Report*. Januray 14, 2011. http://www.usnews.com/news/articles/2011/01/14/10-states-with-the-largest-budget-shortfalls.

Miller, Rich, and William Selway. "U.S. Cities and States Start Spending Again." *BloombergBusinessweek*, January 10, 2013. http://www.businessweek.com/articles/2013-01-10/u-dot-s-dot-cities-and-states-start-spending-again.

Weisman, Jonathan. "After Year of Working Around Federal Cuts, Agencies Face Fewer Options." *The New York Times*, October 26, 2013. http://www.nytimes.com/2013/10/27/us/politics/after-year-of-working-around-federal-cuts-agencies-face-fewer-options.html?_r=0.

Chantrill, Christopher. USGovernmentSpending.com. "Government Spending Details: United States Federal State and Local Government Spending, Fiscal Year 2013." http://www.usgovernmentspending.com/year_spending_2013USbn_15bs2n_20.

Burman, Leonard E., and Joel Selmrod. *Taxes in America: What Everyone Needs to Know*. New York: Oxford University Press, 2012.

Hall, Robert E., and Alvin Rabushka. *The Flat Tax (Hoover Classics)*. Stanford: Hoover Institution Press, 2007.

Kliff, Sarah. "How Congress Paid for Obamacare (in Two Charts)." *The Washington Post: WonkBlog* (blog), August 30, 2012. http://www.washingtonpost.com/blogs/wonkblog/wp/2012/08/30/how-congress-paid-for-obamacare-in-two-charts/.

Matthews, Dylan. "America's Taxes are the Most Progressive in the World. Its Government is Among the Least." *The Washington Post: WonkBlog* (blog). April 5, 2013. http://www.washingtonpost.com/blogs/wonkblog/wp/2013/04/05/americas-taxes-are-the-most-progressive-in-the-world-its-government-is-among-the-least/.

Eisner, Robert. *The Great Deficit Scares: The Federal Budget, Trade, and Social Security*. New York: Priority Press Publications, 1997.

Weisman, Jonathan, and Ashley Parker. "Republicans Back Down, Ending Crisis Over Shutdown and Debt Limit." *The New York Times*, October 16, 2013. http://www.nytimes.com/2013/10/17/us/congress-budget-debate.html.

Wessel, David. *Red Ink: Inside the High-Stakes Politics of Federal Budget*. New York: Crown Publishing Group, 2013.

Alesina, Alberto, and Francesco Giavazzi. *Fiscal Policy after the Financial Crisis (National Bureau of Economic Research Conference Report)*. Chicago: University Of Chicago Press, 2013.

Martin, Fernando M. "Fiscal Policy in the Great Recession and Lessons from the Past." Federal Reserve Bank of St. Louis: *Economic Synopses*. no. 1 (2012). http://research.stlouisfed.org/publications/es/12/ES_2012-01-06.pdf.

Bivens, Josh, Andrew Fieldhouse, and Heidi Shierholz. "From Free-fall to Stagnation: Five Years After the Start of

This OpenStax book is available for free at http://cnx.org/content/col12122/1.4

the Great Recession, Extraordinary Policy Measures Are Still Needed, But Are Not Forthcoming." *Economic Policy Institute*. Last modified February 14, 2013. http://www.epi.org/publication/bp355-five-years-after-start-of-great-recession/.

Lucking, Brian, and Dan Wilson. Federal Reserve Bank of San Francisco, "FRBSF Economic Letter—U.S. Fiscal Policy: Headwind or Tailwind?" Last modified July 2, 2012. http://www.frbsf.org/economic-research/publications/economic-letter/2012/july/us-fiscal-policy/.

Greenstone, Michael, and Adam Looney. Brookings. "The Role of Fiscal Stimulus in the Ongoing Recovery." Last modified July 6, 2012. http://www.brookings.edu/blogs/jobs/posts/2012/07/06-jobs-greenstone-looney.

Leduc, Sylvain, and Daniel Wilson. Federal Reserve Bank of San Francisco: Working Paper Series. "Are State Governments Roadblocks to Federal Stimulus? Evidence from Highway Grants in the 2009 Recovery Act. (Working Paper 2013-16)." Last modified July 2013. http://www.frbsf.org/economic-research/files/wp2013-16.pdf.

Lucking, Brian, and Daniel Wilson. "FRBSF Economic Letter-Fiscal Headwinds: Is the Other Shoe About to Drop?" *Federal Reserve Bank of San Francisco*. Last modified June 3, 2013. http://www.frbsf.org/economic-research/publications/economic-letter/2013/june/fiscal-headwinds-federal-budget-policy/.

Recovery.gov. "Track the Money." http://www.recovery.gov/Pages/default.aspx.

Bastagli, Francesca, David Coady, and Sanjeev Gupta. International Monetary Fund. "IMF Staff Discussion Note: Income Inequality and Fiscal Policy." Last modified June 28, 2012. http://www.imf.org/external/pubs/ft/sdn/2012/sdn1208.pdf.

The Impacts of Government Borrowing

The White House. "This is why it's time to make college more affordable." Last modified August 20, 2013. http://www.whitehouse.gov/share/college-affordability.

Rubin, Robert E., Peter R. Orszag, and Allen Sinai. "Sustained Budget Deficits: Longer-Run U.S. Economic Performance and the Risk of Financial and Fiscal Disarray." Last modified January 4, 2004. http://www.brookings.edu/~/media/research/files/papers/2004/1/05budgetdeficit%20orszag/20040105.pdf.

U.S. Department of Commerce: Bureau of Economic Analysis. "National Data: National Income and Product Accounts Tables." Accessed December 1, 2013. http://www.bea.gov/iTable/iTable.cfm?ReqID=9&step=1#reqid=9&step=3&isuri=1&910=X&911=0&903=146&904=2008&905=2013&906=A.

Board of Governors of the Federal Reserve System, "Selected Interest Rates (Daily) – H.15." Accessed December 10, 2013. http://www.federalreserve.gov/releases/h15/data.htm.

The White House. "Fiscal Year 2013 Historical Tables: Budget of the U.S. Government." Accessed December 12, 2013. http://www.whitehouse.gov/sites/default/files/omb/budget/fy2013/assets/hist.pdf.

The National Science Foundation. Accessed December 19, 2013. http://www.nsf.gov/.

Macroeconomic Policy Around the World

International Labour Organization. "Global Employment Trends for Youth 2013." http://www.ilo.org/global/research/global-reports/global-employment-trends/youth/2013/lang--en/index.htm

International Monetary Fund. "World Economic and Financial Surveys: World Economic Outlook—Transitions and Tensions." Last modified October 2013. http://www.imf.org/external/pubs/ft/weo/2013/02/pdf/text.pdf.

Nobelprize.org. "The Prize in Economics 1987 - Press Release." *Nobel Media AB 2013*. Last modified October 21, 1987. http://www.nobelprize.org/nobel_prizes/economic-sciences/laureates/1987/press.html.

Redvers, Louise. BBC News Business. "Youth unemployment: The big question and South Africa." Last modified October 31, 2012. http://www.bbc.co.uk/news/business-20125053.

The World Bank. "The Complete World Development Report Online." http://www.wdronline.worldbank.org/.

The World Bank. "World DataBank." http://databank.worldbank.org/data/home.aspx.

Todaro, Michael P., and Stephen C Smith. *Economic Development (11ᵗʰEdition)*. Boston, MA: Addison-Wesley: Pearson, 2011, chap. 1–2.

"Shinzo Abe's Government Looks Likely to Disappoint on Fiscal Consolidation." *The Economist*, May 4, 2013. http://www.economist.com/news/finance-and-economics/21577080-shinzo-abes-government-looks-likely-disappoint-fiscal-consolidation-dont.

Banerjee, Abhijit V., and Esther Duflo. *Poor Economics*. "About the Book: Overview." http://pooreconomics.com/about-book.

CARE International. "About Us." Accessed January 14, 2014. http://www.care-international.org/about-us.aspx.

Central Intelligence Agency. "The World Factbook: Africa, Burundi." Last modified November 12, 2013. https://www.cia.gov/library/publications/the-world-factbook/geos/by.html.

Central Intelligence Agency. "The World Factbook: Africa, Democratic Republic of the Congo." Last modified November 12, 2013. https://www.cia.gov/library/publications/the-world-factbook/geos/cg.html.

Easterly, William. *The White Man's Burden: Why the West's Efforts to Aid the Rest Have Done So Much Ill and So Little Good*. Penguin Group (USA), 2006.

Goel, Vindu. "Facebook Leads an Effort to Lower Barriers to Internet Access," *The New York Times*. Last modified August 20, 2013.

Google. "Project Loon." http://www.google.com/loon/.

GOV.UK. "Department for International Development." https://www.gov.uk/government/organisations/department-for-international-development.

The World Bank. "Millennium Development Goals." http://www.worldbank.org/mdgs/.

Todaro, Michael P., and Stephen C Smith. *Economic Development (11th Edition)*. Boston, MA: Addison-Wesley: Pearson, 2011, chap. 3.

Vercillo, Siera. "The Failures of Canadian Foreign Aid: Tied, Mismanaged and Uncoordinated." *The Attaché Journal of International Affairs*. (2010). http://theattachejia.files.wordpress.com/2013/10/the-attache-2010-issue.pdf.

Viscusi, Gregory, and Mark Deen. "Why France Has So Many 49-Employee Companies." *Business Week*. Last modified May 3, 2012. http://www.businessweek.com/articles/2012-05-03/why-france-has-so-many-49-employee-companies.

Edwards, S. (n.d.). "America's Unsustainable Current Account Deficit." *National Bureau of Economic Research Digest*. http://www.nber.org/digest/mar06/w11541.html. http://www.ustr.gov/trade-agreements/free-trade-agreements/north-american-free-trade-agreement-nafta.

New Country Classifications | Data. (n.d.). Accessed January 14, 2014. http://data.worldbank.org/news/new-country-classifications.

Office of the United States Trade Representative: Executive Office of the President. "North American Free Trade Agreement (NAFTA)."

Why India's Labour Laws are a Problem. (2006, May 18). *BBC*. May 18, 2006. http://news.bbc.co.uk/2/hi/south_asia/4984256.stm.

International Trade

Krugman, Paul R. *Pop Internationalism*. The MIT Press, Cambridge. 1996.

Krugman, Paul R. "What Do Undergrads Need to Know about Trade?" *American Economic Review* 83, no. 2. 1993. 23-26.

Ricardo, David. *On the Principles of Political Economy and Taxation*. London: John Murray, 1817.

Ricardo, David. "On the Principles of Political Economy and Taxation." *Library of Economics and Liberty*. http://www.econlib.org/library/Ricardo/ricP.html.

Bernstein, William J. *A Splendid Exchange: How Trade Shaped the World*. Atlantic Monthly Press. New York. 2008.

U.S. Census Bureau. 2015. "U.S. International Trade in Goods and Services: December 2014." Accessed April 13, 2015. http://www.bea.gov/newsreleases/international/trade/2015/pdf/trad1214.pdf.

U.S. Census Bureau. U.S. Bureau of Economic Analysis. 2015. "U.S. International Trade in Goods and Services February 2015." Accessed April 10, 2015. https://www.census.gov/foreign-trade/Press-Release/

current_press_release/ft900.pdf.

Vernengo, Matias. "What Do Undergraduates Really Need to Know About Trade and Finance?" in *Political Economy and Contemporary Capitalism: Radical Perspectives on Economic Theory and Policy*, ed. Ron Baiman, Heather Boushey, and Dawn Saunders. M. E. Sharpe Inc, 2000. Armonk. 177-183.

World Trade Organization. "The Doha Round." Accessed October 2013. http://www.wto.org/english/tratop_e/dda_e/dda_e.htm.

The World Bank. "Data: World Development Indicators." Accessed October 2013. http://data.worldbank.org/data-catalog/world-development-indicators.

Globalization and Protectionism

Bureau of Labor Statistics. "Industries at a Glance." Accessed December 31, 2013. http://www.bls.gov/iag/.

Oxfam International. Accessed January 6, 2014. http://www.oxfam.org/.

Bureau of Labor Statistics. "Data Retrieval: Employment, Hours, and Earnings (CES)." Last modified February 1, 2013. http://www.bls.gov/webapps/legacy/cesbtab1.htm.

Dhillon, Kiran. 2015. "Why Are U.S. Oil Imports Falling?" Time.com. Accessed April 1, 2015. http://time.com/67163/why-are-u-s-oil-imports-falling/.

Kristof, Nicholas. "Let Them Sweat." *The New York Times*, June 25, 2002. http://www.nytimes.com/2002/06/25/opinion/let-them-sweat.html.

Kohut, Andrew, Richard Wike, and Juliana Horowitz. "The Pew Global Attitudes Project." *Pew Research Center*. Last modified October 4, 2007. http://www.pewglobal.org/files/pdf/258.pdf.

Lutz, Hannah. 2015. "U.S. Auto Exports Hit Record in 2014." Automotive News. Accessed April 1, 2015. http://www.autonews.com/article/20150206/OEM01/150209875/u.s.-auto-exports-hit-record-in-2014.

United States Department of Labor. Bureau of Labor Statistics. 2015. "Employment Situation Summary." Accessed April 1, 2015. http://www.bls.gov/news.release/empsit.nr0.htm.

United States Department of Commerce. "About the Department of Commerce." Accessed January 6, 2014. http://www.commerce.gov/about-department-commerce.

United States International Trade Commission. "About the USITC." Accessed January 6, 2014. http://www.usitc.gov/press_room/about_usitc.htm.

E. Helpman, and O. Itskhoki, "Labour Market Rigidities, Trade and Unemployment," *The Review of Economic Studies*, 77. 3 (2010): 1100-1137.

M.J. Melitz, and D. Trefler. "Gains from Trade when Firms Matter." *The Journal of Economic Perspectives*, 26.2 (2012): 91-118.

Rauch, J. "Was Mancur Olson Wrong?" *The American*, February 15, 2013. http://www.american.com/archive/2013/february/was-mancur-olson-wrong.

Office of the United States Trade Representative. "U.S. Trade Representative Froman Announces FY 2014 WTO Tariff-Rate Quota Allocations for Raw Cane Sugar, Refined and Specialty Sugar and Sugar-Containing Products."Accessed January 6, 2014. http://www.ustr.gov/about-us/press-office/press-releases/2013/september/WTO-trq-for-sugar.

The World Bank. "Merchandise trade (% of GDP)." Accessed January 4, 2014. http://data.worldbank.org/indicator/TG.VAL.TOTL.GD.ZS.

World Trade Organization. 2014. "Annual Report 2014." Accessed April 1, 2015. https://www.wto.org/english/res_e/booksp_e/anrep_e/anrep14_chap10_e.pdf.

This OpenStax book is available for free at http://cnx.org/content/col12122/1.4

INDEX

This OpenStax book is available for free at http://cnx.org/content/col12122/1.4